MODERN LAND LAW

MODERN LAND LAW

Fifth Edition

**MARK P. THOMPSON LL.B (Leicester);
LL.M (Keele)**

Professor of Law and Senior Pro-Vice-Chancellor, University of Leicester

OXFORD
UNIVERSITY PRESS

OXFORD
UNIVERSITY PRESS

Great Clarendon Street, Oxford, OX2 6DP,
United Kingdom

Oxford University Press is a department of the University of Oxford.
It furthers the University's objective of excellence in research, scholarship,
and education by publishing worldwide. Oxford is a registered trade mark of
Oxford University Press in the UK and in certain other countries

British Library Cataloguing in Publication Data
Data available

Library of Congress Cataloging in Publication Data
Data available

ISBN 978-0-19-964137-6

Printed in Great Britain by
Ashford Colour Press Ltd, Gosport, Hampshire

Preface

The three years since the publication of the previous edition of this book have seen significant judicial developments in the law, which has led to a significant amount of rewriting of the text and, to a limited extent, some restructuring of the book. As well as the normal flow of decisions in the High Court and Court of Appeal, I would draw particular attention to the activity of the House of Lords/Supreme Court, which has been very active in areas relevant to this book, and has made a number of important contributions to the development of the law. In part, some of these developments were foreseen. Thus in the Preface to the fourth edition, attention was specifically drawn to three decisions of the House of Lords: *Stack v. Dowden*, *Yeoman's Row Management Ltd v. Cobbe*, and *Moncrieff v. Jamieson*. The reasoning in all of these cases was considered to be problematic, and so it should not occasion great surprise that some of the issues raised have had to be revisited at the highest judicial level. In *Jones v. Kernott*, the Supreme Court revisited issues raised in *Stack v. Dowden* although one is, again, left with the strong feeling that the last word has yet to be said on the issue of the acquisition of interests in the home; a feeling which is strengthened by the continuation of reasoning which applies different legal principles to situations where a house is jointly purchased dependent largely on the relationship between the people who are buying it. A not dissimilar approach, which involves distinguishing between disputes occurring in a commercial rather than a family context, was also taken in *Thorner v. Major*, although the analysis adopted in that case is much to be welcomed, in that it saw a substantial rowing back from the unacceptably narrow exposition of the principles of equitable estoppel in *Yeoman's Row*; an exposition which, if accepted, would have left little scope for the operation of an important and flexible equitable doctrine.

The third case, *Moncrieff*, has not been revisited by the courts, although it has been discussed by the Law Commission in its final report on Easements, Covenants and *Profits à Prendre*, and the Commission's Report and recommendations are analysed in the text. Although I am critical of some of its recommendations, other parts, notably its proposals to simplify the very messy law pertaining to prescription, are to be welcomed. This has also been an area of Supreme Court activity, and the decision in *R (on the Application of Lewis) v. Redcar and Cleveland Borough Council*, albeit in the context of village greens, contains an important discussion of the issue of permissive user.

The Court has, in addition to the above, in *Star Energy Weald Basin Ltd v. Bocardo SA*, also undertaken a rare judicial discussion of the extent of subterranean ownership of land. More importantly, however, in *Manchester City Council v. Pinnock* (together with *Hounslow London Borough Council v. Powell*), it has resolved the long-running debate as to whether an occupier can rely on the Human Rights Act to resist a possession action brought by a local authority which, under domestic property law, has an unqualified right to possession. The decision that he can is of considerable theoretical importance. Although my view is that the practical consequences of this decision are unlikely to be great and that, in particular, the reach of the Act does not extend to affecting the rights of private landowners, the conceptual significance of the decision is considerable and has led me to recast Chapter 3 to include for the first time a discrete treatment of human rights, as opposed to the approach in the past, which was to discuss these issues as and where they arose.

Finally, mention should be made of the landmark decision in *Berrisford v. Mexfield Housing Co-operative Ltd*. This decision, which relied upon an analysis which had been widely overlooked, was able, entirely convincingly, to limit the effect of the earlier decision in *Prudential Assurance Co. Ltd v. London Residuary Body* with the effect that purported leases between individuals will not now fail because the agreement is for an uncertain term. That prospect does, however, remain in respect of corporate tenants, a consideration which strengthens the case for legislative reform, notwithstanding the significant recasting of the law occasioned by the decision in *Berrisford*.

In writing this new edition, I have incurred a number of debts which I am happy to acknowledge. Thanks are due to staff at OUP, in particular Caroline Davidson and Emma Wilson, who, amongst other things, have displayed considerable patience while waiting for the work finally to be completed. Thanks are also due to Deborah Renshaw and Sarah Nattrass for help with copy-editing and proofreading respectively. Above all, however, I am grateful to my wife, Kathy, who has been a constant source of support and encouragement to me while I was working on the completion of the manuscript, and helped to ensure that the patience of Caroline and Emma was not tested to an even greater extent than I fear was actually the case.

I have attempted to state the law as I understand it to have been at the end of January 2012. I am solely to blame for any failure to do so.

Mark P. Thompson
University of Leicester
20 April 2012

Outline Contents

Detailed Contents

Table of Cases

Table of Statutes

Foreign Statutes

Statutory Instruments

1

The Scope of the Subject

When people refer to property, they frequently mean a particular object. Thus, a person may point to a car or a watch and simply state that this is their property. While it does no great harm to describe objects in this way, it does tend to obscure the notion of what is meant by property. Instead of referring to the item in question, it is more helpful to see the idea of property as involving a person's relationship to a particular item.[1] When one states that one owns property, one is using a form of shorthand to describe the rights which one possesses.

Land is an important commodity in society. It also differs from other forms of property in that it is both permanent and indestructible. Because of these two features, it is quite possible for more than one person to have a relationship with the land; a phenomenon which, while possible, is less likely to occur with other forms of property.

One of the more important rights which can exist in relation to land is the right, physically, to possess it. This right can be shared amongst different people. Most obviously, more than one person can simultaneously have the right to possess. This will occur when there is concurrent ownership, such as a husband and wife together sharing the matrimonial home.[2] Alternatively, consecutive rights to possess the land can exist, for example, when a person is given the right to possess the land for his lifetime with provision made, in advance, as to who will succeed to the right of possession after the first person has died. This latter phenomenon arose from a long-standing desire, less common today than in the past, to secure intergenerational transfers of wealth and to seek to retain the land within the ownership of the family.[3]

Another common situation where a person cedes physical possession of land to another is when a lease is created. This is a commercial transaction where, for historical reasons, the landlord, or freeholder, is still, legally, regarded as being in possession of the property, his interest in that property being termed a reversion; his right, physically, to possess the land[4] reverts to him on the termination of the tenancy. Nevertheless, it is a transaction which results in more than one person

---

[1] See, generally, K. Gray and S.F. Gray in Bright and Dewar, *Land Law, Themes and Perspectives* (Oxford: Oxford University Press, 1998), 15 *et seq.*

[2] See Chapter 8.   [3] See Chapter 8.

[4] Under the Law of Property Act 1925, s. 201(1)(xix), possession is defined to include the receipt of rents and profits or the right to receive the same, thereby ensuring that, legally, a landlord is still regarded as being in possession of the land.

concurrently owning interests in the property, those interests being akin to a form of ownership of it.

The preceding examples have focused on the possibility of dividing rights to possession of land amongst different people. Because the right to possession of land is regarded as one of the more important incidents of ownership, these types of situations are generally seen as the division of ownership rights between the parties involved. Other rights can, however, be created over land. For example, because of the nature of the property in question, it forms good security for a loan. Consequently, an important, and common, right to create over land is a mortgage, whereby the lender, or mortgagee, in return for his loan, acquires important rights over the borrower's, or mortgagor's, land.

The rights acquired by a mortgagee are sufficiently extensive to be able to regard him as having acquired ownership rights over the property. Indeed, as shall be seen, until 1925, the mortgagee did actually become the legal owner of the mortgaged property.[5]

THIRD PARTY RIGHTS

In addition to having ownership rights in land, whereby a person has the right to possess it, it is common for people to have enforceable rights in other people's land. For example, a person may enjoy a right of way, an example of a right which is termed an easement, across a neighbour's land. Another example of a third party right is where the owner of a house in a residential area covenants with neighbours that the house will only be used as a residence.

THE CONVEYANCING DIMENSION

In view of the foregoing, it is evident that a number of people may, simultaneously, have interests in the same piece of land. A feature of the law of property is that these rights are not binding only upon the parties who were privy to their creation. Rather, the rights which are created can affect successive owners of the relevant land. Thus, a right granted by the owner of a piece of land to a neighbour to cross it would have only limited utility if it was lost when that owner sold the land to another person. Unlike the law of contract, where the liabilities[6] under the contract are personal to the parties who entered into the contract, once a particular right is recognized as part of the law of property, or, as it is also put, a proprietary right, it takes effect against successive

---

[5] See Chapter 12.

[6] Rights can now be conferred on someone who is not a party to the contract: Contracts (Rights of Third Parties) Act 1999, *Prudential Assurance Co. Ltd v. Ayres* [2007] 3 All E.R. 946.

owners of the land in question, who are said to be bound by that right. So, in the above example, if certain conditions are satisfied, the new owner of the land will take subject to the right of way created by the former owner or, as that person is frequently referred to, his predecessor in title.

The fact that certain rights can be enforced against successive owners has a number of consequences, influenced to a large extent by the desire that land be easily transferable. Ownership rights can, as has been seen, be fragmented and divided among different people. Again, a particular piece of land may be subject to a covenant restricting building upon it. From the point of view of a person buying that land, these are matters of major concern. A property developer will obviously not wish to buy a piece of land which is subject to an obligation prohibiting building upon it.

One of the tasks of Land Law is to seek to reconcile competing interests. On the one hand, people who enjoy rights in or over land wish to ensure that such rights remain in existence, whoever currently owns that land. On the other, people who buy land wish to acquire as many rights as possible in it and to be free of other people's rights, or at least be able to discover, as easily as possible, before buying the land, what those other rights are. The greater the protection given to people claiming rights in another's land, the more difficult it can be to enter into commercial transactions involving that land.

To facilitate conveyancing, the law has adopted a number of strategies. First, although landowners are free to enter into whatever personal obligations affecting only themselves as they please, their ability to create proprietary rights, that is rights which are capable of affecting future owners of the land, is limited.[7] The number of proprietary rights recognized by law is limited and it is not open to the parties to fashion new rights which will continue to affect the land through successive periods of ownership.[8] As Lord Wilberforce put it:

'Before a right or an interest can be admitted into the category of property, it must be definable, identifiable by third parties, capable in its nature of assumption by third parties, and have some degree of permanence and stability.'[9]

Although this passage is somewhat circular,[10] the main feature of it, which is intended to limit the number of rights which the law is prepared to recognize as property rights, is the need for such a right to be both certain in its nature[11] and easily identifiable. Consistent with this, as well as the law insisting upon the right in question possessing these, and certain other characteristics, it also insisted upon certain formalities being

---

[7] For a valuable discussion of the distinction between personal and proprietary rights, see M. Dixon in Tee (ed.), *Land Law: Issues, Debates, Policy* (Cullompton: Willan Publishing, 2002), Chapter 1.

[8] See *Keppell v. Bailey* (1833) 2 My & K. 517 at 533 *per* Lord Brougham L.C.; Law of Property Act 1925, s. 4.

[9] *National Provincial Bank Ltd v. Ainsworth* [1965] A.C. 1175 at 247–248. See also S. Bright in Bright and Dewar, op. cit., Chapter 21.

[10] See Gray and Gray, *Elements of Land Law* (5th edn) (Oxford: Oxford University Press, 2009), 97–98; J.-P. Hinojosa [2005] Conv. 114 at 116–122.

[11] Although see the position with regard to estoppel rights, which are now recognized as property rights: Land Registration Act 2002, s. 116. See Chapter 15.

observed before such rights could be created.[12] As a general rule, in order to transfer land or create an interest in it, one must use a deed,[13] a deed being a formal document which explicitly makes clear that it is intended to be a deed, is signed by the person making it, and is delivered as a deed.[14] Similarly, contracts for the sale of land, or an interest in land, are required to be in writing.[15] In the future, such formalities will be satisfied by electronic means,[16] but the essential need for formal requirements to be met will remain.

Also, with a view to facilitating conveyancing, systems of registration were introduced. The two systems, which are mutually exclusive, provide, in one case, for various interests in the land of others to be registered, and, in the other, for the ownership of the land itself to be registered. This latter system of registration, termed registration of title, operates so that the registration entry for a piece of land records not only the registration of the ownership of it, the registration of title, but, subject to a category of interest, termed 'rights' which override registration,[17] also the interests which other people have over that land.

The purpose of the registration systems is to make it as straightforward as possible for a purchaser of land to discover, before buying the property, what rights he will take subject to and, in the case of registration of title, to assure him that the seller actually owns the land he is purporting to transfer. These systems undoubtedly facilitate the conveyancing process, by which is meant that the process of buying and selling land is made as simple a transaction as is possible. This facilitation, however, comes at a price.

If a person has a right over another person's land then, from a conveyancing perspective, it is desirable that such a right is easily discoverable. The process devised to implement such a policy is to make as many rights as possible registrable. A purchaser may then easily discover[18] what rights affect the land which is being bought. If no rights have been registered, then the purchaser is entitled to assume that there are no such rights: the general sanction for a failure to register a registrable interest being that it is void against a purchaser of the land.[19] The difficulty with this is that a person who possesses a right may be quite unaware of registration requirements, particularly if the right in question has arisen in an informal situation. In such situations, especially where the person claiming the right actually lives in the property, the argument that the law should always favour simplification of conveyancing becomes less compelling.

---

[12] For a valuable discussion of the reasons for formal requirements, see P. Critchley in Dewar and Bright, op cit., Chapter 20.

[13] Law of Property Act 1925, s. 52. There are a number of exceptions to this, the most important being a lease for a period of less than three years: ibid., s. 54(2).

[14] Law of Property (Miscellaneous Provisions) Act 1989, s. 1.   [15] Ibid., s. 2. See Chapter 6.

[16] Electronic Communications Act 2000, s. 8(2)(a)(b).   [17] See Chapter 5.

[18] For the defects in the registration system, see Chapter 4.

[19] For a more detailed discussion of this, see Chapter 4.

The task of reconciling the competing interests of those claiming rights in land and the pressure to simplify conveyancing has become an issue of increased importance in modern times. How the law has approached this task will be examined fully, in various parts of this book. In order to do this, it is first necessary to appreciate not only what constitutes land but also the principles upon which the ownership of land, and interests in land, are based.

REAL PROPERTY

Some legal systems, when classifying different forms of property, adopt a division between movable and immovable property. English Law did not do this.[20] Rather, for historical reasons, the essential difference is between real property and personal property, with land coming into the former category.

Origins of the distinction

The basis for the distinction in English law between real property and personal property is rooted in history and rests upon the different remedies available in the event of interference with a person's rights to property. In the case of land, if a person was dispossessed by another he could bring an action to recover the thing itself and did not have to be content with damages for trespass. As what was recovered was the land itself, the type of action involved was termed a real action, that is an action relating to the thing or, as it was put in Latin, the *res*. If, on the other hand, the wrongdoer had dispossessed a person of his horse, there was no right to recover the actual property;[21] the action was for damages only, the measure of those damages being, in general, the value of the property. Because of the nature of the actions, property which could be recovered by an action was termed real property. Other forms of property were categorized as personal property, or personalty.

A further division of types of property is that between tangible and intangible property. The former category is self-explanatory and includes items such as a car or a television. Intangible property, also referred to as a *chose in action*, is capable of ownership but is not a physical entity. Examples of the latter form of property include a debt owed by one person to another and copyright in an artistic or literary work, the essence of such a right being the power to prevent other people exploiting that work without permission.[22] It is normal for that permission to be given in return for payment, so that the owner of the copyright in a book will receive payment, termed royalties, on the sale

---

[20] English Law adopts this classification in cases involving the Conflict of Laws. See Clarkson and Hill, *The Conflict of Laws* (4th edn) (Oxford: Oxford University Press, 2011), 472–474.

[21] See now Palmer, *Bailment* (2nd edn) (Sydney: Law Book Co., 1991), 248–253.

[22] See *Fisher v. Brooker* [2009] UKHL 41 at [8] *per* Lord Hope of Craighead. The recent assertion that a property right has to be physically located, McFarlane, *The Structure of Property Law* (Oxford: Hart

of copies of that book. Intangible property is as much property as tangible property in that its ownership can be transferred from one person to another. Items of personal property are also termed chattels.

Leases

Today, leases are a common form of land holding and very much a part of Land Law. In the earliest days of the development of the subject, however, this was not so. At the outset, Land Law was based upon the feudal system.[23] One held land from a superior lord in return for the performance of various duties. How one held the land was indicative of one's status in society. A lease was seen as a commercial transaction and, as such, did not fit into the feudal system of landholding. Because of this, the relationship between the landlord and the tenant was not seen as being part of Land Law. A tenant who had been dispossessed could not, therefore, recover the land by bringing a real action and, as a result, a lease was classified as personal property.

In time, and in particular when the feudal system began to decay, it became increasingly unrealistic to view the lease in this way. Nevertheless, they were still regarded as being part of the law of personalty but, in recognition of the importance of the lease with regard to land, they are now termed chattels real. The term 'chattel' reflects the fact that leases were originally regarded as personal property, and the addition of the word 'real' recognizes the importance of the lease in Land Law.

The distinction today

The main reason for distinguishing between real property and personal property used to be that different rules of inheritance applied to the two types of property in the event of a person dying intestate. This is no longer the case and section 46 of the Administration of Estates Act 1925 now provides for the devolution of a deceased's property upon intestacy. If a testator makes a will leaving real property to one person and personal property to another,[24] then the distinction will be important. Aside from that, the term 'real property' is used essentially to differentiate between what the law considers to be land and other forms of property.

THE MEANING OF LAND

Land is defined elaborately by section 205(1)(ix) of the Law of Property Act 1925 to include not just the physical entity itself. Also within the definition are things such as mines and minerals found underneath the land, buildings on the land, and rights over

---

Publishing, 2008), 132, is unsupportable. For a discussion of Intellectual Property in this context, see Penner, *The Idea of Property in Law* (Oxford: Oxford University Press, 2000), 118–120.

[23] See Chapter 2.   [24] See e.g. *Re Kempthorne* [1930] 1 Ch. 268.

land, such as easements, as well as some archaic rights derived from the feudal system such as an advowson, which is the right to present a clergyman to a living, which, for some reason, was classed as real property. The extent of ownership of land can now be more fully considered.

The extent of ownership

The extent of one's ownership of land is encompassed in the somewhat misleading Latin phrase, which dates back at least to the thirteenth century,[25] that: *cuius est solum eius est usque ad coelum et ad inferos*, which means that he who owns the land owns everything 'up to the sky and down to the centre of the earth'.[26] Not surprisingly, such an extreme statement is not, particularly in the modern world, without its problems, and Lord Wilberforce commented that it was 'so sweeping, unscientific and unpractical that it is unlikely to appeal to the common law mind'.[27] More recently, in *Bocardo SA v. Star Energy UK Onshore Ltd*,[28] Aitkens J. asserted that the maxim did not represent English law, however, on appeal, Lord Hope expressed the view that it was a little hasty to assert that the maxim was not part of the law, although he did concede that the principle was neither absolute nor consistent in its application between downward and upward ownership.[29]

In terms of downward ownership,[30] this means that the landowner owns the mines and minerals contained in the land. This is subject to statutory exceptions, so that coal, gas and petroleum found under land are now subject to public ownership.[31] In *Bocardo*, the defendant had a licence to drill for oil. To extract the oil, it drilled under the claimant's land, at depths of up to 3,000 feet, and the claimant brought an action for trespass. This claim was upheld by the Supreme Court although, by a majority, only relatively nominal damages were awarded. In holding that the action, which occasioned no damage to the claimant's land, amounted to trespass, the argument that the land was not owned by the claimant was rejected. Lord Hope accepted that the maxim could not apply literally, but that the facts of the instant case did not get anywhere near to approaching the point of absurdity. Where, as here, there were substances which could be exploited, this raised the question as to who, if anyone, was the owner of the strata where those substances were to be found. In his view, the only plausible

---

[25] See the analysis in *Bocardo SA v. Star Energy UK Onshore Ltd* [2011] 1 A.C. 380 at [18]–[28] *per* Lord Hope.

[26] *Corbett v. Hill* (1870) L.R. 9 Eq. 671 at 673 *per* Sir William James V.-C. (column of air above a room). See also *Mitchell v. Manley* [1914] 1 Ch. 438 at 450 *per* Cozens-Hardy M.R.

[27] *Commissioner for Railways v. Valuer-General* [1974] A.C. 328 at 351.

[28] [2010] 1 All E.R. 26 at [59].

[29] *Bocardo SA v. Star Energy Weald Basin Ltd* [2011] 1 A.C. 380 at [14].

[30] See J. Howell (2002) 53 N.I.L.Q.268. For an interesting account of the extent of subterranean ownership of land, with particular reference to the Post Office, see A. Turner [2011] Conv. 465.

[31] Petroleum Act 1998, s. 2 (replacing earlier legislation); Coal Industry Act 1994, s. 9.

candidate was the registered owner of the land above, a conclusion which was exactly in line with the maxim.[32]

As well as the strata beneath the surface of the land, items found buried in the soil, unless constituting treasure trove,[33] in which case the treasure belongs to the Crown, belong to the owner of the land, unless the previous owner of the object can be found. So, for example, in *Elwes v. Brigg Gas Co.*,[34] a prehistoric boat buried six feet below the surface of the land was held to belong to the landlord, as opposed to the tenant who had discovered it. The basis of this is that, as the landlord was in possession of the land, including that below the surface, at the time when the lease was granted, he was regarded as being in possession of the chattel, and so had a better claim to it than the tenant.[35]

Items found on the land

Although not directly relevant to the issue of the extent of land ownership, it is convenient at this stage to consider the related issue of the ownership of chattels found on the land. In the case of objects found on the surface of the land, a distinction is drawn between situations when the object is found by a person who is on the land lawfully and where it is found by a trespasser. This issue was fully reviewed by the Court of Appeal in *Parker v. British Airways.*[36] The plaintiff was in the executive lounge at an airport when he found a bracelet on the floor. He handed it in to one of the airport staff, together with his name and address, and asked them to contact him if the owner could not be found. He later discovered that the defendants had sold the bracelet for £850 and he claimed to be entitled to the money. His claim succeeded.

To the evident surprise of Donaldson L.J., who gave the leading judgment, the law with regard to this issue was unclear. Having reviewed the authorities, he first of all recognized that, if the true owner of the property came forward, that person would have the best claim of all to the property.[37] The contest, therefore, is not generally to determine, absolutely, who is the owner of the chattel in question. The issue is simply, as between two claimants, which of them has the better right to it. As will be seen, this is an approach applied generally in disputes to rights to possession in Land Law cases.[38] He then articulated the relevant principles to be applied.

---

[32] [2011] 1 A.C. 380 at [15].

[33] For the definition of which, see Treasure Act 1996, ss 1–3. *Ex gratia* payments are normally made to the finder of treasure trove by the Secretary of State.

[34] (1886) 33 Ch.D. 562. See also *South Staffordshire Water Co. v. Sharman* [1896] 2 Q.B. 44 (rings found in mud at the bottom of a pond were part of the land).

[35] See Hickey, *Property and the Law of Finders* (Oxford: Hart Publishing, 2010), 28–49.

[36] [1982] Q.B. 1004. See S.A. Roberts (1982) 45 M.L.R. 683.

[37] *Moffatt v. Kazana* [1969] 2 Q.B. 152.   [38] See Chapter 7.

First, he stated that the finder of a chattel acquires no rights over it unless it has been abandoned[39] or lost and then taken into his care and control.[40] If the finder is a trespasser, or has a dishonest intent, then, in his view he acquires only very limited rights. The weakness of these rights is manifest only against the true owner of the property and, it seems, the occupier of the land. As against other people, the fact of possession confers on the person a possessory title, which is good against them. This latter point is illustrated by *Costello v. Chief Constable of Derbyshire Constabulary*.[41] The police lawfully took possession of a car in the belief that it had been stolen. At the time when they did this, the car was in the possession of the claimant. When, in 1997, the statutory purpose for which the police were authorized to hold the car had been exhausted, the claimant demanded its return. The police refused to return the car on the ground that the claimant knew it to have been stolen. The Court of Appeal decided in favour of the claimant. According to Lightman J.:

'The fact of possession of a chattel of itself gives to the possessor a possessory title and the possessor is entitled to rely on such title without reference to the circumstances in which such possession was obtained; his entitlement to do so is not prejudiced by the fact that he obtained such possession unlawfully or by an illegal transaction.'[42]

On this basis, it was held that the claimant had a better right to the car than did the police and they were ordered to return the car to him.

Ultimately, the issue in cases of this nature is who has the better right to the chattel in question. The finder of a lost or abandoned chattel will have a better right to it than everyone other than the true owner of the property,[43] unless the occupier of the land on which the item was found has better right to it. To establish a better right than the finder, the occupier must have manifested an intention to exercise control over the land[44] and the things which might be found upon it.[45] On the facts of *Parker*, the claim by British Airways failed because, although access to the executive lounge was limited to first class customers, no attempt was made to search for lost articles and there was, therefore, no attempt to exert control over such property.

---

[39] For an interesting, comparative, analysis of the proprietary consequences of abandonment, see J. Griffiths-Baker (2007) 36 C.L.W.R. 16. See also, A.H. Hudson (1984) 100 L.Q.R. 110. For the problems associated with the practice known as freeganism, that is taking goods which appear to be abandoned, see S. Thomas (2010) 30 L.S. 98.

[40] [1982] Q.B. 1004 at 1017. For justified criticism of the need for the chattel to have been lost or abandoned with respect to a claimant who asserts title after the chattel has been found, see Hickey, op. cit., Chapter 3; Roberts, loc. cit., 687.

[41] [2001] 3 All E.R. 150. See also *Webb v. Chief Constable of Merseyside Police* [2000] Q.B. 427. See G. Battersby (2002) 65 M.L.R. 603.

[42] Ibid. at 157. Contrast *Hibbert v. McKiernan* [1948] 2 K.B. 142, where the notion that a thief could obtain any sort of title was regarded as 'fantastic': at 151 *per* Humphreys J.

[43] See *Armorie v. Delamirei* (1722) 1 Str. 505.

[44] For examples of such a degree of control, see *Hibbert v. McKiernan* [1948] 2 K.B. 142; *City of London Corporation v. Appleyard* [1963] 1 W.L.R. 982. Contrast *Bridges v. Hawkesworth* (1851) 21 L.J.Q.B. 75 (banknotes dropped in common part of shop).

[45] *Parker v. British Airways Board* [1982] Q.B. 1004 at 1007–1008 *per* Donaldson L.J.

The issue of claims to chattels found on another person's land was considered again in *Waverley Borough Council v. Fletcher.*[46] The plaintiff council owned an open access park. It was council policy not to allow people to use metal detectors in the park and this policy was implemented not by the enactment of byelaws, but by placing prohibitory notices in the park, although it was admitted that these notices were often pulled down. The defendant, who was unaware of the council's policy, used his detector in the park and was thus able to discover a medieval bronze brooch some nine inches below the surface of the land, which he recovered by digging it up. He offered it to the coroner as treasure trove but the offer was declined. The council then claimed to be entitled to the brooch and the action was resisted by the defendant. The Court of Appeal found in favour of the council.

Auld L.J. restated the views expressed in *Parker.* He said that where an article is found in or attached to the land then, as between the owner or lawful possessor of the land and the finder of the article, the owner or possessor of the land has the better title to it. When the article is unattached to the land then, as between these two rival claims, the finder has the better right to the article unless the possessor of the land has exercised such manifest control over the land as to indicate an intention to control the land and anything which might be found upon it.[47] In the present case, the finder lost his claim on two grounds. First, because the brooch was found under the ground this, of itself, meant that the owner of the land had the better right to it. Secondly, although the public had a right of general access to the park, that right did not extend to digging,[48] so that activity of this sort, which was outside the scope of the general licence to use the park, made the claimant a trespasser, with the result that any claim by the finder to the chattel was weaker than that of the occupier of the land.

Trespassers

It will be observed that, in both *Parker v. British Airways* and *Waverly Borough Council v. Fletcher*, the status of the finder was considered to be important; if the finder was a trespasser then his claim to the chattel is said to be weaker than that of the occupier of the land.[49] This seems highly questionable. As has been pointed out, if in *Parker*, the finder had simply put the brooch in his pocket and had not alerted the British Airways staff of his find then, although he might be said to have been behaving dishonestly, it is difficult to see why that should enhance the claim of British Airways to the brooch.[50] Similarly, if a friend of Mr Parker, who was flying economy class, accompanied him into the executive lounge, where he was not entitled to be, and he found the brooch, it is not at all obvious why his claim to it, as against British Airways, should fail. It is true that in cases of trespass, the occupier of the land may find it easier to show the requisite degree of control to establish possession of the chattel and to be able to assert

46 [1996] Q.B. 334. See J. Stevens [1996] Conv. 216.
47 *Waverly Borough Council v. Fletcher* [1996] Q.B. 334 at 336.
48 Cf. *The Calgarth* [1927] P. 93 at 110 *per* Scrutton L.J.
49 In *Parker*, Sir David Cairns reserved his opinion on this matter: see [1982] Q.B. 1004 at 1021.
50 Battersby, loc. cit., 604–605. See also Roberts, loc. cit., 687–688; Hickey, op. cit., 132–135.

a stronger title to it than the finder, but if he cannot do this, then the title of the finder should be stronger than that of the occupier of the land regardless of the legal status of the finder. Distaste for dishonest people and for trespassers should not alter the general principles applicable when resolving disputes between the occupier of land and a person who finds chattels on that land as to who has the better title to the particular object in question.

Airspace

In this context, the maxim that he who owns land does so up to the sky and down to the centre of the earth is particularly apt to mislead, and it has been accepted that it is not generally applicable in respect of upwards ownership.[51] Nevertheless, it has long been accepted that a physical incursion into the airspace over a person's land is capable of amounting to a trespass. So, in *Kelsen v. Imperial Tobacco Co. (of Great Britain and Ireland) Ltd,*[52] a mandatory injunction was granted to secure the removal of an advertising sign which infringed the airspace above the plaintiff's single-storey shop.

It was made clear that the basis of the cause of action was in trespass rather than nuisance;[53] that it was in respect of the intrusion onto the property and not because it affected the enjoyment of the land in any way. On this basis, it was accepted that a landowner had the right to object to someone putting anything, such as a wire, over his land at any height.[54] Similarly, a landowner, provided he does not, himself, have to trespass on his neighbour's land to do it, has the right to lop overhanging branches[55] but, if this is done, any fruit, or suchlike, remains the property of the neighbour.[56]

Aircraft

If one takes the maxim to its logical extreme, difficulties would be faced in the context of overflying aircraft. In the case of civil aircraft, the matter is regulated by statute. Section 76 of the Civil Aircraft Act 1982 provides that no action for trespass or nuisance lies only for the flight of aircraft over land at a reasonable height, provided that the proper regulations have been observed. This would seem to reflect the general law, because as long ago as 1815, in a judgment which was admittedly unsympathetic to the

[51] *Bocardo SA v. Star Energy UK Onshore Ltd* [2011] 1 A.C. 380 at [26] *per* Lord Hope.
[52] [1957] 2 Q.B. 334. It remains a matter of discretion as to whether an injunction is an appropriate remedy on the facts. See *Woolerton & Wilson Ltd v. Richard Costain Ltd* [1970] 1 W.L.R. 411 and *Trenbath Ltd v. National Westminster Bank Ltd* (1979) 39 P & CR 104.
[53] *Kelsen v. Imperial Tobacco Co. (of Great Britain and Ireland) Ltd* [1957] 2 Q.B. 334 at 345 *per* McNair J., disapproving *dicta* in *Pickering v. Rudd* (1813) 4 Camp. 219. See also *Gifford v. Dent* [1926] W.N. 336.
[54] See *Wandsworth District Board of Works v. United Telephone Company Co. Ltd* (1884) 13 Q.B.D. 904 at 919 *per* Bowen L.J. The case turned on the meaning of 'street'.
[55] *Lemmon v. Webb* [1895] A.C. 1. Owing to the differing size of a tree over the requisite 20-year period, it is very difficult to obtain a prescriptive right to have branches overhanging a neighbour's land: ibid. at 6 *per* Lord Herschell L.C. For prescription, see Prescription, pp. 565–573.
[56] *Mills v. Brooker* [1919] 1 K.B. 555. It is immaterial whether the fruit falls off the tree naturally or by the result of some physical act: ibid. at 558 *per* Lush J.

notion that a landowner also owns the airspace over the land, it was said that a bal-loonist would not be liable in trespass for flying over a person's land.[57]

This issue was considered in *Bernstein of Leigh (Baron) v. Skyviews & General Ltd*.[58] The defendant flew a light aeroplane over the plaintiff's country house to photograph it and then sell the photograph to him. The plaintiff sued for trespass and breach of privacy. He lost. Starting from the premise that it would be an absurdity to imagine that an action for trespass could be brought each time a satellite passes over a subur-ban garden,[59] Griffiths J. thought that the maxim could not be applied literally and that what was involved was 'to balance the rights of an owner to enjoy the use of his land against the rights of the general public to take advantage of all that science now offers in the way of air space'.[60] In determining where that balance lay, relevant criteria would include the height at which the plane flew and whether or not what occurred amounted to a form of constant surveillance which, he thought, might be actionable in nuisance.[61] While an argument based upon trespass would still fail on the facts if they recurred today, it is possible, depending upon what was actually photographed, that an action could now be brought either for breach of confidence[62] or under the emerg-ing tort of breach of privacy.[63]

Flats

Particular problems can arise when a building is divided horizontally rather than ver-tically, the normal situation when one is considering a flat. In such cases, unless one is talking about a ground floor flat, what is in question is the ownership of a block of space[64] surrounded by other flats. While it is possible for such property to be owned in the same way as a house, such a form of ownership being, in the present context, known as a flying freehold,[65] there are serious practical problems relating to owner-ship of this type of property.[66] The principal problem is, when considering properties of this nature, that it is desirable to create a system of mutual obligations, such as the liability to contribute to the cost of maintenance of the common parts of the build-ing and the lift. Insofar as freehold ownership is concerned, it is extremely difficult to

---

[57] *Pickering v. Rudd* (1815) 4 Camp. 219 at 221 *per* Lord Ellenborough.   [58] [1978] Q.B. 474.
[59] Ibid. at 487.   [60] Ibid. at 488.   [61] Ibid. at 489.
[62] See *Hellewell v. Chief Constable of Derbyshire* [1995] 1 W.L.R. 804 at 807 *per* Laws J.; M.P. Thompson [1995] Conv. 404. For recent discussions of the impact of the Human Rights Act 1998 and the relationship between breach of confidence and privacy, see *Douglas v. Hello! Ltd* [2001] Q.B. 967. Contrast *A v. B (a com-pany)* [2002] 2 All E.R. 545. See now *Campbell v. Mirror Group Newspapers Ltd* [2004] 2 A.C. 457; *Mosley v. News Group Newspapers Ltd* [2008] EWHC 1777 (Ch).
[63] See, e.g., Murphy, *Street on Torts* (12th edn) (Oxford: Oxford University Press, 2007), Chapter 15.
[64] See K. Gray [1991] C.L.J. 252.
[65] For the position in Lincoln's Inn, see Lincoln's Inn Act 1860. For discussion of the meaning of the term 'freehold', see Chapter 2.
[66] See *Stadium Capital Holdings v. St Marylebone Properties Co Plc* [2009] EWHC 2942 (Ch) at [26], where Sir Donald Rattee considered the ownership of airspace separate from ownership of the land underneath 'a very strange concept'.

ensure that such obligations remain binding upon successive owners of the flats[67] and, for this reason, it is usual to find that such properties are dealt with by the creation of a lease.[68] In the future, some of these problems may be resolved by the implementation of the new scheme of landholding, termed commonhold.[69]

Water

Water lying on the land itself is not regarded as being capable of separate ownership, so that any right of public navigation is not regarded as a right over the water but as a right over the land underneath the water.[70] That said, the owner of land upon which there is water does have rights over that water, such as the right to fish. Where a river flows between two plots of land, the owner of each bank has rights up to the middle of the river. In terms of the abstraction of water, this is now governed by the Water Resources Act 1991, which limits the amount of water which can be abstracted.

In cases where the land is bounded with water which, over the years, ebbs and flows, then if there is a fixed boundary, that is conclusive of the matter.[71] If this is not the case, then the boundary will move with the water, so that the land will either increase or diminish in size accordingly,[72] a process known as accretion, or diluvion, respectively.

Wild animals

Wild animals do not belong to anyone. The owner of the land on which they are does have the right to catch or kill such animals and, when killed, the carcass belongs to the landowner, regardless of who killed it.[73]

ITEMS ATTACHED TO THE LAND

It is a general maxim of English Land Law that 'quicquid planatur solo, solo cedit',[74] the meaning of which is that whatever is attached to the soil becomes part of it. The application of this maxim leads to an important distinction between what are known

---

[67] See Positive covenants, pp. 590–594.

[68] This, too, is not without its problems. See D. Clarke in Dewar and Bright, op. cit., Chapter 15.

[69] See Commonhold and Leasehold Reform Act 2002 and Chapter 14.

[70] Attorney-General, ex rel. Derwent Trust Ltd v. Bortherton [1992]1 A.C. 425 at 441 per Lord Goff of Chieveley.

[71] Baxendale v. Instow Parish Council [1982] Ch. 14.

[72] Southern Centre of Theosophy Inc. v. State of South Australia [1982] A.C. 706. See R.E. Annand [1982] Conv. 208; W. Howarth [1986] Conv. 247.

[73] Blade v. Higgs (1865) 11 H.L.C. 349.

[74] A maxim apparently first coined in Marshall v. Lloyd (1837) 2 M. & W. 450 at 459 per Parke B. See P. Luther (2004) 24 O.J.L.S. 597 at 600.

as fixtures and fittings. The essence of the distinction between the two is that a fixture is something which, due to the manner and purpose of its attachment to the land, becomes part of the land itself, whereas fittings are chattels which are physically in the property and, in some cases, attached to it, but are not considered to be a part of it. As will be seen, an important aspect in deciding whether or not a particular item is a fixture is the degree of physical attachment to the land. Before considering the distinction between the two, it is necessary to have regard to a third category; items which are brought onto the land and become part of it, without properly being regarded as fixtures at all.

The issue arose in *Elitestone Ltd v. Morris*.[75] The plaintiffs owned land on which were constructed wooden bungalows. The bungalows rested upon concrete pillars which were attached to the land and to remove them from the land would have required their demolition. The issue arose as to whether the defendant's bungalow was a building or a chattel. The House of Lords held unanimously that the building was part of the land. Lord Lloyd of Berwick adopted the tripartite analysis put forward in a leading text that:

'An object which is brought onto land may be classified under one of three broad heads. It may be (a) a chattel; (b) a fixture; or (c) part and parcel of the land itself. Objects in categories (b) and (c) are treated as being part of the land.'[76]

Pointing out expressly that the building in question was not like a Portakabin or a mobile home,[77] Lord Lloyd took the view that it was not really apposite to consider whether or not the bungalow was a fixture. He thought that the issue of whether an item was a fixture arose when it was attached to a building; when one was considering whether the structure, itself, was part of the land, different considerations apply. This point was also made in *Holland v. Hodgson*,[78] where Blackburn J. explained that:

'blocks of stone placed one on top of another without any mortar or cement for the purpose of forming a dry stone wall would become part of the land, though the same stones, if deposited in a building yard and for convenience sake stacked on top of each other in the form of a wall, would not'.

The issue in cases of this nature seems to be the intention of the party constructing the item in question and the damage which would be caused to it by removing it. With regard to fixtures, an important issue will be the damage that would be done to the remaining property by removing the particular item.[79]

---

[75] [1997] 1 W.L.R. 687; H. Conway [1998] Conv. 418; P. Luther (2008) 28 L.S. 574.

[76] Woodfall, *Landlord and Tenant* (London: Sweet & Maxwell, Looseleaf), Vol. 1, para. 13.131, cited at [1997] 1 W.L.R. 687 at 691.

[77] Ibid. at 690. Similarly, a moveable houseboat is not regarded as being part of the land. See *Chelsea Yacht and Boat Co. Ltd v. Pope* [2000] 1 W.L.R. 1941; M.P. Thompson [2001] Conv. 417. For a more marginal example of this, see *Mew v. Tristmere Ltd* [2011] EWCA Civ. 912.

[78] (1872) L.R. 7 C.P. 328 at 335.

[79] See, generally, *Wessex Reserve Forces and Cadets Association v. White* [2005] EWHC 982 (Q.B.) at [21]–[61] *per* Mr Michael Harvey Q.C., affmd [2005] EWCA Civ. 1744.

FIXTURES

The issue of whether a particular item is regarded as being a fixture is potentially important to a number of people. If a person has contracted to sell a house, then it is quite clear that, after the contract has been made, the seller cannot remove any items from the property and is liable to the purchaser should he do so.[80] Rather more contentiously, in *Taylor v. Hamer*,[81] the majority of the Court of Appeal held that the seller was liable for the removal of flagstones, which were undoubtedly fixtures, the stones being removed after an agreement in principle had been reached concerning the sale of the property but before a binding contract had been entered into. This decision goes further than previous authority, but is unusual. A few days before the contract had been formed, the vendor gave a highly misleading answer to a question directly concerning the disputed flagstones and this aspect of the case clearly weighed heavily with the majority of the court. Indeed, subsequently, this was seen as being an integral part of the reasoning and the proposition that there is a wider principle that a vendor may not remove fixtures prior to the formation of a contract of sale was denied.[82] Despite some wide statements made in *Taylor*[83] that a vendor may not remove fixtures prior to entry into a contract, this is unlikely to be followed, particularly as the leading work on the subject has said of the case that 'it seems so anomalous, although meritorious, that it cannot comfortably be incorporated into any existing account of the law...'[84] Clearly, however, the avoidance of disputes of this nature is desirable, and it is now normal practice, as part of the Conveyancing Protocol, for the seller to complete, prior to entry into the contract, a questionnaire detailing which common household items are to be included in the sale, and this then becomes the basis of what is included in the contract.

If the property is mortgaged, then the mortgage extends to all fixtures,[85] even those which were affixed after the mortgage was created.[86] Again, if a situation, termed a settlement, is in existence, whereby, for example, land is left to A for life, thereafter to B, on A's death, fixtures will pass to B and will not pass under A's will, or upon his intestacy. Finally, when property is leased, items which are fixtures become part of the land and will pass to the landlord on the termination of the lease. In the latter two cases, however, although fixtures become part of the land, there exists a right to remove certain types of fixture.

---

[80] See, e.g., *Phillips v. Lamdin* [1949] 2 K.B. 33 (ornate Adam door).
[81] [2003] 1 E.G.L.R. 103. For criticism, see C. McNall [2003] Conv. 432.
[82] *Sykes v. Taylor-Rose* [2004] EWCA Civ. 299 at [15] *per* Sir William Aldous, quoting the trial court judge. This aspect of the decision was not appealed. See also, to similar effect, *Wickens v. Cheval Property Developments Ltd* [2010] EWHC 2249 (Ch).
[83] [2003] 1 E.G.L.R. 103 at [93] *per* Sedley L.J.
[84] Emmet and Farrand, *On Title* (17th edn) (London: Sweet & Maxwell, Looseleaf) para. 4.001.
[85] Law of Property Act 1925, s. 62(1); *Botham v. TSB Bank plc* (1997) 73 P. & C.R. D1.
[86] *Reynolds v. Ashby & Son* [1904] A.C. 466.

The distinction between fixtures and fittings

In answering the question as to whether a particular item is a fixture it is traditional to consider two issues:

(i) the degree of annexation of the object to the land; and

(ii) the purpose of annexation.[87]

The degree of annexation

As a general rule, unless an item is physically attached to the land, it will not be considered to be a fixture. Items which rest on the property by their own weight, such as a 'Dutch barn',[88] are unlikely to be regarded as fixtures. Similarly, a greenhouse which is not physically attached to the land is also not likely to be seen as a fixture and this is particularly true if it is normal practice to move the greenhouse periodically to various sites on the land.[89] It is not the case, however, that physical attachment is necessarily essential for an item to be regarded as being part of the land. As has been seen, if a structure, such as a dry stone wall or a pre-constructed bungalow, cannot be removed without destroying that structure, then it is likely that it will be regarded as being a part of the land, it not being regarded as helpful to describe it as a fixture.[90] It is also possible that self-standing objects, such as statues, could be regarded as fixtures, but this will only be the case if they are regarded as an integral part of the architecture,[91] although in the light of the modern approach to this issue, it is probable that this will not be held to be the case.[92]

The purpose of annexation

Although it is generally true to say that an item will not be regarded as a fixture unless it is physically attached to the land, that alone is insufficient; the court will also look at the purpose of the annexation to determine whether something is, or is not, a fixture and, in deciding this matter, how the parties choose to describe a particular object is not determinative.[93] The court will take an objective view of the matter. This can cause problems for suppliers of goods on hire-purchase agreements, who seek to retain ownership of the product until all the payments have been made. If the installation of the chattel in question is such that it becomes a fixture, then it will become part of the land and, consequently, part of the security of the house if the house is

---

[87] See *Holland v. Hodgson* (1872) L.R. 7 C.P. 328 at 334 *per* Blackburn J. For an interesting historical account of the development of this test, see P. Luther (2004) 24 O.J.L.S. 597.

[88] See *Wiltshear v. Cottrell* (1853) 1 E. & B. 674.

[89] See *H.E. Dibble Ltd v. Moore* [1970] 2 Q.B. 181 at 187 *per* Megaw L.J. See also *Deen v. Andrews* [1986] 1 E.G.L.R. 262. As a general proposition, when it is envisaged that an item will regularly be moved, it is unlikely that that item will be regarded as being a fixture. See *Hynes v. Vaughan* (1985) 50 P. & C.R. 444 (growing frame and garden sprinkler).

[90] *Elitestone Ltd v. Morris* [1997] 1 W.L.R. 687.

[91] See *D'Eyncourt v. Gregory* (1866) L.R. 3 Eq. 382; *Re Lord Chesterfield's Settled Estate* [1911] Ch. 237.

[92] See *Berkley v. Poulett* [1977] E.G.D. 754.

[93] *Melluish v. B.M.I. (No. 3) Ltd* [1996] A.C. 454 at 473 *per* Lord Browne-Wilkinson. The approach taken to this issue in *Hamp v. Bygrave* [1983] E.G.D. 1000 must now be regarded as wrong.

mortgaged.[94] Nevertheless, how the parties regard a particular item can have some effect, so that if a vendor and purchaser agree that certain items are fixtures, the vendor will not, after a contract of sale has been made, be able to remove them.[95]

In drawing the line between fixtures and fittings, the modern tendency is to place considerably more emphasis on the purpose of annexation than on the method of attachment, although the issue remains whether the item in question is properly to be regarded as part of the building.[96] In determining this matter, attitudes have changed to reflect the fact that the manner in which ornaments have been put up is different from that which occurred in the past, with the result that less disruption is now necessary to the building in order to remove them than was previously the case.[97] So, in *Leigh v. Taylor*,[98] a tapestry attached by tacks to wooden frames was held not to be a fixture, the purpose of the attachment to the building being to enable the tapestry to be enjoyed as an ornament rather than to enhance the building.

This approach was continued in *Berkley v. Poulett*,[99] where the principal issues of dispute were whether paintings screwed in to recesses in a wall, a large sundial on a plinth, and a statue weighing half a ton were fixtures. The Court of Appeal held that they were not. Scarman L.J. considered that the starting point in determining this issue was *Leigh v. Taylor* and the essential issue to be determined was whether the purpose of the annexation was to enjoy the pictures as pictures or to enhance the structure of the building. Conceding that the law in this area was frequently more difficult to apply than to state, and that 'a degree of annexation which in earlier times the law would have treated as conclusive may now prove nothing',[100] he concluded that the pictures remained as chattels. They were put on the wall to be enjoyed as pictures and how a workman chose to solve the problem of how they should be fixed to the walls was not decisive in determining their status. That they could be removed with comparative ease and without significant damage to the building[101] militated against them being fixtures. Similarly, the statue and sundial, which both rested by their own weight, were also regarded as chattels.

The most detailed consideration of which ordinary household items were fixtures occurred recently in *Botham v. TSB Bank plc*,[102] where the Court of Appeal had to consider the status of some 109 different items in a flat, the issue being whether they were included as part of the security for a loan, which would have been the case if the items were fixtures. The items were placed into nine different categories, of which eight were in dispute. It is not essential to enumerate each item to obtain the gist of the approach taken. The more important items were fitted carpets, curtains, light fittings, gas fires,

[94] *Botham v. TSB Bank plc* (1977) 73 P. & C.R. D1; *Melluish v. B.M.I. (No. 3)* [1996] A.C. 454.
[95] *Hamp v. Bygrave* [1983] E.G.D. 1000.
[96] *D'Eyncourt v. Gregory* (1866) L.R. 3 Eq. 382 at 396 *per* Lord Romilly M.R.
[97] *Leigh v. Taylor* [1902] A.C. 157 at 161 *per* Earl of Halsbury L.C.
[98] [1902] A.C. 157. See also *Re Falbe* [1901] 1 Ch. 523.   [99] (1976) 241 E.G. 911.
[100] Ibid. at 913.
[101] In contrast, some Chinese prints which were stuck to the wall and could not be removed without ripping off the wallpaper were conceded to be fixtures.
[102] (1997) 73 P. & C.R. D1. See M. Haley [1998] Conv. 137.

kitchen appliances, and bathroom items such as towel rails, lavatory roll holders, and soap dishes.

Quoting extensively from *Berkley v. Poulett*, Roch L.J. giving the leading judgment, approached the problems by asking, in essence, whether the purpose of the attachment was to allow the chattel to be enjoyed as a chattel or was designed to improve the building. On this basis, items such as fitted carpets,[103] which can easily be removed, and curtains, were seen as chattels. Conversely, the various items of bathroom furniture, compendiously described as ironmongery, were regarded as fixtures, as their purpose was to improve the bathroom as a bathroom and, indeed, make it usable as such. Other items came into a greyer area.

With regard to kitchen equipment, gas fires, and lighting, much depended upon how they were fitted. For example, an oven can be free-standing and attached to the building by either an electricity cable or gas pipe, or it can form an integrated part of the kitchen, as is the case where it is a fitted unit. If the former is the case, the item will remain a chattel; if the latter, which will require considerable damage to the fabric of the kitchen to secure its removal, it will be regarded as a fixture. An essentially similar test is applied to items such as fires and lights. If the item in question is integrated into the structure of the building, so that its removal will occasion difficulty, then the item would, *prima facie*, be a fixture.[104]

What the cases show is that, where possible, it is highly desirable to stipulate in a contract of sale which items are to be included and which are to be excluded from the sale.

The removal of fixtures

The effect of a chattel becoming a fixture is that, if the person who attaches the item to the property has only a limited interest in that property, which will be the case if that person has only a lease, or is entitled to that property only for his lifetime, that person being termed a tenant for life or life tenant, then they will lose the ownership of that item. Either the landlord or the person entitled to the land after the death of the tenant for life will acquire the item after the termination of the prior interest. This may not, however, be universally desirable in that the rule may provide a disincentive for certain limited owners of property to use the land to its best effect. This is particularly the case with regard to tenancies when, in order to pursue a business, a tenant may wish to install equipment or other items which would ordinarily become fixtures. If these passed to the landlord on the termination of the lease, a tenant may be disinclined to do this. To avoid this difficulty certain limited owners have the right to remove certain fixtures.

Tenant's fixtures

As a general rule, if a tenant attaches items to the property which is being leased in such a way that they become fixtures, then they will become part of the land and so

---

[103] *Young v. Dalgety plc* [1987] 1 E.G.L.R., which accepted fitted carpets as being fixtures, was disapproved.
[104] See also *Hamp v. Bygrave* [1983] E.G.D. 1000, where patio lights were conceded to be fixtures.

the landlord will be entitled to them at the end of the lease. To avoid this consequence, certain items are designated as 'tenant's fixtures', which the tenant is entitled to remove during the subsistence of the lease. They can also be removed at the end of the lease and, indeed, thereafter, if the tenant remains in possession of the property under statute.[105] Where the tenancy is terminated without giving the tenant a reasonable time to remove the fixtures, then that time is afforded to him to effect their removal.[106] Any damage done by the tenant in either installing or removing the fixtures must be made good.[107] If the tenant does not exercise his right to remove such fixtures, then the items will be regarded as belonging to the landlord.

Tenant's fixtures are divided into three types: trade fixtures, ornamental fixtures, and agricultural fixtures.

Trade fixtures

There is a tendency when considering what amounts to a tenant's fixture to run together the separate questions of whether the particular item is a fixture at all and whether or not it can be removed. While this is understandable when the issue is as to whether the landlord or the tenant is entitled to a particular item, it is not without its difficulties. First, it can lead to subsequent confusion, outside the context of landlord and tenant, as to the status of a particular item.[108] Secondly, it can be important from a tax point of view to determine who owns a particular item at a given time,[109] and, thirdly, the issue may be relevant in the context of rent reviews. Rent review clauses are common in commercial leases. They are included in long leases, so that the rent which was originally agreed to be payable can be adjusted, in order to reflect the prevailing market conditions. If specific mention is made in a rent review clause to fixtures,[110] then the task of determining what are actually fixtures is obviously important.

It has long been accepted that items attached to the land in order that the tenant can carry out his trade can be removed and so, it has been held, the fittings of a public house can be removed by the tenant.[111] Other examples of trade fixtures are vats, steam engines, and boilers and other articles of this type.[112]

Ornamental fixtures

An article which can be removed whole, without substantial damage to the building, has traditionally been regarded as an ornamental fixture, which the tenant can

---

[105] See *Poster v. Slough Estates Ltd* [1969] 1 Ch. 495; *New Zealand Government Property Corporation v. H. M. & S. Ltd* [1982] Q.B. 1145.

[106] *Smith v. City Petroleum Co. Ltd* [1940] 1 All E.R. 260.

[107] *Mancetter Developments Ltd v. Garmanson Ltd* [1986] Q.B. 1212.

[108] See the discussion of *Webb v. Frank Bevis Ltd* [1940] 1 All E.R. 247 in *Elitestone Ltd v. Morris* [1997] 1 W.L.R. 687 at 691 *per* Lord Lloyd of Berwick.

[109] See *Melluish v. B.M.I. (No. 3) Ltd* [1996] A.C. 454.

[110] See, e.g., *National Grid Co. plc v. M25 Group Ltd* [1999] 1 E.G.L.R. 65. *Prima facie* a rent review should not take account of the value of tenant's fixtures: *Young v. Dalgety plc* [1987] 1 E.G.L.R. 116.

[111] *Elliott v. Bishop* (1854) 10 Exch. 496.

[112] See Harpum, Bridge, and Dixon, *Megarry and Wade's Law of Real Property* (7th edn) (London: Sweet & Maxwell, 2008), 1072–1073.

remove.[113] In view of the modern approach to fixtures, which emphasizes the purpose of annexation, it is likely that this would not, today, be regarded as a proper exception, the real question being whether the item is a fixture at all.

Agricultural fixtures

The position of a farm tenant is governed by section 8 of the Agricultural Tenancies Act 1995, a provision which gave greater rights for tenants to remove fixtures than had previously been the case.[114] Under the section, the tenant can, subject to certain exceptions, remove any fixture (of whatever description), affixed, whether for the purposes of agriculture or not, to the holding under a business farm tenancy, and any building erected by him on the holding.

This right may be exercised at any time during the subsistence of the tenancy, or at any time after its termination, provided that he remains in possession as a tenant. Unlike the position with other tenancies, the fixtures remain the property of the tenant while he continues to have the right to remove it. When removing the fixture, he must not cause avoidable damage and, in any event, must make good any damage caused by the removal of the fixture.[115]

Life tenants

A person who has a life interest in property—a life tenant—is in much the same position as a tenant under a lease, save that the provisions of the Agricultural Tenancies Act 1995 will not apply.

INCORPOREAL HEREDITAMENTS

The previous discussion has related, with the possible exception of airspace, to tangible property. The definition of land extends also to intangible rights, known as incorporeal hereditaments. This, in essence, refers to rights over another person's land. A good example of such a right is an easement, an example of which is the right to cross a neighbour's land. Such a right is regarded as being land, so that if the owner of the land with the right to cross his neighbour's property conveys his land to another person, that person, termed the successor in title, will acquire, together with that land, the right to cross the neighbour's land.[116] A separate issue which can then arise is to consider the circumstances where a person who acquires the land over which the right is enjoyed must also give effect to that right. This issue is considered elsewhere in the book.

---

[113] *Martin v. Roe* (1857) 7 E. & B. 237.   [114] Cf. Agricultural Holdings Act 1986, s. 10.
[115] Agricultural Tenancies Act 1995, s. 8(3), (4).   [116] Law of Property Act 1925, s. 62(1).

2

Tenure and Estates

When people describe their relationship with property, it is common to speak of ownership of the item in question. With regard to land, although such usage is normal, technically it is inaccurate. This is because of the doctrines of tenure and estates. The former notion is now, essentially, of historical interest and of little contemporary significance; the latter concept remains, however, a theoretical pillar of Land Law.

TENURE

In the early eleventh century, there existed a rudimentary system of strip farming in England. After the Norman invasion in 1066, a rigorous feudal structure was imposed upon the country. Central to it was the notion that all the land belonged to the Crown. The king then proceeded to grant tracts of land to his principal supporters, who held the land from the Crown. In return for this grant, they provided various services.[1]

The people to whom land was granted directly by the king were termed tenants in chief.[2] They, in turn, granted part of the land to someone else, again in return for feudal services. This process could then be continued to create further holdings, a process known as subinfeudation. This process led to the formation of a feudal pyramid or ladder, which is illustrated in Figure 1:

Fig. 1 The feudal pyramid or ladder

---

[1] See, generally, Simpson, *An Introduction to the History of Land Law* (Oxford: Oxford University Press, 1961), Chapter 1. [2] These people were the subject of the Domesday Book.

The person at the bottom of the ladder was termed the tenant in demesne and those between that person and the tenant in chief were termed mesne[3] lords. Central to the system was that the land was enjoyed in return for services. A person held land from another, this being the origin of the term 'tenure', which derives from the Latin *tenere*, to hold. These terms on which the land was held varied both in nature and in prestige. The types of tenure were divided into free and unfree tenures.

Free tenures

Free tenures were divided into tenures of chivalry, spiritual tenures, and socage.

Chivalry

This form of tenure was divided into two main types: grand sergeanty and knight's service. The former involved the tenant performing personal tasks for the king and were, in the main, regarded as being highly honourable.[4] Knight service was, as the name suggests, the provision of armed knights for a period of a year.

Spiritual tenancies

This, again, as the name implies, was the holding of lands in return for the performance of divine services for the grantor.[5]

Socage

This was a form of tenure which, in essence, did not fall into any of the other categories and consisted principally of the provision of agricultural services, but could also involve non-personal services for the king. Over time, it became the most common form of tenure.

Unfree tenures

The essence of an unfree tenure was that the services of the tenant were not known from day to day; the tenant had to perform such tasks as he was instructed to do. Originally, this was known as villein tenure, but this form of landholding gradually died out to be superseded by copyhold, a form of landholding which did not finally disappear entirely until 1925.[6]

---

[3] Pronounced 'mean'.

[4] For amusing and outlandish forms of tenure, some of which were certainly not honourable, see Megarry, *Miscellany-at-Law* (London: Stevens & Sons Ltd, 1955), 154–157. Services of a non-personal kind were referred to as petty sergeanty.

[5] This form of service was subdivided into divine service and frankelmoign. See Harpum, *Megarry and Wade's Law of Real Property* (6th edn) (London: Sweet & Maxwell, 2000), 21–22, a fuller account than is contained in the 7th edn.

[6] Law of Property Act 1925, s. 202. For details of these and other forms of miscellaneous tenures, see Harpum, Megarry, and Wade, op. cit., 22–28.

INCIDENTS OF TENURE

The feudal system carried with it a number of consequences which helped shape modern law. In addition to the services which had to be performed in return for the grant of land,[7] the superior lord was also entitled to a number of benefits upon the death of the tenant. As shall be seen, it was a desire to avoid such death duties that was a powerful spur to the creation of the trust.[8] A further feature of the system was the doctrine of escheat, whereby land reverted to the superior lord. This occurred originally on the commission of an offence by the tenant,[9] and also when the tenant died without heirs; this latter form of the doctrine still has the capacity to emerge occasionally in respect of a person dying without heirs prior to 1925,[10] or when the liquidator of a company disclaims the freehold, pursuant to section 178 of the Insolvency Act 1986.[11]

THE DISMANTLING OF TENURE

The feudal system of landholding had a number of disadvantages, a notable one being its cumbersome nature. To collect undelivered incidents, which increasingly became the most important aspect of the feudal system, an action had to be brought against the person in possession of the land. That person then had a remedy against his lord. As the rungs grew in the feudal ladder, the system became increasingly unwieldy, with the result that further subinfeudation became increasingly unpopular and led to the enactment of the statute, *Quia Emptores* 1290. This provided for the substitution of tenants rather than the creation of a further rung in the feudal ladder. The statute effectively put an end to any further process of subinfeudation.

This statute, together with the increased commutation of feudal services by the payment of money, such payments being termed quit rents, led to the withering away of the rungs in the ladder. Over time, the quit rents ceased to be worth collecting, and therefore lapsed. Coupled with the conversion of all tenures, except frankelmoign and copyhold (respectively, a form of spiritual tenure and a form of tenure peculiar to certain manors), into free and common socage by the Tenures Abolition Act 1660, the end of the feudal pyramids became inevitable, so that, today, a person who owns a house is,

---

[7] Some of which are still referred to in current legislation. See, e.g., Land Registration Act 1925, s. 70(1)(a); Land Registration Act 2002, Scheds 1 and 3.

[8] See Chapter 3.

[9] For the erosion of this, see Corruption of Blood Act 1814; Forfeiture Act 1870.

[10] See *Re Lowe's Will Trusts* [1973] 1 W.L.R. 882 in which, 'by a happy chance the topic has arisen from the past in connection with premises known as The Phoenix Inn'. Ibid. at 884 *per* Russell L.J. See also *Re Strathblaine Estates Ltd* [1948] Ch. 228. See now Administration of Estates Act 1925, s. 4; Land Registration Act 2002, s. 82.

[11] *Semlla Properties Ltd v. Gesso Properties (BVI) Ltd* [1995] B.C.C. 793, a decision containing a thorough review of escheat.

in fact, a tenant in chief holding from the Crown. It is readily assumed that if a person died without heirs, he was not holding the land from another lord and so the land will pass to the Crown.[12]

One, perhaps surprising, paradox concerns leasehold property. The feudal system of landholding had, as an important element of it, the identification of one's status in society: that status being coloured to a large extent by where one was in the feudal pyramid and the nature of the services that the tenant was required to provide. The lease, whereby the land was used for exclusively commercial purposes, was outside this system with the consequence that a lease was not originally regarded as being real property at all.[13] Therefore, the statute *Quia Emptores* did not apply to leasehold property and so did not prevent a different process of subinfeudation, where sub-leases are created. So, a person who has a ninety-nine-year lease can carve out of that interest a lesser interest, say, of fifty years, the result being described diagrammatically in Figure 2:

Landlord → Tenant 99 Years
↓
Sub-tenant 50 years

Fig. 2 Lease and sub-lease

The tenant occupies a position akin to that of a feudal mesne lord; he holds as tenant from the head landlord but is, himself, the landlord of the sub-tenant.

With regard to holdings within the feudal system, the rungs between the person in possession of the land and the Crown withered away and it is now assumed that an owner of land holds directly from the Crown as tenant in chief but without the provision of any services in respect of that holding. To that extent, the interest of the Crown is vestigial, the land reverting to the Crown by escheat on the termination of the holding. The effect of the statute *Quia Emptores* is that, when a house is sold, the purchaser replaces the vendor as the tenant in chief, holding the land directly from the Crown.

ESTATES

The doctrine of tenure is now almost entirely of historical interest. The main reasons for saying anything about it today are, first, to point to the different importance attached to one's relationship with land. While it was, of course, a source of wealth, it was also indicative of one's status in society. Its other principal value, however, is to allow one to become accustomed to the idea that land ownership is not an absolute thing. It remains theoretically true to say that all land is held from the Crown. The

---

[12] See *Re Lowe's Will Trusts* [1973] 1 W.L.R. 882.   [13] See Leases, p. 6.

idea that one does not actually own the thing itself but rather has an interest in it, is also what underlies the theoretical basis of landholding in this country: the estate, the development of which in part at least, it has been said,[14] was forced upon the common lawyers by the theoretical difficulties caused by the doctrine of tenure. An estate is an abstract entity which defines the rights that the owner of an estate has in relation to the land in question.

THE NATURE OF AN ESTATE

It is common to talk of a person owning an item of property. The use of such a term is a form of shorthand; it is a means of describing the rights which a person has over a particular item. If one speaks of ownership of a car, then one can readily appreciate the rights which one has over it. The owner can drive it, sell it, lend it to others, and maintain an action against any person who damages it, or otherwise infringes his ownership rights. There are, of course, restrictions on what the owner of a car can do with it. Such restrictions are not so much a matter of private ownership; rather they are matters imposed by the state or by the general law. So, for example, a car must be taxed and insured; the speed limits must be observed; one should not drive having consumed more than a specified amount of alcohol; and, in driving the car, one must take reasonable care not to injure other people or other people's property.

Similar observations can be made about land ownership. The 'owner' of land can exercise a wide variety of rights over it, the range of these rights, owing to the physical nature of the property in question being, in practical terms, rather wider than those enjoyed by a car owner. For example, although car leasing arrangements certainly exist, such arrangements are far less prevalent than is the case with land. Similarly, a long-term mortgage of land is a commonplace, something not really possible with cars. Again, however, there are restrictions on how one can enjoy the land. In the main, these, again, are matters imposed by the state and the general law. Thus, for example, there are restrictions imposed by planning legislation on how one can develop land or alter its use. In terms of the general law, an owner of land is restricted by the law of nuisance as to how the land is enjoyed; its use must not cause unreasonable interference with the enjoyment of land by a neighbour.

One speaks of ownership of a car yet, in the context of land, one does not, technically, refer to ownership of the land; instead, an abstract entity, known as an estate,[15] was created and one's ownership rights are defined by this abstract entity. The main defining aspect of the estate is its temporal nature; the length of time that the land

---

[14] Simpson, op. cit., 1.
[15] See Lawson, *Introduction to the Law of Property* (Oxford: Oxford University Press, 1958), 67.

would be enjoyed.[16] A natural question is why this occurred; what is the point of this abstract entity?

First, the doctrine of estates seems to be a logical consequence of tenure. As the theory underpinning English Land Law is that all land is owned by the Crown and that people held the land from the Crown,[17] originally, in return for the performance of services, it is difficult to say that the tenants actually owned the land itself; rather, they held an interest, or estate in the land. The second reason is more practical. This is that certain incidents of ownership can be divided between different people at different times. The doctrine of estates facilitates this process.

FREEHOLD ESTATES

Traditionally, estates are defined in terms of their duration. A freehold estate is one whose actual duration cannot be known, with certainty, at the outset. One knows its theoretical duration but cannot know, in advance, when the event will occur which will cause the estate to end. Originally, at common law, there were two freehold estates: the fee simple and the life estate. To these estates, a third, the fee tail, was later added by statute.

The fee simple

The word 'fee', in the context of estates, means that it is inheritable. The word 'simple' indicates that the right to inherit the property is unrestricted. This means that, if a person with a fee simple estate dies intestate, the land can be inherited by any heir. This includes lineal heirs such as sons, daughters, and grandchildren, as well as collateral heirs, such as cousins, nephews, and nieces.

Because the fee simple could pass to any heir, however remote, it is highly unlikely that it would ever end. In consequence, it is the largest estate that it is possible to own and, in reality, is akin to outright ownership of the land. As such, the owner of the fee simple is, in general, unrestricted as to what he can do with the land. Such restrictions as there are derive in the main from the general law relating to planning[18] and nuisance.

---

[16] See P. Birks in Bright and Dewar, *Land Law, Themes and Perspectives* (Oxford: Oxford University Press, 1998), 462–467.

[17] To improve the accuracy of the register of title, the Queen may now grant an estate to herself: Land Registration Act 2002, s. 79. See Crown land, p. 117.

[18] Such public control of land which restricts the rights of owners will, in the future, have to be considered in the context of the European Convention on Human Rights, now incorporated into English law by the Human Rights Act 1998. See J. Howell [1999] Conv. 287; K. Gray in Tee, *Land Law: Issues, Debates, Policy* (Cullompton: Willan Publishing, 2002), Chapter 7.

Some restrictions on the enjoyment of the land can be caused by the creation of third party rights over it. For example, the owner of a fee simple in land has the right to sue people who trespass on that land. If, however, he has granted a neighbour a right of way over the land, then clearly, he cannot bring an action in trespass against the person who exercises that right. To that extent, he has modified one of the rights of the fee simple owner, which is to restrain all other people from coming on to the land,[19] because he has given his neighbour the right to cross the land in accordance with the right. Similarly, the owner of the fee simple may covenant with a neighbour that the property will only be used as a private residence. The effect of this is that the right, which is normally an incident of ownership of the fee simple, to use the land for whatever purpose one likes, has, to an extent, been lost. On the other side of the same coin, the neighbour, as part of his ownership of land, has acquired a right over the affected land; in the first instance a right to cross another person's land and, in the second, the right to restrain his neighbour's use of that land.[20] One can envisage an estate as a metaphorical receptacle, the ownership of which carries various rights over the land in question. Various rights can, however, be removed from that receptacle and given to holders of other estates.

The position of heirs

The fee simple is defined in terms of its potential duration. In theory, it is likely never to end as it can be passed to any heir of the owner of it. This is not to say that the potential heirs have any rights in the property while the owner of the fee simple is alive. They merely have a hope[21] of succeeding to the property. As such, they have no right to control how the holder of the fee simple uses the land. This point is reflected in the difference between words of purchase (purchase here not being used in its normal meaning of buying but meaning, instead, taking hold of) and words of limitation.

Traditionally, the way in which a fee simple was created was to grant the land 'to A and his heirs'. This gave no estate to A's heirs; rather it defined the estate that A has. The first part of the phrase is regarded as words of purchase, the words which grant the estate to A; the latter part are words of limitation—they define the estate that A has.

In the past, a good deal of technicality hinged upon the correct wording being used and a failure to do so resulted in lesser estates than a fee simple being created.[22] Happily, these difficulties are a thing of the past because section 60 of the Law of Property Act 1925 provides that a conveyance of freehold land to any person without words of limitation, or any equivalent expression, shall pass to the grantee the fee simple or other the whole interest which the grantor had power to convey in such land, unless a contrary intention appears in the conveyance. This means simply that, whatever interest the grantor has, a conveyance will, unless there are words to the contrary

[19] The right to exclude other people from interfering with the subject matter is an essential element of property: see Penner, op. cit., Chapter 4.
[20] For the substantive law of easements and covenants, see Chapters 13 and 14.
[21] Sometimes referred to by its Latin form as a *spes*.
[22] See Megarry and Wade, op. cit., 49–50 and App. 2.

in that conveyance, operate to transfer that interest. The distinction between words of purchase and words of limitation does retain some importance, however, in that, technically, a person who is granted land by the act of another party is a purchaser. This, contrary to common parlance, does not mean that the grantee has necessarily given value for the transfer. To signify that value or consideration has been given for the transfer, the correct expression is 'sold and conveyed'.

A second point concerning the position of heirs with regard to the fee simple estate concerns the situation where that estate is transferred. Logically, if A holds a fee simple in land and transfers it to B then the duration of the estate should be determined by the continued existence of A's heirs rather than those of B. Presumably, for practical reasons, this position was abandoned by 1306,[23] so that in the example given above, the measuring aspect of the estate becomes B's heirs and not those of A.

Qualified fees simple

The fee simple outlined above is not qualified, or cut down in any way. It is therefore referred to as a fee simple absolute. It is possible, however, for the fee simple to be cut down. As an example of this, land can be granted to a person in fee simple or until he becomes a solicitor. Such a grant may, in fact, be absolute because the determining, or terminating, event may never happen. If the person does become a solicitor, however, his interest will terminate and the land will pass to someone else. That person has a contingent interest in the land; it is contingent upon that determining event actually occurring. Because the original estate which was granted is liable to be terminated for a reason other than the death without heirs of the holder of it, it is not a fee simple absolute but is a qualified fee simple.

In modern times, it is quite rare for such an interest to be created with respect to land. More commonly, such interests are created in respect of money, where a person is given a life interest in money determinable upon that person becoming bankrupt or suffering any act or thing which causes him to cease to be entitled to the income, such interests being known as protective trusts.[24]

A further example of a contingent interest would be where a testator leaves land in his will 'to the first of my children to become a barrister'. When the testator dies, he may have a number of children, none of whom, as yet, have qualified to be a barrister. As such, none of them are entitled to the land; they merely have a hope of one day satisfying the condition inherent in the will and taking the land. Until that event occurs, some other person is entitled to the land. That person would be either the person identified in the will or, if there is no such person, whoever is entitled, on intestacy, to the deceased person's property. That person's interest in the property is also determinable,

---

[23] See Harpum, Bridge, and Dixon, *Megarry and Wade's Law of Real Property* (7th edn) (London: Sweet & Maxwell, 2008), 38.

[24] See Trustee Act 1925, s. 33. For the concept of the trust, see Chapter 3.

in that as soon as one of the testator's children qualified as a barrister, that person would become entitled to the land and would acquire a fee simple absolute.

A problem with transactions of this nature, particularly when the contingencies in question are more complicated than the example just referred to, is that one might have to wait a considerable period of time to see whether or not the contingency has occurred and the person entitled to the land upon the event occurring has the estate vested in him. To circumvent this problem, a complex body of law, which is a combination of common law and statute,[25] developed to fix a time limit by which the contingency must occur. The details of these rules are outside the scope of this book.[26] The Law Commission recommended a legislative simplification of this highly complex body of law[27] and, in respect of instruments taking effect after the Perpetuities and Accumulations Act 2009 came into force, a more straightforward perpetuity period of 125 years has been introduced.[28]

The life estate

One of the more important rights that the owner of a fee simple has is the right, physically, to possess the land. One of the principal flexibilities of the doctrine of the estate is that particular rights can be separated out from the bundle of rights that the fee simple owner has and become, themselves, the subject of ownership. The right to possess the land is one of the more important rights which a landowner has. This right can be separated from the bundle of rights and become, itself, the subject matter of ownership. Thus, A can be given a life estate in land, remainder to B in fee simple. This means that, for the duration of A's life, it is A who has the right to possess and enjoy the land.

The duration of the life estate is self-explanatory; it continues for as long as A, who is termed the life tenant or tenant for life, continues to live. Various consequences flow from the existence of this more limited estate. First, the principal right that the tenant for life enjoys is the right, physically, to possess and enjoy the land in his lifetime. Upon his death, however, that right will pass to B. Unlike the position considered earlier, where land is settled to the first of a person's sons to become a barrister, where that qualifying event is not certain to happen, it is inevitable that A, at some time, will die and that B or his heirs will become entitled to the property. B does not, therefore, have a contingent interest in the property. The only element of futurity about B's interest in the land is his right, physically, to possess it. To distinguish his position from that of the holder of a contingent interest in land, B's estate is said to be vested in interest. Because, unlike the holder of a contingent interest, B's right to possess the land at some time in the future is certain, his estate is said to be vested in interest, and is termed a

---

[25] Perpetuities and Accumulations Act 1964.

[26] For details of the rules, see Megarry and Wade, op. cit., 238–311; Maudsley, *The Modern Law of Perpetuities* (London: Butterworths, 1979).

[27] (1998) Law Com. No. 251. See P. Sparkes [1995] Conv. 212; (1998) 12 Trust Law International 148.

[28] Perpetuities and Accumulations Act 2009, ss 5, 15.

fee simple in remainder. A, as the person entitled to possess the property during his lifetime, is said to have an interest in possession. When A dies, the prior estate comes to an end and B's estate is now said to fall into possession. His fee simple is no longer subject to any qualification and becomes absolute.

A second element of the life estate is that, unlike the position with the fee simple, the determining event of A's estate is quite simple to identify. Whereas, if land is granted to X in fee simple, it will not be practical to consider when all X's heirs have died, so that, if X transfers his fee simple to Y, the duration of Y's estate is determined by the continued duration of Y's heirs and not X's, this is not the case with the life estate. It is easy to determine when the life tenant dies so that if A transfers his life estate to C, the rights that C obtains are determined by the longevity of A, not C. What C has acquired is termed an estate *pur autre vie*: an estate for the life of another.

A final point to make about the nature of the life estate is that, because A's right to enjoy the land is limited to his lifetime, his rights over that land are correspondingly limited. As it is certain that B will be entitled to the land upon A's death, B has legitimate concerns as to how A uses the property during his lifetime. To protect B's interest, the doctrine of waste was developed.

Waste

Technically, what is meant by waste is a change in the use of land. Such a change can amount to an improvement in the land, known as ameliorating waste, or it can cause the property to deteriorate. A life tenant is not liable for ameliorating waste.[29] Neither is he liable, unless the contrary is specifically stated,[30] for what is termed permissive waste. What is meant by permissive waste is the natural deterioration of the property caused, for example, by the failure to repair buildings or clean out ditches.[31] He is, however, liable for voluntary waste, which is, as the name suggests, an act performed by the life tenant, such as felling timber, which reduces the value of the property.[32]

It was not uncommon, however, when creating a life estate, to stipulate that the life tenant was not impeachable; that is, liable for waste. Such a clause did not, however, give the life tenant *carte blanche* to enjoy the property. The body of law known as equity, which developed to modify the common law,[33] would intervene to make liable a life tenant who was unimpeachable for waste if what was done amounted to devastation of the property. An example of equitable waste occurred in *Vane v. Lord Barnard*,[34] where the life tenant was held liable for stripping a house of lead, iron, and glass, the value of which was the then massive sum of £3,000.

---

[29] *Doherty v. Allman* (1879) 3 App. Cas. 709.   [30] *Re Cartwright* (1899) 41 Ch.D. 532.

[31] *Sticklehorne v. Hatchman* (1586) Owen 43; *Powys v. Blagrave* (1854) 4 De G.M. & G. 448.

[32] See *Honywood v. Honywood* (1874) L.R. 18 Eq. 306, a decision which contains an interesting account as to which trees constitute timber, at 309–311 *per* Sir George Jessel M.R. See also *Pardoe v. Pardoe* (1900) 82 L.T. 549.

[33] For the development of equity, see Chapter 3.   [34] (1716) 2 Vern. 738.

The fee tail

The only freehold estates which existed from the outset were the fee simple and the life estate. Neither of these estates permitted the realization of what was for some a strongly held aspiration, which was to ensure that land remained within the family from generation to generation. To accommodate this desire, the Statute *De Donis Conditionalibus* 1285 was enacted, its effect being to create a new estate, the fee tail. The term 'fee' again indicates that the estate is inheritable; the word 'tail', which derives from the French word '*taille*', indicates that the range of those who may inherit the estate is cut down. In the case of the fee simple, any relation of the holder of the estate can inherit it on his death. In the case of the fee tail, only lineal descendants can inherit. The range of potential descendants could be cut down further, for example by stipulating that only the male heirs can own the property, such a settlement being termed a tail male.

The introduction of the fee tail led to a conflict of aspirations with regard to the use of the land. On the one hand was the aspiration which prompted the enactment of the Statute *De Donis* in the first place, the wish for a legal mechanism to be created which would facilitate the intergenerational transfer of a particular parcel of land within the same family; on the other was the emerging desire for land to be freely alienable. Once a fee tail had been created then, unless it could somehow be upgraded into a fee simple, its transferability was limited. The reason for this was that, *mutatis mutandis* with the situation pertaining to the life estate, if A had a fee tail and transferred it to B, its duration would be measured by the continuation of A's heirs, not by those of B. What B would acquire was termed a base fee.

To enable land to be freed from the constraints imposed by the existence of a fee tail, two devices were developed to enable a fee tail to be enlarged into a fee simple. The process involved is termed barring the entail. The two devices, which were both highly artificial, were known respectively as suffering a recovery or levying a fine. The essential difference between the two actions lay in the identity of the person seeking to bar the entail. If a settlement was created whereby the land was granted to A in fee tail, remainder to B, then A, whose interest was in possession, could suffer a recovery. The effect of this was to enlarge A's interest into a fee simple, thereby defeating any chance B might have of succeeding to the property. If, however, the settlement was to A for life, remainder to B in fee tail, then B is not in possession of the land. Unless B could secure A's co-operation, his only recourse, while A was alive, was to levy a fine and this would create a base fee.[35] Although entirely artificial, these methods of barring entails were popular in that they enabled people to enlarge their estates into a fee simple. To reflect this, the law was put on a statutory footing by the Fines and Recoveries Act 1833, which provided new methods of barring an entail but with the same effects as described above. It was not then possible to bar an entail by will, but this was later made possible by section 176 of the Law of Property Act 1925.

---

[35] For a fuller account, see Harpum, Bridge, and Dixon, *Megarry and Wade*, op. cit., 75–76.

It is the case today that the desire to attempt to secure intergenerational transfers of land by the use of the fee tail is not nearly as strong as was previously the case. Acknowledging this, it is no longer possible to create a new fee tail, and any attempt so to do will instead create a fee simple.[36] Existing fees tail are not affected by this legislation.

Unbarrable entails

The whole process of barring entails was to enable land to become more freely alienable, a fee simple being far more attractive to a potential purchaser than a base fee. The effect of barring the entail, of course, affected later generations, who could no longer rely upon the land descending down the family line. It was not possible for individuals to create an unbarrable entail but certain entails became unbarrable by statute. Instances of this are, first, when, as a reward for services rendered, a fee tail was created by the Crown, in whom the fee simple in remainder was vested and, secondly, when a special Act of Parliament is passed to create an unbarrable entail, as occurred to reward the first Duke of Marlborough.[37] The existence of such an entail can create problems, however, where the heir apparent is unsuitable to manage the estate on the death of his father, and in such situations the court has jurisdiction under section 64 of the Settled Land Act 1925 to vary the settlement.[38]

THE CO-EXISTENCE OF ESTATES

It is fundamental to the understanding of the doctrine of estates to appreciate that they co-exist simultaneously with regard to the same plot of land. The largest estate is the fee simple and it is from this estate that the smaller estates are carved. Some examples can be given.

1. X has a fee simple in land and grants his son, S, a life interest in it. That settlement does not exhaust X's interest in the property, so that, on S's death, the land will revert back to X or if, as is likely, X has already died, to whoever is next entitled in descent from X. Diagrammatically, the position is shown in Figure 3A:

S (Life Interest) → X (Fee Simple in Reversion)

Fig. 3A Life interest

[36] Trusts of Land and Appointment of Trustees Act 1996, Sched. 1, para. 5. But see E. Histed (2000) 116 L.Q.R. 445.

[37] 3 and 4 Anne, c. 6 (1704); 5 Anne, c. 3 (1706).

[38] *Hambro v. Duke of Marlborough* [1994] Ch. 158. See E. Cooke [1994] Conv. 492.

2. X has a fee simple and, by will, leaves the land to his widow, W, for life, thereafter to his son, S, in fee simple. Such a settlement will, on X's death, exhaust his interest in the property, leaving W with a life estate and S with a fee simple in remainder. The term remainder is used, as opposed to reversion, because S's interest is what remains out of the settlement made by X, whereas in the first example, X's interest in the land reverts back to him. Diagrammatically, the position is shown in Figure 3B:

W (Life Interest) → S (Fee Simple in Remainder)

Fig. 3B Life interest and fee simple

3. X has a fee simple and creates a settlement under which he grants the land to his wife, W, for life, thereafter to his son in fee tail. In this situation, X has not exhausted his fee simple; what he has created is a life estate for W, a fee tail in remainder for S and a fee simple in reversion for himself. Diagrammatically, the position is shown in Figure 3C:

W (Life Interest) → S (Fee Tail in Remainder) → X (Fee Simple in Reversion)

Fig. 3C Life interest and fee tail

It is important to realize that in all the examples given the parties each have estates in land, although in the case of some of them their right, physically, to possess that land will not arise until the future. Their interests exist, however, from the date of their creation. So, for instance, in the first example, X has a fee simple in reversion. If, before the death of himself and his son, he makes a will leaving all his property to Y, then, on his death, that reversion will pass to Y, so that on S's death, Y will be entitled to the land.

Again, if one considers example 2, both W and S have interests in the land which they are free to deal with. W could, for example, sell her interest to P. P's right to the land is determined by W's lifetime, it is a tenancy *pur autre vie* and, as such, is unlikely to be an attractive proposition to a purchaser. S, who has the fee simple in remainder, has the more valuable interest, but a purchaser would not be able to possess the land until W dies. Its potential value to a purchaser would depend upon an actuarial assessment of W's life expectancy.

Finally, in example 3 all the parties, X, W, and S, have estates in the property. X's interest, while existing, is of minimal value as the fee tail may not come to an end, thereby causing the fee simple to fall into possession. Moreover, after W's death, it would always be possible for S, or one of his successors, to bar the entail which would convert the fee tail into a fee simple and put an end to X's reversionary interest.

A final point to make in the present context is that, whenever there exists a succession of interests, the finishing point is always the fee simple. The reason for this is, simply, because it is the largest estate out of which all other estates are carved. So, in example 3, X has a fee simple in reversion because, having initially had vested in him a fee simple in possession, he has failed to dispose entirely of his interest in the property. In the second example, on the other hand, he has divested himself entirely of his interest in the land. A succession of estates will, therefore, always end with a fee simple, which will either be in reversion or in remainder.

POSSESSION

The foregoing discussion of estates has tended to presuppose that the person creating the various estates in land was, in fact, entitled to do so. For various reasons, however, this might not be the case. English law has never embraced the concept of absolute ownership of land. The closest it has come to doing so is when a person is registered as the proprietor of land with an absolute title. Even then, however, as will be seen, that person's title is not indefeasible.[39] Where title to the land is unregistered, this is even more the case. All that a person can do is to demonstrate that he has the better right to possess the land than anyone else. To do this, he must show a convincing documentary title to the property, which will establish how, through various transactions in the past, the land came to be vested in him. Even such a process cannot, however, prove conclusively that no better title to the land exists. This proposition was explained engagingly in the following terms:

'To make better rights impossible the proof would have to start with the grant to Adam and Eve, but even then this was save and except the Garden of Eden, and one is not even sure if they took as joint tenants or tenants in common...'[40]

English law has traditionally adopted a pragmatic approach to ownership rights with regard to land, although that tradition is changing with the spread of registration of title. The traditional approach was to afford particular importance to the issue of who was in possession of it. The importance of possession was reflected in the medieval doctrine of seisin, so that the person who was in peaceful possession of the land was said to be seised of it. This was particularly important during the feudal period, because the various feudal incidents were levelled against the person who had seisin.[41]

This element of seisin is no longer of any consequence, but the importance of possession of the land remains, in that it is assumed that the person in physical possession

---

[39] See Chapter 5.

[40] Farrand, *Contract and Conveyance* (4th edn) (London: Oyez Longman, 1983), 85. For the distinction between joint tenants and tenants in common, see Chapter 10.

[41] See Megarry and Wade, op. cit., 45–47.

of the land is rightfully there. Such a person can bring an action against anyone who interferes with his enjoyment of the land, except someone who can show a better right to possess it. In that sense, title to land is relative.[42] If A sues B for trespass, it is no defence to argue that A is not entitled to be in possession of the land. As the person in possession, A has a better right to the land than B. Possession, therefore, raises the presumption that the possessor of the land has a fee simple in that land,[43] unless and until some other person establishes a better right to it.[44] In time, the possession, originally wrongful, may be sufficiently prolonged to prevent anyone else from successfully challenging the possessor's right to the land, although, as will be seen, this principle has been drastically curtailed by the provisions of the Land Registration Act 2002.[45]

LEASEHOLD ESTATES

The other estate known to the law is the leasehold estate. As the law developed in the context of the feudal system, the lease, being a commercial transaction, was not regarded as being an estate at all. It was seen as personal property and the tenant was not regarded as being seised of the property. The owner of the freehold estate, who created the lease—the landlord—was regarded, legally, as being in possession of the land, something which is true to this day, as possession is defined to include the receipt of rents and profits or the right to receive the same.[46] Somewhat misleadingly, however, when compared to the use of the term in the context of freehold estates, the landlord's interest is described as a reversion. Although, legally, he is considered to be in possession of the land, while the lease continues, he cannot possess the land physically.

Despite the historical origins of the lease being outside the law of real property, it has been recognized for a considerable period of time that it is an important form of landholding. To reflect this fact, leases are now classified as chattels real, are invariably regarded as forming part of the law of real property, and will be considered in a subsequent chapter of this book.[47]

---

[42] See *Asher v. Whitlock* (1865) L.R. 1 Q.B. 1 at 5 *per* Cockburn C.J. *Ocean Estates Ltd v. Pinder* [1969] 2 A.C. 19 at 24–25 *per* Lord Diplock. See also *Dutton v. Manchester Airport plc* [200] 1 Q.B. 133.

[43] See E. Cooke (1994) 14 L.S. 1 at 4–5.

[44] See *Alan Wibberley Building Ltd v. Instey* [1999] 1 W.L.R. 894 at 898 *per* Lord Hoffmann.

[45] See Chapter 7.   [46] Law of Property Act 1925, s. 205(1)(xx).   [47] See Chapter 11.

3

Law, Equity and Human Rights

The concepts of tenure and estates are the essential building blocks upon which Land Law is constructed. A further fundamental aspect of the law is the impact of equity, a proper understanding of which is essential to the subject.

THE HISTORICAL BASIS OF EQUITY

As the English Legal System developed, it was based upon local courts and the Royal Courts: the Courts of Common Law. At the outset, the system was bedevilled by excessive formality. As is the case today, an action had to be initiated by the service of a writ. Unlike modern times, however, this, in medieval times, was a highly technical process. Writs were issued through the office of the Chancellor, at the time the King's chief minister and legal adviser. In order to seek different sorts of relief, different writs had to be issued. This caused difficulty, because fitting one's case into a particular legal form of relief was not always straightforward and, if the wrong writ was issued, the action would be discontinued and the litigant would have to recommence the action.[1] Further problems arose if there was not in existence an appropriate writ with which to initiate the particular action. Even if the Chancellor could be persuaded to issue a new writ, and his power to do so was limited,[2] it was not certain that a court would accept its validity.

In addition to the problems caused by the excessive formality, which was an inherent part of the system, difficulties also arose because of the nature of the local courts. The possibility arose that certain powerful opponents could exert undue influence in a particular case, with the possibility that a litigant might have the law on his side, but be unable to vindicate that right in the local court.

---

[1] This degree of formality died out as a result of the Common Law Procedure Act 1852 and the Judicature Acts 1873–1875.

[2] See Harpum, *Megarry and Wade's Law of Real Property* (6th edn) (London: Sweet & Maxwell, 2000), 96.

Petitions to the King

Because of the problems inherent in the legal system, a good deal of dissatisfaction with it developed. As a result of this sense of grievance, disappointed litigants began the process of petitioning the King directly, the King being regarded as the fount of justice. These petitions were heard by the King's Council, of which the Chancellor was a prominent member. In time, these petitions were addressed directly to the Chancellor, who would determine the case.

The office of Chancellor was frequently held by an ecclesiastic.[3] This background was important because cases were frequently decided on the basis of an appeal to conscience and, as an ecclesiastic, often trained in 'canon' or church law, the Chancellor would be familiar with disputes concerning the state of a man's soul, or good conscience. Such an approach to the exercise of jurisdiction was, of course, unpredictable in nature. What is unconscionable to one mind may be acceptable to another. Such a system, which gave a seemingly unfettered discretion to the Chancellor, could not be tolerated as a rational system of law, and so the principles upon which the Chancellor would intervene became established and developed into a coherent body of law, known as Equity.[4] The origin of Equity, as a body of law based upon the notion of conscience, nevertheless continues to have an important effect.

As well as the principles upon which Equity would intervene becoming systematized, so the administration of the jurisdiction was also put on a more organized footing. The task of resolving disputes of this nature was not confined to the Chancellor. Various judges were appointed to exercise the equitable jurisdiction, sitting in what became known as the Court of Chancery. Later, when the court system was reformed, what was the Court of Chancery became a separate division of the High Court and is termed, simply, the Chancery Division.[5]

Equity acts *in personam*

In order to grasp the nature of equitable intervention, it is necessary to appreciate the technique employed, first by the Chancellor, and then by the Court of Chancery. What did not occur was for the Chancellor to disregard the common law. To the contrary, the common law position would be recognized and regard then had to the merits of the particular case to determine if it was conscionable for one party to rely on the legal position. If not, then that party would be ordered, personally, either to do, or refrain from doing, something.

---

[3] Probably the best known of the holders of the Office of Chancellor was Sir, later St, Thomas More, who, perhaps ironically, was not, himself, from an ecclesiastical background.

[4] For the comments of Lord Eldon L.C. on the demise of a general discretionary approach, see *Gee v. Pritchard* (1818) 2 Swans. 402 at 414.

[5] Supreme Court Act 1981, s. 5.

A good example of this occurred in *Penn v. Lord Baltimore*.[6] A dispute arose as to the boundary between Maryland and Pennsylvania and this led to an agreement being arrived at between the plaintiff and defendant. When the plaintiff sought to enforce the agreement, the argument was raised that the court lacked the jurisdiction to determine a boundary dispute in land situated overseas.[7] This was not, however, seen as a major problem. Lord Hardwicke L.C. said: 'The conscience of the party is bound by this agreement and being within the jurisdiction of this court...which acts *in personam*, the court may properly decree it as an agreement.'[8] In other words, because the defendant's conscience was affected by the agreement, he was ordered, personally, to implement it, this order now being known as specific performance.

This case is illustrative of a number of things. First, the nature of the remedy can be seen to be an order directed specifically at an individual: an instance of equity acting on the person. Secondly, it was made clear in the judgment that the reason why equity intervened was because the common law was inadequate to provide a solution; damages, which is a monetary form of compensation, and is the only remedy which the common law could grant, would not have been adequate.[9] Finally, it points to what became a source of tension and conflict within the legal system. The more that the Chancery judges intervened when the common law was perceived to be inadequate, the greater was the irritation of some common law judges; a factor which led to a struggle between judges as to which system was to have supremacy, law or equity.[10]

Conflict between law and equity

This, in truth, was a somewhat arid debate, as, for equity to have any role at all, it must have precedence when common law and equity took a different view of a situation. This proposition is what lay behind Maitland's oft-quoted proposition that equity had come not to destroy the law, but to fulfil it.[11] By this is meant that equity recognizes what the position is but intervenes to modify its effect in the exercise of its jurisdiction. Equity could not operate without the prior existence of the law; its role then became to intervene to complement the law.

As equity developed, it was administered in a different court from the common law courts, thereby leading to prolonged litigation; a case being brought, first, in the common law court and then the action continuing until its final resolution in Chancery. This was clearly inefficient, and to obviate this moves were made to fuse the administration of the two systems,[12] culminating in the Judicature Acts 1873 and 1875.

---

[6] (1750) 1 Ves. Sen. 444. See also *Luxe Holding Ltd v. Midland Resources Ltd* [2010] EWHC 1908 (Ch) at [28]–[46] *per* Roth J.

[7] With regard to this land, that jurisdiction rested with the King in council.

[8] (1750) 1 Ves. Sen. 444 at 447–448.   [9] Ibid. at 446. See *post*, pp. 40–41.

[10] See Hanbury and Martin, *Modern Equity* (18th edn) (London: Sweet & Maxwell, 2009), 12–13.

[11] Maitland's *Equity* (2nd edn) (London: Cambridge University Press, 1936), 19.

[12] See Hanbury and Martin, op. cit., 15–18.

Under the Acts, now superseded by the Supreme Court Act 1981, the separate courts were abolished to be replaced by the Supreme Court of Judicature, consisting of a High Court made up of Divisions, the assignment of the workload being done on the basis of convenience, the determining factor being the subject matter of the dispute. However, whatever the nature of the dispute, any point of law or equity could be determined by any Division. Moreover, it was provided by section 25(11) of the Supreme Court of Judicature Act 1873 that:

'Generally, in all matters not hereinbefore particularly mentioned in which there is any conflict or variance between the rules of equity and the rules of common law with reference to the same matter, the rules of equity shall prevail.'

The effect of this provision, which finally determined the supremacy of equity, is well illustrated in the leading case of *Walsh v. Lonsdale*.[13] The defendant, the landlord, agreed in writing to grant the plaintiff, the tenant, a seven-year lease. It was a term of the lease that the landlord could demand one year's rent in advance. A deed was not executed so that, at law, there was not a seven-year lease. The tenant, nevertheless, took possession and paid rent quarterly in arrears. The landlord then, as the agreement envisaged, demanded payment of a year's rent in advance and, when the tenant refused, he purported to exercise the remedy of distraint, that is the seizing of the tenant's goods to the value of the rent which was owed. The tenant disputed the landlord's right to do this and sued for trespass.

The competing arguments of the two parties rested on the different view taken of the transaction by law and equity. At law, because there was no deed, there could not be a seven-year lease. Because the tenant had gone into possession and paid rent, the law implied that there was a periodic tenancy from year to year, which could be terminated by giving six months' notice to quit.[14] The requirement to pay a year's rent in advance was inconsistent with the tenant's ability to terminate the lease by giving six months' notice to end the lease and, therefore, it was argued that the distress was unlawful. Equity, on the other hand, takes a more relaxed view as to the need for formality and considered that there was a valid seven-year lease. Insofar as law and equity differed as to how the transaction was viewed, equity prevailed. A seven-year equitable lease existed and, consequently, what the landlord had done was lawful. As Sir George Jessel M.R. put it: 'There is only one court and the equity rules prevail in it.'[15]

Although this is, rightly, considered to be a leading case on the effect of the Judicature Acts in fusing the administration of law and equity, it should be appreciated that the result would have been the same prior to the Act: the litigation would simply have been more prolonged. The plaintiff would have brought his case in the common law courts and won. The defendant would then have sought in Chancery an injunction to restrain him from enforcing his judgment and would also have won. The outcome therefore, is

---

[13] (1882) 21 Ch.D. 9. The case is discussed further, see Equitable leases, pp. 425–429.
[14] For this aspect of the case, see Termination of tenancies, pp. 453–454.   [15] (1882) 21 Ch.D. 9 at 14.

that by fusing the administration of the two systems,[16] the case is finally disposed of by one court.

Equitable remedies

A central feature of equitable intervention is the nature of the remedies afforded. Equity acts on the person by issuing an order to do something or to refrain from doing something. The former remedy is most commonly associated with specific performance, whereby one party to a contract is ordered to fulfil the obligations which have been created, but can also be the subject of a mandatory injunction, whereby the defendant is ordered to undo a wrong he has committed, such as building in contravention of a restrictive covenant.[17] The latter remedy is the grant of an injunction. In the event of non-compliance with either order, the defaulting party is in contempt of court and, as a result, is subject to punitive sanctions.

The principal equitable remedies of specific performance and the injunction are integral parts of the equitable process. The availability of either remedy is predicated upon the common law being unable, through the award of damages, to provide an adequate remedy for the wronged party. If, for example, A contracts with a car dealer to buy a mass-produced car and, in breach of contract, the dealer fails to deliver it, A is adequately compensated by an award of damages; he can easily use the monetary award to buy a car of the same type from another source. If, however, the subject matter of the contract is for the purchase of a rare item, such as an original Van Gogh, then damages cannot compensate entirely for the failure to deliver. The buyer wants the actual painting. In recognition of this fact, equity would normally award specific performance of this type of contract and the seller would be ordered to deliver the painting in return for the purchase price.[18] In the context of land, it has long been assumed that damages are not an adequate remedy for the non-performance of a contract of sale and so a contract to create, or transfer, an interest in land is, *prima facie*, liable to be enforced by a decree of specific performance.

Although specific performance is generally available as a remedy for contracts for the sale of land, or the creation of interests in land, the decree is not automatic. Equitable remedies are discretionary, although that discretion is exercised judicially.[19] Factors

---

[16] The much-debated issue as to whether there has been a substantive fusion of law and equity is beyond the scope of this book. See Hanbury and Martin, op. cit., 22–29, where many of the conflicting authorities are considered. For a stimulating discussion of the general role of equity and its relationships with law, see Worthington, *Equity* (2nd edn) (Oxford: Oxford University Press, 2006).

[17] See, e.g., *Wakeham v. Wood* (1982) 43 P. & C.R. 40.

[18] Contrast *Cohen v. Roche* [1927] 1 K.B. 169, where specific performance of a contract to deliver ordinary chairs was refused with *Behnke v. Bede Shipping Co.* [1927] 1 K.B. 649, where specific performance of a contract to sell a ship was ordered, regard being had to the particular value of the ship to the plaintiff.

[19] See *Haywood v. Cope* (1858) 25 Beav. 140 at 141 *per* Sir Samuel Romilly M.R.; *White v. Damon* (1801) 7 Ves. Jun. 31 at 35 *per* Lord Eldon L.C.

may be present which would cause a court to decline to order specific performance. For example, if the completion of a contact to sell land to B would entail the breach of a prior contract to sell that land to A, then specific performance will not be ordered in favour of B.[20] Alternatively, if performance of the contract would require constant supervision by the court,[21] or such an order would cause exceptional hardship,[22] the remedy will also be refused.

The availability of specific performance in the context of contracts for the sale of land is important. This is because equity takes the view that what ought to be done should be regarded as already having been done. This is the basis of the decision in *Walsh v. Lonsdale*[23] where, it will be recalled, it was held that, because there was a contract to grant a seven-year lease, this gave rise, in equity, to a seven-year lease. The basis of this was that equity would have awarded specific performance of this contract. Pending the actual award of the decree, which would, of course, have led to the creation of a legal lease, equity anticipates the making of such an order and considers the lease already to have been created. This doctrine, which is applicable to contracts to create other interests in land,[24] is an important source of the creation of equitable interests in land, that is interests in land whose existence depends upon the rules of equity rather than those of the common law. An essential part of the reasoning process is that for the equitable interest to arise, the remedy of specific performance must be available. Because all equitable remedies are discretionary,[25] a reason may exist why that remedy is not available and, if this is the case, the equitable interest in question will not be created.[26]

THE TRUST

The original basis upon which equity intervened was to enforce obligations of conscience and to redress defects in the common law. What also emerged from the intervention of equity was its most important theoretical and practical development: the trust.

---

[20] See *Warmington v. Miller* [1973] 2 All E.R. 372.

[21] *Co-operative Insurance Society Ltd v. Argyll* [1998] A.C. 1. For a valuable critique of this decision, see A. Tettenborn [1998] Conv. 23.

[22] *Patel v. Ali* [1984] Ch. 283.   [23] (1882) 21 Ch.D. 9.

[24] See *McManus v. Cooke* (1887) 35 Ch.D. 681; *United Bank of Kuwait v. Sahib* [1997] Ch. 107, where there was held not, in fact, to be a contract to create a mortgage.

[25] The court has a jurisdiction, in appropriate cases, to award damages in lieu: Chancery Amendment Act 1858 (Lord Cairns' Act); Supreme Court Act 1981, s. 50. For the award of such damages, see *Shelfer v. City of London Lighting Co.* [1895] 1 Ch. 287; *Jaggard v. Sawyer* [1995] 1 W.L.R. 269. See J.A. Jolowicz [1975] C.L.J. 224; P.H. Pettit [1977] C.L.J. 369, [1978] C.L.J. 51.

[26] See *Bell Street Investments v. Wood* [1970] E.G.D. 812; *Warmington v. Miller* [1973] 2 All E.R. 272. See Specific performance, p. 427.

The use

The precursor of the trust was a device termed the use. From early days, the practice developed of land being conveyed to a person, T, for the use of another person, B. The effect of this at law was quite straightforward. T was the legal owner of the property and the obligation accepted on behalf of B was disregarded by the common law. Equity, however, took a different view of the matter. Because T had accepted the undertaking to hold the land to the use of B, it was considered unconscionable for T to renege on that obligation. His conscience was affected and equity compelled T to comply with the use. In this way, equity ensured that B enjoyed the benefit of the land.

Before considering how the early use developed into the modern trust, it is as well to question why people should have adopted this procedure. If it was intended that B should benefit from the land, the obvious question is why not transfer the land to him directly and forego the somewhat artificial procedure of transferring the land to T to be held to the use of B. There were a number of reasons why this procedure was adopted. Some had a slightly romantic air to them; others were more prosaic.

Reasons for the use

One of the reasons for putting land into use was when the owner of it was going to go abroad to fight in the crusades. In such circumstances, the land was transferred to a nominee to hold the property for the use of the departing knight. A second, rather more meretricious, reason concerned certain people who were in religious orders. Some religious orders had taken vows of poverty and, because of such a vow, the monks could not own land. To circumvent this difficulty, land could be conveyed to a nominee to be held to the use of the monks. Technically, therefore, because the legal title was not vested in the monks, the legal ownership being in the nominee, the vow of poverty had not been broken but they, nevertheless, enjoyed the benefit of the land because equity would enforce the use. The third main reason for employing the use was tax.

Feudal dues

An inherent part of the feudal system was that when land passed by inheritance, various feudal dues became payable to the superior lord. The feudal dues, which may be likened to an early form of inheritance tax, could be quite swingeing in nature. The device of the use was an important weapon in the armoury of those seeking to avoid paying these dues, the object being to avoid land passing by succession.

The scheme adopted was for land to be transferred to a number of people, say, T1, T2, T3, and T4, to be held to the use of B and his heirs. The effect of this was that the legal title to the land would be vested in the name of these four people subject to their obligation, enforceable in equity, to honour the use in favour of B. When B died, because the use was in favour of B and his heirs, the land would now be held for the benefit of that heir. The important point was that, at law, nothing of significance had happened. The legal title remained vested in T1, T2, T3, and T4. Consequently, although the actual benefit of the land had passed, by inheritance, to B's heir, because this had not happened at law, the feudal incidents were not payable.

Of course, T1, T2, T3, and T4 were not immortal. It was unlikely, however, that all of them should die simultaneously, thereby causing the legal title to pass by inheritance. Instead, when one of the legal owners died, the remaining three would retain the legal ownership or title to the land[27] and the person would simply be replaced. So, on the death of T1, the position would be that T2, T3, and T4 would be the legal owners of the land. T5 would then be added to the number of legal owners. By topping up the legal owners in this way, it was ensured that, barring catastrophe, the payment of the feudal dues incident upon death was avoided.

The Statute of Uses 1535

For the leading barons, the use was a very welcome device in that it enabled them to avoid paying feudal incidents to the King. While it was true that their own tenants could utilize the use to avoid similar payments, the use was, nevertheless, highly popular. For the King, however, the use had no advantages. As the King was at the apex of the feudal pyramid, the ultimate lord and tenant of no one, the employment of the use deprived him of valuable resources, while conferring no advantages upon him. In an effort to emasculate the use, Henry VIII forced through Parliament the Statute of Uses 1535.

The effect of the statute was to 'execute' the use. If land was conveyed to T1, T2, T3, and T4 to the use of B and his heirs, then the statute operated to execute the use and cause the legal title to the land to vest in B. So, when B died, the land would pass by inheritance to his heir and feudal dues would now be payable.

The use upon a use

Faced with a potentially lethal attack upon a popular concept, lawyers employed a degree of ingenuity to side-step the statute and to resurrect the use. The method adopted was to employ two uses: the use upon a use. What this amounted to was that if one was trying to ensure that C obtained the benefit of the land, it would be conveyed to A and his heirs to the use of B and his heirs to the use of C and his heirs. It was eventually held that while the statute operated to execute the first use, thereby transferring the legal title to B, it did not operate to execute the second use, with the result that equity recognized the obligation imposed upon B.

The acceptance of this device demonstrated the enthusiasm of lawyers to reintroduce a popular device, because the reasoning employed to achieve this goal is manifestly threadbare. This reasoning was less controversial than might be supposed in that, with the decline in the feudal system, the avoidance of feudal dues was less of

---

[27] This depended upon the land being conveyed to them as joint tenants, a concept which will be fully explained in Chapter 10.

a motivation for the employment of the use than was previously the case. Be that as it may, it enabled the use to continue to be used. In time, however, the second use changed its name and the practice developed of terming the second use a trust. Land was then conveyed to A and his heirs unto the use of B and his heirs on trust for C and his heirs. The Statute of Uses was repealed in 1925[28] and what one does now is simply convey the land to B in fee simple upon trust for C. B is termed the trustee and C the beneficiary.

Formality

To create a trust of personalty, no formality is required. A trust can be created orally. All that is necessary is for a court to be satisfied that the person intended to create a trust.[29] Provided, then, that the subject matter and the objects of the trust are sufficiently certain,[30] a trust will be created. This is not the case with land. Section 53(1)(b) of the Law of Property Act 1925 provides that:

'a declaration of trust respecting any land or interest therein must be manifested and proved by some writing signed by some person who is able to declare such trust or by his will.'

This formal requirement, it should be noted, is evidentiary, so that it is not necessary that the declaration itself should be in writing. More importantly, resulting and constructive trusts are exempt from the requirement that there be written evidence of the trust.[31] These trusts have particular importance in the context of disputes as to ownership of the family home,[32] but are relevant also to some other areas of Land Law. Although the operation of these trusts will be considered in detail later in the book, it is convenient to say something about the nature of these trusts at this stage.

Resulting trusts

The essential nature of the resulting trust is that it arises when the legal title is put into the name of one person but where it is not intended to make an out and out gift to that person.[33] In the context of Land Law, the main relevance of the resulting trust is when land is conveyed into the name of one person but another person has contributed to the purchase price. So, if a house is bought outright for £100,000 and A provides £10,000 and the balance of £90,000 is supplied by B, into whose name the house is conveyed, equity presumes that A did not intend to make B a gift of the £10,000. Despite the lack of writing normally required to create a trust, a resulting trust will arise, whereby A will get an equitable share in the property commensurate with the size of

---

[28] Law of Property Act 1925, Sched. 7.

[29] See, e.g., *Paul v. Constance* [1977] 1 W.L.R. 527; *Rowe v. Prance* [1999] 2 F.L.R. 787. For criticism of the latter decision, see S. Baughen [2000] Conv. 58.

[30] See Hanbury and Martin, op. cit., 101–121.   [31] Law of Property Act 1925, s. 53(2).

[32] See Chapter 9.

[33] See Chambers, *Resulting Trusts* (Oxford: Clarendon Press, 1997), 5. Contrast W. Swadling (2008) 124 L.Q.R. 72 at 85 *et seq.*

the contribution to the purchase price. In this case, B will hold the property on trust for himself and A in the proportion of ninety per cent to ten per cent.[34]

Constructive trusts

The constructive trust is a trust imposed by equity as a response to inequitable conduct on the part of the holder of the legal title to the property.[35] This, it will be appreciated, is a somewhat vague definition which says nothing of when conduct will be regarded as being inequitable. The constructive trust has a wide role to play in the resolution of disputes concerning all types of property. In the context of Land Law, its main role, traditionally, was to prevent one person, C, going back on an undertaking that land will be held for the benefit of another person, D, in circumstances when it would be unconscionable to allow C to rely on the lack of writing which would normally be required to create a trust in D's favour.[36] More recently, however, the House of Lords, in *Stack v. Dowden*,[37] has adopted a rather wider rationale for the imposition of a constructive trust. The ramifications of this will be considered fully in the discussion of ownership of the family home.[38]

Equity follows the Law

It is important to appreciate that, as the trust concept developed, equity never disputed that the trustee was the legal owner of the land. Equity took the view, however, that the trustee was required to use the land for the benefit of the beneficiary. From there it was but a short step, when land is conveyed to T on trust for B, to say that, although T was the legal owner of the land, because the real enjoyment of the land belonged to B, B was regarded as the equitable owner of it. Various consequences flowed from this. T is the legal owner of the property but is required to use that property for B's benefit. To ensure that this was the case, equity imposes various obligations, termed fiduciary obligations, on the trustee as to how that property is used. For example, T cannot use his position as the legal owner of the property for personal gain and, if he does, equity will require him to hold that profit on a constructive trust for the beneficiary because his action is regarded as an abuse of his fiduciary position.[39]

Having accepted the notion of equitable ownership of land, the next question is to determine the nature of that ownership. At law, a person does not actually own the land itself; rather he owns an estate in land, originally either a fee simple, a fee tail, or a life estate. Equity followed the same theoretical framework. So, as the common law enabled land to be settled upon A for life, to B in fee tail, remainder to C in fee simple,

---

[34] See, e.g., *Re Rogers' Question* [1948] 1 All E.R. 328. The role of the resulting trust in the context of the family home has become much diminished. See Chapter 9.

[35] See P. Millett (1995) 9 Trust Law International 35 at 39.

[36] See *Rochefoucauld v. Boustead* [1897] 1 Ch. 196; *Grant v. Edwards* [1986] Ch. 638.

[37] [2007] 2 A.C. 432.   [38] Chapter 9.

[39] See *Boardman v. Phipps* [1967] 2 A.C. 46, which involved a very strict application of this principle. See, generally, *Attorney-General of Hong Kong v. Reid* [1994] 1 A.C. 324.

equity also allowed these interests to be held on trust. The effect of this is that legal estates had their counterparts in equity, so one could have equitable life estates, fees tail, and fees simple. This mirroring of the common law estates is an application of an important principle, applicable to many areas of Land Law, that principle being that Equity follows the Law.

The trust is a legal device which is widely used and embraces all sorts of property and not just land. It nevertheless occupies a pivotal role in Land Law. Although it is commonly the case that a legal owner of land does not hold the land on trust for anyone, this is not necessarily the case. If the legal owner of the property does not hold on trust for anyone else, it is misleading to refer to him as the owner in equity as well as at law because in this situation there is no trust in existence, and consequently no separate equitable title.[40] To emphasise that there is no trust in existence, it is common to refer to this person as being the legal and beneficial owner of the land. While the legal owner may be solely entitled to the land for his own benefit, this is not necessarily the case. He may hold the land on trust for another person altogether,[41] or for himself and another person, a case where there is sole ownership at law but co-ownership in equity.[42] In these cases, the legal owner is not the sole beneficial owner and it is then necessary to locate the equitable ownership of the property.

Normally, if the legal owner, or owners, of the property are also beneficially entitled to that property, it is misleading to talk of them being the equitable owners as, ordinarily, there would not be a trust in existence as there are no outstanding equitable interests. An exception to this occurs in the case of co-ownership at law. In this case a trust of land is imposed by statute, so that if A and B are co-owners at law, they hold the land on trust for themselves in equity.[43] The reason for this derives from the nature of co-ownership. In the case of co-owners of land, the co-owners can be either joint tenants or tenants in common. These concepts will be explained more fully in a later chapter.[44] For present purposes, it is sufficient to say that if a joint tenancy is in existence, the co-owners are regarded as being one legal unit and, as individuals, they own no specific share in the property. If they are tenants in common, they do own separate shares in the property, but those shares are not physically divided. For example, A can own a 60 per cent share of the property and B a 40 per cent share and, when the property is sold, they will divide the proceeds of sale in those proportions. At law, it is only possible for co-owners to hold the property as joint tenants, whereas, in equity, they can be either joint tenants or tenants in common. To recognize this, a trust is always imposed in the case of legal co-ownership, even when the only beneficiaries are the legal co-owners. So, it is quite possible, and indeed common, for A and B, who are joint tenants at law, to hold a house on trust for themselves as joint tenants in equity.

---

[40] See *Westdeutsche Landesbank Girozentrale v. Islington London Borough Council* [1996] A.C. 669 at 706 *per* Lord Browne-Wilkinson.

[41] See, e.g., *Hodgson v. Marks* [1971] Ch. 892.

[42] See, e.g., *Williams & Glyn's Bank Ltd v. Boland* [1981] A.C. 487.

[43] Trusts of Land and Appointment of Trustees Act 1996, s. 5, Sched. 2.   [44] See Chapter 10.

OTHER EQUITABLE INTERESTS

Although the trust is probably equity's greatest creation, the intervention of equity was not limited to that. There were other areas of Land Law, where the common law position was considered to be defective or oppressive and so equity intervened to mitigate the harshness of the law. A notable example is the law of mortgages.[45] As well as modifying the common law, equity also recognized other rights which did not amount to the beneficial entitlement to the land.

The creation of equitable rights

There are a number of ways in which an equitable interest can be created. These can be enumerated here and elaborated hereafter.

1. **Lack of formality**. As a general proposition, in order to create a legal interest in land, a deed must be used.[46] Equity, however, takes a more relaxed view of formalities. An attempt to create a legal interest which fails due to the lack of a deed is, by a fiction, regarded as a contract to create that interest.[47] Provided specific performance was available, then, on the basis that equity looks on that which ought to be done as already being done,[48] an equitable right would be created. For such a view to be taken, however, it is essential that there is in being a contract. For this to be the case, it is necessary that the agreement is in writing and is signed by both parties.[49] If this level of formality is not present, then there will be no contract and, in consequence, an equitable right will not be created in this way,[50] although rights may be acquired through the medium of estoppel.[51]

2. **Possession of an equitable interest**. If a person has only an equitable estate in land, then the only interests he can create over that land are, themselves, equitable. The holder of an equitable estate cannot, as a matter of general principle, create a legal estate or interest.[52]

3. **Time**. As will be seen in Chapter Four, the legislation of 1925 provided that, to exist as a legal interest, the right in question must exist for the equivalent of a fee simple absolute in possession or a term of years. If, for example, a person purports to create a right of way for life, that easement can only be equitable.

---

[45] See Chapter 12.   [46] Law of Property Act 1925, s. 52(1).
[47] *Parker v. Taswell* (1858) 2 De G. & J. 559.   [48] See The trust, p. 41.
[49] Law of Property (Miscellaneous Provisions) Act 1989, s. 2.
[50] *United Bank of Kuwait plc v. Sahib* [1997] Ch. 107. For criticism, see M.P. Thompson [1995] Conv. 465, commenting on the decision at first instance.
[51] See *Halifax Plc v. Curry Popeck (A Firm)* [2008] EWHC1692 (Ch) at [15] *per* Norris J. and Equitable estoppel, pp. 609–644.
[52] *Cook v. The Mortgage Business Plc* [2012] EWCA Civ.17 at [59] *per* Etherton L.J.

4. **Right only recognized in equity**. There are certain recognized property rights which were the creation of equity. A good example of such a right is a restrictive covenant where, for instance, one landowner covenants with his neighbour that he will only use the land as a private residence. Such a covenant is capable of existing as a property right[53] but has only ever been recognized in equity.

THE ENFORCEABILITY OF LEGAL AND EQUITABLE RIGHTS

In the Law of Contract, the doctrine of privity was to the effect that only the parties to a contract could sue or be sued upon it. Nowadays, with regard to who can sue on the contract, the position has been changed considerably by the Contracts (Rights of Third Parties) Act 1999 so as to enable a person who is not a party to the contract, but for whose benefit the contract is made, to bring an action on it. It remains axiomatic, however, that a person who is not a party to a contract cannot be sued upon it.[54] In Land Law, however, this is not the case. If something is recognized as a property right, then parties other than those who are privy to its creation will be affected by it. If a right of way has been created, successive owners of the land affected by that right will have to give effect to it or, as is also said, will take subject to the right or be bound by it. On the other side of the coin, the issue will arise as to the circumstances when a person who acquires land acquires, also, rights over another person's land. Of these two issues, it is the circumstances when a person takes subject to rights which is the most contentious and, in determining this issue, it was always vital to distinguish between legal and equitable rights, although this previously fundamental distinction is less important under the system of registration of titles to land.

LEGAL RIGHTS

If a legal right affects land then any person who acquires that land will be bound by that right. It is immaterial whether or not he had prior notice of that right. A legal right binds the world. This is well illustrated by *Wyld v. Silver*.[55] A property developer bought land and had obtained outline planning permission to build five houses. It then transpired that, under a private Act of Parliament of 1799, the villagers had been given the right to hold an annual fair or wake on the land on the Friday in Whit week, although the last known occasion when this right had been exercised was in 1875. It

---

[53] *Tulk v. Moxhay* (1843) 2 Ph. 773. See Chapter 14.   [54] *Dunlop v. Selfridge* [1915] A.C. 847.
[55] [1963] Ch. 243.

was nevertheless held that an injunction should be granted to restrain the planned building, so as not to interfere with the legal right of the villagers to hold a fair. The fact that the purchaser neither knew, nor should have known, of this right was immaterial. Because it was a legal right, the purchaser, despite enjoying the unqualified sympathy of Russell L.J.,[56] was bound by it.

The case also illustrates a second point. In *Wyld v. Silver*, the builder had acquired outline planning permission to build. Although this is necessary in order for the proposed development to be lawful, alone it is not sufficient. The fact that planning permission has been granted will not override an individual's property right to object to what has been permitted by the local authority.[57]

EQUITABLE RIGHTS

Unlike legal rights, equitable rights are not automatically binding on a successor in title to the land affected. The original basis of equitable intervention was that the conscience of a landowner had been affected by some undertaking which had been entered into. The next question which arose was to determine the circumstances in which the conscience of a successor in title would also be regarded as being affected by the particular obligation. The answer to this came really in a negative form. An equitable interest would be binding upon the whole world, except a bona fide purchaser of a legal estate for value without notice of the equitable interest.

In *Pilcher v. Rawlins*,[58] the legal owner of land, which was already subject to an equitable mortgage, created a legal mortgage and the issue was whether the second mortgagee, who had a legal estate in the land, took subject to the first mortgage, which was an equitable interest in the land. When creating the legal mortgage, the landowner had, by suppressing relevant documents, been able to create the impression that the land was free of any incumbrance; the second mortgagee neither knew of, nor had any means of discovering, the prior equitable mortgage, which was held to be void against him. The position was that 'such a purchaser's plea of a purchase for valuable consideration without notice is an absolute, unqualified plea to the jurisdiction of this court'.[59] To sum up, the essential difference between legal and equitable rights is that legal rights are enforceable against the whole world, whereas equitable rights are enforceable against the whole world, except the bona fide purchaser of the legal estate for value without notice. What must now be considered is what must be established before a person is regarded as being a bona fide purchaser (as the term is usually abbreviated).

---

[56] Ibid. at 268.

[57] See also *Wheeler v. J.J. Saunders Ltd* [1996] Ch. 19; *Turner v. Pryce* [2008] 1 P. & C.R D. 52. See M.P. Thompson [1995] Conv. 239 at 242–244.

[58] (1872) 7 Ch. App. 259.   [59] Ibid. at 268–269 *per* James L.J.

Bona fide

Although it has been said that good faith is an independent part of the definition,[60] no example appears to exist where this seems to play any separate role. All that it appears to do is to emphasize that the purchaser must be without notice of the relevant equitable interest.

Purchaser for value

As was explained in Chapter 2,[61] the term 'purchaser' is a technical term and does not, as it does in common parlance, carry the necessary implication that the transfer was for value. A purchaser is a person who acquires property through the act of the parties and not by operation of law. A person who acquires property under a will is, therefore, a purchaser but someone who succeeds to property on intestacy is not. In neither case, however, has the person given value and will, therefore, be bound by any equitable interests regardless of notice.

Value includes more than money and this can be anything that the common law would regard as being good consideration. As is the case in the law of contract, the consideration need not be adequate, so that a purchase at an undervalue is, nevertheless, for value.[62] In addition to what common law regards as consideration, equity regards an ante-nuptial agreement made in contemplation of marriage to transfer property as being for value. Such agreements must, today, be very rare.

Legal estate

To take free of an equitable interest, the purchase must be of a legal estate. This obviously includes the purchase of a freehold estate, but also includes the purchase of a lease and, most importantly, a mortgage. This is because a mortgage, when it has been created by a charge by deed expressed to be by way of legal mortgage, which is the usual method of creating a legal mortgage, is given the same protection as if the mortgage had been created by a 3,000-year lease[63] and, as a result, is treated as being a purchase of a legal estate.

If the purchaser acquires only an equitable estate, such as would be the case upon the creation of an equitable mortgage,[64] the contest for priority is between two equitable rights. In such a case, the normal rule is that, when the equities are equal, the first in time will prevail.[65] What will cause the equities to be unequal is when the holder of the first equitable interest allows the holder of the legal estate to appear to be

[60] *Midland Bank Trust Co. Ltd v. Green* [1981] A.C. 513 at 528 *per* Lord Wilberforce.
[61] See The position of heirs, p. 28.
[62] *Bassett v. Nosworthy* (1673) Rep. T. Finch 102; *Midland Bank Trust Co. Ltd v. Green* [1981] A.C. 513.
[63] Law of Property Act 1925, s. 87(1)(a). See Legal mortgages, pp. 468–469.
[64] See *McCarthy & Stone Ltd v. Julian S. Hodge & Co. Ltd* [1971] 1 W.L.R. 1547 at 1555.
[65] Ibid. at 1554 *per* Foster J. See also *Flinn v. Pountain* (1889) 60 L.T. 484 at 486 *per* North J.; *Sainsbury's Supermarkets Ltd v. Olympia Homes Ltd* [2005] EWHC 1235 (Ch) at 79 *per* Mann J.; *Halifax Plc v. Curry*

absolutely entitled to the property, thereby allowing the subsequent person to act to his detriment.[66] An example of this occurred in *Freeguard v. Royal Bank of Scotland plc.*[67] Mr and Mrs Freeguard owned land situated near other land which they had sold to a Mr Edgar, a property developer. To disguise their interest in the retained land, they sold it to the developer, having lent him the money to finance the purchase. They were granted an option to repurchase the land, but did not protect that option in the appropriate manner by registration. He subsequently created an equitable mortgage in favour of the bank and the issue was whether the equitable interest which arose as a result of the creation of the option had priority over the, later, equitable mortgage. It was held that it did not. While refusing to stigmatize the transaction between the Freeguards and Mr Edgar as a sham,[68] Robert Walker L.J. considered it to be 'designed, if not to deceive, at any rate to give to the world . . . the impression that he was the unencumbered owner of the . . . strip and could deal with it as he pleased'.[69] This conduct caused the normal priority rule to be displaced, so that the bank took free from the prior equitable interest.

There are three exceptions to the normal rule whereby, as between two competing equitable interests, the first in time prevails. These are:

1. **Better right to legal estate**. If the purchaser of an equitable estate has, as a result of his purchase, a better right to the legal estate than the holder of the prior equitable interest, he will take free from it. An example of this occurred in *Assaf v. Fuwa*,[70] where land was conveyed to a trustee, who is, it will be recalled, the legal owner of the property and so can be classed as a bona fide purchaser. The trustee did not have notice of the equitable interest, and so the beneficiary under the trust, who had the right to have the legal estate conveyed to him, was held to take free of it.

2. **Later acquisition of the legal estate.** A purchaser of an equitable estate without notice will take free from a prior equitable interest if he subsequently acquires the legal estate, even if, when he does so, he then has notice of it.[71] This is so unless he knowingly acquires the legal estate in breach of trust, in which case he will take subject to the interests under that trust.[72]

3. **Mere equities**. A purchaser of an equitable estate will take free of 'mere equities' of which he has no notice. Mere equities are equitable rights which fall short of being a full equitable interest in land[73] and, in essence, amount to claims to equitable relief. Examples of such equities are the right to have an instrument set

---

Popeck (A firm) [2008] EWHC 1692 (Ch) at [24]–[25] *per* Norris J. See also Land Registration Act 2002, s. 28.

[66] See *Abigail v. Lapin* [1934] A.C. 491 at 507 *per* Lord Wright.   [67] (2000) 79 P. & C.R. 81.

[68] Ibid. at 84 *per* Robert Walker L.J. For sham transactions, see Fraud, p. 167.   [69] Ibid. at 89.

[70] [1955] A.C. 215.   [71] *Bailey v. Barnes* [1894] Ch. 25.

[72] *McCarthy & Stone Ltd v. Julian S. Hodge & Co. Ltd* [1971] 1 W.L.R. 1547.

[73] Where title is registered, these equities are interests capable of binding successors in title: Land Registration Act 2002, s. 116. See Rights, p. 138.

aside on the ground of mistake,[74] or a transaction set aside because of fraud.[75] While such an equity is capable of binding a purchaser,[76] a purchaser of an equitable estate without notice will take free from it.[77]

Without notice

The final element of the notion of the bona fide purchaser is that he is without notice. This is also the part which has generated the greatest debate. There are three forms of notice: actual notice, constructive notice, and imputed notice, which will be examined in turn.

Actual notice

As a result of the system of registration of land charges, to be discussed in Chapter 4, actual notice has increased in importance because the effect of registration is that a purchaser is deemed to have actual notice of any matter which has been registered.[78] Traditionally, however, this form of notice was less important than other sources of notice, since disputes normally centred on what a purchaser should have known rather than what he did know. A person was regarded as having actual notice of a matter if information about it had come to his attention from a reputable source and not, simply, from casual conversations.[79]

Constructive notice

If a purchaser of a legal estate was only bound by equitable interests, the existence of which he was actually aware, then it would be in his interest to know as little as possible prior to making the purchase. This would make equitable interests highly vulnerable. To avoid this, equity developed the doctrine of constructive notice. Under this doctrine the question which had to be considered is what the purchaser should have known.[80] The test which came to be adopted, and which was confirmed by statute,[81] was to consider what a purchaser should have discovered by making reasonable enquiries. The relevant test is now that contained in section 199 of the Law of Property Act 1925, which provides that:

'a purchaser is not to be prejudicially affected by notice of…any instrument or matter unless it is within his own knowledge, or would have come to his knowledge if such inquiries and inspections had been made by him as ought reasonably to have been made by him.'

---

[74] *Smith v. Jones* [1954] 2 All E.R. 823.   [75] *Ernst v. Vivian* (1863) 33 L.J. Ch. 513.
[76] See, e.g., *Blacklocks v. J.B. Developments (Godalming) Ltd* [1982] Ch. 183.
[77] See, generally, *Latec Investments Ltd v. Hotel Terrigal Pty Ltd* (1965) 113 C.L.R. 265.
[78] Law of Property Act 1925, s. 198.   [79] *Lloyd v. Banks* (1868) L.R. 3 Ch. App. 488.
[80] For an historical account, see J. Howell [1997] Conv. 431.
[81] Conveyancing Act 1882, s. 3(1). This was regarded as being confirmatory of the general law in *Hunt v. Luck* [1901] 2 Ch. 428 at 435 *per* Vaughan-Williams L.J.

The issue to be addressed is what enquiries a purchaser ought reasonably to make, assuming that such enquiries would have revealed the necessary knowledge.[82] The two main sources of information were investigation of title and a physical inspection of the property.

Investigation of title

It should be said at the outset that this form of notice has substantially diminished in importance because of the introduction of a system of registration of land charges and the spread of registration of title. What this source of notice entailed is the requirement that a purchaser conducts a proper investigation of the vendor's title.

When title to land is unregistered, the fact that a person is in possession of land is indicative of his ownership of a fee simple. He is assumed to be rightfully in possession of the land and he can bring an action against anyone who interferes with his enjoyment of the land except someone who can establish a better right to it.[83] Therein lies the rub. A large number of different interests could exist simultaneously with regard to the land and, although possession of land is, itself, evidence of the ownership of the land in fee simple, 'no man in his senses would take an offer of purchase from a man merely because he stood on the ground'.[84] The person in question could be a tenant, or even a squatter. To prove that he in fact owns what he is purporting to sell, the vendor must, by documentary evidence, give a convincing account of how the land came to be vested in him.

The process of proving his right to sell the property, known as deducing title, begins with the vendor showing how he came by the property. This starts with the conveyance of the land to him. A purchaser may then wish to be satisfied that the person who conveyed the land to the vendor was, himself, entitled to the land. This process could then be repeated by wanting to see how that person was entitled to the land, which would, again, require an examination of the conveyance of the land to him. And so on, potentially back to when time began.

For obvious reasons, some limit had to be imposed upon how far back a purchaser should be required to go and, indeed, how much evidence a vendor should be required to provide. The original period established at common law was sixty years, but this was reduced to forty years in 1874, to thirty years in 1925, and to its present length of fifteen years in 1969.[85] It is unlikely that a conveyance exactly fifteen years old will be in existence, and so, what the purchaser must do is to investigate the title by examining all title documents starting with a conveyance on sale which is *at least* fifteen years old. If there are conveyances which are twelve years old and twenty years old, the starting point is the one which is twenty years old, this conveyance being termed the root of title.[86]

---

[82] See *Kemmis v. Kemmis* [1988] 1 W.L.R. 1307 at 1319 *per* Purchas L.J.

[83] See Possession, pp. 34–35.

[84] *Hiern v. Mill* (1806) 123 Ves. 113 at 122 *per* Lord Erskine.

[85] Vendor and Purchaser Act 1874, s. 1; Law of Property Act 1925, s. 44(1); Law of Property Act 1969, s. 23.

[86] See *Re Cox and Neve's Contract* [1891] 2 Ch. 109 at 118 *per* North J.

The relevance of this for the purpose of constructive notice is that a purchaser would be considered to have had constructive notice of all equitable interests which he would have discovered had he inspected all the documents comprising the relevant title, these documents being compendiously termed the title deeds, starting with a root of title of the appropriate age.[87]

It should be stressed, however, that this form of constructive notice is now almost entirely obsolete, having been almost entirely superseded by the system of registration of land charges[88] and the spread of registration of title.[89] It is included to give an historical perspective of what the new systems were designed to replace.

Inspection of the land

Possibly the first judicial recognition that a purchaser may be regarded as having constructive notice of the rights of occupiers of the land occurred in *Taylor v. Stibbert*,[90] where it was recognized that when land was occupied by tenants, a purchaser was bound to enquire as to what rights the tenants had in the property. This approach was confirmed and became known as the rule in *Hunt v. Luck*, where it was said that:

'...if a purchaser or a mortgagee has notice that the vendor is not in possession of the property, he must make enquiries of the person in possession—of the tenant in possession—and find out from him what his rights are, and if he does not choose to do that, then, whatever title he acquires as purchaser or mortgagee will be subject to the title or right of the tenant.'[91]

The rule in *Hunt v. Luck*, whereby a person is fixed with constructive notice of the rights of persons in actual possession of the land, seems eminently sensible. In the situation in which the rule was formulated, the vendor himself did not physically occupy the land which was being sold.[92] As a matter of common sense, in this situation one would enquire of the people who did possess the land what their rights were and, if a purchaser did not do this, then it is perfectly reasonable to hold that he has constructive notice of those rights. What caused rather greater problems is the situation where the vendor was in occupation of property which he shared with others. The question was whether a purchaser should make enquiries of these other occupiers or, put another way, whether he would have constructive notice of any rights that those people possessed.

Shared occupation

There can be little doubt that, as the doctrine of constructive notice was being developed, a purchaser would not have been expected to make enquiries of occupiers of the property other than the vendor when the vendor was also in occupation of the land.[93]

---

[87] *Re Nisbett and Pott's Contract* [1906] 1 Ch. 386.   [88] Chapter 4.   [89] Chapter 5.
[90] (1794) 2 Ves. Jr. 438 at 440 *per* Lord Loughborough. See also *Barnhart v. Greenshields* (1853) 9 Moo. P.C. 18 at 32–33.
[91] [1901] 2 Ch. 428 at 433 *per* Vaughan-Williams L.J.
[92] See also *Daniels v. Davison* (1809) 16 Ves. Jun. 249 at 252.
[93] See R.H. Maudsley (1973) 36 M.L.R. 25 at 33; M.P. Thompson [1984] Conv. 362 at 367.

The problem did not seem to have arisen, however; the reason probably being that, in the nineteenth century, it would have been highly unlikely that a person sharing a house with a vendor would have had an equitable interest in it. In modern times, however, it is common for wives, or unmarried partners, to go out to work and contribute to the purchase of the house[94] and so the issue became very much a live one.

Caunce v. Caunce[95] involved what was to become a familiar scenario. A matrimonial home was legally in the sole name of Mr Caunce but his wife, having contributed to the purchase of it, was an equitable co-owner of it.[96] He mortgaged the house to the bank without telling her that he had done so. The bank, when granting the mortgage, made no enquiries of her. When he defaulted on the mortgage and the bank sought possession, the issue was whether or not the bank was bound by her equitable interest, which turned, of course, on whether it had constructive notice of her interest in the property.

In a judgment which was warmly welcomed by conveyancers,[97] Stamp J. held in favour of the bank. In his opinion, it was quite unreasonable to expect a bank to make enquiries beyond the legal owner of the property, taking the view that 'it is not in the public interest that bank mortgagees should be snoopers and busybodies in relation to wholly normal transactions of mortgage'.[98]

The appeal to public interest in this case involves the reiteration of a policy statement articulated previously in the House of Lords. In *National Provincial Bank Ltd v. Ainsworth*,[99] Lord Upjohn famously remarked that, 'It has been the policy of the law for over a hundred years to simplify and facilitate transactions in real property.' What this means, in the present context, is that it is contrary to this policy to allow people with informally created rights in land to assert those rights against institutions who lend money against the security of a house. To decide in favour of banks in situations such as these means that their task when lending money is easier than it would otherwise be. Provided that the legal owner lives in the property in question, enquiries need not be addressed to any other occupier. This reduces the transaction costs involved and enhances the security of the mortgagee's position. On the other hand, it necessarily involves reducing the residential security of those who, for whatever reason, are equitable rather than legal co-owners of the property,[100] and have not been consulted about the transaction in question.

The approach taken by Stamp J. was consistent with the view that was taken in the early development of constructive notice and was that, 'the vendor being in

---

[94] See the comment in *Williams & Glyn's Bank Ltd v. Boland* [1981] A.C. 487 at 508 *per* Lord Wilberforce.

[95] [1969] 1 W.L.R. 286.   [96] See Contributions and resulting trusts, pp. 325–335.

[97] See Barnsley, *Conveyancing Law and Practice* (1st edn) (London: Butterworths, 1973), 333.

[98] [1969] 1 W.L.R. 286 at 294.   [99] [1965] A.C. 117 at 1233.

[100] The fact that Mrs Caunce was not a legal co-owner seemed to influence the judge against her, in that she allowed a position to exist whereby her husband could present himself to the world as the absolute owner of the property: see [1969] 1 W.L.R. 286 at 290 and 292. See also *Abbey National Building Society v. Cann* [1991] 1 A.C. 56 at 94 *per* Lord Oliver of Aylmerton and the position where the contest is between two equitable interests. See Legal estate, pp. 50–51.

possession, the presence of his wife or guest or lodger is not inconsistent with the title offered'.[101] This view, which found a ready echo in some quarters,[102] construed the ambit of constructive notice narrowly. In so doing, his approach was to take the view that section 199 of the Law of Property Act 1925, and its predecessor, section 3(1) of the Conveyancing Act 1882, had been intended to restrict rather than extend the scope of constructive notice,[103] with the result that his conclusion appeared, as a matter of analysis, to have been amply justified in terms of what would, in the nineteenth century, have been considered to be the extent of reasonable enquiries. It failed, however, to give weight to the idea that notions of reasonableness may change over time, as the nature of society changes. In particular, it gave little weight to the expectation of security in a home that a co-owner might legitimately hold. It was perhaps unsurprising that what might be regarded as the conservative conveyancing-based approach did not ultimately prevail.

The retreat from Caunce

Soon after *Caunce* was decided, the position of occupiers who shared the property with the legal owner was reconsidered, albeit in a different context. In *Hodgson v. Marks*,[104] a man, who was originally a lodger in the house in question, became the legal owner of it, but he held the property on trust for an elderly woman, who had previously held the legal title and who lived in the house at all material times. He transferred the house to a purchaser who, in turn, created a mortgage over it. The issue was whether the woman's equitable interest in the house was binding upon the purchaser.

Because the title to the house in question was registered, the determination of this issue raised a similar, but not identical, question to that which was addressed in *Caunce*. Whether or not the woman's interest was binding upon a purchaser depended upon whether she was to be regarded as having been in actual occupation of the house, within the meaning of section 70(1)(g) of the Land Registration Act 1925, rather than whether reasonable enquiries would have revealed the existence of her interest.[105] Reversing the first instance decision, which was based on the interpretation of 'actual occupation' as meaning 'actual and apparent occupation', the Court of Appeal held that she was and that the purchaser took subject to her interest.

Although Russell L.J. was prepared, without deciding, to construe the phrase 'actual occupation' in such a way that it would equate with the ambit of constructive notice,[106] he did not think that this would help the purchaser. He thought, as a matter of fact, that the woman was in actual occupation of the land and that the addition of the adjective 'apparent' added little if anything to the meaning of the words 'actual occupation'. Had the issue been whether the purchaser had constructive notice of the woman's

[101] [1969] 1 W.L.R. 286 at 294.
[102] See *Bird v. Syme-Thomson* [1979] 1 W.L.R. 440 at 444 *per* Templeman J., who regarded occupation of a home by a wife as being the shadow of her husband.
[103] [1969] 1 W.L.R. 286 at 293.   [104] [1971] Ch. 892.
[105] See Actual occupation, pp. 141–144.   [106] [1971] Ch. 892 at 931.

rights, it is fairly clear that he would have held that he did because, when commenting on *Caunce*, he said:

'In that case the occupation of the wife may have been rightly taken to be not her occupation but that of her husband. In so far, however, as some phrases in the judgment might appear to lay down a general proposition that inquiry need not be made of any person on the premises if the proposed vendor himself appears to be in occupation, I would not accept them.'[107]

Although prepared to accept the actual result in *Caunce*, it was clear that the Court of Appeal was not prepared to accept as a general proposition that the ambit of reasonable enquiries did not extend to asking occupiers of the land what, if any, interests they had in it. The exclusion of wives from the class of people to whom questions needed to be addressed was unlikely to survive for long. Leaving aside the inherent unattractiveness of singling out one particular type of occupier in this way, to do so was not very heplful to a purchaser because this exclusion of wives would necessitate an enquiry as to whether an occupant was in fact married to the vendor or was merely living with him; not the sort of enquiry that the law should require a purchaser to make.[108]

The criticisms made of *Caunce* in *Hodgson v. Marks* found strong support in the House of Lords in *William & Glyn's Bank Ltd v. Boland*,[109] a case involving substantially the same facts as *Caunce* but which, again, concerned registered land. Lord Wilberforce, in deciding that Mrs Boland was in actual occupation of the house, aligned himself with the criticisms made of *Caunce*. He was also quite unprepared to treat wives as being, legally, the shadow of their husbands, thereby effectively removing the cautiously stated qualification expressed by Russell L.J.[110] Lord Scarman, while recognizing that he did not have to decide the point, expressed himself to be far from certain that *Caunce* had been correctly decided.[111] The upshot was that it became overwhelmingly apparent that a purchaser would, in principle, have constructive notice of the rights of occupiers who shared the property with the vendor.

There was soon afterwards an acceptance by the Court of Appeal that the *dicta* in *Boland* had had the effect that the restrictive approach taken in *Caunce* was no longer applicable and that the ambit of reasonable enquiries extended to making enquiries of all occupiers of the property, despite the vendor also being in occupation.[112] The full extent of the purchaser's task was considered in *Kingsnorth Trust Ltd v. Tizard*.[113] A house was in the sole name of Mr Tizard, although it was conceded that his wife was an equitable co-owner of it. They had separated and she lived with her sister and only

[107] Ibid. at 934–935.

[108] *National Provincial Bank Ltd v. Ainsworth* [1965] A.C. 1175 at 1234 *per* Lord Upjohn. See Response to *Boland*, p. 487.

[109] [1991] A.C. 487.   [110] [1991] A.C. 487 at 505.   [111] Ibid. at 511.

[112] *Midland Bank Ltd v. Farmpride Hatcheries Ltd* [1981] 2 E.G.L.R. 147. The interest claimed in this case has since been held not to be an interest in land and so the point need not actually have arisen: *Ashburn Anstalt v. W.J. Arnold* [1989] Ch. 1. For contemporary comment, see R.E. Annand [1982] Conv. 67.

[113] [1986] 1 W.L.R. 783.

stayed in the house when he was not there. She did, however, visit the house on a daily basis to collect their two children for school. He applied for a loan to be secured by a mortgage against the house. On his application form, he stated that he was single. A surveyor was instructed to inspect the house and to interview Mr Tizard, where he was told that the house was untidy because Mrs Tizard had recently left. In his report, the agent stated that Mr Tizard was single and occupied the house with his two children. After the mortgage was granted and Mr Tizard had defaulted on the repayments, it was held that the mortgagee was bound by Mrs Tizard's equitable interest on the basis that it had constructive notice of it.

Of more general importance, it was held that, in the light of the approach taken in *Boland*, the decision in *Caunce* could no longer stand. It was accepted that reasonable enquiries now embraced making enquiries of all occupants of the house, whether or not the vendor was himself in occupation of it. This seemed inevitable and represents a welcome recognition that people living with the legal owner of a house may have an interest in it and that those rights are deserving of protection when the property is mortgaged without their consent. Less welcome were some of the judge's comments on the ambit of reasonable enquiries. He expressed the view that, if the purpose of an inspection of the property is to ascertain the existence of other occupiers, then an inspection at a time pre-arranged with the vendor might not be sufficient.[114] This goes too far. While the actual decision might, on the facts, have been justified, in that the agent was put on notice that Mrs Tizard had only recently left the house and so might well have had an interest in it,[115] the requirement that an inspection of the property should take place at an unannounced time goes well beyond what might be regarded as a reasonable enquiry.

On the other hand, what seems to be an unduly relaxed view as to the ambit of constructive notice was taken in *Le Foe v. Le Foe*.[116] One of the issues in this case was whether a mortgage created by Mr Le Foe should be set aside under section 37 of the Matrimonial Causes Act 1973 on the basis that the bank had notice of his intention to defeat his wife's claim for financial relief under that Act.[117] The judge held that it did not but considered, also, whether the bank would have had constructive notice of her presence in the house. As to this, despite expressing the view that the person who inspected the property on behalf of the bank could hardly have failed to notice evidence of her presence in the house,[118] he considered that it would not have done. The reason for this surprising conclusion appeared to be that the remit of the person instructed to inspect the house was limited to assessing its value. On this basis the judge expressed the view, albeit *obiter*, that, had the point been in issue, he would not

---

[114] [1986] 1 W.L.R. 783 at 794–795.   [115] See M.P. Thompson [1986] Conv. 283 at 285.

[116] [2001] 2 F.L.R. 970. Permission to appeal was originally granted, [2001] EWCA Civ. 1789 but subsequently withdrawn: [2001] EWCA Civ. 1870.

[117] For the relevance of constructive notice in this context, see *Kemmis v. Kemmis* [1988] 1 W.L.R. 1307. See J.E.S. Fortin [1989] Conv. 204.

[118] [2001] 2 F.L.R. 970 at 988 *per* Nicholas Mostyn Q.C.

have considered the bank, through its representative, to have had constructive notice of her presence.[119]

This seems remarkably generous to the purchaser,[120] and is out of line with recent authority. When, as in this case, it is evident that the borrower is sharing accommodation with another person then, as between the bank and that person, reasonable enquiries should extend to asking that person what, if any, interest, they have in the property. The instructions given by the bank to its representative, should not limit what are, for the purposes of constructive notice, reasonable enquiries.

Although the importance of the doctrine of constructive notice has receded considerably as a consequence of the spread of registration of title,[121] the question of what is comprehended by reasonable enquiries remains important. This is because on a transfer of land when title is registered, the transferee will take the land subject to an interest of a person in actual occupation of the land, provided that the fact of occupation would have been obvious on a reasonably careful inspection of the land.[122] The *dicta* in *Tizard* appear to take too stringent a view of what is reasonable, whereas those in *Le Foe* appear to err in the other direction.

The nature of the transaction

The doctrine of notice is traditionally concerned with determining whether or not a purchaser of a legal estate is bound by a prior equitable interest. Its role may, however, be wider than this[123] and involve situations where what is in issue is where a transaction is entered into in circumstances where some wrong, such as misrepresentation or undue influence, has been exerted on one of the parties to it.

The use of the doctrine of notice with regard to particular transactions was developed in *Barclays Bank plc v. O'Brien*.[124] A matrimonial home was in the joint names of Mr and Mrs O'Brien. A company with which he was closely involved had serious financial problems and Mr O'Brien agreed with the bank that he would act as guarantor for its overdraft. When the overdraft reached £60,000, the bank required security for its loan, that security being the matrimonial home. Because her husband had misrepresented the nature of the mortgage to his wife, she thought, when signing the mortgage, that it was to secure a short-term loan of a fixed amount, that amount being £60,000. In fact, it secured the total and open-ended indebtedness of the company to the bank. None of this was explained to her by the bank and, although she signed both the mortgage and a letter to the effect that she had fully understood the transaction, she had not actually read either document prior to signing them. When the bank sought possession of the house to enforce its security, the amount owing by the company then standing at some £154,000, she argued, successfully, that the mortgage was void as against her.

---

[119] Ibid. at 989.   [120] See M.P. Thompson [2002] Conv. 273 at 283–284.   [121] Chapter 5.
[122] Land Registration Act 2002, ss 29 and 30; Sched. 3, para. 2. See Unregistered interests which override registered dispositions, pp. 145–148.
[123] See J. Howell [1996] Conv. 33.   [124] [1994] 1 A.C. 180.

The approach of the House of Lords was to employ the doctrine of notice, a doctrine which Lord Browne-Wilkinson considered to be 'at the heart of equity'.[125] In seeking to apply that doctrine in the present context, he said:

'... if the party asserting that he takes free of the earlier rights of another knows of certain facts which put him on inquiry as to the possible existence of rights of that other and he fails to make such inquiry or take such steps as are reasonable to verify whether such earlier right does or does not exist, he will have constructive notice of that earlier right and take subject to it.'[126]

In the instant case, the fact that the transaction involved a husband and wife and was not for her financial benefit was sufficient to put the bank upon notice that her consent to the transaction had been secured by some equitable wrong. Because the bank had not taken sufficient precautions to ensure that no such wrong had occurred, it was bound by her equity to set the transaction aside.

The decision in O'Brien, and the ensuing litigation which followed it, is of the utmost importance in the law of mortgages.[127] For present purposes, it suffices to show that notice can be derived from factual situations and not simply from traditional sources such as investigation of title and inspection of the property. The role of notice is, however, different in this context from the role which it normally plays.[128] Normally, notice is relevant when the issue to be determined is whether a purchaser is bound by an existing equitable interest. This, indeed, is how the role of notice in this type of case was originally explained, the analysis being that as between the husband and wife, the latter had, in equity, a right against the former to set the transaction between them aside and the question was whether or not the lender had notice of that equity.[129] It soon became apparent, however, that notice was not being used in this sense. This was because there was not a separate transaction between husband and wife, followed by a mortgage of the property to the lender.[130] Consequently, there was no question of the lender being bound by a pre-existing equity.[131] Instead the issue came to be seen as being to determine the circumstances when a lender is to be regarded as being put on notice that the transaction which it is entering into is tainted by the possible use of some species of equitable fraud. Although notice is still relevant, it is being used in a different way; it is not being used to determine the priority of property rights but is, instead, being used as part of the law of contract.[132]

---

[125] [1994] 1 A.C. 180 at 195.

[126] Ibid. at 195–196. For constructive notice to be relevant, the facts must point to something which affects the purchaser's title and not simply be relevant to the financial status of one of the parties: Abbey National plc v. Tufts [1999] 2 F.L.R. 399.

[127] For a full analysis, see Vitiating factors, pp. 492–510.

[128] For a debate as to the role of notice in this context, see M.P. Thompson [1994] Conv. 140; M. Dixon and C. Harpum [1994] Conv. 421; P. Sparkes [1995] Conv. 250.

[129] See CIBC Mortgages plc v. Pitt [1994] 1 A.C. 200 at 210 per Lord Browne-Wilkinson.

[130] See, particularly, Dixon and Harpum, loc. cit.

[131] See Barclays Bank plc v. Boulter [1999] 4 All E.R. 513; M.P. Thompson [2000] Conv. 43 at 47–48.

[132] See Royal Bank of Scotland v. Etridge (No. 2) [2001] 4 All E.R. 449 at 498 per Lord Scott of Foscote. Notice, p. 504.

Imputed notice[133]

Under section 199(1)(ii)(b) of the Law of Property Act 1925, a purchaser will be regarded as having notice of any matter which has, in respect of the same transaction in which the question arises, come to the knowledge of his solicitor or other agent or would have come to the knowledge of the solicitor or agent had that person made such enquiries as should reasonably have been made.

Ordinarily, the person most likely to acquire notice is the purchaser's solicitor.[134] As the section makes clear, however, knowledge which has either been acquired, or should have been acquired, by any agent, will be imputed to the principal. So, in *Kingsnorth Trust Ltd v. Tizard*,[135] notice was imputed to the finance company on account of constructive notice acquired by a surveyor instructed by them to inspect the property.

A limitation on imputed notice is that the notice must have been acquired in respect of the same transaction. This was introduced because otherwise, if a solicitor had acquired notice in a previous transaction, this notice could be imputed to his present client,[136] an undesirable state of affairs[137] which could dissuade purchasers from employing local solicitors who may have acquired notice of matters when dealing, in the past, with the property in question.

The requirement that notice be acquired in the same transaction would mean that, if a solicitor is acting for both parties, any notice he acquires will be imputed to them both.[138] Some difficulty has arisen, however, when a solicitor acts for both parties but when his involvement with each of them occurs at a different stage in the transaction, or when he performs different roles for the two parties. In *Halifax Building Society v. Stepsky*[139] a solicitor knew that the stated reason being given by a married couple for a loan was not true, where, if the real reason had been known, the mortgagee would have been put on notice that the wife's agreement to the proposed mortgage might have been obtained by misrepresentation or undue influence. When, subsequently, the same solicitor was instructed to act for the bank in respect of the mortgage, he did not inform the bank of what he knew and that knowledge was not imputed to them. This seems correct, in that, although the solicitor was acting for both parties to a transaction, he did so at significantly different times and when he acted for the wife, he was not, at the time, also the agent for the bank.[140]

---

[133] See S. Nield [2000] Conv. 196.

[134] For an example, see *Bank of Credit and Commerce International SA v. Aboody* [1990] 1 Q.B. 923 at 971 *per* Slade L.J.

[135] [1986] 1 W.L.R. 743.   [136] *Hargreaves v. Rothewell* (1836) 1 Keen 154.

[137] See *Re Cousins* (1886) 31 Ch.D. 671 at 676–677 *per* Chitty J.

[138] *Sharpe v. Foy* (1868) 4 Ch. App. 35; *Meyer v. Chartres* (1918) 34 T.L.R. 589.

[139] [1997] 1 All E.R. 46.

[140] See also *Midland Bank plc v. Serter* [1995] 1 F.L.R. 1034 at 1045 *per* Glidewell L.J., although contrast *Barclays Bank plc v. Thomson* [1997] 4 All E.R. 816 at 826 *per* Simon Brown L.J., criticized by M.P. Thompson [1997] Conv. 216 at 219.

The role of imputed notice can be confused in cases of this nature. In *Barclays Bank plc v. Thomson*,[141] a wife claimed that a mortgage was not binding on her as she claimed that the bank had notice of the fact that her signature to the mortgage had been obtained by misrepresentation and undue influence. The bank had instructed the solicitor who was acting for the husband to explain the charge to the wife and also to secure its registration. She claimed that the advice given to her by the solicitor was deficient and that knowledge of that deficiency should be imputed to the bank.

In deciding in favour of the bank, the Court of Appeal rejected the argument that knowledge of the deficiency of the advice should be imputed to the bank. Such a conclusion seems inevitable as imputed notice should not be relevant to a situation such as this and it is, perhaps, unfortunate that the case was presented, at least in part, on this basis. Whether a solicitor ought to know that his advice is inadequate is hardly knowledge that can be imputed to the bank.[142] Rather, the case is really about whether or not the bank took adequate steps to ensure that she received proper, independent advice, as to which, the decision was arguably overly lenient to the bank.[143]

Successors in title

If land has been conveyed to a bona fide purchaser who consequently is not bound by a prior equitable interest, the question can arise as to whether a subsequent purchaser who does have notice of it will be bound; whether the equitable interest will be revived. This point arose in *Wilkes v. Spooner*,[144] where the court held that it was not. Once the land has been conveyed to a bona fide purchaser, any equitable interests are overridden and, thereby, removed from the land. The only exception to this is when the land is subsequently conveyed to a person who had previously owned the land and who was, at that time, bound by the interest in question.

HUMAN RIGHTS

A further, more recent, influence on Land Law is the human rights legislation.[145] Under section 3(1) of the Human Rights Act 1998, which incorporated the European Convention on Human Rights into English law, a court is obliged to read primary and secondary legislation in a way which is compatible with Convention rights. This has

---

[141] [1997] 4 All E.R. 816.

[142] See ibid. at 829 *per* Morritt L.J. See also *Royal Bank of Scotland v. Etridge (No. 2)* [2001] 4 All E.R. 449 at 472 *per* Lord Nicholls of Birkenhead.

[143] See M.P. Thompson [1997] Conv. 216 and Obligations of the mortgagee, p. 507.

[144] [1911] 2 K.B. 473.

[145] See generally Allen, *Property and the Human Rights Act* (Oxford: Hart Publishing, 2005).

entailed the courts adopting a new approach to statutory interpretation.[146] In *Ghaidan v. Godin-Mendoza*,[147] Lord Nicholls of Birkenhead said that:

'the application of section 3 does not depend upon the presence of ambiguity in the legislation being interpreted. Even if construed according to ordinary principles of interpretation, the legislation admits of no doubt, the section may none the less require the legislation to be given a different meaning.'

On this basis, the expression 'living with the tenant as his/her wife or husband'[148] was interpreted, Lord Millett dissenting, to include a cohabiting homosexual couple. The reason for this was that an interpretation which limited the meaning of this phrase to heterosexual couples would have been discriminatory, contrary to article 14 which prohibits discrimination on, *inter alia*, grounds of sexual orientation.

While it is clear that the section can have a significant effect on the tenets of statutory interpretation, it does not empower the courts to disregard clear statutory provisions. Thus, under section 89 of the Housing Act 1980, after making a possession order, the giving up of possession may not be postponed for more than 14 days or, in cases of exceptional hardship, to a date no later than six months after the making of the order. Even were this to be considered incompatible with the Convention, it would not be possible, in the teeth of such clear language, to construe this provision in a way so as to extend the period of postponement.[149] This limitation on the width of the new approach to statutory interpretation needs to be borne in mind when regard is had to some of the wider views of the approach to be taken to the effect of section 3. An articulation of such an approach occurred in a dissenting speech in *Hounslow London Borough Council v. Qazi*,[150] where Lord Steyn was critical of an approach which allowed domestic notions of title, legal and equitable rights and interest, to colour the interpretation of article 8.[151] Instead, he considered that:

'Nowhere in our legal system is a literalistic approach more inappropriate than when considering whether a breach of a Convention right may be removed by interpretation under section 3. Section 3 requires a broad approach concentrating, amongst other things, in a purposive way on the importance of the fundamental right involved.'[152]

Should this approach be followed, it has the potential to alter significantly our traditional understanding of property rights, which have been developed over centuries. It raises the prospect of a decision being arrived at on the application of normal principles of property law, and then that decision being trumped by an appeal to a Convention right. The extent to which that has, or may, occur needs consideration.

---

[146] See A. Kavanagh (2004) 24 O.J.L.S. 259. It is clear that, although the Act refers to legislation, this principle applies to domestic law as a whole: see *Doherty v. Birmingham City Council* [2009] A.C. 367 at [67] *per* Lord Scott of Foscote.

[147] [2004] 2 A.C. 557 at 572. See also *R. v. A. (No.2)* [2002] 1 A.C. 45.

[148] Rent Act 1977, Sched. 2, para. 2(2).

[149] *London Borough of Hounslow v. Powell* [2011] UKSC 8 at [62] *per* Lord Hope.

[150] [2004] 1 A.C. 983.   [151] Ibid. at [27].

[152] Ibid. at [41]. For a strong, and convincing, critique of this dictum, see J. Howell (2007) 123 L.Q.R. 618.

Convention rights

Of the various rights contained within the Convention, there are two,[153] in particular, which may be engaged in disputes pertaining to matters within the scope of this book. The first is article 1 of the First Protocol, which provides that, subject to some qualifications, everyone is entitled to the peaceful enjoyment of his possessions. Secondly, and of considerable significance, is article 8. Article 8 provides that:

(1) Everyone has the right to respect for his private and family life, his home and his correspondence;

(2) There shall be no interference by a public authority with the exercise of this right except such as in accordance with the law and is necessary in a democratic society in the interests of national security, public safety or the economic well-being of the country, for the prevention of disorder or crime, for the protection of health or morals, or for the protection of the rights and freedoms of others.

Reliance has been placed on this provision in a number of different contexts, and will be dealt with as and when they arise, rather than being collected in a somewhat miscellaneous group. Recent developments have, however, necessitated a discussion of the general approach to the issue of the impact of human rights considerations on the law of property and, in particular, on the question of the right to possession.

Possession actions and human rights

A fundamental issue which has repeatedly exercised the courts has been when a local authority brings an action for possession in circumstances when, as a matter of general property law, the occupier has no legal right to remain in the property. The question which has arisen is whether, despite the property law entitlement to possession, a defence can be raised on the basis of article 8. After a prolonged debate at the highest judicial level, the question has been answered in the affirmative by the Supreme Court in *Manchester City Council v. Pinnock*.[154] In 1978, Mr Pinnock was granted a secure tenancy of a property, where he lived with this partner and, from time to time, their children. In 2005, the council brought possession proceedings, this action being prompted as a result of serious antisocial behaviour by his children and partner. Perhaps as a consequence of his prolonged residence and the fact that he had not, himself, been guilty of antisocial behaviour, a possession order was not granted and, instead, a demotion order was made. This type of order,[155] which can only be made if one of a number of criteria relating to antisocial behaviour is satisfied and it is, separately, considered to be reasonable to make the order, has the effect of removing secure

---

[153] Article 6, which affords the right to a fair and impartial trial may also be relevant, but is not of central concern to the issues considered in this section.

[154] [2010] UKSC 45. See also *London Borough of Hounslow v. Powell* [2011] UKSC 8; M.P. Thompson [2011] Conv. 421.

[155] Introduced by the Anti-social Behaviour Act 2003, s. 15.

status from the tenant for a period of one year. During that period, the council can bring possession proceedings and, if it does so, must follow a prescribed procedure,[156] which involves giving reasons why the proceedings are being brought and notification of a right to request a review. It is then for the county court to make an order for possession and it is provided by section 143D of the Housing Act 1996 that the court must make an order if it is satisfied that the statutory procedure has been followed. In the present case, following further misconduct on the part of members of Mr Pinnock's family, this procedure was followed and an order for possession was made. Mr Pinnock appealed, contending that his rights under article 8 had been violated. This contention was upheld by the Supreme Court although, on the facts, the appeal was dismissed.

The point of principle centred on the role of the county court. Under the legislation, it appeared that this was confined to ascertaining that the correct procedure had been followed by the local authority. If it had been, a possession order had to be made: the local authority had an absolute right to possession. The argument for the tenant, which was accepted by the Supreme Court, was that, even when a local authority had an absolute right to possession, in order to satisfy article 8(2) of the Convention, the question as to whether the grant of possession was necessary or, as the test has become, whether making such an order was proportionate was relevant. The actual appeal was, however, dismissed, it being held that, as the facts were largely undisputed, there was no need to remit the case to the county court to consider the proportionality of the possession order; on the facts, such an order was considered to be amply justifiable.

It is now clear that, at least so far as actions brought by public bodies are concerned, it will be possible for an occupier of land, who has no legal right to possession, to be able to defend a possession action on the basis that an order for possession is disproportionate. It is now necessary to consider how far reaching this decision is and, in particular, what, if any, impact, this decision has on private landowners. To do this will necessitate some consideration of how the law has come to recognize the potential applicability of article 8.

The increased recognition of human rights

In arriving at the position that occupiers of land may be able to rely on an article 8 defence to possession proceedings, there has been a considerable prior debate involving both the English courts and the European Court of Human Rights. One can take as a starting position, the House of Lords decision in *Harrow London Borough Council v. Qazi*.[157] One of two joint tenants of a council house left the property and, having done so, served a notice to quit on the landlord. This had the effect of terminating the tenancy,[158] with the result that the remaining joint tenant had no legal right to remain. The House of Lords was unanimous that, as Mr Qazi occupied the house as his home, article 8 was engaged. By a bare majority, it was held that there was no need to remit

---

[156] Housing Act 1996, s. 143.   [157] [2004] 1 A.C. 983. See S. Bright (2004) 120 L.Q.R. 398.
[158] See Notice to quit, pp. 360–362.

the case to the county court to consider whether the grant of possession could be justified under article 8(2). This was because 'article 8(2) *is* met where the law affords an unqualified right to possession on proof that the tenancy has been terminated'.[159] Put another way, the balancing act envisaged by article 8(2) is carried out by the law of property and, once that has provided the answer, there is no further balancing to do.[160] That said, the action of the local authority in bringing possession proceedings was, as is the case with other actions by public bodies, amenable to judicial review; an important caveat, in that this remedy is not available to regulate the actions of private individuals—and, also, to establish the grounds on which the courts could intervene. The minority took the view that, even when a proprietary right to possession had been established, it would still be possible for an individual to argue, on the particular facts of a case, that article 8(2) could require the issue of proportionality to be addressed, although it was conceded that it would only be in exceptional cases that such an argument would succeed.[161] This aspect of the law will be considered shortly. What the majority decision clearly established, however, was that 'as a matter of human rights law, Art.8 is not available as a defence to possession proceedings brought to enforce the ordinary property rights of a local authority.'[162]

The retreat from *Qazi*

The position laid down in *Qazi* soon had to be modified. This was as a result of the decision of the European Court of Human Rights in *Connors v. United Kingdom*.[163] This case arose out of a decision by a local authority to bring possession proceedings against a gypsy, who had been living, save for a short interruption, on the authority's land for over 16 years. He occupied the land under a licence agreement which, when revoked, meant that he had no legal right to remain. Following an unsuccessful application for permission to seek judicial review, the county court granted a possession order and Mr Connors brought proceedings in Strasbourg alleging an infringement of his human rights. The European Court upheld his claim.

Underlying the decision of the council to seek possession was its view that Mr Connors and his family had been guilty of various acts of antisocial behaviour, although this was strongly contested. No opportunity was given for a court to determine the actual facts, because the procedure adopted by the council of determining the licence and seeking summary possession obviated the need to do this. As a matter of law, it was entitled to possession because, unlike other occupiers of mobile homes, gypsies occupying local authority property did not enjoy security of tenure. The European Court was critical of a situation whereby a local authority could obtain possession of a person's home without any investigation of the factual position and concluded that his rights had been infringed.

---

[159] [2004] 1 A.C. 983 at [78] *per* Lord Hope of Craighead. Lord Hope's italics.
[160] Ibid. at [103] *per* Lord Millett.   [161] Ibid. at [25] *per* Lord Bingham of Cornhill.
[162] *Birmingham City Council v. Bradney* [2004] H.L.R. 27 at [15] *per* Mummery L.J.
[163] (2005) EHHR 9.

The impact of the decision in *Connors* was first considered by the Court of Appeal in *Leeds City Council v. Price*,[164] a case also involving gypsies, and it was considered that, as a result of that case, the decision in *Qazi* was, itself, incompatible with the Convention. The Court, nevertheless, considered itself to be bound by *Qazi* and followed it: a course of action expressly approved by the House of Lords.[165] As to the merits, this was reconsidered by a seven-member panel of the House of Lords in the conjoined appeals in *Price* and *Kay v. London Borough of Lambeth*.[166]

In *Price*, the House unanimously rejected the argument that article 8 had been infringed. This was because the occupation in this case had only been for a period of two days and this was insufficient to establish that the property was occupied as a home: article 8 was not, therefore, engaged at all. In *Kay*, however, there had been sufficiently prolonged occupation of the property to establish that it was the defendant's home, and the issue of whether the reasoning employed in *Qazi* could survive the decision in *Connors* had to be addressed. With some modification of the earlier decision, a bare majority held that it could.

The gateway approach[167]

Kay involved a situation where, as a matter of law, the local authority had an unqualified right to possession and the occupier ran the same argument that had failed in *Qazi*: that to grant possession without adverting to his personal circumstances infringed his rights under article 8. The leading speech, which rejected this argument, was given by Lord Hope of Craighead. Upholding the essential reasoning in *Qazi*, he nevertheless, to an extent, modified it. In his view, article 8 could be relied upon in two situations, later termed gateways (a) and (b). Under the first of these gateways, the occupier could argue that the substantive law which afforded the authority the right to possession was, itself, challengeable as being inconsistent with the Convention. In such circumstances the court should, if possible, apply section 3 of the Human Rights Act 1998 and construe the legislation in a way which was compatible with the Convention. If that was not possible, the proceedings should be adjourned to the High Court to determine the issue of compatibility with the Convention and, if the law was not so compatible, a declaration to that effect should be made.[168] The alternative argument, gateway (b), was to challenge the decision of the local authority, notwithstanding its unqualified right to possession, to seek to enforce that right, the basis of that argument being that this would amount to an abuse of its powers.[169] Such an attack on the decision making process could only succeed, however, if the decision was one which no reasonable person would consider to be justifiable: the public law

---

164 [2005] 3 All E.R. 573.
165 *Kay v. London Borough of Lambeth* [2006] 2 A.C. 465 at [43] *per* Lord Bingham of Cornhill.
166 [2006] 2 A.C. 465.
167 See I. Loveland [2009] Conv. 396; M. Davis and D. Hughes [2010] Conv. 57.
168 See Human Rights Act 1998, s. 4.   169 *Kay v. London Borough of Lambeth* [2006] 2 A.C. 573.

test of *Wednesbury* unreasonableness.[170] Applying this to the facts of *Connors*, both gateways appeared to be open. First, the legislative regime which was then in place discriminated against gypsies who, unlike other occupiers of mobile homes, were not afforded any security of tenure,[171] a position which could amount to an infringement of article 14.[172] Secondly, although the council had the right to terminate the licence, the view was expressed that, given the length of the period of occupation, it would be grossly unfair to take such action without having to make good any underlying reason for doing so.[173]

An important point to stress about this reasoning is that it should be appreciated that if the substantive law affords a local authority an unqualified right to possession, that does not entail, of itself, that that law is incompatible with the Convention. Were this to be the case, then gateway (b) would be redundant. There would be no reason to insist that the decision to enforce this right was an abuse of power: the very existence of the right would contravene the Convention. For gateway (a) to be an issue, it must have been the case that the substantive law infringed some other Convention right: an important point to appreciate when assessing the impact of the decision in *Pinnock*.

The widening of the grounds for review

Prior to the Supreme Court finally abandoning the position laid down in *Qazi*, the House of Lords had a final opportunity to review this area of law in *Doherty v. Birmingham City Council*.[174] The Council brought summary possession proceedings against a gypsy family who had occupied council property for over 17 years, it having terminated their licence to occupy. The reason why the council had done this was not because of any misconduct on the part of the family, but because it wanted to redevelop the land. Following *Qazi*, possession was ordered and the defendants appealed. The appeal was allowed, and the case was remitted to a High Court judge to consider the reasonableness of the council's actions having regard to its stated reason for seeking possession and the length of occupancy of the defendants: in effect gateway (b). As to the more substantive element of the decision, despite some forthright statements, the effect of the judgments was not that easy to state.

In deciding whether a court was required to have regard to the issue of proportionality when considering whether a council had an unqualified right to possession, the House was pressed with another decision of the European Court, *McCann v. United Kingdom*.[175] In that case, following issues concerning domestic violence,

---

[170] *Associated Provincial Picture Houses Ltd v. Wednesbury Corp* [1948] 1 K.B. 223.

[171] This position has now been remedied by the Housing and Regeneration Act 2008, s. 318, Sched. 16.

[172] See *Doherty v. Birmingham City Council* [2009] A.C. 367 at [25] *per* Lord Hope, albeit conceding that the European Court had not decided that this was the case.

[173] *Kay v. London Borough of Lambeth* [2006] 2 A.C. 367 at [210] *per* Lord Brown of Eaton-under-Haywood.

[174] [2009] A.C. 367.   [175] [2008] H.L.R. 40.

Mrs McCann left the council house which she had shared with her husband. At the instigation of the council, she served a notice to quit, thereby terminating the tenancy. The council then obtained possession and Mr McCann pursued the matter in Strasbourg, where it was held that there had been an infringement of his right under article 8.

In upholding the claim, the Court noted that, by persuading Mrs McCann to serve a notice to quit, the council had sidestepped the need to bring possession proceedings under section 84 of the Housing Act 1985, thereby obviating the need to satisfy a court that an order for possession was reasonable: a task which would have required the facts to be ascertained and the merits of the case to be assessed.[176] It went further than this, however, commenting that the decision in *Connors* was not confined to gypsies or to cases where the substantive law was challenged as being incompatible with the Convention. Instead, it considered that the loss of one's home was a major interference with a person's right and this should require the proportionality of the measure to be determined by an independent tribunal, notwithstanding that, under the general law, the occupier had no legal right to be on the property.[177] Having said that, however, the actual decision that there had been a violation of article 8 was based on the procedural aspect only, and it was stressed that it was far from clear that had a domestic tribunal been in a position to assess the proportionality of the eviction that the possession order would not still have been granted.[178]

While the writing on the wall of the Strasbourg jurisprudence seemed to be clear that the philosophy underlying *Qazi* was not acceptable, the House of Lords in *Doherty* made one last ditch attempt to hold the line it had previously laid down. *McCann* was given fairly short shrift. Lord Hope considered that the failure of the European Court to articulate any criteria as to what the exceptional circumstances might be which could cause a court to refuse to grant possession made the guidance almost useless,[179] and indicated that English courts should continue to follow the decision in *Qazi*. He reiterated that, if a local authority had an unqualified right to possession, then, unless that right could be challenged on the basis that the relevant legislation was, itself, incompatible with the convention, it 'is not open to the court...to hold that the exercise of that right should be denied because of the occupier's personal circumstances.'[180] Any such challenge must be on public law grounds, that is that the decision of the public authority amounted to an abuse of its powers on the basis that it was a decision that no reasonable person would consider to be justifiable: that it was *Wednesbury* unreasonable.

---

[176] This was considered to be an important consideration in *Wandsworth London Borough Council v. Dixon* [2009] EWHC 27 (Admin) at [51] *per* Judge Bidder Q.C.

[177] *McCann v. United Kingdom* [2008] H.LR. 40 at [50].   [178] Ibid. at 59.

[179] *Doherty v. Birmingham City Council* [2009] A.C. 367 at [20]. See also the comments, at [82], of Lord Scott of Foscote on the failure of the European Court to appreciate the procedural protection which was already available in England in this type of case.

[180] Ibid. at [22].

Having reaffirmed the essential approach in *Qazi*, as modified by what he had said in *Kay*, however, Lord Hope appeared to widen the basis on which a public law challenge could be made. He said:

I think that…it would be unduly formalistic to confine the review strictly to traditional *Wednesbury* grounds. The considerations that can be brought into account in this case are wider. An examination of the question whether the council's decision was reasonable, having regard to the aim which it was pursuing *and to the length of time that the first defendant and his family have been living on the site would be appropriate.*[181]

It will be appreciated that, although Lord Hope had expressly discounted the relevance of the personal circumstances of the occupier, his acceptance that the length of the period of residence was a relevant consideration in determining the reasonableness of the council's action does actually amount to a consideration of one such personal circumstance. This, together with the comments of Lords Walker of Gestingthorpe and Mance that the decisions of local authorities to enforce an unqualified right to possession could be challenged on grounds wider than the traditional test of *Wednesbury* unreasonableness,[182] meant that, despite the strong reaffirmation of *Qazi*, English law was moving towards an approach more consistent with that taken in Europe.

The abandonment of *Qazi*

Despite protestations to the contrary, it seems evident that English law was moving towards an approach to this matter which was more consistent with that taken in Europe than had previously been the case, although the extent of convergence was unclear. Thus in *Taylor v. Central Bedfordshire Council*,[183] Waller L.J. said 'that the question whether a decision of a public body is "reasonable" post-*Doherty* goes beyond the question whether it is rational', but commented that there 'does appear to have been a tension between the House of Lords as to the proper approach to Article 8, and those of ECtHR, but hopefully the divergence is less serious than some would suggest.'[184] How far the divide might have been bridged by the English courts acting alone is speculative, but also became academic, in the light of the decision of the European Court of Human Rights in *Kay v. United Kingdom*,[185] which, following the dismissal of his appeal by the House of Lords, held that there had been an infringement of his rights under article 8 and awarded him compensation.

While the European Court accepted that the distance between conventional judicial review grounds and Human Rights Act grounds appeared to have narrowed, it

---

[181] Ibid. at [55]. Emphasis supplied. For the importance of the length of occupation, see *Stokes v. London Borough of Brent* [2009] EWHC 1426 (Ch) at [49]–[50] *per* King J.

[182] Ibid. at [135] and [162]. For an example of such a case based upon procedural defects, see *Eastlands Homes Partnership Ltd v. Whyte* [2010] EWHC 695 (QB).

[183] [2010] 1 W.L.R. 446 at [44].

[184] Ibid. at [26], although see *Salford City Council v. Mullen* [2010] EWCA Civ.336 at [61] *per* Waller L.J.

[185] [2011] H.L.R. 2. See S. Nield [2010] Conv. 498.

was also noted that the extent to which those grounds could be said to encompass proportionality was unclear.[186] Moreover, it was critical that the facts which it considered to be relevant to that issue had not been considered by the county court. The matters to which the court considered that regard should have been had included such things as the lengthy period of occupation, the improvement works carried out to the property, the factual correctness (or otherwise) of the authority's reasons for seeking possession and whether there actually was a need for vacant possession. The overriding principle was stated as being that:

'Any person at risk of an interference of this magnitude should…be able to have the proportionality of the measure determined by an independent tribunal in light of the relevant principles under Article 8 of the Convention, notwithstanding that, under domestic law, his right to occupation has come to an end.'[187]

This decision meant the English courts had to accept either that there was a rift between English law and the European Court of Human Rights as to the scope of article 8 of the Convention, or it had to accept that the law as laid down in *Qazi* was wrong. Accepting the seemingly inevitable, a nine-member panel of the Supreme Court in *Manchester City Council v. Pinnock*[188] took the latter option.[189] In so doing, a number of issues emerged, which will be considered in turn.

Introducing proportionality

Having accepted that, as a result of the European ruling in *Kay*, the proportionality of making a possession order was now an issue, the first question which arose was how to introduce this in the context of the legislative provisions relevant to the demoted tenancy procedure. It will be recalled that under the Act, the role of the county court was to ascertain that the local authority had followed the correct procedure. If it was satisfied that this was the case, then under section 143D of the Housing Act 1996 the court must make an order for possession. Giving the judgment of the Court, Lord Neuberger found a neat solution. When deciding whether to institute possession proceedings and, where requested, to establish a review, the local authority is under a duty, as a public body, to consider whether it is proportional that possession be obtained. The role of the county court is to establish that the correct procedure has been lawfully carried out. To this end, it must, itself, be able to satisfy itself that the making of an order was proportionate. Accordingly, section 149D of the Act was construed to allow the county court 'to consider and, where appropriate, to give effect to, any article 8 defence which the defendant raises in the possession proceedings'.[190] In short, it is now open to county court judges to consider the factual basis of an authority's action and to consider, notwithstanding that, under domestic law, the authority has an unqualified

---

[186] Ibid. at [54].   [187] Ibid. at [68].   [188] [2010] 3 W.L.R. 1441.

[189] For the reasons, see at [48] *per* Lord Neuberger.

[190] Ibid. at [79]. See also in respect of the similar legislative provisions with respect to introductory tenancies *London Borough of Hounslow v. Powell* [2011] 2 W.L.R. 287 at [56] *per* Lord Hope.

right to possess the property, whether the making of a possession order is proportion-ate. This gives rise to the related questions as to the impact of this on the conduct of possession proceedings, and to what matters the court will have regard in considering proportionality.

Assessing proportionality

In *Qazi* Lord Millett stressed that the issue of principle which divided the House was a narrow one, but one which he considered to be of considerable practical impor-tance.[191] The practical issue was articulated by Lord Hope who said the point of automatic possession proceedings was to provide a quick and reliable way of evict-ing tenants whose leases have terminated, and that the conferring on county court judges a discretion to not order possession on the ground of proportionality would be inimical to that policy.[192] While it is true that the possession proceedings may be complicated to an extent by the admission of a criterion of proportionality as a poten-tial defence, Lord Neuberger in *Pinnock*[193] was clearly mindful of this consideration when he considered how such cases should proceed. In his view, article 8 need only be considered by the court if it is raised by the residential occupier. If it is not, it would seem that summary judgment should be given. If, however, the matter is raised, the judge should consider the matter on a summary basis and:

'if, as no doubt will often be the case, the court is satisfied that, even if the facts relied on are made out, the point would not succeed, it should be dismissed. Only if the court is sat-isfied that it could affect the order that the court might make should the point be further entertained.'[194]

Throughout the debate as to the applicability of an article 8 defence, it has been stressed that, if as a matter of property law, a local authority is entitled to possession, it will only be in exceptional cases that that defence would prevail.[195] Although Lord Neuberger preferred to eschew the use of the expression, 'exceptional circumstances',[196] the general tenor of his remarks made it clear that, as a defence, it was unlikely to be of widespread application. He distinguished cases where, in order to obtain a pos-session order, the local authority must satisfy the court that it is reasonable to make such an order. In such instances, he expressed the view that there was no room for a separate defence of proportionality, as this criterion is an integral part of assessing reasonableness.[197] This must be right. In cases where there is no independent require-ment that it must be reasonable to make an order, the starting point is to recognize that unencumbered rights, even when they are enjoyed by a local authority, are of real weight when it comes to assessing proportionality, as is the right and obligation of a local authority to determine who should occupy its property. Accordingly, he

---

[191] *Harrow London Borough Council v. Qazi* [2004] 1 A.C. 983 at [85].   [192] Ibid. at [38].
[193] *Manchester City Council v. Pinnock* [2010] UKSC 45.   [194] Ibid. at [61].
[195] *Harrow London Borough Council v. Qazi* [2004] 1 A.C. 983 at [25] *per* Lord Bingham of Cornhill.
[196] *Manchester City Council v. Pinnock* [2010] UKSC 45, at [64].   [197] Ibid. at [55]–[56].

considered that 'in virtually every case where a residential occupier has no contractual or statutory protection, and the local authority is entitled to possession as a matter of domestic law, there will be a very strong case for saying that making an order
for possession would be proportionate. However, in some cases there may be factors
with would tell in the other way.'[198]

The bar for an occupier to surmount in order to successfully rely on article 8 is very
high, and the authority's case that the granting of possession is proportionate is supported by the fact that the gaining of possession would enable it to comply with its
duties in relation to the distribution and management of its housing stock. Relevant
factors in doing this would include the fair allocation of its housing, the redevelop-
ment of the site, the refurbishing of sub-standard accommodation, the need to move
people who are in accommodation that exceeds their needs, the need to move vulnerable people into sheltered accommodation and, in some cases, the need to remove a
source of nuisance to neighbours.[199]

Evidently it will be very difficult for occupiers to clear this bar. Little guidance as
to how this may be done was given, however, beyond saying that this was a matter
which 'is best left to the good sense and experience of the judges sitting in the County
Court'.[200] A little more substance was provided, however, when Lord Neuberger
accepted as well made the argument put forward by the Equality and Human Rights
Commission that proportionality may become a live issue in the case of occupiers who
are vulnerable by reason of mental illness, ill-health and frailty.[201]

To conclude, it is unlikely that the acceptance of article 8 as a potential defence to
possession proceedings brought by local authorities will have much impact on the
outcome of such cases, and so the importance of the decision is likely to be of more
theoretical than practical significance. It may have a role to play when a local authority
instigates the service of a notice to quit by one joint tenant who has left the property,
as this can be seen as a way of avoiding a different possession procedure, where it
otherwise may have to satisfy a court that to order possession was reasonable. Other
than that, it is likely to be the case that very strong personal circumstances will need
to be shown by the occupier to resist a possession action brought by a public body with
a proprietary right to possession.

Proportionality and private landlords

The discussion to date has centred solely on possession actions brought by public bodies. Now it has been established that an article 8 defence can be run to defend such possession actions, the question arises as to whether the same is true of actions brought by
private individuals. As the jurisprudence relating to this area developed, it was made
clear that the analysis was being applied only to public authorities. Lord Bingham, in

[198] Ibid. at [62].
[199] Ibid. at [52]. See also *London Borough of Hounslow v. Powell* [2011] UKSC 8 at [36].
[200] Ibid. at [57].   [201] Ibid. at [64].

Qazi, was explicit that 'nothing I have said in this opinion should be understood as applying to any landlord or owner which is not a public authority'.[202] Lord Neuberger in *Pinnock* also reserved his opinion on this matter, expressly leaving open whether the reasoning of the Supreme Court applied to private landowners, although pointing out that, in the case of private landowners, any argument that it did would raise issues concerning article 1 of the First Protocol.[203]

Substance or procedure?

To answer this important question, it is important to be clear as to the basis on which the courts have introduced the article 8 defence of proportionality. One way of looking at the impact of article 8 is to see the effect of *Pinnock* as altering the substantive law by creating, in effect, a freestanding defence to possession actions based upon proportionality. If this was the case, and such an argument was flatly rejected by the House of Lords in *Kay*,[204] then its effect would be to 'create an extensive reservoir of entitlement which would wreak havoc within substantive property law'.[205] This is because the substantive law would not differ with regard to this matter whether the claimant was a public or a private body. This argument has been advanced, it having been argued that the effect of article 8 is to modify the general principles of property law, it being said that the identity of the claimant is irrelevant; the real 'defendant' is the law.[206] It is suggested that this argument is supported neither by precedent nor principle.

As the debate as to this issue went on, the substance of it has related to the supervisory role of the courts. In *Qazi*, the scope of that intervention was limited by the majority to that of traditional judicial review of the decision to enforce the right to possession.[207] As the indirect dialogue with the Court in Strasbourg continued, the grounds on which such intervention could take place progressively widened, but it remained the case that the focus of attention was the enforcement of the right, unless, separately, an attack could be made on the substantive law which afforded the right to possession: a state of affairs which led to the creation of the dual track approach of gateways (a) and (b). This dichotomy would have been completely unnecessary had the argument been that the effect of article 8 was to alter the substantive law so that the absolute right to possession recognized by the law of property had, itself, been diluted. This approach has also been taken by the European Court of Human Rights, whose concern has not been with the substantive law, but with the procedural safeguards afforded to residential occupiers. This was made clear both in *McCann v. United*

---

[202] *Harrow London Borough Council v. Qazi* [2004] 21 A.C. 983 at [23].

[203] [2010] UKSC 45 at [4] and [50].

[204] *Kay v. London Borough of Lambeth* [2006] 2 A.C. 465 at [207] *per* Lord Brown of Eaton-under-Haywood.

[205] See A. Goymour [2006] C.L.J. 696 at 706.

[206] I. Loveland (2011) 2 EHRLR 151 at 158. See also M. Davis and D. Hughes [2010] Conv. 57 at 72.

[207] See *Harrow London Borough Council v. Qazi* [2004] 1 A.C. 983 at [109] *per* Lord Millett.

Kingdom[208] and in *Kay v. United Kingdom*.[209] In the latter case, the Court welcomed the fact that the English courts had widened the judicial review grounds to encompass article 8, but considered that, at the time when the actual case was decided in England, the majority view did not extend to allowing a defendant to argue that the local authority had been acting proportionately and, as a result, there was a breach of the Convention.[210]

It is, of course, true that the fact that either a public body or a private individual has the right to possession of land does not mean that that right has to be enforced. In the case of the former, however, the decision making process to decide to enforce that right has always been amenable to judicial review and, now, as a result of *Pinnock*, it is clear that public bodies must apply a Convention-compliant policy.[211] In the case of private landowners, in principle there should be no such constraint. This was spelled out explicitly in *Central Bedfordshire Council v. Taylor*.[212] Waller L.J. commenting on the decision in *Doherty* said:

'I can start by emphasising that if the landowner were a private landowner there would be no question of that landowner being required to take account of the personal circumstances of the trespassers. The court would be bound to make an order for possession. It is because the council are a public authority and its decisions are susceptible to judicial review that there can be any question of the appellants being able to raise what is loosely called an Article 8 defence.'

This is consistent with the normal approach to the enforcement of private property rights. In such cases, it has been said that:

'There is no concept that is more fundamental than a right of property. Where it exists, it is for the owner to exercise it as he pleases. He does not need the permission of the court, nor is it subject to court's discretion.... These are rights which the court must respect and which it will enforce if it is asked to do so.'[213]

Where private landowners are concerned, it is thought that this remains the position notwithstanding article 8 of the European Convention. To this argument of principle can be added the consideration alluded to by Lord Neuberger in *Pinnock*, that to hold that a possession action brought by a private landowner is subject to a test of proportionality and would involve a counter-argument based on article 1 of the First Protocol.[214] This article protects people from being deprived of their possessions and, it would seem, would be potentially infringed if a court prevented a private landowner from exercising a right to possession which domestic law afforded him.

---

[208] [2008] 47 EHHR 913 at [55].   [209] [2011] HLR 2.   [210] Ibid. at [72]–[74].

[211] See the comments in *Doherty v. Birmingham City Council* [2009] A.C. 387 at [121] *per* Lord Walker of Gestingthorpe.

[212] [2009] EWCA Civ. 613 at [18].

[213] *Fisher v. Brooker* [2009] 1 W.L.R. 1764 at [8] *per* Lord Hope of Craighead, a case concerning intellectual property.

[214] *Manchester City Council v. Pinnock* [2010] UKSC 45 at [50].

Defects in the substantive law

A situation where a private landowner may be restricted in his ability to obtain possession of land is where the law which entitles him to do is, itself, open to objection
on the basis that it contravenes the Convention. A good example of this occurred in
Ghaidan v. Godin-Mendoza.[215] A private landlord sought possession of property after
the death of a tenant. This was resisted by the homosexual partner of the deceased.
Had the couple been heterosexual, the defendant would have succeeded to the tenancy
as the survivor of a couple who had been living together as husband and wife. To avoid
the statute[216] from causing discrimination against the defendant on the ground of
sexual orientation, which would infringe article 14 of the Convention, the House of
Lords, following section 3 of the Human Rights Act 1998, construed the expression
'living together as husband and wife' to include a homosexual couple. This is unexceptional, and is illustrative of how the Human Rights Act can modify the substantive
law, and arguments such as this will be encountered elsewhere in this book. It does
not, however, support the wider view that article 8 should have this effect so as to convert absolute proprietary rights to rights which are subject to an overriding criterion
of proportionality.

[215] [2004] 2 A.C. 557.   [216] Rent Act 1977, Sched. 1, paras 2, 3.

4

The 1925 Legislation

In 1925, substantial legislation was enacted which recast Land Law in this country. Surprising though this may seem, this legislation provided the skeleton on which modern Land Law was developed for over seventy-five years. Of course, over the years, many developments, both statutory and judicial, have occurred since that date, but the essential framework remained intact until the enactment of the Land Registration Act 2002, legislation which replaced, and substantially modified, the Land Registration Act 1925. Despite this new legislative reform, the system put in place by the 1925 legislation still remains the bedrock upon which modern Land Law is based. Although the 2002 Act will, for the future, be the principal piece of legislation relating to land ownership in this country, a good deal of the theoretical underpinning of the subject will remain that provided by the 1925 legislation.

THE LEGISLATIVE BACKGROUND[1]

A feature of the doctrine of estates was that it allowed for the fragmentation of ownership rights amongst various people. In addition to the existence of legal estates there existed the equitable counterparts of them. As well as it being quite possible for a number of estates to exist simultaneously with respect to the same plot of land, there could also exist a number of different third party rights, such as easements and restrictive covenants, affecting it. Moreover, there was considerable formality and artificiality involved with the creation of interests in land, with the result that, to quote a memorable phrase attributed to Lord Westbury, titles to land depended on the interpretation of deeds which were 'difficult to read, disgusting to touch, and impossible to understand'.[2] This problem, coupled with the complexity of the substantive law, itself,[3] was the principal reason for a special rule affecting contracts for the sale of land. This

---

[1] See Anderson, *Lawyers and the Making of English Land Law 1832–1940* (Oxford: Oxford University Press, 1992).

[2] See *Wroth v. Tyler* [1974] Ch. 30 at 56 *per* Megarry J.

[3] See Law Reform Commission of British Columbia, Report on the Rule in *Bain v. Fothergill* (1976) 6 cited in (1987) Law Com. No. 166, Appendix C, para. 3.7.

rule[4] limited the damages recoverable for the breach of such a contract by the vendor, if the breach was occasioned by his inability to convey that which he had contracted to convey because his title to the land was defective: that is, the vendor was not able to prove in a satisfactory manner that he actually owned the land which he had contracted to sell, or that the land was subject to some third party right, the existence of which had not been disclosed in the contract of sale.

Various attempts were made to simplify and add security to the conveyancing process, measures which included the registration of deeds[5] and the registration of incumbrances affecting the land. The ultimate goal, however, was to facilitate the registration of title to land, whereby a person's ownership of the land would be entered upon an official register, the third party rights affecting that land also being entered on that register. For this process to happen, however, it was necessary to simplify the substantive law relating to land.[6] To this end, a series of reforming statutes were enacted,[7] culminating in the largely consolidating legislation of 1925, which is sometimes referred to, after its principal architect, as the Birkenhead legislation.[8]

The aim of this chapter is to explain the main strategies of the 1925 legislation. This will focus, principally, on its effect on unregistered land. Although this form of land ownership, whereby a person proves his entitlement to land by reference to the title deeds, will soon be superseded by the universal spread of registration of title, it remains relevant and will continue to do so for a number of years to come. The next chapter will consider the system of registration of title. For many years, the Act concerned with registration of title was the Land Registration Act 1925. This legislation has now been superseded by the Land Registration Act 2002.

LAND LAW AFTER 1925

Lord Birkenhead, who piloted the earlier legislation through Parliament, described its policy in the following terms. He said:

'Its general principle is to assimilate the law of real and personal estate and to free the purchaser from the obligation to enquire into the title of him from whom he purchases, any more than he would have to do if he were buying a share or a parcel of stock.'[9]

---

[4] *Flureau v. Thornhill* (1776) 2 Wm. Bl. 1078; *Bain v. Fothergill* (1874) L.R. 7 H.L. 158. This rule was not finally abolished until 1989: Law of Property (Miscellaneous Provisions) Act 1989, s. 3.

[5] See J. Howell [1999] C.L.J. 366.

[6] Hayton, *Registered Land* (3rd edn) (London: Sweet & Maxwell, 1981), 8–14.

[7] Notably, the Vendor and Purchaser Act 1874, the Conveyancing Act 1881, the Settled Land Act 1882, and the Law of Property Acts 1922 and 1924.

[8] See Campbell, *F.E. Smith First Earl of Birkenhead* (London: Jonathan Cape, 1983), 483–486. The Lord Chancellor when the 1925 legislation was enacted was Lord Cave L.C.

[9] Letter to *The Times*, 15 December 1920, cited in Campbell, op. cit., 485.

To seek to achieve what was probably an unattainable goal, various strategies were adopted. As well as ridding the law of some of the more technical and artificial aspects,[10] various substantive themes can be seen. These can be outlined as follows.

Reduction in legal estates and interests

Prior to 1926, when the legislation came into force, various different estates could exist at law. Section 1 of the Law of Property Act 1925 reduced the number of legal estates which could exist to two: the fee simple absolute in possession and the term of years absolute. The former expression has already been discussed[11] and the latter relates to leases. All other estates in land can now exist only in equity. In addition to this, the number of legal interests, which would bind a purchaser of land, irrespective of notice, was also reduced.

Registration of land charges

The reduction of the number of legal estates and interests in land led to a corresponding increase in the number of equitable interests. Prior to 1925, the question of whether or not a purchaser would be bound by equitable interests turned on whether he was able to establish that he was a bona fide purchaser of a legal estate without notice. This entailed him having to establish that he had made all the enquiries which the law considered ought reasonably to have been made. To facilitate the purchaser's task, and also to assist a holder of an equitable interest to be able securely to protect that right, provision was made for such rights to be made registrable as land charges. The aim of this was to enable a purchaser, by the relatively simple means of requisitioning an official search of the land charges register, to be able to discover to what third party rights the property he was buying would be subject.

Registration of title

As indicated earlier, one of the principal reasons for reforming the substantive law was to promote the spread of registration of title. The traditional method of establishing that the vendor owned the land which he was purporting to sell was to examine the title deeds, the purpose of which was to show a convincing account of the devolution of the property in the past to establish his right to deal with the land. This is a time-consuming business and one where mistakes can be made, so that security of title is not guaranteed. Registration of title is an idea designed to make this process obsolete. Once title to the land is registered, a central idea of the system is that the state will guarantee that the register is accurate in terms of who owns the land.

---

[10] For example, the rule in *Shelley's Case* (1581) 1 Co. Rep. 88b was abolished: Law of Property Act 1925 s. 131 and the Statute of Uses 1535 was finally repealed: Law of Property Act 1925, Sched. 7, thereby making the creation of trusts of land more straightforward.

[11] See The fee simple, p. 26.

In addition, subject to a category of rights, which were formerly termed 'overriding interests' and are now, somewhat less elegantly, called 'unregistered interests which override registration',[12] which as the latter term suggests are rights which will bind a purchaser despite not being noted on the register of title, the register will also indicate to what third party rights the land is subject.

Extension of overreaching

The existence of a large number of freehold estates in relation to the same property was normally indicative of there being a family settlement. A settlement to A for life, to B in fee tail, to C in fee simple would normally take place within a family unit. That being the case, it is unlikely that any of A, B, or C would have paid money to acquire their interests in the land. The effect of the settlement, however, made it extremely difficult for the land to be sold, for the simple reason that none of the estate owners held an estate that would be particularly attractive for a purchaser to buy. If, for example, A sold his interest, then all that a purchaser would acquire was an estate *pur autre vie*; his interest in the land would terminate upon the death of A. Again, if either B or C sought to alienate their interests, then a purchaser would have to wait until that interest fell into possession before the land could actually be enjoyed and, in the case of C, there would be no guarantee that this would necessarily ever happen at all.

To enable land, subject to a settlement such as this, to become marketable, a mechanism was imposed to enable the land to be sold. A, who is termed the tenant for life, is given a legal fee simple but, to safeguard the position of B and C, two trustees had to be appointed to receive the purchase money when the land was sold. The purchaser would take a conveyance from A and pay the purchase money to the trustees. That money would be invested and A would receive the income, that money representing his life interest in the land. On A's death the money would then pass in accordance with the settlement. In this way, the interests in the land are converted into money. This process is termed 'overreaching'.[13]

Reform of co-ownership

It is common for land to be co-owned, the most common situation probably being when a family home is owned by a married couple. Under the law as it existed prior to 1925, it was possible for the legal ownership of the land to become fragmented between numerous people, with obvious attendant conveyancing difficulties. To avoid these difficulties, the law was altered, imposing four as the maximum number of legal owners

---

[12] Land Registration Act 2002, Scheds 1 and 3. For a full discussion of these matters, see Chapter 5.

[13] For settlements created after 1996 a new regime was introduced by the Trusts of Land and Appointments of Trustees Act 1996. See Chapter 8.

of land. The legal owners could then hold the property on trust for any number of equitable co-owners.[14] Provided that the purchase money is paid to the legal co-owners, the purchaser need not concern himself with the interests of the equitable co-owners, whose interests will be overreached,[15] that is, their interests will take effect against the proceeds of sale of the property.

Mortgages

A mortgage is a loan secured against land. Under the old law, the security was given by conveying the land to the mortgagee, the land being reconveyed upon the repayment of the loan. This, of course, was highly artificial and disguised the true nature of the transaction. After 1925, a mortgage could be created either by executing a charge by way of legal mortgage, by which the lender, or mortgagee, acquires the right to take possession of the mortgaged property and, if the mortgage is not repaid, to sell the property, or by creating a 3,000-year lease,[16] although where title is registered, it is no longer possible to utilize the latter method to create a mortgage.[17] In both cases, the fee simple remains with the borrower, the mortgagor.

Capacity

Section 1(6) of the Law of Property Act 1925 provides that a legal estate is not capable of being held by a minor. The general rule is clear that a person below the age of eighteen lacks the capacity to own a legal estate.[18] If, however, by some mistake, a person below that age is registered as the proprietor of land with an absolute title, then the provisions of the Land Registration Act 2002 would appear to clothe that person with the legal title, notwithstanding section 1(6) of the earlier Act.[19]

The Law Commission has recently recommended that letting contracts should be able to be entered into with minors aged sixteen and seventeen.[20] This is sensible when one bears in mind that people of that age can marry each other,[21] and it makes little sense for the law then to preclude them from the legal ownership of a place in which to live.

---

[14] Law of Property Act 1925, s. 34(2). The Law Commission has recommended that, in respect of housing tenancies, this restriction should be abolished: (2003) Law Com. No. 284, para. 11.12.

[15] *City of London Building Society v. Flegg* [1988] A.C. 54; *State Bank of India v. Sood* [1997] Ch. 276. See Overreaching, pp. 297–300.

[16] Law of Property Act 1925, s. 85. See Chapter 12.   [17] Land Registration Act 2002, s. 23(1).

[18] If land is conveyed to a minor before 1997, the land will be regarded as settled land: Settled Land Act 1925, ss 1, 26. If this occurs after this date, the land will be held on a trust of land. See Chapter 8.

[19] See Registration with an absolute title, p. 126.   [20] (2003) Law Com. No. 284, para. 3.18.

[21] See Marriage Act 1949, s. 2.

Reduction in legal estates

Section 1 of the Law of Property Act 1925 provides that the only estates in land which are capable of subsisting or being created at law are:

(a) an estate in fee simple in possession; and

(b) a term of years absolute.

Section 1(2) also limits the number of legal interests in land capable of subsisting or being conveyed. Of these interests, the most important are:

(a) an easement right or privilege in or over land for an interest equivalent to an estate in fee simple absolute in possession or a term of years absolute;

(b) a rentcharge in possession issuing out of or charged on land being either perpetual or for a term of years absolute;

(c) a charge by way of legal mortgage;

(d) rights of entry exercisable over or in respect of a term of years absolute or annexed, for any purpose, to a legal rentcharge.

It is provided by section 1(3) of the Act that all other estates, interests, or charges in or over land shall take effect as equitable interests.

Before elaborating on these crucial definitions, some preliminary points should be made.

Capable of existing as legal estates

Section 1 of the Act lays down which estates are *capable* of existing as legal estates. It is not the case, however, that because a particular interest falls within that definition it will necessarily be legal. In general, to create a legal estate or interest in land one must use a deed.[22] If a deed is not used, then unless the transaction in question is exempt from this formal requirement,[23] no legal estate or interest will be created. The purported grant may, however, take effect in equity. A term of years absolute, or lease, may therefore be either legal or equitable.

Estates and interests

Section 1 of the Act refers separately to estates and interests. This is a helpful division, in that the concept of an estate connotes ownership rights in land, which are possessory in nature, whereas the idea of an interest in land generally means rights over another person's land.

---

[22] Law of Property Act 1925, s. 52(1).

[23] Ibid., s. 53(2). For prescriptive rights, see Prescription, pp. 565–573.

LEGAL ESTATES

The fee simple absolute in possession

A central plank in the strategy was to make the basis of conveyancing the fee simple absolute. Hence this is now the only legal freehold estate which can exist. The nature of a fee simple absolute in possession has already been considered. Outside the definition would be estates such as a life estate, a fee tail, or a base fee, which can now only take effect in equity. Similarly, a fee simple which will determine upon the occurrence of a particular event, for example to A in fee simple or until he becomes a solicitor, is not a fee simple absolute because of the existence of the determining element.

Some problems were occasioned, however, with regard to certain types of determinable fees simple and, in particular, the situation where land was subject to a rentcharge. The practice developed in some parts of the country whereby land would be conveyed subject to a rentcharge, which is an obligation on the part of the landowner to pay an annual sum of money charged on the land. The normal sanction for non-payment was that the owner of the rentcharge had the right to re-enter the land and to determine the fee simple. This type of device would prevent the original fee simple from being legal as, because it was liable to be determined, it was not absolute. This problem was solved by the Law of Property (Amendment) Act 1926, which amended section 7(1) of the 1925 Act to provide that a fee simple subject to a legal or equitable right of re-entry is for the purposes of the Act a fee simple absolute.[24] The importance of this is diminished, however, because the ability to create new rentcharges was severely restricted by section 2 of the Rentcharges Act 1977 and those already in existence at the time that the Act was passed will be extinguished sixty years from the passing of the Act or when the rentcharge first became payable, whichever is the later.[25]

A similar problem arose with regard to land which, by statute, was held for a specific purpose, such as schools and highways, which would revert, usually to the grantor, on the ending of that purpose. A fee simple such as this remains absolute.[26] At the end of the purpose, the land remains vested in the existing owners, who hold the property on a trust of land for those entitled under the reverter.[27]

A fee simple is in possession unless it is subject to some prior freehold estate, such as a life estate. Any fee simple in remainder cannot, therefore, be legal. Possession does not necessarily entail physical possession. If the owner of a fee simple creates a lease, the fee simple remains in possession because possession is defined to include the right to receive rents and profits.[28]

[24] Law of Property (Amendment) Act 1926, s. 7, Sched.   [25] Rentcharges Act 1977, s. 3(1).

[26] Law of Property Act 1925, s. 7.

[27] Reverter of Sites Act 1977, s. 1 as amended by Trusts of Land and Appointment of Trustees Act 1996, s. 5, Sched. 2, resolving the problem revealed by *Re Clayton's Deed Poll* [1980] Ch. 99 and *Re Rowhook Mission Hall, Horsham* [1985] Ch. 62. See D. Evans [1987] Conv. 408. See, also, the discussion of the operation of statutes dealing with this issue in *Fraser v. Canterbury Diocesan Board of Finance* [2006] 1 A.C. 377.

[28] Law of Property Act 1925, s. 205(1)(xix).

The term of years absolute

A term of years absolute is a lease. The definition is somewhat unhelpful as term of years includes periods of less than a year, as well as periods from year to year.[29] This latter concept occurs when a lease is granted initially for a specific period, such as one year, and at the end of that period it is renewed automatically for a further period. Such leases will continue indefinitely until either the landlord or the tenant brings it to an end by a process of serving a notice to quit upon the other. What the definition entails is that there is a term which is either certain at the outset, or is capable of being made certain upon the service of a notice to quit.[30]

The word 'absolute' appears to have no discernible meaning in that a lease which is determinable on the occurrence of a particular event, or is liable to forfeiture—that is where the lease can be brought to a premature end by the landlord consequent upon a breach by the tenant of one of the terms of the lease—is, nevertheless, a term of years absolute.

A term of years need not take effect in possession, so that a lease granted today to commence in five years' time is perfectly valid. A lease which is to take effect more than twenty-one years from the date of its creation is, however, void.[31]

LEGAL INTERESTS

Various interests are capable of taking effect as legal interests in land. They are defined by section 1(2) of the Law of Property Act 1925 and the most important of these are as follows.

Easements, rights, and privileges

An easement, right, or privilege in or over land for an interest equivalent to a fee simple absolute in possession or a term of years absolute is capable of taking effect as a legal interest. An easement is normally a positive right to do something over nearby land, such as the exercise of a right of way over it. Less commonly, it can amount to a restriction on another's use of his own land. This will be the case if there is in existence an easement of light which will restrict a landowner's ability to build on his own land, if the effect of so doing would be to obstruct the flow of light. Also within the definition is a *profit à prendre*. This is the right to go onto another person's land and to take something, for example wood, from it.[32]

---

[29] Ibid., s. 205(1)(xxvii).
[30] *Prudential Assurance Co. Ltd v. London Residuary Body* [1992] 2 A.C. 386. See Restricting service of notice to quit, pp. 417–418.
[31] Law of Property Act 1925, s. 205(1)(xxvii).   [32] For easements and profits, see Chapter 14.

For either interest to be legal, their duration must be the equivalent to a fee simple absolute or to a term of years absolute. An easement for life, if such a right is actually an easement at all,[33] is, therefore, necessarily equitable.

Rentcharges

A rentcharge is a right for the owner of it to receive a periodical payment from the owner of the burdened land. This right is independent of any other interest in the land. To be legal, a rentcharge must be perpetual, the term 'perpetual', for some reason, being used instead of the more normal expression, 'fee simple absolute', or it must subsist 'for a term of years absolute'. While it must also take effect in possession, possession in this context has a wider meaning than normal; it includes a situation where it becomes payable at some time in the future, after its creation, provided that it does not take effect upon the determination of some prior interest.[34]

Subject to limited exceptions,[35] no new rentcharges may be created after 1977 and rentcharges still in existence, having been created prior to that date, will expire, at the latest, by 2033.[36]

A charge by way of legal mortgage

A mortgage is one of the most important interests affecting land and will be considered in Chapter 12.

Rights of re-entry

A right of re-entry is normally annexed to a leasehold estate to enable the landlord to determine the lease upon the tenant's failure to comply with the covenants contained in the lease. A right of re-entry is the normal sanction in respect of a failure to comply with the terms of a rentcharge. On the exercise of that right the fee simple against which the rentcharge takes effect is terminated.

EQUITABLE RIGHTS

Unless a right in land falls within one of the definitions given above, it cannot be a legal right and must, therefore, be equitable. The types of equitable interests in land, however, differ in nature. Although there is no formal statutory division of equitable interests, they fall within two broadly defined groups: family interests and commercial interests. The general scheme of the legislation was to make the former type of interest overreachable and the latter type registrable.

---

[33] For the view that it is not, see D.G. Barnsley (1999) 115 L.Q.R. 89.
[34] Law of Property (Entailed Interests) Act 1932, s. 2.   [35] See Rentcharges, p. 592.
[36] Rentcharges Act 1977, ss 2, 3.

Family interests

If one returns to the settlement considered earlier, where land is settled on A for life, to B in fee tail, remainder to C in fee simple, it should be apparent that, after 1925, neither A, B, nor C have legal interests in the property. A and B do not have a fee simple and C has a fee simple but it is not in possession. The effect of section 1 of the Law of Property Act 1925 was to ensure that all three would now have equitable estates in the land.

The fee simple absolute in possession was made the only legal, freehold estate in land and was intended to be the subject matter of a conveyance. Yet, in this situation, nobody would be entitled to such an estate in his own right. To fill this gap, the original solution[37] imposed by the Settled Land Act 1925 was to require a vesting deed to be executed, the effect of which would be to vest in A, the tenant for life, a legal fee simple, that fee simple being held by A on trust for those, including himself, entitled under the settlement. To prevent A from selling the property and then misapplying the purchase money, two trustees would be appointed and any purchase money paid to them. On a conveyance by A, the purchaser, provided that he paid the money to the trustees, would take free of the interests behind the settlement which would attach to the proceeds of sale. What this means is that the trustees would invest the capital money which was realized by the sale of the land. They would then pay the interest to A, this representing what was his estate in the land. On A's death, B, if still alive, would be entitled to the interest and, on B's death, or, if B had predeceased A, B's lineal heir would be entitled to that money. Provided that the fee tail had not been enlarged into a fee simple then, on the failure of B's lineal heirs, C would be entitled to the capital sum. In this way, the interests which were previously interests in land became interests in money and those interests are said to have been overreached.

The effect of this procedure is that A can, in a sense, occasion the compulsory purchase of the interest of B and C. While, at first sight, this can appear to be harsh on them, this is not really so, because, given the type of interests that the various characters have in the property, it is unlikely that they will have paid to acquire them. The interests will almost inevitably have been created as part of a family settlement and, in the interests of making the land marketable, this procedure was made available to allow the family interests to be overreached.[38]

Commercial interests

A person may own land and covenant with his neighbour that he will only use the land as a private residence. This obligation, termed 'a restrictive covenant', is, if certain

---

[37] Such settlements, if created after 1996, are now governed by the Trusts of Land and Appointment of Trustees Act 1996, s. 2.

[38] Overreaching can also occur in different contexts, most notably on a sale by a mortgagee. See Law of Property Act 1925, s. 104, see The effect of a sale, p. 525.

criteria are satisfied,[39] capable of creating an equitable burden affecting the land of the covenantor and is able to affect subsequent purchasers of the land. It should be apparent that this type of right, which affects the value of the burdened land, is unlikely to have been granted for nothing. It will have been paid for, either as an independent transaction or, more likely, as part of a commercial transaction involving the sale of the land in question. Moreover, it is not the sort of right which can sensibly be transferred to money.[40] While it can readily be seen that one can have a life interest in a capital fund, the effect of which is that the tenant for life enjoys the income produced by the investment of that fund, one cannot sensibly be said to enjoy a restrictive covenant over money. To retain its utility, it must remain attached to the land through successive periods of ownership. It is a commercial interest in land which cannot be overreached, and its enforceability is made dependent upon registration.

A basic strategy of the 1925 legislation was to categorize equitable interests into family interests which, by implementing the correct conveyancing procedure, can be overreached and commercial interests, which would depend for their enforceability upon registration. If such a scheme was all-embracing, the purchaser's task would be relatively straightforward. Where land was subject to family interests, his task would be simply to ensure that the correct procedures are followed; in the case of commercial interests, he would simply have to ascertain what interests had been registered, in order to know, before buying the land, to what incumbrances it would be subject. As will be seen, however, this dichotomy is not exhaustive of equitable interests. There exists a third category of interest which is neither overreachable nor registrable, the enforceability of which depends upon the traditional doctrine of notice.

LAND CHARGES REGISTRATION

An aim of the legislation was to make the enforceability of various rights dependent upon registration. To this end, the Land Charges Act 1925, which has since been superseded by the Land Charges Act 1972, was enacted. This Act established five separate registers, of which the most important is the land charges register. The remainder of this chapter will be confined to this most important category established by the land charges legislation, the land charges register.[41]

Before considering the structure and working of the system, a number of preliminary points may be made. First, one must distinguish land charges registrable under the 1972 Act from local land charges registrable under the Local Land Charges Act

---

[39] See Chapter 14.

[40] See *Birmingham Midshires Mortgage Services Ltd v. Sabherwal* (1999) 80 P. & C.R. 256 at 263 *per* Robert Walker L.J.

[41] For the other registers, see Thompson, *Barnsley's Conveyancing Law and Practice* (4th edn) (London: Butterworths, 1996), 390–391.

1975. Local land charges relate to various charges, normally either of a financial nature or restrictive of land use, imposed on land in favour of local authorities. Second, and more importantly, it is essential not to confuse the registration of land charges with registration of title. The registration of land charges concerns land where the title is still evidenced by deeds. Registration of title is a system of land ownership whereby the actual title to the land is registered and where recourse to the deeds is no longer necessary, or indeed possible. Under this system, which will eventually replace almost entirely the unregistered, or deeds-based system of land ownership, the register gives an authoritative version of the ownership of the land itself and, subject to a category of rights, originally termed 'overriding interests', will reveal the obligations to which the land is subject,[42] so that a separate register of third party rights affecting the land is unnecessary.

Ultimately, the land charges system will become obsolete, as virtually all titles become registered; indeed, all transactions conducted under the old system of establishing title to the land by reference to the title deeds, where searches in the land charges register are necessary, are now, by force of law, to be followed by the immediate registration of title, so that the deeds will never again be used in respect of the land in question. At present, and indeed for some time to come, the system remains important. In 2010/2011, there were over 140,000 registrations of new land charges, and over 353,000 full official searches made.[43] The remainder of this chapter is concerned with the operation of the system of land charges, and relates to land where the title is not registered.

Basic principles

It may be helpful, at the outset, to state the two basic principles which apply to the registration of land charges. These are that:

(i)   the registration of a land charge constitutes actual notice of the interest registered;[44] and

(ii)   non-registration of an interest against a particular type of purchaser will make it void against certain types of purchaser.[45]

REGISTRATION UNDER THE LAND CHARGES ACT

Under section 1 of the Land Charges Act 1972, the registrar is required to keep five registers and an index. The five registers are:

(i)   a register of land charges;

(ii)   a register of pending land actions;

---

[42] See Chapter 5.   [43] Land Registry Annual Report 2010/11, (HCP 1158), 15.
[44] Law of Property Act 1925, s. 198.   [45] Land Charges Act 1972, s. 4.

(iii) a register of writs and orders affecting land;

(iv) a register of deeds of arrangement affecting land;

(v) a register of annuities.

The five registers are kept in computerized form at the Land Charges Department at the Land Registry in Plymouth.[46] Of the five registers, the most important is the first named, the land charges register, and this is the only one of the registers which will be discussed.

Land charges

This is far and away the most important of the registers. Matters registrable as land charges are placed into one of six categories, labelled A to F, some of these categories themselves being subdivided. The various land charges are defined in section 2 of the Act.

Class A

This class consists of financial charges on land created pursuant to a statute on the application of some person. An example is a charge obtained by a landlord in respect of compensation paid to his tenant for improvements to business premises.[47]

Class B

This group consists of charges, not being local land charges, which are imposed automatically by statute, an example being the legal aid charge in favour of the Legal Services Commission in respect of property recovered or preserved by a legally aided litigant.[48]

Class C

This category is one of the most important classes of land charge and is subdivided into four subcategories.

Class C(i): A puisne mortgage[49]

A puisne mortgage is a mortgage not protected by a deposit of title deeds relating to the legal estate affected. This type of mortgage is a legal interest in land but, for it to be enforceable against purchasers of the estate affected, it must be protected by registration. As such, this is an exception to the general principle that legal rights bind the world, regardless of notice. The reason for this exception is entirely pragmatic.

---

[46] For an account of how the system worked prior to computerization, see *Oak Co-operative Building Society v. Blackburn* [1967] Ch. 730 at 741 *per* Russell L.J.

[47] Landlord and Tenant Act 1927, s. 12 and Sched. 1, para. 7. The full list of such charges is contained in Land Charges Act 1972, Sched. 2.

[48] Legal Aid Act 1988, s. 16. See *Hanlon v. Law Society* [1981] A.C. 124; *Curling v. Law Society* [1985] 1 W.L.R. 470; *Parkes v. Legal Aid Board* [1996] 4 All E.R. 271.

[49] Pronounced 'puny'.

Prior to 1925, the traditional way of creating a mortgage was to convey the land to the mortgagee as security for the loan, the land to be reconveyed when the loan was repaid. As the legal owner of the land, the mortgagee was entitled to the title deeds. Moreover, if land had been mortgaged in this way, it was not possible to create a second legal mortgage as, the land having already been conveyed to the first mortgagee, it could not be conveyed a second time to a subsequent lender. After 1925, to create a legal mortgage, one executes a charge by way of legal mortgage[50] and the mortgagor retains the legal estate. It is possible, therefore, for him to create subsequent legal mortgages.

The first mortgagee is entitled to possession of the title deeds and this alerts subsequent lenders to the fact that the land is already subject to a mortgage. Unless any subsequent mortgages were registered, however, one could not know if the land was subject to more than one mortgage and it would be unsafe to lend money against the security of the land. For this reason, a legal mortgage not protected by a deposit of title deeds is registrable as a land charge.

Class C(ii): A limited owner's charge

A limited owner's charge is an equitable charge acquired by a tenant for life or statutory owner when that person discharges tax liability[51] payable on the death of the previous tenant for life out of his own resources rather than from the settled property.

Class C(iii): General equitable charge

This is a residuary category which is defined in a negative way, by reference to what it is not. It is an equitable charge which:

(a) is not secured by a deposit of documents relating to the legal estate affected; and

(b) does not arise or affect an interest arising under a trust of land or a settlement; and

(c) is not a charge given by way of indemnity against rents equitably apportioned on land in exoneration of other land and against the breach or non-observance of other covenants or conditions; and

(d) is not included in any other class of land charge.[52]

As can be seen, this is something of a 'sweeper' category. It includes an unpaid vendor's lien,[53] which is a charge that a vendor has against the land which he has sold in respect of which some, or all, of the purchase money remains outstanding and

---

[50] Law of Property Act 1925, s. 85. See The creation of mortgages, pp. 467–469.

[51] Land Charges Act 1972, s. 3(4)(ii) as amended by Capital Transfer Tax Act 1984, Sched. 8, para. 3. The tax is now termed Inheritance Tax: Finance Act 1986, s. 100.

[52] Land Charges Act 1972, as amended by Trusts of Land and Appointment of Trustees Act 1996, s. 25, Sched. 3, para. 12(1)(2).

[53] *Uziell-Hamilton v. Keen* (1971) 22 P. & C.R. 655. For a discussion of this lien, see D.G. Barnsley [1997] Conv. 338.

also annuities created after 1925. An annuity is a charge against land to produce an annual income and is rarely, if ever, encountered today.

Class C(iv): Estate contract

The estate contract is one of the more important categories of land charge. It is defined by section 2(4)(iv) of the Act as being:

'...a contract by an estate owner to have a legal estate conveyed to him to convey or create a legal estate, including a contract conferring either expressly or by statutory implication a valid option to purchase, a right of pre-emption or any other like right.'

A contract to purchase land is obviously within the terms of the definition. In the case of contracts made after 1989, it is now essential that they be made in writing and signed by both parties[54] and an agreement which does not comply with these formalities is non-contractual in nature and cannot be registered. A conditional contract, such as where the contract is conditional upon the purchaser obtaining planning permission,[55] is apparently registrable[56] even though the condition has not, at the time, been satisfied.[57]

A contract to create a lease is registrable as a C(iv) land charge, so that a lease which should have been granted by deed and which satisfies the formal requirements of section 2 of the Law of Property (Miscellaneous Provisions) Act 1989, which means that it must be in writing and signed by both landlord and tenant, will be registrable.

Options to purchase

An option to purchase is a right given by the owner of land to another person, within a stated period of time, to purchase the land. Upon the grant of the option neither side is committed to a purchase. The contract of sale arises when the grantee of the option exercises it, thereby causing a binding contract to be created between the landowner and the grantee of the option. An option to purchase is registrable as a land charge, although once it has been registered, it is unnecessary to register, separately, the contract of sale which is created upon the exercise of the option.[58]

A lease may give to the tenant the option at the end of the period granted the right to renew that lease for a further term. Although it has been argued that it should not be necessary for such an option to be registered,[59] it is now clear that, for such an option to bind a purchaser of the landlord's reversion, the option must be registered

---

[54] Law of Property (Miscellaneous Provisions) Act 1989, s. 2.

[55] See, e.g., *Batten v. White* (1960) 12 P. & C.R. 66.

[56] *Haselmere Estates Ltd v. Baker* [1982] 1 W.L.R. 1109 at 1118–1119 *per* Sir Robert Megarry V.-C. See also *Williams v. Burlington Investment Ltd* (1979) 121 S. J. 424.

[57] For an argument that such a contract should not be regarded as registrable, see R.J. Smith [1974] C.L.J. 311 at 314.

[58] *Armstrong & Holmes v. Armstrong and Dodds* [1994] 1 All E.R. 826. See N. Gravells [1994] Conv. 483.

[59] See M.P. Thompson (1981) 125 S. J. 816. See Touching and concerning the land pp. 449–450.

as a land charge.[60] Similarly, a lease may contain a term that, if the tenant wishes to assign his lease, that is to transfer it to another person, he must first offer to surrender it, that is give it up, to the landlord. Such a clause is also registrable as a C(iv) land charge.[61]

Rights of pre-emption

Although express reference is made in the Act to a right of pre-emption, that is a right of first refusal should an owner of land decide to sell it, the position is not straight-forward. In *Pritchard v. Briggs*,[62] the Court of Appeal held that, contrary to what the framers of the legislation had thought, a right of pre-emption is not an interest in land. This was because, unless the owner of the land decides that he will sell it, the holder of the right of pre-emption has no right to insist upon the land being conveyed to him. This contrasts with an option to purchase where, on the exercise of the option, the grantee has a contractual right to the property. The majority[63] further held, however, that, when the condition precedent to the right of pre-emption becoming enforceable is satisfied, that is when the vendor decides to sell the land, the right does then become an interest in land and is, therefore, registrable.

In the case, itself, an option to purchase was granted subsequent to the creation of a right of pre-emption. Despite the right of pre-emption having been registered, it was held not to be binding on the grantee of the option. On the exercise of the option, the condition precedent to the right of pre-emption was not satisfied as the vendor had not decided to sell the land; he was required to sell it by the exercise of the option by the grantee. In most cases, however, registration of the right of pre-emption will adequately protect the holder of the right because, if the vendor chooses to sell the property, the condition precedent to the right of pre-emption will be satisfied and the holder of that right is now in a position to enter into a binding contract for the sale of the land in question.

Mortgage by deposit of title deeds

A traditional method of creating an equitable mortgage was to deposit with the lender of money the title deeds to land, such a deposit acting as security for the loan. The basis of such a transaction being regarded as an equitable mortgage is that, provided the necessary statutory formalities are complied with,[64] it is seen as a contract to create a

---

[60]   *Beesly v. Hallwood Estates Ltd* [1960] 2 All E.R. 314, affirmed on other grounds [1961] Ch. 105; *Taylors Fashions v. Liverpool Victoria Trustees Ltd* [1982] 1 Q.B. 133n; *Phillips v. Mobil Oil Co. Ltd* [1989] 1 W.L.R. 888; *Markfaith Investments Ltd v. Chap Hua Flashlights Ltd* [1991] 2 A.C. 43 at 58–59 *per* Lord Templeman.

[61]   *Greene v. Church Commissioners for England* [1974] Ch. 467.

[62]   [1980] Ch. 338. See H.W.R. Wade (1980) 96 L.Q.R. 488; J. Martin [1980] Conv. 433. But contrast *Dear v. Reeves* [2002] Ch. 1, a case on the Insolvency Act 1986, s. 436, where it was said that the reasoning in the judgments in *Prichard v. Briggs* may need reconsideration: [2002] Ch. 1 at 10 *per* Mummery L.J.

[63]   Templeman and Stephenson L.J.J.; Goff L.J. dissenting.

[64]   Law of Property (Miscellaneous Provisions) Act 1989, s. 2.

legal mortgage.[65] As such it is a contract to create a legal estate and is registrable as a C(iv) land charge and is not registrable as a C(iii) land charge.[66]

Class D(i): HMRC land charge

The Commissioners for HMRC may register a charge for unpaid inheritance tax in respect of freehold land.[67]

Class D(ii): restrictive covenants

A restrictive covenant is registrable as a D(ii) land charge. This does not include either covenants created before 1926 or covenants between landlord and tenant.[68] The enforceability of the former category depends upon the old doctrine of notice. In the case of restrictive covenants contained in leases, their enforceability will depend either upon the rules which relate to the running of covenants in leases[69] or, if these do not cause the burden of the covenant to run, upon the doctrine of notice.

There is some disagreement as to whether restrictive covenants arising under a scheme of development are registrable as land charges. A scheme of development, to be discussed in a later chapter,[70] involves a situation where land is sold off in individual lots and an attempt is made to impose mutually enforceable restrictive covenants upon the purchasers of the individual lots. While there are practical arguments for suggesting that they are not registrable,[71] there is nothing actually in the Act to exclude such covenants which, in principle, would seem to be registrable.[72]

Class D(iii): Equitable easements[73]

An equitable easement is defined as being an easement, right, or privilege affecting land created or arising on or after January 1, 1926, and being merely an equitable interest. This will include easements which are not equivalent to a fee simple absolute in possession or a term of years. An easement for life will, if contrary to the views of some it is capable of existing as an easement at all,[74] therefore, be registrable. Also registrable will be a specifically enforceable contract to create an easement.[75]

The definition of this category of land charge includes a 'right or privilege affecting land'. These words are construed narrowly so that the right in question must have the essential characteristics of an easement[76] in order to be registrable. Accordingly, a

---

[65] *Habib Bank of Kuwait plc v. Sahib* [1996] 3 All E.R. 215. See Deposit of title deeds, p. 470.

[66] An equitable charge on an equitable interest is registrable as a Class C(iii) land charge: *Property Discount Corpn Ltd v. Lyon Group Ltd* [1981] 1 All E.R. 379 at 383 *per* Brightman L.J.

[67] Land Charges Act 1972, s. 2(5) as substituted by the Inheritance Tax Act 1984, s. 276, Sched. 8, para. 3.

[68] Land Charges Act 1972, s. 2(5).   [69] See The enforceability of covenants, pp. 447–453.

[70] See Chapter 14.   [71] Thompson, op. cit., 388–389.

[72] R.G. Rowley (1956) 20 Conv. (N.S.) 370 at 371–373.   [73] See D.G. Barnsley (1999) 115 L.Q.R. 89.

[74] Ibid.

[75] See *E.R. Ives Investment Ltd v. High* [1967] 2 Q.B. 379. Arguably, it is also registrable as an estate contract. See *Huckvale v. Aegean Hotels Ltd* (1989) 58 P. & C.R. 163 at 165; E.O. Walford (1947) 11 Conv. (N.S.) 165 at 176.

[76] See Chapter 13.

requisition of land under Defence Regulations,[77] a right to remove fixtures at the end of a lease,[78] and an equitable right of re-entry to secure compliance with covenants contained in an assignment of a lease[79] have all been held not to be registrable as equitable easements. Neither has a claim arising under the principles of estoppel.[80] The enforceability of such rights against a purchaser is dependent upon the old doctrine of notice.

Class E

This is an annuity created before 1926 and not registered in the register of annuities.

Class F: A spouse's statutory right of occupation

The Class F land charge was created as a legislative response to the House of Lords decision in *National Provincial Bank Ltd v. Ainsworth*.[81] Prior to this decision there had been a controversial line of authority[82] where it was held that a wife who had been deserted by her husband had an equitable right to remain in the matrimonial home. This right, which had been considered to be some form of equitable property right, was held to be binding upon mortgagees. In *Ainsworth*, however, the House of Lords held that there was no such right known to law and, therefore, no possibility of mortgagees being bound by it.

This decision was seen as leaving wives in an unacceptably exposed position and a Private Member's Bill was guided through Parliament to become the Matrimonial Homes Act 1967.[83] Under the terms of this Act a spouse, and now also a person in a registered civil partnership,[84] was given a statutory right not to be excluded from the matrimonial home and, if not in possession of it, the right, with the leave of the court, to enter the matrimonial home.[85] This right will, if registered,[86] be binding also upon a purchaser and on a trustee in bankruptcy.[87]

The court has the power to regulate the statutory right, so that if registration is motivated by spite, the court will order its removal.[88] The court has wide regulatory powers in respect of matrimonial rights[89] and, in exercising these powers the court is directed to have regard to various factors, including the housing needs and resources

---

[77] *Lewisham Borough Council v. Moloney* [1948] 1 K.B. 50.

[78] *Poster v. Slough Estates Ltd* [1969] 1 Ch. 495.   [79] *Shiloh Spinners Ltd v. Harding* [1973] A.C. 691.

[80] *E.R. Ives Investment Ltd v. High* [1967] 2 Q.B. 379. For the doctrine of equitable estoppel, see Chapter 15.

[81] [1965] A.C. 1175.

[82] *Bendall v. McWhirter* [1952] 2 Q.B. 406; *Street v. Denham* [1954] 1 W.L.R. 624. See R.E. Megarry (1952) 68 L.Q.R. 379.

[83] The relevant legislation is now the Family Law Act 1996. See, generally, M.P. Thompson in Meisel and Cook (eds), *Property and Protection: Essays in Honour of Brian Harvey* (Oxford: Hart Publishing, 2000), 157 at 158–161.

[84] Civil Partnerships Act 2004, s. 101.   [85] Family Law Act 1996, s. 32.

[86] The right can be registered before a court has granted leave: *Watts v. Waller* [1973] Q.B. 133. See, generally, D.G. Barnsley [1974] C.L.P. 76; D.J. Hayton [1976] C.L.P. 26.   [87] Insolvency Act 1986, s. 336(2).

[88] *Barnett v. Hassett* [1981] 1 W.L.R. 1385.   [89] Family Law Act 1996, s. 33(3).

of the parties[90] and any relevant child, the health, safety, and well-being of the parties and any relevant child, and the conduct of the parties towards each other.[91]

The 1967 Act provided some modest reform of this area and afforded some protection to spouses who are not legal co-owners of the matrimonial home. The statutory right of occupation can be a powerful weapon in the hands of a spouse, giving her potentially a power of veto over a proposed transaction affecting the matrimonial home.[92] On the other hand, however, the enforceability of this right as against a purchaser is made dependent upon registration. Unless the wife (or husband) is in receipt of legal advice, the most likely occasion for this being if there are marital difficulties, she is highly unlikely to have heard of the statutory right of occupation, let alone the need to protect it by registration. By the time this has been discovered, the house may already have been mortgaged, in which case her right will not be binding upon the mortgagee.

The history of the Class F land charge reveals an underlying tension between protecting the rights of occupiers and promoting the security of conveyancing transactions. Had the existence of the deserted wife's equity been upheld in the House of Lords, there would have been recognized an informal right in land which was potentially binding upon a purchaser but was not registrable. The purchaser could not then rely on the simple expedient of searching the register to discover the existence of all equitable rights to which the property was subject. Instead, he would need to make additional enquiries, thereby complicating the conveyancing process. It is clear that a desire to avoid any such complication was an important factor in the decision-making process in *Ainsworth*, Lord Upjohn commenting that it had been the policy of the law for over a hundred years to simplify and facilitate the conveyancing process;[93] a policy objective which would have been hindered had the case been decided the other way.

The legislative response to the decision was consistent with this general policy. Although a wife is given the statutory right to occupy the matrimonial home, its enforceability is made dependent upon registration. The effect of this is that, in general, the conveyancing process will continue to operate smoothly and the reliability of the register of land charges is enhanced. There is a cost to this, however, which is that people who are not familiar with the registration system are, through a failure to protect their rights by registration, at risk of losing those rights, and also their homes, because of ignorance of the need to register. As will be seen, this tension between the competing interest of protecting the rights of occupiers and enhancing the security of conveyancing transactions has continued to be an important one in the law.

---

[90] This would seem to include a purchaser who has taken subject to the right: *Kashmir Kaur v. Gill* [1988] Fam. 110.

[91] Family Law Act 1996, s. 33(6).   [92] For a graphic example, see *Wroth v. Tyler* [1974] Ch. 30.

[93] [1965] A.C. 1175 at 1233.

THE REGISTRATION OF LAND CHARGES

Having considered the different classes of land charge, it is now necessary to consider the system in operation.

The effect of registration

The effect of registration of a land charge is determined by section 198 of the Law of Property Act 1925, which provides that:

'The registration of any instrument or matter . . . shall be deemed to constitute actual notice of such instrument or matter, and of the fact of such registration, to all persons and for all purposes[94] connected with the land affected, as from the date of registration or other prescribed date and so long as the registration continues in force.'

This important provision is central to the working of the Act. If an interest has been registered correctly as a land charge, then, subject to one exception,[95] a purchaser cannot claim not to have notice of it. Registration constitutes notice. The purpose of the legislation is to do away with the uncertainties attendant on the old doctrine of notice in respect of matters which are registrable. Registration supplies a different form of notice. If, however, something is registered as a land charge, this does not guarantee the validity of the right in question, so that, if something is registered which is not actually an interest in land, registration will not confer validity upon it.[96]

Registration against names

The most serious defect in the whole system of registration of land charges is the method of registration. Section 3(1) of the Land Charges Act 1972 provides that:

'A land charge shall be registered in the name of the estate owner intended to be affected.'

The requirement that a land charge be registered against the owner of the land, at the time when the charge was created, rather than against the land itself, has created a number of avoidable difficulties. Even without these difficulties, this requirement does not avoid both the registration and the application for a search having to give the accurate address of the property, as it will be appreciated that registration against the name of John Smith, without any description of the property to be affected, would be pointless.

---

[94] There are statutory exceptions to this: Law of Property Act 1969, s. 24, removing the problem caused by the decision in *Re Forsey and Hollebone's Contract* [1927] 2 Ch. 379, a decision disapproved in *Rignall Developments Ltd v. Halil* [1987] 1 E.G.L.R. 193; s. 25(2) (compensation for undiscoverable land charges).

[95] See Wrong certficates, p. 105.

[96] Cf. *Cator v. Newton* [1940] 1 Q.B. 415 (registration of a positive covenant on the register of title).

What name?

Registration of a land charge must be against the correct name of the estate owner. This has been held to mean the version of the name, or names, as it appears in the title deeds and not as it may appear in other contexts, such as a birth certificate.[97] This may be easier said than done. In *Diligent Finance Co. Ltd v. Alleyne*,[98] a wife sought to register a Class F land charge against her husband, whom she knew by the name Erskine Alleyne. Unknown to her, he had a middle name, Owen. The finance company searched against the full, correct version and obtained a clear certificate of search, and her attempted registration was held to have been ineffective.

The problems involved in getting the names right, a problem described as 'the tip of a fairly large iceberg',[99] emerged again in the near farcical case of *Oak Co-operative Building Society v. Blackburn*.[100] Mr Blackburn's real name was Francis *David* Blackburn. A land charge was registered against the name Frank David Blackburn, which was the name under which he traded. A search was then requisitioned against the name, Francis *Davis* Blackburn; in other words, both the registration and the search used the wrong names. It was held that a purported registration against what can be regarded as a fair approximation of the estate owner's correct name will be effective against a person who either does not search at all, or requisitions a search against an incorrect version of the name.

This is a pragmatic rather than a logical solution. If a person has registered a land charge against the wrong name then, unless the person requisitioning the search replicates the error, the land charge cannot be discovered. Yet, the result is not unreasonable as the task of the person seeking to register may be more difficult than is the task for the person making the search. A person registering a land charge against a person may not have the latter's co-operation in so doing. It may be a hostile act, in which case access to the title deeds will not be available and the prospect of getting the name wrong is increased. A person requisitioning a search would normally be engaged in a transaction with the estate owner, who will be co-operative and allow him access to the deeds. There is, therefore, very little excuse for the person searching to get the name wrong. This problem would not have occurred, however, if registration was against the land rather than the estate owner.

Who is the estate owner?

A second, related, problem is to establish who the estate owner actually is at the relevant time. This problem was seen in *Barrett v. Hilton Developments Ltd*,[101] where A contracted to sell land to B, who, before the completion of that contract, had contracted to sell the same land to C. C registered his estate contract against B but this was invalid because the estate owner at the time was not B but A. A similar difficulty could occur when an estate owner died, in that registration should be against his personal

[97] *Standard Property Investment plc v. British Plastics Federation* (1985) 53 P. & C.R. 25.
[98] (1972) 23 P. & C.R. 346. [99] Ruoff, *Searching without Tears* (London: Oyez, 1974), 49.
[100] [1968] Ch. 730. [101] [1975] Ch. 237.

representatives.[102] If he died intestate, until 1995 it was the case that the deceased's property vested in the President of the Family Division of the High Court and so any land charge would need to be registered against that person. Thereafter the property vests in the Public Trustee.[103] This particular problem has now been eradicated in that section 15 of the Law of Property (Miscellaneous Provisions) Act 1994 amended the Land Charges Act 1972 to permit registration of a land charge against a person who has died.[104]

Undiscoverable land charges

A further difficulty that was caused by requiring land charges to be registered against the name of the estate owner is that the possibility may arise of a purchaser being deemed to have notice of a land charge which he could not actually discover. This possibility arises owing to a combination of registering against names, the effect of section 198 of the Law of Property Act 1925, and the method of investigating title to unregistered land. The problem is best illustrated by an example.

1925	A conveys to B
1935	B conveys to C
1945	C conveys to D
1955	D conveys to E
1965	E conveys to F
1975	F conveys to G
1996	V inherits the property from G[105]
2012	V contracts to sell the property to P.

In this example, the entire list of transactions affecting the land since 1925 is given. It is possible that a land charge was registered against any of the different people from that date, when they owned the land. Suppose, for example, that the conveyance in 1935 from B to C contained a restrictive covenant and that that covenant was duly registered against the name of C. The fact that the land charge had been properly registered means that P will be deemed to have actual notice of it. This means that, on completion of the V–P transaction, P will be bound by the covenant. The problem is that he may have had no way of discovering it.

When investigating title, a purchaser must go back to a good root of title which is at least fifteen years old.[106] In the example given above, this is the 1975 conveyance between F and G. Although this conveyance is thirty-seven years old, it is the first

---

[102] These are the people in whom the property of a deceased will vest pending the implementation by them of his will.

[103] Administration of Justice Act 1925, s. 9, as substituted by the Law of Property (Miscellaneous Provisions) Act 1994, s. 14(1). For a discussion of the difficulties caused by death, see A.M. Prichard [1979] Conv. 249.

[104] Land Charges Act 1972, s. 3(1)(A).

[105] At that time, the transmission of land by means of an assent, the procedure by which land is transferred on death, did not trigger compulsory registration of title. See Triggering events, pp. 119–121.

[106] Law of Property Act 1969, s. 23.

conveyance which is at least fifteen years old. He will then discover that, at various times, F, G, and V were estate owners of the land and be able to requisition searches against them. He will not, however, discover who owned the land previously and will be unable to search against them. He runs the risk, therefore, of being bound by a land charge, the existence of which he could not have discovered. This risk grows as the period of time between 1925 and what will constitute a good root of title grows.[107]

This problem, which was a direct consequence of registration being against names of estate owners rather than against the land itself, was appreciated a long time ago and the only palliative for it was seen to be compensatory, it not being realistic to unscramble the whole system.[108] A compensation scheme was established in 1969.

Compensation

Under section 25 of the Law of Property Act 1969, a purchaser may claim compensation if various conditions are satisfied, the principal ones being that he had no actual knowledge of the charge[109] and that the charge was registered against the owner of an estate who was not, as owner of any such estate, a party to any transaction, or concerned in any event, comprised in the relevant title. This means that the purchaser has investigated back to a good root of title and could not have discovered the land charge by searching against the names of people revealed to have been estate owners from then to the present day. In the example given above, because C is not a name which would be revealed by an investigation of the relevant title, P would be entitled to compensation under the Act.

Given the scale of the theoretical risk of undiscoverable land charges, it may, at first sight, seem surprising that there appear to have been very few claims for compensation under this legislation.[110] There appear to be two main reasons for this. First, on each transaction involving the land since 1925, the purchaser would have made a land charges search and would discover land charges registered at an earlier time and this information could be passed on to later purchasers. Secondly, the problem has been assuaged by the spread of registration of title. It has been the case that, since 1989, every conveyance on sale of unregistered land must be completed by registration of title.[111] If, as is likely, the land charge is not discovered when title is registered, it will not be entered on the register, with the result that the registered proprietor will take free from it. If it is sought subsequently to enforce the right protected by the land charge, the

---

[107] The problem has been likened to 'the conveyancing equivalent of a Franckenstein's [sic] monster, which with the passing years would become not only more dangerous but also more difficult to kill': H.W.R. Wade [1956] C.L.J. 216.

[108] Report of Committee on Land Charges 1956 (Cmd. 9825) (The Roxburgh Committee).

[109] The effect of Law of Property Act 1925, s. 198, which deems a person to have actual notice of any matter registered as a land charge, is disregarded in determining whether a purchaser actually knew of the land charge: ibid., s. 25(2). Whether the purchaser knew of the matter is a matter of fact decided without reference to s. 198.

[110] For the first such claim, see Chief Land Registrar's Report (1988–89), para. 56.

[111] See Triggering events, pp. 119–126.

person seeking to enforce the right will have to proceed by way of rectification of the register[112] and the compensation scheme devised by the 1969 Act will not be relevant.

The rule in Patman v. Harland

A grantee of a lease does not have the right to insist upon investigating the title of his landlord.[113] Nevertheless, although he could not, as a matter of general law, insist upon doing this, he could, by a clause in the contract, attain such a right. Unless a lease is being granted for a lump sum, however, it is not usual to do this. In *Patman v. Harland*,[114] it was held that, because a purchaser could have negotiated a clause in the contract to allow him to investigate the lessor's title, he would be regarded as having notice of all matters which he would have discovered had he done so.

This rule was considered to cause hardship. So, in a reform which has been described as being 'more soft-headed than soft-hearted',[115] the position was reversed by legislation. Under section 44(5) of the Law of Property Act 1925, an intended lessee who is not permitted to investigate his landlord's title is not to be regarded as having notice of any matter which he would have discovered had he negotiated a clause in the contract entitling him to do this. The reason why this reform was described as being soft-headed is that it could have led to the loss of equitable interests, depending upon whether or not the intending lessee had negotiated to obtain the right to investigate the landlord's title. Much of the potential sting of this reform has, however, been removed because, in respect of matters which are registrable as land charges, the effect of section 198 of the Law of Property Act 1925 is to fix the intending lessee with actual notice of any matter which has been registered. If a land charge has been registered against a predecessor in title of his landlord, the tenant will be bound by it, regardless of whether or not he could have discovered who that person was. Moreover, for no apparent reason, such a tenant is excluded from the statutory compensation scheme.[116] Had land charges been registrable against the land, rather than the owner of an estate in it, this problem would not have arisen.

The effect of non-registration

Just as the effect of registration of land charges is clear, so, too, is the consequence of non-registration. Although there are some differences between the different classes of land charge, the essential consequence of non-registration is that the particular land charge becomes void for non-registration against a purchaser for value,[117] such persons including, of course, a lessee and a mortgagee.[118] The differences relate to the different type of purchaser with respect to particular land charges. Some land charges are void for non-registration against a purchaser for value of any interest in the land,

---

[112] See Alteration and indemnity, pp. 171–182. See, also, *Horrill v. Cooper* (2000), Unreported, Court of Appeal.

[113] Law of Property Act 1925, s. 44(2).   [114] (1881) 17 Ch.D. 353.

[115] Farrand, *Contract and Conveyance* (4th edn) (London: Oyez, 1983), 134.

[116] Law of Property Act 1969, s. 25(9).   [117] Land Charges Act 1972, s. 4.   [118] Ibid., s. 17(1).

whereas, in the case of other land charges, they are void against the purchaser of a legal estate for money or money's worth. Class C(iv) and Class D[119] fall into the latter category. This division seems needlessly complex, although no particular problems seem to have arisen in consequence of it.

Two initial points can be made. If the purchaser has not given value, perhaps because he has inherited the property, or has been given it, then he will still be bound by an interest which is registrable but not registered. Second, if the land charge is void for non-registration as against a purchaser for value, it will not be binding on a successor in title of that purchaser, even if that person is not, himself, a purchaser for value.

The consequence of a land charge being void for non-registration is underlined by section 199(1) of the Law of Property Act 1925, which provides that:

'A purchaser shall not be prejudicially affected by notice of—

any instrument or matter capable of registration under the provisions of the Land Charges Act 1972…which is void or not enforceable as against him under that Act…by reason of the non-registration thereof.'

The operation of these provisions was considered by the House of Lords in the leading case of *Midland Bank Trust Co. Ltd v. Green*.[120] Walter Green granted his son, Geoffrey, an option to purchase agricultural land, of which he was a tenant, for the sum of £22,000. This option was exerciseable for a period of ten years. Some six years later, when the value of the land had nearly doubled in value, Walter then 'met a lawyer somewhere or other and told him of the option'.[121] After this meeting he consulted another solicitor and, within three days thereafter,[122] he conveyed the land to his wife, Evelyne, for £500. The principal issue in the litigation was whether the option to purchase the land, which by then was worth in excess of £450,000, was binding upon Evelyne who, it was accepted, knew of the existence of the option, despite it having not been registered.

The majority of the Court of Appeal had held the option to be enforceable despite it not having been registered. One basis for this decision was that, because £500 was a substantial undervalue, Evelyne should not be classified as a purchaser for money or money's worth.[123] An alternative reason was that one could not rely upon the statute as to do so would have been fraudulent; fraud in this context, according to Lord Denning M.R., being 'any dishonest dealing done so as to deprive unwary innocents of their rightful dues'.[124] The House of Lords unanimously reversed this decision and held that the option was void for non-registration.

[119] Except for the Class D(i) charge, which is void against a purchaser of any estate: ibid., s. 4(6).
[120] [1981] A.C. 513. See also *Hollington Bros v. Rhodes* [1951] 2 All E.R. 487; *Markfaith Investments Ltd v. Chap Hua Flashlights Ltd* [1991] 2 A.C. 43.
[121] *Midland Bank Trust Co. Ltd v. Green* [1980] Ch. 590 at 620 *per* Lord Denning M.R.
[122] 'Never in the history of conveyancing has anything been done so rapidly': ibid. at 621 *per* Lord Denning M.R. Cf. *Miles v. Bull* [1969] 1 Q.B. 255. at 260, where contract and completion occurred on the same day.
[123] [1980] Ch. 590 at 624 *per* Lord Denning M.R.; at 628 *per* Eveleigh L.J.
[124] Ibid. at 625.

The irrelevance of good faith

The only speech was delivered by Lord Wilberforce, who applied traditional concepts of the doctrine of consideration and refused to consider its adequacy. In his view, £500 clearly represented money or money's worth.[125] He also declined either to read the notion of good faith into what he regarded as clear legislation or to disallow the purchaser from relying on the legislation on the basis that the transaction was fraudulent. By fraud was meant something similar to the more colourful language of Lord Denning that, if the motive underlying the transaction was to defeat an unregistered interest, then this was fraudulent.[126] Taking the view that there may be mixed motives underlying a particular transaction,[127] Lord Wilberforce saw such a test as being unworkable. Accordingly, the legislation was given its plain meaning with the result that, despite having actual knowledge of the unregistered land charge, the purchaser took free from it.

Not surprisingly, this decision attracted criticism, one commentator asking when discussing a case raising a similar issue,[128] 'would it really cause the collapse of civilised conveyancing if the...statutes were altered to make actual notice of an unprotected interest binding upon a purchaser?'[129] While such views are readily understandable, in that the mother's case seemed to be short of merit and that the land charges legislation was being construed in what might be termed an amoral way, there is also a good deal to be said in favour of the approach taken.

First, the decision brings certainty into this branch of the law. While certainty is not necessarily an overriding goal, and the facts of *Green* were such that one would instinctively sympathize with the plaintiff, other cases where issues of good faith might arise may well involve less dramatic facts and a less substantial undervalue. In such circumstances, the temptation to water down the clarity of the legislative provision of the legislation may be less strong and the results less predictable.

A second point is that the plaintiff is usually not without a remedy in this type of case. In *Green* itself, as one would expect in a commercial transaction of this nature, legal advice had been taken. Insisting that rights such as an option to purchase should be registered if they are to be enforceable against third parties should not cause undue hardship, as one would expect a competent solicitor to ensure that it was protected by registration. Indeed, the failure to do so led to a successful action for substantial damages.[130] It should also not be forgotten that the father who, in breach of his obligation to his son, conveyed the land to his wife would also have been personally liable to

---

[125] [1981] A.C. 513 at 532. Cf. *Nurdin & Peacock plc v. D.B. Ramsden & Co. Ltd* [1999] 1 E.G.L.R. 119 at 123 *per* Neuberger J.

[126] *Re Monolithic* [1915] 1 Ch. 643 at 669–670 *per* Phillimore L.J. See also M.P. Thompson [1985] C.L.J. 280 at 280–284.

[127] [1981] A.C. 513 at 530. See also [1980] Ch. 590 at 625 *per* Eveleigh L.J.

[128] *Peffer v. Rigg* [1977] 1 W.L.R. 285. See Notice of unprotected interests, pp. 166–171.

[129] S. Anderson (1977) 40 M.L.R. 600 at 606. See also B. Green (1981) 97 L.Q.R. 518 at 520.

[130] See *Midland Bank Trust Co. Ltd v. Hett, Stubbs and Kemp* [1979] Ch. 384. See also *Midland Bank Trust Co. Ltd v. Green* [1981] A.C. 513 at 526 *per* Lord Wilberforce, although contrast *Bell v. Peter Browne & Co.* [1900] 2 Q.B. 495.

his son for breach of contract although, admittedly, given the sums involved, this was probably not a cause of action worth pursuing.

The economic torts

A final potential cause of action, which was assumed to be available on the facts of *Green*, was to pursue an action in tort against the parents for conspiracy,[131] although this assumption seems questionable for two reasons. First, an essential ingredient of that tort is to be able to identify a predominant intention to injure.[132] Yet, it was precisely the difficulty in isolating an intention of this type that led to Lord Wilberforce rejecting the test of fraud as being an intention to defeat an unregistered interest, thereby injuring the holder of the right. Isolating this intention can be no easier a task if the cause of action is in tort. Secondly, the land charges legislation is designed to answer questions as to when a purchaser takes subject to a prior interest in land. It makes little sense to hold, as a matter of Property Law, that the purchaser takes free from an interest and then to hold that person liable in tort in respect of the same right. It is suggested that the economic torts should not have a role to play in this context.[133]

Payment of purchase price

Midland Bank Trust Co. Ltd v. Green was followed recently in a less clear context in *Lloyds Bank plc v. Carrick*.[134] Mrs Carrick contracted orally[135] to buy a long leasehold of a maisonette from her brother-in-law. She paid the purchase price in full and went into sole possession.[136] The legal title was never, however, conveyed to her. Some time later, the brother-in-law mortgaged the property to the bank and, when he defaulted on the repayments, the bank sought possession; an action resisted by Mrs Carrick. It was held, following *Green*, that the contract was void against the bank for want of registration and so the bank was entitled to possession.

Had the contract in this case been entirely executory, then the case would, indeed, have been on all fours with *Green*. It is suggested, however, that the fact that the purchase price had, in this case, been paid in full should have made a material difference to the decision. While it is true to say that the existence of an enforceable contract of sale did, in itself, give rise to an equitable interest in favour of Mrs Carrick,[137] the fact that she had paid the entire purchase price meant that her brother-in-law would hold the property on a bare trust for her, thus making her the equitable owner of the

---

[131] *Midland Bank Trust Co. Ltd v. Green (No. 3)* [1982] Ch. 529.

[132] See *Lonhro Ltd v. Shell Petroleum Co. Ltd* [1982] A.C. 173 at 189 *per* Lord Diplock. See, also, *Meretz Investments N.V. v. ACP Ltd* [2007] EWCA Civ. 1303 at [172] *per* Toulson L.J.

[133] See R.J. Smith (1977) 41 Conv. (N.S.) 318; M.P. Thompson [1985] C.L.J. 280 at 293–295.

[134] [1996] 4 All E.R. 630. See M.P. Thompson [1996] Conv. 295; P. Ferguson (1996) 112 L.Q.R. 549.

[135] The agreement pre-dated the coming into force of the Law of Property (Miscellaneous Provisions) Act 1989, s. 2, when oral contracts for the sale of land could be made. See Chapter 6.

[136] For a similarly cavalier approach to the conveyancing process by the late actor, Kenneth More, see Kenneth More, *More or Less*, an autobiography, 194, cited by Farrand, op. cit., 6–7.

[137] See The effect of the contract, pp. 220–225.

lease.[138] The nature of this interest is different in nature from that which arises from an enforceable contract of sale and, it is thought, the bank should have been held to have been bound by this interest, which would not have been registrable.

Actual occupation

A feature of both *Midland Bank Trust Co. Ltd v. Green* and *Lloyds Bank plc v. Carrick* is that, in each case, the person seeking to enforce the right was in actual occupation of the land at all material times. The fact that this had no bearing on the outcome of the litigation highlights, as was pointed out in *Carrick* itself,[139] an anomalous difference between the unregistered and registered land systems. Had title to the land been registered, then the fact that Mrs Carrick was in actual occupation of the land would have meant that her interest in the land would have been binding on the bank; the existence of her right, coupled with actual occupation of the land would have meant that she would have had an overriding interest,[140] or, as this concept is now termed, an unregistered interest which overrides a registered disposition.[141]

When title to the land is registered then, in general, if the person with a right over another's land is in actual occupation of that land, this is an alternative to registration as a means of ensuring its enforceability against purchasers.[142] As such, the importance of actual occupation is that it provides a form of safety net against the consequences of non-registration of rights. Where title to the land is unregistered, almost certainly as a result of a legislative mishap,[143] no such alternative form of protection is available.

The result of this is that, if an interest is registrable but not registered, the fact that the owner of that interest is in actual occupation of the relevant land is irrelevant. It is unfortunate that a morally neutral matter such as whether or not title to land is registered should have such a decisive effect on the outcome of disputes of this nature. It is suggested that the registered land position is preferable, reflecting as it does the modern tendency to afford greater protection to the rights of people who actually occupy the land.

The system in operation

So far as a purchaser is concerned, the central aspect of the system is the requisitioning of an official search. A purchaser should requisition an official search[144] against the name of every estate owner revealed to have owned the land. The search application

---

[138] See *Bridges v. Mees* [1957] Ch. 475.   [139] [1996] 4 All E.R. 630 at 642 *per* Morritt L.J.

[140] Land Registration Act 1925, s. 70(1)(g). See *Bhullar v. McArdle* [2001] EWCA Civ. 557, where such a claim failed because the person was not in actual occupation of the land.

[141] Land Registration Act 2002, Sched. 3.

[142] Land Registration Act 1925, s. 70(1)(g); *Williams & Glyn's Bank Ltd v. Boland* [1981] A.C. 487. See The upgrading of rights, pp. 139–141.

[143] Earlier legislation did provide protection for people in actual occupation. See Law of Property Act 1922, ss 14, 32, Sched. 7; H.W.R. Wade [1956] C.L.J. 216 at 228.

[144] Land Charges Act 1972, s. 10(1).

should also include the correct address of the property in question. Once a search has been properly requisitioned, it is then provided by section 10(4) of the Land Charges Act 1972 that, in favour of an intending purchaser, an official search certificate shall be conclusive, affirmatively or negatively, as the case may be. Two issues arise from this. These are, first, the consequences of an incorrect certificate of search and, secondly, the length of time for which a clear certificate can be relied upon.

Wrong certificates

If the official certificate of search states there to be no subsisting entries then the search will be conclusive and the purchaser will not be bound by a correctly registered land charge. Although it has been said that 'one would have expected section 198(1) of the Law of Property Act to contain some warning that actual registration will not prevail against a negative certificate',[145] that is the effect of section 10(4) of the Land Charges Act 1972. This, then, is the only exception to the effect of section 198, which provides that registration is deemed to constitute actual notice to all persons for all purposes. The only remedy for the person who, as a result of the error made in the issuing of an erroneous certificate, has lost his interest in the land, is to sue the Land Registry in negligence.[146]

The conclusive nature of the certificate is, however, dependent upon the search being against the correct name of the estate owner and the correct description of the relevant land.[147] In *Horrill v. Cooper*,[148] the plaintiff had the benefit of a restrictive covenant, which had been properly registered as a D(ii) land charge.[149] The defendants purchased the land. Prior to the conveyance, a clear official search certificate was obtained. Unfortunately, the application for the search incorrectly identified the land in question. The consequence was that the defendants were bound by the covenant. However, subsequently, the defendants were registered as proprietors of the land, following an application for first registration of title. The covenants were not entered onto the register of title. As matters were now governed by the provisions of the Land Registration Act 1925, the effect was that the covenants, not being on the register of title, were no longer binding on the defendants. The plaintiffs successfully brought an action for rectification of the register, the effect of which was that the covenants were entered onto the registered title.[150]

Period of protection

A purchaser will requisition a search prior to completion of the transaction. The question then arises as to how long he can rely upon the certificate being conclusive. The answer is provided by section 11(6) of the Act, which affords the purchaser priority in

---

[145] *Du Sautoy v. Symes* [1967] Ch. 1146 at 1165 *per* Cross J.

[146] *Ministry of Housing and Local Government v. Sharp* [1970] 2 Q.B. 223. See also *Murphy v Brentwood District Council* [1991] 1 A.C. 398 at 486 *per* Lord Oliver of Aylmerton.

[147] *Du Sautoy v. Symes, supra,* at 1166.   [148] (2000), Unreported, Court of Appeal.

[149] Reversing the first instance decision at (1999) 78 P. & C.R. 336 on this point.

[150] See, Mistake, p. 173.

respect of land charges registered after he has obtained a certificate provided that the transaction is completed within fifteen working days.

Priority notices

It is usual for the purchase of land to be financed by a mortgage. A potential difficulty which can arise occurs when land is being sold to a purchaser and it is sought, on the occasion of the purchase, to register a land charge, for example a restrictive covenant, against him. The problem is that the conveyance to the purchaser and the mortgage granted by him will be simultaneous transactions so that the risk is that the mortgagee, as a purchaser of a legal estate for money or money's worth, would necessarily take free from the covenant which has to be registered against the estate owner, who is P. To overcome this difficulty, provision is made for the registration of a priority notice. What this entails is that the person seeking to effect registration should apply for the registration of a priority notice at least fifteen days prior to the creation of the covenant. On so doing, provided that the charge is registered within thirty working days of the entry of the priority notice, then the registration will date back to the creation of the covenant, which will be binding upon the mortgagee.[151]

UNREGISTRABLE INTERESTS

In reforming the substantive law as it affects unregistered land, a principal stratagem was to fit equitable interests into one of two categories: those which were overreachable and those which were registrable. Had this compartmentalization been complete, a purchaser of land would be able to be assured that, provided where necessary he operated the overreaching machinery correctly, he would take subject only to those equitable interests which had been correctly registered and the limited number of legal interests which remained in existence. He could be unconcerned with any other rights. This scenario has not occurred, however, as not all equitable rights fall into one of these categories.

It can be stated at the outset that the legislation itself envisaged that some equitable interests would fall into a residuary category where their enforceability against a purchaser was made dependent upon the unreformed doctrine of notice, an example being a restrictive covenant created before 1926.[152] Other rights, however, came to be recognized as having the capacity to affect purchasers without being registrable. At first, such rights were limited to relatively arcane matters, such as a tenant's right to remove fixtures at the end of the lease[153] or an equitable right of re-entry.[154] Of

---

[151] Land Charges Act 1972, s. 11(1)(3)(6).   [152] Ibid., s. 2(5)(iii).
[153] *Poster v. Slough Estates Ltd* [1969] 1 W.L.R. 1807.
[154] *Shiloh Spinners Ltd v. Harding* [1973] A.C. 691. See P.B. Fairest [1973] C.L.J. 218.

much greater significance were rights arising under trusts and rights arising through estoppel.

Informal rights

A phenomenon which, in recent times, has frequently exercised the courts is where a house has been conveyed into one person's name but another person has an equitable interest in it. This situation will most frequently arise where the two parties are either married or are involved in a stable relationship. The normal scenario is when the legal title to a house is in the name of the man and his partner is an equitable co-owner of it. He then, without consulting her, mortgages the property and then defaults on the mortgage repayments. The issue then becomes whether or not her interest is binding upon the mortgagee.

The difficulty for the mortgagee is that the framework of co-ownership of land is predicated upon the notion that the legal title is vested in two legal owners. If that is the case then, on a conveyance by the two legal owners, any equitable co-ownership interests will be overreached and attached to the purchase money.[155] Where the correct overreaching machinery is not operated, which will be the case when there is only one legal owner of the land, there is no land charge which would include the rights of an equitable co-owner.[156] The determination of the issue of whether such an interest is binding on a purchaser is then governed by the traditional doctrine of notice.

Where a person has become an equitable co-owner, in circumstances such as those outlined above, she will have acquired her interest under a trust. This trust will normally have arisen as a result of her contributing financially to the acquisition of the house, for example by using her salary to help meet the mortgage repayments.[157] It is also possible that an interest may be acquired in the property without making direct contributions to the purchase of the house, relying on this occasion on the doctrine of equitable estoppel which, in the present context, is a doctrine which bears a close affinity to the law of trusts.[158]

Equitable estoppel, which will be examined in depth in subsequent chapters, is a flexible doctrine, whereby one person acquires rights over another's land by relying upon the expectation either that they will acquire, or already have, an interest in that person's land, in circumstances when it would be inequitable for the latter to deny some effect to such an expectation. Although not entirely uncontroversial,[159] it seems probable that such rights are capable of binding purchasers and that their enforceability will depend upon the doctrine of notice. This view is reinforced by the recognition in section 116 of the Land Registration Act 2002 that such rights are, for the

---

[155] *City of London Building Society v. Flegg* [1988] A.C. 54. See Extension of overreaching, p. 80 and Overreaching, pp. 297–300.

[156] This is also true in the rarer situation where a legal owner holds the land on a bare trust for another. Cf. *Hodgson v. Marks* [1971] Ch. 892.

[157] See Chapter 9.   [158] See Chapter 13.   [159] See Chapter 15.

purposes of registered land, capable of binding purchasers of that land. It is unlikely that a different view will be taken when title is unregistered.

When faced with the question of the enforceability of rights of this nature, the original judicial attitude was to give the doctrine of notice a narrow ambit, holding that a purchaser did not have notice of the rights of a person who was sharing occupation of a house with the legal owner of it, thereby enhancing the security of the conveyancing transaction.[160] Latterly, however, a different line has been taken, with the courts being prepared to hold a purchaser to be fixed with notice of the rights of such occupiers.

The recent trend of judicial decisions has been to protect the rights of occupiers of land. Such a trend could be reversed by legislation, by making rights of this nature registrable so that, if not registered, they would be void as against purchasers. If such a course was taken, it would give priority to the conveyancing dimension and make it more true than it is currently to say that equitable rights are either overreachable or registrable. To adopt such a course would necessarily entail a number of people having their homes put at risk through the activities of the person with whom they share the property. Cases of this type tend, generally, to involve the acquisition of rights through highly informal transactions of a non-commercial nature, where it is highly unlikely that legal advice would be taken. To insist upon such rights being registrable would, in most cases, mean that they would not be binding upon mortgagees. Clearly, this involves a policy issue as to which of two competing interests should be afforded priority and, indeed, where the balance should be struck between them. The resolution of this issue has underpinned a considerable amount of litigation in this area and will be considered in detail when considering the law relating to mortgages.[161]

THE CLASSIFICATION OF INTERESTS

Having analysed the legislative reform of unregistered land, it may be useful to tabulate how the various interests can be classified resulting from the reduction of the number of legal estates and interests and the treatment of equitable interests.

(i)   **Legal estates.** These are the fee simple absolute in possession and the term of years absolute.

(ii) **Legal charges.** These are mortgages.

(iii) **Legal interests.** This group principally involves easements and profits.

(iv) **Equitable interests.** This group divides into three categories:

   (a) **Overreachable interests.** These family-type interests will be transferred from land to money, provided that the correct machinery is employed.

---

[160] See Shared occupation, p. 54.   [161] See Chapter 12.

(b) **Registrable interests.** These equitable interests will, if registered, bind a purchaser. If not registered, they will be void against a purchaser for money or money's worth.

(c) **Residuary category.** This is a category of equitable right which is neither overreachable nor registrable but depends for its enforceability against purchasers on the traditional doctrine of notice.

5

Registration of Title

As was discussed in Chapter 4, one of the aims of the 1925 legislation was to encourage the development of the registration of title to land. To this end, it was necessary to simplify the basic doctrines of substantive Land Law. Thereafter, the ultimate goal has been to arrive at a situation where all titles to land in England and Wales are registered. Although substantial progress has been made towards the achievement of this objective, there is still a considerable way to go before this outcome is attained. This can be seen from the Land Registry's Annual Report of 2010/11,[1] in which it is revealed that land registration covers only around seventy-five per cent of England and Wales. The upshot is that it will remain necessary for a number of years to come to have regard to the principles of unregistered land, although it is anticipated that, in the not too distant future, those principles will have become obsolete. When that occurs, the ownership of land will be governed almost exclusively by the provisions of the Land Registration Act 2002. One benefit of this is that the somewhat flawed Land Charges legislation will cease to be relevant to the question of the enforceability of third party rights.

Systems of registration of title have been in existence for many years. At first, what was in place was a regime which allowed for the voluntary registration of titles. Perhaps unsurprisingly, this was not a great success. Compulsion to register titles was first introduced with respect to London in 1898.[2] It was not until the enactment of the Land Registration Act 1925, however, that the principle of compulsory registration of title was introduced into England and Wales. For reasons which will become apparent, however, it has taken many years for this principle to be implemented and it remains the case that not all titles to land are registered. The past few years have seen a concerted legislative attempt to accelerate the process of ensuring that the title to all land in England and Wales is registered, and it is anticipated that this process will be completed within a comparatively short space of time.

For over seventy-five years, the law governing land registration was underpinned by the Land Registration Act 1925, as amended.[3] Pursuant to a joint report by the Law Commission and the Land Registry,[4] a radical overhaul to the system was

---

[1] 2010/11 HCP 1158, 5.

[2] Land Transfer Act 1887. See Hayton, *Registered Land* (3rd edn) (London: Sweet & Maxwell, 1981), 14.

[3] The main amendments were implemented by the Land Registration Acts 1936, 1986, 1988, and 1997.

[4] (1998) Law Com. No. 254.

proposed. Following consultation, a further joint report was published, entitled: *Land Registration for the Twenty First Century: A Conveyancing Revolution*.[5] As the title to this report suggests, the changes introduced are intended to be substantial and these changes have now been implemented by the Land Registration Act 2002.[6] While it may be an overstatement to say that the changes made by the Act 'are likely to be more far-reaching than the great reforms of property law that were made by the 1925 legislation',[7] it is undoubtedly the case that the Act and, in particular, the introduction of compulsory electronic conveyancing, which has yet to be implemented, will reshape the terrain of modern Land Law.

The main provisions of the Act came into force towards the end of 2003, but it was not intended to bring in the provisions relating to electronic conveyancing until later in the decade, although that ambition has yet to be realized. The Act has repealed the Land Registration Act 1925 in its entirety.[8] Some reference will still need to be made to the earlier legislation, however, in order both to understand the new law and to explain the effect of some of the transitional provisions contained in the new Act.

THE BASICS OF REGISTRATION OF TITLE

The principal ambition of registration of title is to facilitate the security of land ownership and transfer:

'The essential purpose of the scheme created by the Act...is to provide a system of state-guaranteed registered title. Subject to exceptions, the register is intended to provide a comprehensive and accurate reflection of the title to registered land at any given time, so that it is possible to investigate title on line with the 'minimum of additional enquiries and inspections.'[9]

Under the unregistered system, when selling land, the seller has to give a convincing historical account of his right to sell it. This entailed an inspection of the title deeds to prove, so far as possible, that the purchaser's right to enjoy the land would not subsequently be disturbed by others. Furthermore, elaborate enquiries, admittedly made easier by the system of the registration of land charges, had to be made to discover what third party rights affected the land in question. This process was repetitive and not entirely secure. For example, a purchaser would be bound by legal third party rights

---

[5] (2001) Law Com. No. 271, referred to hereafter as the joint report.

[6] For helpful accounts of the new law, see Harpum and Bignell, *Registered Land, The New Law* (Bristol: Jordans, 2002) and Abbey and Richards, *Blackstones Guide to the Land Registration Act 2002* (Oxford: Oxford University Press, 2002). See also E. Cooke, *The New Law of Land Registration* (Oxford: Hart, 2003) and E. Cooke [2002] Conv. 11. The first named author of the first cited book was a member of the Law Commission throughout the period when these reports were prepared.

[7] (2001) Law Com. No. 271, para. 1.1.   [8] Land Registration Act 2002, s. 135, Sched. 13.

[9] *Chief Land Registar v. Franks* [2011] EWCA Civ. 772 at [25] *per* Rimer L.J.

regardless of whether he knew, or even could have known, about them[10]. To replace this laborious process, the fundamental idea behind the system of registration of title was that, as opposed to the land charges system, whereby third party rights affecting land are registered, it is the title to the land itself which is registered. The registered title replaces the evidence of entitlement to the land which was previously provided by the title deeds. In addition, third party rights affecting the land would be entered on to the register so that, by the relatively simple process of inspection of the register, a purchaser could ascertain both who owned the land and the rights to which it would be subject. Finally, the accuracy of the register would be backed by a state guarantee.

The basic principles were listed by a former Chief Land Registrar, Theodore Ruoff, as being:

(i)   the mirror principle;

(ii)   the curtain principle;

(iii) the insurance principle.[11]

Put briefly, the mirror principle is that the register should reflect accurately the position with regard to the ownership of land and the third party rights affecting it. This principle was recently restated in the joint report, where it is said that:

'The fundamental objective of the [Act] is that, under the system of electronic dealing with land that it seeks to create, the register should be a complete and accurate reflection of the state of the title to land at any given time, so that it is possible to investigate title to land on line, *with the absolute minimum of additional enquiries and inspections.*'[12]

The italicized part of this quotation reflects, what was recognized by Ruoff himself, that the mirror principle is not an inviolate one. It has always been the case that a certain category of interests, first termed overriding interests, and now referred to as interests which override either first registration or registered dispositions,[13] will bind a purchaser of registered land. This category of interests are interests which do not appear on the register of title but to which the registered proprietor will be subject. In the joint report, it was recognized that this category of interest was a major impediment to the achievement of the aim mentioned above.[14] It was also recognized, however, that there are certain types of right which it is not reasonable to expect to be protected on the register.[15] The existence of this category of right is, therefore, a fairly large exception to the mirror principle.[16]

---

[10] See, e.g. *Wyld v. Silver* [1963] Ch. 243, Legal rights, pp. 48–49.

[11] Ruoff, *An Englishman Looks at the Torrens System* (Sydney: Law Book Co., 1957), 8.

[12] (2001) Law Com. No. 271, para. 1.5. Emphasis supplied.

[13] Land Registration Act 2002, Scheds 1 and 3.

[14] (2001) Law Com. No. 271, para. 2.24. See also *Secretary of State for the Environment, Transport and the Regions v. Baylis (Gloucester) Ltd* (2000) 80 P. & C.R. 324 at 338 *per* Mr Kim Lewison Q.C., sitting as a High Court judge.

[15] (2001) Law Com. No. 271, para. 2.25.

[16] See Unregistered interests which override registration, pp. 135–157.

As was explained in Chapter 4, equitable interests in land can broadly be divided into commercial interests and family interests.[17] The latter type of interest will, provided that the correct machinery is operated, be overreached on a conveyance of the land and will not prejudicially affect a purchaser. The curtain principle in registered land is an application of this division. The details of interests affecting registered land which will be overreached by a disposition of that land are kept off the register of title. Their existence is protected by alerting the purchaser to what formalities have to be complied with to ensure that the interests are overreached.[18]

The third principle underlying registered land is the insurance principle. This is that the state provides a guarantee of the accuracy of the register and will compensate any person who suffers loss as a result of any errors contained in it.

As noted above, these principles are not inviolate, but it is nevertheless worth bearing them in mind when considering the operation of the system.

A second, preliminary, point to make concerns the interrelationship between the substantive law underlying the unregistered and registered systems. The traditional view was that, to some extent, the regime of registration of title was superimposed upon the framework of unregistered land. Increasingly, however, it came to be recognized that problems involving registered land may involve different outcomes than would have been the case had title not been registered.[19] Because the registered system is based upon registration rather than, as is the case with unregistered land, possession, this is almost inevitably going to be the case.[20] Increasingly, the registration system will be based upon principles of its own and the law relating to unregistered land, and in particular the sharp division between legal and equitable interests, will cease to be relevant.[21]

The Land Registry

Section 1 of the Land Registration Act 2002 provides that there shall continue to be maintained a register of title kept by the registrar. The business of registration under the Act is carried out by an office termed Her Majesty's Land Registry. The Land Registry consists of the Chief Land Registrar, who is appointed by the Lord Chancellor, and the staff appointed by the Registrar.[22] Until 1990, the Chief Land Registrar had to be a solicitor or barrister of at least ten years' standing, and he played an important role in the resolution of disputes and the interpretation of the legislation.[23] Upon the Land

---

[17] See Equitable rights, pp. 85–87.   [18] See Restrictions, pp. 130–131.

[19] See, e.g. *Lloyds Bank plc v. Carrick* [1996] 4 All E.R. 630 at 642 *per* Morritt L.J.; Harpum, Bridge, and Dixon, *Megarry and Wade's Law of Real Property* (7th edn) (London: Sweet & Maxwell, 2008), 146–147.

[20] See (2001) Law Com. No. 271, para. 1.13.

[21] See R.J. Smith in Tee (ed.), *Land Law: Issues, Debate, Policy* (Cullompton: Willan Publishing, 2002), Chapter 2.

[22] Land Registration Act 2002, s. 9(9).

[23] Successive holders of this office published a regularly updated reference work on Land Registry law and practice. The current edition is Ruoff and Roper, *The Law and Practice of Registered Conveyancing* (London: Sweet & Maxwell, 2008, looseleaf).

Registry becoming an executive agency, however, the requirement that the Chief Land Registrar be legally qualified was removed.[24] This change reflected the fact that the essential role of the office is now a managerial one and the principal legal tasks once performed by that official were undertaken by the Solicitor to the Land Registry.[25] This role has now been superseded by the creation of a new office, independent from the Land Registry, which is led by an official with the title of the Adjudicator, who must be a solicitor or barrister of at least ten years' standing.[26] In October 2003, Mr Edward Cousins was the first person to be appointed to this office.[27]

The Head Office is not actually responsible for any particular area and does not deal with applications for registration. That task was performed by District Land Registries, which were established by section 132 of the Land Registration Act 1925. The 2002 Act does not deal expressly with District Land Registries, it simply being provided that the Lord Chancellor may by order designate a particular office of the Land Registry as the proper office for the receipt of applications or a specified description of application.[28]

At the various Land Registry offices are kept and maintained a register of title to freehold and leasehold land which, since 1982, need not be kept in documentary form;[29] a provision which enabled the expansion of the computerization of the Registry. The advent of electronic conveyancing will, in time, lead to its complete computerization. It is also important for people dealing with land to know if it is already registered. To this end, kept also at the registry is a map, formerly known as the public index map, but now simply termed the Index. The purpose of the Index is to enable it to be ascertained whether any registered estate relates to the land and how any registered estate which relates to the land is identified for the purposes of the register.[30]

Open register

For many years, the register, as opposed to the public index map, was not open to public inspection; it could only be inspected with the written authority of the proprietor or his solicitor.[31] Following an earlier Law Commission Report,[32] the position was changed by section 1(1) of the Land Registration Act 1988 to enable open access to the register. This provision, which was seen as being a necessary springboard to the

---

[24] Courts and Legal Services Act 1990, s. 125(2)(7), Sched. 17, para. 3; Sched. 20, replacing Administration of Justice Act 1956, s. 53.

[25] Land Registry (Solicitor to HM Land Registry) Rules 1990, rr. 3, 4; Land Registration (Conduct of Business) Regulations 2000, reg. 3.

[26] Land Registration Act 2002, s. 107. The Adjudicator is empowered to appoint such staff as he sees fit to assist in the carrying out of his duties: ibid., Sched. 9, paras 2, 3.

[27] Land Registry Annual Report and Accounts 2003–2004, p. 57.

[28] Land Registration Act 2002, s. 100(3).

[29] Land Registration Act 1925, s. 1 as amended by Administration of Justice Act 1982, s. 66. The form in which information included in the register is to be kept will be governed by Land Registration Rules made under the Act: Land Registration Act 2002, s. 1(2).

[30] Land Registration Act 2002, s. 68(1).

[31] Land Registration Act 1925, s. 112, as originally enacted.   [32] (1986) Law Com. No. 148.

development of electronic conveyancing,[33] has, itself, been extended in some respects by the 2002 Act.[34]

It is now provided by section 66(1) of the Act that any person may inspect and make copies of, or any part of, the register of title, any document kept by the registrar which relates to an application to him, or the register of cautions against first registration.[35] This right is subject to the exception that the registrar may, upon an application by a person, designate a relevant document as an exempt information document if it contains prejudicial information.[36] This exemption is principally included in order to protect commercially sensitive information. The opening up of the register is designed to facilitate online searches by direct access, without the need to secure the consent of the registered proprietor.[37]

The register of title

The register of title is divided into three constituent parts: the Property Register, the Proprietorship Register, and the Charges Register.

The property register

This part of the register gives a verbal description of the property. This comprises a physical and legal description of the property. The former aspect of the description makes reference to a filed plan. The description of the property will note the boundaries although, unless the boundaries are shown as being fixed, which is extremely rare,[38] then the boundaries are general boundaries: that is they do not determine the exact line of the boundary.[39] In the event of a boundary dispute, the conveyance of the property prior to registration of title may then be relevant,[40] as will the normal presumptions made for the resolution of such disputes.[41] The fixing of boundaries does not prevent the operation of accretion or diluvion,[42] the former being the situation when land is bounded by water and that water recedes, the latter being the converse situation. The boundary then moves to where the new waterline is.[43]

---

[33] (2001) Law Com. No. 271, para. 9.37.

[34] For criticism of this, on the ground that it facilitates the commission of fraud, see P. Matthews (2008) 124 LQ.R. 351.

[35] See Cautions against first registration, p. 124.

[36] Land Registration Act 2002, s. 66(2); Land Registration Rules 2003, r. 136.

[37] See (2002) Law Com. No. 271, para. 9.37.

[38] Rules to govern fixing the exact boundaries have been made under the Land Registration Act 2002, s. 60(3). See Land Registration Rules 2003, Part 10.

[39] Land Registration Act 2002, s. 60(1)(2).

[40] See *Lee v. Barrey* [1957] Ch. 251; *Derbyshire County Council v. Fallon* [2007] EWHC 1326 (Ch.); *Wilkinson v Farmer* [2010] EWCA Civ. 1148.

[41] See *Alan Wibberley Buildings Ltd v. Instey* [1999] 1 W.L.R. 894 (the hedge and ditch presumption); J. Cross and G. Broadbent [2000] Conv. 61.

[42] Land Registration Act 2002, s. 61(1).

[43] See *Southern Centre of Theosophy Inc. v. State of South Australia* [1982] A.C. 706 at 712 *per* Lord Wilberforce.

The legal description of the property will indicate the interest which is held and any appurtenant rights, such as the benefit of easements or covenants. If mines and minerals have previously been excluded, this will be recorded in this part of the register.

The proprietorship register

This part of the register states the name and address of the proprietor and the nature of the title. In the case of freehold land, this will indicate whether it is absolute, qualified, or possessory. In the case of leasehold titles, there is a similar gradation, in that case the title being either absolute, good, qualified, or possessory leasehold.[44] Also included in the proprietorship register are any restrictions which affect the ability of the proprietor to deal with the property.

The charges register

This part of the register is concerned with third party rights which adversely affect the property, such as covenants, easements, and mortgages. Matters which are registrable as land charges, where title to the land is unregistered, should appear in this section of the register. It is important to appreciate that, when title is registered, the enforceability of such rights no longer depends upon the registration of that interest as a land charge; the enforceability of such rights depends upon it either being entered on the register or it taking effect as an interest which overrides registration. The two systems are mutually discreet and, for this reason, the problems inherent in the land charges system, caused by registration being against the name of the estate holder, will become obsolete.

REGISTRABLE INTERESTS

Although it is common, as a form of shorthand, to speak of registered land, this technically is inaccurate. What is registered is not the land, itself, but title to the land. Only certain estates and interests are registrable with separate titles. One must keep separate the ideas of registration with an independent title and matters which can be registered so as to affect that title.

Traditionally, it was the case that only certain legal estates in land and rentcharges could be substantively registered with a separate title.[45] The list has now been expanded and the following interests are now capable of registration:

(i)   estates in land;

(ii) a rentcharge;

(iii) a franchise;

(iv) a *profit à prendre* in gross.

---

[44] See Titles less than absolute, pp. 157–159.   [45] Land Registration Act 1925, s. 2.

It was previously the case that neither a franchise nor a profit could be registered with its own title. A franchise is 'a royal privilege or branch of the royal prerogative subsisting in the hands of a subject, by grant from the King'.[46] Apparently, the most common forms of such rights are those to hold a market or fair, or to charge tolls.[47] A *profit à prendre* is the right to go on to someone else's land and take something from it, such as fish. A profit can exist in gross, which means that the owner of it does not have to own land, himself; the right can exist separately from ownership of land. Both of these types of right can be valuable and can be bought and sold. Consequently, provision is now made for these rights to be registrable with their own titles. Registration of rentcharges, franchises, and profits is voluntary and not the subject of compulsion. Once registered, however, any subsequent disposition of them must be completed by registration.

Crown land

As a matter of feudal theory, all land is ultimately held by the Crown.[48] Furthermore, the land registration provisions were based upon the registration of estates and the Crown does not hold estates in land. For these reasons, no provision was made for the Crown to be registered as the proprietor of land. It is the case, however, that large tracts of land, most notably foreshore land around the coast, are held by the Crown and nobody has an estate in that land. In other words, the Crown holds the land in demesne.[49] This will also be the case where land has reverted to the Crown by escheat.[50]

The fact that the Crown could not be registered as proprietor of such land was considered to be unsatisfactory.[51] Section 79(1) of the 2002 Act solves this problem by enabling Her Majesty to grant an estate in fee simple absolute in possession out of demesne land to herself. Unless an application for registration is made within two months from the date of the grant, then the grant made under subsection 1 is to be regarded as not having been made.[52]

Freehold estates

A person who holds a freehold estate in unregistered land may apply to be registered as proprietor of that estate. Under section 3(2) of the Act, a person who is entitled to have a legal estate vested in him may also apply to be registered. So if land is held on a bare trust for a person, the beneficiary may apply to be registered as proprietor. This

---

[46] *Spook Erection Ltd v. Secretary of State for the Environment* [1989] Q.B. 300 at 305 *per* Nourse L.J.
[47] (2001) Law Com. No. 271, para. 3.19.   [48] See Tenure, p. 48.
[49] See Tenure, p. 23.
[50] There are, apparently, some 500 cases of escheat involving freehold land a year: (2001) Law Com. No. 271, para. 11.22.
[51] Ibid., paras 11.1–11.38.
[52] Land Registration Act 2002, s. 79(2)(3). This period may be extended by the registrar: ibid., s. 79(4).

does not extend, however, to a person who is entitled to have an estate vested in him by reason of a contract to purchase that land.[53] Such a person should first have the land conveyed to him, pursuant to the contract, and then apply for registration.

Leasehold estates

In unregistered land, provided that the lease in question satisfies the definition of a term of years absolute, it can subsist as a legal estate in land. One of the purposes of registration of title is to facilitate dealings in land. As short leases are frequently not the subject of dealings, it would make little sense to make all such leases registrable. In any event, to make any lease, of whatever duration, registrable would clog up the system.[54] Accordingly, only certain leases are registrable.

At one time, the position with regard to the registration of leases was unnecessarily complex It was simplified in 1996, however, so that the position which was then introduced was that a leasehold interest of not less than twenty-one years was registrable.[55] This period was, however, considered to be too long by the Law Commission and the Land Registry. In particular, it was noted that many commercial leases are granted for a shorter period and it was considered to be undesirable that many such leases were outwith the registration system.[56] Consequently, it is now the case that, since the Act came into force, leases of more than seven years are registrable with their own title.[57] Shorter leases which are discontinuous, which is the case with time-sharing agreements, are also made registrable. The Lord Chancellor is empowered, after consultation with such persons as he considers to be appropriate, to reduce this term,[58] and it is envisaged that, when electronic conveyancing becomes compulsory, the term will be reduced to three years.[59]

As will be seen, provision for certain other leases to be registered is made and these will be considered shortly. One type of lease which is envisaged as being of over seven years' duration is not registrable. These are PPP leases, that is Public–Private Partnership agreements,[60] which are intended as the means of landholding for the London Underground. The practical difficulties in registering such leases are considered to be too great and they cannot be registered voluntarily and are not subject to compulsory registration of title.[61]

---

[53] Land Registration Act 2002, s. 3(2)(6).

[54] This reason will be less cogent when electronic conveyancing is made compulsory.

[55] Land Registration Act 1986, s. 2, replacing Land Registration Act 1925, s. 8, implementing proposals contained in (1983) Law Com. No. 125.

[56] See (2001) Law Com. No. 271, paras 3.16–3.17.

[57] Unless the leasehold estate is vested in him as mortgagee where there is a subsisting right of redemption: Land Registration Act 2002, s. 1(5). See Triggering events, pp. 119–121.

[58] Land Registration Act 2002, s. 118(1)(3).   [59] (2001) Law Com. No. 271, para. 3.17.

[60] As defined by the Greater London Authority Act 1999, s. 218.

[61] Land Registration Act 2002, s. 90.

FIRST REGISTRATION OF TITLE

Although the principle of compulsory registration of title was introduced in 1925, the registration of all titles to land did not, of course, happen overnight. It was provided by section 120 of the Land Registration Act 1925 that, by Order in Council, a particular area could be designated as an area of compulsory registration of title. Over time, the areas of compulsory registration were extended, the process resembling the construction of a patchwork quilt. This process was completed on 1 December 1989, when the whole of England and Wales was designated as an area of compulsory registration of title,[62] each geographical area being served by a District Land Registry.

Voluntary registration

It has never been the case that, simply because land is situate in an area of compulsory registration of title, the landowner is required to register the title to it. The compulsion to do so applies only on the occurrence of certain transactions.[63] It has always been possible to register the title voluntarily, however, and inducements are provided in the form of reduced fees to encourage people to do this, thereby helping to accelerate the spread of registration of title.[64]

Triggering events

The fact that land is situate in an area of compulsory registration does not mean that the owner of that land must forthwith apply for registration of title to it. Registration is made compulsory only upon the occurrence of a specified transaction involving the land. For many years, this triggering event was either a conveyance on sale of a fee simple, or the grant or assignment of a lease of more than twenty-one years. The limitation of the requirements for compulsory registration of title had the result that land could be in an area of compulsory registration of title for a very long time before there was any requirement for title to it to be registered. The land might remain unsold for many years and pass down the family by inheritance. In order to accelerate the spread of registration of title,[65] the number of transactions which would trigger the compulsory registration of title was extended considerably by section 1 of the Land Registration Act 1997. In particular, the requirement to register title was extended to occasions when land passed by inheritance;[66] a factor which will obviously acceler-

---

[62] Registration of Title Order 1989 (S. I. 1989, No. 1347).

[63] See Triggering events, p. 119.

[64] Land Registration Fees Order 2001 (S. I. 2001, No. 1179), art. 2(5). For the power of the Lord Chancellor to prescribe fees, see Land Registration Act 2002, s. 102.

[65] (1995) Law Com. No. 154, a paper published jointly by the Law Commission and the Land Registry.

[66] Land Registration Act 1997, s. 1(6).

ate the achievement of the goal of universal registration of title.[67] The requirement to register title was further extended by the 2002 Act and the list of triggering events is now to be found in section 4.[68]

Under section 4(1) of the Act, the requirement of registration applies on the occurrence of any of the following events:

(a) the transfer of a qualifying estate—
  (i) for valuable or other consideration, by way of gift or in pursuance of an order of any court, or
  (ii) by means of an assent (including a vesting assent);[69]

(b) the transfer of an unregistered legal estate in land in circumstances where section 171A of the Housing Act 1985 applies (disposal by landlord, which leads to a person no longer being a secure tenant);

(c) the grant out of a qualifying estate of an interest in land—
  (i) for a term of years absolute of more than seven years from the date of the grant, and
  (ii) for valuable or other consideration, by way of gift or in pursuance of an order of any court;

(d) the grant out of a qualifying estate of an estate in land for a term of years absolute to take effect in possession after the end of a period of three months beginning with the date of the grant;

(e) the grant of a lease in pursuance of Part 5 of the Housing Act 1985 (the right to buy) out of an unregistered legal estate in land;

(f) the grant of a lease out of an unregistered legal estate in land in such circumstances as are mentioned in paragraph (b);

(g) the creation of a protected first legal mortgage of a qualifying estate.

Section 4(2) of the Act defines a qualifying estate as being an unregistered legal estate, which is either a freehold estate in land, that is a fee simple absolute in possession, or leasehold estate in land for a term which, at the time of the transfer, grant or creation, has more than seven years to run.

Before expanding on this definition, it is convenient to mention some events which are specifically excluded from being triggering events. These are the assignment of a mortgage term, or the assignment or surrender of lease to the owner of the immediate reversion where the term is to merge in that reversion.[70] The latter event is a means by which a lease can come to an end, the tenant giving up, and the landlord accepting, the

[67] This may still not be achieved for some time, as companies can hold unregistered land for prolonged periods and there will not be an inheritance of it. This is also true of local authorities.

[68] The Lord Chancellor is empowered to add to the triggering events: Land Registration Act 2002, s. 5(1).

[69] An assent is the process by which the personal representatives of a deceased person vest the property in the person entitled under the will. In cases of intestacy, the assent is executed by the administrators of the estate.

[70] Land Registration Act 2002, s. 4(4).

lease prior to its coming to the end of its natural term.[71] A further excluded event is the creation of a lease in order to create a mortgage. One way of creating a legal mortgage was by the creation of a long lease in favour of the lender, the mortgagee. It is no longer possible to create a mortgage of registered land in this way.[72]

The Act goes on to give further definition as to what constitutes a triggering event. First, if the estate transferred or created has a negative value, it is nevertheless to be regarded as having been transferred or granted for valuable consideration.[73] Such an event is likely to occur when the extent of the repairing obligations in a lease means that the cost of complying with such obligations exceeds the value of the lease itself. Second, a transfer or grant by way of gift expressly includes the constitution of a trust where the settlor does not retain the whole of the beneficial interest. This would include a situation where a person, who is the sole owner of a house, on getting married, transfers the house into their joint names. A further event which triggers compulsory registration is a transaction uniting the legal and beneficial titles where the settlor, on the constitution of the trust did not retain the entire beneficial interest.[74]

Protected mortgages

A protected mortgage is defined by section 4(8) of the Act as being a legal mortgage if it takes effect on its creation as a mortgage to be protected by the deposit of documents relating to the mortgaged estate and a first legal mortgage is one which, on its creation, ranks in priority ahead of any other mortgages then affecting the mortgaged land. This aspect of the law of mortgages will be explained in Chapter 12.

Reversionary leases

One of the main changes introduced by the Act was to reduce the length of leases which are required to be registered from twenty-one years to a period of seven years. What should not be overlooked, however, is that on the grant of lease to take effect in possession after the end of the period of three months beginning with the date of the grant, this lease is required by section 4(1)(d) of the Act to be registered. This type of lease is termed a reversionary lease and it is immaterial for how long the lease is to last. The width of this provision is unfortunate. It is by no means uncommon for student leases to be granted in March or April, to take effect in possession in September and to be for a period of one year.[75] Such a lease is now the subject of compulsory registration. One suspects strongly that this will not occur.

---

[71] See Surrender, p. 459.   [72] Land Registration Act 2002, s. 23(1).   [73] Ibid., s. 4(6).
[74] Ibid., s. 4(7).
[75] This point is also taken by Smith, *Property Law* (7th edn) (Harlow: Longman, 2011), 236. For other problems with this type of lease, see In possession, pp. 424–425.

Duty to register

Section 6 of the Act imposes a duty to register on the occurrence of one of the events specified in section 4. This duty is generally imposed upon the transferee of the relevant estate. In the case of the creation of a protected first mortgage, section 4(1)(g) of the Land Registration Act 2002 imposed the obligation to apply for registration upon the mortgagor (that is, the borrower). This potentially created a problem for the mortgagee in ensuring that the mortgagor did this.[76] This potential difficulty has been removed as under a rule made under section 6(6) of the Act, the mortgagee may make an application in the name of the mortgagor for the estate charged to be registered, whether or not the mortgagor consents.[77]

Sanction for non-registration

The Act makes registration of title compulsory on the occurrence of one of the events set out in section 4 of the Act. The original legislation simply enacted that if, after two months from the date of the conveyance no application had been made for registration, then the conveyance would be void. This provision was thought to give rise to potential problems.[78] The consequence of non-registration was later spelled out more explicitly in amending legislation,[79] and the matter is now governed by section 7 of the 2002 Act.

It is provided that unless, within two months of the disposition,[80] an application is made for registration,[81] then, if the disposition purports to transfer the legal estate, the title to the legal estate will revert to the transferor, who will hold it on a bare trust for the transferee.[82] In the case of grant or creation of a lease or a mortgage, the effect of non-registration is to treat what has happened as a contract for valuable consideration to grant or create the particular interest.[83] If either of these consequences occurs, then the cost of retransferring, regranting, or recreating the legal estate will fall upon the person who failed to register the title.[84]

---

[76] For the considerable problems caused by a failure to make a proper application for first registration, see *Sainsbury's Supermarkets Ltd v. Olympia Homes Ltd* [2005] EWHC 1235 (Ch.).

[77] Land Registration Rules 2003, r. 21.

[78] See D.G. Barnsley (1968) Conv. (N.S.) 391 at 401, although see *Pinekerry Ltd v. Kenneth Needs (Contractors) Ltd* (1992) 64 P. & C.R. 245 at 247.

[79] Land Registration Act 1997, s. 1.

[80] Land Registration Act 2002, s. 6(5). The registrar is empowered by s. 6(5) to extend this period, if satisfied that there is a good reason for so doing. In practice, the registrar is normally willing to grant an extension: Ruoff and Roper, op. cit., 11.13.

[81] A misdescription of the property in the application does not amount to a failure to apply: *Proctor v. Kidman* (1985) 51 P. & C.R. 647.

[82] Land Registration Act 2002, s. 7(2)(a). The possibility of the estate reverting is disregarded for the purpose of determining whether a fee simple is a fee simple in possession: ibid., s. 7(4). See The fee simple absolute in possession, p. 83. For a good example of the reversion of the estate, see *Sainsbury's Supermarkets Ltd v. Olympia Homes Ltd, supra.*

[83] Land Registration Act 2002, s. 7(2)(b).   [84] Ibid., s. 8.

The consequence of a failure to register is that the transferee is in danger of losing priority to an interest which is created subsequent to the disposition. It is true that, in most cases, the transferee will be in actual occupation of the land in question and that occupation will afford protection to the right as against a subsequent transferee of the property,[85] but this is unlikely to be the case where the disposition in question is a mortgage. In that event, a failure to apply for registration of title may cause the mortgagee to be bound by interests created subsequent to the mortgage; a position which would not have happened had a timely application for registration been made.[86]

The extension of compulsion

As noted previously, it has never been the case that, simply because land is situate in an area of compulsory registration, title to it must be registered. The law has always made compulsory registration dependent upon the occurrence of a particular triggering event. The framers of the 2002 Act are committed to speeding up the time when title to all land in England and Wales is registered and, to this end, have recommended that ways in which all remaining land with unregistered title might be brought on to the register should be re-examined five years after the Act is brought into force.[87]

It is hard to see how this could be done. While it is possible to enact that all owners of land to which title is unregistered should have to register title to it, it seems objectionable to impose such an obligation upon people who may have lived in the property for a considerable number of years and are, quite reasonably, unaware of the need to register title to it. Moreover, it is difficult to see what the sanction for non-registration would be. It is clearly not sensible to provide that the legal title would revert to the person who transferred it many years ago. It would seem to be very unlikely that a universal compulsion to register title will be introduced.

The process of registration

Once one of the triggering events has occurred, an application for registration must be made within the two-month period. If the transaction is a conveyance on sale, then the traditional method of investigation of title will be employed; the purchaser will peruse the title deeds and make the normal searches in the land charges registry. When the process has been completed, and the land conveyed to the purchaser, this process is repeated in the registry. If the registrar is satisfied that the title is such as a willing buyer could properly be advised by a competent solicitor to accept, then the applicant for first registration will be registered with an absolute title. In deciding this question, the registrar may disregard the fact that the title may be open to objection if he is of the opinion that the defect will not cause the holding under the title to

---

[85] See Interests of persons in actual occupation, p. 137.

[86] See *Barclays Bank plc v. Zaroovabli* [1997] 1 All E.R. 19, although not a case concerning first registration of title.

[87] (2001) Law Com. No. 271, para. 2.13.

be disturbed.[88] This latter provision is designed to enable the registrar to register the applicant with an absolute title, despite there being technical objections to the title deduced and, apparently, the registrar is prepared to take a robust view as to when a defect is merely technical.[89] Any refusal by the registrar to register the applicant with an absolute title cannot, apparently, be appealed against directly,[90] although the matter would seem to be amenable to judicial review and may, in the future, be dealt with in rules promulgated under the Act.[91] If, in separate proceedings, a court has held a title to be free from objection, and such that it can be forced upon a reluctant purchaser, then it is considered to be inconceivable that the registry will decline to register the purchaser with an absolute title.[92]

Cautions against first registration

An application for first registration of title may affect the rights and interests of other people with interests in the land. Provision is made for people who claim to have certain interests to lodge a caution against first registration of title. The effect of the registration of such a caution is that, when an application is made for registration of title, the registrar must give the cautioner notice of the application for registration and of his right to object to the registration.[93] The cautioner is then given a period of fifteen working days from the issue of the notice to exercise his right to object to the application or to give the registrar notice that he does not intend to do so.[94] The registrar cannot determine an application for first registration until the period specified in the rules has expired. If the period expires without there being any response from the cautioner, then the registrar will proceed to determine the application for registration. If the cautioner objects to the application, then, unless the registrar is satisfied that the objection is groundless, or it can be disposed of by agreement, the matter must then be referred to the adjudicator,[95] who may determine any dispute between the parties.[96]

A person may lodge a caution against first registration if he claims to be either the owner of a qualifying estate or entitled to an interest affecting a qualifying estate. A qualifying estate is either an estate in land, a rentcharge, a franchise, or a profit in gross. In the case of estates in land, in the case of either a freehold or a lease for more

---

[88] Land Registration Act 2002, s. 9(2)(3).
[89] For criticism, see C.T. Emery (1976) 40 Conv. (N.S.) 122.
[90] *Dennis v. Malcolm* [1934] Ch. 244, although see *Quigly v. Chief Land Registrar* [1992] 1 W.L.R. 834 at 837 *per* Millett J.
[91] Land Registration Act 2002, s. 14.
[92] *M.E.P.C. Ltd v. Christian-Edwards* [1981] A.C. 205 at 220–221 *per* Lord Russell of Killowen, a case concerning the enforceability of an uncompleted contract made in 1911 to buy land contracted to be sold in 1973.
[93] Land Registration Act 2002, s. 16(1).
[94] Land Registration Rules 2003, r. 53(1). At the request of the cautioner, this period can be extended to a maximum of thirty working days: r. 53(1)(2).
[95] Land Registration Act 2002, s. 73(2)(6)(7).
[96] See *Jayasinghe v. Liyange* [2010] EWHC 265 (Ch); *Chief Land Registrar v. Silkstone* [2011] EWCA Civ. 801.

than seven years, then these estates could be protected by a caution against registration for a period of two years after the coming into force of the Act.[97] After that date, it was anticipated that a person claiming to be the owner of these estates should apply themselves for first registration.[98] An interest in land is defined by section 132(3)(b) of the Act to mean an adverse right affecting the title to the estate or charge. This will necessarily include matters registrable under the Land Charges Act 1972, and the possibility of lodging a caution against first registration to protect such a right is seen as a means of conferring additional protection upon such rights.

Additional protection

It should be appreciated, however, that the lodging of a caution against first registration is an additional method of affording protection to a matter which is registrable as a land charge, and not an alternative. In *Sainsbury's Supermarkets Ltd v. Olympia Ltd*[99] the claimant sought to protect an option to purchase by the lodging of a caution against first registration but did not also register a land charge. As was pointed out by Mann J., this was insufficient. The reason for this is that the effect of section 4(6) of the Land Charges Act 1972 would be that the option would have become void for non-registration on the occasion of the conveyance for money or money's worth which would have preceded the application for first registration.[100] This point is reinforced by section 16(3) of the Land Registration Act 2002, which specifically provides that a caution against first registration has no effect on the validity of any interest of the cautioner in the legal estate to which the caution relates: that is, it does not confer validity on a claim which is not otherwise valid.[101] What it does is to allow the cautioner to substantiate a claim to have a right in another person's land. The existence of such a caution is revealed by searching the register of cautions, which the registrar is obliged to maintain and in the Index.[102] The existence of a caution against first registration may, however, prejudicially affect the owner of the land to which the caution relates. Its existence may well impair his prospects of selling the land, as no purchaser wishes to buy a law suit. To reflect this, a cautioner owes a statutory duty to the owner of the estate affected not to lodge a caution without reasonable cause.[103] The owner of the estate may also apply for the cancellation of a caution. If this is done, then the registrar must serve notice on the cautioner and must also inform him that, if he does not exercise his right to object within fifteen working days, the caution will be cancelled.[104]

Land certificates

It was previously the case that, on registration of title, the proprietor would be issued with a land certificate, which is a replica of the state of the title at the time of

[97] Ibid., s. 15(3), Sched. 12, para. 14(1)(2).   [98] (2001) Law Com. No. 271, para. 3.58.
[99] [2005] EWHC 1235 (Ch).   [100] Ibid., at para. 53.
[101] See also *Kitney v. M.E.P.C. Ltd* [1977] 1 W.L.R. 981.
[102] Land Registration Act 2002, ss 19, 68(3).   [103] Ibid., s. 77(1)(2).
[104] Ibid., s. 18; Land Registration Rules 2003, r. 53.

registration. These certificates had to be produced on certain specified dealings.[105] This is no longer the case. Additionally, when a mortgage was created, the mortgagee would receive a charge certificate in respect of the mortgage. The Act makes no provision for the issuing of charge certificates, which are abolished.[106]

REGISTRATION WITH AN ABSOLUTE TITLE

The overwhelming majority of applications for first registration of a freehold title result in the applicant being registered as proprietor with an absolute title. The effect of this was formerly governed by section 5 of the Land Registration Act 1925. The key provision is now section 11 of the 2002 Act. This provides that:

'The estate is vested in the proprietor together with all interests subsisting for the benefit of the estate.

The estate is vested in the proprietor subject only to the following interests affecting the estate at the time of registration—

(a) interests which are subject to an entry in the register in relation to the estate,

(b) unregistered interests which fall within any of the paragraphs of Schedule 1, and

(c) interests acquired under the Limitation Act 1980 of which the proprietor has notice.

If the proprietor is not entitled to the estate for his own benefit, or not entitled solely for his own benefit, then, as between himself and the persons beneficially entitled to the estate, the estate is vested in him subject to such of their interests as has notice of.'[107]

This provision is fundamental to the working of the system. It operates at two levels. First, it has a credit side, stipulating what it is that the statute gives to the registered proprietor, and, secondly, it makes clear the rights to which he takes subject. These matters will be considered in turn.

The statutory magic

A central feature of property law in general is encapsulated in the Latin phrase, *nemo dat quod non habet*, which means, one cannot give what one does not own. If, therefore, either by accident or design, a person purports to convey either more land than he actually owns, or land to which he has no title at all, the conveyance is void in respect of that piece of land. Whether or not the purchaser either could, or should, have known of this is quite immaterial. The Act operates to create a major exception to this principle.

---

[105] See 1st edn. 97.   [106] See (2001) Law Com. No. 271, para. 9.89.

[107] Land Registration Act 2002, s. 11(3)(4)(5). The last provision relates to a situation where the proprietor holds the land on trust for others.

In *Re 139 High Street, Deptford*,[108] a vendor purported to convey to a purchaser a shop, together with an annexe. The purchaser was registered as the proprietor with an absolute title of both the shop and the annexe. In fact, the annexe did not belong to the vendor but to a third party. The litigation concerned an attempt by the third party to secure the rectification of the register, so as to have the land returned to him. The point, for present purposes, is that what was once termed 'the statutory magic'[109] had operated to vest in the registered proprietor the legal estate to the land, even though the person who had purported to transfer the land to him did not own the land which he had purported to convey. This is made even clearer under the 2002 Act, as section 58(1) provides that:

'If, on the entry of a person in the register as the proprietor of a legal estate, the legal estate would not otherwise be vested in him, it shall be deemed to be vested in him as a result of the registration.'

As was just noted, the litigation in this case was a claim to have the register rectified to undo the effect of section 5 of the 1925 Act. This action succeeded and the proprietor was deprived of the annexe. He was, however, entitled to be indemnified to compensate for the loss which he had suffered as a result of the register having been rectified.[110] This is illustrative of one of the principles underpinning the system of registration of title: the insurance principle,[111] whereby people are, in general, compensated for loss caused by mistakes made in the registration process.[112]

Equitable title

Section 58 of the Act is quite explicit that the proprietor of a legal estate is deemed to have the legal estate vested in him, notwithstanding that, apart from the fact of registration, that estate would be vested in someone else. Save for limited examples,[113] the fact of registration is conclusive as to the location of the legal title: it is vested in the registered proprietor. Unfortunately, neither the 1925 Act nor the 2002 Act dealt explicitly with the ownership of the equitable title. This issue arose in *Epps v. Esso Petroleum Ltd*.[114] By mistake, a strip of land was purported to be conveyed twice by the same person. On the occasion of the second conveyance, which was of course void, the person to whom the strip had purportedly been conveyed was

---

[108] [1951] Ch. 884.

[109] Ruoff and Roper, op. cit. (5th edn, 1986), 70, a process now, less graphically, termed 'automatic vesting': para. 2.08.

[110] For alteration of the register and indemnity, see Alteration and indemnity, pp. 171–182.

[111] See The basics of registration of title, pp. 111–113.

[112] For a memorable example of the operation of this principle, see the reference to *Haigh's Case*, in Ruoff and Roper, op. cit., para. 40.13, where the notorious 'acid bath murderer' also forged conveyances from his victims and secured himself as proprietor of their properties.

[113] See Ruoff and Roper, op. cit., para. 2.09, instancing matters such as the death or bankruptcy of the proprietor.

[114] [1973] 1 W.L.R. 1071. See also *Gardner v. Lewis* [1998] 1 W.L.R. 1535 at 1538 *per* Lord Browne-Wilkinson. Cf. *Blacklocks v. J.B. Developments (Godalming) Ltd* [1982] Ch. 183.

registered as the proprietor of it. The action was brought by the people who derived title from the person to whom the first conveyance was made: that is the people who, had title not been registered in the name of the wrong person, would have been the owners of it.

One of the arguments employed to secure the restoration of the land to them was that they had an overriding interest in it. Although it was accepted that the effect of section 5 of the Land Registration Act 1925 was to vest the legal title in the registered proprietor, it was contended that the equitable title was not so vested, but, instead, was retained by the first purchaser of the strip and had then passed to them as successors in title. This equitable interest, it was said, when coupled with their actual occupation of the land, was upgraded to an overriding interest and, consequently, was binding upon the registered proprietor.[115] Although the argument failed on the facts, in that it was held that they were not in fact in actual occupation of the disputed strip, the premise upon which it was based appeared to have been accepted. Had Templeman J. not accepted the argument that the effect of registration of the wrong person as proprietor of the land was to vest only the legal title, but not the beneficial ownership, the point as to whether or not the plaintiffs were in actual occupation of the strip would not have arisen. They would not have had any interest in the property. The case seems to accept, therefore, that the curative effect of registration is only to vest the legal title in the person wrongly registered as the proprietor, but not the equitable title.

This is wrong in principle.[116] If the argument that the effect of registration is merely to clothe the registered proprietor with the bare legal title to the land, but, potentially, to leave the beneficial title outstanding is correct, this would have serious consequences. Under the rule in *Saunders v. Vautier*[117] a beneficiary under a bare trust can, if of full age, insist that the trustee transfers the legal title to him. In the present context, this would mean that the person who had lost the legal title to the land as a result of another person being mistakenly registered as the proprietor of it, could simply call for the land to be reconveyed to him. This would undermine completely the whole basis of the conclusiveness of the register. The 2002 Act does not, as it could have done, deal explicitly with this point. Nevertheless, much the better view is that first registration of title vests in the registered proprietor both the legal and the equitable titles to the land.[118]

---

[115] See The upgrading of rights, pp. 139–140.

[116] For a convincing critique, see S.N.L. Palk (1974) 38 Conv. (N.S.) 236. See also the comments in *Malory Enterprises Ltd v. Cheshire Homes Ltd* [2002] Ch. 216 at 232 *per* Arden L.J.

[117] (1841) Beav. 115.

[118] See, generally, C. Harpum in Getzler (ed.), *Rationalizing Property, Equity and Trusts: Essays in Honour of Edward Burn* (London, LexisNexis, 2003), 187. The interesting article on the role of resulting trusts in registered land, D. Wilde [1999] Conv. 382 is not germane to this issue because, *ex hypothesi*, the 'transferor' never held either the legal or equitable titles to the property. See, however, *Collings v. Lee* [2001] 2 All E.R. 332 and *Malory Enterprises Ltd v. Cheshire Homes Ltd, supra*. Neither case involved first registration of title.

THIRD PARTY RIGHTS

Section 11 of the Act operates positively to vest the legal and equitable titles to the land in the registered proprietor. It stipulates, also, to what rights the land is subject. These are entries noted on the register, unregistered interests which fall within any of the paragraphs of Schedule 1, and interests acquired under the Limitation Act 1980, of which the proprietor has notice. These matters must now be considered.

When title is unregistered, as seen in the previous chapter, interests in land can be placed into one of four categories and three subcategories. These are:

1. legal estates;
2. legal charges;
3. legal interests; and
4. equitable interests.

This fourth group can be subdivided into three subcategories:

1. registrable interests;
2. overreachable interests; and
3. interests neither registrable nor overreachable but dependent for their enforceability on the doctrine of notice.

Where title is registered, there is a similar classification, although there are fewer groups and the terminology is different. The groups are:

1. registrable interests;
2. registrable charges;
3. interests which are subject to an entry on the register; and
4. interests which override first registration or registered dispositions.

Category 3, interests which are subject to an entry on the register, can be divided into interests which are overreachable and those which are not.

Registrable interests and charges have already been considered. Attention must now be turned to interests which are subject to an entry on the register, and the different methods of protection, and to interests which override registration.

Interests protected on the register

Under the 1925 Act, third party rights affecting land fell into one of two categories: minor interests and overriding interests. This helpful nomenclature has been abandoned by the 2002 Act, although the essential distinction remains the same. Minor interests were defined by section 3(xv) of the 1925 Act and, save where the holder of the right was also in actual occupation of the land,[119] would only bind a purchaser if protected by an appropriate entry on the register. Overriding interests were listed in section 70 of the 1925 Act and were interests which did not appear on the register of title but would bind a purchaser of the land.

The interests which will bind a purchaser, although not entered on the register, are listed in Schedules 1 and 3 to the 2002 Act. Any interest which is not contained in these Schedules, if it is to bind a subsequent purchaser of the land, will need to be protected in the appropriate manner by registration. In particular, interests registrable as land charges must be entered on the register of title. On first registration, an official search will be made against the names of all people revealed on investigation of title as having been owners of the estate. These matters will then be entered in the charges register of the register of title. It follows that, in the case of land charges which have not been discovered, because they are registered against the name of an estate owner behind the root of title, they will not be entered on the register and the proprietor will take free from them. The person who subsequently learns that the interest, formerly protected by the correct registration of the land charge, has been lost will then have to seek alteration of the register to give effect to the right.[120] The provisions contained in section 25 of the Law of Property Act 1925, to provide compensation for purchasers bound by land charges registered behind the root of title have, therefore, become virtually obsolete.

There were various methods of protecting third party rights on the register. The 2002 Act has reduced these methods to two. Because the new Act operates prospectively, however, it remains necessary to have regard to the old regime as well as to the new.

Protection prior to 2003

Before the changes made by the 2002 Act came into force, there were four ways in which third party interests in land could be protected. These were restrictions, inhibitions, notices, and cautions.

Restrictions

A restriction, as the name suggests, is a limitation on the power of the registered proprietor to deal with the property.[121] Unless the terms of the restriction are complied with, the registrar will not register the disponee of the property. Its function is largely to protect family interests relating to land which can, if the proper machinery is operated, be overreached. Where, for example, land is subject to a settlement, a restriction will be entered to the effect that no disposition by a sole registered proprietor shall be registered unless the capital money which arises is paid to two trustees.

[119] See The upgrading of rights, pp. 139–140.
[120] For a similar situation, see *Horrill v. Cooper* (2000) Unreported, Court of Appeal.
[121] Land Registration Act 2002, s. 40.

Again, when two or more persons are registered as the proprietor of an estate in land, the registrar is obliged to enter a restriction for the purposes of securing that interests which are capable of being overreached on a disposition of the estate are overreached.[122] In these cases, the nature of the beneficial interests is not disclosed; an intending purchaser is simply informed as to how the conveyancing procedure is to be operated for those equitable interests to be overreached. This is what is meant by the curtain principle.

The restriction, as described above, is being used to ensure that the overreaching mechanisms are operated correctly. It can also perform other functions. In particular, the Act itself mentions other situations where a restriction may be registered. These include where notice must be given to a person prior to a disposal of the property, the need to obtain a person's consent to the disposal, and the need for an order by the court or registrar.[123]

Inhibitions

An inhibition was an entry made by the court or the registrar on the application of any person interested in the land.[124] The purpose of such an entry was to inhibit the occurrence of any event specified in the inhibition. Such entries were rare and were intended to provide protection in cases where fraud or suchlike was suspected.[125] In the case of a bankruptcy order, the registrar would automatically enter a bankruptcy inhibition restraining any dealing with the land until the trustee in bankruptcy was registered as the proprietor.[126]

Notices

A notice is the most effective way of protecting an interest in another person's land. A disposition by the proprietor will take effect subject to all entries, rights, and claims which are protected by the entry of a notice on the register.[127] This is subject to an important qualification. This is that the right which is sought to be protected must be a valid right, as the fact that the interest is the subject of a notice does not necessarily mean that the interest which it seeks to protect is valid.[128]

The registration of a notice was generally a co-operative act, in that the registered proprietor had to agree to its registration. Accordingly, it was unusual for there to be any dispute as to the validity of the interest in question. There is now, however, a new type of notice, a unilateral notice, to be discussed below, where the proprietor's consent to its registration is not required and, in this context, disputes have occurred.[129]

---

[122] Ibid., s. 44(1).   [123] Ibid., s. 40(3).   [124] Land Registration Act 1925, s. 57.
[125] See *Ahmed v. Kendrick* (1987) 56 P. & C.R. 120.
[126] Land Registration Act 1925, s. 61, as amended by Insolvency Act 1986, s. 235(1), Sched. 8, para. 5(3).
[127] Land Registration Act 2002, s. 29.
[128] Ibid., s. 32(3). See also *Kitney v. M.E.P.C. Ltd* [1977] 1 W.L.R. 981.
[129] See Unilateral notices, pp. 134–135.

Registrable interests

The 1925 Act contained a list of interests which could be protected by a notice.[130] The new Act lists the interests which cannot be protected in this way. The interests which cannot be protected by the registration of a notice are listed by section 33 of the 2002 Act. They are, first, an interest under a trust of land or a settlement under the Settled Land Act 1925. These are family-type interests which will be overreached on a disposition and should be protected by a restriction. The remaining interests which cannot be protected by the entry of a notice are leases of three years or less, which take effect in possession, a restrictive covenant between landlord and tenant, which relates to the property which has been leased, an interest capable of being registered under the Commons Registration Act 1965, and rights relating to coal or coal mines.

Cautions

The entry of a notice, as has been seen, is frequently effected with the consent of the registered proprietor. A caution, on the other hand, is non-consensual and can been seen as being a hostile act. There are two types of caution, although they perform the same function. First, where title is not registered, a caution may be lodged against first registration.[131] Secondly, when title is registered, a caution could be lodged against dealings. It is this latter form of caution which is the current concern.

The purpose of lodging a caution against dealings is to protect a claimed proprietary right in another person's property, such as a contract to buy the land or a lien over it.[132] The effect of registering a caution is not, of itself, to validate the claim. Once a caution has been registered, no dealing with the land is to be registered until notice of that proposed dealing has been served on the cautioner. He then has fourteen days in which to object to the registration. If the cautioner does not object within that period, then registration will occur and the caution is removed from the register; it is said to have been 'warned off'.[133] If the cautioner responds, then the registrar will determine the matter and either, if the claim cannot be sustained, remove the caution, or, alternatively, an appropriate entry is made on the register to give effect to the interest.

It should be appreciated that the protection afforded by a caution is inferior to that given by a notice. In the case of a notice then, assuming that the interest in question is valid, the notice establishes priority for that interest and ensures that any transferee of the land takes subject to it. In the case of a caution, section 56(2) of the Land Registration Act 1925 provides that a caution has no effect except as is mentioned in the Act. It does not confer priority for the claim[134] and only entitles the cautioner to be heard in order to substantiate the claim.[135]

---

[130] Land Registration Act 1925, s. 49.   [131] See Cautions against first registration, pp. 124–125.
[132] See *Lee v. Olancastle* [1997] N.P.C. 66.
[133] Land Registration Act 1925, s. 54(2); Land Registration Rules 1925, r. 218.
[134] *Clark v. Chief Land Registrar* [1994] Ch. 370.
[135] See *Barclays Bank Ltd v. Taylor* [1974] Ch. 137 at 147 *per* Russell L.J.

Improper cautions

Although an application to lodge a caution had to be supported by evidence of the existence of the right which was being claimed,[136] its entry on the register was no guarantee that the right actually existed. Such an entry is, however, a serious matter for the proprietor as it 'casts a dark shadow on the property. It paralyses dealings in it. No one will buy the property under such a cloud.'[137]

The proprietor can seek to dispel the cloud by applying by motion to have the caution vacated.[138] This procedure is only suitable if it is clear that the cautioner has no interest in the land which can be substantiated, although in *The Rawlplug Co. Ltd v. Karnvale Properties Ltd*,[139] Megarry J. indicated that the courts should take a robust approach to these matters. Where it is necessary for the matter to be resolved at trial, the proprietor may be seriously prejudiced by the delay involved in resolving the doubt affecting his title. In such circumstances, the cautioner may be told that:

'You may keep the caution on the register if you undertake to pay any damages caused by its presence if it was afterwards held that it was wrongly entered. But if you are not prepared to give such an undertaking, then the caution must be vacated.'[140]

This approach seems preferable to pursuing any claim under section 56(3) of the 1925 Act, under which damages may be awarded if a person lodges a caution without reasonable cause. There is no reported case where damages have been awarded under this provision. This relates partly to the difficulty in establishing what is meant by reasonable cause, the view having been expressed that it is at least arguable that a person who genuinely believes that he has a right to specific performance and, having had legal advice, issues a writ seeking such a remedy, has reasonable cause for lodging a caution.[141] The other problem in seeking a remedy under the statute is that, whereas damages may be awarded when the caution was lodged without reasonable cause, no remedy was available for maintaining the registration of the caution, which may be equally as damaging to the proprietor.[142]

---

[136] Land Registration Act 1925, s. 54(2); Land Registration Rules 1925, r. 215(4).

[137] *Tiverton Estates Ltd v. Wearwell* [1974] Ch. 146 at 156 *per* Lord Denning M.R.

[138] R.S.C. Ord. 14. See *Heywood v. B.D.C. Properties Ltd (No. 1)* [1963] 1 W.L.R. 975; *The Rawlplug Co. Ltd v. Kamvale Properties Ltd* (1968) 20 P. & C.R. 32.

[139] (1968) 20 P. & C.R. 32 at 40 (caution to protect contract to purchase when that contract had effectively been rescinded). See also *Woolf Management Ltd v. Woodtrack Ltd* [1988] 11 E.G. 111.

[140] *Tiverton Estates Ltd v. Wearwell Ltd* [1975] Ch. 145 at 161–162 *per* Lord Denning M.R. This approach seems preferable to the use of an interlocutory injunction in *Clearbrook Property Holdings Ltd v. Verrier Properties plc* [1974] 1 W.L.R. 243 at 246 *per* Templeman J. See *Tucker v. Hutchinson* (1987) 54 P. & C.R. 106; *Alpenstow Ltd v. Regalia Properties plc* [1985] 1 W.L.R. 271.

[141] *Clearbrook Property Holdings Ltd v. Verrier* [1974] 1 W.L.R. 243 at 246 *per* Templeman J.

[142] See Thompson, *Barnsley's Conveyancing Law and Practice* (4th edn) (London: Butterworths, 1996), 75.

Protection after 2003

The Law Commission and the Land Registry considered that the methods of protect-ing third party rights on the register were unnecessarily complex and concluded, also, that the system of the registration of cautions against dealings was not satisfac-tory.[143] The 2002 Act has, therefore, established a new regime for the protection of such rights. These changes are prospective. Existing inhibitions and cautions con-tinue to have effect.[144] For the future, however, it will not be possible to register a new inhibition; the role of the inhibition is subsumed into the restriction. Neither will it be possible to register new cautions *against dealings*. It remains the case that cautions against first registration may still be registered.[145] Consequently the only methods available by which to protect third party rights on the register are the restriction and the notice. The role of the restriction has already been considered. What must be examined is the new type of notice introduced by the Act.

Unilateral notices

Under the 1925 Act, the registration of a notice was normally a consensual matter. Under section 34(2), a notice may now be either an agreed notice or a unilateral notice. The agreed notice may only be registered if either the applicant is the registered pro-prietor, or a person entitled to be registered as such proprietor, or, alternatively, if such a person consents to the entry, or the registrar is satisfied as to the validity of the applicant's claim.[146] A unilateral notice is designed to replace the caution against deal-ings, and has been employed to protect an alleged lien over the land,[147] a pending land action,[148] and an alleged contract to purchase the relevant property.[149]

A person may apply for the registration of a unilateral notice. The registrar must then give notice to the registered proprietor of the entry. The registered proprietor, or the person entitled to be so registered, may then apply to the registrar for the cancella-tion of the unilateral notice.[150] If such an application is made, the registrar must serve on the beneficiary of the notice, that is the person who lodged the entry, notice of the application for cancellation. If the beneficiary does not respond to this notice within fifteen working days, the entry will be cancelled.[151] This, effectively, is the 'warning off' procedure which operated under the old system of cautions. The difference is that such matters are now likely to be dealt with before there is any dealing with the land, and so the system is more satisfactory than that which it replaced.

It may be the case that, at a hearing of the matter, issues arise which cannot quickly be resolved. In such cases, in the event of an application to have the notice removed, the approach which is to be taken in determining whether or not to order the vacation

---

[143] See (1998) Law Com. No. 254, paras 6.3–6.9.   [144] Land Registration Act 2002, Sched. 12.
[145] Ibid., para. 4.   [146] Ibid., s. 34(3).
[147] *Donnelly v. Weybridge Construction Ltd* [2006] EWHC 348 (T.C.C.).
[148] *Godfrey v. Torpey* [2006] EWHC 1423 (Ch.).
[149] *Loubatieres v. Mornington Estates (UK)* [2004] EWHC 825 (Ch.).   [150] Ibid., ss 35, 36.
[151] Land Registration Act 2002, s. 36(2)(3). Land Registration Rules 2003, r. 53.

is to decide on the basis of the balance of convenience.[152] If a person either applies for the entry of a caution or restriction, or objects to an application for its removal, without reasonable cause, he is, under section 77 of the Act, liable in damages to anyone who suffers loss as a consequence. If it is clear that there is no sustainable basis for the application to register a notice, then there is no reason why the court should not entertain a claim for breach of section 77 and make appropriate orders.[153] For such a claim to succeed, however, the claimant must establish the loss which he has suffered as a consequence of the wrongful application.[154]

UNREGISTERED INTERESTS WHICH OVERRIDE REGISTRATION

Under the 1925 Act, it was provided that the first registered proprietor with an absolute title would take the land subject to entries on the register and to overriding interests. A similar provision was in place in respect of a transferee for valuable consideration of a registered estate; the proprietor would, again, be subject to entries on the register and to overriding interests.[155] Overriding interests were interests not entered on the register to which the registered proprietor took subject.[156] A list of what constituted overriding interests was contained in section 70 of the Act.

A principal aim of the reformers of the law was to make the register as accurate and reliable as possible. To this end, the existence of a category of rights which will bind a proprietor, despite not being noted on the register, is inimical to this goal. Nevertheless, the abolition of this category of right would not be feasible. In the first place, it would not be possible to engage in wholesale abolition of such rights. As was recognized in an earlier joint report, the removal of overriding status without compensation carries with it the risk of contravening Article 1 of the First Protocol of the European Convention on Human Rights, which has been incorporated into English Law by section 1 of the Human Rights Act 1998. This Article provides that:

'Every natural or legal person is entitled to the peaceful enjoyment of his possessions. No one shall be deprived of his possessions except in the public interest and subject to the conditions provided for by law and by the general principles of international law.

The preceding provisions shall not, however, in any way impair the right of a State to enforce such laws as it deems necessary to control the use of property in accordance with the general interest or to secure the payment of taxes or other contributions or penalties.'

---

[152] *Donnelly v. Weybridge Construction Ltd, supra,* at [18] *per* H.H.J. Peter Coulson Q.C.

[153] *Lombatieres v. Mornington Estates (UK), supra,* at [38] *per* David Richards J.

[154] *Anderson Antiques (UK) Ltd v. Anderson Wharf (Hull) Ltd* [2007] EWHC 2086 (Ch.) at [49] *per* Briggs J.

[155] Land Registration Act 1925, ss 5, 20.   [156] Ibid., s. 3(xvi).

To avoid contravening this Article, a cautious approach to the rationalization of this area had to be taken. Consequently, overriding status was only removed from existing rights[157] if one of the following conditions was met:

(i)   that the rights could fairly be regarded as obsolete;

(ii) those affected consented;[158] and

(iii) there were strong policy grounds for so doing and suitable transitional arrangements were put in place.[159]

In addition to this consideration, it was also accepted that there were certain rights where it was not reasonable to expect the holders of them to have to protect them by registration. Such rights have been retained under the 2002 Act. Under the previous statutory regime, this collection of rights was known, generically, as overriding interests. The terminology has now changed. This, presumably, is to reflect the fact that interests which affect a first proprietor and interests which affect a subsequent proprietor are, unlike the previous position, treated separately. Thus, there are now in existence rights which override first registration and, separately, rights which override registered dispositions. In addition to this division, transitional provisions have also been enacted to deal with pre-existing overriding interests. The result is that, whereas under the old law, regard could be had simply to section 70 of the Act to determine what were overriding interests, the present position is that the relevant provisions are now contained in three separate Schedules to the Act, namely Schedules 1, 3, and 12; a situation which is not the easiest to follow. Although Schedule 3 deals with the effect of unregistered interests on registered dispositions, it is convenient to deal with the impact of unregistered interests together. The scheme of this section is to consider the various rights in question and assess how they are dealt with by the different Schedules.

Leases

Under the 1925 Act, only leases granted for a period of more than twenty-one years were capable of substantive registration. As a corollary to this, it was provided that a lease granted for a period not exceeding twenty-one years took effect as an overriding interest.[160] The word 'granted' was important as this meant that only legal leases came within this category of overriding interest,[161] and this will still be the case under Schedules 1 and 3. Equitable leases are likely to be binding upon a registered proprietor, however, as it is probable that the tenant will be in actual occupation of the land and consequently protected.[162]

---

[157] For the difficulty associated with the deletion of one such right, liability to repair the chancel of a church, see Miscellaneous rights, pp. 156–157.

[158] No such right was identified.   [159] (1998) Law Com. No. 254, para. 4.30.

[160] Land Registration Act 1925, s. 70(1)(k).

[161] *City Permanent Building Society v. Miller* [1952] Ch. 840. See also, in a different context, *Truro Diocesan Board of Finance v. Foley* [2008] EWCA Civ. 1162.

[162] Land Registration Act 2002, Sched. 1, para. 2; Sched. 3, para. 2 discussed below.

Under the 2002 Act, on the grant of a lease for more than seven years, the tenant should apply for registration of the title to that lease.[163] Consistently with the previous treatment of this issue, a lease granted for a period not exceeding seven years will normally override registration and so bind the proprietor, both on first registration[164] and on a subsequent disposition.[165] There are, however, exceptions to this. The grant of certain leases not exceeding seven years triggers the obligation for those leases to be registered with their own titles. These leases are listed in section 4 of the Act, of which the most important concerns a lease which takes effect in possession after the end of a period of three months beginning with the date of the grant.[166] Such a reversionary lease is required to be registered and, consequently, will not override registration.[167] This may cause problems with certain student lets, where it is not uncommon for a lease to be granted in March to take effect in possession in September. This lease should now be registered with its own title,[168] and such a lease will not override registration. So, if a purchaser buys the freehold, prior to the lease falling into possession, he will take free of that lease.

Transitional provisions

The Act makes specific transitional provision for certain leases. If, a year prior to the Act coming into force, a person was granted a fifteen-year lease, that lease would take effect as an overriding interest.[169] This position is retained by paragraph 12 of Schedule 12 to the Act, which continues the overriding status of leases which were previously overriding interests under the 1925 Act. This transitional period will cease to have effect in 2023, that is twenty years after the commencement of the Act.

Interests of persons in actual occupation

The protection of the rights of persons in actual occupation of land is the most important and contentious category of what were formerly termed overriding interests. The original provision dealing with this type of right was section 70(1)(g) of the Land Registration Act 1925, to which it is still necessary to have regard in order to appreciate the effect of the modified versions of the paragraph contained in the 2002 Act.

Section 70(1)(g) defined as an overriding interest 'the rights of every person in actual occupation of the land or in receipt of the rents and profits thereof, save where enquiry is made of such person and the rights are not disclosed'. Its purpose was to provide a safety net in terms of the protection of people who have rights in property and who actually occupy it, or, as it was put by Lord Denning M.R., 'to protect a person in actual occupation from having his rights lost in the welter of registration'.[170]

---

[163] Ibid., s. 4(1)(c).   [164] Ibid., Sched. 1, para. 1.

[165] Land Registration Act 2002, Sched. 3, para. 1.

[166] Ibid., s. 4(1)(d). The other exceptions are contained in paras (e) and (f).

[167] Ibid., Sched. 1, para. 1; Sched. 3, para. 1.   [168] See Reversionary leases, p. 121.

[169] Land Registration Act 1925, s. 70(1)(k).

[170] *Strand Securities Ltd v. Caswell* [1965] Ch. 958 at 979.

There were two components to the operation of this paragraph, and this remains the case under the modified versions of it contained in the 2002 Act. These are the establishment of a right and the requirement that the holder of the right be in actual occupation of the land. These matters will be addressed in turn.

Rights

It is not the fact that a person is in actual occupation of another person's land which gives him an interest overriding registration. He must also establish that he has a right in that property. To ascertain what rights override registration, regard must be had to the general law. If, as a matter of general principle, a right is not regarded as being a property right, then despite the holder of that right being in actual occupation, it will not override registration and will not, therefore, bind the new registered proprietor of the land. So, for example, in *National Provincial Bank Ltd v. Ainsworth*,[171] the House of Lords held that the 'deserted wife's equity' was not an interest in land, a finding which precluded the wife in that case from being able to establish an overriding interest in the property. Similarly, an equitable right which has been overreached cannot override registration, irrespective of whether the person with the prior equitable interest is in actual occupation of the property.[172]

Some difficulty was experienced in determining whether certain rights were capable of existing as overriding interests, these doubts centring on the status of equities and rights arising through the medium of equitable estoppel.[173] Although it had already been held that the right to rectify a deed could exist as an overriding interest,[174] any uncertainty has been dispelled as it is now provided that, for the avoidance of doubt, both an equity arising from estoppel and a mere equity have effect from the time the equity arises as interests capable of binding successors in title.[175]

Rights incapable of overriding

Certain rights are not capable of overriding registration. The 2002 Act specifies two such interests. First, an interest under a settlement under the Settled Land Act 1925 cannot be overriding.[176] This Act deals mainly with successive interests in land and, after 1997, would take effect under a trust of land and could, in principle, be overriding.[177] Second, in the case of a transfer of registered land, a reversionary lease which

---

[171] [1965] A.C. 1175. See L. Tee [1998] C.L.J. 328 at 331 *et seq.*

[172] *City of London Building Society v. Flegg* [1988] A.C. 54; *State Bank of India v. Sood* [1997] Ch. 276. See Overreaching, pp. 297–300.

[173] For a discussion of estoppel rights, see Chapter 15.

[174] *Blacklocks v. J.B. Godalming Ltd* [1982] Ch. 183; *D.B. Ramsden & Co. Ltd v. Nurdin & Peacock Ltd* [1999] 1 E.G.L.R. 119 (rectification of a lease). Cf. *Collings v. Lee* [2001] 2 All E.R. 332 at 338 *per* Nourse L.J. but see *Malory Enterprises Ltd v. Cheshire Homes (U.K.) Ltd* [2002] 3 W.L.R. 1 at 18 *per* Arden L.J., accepting that the right to rectify the register could take effect as an overriding interest. See D. Sheehan (2003) 119 L.Q.R. 31.

[175] Land Registration Act 2002, s. 116. Rights of pre-emption in relation to registered land are also, from the day on which the Act comes into force, capable of binding successors in title: ibid., s. 115.

[176] Ibid., Sched. 1, para. 2; Sched. 3, para. 2(a).

[177] Trusts of Land and Appointment of Trustees Act 1996, ss 1, 2(1). See The trust of land, p. 293.

takes effect in possession more than three months beginning with the date of the grant and which has not taken effect at the time of the disposition cannot override a registered disposition.[178]

There are two further interests which cannot override either registration or a registered disposition. The first of these is a spouse's statutory right of occupation.[179] The spouse's statutory right of occupation was first introduced as a direct response to the decision in *Ainsworth*, where the House of Lords held that the so-called deserted wife's equity was not capable of taking effect as an overriding interest. If it is correct to describe this right as an equity, then, read literally, section 116 of the 2002 Act would appear to allow such a right to override. This was certainly not intended and it is highly improbable that the Act will be construed in this way.[180] Finally, section 20(6) of the Landlord and Tenant (Covenants) Act 1995 provides that the right to what is termed an overriding lease[181] is not capable of being an overriding interest.

The upgrading of rights

The Land Registration Act 1925 divided interests in registered land into either minor interests or overriding interests. What constituted minor interests were defined in section 3(xv) of the Act. An important question which then arose was whether an interest, which was defined as being a minor interest, would be transformed into an overriding interest if the owner of that right was in actual occupation of the land affected by it. This matter was squarely raised in *Williams & Glyn's Bank Ltd v. Boland*.[182] Mr Boland was the sole registered proprietor of the matrimonial home, although it was conceded that his wife[183] was a beneficial co-owner of it. The effect of this was that he held the house on trust for himself and his wife, the type of trust in question being a trust for sale which, at the time, was the legal device employed to accommodate equitable co-ownership.[184] Mr Boland mortgaged the house to the bank. Mrs Boland argued that, as she had an equitable interest in the house and was in actual occupation of it, she had an overriding interest binding on the bank. The bank countered by arguing that, because the type of interest which she had in the land was within the definition of a minor interest, it could not take effect also as an overriding interest. Despite finding this argument to be 'formidable',[185] Lord Wilberforce rejected it. In his view, if a person held a minor interest in land and was also in actual occupation, there was every reason why that right should acquire the status of an overriding interest.[186]

---

[178] Land Registration Act 2002, Sched. 3, para. 2(d).   [179] Family Law Act 1996, s. 31(10)(b).

[180] See also Smith, op. cit., 29.

[181] For the nature of such leases, see Overriding leases, pp. 451–453.   [182] [1981] A.C. 487.

[183] The fact that she was his wife was irrelevant to the decision. Her case was based upon her being an equitable co-owner of the property, not on her status as a spouse.

[184] Settled Land Act 1925, s. 36(4). The property would now be subject to a trust of land: Trusts of Land and Appointment of Trustees Act 1996, s. 25(1), Sched. 3, paras 2(1), 11(b). The nature of this type of trust is explained in Chapter 8.

[185] [1981] A.C. 481 at 506.

[186] Ibid., at 507. As Lord Wilberforce recognized this conclusion was consistent with earlier authority such as *Bridges v. Mees* [1957] Ch. 475 and *Hodgson v. Marks* [1971] Ch. 892.

This seminal decision established, for the purposes of the 1925 Act, an important equation, that:

Minor interest + actual occupation = overriding interest

Under the 2002 Act, this equation exists in substance, but not in form. The old distinction between minor interests and overriding interests has been abandoned. The division is now between interests which are subject to an entry on the register and interests which override first registration or a registered disposition. However, provided that a right is capable of being protected by an entry on the register, and is not specifically excluded from being able to override, then, if the holder of the right is in actual occupation of the property, that right will be protected and will override either first registration or a registered disposition. In other words, the substance of the decision in *Boland* is retained.

There are a number of consequences to this. First, it should be appreciated that the right which is overriding need not, of itself, confer the right of occupation.[187] In *Webb v. Pollmount*,[188] a tenant, as one of his rights under the lease, had the option to purchase the freehold. Because the tenant was in actual occupation of the land, the option was held to be an overriding interest binding upon a purchaser of the landlord's reversion. In other words, the tenant was entitled to purchase the freehold from him. It was immaterial that his right of occupation derived from the lease and not from the option. Provided that the occupier of land has proprietary rights in it, which in this case included the option, then the effect of actual occupation will make those rights overriding.

Difference with unregistered land

A second feature of the decision in *Boland* is to establish a significant distinction between unregistered and registered land with regard to the consequences of non-registration. When title is unregistered, if a person holds an interest in property which is registrable as a land charge, if this is not registered, that interest will be void as against a purchaser. It is immaterial if the holder of the right is in actual occupation of the land affected.[189] Where title is registered, however, if the holder of a right which can be protected by an entry on the register is in actual occupation of the land, non-registration of the right will not be fatal. The interest will override.

The disparity of result is anomalous.[190] It is also, almost certainly, accidental. It seemed that the original intention of the legislature was to establish the same fall-back position with regard to unregistered land as is the case when title is registered, so that, in both cases, if a person had failed to register a particular right, but was in actual occupation of the land, that right would be binding on a purchaser. Because

---

[187] Cf. S. Baughen [1991] Conv. 116.   [188] [1966] Ch. 58.

[189] See *Midland Bank Trust Co. Ltd v. Green* [1981] A.C. 513; *Lloyds Bank plc v. Carrick* [1996] 4 All E.R. 630. See The effect of non-registration, pp. 100–104.

[190] The difference is commented upon, uncritically, in *Lloyds Bank plc v. Carrick* [1996] 4 All E.R. 630 at 642 *per* Morritt L.J.

of a legislative mishap, this position has not been achieved.[191] It is suggested that the position when title is registered is to be preferred. The protection afforded to occupiers by the registered land system recognizes that people who actually occupy property are less likely to feel, or even be aware of, the need to protect their rights by registration than will those who have rights affecting property occupied by others. In the latter situation, it seems more likely that legal advice will be taken, with the result that a strict registration requirement may create less hardship for people in possession of rights than will be the case when the owner of rights in land is also in occupation of that land.

Actual occupation

While actual occupation of land without ownership of a right will not create an interest overriding registration, the converse is also, of course, true; in addition to the possession of a right the person must also be in actual occupation of the land. What was meant by the phrase 'actual occupation' within the meaning of paragraph (g) was a matter of some controversy and, despite the reform contained in the 2002 Act, the matter is not free from doubt.

The meaning of the word 'occupation' has been said to be capable of meaning different things in different contexts,[192] and that it 'can have a variety of different meanings, some of which can differ quite subtly from others, and its precise meaning in any case is thus particularly prone to be governed by its context'.[193] In the present context, initially, the courts were keen to assimilate the meaning of the words 'actual occupation' with the concept of constructive notice. In *Hodgson v. Marks*,[194] the question was whether an elderly woman, who held a beneficial interest in a house, was in actual occupation of it within the meaning of the Act when she shared the accommodation with the registered proprietor. At first instance, Ungoed-Thomas J. held that she was not. He considered that actual occupation should be construed to mean 'actual and apparent occupation'[195] and, because the registered proprietor was also in occupation, he considered her occupation not to be apparent. On appeal, however, this was rejected. Russell L.J. declined to gloss the wording of the Act in this way. He preferred to give the words their literal meaning and treat the question of whether a person was in actual occupation as being one of fact.[196] As, factually, she was in actual occupation of the house, it was held that she had an overriding interest in it.

This approach was continued in *Williams & Glyn's Bank Ltd v. Boland*, where it was held that a wife who shared occupation of the matrimonial home with her husband was in actual occupation of it. The argument that a wife could not, as a matter of law, be regarded as being in actual occupation of the shared matrimonial home in her right,

---

[191] See H.W.R. Wade [1956] C.L.J. 216 at 228.

[192] *RCC v. Newnham College, Cambridge*[2008] UKHL 23 at [9] *per* Lord Hoffmann. See, also, *Madrassa Anjuman Islamia of Kholwad v. Municipal Council of Johannesburg* [1922] 1 A.C. 500 at 504 *per* Viscount Cave; *Southern Water Authority v. Nature Conservancy Council* [1992] 1 W.L.R. 775 at 781 *per* Lord Mustill.

[193] *RCC v. Newnham College, Cambridge, supra*, at [56] *per* Lord Neuberger of Abbotsbury.

[194] [1971] Ch. 892.   [195] Ibid., at 916.   [196] Ibid., at 931–932.

because of a fictitious unity between husband and wife, so that her occupation was to be regarded as being a shadow of his,[197] was condemned as being 'heavily obsolete'.[198] Of more general interest was the approach taken to the construction of the phrase 'actual occupation' as used in the Act.

Lord Wilberforce expressly declined to construe the meaning of actual occupation so as to make it correlate to the ambit of constructive notice in unregistered land. He emphasized this by saying that 'the law as to notice as may affect purchasers of unregistered land, whether contained in decided cases, or in a statute...has no application even by analogy to registered land'.[199] He underlined this still further, by going on to say that, 'In the case of unregistered land, the purchaser's obligation depends upon what he had notice of—notice actual or constructive. In the case of registered land, *it is the fact of occupation that matters.*'[200]

Absolutism or constitutionalism?[201]

The comments of Lord Wilberforce, and by others made in similar vein in other cases,[202] represented the high point of what has been termed the absolutist view of what constituted actual occupation; that the determination of whether or not a person was in actual occupation of land was a matter of fact, and did not depend upon the discoverability of that fact. Others took the view that because paragraph (g) was intended to encapsulate the unregistered land concept of constructive notice, which derives from the rule in *Hunt v. Luck*,[203] in determining whether a person was in actual occupation of land, regard should be had to whether that occupation could be discovered by making reasonable enquiries and inspections.[204] This approach, termed the constitutionalist view, also has judicial support.[205]

In truth, this was probably rather an academic debate in that the scope of constructive notice has widened considerably since the rule in *Hunt v. Luck* was formulated.[206] In particular, it has now been accepted that, if a person with a beneficial interest in a house shares that accommodation with the sole legal owner of it, a purchaser would be fixed with constructive notice of that person's rights unless enquiries had

---

[197] An expression used in *Bird v. Syme-Thomson* [1979] 1 W.L.R. 440 at 444 *per* Templeman J.

[198] *Williams & Glyn's Bank Ltd v. Boland* [1981] A.C. 487 at 504 *per* Lord Wilberforce.   [199] Ibid.

[200] Ibid., emphasis supplied. See also at 511 *per* Lord Scarman.   [201] See Hayton, op. cit., 87–91.

[202] *Hodgson v. Marks* [1971] Ch. 892 at 932 *per* Russell L.J.; *Kling v. Keston Properties Ltd* (1989) 49 P. & C.R. 212 at 222 *per* Vinelott J.

[203] [1902] 1 Ch. 428. See, e.g. *National Provincial Bank Ltd v. Ainsworth* [1965] A.C. 1179 at 1259 *per* Lord Wilberforce; *Abbey National Building Society v. Cann* [1991] A.C. 56 at 87 *per* Lord Oliver of Aylmerton.

[204] P. Sparkes [1989] Conv. 342; Sparkes, *A New Land Law* (2nd edn) (Oxford: Hart Publishing, (2003), 281.

[205] See, e.g., *Lloyds Bank plc v. Rosset* [1989] Ch. 350 at 377 *per* Nicholls L.J.; at 397 *per* Mustill L.J. (dissenting on the facts); at 403 *per* Purchas L.J., reversed on an unrelated point [1991] 1 A.C. 107. For criticism of these views see R.J. Smith (1988) 104 L.Q.R. 507; M.P. Thompson [1988] Conv. 453. See, however, *Malory Enterprises Ltd v. Cheshire Homes (U.K.) Ltd* [2002] 3 W.L.R. 1 at 21 *per* Arden L.J.

[206] See Inspection of the land, pp. 54–59.

been addressed to that occupier.[207] Had the legislation insisted that the occupation had to be actual and apparent, the result in most cases would have been the same.[208] The approach of the 2002 Act, to be considered shortly, in respect of interests which override registered dispositions adopts the constitutionalist view with respect to the binding effect of the right in question[209] while, in respect of the meaning of actual occupation, itself, adopts an absolutist position. This is because it is provided by paragraph 2 of Schedule 3 to the Act that, to bind a purchaser, the interest must belong to a person in actual occupation *and* that occupation must be obvious on a reasonably careful inspection of the land. It must follow that there can be some instances when a person is in actual occupation of land, but that fact was not obvious on a reasonably careful inspection. Consequently, it is no longer the case that the finding that a person was in actual occupation will be determinative of whether the right of that person will override.

Nature of the property and intermittent occupation

Situations which have caused difficulty in the past have arisen where either the nature of the property in question is such that what might be regarded as normal occupation of it may be difficult or, alternatively, the person claiming to have been in occupation is either an intermittent occupier or absent from the property for prolonged periods of time. Where the property in question is not residential, such as a lock-up garage, then the parking of a car in it would be regarded as amounting to actual occupation.[210] Again, when the condition of the property is such that it cannot physically be occupied, the presence of builders under the supervision of the right holder will also amount to actual occupation.[211] It has also been accepted that a person may be in actual occupation through the medium of an agent, such as a caretaker,[212] but not through the presence of a licensee, who is not a representative occupier.[213] In any event, however, to establish actual occupation in the first place, there must be some degree of permanence and not merely a fleeting presence, such as will occur when a prospective purchaser is allowed access to the property prior to its purchase.[214]

---

[207] *Kingsnorth Finance Co. Ltd v. Tizard* [1986] 1 W.L.R.783; *Midland Bank Ltd v. Farmpride Hatcheries Ltd* [1981] 260 E.G. 493. Contrast *Le Foe v. Le Foe* [2001] 2 F.L.R. 970 at 988 *per* Mr Nicholas Mostyn Q.C., sitting as a High Court judge, criticized by M.P. Thompson [2001] Conv. 273 at 283.

[208] See L. Tee [1988] C.L.J. 328.

[209] Although see the counter-argument by N. Jackson (2001) 119 L.Q.R. 660 at 665 *et seq.*

[210] *Kling v. Keston Properties Ltd* (1989) 49 P. & C.R. 212. Cf *Epps v. Esso Petroleum Ltd* [1973] 2 All E.R. 465.

[211] *Lloyds Bank Plc v. Rosset* [189] Ch. 350, reversed on a different point: [1991] A.C. 107; *Thomas v. Clydesdale Bank Plc* [2010] EWHC 2755 (QB). See also *Malory Enterprises Ltd v. Cheshire Homes (UK) Ltd* [2002] Ch. 216 at [82] *per* Arden L.J.

[212] *Abbey National Building Society v. Cann* [1991] A.C. 56 at 93 *per* Lord Oliver of Aylmerton.

[213] *Strand Securities Ltd v. Caswell* [1965] Ch. 958 at 981 *per* Lord Denning M.R. See *Thompson v. Foy* [2009] EWHC 1076 (Ch) at [127] *per* Lewison J., approved in *Link Lending Ltd v. Bustard* [2010] EWCA Civ. 424 at [31] *per* Mummery L.J.

[214] *Abbey National Building Society v. Cann* [1991] A.C. 56 at 93 *per* Lord Oliver of Aylmerton. See, also, albeit in a different context, *RCC v. Newnham College, Cambridge* [2008] UKHL 23 at [31] *per* Lord Hope of Craighead.

Cases where there the person claiming to be in actual occupation of a house but was physically absent from it at the relevant time have also created difficulty. Clearly, it is not necessary for continuous physical presence to be maintained for actual occupation to be established so that, if for example, the transaction occurred when a beneficial co-owner was in hospital having a baby, this would not prevent her from being in actual occupation of the house.[215] This issue was considered by the Court of Appeal in *Link Lending Ltd v Bustard*.[216] In this case the issue arose as to whether a person's beneficial interest in a house was binding on a mortgagee. The case turned on whether or not she was to be regarded as being in actual occupation of it.[217] She had been compulsorily detained in a psychiatric hospital for over a year under section 3 of the Mental Health Act during the relevant period and, so, did not actually live in the property, although she retained some furniture there and made supervised visits to the house on a weekly basis. It was held that she was in actual occupation.

In reaching this conclusion, Mummery L.J. eschewed any attempt to lay down any single test for determining whether a person was in actual occupation, instead advert-ing to various criteria to which consideration should be given. These included the degree of permanence and continuity of presence of the person concerned, the inten-tions and wishes of that person,[218] the length of absence from the property and the reason for it and the nature of the property and personal circumstances of the person concerned.[219] In the present case, the defendant was absent on an involuntary basis from the property and always intended to return to it. By way of contrast, in *Stockholm Finance Ltd v. Garden Holdings Ltd*,[220] a Saudi princess had been absent from the prop-erty for over a year and, although she retained furniture in it, seemed to regard the flat as an alternative home, and this was not sufficient to amount to actual occupation. Thus, it would seem that the intention of the person claiming to be in actual occupa-tion will be an important factor in determining this factor. Intention to occupy on its own, however, should not be enough, and, in the case of prolonged absences, it is thought that, as well as an intention to return, some physical manifestation of that intention should be necessary,[221] although this will also clearly be relevant to the issue of discoverability, to be considered shortly.

First registration of title

The 2002 Act distinguishes between interests which override first registration and interests which override registered dispositions. The former position is governed by paragraph 2 of Schedule 1 to the Act. This provides that 'an interest belonging to a

---

[215] *Chhokar v. Chhokar* [1984] F.L.R. 313.   [216] [2010] EWCA Civ. 424.

[217] The issue of whether the fact of occupation was obvious on a reasonably careful inspection of the property was not properly addressed.

[218] On the issue of the intention of the putative occupier, see B. Bogusz [2011] Conv. 268.

[219] [2010] EWCA Civ. 424 at [27].   [220] [1995] N.P.C. 162.

[221] *Thompson v. Foy* [2009] UKHC 1076 (Ch) at [127] *per* Lewison J. See also *Chhokar v. Chhokar* [1984] F.L.R. 313 at 317 *per* Ewbank J., a point not considered on appeal. See also the helpful discussion of a simi-lar issue in the context of what is now Rent Act 1977, s. 2 in *Brown v. Brash* [1948] 2 K.B. 247 at 254–255 *per* Asquith L.J. and *Hoggett v. Hoggett* (1980) 39 P. & C.R.121 at 127 *per* Sir David Cairns.

person in actual occupation, so far as relating to land of which he is in actual occupation, except for an interest under a settlement under the Settled Land Act 1925' will override first registration.

Little need be said about this provision, which is closely modelled on section 70(1)(g) of the Land Registration Act 1925. Some points can, however, be made. First, the words 'actual occupation' should be construed in the same way as they were under paragraph (g) and the case law just discussed should be directly in point. Secondly, unlike paragraph (g) there is no proviso concerning the situation where enquiry is made of the person in actual occupation and those rights are not disclosed. Under the old law, in such circumstances the person in actual occupation could not assert an overriding interest binding on the registered proprietor. The same result will follow under Schedule 1, as a person who fails to reveal the existence of an interest when asked about it will normally be estopped from subsequently asserting that right. A third point which can be made is more subtle.

Unregistered land charges

Prior to first registration of title, land is transferred by way of conveyance and the principles of unregistered land are applicable. The transferee then applies to be registered as first proprietor. If a third party has a right in the land which is registrable as a land charge, the fact that he is in actual occupation of the land will not cause his interest to override first registration, if that interest has not been registered. An example may assist. A has contracted to sell his land to B and prior to the completion of that contract B is allowed into possession of the land. B does not register the estate contract as a Class C(iv) land charge. In breach of contract, A then sells and conveys the land to C, who applies for first registration of title. On the occasion of the conveyance, B's estate contract will become void as against C for non-registration.[222] The fact that B is in actual occupation at the date of registration will not avail him as he no longer has a right in the land.[223] The anomalous difference between unregistered and registered land, adverted to earlier,[224] will still continue to exist.

Unregistered interests which override registered dispositions

Paragraph 2 of Schedule 3 to the Land Registration Act 2002 provides that an unregistered interest which will override registered dispositions includes:

'An interest belonging at the time of disposition to a person in actual occupation, so far as relating to land of which he is in actual occupation, except for—

(a) an interest under a settlement under the Settled Land Act 1925;

(b) an interest of a person of whom inquiry was made before the disposition and who failed to disclose the right when he could reasonably have been expected to do so;

---

[222] See *Lloyds Bank plc v. Carrick* [1996] 4 All E.R. 630.
[223] A similar point is made in *Sainsbury's Supermarkets Ltd v. Olympia Homes Ltd* [2005] EWHC 1235 (Ch) at [53] *per* Mann J.
[224] See Actual occupation, p. 104.

(c) an interest—

    (i) which belongs to a person whose occupation would not have been obvious on a reasonably careful inspection of the land at the time of the disposition,[225] and

    (ii) of which the person to whom the disposition is made does not have actual knowledge at the time, and

(d) a leasehold estate in land granted to take effect in possession after the end of the period of three months beginning with the date of the grant and which has not taken effect in possession at the time of the disposition.'

The effect of paragraphs (a) and (d) has already been considered.[226] Little need be said about paragraph (b), save for the, perhaps, obvious point that the inquiry should be made to the occupier: 'reliance on the untrue *ipse dixit* of the vendor will not suffice.'[227]. For example, in *HSBC Bank v. Dyche*,[228] the bank was prepared to accept that a forged lease was an adequate explanation of the right of an occupier without actually asking him, and was subsequently held to be bound by his beneficial ownership of the property, the legal owner in fact holding the property on a constructive trust for him. Rather more needs to be said about paragraph (c).

Referring to this paragraph, the leading practitioner text comments that this is 'an extraordinary restriction', which re-introduces the concept of constructive notice.[229] The joint report insists, however, that the 'test is not one of constructive notice of the occupation. It is the less demanding one (derived from the test applicable to intending buyers of land) that it [*sc.* the fact of occupation] should be obvious on a reasonably careful inspection of the land.'[230] It is not at all clear, however, what this means.

When advocating reform of what was section 70(1)(g) of the Land Registration Act 1925, an express parallel was drawn with patent defects in title. This is a term used in conveyancing. What it derives from is the implied obligation imposed on a vendor to show a good title to the land which he is selling. To fulfil this obligation, the vendor is required to disclose in the contract of sale any defects in his title, and this includes any third party rights affecting the land. This obligation of disclosure is not, however, absolute; it is limited to latent defects in title. Defects in title which are patent need not be disclosed as it is assumed, precisely because their existence is patent, that the purchaser agrees to take subject to them.[231]

In determining whether a particular defect in title is patent, and so need not be disclosed by the purchaser, the courts have been reluctant to decide that it is.[232] The

---

[225] It is, perhaps, symptomatic of some of the less than user-friendly drafting of the Act that a double negative is employed.

[226] See Rights incapable of overriding, pp. 138–139 and Leases, pp. 136–137.

[227] *Hodgson v. Marks* [1971] Ch. 892 at 932 *per* Russell L.J., who also commented that he shed no tears for a building society who had done that and had been lied to.

[228] [2009] EWHC 2954 (Ch).

[229] Emmet and Farrand, *Title* (19th edn) (London: Sweet & Maxwell, Looseleaf), 5.105.

[230] (2001) Law Com. No. 271, para. 8.62(2).   [231] See Thompson, op. cit., 153–160.

[232] For a helpful discussion, see Farrand, *Contract and Conveyance* (4th edn) (London: Oyez Longman, 1983), 63–64.

essential test is that, to be patent, it must be visible to the eye, or by necessary implication from something which is visible to the eye.[233] The existence of a marked track on
a property being sold may well be obvious; it does not follow, however, that the existence of a right of way over that track would be regarded as patent, as the track may
be there for the convenience of the landowner.[234] The existence of other occupiers of
property does not, of itself, mean that any rights which they may have in the property
are patent. Such presence may well mean that the purchaser has constructive notice of
those rights; it does not mean that the right is patent.[235] The point is that the case law
is directed to whether the particular *right* is obvious on an inspection of the property.
It is not directed to the different question as to whether or not a person is in actual
occupation of the land.

Obviousness of occupation

The test in paragraph 2, as the joint report was at pains to point out, is not whether the
right is obvious; it is whether the fact of occupation is obvious.[236] The fact that the case
law dealing with what is a patent defect in title is concerned with whether the right is
obvious means that the analogy drawn with it is inapt.[237] This, however, leaves open
the questions of what is a reasonably careful inspection of land and, then, what should
be considered to make the fact of occupation obvious.

As to what constitutes a reasonably careful inspection of the land, the answer to this
must be dependent upon what the inspection is intended to achieve. In this day and
age, an inspection limited solely to ascertain the monetary value of the property[238] will
surely not exhaust what is meant by a reasonably careful inspection. Rather, when one
has regard to the 'extension, beyond the paterfamilias, of rights of ownership following from the diffusion of property and earning capacity',[239] one would anticipate that
a reasonably careful enquiry should extend to seeking to establish whether there is an
occupier of the property other than the registered proprietor. So, if an inspection of
the property reveals some evidence of another person's presence, such as clothes, this
should, it is thought, make the fact of actual occupation obvious within the meaning
of the Act.[240]

The case of *Link Lending Ltd v. Bustard*[241] should have provided an opportunity
to discuss this issue. The registered proprietor of the house was not in occupation
of it, and the beneficial owner, who had left furniture at the house, only visited on
a weekly basis as, for the rest of the time she was detained in a psychiatric hospital.

---

[233] *Yandle & Sons v. Sutton* [1922] 2 Ch. 199 at 210 *per* Sargent J.

[234] See *Ashburner v. Sewell* [1893] 3 Ch. 405. Cf. *Bowles v. Round* (1800) 5 Ves. 508.

[235] See *Nelthorpe v. Holgate* (1844) 1 Coll. 203 at 215 *per* Sir James Knight-Bruce V.-C.; *Caballero v. Henty*
(1874) L.R. 7 Ch. 447.

[236] (2001) Law Com. No. 271, para. 8.62.

[237] Contrary to the view expressed in (1998) Law Com. No. 254, para. 5.72.

[238] Although, see the extremely lax approach adopted with regard to this point in *Le Foe v. Le Foe* [2001]
2 F.L.R. 970 at 989 *per* Mr Nicholas Mostyn Q.C.

[239] *Williams & Glyn's Bank Ltd v. Boland* [1981] A.C. 487 at 508–509 *per* Lord Wilberforce.

[240] See *Le Foe v. Le Foe, supra*, at 988.   [241] [2010] EWCA Civ. 424.

Unfortunately, the bank did not rely on whether or not the occupation would have been obvious on a reasonably careful inspection of the property, because it accepted that the only inspection actually carried out was a 'drive-by' inspection done for the purpose of valuation.[242] This must be wrong. The statute does not require that an inspection be made; it is a requirement that the fact of occupation would have been obvious on a reasonably careful inspection. If it was not, then it should be completely immaterial whether any inspection was cursory, or even non-existent. The establishment of the fact of actual occupation and the determination of the obviousness of that occupation are separate questions.[243]

It is plain that the absolutist view of the meaning of actual occupation no longer represents the law.[244] Although the wording of paragraph 2 is not as clear as it might be, it is suggested that the constitutionalist interpretation employed with regard to section 70(1)(g) of the 1925 Act is now the position and that, despite the protestations of the authors of the joint report, the test of whether a purchaser will take subject to the rights of an occupier is, in substance if not in form, that of constructive notice. If this is correct, then it would seem that the judicial comments favouring the constitutionalist approach remain good law. It would have been preferable, however, if, instead of drawing an unhelpful analogy with the law relating to patent defects in title, the Act had simply said that the fact of occupation must be apparent as well as actual.

Actual knowledge

Finally, it should also be noted that, even if the right would not have been obvious on a reasonably careful inspection of the land, if the person to whom the disposition is made actually knows of the existence of the right held by the person in actual occupation of the land, then the right will override the registered disposition.[245] This was considered in *Thomas v. Clydesdale Bank Plc.*,[246] where the issue arose as to whether a woman had an overriding interest binding on a mortgagee. Ramsey J. thought that, as the bank was aware that the borrower had a new partner who was prepared to contribute in the region of £100,000 to the property, which was to become the family home, she had a reasonable prospect of showing that it had actual knowledge of her interest. This seems right, although the decision itself in favour of the occupier is suspect, in that no attention was paid to the purpose of the loan which, at least in part, was to pay off a mortgage used to finance the acquisition of the property, a consideration which would normally mean that the interest of the bank had priority.[247]

It must be said, however, that this is a very curious provision. First, it seems odd that, in a system which places such emphasis on registration, the state of mind of a purchaser should be an important criterion in the determination of whether or not

[242] Ibid, at [12] *per* Mummery L.J.
[243] See *Thompson v. Foy* [2009] EWHC 1076 (Ch) at [132] *per* Lewison J.; *Thomas v. Clydesdale Bank Plc* [2010] EWHC 2755 (QB) at [40] *per* Ramsey J.
[244] Although see the counter-argument by N. Jackson (2003) 119 L.Q.R. 660 at 665 *et seq.*
[245] Land Registration Act 2002, Sched. 3, para. 2(c)(ii).   [246] [2010] EWHC 2755 (Ch). at [49].
[247] *Equity and Law Home Loans Ltd v. Prestidge* [1992] 1 W.L.R. 137. See Acquisition mortgages, pp. 488–490.

an interest is binding upon him. As will be seen, this is true not only in the case of the rights of occupiers, but applies also to other interests which override registered dispositions.[248] A second point to make is that what is relevant is actual knowledge of the interest, not actual knowledge of the fact of occupation. As will be seen, the fact that a purchaser has actual knowledge of an interest which should have been protected by registration will not mean that he will be bound by that interest. If, however, the owner of that interest is in intermittent, or occasional, occupation of the relevant property, so that the fact of occupation was not obvious on a reasonably careful inspection of the land, then the interest will bind, provided that the purchaser has knowledge of the right. The distinction is more than a little puzzling.

Occupation of part of the property

An issue which arose on the construction of section 70(1)(g) of the Land Registration Act 1925 was whether, if the occupier of land which forms part of a larger plot enjoys rights over that larger part, he also enjoyed an overriding interest over the unoccupied part. Originally, the Court of Appeal in *Ashburn Anstalt v. Arnold*[249] thought not, but on a fuller consideration of this issue, it was held in *Wallcite Ltd v. Ferrishurst Ltd*,[250] that he would. Thus in the case itself, the occupier of premises adjoining a garage, who had a right affecting both the premises and the garage, was held, by dint of its occupation of the premises, to have an overriding interest affecting both the premises and the garage. This conclusion would lead to the somewhat startling, if unlikely, result that if a tenant of a flat in The Barbican had an option to purchase the freehold of the entire complex then that option would be an overriding interest.[251] This was considered to be unacceptable,[252] and the position is now that the right will affect only the part of the land which is actually occupied. This is so, both on first registration and on a registered disposition.[253]

Date of actual occupation

An important issue is that of the date when the person claiming to have a right overriding a registered disposition must be in actual occupation. When land, title to which is registered, is being transferred, this currently is a two-stage process.[254] The transferor executes a document termed a transfer in favour of the transferee. The transferee then applies to be registered as the new proprietor. The legal title will not pass to the transferee until registration occurs.[255] There is a period of time between these two events and the possibility exists that a third person with an interest in the property may go

---

[248] See Registered dispositions, p. 152 and p. 155.

[249] [1989] Ch. 1 at 28 *per* Fox L.J.   [250] [1999] 1 All E.R. 977. See S. Pascoe [1999] Conv. 144.

[251] Ibid., at 990 *per* Robert Walker L.J.   [252] (2001) Law Com. No. 271, para. 8.58.

[253] Land Registration Act 2002, Sched. 1, para. 2; Sched. 3, para. 2. See *Thompson v. Foy* [2009] EWHC 1076 (Ch) at [128]–[129] *per* Lewison J.

[254] When Part 8 of the Land Registration Act 2002 is brought into force and electronic conveyancing is made compulsory, there will only be one stage as the disposition and its registration will be simultaneous. See Electronic conveyancing, pp. 157–163.

[255] Land Registration Act 2002, s. 27(1).

into occupation of it during this period and thereby establish an interest overriding the registered disposition.

This potential problem existed also with respect to section 70(1)(g) of the Land Registration Act 1925 but was resolved by the House of Lords in *Abbey National Building Society v. Cann*,[256] where it was held that, for the purpose of paragraph (g), the relevant date is the date of the transfer and not the date of registration. This is confirmed by paragraph 2 of Schedule 3 to the Land Registration Act 2002, which refers to the person being in actual occupation at the time of the disposition.

This gives rise to a related point. If the person is in actual occupation at the time of the disposition, his interest will continue to override the registered disposition, notwithstanding that, subsequently, the property is vacated,[257] and, although the point was left open in *Thompsn v. Foy*,[258] it would seem that, if the occupier ceased to be in actual occupation between the date of the disposition and that of its registration, the interest will still override.

Receipt of rents and profits

Possession, for the purposes of the Law of Property Act 1925, includes the receipt of rents and profits or the right to receive the same.[259] Perhaps for this reason, section 70(1)(g) of the Land Registration Act 1925 included, in addition to the rights of people in actual occupation of the land, the rights of those in receipt of rents and profits.[260] While one can appreciate why the rights of people who actually occupy land should nevertheless have their unregistered rights in it protected as a consequence of their occupation, it is not easy to see why someone who does not occupy property but instead derives profit from it should be spared the normal consequence of a failure to register a registrable interest.[261] The 2002 Act does not allow the receipt of rent and profits as an alternative to actual occupation of the land. So as not to deprive people in this position of their established rights, however, transitional provisions are in place. Paragraph 8 of Schedule 12 to the 2002 Act introduces two new paragraphs into Schedule 3 to the Act.[262]

The effect of these paragraphs is that, if immediately prior to the coming into force of Schedule 3 to the Act a person held an overriding interest as a result of being in receipt of rents and profits, then that right will continue to override a registered disposition. If, however, a person becomes entitled to rents and profits after the Schedule came into force, then the right which he has in the land will not enjoy overriding status.

---

[256] [1991] A.C. 56. Contrast *Barclays Bank plc v. Zaroovabli* [1977] 1 All E.R. 19, in respect of a different overriding interest (a lease).

[257] *London and Cheshire Insurance Co. Ltd v. Laplagrene Property Co. Ltd* [1971] Ch. 499.

[258] [2009] EWHC 76 (Ch) at [122]–[126].   [259] Law of Property Act 1925, s. 3(xvii).

[260] If rent is reserved but not paid, the person entitled to the rent does not have an overriding interest: *E.S. Schwab & Co. Ltd v. McCarthy* (1975) 31 P. & C.R. 196. See also *Strand Securities Ltd v. Caswell* [1965] Ch. 958.

[261] Although see L. Tee [1998] C.L.J. 328 at 348.

[262] Would the legislation not be more 'user-friendly' if these provisions were contained in Schedule 3 itself, rather than being cross-referenced in this way?

The protection of occupiers

It was undoubtedly the case that the House of Lords decision in *Williams & Glyn's Bank Ltd v. Boland*[263] generated considerable interest and controversy. In particular, it established that occupiers of property, provided that they were adults,[264] could establish an overriding interest in that property despite the fact that the registered proprietor was also in occupation of it. The conveyancing implications of this were regarded as being extremely serious. The reliability of the register was undermined and, to satisfy himself that there were no adverse rights affecting the property, the purchaser would have to depart 'from the easy-going practice of dispensing with enquiries beyond that of the vendor'.[265]

In reaching this decision, the House of Lords was clearly mindful of the tension existing between the conflicting policies of, on the one hand, protecting the rights of people whose principal interest in the property was its use as a home and, on the other, the facilitation of conveyancing; an interest which is enhanced by confining the ambit of interests which override registered dispositions as narrowly as possible. The conclusion reached in *Boland* was to favour the former interest.[266] This tension has permeated the law for a considerable period of time and has usually become apparent when the contest is between the occupier of a home and a mortgagee, who has lent money against the security of a house. This issue will be returned to, therefore, when considering possession actions brought by mortgagees.

Easements and *profits à prendre*

The status of easements and profits was formerly governed by section 70(1)(a) of the Land Registration Act 1925. This was an obscurely drafted paragraph. It came to be established that both legal and equitable easements[267] and profits were overriding interests. The position has been affected considerably by the 2002 Act, which deals differently with the position on first registration of title and registered dispositions and contains also transitional provisions. These will be dealt with in turn.

First registration

A legal easement or profit will override first registration. It was a conscious decision to exclude equitable easements and profits from overriding status on first registration

---

263 [1981] A.C. 487.

264 *Hypo-Mortgage Services Ltd v. Robinson* [1997] 2 F.L.R. 71. The blanket statement denying protection to all minors is probably too sweeping, particularly when regard is had to the fact that minors aged sixteen have the capacity to marry. See also on the capacity to give consent, admittedly in a different context, *Gillick v. West Norfolk and Wisbech Area Health Authority* [1986] A.C. 112.

265 [1981] A.C. 487 at 508 *per* Lord Wilberforce.

266 See, especially, ibid. at 510 *per* Lord Scarman.

267 *Celsteel Ltd v. Alton House Holdings Ltd* [1985] 1 W.L.R. 204 (reversed, in part, on another point: [1986] 1 W.L.R. 512); *Thatcher v. Douglas* (1996) 146 N.L.J. 282; *Sommer v. Sweet* [2005] EWCA Civ. 227. See M.P. Thompson [1986] Conv. 31; M. Davey [1986] Conv. 296.

of title.[268] Although welcome, this was not actually necessary, in that equitable easements could not bind a first registered proprietor. This is because, when title is unregistered, an equitable easement is registrable as a Class D(iii) land charge and would be
void as against a purchaser for money or money's worth[269] and could not, therefore,
take effect as an overriding interest on an application for first registration which followed a conveyance on sale.

Registered dispositions

Easements and profits affecting land, title to which is registered, are affected by section 27 of and Schedules 3 and 12 to the Land Registration Act 2002. The effect of
section 27(d) and (e) is to prevent express grants or reservations of easements or profits
from taking effect as interests which override registration because they are, themselves, dispositions which require to be completed by registration. Excluded from the
effect of this section are easements or profits which are created as a result of the operation of section 62 of the Law of Property Act 1925.[270] This section operates to imply
words into conveyances, with the result that a purchaser of part of a vendor's land
may acquire easements over the land which was retained. This provision will be fully
explained in Chapter 13.

The combined effect of section 27 and Schedule 3 is to reduce significantly the types
of easement and profit which can override a registered disposition. First, only legal
easements and profits can override. Secondly, the express creation of such interests
are registrable dispositions and so cannot override a registered disposition. The effect
of this is that the only legal easements which can override a registered disposition
are those which are created by prescription, that is long user,[271] or by implication. To
repeat, express easements must themselves be completed by registration against the
title of the burdened land.

In the case of easements and profits which are capable of overriding a registered
disposition, the Act imposes further limitations on their ability so to do. Except in the
case of easements or profits which are registered under the Commons Registration
Act 1965, an easement will not override a registered disposition if it was not within
the actual knowledge of the person to whom the disposition is made, and[272] would not
have been obvious on a reasonably careful inspection of the land over which the easement or profit is exercisable. These qualifications do not apply if the person entitled
to the easement of profit proves that it has been exercised in the period of one year
ending with the disposition.[273] The purpose of these provisions is to reduce the likelihood of a purchaser of land being bound by an easement which is difficult to discover

[268] (2001) Law Com. No. 271, para. 8.24.
[269] Land Charges Act 1972, ss 2(5), 4(6). See also *Sainsbury's Supermarkets Ltd v. Olympia Homes Ltd*
[2005] EWHC 1235 (Ch) at para. 53 *per* Mann J.
[270] Land Registration Act 2002, s. 27(7).   [271] See Prescription, pp. 565–573.
[272] Surely, this should have been disjunctive, rather than conjunctive. If a purchaser actually knows of
the easement, why should it matter if its existence is not obvious on a reasonably careful inspection of the
property?
[273] Land Registration Act 2002, Sched. 3, para. 3(1)(2).

and has not been exercised for a long period of time, but has not necessarily been abandoned.[274]

Actual occupation

At one time it was thought to be highly unlikely that an easement could achieve over-riding status as a result of the owner of the right being in actual occupation of the land affected, the servient land, and thus coming within Schedule 3, paragraph (2). This was because the nature of an easement was generally thought to entail the right to do something on the servient land rather than to occupy it.[275] The House of Lords in *Moncrieff v. Jamieson*,[276] however, has widened the scope of the type of right which can qualify as an easement, and it would now seem to be quite possible for an easement to secure overriding status because the holder of it is regarded as being in actual occupa-tion of the servient land. That said, however, in the case of the exercise of an easement such as a right of way, that use will not be regarded as actual occupation of the servient tenement,[277] so that cases where the owner of an easement can be said to be in actual occupation of the servient land are likely to be rare.

Transitional arrangements

Under the new regime, far fewer easements will have overriding status than was pre-viously the case. The changes which have been made are far-reaching. To reflect this, important transitional provisions are in place.

In the case of existing easements and profits which were overriding interests prior to the coming into force of the 2002 Act, they will retain that status even if, had they been created after the Act came into force, they would not have overridden a registered disposition.[278] In other words all easements and profits which qualified as overriding interests under section 70(1)(a) of the Land Registration Act 1925 will continue to bind purchasers of the land, notwithstanding the more restricted treatment of such rights under the 2002 Act. Secondly a period of grace of three years was created in respect of easements and profits created after the coming into force of the 2002 Act. For a period of three years from that date, such easements and profits, in order to have overriding status would not have to be either within the knowledge of the transferee or be obvious to him on a reasonably careful inspection of the land.[279] This period of grace did not extend to express grants or reservations which the Act requires to be registered.

Squatter's rights

Section 70(1)(f) of the Land Registration Act 1925 provided that, 'Subject to the provisions of this Act, rights acquired or in the course of being acquired under the Limitation Acts' take effect as an overriding interest.

[274] See (2002) Law Com. No. 271, paras 8.70–8.73.   [275] See M.P. Thompson [1988] Conv. 31 at 36.
[276] [2007] 1 W.L.R. 2620. See Chapter 13.
[277] See *Chaudhury v. Yavuz* [2011] EWCA Civ. 1314 at [27]–[36] *per* Lloyd L.J.
[278] Land Registration Act 2002, Sched. 12, para. 9.   [279] Ibid., para. 10.

This was an important provision which related to the acquisition of title by adverse possession. What this entailed is that if a squatter occupied another person's land for twelve years then the latter lost his title to that land, his title being extinguished.[280] The squatter would then apply to be registered with a possessory title to the land.[281] The operation of this provision is illustrated by *Bridges v. Mees*.[282] Under an oral contract, the plaintiff agreed to buy a strip of land for £7. He paid a deposit of £2 and went into possession, the following year paying the balance of the purchase price. No transfer of the legal estate ever took place. Some twenty years later, the registered proprietor went into liquidation and the liquidator transferred the strip of land to the defendant, who was registered as the proprietor. It was held that the defendant took subject to the plaintiff's interest. Because he had been in possession of the land for twenty years, he had an overriding interest under paragraph (f).

As the plaintiff was in actual occupation of the land, his claim to an overriding interest would also have succeeded under paragraph (g). Had he abandoned possession of the land prior to the transfer of the land to the defendant, however, he would have succeeded under paragraph (f) but not paragraph (g). The defendant would, therefore, have taken subject to the plaintiff's possessory title, even though he could not have known about it prior to the transfer. This latter position was considered in the joint report to be unacceptable.[283]

The Land Registration Act 2002 makes fundamental changes to the law relating to adverse possession, which will be fully considered in Chapter 7. For present purposes, it will suffice to say that it will no longer be possible to obtain a possessory title against a registered proprietor and, accordingly, what was paragraph (f) is not reproduced in the Act. Provision is, however, made in respect of situations where a squatter had established a possessory title prior to the Act coming into force.

First registration of title

Two provisions are relevant to first registration of title. First, section 11 of the Act, which is concerned with first registration of title, provides that a person registered with an absolute title will take subject to interests under the Limitation Act 1980 of which he has notice. When title is unregistered, and a squatter has been in adverse possession of the land for the requisite twelve-year period, then, if he remains in possession of the land, and that land is then conveyed to a person who is registered as first proprietor, that person will be bound by the squatter's rights which derive from his adverse possession. The second relevant provision is paragraph 7 of Schedule 12 to the Act, which operates to insert paragraph 15 into Schedule 1 to the Act. This provides that, for a period of three years beginning with the date on which Schedule 1 came into force, the first registered proprietor would take subject to a right acquired under the Limitation Act 1980. This second provision would operate regardless of whether the transferee had notice of the right.

---

[280] See Chapter 7.   [281] See Titles less than absolute, pp. 157–159.
[282] [1957] Ch. 475. Cf. *Lloyds Bank plc v. Carrick* [1996] 4 All E.R. 630.
[283] See (1998) Law Com. No. 254, para. 5.47; (2001) Law Com. No. 271, paras 4.6–4.7.

Registered dispositions

When title is registered, the legal title to the land is vested in the registered proprietor. If a squatter established the requisite period of adverse possession against the proprietor, the legal title remained vested in the proprietor. The effect of the adverse possession was that the registered proprietor held the land on trust for the squatter and the squatter could then apply for registration.[284] This trust will no longer arise, but transitional provisions are in place to deal with the situation where, prior to the changes introduced by the 2002 Act coming into force, a possessory title had been achieved against a registered proprietor. It has to be said, however, that these provisions are implemented in a very tortuous manner.

Paragraph 11 of Schedule 12 to the Act introduces a new paragraph 15 into Schedule 3, this being a right under paragraph 18(1) of Schedule 12! The effect of this cumbersome piece of drafting is to replicate the transitional provision which has been put in place in the case of first registration of title. For a period of three years, beginning with the day when Schedule 3 came into force, the interests which override a registered disposition will include the interest of a person entitled to be registered as proprietor of the estate which is held in trust for him under section 75 of the Land Registration Act 1925.[285]

From 13 October 2006, which is three years from when Schedule 3 came into force, this transitional provision ceased to have effect. If a person has acquired a possessory title to registered land prior to the Act coming into force in 2003, the registered proprietor will continue to hold the land on trust for him. For that interest to override a registered disposition, the squatter will have to be in actual occupation of the land, and[286] that occupation should be obvious on a reasonably careful inspection of the land.[287]

Other unregistered interests which will override

The next group of rights is common to both Schedules 1 and 3 and there is no need for transitional provisions. They are divided into separate categories. The first category is contained in paragraphs (4)–(9) of each Schedule, and is:

(4) a customary right;

(5) a public right;

(6) a local land charge;

(7) an interest in any coal or coal mine, the rights attached to any such interest and the rights of any person under section 38, 49, or 51 of the Coal Industry Act 1994;

(8) in the case of land to which title was registered before 1898, rights to mines and minerals (and incidental rights) created before 1898;

---

[284] Land Registration Act 1925, s. 75; see Registered title, pp. 258–260.
[285] See *Chief Land Registrar v. Franks* [2011] EWCA Civ. 772.   [286] See n. 272.
[287] Land Registration Act 2002, Sched. 3, para. 2(c).

(9) in the case of land to which title was registered between 1898 and 1925 inclusive, rights to mines and minerals (and incidental rights) created before the registration of the title.

Miscellaneous rights

The remaining group of unregistered rights which have overriding status are contained in paragraphs (10)–(14) and paragraph 16 of the two Schedules, and are relics of the feudal system of landholding.[288] The list which was originally enacted, that is paragraphs (10)–(14), consisted largely of the re-enactment of rights defined as overriding interests by section 70 of the 1925 Act. These rights are:

(10) a franchise;

(11) a manorial right;

(12) a right to rent which was reserved to the Crown on the granting of any freehold estate (whether or not the right is still vested in the Crown);

(13) a non-statutory right in respect of an embankment or sea or river wall; and

(14) a right to payment in lieu of tithe.

This collection of somewhat arcane and archaic rights is ripe for abolition. Simply to excise them from the list of interests which will override registration was not considered to be appropriate, however, as to do so was thought to carry the risk of contravention of Article 1 of the First Protocol of the European Convention on Human Rights, in that it may have amounted to a deprivation of property.[289] Rather than take this risk by outright abolition, provision was made to phase them out over time. Accordingly, section 117(1) of the 2002 Act provides that paragraphs (10)–(14) of Schedules 1 and 3 to the Act will cease to have effect at the end of the period of ten years beginning with the day on which those Schedules came into force, that is 2013.[290] Applications to lodge either a caution against first registration or the entry of a notice made before the expiration of that period can be made free of charge.[291]

A right which was contained in section 70 of the Land Registration Act 1925, but was not originally included in the 2002 Act, was liability to repair the chancel of a church. The reason for this omission was that, in *Anton Cantlow and Wilmcote Parochial Church Council v. Wallbank*,[292] the Court of Appeal had held that this liability, which on the facts amounted to a charge in excess of £95,000, was, itself, a contravention of Article 1, in that it amounted to an indiscriminate form of taxation. The House of Lords,[293] however, reversed this decision, with the result that the omission of this property right from the Schedules would now contravene Article 1. To remedy this, Rule 2 of the Land Registration Act 2002 (Transitional Provisions) (No. 2) Order 2003 inserts as paragraph 16 of Schedules 1 and 3 to the Act, a right in respect of the repair

---

[288] See E. Nugee (2008) 124 L.Q.R. 586.   [289] See (2001) Law Com. No. 271, paras 8.81–8.85.

[290] For an interesting discussion of these rights, see S. Coveney [2011] Conv. 259.

[291] Land Registration Act 2002, s. 117(2).   [292] [2002] 1 Ch. 51.   [293] [2004] 1 A.C. 546.

of a church chancel.[294] The same transitional period applies to this paragraph as to the other paragraphs in the Schedules.

TITLES LESS THAN ABSOLUTE

Where freehold titles are concerned, in the overwhelming majority of cases when application is made for first registration of title, the applicant is registered with an absolute title. There are, however, lesser titles which can now be considered.

Qualified titles

When an application is made for registration with an absolute title, it may emerge that there is a defect in title such that an absolute title cannot be registered. In such a case, it is provided by section 9(4) of the 2002 Act that, if the registrar is of the opinion that the person's title to the estate has been established only for a limited period or subject to certain reservations which cannot be disregarded, the applicant may be registered with a qualified title. The effect of registration with a qualified title is the same as registration with an absolute title, except that it does not affect the enforcement of any estate, right, or interest which appears from the register to be excepted from the effect of registration.[295]

Possessory titles

A possessory title is applied for when the applicant is unable to produce the title deeds to the property. This will normally be the case when the title is based upon a squatter's adverse possession of unregistered land.[296] The effect of the grant of a possessory title is that, subject to any pre-existing rights, the registration has the same effect as registration with an absolute title.[297] What this means is that there is no guarantee as to what rights the land is subject prior to registration, so that a proprietor with a possessory title will be bound by any existing restrictive covenants.

Leasehold titles

The applicant may also, of course, apply for registration of a leasehold title. There are four classes of leasehold title: absolute, good, qualified and possessory. Of these titles, the only one which is not a counterpart of a freehold title is the good leasehold title.

---

[294] For strong criticism of this potential liability, see J. Naylor (2007) 157 N.L.J. 1500.
[295] Land Registration Act 2002, s. 11(6).
[296] For the position when adverse possession is established against a registered proprietor, see Registered title, pp. 258–260.
[297] Land Registration Act 2002, s. 12(7).

Good leasehold title

An absolute leasehold title can only be registered if the register is satisfied as to the freehold title out of which the lease has been granted. The problem here was that, on the grant of a lease, the tenant, unless the contract provided to the contrary, did not have the right to investigate the freeholder's title[298] and, therefore, could not supply the registrar with the requisite evidence of that title. In this event, the applicant would be registered with a good leasehold title. The effect of registration with a good leasehold title is that there is no guarantee of the landlord's right to grant the lease, and the tenant will take subject to any interests affecting the freehold.[299] This title is, therefore, inferior to an absolute leasehold title.

This problem has been alleviated in two ways. Since 1998, the register of titles has been open to inspection.[300] If the freehold title out of which the lease is to be granted is, itself, registered, then the problem of establishing evidence of the freehold title will disappear. Secondly, paragraph 2 of Schedule 11 to the 2002 Act has altered the rules concerning the investigation of the freehold title on the grant of the lease. The position now is that, on the grant of a lease which will trigger compulsory first registration of title, the tenant will, unless there is a contractual provision to the contrary,[301] be entitled to register the freehold title out of which the lease is being granted. Accordingly, in the future, the registration of good leasehold titles will become less common.

Upgrading of titles

Provision is made by section 62 of the 2002 Act for the registrar, either on his own initiative, or on the application of certain specified people, to upgrade various titles which have already been registered. It was previously the case that only the registered proprietor could apply for title to be upgraded,[302] but, under section 62(7) of the Act, the class of potential applicants has been widened to include a person entitled to be registered as proprietor of the estate, the proprietor of a registered charge affecting that estate, and a person interested in a registered estate which derives from that estate.

If the title is freehold, then a qualified or a possessory title can be upgraded to an absolute title. In the case of a possessory title, if that title has been registered for a period of at least twelve years, it may be upgraded to an absolute title. Where the title is leasehold, then a qualified or possessory title can be upgraded to a good leasehold if the registrar is satisfied as to the title to the estate and to absolute leasehold if he is satisfied both as to the title to the estate and to the title to the freehold. Again, in the case where title to a possessory leasehold title has been registered for at least twelve years, then the registrar may enter it as a good leasehold title if satisfied that the proprietor is in possession of the land.[303]

---

[298] Law of Property Act 1925, s. 44(2).   [299] Land Registration Act 2002, s. 12(6).
[300] Land Registration Act 1998, s. 1. See now Land Registration Act 2002, s. 66.
[301] Law of Property Act 1925, s. 44(11). This presupposes that the grant of the lease is preceded by a contract, which is not always the case.
[302] Land Registration Act 1925, s. 77.   [303] Land Registration Act 2002, s. 62(1)–(6).

The effect of the upgrading of a title is laid down by section 63 of the Act. In the case of registration of either a freehold or leasehold estate being entered as an absolute title, the proprietor ceases to hold the estate subject to any estate, right or interest whose enforceability was preserved by virtue of the previous entry about the class of title. The same applies in the case of the registration of a good leasehold title, except that the entry does not affect the enforcement of any estate, right, or interest affecting the title of the lessor to grant the lease. A consequence of the upgrading of a title may be to cause loss to a person who, prior to the upgrading of the title may have had an interest affecting that property. If this occurs, then the person who suffers loss is entitled to be indemnified.[304]

DEALINGS WITH REGISTERED LAND

When title is registered, future dealings with it must be completed by registration. This is dealt with explicitly by section 27(1) of the 2002 Act, which provides that if a disposition of a registered estate or registered charge is required to be completed by registration, it does not operate at law until the relevant registration requirements are met. Until application is made for registration, the transfer operates only in equity.[305] The dispositions required to be completed by registration are then listed by section 27(2). This includes a transfer, the grant of various leases, the grant of easements and rentcharges, and the grant of a legal charge. With regard to leases, it is important to distinguish between situations when a leasehold estate is registered and when it is not. When a leasehold estate is registered and that lease is then assigned, then that assignment must be registered. It is immaterial how many years remain under the lease. The assignment is a transfer. So if the residue of a registered lease with six years remaining is assigned, that assignment must be completed by registration. Despite the fact that the term is for less than seven years, it will not take effect as an interest overriding registration.[306] When what is in question is the grant of a new lease, the leases which must be completed by registration are those which exist as registrable interests.[307]

Having contracted to purchase the particular estate in question, the purchaser will requisition an official search of the register.[308] Provided that he is in good faith then, provided that the application for registration is made within the priority period,[309] this period currently being thirty working days from the time when the search appli-

---

[304] Land Registration Act 2002, Sched. 8, para. 2. For indemnity, see Indemnity, pp. 180–182.

[305] See *Barclays Bank plc v. Zaroovabli* [1997] Ch. 321 (creation of a mortgage); *Scribes West Ltd v. Relsa Anstalt* [2004] EWCA Civ. 1744 (transfer of freehold reversion).

[306] Ibid., Sched. 3, para. 1(b).   [307] See Leasehold estates, p. 118.

[308] Land Registration Act 2002, s. 70.

[309] It is not sufficient if the transaction is completed within the priority period. An application must be made for registration of title: see *Howell v. Murray* (1990) 61 P. & C.R. 18.

cation is deemed to have been delivered,[310] he will take free from any interests registered between the date of the search and the application for registration.[311] Good faith, in this context, appears to mean only that the purchaser is acting honestly,[312] a requirement which is not precluded simply because he has notice of a competing claim.[313]

If the official search certificate is incorrect, the position is different from that which pertains with regard to unregistered land. When title is unregistered, it is provided by section 10(4) of the Land Charges Act 1972 that the certificate shall be conclusive, so that if the search erroneously fails to reveal the existence of a registered land charge, the purchaser will take free from it.[314] When title is registered, it is the actual state of the register which is conclusive and so, in *Parkash v. Irani Finance Co. Ltd*,[315] a purchaser took subject to a caution even though the search had failed to reveal it. The purchaser's remedy in this situation is to obtain an indemnity.[316]

Electronic conveyancing[317]

The actual transfer of registered land is currently a two-stage process. The registered proprietor executes a document termed a transfer in favour of the transferee. The transferee then applies to the registry to be registered as the proprietor of the estate supporting that application with the transfer document. The Act is explicit that if the disposition of a registered estate or charge is required to be completed by registration, it does not operate at law until the relevant registration requirements are met.[318] This means that, until registration, the transferee will not acquire the legal title to the land. It does not, however, mean that the transfer is totally ineffective; the transfer will operate to vest the equitable title in the transferee and, if that person is then in actual occupation of the land, that interest will override a subsequent registered disposition of the land.

This two-stage process does, however, involve delay, and the creation of a 'registration gap' between the transfer and its registration. The principal motivation for the enactment of the Land Registration Act 2002 was to pave the way for electronic conveyancing, which will do away with such problems. The provisions relating to

---

[310] Land Registration (Official Searches) Rules 1993, r. 3. The Lord Chancellor is empowered to make rules in respect of priority periods: Land Registration Act 2002, s. 72(6)(7).

[311] Land Registration Act 2002, s. 72(1)(2). See *Meretz Investments N.V. v. ACP Ltd* [2007] EWCA Civ. 1303 at [18] *per* Arden L.J.

[312] Land Registration (Official Searches) Rules 1993, r. 2(1).

[313] *Smith v. Morrison* [1974] 1 W.L.R. 659.   [314] See Wrong certificates, p. 105.

[315] [1970] Ch. 101.

[316] Land Registration Act 2002, Sched. 8, para. 1(1)(c). See *Prestige Properties Ltd v. Scottish Provident Institution* [2003] Ch. 1.

[317] For a helpful discussion, not least of the technical aspects of this, see D. Capps [2002] Conv. 443. See also C. Harpum in E. Cooke (ed.), *Modern Studies in Property Law. Vol. 1: 2000* (Oxford: Hart Publishing, 2001), Chapter 1; R. Parry [2003] Conv. 215.

[318] Land Registration Act 2002, s. 27(1).

electronic conveyancing are contained in Part 8 of the 2002 Act. These provisions have not been brought into force at the same time as the rest of the Act.[319]

Formalities

Section 91 of the Act deals with the issue of formalities. It applies to a document in electronic form where the document purports to effect a disposition which falls within subsection (2) and the conditions of subsection (3) are met. The dispositions within subsection (2) are a disposition of a registered charge, a disposition of an interest which is the subject of a notice in the register, or a disposition which triggers the requirement of registration which is of a kind specified by rules.[320] The conditions laid down by subsection (3) are that the electronic document makes provision for the time and date when it takes effect, has the electronic signature of each person by whom it purports to be authenticated, each electronic signature is certified,[321] and any other conditions as rules may provide are met. These electronic documents are then to be regarded as being in writing, signed by each individual, whose electronic signature it has and also as a deed.[322]

Compulsion

Perhaps the most far-reaching change wrought by the 2002 Act is contained in section 93. Part 8 of the Act, when it is brought into force, will not provide an alternative method of transferring or creating interests in land; the electronic procedure will become mandatory. Section 93 is a hugely significant provision. Section 93(2) provides that:

'A disposition to which this section applies, *or a contract* to make such disposition, *only has effect* if it is made by electronic form and, if when the document purports to take effect—

(a) it is electronically communicated to the registrar, and

(b) the relevant registration requirements are met.'[323]

The section applies to the disposition of a registered estate or charge or an interest which is the subject of a notice in the register, where the disposition is of a description specified in the rules.[324] The relevant registration requirements are then listed in Schedule 2 to the Act.

The combined effect of the section and the Schedule is that it will only be possible to create or transfer various interests in the property by electronic means which are

---

[319] For the current progress towards this end, see Dixon *et al*, Ruoff and Roper, *Registered Conveyancing* (London: Sweet & Maxwell, 2011, looseleaf), Chapter 19.

[320] The power to make rules governing communication of documents in electronic form is conferred by s. 95 of the Act.

[321] This entails compliance with s. 7(2)(3) of the Electronic Communications Act 2000: Land Registration Act 2002, s. 91(10).

[322] Ibid., s. 91(4)(5). For the establishment of a land registry network and a system of authorized users, see s. 92 and Sched. 5.

[323] Emphasis supplied.   [324] Land Registration Act 2002, s. 93(1).

communicated to the registrar, it being envisaged that the creation of the electronic document and its communication to the registrar will occur simultaneously.

The transactions to which this provision will apply are:

(i)   a transfer of an estate;

(ii) the grant of a term of years absolute when the lease is required to be registered;

(iii) lease of a franchise or manor;

(iv) creation of independently registrable legal interests. This consists of rentcharges and profits in gross for a period of not less than seven years;

(v)   easements.[325]

Two key points need to be made about these provisions. First, section 93 refers to both dispositions *and* contracts to make dispositions. Secondly, the section makes clear that dispositions to which the section applies, and which do not comply with its requirements, have no effect.

The consequences of non-compliance

For very many years, to create most legal interests in land, it was necessary to use a deed. A failure to do so was not, however, fatal to the creation of an equitable interest. If a deed was not used then, provided other formal requirements were met, the intended transaction was seen as a contract to create whatever interest was intended and, provided specific performance was available, an equitable interest would be created.[326] Such an argument will no longer be sustainable. The distinction between legal and equitable interests will, therefore, to a considerable extent, disappear.

It is not hard to envisage, however, that cases will come before the courts where the parties have not complied with the requirements to use electronic documents and electronically communicated the disposition to the registrar but have, nevertheless, acted in the belief that their intended transaction had legal efficacy. In such circumstances, one would envisage that the principles of estoppel would be applicable, and that there may emerge a proliferation of such claims.[327] Given the highly conservative approach taken in some quarters to allowing the perception that estoppel may be able to outflank the formal requirements of section 2 of the Law of Property (Miscellaneous Provisions) Act 1989—a provision dealing with the formal requirements for the creation of a contract for the sale of land[328]—it may be the case that the courts will not accept this argument, although the better view is that they should do so.

A further point is that these new provisions do not apply to the creation of trusts. It will, therefore, still be open to a person to argue that they have an interest in

---

[325] This does not include easements which arise by implication.

[326] See The creation of equitable rights, p. 47.

[327] See M. Dixon in Cooke (ed.), *Modern Issues in Property Law Vol .2: 2002* (Oxford: Hart Publishing, 2003), Chapter 9. See Chapter 15.

[328] See *Yeoman's Row Management Ltd v. Cobbe* [2008] UKHL 1139 at [29] *per* Lord Scott of Foscote.

another person's land under a trust and such a trust may well override a registered disposition.

The owner's powers

The Land Registration Act 1925 provided quite a detailed list of the powers of a registered proprietor.[329] This important matter is dealt with more succinctly by the 2002 Act. Under section 23(1), the owner's powers in relation to a registered estate consist of:

    (a) power to make a disposition of any kind permitted by the general law in relation to an interest of that description, other than a mortgage by demise or sub-demise, and

    (b) power to charge the estate at law with the payment of money.[330]

A person is entitled to exercise these powers in relation to a registered charge or estate if he is either the registered proprietor or entitled to be so registered.[331] Insofar as the disponee is concerned, section 26 provides that a person's right to exercise an owner's powers in relation to a registered estate or charge is to be taken to be free from any limitation affecting the validity of the disposition, unless that limitation is reflected by an entry in the register or is imposed by the Act.

    The effect of these provisions is to prevent an argument being raised that a particular disposition by a registered proprietor is ineffective on account of a lack of power to implement it. If the consent of a particular person is required for a particular transaction[332] then, unless the need for this consent is referred to in a restriction entered on the register, the title of the disponee will not be impeachable on the ground that the requisite consent has not been obtained. The transferors will be liable to the person whose consent was necessary,[333] but the disponee's title will not be affected.

    One point which should be made concerning this section is that the power which is given by section 26 is to make a disposition of any kind permitted by the general law. This will require that the overreaching machinery is complied with. If there is a sole registered proprietor, but there exists co-ownership in equity, then a disposition by the sole trustee, while sufficient to vest the legal title in the disponee, will not overreach the beneficial interests existing behind the trust.[334] If the beneficiary is in actual occupation of the property, then that interest will override a registered disposition. In other words, the decision in *Williams & Glyn's Bank Ltd v. Boland*[335] remains good law.

---

[329] Land Registration Act 1925, s. 18.

[330] Similar provisions exist in respect of owners of a registered charge: Land Registration Act 2002, s. 23(2).

[331] Ibid., s. 24.

[332] As may well be the case under the Trusts of Land and Appointment of Trustees Act 1996, s. 10. See The rights of beneficiaries, pp. 296–297.

[333] Land Registration Act 2002, s. 26(3).   [334] See One trustee, p. 292.

[335] [1981] A.C. 487.

Effect of dispositions

The position of a purchaser of registered land is governed by section 29 of the 2002 Act. This provides that:

'If a registrable disposition of a registered estate is made for valuable consideration, completion of the disposition by registration has the effect of postponing to the interest under the disposition any interest affecting the estate immediately before the disposition whose priority is not protected at the time of registration.'

Before considering what rights are protected, and consequently binding upon a purchaser, one initial point should be stressed. The protection afforded to a purchaser is dependent upon the disposition being for valuable consideration. This, therefore, excludes voluntary transfers, whether during the transferor's lifetime or by will. It also excludes marriage consideration and a nominal consideration in money.[336]

An interest is protected, that is binding upon the purchaser, if either:

(i)   it is a registered charge or the subject of a notice on the register;

(ii) it falls within any of the paragraphs of Schedule 3; or

(iii) it appears from the register to be excepted from the effect of registration; and

(iv) in the case of a disposition of a leasehold estate, if the burden of the interest is an incident of the estate.

The first two paragraphs are self-explanatory. The purchaser takes subject to interests noted on the register and to interests which override registered dispositions. The third paragraph is relevant to situations where the proprietor is not registered with an absolute title and so the purchaser takes subject to the interests excepted from registration. The final paragraph means simply that the purchaser of a leasehold estate takes subject to the obligations imposed by the lease.

Although these provisions appear to be clear enough, two situations which are not dealt with explicitly by the Act need to be addressed. These are the effects of forgery and the role, if any, of notice in respect of unprotected interests.

Forgery[337]

In *Malory Enterprises Ltd v. Cheshire Homes (U.K.) Ltd*,[338] the facts, somewhat simplified, were that A was the registered proprietor of land. B, by fraud, secured a land certificate in its own name in respect of the land of which A was the registered proprietor. B then executed a transfer of that land to C, who was registered as the proprietor. A then sought and obtained rectification of the register to recover the land.

The Court of Appeal analysed the effect of the forgery in the context of the provisions of the Land Registration Act 1925. Arden L.J. held that the purported transfer

---

[336] Land Registration Act 2002, s. 132(1).

[337] For the relative ease of making fraudulent transfers, see P.H. Kenny [2007] Conv. 195.

[338] [2002] Ch. 216. For critical analysis, see C. Harpum in Getzler (ed.), *Rationalizing Property, Equity and Trusts: Essays in Honour of Edward Burn* (London: LexisNexis, 2003), 187 at 199–203.

could not, in law, have had any effect because B was not the proprietor of the land and, thus, had no right to execute it. C, however, had become the registered proprietor and one then had to consider what the effect of that registration was. This was governed by section 69 of the 1925 Act, which provided that 'the proprietor of land…shall be deemed to have vested in him, where the legal estate is freehold, the legal estate in fee simple'. This section, she observed, unlike section 5 of the Act which dealt with first registration of title, did not state that the fee simple was vested in the proprietor 'together with all rights, privileges and appurtenances'. She, therefore, concluded that C as registered proprietor held the legal estate, but that the beneficial interest was held by A, who was previously the registered proprietor.[339]

This reasoning would seem to apply also to the new legislation. In the first place, the person entitled to exercise owner's powers in relation to a registered estate conferred by section 23 of the Act is either the registered proprietor or the person entitled to be registered as proprietor.[340] Manifestly, this does not include the forger. Secondly, section 26, which is headed 'Protection of disponees', would not appear to be relevant, as this protects the disponee in respect of any limitation of a person's right to exercise owner's powers. This would not seem apt to cover the case where the person purporting to exercise these rights has no power at all to exercise them. Thirdly, the protection afforded to a purchaser of registered land by section 29 proceeds on the basis of there having been a registrable disposition. In *Malory*, the Court of Appeal held that the forged disposition was not a disposition, with the consequence that section 20, which provided protection on a registered proprietor following a disposition to him for valuable consideration, did not apply. The same reasoning would seem to apply to section 29 of the 2002 Act.

Registration of C did, however, occur. Under the 1925 Act, the effect of this was, indisputably, to vest the legal title in it. The same result is confirmed by section 58 of the 2002 Act, which provides that:

'If, on the entry of a person on the register as the proprietor of a legal estate, the legal estate would not otherwise be vested in him, it shall be deemed to be vested in him as a result of registration.'

Beneficial ownership

It will be observed that no mention is made of beneficial ownership. Accordingly, the reasoning employed in *Malory Enterprises Ltd v. Cheshire Homes (U.K.) Ltd* would seem to be equally applicable to the provisions of the 2002 Act. This consequence is disturbing. The result is that if A is the registered proprietor and B forges a transfer in favour of C, who is registered as the new proprietor, C will hold the estate on trust for A. As such, as was pointed out at first instance in *Malory*, C could simply be called upon to execute a transfer to A.[341] C, who it will be assumed, was an entirely innocent

---

[339] [2002] Ch. 216 at 232.   [340] Land Registration Act 2002, s. 24.
[341] See [2002] Ch. 216 at 224 *per* Arden L.J. See also *Barclays Bank Plc v. Guy* [2008] EWCA Civ. 452 at [5] *per* Lloyd L.J.

victim of the fraudster will then lose his estate in the land, despite having paid money for it, and not be entitled to any indemnity to compensate him for his loss,[342] unless the order to reconvey the property was seen as rectification of the register.[343] To avoid what would be an unpalatable conclusion, it may be necessary to construe section 26 of the Act so as to extend protection to a disponee in a situation where the disponor has no title to the land at all. One of the advantages of electronic conveyancing is that this problem will not arise if the transaction is conducted by a person authorized to do so, under a network access agreement, and who uses the network to make a disposition. In these circumstances, he is deemed to be acting with authority,[344] and, so, the disposition will be valid.

Notice of unprotected interests

In any system of registration, the question will arise as to what the position is when an interest which is registrable is not registered, but the purchaser has notice of it. The provisions of the 1925 Act appeared to provide a clear answer: that the purchaser was not bound.[345] Initially, this was also the approach of the judiciary. In *De Lusignan v. Johnson*,[346] a claim that a registered chargee was bound by a unregistered interest, of which he had prior notice, was struck out as disclosing no cause of action. This case was not cited, however, in the almost universally criticized case of *Peffer v. Rigg*.[347]

In *Peffer v. Rigg*, as part of a divorce settlement, a house was transferred from D1 to D2 in consideration of £1, and D2 was registered as proprietor with an absolute title. Prior to the transfer D1 had held the house on trust for P1, a fact of which D2 was aware. It was argued that D2 should take free from P1's interest, which was neither protected on the register nor an overriding interest. Graham J. held that D2 was bound by the unprotected interest.

There were three grounds for the decision. The first, and potentially most far-reaching, relied on a tortuous construction of the 1925 Act, which was demonstrably wrong,[348] the effect of which was to introduce a general requirement of good faith into registered conveyancing. As there are no comparable provisions in the 2002 Act, this need not be explored further. A second reason was that the purchase price of £1 was nominal consideration and section 20 of the 1925 Act, as is the case with section 29 of the 2002 Act, only affords protection to a person registered as proprietor if the disposition was for valuable consideration. This is plausible, although not necessarily convincing, in that as the transfer was part of a divorce settlement one could have looked at matters in the round having regard to such areas as potential liability to pay

---

[342] For the indemnity provisions, see Indemnity, pp. 180–182.
[343] See Land Registration Act 2002, Sched. 8, para. 2(b).
[344] Land Registration Act 2002, Sched. 5, para. 8.   [345] Land Registration Act 1925, s. 20.
[346] (1973) 230 E.G. 499.
[347] [1977] 1 W.L.R. 285. For criticism, see D.J. Hayton [1977] C.L.J. 277; D.C. Jackson (1977) 94 L.Q.R. 239, especially at 242; R.J. Smith (1977) L.Q.R. 341; M.P. Thompson [1985] C.L.J. 280 at 285 and 289. Cf. S. Anderson (1977) 40 M.L.R. 600 at 606.
[348] See the 1st edn of this work at p. 121.

maintenance, when deciding whether the consideration was really only nominal.[349] Finally, the judge considered that, because the land had, to the knowledge of D2, been conveyed in breach of trust, this inequitable behaviour was sufficient to lead to the creation of a new constructive trust.[350]

Fraud

The imposition of a constructive trust in *Peffer v. Rigg* raises the interesting question as to what extent the registration provisions are to be affected by general equitable principles and, in particular, the extent to which notions of equitable fraud are relevant.[351] That there is such a role for notions of fraud is evident from the clear case of *Jones v. Lipman*.[352] In that case, the defendant, in order to escape a contract of sale which he had made, transferred the property to a company which he controlled. As the company was considered to be 'a device and a sham, a mask which he holds before his face in an attempt to avoid recognition by the eye of equity',[353] specific performance of the contract was ordered against the company, despite the original contract not having been protected by registration.

A case such as *Jones v. Lipman*, where the supposed transfer for value is in fact a sham, is a clear case where the supposed purchaser should not take free from an unprotected interest. Rather less clear is the situation which occurred in *Lyus v. Prowsa Developments Ltd.*[354] Land was mortgaged to a bank. The registered proprietor then contracted to sell it to the plaintiff. Before that contract could be completed, however, the bank exercised its power of sale over the property, and sold it to D1, who in turn sold the land to D2. Although it was clearly the case that the bank could have sold the property free from the plaintiff's contractual right, it chose not to do so. Instead, each successive sale was made expressly subject to the rights of the plaintiff. Dillon J. ordered specific performance of the contract.

The reasoning was that, because the purchaser had expressly agreed to take subject to the plaintiff's right, it would be inequitable for him to renege on that undertaking, and so a constructive trust was imposed to prevent him from so doing. While this reasoning appears to be attractive, and has subsequently secured the approval, albeit *obiter*, of the Court of Appeal,[355] it is clear that the reasoning is to be applied narrowly. In *Lloyd v. Dugdale*,[356] Sir Christopher Slade was clear that, for a constructive trust to arise, it is essential that there be an undertaking to give effect to a new obligation, and notice of its existence is not sufficient.[357] Even construed narrowly, however, there are

---

[349] See also the comments in *Miles v. Bull* [1969] 1 Q.B. 258 at 264 *per* Megarry J.

[350] [1977] 1 W.L.R. 285 at 293.

[351] See, generally, M.P. Thompson [1985] C.L.J. 280; E. Cooke and P. O'Connor (2004) 120 L.Q.R. 640; M Harding and M. Bryan in Dixon (ed.), *Modern Studies in Property Law* (Oxford: Hart Publishing, 2009) (Volume 5), Chapter 1.

[352] [1962] 1 W.L.R. 832. See, also, *Buckinghamshire County Council v. Briar* [2002] EWHC 2821 (Ch.).

[353] Ibid., at 836 *per* Russell J.   [354] [1982] 1 W.L.R. 832.

[355] *Ashburn Anstalt v. Arnold* [1989] Ch. 1 at 24 *per* Fox L.J.   [356] [2002] 2 P. & C.R. 13 at [52].

[357] See also *Chattey v. Forndale Holdings Ltd* (1996) 75 P. & C.R. 298 at 317 where Morritt L.J. stressed that notice of a prior interest would, on its own, be insufficient to give rise to a constructive trust.

serious difficulties with it.[358] The essential proposition which was accepted was that if A and B contract, and that contract seeks to confer rights on C, then a constructive trust should be imposed to give effect to that agreement. This would seem to conflict with the doctrine of privity of contract,[359] which prevailed at the time when this case was decided.

The particular problem thrown up by *Lyus v. Prowsa Developments Ltd* would now be resolved by section 1 of the Contracts (Rights of Third Parties) Act 1999. Under this section, where two parties to a contract seek to confer rights upon a third party, then that party may sue upon that contract and the remedies available may include specific performance. The more general issue remains, however, which is the extent to which seemingly clear statutory provisions should be undermined by the application of general equitable principles.

The problem of the role, if any, actual notice of an unprotected interest should play in a system of registration is a thorny one, and in *Chaudhary v. Yavuz*,[360] Lloyd L.J. pointed out that he knew of no English case where the reasoning employed in *Lyus v. Prowsa* had been used to make binding on a purchaser an interest which was void against him for non-registration. In unregistered land, the House of Lords declined to apply a gloss to the provisions of the Land Charges Act 1972, so as to introduce any notion of good faith.[361] *Peffer v. Rigg*, while dealing with the provisions of a different statute, embraces a totally different philosophy from that adopted by the House of Lords and the question remains as to which of the two should prevail, a question which becomes increasingly pertinent as the total replacement of the unregistered land system is now a foreseeable event. In approaching this question, it is pertinent to bear in mind that 'since in matters relating to title to land certainty is of prime importance, it is not desirable that constructive trusts of land should be imposed in reliance on inferences from "slender material"'...'[362]

Personal liability

In its Third Report, the Law Commission did advocate that a purchaser should be required to be in good faith but, beyond a statement that this should not be equated simply with notice of an unprotected interest, little guidance was given as to what this might mean.[363] This approach was not pursued in the most recent report and the 2002 Act does not specifically deal with this issue. What is intended is that the disponee's title should not be impeachable but that he should, in appropriate cases, be personally liable for complicity in any breach of trust. The example which is given is a case where

---

[358] For a different view, see B. McFarlane (2004) 120 LQ.R. 667, although difficulty with privity remains.

[359] See M.P. Thompson [1988] Conv. 201 at 206.   [360] [2011] EWCA Civ. 1314 at [61].

[361] *Midland Bank Trust Co. Ltd v. Green* [1981] A.C. 513.

[362] *Lloyd v. Dugdale* [2002] 2 P. & C.R. 13 at [52] *per* Sir Christopher Slade.

[363] (1987) Law Com. No. 158, paras 4.14–4.17. See R.J. Smith [1987] Conv. 334 at 337; R.J. Smith in Jackson and Wilde (eds), *The Reform of Property Law* (Aldershot: Dartmouth, 1997), 129 at 133–137. For an argument sympathetic to the introduction of notions of good faith, see J. Stevens in Meisel and Cook (eds), *Property and Protection: Essays in Honour of Brian Harvey* (Oxford: Hart Publishing, 2000), 177.

A and B hold land on trust and have limited powers of disposition. They then transfer the property to C in circumstances that were prohibited by the trust. C knows of this. The effect of the statutory provisions is that C's title is unimpeachable, yet, it is argued, there is no obstacle in holding C to be personally liable for the knowing receipt of trust property transferred in breach of trust.[364] It is hoped that, for a number of reasons, this suggestion is not taken up by the courts.

Knowing receipt

It should be said at the outset, that it is perfectly true that a registered proprietor with an absolute title may be subject to personal liability in respect of his acquisition of the title. Where that liability has been recognized, however, is in respect of a wrong committed by the transferee as against the transferor.[365] The point is 'that the continued existence of rights of action of a personal nature, *as between the original parties to a land transaction*, is not inconsistent with the Land Registration Act'.[366] Where the dispute is not confined to the original parties to the transaction, however, the situation is not the same. As was explained in *Creque v. Penn*,[367] '[t]he position as against a third party (such as a mortgagee or a later purchaser deriving title from the original purchaser) would be quite different, because then it would be a matter of title, not personal liability'. This point was also emphasized over a century ago. In *Assets Co. Ltd v. Mere Roihi*,[368] Lord Lindley said:

'If the alleged [beneficiary] is a rival claimant, who can prove no trust apart from his own alleged ownership, it is plain that to treat him as a beneficiary is to destroy all benefit from registration. Here the plaintiffs set up an adverse title and nothing else; and to hold in their favour that there is any resulting or other trust entitling them to the property is, in their Lordships' opinion, to do the very thing which registration is designed to prevent.'

If one returns to the example given above, it should first be emphasized that the principles enshrined in the Act make it clear that, as a matter of Property Law, the disponee takes free from the unprotected interest. To hold that he is personally liable to the holder of the unprotected interest undermines this principle. To say that liability is personal and not proprietary 'masks the reality that the purchaser will barely spot the difference: liability feels the same by which ever route it arrives'.[369] This point can be reinforced by enquiring as to what the effect of this personal liability is. In trust law, a person who receives trust property in breach of trust, and subsequently disposes of that property, can be personally liable to the beneficiary on the basis of knowing receipt. If he still has the property then, unless he is a bona fide purchaser, he will be liable to return the trust property and, pending that return will be bound by the

---

[364] (2001) Law Com. No. 271, para. 4.11.
[365] See *Frazer v Walker* [1967] A.C. 569; *Creque v. Penn* [2007] UKPC 44.
[366] *Creque v. Penn, supra*, at [15] *per* Lord Walker of Gestingthorpe.
[367] Ibid. at [10] *per* Lord Walker of Gestingthorpe.   [368] [1905] A.C. 176 at 204–205.
[369] Smith, op. cit., p. 248.

original trust; he will hold the property on trust for the wronged beneficiary.[370] If a purchaser of registered land is held to be personally liable as a result of his knowledge of an unregistered trust, the effect would seem to be that a constructive trust is imposed. The upshot would be that he now holds the property on trust for the beneficiary whose previous trust interest was not regarded as binding upon him. To respond to this objection by saying that he is subject to a new trust and not bound by the original trust is really a distinction without a difference. Finally, there is the important question of the basis upon which liability is to be imposed. To be liable on the basis of knowing receipt, it is necessary that it is unconscionable for the recipient to retain the property.[371] In the present context, it is far from clear what would constitute the requisite degree of unconscionability. Actual knowledge of the unprotected interest would not appear to be sufficient; the purchaser may quite reasonably believe, and indeed have been advised to this effect, that under the provisions of the Act, that interest can be ignored because it is not registered. In such circumstances, it is clear that the purchaser would not be liable for committing an economic tort,[372] and should not be liable, either, in respect of knowing receipt.

Neither is it helpful to ask if the purpose of the transaction is to defeat an unprotected interest. Precisely such an argument was propounded in the context of unregistered land, to put forward the argument that such a motive amounted to fraud, so that the purchaser could not take free of an unprotected land charge. This was rejected as being unworkable in *Midland Bank Trust Co. Ltd v. Green*,[373] and is no more plausible where title is registered and the same issue arises.

A good example of where there is scope for imposing personal liability occurred in *HSBC Bank Ltd. v. Dyche*.[374] Mr and Mrs Dyche were the registered proprietors of a house, but held it on constructive trust for her father, Mr Collelldevall. As part of a divorce settlement, they transferred the title to her in consideration of £5000. She then mortgaged the house to the bank, having explained her father's presence in it by showing a tenancy agreement with him. This was a forgery. It was held that the bank was bound by Mr Collelldevall's interest in the property. In reaching this conclusion Judge Purle attached significance to the fact that, as Mrs Dyche knew that the transfer to her was in breach of trust, this meant that she was not acting in good faith and, so would not take free from a beneficial interest existing behind a trust of land, as a purchaser normally would if the transfer is executed by two trustees.[375]

---

[370] See Hanbury and Martin, *Modern Equity* (18th edn) (London: Sweet & Maxwell, 2009), 337–345.

[371] See *Bank of Credit and Commerce International (Overseas) Ltd v. Akindele* [2001] Ch. 437 at 455 *per* Nourse L.J. In the context of accessorial liability, see *Twinsectra Ltd v. Yardley* [2002] 2 All E.R. 377, criticized by M.P. Thompson [2002] Conv. 387 at 394–399.

[372] See *Meretz Investments N.V. v. ACP Ltd* [2007] EWCA Civ. 1303 at [146] *per* Arden L.J., [174] *per* Toulson L.J.

[373] [1981] A.C. 513 at 531 *per* Lord Wilberforce.

[374] [2009] EWHC 2954 (Ch). For criticism of the reasoning, albeit not the result, see M. Dixon [2010] Conv. 1; N.P. Gravells [2010] Conv. 169.

[375] [2009] EWHC 2954 (Ch) at [38]–[40].

This reasoning must, however, be read in the context of the facts of the case, and should certainly not be seen as introducing a general requirement of good faith. On the facts, Mrs Dyche was a co-trustee prior to the transaction and cannot use the overreaching machinery to conyey the property to herself to escape her own trusteeship. Quite properly, therefore, after she became the sole proprietor of the house, she continued to be bound by the trust obligation. That obligation was then, quite properly held to be binding on the bank because, as in *Boland*[376], the mortage was executed by only one legal owner, and the beneficial owner was in actual occupation at the relevant time.

It is always tempting to seek to introduce general equitable concepts into registration systems, so as to avoid seemingly unmeritorious purchasers from taking advantage of the registration provisions to take free from unregistered interests of which they were aware prior to the purchase. This temptation should be resisted.[377] It is already the case that the owner of an interest will be protected if he or she is in actual occupation of the relevant property. If the person is not in occupation, it is not unreasonable to insist upon registration. Cases such as *Lyus Investments Ltd v. Prowsa*, where the purchaser expressly agrees to take subject to a right, can now be accommodated by the Law of Contract, in that the third party can now sue on the basis of contracts made for his benefit.[378] In other cases, however, of which *Peffer v. Rigg* is an example, the courts should refrain from seeking to have regard to broad equitable principles to effect what is perceived to be a fair result in an individual case. To succumb to the temptation to do so would introduce unwelcome uncertainty to an area of law where certainty is desirable.

ALTERATION AND INDEMNITY

As has been seen, one of the effects of the Land Registration Act 2002 is to provide certainty as to the ownership of the land. If a person is registered as proprietor with an absolute title then, whatever the position might have been had title been unregistered, the proprietor is the owner of that land. Of course, mistakes may occur, so that the person who has been registered as proprietor may not actually be entitled to the land because the person who conveyed it to him was not, himself, the owner of it.[379] To deal with problems such as this, jurisdiction exists for these matters to be corrected. There is also a complementary jurisdiction to award an indemnity to people who suffer loss as a result of a change being made to the register or, alternatively, such a change being

---

[376] *Williams and Glyn's Bank v. Boland* [1981] A.C. 487.
[377] See also *Halifax Plc v. Curry Popeck (A firm)* [2008] EWHAC (Ch.) at [48]–[52] *per* Norris J.
[378] Law of Contract (Rights of Third Parties) Act 1999, s. 1.
[379] See, e.g., *Re 139 High Street, Deptford* [1951] Ch. 884.

refused. The availability of indemnities is what underpins the insurance principle underlying the registered land system.

Under section 82 of the 1925 Act, there were listed eight different grounds on which jurisdiction to make changes to the register existed. There then were listed four restrictions on this jurisdiction where the registered proprietor was in possession of the land. All of these came under the generic description of rectification. The 2002 Act has substantially changed the terminology which is used. The generic term which is now used is alteration of the register and, under section 65 of the Act, provisions regarding alteration are governed by Schedule 4. This Schedule then draws a distinction between alterations to the register and rectification of it. The term rectification is limited to situations which involve the correction of a mistake and which prejudicially affects the title of a registered proprietor.[380] Alteration is wider than this and includes any changes to the register. Alterations which do not amount to rectification are those which do not prejudicially affect the title of a registered proprietor. This distinction is important because the indemnity provisions contained in Schedule 11 are principally relevant to cases of rectification and not to alterations.

Although the terminology used and the drafting technique employed are very different from that which pertained under the 1925 Act, it was not intended to make substantive changes to the law,[381] so that previous authorities on the jurisdiction to rectify the register will remain relevant.

Jurisdiction to alter the register

Under paragraph 2 of Schedule 4 to the 2002 Act the court may make an order for the alteration of the register in one of three situations. These are:

(i)   correcting a mistake;

(ii)   bringing the register up to date; and

(iii)   giving effect to any estate, right or interest excepted from the effect of registration.

An order made under this paragraph has effect when served on the registrar to impose a duty on him to give effect to it.[382]

Paragraph 5 of the Schedule confers on the registrar the same jurisdiction as is conferred upon the court, by paragraph 2 of the Schedule, with the additional power to remove superfluous entries from the register. If the case comes within either paragraph 2 or paragraph 5, unless there are exceptional circumstances then an order must be made.[383] In applications made to the registrar, if agreement cannot be reached between the parties, then the matter is referred to the adjudicator.[384]

---

[380] Land Registration Act 2002, Sched. 4, para. 1.   [381] See (2001) Law Com. No. 271, para. 10.4.
[382] Land Registration Act 2002, Sched. 4, para. 2.
[383] Ibid., paras 3(3), 5(3); Land Registration Rules 2003, r. 126.
[384] Land Registration Act 2002, s. 73(7).

Mistake

To ascertain what constitutes a mistake under paragraphs 2 and 5, regard must be had to the old law on rectification. Jurisdiction existed to order rectification if a person was aggrieved by an entry or omission on the register.[385] This would be apt to cover the situation to give effect to a land charge which had been registered under the land charges register and which had not been included on the register of title.[386] This may occur when the land charge was behind the root of title and only comes to light, as is likely to be the case, some time after registration of title has occurred. This would now appear to come within the meaning of a mistake, although, as the proprietor is likely to be in possession of the land, it is unlikely that rectification will be ordered.[387] Conversely, although it has been suggested[388] that rectification could have been ordered under section 82 of the 1925 Act to give effect to an unprotected minor interest which had become void for non-registration against a registered proprietor,[389] this always seemed to be unsound as it would make little sense to hold first that a proprietor took free from an interest and then rectify the register to give effect to precisely that interest.[390] This argument seems even less tenable under the 2002 Act as it is impossible to see what mistake has been made.

Wrong owner

It can happen that a person who is not entitled to the land is wrongly registered as the proprietor. Previously, specific provision was made for this.[391] An example occurred in *Re 139 High Street, Deptford*,[392] where, by mistake, a conveyance of land included an annexe which was not owned by the vendor. The effect of registration was to vest the title in the registered proprietor and a claim to rectification succeeded. Such would also be the case under the new Act. If the error is not discovered for some time, and the first proprietor transfers the property to a second proprietor, it is not entirely clear if the register can now be rectified. On the occasion of the second registration, no mistake has been made; the person who transferred the legal title had that title vested in him. In *Barclays Bank Plc v. Guy*[393] it was accepted that a fraudster had procured the registration of a company as proprietor. That company then created a mortgage in favour of a bank, and that charge was duly registered. It was held, unless the bank had actual notice[394] of, or had turned a blind eye to, the prior forgery, it was not argu-

---

[385] Land Registration Act 1925, s. 82(1)(b).

[386] See *Rees v. Peters* [2011] EWCA Civ. 836. *Cf. Horrill v. Cooper* (2000) Unreported, Court of Appeal.

[387] See Restrictions on jurisdiction to alter the register, pp. 177–180.

[388] See R.J. Smith (1977) 93 L.Q.R. 341 at 343–344.

[389] *Orakpo v. Manson Investments Ltd* [1977] 1 All E.R. 666 at 678 *per* Buckley L.J., affirmed without reference to this point: [1978] A.C. 95.

[390] D.C. Jackson (1978) 94 L.Q.R. 239 at 244; M.P. Thompson [1985] C.L.J. 280 at 299–301.

[391] Land Registration Act 1925, s. 82(1)(g).

[392] [1951] Ch. 884. See also *Epps v. Esso Petroleum Ltd* [1971] 1 W.L.R. 1071.

[393] [2008] EWCA Civ. 452.

[394] For an example of this, see *Odugwu v. Vastguide Ltd* [2009] EWHC 3565 (Ch), where it was conceded, wrongly in the light of *Barclays Bank v. Guy* which was not cited, that the registration of a subsequent transaction had been a mistake giving jurisdiction to rectify the register.

able that its registration had been as a result of a mistake.[395] Although it might well be thought that because the original registration occurred as a result of a mistake, jurisdiction to rectify will still exist,[396] it appears that this is not the case:[397] an outcome which is unfortunate.

Fraud

Under section 82(1)(d) of the 1925 Act, rectification of the register could be ordered if the registrar was satisfied that any entry in the register had been secured by fraud. This was construed to mean fraud practiced on the registry, so that if a transfer took place as a result of a fraud practiced on the transferor, rectification would not be ordered under this paragraph.[398] If a conveyance, or more likely a mortgage,[399] is forged, then jurisdiction to rectify would have been available. This should still be the case, and the situation should be seen as one where the forged document has induced a mistake in the registry.

The mistake need not have been induced by fraud. In *Baxter v. Mannion*,[400] B made a statutory declaration that he had been in adverse possession of M's land for ten years and applied to be registered with a possessory title. The effect of this is that the land registry served a notice of this on M indicating that he had 65 working days in which to contest the application. If the application is contested within that period then, subject to the fairly narrow exceptions, the application will be dismissed. If it is not, however, then the applicant is registered with a possessory title.[401] Because of quite compelling personal circumstances, M did not contest the application within the time period and B was registered as proprietor. M then sought alteration of the register to substitute his name as proprietor for that of B's, his argument being that alteration was necessary for the purpose of correcting a mistake, the mistake in this case being that the statutory declaration was incorrect in that ten years adverse possession had not actually been established. On being satisfied that this was the case, the Court of Appeal upheld M's application holding, correctly, that it had jurisdiction to correct a substantive error made at the registry, and was not limited to the correction of procedural errors. There was no reason to limit the jurisdiction to the correction of mistakes which have been caused by fraud: regardless of whether fraud was present the reason for the mistake was that the Registrar had been given false information.[402]

---

[395] [2008] EWCA Civ. 452 at [23] *per* Lloyd L.J.

[396] For a discussion of this issue, see *Fretwell v. Graves* (2005), Unreported at [23]–[24] *per* Judge Langan Q.C.

[397] *Barclays Bank plc v. Guy* [2008] EWCA Civ. 452. Although see the comments in the unsuccessful attempt to reopen this litigation: *Guy v. Barclays Bank Plc* [2010] EWCA Civ. 1396 at [35] *per* Lord Neuberger M.R.

[398] *Norwich & Peterborough Building Society v. Steed* [1992] Ch. 116, not following *dicta* in *Re Leighton's Conveyance* [1936] 1 All E.R. 667. See C. Davis [1992] Conv. 293.

[399] See *First National Securities Ltd v. Hegerty* [1985] Q.B. 550; *Ahmed v. Kendrick* (1987) 56 P. & C.R. 120. Cf. *Mortgage Corporation Ltd v. Shaire* [2001] Ch. 743; M.P. Thompson [2000] Conv. 329 at 331–332.

[400] [2011] EWCA Civ. 120.

[401] Land Registration Act 2002, s. 97, Sched. 6. See Applications for registration, p. 264.

[402] [2011] EWCA Civ. 120 at [29] *per* Jacob L.J.

Bringing the register up to date

This innocuous looking provision is an example of alteration of the register and not rectification, the significance of which is that no indemnity is payable after the register is altered. Because no indemnity is payable if the register is altered under this head, it is important to be clear as to the scope of it. Unfortunately, the matter is not as clear as one would like. The bringing of the register up to date will cover rights which arise after registration, such as when an easement by prescription is established.[403] Perhaps less obviously, it will also include the entry onto the register of what was previously an interest which has overriden registration. The registered proprietor will have taken subject to such a right and the entry of it on the register will only serve to reflect the true position.

The provision will also be relevant in the case of certain types of fraud. If a conveyance or a transfer is executed as a consequence of some type of fraud being perpetrated on the transferor by the transferee, and he succeeds in having the conveyance or transfer set aside, the order restoring his name as the proprietor is a case of bringing the register up to date. It does not come within the first head of alteration, that of correcting a mistake.[404] The position where the transfer is forged by a third party is more problematic.

In *Malory Enterprises Ltd v. Cheshire Homes (UK) Ltd*,[405] A was the registered proprietor of land. By means of forgery, B purported to transfer the land to C, who was registered as the proprietor. In the Court of Appeal, it appeared to be accepted that the effect of registration was to clothe C with the legal title, but that the beneficial ownership remained vested in A. If this is correct, A could simply call on C to transfer the legal title to him, and, so, an order replacing A's name as the proprietor with that of C would appear, simply, to be bringing the register up to date. The difficulty with this is that this order would not appear to adversely affect C's title and, in consequence, he would not be entitled to an indemnity.[406] Such a conclusion would undermine, considerably, the insurance aspect of registration of title. To avoid such an unpalatable conclusion, one needs to accept the argument rehearsed earlier, that registration of title vests both the legal and beneficial title in the registered proprietor, regardless of whether the transfer to whom was by someone who was not entitled to transfer it.[407] If the person who has suffered as a result of the wrongful transfer succeeds in getting the register changed, this should be seen as the correction of a mistake and the innocent proprietor who loses his title would be seen to have had his title adversely affected and be entitled to an indemnity. Such an outcome is consistent with paragraph 1(2)(b) of Schedule 8 to the Act, which provides that the proprietor of a registered estate or charge claiming in good faith under a forged disposition is, where the register is rectified, to be regarded as having suffered loss by such rectification as if the disposition had not been forged. For this provision to have any meaning, the substitution of the

---

[403] See Prescription, pp. 565–573.   [404] See Law Com. No.271, para. 107, n. 23.
[405] [2002] Ch. 216.   [406] See Loss, pp. 180–181.   [407] See Equitable title, pp. 127–128.

proprietor's name with that of the victim of the fraud must be seen as rectification and not alteration to bring the register up to date.

Boundary disputes

When title to land is registered, the land is identified by reference to a filed plan. In the vast majority of cases, the boundaries are what are termed 'general boundaries': that is they do not determine the exact line of the boundary.[408] That is only the case when the boundaries are shown as being fixed. The position of general boundaries and the jurisdiction to alter the register was considered in *Derbyshire County Council v. Fallon*.[409] The council owned land, title to which was unregistered, which adjoined land of which the Fallons were the registered proprietors. They had built up to where the boundary of their land was indicated by the filed plan. Subsequently, the council argued that the boundary on the plan did not accurately indicate where it actually should be, and that the register should be altered to move the boundary, thereby depriving the Fallons of a strip of land which had erroneously been included in their title. Upholding the decision of the Deputy Adjudicator, Mr Christopher Nugee Q.C., sitting as a Deputy High Court judge, declined to alter the register.

In reaching this conclusion, it was first held that the boundary was indeed marked in the incorrect position. As this was within the general boundaries rule, there was no guarantee given that the boundary was accurate and so, to alter the register to move the boundary to its correct position on the plan, would not have prejudicially affected the Fallons' title.[410] In these circumstances, rule 126 of the Land Registration Rules 2003 makes it clear that, save in exceptional circumstances, the register should be altered. Recognizing this, and that 'in the normal case ... if the registrar or Adjudicator has determined that the boundary is in the wrong place, it can be expected that the filed plan will be altered to show the boundary more accurately ...',[411] it was held that the circumstances were exceptional. What made them so were that, first, a contrary outcome may have resulted in the building having to be demolished and, secondly, as planning permission had been granted by the council prior to the building, a strong case of estoppel against the council would have been available to the Fallons.

While, on the facts, this outcome seems reasonable, some of the reasoning regarding the effect of the decision whether or not to alter the register is concerning. The judge seemed to be of the view that altering the register would not have benefited the claimant much, because the newly drawn boundary would, itself, be a general boundary and therefore not guaranteed. Conversely, refusing to alter the boundary left the original general boundary in its original incorrect place leaving the council with a paper title over the adjoining land.[412] This seems wrong. The better view is that, after the decision, the boundary should be regarded as a fixed boundary so that, in

---

[408] Land Registration Act 2002, s. 60(1), (2).
[409] [2007] EWHC 1326 (Ch.). See M. Dixon [2008] Conv. 238.   [410] Ibid., at [23].
[411] Ibid., at [33].   [412] Ibid. at [37]–[38].

the case itself, the council should have, in principle, been entitled to an indemnity to compensate for the loss of its land.

Exceptions from registration

If a person is registered with a title less than absolute, then he takes subject to various interests which were excepted from registration.[413] When it is discovered what those interests are, the register may be altered to enable the register to reflect more accurately the true position.

Removal of superfluous entries

The registrar is given jurisdiction to remove superfluous entries on the register. Examples given of when this jurisdiction may be exercised are when a restriction had been entered on the register to freeze all dealings with a registered estate, but the circumstances which made that precaution necessary had passed, an interest protected by one entry was adequately protected by another, and a restriction on the powers of a registered proprietor had ceased to apply.[414]

Restrictions on jurisdiction to alter the register

As was the case under the 1925 Act, the jurisdiction to order the alteration of the register is seriously limited when the registered proprietor is in possession of the property. Under paragraph 3(2) of the 2002 Act, if an alteration affects the title of a registered estate in land, no order may be made under paragraph 2 without the proprietor's consent in relation to land in his possession unless either he has by fraud or lack of proper care caused or substantially contributed to the mistake or, if for any other reason, it would be unjust for the alteration not to be made.

Before looking more closely at this provision, one important preliminary point should be made. The additional protection afforded to a proprietor in possession extends to rectification of the register; it does not relate to an alteration of the register which does not prejudicially affect him.[415] So, if the land is subject to an interest which overrides a registered disposition, and the register is altered to reflect the true position, the alteration has not affected the title of the registered proprietor. Consequently, alteration will be ordered whether or not the proprietor is in possession. This point was dealt with explicitly under the previous legislation[416] but implicitly by the 2002 Act.

The meaning of possession

Under section 131(1) of the 2002 Act, a registered proprietor is in possession of land if it is physically in his possession, or in that of a person who is entitled to be registered

---

[413] See Land Registration Act 2002, s. 11(6)(7).   [414] (2001) Law Com. No. 271, para. 10.19.
[415] See *Derbyshire County Council v. Fallon* [2007] EWHC 1326 (Ch.) at [27] *per* Mr Christopher Nugee Q.C.
[416] Land Registration Act 1925, s. 82(3).

as the proprietor of a registered estate. The section then goes on to make specific provision for certain relationships. Section 131(2) provides that, when land is in the physical possession of the second named person, then the first named person is to be treated for the purposes of subsection (1) as being in possession. These are:

(a) landlord and tenant;

(b) mortgagor and mortgagee;[417]

(c) licensor and licensee; and

(d) trustee and beneficiary.

A squatter is not regarded as being in possession.[418]

Lack of proper care

As originally drafted, the register could be rectified against a registered proprietor in possession who had contributed to the error. This meant that, if a person lodged an inaccurate conveyance, then he would be regarded as having contributed to the error with the result that he did not enjoy the protection afforded to proprietors in possession.[419] The introduction of the requirement of fraud or lack of proper care removed this difficulty. Although the issue of a lack of proper care relates to the proprietor against whom rectification is sought, if the person seeking rectification has, through a lack of proper care facilitated the dishonest dealings by others, this will militate against an order being made in his favour.[420]

Unjust not to rectify

The onus is on the person seeking rectification against a proprietor in possession to show that it is unjust not to rectify. This is not easy to satisfy. In particular, the mere fact that the wrong person has been registered as the proprietor of the land will not, of itself, mean that it is unjust not to rectify.[421] Instances where it has been considered to be unjust not to rectify the register have included a situation where a purchaser was perfectly well aware of the existence of a land charge which, owing to a mix up, was not revealed by a search in the land charges register.[422] Another occurred in *Johnson v. Shaw*,[423] where the paper title had been held for many years by the person seeking rectification and the land had been continued to be used by him. This, coupled with the fact that the registered proprietor had contributed to the mistake, led to rectification being ordered.[424] Again, in *James Hay Pension Trustees Ltd v. Cooper Estates*

---

[417] This reverses the previous position as exemplified in *Hayes v. Nwajiaku* [1994] E.G.C.S. 106.

[418] Land Registration Act 2002, s. 133(3).

[419] See S. Cretney and G. Dworkin (1968) 84 L.Q.R. 528.

[420] See *Nouri v. Marvi* [2005] EWHC 2996 (Ch.) at [51] *per* Judge Rich Q.C.

[421] See *Epps v. Esso Petroleum Ltd* [1973] 1 W.L.R. 1071; *Kingsalton v. Thames Water Development Ltd* [2002] 1 P. & C.R. 15.

[422] *Horrill v. Cooper* (1998) 78 P. & C.R. 293.   [423] [2004] 1 P. & C.R. 10.

[424] See also the robust approach to this matter in *Mannion v. Baxter* [2011] EWCA Civ. 120 at [41]–[42] *per* Jacob L.J.

Ltd,[425] rectification was ordered to remove a 14-foot strip of land from the title of a proprietor in possession. The reason it was considered to be unjust not to rectify was that the proprietor was 'the accidental owner of a small parcel of land which it never intended to acquire and which is of no use to it save as a means of extracting a ransom payment..., a stand which however legitimate commercially does not commend itself to this court as in any way meritorious'.[426]

The recent decision in *Sainsbury's Supermarkets Ltd v. Olympia Homes Ltd*[427] provides an interesting example of the exercise of this jurisdiction. A Mr Hughes bought land from British Gas and applied for first registration of title. Because he failed to respond to requisitions on title made by the Land Registry, this application lapsed. The consequence of this was the legal title revested in British Gas, leaving Mr Hughes with only the equitable title to the land. A little later, he entered into a complex arrangement with Sainsbury's, the effect of which was to create an option to purchase part of the land. Sainsbury's sought to protect this option by lodging a caution against first registration. This, however, was inapposite. What should have been done was to register a land charge.[428] Later still, a charging order was obtained against Mr Hughes's property in respect of a debt in excess of £3.75 million. The property was then sold to Olympia, who were registered as proprietors of the land. Sainsbury's, on being notified of the application for registration did not respond and the option was not entered onto the register of title. The action arose when Sainsbury's sought rectification of the register to give effect to the option.

Amongst the complications of this case was that Olympia should not have been registered as proprietors at all. This was because when the charging order was made, Mr Hughes did not own the legal estate in the land, the title having revested in British Gas. Consequently when the sale was ordered, all that he could transfer was his own equitable interest in the property. The registration of Olympia as proprietors was a mistake. The whole transaction between the creditor enforcing its security and Olympia was predicated on the basis that the option in favour of Sainsbury's was enforceable, and the purchase price reflected this. To have held the option not to be binding would have occasioned Olympia a considerable windfall, and this was considered to be unjust. Consequently Mann J. ordered rectification. This was not done on the basis simply that Olympia had notice of an unregistered interest. To have done so would undermine the registration provisions, whereby a purchaser takes free of unregistered interests. The facts went beyond that and the case provides a good example of the proper exercise of discretion.

---

[425] [2005] EWHC 36 (Ch.).   [426] Ibid. at [41] *per* Hart J.

[427] [2005] EWHC 1235 (Ch). See M.J. Dixon [2005] Conv. 447.

[428] Whether this should have been registered against Mr Hughes or British Gas would seem to have depended on the precise time when the legal title revested in the latter: a further illustration of the problems of registration of land charges being against the name of the estate owner. See Registration against names, pp. 96–100.

Human rights

If a person fails to secure rectification of the register to reflect the fact that, owing to some mistake, the wrong person has been registered as the proprietor of the land, then the effect will be that he has, as a result of the registration process, been deprived of land which he previously owned. In *Kingsalton v. Thames Water Developments Ltd*,[429] it was argued that this contravened Article 1 of the First Protocol of the European Convention on Human Rights, the argument being that such a decision would deprive the company of its possessions. This was rejected. The power to decline rectification was considered to have been given for the legitimate aim in the public interest of enhancing the security of the land registration system and, having regard to the fact that the unsuccessful claimant would be entitled to an indemnity payment, no breach of the Convention was established.[430]

Indemnity

A remedy, which is complementary to that of alteration of the register, is the payment of an indemnity.[431] Because there is a discretion as to whether or not to alter the register, provision is made both for the payment of an indemnity when loss is suffered as a result of rectification and also when loss occurs when rectification is refused.[432]

Loss due to rectification

A person suffering loss as a result of rectification of the register is, in general, entitled to be paid an indemnity, this indemnity being paid from public funds. Thus, in a case such as *Re 139 High Street, Deptford*,[433] an indemnity was paid to a person who had, wrongly, been registered as proprietor of an annexe, and against whom rectification was ordered to restore the property to the person who, had title not been registered, would have been the owner of it. The position contrasts with that which pertains when title is unregistered. In that case, if a person had purported to convey land which he did not own, the conveyance would have had no effect and the purchaser would have paid money but got no title to the land. Where title is registered, he first gets title to the land and, if he is deprived of that land, by rectification, he is compensated from public funds; this is an example of the insurance principle.

Loss

Schedule 4 to the Act distinguishes between rectification and alteration of the register. Rectification involves the correction of a mistake which adversely affects the title of

---

[429] [2002] 1 P. & C.R. 15.   [430] Ibid., at para. 30 *per* Peter Gibson L.J.; at para. 45 *per* Arden L.J.

[431] In 2010/2011 a total of nearly £9.5 million was paid under the indemnity provisions: Land Registry Annual Report 2010/11 (HC 11580.

[432] Land Registration Act 2002, Sched. 8, para. 1. An indemnity may also be paid when rectification is ordered but the person in whose favour rectification is ordered still suffers loss, thus dealing with the problem illustrated by *Freer v. Unwins* [1976] Ch. 288.

[433] [1951] Ch. 884.

a registered proprietor or, in other words, causes loss. The payment of an indemnity is linked to rectification in the narrow sense used in Schedule 4; an indemnity is payable under Schedule 8 if loss is caused by reason of rectification or by a mistake the correction of which would involve rectification, this latter provision providing for the payment of an indemnity when rectification is refused. Other forms of alteration of the register, that is those which do not cause loss, do not entitle the person against whom the order was made to an indemnity. Consequently, if the register is altered to give effect to an interest which overrides registration, no indemnity is payable.[434] The proprietor was, in any event, bound by that interest and the alteration of the register has the effect only of reflecting the true position.

Fraud or lack of proper care

If a person suffers loss as a result of rectification, he is not entitled to an indemnity on account of his loss suffered as a result of his own fraud or lack of proper care. Where the loss is caused partly by his own lack of proper care, any indemnity payable shall be reduced to such an extent as is just and equitable having regard to his share in the responsibility for the loss; in effect a defence of contributory negligence.[435] An example may assist.

Let us suppose a case where money is borrowed from a mortgagee by a person impersonating the proprietor or one of the proprietors. The signature on the mortgage is forged but, when it is lodged at the registry, the charge is registered. When the fraud is discovered, the application for rectification is successful and the charge is removed from the register. If the mortgagee, who has now lost the security for the loan, seeks an indemnity, then it is thought that much will depend upon the precautions, such as the requiring of the production of passports, which were taken when obtaining the signatures to ensure that the person or persons signing the mortgage deed were who they were claiming to be.

The quantum of indemnity

The amount payable as an indemnity is governed by Schedule 8, paragraph 6, which distinguishes between the amount payable when rectification is ordered and when it is not. In the former situation, the amount payable in respect of the loss of an estate, interest or charge is the value of that interest immediately before rectification is ordered. That is its current market value. When rectification is refused, however, as is likely to be the case when the proprietor is in possession of the land, the amount payable as an indemnity is the value at the time when the mistake was made. While logical, this is arguably unfortunate. It may be the case that the error is not discovered for some time and, if in the exercise of his discretion, the adjudicator declines to rectify the register, the claimant will get an indemnity to reflect the value of the land at the time when the

---

[434] *Re Chowood's Registered Land* [1933] Ch. 574.
[435] Land Registration Act 2002, Sched. 5, para. 5(1)(2). See *Dean v. Dean* (2000) 80 P. & C.R. 457.

original error was made and not the date of the adjudication. Given the substantial rise in the value of land, this may be a significant undervalue.

This problem was more acute as the claim to an indemnity is a contract debt and so liable to become statute barred under the Limitation Act 1980. This occurred in *Epps v. Esso Petroleum Ltd*,[436] where the fact that the claimant for rectification would receive no indemnity if the register was not rectified was unsuccessfully argued to mean that it would be unjust not to rectify the register. This particular problem is now less acute as it is provided by Schedule 8, paragraph 8 that, for the purpose of the Limitation Act 1980, the cause of action arises at a time when the claimant either knows or, but for his own default, might have known of the existence of the claim and rules may be made for the payment of interest on the indemnity.[437] The disparity between indemnity payable in case of rectification and non-rectification is not something which contravenes the European Convention on Human Rights.[438]

---

[436] [1973] 1 W.L.R. 1071.   [437] Land Registration Act 2002, Sched. 8, para. 9.
[438] *Kingsalton v. Thames Water Developments Ltd* [2002] 1 P. & C.R. 15 at para. 45 *per* Arden L.J.

6

The Transfer of Freehold Land

Land may be transferred in a number of ways. It can be given away, or it can form part of a settlement, whereby different interests in the land are given to various people. The most common methods for the transfer of ownership are by sale and upon death and this chapter deals with these two methods of the transfer of land.

SALE

The buying or selling of a house, a process known as conveyancing, is widely regarded as being both one of the most important financial transactions in which an individual takes part and also one of the more stressful. The process, itself, in practice, is a three-stage process. The first part involves the conclusion of negotiations and arrival at an agreement as to the sale of the property. The second stage, which is often the most stressful, involves the formation of the contract and the final part is the actual completion of the transaction when the property is conveyed or transferred to the buyer and the purchase money is paid.

The pre-contract stage

The process of arriving at a stage when a legally binding contract to buy land is created can be a prolonged affair. Apart from the practical problem of finding a property which one likes, and then agreeing a price with a vendor, there are various matters which a purchaser should attend to before committing himself to a contract to buy the land in question. The normal practice when buying a house is, after a price has been agreed, to enter into a 'subject to contract agreement'. Such an agreement has no legal effect. As was said recently 'everybody knows ... that expression ... when used in relation to the sale of land, means that, although the parties have reached an agreement, no legally binding contract comes into existence until the exchange of formal written contracts takes place'.[1] Either party is free to withdraw from the

---

[1] *Secretary of State for Transport v. Christos* [2003] EWCA Civ. 1073 at [34] *per* Lindsay J. See also *Derby & Co. Ltd v. I.T.C. Pension Trust Ltd* [1977] 2 All E.R. 890 at 896 *per* Oliver J.

proposed transaction, and this will, in general, be without incurring liability to the other side.[2]

There are good reasons why the parties enter into subject to contract agreements prior to committing themselves to the transaction. First, the general principle applicable to contracts for the sale of land is *caveat emptor*: let the buyer beware. What this means is that, when selling land, the vendor, unless he expressly agrees to do so, gives no guarantee as to either the physical condition of the property, or that it is legally fit for the purpose which the purchaser has in mind for it.[3] Consequently, prior to committing himself to the contract, the purchaser will require a good deal more information about the property than that which can be obtained from the estate agent's particulars.[4] It was the Government's intention to compel vendors to supply purchasers with a good deal more information pertaining to the property to be sold than has traditionally been the case. To this end the Housing Act 2004 was passed, enabling secondary legislation to be enacted stipulating what information the vendor would be obliged to provide. As will be seen, however, the scheme which was introduced was a considerably watered down version of what was originally planned, and even that more limited obligation has, to most intents and purposes, been suspended so that the vendor's duty of disclosure remains very limited.

The second, and most important reason, why the parties enter into subject to contact agreements is the existence of chains of agreements. It is quite unusual for a contract for the sale of land to be an independent transaction. It will often be the case that the person who is selling the house will be seeking to buy another. The person from whom he is seeking to buy may also be looking to buy a replacement property, and so on. With a number of interrelated transactions in train, it is important to synchronize the entry into a contract to buy with the contract to sell. A failure to do this can lead to the financially catastrophic result of having contracted to buy one house before entering into a contract to sell the existing one. Alternatively, a person can find himself without a home. To avoid either of these outcomes, it is necessary for all the people involved in the chain to synchronize the times when the respective contracts are entered into. To do this, they all enter into subject to contract agreements and then, when everyone is in a position to proceed, a formal process, known as exchange of contracts, is gone through. This is when the contracts are created. The speed of moving from the subject to contract stage to the time when the contract is formed is dependent on the time taken to effect this synchronization, and the delays involved can be considerable.

[2] For a discussion of potential liability, see Subject to contract agreements, pp. 213–216.
[3] See Thompson, *Barnsley's Conveyancing Law and Practice* (4th edn) (London: Butterworths, 1996), 178–180.
[4] Although the estate agent may incur criminal liability under the Property Misdescription Act 1991, s. 1 in respect of misdescriptions, he will not ordinarily be liable in tort to the purchaser. See *McCullagh v. Lane Fox & Partners* [1996] 1 E.G.L.R. 35; J. Hartshorne [1997] Conv. 229.

Gazumping

One of the consequences of the considerable delays which can occur between an agreement 'subject to contract' and the actual formation of a contract is that a practice known as gazumping can occur. This practice, which came to prominence in the 1970s, was a result of rapidly increasing house prices. An example of this may help to explain the practice. P1 offers V £250,000 for his house and this offer is accepted, 'subject to contract'. At this stage, P1 commissions a survey on the house and incurs some other legal expenses. A little later, P2 offers £280,000 for the same house. V can now react in one of a number of ways. First, he may follow what many consider to be the most ethical course of action and reject the higher offer and stick with the original agreement. Alternatively, and this may be a result of his experiencing the same phenomenon with the house he is buying further up the chain, he can inform P1 of the new offer, leaving him with the dilemma of having to match the new offer, or of pulling out of the proposed transaction. If P1 opts to do the latter, he is left out of pocket. In the latter situation P1 is said to have been gazumped, and in both situations is left nursing a sense of grievance. The possibility of gazumping occurring is the consequence of subject to contracts not being legally binding, and the delay occasioned in arriving at the situation where a contract is formed and either party is then free to withdraw from the sale.

Home Information Packs

Although, in the past, various potential solutions to the problem have been canvassed,[5] none have been found that were a satisfactory way to end the practice, the view being expressed that 'all appear agreed that any cure must be worse than the disease'.[6] The Government has attempted not to stamp out the problem, but to alleviate the adverse financial consequences of the practice by the introduction of Home Information Packs, or HIPS.

Section 155 of the Housing Act 2004 places a duty on a seller to have in his possession or control an information pack.[7] The sanction for non-compliance with this duty is a fixed penalty charge, not exceeding £500, to be served by the Trading Standards Authority.[8] When a potential buyer makes a request for a copy of the information pack, it is the duty of the seller or the estate agent to comply with that request within fourteen days of it being made.[9]

Clearly, the aim of these provisions was to reduce the pre-contract cost incurred by a purchaser, so that, if the projected contract fell through, the loss to him would be

---

[5] See (1975) Law Com. No. 75; (1987) Law Commission Standing Committee, *Pre-Contract Deposits.* For the use of a 'lock-out agreement', see *Pitt v. P.H.S.S. Management Ltd* [1994] 1 W.L.R. 327; M.P. Thompson [1994] Conv. 58.

[6] Farrand, *Contract and Conveyance* (4th edn) (London: Oyez, 1983), 17.

[7] Where, as is normal, the property is being sold through an estate agent, this responsibility will rest with the agent: Housing Act 2004, ss 152, 155(2).

[8] Ibid., s. 168, Sched. 8, para. (2).   [9] Ibid., s. 156(1)(9).

less than was previously the case.[10] For this aim to be realized, however, what became important was the content of a HIP: what information the seller is required to give to the buyer. Central to the initial scheme was that the seller should supply to the purchaser a home condition report. A number of criticisms were levelled at this idea,[11] but it is no longer necessary to rehearse them as the plan to make the home condition report part of the HIP was abandoned. The reason for this was that the financial institutions, who provide the money to finance most house purchases through the provision of mortgages, were not prepared to lend money on properties where the only survey provided had been prepared on behalf of the sellers. For a purchaser to obtain a mortgage, therefore, he would need to commission a survey in order to satisfy the lender. It was, therefore, pointless to insist that the vendor should include a home condition report as part of the HIP.

Without the home condition report, HIPs contained very little. Vendors were required to supply to prospective purchasers a sale statement, standard local authority searches, evidence of title, and an energy performance certificate. This very limited duty of disclosure was further diluted when one of the first acts of the Coalition Government, in May 2010, was to suspend the obligation to provide any information other than the energy performance certificate.[12] Even this can be regarded as having more nuisance value to the vendor than providing a valuable service to purchasers. It is also ironic that, given that the purpose of HIPs was to protect the purchaser from the costs of gazumping, their introduction coincided with a major fall in the housing market, so that gazumping is unlikely to reoccur for some time to come. Indeed, currently, the problem is that houses are proving to be very difficult to sell. Because of this downturn, somewhat ironically, the opposite situation is now more likely to occur. That is, once a price has been agreed, subject to contract, the purchaser comes back and offers a lower price than that which had originally been accepted, a practice known as 'gazundering'".

Chain management

It is the existence of chains of transactions which is the principal cause of delays in the formation of the contract of sale. When such delays occur and house prices are volatile, then the vendor may react to that volatility by increasing the asking price or, conversely, if house prices are falling, the purchaser may reduce his offer, a process which has been dubbed gazundering. In an attempt to reduce the delays, the joint Law Commission and Land Registry Report advocated the introduction of a system of chain management conducted by the registry.

When Part 8 of the Land Registration Act 2002 is brought into force, all contracts and dispositions of registered land will have to be effected electronically. What is

[10] For reactions to these measures, see P.H. Kenny [2003] Conv. 262; [2005] Conv. 1, where references to relevant websites can be obtained. See also, M. Garson (2005) 155 N.L.J. 5.
[11] See the 3rd edition of this work at pp. 162–163.
[12] Home Information Pack (Suspension) Order 2010; SI 2010/1456.

envisaged is that, when a solicitor or licensed conveyancer is given instructions to act on the sale or purchase of a registered property, the chain manager in the registry should be informed of this and then kept informed of all steps along the way to the creation of the contract. The chain manager will be able to form a picture of the chain and see where the delays are and then seek to encourage any parties to take any necessary steps to expedite the completion of a chain of binding contracts. It will be interesting to see how efficacious this proposal turns out to be.

FORMATION OF THE CONTRACT

Until 1989, it was true to say that a contract for the sale of land could be formed in the same way as any other contract. For over three hundred years, however, such a contract was not enforceable, unless it satisfied certain formal requirements.[13] The formal requirements were introduced by section 4 of the Statute of Frauds 1677 and replaced by section 40 of the Law of Property Act 1925. That section has, in turn, been superseded by section 2 of the Law of Property (Miscellaneous Provisions) Act 1989. To appreciate fully the change wrought by the new legislative provision, it is necessary to have some regard to the old law.

Contracts made before 27 September 1989

Section 40(1) of the Law of Property Act 1925 provided that:

'No action may be brought upon any contract for the sale or other disposition of land or any interest in land, unless the agreement upon which such action is brought, or some note or memorandum thereof, is in writing and signed by the party to be charged or some person thereunto by him lawfully authorised.'

Evidenced in writing

What should be appreciated is that the section did not require the contract to be in writing; what was insisted upon was that there was adequate written evidence of it. An oral agreement for the sale of land was perfectly valid. The position was that it could not be sued upon unless there was a sufficient memorandum of it. Such a contract could be used as a defence, so if a purchaser had, pursuant to an oral contract, paid an agreed deposit, the vendor could rely on the existence of the oral contract as a defence to an action for its return.[14]

---

[13] For a valuable discussion of the reasons for insisting upon certain formalities, see P. Critchley in Bright and Dewar (eds), *Land Law: Themes and Perspectives* (Oxford: Oxford University Press, 1998), Chapter 20.

[14] *Monickendam v. Leanse* (1923) 39 T.L.R. 445. Where appropriate, this may also be the outcome in cases decided under the new law: see *Sharma v. Simposh Ltd* [2011] EWCA Civ. 1383.

A second point to make was that the section required only that the person to be charged, the defendant, need sign the memorandum. If the vendor alone had signed the memorandum relating to the oral contract, then he could be sued upon it but the purchaser could not.

Part performance

The effect of non-compliance with the formalities imposed by section 40(1) of the Act was not to make the contract void; it rendered it unenforceable by action. Cases could arise, however, where the parties, unaware that their agreement was unenforceable by action, acted on the belief that it was fully binding. In such circumstances, it may become unjust to allow one party, on discovering that the contract is unenforceable, to resist an action being brought upon it.

To deal with such a situation, equity soon developed the doctrine of part performance.[15] The basis of this doctrine was the prevention of fraud; it was considered to be fraudulent for one party to the contract to allow the other to act on the basis that it was enforceable and, then, subsequently, turn round and plead that the contract was unenforceable because it did not satisfy the formal requirements of the statute. In this situation, equity considered that to allow a party to rely on the lack of writing required by the statute would be to use that statute as an instrument of fraud and, to avoid this, enforced the contract.[16] The basis upon which equity intervened was termed the doctrine of part performance and this doctrine was, itself, given statutory recognition in 1925.[17]

The precise basis of the doctrine of part performance was not entirely clear, a result, in part, of the merging of two exceptions to the statute. The first, and original exception, was based upon the prevention of fraud. The second, which was soon to be discredited, was that if there was satisfactory proof of the contract by means other than writing, then the mischief to which the statue was addressed did not apply, and so the contract was enforced.[18] These two exceptions became merged with the result that, to be sufficient, an act of part performance was not based solely on the prevention of fraud, but had, also, to perform an evidential function. What was unclear, however, was whether the acts relied upon had, of themselves, to prove the existence of a contract for the sale of land, or merely the existence of a contractual relationship between the parties.[19] If the acts were sufficient, however, then the court was given a choice 'between undoing what has been done (which is not always possible, or, if possible, just) and completing what has been left undone'.[20] In practice, this meant that if a case of part performance was established, a classic example of which being the taking of

---

[15] See *Hollis v. Edwards* (1683) 1 Vern. 189; *Butcher v. Stapely* (1686) 1 Vern. 363; *Lester v. Foxcroft* (1700) Colles P.C. 108.

[16] See M.P. Thompson (1985) 36 N.I.L.Q. 358 at 359–364.   [17] Law of Property Act 1925, s. 40(2).

[18] See *Hosier v. Read* (1724) 9 Mod. 86.

[19] Contrast *Steadman v. Steadman* [1976] A.C. 536 with *Re Gonin* [1979] Ch. 16. See M.P. Thompson [1979] Conv. 402, an article favouring the latter formulation.

[20] *Maddison v. Alderson* (1883) 8 App. Cas. 467 at 476 *per* Earl of Selborne L.C.

possession by the purchaser of land which he had contracted to buy, then the court would award specific performance of the contract.

The rationale for change

The law governing this area of law was subjected to a critical examination by the Law Commission, who considered it to be unsatisfactory.[21] The idea of a valid, but unenforceable contract, was thought, with some justification, to be confusing. It was also considered to be unfair that a contract could be enforced by only one party to it, which would be the case where only one person had signed the memorandum. In addition, the doctrine of part performance was regarded as being undesirably uncertain. These reasons, collectively, were regarded as sufficient justification for legislative reform, that reform being enacted by section 2 of the Law of Property (Miscellaneous Provisions) Act 1989, a provision which, for no discernible reason, differs significantly from the draft Bill attached to the Law Commission Report.[22] Unfortunately, 'it is not uncommon to find a statutory provision which, in seeking to remedy one mischief, unexpectedly creates another, which cannot be undone by any purposive approach to construction'[23] and, arguably, this has occurred with the present reform, which has led to what has been described by Lord Neuberger as a misconceived piece of legislation, which has left us worse off than we were before.[24]

Contracts made after 26 September 1989

Contracts made prior to the coming into force of the new Act continue to be governed by section 40 of the Law of Property Act 1925,[25] although cases where this will occur will, now, obviously, be rare.[26] For contracts entered into after that date, the new statutory regime is set out in section 2 of the Law of Property (Miscellaneous Provisions) Act 1989,[27] a provision of which it has been said, with considerable justice, that 'it has given rise to a considerable amount of difficulty over its short life'.[28] The section provides that:

'(1) A contract for the sale or other disposition of an interest in land can only be made in writing and only by incorporating all the terms which the parties have expressly agreed in one document or, where contracts are exchanged, in each.

[21] (1987) Law Com. No. 164. A fuller critique can be found in (1985) Law Com. W.P. No. 92.
[22] See C. Harpum in Bright and Dewar (eds), *Land Law, Themes and Perspectives* (Oxford: Oxford University Press, 1998), 151 at 167–169.
[23] *North Eastern Properties Ltd v. Coleman* [2010] EWCA Civ. 277 at [44] *per* Briggs J.
[24] Lord Neuberger [2009] C.L.J. 537 at 546.
[25] Law of Property (Miscellaneous Provisions) Act 1989, s. 2(7).
[26] Equitable leases, options to purchase, and mortgages by deposit of title deeds are the most likely possibilities.
[27] See P.H. Pettit [1989] Conv. 432; M. Haley [1993] A.A.L.R. 498. G. Griffiths in Jackson and Wilde (eds), *Contemporary Property Law* (Aldershot: Ashgate, 1999), 183. This provision may be modified by statutory instrument to permit the formal requirement of writing to be satisfied electronically: Electronic Communications Act 2000, s. 8(1)(2).
[28] *Courtney v. Corp Ltd* [2006] EWCA Civ. 518 at [1] *per* Arden L.J.

(2) The terms may be incorporated in a document either by being set out in it or by reference to some other document.

(3) The document incorporating the terms or, where, contracts are exchanged, one of the documents incorporating them (but not necessarily the same one) must be signed by or on behalf of each party to the contract.

(4) Where a contract for the sale or other disposition of an interest in land satisfies the conditions of this section by reason only of the rectification of one or more documents in pursuance of an order of the court, the contract shall be deemed to have come into being, at such time as may be specified in the order.

(5) This section does not apply in relation to:

  (a) a contract to grant such a lease as is mentioned in section 54(2) of the Law of Property Act 1925 (short leases);
  (b) a contract made in the course of a public auction; or
  (c) a contract regulated under the Financial Services Act 1976;

  and nothing in this section involves the creation or operation of resulting, implied or constructive trusts.'

Before analysing the section, one vitally important point must be made. This is that the section requires contracts for the sale of land *to be in writing*. If an agreement is merely oral, there is no contract at all.[29] Oral agreements now have no contractual effect. It follows from this that the equitable doctrine of part performance has been abolished. As there is no such thing as an oral contract for the sale of land, there cannot be part performance of it.[30] Cases which would, in the past, have been regarded as instances of part performance, will be considered below.

Contracts within the section

The section refers to a contract for the sale or other disposition of an interest in land. This, obviously, will include a contract for sale or a contract to create a lease for more than three years. It will also include a contract to create an easement or a mortgage. In the latter case, this means that a simple deposit of title deeds as security for a loan will no longer be effective to create an equitable mortgage.[31]

Options to purchase

For some time, the position with regard to options to purchase was considered to be controversial,[32] it having been said that it was 'evident that the draftsman of this section did not take account of options'.[33] The principal difficulty was whether or not the

---

[29] See, e.g., *Ravenocean Ltd v. Gardner* [2001] NPC 44.

[30] The suggestion to the contrary in *Singh v. Beggs* (1995) 71 P. & C.R. 120 at 122 is unsound. See S.J.A. Swann [1997] Conv. 293. The correct position was stated in *Yaxley v. Gotts* [2000] 1 All E.R. 711 at 717 *per* Robert Walker L.J. See, generally, G. Griffiths [2002] Conv. 216.

[31] *United Bank of Kuwait plc v. Sahib* [1997] Ch. 107. For criticism, see M.P. Thompson [1994] Conv. 465.

[32] See J.E. Adams (1990) 87 L.S.G. 19.

[33] *Trustees of the Chippenham Golf Club v. North Wiltshire District Council* (1991) 64 P. & C.R. 527 at 530 *per* Scott L.J.

notice exercising the option had to satisfy the section, which would be problematic as it would normally be signed only be the grantee of the option rather than both parties as is envisaged by the Act. This difficulty, which turned largely on whether an option was regarded as being an irrevocable offer to sell property or a conditional contract of sale, was resolved in *Spiro v. Glencrown Properties Ltd*,[34] where Hoffmann J. took the commonsense view that it was sufficient if the option itself satisfied the terms of the section. It was not necessary for the notice exercising it to do so as well.

Boundary agreements

A potent source of disputes between neighbours relates to the precise demarcation of the boundary between their two properties.[35] Large amounts of money can be expended contesting the ownership of very small areas,[36] in one case the dispute being over a strip of land measuring between six and nine inches.[37] To avoid such disputes, which always cost a lot of money and usually generate a lot of ill-feeling,[38] it is clearly desirable that the parties reach agreement between themselves as to the location of the boundary, rather than having recourse to litigation. The question then arises as to whether such agreements come within section 2 of the Act. This issue was considered in *Joyce v. Rigoli*,[39] where a distinction was drawn between two types of agreement. In the first situation, the precise location of the boundary is not clear. The parties agree on where it is to be, although that agreement might appear to one of them to involve ceding land to the other. Because there is a genuine uncertainty over what the true position is, then the agreement to settle the matter is not a contract for the sale of land and section 2 of the Act is not engaged. Where, on the other hand, the boundary is clear and the neighbours agree to move it, then this will involve the transfer of ownership and any agreement will need to be in writing and signed by both parties.

Agreements to contract

It sometimes happens that parties agree to contract at some time in the future. In principle, such agreements are contracts for the disposition of an interest in land and so must satisfy the formal requirements of the Act. In *Daulia Ltd v. Four Millbank Nominees*,[40] there was an oral agreement that if the plaintiff attended the defendants' offices with a draft contract containing the terms previously agreed between them, together with a banker's draft for the amount of the deposit, then the defendants would exchange contracts for the sale of certain property. This oral agreement was held to

---

[34] [1991] Ch. 237.
[35] See the comments in *Alan Wibberley Buildings Ltd v. Insley* [1991] 1 W.L.R. 894 at 895 *per* Lord Hoffmann.
[36] See *Palfrey v. Wilson* [2007] EWCA Civ. 94, where a dispute over the ownership of a garden wall cost an estimated £260,000, excluding VAT!
[37] *Burns v. Morton* [1999] 3 All E.R. 646. This litigation involved a hedge between the properties, which is another cause of friction between neighbours. See now the Anti-social Behaviour Act 2003, Part 8.
[38] *Pennock v. Hodgson* [2010] EWCA Civ. 873 at [46] *per* Mummery L.J.
[39] [2004] EWCA Civ. 79. See also *Nielson v. Poole* (1969) 20 P. & C.R. 909; M.P. Thompson [2004] Conv. 224.
[40] [1978] Ch. 231.

be unenforceable because it did not comply with section 40(1) of the Law of Property Act 1925. The same is true under the 1989 Act. In *Loubatieres v. Mornington Estates (UK)*,[41] it was argued that an oral agreement bound the parties to execute a written document which would comply with the Act. This was rejected on the basis that, if the argument was correct, it 'would render section 2 largely meaningless'.[42]

Where only the two parties are involved in agreements of this sort, it is plain that the first contract is one for the disposition of an interest in land and, now, must be in writing and signed by both parties.[43] A rather different position may occur when the initial agreement is that the property should be sold to a third party. In *Nweze v. Nwoko*,[44] following a dispute between the two parties over the sale of a house, as part of a compromise agreement between them, it was agreed that the house would be put on the market, and, if a buyer were found, a contract with that person would be entered into. It was held that it would be a misuse of language to say that this compromise should be regarded as a contract for the sale or disposition of an interest in land.[45] This seems to be clearly right as, at the time, there was no identifiable buyer of the property. By way of contrast, in *Jelson Ltd v. Derby City Council*,[46] under an agreement between A and B, B had the right to nominate a housing association, C, to whom A could be directed to transfer a number of houses. It was held that the agreement between A and B did not satisfy the requirements of section 2 of the Act because it had not been signed by C. This decision was doubted, but distinguished, in *Nweze v. Nwoko*.[47] While it is thought that the finding in *Jelson* that the contract between A and B would need to satisfy the requirements of section 2 of the Act is clearly correct, the decision that it did not do so, because the document was not signed by C, is not.[48] C was not a party to the contract and should not, therefore, be required to be a signatory to it. A case such as this should, in the future, come within section 1 of the Contracts (Rights of Third Parties) Act 1999, so that C would be able to enforce the contract between A and B. The general position, however, is that an agreement to effect the formation of a contract for the sale of land in the future is, in general, one which must comply with the provisions of section 2 of the Act.

Terms of the contract

Section 2 of the Act provides that all the terms which the parties have expressly agreed must be in writing. This means that the contract must contain what has been termed 'the four Ps': the parties, the property, the price, and any other provisions.[49] What served as adequate descriptions of these matters was the subject of extensive litigation under the old law, and although it has been said that the old authorities are

---

[41] [2004] EWHC 825(Ch.).   [42] Ibid. at [37] *per* David Richards J.
[43] *Sharif v. Sadiq* [2004] EWHC 1931 (Ch.).   [44] [2004] 2 P. & C.R. 33.
[45] Ibid., at para. 26 *per* Waller L.J.   [46] [1999] 3 E.G.L.R. 91.
[47] [2004] 2 P. & C.R. 33 at 34 *per* Waller L.J.; at 35 *per* Carnwath L.J.
[48] See also the cogent criticism by P.H. Kenny [2004] Conv. 4.   [49] Farrand, op. cit., 38.

not necessarily of much, if any, assistance,[50] it is nevertheless felt that much of the previous case law will continue to have relevance as it dealt with essentially similar problems as will arise under the new Act.

Parties

It is essential that the parties to the contract are properly identified.[51] It is not sufficient simply to name the parties. One must be able to determine their respective capacities as vendor and purchaser,[52] although this can be determined by inference, so that a statement of the receipt of money from a person will imply that that person is the purchaser.[53]

The general position is that it is not essential for the actual names of the parties to appear in the document, provided that the description is such as to preclude any fair dispute as their identity.[54] Consistent with this, it is not fatal if an incorrect version of the name is inserted into the contract if the true identity is nevertheless apparent.[55] Again, the courts have held some quite vague descriptions of the parties to suffice, a reference to the vendors as mortgagees being regarded in one case as an adequate description.[56] This, however, goes too far and a description of a person simply as 'vendor, client, and friend' was not sufficient,[57] the essential point being that extrinsic evidence is not admissible if such evidence is necessary to identify the parties to the contract.[58]

One exception to the general rule that the parties must be identified by writing occurs when an agent is involved. In *Davies v. Sweet*,[59] an estate agent signed a receipt for a deposit. It was held that he had authority both to conclude the contract and to sign the memorandum. Although the name of the actual vendor did not appear, it was sufficient that the names of two people bound by the agreement appeared in the memorandum and this was the case as the agent had purported to contract in his own name and would, therefore, have been bound personally by the contract, notwithstanding the agency agreement.

Property

Again, it is clearly necessary for the subject matter of the contract, the land to be sold, to be identified. In the past, the courts have been prepared to allow vague descriptions, such as 'the house in Newport',[60] and 'twenty four acres of land, freehold, at Totmonslow'[61] to suffice as adequate descriptions of the property. Such decisions should, perhaps, now be regarded with some caution as the introduction of parol

---

[50] *Rudra v. Abbey National plc* (1998) 76 P. & C.R. 537 at 541 *per* Robert Walker L.J.
[51] See *Potter v. Duffield* (1874) L.R. 18 Eq. 4; *Francis v. F. Berndes Ltd* [2011] EWHC 3377 (Ch).
[52] *Dewar v. Mintoft* [1912] 2 K.B. 373.   [53] *Auerbach v. Nelson* [1919] 2 Ch. 373.
[54] *Fay v. Miller, Wilkins & Co.* [1941] Ch. 360 at 365 *per* Clauson L.J.
[55] *F. Goldsmith (Sicklesmere) Ltd v. Baxter* [1970] Ch. 85.
[56] *Allen (A.H.) & Co. Ltd v. Whiteman* (1920) 89 L.J. Ch. 534.
[57] *Jarrett v. Hunter* (1866) 34 Ch.D. 182.   [58] *Rudra v. Abbey National plc* (1998) 76 P. & C.R. 537.
[59] [1962] 2 K.B. 300.   [60] *Owen v. Thomas* (1834) 3 My. & K. 353.
[61] *Plant v. Bourne* [1897] 2 Ch. 281; *Harewood v. Ratetse* [1990] 1 W.L.R. 333.

evidence was necessary to identify the property in question. The extent to which such evidence is admissible would appear to depend on the adequacy of the written description so that, in *Freeguard v. Rogers*,[62] a description of 'property known as 9 Graffham Close, Chichester' and identified further by reference to an incorrect title number was adequate because an inspection of the property would make it clear that a garage was included in the sale, the test being to determine what the reasonable man thought he was buying.[63]

As a general proposition, it is not essential for there to be a legal description of the property. In the absence of anything to the contrary, a vendor is taken to be selling a fee simple free from incumbrances.[64] Where a lease is being granted, it is necessary that the contract states accurately the length of the term.[65] It is also essential that the parties, as well as stating the length of the term, state also the date from which the lease is to commence.[66]

Price

As with the parties and the properties, the price agreed upon must also be in writing. It is not, however, essential that the parties have, themselves, agreed upon the price, so long as they have agreed upon a mechanism by which the price will be fixed.[67] Where the parties have agreed upon the method of valuation, this is sufficient and both parties will be bound by that subsequent valuation, even if it is wrong,[68] although if the valuation was carried out negligently the party suffering loss will have a cause of action in tort against the valuer.[69]

Other provisions

Agreement on the property to be sold and the consideration to be paid is the bare minimum necessary to form a contract of sale. To give business efficacy to such a contract, which is termed an open contract, the law will imply certain terms into it, for example, that completion will occur within a reasonable period from the date of the contract. Ordinarily, the parties will not be content to allow the law to imply terms into their contract but will come to an express agreement as to such issues. The basic rule is that, unless these agreed terms are in writing, which satisfies the terms of section 2, then the writing will be defective and there will be no contract.[70]

---

[62] [1999] 1 W.L.R. 375; *Spall v. Owen* (1981) 44 P. & C.R. 36.

[63] *Targett v. Ferguson* (1996) 72 P. & C.R. 106 at 114 *per* Balcombe L.J.

[64] *Timmins v. Moreland Street Properties Ltd* [1958] Ch. 110 at 118–121. Cf. *Freeguard v. Rogers* [1999] 1 W.L.R. 373, where a description of a house by its address was held to be a sufficient description of both the freehold house and a garage held on a long lease. This seems highly questionable.

[65] See *Dolling v. Evans* (1867) 36 L.J. Ch. 474.   [66] See *Harvey v. Pratt* [1965] 2 All E.R. 786.

[67] See *Brown v. Gould* [1972] Ch. 53.

[68] *Campbell v. Edwards* [1976] 1 W.L.R 403; *Baber v. Kenwood Manufacturing Co. Ltd* [1978] 1 Lloyd's Rep. 173.

[69] *Sutcliffe v. Thackrah* [1974] 1 All E.R. 859.

[70] See *North Eastern Properties Ltd v. Coleman* [2010] EWCA Civ. 237 at [81] *per* Longmore L.J. See also, e.g., *Hawkins v. Price* [1947] Ch. 645, where a memorandum which did not include the agreed date for completion was held to be defective.

Under the old law, a memorandum which failed to include all the agreed terms could, nevertheless, be regarded as sufficient in one of two situations. First, if the omitted term was for the sole benefit of one of the parties, for example that the vendor would pay the purchaser's removal expenses, then it was open to the purchaser to waive that term[71] and enforce the contract to the extent that it was evidenced in writing. The converse was also true. If the term omitted from the memorandum was for the sole benefit of the plaintiff, he could enforce the contract as evidenced in writing provided that he submitted to perform the term which was not included in the memorandum.[72] If the omitted term was for the benefit of both parties, neither escape route was possible and the memorandum was simply inadequate.[73]

Under the new law, neither of these possibilities are open as a way of circumventing the inadequacy of writing which fails to contain all the terms agreed between the parties. This is because, under the old law, an oral contract for the sale of land was a valid legal concept, and the question for the court was its enforceability. Under the new law, however, if the agreement is not in writing, it is not contractual, and so the consequence of all the agreed terms not being in writing is potentially fatal to the argument that the agreement amounts to a binding contract.[74] Nevertheless, the courts have shown themselves able, by various routes, to enforce agreements which are not fully recorded in writing, leading to the somewhat paradoxical result that the absence of agreed terms in the written document may be less of an impediment to the enforcement of the agreement than was previously the case.

Collateral contract

In *Record v. Bell*,[75] there was an agreement for the sale of residential property for £1.3 million. At the same time, a separate agreement was entered into for the sale of various chattels. The day before contracts were exchanged, the purchaser's solicitor contacted his opposite number to state that the contract was conditional upon the vendor furnishing office copies from the Land Registry, to show that the vendor was the registered proprietor of the property and that this condition be attached to the contract. Thereafter, this occurred and contracts were exchanged and the office copies did, indeed, reveal the vendor to be the proprietor. Owing largely to the threat of the onset of the first Gulf War, an area where the purchaser did much of his business, he then repented of the contract and refused to complete, arguing that there was no contract. It was contended that section 2 had not been complied with because the term relating to the office copies had not properly been incorporated into the contract. Although Judge Baker Q.C. accepted that the term relating to office copies had not, validly, been

---

[71] *North v. Loomes* [1919] 1 Ch. 378 (payment of legal fees).

[72] *Martin v. Pycroft* (1852) De G.M. & G. 785; *Vouillon v. States* (1856) 25 L.J. Ch. 875; *Scott v. Bradley* [1971] Ch. 850, declining to follow *Burgess v. Cox* [1951] Ch. 383.

[73] *Hawkins v. Price* [1947] Ch. 645; *Heron Garage Properties Ltd v. Moss* [1974] 1 All E.R. 1096; *Tweddell v. Henderson* [1975] 2 All E.R. 1096.

[74] See *Dolphin Quays Development Ltd v. Mills* [2006] EWHC 931(Ch.).

[75] [1991] 4 All E.R. 471. See M. Harwood [1991] Conv. 472.

incorporated into the contract, he nevertheless held it to be enforceable. He did so on the basis that the supply of office copies was a warranty as to title, collateral to the main contract, the consideration for which was entry into the main contract by exchange. On this basis, the contract was held to be enforceable.

The terms of what was held to be a collateral contract had, in this case, been performed. The importance of this was stressed in *Tootal Clothing Ltd v. Guinea Properties Ltd*.[76] A contract for the grant of a lease stated that 'this agreement sets out the entire agreement between the parties'. This was not actually true. It had also been agreed that the landlord would contribute to the cost of shop-fitting works which, it had been agreed, would be carried out by the tenant. This clause was not included in the draft contract. After the lease had been granted, and the tenant had carried out the shop-fitting work, the landlord refused to pay his agreed contribution arguing that, because of section 2, there was no contractual obligation to do this. The argument was rejected. First, it was held that section 2 applied only to executory contracts. Where, as in this case, the contract had been completed by the execution of the lease, the section ceased to be applicable. It was further stated, *obiter*, that even had this not been the case, the agreement would have been enforceable as the agreement regarding the shop-fitting was collateral to the main contract for the lease and, as it was not itself a land contract, need not satisfy the requirements of section 2.[77] This is a conclusion that the courts are likely to favour, if the alternative is to allow one of the parties to disown an apparent contract.[78]

Rectification

In these two cases, there was a degree of separateness between the main agreement and the omitted term which enabled the court, in each case, to regard the clause in question to be a separate collateral contract. In other cases, such a finding may be inappropriate, which leaves the question remaining as to the position when such a clause is not included in the written contract. This occurred in *Wright v. Robert Leonard Developments Ltd*.[79] The case concerned the sale of a show flat, which was fully furnished with carpets, curtains, furniture, and appliances. Prior to exchange of contracts, agreement had been reached on a schedule of items to be included in the sale and that the purchase price for the flat should reflect this. Contracts were then exchanged but the contract made no reference to this schedule. The vendor then proceeded to remove various items and an action was brought for damages. The defence was based upon section 2 of the Act, it being argued that there was no contract because the writing did not include all the terms expressly agreed by the parties. The Court of Appeal found for the purchaser.

---

[76] (1992) 64 P. & C.R. 452. For critical comment, see P. Luther [1993] Conv. 89. See also *Grossman v. Hooper* [2001] 3 E.G.L.R. 662 at 671 *per* Sir Christopher Staughton where, on the facts, the part of the agreement which was not in writing was obviously separate from the land contract.

[77] Ibid. at 456 *per* Scott L.J. This seemed also to be the case with the separate contract for chattels in *Record v. Bell* [1991] 4 All E.R. 471. See also *Lotteryking Ltd v. A.M.E.C. Properties Ltd* [1995] 2 E.G.L.R. 13.

[78] See *North Eastern Properties Ltd v. Coleman* [2010] EWCA Civ. 237.

[79] [1994] E.G.C.S. 69. See M.P. Thompson [1995] Conv. 484.

In reaching this conclusion, it was held that recourse could not be had to the argument that the agreement as to the contents of the flat amounted to a separate collateral contract. Instead, it was seen as being an integral part of the contract for the sale of the flat. It was held, however, that there was convincing proof that this term had been agreed upon by the parties.[80] Owing to the nature of the evidence, the court was satisfied that a case for rectification of the document had been established so the contract, as rectified, was enforced.[81]

The case is important and demonstrates, somewhat paradoxically, that the law may have become less stringent in respect of the consequences of omitted terms than was previously the case. Under the old law, unless the term omitted was for the exclusive benefit of one of the contracting parties, then its omission from the memorandum was fatal to a claim that the contract was enforceable. Where rectification is in issue, however, as is demonstrated by *Wright v. Robert Leonard Developments Ltd*, it is immaterial whether or not the missing term benefits both parties to the contract. The issue is whether the case for rectification has been made out.

The proof sufficient to establish a case for rectification does, however, present a problem. A case may occur where there is a dispute between the parties as to whether a term which is not in writing has been agreed between them. The potential problem is if, on the balance of probabilities, it is found that there was such an agreement. The difficulty is that, for a case for rectification to be made out, the court normally requires convincing proof that the document does not accurately reflect the terms of the agreement which has been reached,[82] which seems to be a higher standard than mere proof on the balance of probabilities. If this is right, a judge could be left with the position that the proof is insufficiently strong to order the rectification of the contract, yet sufficiently strong to establish that the written contract does not contain all the terms expressly agreed between the parties; a position which should lead to the finding that there is no contract. It is suggested that this outcome is likely to be avoided by a finding that the evidence is insufficient to satisfy the court that the written contract does not accurately reflect the antecedent agreement and that the contract, as written, will be enforced.

For rectification to be available, what must be established is that, by a mistake, the document does not accurately record what has been agreed between the parties. If a term which has been agreed upon is deliberately not included in the relevant document, rectification will not be available, with the result that there will be found to be no contract.[83] Where the parties have used a standard form contract, which states that the agreement contains the entire agreement between the parties,[84] then a court

---

[80] See *Josceleyne v. Nissen* [1970] 2 Q.B. 86.

[81] Law of Property (Miscellaneous Provisions) Act 1989, s. 2(4).

[82] *Josceleyne v. Nissan* [1970] 2 Q.B. 86 at 98 *per* Russell L.J.

[83] See *Oun v. Ahmed* [2008] EWHC 545(Ch.) 54 at [41]–[55] *per* Morgan J; *Francis v. F. Berndes Ltd* [2011] EWHC 337 (Ch) at [37]–[44] *per* Henderson J.

[84] National Conditions of Sale (4th edn) 16.3.

is likely to hold any separately agreed term to be part of a collateral agreement, and unaffected by section 2.[85]

Implied terms

Section 2 of the Act requires only that terms expressly agreed between the parties need be in writing. The fact that a term which the law would imply, such as that vacant possession is to be given upon completion, is not in writing will not, of itself, cause a failure to comply with the section.[86]

Signature

Unlike section 40 of the Law of Property Act 1925, section 2 of the 1989 Act requires the document to be signed by both parties to the contract. This means that it is no longer possible for a contract to be enforceable by only one of the parties to it.

In the past, the courts were prepared to adopt a liberal approach as to what constituted a signature. The view was taken that this did not entail the writing of a person's forename and surname. Any mark which identified it as the act of the parties was considered to be sufficient.[87] Consistent with this view, a facsimile of a signature on a rubber stamp has been held to suffice.[88] Similarly, a memorandum which commenced with the words, 'I James Crockford, agree...'[89] was also held to be a valid signature.

Despite the fact that the Law Commission, when reviewing the law relating to formalities relating to contracts for the sale of land, gave no indication of dissatisfaction with the existing law as to what constitutes a signature, the Court of Appeal in *Firstpost Homes Ltd v. Johnson*[90] considered that the enactment of a new statutory provision meant that a new start should be made in determining what should, for the purposes of that provision, amount in law to a signature. The notion that the printing or signing of the name of an addressee in a letter could constitute a signature by the addressee was rejected as being an artificial use of language.[91] Instead, the view was expressed that it would be wrong to encumber the construction of the new Act with the ancient baggage of old case law which had given an extended meaning to the word signature. The meaning of this word should, in the future, correspond to the meaning of the word which the ordinary man would understand it to have.[92]

Manifestly, therefore, what the courts are prepared to countenance as a signature will be much narrower than in the past and so the previous authorities will be of very limited guidance. The requirement that both parties sign the agreement for it to have

---

[85] *North Eastern Properties Ltd v. Coleman* [2010] EWCA Civ. 237.

[86] *Farrell v. Green* (1974) 232 E.G. 587. This point could also have provided a possible solution to the problem in *Record v. Bell* [1991] 4 All E.R. 471.

[87] *Moreland v. Copeland* (1855) 1 C.B. 517 at 535 *per* Maule J.

[88] *Goodman v. J. Eban Ltd* [1954] 1 Q.B. 550.   [89] *Knight v. Crockford* (1794) 1 Esp. 190.

[90] [1995] 1 W.L.R. 1567.   [91] Ibid. at 1575 *per* Peter Gibson L.J.

[92] Ibid. at 1756 *per* Peter Gibson and Hutchison L.J.J.; at 1757 *per* Balcombe L.J.

any contractual effect should mean, however, that it should be only in rare cases that there should be doubt as to this matter.[93]

Agents

Section 2(3) of the Act requires the document to be signed 'by or on behalf of each party to the contract'. With regard to the latter aspect of this, it is clear that the contract may be signed by the agent of a contracting party. Authority to act as an agent need not, itself, be in writing.[94] Where there are more than two parties to a contract, one agent, if authorized to do so, may sign on behalf of all the contracting parties,[95] but one party to the contract cannot sign on behalf of the other party, as to allow this may facilitate fraud.[96] It used to be the case that an auctioneer had authority to sign on behalf of both parties,[97] but as such contracts need not comply with the requirements of section 2, the point is now academic. Neither solicitors nor estate agents have the authority, purely by virtue of their office, to sign on behalf of their clients.[98] For their signatures to bind the principal, there must be actual authority for them to do so.[99]

Variation

In order to effect a variation of a contract, it is necessary for the variation itself to satisfy the requirements of section 2.[100] In *McCausland v. Duncan Lawrie Ltd*,[101] the contract stated the date of completion to be 26 March 1995 and, when it was realized that that was a Sunday, an exchange of letters ensued agreeing a change of date to 24 March. Because the exchange of letters did not comply with section 2,[102] this intended variation was ineffectual.[103] The effect of this was that the parties were bound by the original agreement. To vary an existing contract, it is necessary that either both parties sign the same document which effects the variation or exchange

---

[93] Although see *Jelson Ltd v. Derby City Council* [1999] 3 E.G.L.R. 91, criticized in Agreements to contract, p. 192.

[94] *Heard v. Pilley* (1869) 4 Ch. App. 548; *McLaughlin v. Duffill* [2008] EWCA Civ. 1627.

[95] *Gavaghan v. Edwards* [1961] 2 Q.B. 220.

[96] *Sharman v. Brandt* (1871) L.R. 6 Q.B. 720. One co-purchaser may sign on behalf of the co-purchasers but only if authorized so to do. Cf. *Enfield London Borough Council v. Arajah* [1995] E.G.C.S. 164, where one of three co-purchasers who did sign had no authority to sign for the others, with the result that there was no contract.

[97] *Emerson v. Heelis* (1809) 2 Taunt. 38 at 48 *per* Lord Mansfield C.J.; *Leman v. Stocks* [1951] Ch. 941.

[98] *Wragg v. Lovett* [1948] 2 All E.R. 968 at 969 *per* Lord Greene M.R. (estate agents); *Smith v. Webster* (1876) 3 Ch.D. 49 (solicitors); *James v. Evans* [2000] 3 E.G.L.R. 1 at 4 *per* Wright J. Cf. *Hooper v. Sherman* [1994] N.P.C. 153, where this point was not pleaded and leave to amend was refused.

[99] See *McLaughlin v. Duffill* [2008] EWCA Civ. 1627.

[100] See *Record v. Bell* [1991] 4 All E.R. 471 at 477 *per* Judge Baker Q.C. The same is, apparently, not so in the case of the variation of a mortgage. See *Target Holdings Ltd v. Priestley* (1999) 79 P. & C.R. 305, criticized by M.P. Thompson [1999] Conv. 414.

[101] [1997] 1 W.L.R. 38. See M.P. Thompson [1996] Conv. 366.

[102] See Contracts by correspondence, pp. 201–202.

[103] See also *Morris v. Baron & Co.* [1918] A.C. 1.

identical letters to this effect; something which is likely, in practice, to be very easy to overlook.

The only exception to the principle that a contract can only be varied by writing which, itself, satisfies section 2 is where the purported oral variation is so substantial that it amounts to a wholly new agreement. In such circumstances, the original contract is rescinded.[104]

Joinder and exchange

Under the previous statutory regime, a memorandum could be pieced together by joining together various documents, a process known as joinder. The principle upon which the courts acted was spelled out in *Timmins v. Moreland Street Properties Ltd*,[105] as being:

'...there should be a document signed by the party to be charged which, while not containing in itself all the necessary ingredients of the required memorandum, does contain some reference, express or implied, to some other document or transaction. Where any such reference can be spelt out of a document so signed, then parole evidence can be given to identify the other document referred to, or as the case may be, to explain the other transaction, and to identify the document relating to it.'

What this passage meant was that one started with a document signed by the defendant. If that document referred to another document, then the two documents could be read together and, if together, they satisfied section 40, then the contract would be enforceable. It was immaterial that neither document, individually, would have complied with the statutory provision.

It is abundantly clear that the Law Commission was perfectly happy to retain that aspect of the law[106] and that the draft Bill appended to the Report would have done so. Unfortunately, and for no articulated reason, the Bill presented to Parliament, and subsequently enacted, is significantly different from the Law Commission Bill,[107] with the result that the Commission's intention in this regard has been thwarted.

It will be recalled that section 2(1) requires that the agreed terms of the contract be contained in one document or, where contracts are exchanged, in each. Provision is made for joinder of documents but only where the document signed by both parties, itself, refers to some other document.[108] Where contracts are exchanged, one of the

---

[104] *British & Benningtons Ltd v. N.W. Cachar Tea Co. Ltd* [1923] A.C. 48 at 68. For doubts, see Harpum, Bridge, and Dixon, *Megarry and Wade's Law of Real Property* (7th edn) (London: Sweet & Maxwell, 2008), 638.

[105] [1958] Ch. 110 at 130 *per* Jenkins L.J. See also *Elias v. George Sahely & Co. (Barbados) Ltd* [1983] 1 A.C. 646.

[106] (1987) Law Com. No. 164, para. 4.6.

[107] Comment was made on this during Parliamentary debate, but no explanation for the change was forthcoming: see H.L. vol. 503, col. 503.

[108] For examples of this, see *Jones v. Forest Fencing* Ltd [2001] EWCA Civ. 1700; *Courtney v. Corp Ltd* [2006] EWCA Civ. 518.

documents incorporating the terms (but not necessarily the same one) must be signed by or on behalf of each party.[109] To appreciate the effect of this provision some explanation of the practice of exchange of contracts is necessary.

Exchange of contracts

In conveyancing practice, the normal method of forming a contract of sale is to engage in a process termed exchange of contracts. What this entails is that each party is given a standard form contract[110] which contains numerous conditions that regularly apply to a land contract. The details particular to the individual transaction, such as the price, the date of completion, and any other terms agreed upon are then filled in. Each party then signs the contract. When the parties are ready to bring the contract into being, the two parts are exchanged,[111] those two parts being identical.[112] The purchaser then has a contract signed by the vendor and the vendor has an identical document signed by the purchaser. The main purpose of this method of formation of contracts of sale is to allow related transactions to be synchronized. If A is selling his house to B and buying a house from C, it is important that the two contracts are entered into simultaneously. Exchange of contracts facilitates this, enabling A, by the process of exchange, to form the relevant contract with B and C at the same time. This practice is then catered for by the Act, which also allows joinder of documents to take place. The most usual situation where this will occur is when the contracts exchanged refer to an agreed schedule of items to be included in the sale.

Contracts by correspondence

Under the old law, a memorandum need not take any particular form and could be created by an exchange of letters. An important issue which has since arisen is whether it is any longer possible to create a contract in this way. The point first arose in *Hooper v. Sherman*,[113] where, following a matrimonial dispute, an agreement relating to a matrimonial home was confirmed by an exchange of letters. One of the issues that then arose was as to whether there was a contract between the parties.

Under the old law there would not have been a problem, as the two letters could have been read together and they would have constituted a memorandum sufficient to satisfy the statutory requirement as to formality. The majority of the Court of Appeal in the present case held that, as each side was in possession of a document signed on behalf of the other, section 2 was satisfied and a contract existed.

In reaching this conclusion, the majority relied upon two concessions made by counsel. These were that the term 'exchange of contracts' is not a term of art and that the Act had implemented the Law Commission's proposal that the possibility of entering

---

[109] Law of Property (Miscellaneous Provisions) Act 1989, s. 2(2)(3).
[110] Currently the Standard Conditions of Sale (5th edn).
[111] See *Eccles v. Bryant* [1948] Ch. 93; *Shafiq v. Shah* [2004] EWHC 1913 (Ch.) at [15]–[17] *per* Judge Rich. See, generally, Thompson, op. cit., 219–227.
[112] *Harrison v. Battye* [1975] 1 W.L.R. 58.
[113] [1994] N.P.C. 153. See M.P. Thompson [1995] Conv. 319.

into a contract by correspondence should be retained. In *Commissioner for New Towns v. Cooper (Great Britain) Ltd*,[114] one of the issues in a complex factual dispute was whether or not a contract for the sale of land had been entered into by an exchange of faxes, these faxes amounting to an offer and acceptance. A differently constituted Court of Appeal, declining to follow *Hooper v. Sherman*, held that it had not.

On this occasion, what had been conceded in the earlier decision was contested and both concessions were regarded as having been wrongly made. It was held, first, that the process of exchange of contracts does have a technical meaning; for conveyancers it has always meant the swapping of identical documents. Once this, entirely orthodox, view had been taken then, on the wording of the Act, the inevitable conclusion followed that an exchange of letters, one containing an offer and the other the acceptance, cannot amount to a contract because there does not exist one document containing all the agreed terms which has been signed by both parties. As *Hooper v. Sherman* had been decided upon the basis of concessions, the Court of Appeal was free to depart from its earlier decision.[115]

The decision in *Cooper* seems, on the wording of the Act, to be entirely correct but is extremely unfortunate. First, it is now extremely difficult to see a realistic situation where a contract, to which section 2 applies, can ever be created by correspondence; quite simply it is difficult to envisage a letter being signed by both parties. Yet, it was never intended to preclude the making of contracts by correspondence. Perhaps more serious, however, is that an existing contract cannot now be varied by correspondence. This was the position in *McCausland v. Duncan Lawrie Ltd*,[116] where correspondence agreeing to change the date of completion did not have that effect because the correspondence did not, itself, satisfy the requirements of section 2. This represents a considerable trap, as the need for a minor variation to be effected either by a document signed by both parties, or an exchange of identical letters, is very easy to overlook. Had the original draft Bill not, for some unexplained reason, been altered, this position would have been avoided.

FAILED CONTRACTS

Under the previous statutory regime, the sanction for non-compliance with the formal requirements imposed by section 40(1) of the Law of Property Act 1925 was that the oral contract between the parties was unenforceable. It was not void. What this meant was that, while an action could not be brought upon the contract, there was no bar to its being used as a defence. So, in *Monnickendam v. Leanse*,[117] a purchaser had paid a 10 per cent deposit under an oral contract for the sale of land. Later, relying on

---

[114] [1995] Ch. 295. See also *Ruddick v. Ormston* [2005] EWHC 2547 (Ch.).
[115] See *Joscelyne v. Nissen* [1970] Q.B. 86 at 99 *per* Russell L.J.   [116] [1997] 1 W.L.R. 38.
[117] (1923) 39 T.L.R. 445.

the fact that the contract was oral, he refused to complete and sued for the return of his deposit. This action failed because the vendor was allowed to use the existence of the oral contract as a defence to an action for restitution. Such a result has also occurred under the new law. In *Sharma v. Simposh Ltd*[118]an oral agreement was entered into whereby the claimants had been given an option to purchase property which was then under construction. It was agreed that a deposit would be paid, and that the defendant developers would continue with the construction and remove the property from the market. They did this. When the property market collapsed, the claimants withdrew from the agreement and sought the return of their deposit. This action failed. While recognizing that, because the agreement was oral and, therefore, non-contractual, the Court of Appeal refused the claim to restitution. This was because the oral agreement had been executed and, consequently, there had not been a total failure of consideration. The defendants had done what had been agreed and this was sufficient to defeat the restitutionary action. In cases concerning a simple payment of a deposit under an oral agreement, however, it will normally be the case that the putative purchaser will be able to recover the money which has been paid.

As well as an oral contract being able to provide a defence to an action, circumstances could exist where it was considered to be unfair to allow a defendant to rely on the lack of writing to resist an action brought upon an oral contract. Acting on the principle that equity will not allow a statute to be used as an instrument of fraud, the doctrine of part performance was developed. Under this doctrine, if one party to an oral contract had acted in reliance on that contract being enforceable, in circumstances where it would be inequitable for the other party to deny liability on it, then, notwithstanding the lack of writing, the court would enforce the contract.

The doctrine, which was available to both vendor and purchaser, had become beset with various uncertainties and difficulties. The existence of these problems was one of the reasons why the Law Commission felt that a legislative recasting of the law was appropriate. Unfortunately the method of reform employed has introduced new difficulties in situations where an agreement fails to satisfy the formal requirements introduced by section 2 of the Law of Property (Miscellaneous Provisions) Act 1989.[119]

The abolition of part performance

As noted previously, the effect of section 2 of the Act is, of necessity, to abolish the doctrine of part performance. As there is no longer any such thing as an oral contract for the sale of land, there cannot be part performance of it. As a doctrine, '[i]t is quite clear that it has not survived'.[120] The question which remains is what the position is

---

[118] [2011] EWCA Civ. 1383.

[119] See L. Bentley and P. Coghlan (1990) 10 L.S. 325; C. Davis (1993) 13 O.J.L.S. 99; B. McFarlane [2005] Conv. 501.

[120] *Yaxley v. Gotts* [2000] 1 All E.R. 711 at 717 *per* Robert Walker L.J. See also *Cobbe v. Yeoman's Row Management Ltd* [2005] EWHC 266 (Ch) at [41] *per* Etheridge J. The ultimate reversal of this decision in *Yeoman's Row Management Ltd v. Cobbe* [2008] UKHL 1139 does not affect this point.

when either party to an oral agreement performs what, in the past, would have been regarded as a sufficient act of part performance to make that agreement enforceable.

Estoppel

When advocating reform, the Law Commission was, of course, perfectly well aware that the enactment of its proposal would lead to the abolition of the doctrine of part performance. Consideration was given to the situation where the parties behaved as if there was a binding contract between them, only to discover, subsequently, that this was not the case, and then one party refused to give effect to their non-contractual agreement. In such circumstances, the Commission was clear that the doctrine of estoppel should then be applicable.[121] So, too, was the Lord Chancellor, when introducing the proposed legislation.[122] Unfortunately, the way that this was implemented was the entirely inapt and unnecessary section 2(5) of the Act,[123] which provides that 'nothing in this section affects the creation or operation of resulting, implied or constructive trusts', with the result that the extent to which the doctrine of estoppel may operate to modify or counteract the effect of section 2 has been described as 'a difficult topic'.[124]

The reason why this subsection is described as inapt and unnecessary will be explained shortly. First, one can look at how the courts have approached the situation where, unfortunately, a relatively clear and acceptable position was thrown into considerable doubt by an ill-considered *dictum* in the House of Lords.

At first, the judiciary seemed to be reluctant to accept that estoppel would be relevant to this type of situation. The perceived difficulty was that, to allow a claimant to have rights arising out of estoppel, when a contract had not been created because of a lack of formality, would be wrong. This was because to do so would undermine the social policy underlying the legislation, that policy being to insist that contracts for the sale of land are made in writing.[125] So, initially, the courts were unprepared to countenance an argument that a party may be estopped by convention from relying on the lack of formality as required by the Act.[126] The matter appeared to have been laid to rest, however, in the leading case of *Yaxley v. Gotts*.[127]

---

[121] (1987) Law Com. No. 164, paras. 5.4–5.5.

[122] See H.L. vol. 503, col. 610 *per* Lord Mackay of Clashfern L.C.

[123] For a similar argument, see G. Owen and O. Rees [2011] Conv. 495.

[124] *Sharma v. Simposh Ltd* [2011] EWCA Civ. 1383 at [[56] *per* Toulson L.J.

[125] On the importance of not undermining the policy of a statute, see *Kok Hoong v. Long Cheong Mines Ltd* [1964] A.C. 993 at 1016 *per* Viscount Radcliffe. The comments made in this case, however, were set against the entirely different context of the regulation of money-lending contracts. See *Shah v. Shah* [2002] Q.B. 35 at 42–47 *per* Pill L.J. The *dicta* in the Privy Council are the basis for the cautious treatment of this issue in Goff and Jones, *The Law of Restitution* (5th edn) (London: Sweet &. Maxwell, 1998), 550. Although, see now (7th edn) (London: Sweet & Maxwell, 2007), 578–580.

[126] See *Godden v. Merthyr Tydfil Housing Association* (1997) 74 P. & C.R.D. 1. For a supposed example of estoppel by convention, see *Amalgamated Investments Ltd v. Texas Commerce International Bank Ltd* [1982] Q.B. 84, discussed by M.P. Thompson [1983] C.L.J. 259 at 273–274.

[127] [2000] 1 All E.R. 711. See R.J. Smith (2000) 116 L.Q.R. 22; M.P. Thompson [2000] Conv. 245. See also *Scottish & Newcastle Plc v. Mortgage Corporation Ltd* [2007] EWCA Civ. 684 at [49]–[55] *per* Mummery L.J.

Estoppel and constructive trusts

The claimant had orally agreed with the defendant's father that, if the latter bought a house, then, provided that he, the claimant, did a substantial amount of building work and acted as the managing agent for the entire property, he would have the ground-floor flats. The property was, in fact, bought by the son of the person with whom the claimant had made this agreement, and the son, who was the defendant in these proceedings, was registered as the proprietor with an absolute title. The claimant, who was unaware for quite some time that it was the son who had bought the property, proceeded to do work to the value of about £9,000. When the defendant sought to evict the claimant from the ground-floor flats, which he occupied, the claimant asserted that he had an interest in the property. The Court of Appeal held that he was entitled to a ninety-year lease of the ground floor, free from any ground rent.

In reaching this conclusion, it was agreed that the original agreement was of no legal effect, because it did not comply with section 2 of the Act. While it was true that the original agreement was oral, this, however, did not appear to be the main problem in establishing the existence of a contract. Rather, the problem appeared to be that the original agreement was with the defendant's father and not the actual defendant, who was never a party to any agreement with the claimant. It is difficult to see, therefore, why section 2 was ever considered to be relevant to the dispute.[128] Be that as it may, the Court of Appeal did consider what rights the claimant had acquired in equity, he having performed an act in accordance with an oral agreement to buy land.

In dealing with this matter, there was some difference in approach shown by the different members of the court. Robert Walker L.J., impressed by the argument that equitable principles should not be allowed to undermine the policy embraced by the Act, felt able to decide for the claimant by the imposition of a constructive trust, the principles of which, he felt, in the present context, were essentially the same as those underlying proprietary, or equitable estoppel.[129] Beldam L.J., however, took a more expansive approach. For him, the clear policy enunciated by the Law Commission[130] was that, in cases where an agreement had been reached, but the formal requirements of the Act had not been met, the principles of estoppel should operate. While, in his opinion, the facts of a particular case could justify the imposition of a constructive trust, estoppel is a more flexible doctrine, and he could see no reason why the principles on which estoppel is based should not, generally, be applicable.[131]

---

[128] At first instance, the trial judge had, for this reason, decided the case without reference to the inter-relationship between section 2 of the Act and estoppel. See Thompson, loc. cit., at 247–248.

[129] [2000] 1 All E.R. 711 at 717–721. For his subsequent misgivings as to equating the two concepts, however, see *Stack v. Dowden* [2007] 1 All E.R. 929 at [36]. See Differences between the concepts, pp. 352–353.

[130] Beldam L.J. was the Chairman of the Law Commission when its Report which led to the passing of the Act was published. This was a fact which was considered to be important in *Whittaker v. Kinnear* [2011] EWHC. 1479 (QB) at [29] *per* Bean J.

[131] See [2000] 1 All .E.R. 711 at 735. Clarke L.J. agreed with Beldam L.J.'s approach to the application of estoppel principles: ibid. at 726.

Estoppel and trusts

Although the two approaches differ, the same result was achieved, which might indicate that there is no real difference between them. On a theoretical level, however, this is not so. Because section 2(5) of the Act refers to the section not affecting the creation of resulting, implied, or constructive trusts, it is entirely understandable that the judiciary should seek to employ the constructive trust to arrive at a solution in cases such as *Yaxley v. Gotts*.[132] Nevertheless, it is inapposite.[133] This is because the section is relevant to the creation of contracts, not trusts. The second objection relates to the actual nature of the trust itself.[134]

A trust, be it express, resulting, or constructive, entails that the trustee holds property on behalf of the beneficiary. The normal conception is that the trustee is the legal owner of the property, and the beneficiary is the equitable owner of it.[135] If the contract is to purchase a freehold property, then the use of a constructive trust to circumvent section 2 of the Act is perfectly intelligible: the result is that the vendor holds the land on trust for the purchaser. If, however, the oral agreement is to create an easement,[136] then it is difficult to see how, on orthodox principles, the prospective purchaser could, through the medium of a constructive trust, acquire such a right, whereas there is no such difficulty in such a result occurring in an estoppel case.[137] The better view is, therefore, that cases such as *Yaxley v. Gotts* should be decided on the basis of estoppel, and this appeared to be happening.[138] Unfortunately, considerable doubt has been caused in this important area by a somewhat extraordinary *dictum* in *Yeoman's Row Management Ltd v. Cobbe*.[139]

In this case, the claimant was a property developer. He agreed with the defendant that he would, at his own expense, apply for planning permission for the demolition of an existing property owned by the defendant and the erection of terraced houses in its place. Once planning permission had been granted, the parties agreed that they would enter into a second agreement, whereby he would purchase the site for £12 million, and would be entitled to fifty per cent of the gross proceeds of sale of the new houses if the sales of them realized more than £24 million. A number of terms of this agreement were, however, left outstanding. After the claimant had spent a considerable amount of time and money in obtaining the requisite planning permission, the defendant

---

[132] The same observations are applicable also to the approach taken in *Kinane v. Mackie-Conteh* [2005] EWCA Civ. 45 and *Kilkane Holdings Ltd v. Targetfellow (Birmingham) Ltd* [2004] EWHC 2547 (Ch.) at [203] *per* Lewison J, affirmed at [2005] EWCA Civ. 1355.

[133] See in particular, *Brightlingsea Haven Ltd v. Morris* [2008] EWHC 1928 (Ch.) at [44]–[55] *per* Jack J.

[134] See *Cobbe v. Yeoman's Row Management Ltd* [2005] EWHC 266 (Ch.) at [50]–[51] and [233], reversed without reference to this issue: *Yeoman's Row Management Ltd v. Cobbe* [2008] EWHL 1139. See also McFarlane, loc. cit., at 516–520.

[135] See *Paragon Finance plc v. Thakerer* [1999] 1 All E.R. 400 at 408–409 *per* Millett L.J.

[136] A similar difficulty would seem to arise if the agreement is to create a lease.

[137] See *E.R. Ives Investments Ltd v. High* [1967] 2 Q.B. 379; *Crabb v. Arun District Council* [1976] Ch. 179; *Mayor of the London Borough of Bexley v. Maison Maurice Ltd* [2006] EWHC 3192 (Ch.).

[138] See *Lloyd v. Sutcliffe* [2007] EWCA Civ. 153; *Smee v. Smee* [2007] 1 F.L.R. 1123. See, also, *Oates v. Stimson* [2006[EWCA Civ. 548.

[139] [2008] EWHL 1139.

refused to implement what had been agreed. The developer then claimed to be entitled to a charge on the property to reflect its increased value, which had been derived from the obtaining of planning permission, the basis of this claim being estoppel. Although this claim succeeded at first instance, and in the Court of Appeal,[140] it failed in the House of Lords, where it was held that he was entitled to a sum to compensate him for the value of his work, that valuation being assessed on a *quantum meruit* basis, but not to any interest in the property. Any more expansive claim, based upon either a constructive trust, or estoppel, failed.

In considering the claim that a constructive trust should be imposed, Lord Scott of Foscote, while conceding that it is impossible to prescribe exhaustively the circumstances sufficient to create a constructive trust,[141] nevertheless focused on a line of authority which he considered to be typical.[142] The type of case which he had in mind was one where two parties, A and B, agree on a joint venture to acquire property but, for some reason, it is transferred into the sole name of A. In these circumstances, it may be fraudulent for A subsequently to deny the agreement, and a constructive trust is imposed to give effect to it. This was inapplicable in the present case, as the defendant had already acquired the property in question before there was any sort of agreement or understanding between the parties.[143]

The claimant also argued that he had acquired rights over the defendant's land through the medium of estoppel. This, too, failed. Although Lord Scott, in reaching this conclusion, embarked on an unduly narrow analysis of the principles underlying this doctrine,[144] the real weakness in the argument was highlighted by Lord Walker of Gestingthorpe. This was that both the claimant and the defendant were experienced practitioners in property matters and knew perfectly well that they had not reached a position where either side was bound in any way other than in honour.[145] Consequently, when the claimant spent time and money pursuing the application for planning permission, he did so in the knowledge that that expenditure may turn out to be wasted, and that there might be no final contract. In these circumstances, no rights could be obtained through estoppel.

Estoppel and section 2

In *Yeoman's Row Management Ltd v. Cobbe*, the arguments based on either estoppel or a constructive trust, failed. As there was no concluded oral agreement for the sale of land, section 2 was not relevant. This was recognized in terms by Lord Walker who,

---

[140] [2005] EWHC 266 (Ch.); [2006] EWCA Civ. 1139. Contrast the cautious reaction to this in *BBS Fashion Merchandising v. Urban Regeneration* [2006] EWHAC 2754 (Ch.) at [65] *per* Judge Williams Q.C.

[141] [2008] EWHL 55 at [30].

[142] The main authorities, not all of which were cited in the present case, are: *Chattock v. Muller* (1878) 8 Ch.D. 117; *Pallant v. Morgan* [1953] Ch. 43; *Holliday Inns Inc. v. Broadhead* (1974) 232 E.G. 951; *Banner Homes Groups plc v. Luff Developments Ltd* [2000] 2 All E.R. 117, and *London & Regional Investments Ltd v. TBI Plc* [2002] EWCA Civ. 355. See also *Samad v. Thompson* [2008] EWHC 2809 (Ch). See M.P. Thompson [2000] Conv. 265; N. Hopkins [2001] Conv. 35.

[143] See [2008] EWHL 55 at [31]–[34].   [144] See A stringent test of certainty, pp. 611–612.

[145] [2008] EWHL 55 at [71].

somewhat surprisingly given that he was a party to the decision in *Yaxley v. Gotts*,[146] said: 'I do not think it is necessary or appropriate to consider the issue on section 2 of the Law of Property (Miscellaneous Provisions) Act 1989.'[147] Lord Scott, on the other hand, while explicitly recognizing that, because the parties had not concluded an oral agreement, the section was not relevant, expressed his views on the applicability of estoppel in a forthright manner. He said:

'Section 2 of the 1989 Act *declares to be void any agreement for the acquisition of an interest in land that does not comply with the requisite formalities prescribed by the section.* Subsection (5) expressly makes an exception for resulting, implied or constructive trusts. These may validly come into existence without compliance with the prescribed formalities. Proprietary estoppel does not have the benefit of this exception. The question arises, therefore, whether a complete agreement for the acquisition of an interest in land that does not comply with the section 2 formalities, but would become specifically enforceable if it did, can become enforceable via the route of proprietary estoppel.... *My present view ... is that proprietary estoppel cannot be prayed in aid in order to render enforceable an agreement that statute has declared to be void.* The proposition that an owner of land can be estopped from asserting that an agreement is void for want of compliance with section 2 is, in my opinion, unacceptable. The assertion is no more than the statute provides. Equity can surely not contradict a statute.'[148]

It should be stressed that this passage is, as Lord Scott himself expressly recognized, entirely *obiter*. Moreover, while it is manifestly of high authority,[149] it is submitted that it is wrong in principle and should not be followed. Subsequent cases have, in effect, followed this argument in allowing equitable intervention, despite an agreement failing to satisfy section 2, in circumstances where there has not been a joint venture to acquire property which is subsequently put into one person's name, which is the situation envisaged by Lord Scott as to when a constructive trust should be imposed.[150] The matter was addressed head on in *Whittaker v. Kinnear*.[151] Acknowledging the high authority of what was said in *Cobbe*, Bean J. commented that 'There is force in the dictum of Ungoed-Thomas J. in *Re Grosvenor Hotel (No. 2)*[152] that a battery of howitzers off the target is more impressive than a popgun on it; but also in the retort of Salmon L.J. in the same case that a battery of howitzers off target can cause a great deal of damage.'[153] He concluded that 'notwithstanding Lord Scott's dicta in *Cobbe*,

---

[146] [2000] 1 All E.R. 711.   [147] [2008] EWHL 55 at [93].

[148] [2008] EWHL 55 at [29]. Emphasis supplied.

[149] Lords Hoffmann and Mance simply agreed with the speech of Lord Scott. Perplexingly, Lord Brown of Eaton-Under-Heywood agreed with the speeches of both Lord Scott and Lord Walker, despite Lord Walker's speech being very different in tenor from that of Lord Scott.

[150] See *Brightlingsea Haven Ltd v. Morris* [2008] EWHC 1928 (Ch); *Herbert v. Doyle* [2010] EWCA Civ. 1095. See. also, *McGuane v. Welch* [2008] EWCA Civ. 785 at [37] *per* Mummery L.J., who regarded the matter as uncontroversial, although, admittedly, Lord Scott's views were not cited.

[151] [20011] EWHC 1479 (Ch) See also *Herbert v. Doyle* [2008] EWHC 1950 (Ch.) at [14] *per* Mr Michael Herbertt Q.C., affm'd on appeal at [2010] EWCA Civ. 1095.

[152] [1965] Ch. 1210.   [153] [2011] EWHC 1479 (QB) at [28].

proprietary estoppel in a case involving land has survived the enactment of s.2 of the 1989 Act.'[154]

To explore more fully the merits of this argument, as an initial observation, it is, to say the least, surprising that none of the authorities which have applied principles of estoppel to the type of situation envisaged by Lord Scott[155] are even mentioned. If this *dictum* was correct, and applied, it would seem that they have all been impliedly overruled. It is unusual for Court of Appeal authorities to be overruled *sub silentio*. Secondly, Lord Scott states that equity cannot contradict a statute. This, of course, is true. It is also true that there is a maxim of some antiquity that equity will not allow a statute to be used as an instrument of fraud. Indeed, so well established is that maxim, that there are instances of it being recognized by the very statute in question.[156] To put the matter in the way Lord Scott has done is to ignore this equitable jurisdiction.

Void agreements?

In the italicized part of the passage above, considerable emphasis is laid on the effect of the statute being to make an agreement for the acquisition of an interest in land void if the formal requirements of section 2 have not been met. Accepting for the moment that the effect of the Act is as stated, this is, of itself, not a fatal objection to the operation of estoppel. In *Kok Hoong v Long Cheong Mines Ltd*,[157] Viscount Radcliffe said that, 'On the other hand, there are statutes which, although declaring transactions to be unenforceable or void, are nevertheless not essentially prohibitory and so do not preclude estoppels.' The question as to whether estoppel can be allowed to circumvent a particular statute is determined by issues of public policy.[158] If the policy as to this issue is considered to be doubtful, then regard should be had to the Parliamentary debates,[159] where Lord Mackay L.C. simply said: 'I believe that there is nothing in this Bill to affect the operation of the doctrine of estoppel.'[160] To this, can be added the decision in the seminal case of *Taylors Fashions Ltd v. Liverpool Victoria Trustees Ltd*,[161] which was cited without any hint of disapproval by Lord Scott.[162] In this case, the issue was whether an option to renew a lease had, through the effect of estoppel, become enforceable against a purchaser of the freehold reversion. Although the action failed on the facts, there was no problem with the argument that estoppel could have had this effect. Yet the option itself had, through the explicit effect of the statute, been held to be void as against the purchaser.[163]

---

[154] Ibid at [30].   [155] See Estoppel and constructive trusts, p. 205.

[156] See Law of Property Act 1925, ss 40(2) (part performance) and 53(2) (resulting, implied, and constructive trusts).

[157] [1964] A.C. 993 at 1015.   [158] Ibid. at 1015–1019.   [159] See *Pepper v. Hart* [1993] A.C. 593.

[160] H.L. vol. 503, col. 610.   [161] [1982] Q.B. 133n.

[162] Intriguingly, Lord Scott, as Mr Richard Scott Q.C., had appeared as leading counsel for the plaintiff in this case.

[163] Land Charges Act 1925, s. 13(2). See now Land Charges Act 1972, s. 4(6).

Formation of contracts

As can be seen, therefore, the statement that the effect of non-compliance with section 2 of the Act is to make an agreement for the acquisition of an interest in land void should not, of itself, lead to the conclusion that the doctrine of estoppel should not be applicable. The section does not, however, operate in this way. Contrary to what is said by Lord Scott, it does not say that any such an agreement is void. What it does say is that 'a contract for the sale of land can only be made in writing...', so that to say that the 'relevant question is whether, subject to section 2 of the 1989 Act, there was a valid contract'[164] is wrong. The section does not impose a sanction for non-compliance with the statutory formalities by making invalid something which would otherwise be valid. What the section actually does is stipulate as to how a contract is to be formed. To say that a contract is void for a failure to comply with the requisite formalities is no different from saying that a contract is void for uncertainty, or for a lack of consideration.[165] In each case, this is merely a shorthand way of saying that no contract has been formed between the parties. In *Yeoman's Row Management* itself, there was no contract between the parties, not because the requirements of section 2 had not been met; it was, principally, because there had yet to be final agreement as to the terms of the second agreement. The parties were in a non-contractual arrangement. Any rights which are later acquired are acquired through the doctrine of estoppel, and, in principle, there is no objection to this. Precisely the same argument should apply in cases where there is a concluded agreement, but there is no contract because the formalities insisted upon by section 2 have not been met. If the agreement has been acted upon in circumstances when, ordinarily, an equity would be created under the doctrine of estoppel, it should also arise in this situation. It is not the case that rights are conferred on the parties *by that agreement*. The equity arises due to the reliance on a non-contractual expectation.[166]

Constructive trusts

Section 2(5) of the 1989 Act provides that 'nothing in this section affects the creation or operation of resulting, implied or constructive trusts'. As noted previously, this provision is inapt.[167] It is inapt, first, because the section does not regulate the creation of trusts; it regulates the creation of contracts. This leads to the second point that the formalities required for the creation of a trust of land are quite different from those required for the creation of a contract to acquire an interest in land. In the case of the former, all that is required is that the declaration of trust be manifested and proved by some writing signed by some person who is able to declare such trust.[168] An oral declaration of a trust of land is not invalid; it is unenforceable. This is the same position

---

[164] *Herbert v. Doyle* [2010] EWCA Civ. 1095 at [71] *per* Arden L.J.

[165] See M.P. Thompson [2000] Conv. 245 at 253–254.

[166] See, also, in the analogous case of part performance: *Maddison v. Alderson* (1883) 8 App. Cas. 467 at 475 *per* Lord Selborne L.C.

[167] See Estoppel and constructive trusts, p. 205.   [168] Law of Property Act 1925, s. 53(1)(b).

that pertained with regard to oral contracts for the sale of land prior to the passing of the 1989 Act.

This leads to the third point. If there is an oral declaration of trust and, as a result of the subsequent conduct of the parties, a constructive trust is imposed, the effect of the imposition of the trust is that the original oral declaration becomes enforceable.[169] In the case of a failed contract this is not necessarily the case. The equity which arises as a result of the subsequent conduct does not necessarily lead to the enforcement of what was agreed.[170] Moreover, as was pointed out by Lord Scott, this type of constructive trust normally arises when there is an agreement between the parties as to the ownership of property which is to be acquired.[171] The present context is quite different, involving a putative sale of property owned by one party to the dispute to the other. In short, it is difficult to see this type of constructive trust being relevant to the situation under discussion.

Conclusion

Despite what was said in *Yeoman's Row Management v. Cobbe*, it is submitted that when there is no contract in being as a result of non-compliance with section 2, it remains open, in an appropriate case, for a party who has acted upon an oral agreement to rely upon the doctrine of estoppel. This is also preferable to seeking to argue in favour of a constructive trust, and it is unfortunate that, as a result of poorly thought out draftsmanship, reference was made in the Act to the creation of trusts. It would have been better, albeit unnecessary, had section 2(5) referred to estoppel, rather than trusts.

Electronic conveyancing

This analysis is also relevant to another area where estoppel claims are likely to be generated. When Part 8 of the Land Registration Act 2002 is brought into force, most dispositions involving registered land will be required to be done electronically.[172] To this end, section 93 provides that:

'A disposition to which this section applies, or a contract to make such disposition, only has effect if it is made by means of a document in electronic form and, if when the document purports to take effect—

(a) it is communicated electronically to the registrar, and

(b) the relevant registration requirements are met.'

It is quite likely that there will be occasions when these requirements will not be met, but the parties act on the basis that their transaction had legal efficacy. The disponee

---

[169] See, for example, *Bannister v. Bannister* [1948] 2 All E.R. 133; *Grant v. Edwards* [1986] Ch. 638.

[170] See *Jennings v. Rice* [2003] 1 P. & C.R. 8 at [50] *per* Robert Walker L.J., and, Satisfaction of the expectation, pp. 629–638.

[171] See Estoppel and section 2, p. 207.   [172] See Electronic conveyancing, pp. 160–163.

is then likely to argue that rights have been acquired in estoppel. Provided that the normal requirements of an estoppel claim are satisfied, such a claim should, in principle, be successful. Much the same argument can be raised against such a claim as has been raised, with some success, in the context of section 2 of the 1989 Act. This is that Parliament has laid down how certain transactions are to be implemented and to allow rights to be acquired through estoppel when these statutory requirements have not been met would undermine the policy being implemented by the relevant provision.

Such an argument should be resisted. If, when section 93 of the 2002 Act is in force, a person purports to make a disposition by means other than that laid down by the Act, that purported disposition will be a nullity. If, however, the parties, believing what has been done to have been effective, substantially change their positions as a result of that belief, there is then no reason to deny that estoppel rights have arisen. The argument is not that, notwithstanding the section, the disposition is valid; it is that rights have arisen as a result of the subsequent conduct. The normal estoppel principles should apply.[173]

Application of estoppel

The principles of equitable estoppel will be considered fully elsewhere.[174] For present purposes, it is necessary to give an outline of those principles. Although the principles to be applied are the same when dealing with agreements which do not satisfy the requirements of section 2 of the Act, the context is different from the more frequently encountered estoppel cases, in that the parties are seeking to enter into a contractual arrangement, whereas in the generality of estoppel cases, this is not usually the case.

Acquisition of rights

Equitable, or proprietary, estoppel is a doctrine of some antiquity.[175] The central element of it is that it enables one party, A, to acquire rights over another person's, B's, land.[176] Such rights will be acquired when A has an expectation that he either has, or will acquire, rights over that land, and he has relied upon that expectation in circumstances where it would be unconscionable for B to deny at least some effect to that expectation.[177]

---

[173] See *Shah v. Shah* [2002] Q.B. 35, which supports this view in relation to the formalities concerning deeds. See Deeds, p. 326.

[174] See Chapter 15.   [175] See *Hobbs v. Norton* (1649) Nels. 47.

[176] It is not clear that the doctrine is confined to land. See M.P. Thompson [1983] C.L.J. 257. See, also, *Yeoman's Row Management Ltd v. Cobbe* [2008] UKHL 1139 at [14] *per* Lord Scott of Foscote, where he expressly envisages the acquisition of rights over personal property.

[177] See *Taylors Fashions Ltd v. Liverpool Victoria Trustees Ltd* [1982] Q.B. 133n; *Habib Bank Ltd v. Habib Bank AG Zurich* [1981] 1 W.L.R. 1265; *Lim Teng Huan v. Ang Swee Chaun* [1992] 1 W.L.R. 113.

When faced with a claim based upon estoppel, the court is faced with three questions:

'First is there an equity established? Secondly, what is the extent of the equity if one is established? And, thirdly, what is the relief appropriate to satisfy the equity?'[178]

To establish an equity, one party must first show that he has an expectation of gaining an interest in another person's land.[179] In addition to that, he must also show that it is unconscionable for the other party to deny giving some effect to that expectation. A recurrent difficulty in estoppel cases is to establish the requisite degree of unconscionability. This involves, first, establishing how the claimant came to possess the expectation and, secondly, to establish why the other party bears responsibility for his reliance upon that expectation. With regard to this first issue, one must consider whether one party actively encouraged the other to believe that he would acquire a right,[180] or, alternatively, stood by while the person acted on the belief that he had a particular right, in the knowledge of that person's mistake.[181] More common, however, than the second, more cynical conduct, is the situation where, for some reason, both parties are mistaken as to the correct legal position and acted in accordance with their mistaken beliefs.[182]

Cases occurring in the present context are likely to come into the third category, and also present fewer problems than may occur in other estoppel cases in determining what the parties' expectations were. This is because, *ex hyposethi*, they have made an agreement with respect to the land in question and action has been taken upon the basis of that agreement being a legally binding contract. The issue that will usually arise is as to what type of conduct will be necessary for rights to arise in equity.

Subject to contract agreements

Before considering the nature of the conduct which will suffice to give rise to an estoppel, one particular issue should be addressed as to the nature of the expectation, which can give rise to an equity. This issue is 'subject to contract agreements'.

Prior to the coming into force of section 2 of the Law of Property (Miscellaneous Provisions) Act 1989, it was commonplace when negotiations were in train for the sale of land for correspondence to be headed 'subject to contract'. There were two, related, reasons for this. The first was to prevent any correspondence from, itself, creating a contract. Thus, if A wrote to B offering to buy his house for £200,000 and B replied, accepting that offer, a contract would be created by this correspondence. If, however,

---

[178] *Crabb v. Arun District Council* [1976] Ch. 179 at 193 *per* Scarman L.J.

[179] As to how precise that expectation must be, see The return to principle, pp. 613–614.

[180] See, e.g., *Plimmer v. The Mayor of Wellington* (1884) 9 App. Cas. 699; *Inwards v. Baker* [1965] 2 Q.B. 29; *Gillet v. Holt* [2000] 2 All E.R. 289.

[181] See the discussion in *Willmott v. Barber* (1880) 15 Ch. 95 at 105–106 *per* Fry J.

[182] See, e.g., *E.R. Ives (Investment) Ltd v. High* [1967] 2 Q.B. 379; *Taylors Fashions Ltd v. Liverpool Victoria Trustees Ltd* [1982] Q.B. 133n.

the letters were headed 'subject to contract', this would indicate a lack of intention to create legal relations and no contract would be formed. A second scenario could also occur. In this scenario, C orally agreed with D to buy his land for £200,000. This, under the old law, would amount to a valid, albeit unenforceable, contract. To make that contract enforceable, a written memorandum of it was necessary.[183] Such a memorandum could be produced inadvertently, with correspondence making reference to the previously created oral contract itself constituting such a memorandum, thereby making that contract enforceable. This may have been unwelcome to the parties, particularly if a chain of transactions were involved, in that they may have become mutually bound by the contract before they actually wished to be. To avoid this happening, prior to the formal exchange of contracts, it was normal practice for correspondence relating to an informal agreement to be headed 'subject to contract'.

Although the effect of expressing correspondence in preventing a memorandum of a contract from being created became a matter of some controversy,[184] it was very clear that the intention of the parties when using the formula 'subject to contract' was to avoid binding obligations with respect to the land from being created. Given this context, while it is possible that a subject to contract reservation can be withdrawn, either expressly or by inference from conduct,[185] it is nevertheless very difficult to persuade the courts that reliance on an expectation of gaining rights which were still the subject of negotiation could create estoppel rights.[186] It would be known to the parties that the expenditure of money or other acts of reliance, on the expectation that a binding contract will be created, carries with it an element of risk, and this is particularly the case where they are both experienced practitioners in the property market, and are both aware that either side is free to withdraw from the putative transaction.[187] Cases occurring in the present context are very fact-sensitive,[188] and the essential element is that the parties consider themselves to be creating binding obligations.[189] In a commercial context, where solicitors are involved, and it is envisaged that a formal contract will be drawn up, it will be very difficult to establish any rights arising from estoppel. In a less commercial context, it may be easier to do this.[190]

The formal requirements for the creation of contracts imposed by section 2 are much stricter than was previously the case and are such that it is almost impossible for a binding contract to be created inadvertently. Still less is it the case that an oral

---

[183]   See Evidenced in writing, p. 187.

[184]   Contrast *Law v. Jones* [1974] Ch. 112 with *Tiverton Estates Ltd v. Wearwell* [1975] Ch. 146. See, generally, Barnsley, *Conveyancing Law and Practice* (3rd edn) (London: Butterworths, 1988), 130–131.

[185]   *Yeoman's Row Management Ltd v. Cobbe* [2008] UKHL 1139 at [27] *per* Lord Scott of Foscote.

[186]   See *Attorney-General for Hong Kong v. Humphreys Estates (Queen's Gardens) Ltd* [1987] A.C. 114; *Regalian Properties Ltd v. London Docklands Development Corporation* [1995] 1 W.L.R. 212. Cf. *Salvation Army Trustee Co. Ltd v. West Yorkshire County Council* (1980) 41 P. & C.R. 179 where, on unusual facts, such a claim succeeded.

[187]   See *Yeoman's Row Management Ltd v. Cobbe, supra*, at [93] *per* Lord Walker of Gestingthorpe.

[188]   See *Whittaker v. Kinnear* [2011] EWHC 1479 (QB) at 36 *per* Bean J.

[189]   See *Herbert v. Doyle* [2010] EWCA Civ. 1095 at [17] *per* Arden L.J.

[190]   See the comments in *Thorner v. Major* [2009] 3 All E.R. 945 at [90]–[97] *per* Lord Neuberger.

agreement can be made enforceable by correspondence referring to that agreement: the contract must be in writing and not simply evidenced in writing. Consequently, while in the past it was almost *de rigueur* to invoke the formula 'subject to contract' in all correspondence concerning land agreements, it might be thought that there is no real need to do so today. This formula retains utility, however, in that its use will make it much more difficult for one party to present an argument based upon estoppel.[191]

A good illustration of this is provided by *James v. Evans*.[192] H entered negotiations with E, for the latter to take a ten-year lease of a hill farm and a draft agreement, with one or two matters outstanding, was arrived at. All the correspondence between them was headed 'subject to contract'. E was, however, allowed into possession of the farm to take care of the flock of sheep. When final agreement had been reached, E's solicitor sent E's part of the agreement, duly signed, together with a cheque, to H's solicitor. H, however, had become seriously ill and nobody had authority to manage his affairs and so this cheque, which included payment in respect of the rent, was not accepted. H died shortly afterwards and his sister, J, as administratrix of his estate, then instituted possession proceedings and the Court of Appeal upheld a summary judgment in her favour, E's argument based upon estoppel and constructive trust being regarded as untenable.

E relied, unsuccessfully, on *Yaxley v. Gotts*. He relied on his acts of taking possession,[193] looking after the sheep and paying half of the price of their valuation. This was rejected. A key part of the judgment was that, as the negotiations were 'subject to contract', E could not acquire rights by estoppel as he knew that the effect of this expression was to prevent the creation of legal rights and, additionally, what he relied on was a normal part of the purchase of a hill farm.

The importance of the expression 'subject to contract' as a means of preventing an argument based upon estoppel has, subsequently, been stressed.[194] The rationale for this was explained as being that:

'proprietary estoppel and constructive trust must require: (a) detrimental reliance; and (b) unconscionable conduct. Since the parties must be taken to know that a party who has agreed terms subject to contract is free to withdraw, there can be no question of reliance (*particularly by a commercial enterprise involved in property transactions*) or of unconscionable conduct.'[195]

In the past, the term 'subject to contract' was used to prevent the inadvertent creation of a binding contract of sale. Because the formal requirements imposed by section 2

191 See J.E. Adams [2001] Conv. 449.
192 [2000] 1 E.G.L.R. 1, although for criticism, see L. McMurtry [2001] Conv. 86.
193 In the old law of part performance, the taking of possession was always regarded as a good act: see Megarry and Wade, *The Law of Real Property* (5th edn) (London: Stevens, 1984), 594–595.
194 *Edwin Shirley Productions Ltd v. Workspace Management Ltd* [2001] 2 E.G.L.R. 16; *Taylor v. Inntrepreneur Estates (C.P.L.) Ltd* (2001) 82 P. & C.R.D. 9.
195 *Edwin Shirley Productions Ltd v. Workspace Management Ltd, supra*, at 22 *per* Lawrence Collins J. Italics supplied.

of the 1989 Act are more stringent than was previously the case, the use of this, or an equivalent term, is no longer necessary to achieve this end. It is the case, however, that it will, in most cases, operate to preclude the success of an estoppel claim based on *Yaxley v. Gotts*. Its protection is not, however, absolute.[196] As the italicized part of the judgment makes clear, parties who are not that well versed in the power of the expression may find it less difficult to raise an estoppel argument than would be the case for more experienced players. It may still be the case, however, that an estoppel argument will not be totally precluded, even in situations where the parties are aware that there is no contract in existence.

Reliance

It is essential, in order for estoppel rights to arise, that there must be reliance on the expectation and that the other party is in some way responsible for, or party to, the action in reliance. It is in this context that it is thought that the old law on part performance will remain relevant. In cases of part performance, the expectation which was being acted upon was that there was in existence a binding contract; in the present context, the expectation is the same.[197] In both cases, the issue will then be the sufficiency of the acts relied upon.

In all cases of estoppel, the claimant must show that he has acted in reliance on his expectation; that is, he must be able to point to behaviour on which he would not have embarked but for the existence of that belief.[198] This means that the action must be action taken in the belief that there is in existence a binding contract.

The most convincing act of reliance is likely to be going into possession of the property in question or spending money upon it.[199] Although such action would be the best form of reliance, reliance is not limited to such acts. So, for example, reliance has been held to include selling land to a third party in the belief that the land which was being sold would enjoy the benefit of a right of way,[200] or the giving up of a job and a council house to live near a parent in a house to be provided by that parent.[201] While this type of action, which is in reliance upon an agreement to sell the land is, in principle, acceptable as a sufficient act to raise an equity, it is not as straightforward as an act which seeks, actually, to implement that agreement. This is because acts such as going into possession, or doing building work, necessarily involve the co-operation of both parties to the agreement, whereas acts done simply in reliance on the mistaken belief that there is a contract of sale may be unilateral, in which case, it is difficult to see why the other party cannot resist an action by relying on the agreement having no contractual effect because it fails to satisfy section 2. A unilateral act performed in reliance on

---

[196] See also the comments in *Secretary of State for Transport v. Christos* [2003] EWCA Civ. 1073 at [34] *per* Lindsay J.

[197] See *Kinane v. Mackie-Conteh* [2005] EWCA Civ. 45 at [29] *per* Arden L.J.

[198] For an excellent discussion of this general issue, see A. Lawson (1996) 16 L.S. 218.

[199] See *Yaxley v. Gotts* [2000] 1 All E.R. 711. Cf. *James v. Evans* [2000] 3 E.G.L.R. 1.

[200] *Crabb v. Arun District Council* [1976] Ch. 179.

[201] *Jones (A.E.) v. Jones (F.W.)* [1977] 1 W.L.R. 438. See, also, *Maharaj v. Chand* [1986] A.C. 898.

a belief that there is a contract in existence should not, in principle, raise any equity in favour of the person who acts in reliance on that belief.[202]

Acts by the vendor

A cogent argument has been put that, unlike the position when the doctrine of part performance was still operative, a vendor may not be able to rely on the doctrine of estoppel if he relies on his mistaken belief that there is a valid contract of sale in being.[203] The principal basis of this argument is that estoppel is perceived as a means by which a person may acquire an interest in another person's land. Because the normal expectation of the vendor is simply to acquire the purchase money, it has been argued that estoppel can be of value only to the purchaser. Clearly, there is force in this argument, although in *Yeoman's Row management Ltd v. Cobbe*,[204] Lord Scott of Foscote referred to proprietary estoppel arising if 'the right claimed is a proprietary right, usually a right to or over land but, in principle, equally available to chattels or choses in action'. This should, it is suggested, enable a vendor to claim an interest in the prospective purchase money.

In principle it is thought that a putative vendor should be able to establish an estoppel right. In the first place, as is well known, the doctrine of part performance was, in appropriate cases, available to a vendor.[205] The underlying basis of that doctrine was equitable estoppel[206] and so it should continue to be the case that rights should be available to a putative vendor under the doctrine of equitable estoppel, even though the actual doctrine of part performance has, itself, been abolished. Secondly, while it is true that any claim by the vendor is likely to be for monetary compensation, it has increasingly been recognized that the appropriate solution in estoppel cases, generally, may be to make a financial award.[207] That the claim by the vendor is financial in nature should not, therefore, be a bar to recovery. Finally, it has been held that the doctrine of estoppel is applicable when the expectation is of disposing of land rather than of acquiring an interest in land.[208] For these reasons, it is thought that the doctrine of estoppel is, in principle, available to a vendor of land.

A vendor is, nevertheless, likely to find the doctrine of estoppel potentially less useful than is a purchaser. This is, first, because it may be more difficult for him to establish that the act in question is not a unilateral one, which would not cause any equity to arise, and, secondly, the remedy afforded to him may well be less extensive than that which might be afforded to a purchaser. A situation which might occur, however, is one where the purchaser encourages his vendor, who is part of a chain, to exchange contracts to buy a house, having assured him that exchange will take place on their contract within a few days of his having done so. To then allow the purchaser to pull

---

[202] Although see the somewhat odd comment in *Kinane v. Mackie-Conteh, supra*, at [32] *per* Arden L.J.
[203] C. Davis (1993) 13 O.J.L.S. 99 at 103–105.   [204] [2008] EWHL 55 at [14].
[205] See *Dickinson v. Barrow* [1904] 2 Ch. 339; *Rawlinson v. Ames* [1925] Ch. 96.
[206] See M.P. Thompson (1985) 36 N.I.L.Q. 358 at 359–364.
[207] See, e.g. *Campbell v. Griffin* [2001] EWCA Civ. 990; *Jennings v. Rice* [2003] 1 P. & C.R. 8.
[208] *Salvation Army Trustee Co. Ltd v. West Yorkshire Metropolitan District Council* (1980) 41 P. & C.R. 8.

out of the proposed transaction would seriously prejudice the vendor and, in such circumstances, it is thought that the vendor would have a remedy in estoppel against the purchaser.

Remedies

One of the features of estoppel which distinguishes it from the law of contract is that, whereas in the law of contract, one is, as a general rule, entitled to have the actual agreement enforced, in estoppel cases, once an equity has arisen in favour of a person, it is not necessarily the case that his expectation is then completely fulfilled. The court has a discretion as to how the equity which has arisen should be satisfied.[209] The question for the court is that articulated in *Crabb v. Arun District Council*,[210] namely, 'What is the relief necessary to satisfy the equity?' So, in previous cases, remedies afforded have included the order of an outright conveyance,[211] a conveyance in return for a valuation of the property,[212] and the grant of a lien in respect of expenditure on another person's land.[213] The issue which arises in the present context is that, when the parties have made an agreement in relation to the disposition of an interest in land which does not satisfy the requirements of section 2 of the Act but that agreement has been relied upon in circumstances where an equity will arise, what will be the appropriate remedy?

Under the old doctrine of part performance, while the choice was, in theory, between 'undoing what has been done (which is not always possible, or if possible, just) and completing what has been left undone',[214] the normal outcome of a successful act of part performance was that the previously unenforceable oral contract was enforced. The only real scope for the restitutionary remedy was in cases where the act of part performance relied upon the payment of money, it having been said '[p]ayment of money... raises no equity except possibly a right to have it paid back'.[215] Even in cases where the main act relied upon was the payment of money, however, the more usual response in modern times was to order specific performance of the oral contract.[216]

Under the new law, there is, of course, no oral contract for the court to enforce specifically. That said, there is an obvious temptation, where it is fairly clear what the parties have agreed, to satisfy the equity that has arisen by enforcing that agreement.[217] Such a course might, however, be perceived as being uncomfortably close to ordering specific

---

[209] There is some controversy as to this matter. See Satisfaction of the equity, pp. 629–638.

[210] [1976] Ch. 179 at 193 *per* Scarman L.J.   [211] *Dillwyn v. Llewellyn* (1866) 4 De G.F. & J. 517.

[212] *Duke of Beaufort v. Patrick* (1853) 17 Beav. 60.

[213] *Unity Joint Stock Mutual Banking Association v. King* (1858) 25 Beav. 72.

[214] *Maddison v. Alderson* (1883) 8 App. Cas. 467 at 476 *per* Earl of Selborne L.C.

[215] *Thursby v. Eccles* (1900) 49 W.R. 281 at 282 *per* Bigham J.

[216] See *Steadman v. Steadman* [1976] A.C. 536.

[217] See *J.T. Developments Ltd v. Quinn* (1990) 62 P. & C.R. 33; *Lim Teng Huan v. Ang Swee Chuan* [1992] 1 W.L.R. 113; *Jennings v. Rice* [2003] 1 P. & C.R. 8 at [50] *per* Robert Walker L.J.

performance of a non-existent contract.[218] In *Morritt v. Wonham*,[219] an agreement had been reached whereby, in return for the plaintiff doing work for the defendant, that work being worth in the region of £15,000 to £20,000, the defendant promised to leave that property to the plaintiff by will, the value of the property being in the region of £365,000. The judge held there to have been an oral contract made enforceable by the plaintiff's acts of part performance. He did not, however, order specific performance. Instead, encouraged by the fact that part performance was soon to be replaced by the more flexible doctrine of equitable estoppel, he imposed a trust for sale upon the property, under which the defendant was to have a life interest, remainder to the plaintiff. The defendant was also held to be entitled to a lump sum of £40,000, to be raised either by mortgage or by selling off part of the property.

This re-writing of the parties' oral contract was unjustified under the old law of part performance but may reflect how the courts might approach cases under the new law, where the doctrine of equitable estoppel does permit the court to exercise a discretion as to remedy;[220] a discretion that may well be exercised where, as here, the agreement seems to be unduly favourable to one side.

That the court does have this discretion, however, is also evident from *Yaxley v. Gotts*.[221] The plaintiff in that case claimed, in the alternative, a declaration that he was entitled to either the grant of a long lease of the ground floor, the financial equivalent of such a lease, or the award of a sum of money equal to the value of his work or services. The first two elements of this claim relate to the enforcement of his expectation; the third is a restitutionary remedy. The court ordered the defendant to grant the plaintiff a long lease.

None of the claims made, however, may actually have reflected the true agreement between the parties, in that it was agreed that the ground floor would be his; an agreement which is at least as consistent with an understanding that he should have a fee simple in the property. The grant of a long lease avoided the problems which might otherwise have arisen had a conveyance in fee simple been ordered, however, as such a solution would have resulted in the upper floors being held on the basis of a flying freehold.[222]

In cases such as this, in the future, one cannot be certain as to how the equity which has arisen will be satisfied, and in *Yeoman's Row Management Ltd v. Cobbe*,[223] in the Court of Appeal, the fashioning of an appropriate remedy to satisfy the estoppel which, of course, the House of Lords held subsequently not to have arisen,[224] was perceived to be the most challenging aspect of the case.[225] The agreement may be fulfilled in full, or in part, or, alternatively, the court may order one party to effect restitution to the

---

[218] It is, of course, possible to achieve much the same result by means of the imposition of a constructive trust: *Yaxley v. Gotts* [2000] 1 All E.R. 711.

[219] [1993] N.P.C. 2; M.P. Thompson [1994] Conv. 233.

[220] See *Brightlingsea Haven Ltd v. Morris* [2008] EWHC 1928 (QB) at [56]–[68] *per* Bean J.

[221] [2000] 1 All E.R. 711.   [222] Ibid. at 724 *per* Robert Walker L.J.

[223] [2006] EWCA Civ. 1139.   [224] [2008] UKHL 55.

[225] [2006] EWCA Civ. 1139 at [1] *per* Mummery L.J.

other.[226] The very existence of this discretion makes the results in such cases unpredictable, so that, in time, the uncertainties attached to the old law of part performance may be seen to be preferable to the uncertainties inherent in the application of the principles of equitable estoppel.

THE EFFECT OF THE CONTRACT

Once a contract has been created, the Rubicon has been crossed and neither side is, any longer, free to withdraw from the agreement. It is quite normal, however, for there to be a gap of some weeks between the creation of the contract and the completion of it by the transfer of the legal estate to the purchaser, a principal reason for this being that, during this period, the purchaser effects searches in either the land charges registry or the register of title. During this period, if either side purports to withdraw from the contract, or is unable to complete it, perhaps because the vendor is not able to show good title to the land, or the purchaser is unable to raise the requisite finance, then they will be liable in damages to the other. More significantly, however, a contract for the sale of an interest in land is one where the courts are prepared to assume that damages are an inadequate remedy, with the result that specific performance is normally available. The availability of this remedy has a significant effect on the respective rights and obligations of the parties to the contract pending completion.

The creation of a trust[227]

The availability of the remedy of specific performance has an important consequence. Because equity looks on that which ought to be done as already having been done,[228] it considers that, because there is in existence a specifically enforceable contract of sale, the beneficial ownership in the land passes, from the date of the contract, to the purchaser.[229] This principle applies generally in Land Law so that if, for example, there is a specifically enforceable contract to create a lease or an easement, then the effect of that contract is to give rise to an equitable lease or easement. What complicates matters in the case of contracts for the sale of land is that, unlike the situation which occurs when one is dealing with contracts to create leases or easements, where the purchaser acquires a different type of interest from that which the vendor retains, the purchaser obtains, in equity, the same estate which the vendor has contracted to sell. The result

---

[226] See *Ravenocean Ltd v. Gardner* [2001] N.P.C. 44, although the reimbursement of an architect's fee seems more like compensation than restitution.

[227] For a full exposition of this trust, see (1988) Law Com. W.P. No. 109, Part 1. See also *Englewood Properties Ltd v. Patel* [2005] 1 W.L.R. 1961 at 1971–1978 *per* Lawrence Collins J.

[228] See The creation of equitable rights, p. 47.

[229] See *Lysaght v. Edwards* (1876) 2 Ch.D. 499 at 510, 518 *per* Sir George Jessel M.R.

of this, in short, is that, from the date of the contract, the vendor holds the legal estate on trust for the purchaser.

While it is commonly said that the effect of the formation of a contract of sale is to render the vendor a trustee for the purchaser, this statement is subject to one important qualification. The basis of the creation of the trust is that there is in existence a specifically enforceable contract of sale. If the contract is not one of which the court will award specific performance, then it is not correct to regard a trust as having arisen.[230] If, for example, the right to specific performance has been lost as a result of misconduct by the person seeking to enforce the contract,[231] or the contract is not enforceable because the vendor's title is defective,[232] the vendor will not be regarded as a trustee for the purchaser. Similarly, if specific performance is not available for other reasons, such as a delay in enforcing the contract,[233] or, if to award specific performance in favour of one party would entail breach of a prior contract in favour of another person, the remedy will not be granted and the equitable title will not pass.[234]

The vendor as trustee

The trust imposed upon the vendor is, on any view, unusual.[235] Its unusual nature stems from the fact that, until he receives the agreed purchase money, the vendor has a substantive interest of his own in the property; an interest reflected by the fact that he acquires a lien on the property from the date that a valid contract is formed.[236]

It is the existence of his own interest in the property that is the principal reason why the vendor is not subject to the fiduciary obligations which are normally imposed upon a trustee. In particular, unlike trustees generally, the vendor is entitled to the profits from the property during his trusteeship. Thus, pending completion, it is the vendor and not the purchaser who is entitled to possession of the land[237] and, consistent with that, he is entitled to the rents and profits emanating from the land,[238] and this will include any damages paid by a tenant for breach of covenant[239] and compensation payable on the de-requisitioning of land.[240] Perhaps most significantly, he does not hold any moneys paid under an insurance policy in respect of property damage on

---

[230] See *Howard v. Miller* [1915] A.C. 318 at 326 *per* Lord Parker; *Bushwall Properties Ltd v. Vortex Properties Ltd* [1976] 2 All E.R. 283 at 294 *per* Buckley L.J.; *McLaughlin v. Duffill* [2008] EWCA Civ. 1627 at [25]–[26] *per* Sir Andrew Morritt C.

[231] *Central Trust and Safe Deposit Co. v. Snider* [1916] 1 A.C. 266 at 272 *per* Lord Parker.

[232] *Re Thomas, Thomas v. Howell* (1886) 34 Ch.D. 166.

[233] See *Cornwall v. Henson* [1899] 2 Ch. 710 at 714 *per* Cozens-Hardy J.

[234] *Willmott v. Barber* (1880) 15 Ch.D. 96; *Warmington v. Miller* [1973] Q.B. 877.

[235] See, e.g. *Wall v. Bright* (1820) 1 Jac. & W. 494 at 501 *per* Sir Thomas Plumer M.R.; *Dowson v. Solomon* (1859) 1 Drew. & Sm. 1 at 9 *per* Sir Richard Kindersley V.-C.

[236] *Re Birmingham, Savage v. Stannard* [1959] Ch. 523; *U.C.B. Bank v. France* [1995] N.P.C. 144; *Barclays Bank plc v. Estates and Commercial Ltd* [1997] 1 W.L.R. 415. For a full discussion of the issue, see D.G. Barnsley [1997] Conv. 336, refuting criticism by M.P. Thompson [1996] Conv. 44.

[237] *Phillips v. Silvester* (1872) 8 Ch. App. 173.   [238] *Cuddon v. Tite* (1858) 1 Giff. 395.

[239] *Re Lyne-Stephens and Scott-Miller's Contract* [1920] 1 Ch. 472.

[240] *Re Hamilton-Snowball's Conveyance* [1959] Ch. 308.

trust for the purchaser;[241] a matter which, as will be seen, was a factor in a proposal for reform of this area of law.[242]

Duty to maintain

The main obligation deriving from the vendor's trusteeship relates to his obligation concerning the condition of the property. The general duty imposed upon the vendor has been said to be to take such care of the property as if it were his own.[243] He is, therefore, liable to the purchaser for damage to the property which he causes himself, such as dumping rubbish on the land,[244] or removing fixtures from the property.[245] He is also liable if damage is caused to the property by his failure to take reasonable care of it by, for example, taking care to ensure that the pipes do not freeze during winter.[246] This duty of care extends to the acts of third parties, so that, if the property is damaged by trespassers, the vendor will be liable to the purchaser if he failed, adequately, to prevent such damage occurring.[247] If, however, the purchaser cannot establish[248] that the vendor is at fault, then he will not be liable to the vendor.[249] To make matters worse, it would seem that the purchaser, because he has only an equitable interest in the property, will not be able to sue a person who has damaged the property.[250]

The normal position of a trustee is that he is liable to be indemnified in respect of expenses relating to the upkeep of the property.[251] This is not the position of the vendor, however, who will be responsible, pending completion, for such items as council tax and utility bills.[252] With regard to actual repairs to the property, the position is not entirely clear,[253] but in line with the general position that the vendor is under a duty to keep the property in a reasonable state of repair,[254] it would seem that repairs necessary to stop further deterioration of the property would be the vendor's responsibility, so that he would be liable for repairs such as the replacement of broken windows or roof slates.[255]

---

[241] *Rayner v Preston* (1881) 18 Ch.D. 1.   [242] See Insurance, pp. 223–224.

[243] *Wilson v. Clapham* (1819) 1 Jac. & W. 36 at 38 *per* Sir Thomas Plumer M.R.

[244] *Cumberland Consolidated Holdings Ltd v. Ireland* [1946] K.B. 264.

[245] *Philips v. Lamdin* [1949] 2 K.B. 33. See also *Were v. Verdeberer* (1978) 247 E.G. 1081.

[246] See *Lucie-Smith v. Gorman* [1981] C.L.Y. 2866, but contrast, in the context of landlord and tenant, *Wycombe Health Authority v. Barnett* (1982) 264 E.G. 619.

[247] *Clarke v. Ramuz* [1891] 2 Q.B. 456; *Davron Estates Ltd v. Turnshire* (1982) 133 N.L.J. 937.

[248] The doctrine of *res ipsa loquitur* (the thing speaks for itself) seems not to be applicable. See *Sochacki v. Sas* [1947] 1 All E.R. 344. See, however, J.T. Farrand (1978) 42 Conv. (N.S.) 183.

[249] See *Smith v. Littlewoods Organisation Ltd* [1987] A.C. 241.

[250] *Leigh and Sillivan Ltd v. Aliakmon Shipping Co. Ltd* [1986] A.C. 785. See R.M. Goode (1987) 103 L.Q.R. 433 at 455–458.

[251] See, e.g. *Re Beddoe* [1893] 1 Ch. 547.

[252] See *Re Watford Corporation and Ware's Contract* [1943] Ch. 82, especially at 85 *per* Simmonds J.

[253] See (1987) Law Com. W.P. No. 109, paras 1.36–1.40.

[254] *Royal Permanent Building Society v. Bomash* (1887) 35 Ch.D. 390 at 396 *per* Kekewich J.

[255] The basis of this is that the vendor would appear to be liable to the purchaser for permissive waste. See *Regent's Canal Co. v. Ware* (1857) 23 Beav. 575 at 588 *per* Sir John Romilly M.R.

The purchaser as beneficiary

The normal rule with regard to trust property is that, if, without fault on the part of the trustee, the trust property is damaged or destroyed, then the loss falls on the beneficiary. In the case of contracts for the sale of land, the fact that the vendor is regarded as being a trustee for the purchaser has long been regarded as causing the same result. In *Lysaght v. Edwards*,[256] Sir George Jessel M.R. said:

'If anything happens to the estate between the time of sale and the time of the completion of the purchase it is at the risk of the purchaser. If it is a house that is sold and the house is burnt down the purchaser loses the house. He must insure it himself if he wants to provide against such an accident. If it is a garden, and a river overflows its banks without any fault of the vendor, the garden will be ruined, but the loss will be the purchaser's.'

This view has long been accepted as being the orthodox position, the rationale being that, because the purchaser is the equitable owner of the property, it is he who must bear the risk of accidental damage occurring to it. The theoretical basis of this view is, however, questionable, in that the reason that the purchaser is regarded as being the beneficial owner at all is that specific performance would be ordered of the contract and, as a result, equity, considering that which ought to be done as already having been done, considers the purchaser to be the owner of the property from the date of the contract. The argument that the risk passes depends, therefore, on specific performance being ordered of a contract to sell a house, when that house has been badly damaged, or even destroyed, and it is not at all clear that such an order would be made. The argument that the risk passes to the purchaser as a result of the contract, although long accepted, is not as firmly based as it might appear.[257]

Insurance[258]

Because it has long been the conventional wisdom that the risk of damage to the property passes to the purchaser from the date of the contract, the normal practice is for the purchaser to insure the property from that date. It is not safe for him to rely upon the vendor's insurance policy because any money paid to the vendor under his own policy is not held upon trust for the purchaser.[259] Moreover, because it is accepted that the purchaser is still bound to pay the purchase price in full, notwithstanding that the property has been badly damaged, the vendor has not actually suffered any loss and, consequently, is liable to repay the insurance money to the insurer,[260] a complication which is likely to render ineffective statutory provisions seeking to allow purchasers to recover on the vendor's insurance policy.[261]

---

[256] (1876) 2 Ch.D. 499 at 507.   [257] See M.P. Thompson [1984] Conv. 43.

[258] For a full discussion of the problems and possible solutions, see (1988) Law Com. W.P. No. 109, Part 2.

[259] *Rayner v. Preston* (1881) 18 Ch.D. 1. It is possible, albeit unusual, for the vendor's policy to be taken out for the benefit of the purchaser. Cf. *Lonsdale & Thompson Ltd v. Black Arrow Group plc* [1993] Ch. 361.

[260] *Castellain v. Preston* (1883) 11 Q.B.D. 380.

[261] See Law of Property Act 1925, s. 47(1). Commonwealth authorities dealing with similar problems have held against the purchaser. See *Ziel Nominees Pty Ltd v. V.A.C.C. Insurance Co.* (1975) 7 A.L.R. 667; *Budhia v. Wellington City Corporation* [1976] 1 N.Z.L.R. 766.

To safeguard his own interest, the purchaser should arrange for the property to be insured from the date of the contract. The vendor would be unwise, however, to cancel his insurance from that date. This is because the contract may go off for a reason unconnected with any damage to the property. The purchaser may, for example, be able to rescind the contract because the vendor's title is defective, in which case, the risk of damage to the property would not have passed to the purchaser. The result is that both parties to the contract need, simultaneously, to insure the property against the risk.

Reform

The incidence of duplication of insurance was one of the reasons why the Law Commission recommended provisionally, as one option, legislative change to the law, whereby the risk of damage to the property would remain with the vendor until completion.[262] A second option put forward, that this change be effected by a contractual term,[263] originally met with a positive response from the Law Society. The result was that the Standard Conditions of Sale,[264] which are normally used in conveyancing transactions, provide that the vendor undertakes to transfer the property in the same physical state (fair wear and tear excluded) as it was in at the date of the contract. In other words, the risk of damage to the property, pending completion, remains with the vendor. While the Law Commission remained of the view that the position was still not entirely satisfactory,[265] it, nevertheless concluded that this change of practice made legislative reform unnecessary, although further consideration of this matter was expressly left open, should evidence emerge that this provision was not being widely used.[266] Now that the Standard Conditions of Sale have reverted to the original common law position,[267] it remains to be seen if any further consideration of this issue will be undertaken.

Payment of purchase price

The existence of a valid contract of sale has the effect that, in the eye of equity, the purchaser becomes the beneficial owner of the property from the date of the contract. The odd nature of this trust is further underlined, however, by the fact that the actual payment of purchase money undoubtedly augments the rights of a purchaser as he acquires a lien over the land corresponding to the amount of the purchase price which has been paid. This was explained in *Rose v. Watson*,[268] where the purchase price was paid by instalments. The position was said to be that:

'Where the owner of an estate contracts with a purchaser for the immediate sale of it, the ownership of the estate is, in equity, transferred by that contract. Where the contract undoubtedly is an executory contract, in this sense, namely, that the ownership of this estate is transferred, subject to the payment of the purchase price-money, every payment of the

---

[262] (1988) Law Com. W.P. No. 109, paras 3.12–3.14.   [263] Ibid., paras 3.15–3.19.
[264] (4th edn) G.C. 5.1.1.   [265] (1990) Law Com. No. 191, para. 3.7.   [266] Ibid., para. 3.12.
[267] National Conditions of Sale (5th edn) G.C. 5.1.1.   [268] (1864) 10 H.L. Cas. 672.

purchase-money paid in pursuance of that contract is a part performance and execution of the contract and, to the extent of the purchase-money paid, does, in equity, finally transfer to the purchaser, the ownership of a corresponding portion of the estate.'[269]

Although the position is confusing, it is clear that the payment of purchase money gives the purchaser rights additional to the equitable interest acquired by the mere entry into an executory contract, his lien over the land arising from the fact of his payment of the purchase price rather than the existence of an enforceable contract of sale.[270] So, from being a highly qualified trustee when the contract is entered into, the vendor, on receipt of the full purchase price becomes a bare trustee for the purchaser.[271] Unfortunately, the significance of the actual payment of the purchase price was downplayed in *Lloyds Bank plc v. Carrick*.[272]

The defendant contracted to buy unregistered land from her brother-in-law and paid him the full purchase price and moved into the property. Although she moved into the property, the legal title was never conveyed to her and remained vested in her brother-in-law who, subsequently, mortgaged the property to the plaintiff. In deciding that her equitable interest arising from the contract of sale was void as against the bank for non-registration,[273] the Court of Appeal also held that it was immaterial that she had paid the purchase price in full, in that, having acquired the beneficial interest in the property by virtue of the contract, she could not acquire a further equitable interest as a result of paying the purchase money.[274] While it is understandable to see a reluctance to hold that a beneficial owner of property can acquire a further equitable interest in it, it is suggested that the court should have done so. The beneficial interest acquired as a result of entry into an executory contract of sale is highly qualified. Once the purchase price had been paid in full, however, the legal owner would hold the property on a bare trust for his sister-in-law.[275] This interest should then have been regarded as being exempt from the requirements of registration under the Land Charges Act 1972, with the result that the bank should have taken subject to her interest of which it would, quite clearly on the facts, have had constructive notice.

TRANSMISSION OF THE LEGAL ESTATE

Following exchange of contracts, a number of tasks have still to be performed prior to the completion of the transactions. The essential nature of these tasks is for the purchaser to investigate the vendor's title, by which is meant establishing that the vendor

---

[269] Ibid. at 678 *per* Lord Westbury. See also at 683 *per* Lord Cranworth.
[270] See *Chatley v. Farndale Holdings Inc.* [1997] 1 E.G.L.R. 153 at 156 *per* Morritt L.J.
[271] *Bridges v. Mees* [1957] Ch. 475 at 485.   [272] [1996] 4 All E.R. 630.
[273] See *Midland Bank Trust Co. Ltd v. Green* [1981] A.C. 513.
[274] [1996] 4 All E.R. 630 at 638, 639 *per* Morritt L.J.
[275] Cf. *Hodgson v. Marks* [1971] Ch. 892. See also M.P. Thompson [1996] Conv. 295 at 299–300.

can convey that which he has contracted to convey and to requisition various searches to discover to what incumbrances the land is subject.[276] When this work has been done the transaction is completed and the legal title is transferred.

Deeds

The general position, to which there are exceptions, is that all conveyances of land or of any interest in land are void for the purposes of conveying or creating a legal estate unless made by deed.[277] At common law, a deed had to be on paper or parchment and sealed and delivered,[278] the requirement that, when sealing the document, it also be signed, being introduced in 1925.[279] In respect of deeds executed after 1989, the requirements are those stipulated by section 1 of the Law of Property (Miscellaneous Provisions) Act 1989.

Section 1(1) first abolishes any rule of law which restricts the substances on which a deed may be written, requires a seal for the valid execution of a deed or requires the authority for another person to deliver a deed to be given by deed. The new formalities are then specified by section 1(2) which provides that:

'An instrument shall not be a deed unless—

(a) it makes clear on its face that it is intended to be a deed by the person making it or, as the case may be, by the parties to it (whether by describing itself as a deed or expressing itself executed or signed as a deed or otherwise); and

(b) it is validly executed as a deed by that person or, as the case may be, one or more of those parties.'

Section 1(3) provides that:

'An instrument is validly executed as a deed by an individual if, and only if—

(a) it is signed—

  (i) by him in the presence of a witness who attests the signature; or
  (ii) at his direction and in his presence and the presence of two witnesses who each attest his signature; and

(b) it is delivered as a deed by him or a person authorised to do so on his behalf.'

Although it is clear that documents can be deeds without using the word 'deed', it is apparently not sufficient that the document was intended to be formal and to have legal effect.[280] On this, somewhat strict approach, it is not easy to envisage a document being held to be a deed which does not describe itself as such.

---

[276] For the process of investigation of title, see Thompson, op. cit., Chapters 9–13.

[277] Law of Property Act 1925, s. 52(1).   [278] *Goddard's Case* (1584) 2 Co. Rep. 4b at 5a.

[279] Law of Property Act 1925, s. 73(1), repealed by Law of Property (Miscellaneous Provisions) Act 1989, Sched. 2.

[280] *HSBC Trust Company (UK) Ltd v. Quinn* [2007] EWHC 1543 (Ch.) at [50]–[51] *per* Mr Christopher Nugee Q.C.

Signed

There appears not to be any case which turns on the meaning of a signature in the context of deeds. The Act, itself, defines 'sign' to include making one's mark.[281] Beyond that, there is no further definition. It is thought that, should the point arise, the courts are likely to follow the approach taken in *Firstpost Homes Ltd v. Johnson*[282] and decline to give a strained meaning to this expression.

A second point which can also be made is that, in contrast to the formal requirements of a contract, it is not necessary for both parties concerned with the deed to sign it. It is sufficient for the grantor, or grantors, to sign the deed.

Attestation

At common law, a deed had to be sealed, but it was not necessary for it to be witnessed. The position is now reversed. Sealing is not necessary, so that the statement in *Oun v. Ahmad* [283] that 'The first document describes itself as "this deed" but the document is executed under hand and not under a seal' is, of itself, clearly not an adequate reason for the conclusion that there was no deed. The deed must be witnessed, by one person if the grantor signs the deed personally, and by two witnesses if it is signed under his direction. If the attestation requirements are not met, a person may, however, be estopped from relying on this to deny efficacy to the deed.[284]

Delivery

Delivery of a deed does not mean a physical transfer of it. What it entails is that the person executing the deed signifies an intention to be bound by it.[285] It is immaterial if the grantee knows of the delivery of the deed.[286] Classically, the way to deliver a deed is physically to hand it over, expressing words such as 'I deliver this as my deed.'[287] In practice, this is rare and the courts are willing to infer the delivery of a deed from the conduct of the grantor in signing it.[288]

Delivery of a deed may be absolute or conditional. If it is conditional, the deed does not become effective until that condition is satisfied. The deed is said, then, to have been delivered in escrow.[289]

Registration

Where title is unregistered, the legal title will pass on the conveyance but application must be made for first registration of title within two months of the execution of the deed. If this is not done, the disposition will be void as regards the transfer of a legal

---

[281] Law of Property (Miscellaneous Provisions) Act 1989, s. 1(4).   [282] [1995] 1 W.L.R. 1567.

[283] [2008] EWHC 545 (Ch.) at [4] *per* Morgan J.   [284] *Shah v. Shah* [2002] Q.B. 35.

[285] See *Alan Estates Ltd v. W.G. Stores Ltd* [1982] Ch. 511 at 526 *per* Sir Denys Buckley.

[286] See *Hughes v. Griffin* [1969] 1 All E.R. 460.

[287] *Xenos v. Wickham* (1867) L.R. 2 H.L. 296 at 312 *per* Blackburn J.

[288] *Hall v. Bainbridge* (1848) 12 Q.B.D. 699. But see *Bolton Metropolitan Borough Council v. Torkington* [2003] EWCA Civ. 1634.

[289] See Thompson, op. cit., pp. 449–453.

estate.[290] Where title is registered, the deed takes the form of a transfer and the legal estate does not pass until the transferee applies for registration.[291]

DEVOLUTION ON DEATH

A second method by which title to land is transferred is upon death. This section outlines the procedure by which this takes place.

Testate succession

As a matter of general principle, a person is free to leave his property to whoever he pleases. This is subject to exceptions. First, the testator may, while alive, commit himself to a binding obligation to leave the property to a particular person,[292] either by contract,[293] by entering into a mutual will agreement,[294] or by estoppel.[295] In addition, various persons may make a claim under the Inheritance (Family Provisions) Act 1975,[296] if the testator has failed to make adequate provision for them.

There are no special rules relating to the formality of wills, insofar as the subject matter of the will relates to land and it is not proposed, therefore, to discuss, in detail, the formal requirements of a will.

With a few rare exceptions,[297] to be valid, a will must comply with the requirements of section 9 of the Wills Act 1837, as amended by section 17 of the Administration of Justice Act 1982. The will must be in writing and signed by the testator, or by someone else in his presence and acting under his direction, in the simultaneous presence of two witnesses, who must, themselves, sign the will.[298]

Passing of title

On death, the property of a testate person will vest in his personal representatives,[299] who apply for a grant of probate. Once probate has been granted, the task of the personal representatives is to distribute the property in accordance with the testator's will. Title to land is passed by a document termed an assent. An assent passes the legal title but is not a deed. The formal requirements of an assent are that it is in writing,

---

[290] Land Registration Act 2002, s. 4(1).   [291] Ibid., s. 27.

[292] See, generally, M. Davey (1988) 8 L.S. 92; S. Nield (2000) 20 L.S. 85.

[293] See *Schaefer v. Schuman* [1972] A.C. 572.

[294] See Hanbury and Martin, *Modern Equity* (18th edn) (London: Sweet & Maxwell, 2009), 347–354.

[295] See *Wayling v. Jones* [1995] 2 F.L.R. 1029; *Gillett v. Holt* [2000] 2 All E.R. 289.

[296] As amended by the Law Reform (Succession) Act 1995.

[297] See Wills Act 1837, s. 11; Wills (Soldiers and Sailors) Act 1918, ss 1, 2.

[298] A witness to a will is not entitled to derive any benefit from it: Wills Act 1837, s. 15.

[299] Administration of Estates Act 1925, s. 1.

signed by the personal representative, and names the person in whom the legal title is to vest.[300]

In terms of proving title to land, when title was unregistered, a purchaser would be entitled to see the grant of probate and the assent, but not the will. It is now the case, however, that the requirement of compulsory registration of title applies to a disposition by an assent,[301] so the person entitled under the will will be registered as proprietor.

Intestacy

If a person dies intestate, his property will vest in the Public Trustee until the grant of administration.[302] The person, or persons, to whom letters of administration are granted has all the powers of a personal representative[303] and will distribute the property in accordance with the rules governing intestacy.

---

[300] Ibid.   [301] Land Registration Act 2002, s. 4(1).

[302] Administration of Estates Act 1925, s. 9, as substituted by Law of Property (Miscellaneous Provisions) Act 1994, s. 14.

[303] Administration of Estates Act 1925, s. 21.

7

Possessory Titles

As is the case with other causes of action, an action to possess land can, after a period of time, become statute barred. In the case of actions in contract and tort, the essence of statutes of limitation is that a particular remedy has been lost. In the case of land, the effect of limitation is more profound. The essential reason for this is that once the right to recover possession has been lost, section 17 of the Limitation Act 1980 provides that the title of that person to the land is extinguished.[1] The corollary to this is that the person who has taken possession acquires rights of ownership. As such, although the working of the Limitation Act is essentially negative in nature, operating to extinguish the title of the paper owner of the land, it is also a means of acquiring title to property, albeit in a non-consensual manner.

OWNERSHIP AND POSSESSION

When title is unregistered, it is a central tenet of English Land Law that ownership of land or, more accurately, estates in land, is a relative concept.[2] If a court is faced with a dispute as to the entitlement to possession of land, its task is not to make a definitive determination as to who is the owner of it. Its task is simply to determine which of the two claimants has a better right to possess it. This central point was made over two hundred years ago, when Lord Mansfield said that 'the plaintiff cannot recover but upon the strength of his own title. He cannot found his claim upon the weakness of the defendant's title. For possession gives the defendant a right against every man who cannot show a good title.'[3]

The same point was made more recently in *Ocean Estates Ltd v. Pinder*.[4] The plaintiff brought an action in trespass and the defendant claimed to have acquired a possessory title to the land. When that argument failed, an alternative defence was advanced,

[1] See The effect of adverse possession, pp. 256–260.

[2] In *Berrisford v. Mexfield Housing Co-operative Ltd* [2011] UKSC 52 at [65], this principle was described by Lord Neuberger as being 'the traditional bedrock of English land law'.

[3] *Roe D. Haldane v. Harvey* (1769) 4 Burr. 2484 at 2487.

[4] [1969] 2 A.C. 19. See, also, *Asher v. Whitlock* (1865) L.R. 1 Q.B. 1; *Ezekiel v. Fraser* [2002] EWHC 2066 (Ch.).

which was that the plaintiff's paper title to the land was defective. This defence also failed because, the plaintiff having been in possession of the land before the defendant, he, as between the actual parties to the litigation, had the better right to possession. Giving the advice of the Privy Council, Lord Diplock said:

'Where questions of title to land arise in litigation, the court is only concerned with the relative strengths of title proved by the rival claimants. If party A can prove a better title than party B he is entitled to succeed notwithstanding that C may have a better title than A, if C is neither a party to the action nor a person by whose authority B is in possession or occupation of the land.'[5]

The relativity of title

The essence of this judgment is to emphasize that the court is concerned only to determine the relative strengths of the claims to possession of the land by the two claimants. If A has taken possession, or is entitled to take possession under a licence,[6] then A can recover possession as against B, unless B can show that A's right is, as against him, statute barred. It is quite irrelevant that B can prove that A had no right to possession in the first place, or that his claim to possession did not confer any proprietary right on him,[7] and that C had a better right to possession than either of them.[8] As the person in prior possession, A, has a better right to possess the land than does B and it is this issue with which the court is concerned.

This central tenet of English Land Law was stressed again recently. In *Harrow London Borough Council v. Qazi*,[9] Lord Millett explained the position in the following terms. He said:

'A person who is in actual possession of land is entitled to remain in peaceful enjoyment of the property without disturbance by anyone except a person with a better title to possession. It does not matter that he has no title. A squatter can maintain an action for trespass. He cannot be evicted save at the suit of a person with a better right to possession, and even then that person must rely on the strength of his own title and not the weakness of the squatter's.'

In general, proof that a third party has a better right to the land is immaterial.[10] The only time that such a plea will be relevant is if C is in possession of land and D, who

---

[5] [1969] 2 A.C. 19 at 25. See also *London Borough of Tower Hamlets v. Barrett* [2005] EWCA Civ. 923 at [100]–[103] *per* Neuberger L.J.

[6] See *Dutton v. Manchester Airport plc* [2000] 1 Q.B. 133. See E. Paton and G. Seabrooke [1999] Conv. 535. If a person has, by licence, only a right of access to property, he does not have the right to bring an action for trespass: *Countryside Residential (North Thames) Ltd v. Tugwell* (2000) 34 E.G. 87.

[7] Ibid. Contrast the position in the law of nuisance, where, to bring a claim, the plaintiff must establish a proprietary interest in the land: see *Hunter v. Canary Wharf* [1997] A.C. 635.

[8] See *Marsden v. Miller* (1992) 64 P. & C.R. 239 at 240 *per* Scott L.J., pointing out that in the case before him the identity of the paper owner of the disputed land was unknown.

[9] [2004] 1 A.C. 983 at 1015.

[10] It is relevant if the person in possession shows that he is there as the agent of a person with the paper title to the land. See *Rosenberg v. Cook* (1881) 8 Q.B.D. 162.

has not, himself, been in prior occupation of the land, brings an action to recover it from C. In such a case, C can rely on the fact that D has no right to the land because E is entitled to it. This, however, serves only further to illustrate that the task of the court is to weigh the strengths of the competing claims to the land. As C is in possession, for D to recover the land, he must show a better right to it than C and this he cannot do, if all that C can show is that D has no such right because E has a better right to it. The fact that E might have a better right to the land than C is of no assistance to D's claim to possession.

THE RATIONALE OF LIMITATION

It is not only land actions that can be affected by limitation of actions. An action on a contract is statute barred after six years, as are actions in tort, except for those relating to personal injuries, where the normal limitation period is three years.[11] In the case of actions for the recovery of land, the limitation period in respect of actions based upon the law prior to 2003 is twelve years.[12] In cases governed by the provisions of the Land Registration Act 2002, that period has been reduced to one of ten years.[13] There are, of course, reasons for the existence of periods of limitation. Some of these reasons are common to limitation periods generally but some are specific to limitation of actions for the recovery of land.

General reasons

In the context of legal actions generally, reasons for disallowing them after a specified period of time include the law's reluctance to encourage the bringing of stale claims and to act as a disincentive to people to sleep on their rights, particularly when, after a period of time, a person might, quite reasonably, think that any cause of action that might have been brought against him has been abandoned. To allow an action to be brought some years later might cause hardship.[14] In addition, as a matter of public policy, it has been said that:

'It is desirable that claims which are brought should be brought at a time when documentary evidence is still available and the recollections of witnesses are still reasonably fresh. That is the best way to ensure a fair trial and thus to maximise the chance of doing justice.'[15]

---

[11] Limitation Act 1980, ss 2, 5, 12, 33. The differing limitation periods for different actions have been criticized for lacking coherence: (1997) Law Com. C.C. No. 151, para. 1.2.

[12] Limitation Act 1980, s. 15.   [13] Land Registration Act 2002, s. 97, Sched. 6, para. 1(1).

[14] See *Cholmondeley v. Clinton* (1820) 2 Jac. & W. 139. For an excellent discussion of the rationale of adverse possession, see M. Dockray [1985] Conv. 272.

[15] (1997) Law Com. C.C. No. 151, para. 1.31.

These reasons all apply, to some extent, to actions for the recovery of land. In the context of land, however, there is an additional, important, reason for the role of limitation.

Security of title

When title is unregistered, the method by which a vendor proves to a purchaser his right to sell it is to give an historical account of how title to the property came to be vested in him.[16] At one time, the period of investigation was sixty years. This period of investigation has, over a period of time, been reduced, so that the current period of investigation is one of at least fifteen years.[17] This reform, aimed at facilitating conveyancing, was made possible, in part, by changes to the law relating to limitation periods in respect of land actions.[18] Put shortly, the early law on the subject was such that a purchaser had to engage in a very lengthy investigation of title as, owing to mistakes which might have been made in the past, a person may still, many years later, be able to substantiate a claim to the land. The effect of changes to the law relating to the law of limitation meant that it was safer for a purchaser to accept a shorter period title than it was in the past, secure in the knowledge that any rights accrued in the past would now have been extinguished by the passage of time.[19] The effect of limitation in the case of unregistered land was, therefore, to add security to titles, with the result that it has been described as being 'absolutely fundamental to unregistered conveyancing'.[20]

A second, related, point concerns boundary disputes. A not infrequent bone of contention between neighbours is where, legally, the boundary lies between two adjoining properties. When such disputes arise, they can frequently generate 'a particularly painful form of litigation. Feelings can run high and disproportionate amounts of money are spent.'[21] If a fence is erected in a place other than where the legal boundary actually is, then some of the neighbour's land will have been wrongfully enclosed. At the end of the limitation period, the person whose land is on the wrong side of the fence will find that his action to recover the land will have been statute barred, thereby in most cases avoiding long and expensive litigation to determine the precise location of the boundary.[22]

As against these arguments, the fact remains that the result of the establishment of a possessory title is that one person, the squatter, obtains land from another, the owner of the paper title, without having to pay anything for it. This was put in graphic terms

---

[16] See Investigation of title, pp. 53–54.

[17] Law of Property Act 1925, s. 44, as substituted by Law of Property Act 1969, s. 23.

[18] See Dockray, loc. cit., at 277–284. The Limitation Act 1833 was an important piece of reforming legislation.

[19] See, e.g., *Re Atkinson and Horsell's Contract* [1912] 2 Ch. 1.

[20] Baroness Scotland of Asthal, Hansard, H.L. vol. 627, col. 1379.

[21] *Alan Wibberley Building Ltd v. Insley* [1999] 1 W.L.R. 894 at 895 *per* Lord Hoffmann. See also, *Palfrey v. Wilson* [2007] EWCA Civ. 94; *Haycocks v. Neville* [2007] EWCA Civ. 78 at [22] *per* Lawrence Collins L.J.

[22] For a graphic illustration, involving a very small amount of land, see *Hawkes v. Howe* [2002] EWCA Civ. 1136. See also *Steward v. Gallop* [2010] EWCA Civ. 823, where the parties agreed that the value of the disputed land was nil, but each had incurred costs in excess of £100,000 in fighting the case!

in *Lambeth Borough Council v. Bigden*,[23] where, had the claim to a possessory title succeeded, 'millions of pounds of public housing stock in one of the poorest boroughs in the country [would have] passed gratis into private ownership'. Not surprisingly, this has evoked expressions of distaste, a factor which has been said to have caused the courts to put glosses on the law, to avoid deciding in favour of the squatter.[24] This evident distaste has led to the squatter being described as a 'thief of the land'.[25] In similar vein, unhappiness has been expressed 'with a jurisprudence that allows squatters to acquire title to land knowing full well that the land belongs to another'.[26] Nor are such claims rare. In the debates on the Land Registration Bill, it was revealed that each year there are some 20,000 applications to the Land Registry by people asserting possessory rights, and of those some 15,000 are successful.[27]

Registered land and human rights

When title to land is unregistered, while it is true that the paper owner loses his title to the land without any compensation, there are strong policy reasons in favour of allowing the squatter to acquire a possessory title to land. Although the ability to do the same when title is registered has long been accepted, the justification for this state of affairs is far more problematic. In the case of unregistered land, the basis of title is possession, the question being who, as between two disputants, has the better right to possession. When title is registered, however, this is not the case. Although title can still, to a very limited extent be regarded as relative, in the sense that jurisdiction exists to rectify the register,[28] 'the basis of title is primarily the fact of registration rather than possession'.[29] As such, except in the case of boundary disputes, where the normal position is that the registered title does not guarantee the precise location of the boundaries,[30] there is no curative effect in respect of possessory titles. In fact, the converse is the case. The existence of possessory titles undermines the reliability of the register, in that the person registered as the proprietor and the person entitled to the enjoyment of the land are different.

The lack of a convincing policy rationale for the operation of the acquisition of possessory titles when title is registered is the reason why the Land Registration Act 2002 has curtailed substantially the ability of a person to acquire a possessory title as against a registered proprietor. The enactment of the Human Rights Act 1998 has led to the question being raised as to whether the law regarding limitation of actions in

---

[23] (2000) 33 H.L.R. 478 at 483 *per* Mummery L.J., although one can also point to the sustained neglect in the management of their property which would enable such a claim to succeed. For an interesting discussion of what they term 'urban squatting', see N. Cobb and L. Fox (2007) 27 L.S. 236.

[24] See *Purbrick v. London Borough of Hackney* [2003] EWHC 1871 (Ch) at [7] *per* Neuberger J.

[25] E.J. Cooke [1999] Conv. 136 at 142. See also *J.A. Pye (Oxford) Ltd v. Graham* [2000] Ch. 676 at 709 *per* Neuberger J., views endorsed on appeal at [2003] 1 A.C. 419 at 426 *per* Lord Bingham of Cornhill.

[26] L. Tee [2002] Conv. 50.   [27] Baroness Scotland of Asthal, Hansard, H.L. vol. 627, col. 1332.

[28] See, e.g., *Re 139 High Street, Deptford* [1951] Ch. 884; see also Alteration and indemnity, pp. 171–182.

[29] (2001) Law Com. No. 271, para. 2.73.   [30] See Boundary disputes, pp. 176–177.

respect of land was compatible with the Act and, in particular with Article 1 of the First Protocol to the Convention. Article 1 provides that:

'Every natural or legal person is entitled to the peaceful enjoyment of his possessions. No one shall be deprived of his possessions except in the public interest and subject to the conditions provided for by law and by the general principles of international law.

The preceding provisions shall not, however, in any way impair the right of a State to enforce such laws as it deems necessary to control the use of property in accordance with the general interest or to secure the payment of taxes or other contributions or penalties.'

The question arose, therefore, whether the effect of the limitation provisions insofar as they affected registered land was compatible with this Article. This question must now be considered from the point of view of the registered proprietor of land, but also from that of the squatter, who may be required to leave land which he has occupied as a home.

Registered proprietors

When the issue of whether the law which enabled a registered proprietor of land to lose his title to it as a result of adverse possession infringed the human rights of the proprietor was first addressed, such discussion was *obiter*. This was because the Human Rights Act 1998, which came into force in 2000, did not operate retrospectively, and the cases where the matter arose pre-dated the implementation of the Act. Nevertheless, a consensus emerged that English law was compliant with the Convention. This was either because Article 1 of the First Protocol was not engaged at all,[31] or, even if it was, the law was justifiable in the public interest. The justification was that the law was 'reasonably required to avoid the real risk of injustice in the adjudication of stale claims, to ensure certainty of title and to promote social stability by the protection of the established and peaceable possession of property from the resurrection of old claims.'[32]

Notwithstanding this consensus, in *Beaulane Properties Ltd v. Palmer*,[33] Mr Nicholas Strauss Q.C., sitting as a Deputy High Court judge, came to a different conclusion. Taking the view that 'the pre-2003 law caused hardship to the registered proprietor, and gives unwarranted windfalls to undeserving land thieves',[34] he decided that English law, as it pertained to registered land, was incompatible with the Convention. Having reached this conclusion, he then felt free not to follow a recent House of Lords decision,[35] and, instead, applied a discredited analysis of the law to arrive at a result favourable to the registered proprietor.

The approach taken to this matter in *Beaulane* was, potentially, a source of considerable confusion and is open to the criticism that it is not open to a first instance

---

[31] *Family Housing Association v. Donnallen* [2002] 1 P. & C.R. 34 at [15] *per* Park J.; *J.A. Pye (Oxford) Ltd v. Graham* [2001] Ch. 844 at [822] *per* Mummery L.J.

[32] *J.A. Pye (Oxford) Ltd v. Graham, supra*, at [823], *per* Keane L.J. The comments on the Convention were unaffected by the reversal of the actual decision. [2003] 1 A.C. 419.

[33] [2005] 4 All E.R. 461. See M.J. Dixon [2005] Conv. 345.   [34] Ibid, at 509.

[35] *J.A. Pye (Oxford) Ltd v. Graham* [2003] 1 A.C. 419.

judge to disregard a decision of the House of Lords on the basis that he considers that it is inconsistent with decisions of the European Court of Human Rights.[36] The folly of adopting this course on his own interpretation of the Convention when there was not even a European Court judgment dealing with the matter was highlighted when it subsequently transpired that his interpretation of the Convention was wrong.

In *J.A. Pye (Oxford) Ltd v. United Kingdom*,[37] The Grand Chamber of the European Court of Human Rights considered whether a company, which had, as a result of the Limitation Act 1980, lost title to twenty-five hectares of land[38] to which it was the registered proprietor, had suffered an infringement of its human rights. By a majority of ten votes to seven, and arriving at a different conclusion to that reached by the Chamber of the Court which had heard the case at first instance,[39] the full Court held that it had not.

In reaching this decision, it was held that, as the consequence of adverse possession the proprietor had lost the title to his land, Article 1 of the Convention was engaged. The view which was taken, however, was that the effect of the Limitation Act was not to operate as a deprivation of a person's possessions within the meaning of the second sentence of the first paragraph of Article 1, but as a control of the use of land within the meaning of the second paragraph.[40] The issue then became whether the working of English law was within an acceptable margin of appreciation. As to this, the majority view was that 'the existence of a 12 year limitation period for actions for recovery of land as such pursues a legitimate aim in the general interest',[41] and that, 'Even where title is registered, it must be open to the legislature to attach more weight to lengthy, unchallenged possession than to the formal act of registration.'[42] The argument that the company's rights had been infringed because it had lost the title to its land without compensation received short shrift. The Court took the view that, although the land lost, particularly if it had development potential, would have been worth a substantial amount of money, this could not affect the outcome of the case. This was because, if limitation periods are to fulfil their purpose, this will always be the case, and must apply whatever the size of the claim.[43]

The decision of the Grand Chamber in *Pye (Oxford) Ltd v. United Kingdom* undermines completely the decision in *Beaulane Properties Ltd v. Palmer*. Although in *Ofulue v. Bossert*,[44] Arden L.J. somewhat enigmatically declined to comment on the decision,[45] save to say that leave to appeal out of time was being sought in that case, the

---

[36] See the comments in *Kay v. London Borough of Lambeth* [2006] UKHL 10 at [40]–[45] *per* Lord Bingham of Cornhill. Cf. *Ofulue v. Bossert* [2008] EWCA Civ. 7 at [9] *per* Arden L.J., affmd without reference to this issue: [2009] UKHL 16.

[37] (2007) (Application No 44302/02). See E.J. Cooke (2008) 59 N.I.L.Q. 149.

[38] In the House of Lords, the area of land was said to be 25 hectares, whereas in the European Court it was said to be 23 hectares. Obviously, nothing turned on this.

[39] [2005] 49 E.G. 90.   [40] *Pye (Oxford) Ltd v. United Kingdom, supra*, at [66].   [41] Ibid. at [70].

[42] Ibid. at [74].   [43] Ibid. at [85].

[44] [2008] EWCA Civ. 7 at [54]. See M.J. Dixon [2008] Conv. 160.

[45] The statement in Harpum, Bridge, and Dixon, *Megarry & Wade, The Law of Real Property* (7th edn) (London: Sweet & Maxwell, 2008), 1422 that *Beaulane* was disapproved is wrong.

decision of the House of Lords in *Pye* was followed. It now seems clear that *Beaulane* is wrongly decided, and that the English law of adverse possession as it affects registered land is compliant with the European Convention on Human Rights, and it is also clear that the full authority of the House of Lords in *Pye* has been restored.[46]

Squatters

As will be seen, the reforms enacted by the Land Registration Act 2002 have made it considerably more difficult for a squatter to acquire a possessory title to registered land than was previously the case. This raises the question as to whether a squatter who has occupied property as a home over a prolonged period can, notwithstanding the fact that he has no legal right to be on the land, nevertheless, resist a possession action by the legal owner. The effect of the Supreme Court decision in *Manchester City Council v. Pinnock*[47] is that the answer to this must, in principle, be in the affirmative.

   Pinnock decided that a person who occupies property as a home can rely on Article 8 of the European Convention to resist a possession action, even if he has no legal right to be on the property. The question of proportionality may be raised. While, admittedly, this was held to be the case where the initial possession was lawful, it is hard to see why that fact should disentitle the squatter from raising the same argument. This matter was adverted to by Lord Bingham of Cornhill in *Kay v. Lambeth London Borough Council*[48] where, after referring to the test of proportionality said:

'Rarely, if ever, could this test be satisfied where squatters occupy the land of a public authority which they do not and…never had any right to occupy, *and the public authority act timeously to evict them*…[I]t is very hard to imagine circumstances in which a court could properly give squatters of the kind described above anything more that a very brief respite.'

This, it will be observed, relates to public authorities who act expeditiously to regain possession. When a squatter, perhaps with a family, has occupied local authority property for a period of many years, then it would seem that the issue of the proportionality of the possession proceedings could be raised, and any personal circumstances of the occupiers brought into play.

Limitation under the 1980 Act

Section 15 of the Limitation Act 1980 provides that no action shall be brought by any person to recover any land after the expiration of twelve years from the date on which the right of action accrued to him, or if first accrued to some person through whom

46 See *National Westminster Bank Plc v. Ashe* [2008] EWCA Civ. 55 at [92] *per* Mummery L.J., admittedly without reference to *Beaulane*. See also *Ofulue v. Bossert* [2009] UKHL 16 at [67]–[68] *per* Lord Neuberger of Abbotsbury; *Higgs v. Leshal Maryas Investment Company Ltd* [2009] UKPC 47 at [57] *per* Lord Scott.
47 [2010] UKSC 45. For a full discussion of this decision, see Chapter 3 and M.P. Thompson [2011] Conv.421.
48 [2006] 2 A.C. 465 at [37], italics supplied.

he claims, that person. The Act refers to the right of action accruing to some person through whom the person seeking to recover the land claims. Thus, if A was dispossessed by S four years prior to B acquiring the title from A, B has a further eight years in which to bring his action against S to recover the land. The converse situation is also true. Suppose C was dispossessed by D four years previously and then D is dispossessed by E, who occupies the land for a further eight years. At this stage, C's cause of action will be barred and so he cannot recover the land from E.[49] D, however, who was in possession of the land before E will be able to recover the land from him, provided that he brings the action within the next eight years, as his right of action accrued four years ago.[50] The general period of limitation under the 1980 Act is twelve years. There are some limited exceptions to this, of which the most important is that when the land is owned by the Crown, the period is thirty years.[51]

The accrual of a right of action

For time to begin to run in favour of the claimant, who is normally referred to as the squatter, certain conditions laid down by section 15 of and Schedule 1 to the Act must be satisfied. The two main requirements are that:

(i)   the owner of the land who is entitled in possession has been dispossessed or has discontinued his possession; and

(ii) some other person has gone into adverse possession of the land.

The various issues raised by these requirements will be considered in turn.

Entitled in possession

The Act refers to a person who is entitled in possession. Provision is made for the position of those who have future interests in the land and the squatter went into possession of the land before that interest fell into possession. Section 15(2) of the Act provides that time begins to run from the date when the squatter took possession. No action can then be brought by the holder of the future interest twelve years from that date or six years from the date when his interest fell into possession, whichever is the longer. So, if land is held by A for life, remainder to B in fee simple, and S takes possession while A is still alive, B must bring an action for possession within either twelve years of S taking possession or six years after A's death, whichever is the later. The purpose of this provision is to prevent the interest of the holder of a future interest being barred before it has actually come into possession. In such circumstances, the squatter

---

[49] See *Chambers v. London Borough of Havering* [2011] EWCA Civ. 1576 at [52] *per* Lewison L.J.

[50] See generally, *Asher v. Whitlock* (1865) L.R. 1. Q.B. 1. See also *Sze To Chan Keung v. Kung Kwok Wai David* [1997] 1 W.L.R. 1232, which was, incidentally, the last appeal to the Privy Council from Hong Kong: see at 1233 *per* Lord Hoffmann.

[51] Limitation Act 1980, s. 25; Sched. 1, paras 11 and 12. It is not necessary that the Crown is the owner of the land throughout the thirty-year period. See *Hill v. Transport for London* [2005] 3 All E.R. 677.

may find that, despite having been in adverse possession for longer than twelve years, his right to continued possession is defeated by the holder of a future interest bringing possession proceedings.

Tenancies

A squatter may go into possession when the land is subject to a tenancy. This adverse possession will operate against the tenant but will not do so against the owner of the reversion. Although the landlord is regarded as being in possession of the land, because he is in receipt of the rents and profits,[52] in the present context his claim to physical possession is what is important and so 'the landlord's right of action accrues when, but only when, the lease ends and the landlord's reversionary estate falls into possession'.[53] The position when a squatter defeats the tenant's title is complex and will be returned to later in this chapter.

It is possible for a tenant to be in adverse possession of a property. He cannot, however, acquire a possessory title of the property which is subject to the lease,[54] as he cannot deny his own landlord's title.[55] If he does not pay rent, however, then the landlord's right to bring an action in respect of the arrears will be barred after six years.[56] The tenant can acquire a possessory title against his landlord if he remains in possession of the property, without paying rent, after the lease has terminated. In the case of a written periodic tenancy, time starts to run from the termination of the lease, that occurring when either party has served upon the other a notice to quit.[57] In the case of an oral periodic tenancy, or one arising by implication, time begins to run from the end of the first period or, if rent is paid subsequently, from the last payment of rent.[58] In the case of a tenancy at will, which, as the name suggests, is a lease which either party can, at any time, terminate,[59] time will begin to run in favour of the tenant when the lease is determined.[60]

If a tenant occupies land owned by a third party, there is a rebuttable presumption that the occupation is on behalf of the landlord.[61] So, in *London Borough of Tower Hamlets v. Barrett*,[62] a tenant of a pub occupied adjoining land for the requisite period

---

[52] Law of Property Act 1925, s. 205(1)(xix).

[53] *Chung Ping Kwan v. Lam Island Development Co. Ltd* [1997] A.C. 38 at 46 *per* Lord Nicholls of Birkenhead.

[54] If the person occupies in the mistaken belief that he has a tenancy, he may acquire a possessory title against the freeholder. See *Ofulue v. Bossert* [2008] EWCA Civ. 7.

[55] A tenant in occupation under a tenancy granted contrary to a term in a mortgage will not be in adverse possession as against the mortgagee: see *Carroll v. Manek* (1999) 79 P. & C.R. 173 at 185 *per* Judge Hicks.

[56] Limitation Act 1980, s. 19. If rent is paid to a person other than the landlord, time will begin to run against the owner of the reversion in favour of the person in receipt of the rent: Sched. 1, para. 6.

[57] See Notice to quit, p. 453.   [58] Limitation Act 1980, Sched. 1, para. 5(1)(2).

[59] See Tenancies at will, p. 420.

[60] *Colchester Borough Council v. Smith* [1991] Ch. 448 at 481 *per* Ferris J.

[61] *King v. Smith* [1950] 1 All E.R. 553; *Smirk v. Lyndale Developments Ltd* [1975] Ch. 317 at 323–331 *per* Sir John Pennycuick V.-C., reversed on the facts but approved on this point, ibid. at 337 *per* Lawton L.J.

[62] [2005] EWCA Civ. 923.

of time. It was held that the possessory title was acquired on behalf of the landlord. When, however, the landlord transferred the freehold of the pub to the tenant, this operated also to transfer the area of land to the tenant who was able, therefore, to resist a possession action brought by the local authority. This presumption is rebuttable and the further the land is away from that which is subject to the tenancy, the more likely it is to be rebutted.[63] If the tenant occupies other land, which is also owned by the landlord, a similar presumption applies, so that the land is regarded as being subject to the terms of the original lease.[64]

Trustees

As a matter of general principle, a trustee cannot acquire a possessory title against his beneficiary.[65] A consequence of this is that, because land which is subject to co-ownership is held on trust,[66] one co-owner cannot acquire a possessory title against the other.[67]

Mortgagors

Under the general law of mortgages, the mortgagee—that is the lender—is entitled as from the date of the mortgage, to possess the mortgaged property.[68] Ordinarily, the mortgagee does not exercise this right and, instead, it is the mortgagor, that is the borrower, who is in possession. In *National Westminster Bank Plc v. Ashe*,[69] the mortgagor had been in possession of the property for twelve years, during which time he had neither made any payments under the mortgage or, in any other way, acknowledged the rights of the mortgagee. It was held that 'even though it may come as an unpleasant surprise to the Bank and other mortgagees that their mortgagors are in adverse possession',[70] this was the outcome which had occurred, and the registered charge was removed from the mortgagor's register of title. The bank raised concerns that a decision to this effect could lead to many mortgagees losing their security. This fear was, quite rightly, seen as an exaggeration, in that it will surely not be common for a lender to allow a mortgagor to remain in possession for twelve years without either receiving any payment, or taking other steps to enforce its security. Furthermore, even if a bank is prepared to allow a defaulting mortgagor to remain in the property, it is quite easy for it to prevent the mortgagor from acquiring a possessory title, by ensuring that he acknowledges the mortgagee's title.[71]

---

[63] Ibid. at [31] *per* Neuberger L.J.   [64] *J.F. Perrot & Co. v. Cohen* [1958] 1 K.B. 705.
[65] Limitation Act 1980, s. 22(2); *J.A. Pye (Oxford) Ltd v. Graham* [2003] 1 A.C. 419 at 434 *per* Lord Browne-Wilkinson.
[66] See Chapter 10.
[67] *Re Landi* [1939] Ch. 828. For the different position in Jamaica, see *Wills v. Wills* [2004] 1 P. & C.R. 37.
[68] See *Four-Maids Ltd v. Dudley Marshall (Properties) Ltd* [1957] Ch. 317, and The right to possession, pp. 512–513.
[69] [2008] EWCA Civ. 55.   [70] Ibid. at [88] *per* Mummery L.J.
[71] Ibid. at [6]–[19] *per* Mummery L.J. For acknowledgement of title, see Interruption of time, pp. 254–255.

Disabilities

Although the fact that a person suffering from a disability[72] does not mean that his interest is not in possession, this is relevant to the length of the limitation period and so it is convenient to deal with this matter here. If possession is taken by the squatter prior to the occurrence of the disability of the paper owner, or the person through whom he claims, then the supervening disability does not affect the running of time and the action will be barred after twelve years.

When possession is taken and the paper owner is suffering from a disability, the action for possession may be brought at any time up to six years from when the person ceased to be under a disability or has died[73] (whichever is the longer), notwithstanding that the period of limitation has expired.[74] Section 28(4) of the Act, however, sets a maximum period of thirty years in which an action can be brought from the date of its accrual.

Public Rights

It is not possible to obtain a possessory right as against a public highway,[75] although one can acquire such a right to land beneath the surface of the highway, such as might occur in the case of a cellar.[76] Similarly, one can acquire a possessory right to a river bed, despite there being a public right of navigation on the river, which will continue notwithstanding the position with respect to the land below it.[77]

ADVERSE POSSESSION

For the limitation period to become an issue, a right of action must have accrued and it is provided by the Act that no right of action shall be deemed to have accrued unless the land is in the possession of some person in whose favour the period of limitation can run, that possession being termed, although not defined, as being 'adverse possession'.[78] The concept of adverse possession involves two elements. These are the dispossession or discontinuance of possession by the owner and the requisite possession by the squatter.

---

[72] This relates to minors and persons of unsound mind: see Limitation Act 1980, s. 38(2)(3)(4). As a minor lacks capacity to hold a legal estate in land, this disability can relate only to equitable interests.

[73] If the person who succeeds to the land is also under a disability, there is no further extension of the time period in which to bring an action: Limitation Act 1980, s. 28(3).

[74] Limitation Act 1980, s. 28(1).

[75] *R. (on the application of Smith) v. Land Registry* [2010] EWCA Civ. 200.

[76] Ibid at [19] *per* Arden L.J.

[77] *Roberts v. Swangrove Estates Ltd* [2007] 2 P. & C.R. 326; *Port of London Authority v. Ashmore* [2010] EWCA Civ. 30.

[78] Limitation Act 1980, Sched. 1, para. 8.

Dispossession or discontinuance

The starting point in establishing a claim to adverse possession is to show that the paper owner has either been dispossessed or has discontinued his occupation of the land. In *Rains v. Buxton*,[79] Fry J. explained the fairly obvious distinction between the two as being that 'the one is where a person comes in and drives out the others from possession, the other is where the person in possession goes out and is followed into possession by other persons'.

Adverse possession cases normally involve the latter scenario, as, if a person is forcibly evicted from property, the matter is unlikely to lie uncontested for a period of twelve years. The normal situation is where land has been unused by the owner of it and the squatter then argues that he has taken over the land. Discontinuance must, nevertheless, be established and relatively minor acts by the owner of it are likely to be regarded as negating this requirement,[80] although merely leaving chattels on open land is not enough to maintain possession of it,[81] and neither is the sporadic draining of water on the land in question.[82]

Establishing adverse possession

For the owner's title to be defeated by limitation, more than a mere discontinuance of possession must be shown; a squatter must establish the necessary twelve years' adverse possession. This involves a number of matters. First, the squatter must establish possession as a fact. Secondly, he must show the requisite intention with regard to that possession and, finally, he must show the possession to be adverse, the final requirement overlapping to a degree with the second.

Factual possession

The squatter must establish an appropriate degree of physical control over the property in question[83] in order to be regarded as being in possession of it.[84] In considering what amounts to a sufficient degree of physical control, the courts will apply an objective test, which relates to the nature and quality of the land in question and is not subject to any variation accorded to the resources and status of the individual parties to the case.[85]

---

[79] (1880) 14 Ch.D. 537 at 540.

[80] See *Powell v. McFarlane* (1977) 38 P. & C.R. 450 at 472 *per* Slade J.

[81] See *London Borough of Tower Hamlets v. Baker* [2005] EWCA Civ. 923 at [60] *per* Neuberger L.J.

[82] *J Alston & Sons Ltd v. BOCM Pauls Ltd* [2008] EWHC 3310 (Ch) at [77] *per* H.H.J. Marshall.

[83] In the case of a house, it is possible to establish adverse possession of a discrete part of a house: *Ramroop v. Ishmael* [2010] UKHL 14 at [25] *per* Lord Walker.

[84] *Powell v. McFarlane* (1977) 38 P. & C.R. 450 at 470 *per* Slade J. See also *Tennant v. Adamczyk* [2005] EWCA Civ. 1239 at [22] *per* Mummery L.J.

[85] *West Bank Estates Ltd v. Arthur* [1967] A.C. 665 at 678–679, *per* Lord Wilberforce. See also *J.A. Pye (Oxford) Ltd v. Graham* [2003] 1 A.C. 419.

In applying this objective standard, the most obvious act of possession is the physical enclosure of the land by fencing.[86] Fencing alone will not necessarily be sufficient, however, as if the purpose of erecting gates or fences is to protect a right of way, then the erection of the fences will not be considered to be the taking possession of the land.[87] It may also be the case that the purpose of the fence is to keep livestock from straying. If this is the case, then this will not be regarded as the taking of possession.[88] The reason for this is that '[a] fence is a barrier. It keeps things in and it keeps things out. No doubt it is reasonable to assume that a person who maintains a fence is doing so for both purposes, but that is not necessarily so.'[89]

Although the physical enclosure of the land is, generally, the most unequivocal way of taking possession of it, it is not an essential act; indeed, the property may be such that it is not capable of being enclosed, but a person may, by his acts in relation to it still take possession of it.[90] In *Wata-Ofei v. Danquah*,[91] it was stressed that the acts necessary to take possession of land will vary depending upon the land in question, so that, in the case of vacant and unenclosed land, which is not being cultivated,[92] there is very little that can be done to it to indicate that it has been possessed.[93] Consistent with this, it was held in *Red House Farms (Thorndon) Ltd v. Catchpole*[94] that the use of waste land for shooting was a sufficient act to constitute possession.

Much will depend upon the facts of each case as to whether or not the acts relied upon with respect to the disputed land will be regarded as sufficient to amount to possession of it. It is not necessary for the act relied upon to inconvenience the owner,[95] which is as is to be expected because the more inconvenience caused to the owner the more likely it is that an action will be brought against the squatter within the twelve-year period. Acts which are considered to be trivial acts of trespass will not suffice to constitute possession,[96] unless the nature of the disputed land is such that what otherwise would be regarded as a trivial act is the only sensible use of the land.[97]

---

[86] *Seddon v. Smith* (1877) 36 L.T. 168. If the fence is pulled down by the owner, however, this will be of little use as an act of possession. See *Marsden v. Miller* (1992) 64 P. & C.R. 239.

[87] See *Littledale v. Liverpool College* [1900] 2 Ch. 19; *George Wimpey & Co. Ltd v. Sohn* [1967] Ch. 487.

[88] *Inglewood Investment Co. Ltd v. Baker* [2003] 1 P. & C.R. 23, where the evidence was that, if the livestock had been cattle as opposed to sheep, the fencing would not have been put up. See at [30] *per* Aldous J.

[89] *Trustees of the Michael Batt Charitable Trust v. Adams* (2001) 82 P. & C.R. 406 at 415 *per* Laddie J. See also *Chambers v. London Borough of Havering* [2011] EWCA Civ. 1576 at [37]–[40] *per* Etherton L.J.

[90] See *Prudential Assurance Co. Ltd v. Waterloo Real Estate Inc.* [1999] 2 E.G.L.R. 85 and *Palfrey v. Wilson* [2007] EWCA Civ. 94 (in both cases a party wall was held to have been adversely possessed).

[91] [1961] A.C. 1238.

[92] For possession by cultivation, see *Hicks Development Ltd v. Chaplin* [2007] EWHC 141 (Ch.); *J. Alston & Sons Ltd v. BOCM Pauls Ltd* [2008] EWHC 3310 (Ch.); *Chambers v. London Borough of Havering* [2011] EWCA Civ. 1576 at [48] *per* Lewison L.J., although see Nature of use, pp. 547–548.

[93] *Hicks Development Ltd v. Chaplin* [2007] EWHC 141 (Ch.) at 1243 *per* Lord Guest. See also *Bristow v. Corrican* (1878) 3 App. Cas. 641 at 657 *per* Lord Hatherley.

[94] [1977] 2 E.G.L.R. 125. Contrast *Inglewood Investment Co. Ltd v. Baker* [2003] 1 P. & C.R. 23 at [35] *per* Aldous J.

[95] See *Trealor v. Nute* [1976] 1 W.L.R. 1295; *Williams v. Usherwood* (1981) 45 P. & C.R. 235.

[96] See *Williams Bros District Suppliers Ltd v. Raftery* [1958] 1 Q.B. 159; *Tecbild Ltd v. Chamberlain* (1969) 20 P. & C.R. 633.

[97] See *Mayor of London Borough of Hounslow v. Minchinton* (1997) 74 P. & C.R. 221 at 233 *per* Millett L.J.

Open enjoyment

Although it has been said that adverse possession must be open,[98] it is probable that the better way of putting it is that the possession must not be concealed or fraudulent. If the squatter's action is based upon fraud, deliberate concealment, or the consequence of a mistake, the time will not begin to run, unless the owner has, or could have, discovered the fraud, concealment, or mistake by reasonable diligence[99] and the onus of proof with regard to these matters is on the owner.[100] For adverse possession to be established, it is not necessary that the owner of the land is actually aware of the fact that the land is in another person's occupation.[101] Nevertheless, because of the need for the squatter to prove the requisite intention to possess, it will only be on very rare occasions that a squatter will be regarded as having been in adverse possession when that fact is not readily discoverable from an inspection of the land. It remains the case, however, that the test is simply to ask if the squatter is in possession.

The matter was considered in *Purbrick v. London Borough of Hackney*.[102] The property in question was what appeared to be a burnt out shell of a building which had survived demolition and had stood derelict for years. The squatter made an increasing amount of use of it over the years, although he admitted that, at first, he had sought to maintain a low profile, in case the owner saw him and tried to prevent his activity.[103] It was nevertheless held that the squatter was in possession. Keeping a low profile was not regarded as being the same as either fraud or concealment. The question is essentially factual and, on the facts of this case, it was said that 'to an ordinary speaker of English and, indeed, to any property lawyer—who many would say are not ordinary speakers of English—Mr Purbrick would appear to have been, at least on the face of it, in possession'.[104] Once that was established, this was sufficient to constitute the fact of possession, and any supposed test based upon how the position might have appeared to an objective observer was rejected.[105] Quite simply, it is 'wrong to formulate the legal test by reference to what the paper owner, or anyone else, might have inferred from a visit to the property'.[106]

The intention to possess

As well as factually being in possession of the land, the squatter must also have the requisite intention to possess it: the *animus possedendi*.[107] Quite what it is that the squatter must intend to do, however, has for some time been a matter of contention. In

---

[98] *Browne v. Perry* [1991] 1 W.L.R. 1297 at 1302 *per* Lord Templeman.
[99] Limitation Act 1980, s. 32(1).   [100] *Rains v. Buxton* (1880) 14 Ch.D. 537 at 540 *per* Fry J.
[101] *J. Alston & Sons Ltd v. BOCM Pauls Ltd* [2008] EWHC 3310 (Ch.) at [114] per H.H.J. Hazel Marshall. Cf. *Powell v. McFarlane* (1977) 38 P. & C.R. 452, where the claim of adverse possession failed on the facts.
[102] [2004] 1 P. & C.R. 34. See also, *Wretham v. Ross* [2005] EWHC 1259 (Ch.).
[103] Ibid. at [5] *per* Neuberger J.   [104] Ibid. at [18].
[105] Ibid. at [27]. For an argument to the contrary, see Jourdan, *Adverse Possession* (London: Butterworths LexisNexis, 2002), 155–158.
[106] *Wrotham v. Ross* [2005] EWHC 1259 (Ch.) at p. 3 *per* David Richards J. accepting the argument of counsel.
[107] *Powell v. McFarlane, supra*, at 470 *per* Slade L.J.

Littledale v. Liverpoool College,[108] Lindley L.J., in an influential *dictum*, insisted that the squatter must not intend simply to possess the land; it was necessary to intend also to exclude everyone else, including the true owner, from the property. This requirement was open to both theoretical and practical objections. The former related to the change in the law brought about in 1833. Until the Real Property Limitation Acts of 1833 and 1874, the rights of the owner of the paper title were not regarded as having been interfered with unless he had been ousted by the squatter. Where a squatter had taken possession of land without ousting the true owner, this was considered to be 'non-adverse' possession.[109] In 1833, the cause of action was deemed to accrue on the dispossession of, or discontinuance by, the paper owner[110] and from that time on, the question was simply whether the squatter had taken possession of the disputed land; it was not necessary to show an intention to oust the holder of the paper title.[111]

Despite this, the idea that the squatter must intend to exclude everyone, including the true owner, gained currency.[112] Nevertheless, it was contrary to principle and, moreover, erected an artificial barrier in the way of a squatter seeking to establish a possessory title as it required him to show 'little more than a private intention to do something which [he] is not required to attempt and which, in most cases, he could not lawfully or practically do.'[113]

This latter point is important as, if a squatter knows that the land he is occupying does not belong to him, he knows that he is not able to exclude the true owner. Nevertheless, such a person is able to acquire a possessory title and his willingness to pay for the right to occupy the land, if requested to do so will not prevent the squatter from being in adverse possession.[114] Similarly, an attitude by the squatter that he would leave the property if asked to do so would render him a 'candid squatter',[115] and would not prevent him from having the requisite intention to possess. The practicalities involved led to a more cautious statement of principle in *Powell v. Macfarlane*,[116] where Slade J. said:

'[T]he *animus possedendi* involves the intention, in one's own name, and on one's own behalf, to exclude the world at large, including the owner with the paper title if he be

---

[108] [1900] 1 Ch.D. 19 at 23. For an interesting discussion of the introduction of this requirement, and its origins in German law, see O. Radley-Gardner (2005) 25 O.J.L.S. 727.

[109] See *Paradise Beach and Transportation Co. Ltd v. Price-Robinson* [1968] A.C. 1072 at 1082 *per* Lord Upjohn; M. Dockray [1982] Conv. 256 at 258.

[110] Real Property Limitation Act 1833, s. 3.

[111] See *Culley v. Doe d. Taylerson* (1840) 11 Ad. & El. 1008 at 1015 *per* Lord Denman C.J.

[112] See, e.g., *Battersea Freehold and Leasehold Co. Ltd v. The Mayor and Burgesses of the London Borough of Wandsworth* (2001) 82 P. & C.R. 137 at 144 *per* Rimer J.; *Trustees of the Michael Butt Charitable Trust v. Adams* (2001) 82 P. & C.R. 406 at 412–413 *per* Laddie J.

[113] Dockray, loc. cit., at 261.

[114] *Ocean Estates Ltd v. Pinder* [1969] 2 A.C. 19 at 24. See also, *The Mayor and Burgesses of Lambeth v. Blackburn* (2001) 82 P. & C.R. 494; *J.A. Pye (Oxford) Ltd v. Graham* [2003] 1 A.C. 419 at 429 *per* Lord Browne-Wilkinson.

[115] *J. Alston & Sons Ltd v. BOCM Paul Ltd* [2008] EWHC 3310 (Ch.) at [105] *per* HH Judge Hazel Marshall.

[116] (1977) 38 P. & C.R. 452 at 470. Italics supplied.

not himself the possessor, *so far as is reasonably practicable and so far as the law will allow him.*'

More recent statements as to what it is that the squatter must intend to do, were made in *Buckinghamshire County Council v. Moran*,[117] where Slade L.J. stressed that what is required is that the squatter must intend to possess the land. That position was itself attacked and the argument advanced that not only must the squatter intend to exclude everyone, including the true owner from the land, he must intend actually to own it.[118] This dispute has now been authoritatively resolved by the House of Lords in *J.A. Pye (Oxford) Ltd v. Graham*,[119] where it was held that the requisite intention was the intention to possess.

Intention to possess and not to own

The dispute involved twenty-five hectares of agricultural land in Berkshire of which, at all material times, Pye was the registered proprietor. In 1977, Pye sold farmland, that land being acquired by the Grahams in 1982. The disputed area was retained by Pye, who intended, in the future, to develop it. From 1982, the Grahams used their own farmland together with the disputed land for farming purposes. Early in 1983, Pye and the Grahams entered into a written agreement to confer grazing rights on the land. On the expiry of this agreement, Pye's surveyor wrote to the Grahams requiring them to vacate the land. He also wrote to Pye asking if they could be granted a new tenancy but Pye declined on the basis that they wanted the land to be vacant when they applied for planning permission. Thereafter, the Grahams in 1984 paid Pye £1,100 to buy crops on the land and, on several occasions, wrote to Pye asking for a new licence. None of these letters were answered and the last such letter was written in May 1985. Thereafter, until 1999, the Grahams continued to farm the land and it was held that, by then, a possessory title had been obtained.

Once it had been found that the Grahams were in factual possession of the land,[120] the issue turned to the intention of the occupier and, in particular, that of the Grahams' son, Michael, who, until his death in 1998, had carried out most of the farming activity. It was accepted that Michael was quite well aware that Pye could have repossessed the property and, if asked, would have been prepared to pay to be allowed to continue in occupation of it. The argument that this prevented the acquisition of a possessory title was rejected: what was required was the intention to possess the land. It was not necessary to have the further intention of excluding the owner or of being the owner of the land.[121] On the facts, this intention was plainly established.

---

[117] [1990] Ch. 623 at 636.

[118] L. Tee [2000] Conv. 113. For a convincing refutation, see O. Radley-Gardner and C. Harpum [2001] Conv. 155.

[119] [2003] 1 A.C. 419. See M.P. Thompson [2002] Conv. 480.

[120] This, somewhat remarkably, was found not to be the case in the Court of Appeal: [2001] Ch. 804 at 814–815 *per* Mummery L.J.

[121] [2003] 1 A.C. 419 at 437 *per* Lord Browne-Wilkinson.

To establish the requisite intention to possess the land, it is not necessary that his intention need in any way be hostile to the paper owner. Indeed, it may be the case that he mistakenly believes that he actually owns the land in question, or holds the property under a lease,[122] in which case the requisite intention to possess will be easy to establish.[123] To establish the intention to possess, the squatter must rely on the nature of the acts themselves. His own evidence given at trial as to what his intention was at the time when he started to make use of the land in question is regarded as being of little weight, as it is likely to be self-serving.[124] The acts relied upon 'must be unequivocal in the sense that his intention to possess has been made plain to the world. If his act is equivocal and his intention has not been made plain, his claim will fail.'[125]

Possession must be adverse

The Act requires that, before time will begin to run in favour of a squatter, he must be in adverse possession of the land.[126] What this means 'is possession which is inconsistent with and in denial of the true owner. Possession is not normally adverse if it is enjoyed with the consent of the owner.'[127] Central to the concept is, therefore, permission.

Permission

It is axiomatic that time does not begin to run in favour of a person in possession of another person's land if he is there with the latter's permission,[128] or if he believes that he has the owner's permission.[129] In this situation, he is a licensee and 'time can never run in favour of a person who occupies or uses land by licence of the owner with the paper title and whose licence has not been duly determined...'.[130] So, if a former tenant is given permission on the termination of the lease to remain in the property rent free, he will not be in adverse possession of the land.[131]

The question of whether possession was adverse arose in *Hyde v. Pearce*.[132] A purchaser bid successfully for a property at auction and paid a deposit. He was then allowed into possession. It was clear that, at this stage, he was a licensee.[133] A dispute

---

[122] *Ofulue v. Bossert* [2008] EWCA Civ. 7.

[123] See *Pulleyn v. Hall Aggregates (Thames Valley) Ltd* (1992) 65 P. & C.R. 452.

[124] *Bolton Metropolitan Borough Council v. Musa* (1998) 64 P. & C.R. D.36 at 37 *per* Peter Gibson L.J. See also the remarks in *J.A. Pye (Oxford) Ltd v. Graham* [2003] 1 A.C. 419 at 443 *per* Lord Browne Wilkinson.

[125] *Prudential Assurance Co. Ltd v. Waterloo Real Estates Inc.* [1999] 2 E.G.L.R. 85 at 87 *per* Peter Gibson L.J.

[126] Limitation Act 1980, Sched. 1, para. 8.

[127] *Ramnarace v. Lutchman* [2001] 1 W.L.R. 1651 at 1654 *per* Lord Millett.

[128] See *Hughes v. Griffin* [1969] 1 W.L.R. 23; *J.A. Pye (Oxford) Ltd v. Graham* [2003] 1 A.C. 419 at 434 *per* Lord Browne-Wilkinson.

[129] *Clowes Development (UK) Ltd v. Walters* [2005] EWHC 669 (Ch.) at [40] *per* Hart J.

[130] *Powell v. McFarlane* (1977) 38 P. & C.R. 452 at 459 *per* Slade J. See also *Buckinghamshire County Council v. Moran* [1990] Ch. 623 at 626 *per* Slade L.J.; *Clarke v. Swaby* [2007] UKPC 1 at [11] *per* Lord Walker of Gestingthorpe.

[131] *Smith v. Lawson* (1997) 74 P. & C.R. D.34.

[132] [1982] 1 W.L.R. 560 described as 'an odd little case' at 562 *per* Templeman L.J.

[133] When a person is negotiating to acquire an interest in land goes into possession, it is normal for a court to consider him to be an implied licensee. See *Sandhu v. Farooqui* [2004] 1 P. & C.R. 3; *Colin Dawson Windows Ltd v. King's Lynn and West Norfolk Borough Council* [2005] 2 P. & C.R. 19 at [39] *per* Rix L.J.

arose between the parties because part of the land contracted to be sold had previously been conveyed to another party and agreement could not be reached as to an appropriate abatement of the purchase price, to reflect the fact that the vendor could not comply fully with his contractual obligation. The vendor asked the purchaser to return the keys but he did not reply and there matters rested until, fourteen years later, the vendor, during the temporary absence of the purchaser, sold the property to a third party. The first purchaser claimed to have a possessory title to the land. His claim failed. Despite accepting that the licence to occupy had been terminated, the Court of Appeal held that he was not in adverse possession because he was there under the contract, which had not been terminated, and so had an equitable interest in the land, with the result that his possession was not adverse. This seems highly questionable. As his licence had been revoked, he did not have the right to be in possession of the land and, as he was there without permission, he should, it is submitted, have been held to have established a possessory title. Certainly, the case sits uneasily with *Bridges v. Mees*,[134] where a purchaser went into possession having paid all the purchase money but where the land had not been transferred to him. There, the judge had no difficulty in finding him to have been in adverse possession, although, as the vendor, having received the full purchase price, would have held the property on a bare trust for the purchaser, it is clear that the purchaser in this case had a much stronger right actually to take possession than did the purchaser in *Hyde v. Pearce*.

Licence to occupy

A second issue which can cause difficulty is where the owner purports to grant a licence to an occupier after possession has been taken. This occurred in *B.P. Properties Ltd v. Buckler*.[135] Land had been occupied by the defendant's family since 1916, originally on a yearly tenancy. This lease was surrendered and a new periodic tenancy arose. No rent was paid and, in 1955, a possession order was obtained and enforced against all the property except, for compassionate reasons,[136] a farmhouse and garden. The family remained in possession and, in December 1962, another possession order was issued but not enforced. Early in 1974, possession proceedings were again started but were not pursued. The land was then sold to the plaintiff who, in October 1974, one month short of twelve years from the date of the possession order having been obtained in 1962, wrote to the defendant's mother giving her permission to remain in the property, rent free, for the rest of her life. This offer was neither accepted nor rejected. After she died, the plaintiff brought possession proceedings against the son, who claimed to have a possessory title. His defence failed. The Court of Appeal held that the effect of the letter to his mother was that, from that point, she occupied the property as a licensee and was not, therefore, in adverse possession.

---

134 [1957] Ch. 475, not cited in *Hyde v. Pearce*.
135 (1987) 55 P. & C.R. 337. For cogent criticism, see H. Wallace [1994] Conv. 196, although see *Clowes Development (UK) Ltd v. Walters* [2005] EWHC 669 (Ch.) at [44] *per* Hart J.
136 (1987) 55 P. & C.R. 337 at 339 *per* Dillon L.J.

While the actual decision can just about be justified on the basis that the letter could be construed as the grant to the mother of a life interest in the property,[137] the actual ground for the decision seems to be wrong. Once a person is in adverse possession, it should not be open to the owner to convert the squatter into a licensee by the unilateral act of authorizing his presence. It was said in *Zarb v. Parry*[138] that if the owner of the paper title planted a flag on the disputed land, put up a notice or made an oral declaration of ownership, this would not prevent the squatter from continuing to be in adverse possession and, neither, it is thought, should it convert that possession into permissive occupation. For that to happen, it is thought that it should be necessary for the squatter to accept that he is there with permission.

Implied permission

It is no longer the case that, because the use of the property by a squatter is not inconsistent with some planned future use of the land by the title owner, that possession must be attributed to a licence. It is, nevertheless, possible that a licence to occupy can be implied. This issue was addressed in *J. Alston &. Sons Ltd v. BOCM Paul Ltd*.[139] S was originally a licensee of the disputed land. When that land was transferred to a new owner, the effect was to revoke the licence. Because the original occupation was permissive, it was argued that the continued occupation by the squatter after the licence had ended should be regarded as being under an implied licence and, therefore, permissive. This was rejected.

Judge Marshall accepted as axiomatic that if a person holds over after a permission to occupy has come to an end, the mere fact that the title owner does not object amounts to acquiescence and not implied permission, and that the two are different. Mere acquiescence is not sufficient to defeat a squatter's claim.[140] For a court to find the existence of a licence to occupy, this must be established as a matter of fact.[141] For a licence to be implied there must be some overt evidence of the fact of the licence being communicated with the licensee. Cases where such a licence has been implied without there being direct communication between the owner and the squatter have fallen into two groups.[142] These are when the occupation was pending negotiation of the grant of an interest in the land,[143] or where the history of the matter has shown that there was a specific intention of the owner to evict the occupier, followed by express reconsideration and change of stance, so that it was obvious that the continued occupation was permissive.[144] In cases that do not fall into either of these categories, it will, in most cases, be necessary for the permission to be communicated to the occupier and, it is suggested, the occupier must accept that the occupation is permissive.

---

[137] See Wallace, loc. cit., 203.   [138] [2011] EWCA Civ. 1306 at [43] *per* Arden L.J.
[139] [2008] EWHC 3310 (Ch.).   [140] Ibid at [129].   [141] Ibid at [117].   [142] Ibid at [137].
[143] *Colin Dawson Windows Ltd v. King's Lynn and West Norfolk Borough Council* [2005] 2 P. &.C.R. 19.
[144] *Hicks v. Chaplin* [2007] 1 E.G.L.R. 1.

Intention of the owner

A further difficulty caused by the need for possession to be adverse arose where the owner had a future use in mind for the land, and where the nature of the occupation by the squatter was not inconsistent with that intended use. The point arose in *Leigh v. Jack*.[145] The dispute focused on a strip of land on which the owner, at some time in the future, intended to construct a street. The squatter had stored material from his factory on the strip, thereby making it inaccessible to pedestrians, and erected fences at each end. This was held not to amount to adverse possession. In a much-quoted *dictum*, Bramwell L.J. said:

'...in order to defeat a title by dispossessing the former owner, acts must be done which are inconsistent with his enjoyment of the soil for the purposes which he intended to use it: that is not the case here, where it is the intention of the plaintiff and her predecessors in title not either to build upon or cultivate the land, but to devote it at some time to public purposes.'[146]

Although influential, the meaning of this *dictum* was not clear. It could be taken to establish that, if the owner of the land had some future use for it which was not precluded by the acts of the squatter, then his actions could never amount to adverse possession, although, if that was the case, the basis of any such rule would become important. Alternatively, it may have meant that, in these circumstances, it is merely more difficult for the squatter to establish the requisite *animus possedendi* for his occupation to amount to adverse possession. Various interpretations were put forward in the controversial case of *Wallis & Cayton Bay Holiday Camp Ltd v. Shell-Mex & B.P. Ltd*.[147]

The squatter performed extensive acts on the disputed land which was owned by a petrol company which intended, at a later date, to construct a road and a garage on the land, although the latter plan was subsequently abandoned. After twelve years, the squatter claimed to be entitled to the land, a claim rejected by the majority[148] of the Court of Appeal.

After referring to a number of authorities, including *Leigh v. Jack*, Lord Denning M.R. said:

'The reason behind the decisions is because it does not lie in that other person's mouth to assert that he used the land of his own wrong as a trespasser. Rather his user is to be ascribed to the licence or permission of the true owner.'[149]

---

[145] (1879) 5 Ex. D. 264.   [146] (1879) 5 Ex. D. 264 at 273.   [147] [1975] Q.B. 94.

[148] The cogent dissenting judgment of Stamp L.J. was approved in *Buckinghamshire County Council v. Moran* [1990] Ch. 623 at 640 *per* Slade L.J.

[149] *Wallis & Cayton Bay Holiday Camp Ltd v. Shell-Mex & B.P. Ltd* [1975] Q.B. 94 at 103. Contrast *Buckinghamshire County Council v. Moran* [1990] Ch. 623 at 644 *per* Nourse L.J. accepting that adverse possession is predicated on 'possession as of wrong'.

Ascribed licence

This *dictum* is manifestly heretical; the whole basis of adverse possession is that the squatter used the land as a trespasser and, so, to imply a licence, without any factual basis for so doing, would make it impossible for a claim of adverse possession to succeed.[150] What was less clear, however, was whether what was being done was to introduce a new, and wholly unjustifiable, rule into the law relating to adverse possession, or whether what was being done was to apply *Leigh v. Jack*, by explaining it in a totally unorthodox fashion. One view of that decision was that, if the owner of the land had some future plans for it, and those plans were not precluded by the squatter's activities, then his possession could not be adverse,[151] the basis of this rule being the novel, and fictitious, licence implied by Lord Denning.

The issue of whether Lord Denning's judgment was, in effect, a novel interpretation of *Leigh v. Jack* or, rather, a complete innovation, became important because of the manner of the legislative response to the decision. Schedule 1, paragraph 8(4) to the Limitation Act 1980 provides that:

'For the purpose of determining whether a person occupying any land is in adverse possession of the land it shall not be assumed by implication of law that his occupation is by permission of the person entitled to the land merely by virtue of the fact that his occupation is not inconsistent with the latter's present or future enjoyment of the land.

This provision shall not be taken as prejudicing a finding to the effect that a person's occupation of any land is by implied permission of the person entitled to the land in any case where such a finding is justified on the actual facts of the case.'

The effect of this provision was to make Lord Denning's approach untenable. For a licence to be implied, there must have been 'some overt act by the land owner or some other demonstrable circumstance from which the inference can be drawn that permission was in fact given. It is however, irrelevant whether the users were aware of those matters… [provided that] a reasonable person would have appreciated that the user was there with the permission of the land owner.'[152] Where it was not possible to imply a licence on the facts of the case, however, what was considerably less clear was the continuing status of *Leigh v. Jack*. Put another way, the issue remained whether, disregarding the implied licence theory, a person, whose occupation of land was not inconsistent with the projected use of that land by the owner, would be regarded as being in adverse possession. The issue was fully ventilated in the leading case of *Buckinghamshire County Council v. Moran*.[153]

---

[150] See *Ramnarace v. Lutchman* [2001] 1 W.L.R. 1651 at 1655 *per* Lord Millett.

[151] This was the basis of Ormrod L.J.'s judgment in favour of the petrol company. See also *Williams Bros Direct Supply Ltd v. Raftery* [1958] 1 Q.B. 159 at 173 *per* Sellers L.J.

[152] *Lambeth London Borough Council v. Rumbelow* (2001), unreported *per* Etherton J., approved in *Bath and North Somerset District Council v. Nicholson* [2002] 10 E.G.C.S. 156 *per* Mr Kim Lewison Q.C.; *Colin Dawson Windows Ltd v. King's Lynn and West Norfolk Borough Council* [2005] 2 P. &. C.R. 19 at [34] *per* Rix L.J.; *Bradford Estates (1983) Co. Ltd v. Taylor* [1996] 2 P. &. C.R. 5 at [23] *per* Sir Martin Nourse.

[153] [1990] Ch. 623.

Land owned by the council had been encroached upon for over twelve years by the defendant, an adjoining landowner, and his predecessor in title. Extensive use had been made of the land and access to it was possible only from the defendant's house. The council, who intended to use the land in the future for a proposed road diversion, argued that the defendant had not established adverse possession because the use to which the defendant had put the land was not inconsistent with their proposed future use of it.

This was rejected by the Court of Appeal, who decided in favour of the defendant. It was held that what was crucial was the intention of the squatter, not that of the landowner. What must be established is that the squatter has the relevant intention to possess, in the sense of excluding all other people from the property. In the instant case, the defendant was aware of the planned use of the land by the council[154] but was, nevertheless, held to be in adverse possession of it, the placing of a lock and a chain and a gate amounting to a final unequivocal demonstration of the defendant's intention to own the land.[155] The intention of the paper owner with regard to the future use of the land is relevant only insofar as the squatter is aware of that intention. Even then, as *Moran* itself demonstrates, this knowledge does not preclude the establishment of adverse possession. Rather, its relevance relates to the state of mind of the squatter who, if he actually intends to use the land so as not to interfere with the owner's planned use of the land, is likely not to have the requisite *animus possedendi* to achieve adverse possession.

It has now been made clear by the House of Lords in *J.A. Pye (Oxford) Ltd v. Graham* that the 'suggestion that the sufficiency of the possession can depend on the intention not of the squatter but the true owner is heretical and wrong',[156] and this view has subsequently been endorsed by the Privy Council.[157] The original formulation of this principle in *Leigh v. Jack* was said to be wrong.[158] It was considered to be 'an attempt to revive the pre-1833 concept of adverse possession requiring inconsistent user',[159] and was never a correct statement of the law. In Lord Browne-Wilkinson's view, it would have been better if the term 'adverse possession' had not been used by section 10 of the Limitation Act 1939, and repeated in paragraph 8(1) of the Limitation Act 1980, as its continued use caused the two heresies concerning the respective intentions of the squatter and the paper owner to be perpetuated.[160] While it is now probably too late

---

[154] Ibid. at 640 *per* Slade L.J.   [155] Ibid. at 642 *per* Slade L.J.

[156] [2003] 1 A.C. 419 at 438 *per* Lord Browne-Wilkinson. Considerable reliance was placed on a valuable article by M. Dockray [1982] Conv. 256 and 'a remarkable judgment' at first instance *Powell v. McFarlane* (1977) 38 P. & C.R. 452: ibid. at 432.

[157] *Wills v. Wills* [2004] 1 P. & C.R. 37 at [29] *per* Lord Walker of Gestingthorpe. See also *Chambers v. London Borough of Havering* [2011] EWCA Civ. 1576 at [35] *per* Etherton L.J.

[158] Ibid., approving statements to this effect in *Buckinghamshire County Council v. Moran* [1990] Ch. 623 at 645 *per* Nourse L.J. See also *Mayor of London Borough of Hounslow v. Minchinton* (1997) 74 P. & C.R. 221 at 227 *per* Millett L.J. For the somewhat startling suggestion, based on alternative reports of this decision, that Bramwell L.J. did not actually say what has been attributed to him, see A. Cloherty and D. Fox [2005] C.L.J. 558 at 559.

[159] [2003] 1 A.C. 419 at 438.   [160] Ibid.

to expect the expression ever to disappear from use,[161] the decision in *Pye* has done much to clarify the meaning of the term. It makes clear that what is required is factual possession of land by the squatter, without the permission, express or implied, of the paper owner, with the intention to possess that land.[162] The future plans of the paper owner are not relevant.

Human rights

The position of clarity established by the House of Lords was, temporarily at least, disturbed by the decision in *Beaulane Properties Ltd v. Palmer*.[163] In this case, the limitation period would have expired in the period between the coming into force of the Human Rights Act 1998, that is 2000, and the introduction of a new, more restrictive, regime pertaining to adverse possession which was brought in following the implementation of the Land Registration Act 2002, in 2003. Mr Nicholas Strauss Q.C., sitting as a Deputy High Court Judge, thought that 'the pre-2003 law caused hardship to the registered owner, and gives unwarranted windfalls in favour of undeserving land thieves.'[164] He held that the law as laid down by the House of Lords in *Pye* was incompatible with Article 1 of the European Convention. In order to interpret the provisions of the Limitation Act 1980 in a way which was compatible with the Convention, Mr Strauss felt able to apply the law as stated in *Leigh v. Jack*, despite that approach having been condemned as heretical by the House of Lords in *Pye*.

Beaulane was open to severe criticism both in terms of its analysis of the substantive law, and its approach to precedent.[165] Its underlying premise that the law of adverse possession as it applied to registered land was not compatible with the Convention was demolished, however, by the decision to the contrary by the Grand Chamber of the European Court of Human Rights in *J.A. Pye (Oxford) Ltd v. United Kingdom*.[166] Despite the fact that this decision has not been formally overruled,[167] subsequent statements of principle were derived from the speeches in *Pye*,[168] and, were it not for the somewhat perverse approach[169] of the Land Registry, one could say that it was inconceivable that a court would opt to follow *Beaulane* rather than *Pye*. That approach was to view the decision of the Grand Chamber as not affecting domestic law and to regard *Beaulane* as being good law.[170] Bowing to the inevitable, however, the Land Registry now applies the law in the same way as it would have done prior to the decision in

---

[161] See Land Registration Act 2002, Sched. 6, para. 11(1).

[162] See also *J. Alston & Sons Ltd v. BOCM Ltd* [2008] EWHC 3310 (Ch.) at [99] *per* HH Judge Hazel Marshall.

[163] [2005] 1 All E.R. 46. See M. Dixon [2005] Conv.345.   [164] Ibid at 509.

[165] See the 4th edn of this work at 229–231.   [166] (2007) Application No. 44302/02.

[167] See *London Borough of Tower Hamlets v. Barrett* [2005] EWCA Civ. 923 at [120]-[122] where Neuberger L.J., although describing the reasoning in *Beaulane* as impressive, expressly declined to say whether he agreed with it.

[168] See, e.g., *Ofulue v. Bossert* [2009] UKHL 16 at [67]–[68] *per* Lord Neuberger of Abbotsbury.

[169] This approach was described as 'misconceived and misleading anti-squatter guidance' in Emmet and Farrand, *On Title* (19th edn) (London: Sweet & Maxwell, Looseleaf), Bulletin 45.

[170] Land Registry, Additional Practice Guide 5.

Beaulane,[171] and it can now be regarded as settled that *Beaulane* was wrongly decided and will not be followed in future.

Interruption of time

Once time has begun to run, it does not matter if the first squatter is dispossessed by a second squatter. As against the owner, the two periods of time will be aggregated and, as against him, time will not stop running just because the squatter has, himself, been dispossessed. Where, however, the squatter gives up possession, or possession is recovered by the owner,[172] even temporarily, and he is not replaced by another squatter, the running of time will be interrupted and the full period of time will need to be established from the date when he retakes possession.[173]

Acknowledgement of title

The running of time will also be interrupted if the squatter acknowledges the title of the paper owner or pays part of the principal or interest due under a debt.[174] To be an effective acknowledgement of the owner's title, that acknowledgement must be in writing and signed by the person making it, or his agent, to the person entitled to the land, or to his agent.[175] An oral acknowledgement of the title will not suffice to stop time running; to allow this to have effect would lead to unnecessary disputes as to what was or was not said over the course of a long period of time.[176] The effect of a written acknowledgement of the owner's title is not suspensory. Once such an acknowledgement is made, then, for a possessory title to be established, the full limitation period must be established from that date.[177]

To interrupt the running of time, it is not necessary that the acknowledgement of the owner's title be explicit. Indeed, it is unlikely to be so.[178] An acknowledgement can be implicit, good examples of this being where the squatter offers to purchase the property,[179] or to rent it,[180] or enquires as to whether the owner intends to sell the property.[181] This is so, unless the offer is made 'without prejudice', when such

---

[171] Ruoff and Roper, *Registered Conveyancing* (London, Sweet & Maxwell, Looseleaf) 33.062.

[172] See *Zarb v. Parry* [2011] EWCA Civ. 1306 at [29]–[44] *per* Arden L.J.

[173] *Generay v. The Containerised Storage Co. Ltd* [2005] EWCA Civ. 478. The squatter erected a fence temporarily excluding himself from part of the land he had previously occupied.

[174] Limitation Act 1980, s. 29.

[175] Ibid., s. 30. See O. Radley-Gardner and C. Harpum [2001] Conv. 155 at 164–172.

[176] See *Browne v. Perry* [1991] 1 W.L.R. 1297 at 1301–1302 *per* Lord Templeman.

[177] Limitation Act 1980, s. 29(2)(a). For an example of this, see *J.A. Pye (Oxford) Ltd v. Graham* [2003] 1 A.C. 419.

[178] Although see *Lambeth London Borough Council v. Archangel* [2002] 1 P. & C.R. 18, where a letter from the squatter referred to Lambeth's property.

[179] *Edgington v. Clark* [1964] 1 Q.B. 367.

[180] *Lambeth London Borough Council v. Bigden* (2000) 33 H.L.R. 478. *R. v. Secretary of State for the Environment, ex parte Davies* (1990) 61 P. & C.R. 487, although disapproved in *J.A. Pye (Oxford) Ltd v. Graham, supra,* at 438 *per* Lord Browne-Wilkinson, is defensible on this basis. See also *Rehman v. Benfield* [2006] EWCA Civ. 1392.

[181] *Allen v. Matthews* [2007] EWCA Civ. 216, the background to this case being said to have been 'one of violence and crime' at [6] *per* Lawrence Collins L.J.

correspondence is not admissible as evidence.[182] Similarly, a written request to the owner of the land to take steps to stop the property from being vandalized should suffice to interrupt the running of time. In all of these cases, the requests carry with them an implicit acknowledgement that the addressee has a better title to the land.[183]

Section 29(2) of the Limitation Act 1980 requires that the acknowledgement of the paper owner's title be made by the person in possession of the land. The meaning of this was considered in the interesting case of *London Borough of Tower Hamlets v. Barrett*.[184] The Barretts were the tenants of a pub. Adjoining the property was open land, the registered proprietor of which was the local authority. The Barretts were found to be in adverse possession of the land. One of the issues which arose in the case was the effect of written negotiations between the landlord of the Barretts, Trumans Brewery, and the local authority with regard to Trumans acquiring the land. It was held that this did not amount to a written acknowledgement of the local authority's title. This was because the meaning of possession in the section was taken to mean physical possession and the brewery was not in possession. The Barretts were.[185] While plausible, it is suggested that this is unsound. In the first place, possession is normally defined to include the receipt of rents and profits,[186] and it is not clear why this should not apply in the present context. Secondly, the effect of the adverse possession by the Barretts was to acquire title on behalf of Trumans[187] and it seems to be very strange that the brewery, having acknowledged in writing the title of the local authority, should subsequently be held to have acquired a possessory title to it.[188]

If the paper owner obtains a possession order, this will stop time running,[189] but a letter demanding that the squatter vacate the premises will not.[190] Neither will the service of a writ seeking possession stop time running,[191] unless the action is proceeded with, so that if the writ is served eleven years and six months after the squatter has taken possession, but the case is not actually heard until the full twelve years has elapsed, the service of the writ will be regarded as having interrupted the running of time. The fact that unilateral demands for possession will not stop time running, however, casts further doubt on the proposition accepted in *B.P. Properties Ltd v. Buckler*,[192] that a unilateral permission to occupy, given to a squatter after he has taken possession, can stop time running for the purposes of the Limitation Act 1980.[193]

[182] *Ofulue v. Bossert* [2009] UKHL 16.
[183] Cf. *Pavledes v. Ryesbridge Properties Ltd* (1989) 58 P. & C.R. 459 at 480 *per* Knox J., who seemed to think that such action gave rise to different considerations when considering a person's intention to possess as opposed to an acknowledgement of title. This seems doubtful.
[184] [2005] EWCA Civ. 923.   [185] Ibid. at [95]–[99] *per* Neuberger L.J.
[186] Law of Property Act 1925, s. 205(2)(xix).   [187] Tenancies, pp. 239–240.
[188] This did not actually happen in the present case, as the brewery had transferred the land to the Barretts.
[189] *B.P. Properties v. Buckler* (1987) 55 P. & C.R. 337.
[190] *Mount Carmel Investments Ltd v. Peter Thurlow Ltd* (1988) 57 P. & C.R. 396; *Ramnarace v. Lutchman* [2001] 1 W.L.R. 1651 at 1653 *per* Lord Millett.
[191] *Markfield Investments Ltd v. Evans* [2001] 2 All E.R. 238.
[192] (1987) 55 P. & C.R. 337. See Licence to occupy, pp. 248–249.
[193] See M.P. Thompson [2001] Conv. 341 at 346–347.

THE EFFECT OF ADVERSE POSSESSION

The consequence of a squatter achieving the requisite period of adverse possession is a combination of statute and common law. The statute has a negative impact whereas the common law view is more positive in its impact. The negative side of adverse possession is established by section 17 of the Limitation Act 1980, which provides that 'subject to section 18 of that Act,[194] and section 75 of the Land Registration Act 1925,[195] at the expiration of the period prescribed by this Act for any person to bring an action to recover land . . . the title of that person to the land is extinguished'.

It should be noted that it is not simply the remedy that is extinguished. The effect of the statute is to extinguish the right which previously existed so that, in principle, an acknowledgement by the squatter of the paper owner's title after the limitation period has expired should have no effect; that which has been extinguished cannot subsequently be resuscitated. It is possible, however, for this effect to be achieved indirectly through a genuine compromise agreement to resolve a dispute between the parties after the twelve-year period has elapsed.[196] It is also possible for a squatter to be estopped from asserting a possessory title,[197] although more than the mere acknowledgement of title will be necessary for this result to occur.[198] Under the new law, whereby the period of adverse possession has to be proximate to the application for registration,[199] this latter issue will not arise.

Unregistered land

Although the general underlying position of a squatter is conceptually the same irrespective of whether title to the land is registered, because of legislative provisions relating to the effect of adverse possession when title is registered, there are significant differences in the outcome of certain situations, and so the two systems must be treated separately.

Independent title

The rights acquired by a squatter derive from the relative nature of title to land. A person in possession of land has rights good against anyone except a person with a better right to that land, that person being the rightful owner. If 'the rightful owner does not come forward and assert his title by process of law within the period prescribed by the Statute of Limitations applicable to the case, his right is forever extinguished, and the

---

[194] This relates to settled land and land held upon trust.

[195] See Registered title, pp. 258–260.

[196] *Colchester Borough Council v. Smith* [1992] Ch. 421. For cogent criticism, see A.R.H. Brierly [1991] Conv. 397.

[197] *St Pancras and Humanist Housing Association Ltd v. Leonard* [2010] EWCA Civ. 1442.

[198] See *J. Alston & Sons Ltd v. BOCM Pauls Ltd* [2008] EWHC 3310 (Ch.) at [109] *per* HH Judge Hazel Marshall.

[199] Land Registration Act 2002, Sched. 15, para.1. See Registration of adverse possession, p. 262.

possessory owner acquires an absolute title'.[200] This title is quite independent from the title held by the person who has been dispossessed. In no sense does the squatter obtain a form of 'parliamentary conveyance'[201] of the estate of the person dispossessed.

The squatter occupies the land as a fee simple owner, whose right of occupation is only liable to be defeated by the holder of a person with a better right to the land. This is, until the limitation period has expired, the person with the superior title to the land. When his right to possession has been defeated, the squatter's possessory title is a fee simple, quite independent from that of the person he has dispossessed. He is not, however, a purchaser of the land for value. Accordingly, he will be bound by any equitable interests affecting the land regardless of notice.[202]

Leasehold titles

When a squatter takes possession of land held previously by a tenant, again he takes possession as a fee simple owner and the title of the tenant is extinguished after the requisite twelve-year period. His position with regard to the freeholder is more complicated. What is clear is that time does not begin to run as against the freeholder until the lease has expired; until that time, he has no right to physical possession of the land.[203] When the lease expires, however, then, despite the squatter possessing the land as owner of a fee simple, the landlord will have the right to recover possession from the squatter because the landlord's right to the land is better than his.[204] The position while the lease continues to exist creates more difficulty.

While the lease is subsisting, the original contractual tenant remains liable to the landlord under the terms of that lease because there exists privity of contract between them. Because the effect of adverse possession is not to operate as a parliamentary conveyance, the effect of the squatter barring the title of the tenant is not to make him liable under the covenants contained in the lease.[205] An indirect method of enforcing these covenants is available, however, as, if the lease contains a forfeiture clause, the landlord can forfeit the lease as against the original tenant for breach of covenant, thereby ending that tenancy. The result of doing this is that, as against the squatter, who cannot apply for relief against forfeiture,[206] the landlord is now entitled to possession of the property. What has occasioned rather more controversy is to establish the respective positions of the landlord and the squatter when the tenant purports to terminate the lease after his title has been barred by a squatter.

---

[200] *Perry v. Clissold* [1907] A.C. 73 at 79 *per* Lord Macnaghten.

[201] *Tichborne v. Weir* (1892) 67 L.T. 735 at 737 *per* Bowen L.J.

[202] *Re Nisbet and Potts' Contract* [1906] 1 Ch. 386.

[203] *Chung Ping Kwan v. Lam Island Development Co. Ltd* [1997] A.C. 38 at 46 *per* Lord Nicholls of Birkenhead. See Tenancies, pp. 239–240.

[204] *Taylor v. Twinberrow* [1930] 2 K.B. 16.

[205] *Tichborne v. Weir* (1892) 67 L.T. 735. If the squatter actively takes advantage of covenants in the lease, he may then be estopped from denying that he is liable under other terms of that lease: *Tito v. Waddell (No. 2)* [1977] Ch. 106 at 299–302 *per* Megarry J.

[206] *Tickner v. Buzzacott* [1965] Ch. 426; D.G. Barnsley (1965) 28 M.L.R. 364. For forfeiture of leases, see Forfeiture, pp. 454–459.

Surrender of tenancy

This problem occurred in the leading case of *Fairweather v. St Marylebone Properties Ltd*,[207] where it was held by a bare majority of the House of Lords that a surrender of a lease by a tenant whose title was barred by the adverse possession of a squatter had the effect that the landlord was at that point entitled to possession of the property as against the squatter. This decision has been subjected to what has been termed a 'powerful critique'.[208] The essence of that critique is, indeed, plausible. Its basis is that the effect of the limitation period having expired is that the title of the tenant is extinguished,[209] and therefore he has nothing to surrender to the landlord. As he could not evict the squatter once the limitation period had expired, he should not be able to confer such a right upon the landlord.[210] He cannot transfer what he has not got.[211]

While persuasive, the argument is not compelling. As the majority in *Fairweather* pointed out, although the effect of the Limitation Act is to extinguish the tenant's title, it is evident that the title is not extinguished for all purposes. Were it otherwise, then when the tenant's title was barred by adverse possession, the landlord would be entitled to possession and the tenant would cease to be liable on the covenants in the lease, which, everyone agrees, is not the case. Moreover, if the original lease contained a break clause, giving either side the option to bring a fixed term tenancy to a premature end, and the landlord exercised this clause as against the original tenant whose interest had become statute barred, it should be the case that the landlord is now entitled to possession as against the squatter. The fact that adverse possession operates to extinguish the tenant's title *vis-à-vis* the squatter but does not do so *vis-à-vis* the landlord,[212] does seem to lead to the conclusion reached by the majority that it is open for the original tenant and the landlord to collude to defeat the squatter's title.

Registered title

The effect of adverse possession when title is registered is different from that when title is unregistered, this difference being occasioned by section 75 of the Land Registration Act 1925. This section provides that:

'**75**—(1) The Limitation Acts shall apply to registered land in the same manner and to the same extent as those Acts apply to land not registered, except that where, if the land were not registered, the estate of the person registered as proprietor would be extinguished, such estate shall not be extinguished but shall be deemed to be held by the proprietor for the time being on trust for the person who, by virtue of the said Acts, has acquired title against any proprietor, but without prejudice to the estates and interests of any other person interested in the land whose estate or interest is not extinguished by those Acts.

---

[207] [1963] A.C. 510.

[208] *Chung Ping Kwan v. Lam Island Development Co. Ltd* [1997] A.C. 38 at 47 *per* Lord Nicholls of Birkenhead, referring to H.W.R. Wade (1962) 78 L.Q.R. 541. The Privy Council found it unnecessary to express a view as to whether the decision in *Fairweather* was correct.

[209] Limitation Act 1980, s. 17.   [210] See Wade, loc. cit., at 552.   [211] Ibid., 559.

[212] [1963] A.C. 510 at 544 *per* Lord Denning.

(2) Any person claiming to have acquired a title under the Limitation Acts to a registered estate in the land may apply to be registered as proprietor thereof.'

The reason for the imposition of a trust is that, while the person whose title is barred remains the registered proprietor, he retains title to the land, and although normally the effect of adverse possession is to extinguish the title, this cannot happen until the register has been altered. Nevertheless, the registered proprietor is no longer entitled to the land and the solution to this paradox was to impose a trust upon him, thereby depriving him of the beneficial title.[213]

Although, in the *Fairweather* case, Lord Denning expressed the view that the imposition of the trust was a mere matter of machinery which 'does not alter the substantive law very much',[214] Lord Radcliffe was more cautious. He considered that the meaning of the section 'was not at all easy to discover'[215] and that he was 'not at all satisfied that section 75(1) does create a trust interest in the squatter of the kind that one would expect from the words used'.[216] It has now become apparent that the effect of section 75 is not merely mechanical but has caused there to be substantive differences between registered and unregistered land when considering the effect of adverse possession, in particular when adverse possession has occurred against a tenant.

The effect of registration

Where the title is leasehold, upon the expiration of the limitation period, the lease-hold estate is held upon trust for the squatter. There are difficulties caused by this, these difficulties first being explored in *Spectrum Investment Co. v. Holmes*.[217] The defendant had established a possessory title against a tenant. Some time later she applied for registration. The Land Registry contacted the tenant but received no reply, whereupon the defendant was registered as a leasehold proprietor with a possessory title and the title under which the original tenant had been registered was closed. Some time later, the plaintiff company, who had originally been registered with a possessory freehold title, was registered with an absolute title to the freehold. The position with regard to the defendant then being discovered, the original tenant then purported to surrender the lease to the company who, thereupon, sought possession. Browne-Wilkinson J., distinguishing *Fairweather*, which he accepted was factually indistinguishable from the present case,[218] held in favour of the defendant.

The reason why a different conclusion was reached related to section 75 of the Act. While noting that the section provides that the Limitation Acts are to apply to registered land to the same extent as they do to land which is unregistered, Browne-Wilkinson J. also observed that section 17 of the Limitation Act 1980 operated expressly subject

---

[213] See E.J. Cooke [1999] Conv. 136 at 142. For a penetrating analysis of the effect of adverse possession in registered land, see E. Cooke (1994) 14 L.S. 1. See also G. Battersby in Bright and Dewar (eds), *Land Law: Themes and Perspectives* (Oxford: Oxford University Press, 1998), 487 at 490–494.
[214] [1963] A.C. 510 at 548.   [215] Ibid., at 541.   [216] Ibid., at 542–543.
[217] [1981] 1 W.L.R. 221.   [218] [1981] 1 W.L.R. 221 at 225.

to section 75 of the Land Registration Act 1925. Section 75(2) of the Act entitles the squatter who claims to be entitled to have acquired a title to a registered estate to apply for registration thereof. The word 'thereof'[219] was regarded as significant, as it referred back to section 75(1). The effect of this was that the registration of the defendant with a possessory leasehold title operated to vest in her the estate held by the original tenant. In other words, the registration operated as a form of Parliamentary conveyance of the tenant's estate to the squatter. The consequence of this is that the tenant had nothing to surrender to the landlord, and so a different result was arrived at because title was registered than would have been the case had title been unregistered.

The impact of the trust

In *Spectrum Investment Co. Ltd v. Holmes*, the squatter had applied for registration, and been registered as proprietor, prior to the purported surrender of the lease. The position was expressly left open as to what the result would have been had the surrender occurred after the squatter had established twelve years' adverse possession against a person registered with a leasehold title but before any application had been made for registration by the squatter.[220] This issue fell to be decided in *Central London Commercial Estates Ltd v. Kato Kagaku Co. Ltd*,[221] where it was held that the freeholder still took subject to the squatter's possessory title.

In reaching this conclusion Sedley J. was aware that a squatter, when in adverse possession of land, is, in accordance with general principle, occupying the property as a fee simple owner. The effect of section 75, however, is that when the requisite statutory period has expired, a trust is imposed upon the leasehold estate and so he becomes the owner of that.[222] The upshot is that even if the tenant then surrenders the lease to the landlord, the equitable lease which has arisen in the squatter's favour takes effect as an overriding interest which is, therefore, binding upon the landlord who will not, therefore, be able to obtain possession of the land until the lease is determined: the opposite result to that which occurs when title is unregistered.

THE NEW LAW OF LIMITATION

The ability of a squatter to acquire title to another person's property has always attracted controversy. When title to the land is unregistered, there are strong arguments in favour of such a state of affairs. The existence of adverse possession enables defective titles to be cured and so adds to the security of conveyancing. Where title is registered, however, the converse is true, in that the existence of possessory titles

---

[219] This word is emphasized by Browne-Wilkinson J. in the judgment at [1981] 1 All E.R. 6 at 14 but the emphasis does not appear at [1981] 1 W.L.R. 222 at 230.
[220] [1981] 1 W.L.R. at 231.   [221] [1998] 4 All E.R. 948. See E.J. Cooke [1999] Conv. 136.
[222] [1998] 4 All E.R. 948 at 955.

reduces the reliability of the register of title.[223] It was this latter consideration, in particular, which led the Law Commission and Land Registry[224] to propose radical changes to the law insofar as registered land is concerned and these proposals have been implemented in the Land Registration Act 2002. Before considering the new regime, which will reduce substantially the ability of a squatter to acquire title to another person's land, it is convenient first to consider the necessary transitional arrangements.

Transitional arrangements: unregistered land

The changes effected by the 2002 Act apply where title is registered. Where title is unregistered, the rules of adverse possession will apply as they have always done. What must be considered is the position where the paper owner conveys the land to a purchaser, who is then registered with an absolute title. Under the 1925 Act, the registered proprietor would take subject to the squatter's possessory title as this interest was included within the list of overriding interests.[225] For three years after the Act came into force, this remained the case.[226] Now, after this period of grace has expired, the possessory title will only override first registration if either the squatter is in actual occupation of the land,[227] or the proprietor has notice of the possessory right.[228]

Transitional arrangements: registered land

If before the 2002 Act came into force, a squatter had established adverse possession against a registered proprietor, the proprietor would hold the estate on trust for the squatter.[229] If the registered proprietor transferred the land, then, for a period of three years after the 2002 Act came into force, the squatter's beneficial interest would override the registered disposition.[230] The three-year period having elapsed, the squatter's beneficial interest will now only bind a registered proprietor if the squatter is in actual occupation of the land and that occupation would be obvious on a reasonably careful inspection of the land.[231] In the case of registered dispositions, there is no separate provision in respect of squatters' rights of which the transferee has notice.

The new limitation regime

The 2002 Act has made fundamental changes to the operation of limitation in respect of registered titles. These changes apply only to registered land and do not affect the rights of squatters who have achieved the requisite period of adverse possession prior

[223] See Security of title, pp. 233–234.   [224] (2001) Law Com. No. 271, paras 2.69–2.74.
[225] Land Registration Act 1925, s. 70(1)(g).   [226] Land Registration Act 2002, Sched. 12, para. 7.
[227] Ibid., s. 11(4)(b), Sched. 1, para. 2.   [228] Ibid., s. 11(4)(c).
[229] Land Registration Act 1925, s. 75(1).
[230] Land Registration Act 2002, s. 29, Sched. 12, paras 11 and 18, inserting para. 15 into Sched. 3.
[231] Ibid., s. 29, Sched. 3, para. 2(c).

to the Act coming into force. For the future, therefore, the establishment of when the limitation period expired may be a crucial issue in disputes.

The end of automatic possessory titles

Under the old regime, if a squatter had been in adverse possession of land for at least twelve years then, as has been seen, the effect in unregistered land is that the title of the paper owner is extinguished. In the case of registered land, the land would be held on trust for the squatter who would, therefore, by virtue of his adverse possession of the land, have acquired an interest in it.[232] This is no longer the case. Under section 96 of the 2002 Act, no period of limitation under section 15 of the Limitation Act 1980 shall run against any person, other than a registered chargee, in respect of an estate in land or rentcharge the title to which is registered. As a consequence of this, the title of any person, other than a registered chargee, is not extinguished as a consequence of limitation.[233] The immediate effect of this is that there is no question of any trust arising in favour of a squatter by reason only of his prolonged occupation of another person's land. He acquires no interest as a result of that occupation.

Registration of adverse possession

The 2002 Act does not abolish adverse possession. As explained above, it prevents the automatic acquisition of a possessory title. A person may still apply for registration in respect of his adverse possession of land under section 97 of the Act, in which case the provisions of Schedule 6 take effect. Similarly, if a person is in adverse possession of land, he can also rely, by way of defence to a possession action brought against him, on the provisions contained in that Schedule.[234] The way that the Act operates is to make it far more difficult for a squatter to obtain a possessory title. It achieves this not by changing the substantive law. Rather, it operates to introduce stringent new procedural safeguards to enable a registered proprietor to defeat a claim to a possessory title which, before the Act, would have succeeded. What constitutes adverse possession remains, however, unaltered. This is made clear by paragraph 11(1) of Schedule 6 to the Act, which provides that a person is in adverse possession of an estate in land for the purposes of this Schedule if, but for section 96, a period of limitation under section 15 of the Limitation Act 1980 would run in his favour in relation to the estate.

Under paragraph 1(1) of the Schedule, a person may apply to be registered as the proprietor of a registered estate if he has been in adverse possession of the estate for a period of ten years ending on the date of the application. He may also apply for registration under paragraph 1(2) if he has in the period of six months ending on the date of the application ceased to be in adverse possession because he has been evicted other than by a court order, and on the day before his eviction, he would otherwise have

---

[232] Registered title, pp. 258–260.   [233] Land Registration Act 2002, s. 96(3).
[234] Land Registration Act 2002, s. 98.

been entitled to make an application and the eviction was not as a result of a court order. He may not make an application for registration if either he is a defendant in a possession action or if a judgment for possession has been given against him in the last two years.[235]

Before looking at the operation of the new system, some preliminary points can be made.

Time

The first, fairly obvious, point to make is the limitation period is reduced from twelve years to ten years. Secondly, the period of adverse possession has to be proximate to the application for registration or the bringing of a possession action. In the past, if a person had established adverse possession for the requisite twelve-year period, he would acquire a possessory title. That title would not be lost if he ceased to be in possession of the land. Under the 2002 Act, unless the reason for the person not being in possession is that he has been evicted other than by a court order, he will not have any rights under the Act, however long he had previously been in adverse possession of the land. A third point, which arises as a consequence of paragraph 11, concerns successive squatters.

Successive squatters

Under the old law, the periods of adverse possession of successive squatters could be aggregated, so that if A was in adverse possession of O's land for four years, and A was then dispossessed by B, who remained in adverse possession for a further eight years, O's title would be barred. A would have four years in which to bring possession proceedings against B, but B would have established a possessory title against O.[236] The position with regard to successive squatters has been modified by paragraph 11 of Schedule 6 to the 2002 Act. A person is to be regarded as having been in adverse possession for the requisite period if either he is the successor in title to an estate in land, during any period of adverse possession by a predecessor in title to that estate, or during any period of adverse possession by any other person which comes between, and is continuous with, periods of adverse possession of his own. The meaning of the provisions is best explained by examples.

1. O is the registered proprietor of land. A goes into adverse possession and, after six years, dies. B, who is entitled under A's will or upon his intestacy, goes into possession and remains there for a further four years. B is A's successor in title and the two periods of adverse possession can be aggregated to make up the requisite ten years of adverse possession.

2. O is the registered proprietor of land. He is dispossessed by C, who occupies the land for six years and is then dispossessed by D. D occupies the land for two years

---

[235] Ibid., Sched. 6, para. 1(3).
[236] *Asher v. Whitlock* (1865) L.R. 1 Q.B. 1; *Sze To Chun Keung v. Kung Kwok Wai David* [1997] 1 W.L.R. 1232. See Limitation under the 1980 Act, pp. 237–238.

and is then dispossessed by C, who occupies the land for a further two years. Although C has not been in adverse possession himself for the full ten years, as he is in possession at the relevant time, the period of D's adverse possession can be aggregated to his own to make up the full ten-year period.

3. O is the registered proprietor of land. He is dispossessed by E, who occupies the property for six years. E is then dispossessed by F, who occupies the land for a further four years. F is not a successor in title to E and, therefore, has not established the requisite period of adverse possession and cannot apply for registration.

Applications for registration

A person who has been in adverse possession for a period of ten years may apply for registration. When such an application is made, the registrar is required under paragraph 2 to give notice of the application to the following people:

(a) the proprietor of the estate to which the application relates;

(b) the proprietor of any registered charge on the estate;

(c) where the estate is leasehold, the proprietor of any superior registered estate;

(d) any person who is registered in accordance with rules as a person to be notified under this paragraph; and

(e) such other person as rules may provide.

The notice given under this paragraph must include notice of the effect of paragraph 4.

The effect of this notice is that the people upon whom it is served have a period of sixty-five business days[237] in which to respond to the application. If there is no response, then the applicant is entitled to be registered as the new proprietor of the estate. If that has happened, however, it will still be open to the former registered proprietor to argue that the requirements to establish a possessory title had not been met and, if successful, can then seek alteration of the register to restore the title to him.[238] If the person on whom the notice is served does respond, he may then require that the squatter's application be dealt with under paragraph 5. If this requirement is not made, then the effect of paragraph 4, to which the attention of the recipient of the notice is required to be drawn, is that the applicant must be registered as the new proprietor of the estate. Accordingly, if one of the people on whom the paragraph 2 notice has been served wishes to prevent the applicant from being registered as the new proprietor of the estate, he must require the application to be dealt with under paragraph 5.

Restricted scope of adverse possession

Once an application for registration has been made and the registered proprietor, upon whom notice has been served of the application, requires the application to be dealt with under paragraph 5, then the applicant is only entitled to be registered as the

---

[237] Land Registration Rules 2003, r. 189.   [238] *Baxter v. Mannion* [2010] EWCA Civ. 120.

new proprietor if one of three alternative conditions has been met. In every other case, the application for registration must be rejected. Similarly, if the boot is on the other foot and the registered proprietor seeks possession as against the squatter, a person only has a defence to such an action by virtue of his possession as a squatter[239] if he would have been entitled to make an application for registration under paragraph 1 of Schedule 6 and, had he made such an application the condition in paragraph 5(4) would have been satisfied.[240] These conditions must be considered.

Estoppel

The first condition laid down in paragraph 5 is that it would be unconscionable because of an equity by estoppel for the registered proprietor to seek to dispossess the applicant and the circumstances are such that the applicant ought to be registered as the proprietor. This is a curious exception and one which is apt to mislead. It envisages a situation where a person has gone into possession of another person's property, pursuant to some informal agreement, in circumstances where it would be unconscionable for the proprietor, subsequently, to object to the occupier's claim to the property. While this seems not unreasonable, the difficulty is that the person in occupation of the land is unlikely to be regarded as being in adverse possession at all, because his initial entry on to the land was almost certainly permissive. Moreover, if the dispute between the proprietor and the occupier occurs before there has been occupation of the land for ten years, the occupier will still be able to assert estoppel rights in the property although, in fairness, it should be recognized that this is most likely to occur when the proprietor seeks possession, and estoppel is used as a defence to that action, rather than when it is the occupier who seeks registration.[241]

Entitlement to registration

The second condition is that, for some other reason, the applicant is entitled to be registered as the proprietor of the estate. This would cover a case such as *Bridges v. Mees*,[242] where a purchaser of land paid the purchase price in full and went into possession but the land was never conveyed to him. This seems unexceptional.

Boundary disputes

The third condition provides a means of avoiding expensive boundary disputes and reflects the fact that, in the case of most registered titles, the precise boundaries are not fixed.[243] The condition is that:

(a) the land to which the application relates is adjacent to land belonging to the applicant;

---

[239] He may, of course, rely on any other defences which were open to him: Land Registration Act 2002, s. 98(6).

[240] In respect of the other conditions set out in para. 5, he would, independently of his possession as a squatter, have the right to defend possession proceedings and, therefore, come within s. 98(6).

[241] See S. Nield [2004] Conv. 137.   [242] [1957] Ch. 575.

[243] See The property register, p. 115.

(b) the exact line of the boundary between the two has not been determined under rules under section 60;

(c) for at least ten years of the period of adverse possession ending on the date of application, the applicant (or any predecessor in title) reasonably believed that the land to which the application relates belonged to him; and

(d) the estate to which the application relates was registered more than one year prior to the date of the application.

The third requirement merits some discussion. If a person deliberately moves a fence so as to enclose some of his neighbour's land, he will not be able to rely on this condition to enable his application to be successful, or to resist a possession action brought by his neighbour, because he will not reasonably believe that the land belongs to him. Less obvious, however, is the position when the squatter, originally, had a reasonable belief that he owned the relevant land but, later, circumstances change so that the belief, if still held, is no longer reasonable.

This issue was raised in *Zarb v. Parry*.[244] A disputed strip of land was situated between the land owned by two neighbours. The strip was enclosed by a hedge, which was not situated on the correct boundary between the two properties, so that it had, wrongly, been enclosed by owners of the northern plot. When a dispute erupted between the owners of the northern and southern plots, a surveyor was engaged, and he determined, wrongly, that the hedge marked the correct boundary between the two properties. As the dispute became prolonged and was being litigated, a second survey was ordered, and this determined that the hedge had been wrongly located and that, as a result, the strip had been wrongly enclosed. The Court of Appeal held that the owners of the northern plot had established adverse possession of the plot for the requisite period of time, and were, therefore, entitled to be registered with a possessory title.

One of the issues in the case was whether the owners of the northern plot reasonably believed that they owned the strip. When they acquired the land in the first place, it was clear that they did. Subsequently, however, as the dispute erupted, the question arose as to whether their continued belief was a reasonable one. It was held that it was. Although it was clear that the ownership of the strip had become a matter of dispute, that, in itself, would not prevent the belief being reasonable. As the intial survey supported their view as to the true position, the belief continued to be reasonable. Had that not been the case, however, then the belief would not have been reasonable with the result that reliance could no longer have been placed upon paragraph (c). The moral then would have been to have applied for registration immediately on doubt being cast on their ownership of the disputed strip, in which case they would still have had the requisite ten-year period prior to the bringing of proceedings when they reasonably believed the land to belong to them.[245]

---

[244] [2011] EWCA Civ. 1306.   [245] Ibid at [17] *per* Arden L.J.

Restrictions on applications

Under the old law, provision was made with respect to people suffering from a disability, this relating to minors and people of unsound mind.[246] The 2002 Act extends this protection. Under paragraph 8, no one may apply under Schedule 6 to be registered as the proprietor of an estate in land during any period in which the existing registered proprietor is:

(a) unable because of mental disability to make decisions about issues of the kind to which such an application would give rise or

(b) unable to communicate such decisions because of mental disability or physical impairment.

Under the new procedures, it may well happen that a squatter applies to be registered, and a notice is sent by the registrar to the registered proprietor and no response is received, with the result that the applicant will be registered as the new proprietor of the estate. The reason why there was no response, however, is that unbeknown to either the applicant or the registrar,[247] the registered proprietor comes within one of the two above paragraphs. If this occurred, the former registered proprietor would need to seek alteration of the register.

Repeated applications

It used to be the case that the period of limitation in respect of land was twelve years. Under the 2002 Act, the relevant period has been reduced to ten years. Twelve years may still become a relevant period owing to paragraphs 6 and 7 of Schedule 6. Under paragraph 6(1), a person whose application for registration under paragraph 1 was rejected may apply again to be registered as proprietor of the estate. He may do this if he is in adverse possession of the estate from the date of the application until the last day of the period from the date of its rejection. Paragraph 6(2) provides, however, that he may not apply under this paragraph if either he is a defendant in proceedings which involve asserting a right to possession of land, judgment in possession of the land has been given against him in the last two years,[248] or he has been evicted from the land pursuant to a judgment for possession.[249] If a person makes an application under paragraph 6, paragraph 7 provides that he is entitled to be registered as the new proprietor of the estate.

These provisions are designed to prevent a registered proprietor from sleeping on his rights. If a squatter has applied to be registered as proprietor and, because he

---

[246] See Disabilities, p. 241.

[247] If it appears to the registrar that either of these paragraphs might apply in relation to an estate in land, he may include a note to that effect in the register: Land Registration Act 2002, Sched. 6, para. 8(4).

[248] A judgment for possession of land ceases to be enforceable at the end of two years from the date of the judgment: ibid., s. 98(2).

[249] Presumably in this situation, the applicant would not qualify under para. 6(1).

cannot satisfy any of the conditions set out in paragraph 5, fails in his application, the registered proprietor cannot then afford to do nothing and allow matters to rest. Unless he seeks to remove the squatter from possession by obtaining a possession order then, two years later, the squatter, provided he has remained in adverse possession of the land, can apply again and, this time, his application cannot be resisted by the registered proprietor.

The effect of registration

Under the old law, the effect of adverse possession, as it affected unregistered land, was to operate negatively. The title of the paper owner was extinguished and the squatter had an independent fee simple in the land. This was modified in the case of registered land by the imposition of a trust, whereby the registered proprietor would hold his estate on trust for the squatter.[250] The 2002 Act operates in a very different way.

If the squatter's application for registration is successful, then his name is substituted for that of the former proprietor. The effect is to transfer the estate to him. So if, as was likely to be the case, the person who was the registered proprietor had an absolute title, then this is the title with which the squatter will be registered. If the previous proprietor was a tenant, then the squatter will be registered as the proprietor of that lease and, therefore, unlike the position when title is unregistered, be directly liable on the covenants in the lease.[251] As a corollary to this, the fee simple estate which the squatter had by virtue of his occupation of the land is extinguished.[252] Again as one would anticipate, but subject to one important exception, the squatter, as the successor in title to the person who was previously the proprietor, will take subject to any interests which bound the former owner of the land.[253]

The exception to this latter point concerns registered charges. If a squatter applies to be registered as proprietor, this application may succeed for one of two reasons. These are that there was no objection to the application or that the squatter satisfied one of the conditions set out in paragraph 5. In the former situation, the squatter, when registered as proprietor, will not be bound by any registered charge affecting the estate immediately before his registration.[254] This does not occasion hardship to the chargee, as such a person must be notified by the registrar of the application for registration and can, therefore, serve a notice objecting to the registration.[255] Where the application for registration is contested, then if the application for registration is successful, the squatter, as the new registered proprietor, will take subject to the registered charge.[256]

---

[250] See Registered title, pp. 258–259.
[251] See *Tichborne v. Weir* (1892) 67 L.T. 735. See also Leasehold titles, pp. 257–258.
[252] Land Registration Act 2002, Sched. 6, para. 9(1).   [253] Ibid., para. 9(2).
[254] Ibid., para. 9(3).   [255] Ibid., para. 2(1)(b).   [256] Ibid., para. 9(4).

Adverse possession and easements

Easements, to be fully discussed in Chapter 13, are property rights which one land-owner has over a neighbour's land. The land which enjoys the benefit of the easement is termed the dominant tenement, and the land which is subject to the right is the servient tenement. Typical examples of such rights are a right of way or a right of light over the servient land. Now, necessarily, the existence of an easement acts as a constraint as to what the servient owner can do on his own land, because, 'Every [easement] prevents any use of the servient land, whether ordinary or otherwise, that would interfere with the reasonable exercise of the [easement]. There will always be some use that is prevented.'[257] The question which can arise is as to how extensive that interference can be. This is particularly the case, because one method by which an easement can be acquired is by a process termed prescription; that is, the user of the particular right over a twenty-year period prior to the bringing of an action.[258] Now that it is much more difficult for a squatter to acquire a possessory title than was previously the case, then provided that the use of the servient land has been enjoyed for the longer period required for prescription, the person who has enjoyed the right will find it potentially more advantageous to argue that the use of the land did not amount to adverse possession, but, instead, had led to the creation of an easement.

Although an easement is traditionally seen as the right of one landowner to do something on a neighbour's land, some rights have involved a degree of occupancy of the servient land. Until recently, the approach of the courts was to see the issue as being one of degree, and the greater the aspect of occupancy, the less likely the use in question was to be held to be capable of existing as an easement.[259] This approach has, however, recently been rejected by the House of Lords in *Moncrieff v. Jamieson*:[260] a decision which contains *dicta* which may make it difficult to distinguish between acts of adverse possession and claims to a prescriptive right to an easement.

The issue in *Moncrieff* was whether a right to drive a car over servient land carried with it the ancillary right to park that car on the land. It was held, on the facts, that it did. The main importance of the case was the recognition that a right to park a car was capable of existing as an easement. As such a right is occupational in nature, this led to a general, albeit *obiter*, discussion of the extent to which a right which is occupational can exist as an easement.

Occupational easements

Although Lord Scott of Foscote stressed that 'the right must be such that a reasonable use thereof by the owner of the dominant land would not be inconsistent with the beneficial ownership of the servient land by the beneficial owner',[261] he and Lord

---

[257] *Moncrieff v. Jamieson* [2007] 1 W.L.R. 2620 at [54] *per* Lord Scott of Foscote.
[258] This is discussed in more detail in Chapter 13.
[259] See, e.g., *R. & S. Platt Ltd v. Crouch* [2003] EWCA Civ. 1110 at [45] *per* Peter Gibson L.J.
[260] [2007] 1 W.L.R. 2620.   [261] Ibid., at [47].

Neuberger of Abbotsbury were both prepared to accept that a use which interfered substantially with the use of the servient land could amount to an easement. Thus, Lord Scott, in approving the decision in *Wright v. Macadam*,[262] said that, 'Sole use of a coal shed for the storage of coal does not prevent the servient owner from using the shed for any purposes of his own that do not interfere with the dominant owner's reasonable use for the storage of coal',[263] although it is not clear what sensible use the servient owner could enjoy in respect of a coal cellar filled with someone else's coal. Lord Neuberger, arguably went further, saying that he could see considerable force in the view 'that a right can be an easement notwithstanding that the dominant owner effectively enjoys exclusive occupation, on the basis that the essential requirement is that the servient owner retains possession and control...'[264] This is reinforced by his earlier comment that he was 'not satisfied that a right is prevented from being...an easement simply because the right granted would involve the servient owner being effectively excluded from the property'.[265] The difficulty here is that it is not easy to see how the servient owner retains possession and control, if another person has the legal right to exclusive occupation of it.

Lord Scott did show some appreciation of the potential overlap between a claim to an easement and a claim to have acquired a possessory title. He referred to *Copeland v. Greenhalf*,[266] where Upjohn J. had rejected a claim that an easement had been acquired to allow the defendant to have an extensive right to store vehicles and other objects on the disputed strip of land, because 'it is virtually a claim to possession of the servient tenement, if necessary to the exclusion of the owner...'[267] Commenting on this passage, he said:

'There may be arguments as to whether the facts of the case justified those remarks but, for my part, I would accept that if they did Upjohn J. was right to reject the easement claim and to require the defendant, if he was to succeed in resisting the plaintiff's claim to remove from the land, to establish title by adverse possession.'[268]

With respect, this is somewhat unhelpful. First, in *Copeland v. Greenhalf*, although the user of the disputed strip was extensive, it is clear that Lord Scott was not convinced that the conclusion that this was an adverse possession case was actually justified. Secondly, it is clear from the *dicta* cited above that he and Lord Neuberger are prepared to allow very extensive use of another person's land to come within the ambit of the law of easements. Even when the land is secured by the trespasser, it appears that for Lord Scott the matter is not free from doubt. So, when considering *Wright v. Macadam*,[269] the case concerning the right to store coal in a shed, he said:

'If the coal shed door had been locked with only the dominant owner possessing a key and entry by the servient owner barred...*I would have regarded it as arguable* that the right

---

[262] [1949] 2 K.B. 744.   [263] [2007] 1 W.L.R. 2620 at [55].
[264] Ibid., at [143]. See also at [57] *per* Lord Scott.   [265] Ibid., at [139].   [266] [1952] Ch. 488.
[267] Ibid., at 498.   [268] [2007] 1 W.L.R. 2620 at [56].   [269] [1949] 2 K.B. 744.

granted was inconsistent with the servient owner's ownership and inconsistent with the nature of ... an easement.'[270]

Easements and prescription

Surely, this is more than merely arguable. It cannot be the case that, in these circumstances, the owner of the servient land could be said to retain control of it. Nevertheless, it does show that there is now considerable potential for what have traditionally been seen to be possessory rights to be recognized as easements.[271] The significance of this is that, whereas the scope for a squatter to acquire title to registered land had been severely curtailed by the Land Registration Act 2002, this is not the case for easements. Instances where there may now be doubt as to whether the claim is one of adverse possession or prescription are likely to involve cases where the land in question has been used for storage purposes or for cultivation.[272] Whereas, in the past, such acts have formed the basis of a claim of adverse possession, if the use has exceeded twenty years, and the other requirements for the creation of an easement have been satisfied,[273] one could find the somewhat counter-intuitive position of the paper owner of the land arguing that the use amounted to adverse possession, and the trespasser denying this and, instead, arguing that he was not in possession but that the use was in the nature of an easement. One can envisage that some of the wider *dicta* in *Moncrieff v. Jamieson* may need some re-evaluation in the future.

CONCLUSION

The changes made to the law of limitation by the Land Registration Act 2002 are profound. While the old law relating to adverse possession has not been entirely swept away, its scope has been reduced considerably. This is to be welcomed. Provision is made for situations where a person has, effectively, abandoned land, thereby making it possible for it to be dealt with in the future. This is likely to be the situation when no objection is made to an application by a squatter to be registered as proprietor. Moreover, the new law enhances the reliability of the register, which is also to be welcomed. Finally, it makes it far less likely that a person will be deprived of their ownership of land without compensation; an aspect of the law of adverse possession which

[270] [2007] 1 W.L.R. 2620 at [55]. Emphasis supplied.

[271] In any event, the claim in *Stadium Capital Holdings v. St Marylebone Properties Co Plc* [2009] EWHC 2942 (Ch.) to have acquired a possessory title to airspace on the strength of an overhanging sign should, surely, have been argued on the basis of a prescriptive right to an easement.

[272] See, e.g., *Tennant v. Adamczyk* [2005] EWCA Civ. 1239. *J.A. Pye (Oxford) Ltd v. Graham* [2003] 1 A.C. 419 may, itself, provide an instance of this.

[273] See Chapter 13.

many people have always found to be objectionable. All in all, it can be said that the new law is a considerable improvement on the old and also, in a number of ways, puts it on a more secure and rational footing. Some difficulties do, however, remain. These are the potential overlap of the law relating to adverse possession with that relating to easements, and the continuing reluctance of the Land Registry to recognize that the decision in *Beaulane* is unsupportable. It can be envisaged that both of these matters will need to be addressed in the future.

8

Consecutive and Concurrent Interests in Land

When discussing the doctrine of estates, which still provides the theoretical under-pinning for modern Land Law, what was identified as an important feature of the system was that a number of estates could exist simultaneously with regard to the same piece of land. Land could be settled upon A for life, remainder to B in fee tail,[1] remainder to C in fee simple. To reiterate a point made earlier, the estates are all the subject of present ownership. What the doctrine of estates facilitates is the division of various rights of ownership between the different parties. One of the most important rights, the right physically to possess the land, is granted to A. B, as yet, has no right to possess the land, this right being acquired on A's death. Similarly, C, or more likely his heirs, will not have the right to possess the land until both A's and B's estates have come to an end.[2] Because the right to possess the land is such an important right, the interests of B and C are termed future interests and are regarded as consecutive inter-ests in the land.

As well as consecutive interests existing with regard to the same land, people can have concurrent interests in the land. A typical example would be where H and W jointly own a house together. This chapter deals with the methods by which the law accommodates both consecutive and concurrent interests, focusing, first, on succes-sive interests. Succeeding chapters will then discuss the law relating to co-ownership of land, considering both how one becomes a co-owner and the structure of co-ownership and the respective rights of the co-owners.

SUCCESSIVE INTERESTS

Prior to 1925, a life estate, a fee tail, and an interest in remainder were all capable of existing as legal estates. Because of the operation of section 1 of the Law of Property Act 1925, none of these estates are any longer legal but can only be equitable. As the fee

---

[1] It is no longer possible to create a fee tail: Trusts of Land and Appointment of Trustees Act 1996, Sched. 1, para. 5.

[2] This assumes that B has not enlarged his interest into a fee simple by barring the entail. See The fee tail, p. 31.

simple absolute in possession was to be the focal point of land ownership, steps had to be taken to ensure that a person was identified who was empowered to deal with this estate, free from the family interests which existed under the settlement. For many years, two devices were employed to deal with this type of situation: the strict settlement and the trust for sale. Since 1997, a new regime designed to replace both of the previous legal devices has been introduced by the Trusts of Land and Appointment of Trustees Act 1996. For a number of reasons, however, it remains necessary to have regard to the old law. These are, first, that existing settlements are not affected by the new legislation, so that settlements created between 1925 and 1997 continue to be governed by the old statutory regime and, secondly, the new law is, to a considerable extent, coloured by the law it was designed to replace, so that it is difficult to understand the content of the new, and the reasons why it was introduced, without some reference to the old.

SETTLED LAND

One of the two ways in which the law sought to deal with successive interests in land was through the device of the strict settlement, whereby the intention of the settlor was to prevent the land being disposed of in the future.[3] The definition of a settlement is provided by section 1 of the Settled Land Act 1925. The essence of the definition is that any deed, will, agreement for a settlement, or other agreement under which land stands limited in trust for any person by way of succession is, for the purposes of the Act, a settlement.[4] The Act goes on to give four specific examples of when land is to be a settlement. The first three of these are, strictly speaking, not necessary, as all of them come within the general definition given above. The fourth example does not, it being provided that land limited in trust for a person being an infant, for an estate in fee simple or for a term of years absolute, is also a settlement within the meaning of the Act.[5]

The theme that runs through the definition is that the estates in question must, because of the legislation, exist only in equity. Apart from the lease, the only legal estate now known to the law is the fee simple absolute in possession.[6] If one considers the example of a settlement given earlier, to A for life, remainder to B in fee tail, remainder to C in fee simple, the effect of section 1 of the Law of Property Act 1925 is

---

[3] See Harvey, *Settlements of Land* (London: Sweet & Maxwell, 1973), 6–26; Smith, *Plural Ownership* (Oxford, Oxford University Press, 2005) Chapter 2.

[4] Expressly excluded from the settlement is land held on trust for sale: Settled Land Act 1925, s. 1(7).

[5] Ibid., s. 1(1)(ii)(d). See now Trusts of Land and Appointment of Trustees Act 1996, s. 2; Sched. 1, para. 1(1) and *Hammersmith London Borough Council v. Alexander-David* [2009] 3 All E.R. 1098.

[6] Law of Property Act 1925, s. 1(1)(a).

that none of A, B, or C would have a legal estate in land. Neither A nor B have a fee simple at all. C does have a fee simple but it is in remainder and not in possession. Because the estates are equitable, it follows that the land must be limited in trust by way of succession. Where land is purported to be conveyed to a minor, because such a person lacks capacity to own a legal estate,[7] that estate can also only be equitable, although, on this occasion, the trust is not limited by way of succession.

The object of the Act

Where land was subject to a settlement, without some legislative reform, it would not be possible to deal safely with it. As no one person held the fee simple in the land, then, unless all the people with various interests in it were prepared to co-operate, that estate could not be sold to a purchaser. As the land was not readily sellable, people with limited interests in it would be less inclined to spend money on improvements to it. When land was settled, it was also common to create charges on it, normally by the creation of a rentcharge. The purpose of this was to provide financial provision for other members of the settlor's family.[8] The result of doing this, however, was that land which was subject to a settlement tended to become burdened with debt. As the social and economic conditions in England changed, and it was considered to be less desirable than was once the case for land to be subject to family settlements of this type, pressure grew to allow the casting off of the fetters imposed by them.[9] Building on the reforms brought in by the Settled Land Act 1882, the 1925 Act sought to arrive at a solution whereby such land became readily marketable.

The central plank in the scheme devised by the Act was to vest the legal fee simple in the hands of one person, the tenant for life, and then to give that person extensive powers to deal with that estate. As the person who is given that estate has only a limited beneficial interest in the property, it was also necessary to safeguard the interests of other people with interests in the land, to ensure that the tenant for life could not exercise the powers given to him by the statute to the detriment of those other people. To prevent this from occurring, the Act provides for the appointment of trustees of the settlement who, unusually for trustees, do not hold the legal title to the land, which is vested in the tenant for life. As will be seen, their role is, essentially, to act as watchdogs of the settlement.

The tenant for life

The central character when land is the subject of a settlement is the tenant for life. Section 4(2) of the Act requires that the land shall be conveyed by a vesting deed to the

---

[7] Law of Property Act 1925, s. 1(6).

[8] Such charges were generally known as jointures or portions. The former is an annuity in favour of a widow, and the latter a lump sum paid to children who were not given a direct interest under the settlement.

[9] See *Re Mundy and Roper's Contract* [1895] 1 Ch. 275 at 278 *per* Chitty J.; Harvey, op. cit., 1–5.

tenant for life or, if there is more than one such person, to them as joint tenants. Where the legal title is already vested in the person who is the tenant for life, as would be the case when a person who owned the fee simple settled the land upon himself for life, remainder to his son in fee simple, it is sufficient if the vesting deed simply declares that the land is vested in him for that estate.

Various issues arise. First, the person who is the tenant for life must be identified. Secondly, the powers of the tenant for life must be considered, a task which entails considering the purpose of the vesting deed. Finally, the role of the trustees of the settlement, and the process of overreaching must also be addressed.

Who is the tenant for life?

Section 19(1) of the Act defines the tenant for life as the person being of full age who is for the time being beneficially entitled to an estate or interest in possession.[10] If there are two or more such persons then, together, they constitute the tenant for life.[11] If, for example, land is settled on A for life, to B in fee tail, remainder to C in fee simple, then A, as the person beneficially entitled in possession, is the tenant for life. On A's death, B, or his lineal heir, will then become the tenant for life and, on the termination of the fee tail, C, or, more likely, his heirs, will be entitled to the land, which will cease to be settled, and the land will simply be conveyed to him.

There are two situations where there is nobody who falls within the definition of a tenant for life. One is where there is no person who is entitled in possession to the land, for example, if a discretionary trust has been created,[12] and the other is where the person so entitled is a minor. In such cases, the person who dons the mantle of the tenant for life is termed the statutory owner.

The statutory owner

If the person entitled in possession is a minor, provision is made that, during his minority, if the settled land is vested in a personal representative, then, until a principal vesting deed has been executed, the personal representative shall have the powers of the tenant for life and, in all other cases, the powers shall vest in the trustees of the settlement.[13] In other cases where there is no tenant for life, then the person who can exercise those powers is either the person of full age on whom such powers are expressly conferred or, if there is no such person, upon the trustees of the settlement.[14]

---

[10] For the more elaborate definition in the case of other limited owners, see Settled Land Act 1925, s. 20.
[11] Ibid., s. 19(2).
[12] *Re Galenga's Will Trusts* [1938] 1 All E.R. 106. See also *Re Frewen* [1926] Ch. 580. A discretionary trust occurs when the settlor nominates a class of people as the beneficiaries but leaves it to the trustees to decide which members of that class, and in what proportions, will benefit from the trust.
[13] Settled Land Act 1925, s. 26.   [14] Ibid., s. 26.

THE POWERS OF THE TENANT FOR LIFE

Although the legal estate is vested in the tenant for life, he is not given unfettered power to deal with the land. The constraints come from two sources. First, while he is given the legal estate by the statute, that estate is held upon trust, the beneficial interests under that trust being those carved out by the settlement. Certain proposed transactions may be prevented by others interested in the land if those transactions are in some way improper. The second constraint upon his actions is that, although he, as tenant for life, is endowed with the legal estate, the Act does not simply confer upon him the normal powers incident upon the ownership of a fee simple. Instead, his powers to deal with the estate are elaborated by the Act. As will be seen, difficulties can arise if the tenant for life purports to deal with the land in a way which is not authorized by the Act.

Trusteeship

The tenant for life holds the legal estate on trust and, consequently, is subject to the normal fiduciary obligations imposed upon a trustee in respect of his dealing with trust property. In making such transactions, the tenant for life is obliged to consider the financial interests of the other beneficiaries and so cannot favour his own political or moral preferences where these would conflict with the interests of the beneficiaries.[15] In *Re Somers*,[16] the tenant for life, who was a confirmed teetotaller, sought to grant a lease of a hotel, the lease to contain a covenant prohibiting the sale of alcohol. The trustees of the settlement obtained a declaration that she was not entitled to do this, because the proposed transaction was not in the best financial interests of the other beneficiaries.

Statutory powers

The powers of the tenant for life to deal with the legal estate are conferred upon him by Part II of the Act. The statutory powers can be increased by the settlement but attempts to restrict them are rendered void.[17] Included within the powers of the tenant for life is the power to sell the land, to grant certain leases, and to mortgage the property for certain specified purposes. Before exercising these powers, the tenant for life is required to serve a written notice on the trustees not less than one month before the proposed transaction.[18] This imposition is not, however, particularly onerous, as it is sufficient if the tenant for life simply gives a general notice of his intention from time to time to

---

[15] For the general position of trustees, see *Cowan v. Scargill* [1985] Ch. 270; *Harries v. Church Commissioners for England* [1992] 1 W.L.R. 1241.

[16] (1893) 11 T.L.R. 567. See also *Wheelwright v. Walker (No. 2)* (1883) W.N. 154; *Middlemas v. Stevens* [1901] 1 Ch. 574.

[17] Settled Land Act 1925, s. 106. See Void transactions, p. 278.   [18] Ibid., s. 101(1).

exercise his powers under the Act,[19] and a purchaser, provided that he is in good faith, is not concerned to see that this requirement has been met.[20]

Unauthorized dispositions

Problems can arise if a tenant for life purports to make a disposition which the Act does not authorize him to do. In such situations, one must distinguish between cases where what has sought to be done is totally unauthorized by the Act, and cases where the transaction is one which is authorized but where there is some irregularity in the exercise of the power.

Void transactions

Section 18 of the Act provides that:

'Where land is the subject of a vesting instrument, and the trustees of the settlement have not been discharged under the Act, then—

(a) any disposition by the tenant for life…other than a disposition authorised by this Act…shall be void, except for the purpose of conveying or creating such equitable interests as he has power, in right of his equitable interests and powers under the trust instrument, to convey or create.'

The effect of this section was considered in the leading case of *Weston v. Henshaw*.[21] G sold property to his son, F, who later resold the land to his father. Sometime later, the father settled the land on F for life, remainder to F's sons. F then mortgaged the property for his own benefit, a transaction which is not authorized under the Act. To prove title to the mortgagee, F showed the conveyance to him by his father but suppressed the later documents, so that there was no way that the mortgagee could have known that the land was actually the subject of a vesting deed and that the transaction was being effected by a tenant for life. The issue subsequently arose as to whether the mortgage was valid and Danckwerts J. held that it was not.

In reaching this conclusion, the judge simply applied section 18 of the Act which does, indeed, suggest that this is the correct result. He also, however, rejected an argument based upon section 110 of the Act. This section, which is designed to protect purchasers, provides that:

'On a sale, exchange, lease, mortgage, charge, or other disposition, a purchaser dealing in good faith with a tenant for life…shall, as against all parties entitled under the settlement, be conclusively taken to have given the best price…that could be reasonably obtained…and to have complied with all the requirements of the Act.'

The mortgagee, who undoubtedly was in good faith, argued that he was protected by this section and that, consequently, the mortgage was valid. This argument was rejected on the somewhat curious ground that the section only applied to protect a purchaser if the purchaser knew that he was dealing with a tenant for life which, in the instant case, he manifestly did not.

---

[19] Ibid., s. 101(2).   [20] Ibid., s. 101(5).   [21] [1950] Ch. 510.

Irregularities

The interpretation given to section 110 in *Weston v. Henshaw* was doubted in *Re Morgan's Lease*.[22] In this case, the principal objection to a lease granted by the tenant for life was that the rent that had been obtained was not the best rent reasonably obtainable. So far as the tenants were concerned, however, it was held that the lease was not liable to be set aside. They had acted in good faith and were therefore protected by section 110 of the Act. The criticism of *Weston v. Henshaw* was, therefore, *obiter*. It is also, it is suggested, misplaced.

The fundamental difference between *Weston v. Henshaw* and *Re Morgan's Lease* is that in the former case the person who was actually the tenant for life was purporting to engage in a transaction which was not authorized by the Act. It was *ultra vires*. In *Re Morgan's Lease*, on the other hand, the transaction was one which was permitted by the Act. The problem with the transaction related to the rent which was payable, a matter which is within the scope of section 110.

The conclusion which should follow in cases such as these is that, if the purported transaction is one which is not authorized by the Act, then it is beyond the powers of the tenant for life and, in principle, should be void so far as the creation of a legal estate is concerned.[23] If the problem relates to technical matters relating to an authorized, and therefore intrinsically valid, transaction then, provided that the purchaser has acted in good faith, he will be able to rely upon section 110 of the Act and will get a good title.

The effect of section 18 can be hard on a purchaser who may find, through no fault of his own, that the transaction he has engaged in is void. This result is, however, a direct consequence of the scheme adopted by the Act. Instead of simply giving the tenant for life the legal fee simple, and the powers of dealing inherent with the ownership of that estate, the Act, instead, gives him the estate but limited his powers of dealing with it to those specified in the Act. The consequence of this is to leave an innocent purchaser exposed to the kind of fraud which occurred in *Weston v. Henshaw*.

The real source of the problem in a case such as *Weston v. Henshaw* is that, because title was unregistered, the fraudster could conceal the fact that he was actually a tenant for life rather than, as he presented himself to be, a straightforward owner of a fee simple. This situation is far less likely to occur when title is registered, as a purchaser will see, from searching the register of title, whether or not the registered proprietor is a limited owner and be able to deal with him accordingly. When title is registered, the only time when a purchaser may be at risk is where the transaction is not, itself, completed by registration, as is the case for a lease of less than seven years, when the prospective tenant may proceed with the transaction without searching the register in order to establish the nature of the freeholder's title.[24]

---

[22] [1972] Ch. 1.   [23] See also *Bevan v. Johnston* [1990] 2 E.G.L.R. 33, a decision adopting this view.
[24] Ibid.

Attempts to fetter the powers of the tenant for life

Central to the operation of the Act is to allow settled land to be bought and sold and not to allow the succession of interests to prevent the land being sellable. To this end, the legal fee simple is vested in the tenant for life, who is then given powers of dealing with that estate. To ensure that this policy is not frustrated by the creator of the settlement, provision is made to prevent the powers of the tenant for life from being cut down.

Section 106 of the Settled Land Act 1925 provides that any provision in a settlement which purports, or tends or is intended to have, or would have the effect of either forbidding the tenant for life from exercising his statutory powers or inducing him not to do so will be void. Attempts to discourage a tenant for life from exercising his powers may not always be blatant. In some cases a fund is made available for the tenant for life and it is not always clear whether the existence of this fund is to act as an inducement to him not to exercise his statutory powers or if it is a genuine attempt to provide funds for the upkeep of the property. In the former situation, the clause will be void under the Act,[25] so that the tenant for life can retain the money despite exercising his powers, whereas in the latter situation the clause is valid and the tenant for life's entitlement to the fund will cease when he no longer holds that position.[26]

The operation of section 106 has arisen a number of times in the context of residence clauses, whereby a person is given a life interest determinable on their ceasing to reside at the property. If the reason why the person has ceased to reside at the property is that he has sold the property, then his interest will not be determined by the residence clause, as its effect is to seek to discourage him from the exercise of his powers.[27] If, however, the reason that the tenant for life ceases to reside in the settled property is simply a matter of choice, then the clause has not operated to discourage him from exercising his powers and is valid, with the result that his beneficial interest will determine on his ceasing to reside at the property.[28]

THE STRUCTURE OF SETTLEMENTS

Having looked at the essential definition of a settlement and the role of the tenant for life, it is necessary now to turn to the mechanics of the settlement; how they are created and how the Act operates to enable settled land to be sold. A feature of the system introduced is that it adopts a two-document structure, the documents being

---

[25] See *Re Ames* [1893] 2 Ch. 479.

[26] See the different views expressed in *Re Aberconway's Settlement Trusts* [1953] Ch. 647. See also *Re Patten* [1929] 2 Ch. 276.

[27] See *Re Paget's S.E.* (1895) 30 Ch.D. 161; *Re Orlebar* [1936] Ch. 147.

[28] See *Re Haynes* (1887) 37 Ch.D. 306.

the vesting deed and the trust instrument,[29] the purpose of this structure being to allow the land to be dealt without the necessity of a purchaser having to investigate the beneficial interests existing behind the settlement.

The vesting deed

When a settlement is created, it is necessary for the legal estate to be vested in the tenant for life or, if it is already vested in him, to indicate that the capacity in which he holds that estate has changed. This task is performed by the vesting deed. The vesting deed contains the following information:

(i)   it describes the settled land;

(ii) it declares that the settled land is vested in the person or persons to whom it was conveyed or in whom it is declared to be vested upon trusts from time affecting the settled land;

(iii) it states the names of the trustees of the settlement;

(iv) it states the names of any persons empowered to appoint new trustees of the settlement; and

(v)   it states any additional powers conferred upon the tenant for life by the trust instrument.[30]

The role of the trust instrument will be considered shortly. First, the consequence of a failure to execute a vesting deed will be addressed.

Failure to execute vesting deed

The sanction for failing to execute a vesting deed when a settlement has been created is provided by section 13 of the Act. Under this section, where a person is entitled to have a vesting deed executed in his favour, and this has not occurred, then any purported disposition of the land will not take effect except as a contract to carry out the purported disposition after the vesting deed has been executed. An exception is provided in favour of a purchaser of a legal estate without notice of the tenant for life who is entitled to have a vesting deed executed in his favour.[31] The protection afforded to a purchaser in this situation contrasts markedly with the effect of section 18 of the Act. An example will illustrate this.

S, who holds a legal estate in land, settles the land upon himself for life, remainder to X but does not, as he should, execute a vesting deed indicating the change of capacity in which he now holds the legal estate. He then mortgages the property for his own benefit: a transaction which is not authorized by the Act. Assuming that the

---

[29] Settled Land Act 1925, s. 4(1).   [30] Settled Land Act 1925, s. 5.

[31] Conversely, if the purchaser does have notice, the conveyance should be void with regard to the transfer of the legal estate. Cf. *Binions v. Evans* [1972] Ch. 359, where this point was overlooked.

mortgagee has acted in good faith, the effect of section 13 is to protect him and the mortgage will be valid. If, however, S did execute a vesting deed but, when mortgaging the property, suppressed that deed, thereby concealing the fact that a settlement is in existence, the effect of section 18 is to make this transaction void.[32] Yet, the purchaser is as innocent in the second situation as he is in the first. The disparity between the two situations is indefensible but is an inevitable consequence of the different wording of the two sections.

The trust instrument

The second document essential to the creation of the settlement is the trust instrument which, as its name suggests, deals with the beneficial interests created by the settlement. The trust instrument contains the following:

(i)   it declares the trusts of the settlement;

(ii)   it appoints the trustees of the settlement;

(iii) it contains the power, if any, to appoint new trustees;

(iv)   it sets out any extended powers given to the tenant for life; and

(v)   it bears any *ad valorum* stamp duty which might be payable.[33]

When a settlement is created by will, the personal representatives of the deceased will vest the legal estate in the tenant for life by means of a vesting assent and the will, under which the settlement was created, will operate as the trust instrument.[34]

It will be observed that some of the information contained in the two documents is common to both. The major difference between the contents of the two is that the trust instrument sets out the beneficial interests existing under the settlement, a matter on which the vesting deed is silent. The reason for this strict demarcation is the curtain principle, a principle which is central to the scheme of the Act and to the operation of the overreaching provisions.

The curtain principle

The purpose of the system of having two documents, one dealing with the legal estate and the other detailing the beneficial interests existing under the settlement, is to free the purchaser from the task of having to investigate the beneficial interests existing behind the settlement. The object of the Act is that, if the correct procedure is adopted, those interests will be overreached and will take effect against the purchase money generated by the sale of the land. As the purchaser will not be bound by these interests, he does not need to know what they are. The Act takes this policy to its logical

---

[32] *Weston v. Henshaw* [1950] Ch. 510.   [33] Settled Land Act 1925, s. 4(3).   [34] Ibid., s. 6.

conclusion. Not only is the purchaser discouraged from investigating the beneficial interests behind the settlement, he is actually precluded from doing so. Section 110(2) of the Act provides that a purchaser of a legal estate in settled land is not, save for four situations of varying importance,[35] entitled to call for the production of the trust instrument and he is bound to assume that the particulars contained in the vesting deed are correct. The curtain principle operates, also, where title is registered. In this situation, the tenant for life is registered as the proprietor of the land and a restriction is entered upon the register that no disposition is to be registered unless capital money is paid to the trustees of the settlement. The effect of this procedure is that the beneficial interests are kept off the register.

Although the Act requires a purchaser to assume that the particulars contained in the vesting deed are correct, it does not deal with the situation where this is not the case. This may occur when title is unregistered. The Act provides no clear solution to the problem, which must be resolved by the application of first principles. The situation normally referred to to illustrate this potential problem is if land is settled upon A for life, or until she remarries, remainder to B. A vesting deed has been executed in favour of A who, having remarried, thereby causing the settlement to terminate, purports to exercise the powers of a tenant for life.

Assuming that the trustees of the settlement, to whom the purchase money will have to be paid, are not alive to the problem and prevent the transaction from taking place, it is thought that the purchaser would get a good title. A, because of the vesting deed, would still have the legal title vested in her and the conveyance would seem to operate to transfer the legal estate to the purchaser. As the purchaser would not have notice of the interests behind the settlement, then, as a purchaser without notice, he should, in principle, take free from those interests.[36]

This problem, which is illustrative of one of the difficulties of the curtain principle, is that a purchaser is precluded from discovering matters which may be of relevance to him, cannot occur when title is registered. This is because the tenant for life will be registered as the proprietor of the land subject to a restriction on his power to deal with the property. That restriction will relate to the payment of capital money having been made to the trustees of the settlement. Provided that the purchase money is paid in accordance with the terms of the restriction, then the purchaser will take free from any interests under the settlement.

Settlements and overreaching

The scheme of overreaching operates on a conveyance by the tenant for life and the payment of capital money to, or at the direction of, the trustees of the settlement.[37] On

---

[35] For these exceptions, see Harpum, Bridge, and Dixon, *Megarry and Wade's Law of Real Property* (7th edn) (London: Sweet & Maxwell, 2008), 1487.

[36] See P.A. Stone [1984] Conv. 354. Cf. R. Warrington [1985] Conv. 377.

[37] Settled Land Act 1925, s. 75.

a conveyance by the tenant for life, section 72 of the Act provides that a purchaser can take the land conveyed free from the interests under the settlement but subject to:

(i) all legal estates and charges by way of legal charges having priority to the settlement;

(ii) all legal estates and charges by way of legal mortgage which have been conveyed or created for securing money actually raised at the date of the deed; and

(iii) all leases and grants of other rights (except annuities, limited owner's charges, and general equitable charges) which at the date of the deed are:

(a) binding upon the successors in title of the tenant for life; and

(b) protected by registration, if capable of registration.

These provisions are, perhaps, not as clear as they might be. First, except where the Act provides expressly to the contrary, any right created prior to the creation of the settlement cannot be overreached by a conveyance by the tenant for life. The reference to legal estates and mortgages having priority to the settlement is unnecessary. The Act then makes reference to interests created by the tenant for life, such as a mortgage. Such interests are commercial interests in land which the tenant for life is authorized to make and so, although created under the settlement, cannot be overreached by a subsequent conveyance of the property. An example may assist.

In 1970, land was settled on A for life, remainder to B in fee simple. Prior to the creation of the settlement, a restrictive covenant affecting the land had been created and had been duly registered as a land charge. In 1980, to raise money to improve the land, a legal mortgage was created[38] and in 2012, A conveyed the land to P and the capital money was paid to the trustees of the settlement. The purchaser will take free from A's life interest and B's fee simple in remainder. He will be bound, however, by the prior restrictive covenant and by the authorized mortgage unless, as is very likely to be the case, the purchaser insisted upon its discharge prior to the transfer. When the purchase money is received by the trustees of the settlement, they will, in accordance with the directions of the tenant for life, invest it. The interest, which represents A's life interest, is paid to A and, on A's death, the capital sum is paid to B representing B's fee simple in remainder, which has fallen into possession.

Problems with the Settled Land Act

This thumbnail sketch of the working of the Act is intended to show the essentials of how the legislation was intended to deal with successive interests affecting land and how the law sought, by utilizing the concept of overreaching, to make such land marketable. There are, however, problems with the statutory regime. As has been seen, one problem is that it can throw the risk of fraudulent conduct

[38] Settled Land Act 1925, s. 71.

onto the purchaser, a feature which is inconsistent with the general policy of the 1925 legislation. An additional problem is that the two-document procedure, while providing an effective curtain behind which to shield the equitable rights existing under the settlement, creates, also, a somewhat complex and cumbersome machinery.

Complexity

Integral to the strategy of the Settled Land Act 1925 is the system of basing it upon the existence of two documents and the vesting of the legal title in the tenant for life. A consequence of this is that when changes occur behind the curtain, new documents will need to be executed to reflect these changes, thereby ensuring that the legal estate is vested in the person currently entitled to be the tenant for life. A good illustration of the need for this is provided by the occasion of the death of a tenant for life, where the settlement continues in being. If land is settled upon A for life, remainder to B in fee tail, remainder to C in fee simple then, upon A's death, the land remains settled land.

In this situation, the settled land must be dealt with separately from the rest of A's estate. The part of his estate which is not subject to the settlement will devolve upon his personal representatives in the normal way. The land, however, will vest in the trustees of the settlement as his special personal representatives.[39] They will then vest the settled land in B by way of a vesting assent.[40] The upshot is that different people will be involved in the administration of the deceased's estate; a factor which increases the cost and complexity of dealing with the estate.

Accidental settlements

The desire to create settlements of any complexity is less strong than was once the case, as the wish to create dynastic settlements is much less prevalent than was true in the past,[41] this tendency being reflected by the prevention of the creation of any new fees tail.[42] As people have been less inclined, deliberately, to create settlements governed by the Settled Land Act 1925, there has been a tendency for this result to occur accidentally, sometimes as result of a 'home made' will, whereby a testator dies leaving his house to his widow, thereafter to their children. Such a testamentary statement brought into play the full structure imposed by the Act. Such a consequence could also ensue as a result of an informal arrangement between people with respect to land, it widely being perceived to be inappropriate that the Act should apply to such situations.

---

[39] Settled Land Act 1925, s. 7; Administration of Estates Act 1925, s. 22.

[40] If title is unregistered, this will trigger the need for first registration of title: Land Registration Act 2002, s. 4(1)(ii).

[41] For an example of a long-standing dynastic settlement giving rise to modern-day problems, see *Hambro v. Duke of Marlborough* [1995] Ch. 158 discussed by E. Cooke [1994] Conv. 492.

[42] Trusts of Land and Appointment of Trustees Act 1996, Sched. 1, para. 5.

In the leading case of *Bannister v. Bannister*,[43] the defendant sold two cottages to the plaintiff, her brother-in-law. It was agreed, orally, that she would remain in one of them, rent free, for the rest of her life and the purchase price reflected this agreement. Some time later, the plaintiff sought to evict his sister-in-law from the cottage that she was occupying, his principal argument being that the oral agreement between them was ineffective precisely because it was merely oral.[44] Unsurprisingly, this argument failed. The Court of Appeal held that, were he to be allowed to rely on the lack of writing to defeat the oral agreement, his action would be fraudulent. As, on the basis of the agreement, he had paid less for the cottage than he otherwise would, for him to be able to rely on the lack of writing would have unjustly enriched him at her expense. To prevent this, a constructive trust was imposed. Under that trust, she was held to be entitled to a life interest in the land. This, in turn, led to the conclusion that the land became settled within the meaning of the Settled Land Act 1925 and she was the tenant for life.

A similar issue arose in *Binions v. Evans*.[45] Tredegar Estate owned land upon which was a cottage occupied by Mr and Mrs Evans. Mr Evans, like his father and grandfather before him, had been employed by the Estate for a long time and, on his death, the Estate agreed with Mrs Evans that, if she kept the cottage and the garden in good order, she could remain in the cottage for the rest of her life. The cottage was then sold, expressly subject to this agreement, to Mr and Mrs Binions who, on account of this agreement, paid a reduced price for it. They then sought to evict her from the cottage. The majority of the Court of Appeal, Lord Denning M.R. dissenting on this point,[46] held that, on the proper construction of the agreement, she had a life interest in the property and, accordingly, was the tenant for life within the meaning of the Settled Land Act 1925.[47]

The result of this case was that Mrs Evans was entitled to have a vesting deed executed in her favour. After trustees of the settlement had been appointed, she would then be able to exercise all the powers conferred upon her by the Act including, should she so wish, that of selling the property. It is principally this latter consideration which led to Lord Denning's dissent on this aspect of the case and to academic disquiet.[48] It is, quite simply, regarded as inappropriate that a person in the position of Mrs Evans should be endowed with all the powers conferred by the Act as a result of an act of generosity towards her.

This concern has led to the courts, on subsequent occasions, to seek to craft solutions in similar situations, where it is sought to protect the occupation rights of persons without becoming involved with the complications of the Settled Land Act 1925.[49] In

---

[43] [1948] 2 All E.R. 133.

[44] Law of Property Act 1925, s. 53(1)(b). See Resulting, implied and constructive trusts, p. 307.

[45] [1972] Ch. 359. The case is discussed further, Life interest, p. 604.

[46] He did not, however, dissent from the result, whereby Mrs Evans was permitted to remain in the cottage. See Life Interest, p. 604.

[47] Cf. *Morrs v. Morrs* [1972] Fam. 204.   [48] See, e.g. J.A. Hornby (1977) 93 L.Q.R. 561.

[49] See, e.g. *Dodsworth v. Dodsworth* [1973] E.G.D. 233; *Griffiths v. Williams* [1978] E.G.D. 919.

other cases, however, the courts have felt constrained to arrive at the conclusion that the parties' informal arrangement has created a life interest, with the consequence that the Act is applicable.[50]

The cases dealing with this type of issue are not easily reconcilable and one can understand why concern is felt in some quarters about the application of the Settled Land Act to informal arrangements of this type. The consequences of the Act being applicable stem, however, from the long-standing policy of seeking to prevent land being made unsellable for a prolonged period. If in the above instances the court had been able to fashion a solution which secured the right of indefinite occupation of the person in occupation but without giving that person the statutory powers, this policy would be undermined. This, in modern times, may not necessarily be a bad thing[51] and, under the new law can now be achieved.[52] It can be conceded, however, that the complication that the Act involved did seem a cumbersome way of dealing with such cases and that the new trust of land copes better with such a situation.

TRUSTS FOR SALE

The second legal device which was available as a means of creating settlements was the trust for sale. If land was the subject of a trust for sale, then it was not subject to the provisions of the Settled Land Act 1925.[53] Although the trust for sale has effectively been superseded by the trust of land, it remains necessary to consider it as a legal device, in that much of the new law derives from its antecedents. In doing this, one must consider the meaning of the term 'trust for sale' and when such a trust would be implied by law, and then examine the respective positions of the trustees and the beneficiaries and the operation of overreaching.

The trust for sale

A trust for sale was defined by section 205(1)(xxix) of the Law of Property Act 1925 as being an immediate binding trust for sale with or without a power at discretion to postpone the sale. The legal estate is held by the trustees for sale. There are various aspects of this definition which require elaboration.

Duty to sell

For a trust for sale to arise, the trust must impose a duty upon the trustees to sell the property. If a settlement provided that land was to be held by trustees for various

---

[50] See *Ungarian v. Lessnoff* [1990] Ch. 206; *Costello v. Costello* (1994) 27 H.L.R. 12. Cf. *Dent v. Dent* [1996] 1 W.L.R. 683.

[51] See M.P. Thompson [1994] Conv. 391 at 394–395.

[52] Trusts of Land and Appointment of Trustees Act 1996, s. 8.   [53] Settled Land Act 1925, s. 1(7).

persons in succession, with power for the trustees to sell the land, the trust did not impose a duty upon them to sell the land. The trust was not, therefore, a trust for sale. Instead, a strict settlement would have been created. An important consequence of this was that the legal title should then be vested in the tenant for life rather than, as directed, the trustees. Problems were at one time also caused by settlements which gave the trustees power to sell or retain the land. Such problems were resolved, however, as such provisions were to be construed as creating a trust to sell the property with power to postpone the sale.[54]

Immediate

For land to be held upon a trust for sale, the duty imposed upon the trustees to sell the property had to be immediate. This never meant that the land had actually to be sold forthwith; it meant merely that the duty to sell was an immediate one. That duty to sell was normally modified by the existence of a correlative power to postpone the sale. Such a power to postpone the performance of the duty to sell the property could be express but need not be, as unless the contrary intention was expressed in the trust,[55] a power for the trustees to postpone the sale would be implied by statute.[56] The fact that the overriding duty on the trustees was to sell the property did have an important effect, however, when the trustees were not unanimous as to whether to exercise the power to postpone the sale, one wishing to sell the property and the other being opposed to a sale. Such disputes are now decided by applying the criteria laid out in section 15 of the Trusts of Land and Appointment of Trustees Act 1996, although the express creation of a trust for sale may still be an important factor in the resolution of such a dispute.[57]

Consents

The sale of the property could be made subject to the consent of a given person. In some cases, the need for that consent may be implicit, as where a house was to be held upon trust for sale with a proviso that G was to have permission to reside in it for life or for as long as she desired. It was held that this was a trust for sale subject to G's consent being obtained before any sale took place.[58] Alternatively, the consent of a named individual could be made a prerequisite to the trustees selling the property. Paradoxically, the requirement of a consent to a sale could be used as a device to prevent the land being sold, this being done by requiring the consent of a person who was unlikely to agree.[59] Even this would not, necessarily, be successful to prevent a sale, however, as if that consent was not forthcoming, the court could be petitioned to order a sale, notwithstanding the refusal to give consent.[60]

---

[54] Law of Property Act 1925, s. 25(4).   [55] See *Re Rooke* [1953] Ch. 716.
[56] Law of Property Act 1925, s. 25(1).   [57] See Intention and purpose, p. 388.
[58] *Re Herklots' Will Trusts* [1964] 1 W.L.R. 583. Cf. *Re Hanson* [1928] Ch. 96.
[59] See *Re Inns* [1947] 1 Ch. 576.
[60] Law of Property Act 1925, s. 30; *Re Beale's Settlement Trusts* [1932] 2 Ch. 15.

Implied trusts for sale

The preceding account related to the creation of an express trust for sale. In certain situations, the law would also imply a trust for sale, the most important occasion being in cases of beneficial co-ownership of land. Where land was conveyed to persons as either joint tenants or tenants in common, specific provision was made that the land would be held upon an implied trust for sale.[61] Express provision was not made, however, for the increasingly common situation where land was conveyed to one person alone, but another person had, through contributing to its purchase, acquired an equitable interest in it.[62] This gap was filled in *Bull v. Bull*,[63] where a house had been conveyed to a son but his mother was a beneficial co-owner of it. The effect of this was held by the Court of Appeal to give rise to an implied trust for sale. The reasoning relied upon section 36(4) of the Settled Land Act 1925, which provided that an undivided share in land, which was the interest held by the mother, should not be capable of being created except under a trust instrument or under the Law of Property Act 1925 and should then only take effect behind a trust for sale.

The conclusion that the interrelation of the statutory provisions had the effect that an implied trust for sale was created was subject to criticism.[64] It did, however, provide a convenient solution to a problem which may not have been foreseen by the drafters of the 1925 legislation, and has the express approval of the House of Lords.[65] The upshot was that, unless land was settled land within the meaning of the Settled Land Act 1925, all land which was the subject of co-ownership was subject to a trust for sale; a matter which remains significant under the new statutory regime.

The trustees for sale

A crucial difference between the strict settlement and the trust for sale was the location of the legal estate. In the case of a strict settlement, the legal estate is vested in the tenant for life or the statutory owner. The role of the trustees of the settlement is to act as a watchdog of the settlement and to receive capital money when a transaction has taken place. In contrast to this, when land was held upon a trust for sale, the legal estate was held by the trustees for sale on trust for the beneficiaries. The trustees were then endowed with all the powers of both the tenant for life and the trustees of the settlement.[66] Although, in the case of settled land, it was expressly provided that the powers of the tenant for life could not be cut down,[67] no provision dealt with this issue in the case of trusts for sale. This point is now academic as the issue is addressed squarely by the 1996 Act.[68] Conversely, if the trustees for sale refused to exercise their

---

[61] Law of Property Act 1925, ss 34, 36. For joint tenancies and tenancies in common, see, Chapter 10.
[62] See Chapter 9.   [63] [1955] 1 Q.B. 234.
[64] B. Rudden (1963) 17 Conv. (N.S.) 51; W. Swadling [1986] Conv. 379; [1987] Conv. 451 at 454–457.
[65] *Williams & Glyn's Bank Ltd v. Boland* [1981] A.C. 487 at 507 *per* Lord Wilberforce.
[66] Law of Property Act 1925, s. 28.   [67] Settlement Land Act 1925, s. 106.
[68] Trusts of Land and Appointment of Trustees Act 1996, s. 8. Under the old law, it was probably the case that the powers could not be cut down. See Thompson, *Co-ownership* (London: Sweet & Maxwell, 1988), 7.

powers, then any person interested could apply to the court, which could make such order as it saw fit.[69]

When land was held upon trust for sale, the managerial role with respect to the land rested with the trustees. The person entitled to the income from the land occupied a far less important role than does his counterpart when the land is settled. He is not, however, without rights. Certain rights of management of the property, albeit not the power of sale, could be delegated to him.[70] Secondly, his consent may be a prerequisite to a sale by the trustees. Thirdly, the trustees may be under a duty to consult the beneficiaries, such a duty being imposed when the trust for sale was imposed by statute. That duty was not a particularly strong safeguard for the beneficiaries, however, as the right to be consulted does not carry with it a power of veto and a purchaser was, in any event, not concerned to see that this obligation had been complied with.[71] Finally, depending upon the circumstances surrounding the trust, the beneficiaries, if in occupation, may also have had the right not to be evicted from the property.[72] Ascertaining the rights of the beneficiaries was, however, approached in a somewhat piecemeal fashion and the new legislation has sought to formalize the position.

Conversion

The maxim that equity looks on that which ought to be done as already having been done is one of general application. The trust upon which the land was held was a trust for sale, the duty of the trustees being to sell the property. The application of this maxim in the present context led to the view that, regarding the property as already having been sold, the interests of the beneficiaries were in the proceeds of sale, rather than in the land, itself, an approach known as the doctrine of conversion.[73]

This doctrine is a technical one and, although judicially endorsed,[74] its application tended to be pragmatic. In the context of succession, it was applied so that if a testator left his real property to A and his personal property to B, then his beneficial interest under a trust for sale would be classed as personal property and would pass to B.[75] In other contexts, however, the application of the principle was less predictable. While a contract to sell a beneficial interest behind a trust for sale was, for the formal requirements necessary for such contracts, regarded as contract for the sale of land,[76] this was

---

[69] Law of Property Act 1925, s. 30.   [70] Ibid., s. 29.   [71] Ibid., s. 26(3).

[72] See Re Bagot's Settlement [1894] 1 Ch. 177; G.A. Forrest (1956) 19 M.L.R. 312.

[73] For a penetrating historical analysis of this doctrine, which concludes that its general applicability was overstated, see S. Anderson (1984) 100 L.Q.R. 46. See also H. Forrest [1978] Conv. 194; J. Warburton [1986] Conv. 415.

[74] See City of London Building Society v. Flegg [1988] A.C. 52 at 82–83 per Lord Oliver of Aylmerton.

[75] Re Kempthorne [1930] 1 Ch. 268.

[76] Cooper v. Critchley [1955] Ch. 431; Steadman v. Steadman [1976] A.C. 536. See also the original Law of Property (Miscellaneous Provisions) Act 1989, s. 2(6) now repealed by Trusts of Land and Appointment of Trustees Act 1996, s. 25(2), Sched. 4.

not the view taken with regard to other situations.[77] The doctrine was unpredictable in its application and its abolition[78] has effected a simplification of the law.

Trusts for sale and overreaching

As is the case when land is the subject of a strict settlement, when land was held upon a trust for sale, machinery exists whereby the beneficial interests are overreached. Although it was thought by some that the existence of the doctrine of conversion was, of itself, sufficient to achieve this end, in that as the beneficial interests took effect in the notional proceeds of sale, overreaching in the strict sense did not occur,[79] this view has been refuted.[80] The conveyance by the trustees of sale would convert the interests of the beneficiaries into the actual proceeds of sale, itself a form of overreaching, provided that the transaction was one that the trustees were empowered to make.[81]

The leading case is *City of London Building Society v. Flegg*.[82] Mr and Mrs Maxwell-Brown were the registered proprietors of a house which, by a happy coincidence, was called 'Bleak House', which they held on trust for themselves and for the Fleggs, who were the parents of Mrs Maxwell-Brown. Without informing the Fleggs, they executed a number of mortgages over the property until, finally, they mortgaged the property to the plaintiffs, the money being used to discharge the previous mortgages. When the Maxwell-Browns defaulted on the mortgage, the plaintiffs sought possession and the Fleggs resisted the action. They argued that, as beneficial co-owners of the property in actual occupation of the land, their interests took effect as overriding interests binding on the plaintiffs, in the same way as did Mrs Boland's in *Williams & Glyn's Bank Ltd v. Boland*.[83]

The defence failed. The fact that the Fleggs were in actual occupation of the land was irrelevant. This was because the effect of the mortgage was to overreach their interests. The effect of overreaching in this context was that the legal interest of the society under the mortgage had priority over that of Mr and Mrs Flegg, who did not, therefore, have an interest capable of binding the mortgagee. As the transaction was effected by two trustees for sale, which is the appropriate method of overreaching the interests of equitable co-owners in cases where land is subject to co-ownership, it was irrelevant whether there were four or forty-four beneficial co-owners with interests behind the trust. The result was that, pending a sale of the property, the interest of the Fleggs was in the value of the land subject to the rights of the mortgagee.[84]

---

[77] *Irani Finance Ltd v. Singh* [1971] Ch. 59, where it was held that a charging order (a form of security in respect of a judgment debt) against land could not be made against the interest of a beneficiary behind a trust of sale; a decision necessitating Charging Orders Act 1979, s. 2.

[78] Trusts of Land and Appointment of Trustees Act 1996, s. 3.

[79] See, e.g., J.M. Lightwood [1929] C.L.J. 59 at 65.

[80] See the seminal article by C. Harpum [1980] C.L.J. 277 at 278.   [81] Ibid.

[82] [1988] A.C. 54.   [83] [1981] A.C. 487.

[84] That interest is termed the equity of redemption. See The equity of redemption, pp. 466–467.

Inherent power of overreaching

This result might have been thought to have been dictated by the overreaching provision contained in the Law of Property Act 1925. Section 2 provides that, provided that the provisions of section 27 of the Act respecting the payment of capital money are complied with, then a conveyance made by trustees for sale shall overreach the equitable interests existing behind the trust. Section 27 provides that a purchaser of a legal estate from trustees for sale is not to be concerned with the trusts affecting the land if the proceeds of sale or capital money are paid to no fewer than two trustees for sale.[85] The true position, however, is that these sections did not confer new powers upon the trustees for sale, whose ability to overreach these interests derives from the powers that they have as trustees.[86]

This point is illustrated by *State Bank of India v. Sood*.[87] Trustees for sale created a mortgage to secure future borrowing. Beneficiaries under the trust for sale argued that their interests had not been overreached because, for that to happen, the capital money had to be paid to or at the direction of the trustees. As, in the instant case, no capital money had arisen at the time of the mortgage, it was argued that no overreaching had occurred. This argument was rejected, the essential reason being that the provisions governing the payment of capital money are relevant only when capital money arises. This will not be the case where the transaction in question is a lease, where no premium is paid, or an exchange of land, or, as here, where the land is mortgaged but no capital money has arisen. The point then is whether or not the transaction is *intra vires* the powers of the trustees. If it is, the beneficial interests will be overreached.

One trustee

A vital feature of both *Flegg* and *Sood* was that the mortgages were created by two trustees. In *Williams & Glyn's Bank Ltd v. Boland*,[88] a mortgage was created by the sole registered proprietor, who held the legal title on an implied trust for sale for himself and his wife, who was a beneficial co-owner of the house. It was held that the wife, who was in actual occupation of the house at all material times, had an overriding interest binding upon the bank. An argument, based upon the doctrine of conversion, that she could not have such an interest because her interest was in the proceeds of sale, was considered to be 'just a little unreal'.[89] Because there was only one trustee for sale, he lacked the power to overreach the beneficial interest existing behind the trust and this interest is, therefore, potentially binding upon a purchaser.[90]

---

[85] See also Trustee Delegation Act 1999, s. 2. The 1925 Act, as amended, now refers to trusts of land rather than trusts for sale, a point which is, for present purposes, immaterial.

[86] See Harpum, loc. cit., 293–294.   [87] [1997] Ch. 276. See M.P. Thompson [1997] Conv. 134.

[88] [1981] A.C. 487.   [89] Ibid., at 507 *per* Lord Wilberforce.

[90] For an interesting historical critique of both *Flegg* and *Boland*, see N. Jackson (2006) 69 M.L.R. 214.

TRUSTS OF LAND

The strict settlement and the trust for sale had different origins and different effects. Most particularly, the decisions as to such key matters as whether the land should be sold or mortgaged was vested in different people; in the case of the former, in the tenant for life, in the case of the latter, in the trustees for sale. This, of course, was an important difference and made distinguishing between the two forms of settlement crucial, something which, unfortunately, was not always easy. More fundamentally, however, the question arose whether it was really necessary or desirable to have in place two systems of settlement.

If the preferred view was simply to allow one form of settlement to be retained, then there is little doubt that, of the two systems, the trust for sale was both simpler and more efficient. A principal reason why this was so was the different documentation required to set up either mechanism. Because, under a strict settlement, the legal estate is vested in the tenant for life, every change which occurs behind the curtain which causes a change in the identity of the tenant for life means that a new vesting deed must be executed to effect the necessary change. This can be a cumbersome and expensive business. With a trust for sale, on the other hand, because the legal estate is vested in the trustees, what occurs behind the curtain is of no concern to a purchaser. When one considers also, that the trust for sale could accommodate both successive and concurrent interests in property and, by the process of requiring consents to the sale of property, could be used more effectively than a settlement to ensure that the property was retained, where that was desired, it was manifest that, of the two legal devices, the trust for sale was the preferable of the two.

If, in reforming the law, the choice was simply between abolishing one form of land-holding and retaining the other, then the most sensible option would have been to abolish the strict settlement and to retain the trust for sale.[91] The Law Commission[92] did not, however, adopt this course. Mindful of the artificiality of the concept of a trust for sale and the concomitant doctrine of conversion, the preferred option was to create a new form of trust, ultimately to replace both of the previous forms of landholding. This recommendation has substantially been implemented by the Trusts of Land and Appointment of Trustees Act 1996,[93] although the new trust which has been created bears close similarities to the effect of the trust for sale.

The trust of land

Part I of the Act contains the provisions relevant to the creation of the new trust of land. Its general scheme is, first, to define the trust of land and then to provide when such a trust will exist. The powers and duties of the trustees are then detailed, together

---

[91] See G.A. Grove (1961) 24 M.L.R. 123.   [92] (1989) Law Com. No. 181.
[93] See N. Hopkins [1996] Conv. 411.

with the rights of the beneficiaries, the position of purchasers, and the procedure, and criteria to be applied in the resolution of disputes.

Definition

A trust of land is defined by section 1(1) of the Act as being any trust of property which consists of or includes land, and trustees of land means the trustees of a trust of land. Section 1(2) elaborates this definition, to make clear that the reference to a trust includes all trusts (whether express, implied, resulting, or constructive), including a trust for sale and a bare trust. It is then further provided that, subject to certain exceptions, the Act is retrospective; that is land which was held on trust for sale prior to the Act coming into force is now subject to a trust of land. As a consequence of this, there was a myriad of legislative changes, so that where reference had previously been made in a statute, these have now been amended to refer instead to trusts of land.[94]

Settlements

Although the intention of the Act is to replace the previous dichotomy of strict settlement and trust for sale with the single new device of the trust of land, this could not be done retrospectively for all settlements. Whereas, converting what was a trust for sale into a trust of land would not involve any action on the part of anybody, this is not the case when land is subject to a settlement. In the former case, the legal title was vested in the trustees, whereas, when land was settled the legal title was vested in the tenant for life. It would not be realistic to expect, in all cases, the legal title to be transferred from the tenant for life to the trustees of the trust and, consequently, existing settlements remain subject to the regime imposed by the Settled Land Act 1925.[95]

In the case of new settlements, section 2(1) prohibits the creation of any new settlements for the purposes of the Settled Land Act. If, therefore, after 1997, a settlement is created to A for life, remainder to B, it will take effect as a trust of land. Where a settlement would arise because a conveyance purports to convey land to a minor, the conveyance is inoperative for the purpose of conveying a legal estate but will, instead, operate as a declaration of trust in favour of the minor.[96] There are limited exceptions to the embargo upon the creation of new settlements. These relate to alterations to interests deriving from settlements in existence prior to the commencement of the Act.[97]

Imposition of the trust

After 1997, all new settlements take effect as trusts of land; with respect to other trusts involving land, the new trust is imposed retrospectively. For trusts created after 1997, the position is governed by sections 4 and 5 of the Act. Section 4 is concerned with the creation of an express trust for sale. This is not prohibited, but such a trust, nevertheless, comes within the definition of a trust of land supplied by section 1. Moreover, if

---

[94] Trusts of Land and Appointment of Trustees Act 1996, Sched. 3.
[95] Ibid., s. 1(3). Also exempt from the Act is land held under the University and College Estates Act 1925.
[96] Trusts of Land and Appointment of Trustees Act 1996, s. 2(6), Sched. 1.   [97] Ibid., s. 2(3).

such a trust is created, then, despite any provision to the contrary made by the disposition, the trustees are given the power, at their absolute discretion, to postpone the sale of the land. If an express trust for sale is created, the only potential significance of doing so would appear to be that it might affect how the court might determine a dispute between interested parties as to whether the land should actually be sold.[98]

Section 5 of the Act is concerned with implied trusts of land. Under the old law, a trust for sale was implied by law in certain situations, notably when land was conveyed to joint tenants or to tenants in common.[99] Section 5 of and Schedule 2 to the Act impose a trust of land in the situations where previously a trust for sale would have been implied.

The nature of the trust

Under the old law, the trust was a trust for sale; the duty of the trustees was, subject to their power to postpone the sale, to sell the property. Under the new law, there is no such duty imposed upon the trustees. Instead, section 6 of the Act operates to vest in the trustees all the powers of an absolute owner and, of course, one of the powers of an absolute owner is to sell the property.

Abolition of conversion

Because the trustees are no longer under a duty to sell the property, a logical consequence is that the doctrine of conversion whereby, at least for some purposes, the interests of the beneficiaries was regarded as being in the proceeds of sale, should no longer be applicable. This logical conclusion is spelled out explicitly by section 3 of the Act, a provision that can now apply only to an express trust for sale, which provides that where land is held by trustees subject to a trust for sale, the land is not to be regarded as personal property. The reverse position is also catered for. If personal property is subject to a trust for sale in order that the trustees may acquire land, the personal property is not to be regarded as land.

Powers of the trustees

As stated above, section 6 of the Act confers upon the trustees all the powers of an absolute owner. In contrast to the previous law, there is no prohibition on the restriction of the trustees' powers, it being provided by section 8 that section 6 does not apply in the case of a trust of land being created by a disposition which excludes its effect. It would seem, therefore, that the power of sale can be excluded, although if that is done, it would still be open to any person interested to petition the court for a sale of the property, although the exclusion of the power of sale would be a factor to which the court would presumably have regard in the exercise of its discretion.[100]

A new power given to trustees is a power, when land is subject to a trust of land and each of the beneficiaries is of full age, to convey the land to the beneficiaries even if

---

[98] Ibid., ss 14, 15. See Disputes as to sale, pp. 387–396.

[99] Law of Property Act 1925, ss 34, 36.

[100] Trusts of Land and Appointment of Trustees Act 1996, ss 14, 15.

they have not required the trustees to do so. If the trustees do convey the land to the beneficiaries, they are required to do what is necessary to secure that the legal title vests in them, which means them applying to be registered as proprietors of the land. If the beneficiaries fail to do so a court may make an order requiring them to.[101] As an alternative to conveying the land to the beneficiaries, the trustees may, by power of attorney, delegate their powers to a beneficiary of full age, who is entitled to an interest in possession.[102]

Purchasing land

It was previously the case that difficulties arose as to whether trustees for sale, having sold the land which was subject to the trust, could use the proceeds of sale to purchase other land.[103] This doubt as to the ability of trustees to do this has now been removed by section 6(3),[104] which empowers the trustees to purchase a legal estate in land in England and Wales for the purpose of investment, for occupation by any beneficiary, or for any other reason.

Misuse of powers

The conferment of powers on the trustees is done in a much simpler way than was previously the case by simply conferring upon them the powers of an absolute owner. It is then provided by section 6(6) of the Act that these powers shall not be exercised in contravention of any other enactment or any rule of law or equity. The consequence of trustees exercising their powers wrongfully is controversial and will be considered in the section on overreaching.

THE RIGHTS OF BENEFICIARIES

The Act, having conferred extensive powers to deal with the land upon the trustees, also confers rights upon the beneficiaries to which the trustees, perhaps somewhat unnecessarily, are required to have regard when exercising their powers.[105]

Consultation and consents

Consultation

As was the case when land was held upon trust for sale, the trustees are obliged to consult the beneficiaries prior to the exercise of any function relating to land subject

---

[101] Ibid., s. 6(2).

[102] Ibid., s. 9. The powers of delegation are much wider than was previously the case.

[103] Re Wakeman [1945] Ch. 177. Cf. Re Wellstead's Will Trusts [1949] 1 Ch. 296 at 319 per Cohen L.J. See D. Pollock (1953) Conv. (N.S.) 134 at 137.

[104] As amended by the Trustee Act 2000, s. 8.

[105] Trusts of Land and Appointment of Trustees Act 1996, s. 6(5).

to the trust. The duty to consult is imposed by section 11 of the Act. The trustees are required, so far as is practicable, to consult the beneficiaries of full age and beneficially entitled to the land and, so far as is consistent with the general interest of the trust, give effect to the wishes of those beneficiaries or (having regard to the respective sizes of the beneficial interests) to the majority of the beneficiaries.

The duty to consult does not carry with it an obligation to carry out the wishes of the beneficiaries or the majority of them if, in the opinion of the trustees, the action proposed is not consistent with the general interests of the trust. Where there is such disagreement, application can be made to the court under section 14 of the Act. The orders which the court can make and the criteria to be applied in determining disputes of this nature will be considered fully in a later chapter.[106]

Consents

Provision is made for the exercise of the trustees' powers to be made subject to the obtaining of consents. Section 8(2) of the Act provides that, if the disposition creating a trust of land makes provision requiring any consent to be obtained to the exercise of any power conferred by section 6 or 7, the power may not be exercised without that consent, thereby giving to that person or persons a power of veto over the exercise of the trustees' powers. If the consent of more than two persons is required then the consent of any two of them to the exercise of the function is sufficient in favour of a purchaser.

The position of the purchaser if the trustees do not comply with these provisions will be considered shortly.

Occupation

Most land which is held on a trust of land is the subject of co-ownership and an important aspect of the rights of co-owners relates to the occupation of the property and the regulation of rights of occupation. Detailed provision is made with respect to these issues by sections 12 and 13 of the Act and will be considered in the context of co-ownership of land.[107]

OVERREACHING

It was established by the House of Lords in *City of London Building Society v. Flegg*,[108] that when land was held upon a trust for sale, a conveyance executed by the trustees for sale would overreach the interests of the beneficiaries, regardless of whether or not those beneficiaries were in actual occupation of the land. Although in a separate report from that dealing with trusts of land generally, the Law Commission recommended

---

[106] See Chapter 10.   [107] Ibid.   [108] [1988] A.C. 54.

that *Flegg* be reversed by legislation, it is not readily apparent that the Act either did, or was intended to, have this effect. Nevertheless, it has been argued[109] that, in the case of registered land, the Act has had this effect, and so this issue must be addressed, considering first the position where title is unregistered.

Unregistered land

Where title is unregistered, the first point to note is that the trustees are, by section 6 of the Act, given all the powers of an absolute owner. However, section 6(6) provides that the powers conferred in this section shall not be exercised in contravention of any rule of law or equity. The restrictions that would seem to be relevant would appear to be contained in various provisions, such as section 6(5), which requires the trustees, in exercising their powers, to have regard to the rights of the beneficiaries,[110] and section 8, which provides that where a consent is required for any disposition, the trustees shall not make such a disposition without obtaining the requisite consent; and section 11(1) requires the trustees in the exercise of any function to consult the beneficiaries of full age entitled to possession.

The essential argument put forward is that these restrictions on the exercise of the powers of the trustees limit their powers of dealing with the trust property and, ordinarily, this would therefore invalidate the disposition by the trustees. This is not the case, however, with respect to unregistered land because of the protection afforded by section 16 of the Act. Section 16(1) of the Act provides that:

'A purchaser of land which is or has been subject to a trust need not be concerned to see that any requirement imposed on the trustees by section 6(5), 7(3) or 11(1) has been complied with.'

The section then goes on to afford further protection to a purchaser by stipulating that, where trustees of land conveying land contravene section 6(6) or 6(8) of the Act, the conveyance shall not be invalidated unless the purchaser has actual notice of the contravention; and a similar provision is made in respect of a conveyance made in excess of any limitation imposed by section 8.[111]

It is clear, therefore, that the purchaser of unregistered land will not be bound by beneficial interests existing behind a trust of land provided that the purchase money is paid to or at the direction of the trustees, unless he has actual notice that the disposition is a breach of trust. The argument that a purchaser of registered land will not be

---

[109] G. Ferris and G. Battersby [1998] Conv. 168. For a similar argument advanced some years previously, see S. Clayton [1981] Conv. 18. That article, however, relied heavily on the restrictions imposed upon trustees for sale by Law of Property Act 1925, s. 28, which has now been repealed.

[110] This is a curious provision, as a basic duty of trustees is to have regard to the interests of the beneficiaries. For an interesting discussion which links this duty to the criteria listed in s. 15, see G. Ferris and G. Battersby [2009] Conv. 39.

[111] Trusts of Land and Appointment of Trustees Act 1996, s. 16(2)(3). Cf. similar provisions in respect of the wrongful exercise of a mortgagee's power of sale: Law of Property Act 1925, s. 104(2).

so protected is based upon section 16(7) which provides, simply, that this section does not apply to registered land.

Registered land

The argument that the decision in *Flegg* has been overruled in respect of registered land rests principally on the fact that the protection afforded to purchasers of unregistered land by section 16 is expressly made not to apply to registered land. Accordingly, it is argued that if trustees contravene any of the limitations imposed by the 1996 Act, then a purchaser will not get a good title and will be bound by the rights of the beneficiaries.[112]

As an initial observation, one would anticipate that, were such a conclusion to be intended, then such a change in the law would be signposted in a rather less cryptic way than this. Nevertheless, if one looks at the arguments on the merits, they do not entirely convince. In the case of registered land, the proprietor, by virtue of section 18 of the Land Registration Act 1925, may, subject to any entry on the register, transfer the fee simple in possession. Accordingly, it has been said to be fundamental that:

'In order to deprive registered proprietors of full powers of mortgaging or leasing, for example, there would have to be a restriction on the register expressly preventing them from exercising those powers.'[113]

In other words, the view is that the protection provided by section 16 in the case of unregistered land is, quite simply, unnecessary in the case of registered land because any restrictions on the rights of the trustees to deal with the land must be entered on the register of title. This conclusion is reinforced by the amendment made to section 94 of the Land Registration Act 1925 by the 1996 Act.[114] Section 94(1) requires that, when there is a trust of land, the land shall be registered in the names of the trustees. It is further provided by section 94(4) that there shall be entered on the register such restrictions as may be prescribed, or are expedient, for the protection of the rights of persons beneficially entitled to the land. The clear implication is that, unless the beneficial rights are protected by the entry of a restriction, the purchaser shall not be concerned with them.

Ultra vires *dispositions?*

A final matter is that the argument that *Flegg* has been overruled rests upon the premise that dispositions made by the trustees in contravention on the limitations imposed by the Act have the effect of making such disposition *ultra vires* and, therefore, ineffective to overreach the beneficial interests behind the trust. It is not at all

---

[112] Ferris and Battersby [1998] Conv. 168 at 179–180. For a refutation of this analysis, see N. Jackson [2007] Conv. 120.

[113] Ruoff and Roper, *The Law and Practice of Registered Conveyancing* (London: Sweet & Maxwell, Looseleaf), para. 32.05.

[114] Trusts of Land and Appointment of Trustees Act 1996, Sched. 3, para. 5.

clear, however, that this is the case; it is quite feasible that the limitations on the powers of the trustees are designed to affect the position of the trustees *vis-à-vis* the beneficiaries rather than a purchaser so that if, for example, the trustees sell the land without consulting the beneficiaries this may make them liable to the beneficiaries for breach of trust but not affect the purchaser.[115] Indeed, given that the trustees are not obliged to follow the views expressed by the beneficiaries after consultation if they consider that such views are not in the best interests of the trust,[116] one would expect this conclusion to follow. It can hardly be the case that a mortgage or convey-ance by trustees contrary to the wishes of beneficiaries, who have been consulted, will overreach those interests, whereas the same transactions carried out, without consulting them at all, will not. Consequently, it is submitted that although, to date, judicial views on this matter are inconclusive,[117] if and when the issue is squarely raised, the conclusion will be reached that a conveyance or mortgage of registered land will overreach the beneficial interests existing behind the trust for sale, provided that the purchase money is paid to two trustees and that the decision in *Flegg* remains good law.

Land Registration Act 2002

Although this issue is not explicitly dealt with in the Land Registration Act 2002, it would seem that the matter is put beyond doubt by a combination of sections 23, 24, and 26. Sections 23 and 24 confer owner's powers on the registered proprietor. Section 26(1) then provides that, subject to subsection (2), a person's right to exercise owner's powers in relation to an estate or charge is to be taken free from any limita-tion affecting the validity of the disposition. Section 26(2) provides that section 26(1) does not apply to a limitation reflected by an entry on the register or imposed by, or under, the Act. Unless, therefore, the right of beneficiaries to be consulted is protected by the entry of a restriction, a purchaser will not be affected by failure of the trustees to do so.[118]

---

[115] See M. Dixon [2000] Conv. 267. But see the reply by G. Ferris and G. Battersby [2001] Conv. 221.

[116] See Consultation, p. 296.

[117] See *State Bank of India v. Sood* [1997] Ch. 276 at 290 *per* Peter Gibson L.J., where this point was assumed without argument and *Birmingham Midshires Mortgage Services Ltd v. Sabherwal* (2000) 80 P. & C.R. 256.

[118] See also E. Cooke [2002] Conv. 11 at 23–25.

9

Co-ownership 1: Acquisition of Interests in the Home

It is far less common than was once the case for people deliberately to create settlements, whereby successive estates are carved out of a fee simple. Although settlements in being prior to 1997 are unaffected by the structural changes brought about by the Trusts of Land and Appointment of Trustees Act 1996, any settlements created after that time will now take effect as trusts of land. A much more common situation than the creation of successive interests in land is the existence of concurrent interests in land, where land is subject to co-ownership.

There are a number of situations where co-ownership may be encountered. Perhaps the most usual is where a house is bought together by a husband and wife as the matrimonial home. A similar situation can arise in the increasingly common arrangement whereby a couple live together in a loving relationship but either out of choice,[1] or because, legally, they are unable to do so,[2] they do not marry. People can also share the ownership of property without there being any romantic attachment between them. They could be siblings, or other relations, or simply friends. Co-ownership can also arise when the relationship between the co-owners is a commercial one, as where partners together buy land from which to operate a business.

Co-ownership of land can, therefore, involve a number of quite different relationships. It was, indeed, this considerable variety in the types of relationship that caused the Law Commission, in its long-awaited Report on Sharing Homes, to abandon the task of trying 'to devise a statutory scheme for the determination of shares in the shared home which can operate fairly and evenly across all the diverse circumstances which are now to be encountered'.[3] The type of relationship which has caused the most anxiety, however, is that between cohabiting couples who are in an intimate relationship. The number of such relationships appears to be rising, and the 2002 Census recorded that there were just over two million cohabiting couples in England and Wales,[4] and the 'Government Actuaries Department predicts that the proportion of couples cohabiting will continue to grow from the present one in

---

[1] For the various reasons for this, see S. Duncan, A. Barlow, and G. James (2005) 17 C.F.L.Q. 383.
[2] See, e.g., *Churchill v. Roach* [2004] 2 F.L.R. 989.
[3] (2002) Law Com. No. 278, *Sharing Homes: A Discussion Paper*.
[4] Office for National Statistics, Census 2001, table S006.

six of all couples to one in four by 2003'.[5] The law governing this type of relationship has, however, been stigmatized as being 'uncertain, difficult to apply and can
lead to serious injustice'.[6] Perhaps for this reason, in the aftermath of the Report on
Sharing Homes, the Government referred the matter back to the Law Commission
to consider only this type of relationship. The ensuing Report[7] will be considered at
the end of this chapter.

The essential legal framework imposed whenever there is co-ownership of land is,
however, the same. In all cases, there will be in existence a trust of land. Issues which
can also arise will be to determine the respective beneficial rights of each co-owner
in the property and the resolution of disputes between the co-owners, in particular,
disputes as to occupation and as to when the property should be sold. It is with these
latter issues, in particular, that the different types of relationship involved between
the co-owners will become material. Before considering the legal framework of
co-ownership and the respective rights of the co-owners, which is the subject matter
of Chapter 10, the prior issue arises as to whether co-ownership actually exists. It is
with this issue that this chapter is concerned.

THE CREATION OF CO-OWNERSHIP[8]

There are a number of situations where it may become necessary to establish the actual
beneficial ownership of land. Quite commonly, this issue will arise when the relationship, of whatever nature, between two people breaks down and the question will arise
as to, as between them, who owns what or, on the death of one of them, who owned
what.[9] This question can also arise, however, when a third party is involved, when it is
argued that an occupier of a property has a beneficial interest in it, the argument being
that that interest is binding upon a mortgagee.[10]

Husband and wife

Much of the case law concerning the acquisition of interests in land has arisen in the
context of disputes concerning the ownership of the family home. In the case of the
matrimonial home, such disputes did not become possible until 1882.[11] Prior to this
date, a husband and wife were regarded as being one legal entity, the embodiment of
that entity being the husband. One consequence of this was that her property vested
in him.

---

[5] *Stack v. Dowden* [2007] 2 A.C. 432 at [44] *per* Baroness Hale of Richmond.
[6] (1995) Law Com. No. 234 at para. 34.   [7] (2007) Law Com. No. 307.
[8] See, generally, Mee, *Property Rights of Cohabitees* (Oxford-Portland, Oregon: Hart Publishing, 1999).
[9] See, e.g., *Bindra v. Mawji* [2008] EWHC 1715 (Ch.).   [10] See Co-owners, pp. 485–491.
[11] See Cretney, *Family Law in the Twentieth Century* (Oxford: Oxford University Press, 2003), 90–102.

This somewhat draconian rule was, in fact, alleviated to a certain extent by the doctrine of dower and the judicious use of trusts and marriage settlements. Despite these alleviations, however, pressure grew for the establishment of the principle of separate ownership of property between spouses. Success came with the enactment of the Married Women's Property Act 1882. Section 1 provides that:

'A married woman shall…be capable of acquiring, holding, and disposing by will or otherwise of any real or personal property as her separate property, in the same way as if she was a femme sole,[12] without the intervention of any trustee.'

This provision established the principle of separate ownership of matrimonial property. Although proposals were made to introduce a scheme whereby there would be equal ownership of the matrimonial home,[13] these proposals were never implemented. There is no regime of matrimonial property,[14] and the principle of separate ownership of property remains the cornerstone of the ownership of matrimonial property. The notion of separate ownership of property led, however, to the difficult task of ascertaining who owns what.

Family assets

Under section 17 of the Married Women's Property Act 1882, provision was made for either spouse to apply, in any question as to the title to or the possession of property, by summons or in any summary way to the High Court or county court, which may make such order with respect to the disputed property as it sees fit.

At one time, in determining disputes brought under this section, the Court of Appeal felt free to adopt a generally discretionary approach, this approach seemingly embracing the notion that disputes as to the ownership of a family home should be determined upon different principles depending upon whether or not the couple were married. In *Hine v. Hine*,[15] Lord Denning M.R. expressed the view that, if a house was acquired by joint efforts, which would include a wife looking after the children, then the house would become a 'family asset' and the court had a discretion under section 17 of the Act as to the shares to be awarded in it to each party. The rights arising from the application of legal or equitable principles were not regarded as being a useful factor in the resolution of such disputes.

Rejection of discretion

The resolution of property disputes by regard to the notion of family assets[16] rested upon the premise that section 17 of the 1882 Act allowed the courts, in disputes between married couples, to share the property between them as they saw fit. The existence of such a discretionary power was, however, decisively rejected in the House

---

[12] A single woman.   [13] (1978) Law Com. No. 86.

[14] See the comments in *Charman v. Charman* [2007] EWCA Civ. 503 at [124] *per* Sir Mark Potter P.

[15] [1962] 1 W.L.R. 1124. See also *Appleton v. Appleton* [1965] 1 W.L.R. 25.

[16] For a valuable discussion, see J.G. Miller (1970) 86 L.Q.R. 98.

of Lords.[17] It was held that the jurisdiction given by section 17 was a procedural one to enable disputes of this nature to be resolved speedily. It did not confer upon the courts *carte blanche* to reallocate property between husbands and wives. Following from this, the law to be applied as to the ownership of the family home was the same regardless as to whether the parties were married. The expression 'family assets', as used in this context, was condemned as being 'devoid of legal meaning and its use cannot define legal rights or obligations'.[18] In any application brought under the section, 'the question was—"Whose is this?" and not "To whom shall this be given?".'[19]

That said, 'Who owns what?' may be a very simple question to ask, but 'in a short time the enquirer will find themselves immersed in the off-putting, and sometimes obscure, terminology of the law of trusts and estoppel'.[20]

Similar sentiments were expressed at somewhat greater length, and with more rhetorical flourish, in *Stack v. Dowden*,[21] where Carnwath L.J. said of this area of law:

'To the detached observer, the result may seem like a witches' brew, into which various esoteric ingredients have been stirred over the years, and in which different ideas bubble to the surface at different times. They include implied trust, constructive trust, resulting trust, presumption of advancement, proprietary estoppel, unjust enrichment and so on. These ideas are likely to mean nothing to a layman, and often little more to the lawyers who use them.'

This chapter seeks to separate out some of these various ingredients, in order to elucidate the applicable principles, and then to assess how satisfactory their application is to disputes of this type.

Divorce jurisdiction

Since the House of Lords established that there was no separate property law regime with regard to married couples, the practical position has changed significantly. Section 4 of the Matrimonial Property and Proceedings Act 1970 gave the courts, on granting a decree of divorce, nullity, or judicial separation, the power to order one party to the marriage to transfer to the other party, or to any child of the family, property to which he is entitled, either in possession or reversion. After 5 December 2005, when the Civil Partnership Act 2004 came into force, this jurisdiction to reallocate property has been extended to the dissolution of a civil partnership.[22] A civil partnership can be entered into between same-sex couples,[23] and enables such people to register their partnership.[24] Most of the legal incidents of marriage are then conferred on the couple, including that of reallocation of property on the dissolution of the relationship. It should be stressed, however, that there is no such jurisdiction on the

---

[17] *Pettitt v. Pettitt* [1970] A.C. 777. See also *Stack v. Dowden* [2007] 2 A.C. 432 at [42] *per* Baroness Hale of Richmond.

[18] Ibid., at 817 *per* Lord Upjohn. Cases which employed this reasoning, such as *Hine v. Hine* and *Appleton v. Appleton*, were overruled.

[19] Ibid., at 798 *per* Lord Morris of Borth-y-Gest.   [20] (2002) Law Com. No. 288, para. 1.12.

[21] [2005] EWCA Civ. 857 at para. 75; affmd for different reasons at [2007] 2 A.C. 929. See E. Cooke [2005] Conv. 555.

[22] Civil Partnership Act 2004, s. 72, Sched. 5.   [23] Ibid., s. 1.   [24] Ibid., s. 2.

breakdown of a non-marital relationship. This point deserves emphasis, because it is widely, although erroneously, believed that cohabitation for a period of time confers upon the parties the same legal rights as if they were married.[25] This is not so.[26]

The statutory jurisdiction to adjust property rights on divorce or, since 2005, the dissolution of a civil partnership, which was re-enacted by section 23 of the Matrimonial Causes Act 1973, has transformed the approach to be taken to property disputes between spouses, and civil partners, on the breakdown of the marriage or civil partnership. In making orders under the Act, the court is not constrained by the ownership rights in the property prior to the order being made. Consequently, in such cases it is not of great importance to determine who owned what. This question will, however, be important if the dispute as to the ownership of property occurs outside the context of divorce or dissolution. This might occur if, for religious reasons, there are objections to divorce,[27] or if the dispute occurs after the death of one of the parties.[28] Much more important than this is the not uncommon situation where one party is seeking to assert rights against a mortgagee,[29] or, indeed, other creditors.[30] In such cases, the person who is asserting the claim will first have to establish that she actually has a right in the property,[31] and this is done by the application of equitable principles, which are principally those underlying the law of trusts. In applying these principles, however, it has become apparent that, although those principles have been said to be the same in respect of whether or not a couple is married and although the inferences which may be drawn may be affected by the status of the relationship,[32] this position can no longer be maintained. In particular, it now appears to be the case that, if the property has been put into joint names, there is no presumption of resulting trust arising solely from the fact that the parties have made unequal contributions to the purchase price.[33] This contrasts with the position where the parties have more of an arm's length relationship, in which different considerations may apply.[34] In cohabitation cases it may be in the interests of both sharers of the house to establish that it is co-owned, and so

---

[25] See A. Barlow, C. Burgoyne, E. Clery, and J. Smithson in A. Park, *et al.*, *British Social Attitudes: The 24th Report* (London: Sage, 2008), 12. See also *Churchill v. Roach* [2004] 2 F.L.R. 989, where it appeared that a university teacher thought that cohabitation for seven days a week over six months would lead the law to consider his partner to be his wife: see at 991 *per* Judge Norris.

[26] For an account of how this myth has developed, see R. Probert [2011] Fam Law 283.

[27] See, e.g., *Shinh v. Shinh* [1977] 1 All E.R. 97.

[28] See, e,g., *Re Draper's Conveyance* [1969] 1 Ch. 486 and Form of notice, pp. 371–372.

[29] See *Williams & Glyn's Bank Ltd v. Boland* [1981] A.C. 487.

[30] See *Hosking v. Michaelides* [2004] All E.R. (D.) 147.

[31] See *Lloyds Bank plc v. Rosset* [1991] 1 A.C. 107.

[32] *Stack v. Dowden* [2007] 2 A.C. 432 at [40] *per* Baroness Hale of Richmond, citing with approval *Bernard v. Josephs* [1982] Ch. 391 at 402 *per* Griffiths L.J.

[33] *Jones v. Kernott* [2011] UKSC 53 at [25] *per* Lord Walker and Lady Hale.

[34] *Stack v. Dowden* [2007] 2 A.C. 432 at [69] *per* Baroness Hale of Richmond. See also *Laskar v. Laskar* [2008] EWCA Civ. 347 at [21] *per* Lord Neuberger of Abbotsbury, sitting in the Court of Appeal. For similar observations in the context of estoppel, see *Thorner v. Major* [2009] UKHL 18 at [56] *per* Lord Walker of Gestingthorpe.

the courts will look carefully, and in some instances sceptically, at the evidence to see if the facts warrant the conclusion that the house is actually co-owned.[35]

EXPRESS DECLARATIONS OF OWNERSHIP

By far the easiest way for the parties to avoid disputes in the future is to state, expressly, and in writing, so as to comply with the formal requirements of section 53(1)(b) of the Law of Property Act 1925, what the beneficial interests are in the house when it is being acquired. If the parties make an express declaration as to the beneficial interests in the property then, *prima facie*, that declaration will be decisive.[36] Such a declaration will cease to be decisive only if one of the parties can secure rectification of the document setting out the equitable interests. For example, in *Thames Guarantee Ltd v. Campbell*,[37] a wife had provided the whole purchase price of the property but, out of courtesy to the husband, the solicitors were instructed to convey the property into their joint names. Although it was intended that she should be the sole beneficial owner in equity, by mistake they were described as being joint tenants in law and in equity. This having been proved, she succeeded in having the document rectified to delete the words 'in equity'. The onus of proof to secure rectification is, however, a heavy one.

Subject to any claim to rectification, however, the express statement of the beneficial interests in the property will be conclusive as to those interests at the time that the property was acquired, although those interests may later be varied as a consequence of subsequent events.[38] As such, it is clearly good practice when a house is being acquired by a couple for their intentions with regard to the beneficial ownership to be ascertained and reflected in a document signed by both parties.[39] Much time and expense can be avoided by an express declaration of the beneficial entitlements and judicial exhortations for advisers to make sure that this is done are not hard to find. The latest *cri de coeur* with regard to this emanated from Ward L.J., who said: 'Perhaps conveyancers do not read the law reports. I will try one more time: *always try to agree on and then record how the beneficial interest is to be held*. It is not

---

[35] See *Midland Bank plc. v. Dobson* [1986] 1 F.L.R. 171 at 174 *per* Fox L.J.; *Hosking v. Michaelides, supra,* at [38]–[43] *per* Mr Paul Morgan Q.C.

[36] *Goodman v. Gallant* [1986] Fam. 106; *Turton v. Turton* [1988] Ch. 542; *The Anglo Eastern Trust Ltd v Kermanshahchi (No. 3)* [2003] EWHC 1939 (Ch.). A statement that the survivor may give a valid receipt for the capital money arising on a disposition of the land does not, of itself, amount to a declaration of a joint tenancy: *Harwood v. Harwood* [1991] 2 F.L.R. 274; *Huntingford v. Hobbs* [1993] 1 F.L.R. 376; *Stack v. Dowden, supra,* at [51] *per* Baroness Hale of Richmond. *Post,* p. 351.

[37] [1985] Q.B. 510. See also *Wilson v. Wilson* [1969] 3 All E.R. 345.

[38] See *Jones v. Kernott* [2011] UKSC 53.

[39] See *Robinson v. Robinson* (1977) 241 E.G. 153. Cf. *Pink v. Lawrence* (1977) 36 P. & C.R. 37.

very difficult to do.'[40] A failure to perform this task may leave a legal adviser open to a claim in negligence.[41]

Since 1998, when title is being registered in joint names, the application form, FR1, in the case of first registration of title, and TR1 in the case of transfers, to joint proprietors, which must be completed to enable registration to occur, enables the applicants to tick one of three boxes.[42] The alternatives are that the applicants are holding for themselves as joint tenants; that they are holding for themselves as tenants in common in equal shares; or that they are holding the property (complete as necessary).[43] Unfortunately, it is not mandatory to tick any of the boxes,[44] and despite the strong exhortation by Baroness Hale of Richmond in *Stack v. Dowden*[45] that the rules should be changed to ensure that this is done, the new Land Registration (Amendment) Rules 2008[46] do not do so.

This is to be regretted. Apparently the reason why there is to be no such change is an attempt to shelter micro-businesses from the perceived pernicious effect of bureaucracy. A good deal of property which is purchased in joint names is bought to set up a small business, and the completion of this form is seen as an example of such red tape from which the Government has ordered a moratorium.[47] As has been aptly commented that, while 'it is always good to see bathwater sloshing down the drain,... are we seeing the baby disappearing with it'?[48] Had such a change occurred, disputes as to the beneficial ownership of houses transferred to joint proprietors would have all but disappeared, with the resulting saving of large amounts of money, and a good deal of angst, currently spent in contesting these cases.

RESULTING, IMPLIED, AND CONSTRUCTIVE TRUSTS

Where the parties have failed to state what the beneficial interests in the property are to be, in a subsequent dispute, this issue will fall to be decided by the application, principally, of the law of trusts. To create a trust concerning land, the normal rule as to formality is contained in section 53(1)(b) of the Law of Property Act 1925, which provides that:

'A declaration of trust respecting any land or any interest therein must be manifested and proved by some writing signed by some person who is able to declare such trust or by his will.'

---

[40] *Carlton v. Goodman* [2002] 2 F.L.R. 259 at 273, Ward L.J.'s italics.

[41] See *Walker v. Hall* [1984] F.L.R. 126 at 129 *per* Dillon L.J.

[42] Empirical evidence, however, shows that the actual parties may not understand the import of the effect of this. See G. Douglas, J. Pearce and H. Woodward [2008] Conv. 365 at 372–375.

[43] For the meaning of these terms, see Chapter 10. The beneficial interests of the parties are not revealed on the register of title.

[44] See the discussion at [2007] Conv. 364.   [45] [2007] 2 A.C. 432 at [52].

[46] [2008] SI No. 1919. For critical comment, see M.J. Dixon [2008] Conv. 355.

[47] See E. Cooke [2011] Fam Law 1142 at 1143.   [48] Ibid., at 1144.

A saving clause exists, however, in that section 53(2) of the Act provides that the section does not affect the creation or operation of resulting, implied, or constructive trusts. It is with resulting and constructive trusts with which we are principally concerned, the usual scenario being a situation where the legal title to the house is in the name of one person, usually the male partner, and the other claims subsequently to have a beneficial interest in it. The resolution of problems concerning this type of situation necessitates one 'to climb again the familiar ground that slopes down from the twin peaks of *Pettitt v. Pettitt* and *Gissing v. Gissing*'.[49]

These two decisions of the House of Lords, decided within a short time of each other, formed the theoretical underpinning of this area of law. Since then, much litigation has ensued, including two further decisions of the House of Lords in *Lloyds Bank plc v. Rosset*,[50] and *Stack v. Dowden*,[51] and a decision of the Supreme Court in *Jones v. Kernott*.[52] Although this chapter will attempt to guide a path through this extensively litigated area of law, it is as well to note, at the outset, that 'as is notorious, it is not easy to reconcile every judicial utterance on this well-travelled area of law'.[53] Moreover, *Stack v. Dowden* has been criticized on the basis that it has failed to provide theoretical clarity to the law,[54] and it has been said, with a degree of understatement, that 'There is some debate about the principles underlying the decision of the majority in that case.'[55] That the conceptual debate may not be over, however was, somewhat depressingly, recognized in *Jones v. Kernott* itself, as Lord Kerr, while expressing the hope that the correctness of the decision in *Stack v. Dowden* would not need to be revisited, said that 'should it be necessary, the court (no doubt with a panel of seven or nine) would need much fuller argument (together with citation of the enormous critical literature which the decision has spawned) than was presented to the court on this appeal.'[56]

The original House of Lords' approach

That disputes as to the ownership of the family home were to be resolved by the application of orthodox trust principles was firmly established by the House of Lords in *Pettitt v. Pettitt*[57] and *Gissing v. Gissing*,[58] although securing agreement as to what those orthodox principles were was to prove more difficult.[59]

In *Pettitt v. Pettitt*, a house had been conveyed into the sole name of a wife, the purchase money being derived from the sale of another house owned solely by her. Her husband, on an application under section 17 of the 1882 Act, claimed a beneficial share

---

[49] *Grant v. Edwards* [1986] Ch. 638 at 646 *per* Nourse L.J.   [50] [1991] 1 A.C. 107.
[51] [2007] 2 A.C. 432.   [52] [2011] UKSC 53.
[53] *Drake v. Whipp* [1996] 1 F.L.R. 826 at 827 *per* Peter Gibson L.J.
[54] See M.J. Dixon [2007] Conv. 352; W. Swadling (2007) 123 L.Q.R. 511 at 518. For a more favourable reaction, see N. Hopkins (2009) 125 L.Q.R. 310.
[55] *Bindra v. Mawji* [2008] EWHC 1715 (Ch.) at [86] *per* Etherton J.   [56] [2011] UKSC 53 at [58].
[57] [1970] A.C. 777.   [58] [1971] A.C. 886.
[59] The former decision was described as 'being more Delphic than the Oracle which at least had the advantage that her ambiguities were uttered in only one voice': J. Tiley [1969] C.L.J. 191 at 196. See also the observations in *Jones v. Kernott* [2011] UKSC 53 at [28] *per* Lord Walker and Lady Hale.

in the house, the basis of his claim being the decorating work that he had done to it, this work, he asserted, having enhanced the value of the property by some £1,000. This claim was unanimously rejected by the House of Lords.

While all members of the Appellate Committee agreed that the claim must fail, essentially on the basis that what he had done was of far too ephemeral a nature to entitle him to an interest in the property,[60] thereafter there was considerable disagreement as to the correct principles to be applied. Lord Upjohn sought to emphasize the role of resulting trusts and, in particular, this meant ascertaining what the intention of the parties was with regard to the beneficial ownership of the house when it was acquired. The role of the resulting trust was then seen to be the medium through which that intention was implemented.

To determine the intentions of the parties, he considered the starting point to be if there was any express declaration of trust. If there was, then this, ordinarily, was conclusive. In the absence of such a declaration, one looks to find some agreement as to how the beneficial interest in the house is to be shared, if that, indeed, is to be the case. In the absence of direct evidence as to the intention of the parties, however, one falls back on the normal equitable presumptions to infer what it was that they intended.

JOINT OWNERSHIP OF THE LEGAL TITLE

In *Pettitt*, it was stated that the starting point in determining the beneficial ownership of the home is to look first at the position at law. If the legal title was in joint names, there was a presumption that it was intended to share the beneficial ownership. Conversely, if there was sole ownership at law, the presumption was that this was also the position in equity.[61] The presumptions were relatively easy to rebut, however, and, in cases of joint ownership of the legal estate, the fact that the parties had contributed unequally to the purchase price would tend to the conclusion that the parties intended the beneficial ownership to be shared unequally.[62] The House of Lords in *Stack v. Dowden*[63] has, however, strengthened considerably the force of the presumption, particularly with regard to the position when there is joint ownership at law.

Barry Stack and Dehra Dowden, who were in a relationship for twenty-seven years, had cohabited for a total of nineteen years, during which time they had four children. In 1983, when they first started living together, the house was in her sole name. This house was sold in 1993, and another house was bought, title to which was in their joint names. The purchase price was £190,000. Just over £128,000 came

---

[60] See also *Button v. Button* [1968] 1 W.L.R. 457.

[61] [1970] A.C. 777 at 813–814 *per* Lord Upjohn, who also said that it is seldom that this is determinative, a point ignored in *Stack v. Dowden*.

[62] See *Stack v. Dowden* [2005] EWCA Civ. 857 at [17] *per* Chadwick L.J; affmd on different grounds at [2007] 2 A.C. 432.

[63] [2007] 2 A.C. 432.

from her building society, and the balance from a bank loan to them jointly. This was secured by a mortgage and two endowment policies, one of which was in their joint names, and the other in her name alone. The interest payments on the mortgage and the joint endowment payments were made by Mr Stack, and the capital sum borrowed was repaid by a series of lump sum payments, of which he contributed £27,000, and she just over £38,000. The utility bills were in her name, although he claimed to have paid some of them. Throughout the period of their cohabitation they maintained separate bank accounts, and made a series of separate investments. When they separated in 2002, she remained in possession of the house with the children and litigation ensued as to the beneficial ownership of it. The House of Lords, unanimously—although Lord Neuberger dissented as to the reasoning—held that the beneficial ownership was divided between them in the proportion 65 per cent to 35 per cent in her favour.

Presumption of joint beneficial ownership

The leading speech was given by Baroness Hale of Richmond. She accepted that the task for the court is to determine what the parties intended.[64] In so doing, however, she stressed that:

'Just as the starting point where there is sole legal ownership is sole beneficial ownership, the starting point where there is joint legal ownership is joint beneficial ownership. The onus is on the person seeking to show that the beneficial ownership is different from the legal ownership. So, in sole ownership cases it is upon the non-owner to show that he has any interest at all. In joint ownership cases, it is upon the joint owner who claims to have other than a joint beneficial interest.'[65]

Subsequently, she made it clear that it would be unusual for the courts to find that the intention of the parties was that the beneficial interests in the house should be different from that which pertained at law.[66] This position was stressed in *Jones v. Kernott*,[67] where Lord Walker and Lady Hale, in a joint judgment, made it clear that, when the property is transferred to the parties in joint names, the default position is that the position in law is mirrored by that in equity. Before considering what factors made the present case unusual, and what might make others fall into the same category, an initial issue about the nature of the beneficial joint ownership when the presumption is applicable must first be addressed.

Joint tenancy or tenancy in common?

While it is clear that, as a result of *Stack v. Dowden*, the existence of joint legal ownership carries with it a strong presumption of joint beneficial ownership, it was not made as clear as it should have been whether this is as a joint tenancy or as a

---

[64] Ibid., at [61].   [65] Ibid., at [56].   [66] Ibid., at [69].   [67] [2011] UKSC 53 at [15].

tenancy in common in equal shares. At law, it is only possible for there to be a joint tenancy,[68] whereas, in equity, co-ownership can take the form of either a joint tenancy or a tenancy in common. The distinction between the two will be considered in more detail in the next chapter, but, for present purposes, the main distinction between the two is what happens in the event of the death of one of the co-owners. If there is a beneficial joint tenancy, then the survivor becomes the sole owner of the property. If, on the other hand, there is a tenancy in common then, on the death of one of them, that person's share in the property will pass by will or upon intestacy. Baroness Hale, who emphasized that equity followed the law, said that 'at least in the domestic context, a conveyance into joint names indicates both legal and beneficial joint tenancy unless and until the contrary is proved'.[69] While this is clear, earlier in the same paragraph she said that the issue was whether a conveyance into joint names established a *prima facie* case of joint and equal beneficial shares unless the contrary is established, a statement which indicates that the co-owners hold as equitable tenants in common in equal shares. On balance, the passage quoted supports the view that an equitable joint tenancy had been created, although the alternative view has been assumed to be the case by some commentators.[70] That assumption was supported by Lord Hope of Craighead, who said that in the present context, 'joint beneficial ownership means that the shares are presumed to be divided equally',[71] a statement indicative of a tenancy in common. A similar lack of precision was exhibited in *Fowler v. Brown*,[72] where Arden L.J. said of the effect of the presumption that:

'It provides a default rule that, unless and until the contrary is proved, joint tenants in this context are treated as joint legal and beneficial owners. If the contrary were not proved, the mere fact that the property was transferred into their joint names would be enough to give both parties *an equal beneficial share*.'

The first sentence is consistent with the existence of a beneficial joint tenancy, and the second with a tenancy in common.

While it is disappointing that this important issue should have been left unclear, and such a lack of clarity had the potential to lead to further litigation,[73] it would now seem that this matter has been settled by *Jones v. Kernott*,[74] where Lord Walker and Lady Hale said that when the property is in joint names, the starting point is that 'equity follows the law and they are joint tenants both in law and in equity.'

---

[68] Law of Property Act 1925, s. 1(6).   [69] [2007] 2 A.C. 432 at [58].

[70] See G. Douglas, J. Pearce, and H. Woodward [2008] Conv. 365, 'the presumption is that equity follows the law so that the beneficial interests are held in equal shares'.

[71] [2007] 2 A.C. 432 at [4].

[72] [2008] EWCA Civ. 377 at [34], emphasis supplied. See also the comment by N. Piska [2008] Conv. 452 at 457.

[73] Cf. *Bindra v. Mawji* [2008] EWHC 1715 (Ch.).   [74] [2011] UKSC.53 at [51].

Rebutting the presumption of joint ownership

Prior to *Stack v. Dowden*, the fact that the legal title to a house was in joint names was rarely decisive as to the size of the beneficial shares each party had in the property. While there was certainly a presumption of beneficial co-ownership, the courts would look carefully at the respective contributions to the purchase of the property to determine the quantum of each party's beneficial interest in it.[75] This approach to the problem, which was consistent with the reasoning in both *Pettitt* and *Gissing*, was abandoned in the domestic context.[76] Instead, as indicated above, it was stressed that, while the question of the beneficial ownership is to be decided on the basis of what the parties intended,[77] the starting point is, emphatically, to start from the basis that the house is to be jointly owned. This was stressed by Lord Walker of Gestingthorpe, who considered there to be a heavy burden on a party who sought to argue that the ownership should be other than joint.[78] In similar vein, Baroness Hale remarked that it 'cannot be the case that all of the hundreds of thousands, if not millions, of transfers into joint names using the old forms are vulnerable to challenge in the courts simply because it is likely that the owners contributed unequally to the purchase price'.[79]

It is evident that the reason why the majority held that a transfer into joint names leads to a strong presumption of an intention to share the beneficial ownership equally is to seek to avoid the torrent of litigation that can ensue to establish who owns what. This process can lead to the expenditure of far more money in legal costs than the value of the property warrants,[80] and result in a 'detailed examination of the parties' relationship and finances'.[81] Nevertheless, it is clear that the presumption of a beneficial joint tenancy is not irrebuttable, and attention can now be turned to the situations where such a presumption can be rebutted, as indeed was the case in *Stack v. Dowden* itself.

Stack v. Dowden was considered by Baroness Hale to be 'a very unusual case'.[82] What appeared to make it so was that she had contributed far more than he had done to the acquisition of the house, and it was not a case where they pooled their resources even notionally.[83] In her view, 'there cannot be many unmarried couples who have lived together for as long as this, who have had four children together, and whose affairs have been kept as rigidly separate as this couple's affairs were kept'.[84] The only item of property which was in their joint names was the house. This, quite reasonably, led

---

[75] See *Walker v. Hall* [1984] 1 F.L.R. 126; *Springette v. Defoe* [1992] 2 F.L.R. 511; *Huntingford v. Hobbs* [1993] 1 F.L.R. 376, all of which were disapproved in *Stack v. Dowden*, *supra*, at [65] *per* Baroness Hale of Richmond.

[76] It was this abandonment of the application of orthodox principles which led Lord Neuberger of Abbotsbury to dissent as to the reasoning, if not the result. For comment on the somewhat cavalier approach to precedent, see W. Swadling (2007) 123 L.Q.R. 511 at 517.

[77] How that intention is discerned is a contentious issue. See Presumed intention, pp. 321–323.

[78] [2007] 2 A.C. 42 at [33].   [79] Ibid., at [68].   [80] Ibid.

[81] Ibid., at [33] *per* Lord Walker of Gestingthorpe.

[82] Ibid., at [92]. Lord Walker regarded it as an 'exceptional case': ibid., at [33].

[83] Ibid., at [87] and [90].   [84] Ibid., at [92].

to the conclusion that it was their intention that it was to be jointly owned, although as they were quite meticulous as to separate ownership of other assets, why the fact they did put the house into joint names led to the conclusion that they intended to have unequal shares in it is, in the context of the general approach to the problem, not entirely clear.[85] Nevertheless, the fact this was found to be their intention led to the difficult question of the quantification of their beneficial shares, an issue which will be returned to later in the chapter.

Relevant criteria for unequal ownership

It is not clear that the facts relied upon to rebut the inference of joint beneficial owner-ship are, in truth, that unusual. Baroness Hale gave further criteria which may help to divine the intentions of the parties with regard to the beneficial ownership of the home. Pointing out that, in law, context is everything, and that every case will turn on its own facts, she indicated what factors other than the financial may cast light upon their intentions. This list, which she also pointed out was not intended to be exhaustive,[86] included any advice or discussions at the time of the transfer; the rea-sons why the home was put into joint names; the reason why (if that was the case) the survivor was authorized to give a receipt for capital monies; the purpose for which the house was acquired; and whether they had children for whom they had responsibility to provide a home. She also considered that the individual characteristics of the par-ties may also be relevant in deciding where their true intentions lay, and it may well be the case that, in the context of cohabitation, mercenary considerations may be more to the fore than they would be in a marriage, but it should not be assumed that they always take pride of place over natural love and affection.

Baroness Hale then turned to relevant financial matters. She drew attention to the issue of how the purchase was financed, whether separately or together or a bit of both; how they discharged the outgoings on the property and their other household expenses. She then said that when a couple are joint owners of the house and jointly liable for the mortgage, the inferences to be drawn are very different from the infer-ences to be drawn when only one is the owner of the house. In such cases, she thought that the arithmetical calculation of how much was paid by each is likely to be less important, and it will be easier to draw the inference that each should contribute as much to the household as they reasonably could and that they would share the even-tual benefit or burden equally. Finally, she pointed out that, whatever the intentions of the parties may have been at the outset, these may have changed, an example being where one of the parties has paid for (or constructed himself) a substantial improve-ment to the property.[87] A second situation where such a change of intention may be found is when there is a significant variation in the manner of purchasing behaviour, a

---

[85] See also Lord Neuberger of Abbotsbury in the (2008) Chancery Bar Association Lecture, para. 16.
[86] Ibid., at [69].
[87] Ibid., at [69]–[70]. For improvements, see Matrimonial Proceedings and Property Act 1970, pp. 331–333.

feature of the Supreme Court decision in *Jones v. Kernott*,[88] a decision to be considered shortly.

Despite having listed these various criteria as being examples of matters which may throw light on the parties' intentions, and presumably, therefore, being matters which may rebut the presumption that where there is joint ownership of the legal estate there will also be equal beneficial ownership, Baroness Hale, somewhat surprisingly concluded that cases where there would not be joint beneficial ownership would be very unusual.[89] Hence, although one might have a great deal of sympathy with the hope that, in subsequent cases, there will be a diminishing number where it is necessary to embark on a detailed examination of the parties' behaviour and expenditure, it is difficult to disagree with the view that, whereas a departure from equal division may only be justified in exceptional cases, until the evidence is heard, it is hard to judge whether any given case is exceptional or not.[90] This consideration has led to the justified criticism that 'the judgments of the majority in *Stack* do not disclose any domestic arrangement so exceptional as to suggest why a departure from the principle of equality was appropriate. The main result of the case may simply be to generate discussion of what exactly its implications are.'[91]

The applicability of Stack

The difficult task of deciding what the circumstances are that will justify the non-application of the presumption of joint beneficial ownership has, as is to be expected, fallen on lower courts. Significant factors appear to be the relationship between the parties and the purpose of the acquisition of the property. In *Adekunle v. Richie*[92] the right to buy a council house was exercised and it was transferred into the joint names of a mother, who was the council tenant, and her son. She contributed significantly more to the acquisition of the property than he did. Although Judge Behrens, sitting in Leeds County Court, considered that, although the presumption of equal ownership articulated in *Stack v. Dowden* was applied to a cohabiting couple who were in a romantic relationship, it also applied to a domestic relationship such as this. That said, where, as here, one is not dealing with a couple living together in a relationship akin to one of marriage or civil partnership, it is easier to find the facts to be unusual in the sense that they are not to be taken to have intended a joint tenancy.[93] Because of the disparity of the size of contributions, the fact that there were nine other siblings, and the house was bought primarily as a home for her to occupy, he felt justified in holding that they were entitled in unequal shares.

This was approved and applied by the Court of Appeal in *Laskar v. Laskar*.[94] A mother was a council tenant who exercised her right to buy, the purchase price being reduced as she, as a sitting tenant, was entitled to a discount.[95] The purchase price was

---

[88] [2011] UKSC 53   [89] Ibid., at [69].   [90] R. Probert [2007] Fam. Law 924 at 927.

[91] Ibid., at 929. See also the extra-judicial observations of Lord Neuberger of Abbotsbury in (2008) Chancery Bar Association lecture at para. 17.

[92] (2007) Unreported.   [93] Ibid., at [65].   [94] [2008] EWCA Civ. 347.

[95] See Council house discounts, pp. 326–327.

made up in part by money borrowed by way of mortgage for which the mother and her daughter were jointly liable, and the balance provided by the payment of cash sums by both of them. The house was transferred to them jointly, with no declaration of trust. As was always intended, soon after the transaction had been completed, the mother moved out to live with another daughter, and the property was rented out. In short, it had been bought principally as an investment. When the pair fell out, there was a dispute as to the beneficial ownership. It was held that they had shares of two-thirds and one-third. According to Lord Neuberger of Abbotsbury, the presumption of a beneficial joint tenancy did not apply to a case such as this. The reason was that 'although the parties were mother and daughter and not in that sense in an arm's length relationship, they had independent lives, and ... the purchase of the property was not really for the purpose of providing a home for them.... The property was purchased primarily as an investment.'[96]

Unequal contributions

Prior to *Stack v. Dowden*, even when a house was transferred into joint names, the fact that the two parties made unequal financial contributions to its acquisition would normally give rise, through resulting trust principles, to a beneficial share proportionate to the size of the contribution. This was rejected in *Stack* and, instead it was held that there was a strong presumption of joint beneficial ownership. This was reiterated in *Jones v. Kernott*, where it was said that it was 'not possible at one and the same time to have a presumption or starting point of joint beneficial interests and a presumption (let alone a rule) that the parties' beneficial interests are in proportion to their respective financial contributions.'[97] While that must be the case, as the presumption of joint ownership can be rebutted, the issue of unequal contributions may still be relevant.

The matter was revisited in *Fowler v. Barron*.[98] A twenty-three year relationship ended in 2005. When it started, she was seventeen and he was forty-seven. A house was bought in 1988, and it was deliberately put into joint names. He paid the initial deposit and, although the mortgage was in their joint names, it was paid for entirely out of his pension, he having retired early from the fire service. The balance of the purchase price was provided from the proceeds of sale of his flat. He also paid the council tax and utility bills. They had a daughter in 1994, having previously had a son. She continued to work, while he stayed at home to look after the children. Her wages were spent on herself and the children, miscellaneous items of food, school trips, seasonal gifts, personal clothing, and holidays. At first instance, it was held that she had no interest in the property but, on appeal, it was held that she was entitled to a half share of the beneficial interest.

---

[96] [2008] EWCA Civ. at [15]. See also *Parrott v. Parkin* [2007] EWHC 210 (Admlty) (purchase of a yacht).
[97] [2011] UKSC. 53 at [23] *per* Lord Walker and Lady Hale.
[98] [2008] EWCA Civ. 377. See N. Piska [2008] Conv. 451.

At first blush, it does not seem easy to distinguish this case from *Stack v. Dowden*. In both cases there had been long-term cohabitation, the existence of children, and a failure to pool their resources. Yet *Stack* was seen as being an exceptional case, and this was not. The key to the distinction would seem to lie in the huge disparity between the size of the contribution in the present case as compared to the position in *Stack*, and the large difference in their ages. In the present case, there was a thirty-year age difference between them, and it was a conscious decision to put the house into their joint names. The reason for this, as found by the judge, was that he wanted to ensure that she would benefit in the event of his prior death. This, coupled with evidence that they had made mutual wills, was indicative of an intention that she should have some share in the property, although what that share should be was not discussed. From this, the inference was drawn 'that the parties simply did not care about the respective size of each other's share'.[99] Thus, it is a short step to find an implied intention that the share should not be commensurate with the size of her contribution: were it to be otherwise, as her contribution could best be described as minimal, she would acquire virtually no share in the property, which was not what was intended. On the facts, therefore, it is not unreasonable to apply the presumption and hold that they shared the beneficial interest equally. The main problem with the decision is that, if she had made no contribution to the acquisition of the house, a not unreasonable finding on the facts, it is difficult to see why any sort of trust should have arisen because, it will be recalled, the basic rule is that a trust of land must be evidenced in writing.[100] If he had said to her that he held the house on trust for her and himself in equal shares alone, this would not create an enforceable trust, and an unarticulated intention to that effect should not do so either, unless there was material on which one could base the imposition of either a resulting or a constructive trust.[101] On the facts, it is not obvious as to why either trust should have arisen.

Inference as to intention

Leaving this aside, the issue of unequal contributions was dealt with by Arden L.J. She recognized that, in at least some instances, this fact may lead to the inference that the parties intended their beneficial interests in the house to reflect the respective size of those contributions. She said:

'In a case where the parties have made unequal contributions to the cost of acquiring their home, it is obvious that in some cases there may be a thin dividing line between the case where the parties' shared intention is properly to be inferred to be ownership of the home in equal shares and the case where the parties' shared intention is properly inferred to be that the party who contributed less should have a smaller interest than the other. The resolution of such cases must however all depend on the facts.'[102]

---

[99] Ibid., at [41] *per* Arden L.J. See also *Holman v. Homes* [2007] EWCA Civ. 877 at [16] *per* Lloyd L.J.
[100] Law of Property Act 1925, s. 53(1)(b).   [101] Ibid., s. 53(2).
[102] [2008] EWCA Civ. 327 at [45].

This, of course, does not help to identify where the line is to be drawn. Clearly, however, it is envisaged that in some cases where the main feature of the case is the inequality of contribution, that fact alone can lead to an unequal sharing of the beneficial interest. The suggestions which follow must necessarily be speculative.

Disparity in size of contribution

In *Fowler v. Barron* virtually the entire contribution to the purchase price was made by Mr Barron, and yet the house was put into joint names. This must be indicative of an intention to share the beneficial ownership; otherwise there is no reason for joint ownership at law. If the intention is not to share the beneficial ownership equally, but for the shares to reflect the amount of the contribution, then one of the parties will acquire only a very small share in the property, which is at odds with putting the house into joint names in the first place. So, perhaps counterintuitively, the fact that when the house is put into joint names, and there is a very wide disparity in the size of the respective contributions to the acquisition, may mean that it is more likely to be held to be the case that the presumption of joint ownership of the beneficial interest will apply. Conversely, where there is a significant difference in the size of the contribution, but, as in *Stack*, the contribution of both is substantial, then the presumption of joint beneficial ownership may more easily be rebutted.

Pooling of resources and nature of contribution

Although it has been argued that, in trying to pin down the exceptional nature of *Stack v. Dowden*, one is driven to conclude that what influenced each member of the House was the fact of unequal contributions to the acquisition of the property,[103] there must be more to it than that. If the position were otherwise, the decision becomes, effectively, broken-backed, in that virtually every case would become unusual. Another significant factor in *Stack* was that the couple kept their finances entirely separate. Although this may well not be that unusual, it could, it seems, be taken to amount to an intention that each should, effectively, get what they paid for.[104] If, on the other hand, the parties effectively pool their resources then, even if one of the parties brings in more money than the other, the very fact of sharing resources would seem to indicate that the presumption of shared ownership of the house would be applicable.[105]

A further feature of *Stack* which may be relevant is that, in the purchase of the house, large lump sum payments were made. These were over and above the initial capital contribution to the purchase, and were the principal means by which the mortgage was repaid. This is an unusual method of repayment, and, in such circumstances may add weight to the inference that the parties intended their interests in the house

---

[103] R. Probert (2007) 15 Fem. Leg. Stud. 341 at 348. See also Lord Neuberger of Abbotsbury (2008) Chancery Bar Association Annual Lecture, at paras 15–17.

[104] Although see Household contributions, p. 334 as to the importance of contributions to household expenditure.

[105] See *Stack v. Dowden* [2007] 2 A.C. 432 at [69] *per* Baroness Hale of Richmond. See also *Abbott v. Abbott* [2007] UKPC 55.

to be commensurate with the size of their financial contributions, rather than sharing the beneficial interest equally.

All that said, *Stack v. Dowden* must be seen as representing a missed opportunity to bring clarity to an important area of law. The upshot of it is that it establishes different presumptions depending upon the relationship of the parties, and a distinct lack of clarity as to when the presumption of equality will be rebutted.

SOLE OWNERSHIP OF THE LEGAL TITLE

Of the cases concerning the ownership of the family home, as Baroness Hale pointed out,[106] *Stack v. Dowden* is the only one to reach the House of Lords where the legal title was in the joint names of the parties, although, since then, a second instance of this has occurred in *Jones v. Kernott*.[107] A much more common area of dispute is where the legal title is in the name of one person, usually the man's, and on the breakdown of the relationship, his partner claims to have an interest in the house. This scenario is of considerable practical importance, as a recent survey revealed that only thirty per cent of cohabitants live in accommodation that is in joint names.[108] Unlike the position when the house is in joint names and there is then a presumption of joint beneficial ownership, in this situation the person whose name is not on the title has the burden of establishing that he has any interest in the property at all.[109] A person seeking to establish an interest in the home must rely on the principles of trusts and estoppel, to which attention can now be turned.

Resulting trusts

In *Pettitt v. Pettitt*,[110] the speech of Lord Upjohn sought to employ traditional resulting trust principles to this area of law, and placed the focus very much on ascertaining what the parties intended when the property was acquired. This approach was also taken by Lords Morris of Borth-y-Gest and Hodson, who both stressed the need to find an agreement between the parties as to what the beneficial interests in the land were intended to be.[111] Lords Reid and Diplock, although concurring in the result, effectively dissented from the reasoning. Whereas the majority insisted that the task of the court was to infer from the conduct of the parties what they had agreed upon, the minority took what, at first sight, might appear to have been a more discretionary approach. According to Lord Diplock, this meant that, if the courts were able to infer

---

[106] Ibid., at [40].   [107] [2011] UKSC 53.
[108] J. Huskey (2001) Population Trends 103, cited by R. Probert (2007) 15 Fem. Leg. Stud. 341 at 350.
[109] *Jones v. Kernott* [2011] UKSC 53 at [17] *per* Lord Walker and Lady Hale.   [110] [1970] A.C. 777.
[111] *Pettitt v. Pettitt* [1970] A.C. 777 at 804–805 and 810, respectively.

that the parties had come to an agreement with regard to the beneficial ownership of the property, then effect should be given to that agreement; if not, however, then an intention should be imputed to them on the basis of what reasonable people would have intended.[112]

The emphasis placed upon the need to infer the intentions of the parties with regard to the beneficial ownership of the home, at the time when it was acquired, has been the source of a considerable amount of difficulty in relation to this branch of the law. The first difficulty relates to the issue of intention, itself, for it is here that two quite different things are being confused. In the first type of case, the courts are prepared to draw inferences as to the intentions of the parties from their behaviour with regard to the acquisition of the property. The evidence does not support the conclusion that the parties have actually considered, consciously, the question of the beneficial ownership of the house. This, traditionally, was the domain of the resulting trust. The second type of case involves situations where the parties have engaged in what has been termed 'title talk'.[113] This is where the evidence shows that the parties have come to an actual agreement as to the beneficial ownership of the home, but where that agreement does not comply with the formalities required for the creation of an express trust.[114] In these quite different cases, the issue is whether the circumstances are such as to justify the imposition of a constructive trust to implement the actual agreement.

This point is very clearly made in *Drake v. Whipp*,[115] where Peter Gibson L.J. said that:

'A potent source of confusion, to my mind, has been suggestions that it matters not whether the terminology used is that of the constructive trust, to which the intention, actual or imputed, of the parties is crucial, or that of the resulting trust which operates on a presumed intention of the contributing party in the absence of rebutting evidence of actual intention.'

As will be seen, however, the modern tendency is to conflate the resulting and constructive trust, and to treat the latter concept as the more appropriate analysis in most matrimonial cases,[116] an analysis which has led to a considerable loss of clarity.

A second difficulty is the focus on the actual time of the acquisition of the property. It is a commonplace that most houses are bought with the aid of a mortgage from either a bank or a building society. The repayment of the mortgage occurs over a prolonged period. To consider the matter solely at the time of the actual purchase of the house is unrealistic, and would ignore entirely the not uncommon situation when a

---

[112] Ibid., at 822–823. See also at 796 *per* Lord Reid.

[113] J.W. Harris in Jackson and Wilde, *Contemporary Property Law* (Aldershot: Ashgate, 1999), 97.

[114] Law of Property Act 1925, s. 53(1)(b). See also *Gissing v. Gissing* [1971] A.C. 886 at 905 *per* Lord Diplock.

[115] [1996] 1 F.L.R. 826 at 827.

[116] *Abbott v. Abbott* [2007] UKPC 55 at [3] *per* Baroness Hale of Richmond.

person moves into a house of which another person is already the legal owner. This point was made explicitly in *Gissing v. Gissing*,[117] where Lord Diplock said:

'But it would in my view be unreasonably legalistic to treat the relevant transaction involved in the acquisition of the matrimonial home as restricted to the actual conveyance of the fee simple into the name of the other spouse....The conduct of the spouses in relation to the payment of the mortgage instalments may be no less relevant to their common intention as the beneficial interests in a matrimonial home acquired in this way than their conduct in relation to the payment of a cash deposit.'

A failure always to bear these comments in mind has led to problems which will be considered below, and it is now clear that, in assessing the question of beneficial ownership, conduct occurring after the acquisition of the legal title can be highly relevant.[118]

Intention at acquisition

Subject to the above comments made by Lord Diplock, the emphasis placed by the House of Lords in *Pettitt*, on the need to infer the actual intentions of the parties at the time when the house was acquired, was repeated shortly afterwards in *Gissing v. Gissing*. In this case, a wife made an unsuccessful claim to an interest in the matrimonial home, the basis of that claim having been the expenditure of some £220 on furnishings and laying a lawn, the purchase of some clothes for herself and her son, and some extras around the house. Her husband paid all the mortgage instalments and had supplied the initial down payment on the house.

In unanimously rejecting her claim, all members of the House agreed that, for her to succeed, she had to establish an interest behind either a resulting or a constructive trust. To establish such a trust, it was again emphasized that it must be possible for the court to be able to infer an agreement that she should have a beneficial share in it. An intention could not be imputed to the parties which they had never had but, as reasonable people, they ought to have had.[119] Such an intention could only be inferred from the fact that a financial contribution had been made to the acquisition of the property, which was not so in the instant case.

The debate between whether one inferred what the parties intended with regard to the beneficial ownership of the property or whether, instead, one could impute intentions to parties which, as reasonable people, they ought to have formed was, in truth, something of an arid one, although it is one which has recently been rekindled.[120] Its principal relevance, however, was to the operation of resulting trusts; what the decision

---

[117] [1971] A.C. 886 at 906. See also at 903 *per* Lord Pearson. See also *Stack v. Dowden* [2007] 2 A.C. 432 at [57] *per* Baroness Hale of Richmond.

[118] *Stack v. Dowden* [2007] 2 A.C. 432 *per* Baroness Hale of Richmond; *Jones v. Kernott* [2011] UKSC 53.

[119] *Gissing v. Gissing* [1971] A.C. 886 at 904 *per* Lord Diplock, who expressly recognized that his previously stated view to the contrary in *Pettitt* did not represent the law. Cf. the speech of Lord Reid, who adhered to the minority view that he had expressed in that case.

[120] See Consistency with resulting trusts, pp. 348–350.

in *Gissing* did do, however, was, perhaps surprisingly, to promote the potential importance of constructive trusts. This was due to an influential dictum of Lord Diplock.

When analysing the principles to be applied in cases of this type, Lord Diplock, in
an oft-quoted *dictum*, said:

'A resulting, implied or constructive trust—and it is unnecessary for present purposes to
distinguish between these three classes of trust—is created by a transaction between the
trustee and the *cestui que trust*[121] in connection with the acquisition by the trustee of a
legal estate in land, whenever the trustee has so conducted himself that it would be inequitable...to deny the *cestui que trust* a beneficial interest in the land acquired. And he will be
held so to have conducted himself if by his words or conduct he has induced the *cestui que
trust* to act to his own detriment in the reasonable belief that by so acting he was acquiring a
beneficial interest in the property.'[122]

Although influential, there are problems with this passage. The main difficulty is that
it runs together conceptually different types of trust, a running together which has
become the source of considerable confusion thereafter. A second problem was that
it focused exclusively on the law of trusts as being the only method by which disputes
of this nature could be resolved. More recently, estoppel has been seen to have a role
to play.

Intention and resulting trusts

Despite the running together of resulting and constructive trusts, the development
of the law has, until quite recently, shown a clear distinction between the two types
of trust and, in particular, demonstrates the somewhat arid nature of the debate concerning the role of intention with regard to resulting trusts.

The role of resulting trusts in this context derives from at least 1788, when in *Dyer
v. Dyer*,[123] it was said that:

'The clear result of all the cases, without a single exception is, that the trust of a legal
estate...whether taken in the names of the purchasers and others jointly, or in the names
of others without that of the purchaser; whether in one name or several; whether jointly or
successive, results to the man who advanced the purchase money. This is a general proposition supported by all the cases...It is the established doctrine of a Court of equity, that this
resulting trust may be rebutted by circumstances in evidence.'

Presumed intention

The point about this is that the law is prepared to assume that if A and B, together,
put up the purchase price for a particular item, and the legal title to that item is put
into the name of A alone, then B will have an equitable interest in that property

---

[121] Another term for the equitable owner.   [122] [1971] A.C. 886 at 905.
[123] (1788) 2 Cox. 92 at 93 *per* Eyre L.C.B. See Chambers, *Resulting Trusts* (Oxford: Oxford University
Press, 1997), 12–39.

proportionate to the size of his financial contribution,[124] this conclusion being said to rest upon 'the solid tug of money'.[125] This is so, unless there is evidence that this is not what was actually intended.[126] So if, for example, B has advanced money to A by means of a loan, then B will not acquire a beneficial interest in the property which has been purchased; the presumption of a resulting trust is rebutted by evidence of what was actually intended and B's right will merely be to have the loan repaid.[127]

It is integral to cases of this type that it is unnecessary, in order for a resulting trust to arise, to have regard to the actual intention of the parties in order for the contributor to acquire an interest in the property under a resulting trust. Where a person makes a contribution to the purchase price, the law does not look to see if there was a meeting of minds between the two parties; it is assumed, unless there is actual evidence to the contrary, that the contributor will acquire an interest in the property proportionate to the size of the contribution.[128] The role of this presumption is illustrated by cases where property is put into the name of another to facilitate the implementation of an unlawful purpose, such as the aim of defeating creditors. The presumption of resulting trust may still be relied upon because the person with the unlawful intention need not rely upon his own illegality to show his intention to remain the beneficial owner of the property; he relies upon the presumption which the law will make in any case that this is what was intended.[129]

Although this principle of a contribution to the purchase price of an item giving rise to the presumption of a resulting trust in favour of the contributor is relatively simple to state, it is frequently not easy to apply in the context of the purchase of a house. The main reason for this is that, unlike many items of personal property which can be bought outright, this is not the usual way in which a house is purchased. The normal method of house buying is to make a down payment and to borrow the remainder of the purchase price by way of a mortgage. That mortgage is then repaid over an extended period of time. It can, in such situations, be more difficult than when the purchase is outright to determine whether or not a person claiming to have an interest

---

[124] A new expression coined for this type of resulting trust is a 'money-down resulting trust interest': J.W. Harris in Jackson and Wilde, op. cit., 97. For an unusual instance where one party, who provided the entirety of the purchase price and when the title was put in the sole name of his girlfriend, see *Re Share* [2002] 2 F.L.R. 88, where the Court of Appeal held that she held the house on trust for him.

[125] *Hofman v. Hofman* [1965] N.Z.L.R. 795 at 800 *per* Woodhouse J.

[126] For a bizarre finding of a contrary intention, where a judge found that an older woman had advanced money towards the purchase of a house in the name of a younger man as being in the nature of risk capital advanced to seduce that younger man, see *Pettkus v. Becker* (1981) 117 D.L.R. (3d) 257 at 265 *per* Richie J., who described it as 'gratuitously insulting'. Cf. at 272 *per* Dickson J. For a valuable discussion of this influential Canadian decision, see M. Welstead (1987) 2 Denning L.J. 151.

[127] See *Re Sharpe* [1980] 1 W.L.R. 219. Cf. *Risch v. McPhee* (1990) 61 P. & C.R. 42, where an arrangement which was originally a loan became, as circumstances changed, a contribution to the acquisition of the house.

[128] See *Gissing v. Gissing* [1971] A.C. 886 at 902 *per* Lord Pearson; *Grant v. Edwards* [1986] Ch. 638 at 647 *per* Nourse L.J. See H.K. Bevan and F.W. Taylor (1966) 30 Conv. (N.S.) 354, 438 at 442–443; F. Webb (1976) 92 L.Q.R. 489.

[129] *Tinsley v. Milligan* [1994] A.C. 330; *Lowson v. Coombes* [1999] Ch. 373; *Barrett v. Barrett* [2008] EWHC 1061 (Ch.). See M.P. Thompson [1999] Conv. 242.

in the home actually has made a contribution to its purchase. Nevertheless, the task of the court when seeking to apply resulting trust principles is to ascertain whether such a contribution has been made.

Although the courts have stressed that the task is to determine what the parties intended with regard to the beneficial interest of the house, in many cases the real answer is that the parties have not given the matter any thought at all and so the task of ascertaining that intention has, aptly, been described as being 'simply unreal'.[130] Instead, the task with which the courts are faced is to decide whether or not a person has actually made a contribution to the purchase of the house. This point is reinforced by the fact that although there was an acute division of opinion in *Pettitt v. Pettitt* as to whether the judicial function is to infer what the parties actually intended or to impute intentions to them which, as reasonable people, they should have formed, this is a fairly barren distinction, given that the House of Lords was unanimous that no interest in the house had been acquired. An intention would neither be inferred by the majority nor imputed by the minority unless the claimant had contributed to the acquisition of the house. In this context, it is really a matter of semantics as to which terminology is to be preferred.

This semantic dispute was recently revived when, in *Stack v. Dowden*,[131] seemingly of his own volition,[132] Lord Walker of Gestingthorpe expressed the view that it would have been better had the House of Lords in *Gissing* openly departed from the earlier decision in *Pettitt*, and, effectively, allowed the courts to impute intentions to parties which they had never had.[133] This, with respect, seems to misunderstand the operation of the resulting trust, where intentions are ascribed to parties on the basis of their purchasing behaviour, in circumstances when it is clear that no actual thought has been given to the question of the beneficial ownership. In such circumstances, it really makes no practical difference as to whether one talks of inferring the intentions of the parties, or one talks of imputing intentions to them. What will be important is a consideration of what elements of the parties' behaviour are relevant to the performance of this task.[134]

Constructive trusts

In many cases, when a court is faced with the task of determining the beneficial ownership of a home, the real focus for the decision is whether what the claimant relies

---

[130] M.M. Helsham (1979) 9 Sydney L.R. 571 at 575. See also the reference in *Rathwell v. Rathwell* (1978) 83 D.L.R. (3d) 289 at 297 to the 'meaningless ritual of searching for a phantom intent' *per* Dickson J, and the comment in *Kerr v. Baranow* (2011) 328 D.L.R. (4th) 577 at [26] *per* Cromwell J.

[131] [2007] 2 A.C. 432 at [21].

[132] No trace of such an argument is apparent from the reports of the arguments of counsel.

[133] Contrast Lord Neuberger of Abbotsbury (2008) Chancery Bar Association Annual Lecture at para. 19, where the notion of imputed intention is described as 'heretical'.

[134] See *Jones v. Kernott* [2011] UKSC 53 at [67] *per* Lord Kerr, commenting on the different conceptual approaches to this issue taken by Lord Walker and Lady Hale, on the one hand, and Lord Wilson on the other.

upon will amount to what the law regards as a contribution to the acquisition of the property. In such cases a search for the actual intention of the parties will frequently be a futile exercise. Deciding what amounts to such a contribution is a difficult task and will be considered shortly. In some situations, however, there is evidence that the parties have actually agreed as to what the beneficial interests in the home should be, and it is this type of case which can give rise to the conceptually different constructive trust.

Actual agreement

Where personal property is concerned, no formalities are necessary to create a trust. It is sufficient if there is a manifestation of a sufficient intention to create a trust and this intention can, on occasion, be established on the basis of fairly casual statements.[135] Where land is concerned, however, to establish a trust, it is necessary that the provisions of section 53(1)(b) of the Law of Property Act 1925 are satisfied: the declaration of trust must be proved by some writing. Alone, therefore, a statement by one person to the other that he regards the house as being as much hers as it is his is not sufficient to create a trust.[136] If, however, in reliance on what has been said, she contributes to the purchase of the property, then it would be fraudulent for him to plead the lack of writing to deny that she has a beneficial interest in the property. To do so would entail him being unjustly enriched at her expense. To prevent this, a constructive trust is imposed to enforce the informal statement.

This principle, which is based upon the nineteenth-century decision in *Rochefoucauld v. Boustead*,[137] was illustrated excellently in *Re Densham*.[138] It was found as a fact that it had been orally agreed between a husband and wife that the matrimonial home was to be owned equally. The title was, however, put into his name alone. It was further found that she had made a financial contribution to the purchase price amounting to one-ninth. Goff J. held that, had the dispute been between the husband and wife as to the ownership of the matrimonial home, she would have been entitled to one-half of the beneficial interest. A constructive trust would have been imposed to give effect to the actual agreement between them.[139]

In this case, however, the husband was bankrupt and so the issue was the size of the beneficial share to which the trustee in bankruptcy was entitled. It was held that, had

---

[135] See *Paul v. Constance* [1977] 1 W.L.R. 527; *Rowe v. Prance* [1999] 2 F.L.R. 787. For criticism of the latter decision, see S. Baughen [2000] Conv. 58.

[136] *Austin v. Keele* (1987) 72 A.L.R. 579 at 587 *per* Lord Oliver of Aylmerton; *Lloyds Bank plc v. Rosset* [1991] A.C. 107 at 129 *per* Lord Bridge of Harwich.

[137] [1897] 1 Ch. 196. See also *De Bruyne v. De Bruyne* [2010] EWCA Civ. 519 at [51] *per* Patten L.J.; M.A. Neave (1978) 11 Melbourne U.L.R. 343 at 348; M.P. Thompson (1985) 36 N.I.L.Q. 343 at 348. Cf. Mee, op. cit., 156–164. For an interesting and unusual example of this in the commercial context, see *Banner Homes Holdings Ltd v. Luff* [2000] Ch. 372; M.P. Thompson [2001] Conv. 249; N. Hopkins [2002] Conv. 35; *Cox v. Jones* [2004] 2 F.L.R. 1010 at 1035–1037 *per* Mann J. See R. Probert [2005] Conv. 168.

[138] [1975] 1 W.L.R. 1519.

[139] The distinction between 'money consensus' and 'interest consensus' drawn in *Cowcher v. Cowcher* [1972] 1 W.L.R. 425 at 436 *per* Bagnall J., which had been refuted by A.A.S. Zuckerman (1978) 94 L.Q.R. 26 at 45, was rejected: [1975] 1 W.L.R. 1519 at 1525 *per* Goff J. Contrast Mee, op. cit., 52–58.

there been no antecedent agreement regarding the beneficial interest in the home, she would have been entitled to a share of one-ninth under a resulting trust. On the basis of her financial contribution to the property, the court would have presumed that it was intended that she would acquire a proportionate equitable share in the property and a resulting trust would arise to achieve this result. In the instant case, because there was an actual agreement to share the beneficial interest in the house equally, and she had contributed to the purchase of the house, a constructive trust was imposed to give effect to the actual agreement. As against the trustee in bankruptcy, however, the difference between one-half and one-ninth was regarded as being a voluntary settlement and, as against him, was set aside on that basis.[140]

This decision provides an extremely clear distinction between resulting trusts and constructive trusts.[141] In the case of the former category of trust, the task is to ascertain if the claimant has contributed to the purchase price and, if so, to quantify that contribution and decide that a corresponding equitable share in the property has been obtained.[142] In the latter, the key issue is what the parties have agreed. When there is a specific agreement as to what interest[143] in the property each party is to have in the property then, provided that there has been an appropriate response,[144] it is the actual agreement which is enforced by the imposition of a constructive trust.[145] The quantum of the share is governed by the agreement, and not by the size of the contribution.[146]

CONTRIBUTIONS AND RESULTING TRUSTS

The essence of the approach taken by the House of Lords in both *Pettitt v. Pettitt* and *Gissing v. Gissing* was that one had to determine the beneficial shares in the property by reference to the inferred intentions of the parties at the time when the house was acquired. The reference to inferring what the parties intended is misleading, in that in many cases it is evident that the parties never gave any thought at all to the question of who owned the house. What was meant, however, was that a court would be prepared to make the necessary inference if the claimant could establish that she had made what was considered to be a contribution to the acquisition of the property.

---

[140] Bankruptcy Act 1914, s. 42. See now, Insolvency Act 1986, s. 339.

[141] See also *Grant v. Edwards* [1986] Ch. 635 at 637 *per* Nourse L.J.; *Midland Bank plc v. Dobson* [1986] 1 F.L.R. 171 at 177 *per* Dillon L.J.; *Lloyds Bank plc v. Rosset* [1991] A.C. 107 at 133 *per* Lord Bridge of Harwich.

[142] See *Arogundade v. Arogundade* [2005] EWHC 1766 (Ch.).

[143] The agreement may relate to a life interest as opposed to a concurrent interest. See *Ungarian v. Lessnoff* [1990] Ch. 206; *Buggs v. Buggs* [2003] EWHC 1538 (Ch.).

[144] See The nature of reliance, pp. 350–351.

[145] See *Chan v. Leung* [2003] 1 F.L.R. 23 (51%–49%); *Hyett v. Stanley* [2004] 1 F.L.R. 394, especially at 403–404 *per* Sir Martin Nourse.

[146] See *Wright v. Johnson* [2002] 1 P. & C.R. 15 at para. 17 *per* Sir Martin Nourse.

The determination of what amounted to a qualifying contribution was not, however, always an easy task.[147]

Direct contributions

The easiest type of case to resolve is where the claimant makes a direct cash contribution to the purchase of the house. In the unusual case where a house is being bought outright, and one pays 30 per cent of the price and the other the remaining 70 per cent, the property will be shared in those proportions.[148] A more usual situation is where the property is bought with the aid of a mortgage.[149] In *Re Roger's Question*,[150] a house was bought for £1,000, the wife supplying the initial payment of £100 and her husband being solely responsible for the payments on the mortgage. This was regarded in the same way as if the property had been bought outright, so that the beneficial ownership was shared in proportion to their contributions, that is in a proportion of 9:1 in favour of the husband.

Council house discounts

When a house is bought with aid of a mortgage, the position is quite straightforward if the claimant makes a direct cash contribution to the initial payment.[151] Slightly more problematic is the situation where the property is a council house which is bought by the tenant under the right to buy provisions contained in Part V of the Housing Act 1985.[152] Under this scheme, depending upon the length of residence, the council tenant is entitled to a discount on the value of the property, up to a maximum of 60 per cent. The question is then whether this discount is to be treated as a contribution to the purchase price. The answer to this is that, in general terms, the courts, although aware that a discount is not the same as cash,[153] are prepared, in effect, to treat it in this way. The normal result is that, if the house is being bought by the tenant with financial assistance from another, usually, but not always,[154] the tenant's children, then the beneficial ownership of the house will be shared. The size of the percentage discount will then determine the size of the tenant's beneficial share in the house.[155] As indeed is the case with a direct contribution, it is only a presumption that a discount is to be regarded as entitling the claimant to an equivalent beneficial share in the property.[156] It may be that the actual intention is to make a gift.[157] Perhaps, more commonly, when the property is bought by a combination of the tenant's discount, together with the

---

[147] See the comments in *Bernard v. Josephs* [1982] Ch. 391 at 402 *per* Griffiths L.J.
[148] *Arogundade v. Arogundade* [2005] EWHC 1766 (Ch.).   [149] See P. Sparkes (1991) 11 O.J.L.S. 39.
[150] [1948] 1 All E.R. 328.
[151] This may be satisfied by a wedding gift by the parents of one of the parties. See *Midland Bank plc v. Cooke* [1995] 4 All E.R. 562.
[152] Replacing the Housing Act 1980, Part 1.
[153] See *Evans v. Hayward* [1995] 2 F.L.R. 511 at 516 *per* Staughton L.J.
[154] See *Oxley v. Hiscock* [2005] Fam. 211.
[155] *Marsh v. Von Sternberg* [1986] 1 F.L.R. 26; *Springette v. Defoe* [1992] 2 F.L.R. 511; *Day v. Day* (2005) Case No. HC 04C00445.
[156] *Evans v. Hayward, supra.*   [157] See *Ashe v. Mumford* (2000) 33 H.L.R. 67.

balance of the purchase price being provided by that person's children, an agreement may be made that the tenant can occupy the house for the rest of his life, and, after his death, to go to the children who provided the balance of the purchase money. In such a case, a constructive trust will be imposed, with the result that there will exist consecutive ownership, rather than the concurrent interests which would have arisen under a resulting trust.[158] In the absence of a contrary intention, however, it now seems settled that the discount will be regarded as a direct financial contribution to the purchase of the house.[159]

Mortgage payments

There are, potentially at least, theoretical difficulties when a person makes a claim to a beneficial share in the property on the basis of having made contributions to the payment of mortgage instalments.[160] The main problem is that, if the interests under a resulting trust are to be taken to have crystallized at the time when the property is acquired, a later payment of mortgage instalments occurs after that time and, so, it may be argued, this precludes the acquisition of an interest under a resulting trust. Secondly, the argument can be put that the payment of instalments does not actually contribute to the purchase of the house, which has already been bought. Until very recently, judicially at least,[161] this was not really considered to be a contentious matter, it being assumed that such a person would acquire an interest. In *Curley v. Parkes*[162] a different view was taken.

Andrew Curley and Nicola Parkes cohabited, first in a house in Richmond, and, subsequently, in a house in Luton. Although the subject matter of the dispute was the ownership of the Luton property, central to its resolution was the ownership of the first house, the proceeds of sale of which had helped to finance the second purchase. With regard to the house in Richmond, Ms Parkes was the sole registered proprietor and the mortgage was in her name.[163] When they moved into that house, they set up a joint bank account, into which they paid roughly equal amounts. Out of that account came all of the household expenditure, including the mortgage payments. Nevertheless, the Court of Appeal held that he acquired no interest in that house.

In arriving at what seems a quite remarkable conclusion, Peter Gibson L.J., with whom Sir William Aldous agreed, reasoned as follows:

'The relevant principle is that the resulting trust of a property purchased in the name of another, in the absence of a contrary intention, arises once and for all at the date on which

---

[158] See *Buggs v. Buggs* [2003] EWHC 153 (Ch.); M.P. Thompson [2003] Conv. 411.

[159] See *Laskar v. Laskar* [2008] EWCA Civ. 347 at [22]–[26] *per* Lord Neuberger of Abbotsbury.

[160] See the inconclusive discussion of this issue in *Stack v. Dowden* [2007] 2 A.C. 432 at [120] *per* Lord Neuberger of Abbotsbury.

[161] For a detailed analysis of the problems, see Mee, op. cit., Chapter 3. See also P. Sparkes (1991) 11 O.J.L.S. 39.

[162] [2004] EWCA Civ. 1515.

[163] There was evidence that, because of financial problems emanating from his student days, he would not have been considered to be a suitable borrower by a mortgagee: ibid., at para. 7 *per* Peter Gibson L.J.

the property is acquired. Because of the liability assumed by the mortgagor in a case where monies are borrowed by the mortgagor to be used on the purchase, the mortgagor is treated as having provided the proportion of the purchase price attributable to the monies so borrowed. Subsequent payments of the mortgage instalments are not part of the purchase price already paid to the vendor, but are sums paid for discharging the mortgagor's obligations under the mortgage....'[164]

Because in the instant case there had been found not to have been any actual agreement reached with regard to the beneficial ownership of the house, this precluded the imposition of a constructive trust. This meant that, despite Mr Curley's contributions to the payment of the mortgage, he acquired no interest in the house.

Disregard of authority

This treatment of an important issue prompts a number of observations. First, and quite remarkably, there is no mention at all of any of the numerous *dicta*, admittedly *obiter*, but of the highest authority, which point directly to the opposite conclusion. To the comment of Lord Diplock in *Gissing v. Gissing*, that:

'The conduct of the spouses in relation to the payment of the mortgage instalments may be no less relevant to their common intention as to the beneficial interest in the matrimonial home acquired in this way than their conduct in relation to the payment of the cash deposit.'[165]

may be added those to similar effect by Viscount Dilhorne and Lord Pearson in the same case.[166] In *Lloyds Bank plc v. Rosset*,[167] Lord Bridge of Harwich was equally explicit. He said that, 'direct contributions to the purchase price by the partner, who is not the legal owner, whether initially *or by payment of mortgage instalments*, will readily justify the inference necessary for the creation of a constructive trust'. Again, in *Stack v. Dowden*,[168] there is the unequivocal statement by Baroness Hale of Richmond 'that the payment of mortgage instalments is the equivalent of the payment of purchase price'. In addition to these *dicta*, there is a line of authority, considered later in this chapter,[169] where one party makes indirect contributions to the purchase of the

---

[164] Ibid., at para. 14. In reaching this conclusion considerable reliance was placed on the treatment of this topic in Underhill and Hayton, *Law of Trusts and Trustees* (16th edn) (London: Butterworths LexisNexis, 2003), 351–352.

[165] [1971] A.C. 886 at 906.

[166] Ibid., at 900 and 903, respectively. The payment of isolated instalments would not give rise to a resulting trust: ibid., at 900 *per* Viscount Dilhorne. For discussion of the position with regard to endowment mortgages, see Thompson, *Co-ownership* (London: Sweet & Maxwell, 1988), 52.

[167] [1991] 1 A.C. 107 at 132–133. Italics supplied. Query whether this should refer to a resulting trust. See also *Oxley v. Hiscock* [2005] Fam. 211 at 220 *per* Chadwick L.J., where the payment of mortgage instalments was regarded as a contribution to the purchase of a house. The case was disapproved, without reference to this issue, in *Stack.v. Dowden* [2007] 2 A.C. 432 at [61] *per* Baroness Hale of Richmond.

[168] *Stack.v. Dowden*, at [57]. The statement by David Richards J. in *Barrett v. Barrett* [2008] EWHC 1061 (Ch.) at [7] that there is nothing in the speeches in *Stack v. Dowden* to support the notion that the payment of mortgage instalments should be treated as contributions to the purchase price is clearly wrong.

[169] See Indirect contributions, pp. 333–335.

property, in the sense of facilitating the other to be able to pay the mortgage instalments, and being held, as a result, to have acquired an interest in the home. The decision in *Curley v. Parkes* is not consistent with this line of authority. In short, apart from this decision, judicial opinion seemed to be unanimous that a person who makes regular mortgage payments will acquire an interest in the house.

In addition to being at odds with the overwhelming judicial consensus, the decision fails to convince on its own terms. Peter Gibson L.J. was prepared to hold that a person who takes on responsibility for paying the mortgage is treated as having made a financial contribution to its purchase and so acquires a corresponding proportionate share.[170] It is not clear, however, why being legally responsible for the mortgage payments should make such a big difference. If the person who pays all or part of the instalments is seen as only to be discharging the mortgagor's liability under the mortgage, the house having been purchased with the money which was borrowed from the mortgagee, it is not at all obvious why the same analysis should not apply to a person who has made himself legally responsible to pay the loan. The distinction does not convince.

Practical consequences

A potentially more difficult problem is where a house is in the name of one party, and another person then moves into the house and contributes to the mortgage payments. If, as has frequently been stressed, one acquires an interest under a resulting trust by reference to the intentions of the parties when the house was acquired, then, even if one accepts that the payment of mortgage instalments is potentially effective to enable an interest in the house to be obtained, there is an obvious problem. This is that, when the house was acquired, the only intention was that there should be sole ownership. In such cases, it is quite likely that the parties will come to actual agreement as to the ownership of the house, so as to bring a constructive trust into play. Even if that is not the case, it should still be possible for a resulting trust to arise. An analogy can be drawn with a position where A is buying a car on a hire-purchase agreement and, sometime later, B starts to pay half of the instalments. B has clearly contributed to the acquisition of the car and, in principle, should acquire an interest in it under a resulting trust.

Although the repayment of a mortgage is different in nature from a hire-purchase agreement, it is thought that the analogy is not inappropriate and the same should happen in the context of the purchase of a house. The essential difference between the operation of a resulting trust here, and that envisaged in *Gissing*, is that, in this situation, the resulting trust would operate to vary the initial beneficial interests in the property, rather than to determine from the outset what those beneficial interests are. In other words, there is no compelling reason to hold that the beneficial interests in a

---

[170] This is supported by *Re Roger's Question* [1948] 1 All E.R. 328. See also the comments in *Ulrich v. Ulrich* [1968] 1 W.L.R. 180 at 186 *per* Lord Denning M.R., and at 289 *per* Diplock L.J., and in *Pettitt v. Pettitt* [1970] A.C. 777 at 816 *per* Lord Upjohn.

house are definitively fixed at the date when it is transferred to one person. There is no reason, in principle, why these interests cannot subsequently be varied by the creation of either a resulting or constructive trust. As against this, in *James v. Thomas*,[171] Sir John Chadwick expressed the view that 'a court will be very slow to infer from conduct alone that parties intended to vary existing beneficial interests established at the time of acquisition'. This should not, it is suggested, preclude the establishment of a beneficial share in the property when a person has moved into a house in sole legal ownership and made a regular contribution to the mortgage repayments. This is illustrated by the Supreme Court decision in *Jones v. Kernott*.[172]

In this case, Ms Jones bought a mobile home in 1981, and Mr Kernott moved in with her in 1983, and their first child was born in 1984. In 1985, this property was sold and another one, 39 Badger Hall Avenue, was acquired, and put into joint names. The purchase price of £30,000 was made up of £6,000 from the sale of the mobile home, and the balance by an endowment mortgage which was taken out in joint names. They had a second child in 1986. In that year they took out a further joint loan of £2,000 to finance the buiding of an extension. After nearly eight and a half years of cohabitation, he left the house in 1993. Thereafter she continued to live in Badger Hall Avenue and met all of the outgoings on the house, including the mortgage. This situation continued for the next fourteen and a half years during which time he paid nothing towards the mortgage on the house, and very little towards the maintenance of their children. During this time, he had purchased another house. To finance this, a joint life insurance policy was cashed in, and the proceeds divided between them. He used his share to put down a deposit and took out a mortgage in respect of the balance. He could not have afforded to have done this if he was paying anything towards the mortgage on Badger Hall Avenue. Restoring the first instance decision,[173] and reversing that of the Court of Appeal,[174] the Supreme Court held that the beneficial shares in Badger Hall Avenue were 90 per cent to her, and 10 per cent to him.

In reaching this conclusion, it was first accepted that, had the property been sold when the couple separated, the shares in it would have been equal. This followed from the property being in joint names, and there being insufficient evidence that the parties intended, at that stage, an outcome different from that which the law presumes: that joint ownership at law leads to the same position in equity. The Court of Appeal held that, because there had been no actual agreement to vary the beneficial ownership of the house, the original position of joint ownership remained. The Supreme Court, however, held that under a common intention constructive trust, the shares had been altered.

In reaching this conclusion the Court was prepared to accept an earlier finding that the parties had actually agreed, when the insurance policy was cashed in, thereby enabling him to purchase a property on his own, that the parties had actually agreed to vary their shares in Badger Hall Avenue, thereby making it unnecessary to either imply

---

171 [2007] EWCA Civ. 1212 at [24]. See also *Morris v. Morris* [2008] EWCA Civ. 257 at [36] *per* May L.J.
172 [2011] EWSC 53.   173 [2009] EWHC 1713 (Ch.).   174 [2010] EWCA Civ. 578.

or impute an agreement between them.[175] Even had that not been so, however, the same result would have been reached, either on the basis of an implied or an imputed intention. This, on the facts, seems an eminently sensible conclusion and, in reality, reflected the purchasing behaviour of the parties. So, although the Supreme Court chose to eschew a resulting trust analysis of the facts, preferring instead to develop the law of constructive trusts, the outcome is consistent with an analysis based upon resulting trusts. This is if one applies, as one should, an approach to the entire purchasing behaviour of the property and does not confine one's attention to the acquisition of the legal title.

Curley v. Parkes was not cited *in Jones v. Kernott*. And, although it is distinguishable, it is submitted that it is inconsistent with it and is, in any event contrary to principle, and wrongly decided. It should not be allowed to prevent a person who regularly makes mortgage payments in respect of a house from obtaining an interest in that house. It should not also be necessary to establish an actual agreement with regard to the beneficial ownership. In the absence of such an agreement, the regular payments of mortgage instalments should entitle the person making them to acquire an interest in the property proportionate to the size of those contributions, under a resulting or constructive trust. The true position would appear to be that the parties should be regarded as having pooled their resources[176] in order to buy the house and the beneficial shares allocated accordingly.

Improvements

A perceived problem with the decision in *Pettitt v. Pettitt* was that it could be taken as precluding a person from obtaining an interest in the home as a result of having spent money on improving it. The reason for this concern was that the general position is that, if a person spends money on another person's property, no interest in that property is acquired as a result. This, however, is subject to the important qualification that if the owner of the property encourages this expenditure, as is likely to be the case, then rights can be acquired through estoppel.[177]

Matrimonial Proceedings and Property Act 1970

Insofar as married couples are concerned, the position has been regulated by legislation.[178] Section 37 of the Matrimonial Proceedings and Property Act 1970 provides that where a husband or wife contributes in money or money's worth to the improvement of real or personal property then, if the improvement is substantial and, subject to any agreement to the contrary, the husband and wife shall be treated as having acquired by virtue of his or her contribution either to a share or an enhanced share in the property to such an extent as may have been agreed or may seem in all the circumstances just.

---

[175] [2011] UKSC 53 at [48] *per* Lord Walker and Lady Hale.
[176] See *Pettitt v. Pettitt* [1970] A.C. 777, at 817 *per* Lord Upjohn.   [177] Ibid., at 818 *per* Lord Upjohn.
[178] An identical provision applies also to people who have registered a civil partnership. See Civil Partnership Act 2004, s. 65.

Although the legislation applies only to either married couples, couples who have registered a civil partnership, or an engaged couple whose agreement to marry has terminated,[179] it is declaratory in nature, which suggests strongly that it is restating the existing law;[180] a consideration which would seem to indicate that the principle enshrined in the section is applicable also to couples who are neither married nor in a civil partnership.[181] This impression is reinforced by the comment by Baroness Hale in *Stack v. Dowden*[182] that the initial beneficial shares in the property may be varied as a result of one of the parties financing or constructing a substantial improvement to the property. Detailed consideration was given to the approach to be taken to the section in *Re Nicholson*.[183] A wife had spent money installing central heating into the matrimonial home. The approach taken was to assess the beneficial share that each party had in the house prior to the improvement and then ascertain the additional value of the house after the central heating had been installed, and to credit her with that gain. On this basis, her share increased from one half to 21/41ths of the house. Although this seems to be a principled approach to this issue, and one of general application, a different process was suggested in *Griffiths v. Griffiths*.[184] In this case, Arnold J., although accepting that, on the facts, the valuation of the improvement was largely a matter of guesswork,[185] expressed the view that one should assess the value of the improvements at the time when the house was realized, rather than when they were made. The better view would seem to be that articulated in *Re Nicholson*, in that increases in value to a property over a time is, normally, a matter of house inflation and should not affect the size of the shares of the respective parties.

Substantial improvement

What is clear is that to qualify as a relevant improvement, the improvement has to be substantial. So, in *Re Nicholson*, relatively small sums spent on the installation of two gas fires and a cooker were discounted.[186] Rather more surprisingly, in *Hosking v. Michaelides*,[187] a wife who had contributed £20,000 to the cost of installing a swimming pool, the total cost being £29,000, was held not to have shown that she had made a substantial improvement to the property. The reason for this is that evidence had not been adduced to show that the construction of a swimming pool had added any value to the property and, for this reason, the judge declined to decide between the different approaches to valuation adopted in *Re Nicholson* and *Griffiths v. Griffiths*. This case

---

[179] Law Reform (Miscellaneous Provisions) Act 1970, s. 2.

[180] This point was stressed in *Davis v. Vale* [1971] 1 W.L.R. 1022 at 1026 *per* Lord Denning M.R. See also *Dibble v. Pfluger* [2010] EWCA Civ. 1005 at [25] *per* Ward L.J.

[181] Although see the comments in *Samuels (W.A.)'s Trustee v. Samuels* (1973) 233 E.G. 149 at 151 *per* Walton J.

[182] [2002] 2 A.C. 432 at [70].   [183] [1974] 1 W.L.R. 476.   [184] [1973] 1 W.L.R. 1454.

[185] Ibid., at 1456.

[186] [1974] 1 W.L.R. 476 at 483 *per* Sir John Pennycuick V.-C. See also *Bindra v. Mawji* [2008] EWHC 1715 (Ch.), where a contribution of £2,500 over a nine-year period in respect of a house bought for £231,000 rising to over £400,000 was discounted.

[187] [2004] All E.R. (D.) 147.

does show, however, the need for a claimant to provide valuation evidence of the significance of the improvement.

Indirect contributions

A problem which was also addressed, albeit briefly, in *Gissing v. Gissing* was the issue of indirect contributions to the acquisition of the house. It may be that a cohabiting couple arrange their finances so that one person's salary is devoted principally to paying the mortgage and the other's goes towards meeting the remainder of the household expenditure. In such a situation, the contribution of the latter does not go directly towards the acquisition of the house but it may, nevertheless, be sufficient in order for her to acquire an interest in it, although the circumstances when that would be the case were narrowly circumscribed. For the courts, in circumstances such as these, to be able to infer an agreement that the beneficial ownership in the house be shared, it was considered to be essential for the financial contribution of the claimant to be such that the other person could not have met the mortgage payments without that contribution.[188]

Assistance in business

The strictness of these criteria became highly contentious. Before considering them more fully, one type of indirect contribution to the purchase of property can be considered, that of assistance in a business. Situations may arise where a man acquires a business, the profits of which are used to finance the purchase of a house where he lives with the claimant. The claimant works unpaid, or at a much reduced rate, in the business, thereby contributing to its profitability. In such circumstances, the courts will regard this form of contribution as being indistinguishable from a situation where both parties are in paid employment and their salaries are pooled together and used to buy the house, and she will acquire an interest in it.[189] None of these cases were cited, however, in *James v. Thomas*.[190] Sarah James moved into a house which was legally and beneficially owned by Peter Thomas. He was a building and drainage contractor, and from 1990 until they separated in 2004, she worked in the business for no pay, this work consisting of driving a tipper, digging trenches, laying concrete and gravel, and, along with her partner, the manual work associated with this business.[191] Although the proceeds of the business were used to service the mortgage, somewhat surprisingly, a

---

[188] *Gissing v. Gissing* [1971] A.C. 886 at 903 *per* Lord Pearson, at 909 *per* Lord Diplock. See also *Richards v. Dove* [1974] 1 All E.R. 888; *Burns v. Burns* [1984] Ch. 317 at 330 *per* Fox L.J.

[189] See *Nixon v. Nixon* [1969] 1 W.L.R. 1676; *Muetzel v. Muetzel* [1970] 1 W.L.R. 188; *Re Cummins* [1972] Ch. 62; *Bothe v. Amos* [1976] Fam. 47. Cf. *Ivin v. Blake* [1995] 1 F.L.R. 70, criticized by A. Lawson [1996] Conv. 462. Contrast, also, *Hosking v. Michaelides* [2004] All E.R. (D.) 147, where, although a wife was a director in the family company, she played no active part in its affairs.

[190] [2007] EWCA Civ. 1212. Contrast the not dissimilar Canadian case of *Sorochan v. Sorochan* (1986) D.L.R. (4th) 1.

[191] Ibid., at [4] *per* Sir John Chadwick.

claim under a resulting trust was abandoned,[192] and it was held that she had acquired no interest in the house. It is submitted that this case is wrongly decided.

It should be appreciated that all of these authorities, except *James v. Thomas*, concerning the ability of a claimant to acquire an interest in a house by means of indirect contributions to its purchase are irreconcilable with the decision in *Curley v. Parkes*[193] concerning the payment of mortgage instalments. This consideration reinforces the view that that case was wrongly decided.[194]

Household contributions

The emphasis in resulting trust cases has always been on the need to make a financial contribution to the purchase of the property in question before one will acquire a beneficial interest in it. An attempt was made, however, to liberalize the judicial approach to this issue and thereby enable the courts to have regard to factors other than purely financial considerations. To do this, reference was made to the *dictum* of Lord Diplock in *Gissing*[195] cited earlier, where he referred to resulting, implied, and constructive trusts together in an attempt to construct a new form of trust to be imposed on the basis of broad principles of justice.

In *Hussey v. Palmer*,[196] the issue was whether an elderly lady who had advanced money to her daughter and son-in-law to build an additional bedroom to their house in which she could sleep was entitled to an interest in it. In upholding her claim,[197] Lord Denning M.R. considered whether she was entitled to an interest under either a resulting or a constructive trust and held that she was. He was unconcerned, however, as to which trust was appropriate. In his view:

'this is a matter of words more than anything else. The two run together. By whatever name it is described, it is a trust imposed whenever justice and good conscience require it. It is a liberal process founded upon large principles of equity, to be applied whenever justice and good conscience require it. It is a liberal process, founded upon large principles of equity, to be applied in cases where the legal owner cannot conscientiously keep the property for himself alone, but ought to allow another to have the benefit of it or a share in it.'[198]

The liberal constructive trust

The origin of this wide-ranging equitable jurisdiction was claimed to be the speech of Lord Diplock in *Gissing*, it being said that: 'Equity is not past the age of child bearing. One of her progeny is a constructive trust of a new model. Lord Diplock brought it into the world and we have nurtured it.'[199] This approach was intended to move the law away from resolving disputes of this nature by reference to what the parties intended with regard to the beneficial ownership of the house and, in particular, by reference

---

[192] Ibid., at [10].   [193] [2004] EWCA Civ. 1515.   [194] See Practical consequences, pp. 329–331.
[195] [1971] A.C. 886 at 905. See Intention at acquisition, p. 320.   [196] [1972] 1 W.L.R. 1286.
[197] Cairns L.J. dissented on the basis that the money had been advanced as a loan.
[198] [1972] 1 W.L.R. 1286 at 1289–1290.
[199] *Eves v. Eves* [1975] 1 W.L.R. 1338 at 1341 *per* Lord Denning M.R.

to contributions to its acquisition.[200] This approach was, perhaps, made most explicit in *Hall v. Hall*,[201] where it was said that, in determining the beneficial entitlement to a house which was subject to cohabitation, 'It depends upon all the circumstances and how much she has contributed—not merely in money—but also in keeping up the house and, if there are children, in looking after them.'[202]

THE PURCHASE MONEY RESULTING TRUST

This post-*Gissing* line of cases sought to introduce a new method to the resolution of disputes of this kind, effectively amalgamating the resulting and constructive trust and declining to take a narrow financial view of what, in law, amounted to a contribution to the acquisition of a home. Not surprisingly, it was also highly controversial, both in England[203] and overseas.[204] The reasons for this controversy are not difficult to see. First, the adoption of a discretionary, justice-based approach is difficult to reconcile with the reasoning of the House of Lords.[205] From a substantive point of view, it was also criticized as being unpredictable. To critics of Lord Denning's approach, 'His Lordship's inspiration is a notion of justice, dim and ever-changing, to the eye of the spectator, but to him clear and compulsive of fervent and evangelical adherence.'[206]

It is perhaps no surprise that this approach failed to prosper, and could be seen as being ahead of its time. The focus of Lord Denning was more on the nature of the relationship, rather than the cold calculus of financial contributions to the purchase of the home. After initial hostility to the idea, courts in the Commonwealth have come to adopt an approach which is not dissimilar to that advocated by Lord Denning.[207] In England, some moves have been made to decide the beneficial ownership of the home on the basis of what was perceived to be fair,[208] but this has since been rejected.[209] The task facing a claimant is: first, to establish that she has any interest in the property at all, and having done that, the issue becomes one of quantifying that interest. With regard to the first of these matters, the more liberal attitude of Lord Denning did not survive his retirement.

---

[200] *Hazell v. Hazell* [1972] 1 W.L.R. 301 at 302–304 *per* Lord Denning M.R.

[201] [1982] 3 F.L.R. 379. The couple were unmarried.   [202] Ibid., at 381.

[203] See A.J. Oakley [1973] C.L.P. 17.

[204] See *Allen v. Snyder* [1977] 2 N.S.W.L.R. 685 at 700–701 *per* Samuels J.A.

[205] See *Grant v. Edwards* [1976] Ch. 638 at 654 *per* Sir Nicolas Browne-Wilkinson; D.J. Hayton in Jowell and McAuslan (eds), *Lord Denning: The Judge and the Law* (London: Sweet & Maxwell, 1984), 79 at 83–88.

[206] Meagher, Gummow, and Lehane, *Equity: Doctrines and Remedies* (3rd edn) (Sydney: Butterworths, 1992), para. 306.

[207] See The Canadian approach, pp. 354–355.

[208] See *Oxley v. Hiscock* [2005] Fam. 211 at 247.

[209] *Stack v. Dowden* [2007] 2 A.C. 432 at [61] *per* Baroness Hale of Richmond.

The return to orthodoxy

In *Burns v. Burns*,[210] an unmarried couple began to cohabit in rented accommodation in 1961, where their first child was born. In 1963, when a second child was expected, they moved into another house which was conveyed into the man's name. He provided the initial finance and paid the mortgage instalments. The woman remained at home looking after the children until 1975, when she got a job as a driving instructor, her wages being used to pay the rates, telephone bills, and various items for the house. She also redecorated the interior of the house. In 1980, the relationship ended and she brought proceedings claiming a beneficial interest in the house. The Court of Appeal unanimously[211] rejected her claim. Despite her having cohabited with him for over nineteen years in total and seventeen years in the house which he had bought, during which time she looked after both the house and the family, she had acquired no interest in it.[212]

The reason that her claim failed was because the court, reverting to the principles laid down by the House of Lords in *Gissing*, held that they could not infer a common intention for her to have an interest in the property because there was no 'evidence of a payment or payments...which it can be inferred was referable to the acquisition of the house'.[213] *Dicta*, such as those in *Hall v. Hall*, which allowed a court to adopt a broader perspective as to contributions to the household in assessing whether a person should be regarded as having an interest in the home were regarded as wrong.[214]

Purchasing behaviour

The decision in *Burns* marked a return to orthodoxy with regard to the role of the resulting trust; that orthodoxy being, in essence, that one gets what one pays for. This orthodoxy was confirmed by the House of Lords in *Lloyds Bank plc v. Rosset*.[215] The facts were unusual. The entire purchase price to buy a semi-derelict farmhouse was provided from a Swiss trust fund held for Mr Rosset and, at the insistence of the trustees, the house was registered in his sole name. Unknown to his wife, he also took out a mortgage against the property to secure his overdraft. The bank manager accepted his story that his wife and children would not be living in the house. When he subsequently defaulted on the mortgage, the bank sought possession and she argued that she had an overriding interest on the basis that she had a beneficial interest in the house and was in actual occupation of it at the relevant time. Reversing the decision of the Court of Appeal,[216] the House of Lords decided in favour of the bank on the basis

---

[210] [1984] Ch. 317. For rather different reactions to the decision, see N.V. Lowe and A. Smith (1984) 47 M.L.R. 341 and J. Dewar, ibid., at 735. This decision was cited in *Stack v. Dowden*, but was not referred to in any of the speeches.

[211] This decision was reached reluctantly by Waller L.J. See [1984] Ch. 317 at 326.

[212] An editorial comment on this decision remarked that 'even the most lukewarm feminist can see the injustice of [it]': [1984] Fam. Law 4.

[213] [1984] Ch. 317 at 328 *per* Fox L.J.   [214] [1984] Ch. 317 at 331.   [215] [1991] A.C. 107.
[216] [1989] Ch. 350.

that she had no beneficial interest in the house and could not, therefore, have an over-riding interest in it.

The basis of her claim to an interest in the house was that she and her husband had agreed that the acquisition of the house was to be a joint venture. Relying on this, she asserted not that she had made a financial contribution to the purchase price but that she had carried out physical work in renovating the property, thereby entitling her to an interest under a constructive trust.

The actual agreement constructive trust

Giving the only reasoned speech, Lord Bridge of Harwich recognized that there were two methods by which one could acquire a beneficial interest in the house. The first method, which was argued to be applicable in the present case, was that there was an actual agreement to share the beneficial interest in the home and, in reliance on that agreement, the claimant has altered her position so as to give rise to a constructive trust or to rights in estoppel.[217]

In what can be regarded as the first type of case, Lord Bridge said:

'The first and fundamental question which must always be resolved is whether, independently of any inference to be drawn from the conduct of the parties in the course of sharing the house as their home and managing their joint affairs, there has at any time prior to acquisition, or exceptionally at some later date, been any agreement, arrangement, or understanding reached between them that the property is to be shared beneficially. The finding of an agreement or arrangement to share can only, I think, be based upon evidence of express discussions between the partners, however imperfectly remembered and however imprecise their terms may have been. Once a finding to this effect is made it will only be necessary for the person asserting a claim to a beneficial interest against the partner entitled to the legal estate to show that he or she has acted to his or her detriment or significantly altered his or her position in reliance on the agreement in order to give rise to a constructive trust or a proprietary estoppel.'[218]

Joint ventures

This is a description of the classical constructive trust, and it was contended that this should apply in the present case. This argument was rejected. First, while the view was taken that the Rossets were buying the house as a joint venture, it was not accepted that this was the same thing as agreeing to share the beneficial ownership in it.[219] This, however, is an extremely fine distinction.[220] While, on the facts, it may have been justified, it should, it is suggested, be treated with considerable caution. The money to purchase the house was only released from the trust on the explicit understanding that it was to be in his sole name. In these circumstances, for the Rossets to have agreed to share the beneficial ownership of it was regarded as a form of subterfuge to circumvent

---

[217] [1991] 1 A.C. 107 at 129.   [218] Ibid., at 132.   [219] Ibid., at 130.
[220] See M.P. Thompson [1990] Conv. 314 at 315.

the intention of the trustee. Clearer evidence than that which is normally required to establish an intention to share the beneficial ownership in the property was, therefore, required, and the evidence presented in the case did not do this.[221] This finding, together with Lord Bridge's view that the work relied upon by Mrs Rosset to establish an interest under a constructive trust was 'almost de minimis'[222] meant that her claim failed. The facts were clearly unusual and should not lead to judges, in more usual contexts, to distinguish cases when the parties have agreed to buy a house as a joint venture from those when there has been a discussion as to beneficial ownership.[223] In either case, the position should be seen as being one where the parties have agreed to share[224] the ownership of the house.

The inferred agreement constructive trust

Having analysed the first method by which a person may establish a beneficial share in a family home, Lord Bridge turned to the second. Having referred to cases where there is an actual agreement with regard to the ownership of the home, he continued:

'In sharp contrast with this situation is the very different one where there is no evidence to support a finding of an agreement or arrangement to share, however reasonable it might have been for the parties to reach such an arrangement if they had applied their minds to the question, and where the courts must rely entirely on the conduct of the parties both as the basis from which to infer a common intention to share the property beneficially and as the conduct relied on to give rise to a constructive trust. In this situation direct contributions to the purchase price by the partner who is not the legal owner, whether initially or by payment of mortgage instalments will readily justify the inference necessary to the creation of a constructive trust. But as I read the authorities, it is at least extremely doubtful whether anything less will do.'[225]

Terminology

A number of points can be made about this significant, albeit misleading, passage. The first concerns terminology. Although Lord Bridge, when referring to the second scenario, spoke of the creation of a constructive trust, this could have been regarded as being a slip, in that what is being described is a classic resulting trust. There is no evidence of an actual agreement between the parties, but, instead, one infers their intentions with regard to the beneficial ownership of the property from the fact that they have both contributed to the purchase of it. The supposition that this was a slip is strengthened by the fact he regarded *Pettitt v. Pettitt*[226] and *Gissing v. Gissing*,[227] both of which are authorities on the application of resulting trust principles to this

---

[221] [1991] A.C. 107 at 128.   [222] Ibid., at 131.

[223] This, unfortunately, is what was done in *Buggs v. Buggs* [2003] EWHC 1538 (Ch), criticized by M.P. Thompson [2003] Conv. 411 at 420–421.

[224] There must, in this type of case, be an express or inferred agreement. See, e.g., *Akhtar v. Arif* [2006] EWHC 2726 (Ch.).

[225] [1991] A.C. 107 at 132–133.   [226] [1970] A.C. 777.   [227] [1971] A.C. 886.

area, as being leading cases which fell into the category of case which he had just described. Since then, however, except where the house has not been bought for the purposes of sharing,[228] the courts have repeatedly stressed that the trust which arises in this type of case is a constructive trust;[229] although, as will be seen, in its application, this constructive trust owes much to the principles underlying resulting trusts.

Indirect contributions in inferred agreement constructive trusts

A second point to make about this passage is that it appears to draw the ambit of what constitutes a contribution to the purchase price too narrowly, and in a way which was not warranted by previous authority.[230] In *Gissing*,[231] Lord Diplock was prepared to accept that indirect contributions to the purchase price would suffice in order to enable an interest to be acquired; instancing as an example a situation where one party's income goes to the meeting of household expenses, the effect of which is to enable the other to meet the mortgage repayments. Similarly, if one person has worked without payment in a business, the profits of which are used to purchase a house, then an interest in that house will be acquired as a result of the indirect contribution.[232] At first sight, Lord Bridge's formulation appears, implicitly, to overrule these authorities, although it is doubtful whether in this short passage, and without reference to them, he intended to do so.

That the law has not been narrowed in this way has since become clear. In *Le Foe v. Le Foe*,[233] Mr Nicholas Mostyn Q.C., sitting as a High Court judge said:

'Although I am sure that H earned more than W…I have no doubt that the family economy depended for its function on W's earnings. It was an arbitrary allocation of responsibility that H paid the mortgage, service charge and outgoings, whereas W paid for day-to-day domestic expenditure. I have clearly concluded that W contributed indirectly to the mortgage repayments, the principal of which furnished part of the consideration of the initial purchase price.'

On this basis, notwithstanding what was said in *Rosset*, it was held that W had established a beneficial interest in the house.

That the passage in Lord Bridge's speech was too restrictive as to what would constitute a contribution to the purchase of a house has since been confirmed by the House of Lords in *Stack v. Dowden*, and by the Privy Council in *Abbott v. Abbott*, thus evidencing a trend not to deal with relevant authority on its merits. So, in the former case, it was said that the comments by Lord Bridge were *obiter* and had set the hurdle

---

[228] See *Laskar v. Laskar* [2008] EWCA Civ. 347 at [21] *per* Lord Neuberger of Abbotsbury, citing *Stack v. Dowden* [2007] 2 A.C. 423 at [11] *per* Lord Hope of Craighead.

[229] See *Ledger-Bendell v. Ledger-Bendell* [2006] EWHC 2940 at [247] *per* Mr Nicholas Strauss Q.C.; *Abbott v. Abbott* [2007] UKPC 53.

[230] See M.P. Thompson [1990] Conv. 314 at 317; P. Ferguson (1993) 109 L.Q.R. 114 at 116.

[231] [1971] A.C. 107 at 132.   [232] See Indirect contributions, pp. 333–334.

[233] [2001] 2 F.L.R. 970 at 973. See M.P. Thompson [2002] Conv. 273.

too high in certain respects,[234] and, in the latter, that the law had moved on since this had been said.[235] Somewhat remarkably, in the latest attempt to elucidate the applicable principles, in *Jones v. Kernott*,[236] the decision in *Rosset* was not referred to at all.

That said, the third point which should be made about *Rosset* is that, although the statement that only direct contributions to the purchase price would suffice is too narrow, it was nevertheless clear that, in order to obtain an interest under a trust, where there is no evidence of an anterior agreement to share the beneficial ownership of the house, the conduct relied upon must be of a purchasing nature. The point made in *Burns v. Burns* of the need to establish a direct link between the conduct relied upon to establish an interest in the property and the acquisition of that property was accepted. Unless the claimant is contributing in money, or money's worth,[237] she will not acquire an interest in it. Subsequent developments in the House of Lords and the Supreme Court do not undermine this, because in both *Stack v. Dowden* and *Jones v. Kernott*, the starting position was co-ownership at law, with the corresponding presumption of joint beneficial ownership. When the legal title is in the sole name of one of the parties, the hurdle of establishing any sort of interest in the first place has to be overcome and, to do that, it would seem to remain the case that facts must fit into one of the broad categories set out in *Rosset*.

Common intention trusts

In his speech in *Rosset*, Lord Bridge was careful to distinguish between cases where there is an actual agreement to share the beneficial interest and cases where there is not, the latter type of situation then being resolved by the application of the principles of resulting trusts. The first type of case, sometimes referred to as the 'common intention' trust,[238] involves the imposition of a constructive trust to enforce the anterior agreement.

A classic illustration of such a trust, considered earlier, was *Re Densham*,[239] where a husband and wife had agreed to share the ownership of the house equally and she had contributed one-ninth of the purchase price. Had the dispute not involved the trustee in bankruptcy, she would have been entitled, under a constructive trust, to a one-half share in equity; the constructive trust would have been imposed to enforce the actual agreement, the size of the contribution to its purchase being immaterial.

---

[234] [2007] 2 A.C. 423 at [61] *per* Baroness Hale of Richmond. See also at [26] *per* Lord Walker of Gestinghope.

[235] [2007] UKPC 53 at [3] *per* Baroness Hale of Richmond.   [236] [2011] UKSC 53.

[237] This will include physical labour improving the house: *Eves v. Eves* [1975] 1 W.L.R. 1338. It will not include domestic labour.

[238] For a somewhat hyperbolic criticism of this term, see Mee, op. cit., 117. See also N. Glover and P. Todd (1996) 16 L.S. 325.

[239] [1975] 1 W.L.R. 1519; J. Mee [2007] Conv. 14. See Actual agreement, pp. 324–325.

Agreement

The starting point in cases such as this is to find an agreement or arrangement between the parties with regard to the ownership of the house. An example of this occurred in *Eves v. Eves*.[240] A couple, Stuart and Janet, wished to acquire a house together but he told her that, because she was not yet twenty-one, the legal title could not be in their joint names.[241] She accepted this, and assumed that this was merely an excuse, but he was determined, throughout, that the house should be in his name alone. The purchase was completed after she had attained majority but the house was still conveyed into his name alone. He provided the finance but she did a considerable amount of physical work on the property, which was previously in a dirty and dilapidated state. When they separated, the issue arose as to the beneficial ownership of the house. The Court of Appeal held her to be entitled to a quarter share.

Lord Denning M.R. decided the case on a broad view of constructive trusts and considered this quantum share to be appropriate. Brightman J., with whom Browne L.J. agreed, took a more principled route to this conclusion. In his view, the statement as to why the house was not to be in their joint names led her to believe that this was a mere technicality and that she would, nevertheless, be a co-owner of it. Such an oral understanding would not, of itself, have been sufficient for her to have acquired a beneficial interest in the house, however, because there was no written evidence of this statement as is required by section 53(1)(b) of the Law of Property Act 1925. As there was a link between her conduct and the acquisition of the property, however, the court could impose a constructive trust to give effect to their agreement and he concurred with the outcome that she be entitled to a one-quarter share in the house.

Pretexts

Eves v. Eves is now accepted as being one of a line of cases where a constructive trust is imposed in order to enforce an anterior agreement, or common intention, to share the beneficial ownership of the property.[242] A common theme of these cases is that the legal owner gives the other person a pretext as to why the property is not being put into joint names. In *Eves*, the reason given was that she was too young. In other cases, the reasons have included possible complications in impending divorce proceedings,[243] or alleged tax advantages.[244] The fact that the legal owner has given some excuse or pretext to the other party for the legal title not being in joint names has led to criticism that there is, in fact, no common intention to share the beneficial ownership of

---

[240] [1975] 1 W.L.R. 1338. See also *Williamson v. Sheikh* [2008] EWCA Civ. 990.

[241] At the time this was said, it may well have been true, as the age of majority was reduced to eighteen in 1969, the year in which the house was bought. See Family Law Reform Act 1969, s. 1.

[242] See *Lloyds Bank plc v. Rosset* [1991] 1 A.C. 107 at 133 *per* Lord Bridge of Harwich.

[243] *Grant v. Edwards* [1986] Ch. 638; *Oxley v. Hiscock* [2005] Fam. 111.

[244] *Hammond v. Mitchell* [1992] 2 All E.R. 109. In *Abbott v. Abbott* [2007] UKPC 53, Mrs Abbott, as a Canadian, would have needed a licence to be the legal owner of land in Antigua.

the house at all.[245] The party giving the pretext may never actually intend to share the ownership: 'Excuses are usually made to hide bad intentions, not good ones.'[246]

Objective determination

From the point of view of a subjective enquiry into the actual intentions of the parties, there is obvious force in these criticisms, and, to that extent, the expression 'common intention' may be inapposite. Nevertheless, the better view is that the very fact that a pretext is given as to why the property is not to be in joint names is, itself, indicative of the fact that the person to whom the pretext is given expects to have an interest in the property and the other party knows this. So, while there may not be an actual agreement, in the sense of a bargain, the statement made should be taken, objectively, as a sufficient indication of an intention to share the beneficial ownership.

This argument was accepted in the leading case of *Grant v. Edwards*.[247] Ms Grant and Mr Edwards were involved in a relationship and were looking to buy a house together. The house was conveyed into the names of Mr Edwards and his brother, Mr Edwards having told Ms Grant that it would be inadvisable for her name to be on the title as this might cause her prejudice in divorce proceedings in which she was involved. It was found that she contributed to the acquisition of the house and on this basis was awarded a half share in the house. With regard to the finding of a common intention, Mustill L.J. dealt head on with the problem of the giver of the pretext never intending to share the ownership of the property. He said:

'The reason given for placing the brother's name on the title was simply an untruthful excuse for not doing at once what he never intended to do at all.

That however is not fatal to the claim. Whatever the defendant's actual intention, the nature of the excuse which he gave must have led the plaintiff to believe that she would in the future have her name on the title, and this in turn would justify her in concluding that she had from the outset some kind of right to the house.'[248]

This belief, because it has been induced by the defendant, is sufficient to establish the common intention necessary to give rise to the imposition of a constructive trust.

Quantification of interest

The theory underlying the imposition of the constructive trust is that the trust is imposed to give effect to the common intention of the parties. Where, as in *Re Densham*, that intention is stated expressly, the result is that the courts should give effect to that intention.[249] In *Eves*, however, the claimant was awarded a one-quarter

---

[245] See S. Gardner (1993) 109 L.Q.R. 263 at 264–265, 281–282; L. Clarke and R. Edmonds [1992] Fam. 523; C. Rotherham [2004] Conv. 268 at 277. See also *Van Laetham v. Brooker* [2005] EWHC 1478 (Ch.) at [67] *per* Lawrence Collins J.

[246] U. Rinker [1998] Conv. 202 at 207.   [247] [1986] Ch. 638.   [248] Ibid., at 653.

[249] See also *Stack v. Dowden* [2007] 2 A.C. 432 at [37] *per* Lord Walker of Gestinghope; *Q v. Q* [2008] EWHC 1874 (Fam.) at [113] *per* Black J.

share. This aspect of the decision was regarded by Brightman J. as being the hardest part of the case[250] and is, it is suggested, also the least satisfactory part of it, there being no evidence at all that the parties had agreed that she should have a share of this magnitude.

In cases where some reason is given for the legal title not being shared, so that the reasonable supposition is that the person to whom the excuse is given is to have an interest in the property, the normal starting point should, it is thought, be one-half, a natural inference being that, if the house was in joint names, then it would be owned equally. Similarly, if the person giving the pretext at the time owns only a share in the relevant property, then the claimant would expect to own a half of that share.[251] The point is that the role of the court is to enforce what it is that the parties actually agreed.

A good example of this occurred in *Willliamson v. Sheikh*.[252] A couple met through the internet in 2002, when she was 15 and he was in his thirties. They bought a house together in 2004. She advanced a capital sum towards the purchase, that sum having been inherited from her grandfather. The house was, necessarily, put into his sole name, and he paid the mortgage repayments. A trust deed was prepared to set out their respective entitlements in the house, although this was not signed. The reason for this was that he assured her that there was no need to do this, and that he would see her all right. When the couple separated, it was held that he held the house on trust for her in the proportions set out in the unsigned trust document. She having contributed to the purchase price on the basis of their agreement, a constructive trust was imposed to give effect to the actual intention of the parties.

Inferred and imputed intentions

Where there is an actual agreement to share the beneficial interest in the property then, provided that the claimant has made a contribution to the purchase of the property, the task of the court is straightforward: it is to enforce what has been agreed. Where there is no such agreement, the task is to draw inferences as to what the parties intended, such inferences being drawn from their conduct with regard to the acquisition of the house. This latter situation was traditionally the area of operation of the resulting trust, with the size of the share reflecting the size of the contribution. The reclassification of this form of trust as an inferred constructive trust, as occurred in *Lloyd's Bank plc v. Rosset*,[253] leads to a blurring of the distinction between enforcing an agreement which the parties actually made and inferring intentions from the conduct of the parties, the latter process running the risk of constructing agreements for people which they never had.

---

[250] [1975] 1 W.L.R. 1338 at 1345.

[251] See *Stokes v. Anderson* [1991] 1 F.L.R. 391; *Chan Pui Chun v. Leung Kam Ho* [2002] EWCA Civ. 1075. See also *Hapeshi v. Allnatt* [2010] EWHC 392 (Ch.). Contrast *Ungarian v. Lessnoff* [1990] Ch. 206 (a life interest).

[252] [2008] EWCA Civ. 990.   [253] [1991] A.C. 107.

An holistic approach

A striking example of this occurred in *Midland Bank Plc v. Cooke*.[254] A matrimonial home was purchased in 1971 for £8,500, and the legal title was in his name
alone. The purchase was financed by a mortgage of £6,450 in favour of the Leeds
Permanent Building Society, with the balance provided by a combination of his
savings and a wedding gift to both of them of £1,000 from his parents. Although
she worked, apart from brief periods surrounding the birth of their three children,
her earnings did not go towards paying the mortgage, but was used for general
household expenditure. Later in 1971, they both executed a mortgage in order to
secure an overdraft, and this was redeemed six months later. In 1978, the mortgage
in favour of the Leeds was redeemed using, in part, money provided by a general
mortgage in favour of Midland Bank. This mortgage was executed by him alone,
and was to secure the business overdraft of his company. After the Court of Appeal
decision in *Williams & Glyn's Bank v. Boland*[255] was reported, the bank, concerned
about the enforceability of its security, got Mrs Cooke to sign a consent form agreeing that any interest that she might have in the house be postponed to that of the
bank. Subsequently they created, jointly, a second mortgage over the property and
then, finally, in 1984 she brought county court proceedings against her husband
under the Married Women's Property Act 1964, and a consent order was made
declaring that the house was held by the spouses jointly, and transferring the property into their joint names, holding beneficially as tenants in common. The present
proceeding arose when the bank, following default on the mortgage by Mr Cooke,
brought possession proceedings to enforce the mortgage. Mrs Cooke claimed to
have an interest binding on it.

Priority of interests

Two issues actually arose in this litigation. First, the question arose as to whether
whatever interest that Mrs Cooke might have in the house was binding on the bank
and, secondly, assuming that she had an interest in it, what was the size of her beneficial share. At trial, the main issue was as to the validity of the consent form signed
by Mrs Cooke, and it was held that it was invalid as it had been obtained by undue
influence. On the facts, this seemed unexceptional. In the light of subsequent case law,
however, this should not have had a determinative effect on the outcome of the case.
This was because part of the money borrowed from the Midland Bank was used to pay
off the mortgage in favour of the Leeds, and that mortgage was used to finance the
purchase of the house in the first place. Despite the creation of the mortgage in favour
of the Midland being tainted by undue influence, because the money borrowed from
them was used to redeem the mortgage which was not so tainted, the Midland should

---

[254] [1995] 4 All E.R. 562. For critical comment, see G. Battersby (1996) 8 C. & F.L.Q. 261; M. Dixon [1997]
Conv. 66.
[255] [1979] Ch. 312, affmd at [1981] A.C. 487.

have been regarded as being in the same position as was the Leeds,[256]and so should have been able to obtain possession.

Approach to the quantification of interest

Be that as it may, the main interest in the case was the approach taken to the quantification of Mrs Cooke's interest in the home. At first instance, the judge held her to be entitled to a share of 6.47 per cent. He arrived at that conclusion by attributing to her a financial contribution representing half of the initial wedding present from his parents, and calculating the proportion that this bore to the initial purchase price. The Court of Appeal reversed this finding and held her to be entitled to a half share in the property.

Had the case not been complicated by the involvement of a mortgagee, and had it been decided after the decision in *Stack v. Dowden*,[257] it is thought that this outcome would have occasioned little controversy. As it is now clear that the original interests in the property can be varied,[258] the transfer of the property into joint names would have carried with it the presumption of equal shares in equity. This, however, was not the basis of the reasoning, which proceeded on the basis of an application of a constructive trust.

Common intention constructive trust

The starting point was an express finding that there had been no actual agreement that there was to be a sharing of the beneficial interest in the home. This, therefore, precluded the imposition of a constructive trust on the basis of the first category of case identified by Lord Bridge in *Lloyds Bank plc v. Rosset*.[259] Despite this finding, however, it was held that 'positive evidence that the parties neither discussed nor intended any agreement as to the proportions of their beneficial interest does not preclude the court on general principles, from inferring one'.[260] In approaching the task of inferring what their intentions were, the court expressly rejected the notion that the shares should be proportionate to the size of the financial contributions. Instead, regard was had to the totality of their conduct throughout their marriage, not necessarily related to the acquisition of the property,[261] and, having reviewed this, the conclusion was reached that a common intention could be inferred to share the ownership of the house equally.

Although there may be much to be said for developing the law along these lines, with the focus of attention being an analysis of the nature of the relationship between

---

[256] See *Equity and Law Home Loans Ltd v. Prestidge* [1992] 1 W.L.R. 137. See M.P. Thompson [2004] Conv. 399 at 405, and Acquisition mortgages, pp. 488–490.

[257] [2007] 2 A.C. 432.   [258] See *Jones v. Kernott* [2011] UKSC 53.

[259] See also *Tackaberry v. Hollis* [2007] EWHC 2633 (Ch.), where such a finding was fatal to a claim to an interest under a constructive trust.

[260] Ibid., at 575 *per* Waite L.J.

[261] Ibid., at 574, *per* Waite L.J., followed in *Le Foe v. Le Foe* [2002] 2 F.L.R. 970. For criticism, see M.P. Thompson [2002] Conv. 273 at 277–281.

the parties rather than on their respective purchasing behaviour,[262] it is hard to see that the authorities justified the use of trust law to achieve this end.[263] It proceeds on the basis that, if a direct contribution is made to the acquisition of a house, this operates as a form of springboard to allow the court a broad discretion to allocate shares in the property, without regard to the actual size of the contribution to its purchase.[264] This is done by imputing intentions to parties, who have not considered the matter, on the basis of what they would have agreed had they considered the matter: a line of reasoning which appears to be precluded by both *Pettitt v. Pettitt* and *Gissing v. Gissing*.[265] As there was no actual agreement in *Cooke*, there should have been no question of the imposition of a constructive trust such as that employed in *Grant v. Edwards*.[266] Once that form of trust has been ruled out, the matter should fall to be determined on the application of resulting trust principles. That it is not is the result of the unfortunate terminology employed in *Lloyds Bank plc v. Rosset*,[267] where a classical resulting trust situation was described as being a constructive trust. Where there is no actual agreement between the parties as to the beneficial ownership of the home, principle would seem to dictate that the size of any beneficial share in the property should be determined by the size of the financial contribution to it, albeit that, in assessing the nature of that contribution, regard should be had to contributions throughout the period during which the house is paid for, and not just the position when the legal title is acquired: an holistic approach.

The abandonment of resulting trusts

This reasoning based on resulting trust principles has not, however, been pursued in subsequent case law, although the actual results are consistent with it. In the influential case of *Oxley v. Hiscock*,[268] Mr Hiscock and Mrs Oxley had been in a relationship for many years and had lived together in various houses. The house, which was the subject matter of the litigation, was put into his sole name, the reason for this being to prevent a claim to it being made by her former husband. It was found as a fact that, although they had agreed to share the beneficial ownership of the house, there was no agreement as to what those actual shares should be.[269] The purchase price was derived from a variety of sources, including the proceeds of sale of a house which they

---

[262] See Proposed legislation, pp. 355–357.

[263] Contrast the *dicta* of Dillon L.J. in *Springette v. Defoe* [1992] 1 F.L.R. 388 at 392 and *McHardy & Sons (A Firm) v. Warren* [1995] 4 All E.R. 562 at 572, which might appear to conflict but are not addressed to the same issue. Cf. [1995] 4 All E.R. 562 at 572 *per* Waite L.J., who found the contrast mystifying.

[264] See also *Drake v. Whipp* [1996] 1 F.L.R. 826 at 832 *per* Peter Gibson L.J., which is open to similar objections, but cf. A. Dunn [1997] Conv. 467 at 472.

[265] [1970] A.C. 777 and [1971] A.C. 866, respectively. It also appears to run directly counter to what was said in *Lloyds Bank plc v. Rosset* [1991] 1 A.C. 107 at 132–133 *per* Lord Bridge of Harwich.

[266] [1986] Ch. 638. For the need in cases of this type to show an actual agreement, see *Lightfoot v. Lightfoot-Brown* [2005] EWCA Civ. 201 at para. 27 *per* Arden L.J.

[267] [1991] 1 A.C. 107 at 133 *per* Lord Bridge of Harwich. See Joint ventures, pp. 337–338.

[268] [2005] Fam. 211. See S. Gardner (2004) 120 L.Q.R. 541; M.P. Thompson [2004] Conv. 496; M. Dixon [2005] Conv. 79.

[269] [2005] Fam. 211 at 217–218 *per* Chadwick L.J.

had previously owned. Despite it being clear that she was making a sizeable financial contribution to the purchase of the house, she, very unwisely, turned down advice from her solicitor that the beneficial interests should be stated at the outset, her reason being that she trusted him.[270] At first instance, it was held that the house was owned beneficially in equal shares. On appeal, the Court of Appeal held that the property was shared in proportion 60 per cent/40 per cent in his favour.

In reaching this conclusion, Chadwick L.J., who gave the only reasoned judgment, embarked on an extensive review of the authorities. He accepted that a beneficial interest in a house could be acquired in one of the two situations referred to in *Rosset*. These situations were when there was an actual agreement as to the respective shares which each party was to have in the property, and those when there was not. In the latter situation, the relevant intention to share the beneficial ownership is derived from the contributions made to its purchase. The present case did not fall neatly into either category. This was because, although there was an actual agreement to share the beneficial ownership of the house, the two of them had agreed that the shares would not be equal[271] but had not come to an agreement as to what those shares should be. Consequently, the case was decided on the basis that it fell into the second of the categories laid down by Lord Bridge in *Rosset*. This then led to the issue of the quantification of the beneficial interest, in cases of this type and, in particular, the principles upon which such quantification is to be carried.

The principal argument of Mr Hiscock was that the size of Mrs Oxley's beneficial share in the property should be determined by the size of her contribution to the purchase price. On this basis, it was argued, her share should have been in the region of 22 per cent, that being the assessment of her contribution at first instance. This analysis was rejected.[272] In cases where the parties have not come to an agreement as to the proportions in which they are to share the ownership of the property, a court may infer the requisite intention to share ownership from the fact that the person who is not on the legal title has made direct contributions to its purchase. That is not determinative of the size of the proportionate share. This was stated in terms by Chadwick L.J., who said, 'Direct contributions to the purchase price may lead to an inference that each party should have some beneficial interest without, necessarily, leading to the further inference that their respective shares should be proportionate to the amount of their direct contributions.'[273]

Fairness

This, of course, leaves unresolved how one does determine what those shares should be. The correct approach was said to be that:

'if it were their common intention that each should have some beneficial interest in the property—which is the hypothesis upon which it becomes necessary to answer the second question [sc. the size of that share]—then, in the absence of evidence that they gave any

---

[270] Ibid. at 215–216 *per* Chadwick L.J.   [271] Ibid., at 218 and 248 *per* Chadwick L.J.
[272] It was based, principally, on *Springette v. Defoe* [1992] 1 F.L.R. 388.   [273] [2005] Fam. 211 at 231.

thought to the amount of their respective shares, the necessary inference is that they must have intended that question would be answered on the basis of what was seen to be fair.'[274]

This approach is open to the standard objection that, except in cases where the parties have actually considered the question of the ownership of the house, it perpetuates the myth that what the courts are doing is to gauge what the parties intended when no real thought had been given to the matter at all.[275] It has also met with fierce criticism, on the basis that it gives to the judiciary an unfettered discretion to decide on the beneficial ownership of a family home and leads to 'palm-tree justice'.[276] A good deal of the sting goes out of this criticism, however, when regard is had to how the court determined what was fair.

A wider view of financial contributions

With regard to this issue, it was clear that what was relevant to the court were financial contributions. In this respect, however, what does emerge is a wider, and more welcome, view of what constitutes a financial contribution than had been previously articulated was accepted. This emerges in the following, important passage. Chadwick L.J. said:

'It must now be accepted that (at least as far as this court and below) the answer is that each is entitled to that share which the court considers fair having regard to the whole course of dealing between them *in relation to the property*. And in that context, "the whole course of dealing between them in relation to the property" includes the arrangements which they make from time to time to meet the outgoings (for example, mortgage contributions, council tax and utilities, repairs insurance and housekeeping) which have to be met if they are to live in their property as their home.'[277]

On the basis of this, Mrs Oxley was held to have a forty per cent share. This was arrived at by first assessing the size of their respective initial contributions to the purchase, his contribution being considerably in excess to that provided by her. Regard was then had to the subsequent pooling of their resources and the consequent expenditure related to the house and, in particular, that they contributed equally to the repayment of the debt incurred to finance the purchase of the home.[278] Her share in the house was, therefore, larger than it would have been had attention been confined solely to her initial contribution.

Consistency with resulting trusts

Although the language used in *Oxley v. Hiscock* is that of constructive trust and fairness, the result of the case is entirely consistent with that which would have been arrived at on the application of resulting trust principles. The share she was held to be entitled

---

[274] Ibid., at 247.   [275] See Presumed intention, pp. 321–323.
[276] See G. Battersby (2005) 17 C.F.L.Q. 259 at 263.   [277] [2005] Fam. 211 at 246. Italics supplied.
[278] Ibid., at 220 *per* Chadwick L.J.

to was commensurate with what she had paid.[279] The case does, however, represent a welcome development in the law, in that credit is given for financial contributions made after the date of the actual transfer of the house. This seems an entirely realistic way to view the purchase of a house, which in most cases is a process occupying over twenty years. Moreover, it also pays regard to payments associated with the purchase, such as the payment of council tax. It may be purely a matter of convenience which person's salary goes towards the payment of the mortgage instalments, and which goes to the other expenditure associated with house ownership and it is undesirable that major differences in outcome should depend on such a distinction.[280] Nevertheless, despite protestations to the contrary, the principles applicable to the resolution of this type of dispute do seem to be those underlying resulting trusts, and the size of the share is governed by the size of the financial contribution, albeit what counts as financial contribution is viewed more widely than was once the case. Non-financial contributions, however, despite the approach taken in *Midland Bank plc v. Cooke*,[281] should not, under the law of trusts, enable the person to acquire a share in the property.

When one turns to *Stack v. Dowden*, itself, one can make similar observations that, although the role of the constructive trust was emphasized, the actual result is consistent with that which would have been arrived at on the application of resulting trust principles.[282] Lady Hale disapproved of the statement in *Oxley v. Hiscock* that the task of the court is to determine the size of each person's beneficial interest in the property on the basis of what was fair.[283] She also disapproved of cases which appeared to adopt an arithmetical approach to the calculation of those interests.[284] When turning to the facts of the case itself, however, she was also critical of the approach of the trial judge, in that 'he had looked at their relationship rather than the matters which were relevant to their intentions about this property'.[285] This then leaves the question as to how those intentions are to be discerned. The answer would seem to be that one looks at the financial contributions that each party made to its acquisition, a process which led Lady Hale to conclude that shares of 64 per cent to 36 per cent would have been appropriate, although she was content to accept the reasoning of the Court of Appeal who, by calculating the shares on the basis of contribution, had arrived at proportions of 65 per cent to 35 per cent.[286] This is also the case in *Jones v. Kernott*,[287] where Lord Walker and Lady Hale, despite favouring the notion of inferred intentions, concluded

---

[279] See also *Pinfield v. Eagles* [2005] EWHC 577 (Ch.) at [39], where the adjudication of what was a fair share was based explicitly on the size of the financial contribution, and *Stock v. Dowden* [2005] EWCA Civ. 857 (in the Court of Appeal), and at [2007] 2 A.C. 432 at [107] *per* Lord Neuberger of Abbotsbury. See also S. Gardner (2004) 120 L.Q.R. 541 at 544; M.P. Thompson [2004] Conv. 496 at 502.

[280] See *Pettitt v. Pettitt* [1970] A.C. 777 at 794 *per* Lord Reid.   [281] [1995] 4 All E.R. 562.

[282] See especially [2007] A.C. 432 at [107] *per* Lord Neuberger of Abbotsbury.   [283] Ibid., at [61].

[284] Ibid., at [65], disapproving *Walker v. Hall* [1984] F.L.R. 126; *Springette v. Defoe* [1992] 2 F.L.R. 511 and *Huntingford v. Hobbs* [1993] 1 F.L.R. 376.

[285] Ibid., at [86].

[286] Ibid., at [88] and [92]. Lord Neuberger would have put the proportions at 70% to 30% but, as Ms Dowden had conceded that Mr Stack was entitled to a 35% share, was prepared to leave it at that: see at [122].

[287] [2011] UKSC 53.

that the division of the beneficial interests in the proportion of 90 per cent/10 per cent was, in fact, consistent with their respective financial contributions and whether one says that this reflects their inferred intentions, or the outcome of intentions ascribed, or imputed, to them is, at the end of the day, largely a matter of taste.

It has been argued that *Stack v. Dowden* is moving the law forward by using the constructive trust as a form of proprietary relief for unjust enrichment.[288] It is difficult, however, to see the force of this, because the nature of the unjust enrichment seems simply to be that she contributed more to the acquisition of the house than he did, and for them to share the beneficial ownership equally would amount to his unjust enrichment at her expense.[289] This is, in essence, what the resulting trust is designed to avoid. Consequently, despite protestations to the contrary, it is difficult to see *Stack v. Dowden* as being more than 'an "updated" resulting trust which takes account of all significant contributions to the family home, whether direct or indirect, in cash or in kind'.[290] The insistence on stressing the role of the constructive trust may be because of the perception that a resulting trust arises when the property is acquired, and that conduct subsequent to that is not relevant. Whether this is the case, unfortunately, neither *Stack v. Dowden* nor *Jones v. Kernott* do much to clarify the conceptual basis underlying this area of law. Nor do they give much guidance as to when the presumption of joint ownership is to be rebutted, or how shares in the property are to be quantified when it is.

The nature of reliance

It is quite clear that a mere statement by one party to another that the ownership in the house is to be shared is, on its own, insufficient to generate an equitable interest in the property. It must be relied upon. The question which then arises concerns the nature of the reliance necessary for a constructive trust to be imposed.

The theoretical root of the imposition of the constructive trust in situations of this type is the decision in *Rochefoucauld v. Boustead*,[291] where an oral agreement to hold property on trust was denied despite the purchase price reflecting this oral agreement. A constructive trust was imposed to give effect to that agreement. The underlying basis of the doctrine would appear to be that the trust is imposed to prevent unjust enrichment; were a trust not to be imposed, the purchaser would have retained the whole beneficial interest in the property, having paid less than its worth because of the agreement to hold the property on trust. One would anticipate, therefore, that the nature of the reliance for a trust to arise would be of a type which is contributory in nature, that is that the claimant has contributed to the acquisition of the property, so that, if the legal owner were allowed to deny the oral agreement to share the beneficial

---

[288] T. Etherton [2008] C.L.J. 266.   [289] Ibid., at 280–281.
[290] N. Piska (2008) 71 M.L.R. 120 at 129.
[291] [1897] 1 Ch. 196. See also *Bannister v. Bannister* [1948] 2 All E.R. 133.

ownership, he would be enriched at the claimant's expense. The courts, in the current context, appear to view reliance more broadly than this.

In *Grant v. Edwards*, the reliance by the claimant on what had been said to her was in the nature of indirect contributions to the mortgage and, had there not been this prior statement, it is not clear that she would have succeeded under a resulting trust,[292] although as it had been found that the defendant would almost certainly not have been able to meet the mortgage payments without the plaintiff's indirect financial contributions, it is probable that she would.[293] Nevertheless, the nature of the necessary reliance was not confined to contributions to the acquisition of the house but was put more widely, as being 'conduct on which the woman could not reasonably have been expected to embark unless she was to have an interest in the house'.[294]

Relationship with estoppel

The focus on the expectation of having an interest in the home, rather than concentrating on the need to contribute to its acquisition has led to parallels being drawn between the operation of the constructive trusts in this area and the operation of equitable estoppel.[295] Owing, perhaps, to the attempt to assimilate the role of the constructive trust with that of equitable estoppel in the context of agreements relating to the sale of land which do not satisfy the formal requirements imposed by section 2 of the Law of Property (Miscellaneous Provisions) Act 1989,[296] these parallels have been stressed. Thus, in *Oxley v. Hiscock*,[297] Chadwick L.J. said that: 'I think that the time has come to accept that there is no difference, in cases of this nature, whether the true analysis lies in constructive trust or in proprietary estoppel.' Equally explicit, however, and to directly opposite effect, in *Hyett v. Stanley*,[298] Sir Martin Nourse said that: 'Although it has been suggested more than once...that the principles underlying the law of proprietary estoppel might provide useful guidance both in regard to the conduct necessary to constitute an acting upon the common intention of the claimant and in regard to the quantification of his or her beneficial interest in the property, the two doctrines have not been assimilated....'. Some attempt to clarify this issue, therefore, seems to be appropriate.

Equitable, or proprietary, estoppel, which will be considered in detail in Chapter 15, is a flexible doctrine, whereby rights can be acquired in another person's land. The essence of the doctrine is that one person relies upon an expectation that he either has, or will, acquire rights in that other person's land in circumstances when it is unconscionable to deny some effect to that expectation. The claimant who has acted upon

---

[292] [1996] Ch. 638 at 650 *per* Nourse L.J.   [293] [1996] Ch. 638 at 649.

[294] Ibid., at 648 *per* Nourse L.J.

[295] Ibid., at 656–657 *per* Sir Nicolas Browne-Wilkinson V.-C. See also *Lloyds Bank plc v. Rosset* [1991] 1 A.C. 107 at 132–133 *per* Lord Bridge of Harwich.

[296] See *Yaxley v. Gotts* [2000] 1 All E.R. 711 at 721–722 *per* Robert Walker L.J. For criticism of this, see Estoppel and trusts, pp. 206–207.

[297] [2005] Fam. 211 at 247. See also *Van Laetham v. Brooker* [2005] EWHC 1478 (Ch) at para. 77 *per* Lawrence Collins J.

[298] [2004] 1 F.L.R. 394 at 404.

this expectation acquires rights in equity, and it is for the court to determine, in all the circumstances of the case, what is the appropriate remedy to satisfy the equity which has arisen.

Differences between the concepts

From this outline of equitable estoppel, it is evident that there are close similarities between it and the constructive trust. It is not the case, however, that the two doctrines are identical.[299] The basis of the constructive trust is that there is an agreement that the beneficial ownership of the house will be shared, or at least a statement from which it can reasonably be inferred that this is what was intended. Estoppel is wider than this. It can be relevant in situations when there has been no statement at all, but where both parties are mistaken as to what the true legal position is.[300] More importantly, in constructive trust cases, the agreement is to share the ownership of property; in estoppel cases, the expectation can be that, at some time in the future, property will be transferred to the claimant.[301] It may also occur that, in an estoppel case, there is no expectation of gaining a share in the property at all; rather the expectation may be limited to a right of secure accommodation.[302]

Just as the nature of the expectation can be different in cases of constructive trust and estoppel, what can amount to reliance may also differ. Although, in recent times, the requirements of reliance in the case of a constructive trust have been relaxed, there do not appear to be any examples of a constructive trust being imposed when the reliance has not been in some way related to the acquisition of the house.[303] In estoppel cases, on the other hand, reliance can take many different forms, and can include the giving up of career prospects in reliance on the expectation of obtaining property in the future.[304]

A further, important, distinction exists between cases of constructive trust and equitable estoppel. In cases of constructive trust, there is an agreement between the parties as to the beneficial ownership of the house. Provided that there has been sufficient reliance, then the role of the court is to enforce that agreement.[305] This may well result in a beneficial share in the property being obtained which is considerably larger than the size of the contribution to its purchase.[306] In estoppel cases, on the other

---

[299] See P. Ferguson (1993) 109 L.Q.R. 114 arguing persuasively against an attempt to treat the two doctrines as being coterminous: see D. Hayton [1990] Conv. 370. For support for the former view, see also S. Gardner (2004) 120 L.Q.R. 541 at 546.

[300] See, e.g., *E.R. Ives Investment Ltd v. High* [1967] 2 Q.B. 379; *Taylors Fashions Ltd v. Liverpool Victoria Trustees Ltd* [1982] 1 Q.B. 133n.

[301] See, e.g., *Gillett v. Holt* [2000] 2 All E.R. 289; *Ottey v. Grundy* [2003] EWCA Civ. 1176.

[302] See *Maharaj v. Chand* [1986] A.C. 898; *H. v. M. (Property Occupied by H's Parents)* [2004] 2 F.L.R. 16.

[303] See *Van Laetham v. Brooker* [2005] EWHC 1478 (Ch.) at para. 71 per Lawrence Collins J.

[304] See *Gillet v. Holt* [2000] 2 All E.R. 289; *Ottey v. Grundy* [2003] EWCA Civ. 1176. Cf. *Lissimore v. Downing* [2003] 2 F.L.R. 308.

[305] See *Gissing v. Gissing* [1971] A.C. 886 at 905 per Lord Diplock; *Grant v. Edwards* [1986] Ch. 638 at 657 per Sir Nicolas Browne-Wilkinson V.-C.; *Hyett v. Stanley* [2004] 1 F.L.R. 394 at 404 per Sir Martin Nourse.

[306] See *Re Densham* [1975] 1 W.L.R. 1519; *Wright v. Johnson* [2002] 1 P. & C.R. 15 at para. 17 per Sir Martin Nourse.

hand, once an equity has arisen, the court has a considerable discretion as to how that equity should be satisfied. The court will have regard to both the nature of the expectation and the extent of the detrimental reliance and, in determining the appropriate remedy, will be concerned that there is proportionality between the expectation and the reliance.[307] In an estoppel case, therefore, the claimant may well end up with some award which is less than the full satisfaction of the expectation.[308]

It is, of course, true that there are substantial similarities between the principles underlying constructive trusts and those underlying equitable estoppel. There are also important differences, and it is important that the two doctrines should not be assimilated. Indeed, to do so may inhibit the development of greater flexibility in this branch of the law. Consequently, the recantation by Lord Walker in *Stack v. Dowden*[309] of his earlier views concerning the assimilation of constructive trusts and estoppel is much to be welcomed.

REFORM

It has long been accepted that this area of the law is unsatisfactory. In 1995, the Law Commission published its Sixth Programme of Law Reform, and identified the law relating to home-sharers as one of the areas in which it wanted to work, being of the view that, 'The present rules are uncertain, difficult to apply and can lead to serious injustice.'[310] Seven years on, however, perhaps as a consequence of being unable to devise a scheme which could apply to all types of home-sharers, it had changed its mind. It had, apparently, 'become clear that the current law offers a degree of flexibility which is positively desirable in that it can respond with sophistication to different factual circumstances and to different personal relationships'.[311] Matters were not allowed to rest there, however, and the Government referred back to the Commission the narrower issue of the position of cohabitants who are in a non-marital, intimate relationship, and a Report has now been published which advocates legislative reform.[312]

Before considering these proposals, one can point to a principal problem of the approach of English law to this area in that it has been dominated by the law of trusts. Except in the case of the form of constructive trust which is imposed to give effect to an antecedent agreement to share the beneficial interest in the home, the underlying principles, although currently not the terminology, have derived from the law relating to resulting trusts. This means that, to obtain an interest in the home, there must

---

[307] *Jennings v. Rice* [2003] 1 P. & C.R. 8 at para. 36 *per* Aldous L.J.

[308] See, in particular, the comments in *Q v. Q* [2008] EWHC 1874 (Fam.) at [113] *per* Black J.

[309] [2007] 2 A.C. 423 at [37].   [310] (1995) Law Com. No. 234, para. 34.

[311] (2002) Law Com. No. 278, para. 1.3.

[312] (2007) Law Com. No. 307. For examples of Commonwealth legislation dealing with this issue, see, e.g., De Facto Relations Act 1964 (New South Wales), Property Law (Amendment) Act 1987 (Victoria).

be a direct financial link between the conduct relied upon to generate the beneficial interest and the acquisition of the property in question. This means that, unless the cohabitant who is claiming an interest in the home has been in paid employment, there will be no question of her acquiring an interest under a trust. There will have been no financial contribution referable to the purchase of the home. Insofar as the law of trusts is concerned, the contribution to the *household* is as opposed to a contribution to the *house*, by what might be termed domestic labour, the type of work which some regard as a form of unpaid labour for which the provider should be compensated is ignored.[313] This approach is exemplified by *Burns v. Burns*.[314]

The Canadian approach

Elsewhere in the Commonwealth, a different judicial approach to these matters has been taken, the jurisdiction at the forefront of a changed perspective being Canada.[315] There, after a prolonged judicial debate,[316] the courts abandoned the employment of the resulting trust and, instead, adopted an analysis based upon the constructive trust. Unlike English law, however, the basis of the imposition of the constructive trust was not to give effect to a prior agreement concerning the ownership of the property. The constructive trust in Canada is employed to prevent the unjust enrichment of the legal owner. Its juridical basis has been described in terms very similar to those used by Lord Denning:[317]

'It is imposed without reference to intention to create a trust. And its purpose is to remedy a result otherwise inequitable. It is a broad and flexible equitable tool which permits Courts to gauge all the circumstances of the case, including the respective contributions of the parties, and to determine beneficial entitlement.'[318]

In *Sorochan v. Sorochan*,[319] an unmarried couple cohabited on a farm for over forty years. During this time, she looked after their children, did all the domestic chores, worked long hours on the farm, and, when he was away, working as a travelling salesman, did all the farming chores. The farm was in his name before they began to cohabit and, therefore, she had made no contribution to its initial acquisition. When their relationship ended, and there was a dispute as to the ownership of the property, the Supreme Court of Canada ordered that he transfer part of the land to her, and to

---

[313] See C.S. Bruch (1981) 29 A.J. Comp. Law 217 at 222–223; M. Neave (1991) 17 Mon. L.R. 14 at 22. For a different view, see R.L. Deech (1980) 29 I.C.L.Q. 480 at 486.

[314] [1984] Ch. 317. Although it has been argued that such a situation is, demographically, highly atypical, R. Probert (2001) 13 C.F.L.Q. 275 at 284, recent empirical research revealed that three out of a sample of twenty-four couples were in similar situations to Mrs Burns.

[315] For a good discussion of the jurisprudence in other jurisdictions, see Mee, op. cit., Chapters 7–9.

[316] The start and finish of this debate are the cases of *Murdoch v. Murdoch* (1973) 83 D.L.R. (3rd) 367 and *Sorochan v. Sorochan* (1986) 29 D.L.R. (4th) 1.

[317] *Hussey v. Palmer* [1972] 1 W.L.R. 1286 at 1289–1290. See Household contributions, p. 334.

[318] *Pettkus v. Becker* (1981) 117 D.L.R. (3rd) 257 at 270 *per* Dickson C.J.

[319] (1986) DL.R. 29 (4th) 1.

pay her a lump sum. The basis of this order was the imposition of a constructive trust, that trust being imposed to reverse what would otherwise have amounted to an unjust enrichment. It was accepted by the court that her work on the farm, her domestic labour, and her 'spousal services' conferred a benefit upon him and the order which was made was to effect restitution.

On the facts of *Sorochan* it is possible, but by no means certain,[320] that an English court would also have held her entitled to an interest in the farm under some form of trust, on the basis that, although the house was already in his name when she moved in, the substantial work which she did helped to pay for it. Although it was initially doubted whether domestic labour alone, such as occurred in *Burns v. Burns*, would, even in Canada, have led to the imposition of a constructive trust,[321] it was accepted in *Peter v. Beblow*[322] that it could. The Canadian courts have, therefore, taken a broad view of what constitutes unjust enrichment, and are prepared to accept that contributions to the household as opposed to the house amounts to an unjust enrichment, and that, despite the contribution not being referable to specific property, a constructive trust can be imposed to effect restitution of the benefit conferred on the legal owner, and that trust can affect the house in which the couple lived.[323]

English law has accepted the general principle that an unjust enrichment should trigger a restitutionary response,[324] and it has been powerfully advocated that English law should embrace this approach to house-sharing cases.[325] It would, nevertheless, take a considerable extension to the attitude of the English courts to unjust enrichment for a person's contribution to the household, as opposed to a financial contribution to the purchase of the house to be recognized in this way, and it is doubtful whether such a step will be taken.[326]

PROPOSED LEGISLATION

In 2007, the Law Commission produced a Report advocating a new legislative regime to affect the property rights of certain types of cohabitant.[327] The types of person to whom the proposed legislation would be relevant would be persons who are living

[320] See *James v. Thomas* [2007] EWCA Civ. 1212, for a criticism of which see Indirect contributions, pp. 333–335.
[321] See M. Neave [1991] Mon. L.R. 17 at 47–49.
[322] (1993) 101 D.L.R. (4th) 621. See also *Kerr v. Boronow* (2011) 328 D.L.R.(4th) 577.
[323] For a persuasive argument favouring the adoption of this approach in England, see S. Wong (1999) 7 Fem. L.S. 42.
[324] *Lipkin Gorman (A Firm) v. Karpnale Ltd* [1992] A.C. 548.
[325] D. Hayton [1988] Conv. 259. See also C. Harpum (1982) 2 O.J.L.S. 277. For other thoughtful contributions to the debate, see S. Gardner (1993) 109 L.Q.R. 263; A. Bottomley in Bright and Dewar (eds), *Land Law: Themes and Perspectives* (Oxford: Oxford University Press, 1998) Chapter 8; J. Dewar, op. cit., Chapter 13; A. Barlow and C. Lund (1999) 19 L.S. 468.
[326] See the comments of Lord Walker of Getingthorpe in *Stack v. Dowden* [2007] 2 A.C. 423 at [28].
[327] (2007) Law Com. No. 307. See D. Hughes, M. Davis, and L. Jacklin [2008] Conv. 197.

together in a joint household and are neither married to each other nor civil partners.[328] No attempt to define this concept was made, the Commission being content
to adopt the 'six signposts' currently used in social security law to identify such couples.[329] Thereafter, there would also be eligibility criteria to satisfy before there would
be jurisdiction to make a property order. Before a cohabitant could apply for financial
relief under the proposed legislation, the couple must either have had children,[330] or,
to avoid frivolous applications, the couple must have cohabited for a specified period
of time. The time factor was left for Parliament to decide, the suggested range being
between two and five years.[331]

The meeting of the eligibility criteria would not, of itself, enable a cohabitant to
apply for financial relief. The notion of simply applying the jurisdiction to reallocate
property on a divorce or dissolution of a civil partnership to non-married couples
was rejected.[332] Instead, the claimant would need to prove that the respondent had
a retained benefit from the cohabitation or that she had suffered an economic disadvantage.[333] The former would include non-financial contributions, such as the care of
children, and the latter would encompass factors such as loss of earnings, something
that is a likely consequence of giving up employment to look after children, but could
also include the giving up of secure accommodation to move in with the respondent. Should these criteria be satisfied, it is then proposed that the courts would have
jurisdiction to make a range of property orders, including lump sum payments, property transfers, and pension sharing, subject to the guidelines as to the exercise of its
discretion.[334]

These proposals which, if implemented, are intended to replace the current legal
regime of implied trust, estoppel, and contract,[335] are, no doubt, contentious. Some
would see such reforms as dealing 'with the problems of past generations and not the
position of the modern woman'.[336] Others might object on the basis that, if a couple choose not to marry or enter into a civil partnership, they should not have law
imposed upon them, although it has been said, with much force, by one of the framers
of these proposals that, 'pushed too far, the autonomy argument may leave the vulnerable facing unjustified hardship on separation'.[337] Pending any legislative reform,
however, one way forward is for the courts to develop the scope of estoppel in the
resolution of disputes of this nature.[338] For such arguments to succeed, the courts will
need to proceed on the basis of reasonable expectations with regard to security of
accommodation,[339] which have been relied upon. In terms of what constitutes reliance,
the focus should include a consideration of what the claimant has given up, in terms of

---

[328] Ibid., at 3.14.   [329] Ibid., at 3.19.

[330] The existing jurisdiction to make orders under Sched. 1 to the Childrens Act 1989 was not considered
to be adequate to meet the needs of the situation: ibid., at 2.66–2.74.

[331] Ibid., at 3.63.   [332] Ibid., at 4.5–4.10.   [333] Ibid., at 4.33.   [334] Ibid., at 4.34–4.105.

[335] Ibid., at 4.42.   [336] R. Probert (2001) 13 C.L.F.Q. 275 at 286.

[337] S. Bridge [2007] Fam. Law 911 at 912.

[338] See M.P. Thompson in Jackson and Wilde (eds), *Contemporary Issues in Property Law* (Aldershot:
Ashgate, 1999), 135–137. See Family disputes, pp. 623–626.

[339] See C. Rotherham [2004] Conv. 268 at 284.

career opportunities and secure accommodation, prior to the commencement of the cohabitation:[340] a criterion similar to that proposed by the Law Commission of economic disadvantage. This, it is suggested, is a better avenue to explore than the law of trusts, with its necessary focus on financial contributions to the purchase of the house, particularly as there appears to be little prospect of the Law Commission's proposals being implemented within the foreseeable future.

---

[340] See the observations in *Grant v. Edwards* [1986] Ch. 638 at 648 *per* Nourse L.J.; at 657 *per* Sir Nicolas Browne-Wilkinson V.-C.

10

Co-ownership 2: The Legal Framework of Co-ownership

Whenever land is the subject of co-ownership, a trust is imposed. Originally, this was a trust for sale but now, it is simply a trust of land. The main reason why a trust is imposed is because it is essential to consider, separately, what the position of the co-owners is in law and at equity. This is because of the legal framework under which co-ownership takes place.[1]

JOINT TENANCIES

At one time, there were four different methods by which land could be co-owned. These were joint tenancies, tenancies in common, tenancies by entireties, and coparceny. The latter two forms of co-ownership are now virtually extinct. The former two categories remain important.

The essential nature of the joint tenancy is that the co-owners are, as a group, regarded as a single entity. Collectively, they own the entire interest in the property but, individually, they own nothing.[2] The significance of this is seen when one joint tenant dies. Because the deceased did not, prior to his death, own a specific share in the land, he has nothing to leave either by will, or upon intestacy. The consequence of this is the *ius accrescendi*: the right of survivorship.

The right of survivorship

The right of survivorship is the most significant feature of the joint tenancy. If A, B, and C are joint tenants, and A dies, the effect of the doctrine of survivorship is that the

---

[1] For a valuable discussion, see L. Tee in Tee (ed.), *Land Law Issues, Debates, Policy* (Cullompton: Willan Publishing, 2002), Chapter 5.

[2] It has recently been said that 'this esoteric concept is remote from the realities of life. It should be handled with care and treated with caution': *Burton v. Camden Borough Council* [2000] 1 All E.R. 943 at 947 *per* Lord Nicholls of Birkenhead.

ownership of the land devolves automatically upon B and C. A simply drops out of the picture. It is quite immaterial that A has purported to leave what he might perceive to be his share in the property to another person, D. A did not have a share in the property and, therefore, had nothing on which the will could operate. If B then dies, the same process of survivorship will take place and C will remain as the sole owner of the land. It is because of this process of survivorship that it has been said of each joint tenant that they 'each hold nothing and yet holds the whole'.[3] The last survivor will hold the land absolutely, for his own benefit; the joint tenants who pre-deceased him will have left nothing to their heirs.

Contemporaneous deaths

Because of the right of survivorship, it is important to know which of the joint tenants died first. When they die together, for example in a motor accident, then, this, as a matter of fact, may well be impossible to determine. At common law, this difficulty was resolved by holding that the property remained in joint tenancy in their respective heirs.[4] The matter is now regulated by statute, section 184 of the Law of Property Act 1925 providing that in these circumstances, the older is deemed to have died first, so that the property will devolve with the younger's estate.[5]

The four unities

Joint tenants are viewed by the law as being, collectively, one entity. For such a relationship to be created, it is necessary that what are known as the four unities are present. If the any of these unities are missing a tenancy in common will arise. The four unities are the unities of possession, interest, title, and time.

Possession

A feature common to co-ownership is that the co-owners, being simultaneously entitled to the land, each has the right to possess it. It can happen, however, that one joint tenant forcibly excludes the other from the property. In such circumstances, the tenant in occupation can be ordered to pay an occupation rent to the one who has been excluded from the property.[6]

Interest

As it is the nature of a joint tenancy that none of the joint tenants have specific interests in the property, it follows that one cannot have a larger interest than the other. Thus, if one co-owner has a life interest and the other an entailed interest, they cannot be joint tenants.[7] If there is an element of succession involved, then the co-owners can

---

[3] *Murray v. Hall* (1840) 7 C.B. 441 at 455.   [4] *Bradshaw v. Tolmin* (1784) Dick. 633.

[5] This rule does not apply in the case of a husband and wife who die intestate: Administration of Estates Act 1925, s. 46(3) as inserted into the Act by Intestates' Estates Act 1952, s. 1(4).

[6] See *Dennis v. McDonald* [1982] Fam. 63; *Re Pavlou* [1993] 1 W.L.R. 1046. See Rent, pp. 390–392.

[7] See Harpum, Bridge, and Dixon, *Megarry and Wade's Law of Real Property* (7th edn) (London: Sweet & Maxwell, 2008), 492.

be joint tenants. So, if property is left to A and B for life, remainder to B, then A and B can be joint tenants of the life interest, despite the fact that B also has a fee simple in remainder.[8]

As the joint tenants hold the title together, they must act together with respect to transactions affecting the legal title. This creates some difficulties with regard to lease-hold property.[9] If there is a break clause in the lease, whereby the tenants can bring the lease to a premature end, then, to be effective, the clause must be exercised by all the joint tenants.[10] Similarly, a purported surrender of the lease by only one of two joint tenants is ineffective.[11] The situation where a notice to quit is exercised may appear, at first sight, to be at odds with this principle, but is, in fact, consistent with it.

Notices to quit

In *Doe d. Aslin v. Summersett*,[12] one joint landlord served a notice to quit on a periodic tenant and this was held to be effective to terminate the lease, despite the other joint landlord not being a party to the notice. The reason for this is that, where there is a periodic tenancy,[13] each successive period operates as a renewal of the lease. For this to happen, each of the joint landlords must agree and, if one of them serves a notice to quit, this indicates that he does not do so.

The same reasoning has been applied in the case of the service of a notice to quit by one joint tenant. If one joint tenant serves a notice to quit on the landlord, then this is effective to end the tenancy despite the other joint tenants being opposed to this being done.[14] Such a course of action was taken in *Harrow London Borough Council v. Johnstone*.[15] Mr and Mrs Johnstone were joint tenants of a council house. He had obtained an injunction restraining her from using or threatening violence against him or to exclude or attempt to exclude him from the house. She then served a notice to quit on the council, who brought possession proceedings against him. The claim to possession succeeded in the House of Lords. The role of the injunction was to protect the husband's rights under the existing tenancy; it did not relate to its continued existence.

This result seems inevitable but can, nevertheless, cause hardship to the tenant who wishes to remain. Although it has been suggested that the tenant whose right to remain in occupation has been defeated in this way might have some remedy against

---

[8] *Wiscot's Case* (1599) 2 Co. Rep. 60b.   [9] See J. Martin [1978] Conv. 436.

[10] *Re Viola's Indenture of Lease* [1909] 1 Ch. 244. See also *Meyer v. Riddick* (1989) 60 P. & C.R. 50.

[11] *Leek and Moreland Building Society v. Clark* [1952] Q.B. 788. If the lease contains an option to renew, this option must also be exercised by all the joint tenants: ibid., at 793 *per* Somervell L.J.

[12] (1830) 1 B. & Ad. 135; *Parsons v. Parsons* [1983] 1 W.L.R. 1390.

[13] See Periodic tenancies, pp. 417–419.

[14] *Hammersmith and Fulham London Borough Council v. Monk* [1992] 1 A.C. 478; *Greenwich London Borough Council v. McGrady* (1983) 46 P. & C.R. 223. The doubt as to this expressed in *Howson v. Buxton* (1928) 97 L.J.K.B. 749 at 752 *per* Scrutton L.J. is unfounded, although supported by F. Webb [1983] Conv. 183.

[15] [1997] 1 W.L.R. 459. See M.P. Thompson [1997] Conv. 288.

the other joint tenant,[16] this view was rejected by the Court of Appeal in *Notting Hill Housing Trust v. Brackley*.[17] Any such remedy might, in any event, be of little consolation for the tenant and one suggestion which has been made to deal with this issue is for legislation to be enacted allowing the occupying tenant to take over the tenancy in a situation such as this.[18] Failing that, in cases of matrimonial disharmony, which is where this problem tends to occur, an undertaking can be sought from the spouse who might by a unilateral action terminate the tenancy not to do so, and that undertaking served on the landlord, or, if such an undertaking cannot be obtained, application can be made for an injunction to this effect.[19] Once the joint tenancy has been determined by the unilateral act of one party, however, this is not a disposition which a court can later set aside under section 37(2) of the Matrimonial Causes Act 1973,[20] so any injunctive relief must be sought before the notice to quit is served, because 'the stable door can be bolted if, but only if, the bolt is thrown before the horse has gone'.[21]

Human rights

The cases where one joint tenant has terminated a tenancy by the unilateral service of a notice to quit have involved public sector housing.[22] The sub-text in these cases is that the property is a family home. On the breakdown of a relationship, the mother leaves the property, taking any children with her, leaving the father remaining alone in accommodation which is suitable for occupation by a family. The local authority is prepared to provide accommodation for the mother and children, but also wishes to recover possession of the tenanted property from the individual occupier, who is now occupying a property which is too large for his needs.[23] The departing tenant is then sometimes advised by the council to serve a notice to quit, the effect of this being to end the tenancy and results, as a matter of property law, in the council having an absolute right to possession.

The scenario featured in a number of the cases which dealt with the question as to whether, if a public authority had an absolute right to possession, the occupier could, nevertheless present an argument that her Article 8 rights had been infringed: to argue that the making of a possession order was disproportionate. That debate has now been settled by the Supreme Court decision in *Manchester City Council v. Pinnock*,[24] where it was decided that such a defence was available. It has been argued, however, that the

---

[16] See *Parsons v. Parsons* [1983] 1 W.L.R. 1390 at 1400 *per* Mr Donald Rattee Q.C., but see the strong doubts expressed as to this in *Hammersmith and London Borough Council v. Monk* [1992] 1 A.C. 478, , *per* Lord Browne-Wilkinson.

[17] [2002] H.L.R. 276.   [18] L. Tee [1992] C.L.J. 218 at 220.

[19] *Bater v. Bater, Greenwich London Borough Council v. Bater* [1999] 4 All E.R. 944 at 952–953 *per* Thorpe L.J.

[20] *Newton Housing Trust v. Alsulaimen* [1999] 1 A.C. 313.

[21] *Bater v. Bater* [1999] 4 All E.R. 944, at 953 *per* Thorpe L.J.

[22] For a general discussion of this area, see M. Davis and D. Hughes [2004] Conv. 19.

[23] This was not actually so in the leading case of *Harrow London Borough Council v. Qazi* [2004] 1 A.C. 983, where another woman and her children had moved into the original property.

[24] [2010] UKSC 45. For a full discussion of this debate, see Chapter 3.

substantive law which allows one joint tenant to terminate a periodic tenancy without the other's consent is, itself, in breach of Article 8, the argument being that this principle is not compliant because 'it enables a person's interest in his or her home to be brought to an end without his or her knowledge and without recourse to an independent adjudicatory tribunal to seek due process of law.'[25] This, it is suggested, goes much too far.

In the first place, such a finding would apply not only to the public sector. The substantive law does not alter depending upon the identity of the parties to litigation,[26] and so a finding that one joint periodic tenant in the public sector could not effectively end the tenancy by the service of a notice to quit would apply equally to tenants in the private sector. This, as was pointed out in *London Borough of Wandsworth v. Dixon*[27] would have various repercussions. A change of this nature would mean that the departing tenant would continue to be jointly and severally liable for the rent, despite no longer wishing to live in the property. Alternatively, the remaining tenant would be liable for the whole rent, which would mean the substitution of a joint periodic tenancy for a sole tenancy in favour of the remaining tenant. There is nothing to suggest that the European Convention would justify the re-writing of legal agreements in this way, and much the better view is that the substantive law pertaining to this matter remains as it was.

Title

It follows rationally from the theoretical basis of the joint tenancy of no joint tenant having an individual interest to call his own that they all acquired their collective interest in the same way. This will include a conveyance, an assent, or a joint act of adverse possession.[28]

Time

Again, it follows from the nature of a joint tenancy that every joint tenant should acquire their interest in the property at the same time.

TENANCIES IN COMMON

The tenancy in common differs crucially from the joint tenancy. Each tenant in common owns a separate share in the property. That share is not physically demarcated and that is why a tenancy in common is often referred to as an undivided share in the property. It is perfectly possible and, indeed, not unusual, for these shares to be of

---

[25] M. Davis and D. Hughes [2010] Conv. 57 at 72. See also I. Loveland (2011) 2 E.H.L.R. 151 at 158.
[26] See M.P. Thompson [2011] Conv. 421 at 436–439.
[27] [2009] EWHC 27 (Admin) at [35]–[36] *per* H.H.J. Bidder.
[28] *Ward v. Ward* (1871) 9 Ch. App. 789.

different proportions. If A and B hold land as tenants in common, it may be the case that A has a one-quarter share and B a three-quarter share.

No right of survivorship

Because each tenant in common holds an undivided share in the property, there is no right of survivorship. On the death of one tenant in common, his share does not devolve automatically on the surviving tenants in common. Instead, it will pass either under the deceased's will or upon his intestacy.

Unity of possession

Each tenant in common has an undivided share in the property. Unless it is physically partitioned, each tenant in common has the right to occupy the property. One tenant in common does not have the right to exclude the others. This unity, the unity of possession, is the only unity necessary for a tenancy in common.

CO-OWNERSHIP AFTER 1925

From a conveyancing point of view, there is no doubt that the joint tenancy is far more convenient than the tenancy in common. The reason for this is that the existence of a tenancy in common can lead to the fragmentation of ownership and the proliferation of the number of people interested in the land. If, for example, A and B held land as tenants in common and A died leaving his share to C and D and then C died leaving his share to E and F then, to deal with the legal title, B, D, E, and F would all have to be parties to the conveyance, although E and F held only one-eighth shares in the property.[29] Had A and B been joint tenants then, on A's death, B would have been left as the sole owner of the property.

While, from a conveyancing point of view, there are distinct advantages to the property being held on a joint tenancy, from the point of view of the joint tenants themselves, the doctrine of survivorship may produce results which are unfair or inopportune. Who survives the longest is a matter of chance. If A and B are joint tenants, A may not want on his death for his 'share' of the property to go to B, his preference being to leave it to his own family. One is left with the position that convenience favours the joint tenancy and fairness the tenancy in common. The 1925 legislation sought to accommodate both aspirations and, in doing so, made it absolutely essential to distinguish between the position at law and in equity.

---

[29] See *Higgs v. Leshel Maryas Investment Co. Ltd* [2009] UKPC 47 at [10], where it was found that one legal co-owner of land in the Bahamas, where this legislation does not apply, held a 1/84th share in the property.

Legal joint tenancies

In what has been described as 'the greatest boon that the...statutes could confer',[30] the 1925 legislation abolished the legal tenancy in common. It is provided by section 1(6) of the Law of Property Act 1925 that, 'A legal estate is not capable of subsisting or of being created in an undivided share...' In addition to this reform, it was further provided that the maximum number of legal owners of land is four. If land is conveyed to more than four people, then the conveyance will operate to vest the land in the first four people named.[31] The effect of these provisions is that when land is conveyed to more than one person, they must hold the legal title as joint tenants. A legal tenancy in common is not possible.

Imposition of a trust

When land is subject to co-ownership then, at law, the co-owners must hold as joint tenants. In equity, however, the co-owners can be either joint tenants or tenants in common. The scheme of the legislation was in all cases of legal co-ownership to impose a trust on the land, so that if land was conveyed to A and B, they would, at law, be joint tenants. They would then hold the land on trust, the beneficiaries being either themselves or others.

Until the enactment of the Trusts of Land and Appointment of Trustees Act 1996, provision was made for the imposition of a trust for sale in certain cases of co-ownership. The position is now that, in those situations, a trust of land will be implied. The position where there is co-ownership of the legal estate is dealt with separately.[32]

Conveyance to tenants in common

If land is conveyed to tenants in common, the position is governed by section 34(2) of the Law of Property Act 1925, which provides for the legal estate to be held by the persons named in the conveyance as joint tenants in trust for the persons interested in the land. If land is conveyed to A and B as tenants in common, the effect of this is that A and B hold the legal estate as joint tenants subject to a trust of land for themselves as tenants in common. This may be represented as shown in Figure 1A:

LAW   [A and B]   Joint tenants

Trust of Land

EQUITY   [A] and [B]   Tenants in common

Fig. 1A Conveyance to tenants in common

---

[30] A.H. Cosway (1929) 15 Conv. (O.S.) 82.

[31] Trustee Act 1925, s. 34(2). For suggested reform of this in the case of residential tenancies, see Reform, p. 416.

[32] Where there is sole ownership at law and co-ownership in equity, see Implied trusts for sale, p. 289.

Devise to tenants in common

Where land is left by will to A and B as tenants in common, again the land is held upon trust but there is a difference in the identity of the trustees. In this case, the land vests in the testator's personal representatives, X and Y, who hold the land as trustees.[33] The position is as shown in Figure 1B:

Fig. 1B Devise to tenants in common

Conveyance to joint tenants

If property is conveyed to A and B as joint tenants, the land is, again, made subject to a trust of land but the manner in which this is done is somewhat tortuous. By section 36(1) of the Act the effect of the conveyance is to vest the legal estate in A and B on trust in like manner as if the land had been conveyed to them as tenants in common but not so as to sever their joint tenancy in equity, that is to change the position in equity from a joint tenancy into a tenancy in common. The outcome of this convoluted section is as shown in Figure 1C:

Fig. 1C Conveyance to joint tenants

This position looks curious because the position at law and in equity is identical. What is the purpose of a trust of land in a situation such as this? The main answer to this is that, although at the outset the position at law and in equity is identical, this may not remain the case. The equitable joint tenancy may, in the future, be converted into a tenancy in common. A purchaser, however, neither knows of this nor needs to know of it. Provided that he pays the purchase money to two trustees, he will overreach the

---

[33] Law of Property Act 1925, s. 34(3).

beneficial interests existing behind the trust[34] and so, as far as he is concerned, it does not matter if there has been fragmentation of ownership in equity. The task of dividing the proceeds of sale between the beneficiaries is the task of the trustees; provided that the money is paid to the trustees, the beneficial interests which exist behind the trust are of no concern to the purchaser.

SEVERANCE

As has been seen, the framework of co-ownership is that the legal title is held by joint tenants who hold the land on trust. In equity, the beneficiaries can be either joint tenants or tenants in common. This section is concerned with how one determines which form of tenancy has been created from the outset and then how one converts a joint tenancy into a tenancy in common.

Words of severance

The simplest method of establishing beyond doubt whether the initial holding is as a joint tenancy or a tenancy in common is for there to be an express declaration to that effect. If, at the outset, it is stated that the co-owners are to hold as tenants in common, then this will avoid disputes on the death of one of them as to whether the doctrine of survivorship applies. If the property is being sold by the surviving legal joint tenant, then a purchaser will be alerted that co-ownership may continue to subsist in equity and that it is necessary to appoint an additional trustee.[35]

While it is desirable, if it is intended to create a tenancy in common, to make this clear beyond argument by using these words, it is not essential to do so. Other expressions, these being termed words of severance, contained in a conveyance or a will have been held to have this effect. The following are examples of words sufficient to display an intention to create a tenancy in common:

'in equal shares';[36]

'share and share alike';[37]

'equally';[38]

'to be divided between'.[39]

---

[34] *City of London Building Society v. Flegg* [1988] A.C. 54. See Trusts for sale and overreaching, pp. 291–292.

[35] See Procedure on death, pp. 379–381.   [36] *Payne v. Webb* (1874) L.R. 19 Eq. 26.

[37] *Heathe v. Heathe* (1740) 2 A. & R. 121.

[38] *Lewen v. Dodd* (1595) Cro. Eli. 443; see also *Re Kilvert* [1957] Ch. 388.

[39] *Fisher v. Wigg* (1700) 1 P. Wms. 14.

These are examples of particular expressions which have been construed as giving rise to a tenancy in common. There is no particular magic in these words. Even if an expression such as one of those given above is used, a tenancy in common will not necessarily arise if it is evident from the rest of the document that this is not what was intended,[40] although the presumption in favour of a tenancy in common will be very strong.

The converse is also true; it is not essential to use words that have previously been held to have effected the creation of a tenancy in common in order to achieve this result. The task is to determine from the words of the document whether the general intention is to create a tenancy in common. In construing the documents, there is a judicial tendency to favour the finding of a tenancy in common,[41] so that if, for example, a will envisages only limited rights of survivorship between the co-owners,[42] or in the slightest degree indicates an intention that the co-owners should have shares in the property,[43] a tenancy in common will be created. Examples of this are where trustees are given power to apply income derived from the property for the maintenance of the beneficiaries,[44] or to advance capital to them,[45] in each case this being indicative that the beneficiaries have individual shares behind the trust.

Contradictory statements

It can happen, by inept draftsmanship, that a conveyance or will uses mutually contradictory expressions, such as to A and B as joint tenants in common in equal shares.[46] The traditional means of construction in cases like this was to apply the rule in *Slingsby's Case*,[47] whereby, in such cases, the first words would prevail in a deed but the last in a will. Although this rule of construction has been employed in modern times to resolve a dispute of this nature,[48] it seems unlikely to be taken as a reliable guide today,[49] so that in cases of ambiguity or contradictory statements,[50] it is likely that a tenancy in common will be held to have been created.[51]

---

[40] *Frewen v. Relfe* (1787) 2 Bro. C.C. 220 at 224 *per* Lord Thurlow L.C.

[41] *Re Woolley* [1903] 2 Ch. 206 at 211 *per* Joyce J.   [42] *Ryves v. Ryves* (1871) 11 Eq. 539.

[43] *Robertshaw v. Fraser* (1871) 6 Ch. App. 696 at 699 *per* Lord Hatherley L.C. See also *Surtees v. Surtees* (1871) 12 Eq. 400.

[44] *Re Ward* [1920] 1 Ch. 334.

[45] *L'Estrange v. L'Estrange* [1902] 1 I.R. 467; *Re Dunn* [1916] 1 Ch. 97.

[46] Described as 'a meaningless jumble of words': *Martin v. Martin* (1987) 54 P. & C.R. 238 at 240 *per* Millett J.

[47] (1587) 5 Co. Rep. 186.   [48] *Joyce v. Barker Bros (Builders) Ltd* (1980) 40 P. & C.R. 512.

[49] 'The nonsense of one man cannot be a guide for that of another': *Smith v. Coffin* (1795) 2 Hy. Bl. 444 at 450 *per* Buller J., cited in *Martin v. Martin* (1987) 54 P. & C.R. 238 at 242 *per* Millett J. See also *Slater v. Simm* [2007] EWHC 951 (Ch.) at [14] *per* Peter Smith J.

[50] For an unusual case where the parties agreed on a beneficial joint tenancy while a house was unsold, but a tenancy in common thereafter, see *Chopra v. Bindra* [2009] EWCA Civ. 203.

[51] *Slater v. Simm* [2007] EWHC 951 (Ch.) . See also *Carr v. Isard* [2006] EWHC 2095 (Ch.), where the headnote refers to the parties as being joint tenants in equal shares. In the judgment, they are referred to as beneficial joint tenants.

IMPLIED SEVERANCE

The potential consequence of the creation of tenancy in common is the fragmentation of ownership. This was never favoured at law; 'joint tenancies were favoured for the law loves not fractions of estates, nor to divide and multiply tenures'.[52] Equity, on the other hand, took a different view, principally because it sees the *ius accrescendi* as being potentially unfair. Accordingly, the traditional approach of equity is, where there is any doubt, to lean in favour of a tenancy in common.[53] In particular, there are a number of situations where equity will presume that a tenancy in common has been created.

Partnerships

When two people buy land together as a commercial investment, it is highly improbable that they intend the doctrine of survivorship to operate, so that the survivor of them would end up as the absolute owner. They would wish their shares to devolve upon their own families. Equity recognizes this by presuming that they originally took the property as tenants in common. A joint tenancy is seen as being inappropriate between merchants, so that land acquired for business purposes is presumed to be held on a tenancy in common. If, however, business partners acquire land for purposes unconnected with commerce, there is no presumption that they hold that land as tenants in common.[54] For this presumption to arise, it is not necessary that there is a formal partnership in existence. In *Malayan Credit Ltd v. Jack Chia-Mph Ltd*,[55] two businessmen together took a lease of commercial property. The areas which they occupied were of different sizes and, to reflect this, they paid different amounts in rent. The Privy Council held that they held the lease on a presumed tenancy in common rather than as joint tenants.

Mortgages

For the same reason that business partners are presumed to take as tenants in common, there is a strong presumption that lenders of money take their mortgage security as tenants in common.[56] Although it has been said that this presumption can be rebutted,[57] a joint account clause in the mortgage does not have this effect, it being held

---

[52] *Fisher v. Wigg* (1700) 1 Salk 391 at 392 *per* Holt C.J. (dissenting).

[53] *Burgess v. Rawnsley* [1975] Ch. 429 at 438 *per* Lord Denning M.R.

[54] *Lake v. Craddock* (1732) 3 P. Wms. 157; *Lyster v. Dolland* (1792) 1 Ves. Jun. 432; *Darby v. Darby* (1856) 3 Drew. 495.

[55] [1986] A.C. 549.   [56] *Petty v. Styward* (1632) 1 Ch. Rep. 57; *Vickers v. Cowell* (1839) 1 Beav. 529.

[57] *Steeds v. Steeds* (1889) 22 Q.B.D. 537 at 541 *per* Willes J., instancing trustees, an example which relates to severance at law, which is no longer possible.

that the purpose of the clause was to protect the purchaser rather than to indicate an intention to create a joint tenancy.[58]

Unequal contributions

A beneficial interest in land can be acquired by a contribution to its purchase. Where an interest is acquired under a resulting trust, then it is presumed that the respective size of each party's share will be commensurate to the size of their contribution and, if they contribute unequally, they will have unequal beneficial shares in the property and, consequently, take as tenants in common. If, however, the property is bought as a shared home, and that property is put into joint names, the presumption now is 'that the parties intended a joint tenancy both in law and in equity'.[59] If the parties contribute equally to the purchase of the property, the presumption is that they take as joint tenants.[60]

Rebutting the presumption

In each of the above situations, it should be remembered that there is only a presumption that there is a beneficial tenancy in common and, like all presumptions, it is capable of being rebutted. The most straightforward way of rebutting this presumption is if there is a statement in the conveyance or the will that a joint tenancy is intended.[61] So, in *Barton v. Morris*,[62] a cohabiting couple bought a cottage in their joint names, the purpose being to use it for commercial purposes as a guest house. As the conveyance declared that they held the property as joint tenants, the normal presumption of a tenancy in common was displaced. Similarly, in *Goodman v. Gallant*,[63] a couple had contributed unequally to the purchase price of a house but, because the conveyance declared that they were to hold as joint tenants, this statement was effective to rebut the presumption of a tenancy in common, which would otherwise have arisen.

In the absence of a claim to rectification,[64] a declaration by the parties that they are to hold the property as beneficial joint tenants is conclusive. A somewhat unfortunate distinction is made, however, if the parties make a declaration that the survivor of them is able to give a valid receipt for capital moneys. Such a declaration is apt to indicate to a purchaser that the property has been conveyed to joint tenants but, as

---

[58] *Powell v. Broadhurst* [1901] 2 Ch. 160; *Re Jackson* (1887) 34 Ch.D. 732.

[59] *Jones v. Kernott* [2011] UKSC 53 at [25] per Lord Walker and Lady Hale. Contrast *Laskar v. Laskar* [2008] EWCA Civ. 347. See Presumption of joint beneficial ownership, p. 310.

[60] *Lake v. Gibson* (1729) 1 Eq. Cas. Ab. 391; *Chandler v. Clark* [2003] 1 P. & C.R. 15.

[61] See *Morris v. Barrett* (1829) 3 Y. & J. 384. See, also, *Ward v. Ward* (1871) 9 Ch. App. 789 (joint adverse possession of a farm, held that they took as joint tenants).

[62] [1995] 1 W.L.R. 1257.

[63] [1986] Fam. 106. See also *Pink v. Lawrence* (1977) 36 P. & C.R. 98; *The Anglo Eastern Trust Ltd, Kermanshahchi* [2003] EWHC 1939 (Ch.).

[64] See *Thames Guarantee Ltd v. Campbell* [1985] Q.B. 210. For the possible impact of undue influence, see *Knott v. Day* [2004] EWHC 484 (Ch.).

between the parties themselves, is not conclusive in this respect.[65] Where two parties are applying to be registered as joint proprietors, the current form which has to be completed to make such an application is drafted in such a way as to make the intentions of the parties clear,[66] and so this issue may not reappear.

ACTS OF SEVERANCE

If a beneficial joint tenancy is created at the outset, it is open to the parties, subsequently, to convert that joint tenancy into a tenancy in common. This process is termed severance. The ability to sever a joint tenancy and to create a tenancy in common exists, so it is said, so that if one joint tenant has an 'ill opinion of his own life', he can sever the joint tenancy to ensure that survivorship does not work any hardship.[67]

For severance to take place, it is essential that the process occurs during the lifetime of the joint tenancy. A joint tenancy cannot be severed by will.[68] This latter point is illustrated by *Carr-Glynn v. Frearsons (A Firm)*.[69] A testatrix instructed solicitors to leave her 'share' in a house to her niece. She held the house on a beneficial joint tenancy with her nephew. On her death, it was discovered that the joint tenancy had not been severed with the result that her nephew became solely entitled to the house by survivorship. The solicitors were held liable in negligence to the niece for failing to ensure that severance had occurred prior to the testatrix's death, action which was necessary to ensure that she had a share in the house to leave.

Methods of severance

The process of severance is governed by section 36(2) of the Law of Property Act 1925, which first provides that no severance of a joint tenancy of a legal estate so as to create a tenancy in common shall be permissible but that this subsection does not affect the right of a joint tenant to sever his equitable interest whether or not the legal estate is vested in the joint tenants. The means of severance are then detailed as follows:

'Provided that, where a legal estate (not being settled land) is vested in joint tenants beneficially, and any tenant desires to sever the joint tenancy in equity, he shall give to the other joint tenants a notice in writing of such desire or do such other acts or things as would, in the case of personal estate, have been effectual to sever the tenancy in equity, and thereupon the land shall be held in trust on terms which would have been requisite for giving effect to the beneficial interests if there had been an actual severance.'

---

[65] See *Harwood v. Harwood* [1991] 2 F.L.R. 274; *Huntingford v. Hobbs* [1993] 1 F.L.R. 376; *Stack v. Dowden* [2007] 2 A.C. 432.
[66] See Express declarations of ownership, pp. 306–307.
[67] *Cray v. Willis* (1729) 2 P. Wms. 529.
[68] See, e.g. *Re Caines (dec'd)* [1978] 1 W.L.R. 540 at 545 *per* Sir Robert Megarry V.-C.
[69] [1999] Ch. 326.

It is proposed, first, to deal with the statutory method of severance and then with the methods of severance at common law, which have been preserved by the Act.

Statutory severance

The statutory form of severance makes reference to a situation where the legal estate is 'vested in joint tenants beneficially' which, it has been argued, on a strict construction could be interpreted to mean that the legal and beneficial interests are the same. If this view is correct, it would lead to the result that, if A and B hold on trust for A, B, and C or for A, B, and Y, then the beneficial joint tenants would not be empowered to sever the joint tenancy by this method,[70] a result which would be unfortunate. It is suggested that such a conclusion can be avoided, however, when regard is had to the opening words of the subsection, which provides that 'this subsection does not affect the right of a joint tenant... to sever a joint tenancy in an equitable interest whether or not the legal estate is vested in the joint tenants'. So it is thought that, except for situations specifically excepted, equitable joint tenants can use this method to sever the joint tenancy by use of the statutory method, regardless of the ownership of the legal estate.[71]

Form of notice

To effect severance using the statutory notice, it is necessary that the notice be served upon all of the joint tenants but it is not essential that it complies with any particular form. What is required is the statement of an unequivocal intention to sever.[72] In *Re Draper's Conveyance*,[73] an affidavit in support of a divorce petition asked for the property to be sold and that the proceeds of sale be divided equally. This was held to be sufficient to effect a severance of the beneficial joint tenancy. In contrast, in *Harris v. Goddard*,[74] a married couple held their house as beneficial joint tenants. When their marriage was foundering, a divorce petition was submitted which sought relief in the terms of section 24 of the Matrimonial Causes Act 1973 asking that such order may be made by way of transfer of property in respect of the matrimonial home as may be considered to be just. Shortly before the date of the hearing, the husband died and the issue was whether or not the beneficial joint tenancy had been severed prior to his death. If not, the doctrine of survivorship would operate. It was held that as the petition did

---

[70] Harpum, Bridge, and Dixon, op. cit., 510.

[71] Severance can also be effected using this method even if the statutory notice does not comply with a condition as to severance appearing on the conveyance: *Grindal v. Hooper* [1999] E.G.C.S. 150. See N.P. Gravells [2000] Conv. 461.

[72] For an example of an equivocal and, therefore, ineffective notice, see *Gore and Snell v. Carpenter* (1990) 60 P. & C.R. 456 at 462 *per* Judge Blackett-Ord.

[73] [1969] 1 Ch. 486. The doubts expressed as to the correctness of this decision in *Nielson-Jones v. Fedden* [1975] Ch. 222 at 236 *per* Walton J. were themselves disapproved in *Harris v. Goddard* [1983] 1 W.L.R. 1203 at 1210 *per* Lawton L.J.

[74] [1983] 1 W.L.R. 1203. See S. Coneys [1984] Conv. 148.

not assert a present claim to a share of the property,[75] no severance had occurred, with the result that the wife became solely entitled to the property. Conversely, if a notice asserts the ownership of a half share in the property, but is content for that share to be realized by a later disposal of it, this document will suffice to effect a severance.[76]

Husband and wife

An additional feature of the dispute in *Harris v. Goddard* was the express acceptance of the proposition that there was no restriction on the ability of a husband and wife to sever a joint tenancy. Somewhat surprisingly, this had previously been uncertain owing to a *dictum* of Lord Denning M.R. in *Bedson v. Bedson*[77] that, if a matrimonial home is used as a dwelling, this was not possible. Although this view was described, perhaps without the usual judicial courtesy, as being 'without the slightest foundation in law or in equity',[78] it was repeated six years later.[79] This caused some difficulty, as the opposite, and orthodox, view was consistently preferred at first instance[80] and so the authoritative endorsement in *Harris v. Goddard*[81] of the proposition that there is no theoretical difficulty in either a husband or wife severing a joint tenancy is to be welcomed. It is also logical, as there is no impediment to a husband and wife being beneficial tenants in common in the first place.

Service by post

A statutory notice of severance can be sent by post. If it is sent by registered or recorded delivery, it is regarded as being sufficiently served if it is addressed to the person on whom it should be served and has not been returned as undelivered to the Post Office.[82] Even if it is not sent by recorded delivery, it is regarded as being sufficiently served if the letter is delivered to the address of the recipient, or his last known place of business, this latter expression, for no obvious reason, having been held not to include a person's work address.[83] It does not matter if the letter is not received, even if the sender, upon delivery destroys it,[84] although, if it is intercepted prior to delivery, it would seem that there has not been an effective delivery.

---

[75] See also *Hunter v. Babbage* [1994] 2 F.L.R. 806; *Edwards v. Hastings* [1996] N.P.C. 87; *Chandler v. Clark* [2003] 1 P. & C.R. 15.

[76] *Wallbank v. Price* [2007] EWHC 3001(Ch.). See also *Quigley v. Masterson* [2011] UKHC 2529 (Ch.) (Application to the Court of Protection).

[77] [1965] 2 Q.B. 666 at 678. For the expression of the opposite view, see *Smith v. Smith* [1945] 1 All E.R. 584 at 586 *per* Denning J. For devastating criticism of Lord Denning's later opinion, see R.E.M. (1966) 82 L.Q.R. 29.

[78] [1965] 2 Q.B. 666 at 690 *per* Russell L.J.

[79] *Jackson v. Jackson* [1971] 1 W.L.R. 1539 at 1542 *per* Lord Denning M.R.

[80] *Radziej v. Radziej* [1968] 1 W.L.R. 1928; *Re Draper's Conveyance* [1969] 1 W.L.R. 486; *Cowcher v. Cowcher* [1972] 1 W.L.R. 425.

[81] [1983] 1 W.L.R. 1203 at 1208 *per* Lawton L.J.

[82] Law of Property Act 1925, s. 196(4); *Re 88 Berkeley Road, N.W. 9* [1971] Ch. 648.

[83] *Quigley v. Masterson* [2011] EWHC 2529 (Ch.).

[84] *Kinch v. Bullard* [1999] 1 W.L.R. 423. See also *Wandsworth London Borough Council v. Attwell* [1996] 1 E.G.L.R. 57; *Blundell v. Frogmore Investments Ltd* [2002] EWCA Civ. 573.

Severance at common law

In addition to introducing a new method of severing a joint tenancy by a unilateral notice of severance, section 36(2) of the Law of Property Act 1925 expressly preserved as a means of severing a joint tenancy such things as would prior to the Act have been sufficient to sever a joint tenancy in personal property. The classic statement of the means of effecting a severance at common law was given by Sir William Page-Wood V.-C. in *Williams v. Hensman*.[85] He said:

'A joint tenancy may be severed in three ways: in the first place, an act of any one of the persons interested operating on his own share may create a severance as to that share. The right of each joint-tenant is a right by survivorship only in the event of no severance having taken place of the share which is claimed under the *jus accrescendi*. Each one is at liberty to dispose of his own interest in such manner as to sever it from the joint fund— losing, of course at the same time, his own right of survivorship. Secondly, a joint tenancy may be severed by mutual agreement. And, in the third place, there may be a severance by any course of dealing sufficient to intimate that the interests of all were mutually treated as constituting a tenancy in common. When the severance depends upon an inference of this kind without any express act of severance, it will not suffice to rely on an intention, with respect to the particular share, declared only behind the backs of the other persons interested.'

The three methods of severance described above will be considered in turn, together with a fourth method of severance, homicide.

Operating on one's own share

The most clear-cut method of severance is to alienate one's own interest in the property.[86] Such an alienation must be during the lifetime of the joint tenant and cannot be by will.[87] Such alienation may be involuntary as on bankruptcy, the effect of which is that the joint tenancy will be severed in equity, it not being possible for this to occur at law, and the share of the bankrupt will vest in the trustee in bankruptcy.[88] To constitute an act whereby one operates on one's own share, it is not essential that a formal alienation occurs. If one joint tenant contracts to sell his interest, this will effect a severance of the joint tenancy,[89] and this includes contracts to settle after-acquired

---

[85] (1861) 1 J. & H. 546 at 557–558.

[86] See *Goddard v. Lewis* (1909) 101 L.T. 528, where many of the authorities are collected.

[87] It is arguable that if one joint tenant shows the other joint tenant his will, whereby he purports to leave his 'share' of the property to another, this may amount to the service of a statutory notice of severance because, although one cannot sever a joint tenancy by a will which operates on death, the will is, itself, a written document whereby the testator is asserting an entitlement to an immediate share in the property. Cf., however, *Carr v. Isard* [2006] EWHC 2095 (Ch.).

[88] Insolvency Act 1986, s.306. See *Morgan v. Marquis* (1853) 9 Exch. 145.

[89] *Brown v. Randle* (1796) 3 Ves. 256. If they all agree to sell the property this, apparently, will not of itself constitute severance: *Re Hayes' Estate* [1920] I.R. 207. In such circumstances it would be normal, however, to find an intention to divide up the proceeds of sale and this agreement should amount to severance: *Morris v. Barrett* (1829) 3 Y. & J. 384.

property,[90] that is property which a person does not yet own but anticipates receiving in the future.

Severance by one joint tenant deliberately purporting to deal with his own share in the property is rare. Severance under this head can occur, however, when one joint tenant purports to deal with the legal estate, as when one legal co-owner purports to grant a lease, such a lease being binding upon his own interest.[91] Such a transaction is unusual. Hopefully also unusual is the situation where one joint tenant procures the forgery of the other joint tenant's signature to the mortgage. The effect of this is that the beneficial joint tenancy is severed and the mortgage takes effect only against the forger's beneficial share in the property.[92]

One matter on which there is some uncertainty is whether an oral statement by one joint tenant to the other of a desire to sever is sufficient for this purpose. Although there is support for the view that this would be effective,[93] the better view is that it would not be. It would make little sense to introduce, by statute, a new method of severance by the service of a written notice of severance, if this could already be done orally.[94]

Mutual agreement and course of dealings

Although these are separate methods of severance[95] they are closely related and it is convenient to treat them together. To sever a joint tenancy by mutual agreement, it is not necessary that a binding agreement be entered into. In the leading case of *Burgess v. Rawnsley*,[96] an oral contract between two beneficial joint tenants was entered into for one to buy the other's share in the house. Despite the contract being unenforceable, this contract was held to have severed the beneficial joint tenancy.

In cases where there is a completed agreement, such as where the joint tenants deal with the property in question by the making of mutual wills,[97] there is little difficulty in finding a mutual agreement to sever. The position is less clear when final agreement is lacking. Certainly, it would not appear to be necessary for the parties actually to form a contract, because 'the significance of an agreement is not that it binds the parties; but it serves as an indication of a common intention to sever . . .'.[98] If the facts of

---

[90] *Re Hewett* [1894] 1 Ch. 363.

[91] See *Cantanzarati v. Whitehouse* (1981) 55 F.L.R. 426. See L. Fox [2000] Conv. 208.

[92] *First National Securities Ltd v. Hegarty* [1985] Q.B. 850. See also *Re Ng* [1998] 2 F.L.R. 386 *Mortgage Corpn v. Shaire* [2001] Ch. 743. See S. Nield [2001] Conv. 462.

[93] *Hawkesley v. May* [1956] 1 Q.B. 304 at 311 *per* Havers J.

[94] *Nielson-Jones v. Fedden* [1975] Ch. 222 at 236–237 *per* Walton J. Although the actual decision in this case has been disapproved, this aspect of the judgment seems to be right; *Burgess v. Rawnsley* [1975] Ch. 429 at 448 *per* Sir John Pennycuick.

[95] [1975] Ch. 429 at 447; *Hunter v. Babbage* [1994] 2 F.L.R. 806 at 812 *per* Mr John McDonnell Q.C., sitting as a Deputy High Court judge. See also H. Conway [2009] Conv. 67 commenting on the Australian decision in *Saleeba v. Wilke* [2007] QSC 298.

[96] [1975] Ch. 429. See also *Hunter v. Babbage* [1994] 2 F.L.R. 806, where severance occurred by mutual agreement despite specific performance not necessarily being available.

[97] *Re Wilford's Estate* (1879) 1 Ch.D. 267; *Re Heys* [1914] P. 192.

[98] *Burgess v. Rawnsley,* [1975] Ch. 429 at 446 *per* Sir John Pennycuick.

Burgess v. Rawnsley were to occur today, the lack of writing would not have resulted in the formation of a valid, but unenforceable contract; there would be no contract at all.[99] Yet, it would seem from the fact that there was a concluded agreement that it would still be held that severance had occurred. If the negotiations have not been concluded, however, the position is uncertain.

In *Burgess v. Rawnsley*, Sir John Pennycuick made it clear that, in his view, 'negotiations which, although not otherwise resulting in an agreement, [may] indicate a common intention that the joint tenancy should be regarded as severed'.[100] He also said, however, that one 'could not ascribe to joint tenants an intention to sever merely because one offers to buy out the other for £X and the other makes a counter-offer of £Y'.[101] The problem with this latter view, however, is that it is difficult to see why not. If the two joint tenants are bargaining over the price of the share in the property then, for their conversation to have any meaning, each must regard the other as having a share which is capable of being sold and this should, it is thought, be sufficient evidence of an mutual intention to have separate shares in the property. The decision in *Gore and Snell v. Carpenter*,[102] where abortive negotiations were held not to effect severance does, at first sight, appear to go against this view but the facts were unusual, in that the co-owners were joint tenants of two houses and the negotiations concerned whether, on their separation, each party should become the sole owner of one house each. The negotiations were not, therefore, related to each other's share in the property; had they been so, then it is thought that the better view is that these negotiations should have caused severance to occur.[103] This is particularly the case, when the trend of recent authority supports the policy that a court should lean in favour of severance when it properly can.[104]

Inferred agreements

Where the parties have not concluded an express agreement to sever the joint tenancy, such an agreement can be inferred from the conduct of the parties. For this to occur, each party must have capacity to enter an agreement.[105] Despite the judicial tendency to lean in favour of finding a tenancy in common,[106] the onus of proof is on the person arguing that severance has occurred[107] and to establish the requisite intention the evidence will be sifted carefully and it may transpire that acts which appear to be acts of severance were not carried out with the requisite intention. So, in

---

[99] Law of Property (Miscellaneous Provisions) Act 1989, s. 2.   [100] [1975] Ch. 429 at 447.
[101] Ibid.
[102] (1990) 60 P. & C.R. 456. See also *McDowell v. Hirschfield Lipson v. Rumnery* [1992] 2 F.L.R. 126, where the negotiations in the run up to a divorce were regarded as similar, on the facts, to *Harris v. Goddard* [1983] 1 W.L.R. 1203.
[103] See *Davis v. Smith* [2011] EWCA Civ. 1603.
[104] *Quigley v. Masterson* [2011] UKHC 2529 (Ch.) at [35] *per* Henderson J.
[105] *Re Wilks* [1891] 3 Ch. 59 at 61–62 *per* Stirling J.
[106] See *Burgess v. Rawnsley* [1975] Ch. 429 at 438 *per* Lord Denning M.R.
[107] *Re Denny* [1947] L.J.R. 1029; *Greenfield v. Greenfield* (1970) 38 P. & C.R. 570.

Greenfield v. Greenfield,[108] the property was physically partitioned but severance was held not to have occurred because it appeared that the parties were happy for the doctrine of survivorship to continue to operate. Perhaps, more controversially, in *Barton v. Morris*,[109] joint tenants of a guest house put the proceeds from the business into their separate names and it was, nevertheless, held that the joint tenancy had not been severed. The reason for the decision was that this manner of dealing with the money was employed for tax reasons, although it is questionable whether such evidence should have been admissible to rebut the normal inference which would have been drawn from dealing with the money in this way.[110]

An interesting decision in the context of severance occurred in *Carr v. Isard*.[111] A married couple were beneficial joint tenants of a house. On the same day in 1967 they, separately, saw a solicitor to make their wills, in each case purporting to deal with their interest in the house. The wills were similar but not identical, and it was accepted that there was insufficient evidence to establish an intention to make mutual wills.[112] Neither was there any evidence that they had given their respective instructions in each other's presence. On these facts Mr Michael Furniss Q.C. held that there had been no evidence of an agreement between the parties to sever the joint tenancy,[113] and so, on the death of the husband, his widow was held to be entitled, by survivorship, to the entire beneficial ownership of the house. This seems unfortunate, in that both parties seemed clearly to be acting in the belief that they had separate interests in the property, and it does little credit to the law that their perceptions are thwarted by an overly legalistic attitude to an area of law which affects many people, but where its intricacies are not really appreciated.

Imputed agreements

None of the authorities on the severance of a joint tenancy were cited in *Jones v. Kernott*.[114] A couple originally owned their house, Badger Hall Avenue, as legal and beneficial joint tenants. When they separated, the house was originally put up for sale, but did not sell. Thereafter, they cashed in a joint life insurance policy, the proceeds of which were used for him to put down a deposit on a house which was transferred into his sole name. She remained in Badger Hall Avenue, which remained in joint names, for the next fifteen years, and she paid all the mortgage payments during that period. The Supreme Court held that the beneficial ownership of Badger Hall Avenue was shared in proportion of 90 per cent to her and 10 per cent to him.[115] Although there was not express agreement between them as to the position with regard to Badger Hall Avenue, the Supreme Court held that a logical inference from their behaviour was

---

[108] Ibid.   [109] [1985] 1 W.L.R. 1257.

[110] See P.J. Clarke [1985] All E. Rev. 187 at 198. See also, in a related context, *Tinsley v. Milligan* [1994] 1 A.C. 340.

[111] [2006] EWHC 2095 (Ch.).   [112] Ibid. at [10] *per* Mr Michael Furniss Q.C.

[113] Surely, it could have been inferred that the couple had discussed the disposition of the house, which should have amounted to a severance.

[114] [2011] UKSC 53.   [115] This aspect of the decision is discussed fully in Chapter 9.

that his interest in the property should crystallize at the time when their new plan was formed.[116] This inferred, or imputed, agreement was, therefore, sufficient to sever the joint tenancy, leaving the ultimate shares in the property to be determined in the light of their conduct over the forthcoming years. While it is to be regretted that there was no discussion of the issue of severance, it may be indicative of a more relaxed approach to finding that this has occurred and enable judges to find that abortive negotiations between the joint tenants for one to buy the other out should be regarded as sufficient to effect a severance.

Homicide

A final method of severance not referred to in *Williams v. Hensman*, where severance will occur, is where one joint tenant kills another. The normal rule at common law is that a person who kills another is not permitted to benefit from that person's death. In the case of a murderer who stands to inherit under the will of his victim, to prevent him from profiting in this way, the killer will hold the legacy on a constructive trust.[117] This principle, known as the forfeiture principle, has, except for the case of murder, been modified by legislation, so that, in appropriate cases, the court may give relief against forfeiture under section 2(5) of the Forfeiture Act 1982.

A number of difficulties arose in relation to the forfeiture rule. The first reflected the fact that the moral culpability involved in the involvement of another's death can vary considerably, from premeditated murder to an accidental killing. One of the problems was to determine when the rule operated in the first place and, in particular, in cases where the killer was not considered to be deserving of serious punishment, whether the forfeiture rule still operated.[118] Because the courts now have the jurisdiction to grant relief from the operation of the rule, it is no longer necessary to be too concerned as to this issue as, in the exercise of the jurisdiction under the Act, the courts will have regard principally to the culpability of the offender.[119]

A second difficulty relates to the effect of the forfeiture rule. If one joint tenant kills another, in circumstances when the rule applies, in the Commonwealth, it has long been accepted that the survivor cannot benefit by taking the whole interest by survivorship but will hold subject to a constructive trust, with the result that the estate of the deceased is entitled to a half share.[120] The homicide does not automatically cause the beneficial joint tenancy to be severed. Instead, the doctrine of survivorship operates in the normal way and a constructive trust is imposed to deprive the killer of the gain which he would otherwise have made from the killing.[121] In *Re K*

---

[116] [2011] UKSC 53 at [48] *per* Lord Walker and Lady Hale.

[117] See, e.g., *Re Crippen* [1911] P. 108. For valuable discussions of this area of the law, see T.G. Youden (1973) 89 L.Q.R. 235; T.K. Earnshaw and P.J. Pace (1974) 37 M.L.R. 481.

[118] See *R. v. National Insurance Commissioner, ex parte Connor* [1981] Q.B. 758.

[119] *Dunbar v. Plant* [1998] Ch. 412 (suicide pact). See M.P. Thompson [1997] Conv. 45.

[120] *Schobelt v. Barber* (1967) 60 D.L.R. (2d) 519; *Re Pechar* [1969] N.Z.L.R. 574; *Rasmanis v. Jurewitsch* [1968] 2 N.S.W.R. 166.

[121] See Youdan, loc. cit., 254–255; Earnshaw and Pace, loc. cit., 488–492.

(deceased),[122] however, it was conceded that a wife who was guilty of the manslaughter of her husband had, thereby, severed the joint tenancy which had existed between them, although the court exercised its statutory jurisdiction to relieve against forfeiture, so that she could take under his will.

This concession is perhaps to be regretted in that it can work unfairly in situations where there are more than two beneficial joint tenants. If A, B, and C are beneficial joint tenants and A kills B, under the Commonwealth approach, survivorship would operate, so that the beneficial ownership would devolve upon A and C. A constructive trust would then be imposed upon A, which would then sever the joint tenancy between him and C, leaving C with a half share in the property. Under the English approach, however, if the killing itself occasioned the forfeiture, then C would have only a one-third share in the property. To avoid this result, which seems to be unfair to C, it is suggested that the better approach to this issue is that followed elsewhere in the Commonwealth, where homicide is not regarded as a means of severing a joint tenancy and the problem of unjust enrichment is resolved by the imposition of a constructive trust.

The effect of severance

Before a beneficial joint tenancy is severed, none of the joint tenants have quantifiable interests in the property. Between them, they own the whole interest and the law regards them as together constituting one person. If severance occurs, then, in principle, the joint tenants should have equal interests in the property. At one time, there was doubt as to this because of *dicta* in *Benson v. Benson*,[123] which envisaged ownership in unequal shares after severance had occurred. This was contrary to principle and was repudiated in *Goodman v. Gallant*,[124] where it was held, first, that in the absence of a claim to rectification,[125] an express declaration of a beneficial joint tenancy is conclusive and, secondly, that upon severance the joint tenants will then hold the property as tenants in common in equal shares, regardless of the sizes of their initial contributions to the purchase of the property.

This is, however, subject to an agreement to the contrary. In *Singla v. Brown*,[126] a notice of severance was served, which stated that the property would thereafter be held as tenants in common in unequal shares, ninety-nine per cent for her and one per cent for him; this reflecting the fact that he had contributed virtually nothing to the purchase of the property, which had been put into joint names in the first place at the insistence of the mortgage company.[127] He agreed to this, and this division of the equitable interest was upheld. In the absence of any such agreement, or a successful

[122] [1986] Fam. 180.
[123] [1965] 2 Q.B. 666 at 681–682 *per* Lord Denning M.R.; at 685 *per* Davies L.J.
[124] [1986] Fam. 106.
[125] See *Thames Guarantee Ltd v. Campbell* [1985] Q.B. 210 at 227–229 *per* Slade L.J.
[126] [2007] EWHC 405 (Ch.).
[127] Owing to the high standard of proof required, although still somewhat surprisingly, no claim to rectification was pursued: ibid., at [23]–[26] *per* Mr Thomas Ivory Q.C.

claim to rectification, however, the general rule will apply and the parties will share the beneficial interest equally.[128]

If there are only two joint tenants, then severance by one necessarily effects total severance of the joint tenancy. Where there are more than two joint tenants, however, this result does not automatically follow. Suppose a situation where A, B, C, and D hold the legal title on trust for themselves as beneficial joint tenants. A then serves a notice of severance on the other three. This will not affect the position at law, but will operate to sever the beneficial joint tenancy between A and the others. It will not affect the position as between B, C, and D, who will remain, as between themselves, joint tenants. A will have a one-quarter share, and B, C, and D will, collectively, own a three-quarter share. The position is illustrated in Figure 2A:

Fig. 2A Example of severance where there are more than two joint tenants

If A then dies leaving his property to E, as there can be no severance of the legal joint tenancy, the doctrine of survivorship will operate. As he has severed in equity, his one-quarter share can now pass under his will. The position would be as shown in Figure 2B:

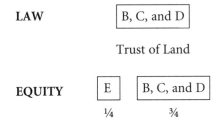

Fig. 2B Position on death of A

Procedure on death

A legal joint tenancy can never be severed but an equitable joint tenancy can be. Suppose a situation where A and B together bought a home in 1980 and that home

---

[128] See also *Hunter v. Babbage* [1994] 2 F.L.R. 806.

was conveyed to them as beneficial joint tenants. In 2012, B died. The effect of this, at law, is that A would, by survivorship, be the sole legal owner. What a purchaser could not know, however, was the position in equity. Prior to B's death, the beneficial joint tenancy might have been severed and his share in the house passed to C. The situation then is that, although A is the sole owner at law, there remains co-ownership in equity and A, acting alone, could not give a good title. On the other hand, however, if severance had not occurred, then A would be the sole owner at law and in equity and perfectly entitled to deal with the property. The difficulty is that, in the nature of things, it is difficult to prove a negative: that severance did not occur. As severance might have occurred, with the result that co-ownership continued to exist in equity, as a counsel of prudence, a purchaser would insist upon the appointment of a second trustee[129] to ensure that, if beneficial co-ownership continued, any beneficial interests would be overreached by a conveyance by two trustees, this procedure being necessary whether or not severance had actually occurred. To obviate this complexity, reform was introduced, that reform being relevant only to unregistered land.

Unregistered land

The Law of Property (Joint Tenants) Act 1964, which applies only to unregistered land, and operates retrospectively,[130] provides by section 1 that, for the purposes of section 36(2) of the Law of Property Act 1925, the survivor of two or more joint tenants shall, in favour of a purchaser, be deemed to be solely and beneficially interested if he conveys as beneficial owner, or the conveyance contains a statement that he is so interested. A purchaser need not, therefore, insist upon the appointment of a second trustee in the circumstances described above, provided that:

(a) a memorandum of severance has not been endorsed on or annexed to the conveyance by virtue of which the legal estate was vested in the joint tenants; or

(b) a receiving order in bankruptcy, or a petition for such an order, has not been registered against any of the joint tenants under the Land Charges Act 1972.

One uncertainty as to the operation of the Act relates to the position where there was no memorandum of severance attached to the conveyance but the purchaser was aware that severance had, in fact, occurred.[131] One argument was that the deeming provision in section 1 was sufficiently strong to ensure that the purchaser would, in these circumstances, still obtain a good title.[132] Recently, however, this uncertainty has been resolved, it having been held in *Grindal v. Hooper*[133] that a

---

[129] This does not seem to offend against the principle that, as between joint tenants, there must be unity of title and time. This is because the title of both A and the new trustee derives from the deed of appointment and so these unities exist. For the opposite view, see D.G. Barnsley [1998] C.L.J. 123 at 127, n. 18.

[130] Law of Property (Joint Tenants) Act 1964, ss 2, 3.

[131] See P. Jackson (1966) 30 Conv. (N.S.) 27.

[132] Thompson, op. cit., 25, an analogy being drawn with *Midland Bank Trust Co. Ltd v. Green* [1981] A.C. 513.

[133] [1999] E.G.C.S. 150. See N.P. Gravells [2000] Conv. 461.

purchaser with actual notice of severance having occurred would be bound by the interest of a beneficial co-owner despite there being no memorandum of severance on the conveyance to indicate that the surviving joint tenant was not the sole beneficial owner.

Registered land

The 1964 Act does not apply to registered land. The reason for this is that the existence of a beneficial tenancy in common is intended to be revealed by a restriction, that restriction being to the effect that the surviving co-owner cannot give a valid receipt for capital money. If there is no such restriction, a purchaser from a surviving joint tenant will normally acquire a good title. A potential problem may arise, however, if beneficial co-ownership continues after the death of one of the legal co-owners. Suppose A and B are registered as proprietors of a house and there is no restriction entered on the register of title. B then marries C, who moves into the house and B then severs the joint tenancy but no restriction is entered on the register. B then dies, leaving his share in the property to C. On a transfer of the house by A, C, as a beneficial co-owner in actual occupation of the property, would appear to have an interest which would override the registered disposition.[134]

The need for beneficial joint tenancies

The abolition of legal tenancies in common has without doubt simplified the structure of co-ownership by preventing the fragmentation of the legal title amongst, potentially, a large number of people; the doctrine of survivorship works well with respect to the legal title. A question which can be asked, however, is whether the existence of an equitable joint tenancy is as welcome.[135]

One of the drawbacks of the joint tenancy is the doctrine of survivorship. If one considers some of the cases on severance discussed above, a number of points may be made. First, this litigation is expensive and would not have been necessary had there have been a tenancy in common in the first place. Secondly, a finding that severance had not occurred will result in the property, on death, going to a person whom the deceased would not have intended to benefit on his death, their relationship having broken down: a consequence of what has aptly been described as 'the survivorship wheel of fortune'.[136] Had they been tenants in common from the outset, and the couple had not been married, then for one tenant in common to leave his property to the

---

[134] Land Registration Act 2002, Sched. 3, para. 2. See E.J. Cooke [2003] Conv. 41.

[135] See S.M. Bandali (1977) 41 Conv. (N.S.) 243; M.P. Thompson [1987] Conv. 29, 375 arguing for abolition and A.M. Prichard [1987] Conv. 272 arguing for the opposite point of view. See also the discussion by Tee, op. cit., at 142–146, which is sympathetic to the abolitionist approach, and N. Piska [2008] Conv. 452 at 457. For a thoughtful discussion, prompted by the Thompson/Prichard debate which comes out against abolition, see Smith, *Plural Ownership* (Oxford: Oxford University Press, 2005), Chapter 5.

[136] S. Nield [2001] Conv. 462 at 463.

other would have required the making of a will. If this was the case then, if the testamentary intention subsequently changed, it would be known that a new will would have to be made. A related point, and one which may not be known to the parties, is that while a joint tenancy subsists neither joint tenant has any share in the property to leave by will. So, if A and B are beneficial joint tenants, and A makes a will leaving 'his share' in the property to C then, unless there had been some act of severance, A will have no share to leave and the will would be ineffective. This is borne out by two recent decisions, where a joint tenant had sought to make a testamentary disposition in relation to the beneficial interest, and in each case, the intended will was ineffective, as there had not been a severance of the joint tenancy,[137] although one does wonder why the solicitors acting in these situations had not ensured that this had been done.[138]

A final point which can be made is that the effect of the severance of a joint tenancy may not be fully appreciated and, in particular, that each tenant in common will receive a half share in the property regardless of each person's initial contribution to the purchase. This may come as an unpleasant surprise if a couple split up shortly after buying a house together as beneficial joint tenants and where one of them has contributed substantially more to the purchase of the property than the other.[139]

As against this, it remains the case that the beneficial joint tenancy remains popular,[140] although whether all the consequences of the property being held in this way are fully explained is perhaps doubtful. When a solicitor is told by a couple buying a house that, on death, they would like their 'share' in it to go to the other, a joint tenancy may then be employed as an alternative to making a will.[141] In any event, any legislative change to the existing position seems unlikely, so one is left to hope that the full pros and cons of this type of beneficial holding are, at the outset, fully explained to the parties by their legal adviser. This may be a pious hope, for, as Ward L.J. recently lamented:

'I ask in despair how often this court has to remind conveyancers that they would save their clients a good deal of later difficulty if only they would sit the purchasers down, explain the difference between a joint tenancy and a tenancy in common and then expressly declare in the conveyance or transfer how the beneficial interest is to be held because that will be conclusive and save all argument.'[142]

---

[137] See *Campbell v. Griffin* [2001] EWCA Civ. 1176 discussed by M.P. Thompson [2003] Conv. 157 at 159–160, and *Carr v. Issard* [2006] EWHC 2095 (Ch.).

[138] Although see *Carr-Glynn v. Frearsons (A Firm)* [1999] Ch. 326.

[139] For empirical research which supports the view that the parties may be unaware of this consequence, see G. Douglas, J. Pearce, and H. Woodward [2008] Conv. 365 at 372–375. See also *Singla v. Brown* [2007] EWHC 405 (Ch.) at [38] *per* Mr Thomas Ivory Q.C.

[140] See the remarkable case of *Bindra v. Mawji* [2008] EWHC 1715 (Ch.), where the parties intended to create a tenancy in common during their lives, to change to a joint tenancy on the death of either: see at [44] *per* Etherton J.

[141] As, if the couple are unmarried, they will certainly need to make a will in respect of their other property, this is, perhaps, a false economy.

[142] *Carlton v. Goodman* [2002] 2 F.L.R. 259 at 273.

DISPUTES BETWEEN CO-OWNERS

When land is acquired by co-owners, then, at the outset, the relationship between them is likely to be harmonious. Disputes can arise subsequently, such disputes generally involving the related areas of occupation and sale. This section considers these matters.

Occupation[143]

The law relating to the rights of occupation of beneficial co-owners prior to the enactment of the Trusts of Land and Appointment of Trustees Act 1996 was quite complex. It was coloured to a considerable extent by the doctrine of conversion. Under this doctrine, for some purposes at least, the interests of the beneficiaries were regarded as being in the proceeds of sale, a proposition which would, *prima facie*, militate against them having the right to occupy the land. This position was, however, modified by reference to the pre-1926 law.

If there was legal co-ownership of the land, either by way of joint tenancy or tenancy in common, then each of the legal co-owners would have the right to possess the land, this right stemming from the unity of possession inherent in co-ownership. This, subject to the abolition of a legal tenancy in common, remains true after 1926. What was regarded as being more problematic was the situation where the beneficiary asserting a right of occupation was not a legal co-owner of the land. This problem occurred in *Bull v. Bull*,[144] where a mother and son had bought a house for their joint occupation but the house was in the sole name of the son. He subsequently sought possession of the property as against her and this action failed.

In reaching this conclusion, Denning L.J. equated the position of the mother, who was a beneficial tenant in common, with that of a legal tenant in common prior to 1926. The importance of this was that a legal tenant in common had, at that time, the right to go into occupation. A legal joint tenancy in common is now no longer possible, this being prevented by statutory provisions.[145] Those provisions are in Part I of the Act, however, and it is provided by section 14 of the Law of Property Act 1925:

'This Part of this Act shall not prejudicially affect the interest of any person in actual occupation of the land to which he may be entitled in right of such possession or occupation.'

Because the mother was in actual occupation, her rights were regarded as being the equivalent of the rights of a legal tenant in common prior to 1926 and so she could not be evicted by her son.[146]

---

[143] See, generally, D.G. Barnsley [1998] C.L.J. 123. See also J.G. Ross Martyn [1997] Conv. 237.
[144] [1955] 1 Q.B. 234.   [145] Law of Property Act 1925, ss 1(6), 36(2).
[146] This was expressly approved in *Williams & Glyn's Bank Ltd v. Boland* [1981] A.C. 487 at 507 *per* Lord Wilberforce. See also *Ramroop v. Ishmael* [2010] UKPC 14 at [14] *per* Lord Walker.

Limits on right

An integral part of the reasoning was the role of section 14 of the Act, which affords protection to people in actual occupation. Accordingly, if a beneficial tenant in common was not in actual occupation, it would not seem that he had the right to insist upon taking possession.[147] In addition, the occupation rights of the beneficiaries appeared to depend upon the underlying purpose of the trust. If, as in *Bull v. Bull*, the property, while held upon a trust for sale, was acquired for the purpose of providing a joint home, then, pending a sale of the property, the beneficiary would have the right to continue in occupation of the land.[148]

This point emerged clearly in *Barclay v. Barclay*,[149] where a bungalow was devised with a direction that it be sold and the proceeds divided between five beneficiaries. One of the five had lived with the testator prior to his death and had continued in possession thereafter. The plaintiff acquired the legal title and brought an action for possession which succeeded in the Court of Appeal. *Bull v. Bull* was distinguished on the basis that, in the present case, 'the prime purpose of the trust was that the bungalow should be sold'.[150] Although the beneficiary was in occupation of the land, because the purpose of the trust was not to provide a home for the beneficiaries, he had no right, as against the owner of the legal title, to remain in the bungalow.

The statutory regime

The Trusts of Land and Appointment of Trustees Act 1996 seeks to set out a comprehensive account of the new law relating to the rights of beneficiaries to occupy the property. It operates by first conferring rights of occupation on the beneficiaries and then by stipulating the circumstances in which the right can be modified or excluded. These sections, it should be added, are directed at the situation where the beneficiary is not a legal co-owner, in which case there is no problem in that that person, as an incident of the legal joint tenancy, has the right of occupation. The right of occupation in respect of beneficial co-owners of the land is conferred by section 12, which provides that:

'12—(1) A beneficiary who is beneficially entitled to an interest in land in possession in land subject to a trust of land is entitled by reason of his interest to occupy the land at any time if at that time—

(a) the purpose of the trust includes making the land available for his occupation (or for the occupation of beneficiaries of a class of which he is a member or of beneficiaries in general), or

(b) the land is held by trustees to be so available.

[147] See *Re Bagot's Settlement* [1894] 1 Ch. 177; G.A. Forrest (1956) 19 M.L.R. 312.
[148] See *City of London Building Society v. Flegg* [1988] A.C. 54 at 81 *per* Lord Oliver of Aylmerton.
[149] [1970] 2 Q.B. 677.
[150] [1970] 2 Q.B. 677 at 684 *per* Lord Denning M.R. For a discussion of this distinction, see M.J. Prichard (1971) 29 C.L.J. 44 at 46; S.M. Cretney (1971) 44 M.L.R. 441 at 443; and A.E. Boyle [1981] Conv. 108.

(2) Subsection (1) does not confer on a beneficiary a right to occupy land if it is either unavailable or unsuitable for occupation by him.

(3) This section is subject to section 13.'

Time at which purpose is assessed

A number of points call for elaboration. The first point is that it would appear from the wording of this subsection that one has regard to the purpose of the trust at the time when a beneficiary seeks to exercise his right to possession and not the time when the trust was created. This purpose may change over time. Suppose, for example, two sisters, A and B, are beneficial tenants in common of a house. B makes a will leaving her share in the property to her nephew, who is shortly to marry, so that, on her death, the nephew and his wife can live in the property. In this situation, subject to section 13 of the Act, it would appear that, on the death of his aunt, the nephew would, under section 12 of the Act, have the right of occupation. This would appear to be the case, unless the unhappily drafted subsection (2) is applicable, in that, if the nephew and A do not get on, it is perhaps the case that the property is not suitable for him.

Subsection (2) denies the beneficiary a right of occupation if the land subject to the trust is unavailable or unsuitable for occupation by him. The former criterion would seem to envisage a situation where the property in question is subject to a tenancy so that the trustees cannot grant others the right of possession. It is the second criterion which may cause difficulty, that is determining whether the property is unsuitable for his occupation.[151] In assessing whether the property is suitable for a person's occupation, regard should be had to the general physical characteristics of the particular property, and also a consideration of the personal characteristics and circumstances of that person.[152] If there is some personality clash between the beneficiary and the other occupiers, this may make the property unsuitable for his occupation.

Restrictions

Section 13(1) of the Act enables the trustees to restrict the right of occupation. If there are two or more beneficiaries, the trustees may restrict or exclude the entitlement of any one or more of the beneficiaries, but not all of them, to occupy the property. In exercising this power, the trustees may not act unreasonably,[153] and are also entitled under section 13(3) of the Act to impose reasonable conditions on any beneficiaries in relation to his occupation. It is possible under this provision for the court to sanction a physical partition of the property, with each beneficial owner entitled to occupy one part and be excluded from the other,[154] although such an outcome is likely to be rare.

---

[151] See Ross Martyn, op. cit., 260.

[152] *Chan v. Leung* [2003] 1 F.L.R. 23 at 48 *per* Jonathan Parker L.J.

[153] Trusts of Land and Appointment of Trustees Act 1996, s. 13(2).

[154] *Rodway v. Landy* [2001] Ch. 703. A jointly owned surgery which could be divided, with each doctor occupying a separate part of the premises.

In the exercise of their power to restrict the right of occupation then, as with the position generally with regard to the exercise of a discretion by trustees, they must act unanimously. This is why a beneficiary, who is also a legal owner of the property, cannot be excluded, against his will, from occupation of the trust property by the other trustees because, in such a case, there is obviously no unanimity amongst the trustees.

Reasonableness

With regard to the issue of reasonableness, certain criteria to which the trustees are to have regard are listed by section 13(4) of the Act. They are:

(a) the intentions of the person who created the trust;

(b) the purpose for which the land is held; and

(c) the circumstances and wishes of each of the beneficiaries entitled to occupy the land under section 12.

In having regard to these criteria, there may be some conflict between (a) and (b). The former relates to the purpose of the trust at the time of its creation and the latter to the current position, so that in the example given above, the nephew who inherits the interest of his aunt might be able to be excluded under paragraph (a) as someone not within the contemplation of the persons creating the trust at the time of its creation, whereas the second criterion would appear to apply to the current purpose of the trust, which is to provide him with a home. It remains to be seen what weight the courts will give to these different criteria.

Conditional occupation

Section 13 of the Act envisages that a beneficiary may be allowed to exercise his right of occupation on various conditions or be excluded from the property. Any conditions imposed upon occupation must be reasonable and can include a condition requiring him to pay any outgoings and expenses in respect of the land, or to assume any other obligation in relation to the land or to any activity which is or proposed to be conducted there.[155] If a beneficiary is excluded from the land, then conditions may be imposed upon those beneficiaries who are in occupation and this may include a requirement to make payments to the beneficiary as compensation for being excluded.[156]

Occupiers of land

The Act draws a distinction between beneficiaries who are not in occupation and who wish to go into occupation and people who are in occupation of land held under a trust of land. Under section 13(7) of the Act, the powers of the trustees to either exclude a beneficiary or to impose conditions on him shall not be exercised so as to prevent any person who is in occupation of land (whether or not by reason of an entitlement to

---

[155] Trusts of Land and Appointment of Trustees Act 1996, s. 13(5).
[156] Ibid., s. 13(6). See Rent, pp. 390–392.

occupy it) from continuing to occupy the land unless either that person consents or a court has given its approval. The court, in determining whether to approve a possession order, has regard to the criteria listed above.[157]

One point which should be noted about this provision is that the person in occupation of the land need not actually be a beneficiary under the trust. It could be the spouse or cohabitant of one of the co-owners of the property.

DISPUTES AS TO SALE

When the beneficial owners under a trust of land are in dispute as to the occupation rights, a factor which is likely to be considered is whether or not the land should be sold and its capital value distributed amongst them. Disputes of this nature are not uncommon; one co-owner wants the house to be sold, while another wants it to be retained for residential purposes. The 1996 Act makes provision for this situation and provides, also, a list of issues to which the court should have regard when faced with such disputes. These matters derive to a considerable extent from the previous case law which will continue to provide a guide to the approach to be taken in such matters, although, as will be seen, the Act has enabled different results to be achieved in some situations than would previously have been the case.

The statutory criteria

Under section 14 of the Act, any person who is a trustee of land or has an interest in property subject to a trust of land may make an application to the court for an order under the section. The court may then make any such order relating to the exercise by the trustees of any of their functions or declare the nature or extent of a person's interest in the property subject to the trust as it sees fit. In making such orders, the court is required to have regard to the following matters, which are listed in section 15 of the Act. These are:

(a) the intentions of the person or persons who created the trust;

(b) the purposes for which the property subject to the trust is held;

(c) the welfare of any minor who occupies or might reasonably be expected to occupy any land subject to the trust as his home; and

(d) the interests of any secured creditor of any beneficiary.

In the case of an application relating to the exercise of powers under section 13 of the Act, the matters to which the court should have regard include the circumstances and wishes of the beneficiaries entitled to occupy the land, and in respect of any other

---

[157] Ibid., s. 13(8).

application the court shall have regard to the circumstances and wishes of the beneficiaries or the majority of them, having regard to the size of their interests.[158]

Intention and purpose

Matters to which the court is to have regard when making an order include the intention of the person or persons who created the trust and the purposes for which the
property subject to the trust is held. These criteria reflect the case law which had developed under the previous legal regime governing co-ownership.

When land was held upon a trust for sale, disputes as to whether or not the property
should be sold were determined on applications to the court under section 30 of the
Law of Property Act 1925. The starting point in such cases was that, as the trust was
a trust for sale, the prime duty of the trustees, subject to their power to postpone the
sale, was to sell the property. If they were not unanimous in exercising their power to
postpone the sale, then, *prima facie*, the property should be sold.[159] This proposition
was, however, subject to a qualification. Where, prior to the acquisition of the land,
there was an agreement between the co-owners that the property should not be sold
unless all the co-owners agreed to this, then the court would not order a sale where
such agreement was lacking.[160]

Cases where there is a prior agreement with respect to how the property is to be
used are now expressly catered for by the Act. In *Charlton v. Lester*,[161] a sitting, protected, tenant bought a house with her son and daughter-in-law on the clear understanding that she could always remain in the house as her home. Despite the couple
having moved out, it was held that, because of the anterior understanding, the house
should not be sold; a decision which would be likely to be arrived at under the statutory provisions.

Such cases afford examples where the initial agreement between the co-owners was
that the house should not be sold. Conversely, it may be the case that the real purpose
of the trust was precisely that the house should be sold and the proceeds of sale divided
between the beneficiaries.[162] Today, if an express trust for sale is created, this would
indicate this intention and, in the event of a dispute between the co-owners, a sale
would be likely to be ordered.

Underlying purpose

The cases where there was an actual agreement with respect to the circumstances in
which the house should be sold were developed by the courts. While recognizing that
the co-owned property was to be held upon a trust for sale, regard was also had to the

---

[158] Ibid., s. 15(2)(3). See *Dear v. Robinson* [2001] EWCA Civ. 1543.

[159] *Re Mayo* [1943] Ch. 302.

[160] *Re Buchanan-Wollaston's Conveyance* [1939] Ch. 738. See also *Re Hyde's Conveyance* (1952) 102
L.J. 58.

[161] [1976] 1 E.G.L.R. 131. See also *Jones v. Jones* [1977] 1 W.L.R. 438; *Chan v. Leung* [2003] 1 F.L.R. 23.

[162] See *Barclay v. Barclay* [1970] 2 Q.B. 677.

underlying purpose of the trust which, at the outset, may well have been to provide a home. A consideration of an underlying purpose may lead to the conclusion that, when a dispute emerged, the result should be that the house be sold. If a house was bought for the purpose of being a 'quasi-matrimonial' home and the couple has split up, then that purpose no longer exists, with the consequence that it is likely that a sale will be ordered.[163] Where the house has been bought for joint occupation and one of the co-owners leaves, then it is likely, subject to the occupying tenant in common being given an opportunity to buy out the other,[164] that the court would order a sale of the property. Where the concept of the underlying purpose was developed further, in order to prevent an immediate sale, was where there were children involved. The idea was that, when the house was acquired, the underlying purpose of the trust was to provide a home not just for the co-owners but also for their children.

Welfare of minors[165]

When a house was subject to co-ownership and was used as a family home, the position of children was a matter to which the courts were used to paying regard. Initially, their existence was regarded as merely an incidental matter in considering whether or not to order a sale.[166] Latterly, however, the prevalent view came to be that the interests of children should be accorded priority and, in so doing, it became apparent that the courts would arrive at solutions similar to those which would result if the case involved a married couple and the property dispute was being resolved under the provisions of the Matrimonial Causes Act 1973.[167]

The approach to be taken in cases where there were children was laid down in *Rawlings v. Rawlings*,[168] by Salmon L.J. who, although ordering a sale on the facts of the case, itself, said: 'if there were young children, the position would be different. One of the purposes of the trust would no doubt have been to provide a home for them, and whilst that purpose still existed, a sale would not generally be ordered.' These sentiments were applied in *Re Evers' Trust*.[169] A couple had been cohabiting in a house with three children, two of whom were hers from an earlier marriage and the third was a child of them both. The parties, who were joint tenants, separated and he petitioned the court for an order that the house, where she continued to live with the children, should be sold. The Court of Appeal refused to make such an order, but instead postponed the sale indefinitely, with liberty to either party to apply for a sale at some time in the future.

---

[163] See [1961] 1 Q.B. 176. See *Bank of Ireland Home Mortgages Ltd v. Bell* [2001] 2 F.L.R. 809 at 815 *per* Peter Gibson L.J. See also *Smith v. Smith and Smith* (1976) 120 S.J. 100, house initially to be used as a joint home for the plaintiff, her brother, and her sister-in-law.

[164] See *Ali v. Hussein* (1974) 231 E.G. 372; *Pariser v. Wilson* (1973) 229 E.G. 786.

[165] See generally Fox, *Conceptualising Home* (Oxford: Hart Publishing, 2007), Chapter 9.

[166] See *Burke v. Burke* [1974] 1 W.L.R. 1063.

[167] See R. Schuz (1982) 12 Fam. Law 108; M. Hayes and G. Battersby [1981] Conv. 404; M.P. Thompson [1984] Conv. 103.

[168] [1964] P. 398 at 419.   [169] [1980] 1 W.L.R. 1327.

The decision to postpone the sale was based upon the view being taken that the underlying purpose of the trust was to provide a home for the family and that this purpose continued to exist. Such reasoning should, however, only be apposite where a family was envisaged, it being quite possible that a couple could begin cohabitation without any intention to have a family, in which case to argue that this was an underlying purpose of the trust would be artificial. The purpose should, however, end in any case when the youngest child no longer needs the house as a residence, which would normally be when he reached a certain specified age. Under the statutory provisions, the first point becomes academic but the second remains relevant.

Under section 15(3) of the Act, one of the matters to which the court is required to have regard is the welfare of any minor who occupies or might reasonably be expected to occupy the land which is subject to the trust as his home. There would be no difficulty, therefore, in refusing to order a sale to take account of the interests of children. When the children have reached eighteen, however, they cease to be minors and so their welfare ceases to be a relevant consideration when considering what order to make.[170] It is also the case that the closer the children come to achieving majority, the less weight will be given to considerations of their welfare than would be done if they were younger.[171]

Rent[172]

Cases where there is a dispute between co-owners as to whether the property should be sold or retained frequently occur in a family context and the court, in resolving the dispute, will have regard to family considerations and, in particular, the interests of any children. The consequence of doing this is that the house may remain unsold for a considerable period with one co-owner deriving no benefit from it and being unable to realize its capital value. To mitigate the hardship that this might cause to the non-occupying co-owner, the courts have been able to combine the postponement of a sale with an order that the occupier pay rent to the other.

Under the old law, although it was sometimes said that the court could simply order one co-owner to pay rent to the other on the basis that this was fair,[173] it was not clear that the courts did have this general power. Rather, the true position was thought to be that a court had jurisdiction to order one co-owner to pay rent to the other only when the former had, effectively, ousted the latter from the property.[174] If one co-owner simply chose not to remain in the property, the one remaining in occupation was not liable to pay rent to the other.[175] This problem was more apparent than

---

[170] See *TSB Bank plc v. Marshall* [1998] 3 E.G.L.R. 100.

[171] *Bank of Ireland Home Mortgages Ltd v. Bell* [2001] 2 F.L.R. 809 at 816 *per* Peter Gibson L.J.

[172] See S. Bright [2009] Conv. 378.

[173] *Chhokar v. Chhokar* [1984] F.L.R. 313 at 332 *per* Cumming-Bruce L.J. See also *Cousins v. Dzosens* (1984) 81 L.S.G. 2855.

[174] See *Dennis v. McDonald* [1981] 1 W.L.R. 810, affirmed in principle: [1982] Fam. 63.

[175] See *McMahon v. Burchill* (1846) 5 Hare 322 and R.E. Annand (1982) 132 N.L.J. 526.

real, however, as it was always open to the court, in an appropriate case,[176] to achieve indirectly what could not be achieved directly; the person seeking to resist an order of sale could be told that, unless she undertook to pay an occupation rent, then a sale would be ordered.[177] This dispute, such as it was, appeared to have been resolved as the courts have since asserted a general right to order the payment of rent where this is necessary to do equity between the parties,[178] and this jurisdiction exists alongside the statutory provisions whereby the payment of rent can be ordered.[179]

In most cases the court will now proceed to assess this matter under the 1996 Act, as if a court has excluded a beneficiary's right of occupation, such exclusion can be on terms that payment by way of compensation be made to that person[180] and such compensation would include the payment of rent.

In *Stack v. Dowden*,[181] although the main issue was the quantification of the beneficial interests in the home, a subsidiary matter was whether, pending the sale of the property, Ms Dowden, who was living in the property with the children, should be required to pay an occupation rent to Mr Stack, who was in alternative accommodation. At first instance, she was ordered to pay him £900 per month but, on appeal, this was set aside, and the House of Lords, Lord Neuberger of Abbotsbury dissenting, confirmed that no rent should be paid. The difficulty is in establishing the reason why.

Baroness Hale of Richmond dealt with this matter very briefly. She criticized the trial judge for not having regard to the criteria listed in section 15 of the Act. She then referred, briefly, to the obligation to maintain the children and the respective outgoings on the properties before concluding that, although she could see that there was a case for him to receive compensation, it should be borne in mind that, in earlier proceedings under the Family Law Act 1996, he had agreed to leave the house. That was coupled with the fact that the house was to be sold as soon as possible mitigated against an order to pay rent. Neither of these reasons is convincing. As Lord Neuberger subsequently pointed out, if the fact that he agreed to leave the house militated against ordering that a rent be paid to him, then this 'appears to reward intransigence and to penalise reasonableness'.[182] He also said, in a convincing dissenting opinion which did relate the facts of the case to the criteria contained in section 15,[183] the fact that it is intended that the house should be sold quickly is irrelevant to the issue as to whether the occupier of it should pay rent to the co-owner who is not in occupation; a consideration which carries greater credence when the housing market is depressed and it is difficult to sell properties.

---

[176] Such a solution should not be seen as a universal panacea to all cohabitation cases. See *Stott v. Rafcliffe* (1982) 79 L.S.G. 643; *Chan v. Leung* [2003] 1 F.L.R. 23.

[177] See M.P. Thompson [1984] Conv. 103 at 110.

[178] *Re Pavlou* [1993] 1 W.L.R. 1046; *Byford v. Butler* [2004] 1 F.L.R. 56; *Murphy v. Gooch* [2007] EWCA Civ. 603.

[179] *French v. Barcham* [2008] EWHC 1505 (Ch.).

[180] Trusts of Land and Appointment of Trustees Act 1996, s. 13(6)(a).   [181] [2007] 2 A.C. 432.

[182] (2008) Chancery Bar Association Annual Lecture, para. 21, where he also expressed his mystification as to why the majority had refused to order that an occupation rent be paid.

[183] [2007] 2 A.C. 432 at [153]–[156].

Because the issue of the payment of an occupation rent was treated in such a cursory manner in *Stack v. Dowden*, it is difficult to see the decision as laying down any principles of general application save that a judge must, in deciding both whether the house should be sold, and whether, pending a sale, the occupier should pay an occupation rent to the party out of occupation, pay regard to the criteria laid down in section 15. Once that has been done, one would envisage that the normal outcome would be that a rent should be paid, and such an order was made in *Murphy v. Gooch*[184], this being considered by the Court of Appeal to be almost a matter of course. In quantifying the rent, however, regard is had to how the outgoings are paid on the co-owned house, so that if the person in occupation is paying the mortgage on that house, credit should be given for this.[185]

Insolvency[186]

The above section was concerned with disputes between the co-owners as to whether the property should be sold. This issue may also arise in a rather different context, when one of the co-owners has financial problems and the pressure for the house to be sold comes from the creditors. In this situation, rather different considerations arise in the exercise of the court's discretion.

Bankruptcy

When one of the co-owners has been declared bankrupt, the effect of the bankruptcy is that the bankrupt's beneficial share in the property will vest in the trustee in bankruptcy. The trustee would then petition the court for a sale of the property, such petitions being made, first, under section 30 of the Law of Property Act 1925, and now under section 14 of the Trusts of Land and Appointment of Trustees Act 1996. The trustee must lodge such a petition within three years of the bankruptcy, because after that period the bankrupt's interest in the home will re-vest in him.[187] A petition may also be lodged, even if the house has been the subject of a matrimonial order to the effect that it should not be sold unless one of a number of events has occurred.[188]

The common law approach

The judicial tone to how such applications should be approached was set in *Re Solomon*.[189] A married couple had held their home as joint tenants. In matrimonial proceedings, she had obtained an undertaking from him not to dispose of the property. He was then adjudicated bankrupt and the trustee petitioned the court for a sale

---

[184] [2007] EWCA Civ. 608 at [22] *per* Lightman J.   [185] Ibid., at [23]–[25].
[186] For critical accounts of the jurisprudence relating to this area, see Fox, op. cit., Chapter 3; R. Probert in Dixon and Griffiths (eds), *Contemporary Perspectives on Property, Equity and Trusts Law*, (Oxford: Oxford University Press, 2007), Chapter 4.
[187] Insolvency Act 1986, s. 283A, a provision inserted by the Enterprise Act 2002, s. 261.
[188] *Avis v. Avis* [2007] EWCA Civ. 748.
[189] [1967] Ch. 573. For criticism, see C. Palley (1969) 20 N.I.L.Q. 132.

of the matrimonial home. Goff J. held that the contest here was not simply between husband and wife but also between the wife and the husband's creditors. In the case of such a contest, he was of the view that the voice of the trustee in bankruptcy should prevail. The house was ordered to be sold, the wife being given a short time in which to order her affairs.

The approach, which favours the order of a sale, has been consistently followed. Although the court has a discretion, that discretion has, almost without fail, been exercised in favour of the trustee. The judicial attitude is that, 'One's debts must be paid, and paid promptly, and if they cannot be paid promptly, then the trustee in bankruptcy must prevail.'[190]

It became abundantly clear that, for a sale to be refused to the trustee in bankruptcy, exceptional circumstances must exist. It has been argued on more than one occasion that, if the effect of a sale being ordered was that the bankrupt's spouse and children would as a consequence lose their home, then a sale should not be ordered. Such an argument has been consistently rejected, this consequence not being seen as exceptional but as being a normal outcome of bankruptcy.[191] Typical of the judicial response is to say that the resulting problems caused to the bankrupt's family are 'yet another case where the sins of the father have to be visited upon the children, but that is the way in which the world is constructed, and one must be just before one can be generous'.[192] In similar vein, they are said to be 'the melancholy consequences of debt and improvidence'.[193]

Until quite recently, there appeared to be only one case where the trustee in bankruptcy was refused a sale of the property as a result of objections by a co-owner. In *Re Holliday*,[194] a matrimonial home was in the joint names of husband and wife. The wife obtained a decree nisi and was seeking ancillary relief, whereupon the husband lodged his own petition for bankruptcy. After the bankruptcy order was made, the trustee petitioned for a sale of the house. Owing to the needs of the wife and their three children, the Court of Appeal postponed a sale of the property for a period of five years.

The case was clearly highly unusual. The creditors, who were essentially the husband's solicitor and a bank, were not pressing for payment and the bankruptcy petition was, in reality, a device to seek to avoid a property adjustment order being made against him. Moreover, the level of indebtedness was such that it was probable that the creditors would be paid at 100 pence on the £1, itself a highly unusual occurrence. The upshot was that it was highly unlikely that the creditors would suffer any hardship because of a postponement of a sale.[195] As such, the case has not subsequently been regarded as providing much guidance as to when a sale of the property should

---

[190] *Re Bailey* [1977] 1 W.L.R. 278 at 283 *per* Walton J. See also *Re Densham* [1975] 1 W.L.R. 1519 at 1531 *per* Goff J.

[191] *Re Lowrie* [1981] 3 All E.R. 353.   [192] *Re Bailey* [1977] 1 W.L.R. 278 at 284 *per* Walton J.

[193] *Re Citro* [1991] Ch. 142 at 157 *per* Nourse L.J. For a very different approach, which did not actually involve the trustee in bankruptcy, see *Abbey National plc v. Moss* (1994) 29 H.L.R. 249, discussed by D.N. Clarke [1994] Conv. 331.

[194] [1981] Ch. 405.   [195] *Re Citro* [1991] Ch. 132 at 157 *per* Nourse L.J.

be refused to protect the interests of a co-owner.[196] The usual approach, albeit one at times applied reluctantly,[197] was that there was a strong presumption that, if a sale was sought by the trustee in bankruptcy, a sale would be ordered.

Insolvency Act

The case law which developed in relation to this issue did so in the context of petitions for sale by the trustee in bankruptcy and represented a consistent judicial approach to the exercise of discretion. The ethos underlying the case law received statutory recognition in the Insolvency Act 1986. Section 335A of the Act provides that:

'(1) Any application by a trustee in bankrupt's estate under section 14 of the Trusts of Land and Appointment of Trustees Act 1996...for an order under that section shall be made to the court having jurisdiction in relation to the bankruptcy.

(2) On such an application the court shall make such order as it thinks just and reasonable having regard to—

(a) the interests of the bankrupt's creditors;

(b) where the application is made in respect of land which includes a dwelling house which is or has been the home of the bankrupt or the bankrupt's spouse or former spouse—

(i) the conduct of the spouse or former spouse, so far as contributing to the bankruptcy,

(ii) the needs and financial resources of the spouse or former spouse, and

(iii) all the circumstances of the case other than the needs of the bankrupt.

(3) Where such an application is made after the end of the period of one year beginning with the first vesting...of the bankrupt's estate in a trustee, the court shall assume, unless the circumstances of the case are exceptional, that the interests of the creditors outweigh all other considerations."[198]

Section 15(4) of the Trusts of Land and Appointment of Trustees Act 1996 provides that, if section 335A of the Insolvency Act 1986 applies, then the criteria to which the court will normally have regard, contained in section 15, do not apply. In other words, if, a year after the bankruptcy, the trustee petitions for a sale of the bankrupt's home, the interests of the creditors will, unless the circumstances are exceptional, prevail, and an order for sale will be made.

Human rights

It has been suggested that this section may be incompatible with Article 8 of the European Convention on Human Rights,[199] although the opposite view has also been

---

[196] See *Re Lowrie* [1981] 3 All E.R. 353 at 356 *per* Walton L.J.; *Harman v. Glencross* [1986] Fam. 81 at 95 *per* Balcombe L.J.

[197] *Re Citro* [1991] at 161 *per* Bingham L.J.

[198] Section inserted by Trusts of Land and Appointment of Trustees Act 1996, s. 25(1), Sched. 3, para. 23.

[199] *Jackson v. Bell* [2001] EWCA Civ. 387 at [24] *per* Sir Andrew Morritt V.-C.; *Barca v. Mears* [2004] EWHC 2170 (Ch.) at [39] *per* Mr Nicholas Strauss Q.C. See M. Dixon [2005] Conv. 161 at 165–167; A. Barker [2010] Conv. 352.

asserted.[200] It is thought that the latter view is considerably more convincing. Although it is clear that the trustee in bankruptcy is a public body and, as a consequence, a court must be able to determine whether the making of a possession order is proportionate, it is suggested that, in the present context, this test will be satisfied. This is because the Act expressly makes provision for the personal circumstances of an occupier to be taken into account. While it is true that the family dislocation inherent in a forced sale is seen as the default position, and is regarded as being one of 'the melancholy consequences of debt and improvidence',[201] it is clear that an order for possession is not an inevitable conclusion in such cases. While one might argue that the balance struck by English law is too favourable to the trustee, acting on behalf of creditors, and insufficiently sympathetic to the problems of occupiers, such an argument is unlikely to lead to the conclusion that the approach taken under English law is outside the margin of appreciation afforded to individual states. As is the situation concerning the right of a mortgagee to obtain possession, which is not incompatible with the Article,[202] it is thought that this section will, if the matter is fully argued, be held to be compliant with the Convention.

Exceptional circumstances

Because the criteria listed by section 15 of the 1996 Act do not apply to applications for a sale made by the trustee in bankruptcy, it is evident that the previous case law remains a reliable guide to the exercise of the court's discretion in such cases. The onus is therefore very much on the person seeking to obtain a postponement of the sale to establish that the circumstances are exceptional.

In determining what are exceptional circumstances, the courts have wisely refused to lay down general guidelines as to what these might be, preferring to treat each case on its merits.[203] But it remains the case that the family disruption, which is the normal result of a forced sale of a family property will not be so regarded, even in situations where, given the size of the bankrupt's share in the house, little will be generated for the creditors by the sale, the proceeds of which being sufficient only to meet the costs of the trustee in bankruptcy.[204] What can change the courts' perspective is illness.

The illness or disability of the bankrupt's spouse or children may disincline the court to order a sale, one example which has been given being where the house is specially adapted to meet the physical needs of a disabled child, in which case the court would hesitate long before ordering an immediate sale.[205] More recently, the sale of a house was postponed for a year when the bankrupt's wife suffered from paranoid

---

[200] *Hoskings v. Michaelides* [2004] All E.R. (D.) 147 [70], Mr Paul Morgan Q.C. See also *Nicholls v. Lan* [2006] EWHC 1255 (Ch.) at [42]–[44] *per* Mr Paul Morgan Q.C.

[201] *Re Citro* [1991] Ch. 142 at 147 *per* Nourse L.J.

[202] *Wood v. United Kingdom* (1997) 24 E.H.R.R. C.D. 69.

[203] See *Claughton v. Charalambous* [1999] 1 F.L.R. 740 at 744, 745 *per* Jonathan Parker J.

[204] *Trustee of the Estate of Bowe v. Bowe* [1998] 2 F.L.R. 439; *Harrington v. Bennett* [2000] E.G.C.S. 41.

[205] *Re Bailey* [1977] 1 W.L.R. 278 at 284 *per* Walton J.

schizophrenia, a condition which made the impact upon her of adverse events, such as having to leave her home, particularly distressing.[206] Although the circumstances of the bankrupt personally are not a relevant consideration, they may become so indirectly, so that in *Re Bremner*,[207] the bankrupt had terminal cancer and a life expectancy of six months and the court postponed a sale of the matrimonial home until three months after his death, the exceptional circumstance being the wish of his wife to care for him during the latter stages of his life. It is evident, however, that it will require something out of the ordinary for the court to refuse a sale on the petition of the trustee in bankruptcy.

Secured creditors

Prior to the enactment of the Trusts of Land and Appointment of Trustees Act 1996, the courts used to adopt the same approach to petitions for sale brought by a secured creditor as they did if it had been brought by a trustee in bankruptcy,[208] an approach which meant that a sale of the property would normally be ordered.[209] Section 15 of the Act, however, when listing the matters to which the court should have regard when considering whether to order a sale, simply includes the interest of any secured creditor of any beneficiary as one factor to be considered. The interests of a secured creditor would not seem any longer, therefore, to be a decisive consideration, a view confirmed in *Mortgage Corporation Ltd v. Shaire*.[210] Nevertheless, the voice of the creditor will be a powerful one, particularly, as was the case in *Bank of Ireland Home Mortgages Ltd v. Bell*,[211] if there is little, if any, equity in the house and no prospect of any payments being made to reduce the debt. It should also be remembered that, if the court refuses to order a sale at the behest of a secured creditor, that creditor can then petition for the debtor's bankruptcy and, if the debtor is declared bankrupt, the trustee in bankruptcy will petition the court for a sale of the property and, unless there are exceptional circumstances, the court will, a year after the bankrupt's property has vested in him, order that the property be sold.[212]

[206] *Re Raval* [1998] 2 F.L.R. 718. See also *Claughton v. Charalambous* [1999] 1 F.L.R. 740, where an indefinite postponement was ordered on account of the bankrupt's wife suffering from renal failure and arthritis, although, on the facts, a sale of the property would not have benefited the creditors; *Judd v. Barr* [1988] 2 F.L.R. 368 (cancer), reversed with respect to the non-matrimonial property: [1999] 1 F.L.R. 1191. *Hoskings v. Michaelides* [2004] All E.R. (D.) 147; *Nicholls v. Lan* [2006] EWHC 1255(Ch.) (mental health).

[207] [1999] 1 F.L.R. 912.

[208] *Lloyds Bank plc v. Byrne* [1993] 1 F.L.R. 369; *Barclays Bank plc v. Hendricks* [1996] 1 F.L.R. 258. See N.S. Price [1996] Conv. 464.

[209] But see *Abbey National plc v. Moss* (1993) 26 H.L.R. 249, a decision which was out of line with the rest of the authorities.

[210] [2000] 2 F.L.R. 222. Although criticized by S. Pascoe [2000] Conv. 315, the actual wording of the section does lead to this conclusion. See M.P. Thompson [2000] Conv. 329; L. Tee, op. cit., 152.

[211] [2001] F.L.R. 809. See also *First National Bank plc v. Achampong* [2004] 1 F.L.R. 18 and M.P. Thompson [2003] Conv. 314 at 320–325.

[212] See *Zandfarid v. BCCI International S.A.* [1996] 1 W.L.R. 1420; *Re Ng* [1998] 2 F.L.R. 386; *Judd v. Brown* [1999] 1 F.L.R. 1191.

11

Leasehold Estates

The lease is now a familiar part of landholding, it being encountered in various forms and being used for quite different purposes. Originally, it was not perceived as being within Land Law at all. The reason for this view was that the lease was principally a commercial relationship, whereas the doctrine of tenure, which dominated the development of early Land Law, was concerned rather more with a person's status in society. The impact of this early classification is essentially historical, it having long been accepted that the lease is a recognized estate in land. Nevertheless, the underlying basis of the lease is a contractual one, a factor which has led, at times, to some tension as to whether the relationship between landlord and tenant should be regarded as the incidents of that estate, or should be governed by normal contractual principles.

The three main areas where leases are employed are residential property, commercial property, and agricultural property. Within the residential context, the type of lease can vary considerably. One obvious divide is between the private and the public sector. Even within the private sector, however, there is variation as to the type of lease involved. One can have a short-term let, where a person takes a lease of a property for a term of six months. Alternatively, a very long lease of, say, 999 years can be created, one object of which is, effectively, to give the leaseholder the rights of a freeholder. The lease is employed instead of a freehold estate so as to make it possible for the burden of certain covenants to attach to the land in question, this being difficult to do if the property is actually freehold, unless the new commmonhold scheme is employed.[1]

The lease is therefore used for many different purposes. It is also an area of law where there has been extensive statutory regulation, different statutory codes applying to different types of lease. A consequence of this is that the law of landlord and tenant has become an increasingly specialized area. This specialization has extended not only to the comprehensive coverage of the topic but to extensive treatments of different areas of statutory regulation. In a work of this nature, it is not possible to attempt a proper coverage of the different statutory regimes which exist in the leasehold sector; rather, this chapter will seek to explain the general principles underlying the subject.

---

[1] See Chapter 14.

TERMINOLOGY

Before examining the essentials of a lease, it is perhaps helpful at the outset to explain some of the terminology which is commonly used. The term 'demise' is often used instead of the word lease. Similarly, the expressions 'term of years', 'tenancy', and 'lease' are frequently used interchangeably. They mean the same thing.

The person who grants the lease is referred to as the lessor or the landlord. The landlord carves the leasehold estate out of his freehold interest, which he retains. While the landlord, as the person in receipt of rents and profits, is legally regarded as being in possession,[2] physically he does not have the right to possess the property. The landlord's interest is termed the reversion. This estate can be assigned, the person to whom it is assigned being termed the assignee of the reversion.

The tenant also has an estate in the land. This, too, can be assigned to an assignee. Because leases were not originally regarded as land, the statute Quia Emptores 1290[3] did not apply and so, instead of transferring his entire estate the tenant can carve a smaller lease out of it. So, if he holds a ninety-nine-year lease of property, the tenant can create a sub-lease of, say, fifty years. The person to whom the sub-lease is granted is termed the sub-tenant and the lease out of which the sub-tenancy was created is termed the head lease. The head tenant occupies a dual role; under the head lease he is the tenant but, with regard to the sub-lease, he is the sub-landlord. Diagrammatically, this can be represented as shown in Figure 1:

```
L --------- R
|
| 99 years
|
T --------- A
            |
            | 50 years
            |
            ST
```

Fig. 1 Freehold estate, lease and sub-lease

The original lease is a ninety-nine-year lease between L and T. L has assigned his reversion to R. T has assigned his interest to A who has, in turn, created a fifty-year sub-lease in favour of ST.

---

[2] Law of Property Act 1925, s. 205(1)(xix).   [3] See The dismantling of tenure, pp. 23–24.

THE CONTEXT OF LEASES

It has already been observed that the lease is employed in a number of situations. It is used principally in relation to residential tenancies, business tenancies, and agricultural tenancies. In each case, the landlord and tenant relationship is governed by a complex statutory regime, the details of which are beyond the scope of this book. A little must be said, however, about the statutory regulation of the private sector. This is because this forms the backdrop against which the law relating to the creation of leases has had to operate and which had a significant impact upon the legal concept of a lease.

The Rent Acts

Since 1915, there has been in existence legislation affecting the relationship between landlord and tenant in the private sector, this legislation being known, collectively, as the Rent Acts.[4] This legislation was designed to improve the position of tenants *vis-à-vis* their landlords. It did this by focusing on two central elements, the rent which could be charged, and the security of the tenant.

One of the key elements in the strategy adopted by the Rent Acts was to control the rent which had to be paid by the tenant. Whatever the contractually agreed rent might be, if the tenant was protected under the Acts, he could refer the rent to a rent officer, who would then assess and register a fair rent for the property.[5] The consequence of the registration of a fair rent, which was almost invariably lower than the rent specified in the lease, was that the landlord was precluded from collecting more than that sum from the tenant. The second main form of protection afforded by the Acts was to confer upon the tenant security of tenure. This meant that additional hurdles were placed in the way of a landlord seeking to recover possession of the property from the tenant upon whom was conferred what has been described as a 'status of irremovability'.[6] The security conferred upon tenants was such that, in many cases, it would be nigh on impossible for the landlord to regain possession of the property, notwithstanding that the original lease had expired some years previously.

The impact of the Rent Acts upon landlords was considerable. They prevented landlords from being able to secure a commercial return on property which was let in the private sector and, as a result, affected significantly the capital value of that property. If a house was subject to a protected tenancy, it would be difficult to sell the freehold to anyone else, as any purchaser would also be precluded from obtaining a commercial return on the property. Consequently, many owners of property sought

---

[4] The first such Act was the Rent and Mortgage Interest (War Restrictions) Act 1915.
[5] Rent Act 1977, s. 67.
[6] *Jessamine Investments Co. v. Schwartz* [1978] Q.B. 264 at 277 *per* Stephenson L.J.

to enter contractual relationships affecting the property without creating a tenancy which would attract the protection of the Rent Acts and considerable ingenuity was expended towards the achievement of this aim.[7]

The desire to avoid the Rent Acts is the backcloth against which many of the cases involving the distinction between a lease and a licence have been fought. Since the enactment of the Housing Act 1988, however, the degree of protection afforded to private sector tenants has diminished substantially. As a result, there have been far fewer attempts to create residential occupancy agreements which are not tenancies. The cases which have involved such attempts can only properly be understood, however, if one appreciates some of the motivation on the part of landowners.

THE ESSENTIALS OF A LEASE

There are two estates which are capable of existing at law, the fee simple absolute in possession and the term of years absolute.[8] The second of these estates is the lease. The term of years absolute is defined, somewhat unhelpfully, as, in effect, a term of years certain and one which can also include terms of less than a year.[9]

Certainty

A key element of the definition of a lease is that it is for a term certain. Provision is also made to cater for leases which can be brought to a premature end. This can occur if the lease is expressly made determinable upon the occurrence of a specified event. Alternatively, in a long lease either side may be given the right to terminate the lease on specified occasions. Clauses allowing the parties to do this are termed break clauses. What may also occur is that a periodic tenancy is created. In such cases, the original period is agreed, and that period will recur until either of the parties to the lease brings it to an end.[10] The essential idea remains, however, that the parties have agreed upon the term of the lease. If the period of time agreed upon is uncertain, then the intended lease will be void. In *Lace v. Chantler*,[11] a lease was expressed to be granted for the duration of the war. As, when the lease was granted, it was uncertain as to what the length of the term was to be, the agreement was void.

Such wartime leases were, apparently, quite common and were rescued by statute by being converted into ten-year leases determinable by either party giving one month's notice to the other to determine the lease upon the end of hostilities.[12] This provides an example of a lease where there is a term certain, in the sense of there being a maximum

---

[7] For a penetrating discussion, see S. Bright [2002] C.L.J. 146.   [8] Law of Property Act 1925, s. 1(1).
[9] Ibid., s. 205(1)(xxvi).   [10] See *Periodic tenancies*, pp. 417–419.   [11] [1944] K.B. 368.
[12] Validation of Wartime Leases Act 1944, s. 1.

period agreed upon at the outset but where the lease may be brought to a premature end. The general principle, however, was unaffected, which is that, to be a valid lease one must know at the outset what the period of it is. Consistent with this, if, although the length of the term is agreed, there is no agreed starting date for it, then the purported lease will be void.[13]

This principle was subject to direct challenge in *Prudential Assurance Co. Ltd v. London Residuary Body*.[14] In 1930, the then owner of a strip of land fronting a highway sold it to the council and took a lease back of it, that lease being expressed to continue until the land was required by the council for the purpose of widening the highway. The council abandoned its road-widening plan and the reversion passed to the defendant and the lease was assigned to the plaintiff. The defendant purported to terminate the tenancy by the service of a notice to quit and the plaintiff sought a declaration that the lease could only be terminated when the highway was widened. The declaration was refused. The House of Lords held that the purported lease was void for uncertainty. That being the case, the position was that, as the person to whom the grant was made had gone into possession and paid rent, a yearly tenancy arose by implication and the landlord could terminate this lease by serving an appropriate notice to quit.[15] Lord Templeman considered that 'the principle in *Lace v. Chantler*, reaffirming 500 years of judicial acceptance of the requirement that a term must be certain, applies to all leases and tenancy agreements'.[16] As the widening of the road was an uncertain event which may, indeed, never happen, a lease calculated by reference to such a contingency was void for uncertainty.

This result was reached with reluctance by some members of the House. Lord Browne-Wilkinson, with whom Lords Griffiths and Mustill agreed, described the result as 'bizarre' and 'resulting from the application of an ancient and technical rule which requires the maximum duration of a lease to be ascertainable from the outset'. He went on to say that: 'No one has produced any satisfactory rationale for the genesis of this rule. No one has been able to point to any useful purpose that it serves at the present day.'[17]

Leases for life

These critical comments, unsurprisingly, generated a debate with arguments being put for and against the rule.[18] The general rule has now, however, been substantially modified by the decision of the Supreme Court in *Berrisford v. Mexfield Housing*

---

[13] *Harvey v. Pratt* [1965] 1 W.L.R. 1025. Cf. *Canada Square Corp. Ltd v. Versafood Services Ltd* (1980) 101 D.L.R. (3d) 743. A lease to start on the substantial completion of a rooftop restaurant was regarded as having a sufficiently certain starting date. See also *Liverpool City Council v. Walton Group plc* [2002] 1 E.G.L.R. 149; *Ahmed v. Wingrove* [2007] EWHC 1918 (Ch.) at [16]–[17] *per* Mr Michael Toulson Q.C.

[14] [1992] 2 A.C. 386.

[15] [1992] 2 A.C. 386 at 392 *per* Lord Templeman. See Notice to quit, pp. 453–454.   [16] Ibid., at 394.

[17] Ibid., at 396. For a spirited critique of this decision, see J. Roche [2011] Conv. 444.

[18] See P. Sparkes (1993) 109 L.Q.R.103, supporting the rule, and S. Bright (1993) 13 L.S. 38, opposing it.

Co-operative Ltd.[19] Mexfield was a housing co-operative body which effected mort-gage rescues. To do this, it bought property from borrowers who were in financial dif-ficulties, and then let them back to them. In 1993 it entered such an arrangement with Ms Berrisford. She signed an Occupancy Agreement which continued from month to month until determined as provided by the Agreement. The Agreement provided by Clause 5 that Ms Berrisford could determine the tenancy by giving one month's notice to quit. Mexfield, on the other hand, could by Clause 6 only determine the lease on one of four grounds, of which mention need only be made to the first two: that there were rent arrears; or that she had neglected to perform any terms of the agreement. Neither condition was applicable. Nevertheless, Mexfield sought to terminate the lease by the service of a notice to quit. The argument was that the original agreement was ineffective to create a lease because its duration was, from the landlord's perspective, uncertain; it was unclear as to when, if ever, it could terminate the lease. As she was in possession paying rent, it was argued that there was an implied periodic tenancy which could be ended by an appropriate notice to quit, despite the Agreement preclud-ing it from doing so. The Supreme Court rejected this argument.

Although the members of the Court were highly critical of the certainty rule as reaffirmed in *Prudential*, they declined to overrule it, so the intended lease could not take effect.[20] Nevertheless, this was not considered to be determinative of the mat-ter. The argument was advanced that, prior to 1925, a lease for an individual for an uncertain term took effect as a lease for life, and this was accepted as being correct.[21] Of course, since 1926, such a life interest cannot take effect at law.[22] Such interests are normally granted as part of a family settlement and, as such, provision was made for them to be overreached, first by the Settled Land Act 1925 and, latterly, by the Trusts of Land and Appointment of Trustees Act 1996. It may be, however, that as part of a commercial transaction, a life interest is created either deliberately[23] or, as in the present case, by implication of law and, in such circumstances, overreaching is not appropriate. To deal with this situation, section 149(6) of the Law of Property Act 1925 provides that a lease for life at a rent or in consideration of a fine shall take effect as a ninety-year lease, determinable upon death. This statutory solution overcomes the difficulty that otherwise such a lease would be void for uncertainty. Subject to any question of formalities,[24] such a grant will take effect as a determinable ninety-year lease. So, in the present case, Ms Berrisford had a legal ninety-year lease, determinable upon her death, the service of a one month's notice to quit by her, or a notice served by Mexfield in accordance with the terms of the Agreement. It is, of course, true that

[19] [2011] EWSC 52. This was an important test case as a considerable number of identical agreements had been entered into.
[20] See ibid., at [23]–[37] *per* Lord Neuberger.
[21] Ibid. at [42] *per* Lord Neuberger. See also at [116] *per* Lord Dyson, citing Williams, *Law of Real Property* (23rd edn) (London: Sweet & Maxwell, 1920) 135.
[22] Law of Property Act 1925, s. 1.
[23] See *Skipton Building Society v. Clayton* (1993) 96 P. & C.R. 223.
[24] See *Hardy v. Haselden* [2011] EWCA Civ. 1387 where, somewhat surprisingly, no argument based on estoppel was raised.

the same analysis would have been applicable in *Lace v. Chantler*, itself, and had it been employed, there would have been no need for the amending legislation. The short response to this is that given by Lord Neuberger in *Berrisford*;[25] the argument was never raised and, indeed, perhaps surprisingly, has not been prior to it being successfully argued in the present case.

Contractual licence

Although the argument concerning a life tenancy was accepted in *Berrisford*, and this was enough to determine the outcome of the appeal, the Supreme Court also considered a second argument. This was that, even if the original tenancy had been void for uncertainty, there would still be in existence an enforceable contractual licence between the parties, and Mexfield could have been prevented by equitable relief from breaking that contract. Such an argument had been raised, but rejected, in *Lace v. Chantler*,[26] where Lord Greene M.R. thought it impossible to construe the agreement in this way. In his view, if the parties intended to create a lease, and the law says that it is bad as a tenancy, it cannot be construed as a licence. In *Berrisford*,[27] however, Lord Neuberger did not think that these observations could withstand principled analysis. Instead, he thought the true position to be that, 'If the Agreement is incapable of giving rise to a tenancy for some old and technical rule or property law, I do not see why, as a matter of principle, that should render the Agreement invalid as matter of contract.'

On this analysis, if an intended lease fails for uncertainty, then that same agreement will take effect as a contractual licence. As between the parties, themselves, this may not be that important and, in particular, the landlord will be unable to terminate the occupancy in a way which is not envisaged by the contract. Unlike a lease, however, this licence does not create an interest in land. As was explained in *Berrisford*,

'If the Agreement does not create a tenancy for technical reasons, namely because it purports to create an uncertain term, it is hard to see why, as a matter of principle, it should not be capable of taking effect as a contract, enforceable as between the parties personally, *albeit not capable of binding their respective successors, as no interest in land or other proprietary interest would subsist.*'[28]

The finding of a contractual licence to exist when an intended lease fails for uncertainty will affect companies rather than human tenants. This is because a company is not capable of holding a life interest in property, and so the argument that an uncertain lease can take effect as a lease for life, which is then converted by section 149(6) of the Law of Property Act 1925 into a determinable ninety-year lease is not tenable. That this is the result of the refusal to overrule *Prudential* was recognized in terms by Lord Collins, who considered it to be a mystery as to why, in 2011, the position of a tenant who is a human being and a tenant which is a company should, in this respect, be different.[29] It is easy to sympathize with this view, and it would seem that this area

---

[25] [2011] EWSC 52 at [53].   [26] [1944] K.B. 368 at 372.   [27] [2011] UKSC 52 at [62]
[28] Ibid., at [60]. Emphasis supplied. See Chapter 15.   [29] Ibid., at [105].

of law is one, as all the Supreme Court Justices recognized, would benefit from an examination by the Law Commission, with a view to changing a rule which appears to have outlived its usefulness.

EXCLUSIVE POSSESSION

Section 1 of the Rent Act 1977 provides that:

'Subject to this Part of this Act a tenancy under which a dwelling-house (which may be a house or a part of a house) is let as a separate dwelling is a protected tenancy for the purposes of this Act.'

Central to the definition is that the dwelling-house is '*let*'. To avoid the occupancy agreement, to use a neutral term, attracting the protection afforded by the Act, attempts were made to create such agreements without creating a lease, the aim instead being to create a licence. A key element in the distinction between a lease and a licence is the concept of exclusive possession. As a lease is an estate in land, the tenant, as the holder of that estate, has the right to exclude everyone else, including the landlord, from the property. Whether or not exclusive possession was granted became, therefore, a central feature in determining whether a lease had been created, although the true meaning and importance of this concept came to be somewhat obscured.

Single occupancy

In considering the question as to whether a particular transaction created a lease or a licence, it is necessary to distinguish between cases where the property is occupied by one person and cases where there is more than one occupier, because different considerations arise.

At first, the presence of exclusive possession was regarded as being conclusive as to whether or not there was a lease.[30] Subsequently, however, its importance seemed to be downplayed. In *Marchant v. Charters*,[31] a single man occupied a room in a large house, that house having been converted into bedsits. There was a gas ring, for cooking, in the room, and the toilet and bathroom were shared with other occupants. A housekeeper cleaned the room on a daily basis and the linen was changed once a week. The occupier applied to the rent officer for the registration of a fair rent and the owner of the house responded by serving on him a notice to quit. Central to the case was whether the occupier was a tenant or a licensee. The Court of Appeal unanimously held him to be a licensee.

---

[30] See *Lynes v. Snaith* [1899] 1 Q.B. 466.   [31] [1977] 1 W.L.R. 1181.

Lord Denning M.R. sought to explain how one decides these matters. He said:

'What is the test to see whether the occupier of one room in a house is a tenant or a licensee? It does not depend on whether he has exclusive possession or not. It does not depend on whether the room is furnished or not. It does not depend on whether the occupation is permanent or temporary. It does not depend on the label which the parties put on it. All these are factors which may influence the decision but none of them is conclusive. All the circumstances have to be worked out. Eventually the answer depends upon the nature and quality of the occupancy. Was it intended that the occupier should have a stake in the room or did he have only permission for himself personally to occupy the room, whether under a contract or not? In which case he is a licensee.'[32]

Exclusive occupation

While the decision in this case was undoubtedly correct, the language used in this passage is unhelpful, in that it regards the grant of exclusive possession as being merely one factor in the determination of whether a lease or a licence has been created. As to the first issue, it is quite possible that Lord Denning was using the term 'exclusive possession' loosely, to mean exclusive occupation, which is a factual description of the situation where a room is not actually shared.[33] Exclusive occupation is not an expression which is determinative of the question as to whether the occupier has the right to exclude all others, which is a legal concept.[34] Secondly, it appears to give undue weight to the stated intention of the parties not to create an interest in land.[35] Whereas, Lord Denning was clear that the parties could not convert a lease into a licence simply by attaching that title to the relevant document, his remarks, if taken at face value, would seem to indicate that one could achieve the same result by the statement of an intention to create only a personal interest in the property.

The primacy of exclusive possession

Whatever the correct reading of this passage, greater clarity was re-established by the House of Lords in the leading case of *Street v. Mountford*,[36] a decision which re-established the primacy of exclusive possession and downplayed the stated intentions of the parties. Mrs Mountford[37] signed an agreement, termed a licence agreement, whereby she was given the right to occupy two rooms for a weekly licence fee of £37. At the foot of the document was a statement, signed by her, which read: 'I understand and accept that a licence in the above form does not and is not intended to give me a

---

[32] Ibid., at 1185. For an unwelcome echo of this approach, see *Mehta v. Royal Bank of Scotland* [1999] 3 E.G.L.R. 153 at 156 *per* Mr Richard Southwell Q.C.

[33] For a more recent example of this, see *Vesely v. Levy* [2007] EWCA Civ. 367 at [43] *per* Mummery L.J.

[34] For a valuable discussion of this matter, see M.C. Cullity (1965) 28 Conv. (N.S.) 336.

[35] For a general discussion of the role of intention in the creation of interests in land, see M. Howard and J. Hill (1995) 15 L.S. 356.

[36] [1985] A.C. 809. See S. Anderson (1985) 48 M.L.R. 712; D.N. Clarke [1986] Conv. 39. For a critical reaction by the draftsman of the document, and the loser in the litigation, see R. Street [1985] Conv. 328.

[37] The headnote refers to her husband occupying the rooms but no mention of him appears in the speech of Lord Templeman and the case is treated throughout as a single occupancy agreement.

tenancy protected under the Rent Acts.' She then sought to have a fair rent registered, whereupon the owner of the house sought a declaration that she was a licensee and not a tenant. The House of Lords held her to be a tenant.

A key concession was made. It was conceded that the agreement gave Mrs Mountford exclusive possession of the rooms. Nevertheless, it was argued that, because there was no intention to create a lease, the agreement operated only to create a contractual licence. This argument was rejected. Lord Templeman, who gave the only speech, was at pains to re-assert the role of exclusive possession. He said:

'the court must decide whether upon its true construction, the agreement confers upon the occupier exclusive possession. If exclusive possession at a rent for a term[38] does not constitute a tenancy then the distinction between a contractual tenancy and a contractual licence of land becomes wholly illusory.'[39]

As it had been conceded that Mrs Mountford had exclusive possession for a term at a rent, it followed that she was a tenant. The fact that the parties had stated that their intention was to create a licence was irrelevant. Intention is relevant only insofar as it indicates an intent to grant exclusive possession. Once an agreement has been made, the consequences of that agreement have to be determined as a matter of law. 'If the agreement satisfied all the requirements of a tenancy, then the agreement produced a tenancy and the parties cannot alter the effect of the agreement by insisting that they only created a licence. The manufacture of a five-pronged implement for digging results in a fork even if the manufacturer, unfamiliar with the English language, insists that he intended to make and has made a spade.'[40]

Rent

Before considering more closely the analysis contained in the decision, an initial point can be made concerning rent. On more than one occasion, Lord Templeman emphasized the importance to the finding that where there is a lease there is a payment of rent, seemingly indicating that, for a lease to be created, a rent must be reserved.[41] This, however, is not correct, in that the statutory definition of a lease expressly includes situations where there is no payment of rent[42] and so it is possible for a tenancy to be created when no rent has been reserved.[43] The absence of rent may, however, militate against the finding of a lease because, unless there is some other form of consideration, there will be no contract and, consequently, no lease.

---

[38] For the need for a certain term, see *Berrisford v. Mexfield Housing Co-operative* [2011] UKSC 52, and see Certainty, pp. 400–403.

[39] [1985] A.C. 809 at 825.

[40] Ibid., at 819 *per* Lord Templeman. See also *Addiscombe Garden Estates Ltd v. Crabbe* [1958] 1 Q.B. 513 at 533 *per* Jenkins L.J.

[41] Ibid., at 816, 818, 825.   [42] Law of Property Act 1925, s. 205(1)(xxvii).

[43] *Ashburn Anstalt v. Arnold* [1989] Ch. 1 at 9–10 *per* Fox L.J. This aspect of the case is not affected by the overruling of the decision in *Prudential Assurance Co. Ltd v. London Residuary Body* [1992] 2 A.C. 386.

On the other hand, the fact that money is paid in respect of occupation does not necessarily mean that this payment constitutes rent, or that there is necessarily an intention to create legal relations. In *Leadenhall Residential 2 Ltd v. Stirling*,[44] a possession order was made against a tenant on the ground of non-payment of rent. Liberty was given to the landlord to accept some £411.66 per month as mesne profits until possession was given. The tenant was allowed to continue in occupation and paid this sum, together with £100 per month in respect of the accumulated arrears. The Court of Appeal held that there was no payment of rent. The landlord had allowed the tenant to remain in the property as an act of kindness and there was no intention to create legal relations.[45] The monetary payment was in lieu of damages for trespass.

Leases and lodgings

In his analysis of the previous case law, Lord Templeman shifted the focus from the intention of the parties with regard to what it was that the agreement created, to the central issue of whether or not the agreement conferred exclusive possession in the sense of the right to exclude all others from the property. In determining whether or not exclusive possession had been granted, he distinguished between a lease and lodgings. He said:

'In the case of residential accommodation there is no difficulty in deciding whether the grant confers exclusive accommodation. An occupier of residential accommodation at a rent for a term is either a lodger or a tenant. The occupier is a lodger if the landlord provides attendance or services *which require the landlord or his servants to exercise unrestricted access to and use of the premises*. A lodger is entitled to live in the premises but cannot call the place his own.'[46]

This passage explains why the decision in a case like *Marchant v. Charters* is correct, although the language used in it is not. In that case, the occupant's room was cleaned on a daily basis and fresh linen supplied weekly. The real reason why this was not a tenancy was that the occupier did not have exclusive possession; the provision of services was such that the landlady's employee required unrestricted access to the property and so, in Lord Templeman's terminology, the occupier was a lodger.

In the residential context,[47] it is often fairly straightforward to determine whether the agreement confers exclusive possession on the occupier. The level of access necessary for the provision of services is a decisive factor, so that a student in a hall of residence or an occupant in a hotel will, although in exclusive occupation of the room in question,

---

[44] [2002] 1 W.L.R. 499.

[45] The relevant intention is to create legal relations, not an intention to create a lease, contrary to what was said in *Vesely v. Hart* [2007] EWCA Civ. 367 at [49] *per* Mummery L.J.

[46] [1985] A.C. 809 at 817–818, emphasis supplied.

[47] For more problematic cases in the commercial sector, see *Addiscombe Garden Estates Ltd v. Crabbe* [1958] 1 Q.B. 513; *Shell-Mex and B.P. Ltd v. Manchester Garages Ltd* [1971] 1 W.L.R. 612.

not have exclusive possession.[48] What can present rather more difficulty is where it is not clear that the terms of the agreement represent the reality of the situation. This can involve 're-routing the legal relationship so as to take it outside the remit of the protective legislation'.[49] This process frequently involves an attempt to create a licence rather than a lease, but can involve the inclusion of wholly unrealistic clauses into the agreement. An example of this is a rent review clause enabling the landlord to raise the rent paid by tenants on housing benefit from £4,690 per annum to £25,000 per annum,[50] designed, in this case unsuccessfully, to deprive tenants of their statutory protection.

Shams

In *Crancour Ltd v. Da Silvaesa*,[51] one of the terms of a 'licence' agreement required the occupants to vacate their rooms between 10.30 a.m. and noon on each day to enable cleaning to take place. Such a term was, in the context of the case, regarded with suspicion and was arguably a sham, so that a summary order for possession was not regarded as appropriate. The agreements also provided for the provision of extensive services, although it was not clear that these were actually provided. In the circumstances, it was not clear whether the written agreement reflected the actuality and so, before deciding whether the agreement was for a lease or lodgings, further factual investigation was necessary.

When the agreement envisages the provision of services which require the landlord to be able to go in and out of the lodger's rooms at his convenience,[52] a question arises as to the position if such services are not provided. If they are provided at the outset but their provision subsequently drops off, then the case is still likely to be regarded as involving lodgings, with the lodger having the right to insist upon their resumption.[53] Where the services are never provided, although under the agreement the occupier could presumably insist upon them, another way of looking at the situation is to regard the clause as being inserted solely to seek to prevent the creation of the tenancy and not reflecting the reality of the situation, in which case a tenancy is likely be the result of the agreement.[54]

Access and the provision of services

The key issue in such cases is whether the clause in the contract relating to access is genuine. The matter was explained thus, by Peter Gibson L.J., in *Uratemp Ventures Ltd v. Collins*:[55]

'The crucial matter is whether the occupier has exclusive possession. If the owner of the building is contractually obliged to provide attendance or services that require entry into

---

[48] See *Isaac v. Hotel de Paris Ltd* [1960] 1 W.L.R. 238; *Abbeyfield (Harpenden) Society Ltd v. Woods* [1968] 1 W.L.R. 374.

[49] S. Bright, loc. cit., at 147–148.

[50] *Bankway Properties Ltd v. Pensfold-Dunsford* [2001] 1 W.L.R. 1369.   [51] (1986) 18 H.L.R. 265.

[52] Ibid., at 273 *per* Ralph Gibson L.J.   [53] See *Huwyler v. Ruddy* (1995) 28 H.L.R. 550.

[54] See *Crancour Ltd v. Da Silvaesa* (1986) 18 H.L.R. 265 at 278 *per* Ralph Gibson L.J.; *Grimsby College Enterprises Ltd v. HMRC* [2010] UKUT at [22]–[23] *per* Briggs J.

[55] [2000] 1 E.G.L.R. 156 at 157 reversed without reference to this issue: [2002] A.C. 301.

the room, then the retention of a key for that purpose is a strong indication that the occupier of the room is only a lodger under a licence, without exclusive possession. The fact that an occupier chooses not to avail himself of the attendance or services to which he is entitled cannot convert a licence into a tenancy.'

The point here is choice. If it is never envisaged that the services will be provided, then the arrangement will be a tenancy. If the occupier genuinely declines to accept the services to which he is entitled, the occupancy will be as a lodger.

The extent of the degree of access can be important. One of the issues which arose in *Mehta v. Royal Bank of Scotland*,[56] was the status of a long-term resident of a hotel, who had been wrongly evicted from his room. Under the terms of the agreement, the occupier was entitled to have his linen changed and his room cleaned every fortnight. In approaching the question as to whether the plaintiff was a tenant or a licensee, Mr Richard Southwell Q.C., sitting as a Deputy High Court judge, said:

'Like Lord Templeman, I have concerns as to how contractual tenancies and licences are, in general, to be distinguished but, in my judgment, there is no simple all-embracing test for such a distinction. The search for such a test would be a chimera. What each court, faced with the need to make the distinction, has to do is to weigh all the relevant and significant factors and decide in the light of them on which side of the line the particular case falls.'[57]

Applying this, seemingly intuitive, process, the judge concluded that the claimant was a licensee.[58]

It is suggested that this approach to the problem is entirely misconceived and flies in the face of *Street v. Mountford*. The issue in the case should have been whether the plaintiff actually had exclusive possession. This, in turn, should have depended upon whether the degree of access necessary for the provision of attendance meant that, in Lord Templeman's terms, the occupier was a lodger. That degree of access was regarded by the judge as being 'almost minimal'.[59] If that truly was the case, then the occupier should have been regarded as being a tenant: if not, a licensee. It is to be hoped that this decision does not mark a return to the uncertainties which bedevilled this branch of the law prior to the landmark decision in *Street v. Mountford*.

New occupiers

Subject to what has just been said, in the context of residential property, the easiest way of distinguishing between a lease and a licence is the provision of services and the resulting need of access by the landlord or his representatives. Another method which has been employed in an attempt to create a licence is to seek to insist upon the right to introduce new occupiers into the property or to be able to move the occupier into alternative accommodation. In the private sector, such a clause is unlikely to be

---

[56] [1999] 3 E.G.L.R. 153.   [57] Ibid., at 156.

[58] Reliance was placed on *Luganda v. Service Hotels* [1969] 2 Ch. 209 and *Marchant v. Charters* [1977] 1 W.L.R. 1181, both of which have to be read in the light of Lord Templeman's speech in *Street v. Mountford*.

[59] [1999] 3 E.G.L.R. 153 at 155.

successful as a means of preventing the creation of a tenancy. In *Aslan v. Murphy*,[60] an occupier of a basement measuring 4'3" by 12'6" was required by the document he had signed to share the accommodation with another occupier and to vacate the property for one hour and thirty minutes each day. Both clauses were regarded as being 'wholly unrealistic and were clearly pretences'.[61] They were disregarded and the occupier was held to be a tenant. In the public sector, on the other hand, clauses requiring occupiers to share rooms with others and to move to a different room when required to do so were regarded by the House of Lords in *Westminster City Council v. Jones*[62] as being quite genuine in the context of the provision of shelter for homeless men, with the result that exclusive possession had not been granted and such agreements were regarded as licences.

Other relationships

Although Lord Templeman, in *Street v. Mountford*, accepted that the grant of exclusive possession was one of the hallmarks of a lease, he accepted also that situations could exist where exclusive possession had been granted but a lease had not been created. Examples of this were given as including an owner in fee simple, a trespasser, a mortgagee in possession, an object of charity, or a service occupier.[63]

Of these examples, some, such as the owner in fee simple, obviously do not involve the relationship of landlord and tenant but others seem to misuse the term 'exclusive possession' in that the nature of the relationship is such that the occupier does not have the right to exclude others from the property. Thus, for example, a trespasser has the right to exclude all others but the actual owner from the property and the issue which can then arise is whether the acceptance of payment in respect of the occupation will give rise to a tenancy.[64]

Charity

There have been a number of cases where a person has been allowed exclusive use of property but no tenancy has been created, the reason being that the arrangement was based upon an act of charity. In *Booker v. Palmer*,[65] the owner of a cottage allowed a person who had been bombed out of her own home to occupy the cottage for the duration of the war. It was held that a licence had been created, the reason being that there was no intention to enter into legal relations or, put another way, there was no contractual relationship between the parties at all.[66]

---

[60] [1990] 1 W.L.R. 766.   [61] Ibid., at 773 *per* Lord Donaldson of Lymington M.R.
[62] [1992] 2 A.C. 288.
[63] [1985] A.C. 809 at 818; *Ramnarace v. Lutchman* [2001] 1 W.L.R. 1651 at 1656 *per* Lord Millett. That the landlord is fulfilling a social function in providing accommodation for the homeless or lacks title to grant a tenancy are not special considerations preventing the formation of a lease: *Bruton v. London and Quadrant Housing Trust* [2000] 1 A.C. 406.
[64] Cf. *Westminster City Council v. Basson* (1990) 62 P. & C.R. 57 and *Tower Hamlets London Borough v. Ayinde* (1994) 26 H.L.R. 631.
[65] [1942] 2 All E.R. 674. See also *Heslop v. Burns* [1974] 1 W.L.R. 1241.
[66] See also *Marcroft Wagons Ltd v. Smith* [1951] 2 K.B. 496.

Such cases are, by their nature, unusual and are very unlikely to occur when the parties are, at the outset, dealing with each other at arm's length.[67] Even in cases where the parties are related, this does not preclude a contractual relationship being created.[68] The type of case where a licence is found is where 'there has been something in the circumstances, such as a family arrangement, an act of friendship or generosity, or such like, to negative any intention to create a tenancy...'.[69] In such cases, the occupier, as a gratuitous licensee, does not have exclusive possession at all, as he can be evicted by the owner on the giving of reasonable notice.

Service occupancy

An occupier will not be a tenant if he is required to live in particular accommodation for the better performance of his employment.[70] An example of such a relationship would be a farm worker living in a tied cottage and, perhaps less obviously, a university vice-chancellor who may be required, contractually, to live in a house owned by the university.

Purchasers

In *Street v. Mountford*,[71] Lord Templeman accepted that a purchaser who entered into possession after the entry into a contract to buy the property would occupy as a licensee. To come within this exception the occupation must be under the contract and not in contemplation of the making of such a contract in the future.[72]

Multiple occupancy

In most cases of single occupancy, the test of whether the occupier has exclusive possession relates to whether the provision of services requires the landlord to have unrestricted access to the property; the distinction is between leases and lodgings. In cases of multiple occupancy, the issue of whether or not exclusive possession has been granted remains of central importance. In deciding this matter, however, the degree of access required by the landlord in order to provide services is not the main point of contention. Rather, it is the relationship of the occupiers with each other which can determine whether they are tenants or licensees.

In *Somma v. Hazelhurst*,[73] a cohabiting couple agreed to take a one-room bedsit, which contained two single beds. They signed separate agreements under which each of them agreed to pay a specified sum of money by weekly instalments. The agreements, entitled licences, which they each signed, were identical. Under the terms of the licences, each licensee was required to share the room with the licensor and such other licensees as the licensor should permit to occupy it. The question arose as to their

[67] See *Facchini v. Bryson* [1952] 1 T.L.R. 1386.   [68] See *Nunn v. Dalrymple* (1989) 21 H.L.R. 569.
[69] *Facchini v. Bryson* [1952] 1 T.L.R. 1386 at 1389–1390 *per* Denning L.J. See also *Holt v. Wellington* (1996) 71 P. & C.R. D.40.
[70] *Glasgow Corporation v. Johnstone* [1965] A.C. 609; *Wragg v. Surrey County Council* [2008] H.L.R. 30.
[71] [1985] A.C. 809 at 827.   [72] *Bretherton v. Paton* (1986) 18 H.L.R. 257.
[73] [1978] 1 W.L.R. 1014.

status and the Court of Appeal rejected the argument that they were joint tenants and, instead, held that they were licensees.

Liability to pay rent

The crucial aspects of the reasoning were the reservation of the right by the licensor to move into the room with the couple, this not being regarded as being contrary to public policy, and the provisions regarding the payment for the room. If the couple were joint tenants, then each, as an incident of the joint tenancy, would be jointly and severally liable for the rent; either of them could be pursued by the landlady for the entire rent payable for the room. In the present case, however, each was only liable to pay a specified sum, which amounted to half of the total consideration payable. As they were not jointly and severally liable, this was considered to be fatal to the claim that they were joint tenants. As they were not joint tenants, the result was that they did not form one legal entity enjoying exclusive possession;[74] neither did they, as individuals, enjoy exclusive possession, as each was required to share with the other. The result was that they were licensees.

The effect of this decision was potentially very wide-ranging as it enabled landlords in cases of multiple occupancy arrangements to avoid creating tenancies by the simple expedient of entering into separate agreements with each of the occupiers.[75] As such, it meant that it was facile for the Rent Acts to be neatly avoided in this type of situation. For this reason, there was some relief when *Somma* was overruled in *Street v. Mountford*. Unfortunately, however, when overruling this decision, Lord Templeman did not address the reasoning employed in the case. Instead, he based his disapproval of the decision on his view of the separate licences being a sham. He regarded the couple as being joint tenants. As to the notion that, realistically, the couple could be expected to share the room with such other person as the landlady might nominate, he was scathing. In his view, 'The sham nature of this obligation would have only been slightly more obvious if H and S had been married or if the room had been furnished with a double bed instead of two single beds.'[76]

As the documents signed separately by the couple bore no relation to the reality of the situation, the situation was analysed as being a straightforward case of a joint tenancy.

Genuine sharing arrangements

This view of *Somma v. Hazelhurst* was entirely understandable. What was unfortunate was that the reasoning provided no assistance in cases where such agreements were, at

---

[74] For an argument that they could have been regarded as joint tenants at law, but tenancies in common in equity, see Thompson, *Co-Ownership* (London: Sweet & Maxwell, 1988) 63–64.

[75] For attempts to do this which failed on the facts, see *Demuren v. Seal Estates Ltd* (1978) 249 E.G. 440; *O'Malley v. Seymour* (1978) 250 E.G. 1083, which, for different reasons, were considered to be shams. For successful attempts, see *Aldrington Garages Ltd v. Fielder* (1978) 248 E.G. 557; *Sturulson & Co. v. Weniz* (1984) 17 H.L.R. 740.

[76] [1985] A.C. 809 at 825.

least arguably, genuine. A number of cases such as this occurred subsequent to *Street v. Mountford* and it was found that the simple disapproval of *Somma* on the basis that it was a sham provided little assistance.[77] In sharing cases, one could not determine whether or not a lease had been created simply by distinguishing between leases and lodgings. In *Hadjiloucas v. Crean*,[78] two friends agreed to rent an unfurnished two-roomed flat. Each signed separate, but identical, licence agreements which required each of them to share the flat with one other licensee. After one of the licensees had left, the question arose as to the status of the other and whether a tenancy or a licence had originally been created.

The Court of Appeal remitted the case for a retrial so that the actual facts of the case could be more clearly established. It was considered, however, that Lord Templeman's speech should be read principally in the context of single occupation where exclusive possession was conceded,[79] and that cases such as the present one needed a more careful factual analysis. Mustill L.J. considered that, in cases of this type, there were three possibilities. These were that the occupiers were licensees or that one of two forms of tenancy had been created. The first involved all the occupiers being joint tenants and the second involved each occupier having a separate tenancy of part of the house—that is their own room—with the landlord.[80]

The matter was revisited by the House of Lords in the conjoined appeals in *A.G. Securities Ltd v. Vaughan* and *Antoniades v. Villiers*.[81] The facts of the two cases were very different. In *Vaughan*, the property in question was a furnished four-bedroom flat. Individual agreements were entered into with each occupier. Under these agreements, the rent payable by each occupier was different from that paid by the others and, in some cases, the period of occupation also differed. When one occupant left, he was replaced by another who entered into a new, and separate, agreement with the freeholder. In *Villiers*, the facts were virtually identical to those of *Somma v. Hazelhurst* and it was clear that the agreements signed by the occupants were modelled on those used in *Somma*. Each licence agreement gave the 'licensor' the right to introduce a third occupier into the flat. The only distinction between this case and *Somma* was that here there were two bedrooms, so that the possibility of introducing a third person into the flat was rather more feasible than was the case in *Somma*. The House of Lords, in each case reversing decisions of the Court of Appeal, held that in *Vaughan* the occupiers were licensees and in *Villiers* they were joint tenants.

Independent and interdependent agreements

The difference between the two cases was that in *Vaughan*, the documents reflected the reality of the situation, whereas in *Villiers* they did not. In *Vaughan*, the reality of the situation was that these were genuinely independent agreements to cater for a fluctuating body of people occupying the same household.[82] While it was accepted

---

[77] See *Stribling v. Wickham* [1989] 2 E.G.L.R. 35; *Brooker Estates Ltd v. Ayres* (1986) 19 H.L.R. 1375.
[78] [1988] 1 W.L.R. 1006.   [79] Ibid., at 1013 *per* Purchas L.J.   [80] Ibid., at 1023.
[81] [1990] 1 A.C. 417.   [82] See also *UHU Property Trust v. Lincoln City Council* [2000] R.A. 419.

that there could have been separate tenancies of a part of the house,[83] this did not occur in the present case, perhaps because the practice was that, when one of the occupants left, the remaining occupants chose whether they wished to move into the vacated room. Neither could they, collectively, be seen as joint tenants, as there was no unity of time, title or interest between them. In *Villiers*, on the other hand, the view was taken that 'the two agreements were interdependent. Both would have signed or neither. The two agreements must therefore be read together.'[84] Reading them together, the effect was that the couple were joint tenants, each being jointly and severally liable for the rent. The provision in the agreements to introduce a third person into the property was seen as being quite unrealistic and, in any event, as the original agreement had been held to create a joint tenancy, the introduction of a third person was not something which the landlord could do. To do this would have involved the termination of the original lease and the creation of a new licence and this is not permitted by the Rent Act 1977.[85]

In a case such as *Villiers*, where the couple are in a neo-marital relationship, it is relatively easy to conclude that the agreements are interdependent and should be read together as a composite whole. Other sharing arrangements may occur, however, where the occupants of the property are not linked together in this way, for example if a group of students rent a house together and are made to sign separate documents. It may then be difficult, on the facts, to determine whether the agreements should be regarded as genuinely independent or interdependent.[86] Perhaps ironically, it is now more in the landlord's interest to ensure that the occupiers are, in fact, joint tenants. This is because the statutory regime now in operation is far less onerous to landlords and the desire to avoid the creation of a tenancy is far less strong than was previously the case. A joint tenancy is now preferable because, if one of the occupiers leaves before the end of the term, the landlord can, if the group were joint tenants, look to the remaining occupants for the rent on the property and not have to pursue the person who left prematurely for the money he had agreed to pay. It is noticeable that with the reduction in the protection afforded to residential tenants, cases involving the lease/licence distinction have become far less common than was previously the case.

Reform

As indicated previously, the backcloth against which much of this litigation took place was that of a high degree of regulation of the rental sector. Landlords were very keen to avoid creating agreements which conferred the protection of the Rent Acts on residential occupiers and, to this end, expended considerable ingenuity in seeking to craft agreements which fell outside the terms of the legislation. A favourite device

[83] [2000] R.A. 419 at 460 *per* Lord Templeman.   [84] Ibid.
[85] Ibid., at 462 *per* Lord Templeman. See also *Duke v. Wynne* [1990] 1 W.L.R. 766 at 775–776 *per* Lord Donaldson of Lymington M.R.
[86] See *Mikeover v. Brady* (1989) 21 H.L.R. 513 (an unfortunate decision on the facts).

employed to achieve this aim was to attempt to create a contractual occupancy licence, as opposed to a lease. Since the changes introduced by the Housing Act 1988, much of the heat has been removed from this area with the result that, as between the parties to the agreement, the significance of the agreement being a lease, as opposed to a licence, has declined significantly. In recognition of this, the Law Commission has proposed that this once fundamental divide be to a large extent abrogated.

What is proposed is that, in the residential sector,[87] the rights and obligations of the parties will be governed by the residential contract which they enter into. As between the parties themselves,[88] it will be immaterial whether the contract creates a lease or a licence. It is the contract itself which will govern the relationship between the parties. The contents of those contracts will then be regulated by a consumer approach, so that respective rights and obligations of the parties to it will be substantially the same as those which exist already with regard to residential tenancies.[89] The implementation of these proposals will remove from the sphere of litigation the perennially contentious dispute as to whether an agreement has created a lease or a licence. Given the substantial deregulation of the residential leasehold sector, this reform is to be welcomed. As yet, however, there appears to be little sign of its implementation.

Contracting parties

Under the existing law, because a lease creates a legal estate in land, a minor lacks the capacity to become a legal tenant.[90] It is now proposed that residential contracts can be entered into by people aged sixteen and seventeen.[91] The reason given for this proposal is that the present law presents problems, in particular for social landlords who want to provide secure accommodation for people in this age group.[92] To this reason can be added a second, that people of this age do have the capacity to marry but, under the existing law, lack capacity to own a legal estate in their matrimonial home.

Minors

The potential problems inherent in this area were highlighted in *Hammersmith and Fulham London Borough Council v. Alexander-David*.[93] A local authority granted a tenancy to a homeless 16 year old girl, who had a priority need. A year later, following various complaints concerning her conduct, the authority served a notice to

---

[87] Agreements such as business tenancies or agricultural tenancies will be excluded from the new scheme, as will certain types of agreement excluded on social grounds. See (2003) Law Com. No. 284, paras 3.15 and 6.26–6.29.

[88] As is recognized in the Report, itself, this distinction will remain important insofar as third parties are concerned: ibid., at para. 6.20. See also *Berrisfield v. Mexfield Housing Co-operative Ltd* [2011] UKSC 52. See Contractual licences, pp. 597–601. and Contractual licences and third parties, pp. 602–609.

[89] (2003) Law Com. No. 284, Part VIII.   [90] Law of Property Act 1925, s. 1(6).

[91] (2003) Law Com. No. 284, para. 3.18.

[92] See J. Morgan in Cooke (ed.) *Modern Studies in Property Law, Volume 2* (Oxford: Hart Publishing, 2002) Chapter 13.

[93] [2009] 3 All E.R. 1098.

quit. This was held to be invalid. The reason was that, because the lease purported to be granted to a minor, under paragraph 1(1) of Schedule One of the Trusts of Land and Appointment of Trustees Act 1996 this was ineffective to pass a legal estate, and, instead, took effect as a declaration of trust in favour of the minor. Because the authority was a trustee, it was not open to it to serve a notice to quit, thereby terminating the beneficial interest which had been created. Pending any change in the law relating to minors, the solution to this practical problem would appear to be for the local authority to provide sufficient services to the minor so as to create a licence as opposed to a lease, such an arrangement not creating a trust.[94]

Number of tenants

Under the current law, the maximum number of people who can own a legal estate is four.[95] The Law Commission sees this restriction on estate ownership as being irrelevant to housing law, and recommends that, subject to the statutory rules on overcrowding, this restriction should be lifted, so that any number of people can be party to an occupation agreement. Again, this seems sensible. It is commonplace for more than four students to take a tenancy of a house, little realizing that, under the existing law, only the first four named in the agreement are actually legal tenants of the property, holding on trust for their fellow occupants.[96]

TYPES OF TENANCY

There are a number of different types of tenancy which can be created, which will be considered in turn.

Fixed term tenancy

As the name suggests, this form of tenancy occurs when the start and finish of the lease is set out in advance. A fixed term tenancy can be of any length. As a term of years is defined to include terms of less than a year,[97] a fixed term tenancy of a week is a perfectly valid, if unusual, concept. At the other extreme, one can have a fixed term tenancy of two thousand years. The parties are free to choose whatever length of term that they please.

Once a fixed term tenancy has been created, it is not open to one party, unilaterally, to determine it. This is so unless the lease contains a break clause entitling either side, on complying with the conditions, if any, set out in the clause, to terminate the lease. It is not open for the tenant to seek simply to abandon the tenancy, and the landlord is not under any obligation in order to mitigate his loss to forfeit the lease for

---

[94] Ibid., at [37] *per* Sullivan L.J.   [95] Law of Property Act 1925, s. 34(2).   [96] Ibid.
[97] Law of Property Act 1925, s. 205(1)(xxvii).

non-payment of rent,[98] and it is, in any event, unclear whether a landlord who adopts this course could sue for the future rent.[99] In the case of long leases at a rent, the rent originally reserved by the lease will, in time, cease to reflect the prevailing economic conditions. For this reason, it is usual for commercial leases to contain rent review clauses to provide a machinery whereby the rent can be recalculated periodically during the duration of the lease.

A lease need not take effect in possession. A lease created in 2012 may take effect in 2013. Such a lease is termed a reversionary lease. Such a lease, if granted at a rent or in consideration of a fine, must take effect in possession not more than twenty-one years from the date of the grant and otherwise will be void. Similarly, a contract to create such a lease will also be void.[100] A lease granted in 2012 to take effect in possession in 2033 is therefore void, as is a contract in 2012 to create a lease in 2013 to take effect in possession in 2033. Perhaps somewhat oddly, a contract in 2012 to create a lease to take effect in possession in 2033 is not void as the lease to be created at that date is not a reversionary lease.[101]

Periodic tenancies

A periodic tenancy is a tenancy created initially for a given period but that period will recur until the lease is brought to an end. Thus, if a yearly tenancy is created, then at the end of the first year, a new period of a year will automatically be created and this process will be repeated at the end of the second year, and so on. A periodic tenancy can, therefore, in theory run indefinitely.

An obvious objection to such a lease is the requirement that, to be valid, a lease must be for a term certain. At the start of a periodic tenancy, one cannot know in advance for how long the landlord and tenant relationship will continue.[102] The answer is that the original uncertainty can be made certain by the act of either of the parties; the periodic tenancy will continue to recur until either party brings it to an end by the service of a notice to quit. It is not dependent upon the occurrence of some external event, the happening of which is not necessarily in the control of either party. For this reason, the courts have had difficulties with agreements which have the effect of fettering of the power of one of them, normally the landlord, to end the periodic tenancy by the service of a notice to quit.

Restricting service of notice to quit
The ability of either side to end a periodic tenancy by the service of a notice to quit was seen as a vital element in such a tenancy being considered to be sufficiently certain so

[98] *Reichman v. Beveridge* [2006] EWCA Civ. 1659. For forfeiture, see Forfeiture, pp. 454–459.
[99] Ibid., at [22]–[28] *per* Thomas L.J.   [100] Ibid., s. 149(3).
[101] *Re Strand and Savoy Properties Ltd* [1960] Ch. 582.
[102] See *Berrisford v. Mexfield Housing Co-operative Ltd* [2011] UKSC 52 at [87]–[88] *per* Lady Hale, who described the rules as having an 'Alice in Wonderland quality'.

as to constitute a valid lease. As Lord Templeman put it in *Prudential Assurance Co. Ltd v. London Residuary Body*:[103]

'A term must be either certain or uncertain. It cannot be partly certain because the tenant can determine it at any time and partly uncertain because the landlord cannot determine it for an uncertain period. If a landlord does not grant and the tenant does not take a certain term the grant does not create a lease.'

On the basis of this reasoning, a restriction on the ability of either side to serve a valid notice to quit, thereby bringing the periodic tenancy to an end would cause the lease to fail.[104] In *Berrisford v. Mexfield Housing Co-operative Ltd*,[105] however, the supreme Court modified this principle considerably but, although out of sympathy with the underlying reasoning, declined to overrule the earlier House of Lords decision in *Prudential*.

In approaching this issue, it was first noted that a periodic tenancy with a fetter on the service of a notice to quit for a specified period was valid. In *Breams Property Investment Co. Ld v. Stroulger*[106] it was agreed that there should be a quarterly tenancy, but that the landlord would be restrained from serving a notice to quit for the first three years unless the premises were required by the landlord for its own occupation. This was upheld as a valid lease, it being explained as being a fixed three-year term terminable by notice served by the tenant, to be followed by a normal quarterly tenancy.[107] If the fetter was for an indeterminate period, however, this reasoning could not apply. The solution, therefore, was to hold that such an agreement was effective to create a lease for life. This, in turn, was converted by section 149(6) of the Law of Property Act 1925 into a ninety-year term determinable on either the death of the tenant, or an appropriately served notice to quit.

Corporate tenants

This reasoning is applicable only to human tenants, it being accepted that a company, albeit an entity with legal personality, cannot possess a lease for life. In the case of such an agreement, however, the Supreme Court accepted that, despite the agreement not being a lease, the parties would, as a matter of contract law, be bound by what had been agreed. The effect of this is that the freeholder will be precluded from terminating the licence except on the terms set out in the agreement. The licensee will be vulnerable, however, if the freeholder sells the land to a purchaser, who will not be bound by the licence.[108]

Express or implied periodic tenancies

A periodic tenancy may arise either expressly or by implication.

---

[103] [1992] A.C. 386 at 395.

[104] *Cheshire Lines Committee v. Lewis & Co.* (1880) 50 L.J.Q.B. 121; *Centaploy Ltd v. Matlodge Ltd* [1974] Ch.1; *Re Midland Railway Co.'s Agreement* [1971] Ch. 725 and *Ashburn Anstalt v. Arnold* [1989] Ch. 1 to the contrary were all overruled in the *Prudential Case*: [1992] A.C. 386 at 395 *per* Lord Templeman.

[105] [2011] UKSC 52.   [106] [1948] 2 K.B. 1.   [107] [2011] UKSC 52 at [88] *per* Lady Hale.

[108] See Chapter 15.

Express periodic tenancies

An express periodic tenancy would arise by a statement such as the tenancy to be granted is a yearly tenancy or a tenancy from year to year and the earliest date on which a notice to quit can be given is at the end of the first period, that is one year from the creation of the tenancy. If, however, the grant is for a year and then from year to year, this takes effect as a fixed term tenancy of one year, followed by a yearly periodic tenancy and, so notice to quit can only be served two years from the commencement of the term.[109]

Implied periodic tenancies

When a person goes into possession and pays rent to the freeholder, the law will imply a periodic tenancy.[110] This situation can occur in more than one situation. First, there is a situation where there is no actual agreement between the parties and a periodic tenancy is implied. Secondly, the purported lease may, for some reason, be void. This occurred in *Prudential Assurance Co. Ltd v. London Residuary Body*,[111] where the purported lease was held to be void for uncertainty but the tenant had gone into possession and had paid rent. 'The tenant entering under a void lease became by virtue of possession and the payment of a yearly rent, a yearly tenant holding on the terms of the agreement so far as those terms were consistent with the yearly tenancy.'[112] As the tenancy was a periodic tenancy, it could be terminated upon the service by the landlord of an appropriate notice to quit. In the light of the decision in *Berrisford*, however, such a situation will now be rare.

The period

The way that the period on which the periodic tenancy is based is arrived at by having regard to the method by which the rent is quantified. If the rent is £104 per annum, paid at £2.00 per week, then the tenancy is a yearly tenancy because the rent is measured by the year. If, however, the rent is simply £2.00 per week, then a weekly tenancy is created.[113] The length of the period is important as it is determinative of the length of the notice to quit which must given to terminate the lease.

Options to renew

What, at first sight, may appear to be similar to a periodic tenancy is a tenancy which contains an option for the tenant to renew the lease. Such a position is, in fact, the opposite of a periodic tenancy in that, whereas a periodic tenancy will continue in being until either party brings it to an end by the service of a notice to quit, a lease

---

[109] *Re Searle* [1912] 1 Ch. 610.   [110] *Doe d. Rigg v. Bell* (1793) 5 Durn. & E. 471.
[111] [1992] 2 A.C. 386.   [112] Ibid., at 392 *per* Lord Templeman.
[113] See *Ladies' Hosiery and Knitwear Ltd v. Parker* [1930] 1 Ch. 304 at 328–329 *per* Maugham J.; *Adler v. Blackman* [1953] 1 Q.B. 146.

with an option to renew will end naturally, unless the tenant exercises the option.[114] Care must be taken when drafting such an option. In particular, the option should not be worded so as to state that the new lease which will be created by the exercise of the option will be on the same terms as the original lease. The effect of such a clause is that the lease created on the exercise of the option will, itself, confer upon the tenant an option to renew, again on the same terms as the original lease. Such a lease is regarded as being perpetually renewable,[115] and such leases are converted by statute into a 2,000-year fixed term lease;[116] potentially a disastrous outcome for the landlord. It has been said, with justice, that this is 'an area of law where the courts have manoeuvred themselves into an unhappy position'.[117]

Tenancies at will

A tenancy at will involves a situation where a person is let into possession of property as a tenant but the agreement is such that the tenancy can be determined by either side, at will. The normal situation where such a tenancy will arise is where a person who is minded to purchase the property is allowed into possession.[118] If rent is paid by the tenant after entry, a periodic tenancy will be implied,[119] unless it is clear that both parties intend the relationship to remain as a tenancy at will.[120]

The tenancy at will is a personal relationship between the parties.[121] As such, it cannot be assigned or pass on death. If the tenant at will purports to assign the tenancy this will, on giving notice to the landlord, terminate the tenancy.[122]

Tenancy at sufferance

This term is used to describe what is not really a tenancy at all. A tenancy at sufferance arises when a tenant holds over after the lease has expired with neither the landlord's assent or dissent. The only difference between him and a trespasser is that the initial occupation of the land was lawful. If the holding over follows the service by the tenant of a notice to quit then, under ancient legislation, he is liable to pay double rent for the period of the holding over after the notice has expired.[123]

---

[114] Where title is unregistered, such an option will only bind a purchaser of the reversion if it has been registered as a land charge: *Phillips v. Mobil Oil Co. Ltd* [1980] 1 W.L.R. 888. If title is registered and the tenant is in actual occupation of the land, then the option will take effect under Land Registration Act 2002, Sched. 3, para. 2 as an interest overriding a registered disposition: *Webb v. Pollmount* [1966] Ch. 584.

[115] *Parkus v. Greenwood* [1950] Ch. 33; *Caerphilly Concrete Products Ltd v. Owen* [1972] 1 W.L.R. 372.

[116] Law of Property Act 1922, s. 145, Sched. 15.

[117] '*Caerphilly Concrete Products Ltd v. Owen* [1972] 1 W.L.R. 372 at 376 *per* Sachs L.J.

[118] See *Ramnarace v. Lutchman* [2001] 1 W.L.R. 1651.

[119] *Walji v. Mount Cook Land Ltd* [2002] 1 P. & C.R. 13.

[120] See *Javad v. Aqil* [1991] 1 W.L.R. 1007.

[121] See *Wheeler v. Mercer* [1957] A.C. 426 at 427–428 *per* Lord Morton.

[122] *Pinhorn v. Souster* (1853) 8 Exch. 763 at 772–773 *per* Parke B.

[123] Distress for Rent Act 1737, s. 18.

In cases of tenancies at sufferance, the normal position is that, if the relationship becomes consensual, a new tenancy will arise.[124] In the public sector, however, when a local authority, having obtained a possession order against a tenant, nevertheless allows the tenant to remain in the property, and accepts payment, the former tenant is treated as a 'tolerated trespasser'.[125] This is an anomalous relationship, the consequences of which have yet to be fully worked out.[126]

Tenancies by estoppel

On the grant of a tenancy, both landlord and tenant are mutually estopped from denying the validity of the transaction. It is no defence for a tenant, sued by the landlord, to argue that the landlord had no title to grant a lease.[127] As between the parties to the agreement, the lease is perfectly binding and the tenancy is referred to as a tenancy by estoppel. It is not entirely clear, however, what the value is in describing the lease in these terms. In *Bruton v. London and Quadrant Housing Trust*,[128] a local authority had compulsorily acquired a block of flats with a view to demolishing them and redeveloping the land. Pending this, the council granted a licence to the Trust, which was a charitable organization, to use the property for the purposes of housing the homeless. The licence did not purport to grant the Trust any proprietary interest in the flats, something which the council did not have the power to do.[129] The Trust then entered into an agreement with Mr Bruton, termed a licence, whereby he gained the occupancy of a flat in return for a weekly payment. The issue in the case was whether the Trust was liable for certain repairs under section 11 of the Landlord and Tenant Act 1985, which would only be the case if a tenancy had been created.[130] The argument for the Trust was that, as both parties knew that it did not own the land, and therefore lacked the power to create tenancies, the agreement could not take effect as a lease. While plausible, this was rejected by the House of Lords, who held that Mr Bruton was a tenant.

The central reason was that the agreement between the Trust and Mr Bruton conferred upon him exclusive possession for a term at a rent, a finding which, unless there are exceptional circumstances, leads to the conclusion that, whatever the

---

[124] See *Dougal v. McCarthy* [1892] 1 Q.B. 736.

[125] See *Burrows v. Brent London Borough Council* [1996] 1 W.L.R. 1448.

[126] See the valuable analysis by S. Bright (2003) 119 L.Q.R. 495, where it is also pointed out that this concept applies only in the public sector: ibid., at 496. See also I. Loveland (2007) 123 L.Q.R. 455.

[127] See *Cuthbertson v. Irvine* (1859) 4 H. & N. 742 at 754–755 *per* Martin B.

[128] [2000] 1 A.C. 406. See D. Rook [1999] Conv. 517; P. Routley (2000) 63 M.L.R. 424, where some of the reasoning but not the result is criticized. See also J.P. Hinojosa [2005] Conv. 114; M. Lower [2010] Conv. 38.

[129] Housing Act 1985, s. 32. If a statutory body lacks the power to grant a lease, estoppel principles cannot confer validity on something which the body has no power to do. See *Rhyl Urban District Council v. Rhyl Amusements Ltd* [1959] 1 W.L.R. 465.

[130] For these obligations, see Statutory obligations, pp. 439–444.

parties may choose to call the agreement, a lease has been created. According to Lord Hoffmann:

> 'the term "lease" or "tenancy" describes a relationship between two parties who are designated landlord and tenant. It is not concerned with the question of whether the agreement creates an estate or other proprietary interest which may be binding upon third parties. A lease may, and usually does, create a proprietary interest called a leasehold estate, or more technically, a "term of years absolute". This will depend upon whether the landlord had an estate out of which he could grant it.'[131]

The Bruton *tenancy as an estate*

The conclusion that Mr Bruton held a tenancy in the land rests upon the essential relativity of title upon which Land Law is based, and seems to be entirely correct.[132] The difficulty with this passage, however, is the comment that the lease might not create a proprietary interest in the land. This is not so.

If a person goes into possession of freehold land, he occupies the land as the holder of an estate in fee simple. His title is good as against anyone except a person with a better title.[133] It is open to him to convey his possessory title to anyone else, in which case that person's title will be as good as that of the squatter. That is, his right to possession is only liable to be defeated by the owner of the paper title to the land. If, instead of conveying the land to a purchaser, the squatter purports to grant a lease of it, then similar reasoning should apply. As between the squatter and the tenant, the lease is perfectly valid, and the tenant's right of occupation can only be upset by title paramount, that is an action brought by the true owner of the land.[134] Whether or not the parties to the original lease knew that the landlord had no title to the land should be quite irrelevant. If the squatter transfers his title to a purchaser, than, as a person deriving title from the squatter, the purchaser will be in no better position than the squatter and so the tenancy will be binding on him.[135] On this analysis, it should make no difference if the person purporting to create a licence is himself a licensee rather than a squatter. In both cases, one should look to the agreement between the parties to see if it is consistent with a lease or a licence.

In this sense, *pace*, Lord Hoffmann, the lease created by the squatter does create an interest in land: it is an estate, however, that is vulnerable in that it can be defeated by a better title to that land. The vulnerability of the tenant's position when a *Bruton* tenancy has been created has since been demonstrated in *London Borough Council of Islington v. Green*.[136] Islington Council granted Patchwork Community Housing Association a licence to use its property as temporary accommodation. In the same way as occurred in *Bruton*, the Association purported to create a licence to occupy

[131] [2000] 1 A.C. 406 at 415.
[132] See also *Berrisford v. Mexfield Housing Co-operative Ltd* [2011] UKSC 53 at [65] *per* Lord Neuberger.
[133] See Ownership and possession, pp. 230–231.
[134] See *Kay v. London Borough of Lambeth* [2006] UKHL 10 at para. 144 *per* Lord Scott of Foscote.
[135] Contrast M. Dixon [2000] C.L.J. 25 at 26.
[136] [2005] EWCA Civ. 56. See also *Kay v. Lambeth London Borough Council, supra.*

the property to Ms Green and Mr O'Shea. When the council terminated the licence given to the Association, Mr O'Shea had no defence to a possession action brought by the council. Although the agreement between the Association and Ms Green, who had since left the property, and Mr O'Shea created a tenancy, this tenancy was not binding on the council, who were not transferees of the Association's interest and were not parties to the agreement. Accordingly, the case succeeded on the basis of title paramount.

The same point has since been made by Lord Neuberger in *Berrisford v. Mexfield Housing Co-operative Ltd.*[137] Commenting on the *Bruton* case, he said:

'The point being made by Lord Hoffmann was that the fact that the trust was only a licensee, and therefore could not grant a tenancy binding on its licensor, did not prevent the agreement with Mr Bruton amounting to a tenancy as between him and the trust. The tenancy would thus have been binding as such not only on Mr Bruton and the trust, *but also on any assignee of Mr Bruton or the trust.*'

In other words, the real unorthodoxy in Lord Hoffmann's remarks is to deny that the agreement created an estate. In all aspects it resembles a tenancy by estoppel. Such tenancies are binding between the parties to it, and on those who derive title from them. It is not binding on a person with a better title to the land than the person purporting to create the lease.

Feeding the estoppel

If a tenancy is created by someone who lacks the legal title, the landlord may subsequently acquire the legal title. This is likely to occur when a purchaser of land creates a tenancy prior to the land being conveyed to him. In this situation, the estoppel is said to be fed. What happens is that upon the landlord acquiring the legal title the tenant is clothed automatically with the legal title without any further action by anyone.[138] At one time, this caused problems if the purchase was being financed by a mortgage as it was held that the estoppel was fed immediately the landlord acquired title and then the mortgage, being a separate transaction, was created a fraction of a second later, the so-called *scintilla temporis*, the result being that the mortgagee would be bound by the tenancy, which was a prior legal estate.[139] While this reasoning had a logical charm to it, the conclusion was highly inconvenient and it has now been held by the House of Lords that the conveyance to the landlord and the mortgage are contemporaneous events, so that the tenancy created in these circumstances would not be binding upon the mortgagee.[140]

---

[137] [2011] UKSC 52 at [65]. Emphasis added.

[138] *Maclay v. Nutting* [1949] 2 K.B. 55. For a helpful discussion, albeit in the context of a legal charge, see *First National Bank plc v. Thompson* [1996] Ch. 231 at 236–240 *per* Millett L.J.

[139] *Church of England Building Society v. Piskor* [1954] Ch. 553 at 559 *per* Sir Raymond Evershed M.R. See The effect of the tenancy, pp. 481–482.

[140] *Abbey National Building Society v. Cann* [1991] 1 A.C. 56.

FORMALITIES

A lease is a legal estate in land and, as such, the normal position is that to create a legal lease a deed must be used. An exception to the rule that legal leases must be created by deed is provided by section 52(2)(d) of the Law of Property Act 1925, which refers to leases or tenancies not required by law to be in writing. These leases which, it should be noted, can be created orally, are set out in section 54(2) of the Act as being leases taking effect in possession for a term not exceeding three years (whether or not the lessee is given power to extend the term) at the best rent which can be reasonably obtained without taking a fine. A contract to create such a lease is also exempt from the normal requirements of formality imposed upon land contracts.[141]

Some comments can be made as to this provision.

Term

First, the Act itself provides that a lease which the tenant has power to extend beyond three years need not be by deed. This would cover the situation where there is a two-year lease which confers on the tenant the option to renew it for a further two years. The Act makes no mention of periodic tenancies, which will last for considerably longer than three years if neither side serves a notice to quit. Such tenancies are not required to be made by deed, however, the reason being that the original term is that specified in the grant, so that a yearly tenancy is seen as an initial grant of one year and so need not be made by deed.

Rent

The lease must be for the best rent which can be reasonably obtained without taking a fine. A fine is a lump sum or premium and it is very unusual for such a payment to be sought on the grant of a short lease.

In possession

To be exempt from the requirement that a deed is necessary to create a legal lease, the lease must take effect in possession. This is an extremely unfortunate requirement. It was held in *Long v. Tower Hamlets London Borough Council*[142] that a quarterly tenancy created at the start of September to begin later in the month did not take effect in possession and must, therefore, to be legal be created by deed, which was not the case. This result seems to be an inevitable consequence of the wording of the Act but is extremely inconvenient.[143] Many short leases are created without using a deed. If

---

[141] Law of Property (Miscellaneous Provisions) Act 1989, s. 2(5)(a).   [142] [1998] Ch. 197.

[143] See S. Bright [1998] Conv. 229, who accepts the reasoning as correct, but points to the serious consequences which may arise because of it.

possession is not granted from the date of the lease, then a deed is necessary. Many students rent accommodation in the private sector and sign agreements at the beginning of the summer to begin in September. These agreements are highly unlikely to be contained in deeds and, because the leases which they purport to create do not take effect in possession, they will be ineffective to create legal tenancies. The removal of the requirement in section 54(2) of the Act that the lease take effect in possession would be desirable.

Assignment

Although certain short leases can be created either orally or in writing, to assign an existing lease, a deed must be used.[144] A letter is insufficient.[145] When the leasehold interest is registered, then the assignment must be completed by registration.[146]

EQUITABLE LEASES

If a person fails to use a deed to create a lease when one is required, the position is looked at differently by law and equity. At law, if, as is likely, the tenant takes possession of the property and pays rent, there will be an implication that he holds under a periodic tenancy, the period being calculated by reference to how the rent is measured.[147] Equity, however, takes a quite different view of the matter.

If L purports to grant T a seven-year lease, but does not execute a deed, then there can be no seven-year lease at law. By means of a fiction, however, the ineffective attempt to create the legal tenancy is viewed as a contract to create one.[148] That this is a fiction should be manifest. L has purported to grant a lease; he has not promised to create one in the future. Nevertheless, the fiction is well established. Starting from the fictitious premise that the attempt to grant a lease takes effect as a contract to create a lease, the next step in the reasoning process is that such a contract is one which a court would normally enforce by a decree of specific performance. Applying the maxim that equity looks upon that which ought to be done as already having been done, the consequence is that, in equity, there is a valid seven-year lease.

The leading case is *Walsh v. Lonsdale*.[149] L, by a document in writing, purported to grant a seven-year lease of a mill to T. It was a term of the lease that T should pay a year's rent in advance. T went into possession and paid rent on a quarterly basis for a year and a quarter, whereupon L insisted that he pay a year's rent in advance as had

---

[144] *Crago v. Julian* [1992] 1 W.L.R. 372; *Trustees of St John's Hospital v. Keevil* [2001] EWCA Civ. 1730.

[145] *Camden London Borough Council v. Alexandrou* (1997) 30 H.L.R. 534.

[146] Land Registration Act 2002, s. 27; *Brown & Root Technology Ltd v. Sun Alliance and London Assurance Co. Ltd* [2001] Ch. 733.

[147] See The period, p. 419.   [148] *Parker v. Taswell* (1858) 2 De G. & J. 559.

[149] (1882) 21 Ch.D. 9.

been agreed. T refused to pay and L responded by seizing L's goods in lieu of such payment and T sued him in trespass. T's argument was that the remedy of distress, the seizing of goods for non-payment of rent, is a legal remedy. At law, because he had gone into possession and paid rent, he was a yearly tenant. As such, he could terminate the lease by giving six months' notice to quit.[150] The obligation to pay a year's rent in advance was inconsistent with his ability to end the lease by giving the requisite notice to quit and it, therefore, followed that what L had done was unlawful.

As a statement of the effect of what had happened at law, this was perfectly accurate. It ignored, however, the view which equity took of the situation. There was not a legal seven-year lease but, in the view of equity, there was a perfectly valid contract to create such a lease and specific performance would be granted to enforce that contract. Taking the view that what ought to be done should be regarded as having been done, in equity there was a seven-year lease in existence and, under the terms of that lease, what L had done was perfectly lawful. T's claim, therefore, failed.

Although the actual decision is controversial, in the sense that it is not clear that distress, as a remedy, was available in equity,[151] the case presents an excellent example of the role of equity when the formal requirements at law have not been complied with. From this, it might be seen that an equitable lease is as good as a legal lease. For a number of reasons, this is not so.

Contract

The starting point in the evolution of the equitable tenancy is that the informal grant of a lease is viewed as being a contract to create a lease. Because section 2 of the Law of Property (Miscellaneous Provisions) Act 1989 requires contracts to create an interest in land to be in writing and signed by both parties then, unless the purported grant complies with the requirement of the section, there will be no contract to create a lease and the basis of the equitable lease will be gone.[152] If the tenant goes into possession of the property and pays rent, then a court may seek to fashion such remedy as seems appropriate, using estoppel principles,[153] or, alternatively, regard the relationships as being governed by law, which would imply a periodic tenancy in these circumstances. It is perhaps as well that this problem is unlikely to occur because, whereas the parties may neglect to use a deed, it is normal for a lease of this length at least to be in writing and signed by both landlord and tenant so that the requirements of section 2 will be met. When Part 8 of the Land Registration Act 2002, which will make compulsory

---

[150] See Notice to quit, pp. 453–454.

[151] See Harpum, Bridge, and Dixon, *Megarry and Wade's Law of Real Property* (7th edn) (London: Sweet & Maxwell, 2008), 752–753. The ancient common law remedy of distress has, in respect of residential property, now been abolished: Tribunals, Courts and Enforcement Act 2007, s. 71. A new system in respect of commercial property has been introduced: ibid., s. 72.

[152] See in the context of equitable mortgages, where the same argument is used, *United Bank of Kuwait plc v. Sahib* [1997] Ch. 107.

[153] See *Yaxley v. Gotts* [2000] 1 All E.R. 711. Contrast *Yeoman's Row Management Ltd v. Cobbe* [2008] UKHL 55, Estoppel and trusts, pp. 206–207.

electronic conveyancing, is brought into force, however, this issue will become very much a live one. This will be considered after other aspects of equitable tenancies have been dealt with.[154]

Specific performance

For an equitable lease to be created, it is necessary for there not only to be a contract to create a lease but that that contract is specifically enforceable. If the contract is to create a sub-tenancy and there is a covenant in the head lease which prohibits the granting of sub-tenancies, then specific performance will not be granted of the contract and an equitable sub-tenancy will not arise.[155] The case of *Bell Street Investments Ltd v. Wood*[156] is instructive. A landlord had purported to grant a seven-year lease of a yard but had not used a deed. The yard was in a dilapidated condition owing, in part, to various breaches of covenant by the tenant. In possession proceedings brought by the landlord, one of the issues to be determined was the status of the tenant. Because there was no deed, there was no legal seven-year lease. Because of the misconduct of the tenant, specific performance was not available, he having behaved inequitably himself. As a result, there was no equitable seven-year lease. The tenant had gone into possession and paid rent, however, thus giving rise to an implied periodic tenancy at law. As there was now no conflict between law and equity, his position was governed by the incidents of that periodic tenancy.

Third parties

In common with all equitable rights, the equitable lease is vulnerable to being defeated if the property gets into the hands of a bona fide purchaser, although one must distinguish between unregistered and registered land.

Unregistered land

Where title is unregistered, an equitable lease is registrable as a land charge. As a contract to create a legal estate, the lease, it is registrable as a Class C(iv) land charge. This will be void for non-registration against a purchaser for value of the reversion.[157] If the tenant has gone into possession and has paid rent, the equitable lease will still be void for non-registration,[158] but there will now be in existence an implied legal periodic tenancy which will be binding upon the purchaser.

Registered land

An equitable lease is an interest affecting registered land and, as such should be protected by the entry of a notice. Although most leases granted for a term of less than

---

[154] See Electronic conveyancing, pp. 428–429.
[155] *Warmington v. Miller* [1973] 2 All E.R. 372.   [156] [1970] E.G.D. 812.
[157] Land Charges Act 1972, s. 4(6).   [158] See *Lloyds Bank plc v. Carrick* [1996] 4 All E.R. 630.

seven years are interests which will override a registered disposition,[159] this definition does not include an equitable lease because, as there is no deed, there is no grant.[160] If, however, as is likely to be the case, the tenant has gone into possession, then the equitable lease will override a registered disposition under Schedule 3, paragraph 2 of the Land Registration Act 2002, a further example of the superior protection afforded to the rights of occupiers where title is registered than when it is not.

Easements

On a conveyance of land, easements will, in certain situations, be implied into the conveyance.[161] Because the creation of an equitable lease does not involve a conveyance, there is no such statutory implication in the case of equitable tenancies, although some easements may be acquired under the common law rules.[162]

Covenants

In the case of leases created before 1995, on the assignment of the lease or the reversion, certain covenants would run with that estate, so that the assignee could sue and be sued upon them. For this to occur there had to exist privity of estate between the parties to the action, and this did not occur in the case of equitable tenancies. With the enactment of the Landlord and Tenant (Covenants) Act 1995, this distinction has now been removed, so that covenants in a legal lease and in an equitable lease will run on the same basis.[163]

Electronic conveyancing

Part 8 of the Land Registration Act 2002, when brought into force, will make compulsory electronic conveyancing. Crucially, section 93(2) provides that 'a disposition to which this section applies, *or a contract to make such a disposition*, only has effect if it is made in a document in electronic form and, if when the document purports to take effect, it is electronically communicated to the registrar and the relevant registration requirements are met'.[164] Dispositions to which this section applies include the disposition of a registered estate and a disposition which triggers the requirement of registration.[165] In the present context, this means that the section will apply to the assignment of leases which are already registered and the grant of certain leases which will trigger the requirement of registration. The grant of a lease of more than seven years from the date of the grant and the grant of a lease of any length for a term of years

---

[159] Land Registration Act 2002, Sched. 3, para. 1.
[160] *City Permanent Building Society v. Miller* [1952] Ch. 840.   [161] See Conveyance, p. 560.
[162] See *Borman v. Griffith* [1930] Ch. 493. See The rule in *Wheeldon v. Burrows*, pp. 561–562.
[163] See Post-1996 tenancies, pp. 450–453.   [164] Emphasis supplied.
[165] Land Registration Act 2002, s. 91(2).

absolute to take effect in possession after the end of a period of three years beginning with the date of the grant are required to be registered.[166] The effect of these provisions on 'the rather quaint, if well established doctrine in *Walsh v. Lonsdale*'[167] must now be considered.

The first point is that, unless and until the Lord Chancellor exercises his power under section 5 of the Act to make the grant of a lease for a period of more than three years a triggering event, then the doctrine will be unaffected in the case of leases of more than three years and not more than seven years. Such leases will still need to be created by deed but are not required to be registered. In the case of leases for more than seven years, however, it would seem to be a necessary consequence of section 93(2) of the Act that the doctrine of *Walsh v. Lonsdale* has been abolished. This is because the underlying basis of the creation of an equitable lease is that the purported grant, which is inoperative to create the intended legal lease, is seen as a contract to create that lease. If, as is usually the case, that contract is specifically enforceable, then, on the basis that equity looks on that as done which ought to be done, an equitable tenancy is considered to have arisen.[168] As section 93(2) of the Act makes clear, however, contracts to make certain dispositions are also required to be made by electronic documents and communicated electronically to the registrar. A failure to comply with this requirement means that the purported disposition is entirely ineffective. Consequently, if a landlord purports to grant a twelve-year lease and does not do this electronically, the deed, or whatever document has been used, will have no effect whatsoever, either at law or in equity.

In such circumstances, if the purported tenant goes into possession and pays rent, there seems to be no reason why, on normal principles, a legal periodic tenancy should not be implied. As to whether any greater rights will be acquired, this will depend upon the willingness of the courts to apply estoppel principles: that the parties, or one of them, having acted to their detriment on the belief that there was in existence a valid twelve-year lease, should have rather greater rights than merely a periodic tenancy. A similar issue arose in *Liverpool City Council v. Walton*.[169] In this case, it was argued that a contract to create a 999-year lease was void for uncertainty. Although this argument failed, Neuberger J. considered what the position would have been had that not been the case. The prospective tenant had, in reliance on the agreement, spent some £1 million pounds in circumstances where it would have been inequitable for the landlord to deny him some effect to his expectation. In these circumstances the judge expressed the view that, to satisfy the equity which had arisen, he would have ordered the grant of the agreed lease, but he also made it clear that this would not be the appropriate remedy in all cases.[170] This is an area where uncertainty is likely to prevail.

---

[166] Ibid., s. 4(1)(c)(d).
[167] *Liverpool City Council v. Walton* [2002] 1 E.G.L.R. 149 at 154 *per* Neuberger J.
[168] See Contract, p, 426.   [169] [2002] 1 E.G.L.R. 149.   [170] Ibid., at 156.

Reversionary leases

When Part 8 of the 2002 Act is brought into force, it is likely that, in the vast majority of cases, problems of non-compliance will not arise; a lease of more than seven years is a commercial transaction and advice is likely to be taken and the formal requirements will be met. Where one can envisage problems is with regard to certain reversionary leases. Any lease to take effect in possession more than three months after the date of the grant is required to be registered. A purported let to a group of students granted in March, to take effect in September, will require registration. When section 93 of the Act is in force, unless this transaction is effected electronically and communicated in that form to the registrar, it will have no effect at all. One suspects that non-compliance in these circumstances will not be uncommon. A useful reform in this area might be to exempt reversionary leases of less than three years from compulsory registration.

RIGHTS AND DUTIES UNDER A LEASE

A lease is an estate in land. It is, however, also a contractual relationship and, as such, the parties are free to include in the lease such contractual terms, or covenants, as they see fit. In addition to the terms which the parties actually agree upon, certain obligations are implied into the agreement, sometimes by statute and sometimes by the common law. This section deals with the covenants or obligations commonly found in leases.

Quiet enjoyment

There is implied into every lease a covenant by the landlord that the tenant shall enjoy quiet enjoyment of the property.[171] The scope of this covenant involves the actions of the landlord and the lawful acts of his other tenants. The landlord, unless he expressly covenants to prevent acts of nuisance committed by his other tenants, will not be liable for such acts.[172] Neither will acts of third parties come within the terms of the covenant, so if the tenant is evicted by title paramount, the tenant will have no remedy for breach of the covenant for quiet enjoyment.[173]

It was at one time thought that the covenant for quiet enjoyment extended only to some physical interference with the tenant's enjoyment of the property. This matter was considered by the House of Lords in *Southwark London Borough Council v.*

---

[171] *Budd-Scott v. Daniel* [1902] 2 K.B. 351.

[172] *Baxter v. Camden London Borough Council* [1999] 2 W.L.R. 566. See also *Smith v. Scott* [1973] Ch. 314.

[173] *Jones v. Lavington* [1903] 1 K.B. 523. In the case of leases granted after 1995, when a full title guarantee is given, the landlord will be liable on the covenants for title if the tenant is evicted for this reason: Law of Property (Miscellaneous Provisions) Act 1994, s. 1(1).

Mills.[174] The tenants lived in a block of flats which had been constructed in 1919. The tenants complained that the sound insulation between the flats was inadequate, so that the normal activity of tenants in adjoining flats could clearly be heard. This, it was argued, was a breach of the covenant for quiet enjoyment. This argument was rejected.

Lord Hoffmann observed that the covenant could not be read literally. In the instant case 'the flat is not quiet and the tenant is not enjoying it'.[175] It was accepted, however, that, in principle, excessive noise could amount to a breach of the covenant.[176] It did not do so, however, in the present case. The level of noise did not amount to a nuisance, because the ordinary use of residential premises is not being capable of amounting to a nuisance.[177] More importantly, however, the problem was caused by the way that the property was initially built. The landlord had not done anything after the initial grant of the lease to make the position worse.[178] As there is no implied condition that the property is fit for the purpose for which it is let,[179] the covenant did not extend to interference with the tenant's enjoyment of the property which resulted from the condition of the property before the grant was made. For the same reason, neither did the covenant extend to the use of parts of the building let by the landlord, which the parties must have contemplated before the lease was granted. As it was clear that the other flats in the building would also be let, the tenant could not complain in respect of normal activity of the other tenants which took place in those other flats.

Although the covenant for quiet enjoyment can be broken by acts other than an act of physical interference with the tenant's enjoyment of the property, most acts which have been held to amount to a breach have involved such behaviour. Acts which have been held to amount to breaches of the covenant for quiet enjoyment include subsidence caused by mining,[180] the removal of the tenant's door,[181] and general intimidation to persuade the tenant to leave.[182]

Remedies

If the landlord is committing a breach of the covenant for quiet enjoyment, then the tenant may obtain an injunction to restrain his behaviour. He may, moreover, succeed also in obtaining an award of damages. The damages are assessed on the principles governing the award of damages in the law of contract. Such damages do not, however, include the possibility of the award of exemplary damages. Such a limitation on the

---

[174] [2001] A.C. 1.   [175] Ibid., at 10.

[176] Cf. *Jenkins v. Jackson* (1888) 40 Ch.D. 71 at 74 *per* Kekewich J.

[177] *Baxter v. Camden London Borough Council* [1999] 2 W.L.R. 566 at 574 *per* Tuckey L.J.

[178] See also *Long v. Southwark London Borough Council* [2002] EWCA Civ. 403 at paras. 60–64 *per* Arden L. Cf. *Sampson v. Hodson-Presinger* [1981] 3 All E.R. 710, where a subsequent conversion of the property exacerbated the noise problem.

[179] See *Hart v. Windsor* (1843) 12 M. & W. 68 at 77–78 *per* Parke B.; *Edler v. Auerbach* [1950] 1 K.B. 359 at 374 *per* Devlin J.

[180] *Markham v. Paget* [1908] Ch. 697.   [181] *Lavender v. Betts* [1942] 2 All E.R. 72.

[182] *Kenny v. Preen* [1963] 1 Q.B. 499.

award of damages could act as an inducement to unscrupulous landlords to bully tenants who enjoy statutory protection into leaving the property, it being impossible, or at least very difficult, to evict such tenants lawfully. This unacceptable practice, known after its most famous practitioner, was termed 'Rachmanism'.

Exemplary damages, to punish the wrongdoer, can, however, be awarded in tort, one of the circumstances being when a tortfeasor calculates that he stands to make more money out of committing the tort than he would be liable to pay in damages.[183] That this could apply in the present context was made clear by Lord Hailsham L.C., who, when discussing the principles upon which exemplary damages are awarded, said:

'How, it may be asked, about the late Mr Rachman, who is alleged to have hired bullies to intimidate statutory tenants by violence or threats of violence into giving vacant possession of their premises and so placing a valuable asset in the hands of the landlord? The answer must be that if this is not a cynical calculation of profit and cold-blooded disregard of a plaintiffs' rights, I do not know what is.'[184]

Following this very clear steer, in *Drane v. Evangelou*,[185] a landlord was held liable to pay exemplary damages to a tenant, who, when he was out, returned to find that his belongings had been thrown into the street and his access to the house blocked by a large man standing in the doorway. In addition to a breach of the covenant, the landlord had also committed the tort of trespass and, for this, exemplary damages were available.

Statutory liability

In any claim for exemplary damages, the tenant must show that the landlord has calculated that he will stand to gain more from unlawfully evicting the tenant than he would have to pay him in damages. This may prove to be difficult. A tenant is more likely now to use the civil remedy contained in section 27 of the Housing Act 1988.

This section provides for the civil liability of the landlord in tort if he, or any person acting on his behalf, unlawfully deprives the residential occupier of any premises of his occupation of the whole or part of the premises. He is also liable if he attempts unlawfully to deprive the residential occupier of any premises of his occupation of the whole or part of the premises or, knowing or having reason to believe that the conduct is likely to cause the occupier to give up the premises in whole or in part, or to refrain from exercising any right or pursuing any right or pursuing any remedy in respect of the premises, does acts likely to interfere with the peace and comfort of the residential occupier or members of his household, or persistently withdraws or withholds services reasonably required for the occupation of the premises as a

---

[183] *Cassell & Co. Ltd v. Broome* [1972] A.C. 1027 (a libel case involving a book written by David Irving).

[184] [1972] A.C. 1027 at 1074.

[185] [1978] 1 W.L.R. 455. See also *Guppy's (Bridport) Ltd v. Brookling* (1983) 14 H.L.R. 1; *Mehta v. Royal Bank of Scotland* [1999] 3 E.G.L.R. 153.

residence and as a result the occupier gives up his occupation of the premises as a residence.[186]

The damages, which can be reduced if the conduct of the residential occupier is such that it is reasonable to mitigate the damages,[187] are measured by the difference between the value of the interest of the landlord in default, on the assumption that the occupier continues to have the same right to occupy, and the value of that interest determined on the basis that the occupier ceased to have that right.[188] In other words, the damages payable to the tenant are assessed on the basis of the profit made by the landlord for his unlawful eviction.[189] It should be noted, however, that damages are only payable if the occupier gives up occupation. If he resists the acts of the landlord and remains in occupation, there is no civil liability under the statute and the tenant's remedies would appear to lie in an action on the covenant for quiet enjoyment and, possibly, trespass. The operation of the Act is illustrated by the interesting case of *King v. Jackson*.[190]

On 20 March 1994, the tenant was granted a six-month fixed term tenancy at a rent of £75.00 per week. By 6 April, she found that she was unable to afford the rent and wrote to the landlady purporting to give four weeks' notice to terminate the lease, something which she was not entitled to do. This notice would, however, expire on 12 May, and both parties assumed that she would leave on that date. She paid no further rent. The landlady, assuming the flat would be vacant, advertised for a new tenant and, when someone responded to the advert, that person was shown around with the co-operation of the tenant. On 5 May, however, the landlady asked the tenant to leave the property on that day. The landlady brought her boyfriend around with her, he posing as a prospective tenant. The atmosphere became tense and the tenant left, intending to return later. When she did return, she found that the locks had been changed and she sued the landlady for unlawful eviction. At first instance, she was awarded £11,000 damages but, on appeal, this was reduced to £1,500. The award at first instance reflected the gain to the landlady of having terminated the fixed term tenancy much earlier that she would otherwise have able to do. The Court of Appeal, however, held that, by the tenant's actions, an estoppel had arisen against her, the landlady having acted on her belief that she would be entitled to possession on 12 May. Accordingly, the damages for the breach of quiet enjoyment, rather than damages under the Act in respect of the wrongful eviction, were assessed to reflect the loss of six days under the lease.

Criminal liability

In addition to the imposition of civil liability in respect of unlawful eviction, criminal sanctions are also imposed in respect of harassment committed by the landlord. Separate criminal offences are created by section 1 of the Protection of Eviction Act

---

[186] Housing Act 1988, s. 27(1)(2).
[187] Ibid., s. 27(7). See *Regalgrand Ltd v. Dickerson* (1996) 74 P. & C.R. 312.
[188] Housing Act 1988, s. 28.   [189] See *Melville v. Bruton* [1996] 1 E.G.C.S. 57.
[190] (1977) 30 H.L.R. 541.

1977[191] in respect of unlawful eviction and harassment of a residential occupier. It is also unlawful for the owner of property which has been subject to a tenancy which has come to an end, but where the occupier continues to occupy the premises as a residence, to seek to enforce his right to possession otherwise than by court proceedings.[192]

Derogation from grant

What at one time was thought to be a separate obligation from the covenant for quiet enjoyment implied upon the landlord was the obligation not to derogate from his grant.[193] The essential idea is that, if the property has been let for a particular purpose, then the landlord may not do acts which interfere with that purpose. A reason for seeing the two obligations as being separate was that, originally, the former obligation was seen as being confined to physical acts interfering with the tenant's enjoyment of the property. The present view, however, is that 'The principle is the same in both cases: a man must not give with one hand and take away with the other'.[194]

The essence of the doctrine is the purpose of the letting. In *North Eastern Railway Co. v. Elliot*,[195] the principle was expressed as being:

'If a landowner conveys one of two closes to another, he cannot afterwards do anything to derogate from his own grant; and if the conveyance is made for the express purpose of having buildings erected upon the land so granted, a contract is implied on the part of the grantor to do nothing to prevent the land being used for the purpose for which to the knowledge of the grantor the conveyance was made.'

This principle has been applied to situations where land has been let for the purpose of a particular business and the proposed use by the landlord of his other property would interfere with the tenant's use of his land. In one case, land was let for the purpose of use as a timber merchant and the landlord was restrained from building so as to obstruct the flow of air to the sheds used for the drying of timber.[196] Similarly, when land was let for the storing of explosives, the landlord was restrained from building on his own land when the proximity of those buildings would affect the licence granted to the tenant in respect of the explosives.[197] Again, in *Owen v. Gadd*,[198] premises were let for business purposes. The landlord then erected scaffolding, the effect of which was to make it difficult for customers to access the property and this was held to amount to a breach of the covenant for quiet enjoyment. By way of contrast, however, in *Browne*

---

[191] As amended by Housing Act 1988. ss 27, 28.   [192] Protection from Eviction Act 1977, s. 3.

[193] See, generally, D.W. Elliott (1964) 80 L.Q.R. 244.

[194] *Southwark London Borough Council v. Mills* [2001] 1 A.C. 1 at 23 *per* Lord Millett. For a fuller statement, see *Platt v. London Underground Ltd* [2001] 2 E.G.L.R. 121 at 122 *per* Neuberger J.

[195] (1860) 1 J. & H. 145 at 153 *per* Sir William Page Wood V.-C.

[196] *Aldin v. Latimer, Clark, Muirhead & Co.* [1894] 2 Ch. 437. See also *Chartered Trust plc v. Davies* (1997) 76 P. & C.R. 396.

[197] *Harmer v. Jumbil (Nigeria) Tin Areas Ltd* [1921] 1 Ch. 200. See also *Carter v. Cole* [2009] EWCA Civ. 410 (a case concerning the grant of an easement).

[198] [1956] 2 Q.B. 99.

v. Flower,[199] the plaintiff was the tenant of a flat and the landlord then built an outside staircase, this having the effect that, whenever the landlord used it, he could see into the tenant's living room. This was held not to be a breach of the covenant of quiet enjoyment, the act of the landlord not being considered to make the premises materially less fit for the purpose for which they were let. Given the greater importance attached to privacy today, such a case may well be viewed differently now. What is clear from the case law, however, is that for the landlord to be liable he must do some act after the commencement of the lease which affects the tenant's enjoyment of the land. This obligation will not operate to prevent the landlord from competing with the tenant's business,[200] although, if the property is let as part of a specifically designed commercial operation, such as a shopping mall, if the landlord permits activity inconsistent with that design, he may be found to have derogated from his grant.[201] The fact that, from the outset, the land was not fully fit for the purpose for which it was let will not be sufficient to afford the tenant any remedy.

Rent

Although, strictly speaking, it is not necessary for the creation of a lease that a rent be reserved, it is almost universally the case that this will happen. While a lease is clearly a contractual relationship, it is also an estate in land. Because of this, it was considered to be doubtful if the lease could be ended only by methods appropriate to the termination of that estate, or whether the normal contractual rules are applicable to the ending of the relationship.

Frustration

For quite some time, it was uncertain whether, like other contracts, a lease could be frustrated. The House of Lords in *Cricklewood Property and Investment Trustee Ltd v. Leighton's Investment Trust Ltd*,[202] divided evenly on the issue of principle, with two saying yes, two saying no and the fifth member of the Appellate Committee reserving his opinion. As a matter of principle, this matter was resolved in *National Carriers Ltd v. Panalpina (Northern) Ltd*,[203] it being considered that, in rare cases, a lease could be frustrated. The doctrine was not applied in the case, itself, however, where the inaccessibility of a warehouse for twenty months of a ten-year lease did not amount to frustration. It would seem that some truly cataclysmic event, such as the destruction of a flat in a block caused by landslip,[204] or the falling of a hotel into the sea caused by

---

[199] [1911] 2 Ch. 219.   [200] *Romulus Trading Co. Ltd v. Comet Properties Ltd* [1996] 2 E.G.L.R. 70.
[201] See *Petra Investments Ltd v. Jeffrey Rogers plc* [2000] 3 E.G.L.R. 120, where this argument failed on the facts.
[202] [1945] A.C. 221.   [203] [1981] A.C. 675.
[204] See *Wong Lai Ying v. Chinachem Investment Co. Ltd* (1979) 13 B.L.R. 81.

coastal erosion,[205] would be necessary before a lease of any length would be held to be frustrated.

Repudiation

As a normal incident of a contractual relationship, if one party commits a sufficiently serious breach of the contract, it is open to the other to terminate the contract, he being discharged from his own obligations by the repudiatory breach of the other. It was first accepted, at county court level, that it was open to the tenant to regard the lease as being repudiated by the landlord's breach of his own obligations[206] and, independently of this decision, the same conclusion has been accepted by the Court of Appeal.[207] It will not be every breach of covenant by the landlord which will have this effect, however; it would seem to be necessary for the breach to deprive the tenant, substantially, of the whole benefit of the lease.[208] Whether the landlord can adopt this course is unclear[209] but it seems unlikely given the statutory procedures which are normally required to be followed in respect of termination of a lease in the event of breaches of covenant by the tenant.[210]

Repair

Obligations to repair can be express or implied and can be imposed, depending upon the lease in question, upon either the landlord or the tenant.

Express covenants

As a general proposition, the parties are free to deal with the question of liability for repairs to the property as they choose. As will be seen, this freedom is qualified in respect of certain tenancies, where certain obligations are imposed upon the landlord. Where this is not the case, the main difficulties relate to the ambit of the covenant which, in turn, can relate to matters of construction.

As a general matter of construction, if the covenant requires the tenant to keep the property in good repair, this carries an obligation to put the property in good repair if that is not currently the case.[211] The actual words used do not, however, materially affect the content of the covenant, so that expressing the obligation as being to put the property in good repair, or tenantable repair, or even perfect repair, does not affect what is expected of the tenant. What constitutes such a state of repair is judged,

---

[205] Cf. *Holbeck Hall Hotel Ltd v. Scarborough Borough Council* [2000] 2 All E.R. 705, where the point was not argued.

[206] *Hussein v. Mehlman* [1992] 2 E.G.L.R. 87 (covenant to repair).

[207] *Chartered Trust plc v. Davies* (1997) 76 P. & C.R. 396 (derogation from grant).

[208] See *Nynehead Developments Ltd v. R.H. Fireboard Containers Ltd* [1999] 02 E.G. 139 discussed by M. Pawlowski and J. Brown [1999] Conv. 150.

[209] The point was left open in *Reichman v. Beveridge* [2006] EWCA Civ. 1659 at [10] *per* Lloyd L.J.

[210] See Forfeiture, pp. 454–459.   [211] *Proudfoot v. Hart* (1890) 25 Q.B.D. 92.

however, by the condition of the property and its environs at the date of the lease and not the date of the dispute, so if surrounding property has deteriorated since then, this does not reduce the obligation placed upon the tenant.[212]

The main bone of contention in determining whether a particular item comes within the ambit of a covenant to repair is whether the work in question amounts to a repair or an improvement. This distinction may be easier to state than to apply as, frequently, a repair will also involve the improvement of the property. In deciding this issue, a broad rule of thumb may be taken to be that the replacement of an item which is defective is a repair, while the installation of something new is an improvement and so not a repair. On this basis, the installation of a damp course in a building which does not have one is likely to be seen as an improvement, and, consequently, outside the scope of a covenant to repair,[213] whereas the replacement of an existing course which has broken down would be a repair, even though what would now be installed would be an improvement on the original.[214] In similar vein, the fact that part of a building does not perform its principal task does not mean that it is necessarily in disrepair. So, for example, in *Post Office v. Aquarius Property Ltd*,[215] the basement of an office was built of porous cement so that, whenever the water table rose, the basement was ankle deep in water. No damage was caused by the incursion of water, however, and the Court of Appeal held that the tenant's covenant to repair did not extend to the correction of design faults in the building, as originally constructed.

Two issues arise from this case. First, the notion of disrepair involves some element of damage. In *Quick v. Taff-Ely Borough Council*,[216] the lack of insulation around single glazed windows caused serious condensation problems, the problems being such that the house was uninhabitable at various times of year, yet little actual damage to the house occurred. The fact that the design of the windows was totally inadequate did not mean that they were in a state of disrepair and so within the ambit of the landlord's covenant to repair. This would only have been the case if the design fault had led to actual physical damage.[217] The second point is that the damage can be the result of an inherent flaw in the building and so, to repair the damage, correction of this flaw will result in an improvement of the property. Such correction will then amount to a repair.

Although it has been said that the covenant to repair extends to the restoration of a house to its previous condition and does not entail making it better than it previously

---

[212] See *Anstruther-Gough-Calthorpe v. McOscar* [1928] 1 K.B. 726.

[213] *Wainwright v. Leeds City Council* (1984) 82 L.G.R. 657; *Eyre v. McCracken* (2000) 80 P. & C.R. 220.

[214] *Pembury v. Lamdin* [1940] 2 All E.R. 434; *Elmcroft Developments Ltd v. Tankersley-Sawyer* [1984] 1 E.G.L.R. 47. See also *Creska Ltd v. Hammersmith London Borough Council* [1998] 3 E.G.L.R. 35 (underfloor heating).

[215] [1987] 1 All E.R. 1055.

[216] [1986] Q.B. 821. See also *Mullaney v. Maybourne Grange (Croydon) Management Co. Ltd* [1986] 1 E.G.L.R. 70; *McErney v. Lambeth London Borough Council* (1988) 21 H.L.R. 188.

[217] See *Stent v. Monmouth District Council* (1987) 54 P. & C.R. 193; *Staves and Staves v. Leeds City Council* (1990) 23 H.L.R. 107.

was,[218] a repair, properly called, may have this effect. In *Ravenseft Properties Ltd v. Davstone (Holdings) Ltd*,[219] a block of flats was built and stone cladding had been attached. When the flats were built, expansion joints had not been fitted, the result of this deficiency being that the stones were in danger of falling off the building and, in the interest of safety, this defect had to be remedied. The issue was who had to pay for this work, and this depended upon whether such work was within the scope of the tenant's covenant to repair. It was held that it was. In deciding whether a particular matter constitutes a repair or an improvement,

'The true test is…that it is always a question of degree whether that which the tenant is being asked to do can properly be described as repair, or whether on the contrary it would involve giving back to the landlord a wholly different thing from that which he demised.'[220]

One factor which is then relevant is the cost and the physical scale of what is necessary,[221] so that, in *Ravenseft*, the fact that the cost of the work was in the region of £55,000, when set against a rebuilding cost of £3 million tended to the conclusion that what was involved was a repair. The fact that the problem stemmed from an inherent fault in the building did not alter this conclusion.

Implied terms

As stated previously, it is normally the case that the parties are free to negotiate as to who should bear the burden of repairs. In certain situations, however, there are obligations implied as to this matter, either at common law or by statute.

Common law

The common law has traditionally been loath to imply terms relating to the physical quality of the property in to a lease, the standard position being that:

'A landlord who lets a house in a dangerous state is not liable to the tenant's customers or guests for accidents happening during the term; for fraud apart, there is no law against letting a tumble-down house; and the tenant's remedy is upon his contract, if any.'[222]

The only general modification to this at common law is that, if the letting is of a furnished house, then there is an obligation on the landlord that the house is, at the outset of the tenancy, fit for human habitation.[223] Even this, somewhat limited,

---

[218] See *Quick v. Taff-Ely Borough Council* [1986] Q.B. 809 at 821 *per* Lawton L.J.; *Southwark London Borough Council v. Mills* [2001] 1 A.C. 1 at 8 *per* Lord Hoffmann.

[219] [1980] Q.B. 12. See also *Brew Brothers Ltd v. Snax (Ross) Ltd* [1970] 1 Q.B. 12.

[220] Ibid., at 21 *per* Forbes J.

[221] Cf. *Lurcott v. Wakely* [1911] 1 K.B. 905 (rebuilding a wall held to be a repair) with *Sotheby v. Grundy* [1947] 2 All E.R. 761 (house condemned, rebuilding of it on proper foundations not a repair).

[222] *Robbins v. Jones* (1863) 15 C.B. (N.S.) 221 at 240 *per* Erle C.J. See also *Carstairs v. Taylor* (1871) L.R. 6 Exch. 217 at 222 *per* Martin B. See now Defective Premises Act 1972, s. 4.

[223] *Smith v. Marrable* (1843) 11 M. & W. 5 (bug infestation).

obligation is construed narrowly, there being no implied obligation that the property remains fit for human habitation throughout the lease.[224]

The other source of liability is where a court will imply a term as to liability for repair if to do so it is necessary to give business efficacy to the contract. In *Liverpool City Council v. Irwin*,[225] the council was the landlord of a block of flats, the tenants being subject to various obligations imposed by their agreements. To interpret the lease, the House of Lords held that, by necessary implication, the landlord was under an obligation to take reasonable care to keep the common parts of the building, including the lift, in a state of repair. It was not open to the courts to imply terms on the basis that it was reasonable to do so; the test is one of necessity, a finding which is more likely to be achieved when the term to be implied is correlative to an obligation accepted by the tenant.[226]

Statutory obligations

In respect of certain residential leases, certain statutory obligations are imposed upon the landlord.

Fitness for human habitation

In the case of a house which is let for a period of not more than three years, there is imposed upon the landlord by section 8 of the Landlord and Tenant Act 1985 an obligation that the house will, at the time of the letting and thereafter, be fit for human habitation.[227]

The problem with this provision is that it applies only to tenancies where the annual rent is no more than £52.00 per annum outside London and no more than £80.00 per annum in London. In short, it is clear that this provision is not going to affect any lease[228] and, not surprisingly, there have been pleas for the rent ceilings to be raised from the levels first set in 1957[229] in order for the obligation to have any relevance to today's society.[230] The fact that they have not been raised is interesting and has been used as a reason for judicial caution in not developing the law on a case-by-case basis. In *McErney v. Lambeth London Borough Council*,[231] Dillon L.J. commented, in a case where a flat was badly affected by damp, that:

'Parliament has conspicuously refrained from updating the [rent] limits in the 1985 Housing and Landlord and Tenant Acts. In these circumstances, in my judgment, this is an area where it is for Parliament to extend the duties imposed upon landlords of council flats or houses or other low standard accommodation. It is not for the judges.'

---

[224] *Sarson v. Roberts* [1895] 2 Q.B. 395 (outbreak of scarlet fever).   [225] [1977] A.C. 239.

[226] Ibid., at 254 *per* Lord Wilberforce. See also *Barrett v. Lounava (1982) Ltd* [1990] 1 Q.B. 348, but contrast *Demetriou v. Poolaction Ltd* [1981] 1 E.G.L.R. 100.

[227] For a list of the criteria to be applied in determining this issue, see Landlord and Tenant Act 1985, s. 10.

[228] The provision has been described as 'completely dead letters': *Issa v. Hackney London Borough Council* [1997] 1 W.L.R. 956 at 964 *per* Brooke L.J.

[229] Housing Act 1957, s. 6.   [230] See, e.g., [1986] Q.B. 809 at 821 *per* Lawton L.J.

[231] (1988) 21 H.L.R. 188 at 194.

These sentiments were endorsed in *Southwark London Borough Council v. Mills*,[232] when, in refusing to extend the reach of the covenant for quiet enjoyment to cover the lack of effective soundproofing in a block of flats, it was noted that, although the Law Commission has recommended that landlords should be under an obligation that properties should be fit for human habitation,[233] the criteria to apply in assessing such fitness did not extend to soundproofing. As to the prospects of such an obligation being imposed, perhaps by raising the rent ceilings to realistic levels, so that at least some tenancies are subject to the existing statutory levels, one is forced to be pessimistic. Lord Millett noted the estimate provided by the council that to bring the housing stock within the authority up to modern standards would cost them in the region of £1.271 billion.[234] While such modernization would presumably not be essential to render such properties fit for human habitation, it is a sad testimony to the state of public sector housing stock and may also explain why this redundant statutory provision remains in its unaltered form on the statute book.

Liability to repair

A rather more useful provision than section 8 of the Landlord and Tenant Act 1985 is contained in section 11 of the Act. The obligations contained in this section apply to a lease of a dwelling-house, granted after 24 October 1961, of not more than seven years.[235] This time limit means that in the case of leases such as that seen in *Berrisford v. Mexfield Housing Co-operative Ltd*,[236] where what purported to be a periodic tenancy which, because of the restraints on the landlord's ablity to serve a notice to quit, took effect as a determinable ninety-year lease, this provision will, seemingly, not apply. Any attempt to exclude, or vary, the liability imposed is void unless such a term has been approved by the county court.[237] Under section 11, there is an implied covenant by the lessor—

'(a) to keep in repair the structure and exterior of the dwelling-house (including drains, gutters and external pipes);

(b) to keep in repair and proper working order the installations in the dwelling-house for the supply of water, gas and electricity and for sanitation (including basins, sinks, baths and sanitary conveniences, but not other fixtures, fittings and appliances for making use of the supply of water gas and electricity); and

(c) to keep in repair and proper working order the installations in the dwelling-house for space heating and heating water.'

A number of points can be made concerning this provision. First, the landlord is only liable under the covenant if he is given notice by the tenant of the defect in question.[238] Secondly, the covenant is qualified by the obligation, which is in any event imposed

---

[232] [2001] 1 A.C. 1 at 9–10 *per* Lord Hoffmann.   [233] (1996) Law Com. No. 238, para. 11.16.
[234] [1999] 3 W.L.R. 939 at 960.   [235] Landlord and Tenant Act 1985, s. 13.
[236] [2011] UKSC 52. See Leases for life, pp. 401–403.   [237] Landlord and Tenant Act 1985, s. 12.
[238] *O'Brien v. Robinson* [1973] A.C. 912.

upon a periodic tenant, to use the property in a tenant-like manner.[239] The ambit of this duty is to perform routine acts of maintenance around the house, doing all the jobs, such as unblocking the sink and taking precautions against freezing pipes in winter, that a reasonable tenant would do.[240] Thirdly, the obligation relates to the keeping in repair of various services and installations. This would not appear to impose any liability for a failure to supply them, so that, if a house has no central heating in the first place, the landlord would be under no duty to install it.

The ambit of the landlord's covenant in respect of services and installations was recently considered in *O'Connor v. Old Etonian Housing Association Ltd*,[241] a case concerning an express covenant but one to the same effect as the statutory obligation. The problem was that the pipes were too narrow in diameter to enable the proper circulation of water for the heating system to work adequately for tenants in upper storey flats. The first point which was made was that the obligation is to keep the installations in proper working order. This means that, if the system is not working because of some design defect, it is not in proper working order and it is the landlord's responsibility to rectify the problem.[242] The next issue is the effect of changes to the supply of water, gas, or electricity. The view was taken that the installations would be in proper working order if they were able to function under those conditions of supply that it would be reasonable to foresee would prevail during the subsistence of the lease. If there was a change in the manner of supply then, if this was the result of a deliberate change due to technological advances or business efficacy, for example the change from coal gas to natural gas, or a change in the voltage supply, the responsibility would rest on the landlord to ensure that the installation would be able to work properly in the new conditions. If there were unplanned changes to the supply, then, whether or not the landlord has to do anything to the installations will depend upon the nature of the change and, in particular, its likely duration For example, if there was a fall in the water pressure as result of the collapse of a reservoir or a drought, it may not be necessary for the landlord to have to make expensive alterations to the installations.[243]

Structure and exterior

As a matter of construction, the issue which can give rise to difficulty is to ascertain what is meant by the structure and exterior of the dwelling-house. Useful guidance was provided in *Re Irvine's Estate v. Moran*,[244] where the view was expressed that

[239] Landlord and Tenant Act 1985, s. 11(2)(a).
[240] See *Warren v. Keen* [1954] 1 Q.B. 15 at 22 *per* Denning L.J. Cf. *Wycombe Health Authority v. Barnett* (1982) 47 P. & C.R. 392, criticized by M.P. Thompson (1984) 81 L.S.G. 3408.
[241] [2002] 2 All E.R. 1015. See also *Niazi Services Ltd v. van der Loo* [2004] 1 W.L.R. 1254; M.P. Thompson [2003] Conv. 80.
[242] [2002] 2 All E.R. 1015 at 1019 *per* Lord Phillips of Worth Matravers M.R., who pointed out at 1020 that there is a difference between keeping something in repair and keeping something in working order.
[243] Ibid., at 1023.
[244] (1992) 24 M.L.R. 1. See also *Ibrahim v. Dovecom Reversions Ltd* [2001] 30 E.G. 116; *Marlborough Park Services Ltd v. Rowe* [2006] H.L.R. 30.

structure is not confined to load-bearing parts. It must, however, be a material or significant element of the property. Although windows, window frames, and sashes were part of the structure, the internal plastering was considered not to be, this being in the nature of a decorative finish. This aspect of the decision was not followed, however, in *Grand v. Gill*,[245] where the landlord was held liable in respect of damage caused to the plasterwork by damp, this being contributed to by a lack of adequate heating as a result of a defective boiler. As to matters decorative, depending on the length of the lease, the obligation to decorate could be placed upon the tenant.

With regard to the outside, however, because external decoration provides a protective function against rot being caused by the weather, this would come within the implied covenant by the landlord.[246] A further matter relating to the exterior of the property was clarified by an amendment to the legislation to make clear that, if the dwelling-house forms part of a building, and the landlord either owns or has an interest in the other part, then the implied covenant extends to that part of the building also.[247]

Although the Act provides welcome protection for tenants of residential property held on short leases, it is not all-embracing and has its limitations. In particular, it must be stressed that the structure of the house must be in disrepair. While it may be surprising that a door which cannot perform its primary function of keeping out the rain is not, for that reason alone, in a state of disrepair,[248] the position is that, unless the ingress of water occasions damage to relevant parts of the property, the tenant has no remedy under the section.[249]

This issue was recently reviewed in *Lee v. Leeds City Council*.[250] The case involved two appeals raising the same issue. In each case, owing to a design fault, the interiors of both houses, which were let by local authorities, suffered severe condensation leading to mould. The effect of this problem was that the houses were unfit for human habitation and a danger to health. The tenants brought proceedings against the local authorities, which failed. The statutory obligation with respect to fitness for human habitation imposed by section 8 of the Landlord and Tenant Act 1985[251] was inapplicable as the rent paid exceeded the statutory limits. The main issue was whether the condensation and mould amounted to a breach of the obligation under section 11 of the Act. The Court of Appeal held that it did not. Following the earlier decision

---

[245] [2011] EWCA Civ. 354.

[246] This would seem to be a better explanation of *Barrett v. Lounava (1982) Ltd* [1990] 1 Q.B. 348.

[247] Landlord and Tenant Act 1985, s. 1A inserted by Housing Act 1988, s. 116. The problem may, however, be caused by a defective roof or guttering in which the landlord does not have an interest: see *Grant v. Gill* [2011] EWCA Civ. 354.

[248] See *Stent v. Monmouth District Council* (1987) 54 P. & C.R. 193 at 209 *per* Stocker L.J.

[249] *Quick v. Taff-Ely Borough Council* [1986] Q.B. 809.

[250] [2002] 1 W.L.R. 1488. See M.P. Thompson [2003] Conv. 80; P.F. Smith [2003] Conv. 112.

[251] For an account of the history of this provision from its origin in the Housing of the Working Classes Act 1885, s. 12, see [2002] 1 W.L.R. 1488 at 1492–1493 *per* Chadwick L.J.

in *Quick v. Taff-Ely Borough Council*,[252] Chadwick L.J. explained the position in the following terms:

'The cases show that, where there is a need to repair damage to the structure, the due performance of the obligation to repair may require the landlord to remedy the design defect which is the cause of the damage. They do not support the proposition that the obligation to repair will require the landlord to remedy a design defect which has not been a cause of damage to the structure; notwithstanding that the defect may make the premises unsuitable for accommodation or unfit for human habitation.'[253]

Human rights

A final argument pressed by the tenants was based upon the Human Rights Act 1998. Section 3(1) of the Act, requires, so far as it is possible to do so, primary legislation to be read and given effect in a way which is compatible with Convention rights. The tenants argued that section 11 of the Landlord and Tenant Act 1985 should be read in a way which is compatible with Article 8 of the Convention and that, as section 6(1) of the Act makes it unlawful for public authorities to act in a way which is incompatible with Convention rights, the local authorities should be under a duty to ensure that the properties which they rented out were fit for human habitation. These arguments failed. It was accepted that Article 8(1) of the Convention, which provides that everyone has a right to respect for his private and family life, his home, and correspondence was, in principle, applicable, in that severe environmental pollution may have the effect of adversely affecting a person's right to private life and to enjoy their homes. However, the obligation imposed by Article 8(1) is not absolute; due regard must also be had to the needs and resources of the community. Accordingly, regard must also be had to striking a balance between the rights of individual tenants and the resources of local housing authorities. So, while Chadwick L.J. was not prepared to rule out totally that the condition of a house may be so bad as to amount to a violation of Article 8, he was not prepared to imply a general and unqualified obligation on local authorities in respect of their housing stock.[254] Unless the design default causes damage to the structure of the house, it is difficult to see an argument based on the condition of the house being successful.

Personal injury

The imposition of liability upon the landlord in respect of certain repairs impacts also on his liability to all persons who might reasonably be expected to be affected by defects in the property. Under section 4(1) of the Defective Premises Act 1972, the landlord is liable to such people in respect of personal injury or damage to their property if he fails in his duty to take reasonable care to see that the premises are reasonably safe from such damage. The duty is owed when the landlord knew, or ought to have known, of the relevant defect or has a right to enter the premises to carry out

---

[252] [1986] Q.B. 809.   [253] [2002] 1 W.L.R. 1488 at 1496.   [254] [2002] 1 W.L.R. 1488 at 1506.

repairs.[255] Under section 11(6) of the Landlord and Tenant Act 1985, the landlord has a right at reasonable times in the day and, on giving twenty-four hours' notice in writing, to enter the property for the purpose of viewing their condition and state of repair.

Remedies

It may be the case that the disrepair is sufficiently serious to allow either party to terminate the lease, the landlord by forfeiture or the tenant by accepting that the land-lord's breach of covenant is sufficiently serious to amount to a repudiatory breach of the lease.[256] There are other, less extreme, remedies.

Damages

The recovery of damages by the landlord is regulated by statute. The landlord is not able to recover more in damages than the diminution of the value of the reversion caused by the lack of repair and, if it is proposed to demolish the buildings at the end of the lease, then no damages are recoverable.[257] For leases granted initially for more than seven years, of which there are more than three years to run, then the landlord's ability to enforce repairing covenants is regulated by the Leasehold Property (Repairs Act) 1938, which relates to issues of forfeiture of the lease.

The tenant may also, of course, claim damages for breach of the landlord's covenant to repair and such a claim may, depending upon the seriousness of the breach, include the cost of alternative accommodation.[258]

Specific performance

Although specific performance is generally available to enforce a contract to create a lease, it does not follow that this remedy will be available in respect of particular covenants in leases. For example, in *Co-operative Insurance Society Ltd v. Argyll Stores (Holdings) Ltd*,[259] the House of Lords refused to grant specific performance of a covenant by a tenant to keep open a store during the currency of the lease, the main reason for this being the reluctance to grant this remedy when its performance would require constant supervision by the courts.[260] In the context of repairing covenants, the courts have, in the case of express covenants, specifically enforced covenants by the landlord[261] and, in the case of repairing covenants implied under the Landlord and Tenant Act 1985, it is provided specifically that specific performance may be ordered, notwithstanding any equitable rule restricting the scope of the remedy as against the tenant.[262] It has recently been held that this remedy is also, in principle, available to

---

[255] Defective Premises Act 1972, s. 4(2)(4).

[256] See Forfeiture, pp. 454–459 and Repudiation, p. 436.

[257] Landlord and Tenant Act 1927, s. 18.   [258] See *McGreal v. Wake* [1984] 1 E.G.L.R. 42.

[259] [1998] A.C. 1. Contrast *Capita Trust Co. (Channel Islands) Ltd v. Chatham Maritime J3 Developments Ltd* [2006] EWHC 2956 (Ch) at [27] *per* Pumfrey J.

[260] For cogent criticism, see A. Tettenborn [1998] Conv. 23.

[261] *Jeune v. Queen's Cross Properties Ltd* [1974] Ch. 97; *Gordon v. Selico Co. Ltd* [1985] 2 E.G.L.R.79.

[262] Landlord and Tenant Act 1985, s. 17.

landlords[263] but the facts of the case were unusual and it is unlikely to be a remedy of general application.

Self-help

Although specific performance is available in respect of the landlord's repairing obligations, this may not be the ideal remedy for him. If a tenant, particularly one holding on a short lease, complains that the house is in disrepair, perhaps as a result of storm damage finding that the roof has been damaged and is leaking, he may find that the landlord is dilatory in effecting the repair. As an alternative to bringing an action for specific performance, which will obviously take time, one possible course of action, in these circumstances, is for the tenant to do, or pay for, the work himself and then deduct the cost of the work from future payments of rent.[264] Before this course of action is taken, however, it is necessary to notify the landlord that this will be done.[265]

Assignment and sub-letting

As a general proposition, a tenant, as the holder of an estate in land, is perfectly free either to assign it or to create sub-tenancies, if he so chooses. It is common, however, for the landlord, by the insertion of a covenant in the lease, to curtail the tenant's right to do this. The most complete form of covenant will be a covenant restricting the tenant from assigning, underletting, or parting with possession of the property. If the covenant is more limited, for example a covenant only against assignment, then it may become a matter of law whether a particular transaction operates in this way. For example, a purported sub-tenancy which is longer than the existing lease will take effect as an assignment[266] and so, somewhat surprisingly, is a release by one joint tenant to the other of his interest under the lease.[267]

Absolute and qualified covenants

A covenant against assignment, to use this as shorthand for the full covenant, may be absolute or qualified. An absolute covenant, as its name suggests, simply prohibits the tenant from assigning the lease. Should he, nevertheless, assign, the assignment is effective to transfer the estate[268] but is, automatically, a breach of covenant. It is unusual to find an absolute prohibition of this type in a commercial lease.

---

[263] *Rainbow Estates Ltd v. Tokenhold Ltd* [1999] Ch. 64. See M. Pawlowski and J. Brown [1998] Conv. 495.

[264] *Lee-Parker v. Izzet* [1971] 1 W.L.R. 1688; *Asco Developments Ltd v. Gordon* [1978] E.G.D. 376.

[265] See, generally, A. Waite [1981] Conv. 199.

[266] See *Milmo v. Carreras* [1946] K.B. 306.

[267] *Burton v. Camden London Borough Council* [2000] 1 All E.R. 943, criticized by S. Bridge [2000] Conv. 474.

[268] See *Old Grovebury Manor Farm Ltd v. W. Seymour Plant Sales and Hire Ltd (No. 2)* [1979] 1 W.L.R. 1397.

It is more common to find that the covenant is qualified, that qualification being that the lease should not be assigned without the landlord's consent. In such cases, it is provided by section 19 of the Landlord and Tenant Act 1927 that such consent shall not be unreasonably withheld.[269] Even though the landlord must not unreasonably withhold consent, it is nevertheless a breach of covenant to assign without first seeking it.[270]

The obtaining of such consent became, in practice, a considerable problem, and the delays involved in obtaining such consents were a considerable source of frustration.[271] To alleviate this problem, pursuant to the recommendation of the Law Commission,[272] what has been described as 'this curious little Act',[273] the Landlord and Tenant Act 1988, was enacted.

Under section 1(3) of the Act, the landlord, upon receipt of a written request for consent to assignment is under a duty, within a reasonable time, to give consent, unless it is reasonable not to give that consent. If consent is withheld, written notice must be served on the tenant as to the reasons,[274] and, if the consent is made subject to any conditions, those conditions must themselves be reasonable.[275] A failure to comply with the obligations imposed by the Act leads to liability in tort for breach of statutory duty.[276] This may lead to an award of exemplary damages if the landlord seeks to profit by an unreasonable refusal to give his consent to an assignment.[277]

There is no definition of what is a reasonable time. The starting point in the assessment of what is reasonable is the date on which the tenant serves his request. That does not mean, however, that one can determine conclusively what would be a reasonable time from the date when the application is made. Regard must be had to all the circumstances of an individual case, including negotiations between the landlord and tenant prior to the landlord giving his decision.[278] The onus of proof is on the landlord to establish both that the time taken to reply, and the grounds for a refusal of consent, are reasonable.[279] If the landlord seeks to argue that his refusal of consent is reasonable, he can rely only on those grounds which existed at the end of the reasonable period of time from the making of the request,[280] and he is also limited to the reasons actually given.[281]

---

[269] This qualification does not apply to a covenant to offer to surrender the lease to the landlord prior to any assignment: see *Bocardo S.A. v. S. & M. Hotels Ltd* [1980] 1 W.L.R. 17.

[270] *Eastern Telegraph Co. Ltd v. Dent* [1899] 1 Q.B. 835.

[271] See the observations in *29 Equities Ltd v. Bank Leumi (U.K.) Ltd* [1987] 1 All E.R. 108 at 114 *per* Dillon L.J.

[272] (1987) Law Com. No. 261.

[273] *Venetian Glass Gallery Ltd v. Next Properties Ltd* [1989] 2 E.G.L.R. 42 at 46 *per* Harman J.

[274] This is not satisfied by giving oral reasons: *Footwear Corp. Ltd v. Amplight Properties Ltd* [1999] 1 W.L.R. 551.

[275] Landlord and Tenant Act 1988, s. 1(3).   [276] Ibid., s. 4.

[277] *Design Progression Ltd v. Thurloe Properties Ltd* [2004] EWHC 324 (Ch.).

[278] See *Go West Ltd v. Spigarolo* [2003] 2 All E.R. 141 at 149–151 *per* Mumby J.

[279] Landlord and Tenant Act 1988, s. 1(4)(c).

[280] *Norwich Union Life Insurance Co. Ltd v. Shopmoor Ltd* [1991] 1 W.L.R. 531 at 545 *per* Sir Richard Scott V.-C.; *Go West Ltd v. Spigarolo, supra.*

[281] *Southern Depot Co. Ltd v. British Railway Board* [1990] 2 E.G.L.R. 39 at 44 *per* Morritt L.J.

Reasonableness

As to what is reasonable, much will depend on the facts of a given case, and the authorities dealing with this issue are generally only of illustrative value,[282] although, if the landlord reasonably suspects that the proposed assignee will breach the user conditions in the lease, a refusal to consent will be reasonable.[283] The essential test which the courts will apply is that 'a landlord is not entitled to refuse his consent on grounds which have nothing to do with the relationship of landlord and tenant in regard to the subject matter of the lease…',[284] and it is not reasonable to refuse consent to an assignment on terms which will give the landlord greater rights than he enjoyed under the original lease.[285] Ultimately, in determining whether a refusal of consent is reasonable, that expression should be 'given a broad common sense meaning',[286] although under the Landlord and Tenant (Covenants) Act 1995, the landlord is entitled to stipulate in advance that his consent is subject to undertakings relevant to the operation of that Act.[287] Where the reasonableness of the refusal is in issue, the safest course for the tenant to take is to refer the matter to the court for a declaration as, although if the refusal is unreasonable, the assignment will not amount to a breach of covenant, if it is found that the refusal was reasonable, then a breach will have occurred.

THE ENFORCEABILITY OF COVENANTS

An important issue, particularly in the case of long leases, is that of who can enforce the covenants contained in a lease and against whom. In determining this matter it is necessary to consider the position of the original parties to the lease and, also, the position of assignees of either the lease or the reversion. It is also essential to distinguish between leases created before 1996 and those created after that date.

Pre-1996 leases

The liability of various parties with respect to leases created prior to 1 January 1996 was dependent upon an amalgam of common law and statute. Attention will be given, first, to the position of the original parties to the lease and then to the position of assignees and sub-tenants.

[282] *Ashworth Frazer Ltd v. Gloucester City Council* [2001] 1 W.L.R. 2180 at 2183 *per* Lord Bingham of Cornhill.

[283] Ibid., overruling *Killick v. Second Covent Garden Property Co. Ltd* [1973] 1 W.L.R. 658.

[284] *International Drilling Fluids Ltd v. Louisville Investments (Uxbridge) Ltd* [1986] Ch. 513 at 520 *per* Balcombe L.J. See also *Houlder Bros & Co. Ltd v. Gibbs* [1925] Ch. 575 at 587 *per* Sargent J.

[285] *Mount Eden Land Ltd v. Straudley Investments Ltd* (1996) 74 P. & C.R. 306; *Landlord Protect Ltd v. St Anselm Development Co. Ltd* [2009] EWCA Civ. 99.

[286] *Ashworth Frazer Ltd v. Gloucester City Council* [2001] 1 W.L.R. 2180 at 2183 *per* Lord Bingham of Cornhill.

[287] See Consent to assignment, p. 451.

Original parties

At common law, the liability of the original parties to the lease was governed by the principles of contract law. Quite simply, this meant that, as signatories to the original tenancy, each remained liable to the other for the duration of the term, notwithstanding that their interest had subsequently been assigned. This presented considerable problems for the tenants of commercial properties.[288] Even after the tenant had assigned the lease, he remained liable to the original landlord in respect of the rent for the remainder of the term,[289] so that, if the assignee became insolvent, the landlord could look to the original tenant, maybe some years after the lease had been assigned, for payment[290] and this liability would extend to rent increased pursuant to a rent review clause in the lease.[291] For one large company, this potential liability was estimated as being in the region of £50 million.[292] This aspect of the law was considered to represent a considerable trap and to be unfair. Reforms have been implemented, although not in the form originally proposed.

Assignments and sub-letting

The mutual liability of the original parties to a lease stems from privity of contract. When either the lease or the reversion has been assigned, the question which then arises is as to the liability of the assignees. The basis of liability, derived from *Spencer's Case*,[293] depended upon two issues: privity of estate and whether or not the covenant in question touched and concerned the land. If both conditions were satisfied, then there would be mutual liability between the parties. The covenants are said to run with the lease.

Privity of estate

What is meant by privity of estate is that a direct relationship of landlord and tenant exists between the two parties. If one starts with a lease between L and T, there exists both privity of contract and privity of estate between the two, the latter meaning that the relationship of landlord and tenant exists between them. If T assigns the lease to A, then, as between L and A, there is no privity of contract but there is privity of estate; L is A's landlord. Similarly, if it was L who assigned the reversion to R, then there would now exist privity of estate between R and A, there being a direct landlord and tenant relationship between them. If, subsequently, A assigns the lease to A2, there is now

---

[288] See K. Reynolds and S. Fogel (1984) 81 L.S.G. 2214.

[289] He would not be liable in respect of a statutory extension of that term. See *City of London Corp. v. Fell* [1994] 1 A.C. 458.   [290] See *Hindcastle Ltd v. Barbara Attenborough Associates Ltd* [1997] A.C. 70.

[291] See *Centrovincial Estates plc v. Bulk Storage Ltd* (1983) 46 P. & C.R. 393; *Selous Street Properties Ltd v. Oronel Fabrics Ltd* [1984] 1 E.G.L.R. 50. Where the terms of the lease are subsequently varied, the liability of the original tenant depended upon whether the variation was so substantial as to amount to a surrender and regrant of a new lease. See *Friends Provident Life Office v. British Railways Board* [1996] 1 All E.R. 336. See S. Bright in Jackson and Wilde (eds), *The Reform of Property Law* (Aldershot: Ashgate, 1997), Chapter 5.

[292] (1988) Law Com. No. 174, 15.   [293] (1583) 5 Co. Rep. 16a.

privity of estate between R and A2 but, as between R and A, there is no relationship at all. There never was privity of contract and there is no longer privity of estate as R is not A's landlord. A is not, therefore, liable to R in respect of breaches of covenant committed after he assigned the lease.

If the original lease was between L and T and, this time, instead of assigning the lease, T created a sub-tenancy in favour of ST then, as between L and ST, there was neither privity of contract nor privity of estate. ST's landlord was T and not L. Unless the covenant in question was negative in nature and enforceable by other means,[294] the lack of either privity of contract or of estate between L and ST meant that L could not sue ST directly in respect of any breach of covenant. In practice, this did not cause difficulties because T would be liable to L in respect of any breaches of covenant, albeit committed by ST, contained in the head lease and, so, it would be in T's own interest to ensure that the covenants contained in the sub-lease were at least as stringent as those which were in the head lease, in order to avoid liability in respect of ST's actions.

Touching and concerning the land

Parties to a lease are, as a general proposition, free to include within it such terms as they please. For the rights and obligations created by these covenants to run with the lease, however, it is necessary that these obligations are not regarded as being merely personal. For them to run due to the existence of privity of estate, it is necessary that those covenants touch and concern the land or, to put the matter into modern parlance, affect the landlord in his capacity as landlord and the tenant in his capacity as tenant.[295] What this means was elaborated by the House of Lords in *P. & A. Swift Investments v. Combined English Stores Group.*[296] A covenant by a tenant will touch and concern the land if (i) it is beneficial to the reversioner only for the time being; (ii) it affects the nature, quality, mode of user, or value of the reversioner's land; and (iii) it is not expressed to be merely personal in nature. A similar test is imposed concerning covenants by the landlord.

Despite the articulation of these criteria to determine whether a covenant touched and concerned the land, it is widely accepted that the distinction between those which do and those which do not is largely arbitrary and has been described as being 'quite illogical'.[297] The removal of this criterion[298] to determine whether or not covenants will run with the lease is therefore welcome.

Assignment of the lease

The rules concerning the running of covenants on the assignment of a lease derive from *Spencer's Case* and, as a common law rule, certain consequences followed. First, the lease had to be a legal lease. The doctrine of privity of estates does not

---

[294] See Chapter 14.   [295] *Breams Property Investment Ltd v. Stroulger* [1948] 2 K.B. 1.
[296] [1989] A.C. 632 at 642 *per* Lord Oliver of Aylmerton.
[297] *Grant v. Edmondson* [1931] 1 Ch. 1 at 29 *per* Romer L.J.
[298] Landlord and Tenant (Covenants) Act 1995, s. 2.

apply to equitable tenancies.[299] Secondly, the basis of the common law rule was that of privity of estate. This explains why a sub-tenant is not liable under the common law rules, in that there is no privity between him and the landlord of the head lease. For the same reason, the lack of privity of estate, a squatter who acquires a possessory title against a tenant is not liable to the landlord in respect of covenants in the lease.[300]

Assignment of the reversion

When the landlord assigns the reversion, the original position at common law was that, subject to certain limited exceptions, the assignee could neither sue nor be sued on the obligations contained in the lease. This position was modified by statute, the position now being governed by sections 141 and 142 of the Law of Property Act 1925. The position is, *mutatis mutandis*, essentially the same as that arrived at when it is the lease which has been assigned, but there are some differences.

Section 154 of the Landlord and Tenant (Covenants) Act 1995 provides that the Part of the Act which includes sections 141 and 142 applies to leases created before or after the commencement of the Act and includes an under-lease or other tenancy. This latter expression would seem to be sufficiently wide to include an equitable tenancy so that, on the assignment of the freehold reversion of an equitable lease, the benefit and burden of the covenants contained in the lease will run.

A second point concerns remedies for breaches of covenant occurring prior to the assignment. On an assignment of the reversion, the assignee acquires the benefit of all covenants. This means that the assignee acquires the right to sue for breaches of any covenant made by the tenant. Even after assignment, however, the landlord remains liable to the original tenant for breaches of covenant committed while he was in possession of the land.[301]

Post-1996 tenancies

The subject of covenants in leases was subject to review by the Law Commission, who proposed wide-ranging reform.[302] After considerable consultation, the central thrust of these proposals, subject to considerable alteration,[303] was implemented by the Landlord and Tenant (Covenants) Act 1995.[304] For present purposes, the principal changes introduced by the Act relate to the continuing liability of the tenant through the operation of privity of contract and the nature of covenants which will run with the lease.

---

[299] *Elliott v. Johnson* (1866) L.R. 2 Q.B. 120.   [300] *Tichborne v. Weir* (1892) 67 L.T. 735.
[301] See *City and Metropolitan Properties Ltd v. Greycroft Ltd* [1987] 1 W.L.R. 1085.
[302] (1988) Law Com. No. 174.
[303] For an interesting discussion by one of the responsible Law Commissioners of the process of the implementation of these proposals, see T.M. Aldridge in Jackson and Wilde, op. cit., Chapter 2.
[304] For excellent discussions of the background and the changes introduced by the Act, see S. Bridge [1996] C.L.J. 313; M. Davey (1996) 59 M.L.R. 78.

Liability of tenant

One of the principal objections to the old law was that the original tenant would continue to be liable to the original landlord on the covenants contained in the lease throughout the agreed term. Under the Act, which is not retrospective, when a tenant assigns the entire property comprised in the lease, he is released from the tenant's covenants contained in the lease and ceases to be entitled to the benefit of the landlord's covenants. Upon assignment of part of the property the release operates with respect to the part contained in the assignment.[305] This release does not, however, absolve him from liability in respect of breaches of covenant committed prior to the assignment.[306]

Consent to assignment

Although it is not possible to contract out of the Act,[307] as a major concession to commercial landlords, provision was made to safeguard their position on an assignment of a post-1996 lease. Under section 16 of the Act, the landlord is not precluded from obtaining from the tenant, when assigning the lease, a guarantee of the performance of the covenants in the lease. For such a guarantee to be valid, the lease must contain a qualified covenant against assignment and the condition imposed for consent to be given is that the tenant enters into an agreement guaranteeing the performance of the covenants by the assignee. Section 22 of the Act then amended section 19 of the Landlord and Tenant Act 1927, to provide that, if a landlord refuses consent to an assignment on the ground that the tenant will not give such a guarantee, then that refusal is reasonable.

Overriding leases

The ability of the landlord to seek a guarantee from the tenant that the assignee will perform the covenants in the lease means, in effect, that if such a guarantee is imposed the tenant will continue to be liable under the covenants contained in the lease for the duration of the term, just as was the case prior to the introduction of the Act. To meet both these situations, the tenant is given the right to have granted to him what is termed an overriding lease. Under section 19 of the Act, when a tenant has met in full payment which he has been required to make under either the original lease, when such a lease was created before the implementation of the Act, or under a guarantee covenant,[308] he is entitled to have the landlord grant him an overriding lease. This lease is a tenancy of the reversion expectant on the tenancy, the meaning of which is that the tenant becomes, directly, the landlord of the assignee. This lease is subject to the same covenants as the original lease. The point of this is that, if, in the future, the assignee commits further breaches of covenant, the original tenant is now the landlord of the assignee and can pursue remedies against him including, where appropriate, forfeiture of the lease.

---

[305] Landlord and Tenant (Covenants) Act 1995, s. 5.   [306] Ibid., s. 24.   [307] Ibid., s. 25.
[308] Ibid., s. 17.

Liability of landlords

While the Act operates to release the tenant from liability under the covenants in the lease after it has been assigned, it does not work in the same way insofar as the landlord is concerned upon an assignment of the reversion. He will remain liable on the covenants unless he is released from them. To obtain a release, he must, within four weeks of the assignment, serve a notice on the tenant informing him of the assignment and seeking a release from the covenants. If the tenant does not respond within four weeks of the service of the notice, the landlord will be released from his covenants. If the tenant does object, the matter can be referred to the court to determine if such a refusal is reasonable.[309]

Care must be taken in the case of sub-tenancies. In *London Diocesan Fund v. Phithwa*,[310] a company acquired the lease of a unit of seven shops. Under the terms of the lease, which was for a period of ninety-nine years, the rent payable was £16,700 per annum, subject to review. The company then granted sub-leases of six of the units. The sub-leases were of virtually the same duration as the head lease. On the creation of the sub-tenancies, the sub-tenants paid a premium and only a peppercorn rent was reserved. In the sub-leases, the company covenanted to pay the rent reserved in the head lease, but its liability to do so was limited to the period when it held the reversion on the sub-tenancies. The company then assigned the reversion to an individual, who was impecunious. The owner of the freehold could, of course, have sued that individual in respect of the rent but, because of his financial situation, this was not worth pursuing. Forfeiture proceedings were then brought to terminate the head lease. The sub-tenants, as persons deriving interests under that lease sought relief against forfeiture,[311] and this was granted on terms that they paid the rent reserved in the head lease. The sub-tenants sought damages from the company in respect of the payment of rent.

In deciding in favour of the company, the House of Lords exposed a trap into which the tenants had fallen. The liability of the company to the owner of the freehold in respect of the payment of rent terminated when it assigned the head lease. The covenant contained in the sub-lease was limited to the period when the company held the reversion on the sub-tenancies. Thus, when it assigned the head lease it was liable neither to the freeholder, not to the sub-tenants. The potential for this to occur, however, should have been spotted by the conveyancers dealing with the creation of the sub-leases,[312] and is a forceful warning of the need to take care when drafting sub-leases to ensure that the position of the sub-tenants is adequately protected.

Landlord and tenant covenants

For centuries, a key factor in determining whether a particular covenant ran with a lease was if it touched and concerned the land. Now, the position is that, unless

---

[309] Ibid., ss 7, 8.   [310] [2006] 1 All. E.R. 127.   [311] See Parties, p. 459.
[312] [2006] 1 All E.R. 127 at 133 *per* Lord Nicholls of Birkenhead.

covenants are expressed to be personal to the parties,[313] the benefit and burden of all landlord and tenant covenants will pass on assignment, whether or not such covenants have reference to the subject matter of the tenancy.[314]

TERMINATION OF TENANCIES

There are a number of ways in which a lease can be determined. This section deals with the most important of them. What should be stressed is that this section deals with the termination of tenancies under the general law. In many instances, the tenant will continue to enjoy security of tenure under various statutory provisions. Unless the lease has come to an end under the general law, these provisions will not come into play. In other words, the various provisions conferring security of tenure upon tenants represent additional hurdles for a tenant to surmount before he is enabled, physically, to regain possession of the land.

Effluxion of time

When a fixed term tenancy has been created, then the lease will end at the term date. This is termed effluxion of time. In the case of such tenancies, unless such a right is conferred by the lease, neither side has the right, unilaterally, to bring the tenancy to a premature conclusion.

Notice to quit

The nature of a periodic tenancy is that an original period is agreed between the parties and this period will continue to recur until either side puts an end to this process by the service of a notice to quit.

In the case of a yearly tenancy, the period of notice is at least half a year, expiring upon the end of a completed year of the tenancy. With respect to other periodic tenancies, such as a monthly or weekly tenancy, the period of notice is one full period, expiring at the date of the completion of a period. In the case of residential tenancies, however, a minimum of four weeks' notice in writing must be given.[315]

As was discussed in an earlier chapter, in the case of either joint landlords or joint tenants, a notice to quit served by one of the joint owners will be sufficient to determine the tenancy.[316] To obviate some of the problems caused by this, the Law

---

[313] Landlord and Tenant (Covenants) Act 1995, s. 3(3). See *BHP Petroleum Great Britain Ltd v. Chesterfield Properties Ltd* [2000] Ch. 234.

[314] Ibid., ss 7, 8.   [315] Protection from Eviction Act 1977, ss 3A, 5; Housing Act 1988, ss 31, 32.

[316] See Notices to quit, pp. 360–362.

Commission has proposed that, where one joint tenant serves notice to quit, this should terminate the interest of that person alone, and not the other.[317]

Forfeiture

It is normally the case that a lease contains a number of covenants by the tenant. If the tenant breaches any of these covenants then, subject to the possibility of specific performance being available, which will only be the case in limited circumstances,[318] the landlord's remedy will lie in damages. He is limited to that remedy, however, unless, as is normally the case, the lease contains a clause, termed a forfeiture clause, which enables the landlord to terminate the lease. A forfeiture clause reserves to the landlord the right to re-enter the property upon a breach of covenant and to determine the lease. Alternatively, but less commonly, the lease may be made conditional upon the tenant adhering to the covenants in the lease, in which case, if the tenant is in breach of covenant, the lease becomes voidable at the instance of the landlord.[319]

Termination of a lease, either by forfeiture or by peaceable re-entry, is an area of the law which is dogged by complexity and is an amalgam of statutory regulation and judicial development. The result is that it is necessary to consider, first, the circumstances when a landlord may lose the right to forfeit the lease and then the procedures to be adopted upon the breach of different covenants. Finally, the jurisdiction of the courts to grant relief against forfeiture must be examined.

Waiver

The landlord will lose his right to forfeit the lease if he has waived the breach of the covenant complained of. A waiver may be express but, more usually, is implied. An implied waiver of the breach will occur when the landlord, with knowledge of the breach, does some act which, unequivocally, recognizes the continuing existence of the lease.[320]

There are, therefore, two aspects of waiver which must both be present. First, the landlord must know of the breach, and he will be regarded as having knowledge of matters which are known to his agents.[321] Mere suspicion that there has been a breach of covenant is said not to be enough to constitute knowledge.[322] Yet, in *Van Haarlem v. Kasner*,[323] a landlord was considered to have knowledge of a tenant's breach of a covenant not to use the property for illegal or immoral purposes on the basis that he knew that the tenant had been arrested upon suspicion of spying; a decision which seems to be unduly harsh upon the landlord.

Mere knowledge that the tenant has committed a breach of covenant is, obviously, not of itself sufficient to amount to a waiver of that breach by the landlord. He must

---

[317] (2003) Law Com. No. 284, para. 11.27.   [318] See Specific performance, pp. 444–445.

[319] See *Doe d. Lockwood v. Clarke* (1807) 8 East 185.

[320] *Matthews v. Smallwood* [1910] 1 Ch. 777 at 786 *per* Parker J.

[321] See *Metropolitan Properties Co. Ltd v. Cordery* (1979) 39 P. & C.R. 10.

[322] *Chrisdell Ltd v. Johnson* (1987) 54 P. & C.R. 257.   [323] [1992] 2 E.G.L.R. 257.

also do some act which unequivocally recognizes the continued existence of the lease. The clearest, and most usual, act which is regarded as constituting waiver is a demand or acceptance of rent after the landlord has notice of the breach, and in *Greenwood Reservations Ltd v. World Environment Ltd*,[324] Thomas L.J. was prepared to assume, without necessarily deciding, that an unqualified demand for future rent would always operate as a waiver. Even if a demand is made as a result of clerical error by the landlord's agent, this will amount to a waiver.[325] In the case of negotiations between the landlord and tenant, difficulties may also arise. Such negotiations are themselves capable of amounting to waiver but will not do so if they are conducted against a background of threatened forfeiture proceedings.[326] It is an area where the landlord must tread very carefully if he is not to lose the right to forfeit the lease.

The doctrine of waiver relates principally to the right to forfeit the lease. While it is possible for the conduct of the landlord to preclude him from obtaining any remedy at all,[327] this will only occur in cases where there is a very clear representation to this effect. The normal impact of waiver is that it relates only to the right of forfeiture; the landlord will still be able to recover damages in respect of the breach.[328] Secondly, waiver operates only in respect of existing breaches of covenant. In the case of a continuing breach, or a subsequent breach of covenant, the landlord will not be prevented by a previous waiver from instituting forfeiture proceedings.

Forfeiture proceedings

To forfeit a lease, the landlord will normally issue a writ seeking possession of the property. It is also possible to terminate the lease by effecting a peaceable re-entry of the property. Except in the case of non-payment of rent, notice must first be served upon a tenant of the intention to re-enter.[329] In the case of residential property, it is very unwise for a landlord to seek to terminate a lease by re-entry as, if he does, he runs the considerable risk of committing a criminal offence.[330] In the case of forfeiture actions, generally, the landlord must follow a statutory procedure laid down by section 146(1) of the Law of Property Act 1925. This procedure does not apply, however, in the case of forfeiture for non-payment of rent,[331] to which different rules apply.

Non-payment of rent

When a landlord seeks to forfeit a lease for non-payment of rent, he must first make a formal demand for payment. The nature of a formal demand is that the landlord must demand the exact sum due, on the day it falls due, at such convenient time before

---

[324] [2008] H.L.R. 31 at [27].

[325] *Central Estates (Belgravia) Ltd v. Woolgar (No. 2)* [1972] 1 W.L.R. 1048. A demand for the payment of insurance will not have this effect: *Yorkshire Metropolitan Properties Ltd v. Co-operative Retail Services Ltd* [2001] L. & T.R. 26.

[326] *Expert Clothing Services & Sales Ltd v. Hillgate House Ltd* [1986] Ch. 340.

[327] See, e.g., *Brikom Investments Ltd v. Carr* [1979] 1 Q.B. 497 (estoppel).

[328] See *Greenwich London Borough Council v. Discreet Selling Estates Ltd* (1990) 61 P. & C.R. 405.

[329] Law of Property Act 1925, s. 146(1).   [330] Criminal Law Act 1977, s. 6.

[331] Law of Property Act 1925, s. 146(11).

sunset as to allow the tenant to count out the exact sum due before sunset. To avoid having to comply with this arcane procedure, it is normal for the lease to stipulate that the landlord may forfeit the lease for non-payment of rent, whether the rent has been lawfully demanded or not. This wording is unfortunate, in that it may give the tenant a rather misleading impression of what rent the landlord is entitled to demand, rather than relating, as it does, to the formal requirements of how the demand is made. If half a year's rent is in arrears and no goods are available to the landlord to sell in order to clear off those arrears, then under section 210 of the Common Law Procedure Act 1852, the landlord need not make a formal demand for rent before forfeiting the lease.

Once the landlord has instituted forfeiture proceedings for non-payment of rent, the tenant may seek relief against forfeiture. If, before the trial, the tenant pays off all the arrears and costs, the possession proceedings must be stayed.[332] If a possession order has been made, the tenant may, within six months of the order, apply for relief against forfeiture,[333] at the end of which time the tenant loses his right to relief.[334] In deciding whether to relieve against forfeiture, the court will have regard to whether the arrears have been repaid, if the landlord has been compensated for any expenses he has incurred, and whether it is just and equitable to grant relief.

Breaches of other covenants

In the case of covenants other than the covenant to pay rent, the landlord, to forfeit the lease, must follow the procedure laid down by section 146(1) of the Law of Property Act 1925.[335] Under this section a right of re-entry or forfeiture shall not be enforceable unless the landlord has served on the tenant a notice:

(a) specifying the particular breach complained of; and

(b) if the breach is capable of remedy, requiring the lessee to remedy the breach; and

(c) in any case, requiring the lessee to make compensation in money for the breach;

and the lessee fails, within a reasonable time thereafter, to remedy the breach, if it is capable of remedy, and to make reasonable compensation in money, to the satisfaction of the lessor, for the breach.

Negative covenants

The principal difficulty with complying with the requirements of the section has concerned the question of whether or not a particular breach of covenant is capable of remedy, as, if it is not, then it is not necessary for the notice to require the tenant to

---

[332] Common Law Procedure Act 1852, s. 212. See *Thomas v. Ken Thomas Ltd* [2006] EWCA Civ. 1504 at [53]–[59] *per* Neuberger L.J.

[333] Ibid., s. 210; County Courts Act 1984, s. 138.

[334] *U.D.T. Ltd v. Shellpoint Trustees Ltd* [1993] 4 All E.R. 310.

[335] There are five specified cases where the landlord need not comply with this procedure. See Law of Property Act 1925, s. 146(9).

remedy it. One view is that if the covenant is negative in terms then, if the tenant has done what he has covenanted not to do, the breach is incapable of remedy.[336] With the apparent exception of a covenant against assignment,[337] this view is seen as being too extreme[338] and it is possible that what has been done can be undone. In some situations, however, the courts will consider that the breach of a negative covenant cannot be remedied, for example if, in breach of a covenant not to use the premises for illegal or immoral purposes, the property has been used for the purposes of prostitution, a stigma may attach to the property with the result that the breach may be regarded as irremediable by the tenant.[339] If by taking prompt action to stop the prohibited use of the property, the tenant succeeds in removing the stigma which would otherwise attach to the property, then the breach may be regarded as being remediable.[340] If there is any doubt as to this matter, then much the safest course of action for the landlord to take is to require the tenant to remedy the breach 'if it is capable of remedy'.[341]

Time

Section 146(1) of the Law of Property Act 1925 requires the landlord's notice to give the tenant a reasonable time in which to remedy the breach. What is reasonable will depend upon the facts of the case and the nature of the breach in question. If the breach is not capable of being remedied, it might be thought that no time need be given, but it has been held that, even then, the tenant should be given some time in which to consider his position.[342] The time given can, however, be as little as fourteen days.[343]

Compensation

Although the wording of the section is mandatory, requiring the tenant to compensate the landlord, a section 146 notice is not defective if a claim for compensation is omitted.[344]

Repairing covenants

The position with regard to repairing covenants is regulated by the Leasehold Property (Repairs) Act 1938. The Act applies to non-agricultural leases of seven years or more which have more than three years left to run.[345] The aim of the Act is to

---

[336] See *Rugby School (Governors) Ltd v. Tannahill* [1934] 1 K.B. 695 at 701 *per* Mackinnon J.

[337] *Scala House & District Property Co. Ltd v. Forbes* [1974] Q.B. 575.

[338] *Rugby School (Governors) Ltd v. Tannahill* [1935] 1 K.B. 87. See also *Savva v. Hussein* (1996) 64 P. & C.R. 214; *Akici v. L.R. Butlin Ltd* [2005] EWCA Civ. 1296 at paras 62–71 *per* Neuberger L.J.

[339] *Rugby School (Governors) Ltd v. Tannahill* [1935] 1 K.B. 87; *British Petroleum Pension Trust Ltd v. Behrendt* (1985) 52 P. & C.R. 117. See also *Van Haarlem v. Kasner* [1992] 2 E.G.L.R. 59 (spying).

[340] *Glass v. Kencakes Ltd* [1966] 1 Q.B. 611.

[341] Ibid., at 629 *per* Paull J. See also *Expert Clothing Service & Sales Ltd v. Highgate House Ltd* [1986] Ch. 340.

[342] *Horsey Estate Ltd v. Steiger* [1899] 2 Q.B. 79.

[343] *Scala House & District Land Property Co. v. Forbes* [1974] Q.B. 575. Contrast *Courtney Lodge Management Ltd v. Blake* [2004] EWCA Civ. 975 (four working days was too short).

[344] *Rugby School (Governors) Ltd v. Tannahill* [1935] 1 K.B. 87.

[345] Leasehold Property (Repairs) Act 1938, ss 1(1), 7.

prevent people from buying the reversion of such leases and then forfeiting the lease due to breach of a repairing covenant and, in the process, making a considerable profit. The Act provides that if a section 146 notice is served upon a tenant in respect of a repairing covenant, then that notice must inform the tenant of his right to serve a counter-notice under the Act. The tenant then has twenty-eight days in which to serve a counter-notice on the landlord[346] and, if he does so, the landlord is precluded by section 1(3) of the Act from pursuing the action for forfeiture, re-entry, or damages without the leave of the court. A number of criteria are then set out in section 1(5) of the Act, one of which must be established by the landlord if leave is to be given.[347] The general theme of the criteria is that the property is in urgent need of repair.

Relief against forfeiture

After a reasonable time has elapsed after the section 146 notice has been served, the landlord may proceed to enforce the forfeiture. While the landlord is proceeding to enforce a right of re-entry or forfeiture, the tenant may apply to the court for relief against forfeiture.[348] It is then a matter for the court's discretion as to how this jurisdiction is to be exercised and a relevant factor will be the seriousness of the breach and the circumstances of the parties.[349] Another relevant factor will be the value of the property. In *Van Haarlam v. Kasner*,[350] a tenant was in breach of a covenant not to use the property for illegal or immoral purposes having been convicted of spying and sentenced to ten years' imprisonment, with an order that he be deported upon his release. Harman J. would, nevertheless, have granted him relief against forfeiture. The reason was that the lease was for eighty years and had been bought by the tenant some four or five years previously for £36,000. To have refused relief against forfeiture would have deprived the tenant of a valuable asset, a consequence which the judge considered would have amounted to a double punishment.

The statutory jurisdiction to grant relief against forfeiture is conferred by the Act when the landlord 'is proceeding...to enforce...a right of re-entry or forfeiture'. This raised the question of whether a court could grant relief when the landlord had already forfeited the lease by effecting a peaceable re-entry of the property. The House of Lords, in *Billson v. Residential Properties Ltd*,[351] construed the words 'is proceeding' to mean also 'has proceeded' and so, in these circumstances had jurisdiction under the Act to grant relief. Where, however, the court has made a forfeiture order and the landlord has taken possession, then the tenant can no longer seek relief.

---

[346] Ibid., s. 1(2).   [347] See *Associated British Ports v. C.H. Bailey plc* [1990] 2 A.C. 703.

[348] Law of Property Act 1925, s. 146(2). Relief may be granted in respect of a part of a building where there is a physical division. See *G.M.S. Syndicate Ltd v. Gary Elliott Ltd* [1982] Ch. 1.

[349] See *Central Estates (Belgravia) Ltd v. Woolgar (No. 2)* [1972] 1 W.L.R. 1048. Cf. *Bathurst (Earl) v. Fine* [1974] 1 W.L.R. 905.

[350] [1992] 2 E.G.L.R. 59. See also *Ropemaker Properties Ltd v. Noonhaven Ltd* [1989] 2 E.G.L.R. 50. This is, however, only one factor to be considered: see *Greenwood Reservations Ltd v. World Environment Ltd* [2008] H.L.R. 31 at [33]–[38] *per* Thomas L.J.

[351] [1992] 2 A.C. 494.

Parties

When a landlord is seeking to forfeit a lease, it is not only the immediate tenant who may be affected by this action. Other people, such as a sub-tenant or a mortgagee, may have derivative interests in the property.[352] If the lease is forfeited, then their interests, which derive from the lease, will be destroyed. Consequently, such parties may seek relief against forfeiture.[353]

Recommended reform

Few could deny that the current law relating to forfeiture of leases is unnecessarily complicated. The Law Commission has recommended wide-ranging reform, which would simplify considerably the existing law.[354] No distinction would be made between covenants relating to rent and other covenants and the existing procedure would be considerably simplified and the law on waiver would be reformed, so that a mere acceptance of rent would no longer prevent the landlord from forfeiting a lease. The court could make an absolute or remedial termination order, the latter being designed to allow the tenant to remedy the breach complained of. It is unfortunate that these proposed reforms have yet to be enacted.

Surrender

In the absence of a break-clause neither party to the lease has the right, unilaterally, to end a fixed term tenancy prior to the term date. Surrender involves the tenant giving up the lease to the landlord, who accepts this action. A surrender should be by deed, but a contract to surrender should have the same effect in equity.[355] If, however, the tenant gives up possession, and this is accepted by the landlord, then each party will be estopped from denying that a surrender has taken place.[356]

Merger

Merger is, in effect, the opposite of surrender. Merger will occur when the tenant acquires the landlord's reversion. As the tenant cannot be his own landlord, the lease is said to merge in the reversion.

---

[352] For the rights of such parties to be informed of forfeiture proceedings, see Harpum, op. cit., 829–830.

[353] Law of Property Act 1925, s. 146(5).

[354] (1985) Law Com. No. 142; (1994) Law Com. No. 221. See P.F. Smith [1986] Conv. 165; H.W. Wilkinson [1994] Conv. 177. See now (2006) Law Com. No. 303.

[355] Such a contract would need to comply with the Law of Property (Miscellaneous Provisions) Act 1989, s. 2.

[356] See *Oastler v. Henderson* (1877) 2 Q.B.D. 575.

12

Mortgages

It can be asserted with some confidence that most adults in this country have a general idea of the nature of a mortgage, it being a form of security for a loan. The purpose of the loan is often to finance the purchase of a house, a type of mortgage which can be termed an acquisition mortgage. Alternatively, the house can be used as security for other borrowing, for example to pay for an extension to a house, or to act as security for the provision of finance for a small business. Such mortgages are normally second, or even third, mortgages. Although property other than land can be mortgaged, the main context of mortgages is as a security over land and, certainly, this is the form of property to which most people would have regard when considering the role of the mortgage.

When one creates a mortgage, the person who creates the mortgage is termed the mortgagor and the person in whose favour it is created is termed the mortgagee. The mortgagee is a secured creditor and the interest which is acquired is a proprietary right over the land. Consequently, the mortgagee can transfer the mortgage to another person and, if the mortgagor sells the land to a purchaser, then, unless the mortgage is redeemed by repaying the loan, the purchaser will, generally speaking, take the land subject to that mortgage.

The concept of security for a loan is not a complex one to grasp. If the borrower cannot repay the loan, then the creditor may sell the property in question in order to recover what he is owed. This is true in the case of land mortgages. While this general concept is straightforward, it is, unfortunately, the case that the modern law of mortgages, in appearance at least, disguises its real nature; so much so, that it has famously been said that 'No one … by the light of nature ever understood an English mortgage of real estate.'[1] While it is always undesirable that the legal form should not accord with the reality of a transaction, this is particularly so in the present context. A mortgage transaction is one of the most important commercial transactions with which most people will be involved, and it is much to be regretted that the form of the transaction is mystifying, and, at times, positively misleading to those who enter into it. The reasons for this obfuscation are largely historical and will be considered shortly. First, some account of the modern role of the mortgage will be given.

---

[1] *Samuel v. Jarrah Timber and Wood Paving Corp. Ltd* [1904] A.C. 323 at 326 *per* Lord Macnaghten. For recommendations for reform, see (1991) Law Com. No. 204.

THE ROLE OF MORTGAGES

The nature of home ownership changed considerably over the course of the twentieth century. At the outset of the century, the majority of the population lived in rented accommodation. This changed markedly during that century, so that in 2009 owner-occupation accounted for nearly seventy per cent of the housing stock in England and Wales, a figure which is twentieth out of the countries of the European Union.[2] There are a number of reasons for this change in the nature of occupation. An important reason was the rise of the building society movement, a principal purpose of which was to make funds available for the purpose of house buying. The greater availability of funds, together with active encouragement by central government for people to buy their own homes, this encouragement coming in the form of tax relief on interest payments under the mortgage and the introduction of the right of certain council tenants to buy their homes, introduced, originally, by the Housing Act 1980,[3] has led to the shift from occupiers of homes being tenants to their being owners of the property.

The money to finance the purchase of the home came, principally, from borrowing the money from a bank or a building society, the money to be repaid, with interest, over a prolonged period of time to the mortgagee. The loan was then secured by way of a mortgage. The mortgage operates to secure the amount, with interest, that has been borrowed. The mortgagee does not get a proportionate share in the property, so that if the value of the house increases, the mortgagee derives no direct benefit from this; the rise in value accrues for the benefit of the mortgagor. This means that, over time, despite being already mortgaged, the house may provide good security for further borrowing, the borrowing, in this case, not being for the purpose of acquiring the house. Accordingly, it is not uncommon for a house to be subject to more than one mortgage.

The credit crunch

A major activity of banks is to lend money to enable people to buy houses. Unfortunately, the practices adopted led to a major banking crisis in 2008/2009. In the United States, banks lent vast amounts of money in what has been termed the 'sub-prime' market. By this is meant lending money to people whose income was not sufficient to service the loan. Similarly, on this side of the Atlantic, as a response to the boom in the housing market, loans were made to people of amounts which were many times their annual incomes, with the result that a failure to meet the payments became a very real possibility. To this practice was added the willingness of banks to lend more than the

[2] (2009) Social Trends (41st edn), 241. Of this housing, 37% was being bought with the aid of a mortgage, and the remainder was owned outright: ibid., at 236.
[3] The provisions are now contained in the Housing Act 1985, Part V.

properties were worth, a loan of 125 per cent of the value of the property not being uncommon.

This form of lending carried considerable risks for the lending institutions. These risks were exacerbated by the practice of selling these securities to other banks. This led to many banks being exposed to the risk of a collapsing housing market. This collapse duly occurred, first in the United States, and then in this country. A direct consequence of this was that major banks found that they had very large loans on their account books, and inadequate security to underpin them. Because of the complexity of some of the financial instruments used to bundle up the various loans made by the banks, a crisis of confidence ensued. Banks, concerned about the financial soundness of each other's positions, became reluctant to lend to each other. This led to the so-called credit crunch, and a resultant financial crisis. Deep concern came to be felt about the liquidity, and indeed, solvency of major financial institutions. These concerns were made worse by the actions of speculators trading in the shares of these institutions. To avoid the collapse of the financial sector, the Government took powers under section 3 of the Banking (Special Provisions) Act 2008 to nationalize authorized UK deposit takers, and, to date, the Northern Rock and Bradford and Bingley have been taken into public ownership. Moreover, the Government has also felt it necessary to invest large amounts of capital in other major banks in return for a share in the companies, a practice which has been adopted overseas, where this crisis has also been felt. The effects of the financial crisis brought about principally by the practices in relation to mortgage lending will be felt globally for years to come.

Repossessions

A related aspect of this irresponsible lending policy has been a concomitant rise in the enforcement by banks of their securities. Debts must be repaid. It is sadly the case that, in recent times, the incidence of failure on the part of mortgagors to meet the financial commitments arising from their mortgages has become a serious problem. Mortgagees sought to realize their securities by, first, taking possession of the properties in question and then selling them. The problem is a serious one, although the recent evidence published on the Ministry of Justice website[4] reveals that the number of possession actions brought by lenders, having increased every year from 2002 to 2008, has since fallen back. This fall in the number of possession actions is attributed largely to the introduction of the Mortgage Arrears Pre-Action Protocol, which came into effect in November 2008. It is not clear to what extent the agreement reached with a number of leading banks by the previous Government in 2008 has impacted on this matter. This agreement was to allow householders who have experienced a significant loss of income, as a result of redundancy or as a consequence of the financial downturn, to defer payment of interest for up to two years, with the Government providing

---

[4] Published in November 2011.

a guarantee to the banks against any loss which they might suffer as a consequence of this agreement.[5]

This phenomenon of rising mortgage repossessions has brought in its wake a significant increase in the amount of litigation relating to this issue. This litigation has involved a number of common themes. These concern the protection of the mortgagor, himself, when faced with an action which will result in the loss of his home and, also, the rights of other persons who live in the property and claim to have an interest in it. The action for possession, and the related issue of the sale of mortgaged property, has become the dominant theme in the modern law of mortgages and this chapter will concentrate on these matters. Other matters also arise, however, in the context of mortgages, most notably, how the law has regulated the mortgage relationship itself. To understand how the law has developed, it is necessary to grasp the theoretical basis of the mortgage, which was developed at a time when the role of mortgages was rather different to what it is in the present day. Before considering this, however, it may be helpful to consider briefly the types of mortgage most commonly encountered in modern times.

TYPES OF MORTGAGE

When land is mortgaged, this is usually done for one of two reasons and the purpose of the loan may affect the type of mortgage which is created.

Acquisition mortgages

It is very common for the purchase price of the home to be raised by a combination of a down payment of, say, ten per cent of the purchase price being provided by the purchaser and the balance by the mortgagee. This loan, together with interest, is then repaid over a prolonged period, commonly twenty-five years. This type of mortgage is usually one of two types.

Repayment mortgage

Under a repayment mortgage, a sum of money is borrowed which, it is agreed, is to be repaid over a substantial period of time, say, twenty-five years. The total interest to be paid on the loan over that period is calculated and a schedule of payments is then worked out which, by monthly instalments, will be sufficient to repay the loan plus interest over the entire period. At the outset, the monthly instalments will consist almost entirely of payments of interest, so that there is very little reduction in the capital indebtedness. As time goes on, the amount of capital repayments will increase steadily and, towards the end of the loan, the instalments will consist very largely of capital repayments. When tax relief was granted to mortgage repayments, this was

---

[5] *Hansard*, vol. 485, col. 34.

granted in respect of payments of interest, so that a mortgagor got most tax relief at the early stages of the mortgage. Now that there is no longer tax relief granted on mortgages, this is no longer an issue.

Endowment mortgages

The main alternative to the repayment mortgage is the endowment mortgage. Under this scheme, there is no repayment of any capital until the end of the agreed mortgage period. The only payment made to the mortgagee during the subsistence of the mortgage is in respect of interest payments. The mortgagor is also required to take out an endowment policy, which is assigned to the mortgagee. This policy is scheduled to mature at the end of the mortgage period and produce a lump sum sufficient to pay off the capital sum which had been borrowed. In some cases, the lump sum envisaged to be payable on the maturation of policy would be calculated to exceed the sum borrowed, the balance being paid to the mortgagor. Such a policy is known as a 'with profits' policy. As part of the policy, there would also be a life assurance policy, so that, if the mortgagor died during the subsistence of the mortgage, the capital amount borrowed would become payable under the terms of the policy.

Such mortgages are now less popular than they once were. One reason for their initial popularity was that, because the borrower was paying only interest to the mortgagee throughout the mortgage, this maximized his tax relief. This reason no longer exists. A second reason why this type of mortgage has declined in popularity is that everything depended upon the return on the endowment policy, when it matured, producing a sufficient lump sum to pay off the mortgage. This was not guaranteed. Whether it would do so depended on the success of the investment policy of the company with whom the policy was held. Endowment mortgages, therefore, carry an element of risk, and, in recent times, a considerable number of people have had to face up to the prospect that there will still be money owing on the mortgage after the endowment policy has matured. This, in turn, has led to allegations of malpractice against companies selling such policies. For these reasons, endowment mortgages are less popular today than once was the case.

Non-acquisition mortgages

When a house is used as security for borrowing after the house has been acquired then, in principle, either of the two forms of mortgage considered above can be used; an original mortgage can be extended, or a new mortgage can be created. The terms governing repayment may differ, however, from those normally encountered in an acquisition mortgage. If a property is used as security for a bank overdraft, it may be the case that it is envisaged that the loan will be repayable upon demand. Such an arrangement may affect significantly the ability of the mortgagor to resist a possession action if he defaults on the mortgage.[6]

---

[6] See Mortgages to which the Acts apply, pp. 515–516.

THE NATURE OF MORTGAGES

The modern form of the mortgage, and certain of its characteristics, derives from its historical development,[7] which initially, at least, was a device to avoid the usury laws which prevented the creation of loans at a fixed rate of interest. To avoid this, the mortgagor, originally in consideration of a loan, granted a lease of the property to the mortgagee. If the income from the land was used to discharge the loan, the transaction was termed a *vivum vadium*, or living pledge. Alternatively, the mortgagee could retain the income, leaving the loan outstanding. This was known as a *mortuum vadium* or dead pledge, from which the term 'mortgage' derives. In both cases, if the loan was not repaid by the time agreed, the mortgagee would have the right to have the leasehold interest enlarged into a freehold.

Conveyance

By around the fifteenth century, the method of mortgaging land by granting a lease of it to the mortgagee had changed. What then happened was that, in return for the loan, the mortgagor would convey the land to the mortgagee who, as a result, had security for the loan. A date would be set by the mortgage agreement for the repayment of that loan. If the mortgagor was not able to repay the loan upon the agreed date, then he lost his right to have the land conveyed back to him. Still worse, he remained liable to repay the loan, the upshot being that the mortgagor had lost his land to the mortgagee and still owed him the money which had originally been borrowed. This outcome seems manifestly unjust and, as was to be expected, equity intervened to temper the harshness of the common law.

The equitable right to redeem

The common law took a straightforward view of a mortgage. The land had been conveyed to the mortgagee in return for a loan and, under the contract, there was an agreed date on which that loan was to be repaid. That date is termed the contractual date of redemption, whereby the money is repaid and the land conveyed back to the mortgagor: a process known as redeeming the mortgage. If that date passed, then the mortgagor's right to have the land conveyed back to him had also passed. Equity, however, took a different view. In the eye of equity, the reality of the position was that the mortgagee had security for a loan. If the money had not been repaid by the date agreed, then his security remained good; generally speaking, his position had not been prejudiced. Equity, therefore, was prepared to allow the mortgagor to repay the loan after the contractual date for repayment had passed. This right, which arises

---

[7] For a fuller account, see Harpum, Bridge, and Dixon, *Megarry and Wade's Law of Real Property* (7th edn) (London: Sweet & Maxwell, 2008), 1079–1083.

only once the contractual date for redemption has passed, is termed the equitable right to redeem.

This right remains relevant today and is relied upon when, not uncommonly, the mortgage agreement stipulates that the mortgagor will repay the loan within six months of that loan having been granted. The reason why such an unrealistic clause is inserted into a modern mortgage agreement will be explained below.[8] From that date, however, the right of the mortgagor to redeem the mortgage exists in equity.

The equity of redemption

At common law, the owner of mortgaged property was the mortgagee. Equity, however, looked to the substance of the transaction, which was that the mortgagee was simply a secured creditor. Consistent with this view, equity considered that, subject to the rights of the mortgagee as a secured creditor, the true owner of the property was the mortgagor.[9] To reflect that view, the sum total of the rights of the mortgagor, which consist of the rights of the mortgagor as beneficial owner of the property, minus the rights of the mortgagee as a secured creditor, is termed the equity of redemption. The equity of redemption, which includes the equitable right to redeem, comes into existence from the moment that the mortgage is created; the equitable right to redeem, which is, admittedly, one of the more important rights owned by the mortgagor, comes into being only when the date of redemption has passed.

The equity of redemption, which is commonly referred to in its abbreviated form as the equity, is a valuable asset. 'It constitutes an interest in the mortgaged property and, in terms of value, is the principal element of that which the mortgagor retains after the grant of the mortgage. Thus when a house owner describes himself as having an equity of £300,000 in a property worth £500,000 mortgaged to secure a debt of £200,000, it is strictly the equity of redemption to which the owner refers.'[10] A further mortgage can then be created against the security of the equity of redemption, a process which has been termed asset mobilization, the effect of which is that the 'mortgage is a mechanism that transforms "passive" land value into "active" value in that it allows the value of land to be released for other purposes while the freeholder or leaseholder is still able to enjoy the benefits of physical occupation or possession'.[11]

The equity of redemption can increase in value in one of two ways. First, under a repayment mortgage, the payment of the mortgage instalments will, over time, reduce the level of indebtedness and cause a corresponding rise in the value of the equity. More importantly, the house can simply increase in value. If the house was originally bought for £500,000 with the help of a £200,000 mortgage, the original value of the

---

[8] See Power arising, p. 524.   [9] See, e.g., *Re Sir Thomas Spencer Wells* [1933] Ch. 29.

[10] *Horsham Properties Group Ltd v. Clark* [2009] 1 W.L.R. 1255 at [22] *per* Briggs J.

[11] See M. Oldham in Tee (ed.), *Land Law: Issues, Debates, Policy* (Cullompton: Willan Publishing, 2002), 169–170.

equity was £300,000. If the value of the house doubles to £1 million, there is also an increase in the value of the equity to £800,000. The mortgagee does not share in the benefit of the rise in value of the house. If, on the other hand, property prices fall, the position may be arrived at where the size of the mortgage exceeds the value of the house. If, to change the facts of the example given above, the value of the house had fallen to £150,000 then the position is that the mortgagor has what is known as negative equity, in this case £50,000. The existence of negative equity, which is a fairly recent phenomenon, is a considerable social and economic problem,[12] and has, in the light of the financial crisis affecting banks and the resultant collapse of the housing market, made an unwelcome return, making it extremely difficult for people in this position to be able to sell their houses because the purchase price would not be sufficient to discharge the mortgage.

THE CREATION OF MORTGAGES

The pre-1925 method of mortgaging land was manifestly artificial, the artificiality of the position being accentuated by the approach of equity to the subject. The pre-1925 position, where the legal owner of the land was the mortgagee but the equitable owner was the mortgagor, was abandoned by the 1925 legislation to enable the legal position to reflect more accurately the reality of the situation.

Legal mortgages

After 1925, it was no longer possible to create a legal mortgage of land by conveying the estate to the mortgagee. In the case of freehold, unregistered land, a legal mortgage can now only be created in one of two ways. Under section 85 of the Law of Property Act 1925, a mortgage of an estate in fee simple can only be created by:

(i) a demise for a term of years absolute, subject to a provision for cessor on redemption;[13] and

(ii) a charge by deed expressed to be by way of legal mortgage.

It is further provided by section 85(2) of the Act, that any purported conveyance of the fee simple by way of mortgage shall operate to create a 3,000-year lease subject to cessor on redemption.

In the case of a mortgage of leasehold property, similar provisions exist, so that the method of creating a mortgage is either to create a sub-lease in favour of the mortgagee

---

[12] See Dorling, Gentle, and Cornford, *Housing Crisis: Disaster or Opportunity* (1992), University of Newcastle upon Tyne, C.U.R.D.S., Discussion Paper, No. 96.

[13] This means that the lease will determine when the mortgage is redeemed.

of a period not less than one day shorter than the head lease or, alternatively, to execute a deed expressed to be a charge by way of legal mortgage.[14] If, instead of using one of these methods, the mortgagor purports to mortgage the lease by assigning it to the mortgagee, then the assignment will not be effective as such, but will, instead, operate to create a sub-lease ten days shorter than the lease which was purported to be assigned.[15]

Charge by way of legal mortgage

The charge by way of legal mortgage was a new method of mortgaging land created in 1925. Its effect is defined by the Act as being that, in the case of a mortgage of freehold land, the mortgagee is given the same rights and powers as if he had been granted a 3,000-year lease and, in the case of leasehold land, as if he had been granted a sub-lease, one day less than the lease which was mortgaged.[16]

It is now the case that, whenever a legal mortgage is created, then either the fee simple or the original lease remains vested in the mortgagor and, in that sense, the position reflects more accurately the actual position than was the case prior to 1925. The legal position continues, however, to give a misleading picture of the reality of the situation. The actual position, at law, of the mortgagor of freehold land is that he holds the reversion on a 3,000-year lease, that lease being one which will determine when the loan is repaid and the mortgage is redeemed. Ordinarily, such a reversionary lease would be of little intrinsic value and yet the mortgagor continues to hold a valuable interest in the property, the true value of that position arising in equity and being the value of his equity of redemption. The equity of redemption continues to exist despite the original reason for its creation, that the legal fee simple had been conveyed to the mortgagee, no longer existing. The reality of the position is that, 'The owner of property entering into a mortgage does not by entering into that mortgage cease to be the owner of the property any further than is necessary to give effect to the security he has created.'[17]

Under the Land Registration Act 2002, on the creation of a protected first legal mortgage on unregistered land, the mortgagor is required to register his estate.[18] A protected first legal mortgage is one which takes effect on its creation as a mortgage to be protected by the deposit of title deeds,[19] and ranks in priority ahead of any other mortgages then affecting the mortgaged estate.[20] Although the Act places the onus to register on the mortgagor, under rule 21 of the Land Registration Rules 2003, the mortgagee may make an application in the name of the mortgagor for registration of the mortgagor's estate.

---

[14] Law of Property Act 1925, s. 86(1).

[15] Ibid., s. 86(2). See *Grangeside Properties Ltd v. Collingwood Securities Ltd* [1964] 1 W.L.R. 139.

[16] Law of Property Act 1925, s. 87(1).

[17] *Downsview Nominees Ltd v. First City Corporation Ltd* [1993] A.C. 295 at 311 *per* Lord Templeman.

[18] Land Registration Act 2002, ss 4(1)(g), 6(2).   [19] See Priority of mortgages, pp. 531–537.

[20] Land Registration Act 2002, s. 5(8).

Registered land

When mortgaging property, it is now far more common for it to be done by the creation of a charge by way of legal mortgage than by the creation of a long lease. The reason for this is essentially pragmatic, it being rather easier to explain to a purchaser of a house that a legal charge is being created in favour of a building society rather than that they are having to create a 3,000-year lease of the property that they have just bought as a home. Where title to land is registered, the reality of the situation is recognized and section 23(1) (a) of the Land Registration Act 2002 provides that it is no longer possible to create a mortgage by either a demise or a sub-demise.

Purchaser of a legal estate for value

Because the effect of the creation of a charge by way of legal mortgage is that the mortgagee is treated as if a 3,000-year lease had been created in his favour, he is a purchaser of a legal estate for value. This means that the mortgagee will take free of prior equitable interests, unless either such interests have been protected by registration, or the nature of the interest is such that it will be binding, either as an interest which overrides a registered disposition or under the doctrine of notice, depending upon whether or not title is registered.

Equitable mortgages

Traditionally,[21] an equitable mortgage could be created in one of two ways.

Equitable interest

If a person has only an equitable interest in land, then he can only create an equitable mortgage over that interest. If land is held upon a trust for a person, that person can mortgage his beneficial interest in the land by using the pre-1925 method of mortgaging land: that is, he can assign his interest to the mortgagee, with provision for it to be re-assigned upon the repayment of a loan. To be effective, a mortgage of this type need not be created by deed; the assignment must, however, be in writing and signed by the mortgagor or his agent.[22]

A second way in which a mortgage of an equitable interest can occur is in the event of forgery. In *First National Securities Ltd v. Hegerty*,[23] a legal co-owner of a house got someone to impersonate his wife, who was the other co-owner, and she forged the wife's signature on the mortgage. The forged document did not create a legal mortgage but operated to sever the equitable joint tenancy and the mortgage took effect against his equitable half share in the property. When title is registered, the position is slightly more complex. If the mortgage is registered on the title of the joint proprietors then,

---

[21] For the consequence of a failure to register a charge, see Non-registrable charges, p. 532.
[22] Law of Property Act 1925, s. 53(1)(c).   [23] [1985] Q.B. 850.

despite the mortgage having been forged, the borrower would appear to have a legal mortgage. The innocent co-owner should then seek alteration of the register.[24] The effect of this is that the mortgage would be removed from the register of title and the forged mortgage would then operate as a charge against the forger's beneficial interest in the property.[25]

Deposit of title deeds

A traditional method of creating an equitable mortgage was, in order to secure a loan, to deposit the title deeds with the creditor.[26] The theoretical basis of this type of transaction being recognized as an equitable mortgage, and it had been so recognized for centuries,[27] was that it was seen as a contract to create a mortgage and that the deposit of title deeds was seen as a mutual act of part performance by the lender and the borrower. As there existed a specifically enforceable contract to create a mortgage, then equity, looking on that which ought to be done as already having been done, considered that an equitable mortgage had been created.

The effect of section 2 of the Law of Property (Miscellaneous Provisions) Act 1989 is that there can be no such thing as an oral contract to create a legal mortgage and, as a consequence, there is no room for the doctrine of part performance. Unless the means of creating equitable mortgages, simply by the deposit of title deeds, was to be regarded as *sui generis*, that is not resting upon the theory that their creation is dependent upon the existence of an enforceable contract to create a mortgage, then an equitable mortgage can no longer simply be created in this way. There must be writing sufficient to comply with the provisions of the section and, strictly speaking, the deposit of title deeds would not then be necessary. In *United Bank of Kuwait v. Sahib*,[28] the Court of Appeal held that the theory underlying an equitable mortgage by deposit of title deeds was, indeed, the existence of a specifically enforceable contract to create a mortgage, which means that the provisions of section 2 must be complied with. A deposit of title deeds with the intention of providing security for a loan will no longer give rise to an equitable mortgage although, as between the parties themselves, it may give rise to rights arising out of estoppel.[29]

Registered land

A mortgage of registered land is effected by a registered charge. Such a charge will not operate at law until registered.[30] Until the charge is registered, the charge will only be effective in equity and will, therefore, need to be protected by the registration of a notice. When electronic conveyancing is made compulsory, this will cease

[24] This was overlooked in *Mortgage Corporation v. Shaire* [2001] 1 F.L.R. 273. See M.P. Thompson [2000] Conv. 329 at 331.
[25] See *Bank of Ireland Home Mortgages Ltd v. Bell* [2001] 2 F.L.R. 809.
[26] See *Re Wallis & Simmonds (Builders) Ltd* [1974] 1 W.L.R. 391.
[27] See *Russel v. Russel* (1793) 1 Bro. C.C. 269.   [28] [1997] Ch. 107.
[29] See M.P. Thompson [1994] Conv. 465 at 468–469; P. Critchley [1998] Conv. 502.
[30] Land Registration Act 2002, s. 27; *Grace Rymer Investments Ltd v. Waite* [1958] Ch. 831. See also *Barclays Bank plc v. Zaroovabli* [1997] Ch. 321.

to be an issue as the creation of the charge and the notification of the registrar will be simultaneous.[31]

RIGHTS OF THE MORTGAGOR

This and the following sections deal with the respective rights of the parties to the mortgage. They do not purport to be an exhaustive account; what will be focused upon are the more important issues of contemporary relevance, starting, first, with the rights of the mortgagor.

No clogs on the equity of redemption

The equity of redemption was introduced essentially for two reasons. First, equity was giving recognition to the reality of the transaction. While, at law, the transaction took the form of a conveyance of the property to the mortgagee, the substance of the arrangement was that the mortgagee was to have security for his loan. Recognizing this, equity viewed the true owner of the property as being the mortgagor, that ownership being subject, of course, to the secured rights of the mortgagee. A related reason was that equity saw the mortgage transaction as being, potentially, an instrument of oppression. The most obvious aspect of this was that, if the loan was not repaid on time, the mortgagor would lose his land and still be liable to repay the loan. This was prevented by the introduction of the equitable right to redeem. Other aspects of the mortgage transaction were also potentially onerous to the mortgagor, however, and equity intervened to afford him protection, that protection being embraced compendiously within the doctrine that there should be no clogs on the equity of redemption.

In approaching this area of law, it is as well to point out at the outset that a number of the cases are not easy to reconcile with each other. The reason for this is that there are two competing pressures at work, each of which has been afforded different priority at different stages of history. The first pressure is the desire to adopt a paternalist approach to the mortgagor to protect him from oppressive terms in the mortgage. The second is the general policy of freedom of contract, where the courts give effect to what the parties have agreed. In modern times, rather greater priority, in this area at least, is afforded to the latter policy and it is arguable that the doctrine of clogs and fetters has now outlived its usefulness.

Broadly speaking, there are three types of clause in a mortgage which are open to attack as being a clog on the equity of redemption. These are attempts to restrict the mortgagor's right to redeem the mortgage, clauses giving the mortgagee the right to acquire the mortgaged property, and collateral advantages afforded to the mortgagee by the mortgage. These will be considered in turn.

---

[31] Land Registration Act 2002, s. 93(1)(2).

Restricting the right to redeem

The first problem area concerns attempts by the mortgagee to restrict the mortgagor's right to redeem the mortgage. A very early example of a clause of this type is provided by *Howard v. Harris*,[32] where the mortgage agreement provided that the mortgage could be redeemed only by the mortgagor and his heirs male. As the effect of such a clause would have been to prevent the mortgagor from assigning his interest in the land, because the assignee would not have been able to redeem the mortgage, this was regarded as being an unacceptable restriction on the right to redeem and, consequently, was struck out as being a clog on the equity of redemption.

A more modern example is provided by *Fairclough v. Swan Brewery Ltd*.[33] The mortgaged property was held on a twenty-year lease. It was a term of the mortgage agreement that the mortgagor could not redeem the mortgage until a date six weeks prior to the end of the lease. Despite this clause, the mortgagor was permitted to redeem the mortgage at an earlier date, the reason being that:

'equity will not permit any device or contrivance being part of the mortgage transaction or contemporaneous with it to prevent or impede redemption...[A] mortgage cannot be made irredeemable.'[34]

This case does not decide that a postponement of the right to redeem will always be regarded as being a clog and, therefore, liable to be struck out. In *Knightsbridge Estates Ltd v. Byrne*,[35] a company had created a mortgage over freehold property, it having been agreed that the loan would be paid by eighty, six-monthly, instalments; in other words, the mortgage could not be redeemed for forty years. The mortgagor wished to redeem the mortgage earlier, so that he could create a new mortgage at a lower rate of interest than that which he was obliged to pay under the existing mortgage. It was held that he could not do so. The clause postponing the right to redeem was not a clog on the equity of redemption and, instead, the court upheld the terms of a freely negotiated commercial bargain. What distinguished the case from *Fairclough* was that the right to redeem had not been rendered illusory. The property was freehold and not leasehold. Secondly, the term was not unconscionable. The decision is also representative of the emerging trend for the court to give effect to the policy of freedom of contract and a resulting unwillingness to set aside terms which the parties have freely agreed.

Penalties

In the residential sector, one is unlikely to encounter terms in the mortgage which bluntly postpone the mortgagor's ability to redeem at all. More common is the situation where a financial penalty is imposed upon the mortgagor should he seek to redeem the mortgage within a certain period from the date of the mortgage. Such clauses are usually found when the payments for an agreed number of years are at a fixed rate

---

[32] (1681) 1 Vern. 33.   [33] [1912] A.C. 565.
[34] [1912] A.C. 565 at 570 *per* Lord Macnaghten. See also *Re Wells* [1933] Ch. 29 at 52 *per* Lawrence L.J.
[35] [1939] Ch. 441, affirmed on other grounds at [1940] A.C. 613.

of interest, such offers being common and are intended to act as an inducement to a potential borrower to take this particular form of mortgage, safe in the knowledge that he will be sheltered from the consequences of a general rise in interest rates. Although such penalty clauses do give rise to complaints, none has yet featured in litigation. It is thought that such a clause is unlikely to be considered to be a clog, unless the period specified upon which a penalty can be levied is regarded as unconscionable, or is made to extend for the entire period of the mortgage. In the cases of mortgages created after 2004, matters such as this will fall to be dealt with under the regulatory scheme introduced under the Financial Services and Marketing Act 2000.[36]

Options to purchase

A second type of clog on the equity of redemption is the grant to the mortgagee of an option to purchase the mortgaged property. Such a clause was struck out with a marked lack of enthusiasm by the House of Lords in *Samuel v. Jarrah Timber and Wood Paving Corporation Ltd.*[37] A mortgage of certain stock gave the mortgagee the option to purchase that stock at any time within twelve months of the date of the mortgage. Even though this term was in no way oppressive, it was held to be a clog on the equity of redemption. This was because it was a term contained in a mortgage which enabled the mortgagee to buy the mortgaged property; it was a right which, if exercised, would prevent the mortgagor from redeeming the mortgage. It was, therefore, struck out as being, in the words of the Earl of Halsbury, 'contrary to a principle of equity the sense or reason of which I am unable to understand'.[38]

Separate agreements

A distinction is drawn if the option to buy the mortgaged property is not contained in the actual mortgage but is part of a separate agreement. Thus, in *Reeve v. Lisle*,[39] a ship had been mortgaged and, twelve days after the creation of the mortgage, the mortgagee was granted an option to purchase it. Because this option was not contained in the mortgage agreement, itself, but was separate from it, the option was upheld. The essential aspect of the rule remains in force, however, so that if the mortgage gives the mortgagee the option to purchase the mortgaged property, this will be struck out as a clog on the equity of redemption.[40] This rule has nothing to do with the fairness, or otherwise, of the particular clause. Another, more recent, example of this form of clog occurred in *Jones v. Morgan*.[41] Three years after a mortgage was created, a second

[36] See M. Oldham, op. cit., 185–206. See Statutory regulation, pp. 477–478.
[37] [1904] A.C. 323. For contemporary criticism of a decision to the same effect of the Court of Appeal, [1903] 2 Ch. 1, see F. Pollock (1903) 19 L.Q.R. 359, describing the doctrine as 'anachronistic'.
[38] [1904] A.C. 323 at 325.   [39] [1902] A.C. 461.
[40] See *Lewis v. Frank Love Ltd* [1961] 1 W.L.R. 261; P.V. Baker (1961) 77 L.Q.R. 163.
[41] [2002] 1 E.G.L.R. 125; M.P. Thompson [2001] Conv. 502. Contrast *Warnborough Ltd v. Garmite Ltd* [2006] EWHC 10 (Ch.), where the transaction in question was held not to be a mortgage. See also *Brighton & Hove City Council v. Audus* [2009] EWHC 340 (Ch.).

agreement was entered into between the parties. Under the terms of that agreement, the mortgagee acquired the right to purchase some of the mortgaged land. Although the Court of Appeal was unanimous that this clause should not be struck out on the basis that it was either an unconscionable bargain or had been secured by duress, the majority held the clause to be void as constituting a clog of the equity of redemption. This was because the second agreement was seen as being a variation of the mortgage, a view which on the facts appeared to be correct, rather than a separate, independent contract. As such, because it gave the mortgagee the right to purchase the mortgaged property, it was automatically void, regardless of the fairness or otherwise of the agreement.

The origin of this rule lay in the inequality of the bargaining positions of the mortgagor and the mortgagee, the result being that unconscionable terms could be imposed upon the former by the latter, an example of such a term being that the mortgagee should have the right to purchase the mortgaged property. Because such a clause is, technically, a clog, it will be struck out regardless of the lack of any oppression and is an unfortunate relic of a doctrine of equity which has now a propensity to upset unexceptional contracts.

Collateral advantages

Typically, a mortgagee will seek more than security for a loan. A mortgage is, of course, a business transaction and the lender will charge interest on the loan. During the development of the law of mortgages, the mortgagee would frequently seek to recover more than interest on the loan. Quite commonly, the mortgagee was a brewery who, as part of the mortgage transaction, would seek to tie the mortgagor to buying its product, such a clause being known as a *solus* agreement. More recently, this issue has arisen with mortgages of garages, whereby the mortgagee seeks to tie the mortgagor to the purchase of its petroleum products. Traditionally, the efficacy of such clauses, and other provisions conferring collateral advantages on the mortgagee, was considered as part of the equitable doctrine of clogs and fetters. It is this area of the law of mortgages where there has been the greatest shift in the judicial attitude as to when to intervene to invalidate a particular clause in a mortgage.

Duration of advantage

The traditional approach was to distinguish between cases where the collateral advantage would continue for only as long as the mortgage was in being and those where the advantage was to endure for a longer period. In *Noakes v. Rice*,[42] the mortgagor of a public house agreed with the mortgagee that he would purchase the latter's beer for the duration of his lease of the property. This agreement was held to be invalid. The effect of this clause was that, what was a free house prior to the mortgage, would, on the redemption of the mortgage, remain as a tied house and this was held to be a clog on the equity of redemption. By way of contrast, in *Biggs v. Hoddinott*,[43] the

---

[42] [1902] A.C. 24.   [43] [1898] 2 Ch. 307.

mortgage agreement provided that the mortgage would not be redeemed for a period of five years and, during that period, the mortgagor would buy only the mortgagee's products. It having been held that the postponement of the right to redeem for five years was acceptable, the *solus* agreement limited to that period was also valid.

This essential distinction was upheld by a bare majority of the House of Lords in *Bradley v. Carritt*,[44] where, after redemption of a mortgage of shares, a clause requiring the mortgagor to employ the mortgagee as a broker was struck down as a clog on the equity of redemption. This may be seen as the high point of the doctrine as it is applied to the area of collateral advantages and the turning point in the judicial approach to this issue occurred in *Kreglinger v. New Patagonia Meat and Cold Storage Co. Ltd.*[45] Under the terms of a mortgage entered into by a wool company, the mortgagee was to have, for a period of five years, a right of pre-emption, that is a right of first refusal, in respect of sheepskins produced by the mortgagor. It was argued that this provision could not be enforced once the mortgage had been redeemed, the redemption having occurred before the five-year period had elapsed. This argument was unanimously rejected by the House of Lords.

Although it is possible to find technical distinctions between *Bradley v. Carritt* and *Kreglinger*, it is quite evident that the House of Lords was keen to limit the scope of the equitable doctrine and, instead, to enforce a freely entered contractual agreement. This enthusiasm was marked by the speech of Lord Mersey, who likened the equitable doctrine to 'an unruly dog which, if not securely chained to its kennel is prone to wander into places where it ought not to be'.[46] *Kreglinger* involved an entirely normal commercial contract, which the House of Lords was anxious to uphold. To that end, it was held that there was no rule of equity which prohibited the mortgagee from stipulating in a mortgage for a collateral advantage which will continue after the mortgage has been redeemed. Such a clause will be struck out only if it is unfair or unreasonable; if it operates in the nature of a penalty, clogging the equity of redemption; or it is inconsistent with or repugnant to the contractual or equitable right to redeem.

Unconscionability

Today, the test to decide whether a clause in a mortgage should be struck out is more stringent, and is one of unconscionability. In *Cityland Holdings Ltd v. Dabrah*,[47] at a time when the base lending rate was 7 per cent, the annual rate of interest under the mortgage in question was 19 per cent and, if there was default in payment, the rate of interest would have been 57 per cent. This was considered to be a penal rate of interest and a rate of 7 per cent was substituted for that which had been agreed in the mortgage.

---

[44] [1903] A.C. 307.

[45] [1914] A.C. 25. The speech of Lord Parker of Waddington contains a valuable review of the law of clogs and fetters.

[46] Ibid., at 46.   [47] [1968] Ch. 166.

That the mortgagor was an individual had a bearing on this decision. In *Multiservice Bookbinding Co. Ltd v. Marden*,[48] a small company borrowed money by way of mortgage. Under the terms of the mortgage, the interest payable was index-linked to the Swiss franc, the consequence of this being that, when the value of the pound plummeted as against the Swiss currency, the amount of interest payable rose dramatically. The clause was, nevertheless, upheld. Although it was a hard bargain, the clause was not unconscionable and, for a collateral advantage contained in a mortgage to be struck out, it is not sufficient to show that it was unreasonable; the test is one of unconscionability.[49] To establish unconscionability, the relative strength of the bargaining position of the two parties is a relevant, if not necessarily a decisive, factor. In the instant case, unlike *Dabrah*, the parties had relative equality of bargaining position and, so, the mortgagor was unable to establish that the objectionable term had been imposed in a morally reprehensible way so that the conscience of the mortgagee was affected, this being the test which had to be satisfied.[50]

More recently, clauses in mortgage agreements allowing the mortgagee to vary interest rates, where that variation is not governed by changes in the rates set by the Bank of England, have come under attack. Such clauses are not immune from challenge, but it will be only rarely that such a challenge will be successful. In *Paragon Finance plc v. Nash*,[51] Dyson L.J. accepted that such a power was not completely unfettered.[52] A variation would only be liable to challenge, however, if the lender acted in a way that no reasonable lender, acting reasonably, would do. The fact that the rate which has been set may be regarded as being unreasonable is not a sufficient basis on which to invalidate the rate which has been set. The reason for this is that, although such a rate may be unreasonable from the borrower's point of view, it may be commercially necessary for the lender, and therefore reasonable from its point of view, to set such a rate.[53]

The Consumer Credit Acts

Under section 137 of the Consumer Credit Act 1974, the court is empowered to reopen certain extortionate credit arrangements, such arrangements being where the borrower is an individual. To judge whether or not a transaction is extortionate, the court is required to have regard to certain criteria laid down by section 138 of the Act. These criteria include the prevailing level of interest rates when the loan was made, the age, experience, business capacity, and state of health of the debtor at the time of the loan, and, also the degree of financial pressure he was under at the time and the nature of that pressure. From the creditor's point of view, the court must have regard, *inter alia*, to the degree of risk undertaken by him, having regard to the value of any security offered.

---

48 [1979] Ch. 84.   49 Ibid., at 108 *per* Browne-Wilkinson J.
50 Ibid., at 110 *per* Browne-Wilkinson J.
51 [2002] 1 W.L.R. 685. See also *Paragon Finance plc v. Pender* [2005] EWCA Civ. 760.
52 Ibid., at 699.   53 [2002] 1 W.L.R. 685 at 702.

To date, the courts have not interfered in the case of mortgages, even in cases where the interest rate was over 40 per cent.[54] In both cases, however, the debtor had a poor record as a repayer of debts and the increased risk of default meant that arrangements of this type were normal for risks of this kind. Although there has not been intervention under the Act, the jurisdiction under it, and the criteria laid down, seems a preferable way of approaching issues of this nature rather than reliance on a general principle of equity developed many years ago.

Under the 1974 Act, the criterion that had to be satisfied for the court to intervene was that the credit arrangement was extortionate. Section 19 of the Consumer Credit Act 2006 has added a new section 140A to the original Act, and the test is now that of an unfair relationship, although it is thought that the judicial approach to this issue will remain the same.

Restraint of trade

The issue of *solus* agreements contained in mortgages was considered by the House of Lords in *Esso Petroleum Ltd v. Harper's Garage (Stourport) Ltd.*[55] Two mortgages were in issue. One of them concerned a *solus* agreement of five years; the other an agreement for twenty-one years. The first tie was upheld, but not the second. The decisions were made, however, on the basis of the common law doctrine of restraint of trade[56] and not by reference to the equitable principles of clogs and fetters on the equity of redemption. As Diplock L.J. put it in the Court of Appeal,

'I am not persuaded that mortgages of land are condemned today to linger in a jurisprudential cul-de-sac built by the Courts of Chancery before the Judicature Acts from which the robust doctrines of the common law are excluded.'[57]

The use of the common law doctrine of restraint of trade seems a more apposite way of resolving disputes of this kind than having to apply the somewhat anachronistic equitable rules which were developed centuries ago.

Statutory regulation

Until 2004, the only statutory regulation of terms in mortgages was that contained in the Consumer Credit Act 1974. In respect of regulated mortgages, the terms of mortgage agreements after 31 October 2004 are governed by a code of conduct promulgated by the Financial Services Authority acting under the terms of the Financial Services and Markets Act 2000.

One of the objectives of the Act is to provide protection for consumers.[58] In securing the appropriate degree of protection for consumers the Authority was empowered to make regulations,[59] and, in so doing, regard must be had to the different degrees of

---

[54] *A. Ketley Ltd v. Scott* [1980] C.C.L.R. 47, 41; *Woodstead Finance Ltd v. Petrou* [1986] C.C.L.R. 47.

[55] [1968] A.C. 269.

[56] For the possible impact of European Law on *solus* agreements, see T. Frazer [1994] Conv. 150.

[57] [1966] 2 Q.B. 514 at 577–578.   [58] Financial Services and Markets Act 2000, s. 2(2)(c).

[59] Ibid., s. 138.

risk affecting the parties to the transaction, the different degrees of experience and expertise, and the need for consumers for advice and accurate information. This is, however, subject to the general principle that consumers should take responsibility for their actions.[60] The Financial Services Authority has published a Handbook, *Mortgages: Conduct of Business*, which relates to regulated mortgage agreements. Failure to comply with the Code of Practice does not invalidate the mortgage, but can lead to the imposition of various sanctions against the mortgagee.[61] Regulated mortgage agreements include most first mortgages, and the purpose of the Code of Practice is to ensure that borrowers are given adequate information concerning the content of mortgage agreements. This, coupled with the power to re-open extortionate credit bargains, is a much better way of regulating mortgage agreements than the use of the anachronistic doctrine of clogs and fetters. This doctrine was recently described as 'an appendix to our law that no longer serves any useful purpose and would be better excised'.[62]

Pursuing this, and adapting previously employed metaphors, Jonathan Parker L.J. recently opined that 'the unruly dog is still alive (although one might reasonably expect its venerable age to inhibit it from straying too far from its kennel); and that however desirable an appendectomy might be thought to be, no such relieving operation has as yet been carried out'.[63] Given the available methods of providing consumers with protection against unconscionable bargains, it is to be hoped that the doctrine is soon done away with. Its only remaining scope appears to be to upset transactions, otherwise regarded as unobjectionable, whereby a mortgagee acquires the right to purchase the mortgaged property.

Power to lease

The mortgagor is empowered by section 99 of the Law of Property Act 1925 to grant certain leases which will be binding upon the mortgagee. This is, however, subject to that power not having been excluded by the mortgage agreement. It is almost universal practice for this power to be excluded. The effect on the mortgagee of leases granted by the mortgagor will be considered shortly when considering possession actions brought by the mortgagee.

ENFORCING THE SECURITY

Having considered some of the general rights of the mortgagor, attention can now be turned to the rights of the mortgagee. The mortgagee is a secured creditor and the rights which he has relate to his ability to realize that security to protect his loan. The

[60] Ibid., s. 5.   [61] Ibid., Part XIV.
[62] *Jones v. Morgan* [2002] 1 E.G.L.R. 125 at 136 *per* Lord Phillips of Worth Matravers.
[63] *Warborough Ltd v. Garmite Ltd* [2003] EWCA Civ. 1544 at para. 72.

rights he has as a secured creditor are rights which he possesses against the mortgagor. Before the nature of those rights comes into question, however, the preliminary question can arise as to whether other people have rights binding upon the mortgagee. This issue will be considered first, and attention will then be turned to the position as between the mortgagor and the mortgagee.

If the mortgagor has defaulted on the mortgage, the main way in which the mortgagee will seek to recover the money which he is owed is to secure a sale of the property. In practice, for him to do this, he will need to secure vacant possession of the property, as few purchasers will be prepared to buy a property with other people living in it. Before considering his right to possession as against the mortgagee, therefore, the anterior question can arise as to whether other occupiers of the property have rights binding upon him which, whatever the position might be as between the actual parties to the mortgage, will mean that possession cannot be obtained.

The enforcement of third party rights

In considering the rights of other occupiers of mortgaged property, the mortgagee is, in general, likely to be concerned with two sorts of occupier: tenants and co-owners. These types of occupiers will be considered in turn.

Tenants

Whether or not a mortgagee will be bound by the interest of a tenant will depend to a large extent on when the tenancy was created: that is whether it came into being prior to the mortgage or subsequent to it. With regard to tenancies created before the mortgage and so, *prima facie*, binding upon the mortgagee, it may make a difference as to whether or not title is registered.

Lease prior to mortgage

In the case of leases granted prior to the creation of the mortgage, the principal issue when title is unregistered is whether the lease is legal or equitable. If it is a legal lease then, in accordance with general principles, that lease will be binding on the mortgagee, who will be unable to obtain possession as against the tenant. If the lease is equitable, then to be enforceable as against the mortgagee, it must be protected by the registration of a C(iv) land charge, an equitable lease being an estate contract: a contract to create a legal estate. If it has not been registered, it will be void against the mortgagee.[64] If, as is likely, the equitable tenant has gone into possession and paid rent, the equitable lease will still be void for non-registration, but a legal periodic tenancy will have arisen by implication and that tenancy will be binding upon the mortgagee.[65]

---

[64] *Hollington Bros Ltd v. Rhodes* [1951] 2 T.L.R. 691.
[65] Cf. *Bell St Investments Ltd v. Wood* [1970] E.G.D. 812.

Registered land

Where title is registered, the issue is whether the lease has to be protected by registration or will take effect as an interest overriding a registered disposition. In the case of a lease granted for a term not exceeding seven years, this takes effect under Schedule 3, paragraph 1 of the Land Registration Act 2002 as an interest which overrides a registered disposition. The word 'granted' is important in this context as it presupposes that the lease is a legal lease and so an equitable tenancy of less than seven years will not automatically override a registered disposition.[66] If, however, the tenant is in actual occupation of the land then, under Schedule 3, paragraph 2, the interest will override a registered disposition. A lease of more than seven years is not an interest which will override a registered disposition, and should, itself, be registered with an independent title and its existence protected by a notice on the register of the freehold title. Again, however, if the tenant is in actual occupation of the property it will override a registered disposition and so be binding on a mortgagee.

Time of the mortgage

For the lease to be binding upon the mortgagee, it is important that it was created before the mortgage. Determining this matter is usually no problem, but can sometimes become an issue. The first potential problem arose from tenancies by estoppel.[67] In *Church of England Building Society v. Piskor*,[68] a purchaser of a house, who was financing its purchase with a mortgage, purported to grant a tenancy before the conveyance had taken place. As at the time when the purported grant took place the grantor did not have a legal title to the land, the grant operated to create a tenancy by estoppel, whereby both landlord and tenant are estopped from denying the validity of the transaction. The conveyance and mortgage occurred subsequently. It was held that technically the conveyance which vested the legal title in the purchaser and the mortgage were two separate transactions, the conveyance, which vested the legal title in the purchaser preceding, albeit momentarily, the grant by the purchaser of the legal mortgage. The conveyance to the landlord vested in him the legal fee simple and, automatically, by a process termed feeding the estoppel, the effect of this was that the tenant's tenancy by estoppel became a legal lease. As this legal lease was created a split second prior to the creation of the legal mortgage, the mortgagee was bound by the tenancy.

While there is a logic to this reasoning, it was manifestly inconvenient in that it put the security of the mortgagee at risk in circumstances where it was difficult to see how he could protect his own position. For this reason, *Piskor* was overruled in *Abbey National Building Society v. Cann*,[69] so that, in this type of situation, the tenancy would not be regarded as having been created before the mortgage.

---

[66] *City Permanent Building Society v. Miller* [1952] Ch. 840.
[67] See Tenancies by estoppel, pp. 421–423.   [68] [1954] Ch. 553.   [69] [1991] 1 A.C. 56.

This reasoning was applied in *Cook v. The Mortgage Business Plc*,[70] a test case affecting potentially over a hundred similar disputes. The case involved a number of equity release schemes. What they involved was that a registered proprietor of a house agreed to sell it to a nominee of NEPB. The price was the market value of the property, although a significant part of the purchase price was then repaid to NEPB. The nominee would then lease the property back to the former registered proprietors, who paid rent to the nominees. To finance the purchase of the properties, the nominees borrowed the money, and at the time of the transfers, mortgages were created in favour of the lenders. When the nominees defaulted on the mortgages, the mortgagees sought possession and were met with the defence that the leases were binding on them. This defence failed. Applying *Cann*, the Court of Appeal held that the transfer and the mortgage were simultaneous transactions, so that the purchaser, in this case the nominee of NEPB, never acquired an unencumbered fee simple; what it acquired was, in substance, an equity of redemption. It was not, therefore, in a position to create an interest, in the case the leaseback to the vendor which had priority over the mortgage.

Delayed registration

A rather different issue occurred in *Barclays Bank Plc v. Zaroovabli*.[71] A married couple were registered as joint proprietors of a house in April 1988. In May of that year they created a mortgage in favour of the bank, it being a term of the mortgage that the mortgagors' power to grant leases was excluded. For some inexplicable reason, the bank did not apply for registration of the mortgage until 1994. Without seeking the consent of the bank, the mortgagors had earlier let the property to the tenant who, at the time of the action, was still in occupation of the property enjoying the security of tenure conferred upon her by the Rent Act 1977, the original contractual tenancy having ended. When the bank sought possession of the property, the issue was whether it was bound by the tenancy. Sir Richard Scott V.-C. held that it was. The reason for this finding was that, because of the delay in applying for registration of the mortgage, the bank only acquired a legal charge from the date when it applied for registration. In law, therefore, the lease, admittedly created in contravention of the mortgage agreement, arose before the mortgage and took effect as an overriding interest with the result that the mortgagee was bound by it; a consequence of the bank's own fault in not applying for registration of the mortgage until some considerable time after its creation.

The effect of the tenancy

The general position is that a mortgagee will be bound by a tenancy created before the mortgage. What is also true is that, owing to the statutory rights conferred upon certain tenants, a tenant cannot waive any rights which he may have, thereby effectively

---

[70] [2012] EWCA Civ. 17. The earlier decision in *Redstone v. Welch & Jackson* [2009] E.G. 98 was not followed.

[71] [1997] Ch. 321.

precluding the owner of it from using the property as security for a loan. In *Woolwich Building Society v. Dickman*,[72] a large leasehold flat was owned by the mortgagors but occupied under a tenancy agreement by their in-laws. The mortgagors wished to borrow money on the security of the house. Ordinarily, the society would not lend money on a house which was occupied by tenants but, for some reason, regarded them as being beneficial co-owners rather than tenants. Forms were sent to the tenants seeking their consent to their interest in the property being postponed to that of the society. Although the consent forms were appropriate for co-owners rather than tenants to sign, this, on the facts, was not considered to be a material error. The tenants signed the forms but, when the society sought possession of the property, they claimed that their tenancy was binding upon the society. The Court of Appeal held in favour of the tenants. Their tenancy was an overriding interest within section 70(1)(k) of the Land Registration Act 1925 and, therefore, binding upon the society. Because the tenancy was protected under the Rent Act 1977, such a tenancy could only be terminated on the grounds laid down in that Act and it is not open to the parties, by agreement or otherwise, to contract out of the protection afforded by the Act. Consequently, despite the fact that they had expressly consented to the mortgage, the tenants were not precluded from relying on their statutory rights. It was originally proposed that a person could not assert that his right was an overriding interest if enquiry was made of him and the right was not disclosed.[73] The 2002 Act, however, relates the relevance of enquiry only to the rights of people in actual occupation and does not extend that proviso to the holders of other overriding interests, with the result that the decision in *Dickman* is unaffected.

While the reasoning is hard to fault, the decision is inconvenient. If a person owns the freehold of a large property, the upper floor of which is occupied by others, then it is not safe for a mortgagee to lend against the security of the entire property. The occupiers of the upper floor could be co-owners, in which case, they are able to consent to the lender's security having priority to their interest or, alternatively, if there are two legal owners of the property, their interests can be overreached. If they are tenants, however, and entitled to statutory protection, then the protection afforded by the statute means that, in enforcing its security, the mortgagee will be unable to obtain possession as against them, whatever the tenants may have said prior to the creation of the mortgage.

Unauthorized leases

As stated previously, one of the rights of a mortgagor is to create leases of the mortgaged property. This power is subject, however, to the expression of a contrary intention in the mortgage deed or otherwise in writing.[74] If there is no contrary intention expressed, then any lease created by the mortgagor will be binding upon the mortgagee.

---

[72] [1996] 3 All E.R. 204.   [73] (1998) Law Com. No. 254, para. 5.69.
[74] Law of Property Act 1925, s. 99(1)(13).

In practice, however, it is normal for the mortgage to exclude the power of the mortgagor to create leases. The question then arises as to the position of the tenant when, notwithstanding such a clause in the mortgage, the mortgagor does let the mortgaged property.

The general position is that, while, as between the mortgagor and the tenant, the lease is entirely valid, the lease is not binding upon the mortgagee, who will, therefore, be able to obtain possession as against the tenant.[75] The tenant's position is not improved by the statutory protection afforded to residential tenants. This point was considered in *Britannia Building Society v. Earl*,[76] where despite a clause in the mortgage excluding the mortgagor's power to create leases, the mortgagor did create a tenancy. When he defaulted on the mortgage, the mortgagee sought possession and this action was resisted by the tenants. Their principal argument was that, as they were protected by the Rent Act 1977, possession could be obtained only on one of the grounds stipulated in that Act. This was rejected. The lease was not binding upon the mortgagee and, consequently, the statutory code regulating possession actions was not relevant to the action brought by him.

Limits to right of possession

The decision in *Earl* demonstrates the vulnerable position of a tenant who, having entered into the lease in good faith and performed his obligations under the tenancy, may find himself being forced to leave property at the behest of the mortgagee, almost certainly as a result of default on the mortgage by his landlord, a result which can appear harsh.[77] One's view as to the harshness of this should be tempered, however, by the consideration that the opposite result would be hard on a mortgagee, who would be unable to gain possession of property because of the creation of an interest which he had expressly tried to prevent from being created. The decision in favour of the mortgagee is consistent with principle and establishes the general right of the mortgagee to possession as against a tenant, whose lease was created by a mortgagor in contravention of the terms of the mortgage. The mortgagee's right is not unqualified, however, there being two situations where a possession action may fail.

Collusive actions

The first situation where a mortgagee may fail in an action for possession against a tenant is where such an action is seen as being essentially collusive. In *Quennell v. Maltby*,[78] a husband owned a property subject to a small mortgage in favour of a bank. The mortgage deed excluded the power to create leases. Nevertheless, he created a lease of the property. Later, he wished to sell the property but would have found it difficult to do so as it was occupied by tenants who were protected under the Rent Acts, and were unwilling to leave. To obtain possession, he approached the bank and

---

[75] See *Corbett v. Plowden* (1884) 25 Ch.D. 678 at 681 *per* Lord Selborne L.C.; *Dudley and District Building Society v. Emerson* [1949] Ch. 707.

[76] [1990] 1 W.L.R. 422. [77] See P. Smith (1977) 41 Conv. (N.S.) 197. [78] [1979] 1 W.L.R. 318.

sought to persuade it to bring possession proceedings, the tenancy not being binding upon it. The bank, however, taking the view that its security was safe, declined to do so. The mortgagor's wife then paid off the sum owing under the mortgage and the mortgage was then transferred to her. She then, standing in the shoes of the bank, sought to evict the tenants. The action failed. Although it was accepted that the bank could have obtained possession, on the facts of the case, the wife was acting as her husband's agent. As he could not have obtained possession, neither could she. To have held otherwise would have opened the door to a facile means of evading the Rent Acts.

Adoption

The situation where the possession action is seen as collusive is probably not of general importance. Potentially, a more serious issue for mortgagees is where a lease is regarded as having been adopted. This occurred in *Stroud Building Society v. Delamont*.[79] A mortgagor created an unauthorized mortgage. Sometime later, he was declared bankrupt. Although the mortgagee served a notice to quit on the tenant, this was not complied with and, thereafter, rent was paid to the mortgagor's trustee in bankruptcy. A little later, the mortgagee appointed a receiver,[80] who instructed the tenant to pay the rent to him. After that, the society, replying to a letter it had received, wrote to the tenant, informing her that she held on the same terms as she had previously. When a possession action was brought on behalf of the society against the tenant, it failed, it being held that the action of the society had caused the relationship of landlord and tenant to arise between it and the tenant.

It was accepted that the society could, at the outset, have treated the tenant as a trespasser on the basis that the lease was unauthorized and so not binding upon it but it did not do so. If the society had done nothing, but simply allowed the tenant to remain in possession, this would not, of itself, have prevented it from seeking possession, because something more than mere knowledge of the tenancy is required if the mortgagee is to lose his right to evict the tenant.[81] In this case, the terms of the correspondence amounted to a consent to the tenancy, thereby creating the relationship of landlord and tenant between them. To avoid such a consequence, the mortgagee should avoid taking rent directly from the tenant.

Appointing a receiver

The refusal of a mortgagee to accept rent from a tenant when the lease is unauthorized may, understandably, occasion some distress to the tenant when faced with a possession action arising as a consequence of default by his landlord. Yet the reluctance of the landlord to accept payment is, in his own interest, entirely understandable. One solution is to appoint a receiver. A receiver, when appointed, is the agent

---

[79] [1960] 1 W.L.R. 431. See also *Chatsworth Building Society v. Effion* [1971] 1 W.L.R. 144.
[80] For the power to appoint a receiver, see Appointment of a receiver, pp. 522–523.
[81] See *Nijar v. Mann* (1998) 30 H.L.R. 223 at 227 *per* Ward L.J.

of the mortgagor,[82] and so his receipt of rent from the tenant, although paid to the mortgagee, will not amount to the adoption of the tenancy. A potential difficulty here, as pointed out by Cross J., is that 'the idea that a mortgagee can through the medium of receivership get the benefit of the rent while remaining at liberty to treat him as a trespasser is a highly artificial one which would not readily occur to a layman or even a good many lawyers'.[83] Accordingly, the conduct of the receiver towards the tenant may quite easily amount to an adoption of the tenancy.[84] If the mortgagee is willing to allow the tenant to retain possession, he should make it clear that the receipt of rent by a receiver is done without prejudice to his position. Alternatively, as the appointment of a receiver in respect of domestic property is uncommon, it is hoped that the courts would accept that the receipt of rent directly from the tenant, on the basis that that receipt is without prejudice, should not result in the tenancy being held to have been adopted as this would ensure that his right to possession is not prejudiced, while also ensuring that the tenant does not have to leave the property at short notice.

Statutory reform

Unless a tenant could argue that the possession action was collusive, or that the tenancy had been adopted, he could be faced with summary eviction from his home, through no fault of his own. To alleviate this position, under s.1(4) of the Mortgage Repossessions (Protection of Tenants etc) Act 2010, a court may stay or suspend a possession order against an unauthorized tenant for a period of up to two months. While not necessarily perfect from the point of view of the tenant, this legislative reform does afford him some time to find suitable alternative accommodation when faced with a possession action brought by a mortgagee.

Co-owners

Perhaps the most likely person to claim to have an interest in mortgaged property which has priority to that of the mortgagee is a co-owner of that property. This is an area of law which has seen considerable development over a comparatively short period of time. It has seen the courts seeking to strike a balance between two competing interests. On the one hand, one must consider the position of mortgagees. They lend money as part of a commercial enterprise. For them, the ability, in cases of default, to be able to realize their security by gaining possession and subsequently selling the property is paramount. On the other hand, one must consider the position of people, other than the mortgagor, who use the property as their home, and who have interests in that property, whose principal concern is not to lose their home as a result of the mortgagor using the house as security for a loan. In the course of the

---

[82] Law of Property Act 1925, s. 109(2). See Appointment of a receiver, pp. 522–523.

[83] *Stroud Building Society v. Delamont* [1960] 1 W.L.R. 431 at 435. In *Nijar v. Mann* (1998) 30 H.L.R. 223 at 228, Ward L.J. confessed 'with hardly a tinge of shame, that until I read the papers in this case I was also one of that merry ignorant band'.

[84] See *Nijar v. Mann* (1998) 30 H.L.R. 223.

judicial development of this aspect of the law of co-ownership and mortgages, various different situations have arisen. Put broadly, one must consider whether there was sole ownership or co-ownership at law and, also, the type of mortgage involved. As will be seen, it is particularly important to determine whether the purpose of the loan is for the acquisition of the house or, at least, for the mutual benefit of the co-owners, or whether the house is being used as security for loans for the sole, or principal, benefit of the mortgagor.

Sole legal ownership

In *Williams & Glyn's Bank Ltd v. Boland*,[85] a matrimonial home was in the sole name of Mr Boland, but it was conceded that Mrs Boland was a beneficial co-owner of it. He mortgaged the house to the bank who, when he defaulted on the mortgage, sought possession. It was held by the House of Lords that her equitable interest in the house, coupled with the fact that she was in actual occupation of it, meant that she had an overriding interest and that, as against her, the bank was not entitled to possession. *Boland* was a case concerning registered land. Where title is unregistered, the same result would also have occurred, it being clear that a mortgagee would, in circumstances such as those which occurred in *Boland*, be fixed with constructive notice of her right and, therefore, be bound by it.[86]

The upshot of this is that, although as a matter of law, the husband, as the borrower in default, has no defence to an action for possession, it is pointless for a mortgagee to seek to oust him from the property. This is because, as his wife has the right to remain in the property, vacant possession cannot be obtained, and so the house could not be sold. This consideration led the Court of Appeal in *Albany Home Loans Ltd v. Massey*[87] to decline to order possession against the husband in these circumstances, particularly as the effect of such an order would be to prevent a husband from living with his wife, on pain of being in contempt of court should he flout such an order.[88] Understandably, this was not something that the court was prepared to do. As the house cannot be sold in these circumstances, it may be thought that the outcome would be that both of them could continue living in the house, presumably without making further payments on the mortgage. This is not so, however, because the mortgagee will be able to pursue a personal action against the mortgagor, the end result of which is likely to be that the house is ultimately sold.[89]

Although, with the benefit of hindsight, the decision in *Boland* might appear to be uncontroversial, it was not viewed in this way at the time.[90] Alongside the traditional conveyancing response, which is that to hold that such interests fall within the category of overriding interests is undesirable because it undermines the reliability of the register and, consequently, increases the need for conveyancers to make

---

[85] [1981] A.C. 487.   [86] See *Kingsnorth Trust Ltd v. Tizard* [1986] 1 W.L.R. 783.
[87] [1997] 2 All E.R. 609.   [88] Ibid., at 612 *per* Schiemann L.J.
[89] See The covenant to repay, pp. 511–512.
[90] For a hostile response, see S. Freeman (1980) 43 M.L.R. 692, but contrast the more measured reaction by J. Martin [1980] Conv. 361.

actual enquiries of occupants, the principal concern of the lending institutions was with one particular situation. This situation was where a single person, normally a man, would approach a potential mortgagee to agree a mortgage. Unbeknown to the lender, however, he was planning to cohabit and his partner would contribute to the initial down payment on the house, thereby acquiring a beneficial interest in it but, for some reason, was not to be a legal co-owner of the property. The fear was that her interest in the house would be binding upon the mortgagee, this concern being exacerbated in the case of registered land because of the gap between the transfer of the property and the subsequent application for registration. In this period, it was thought that, if the equitable co-owner, as would be normal, went into actual occupation of the house, she would, at the time when the mortgage was registered, be able to establish an overriding interest binding upon the mortgagee, who would have little opportunity to discover its existence.

Response to Boland

As will be seen, these fears have proved to be exaggerated but, at the time, were keenly felt, so much so, that the matter was referred to the Law Commission, who recommended that the decision in *Boland* be reversed by legislation, so that the interest of a beneficial co-owner should only bind a purchaser including, of course, a mortgagee, if it was protected by registration.[91] The proposed legislative response was unfortunate. Under the provisions of the misguided Land Registration and Law of Property Bill 1985, the beneficial interest of a wife who was in actual occupation of the home would, unless she had consented to the mortgage, continue to take effect as an overriding interest, whereas if the occupier was not married to the legal owner, the same interest would only bind a mortgagee if it was registered. Leaving aside the desirability, or otherwise, of discriminating against non-married cohabitees in this way, this solution, if implemented, would have introduced the need for an enquiry to be made as to the marital status of any person who shared the house with the legal owner of it. If the couple were married, an enquiry would need to be addressed to her as to whether she had a beneficial interest in the house and, if so, whether she consented to the transaction;[92] if they were not married, then no further enquiries would need to be made as her interest could only be binding if it had been registered. This would seem to be a conveyancing absurdity.[93] Fortunately, the Bill was not enacted and the issues involved were left for resolution by the courts.

Limits on Boland

Subsequent case law has done much to clarify the position with regard to the rights of beneficial co-owners when the property has been mortgaged. The general impact of the decisions has been to limit the potential impact of *Boland*, albeit in a way that,

---

[91] (1982) Law Com. No. 115.   [92] For the issue of consents, see Vitiating factors, pp. 492–510.
[93] See the critical comments on the need for enquiries such as this in *National Provincial Bank Ltd v. Ainsworth* [1965] A.C. 1175 at 1234 *per* Lord Upjohn.

in general, would seem to strike a fair balance between the competing interests of secured creditors, on the one hand, and residential occupiers, on the other.

Acquisition mortgages

As noted previously, a principal concern of lending institutions was that, if they lent money to a single person to finance the purchase of a house, they could find that a person cohabiting with him had acquired a beneficial interest in the property which would be binding upon them; a matter which, in the case of subsequent mortgage default, would seriously affect their ability to realize their security by selling the house. This issue first arose in *Bristol and West Building Society v. Henning*.[94] A house was conveyed into the sole name of Mr Henning. The purchase price was £12,900, of which £11,000 was borrowed by way of mortgage from the building society. The balance of the purchase price was raised from the proceeds of sale of another house which had been co-owned by him and Mrs Henning.[95] As she was a beneficial co-owner of the first house, it followed that she was also a co-owner of this house. The society had no idea that the house was going to be shared and did not, therefore, address any questions to her. When he defaulted on the mortgage, the society sought possession and she argued that it was bound by her beneficial interest in the property. This defence failed. The Court of Appeal held that, because Mrs Henning knew that a mortgage was being created, and had benefited from it, in that the house could not have been acquired at all without the finance provided by the society, the intention would be imputed to her that the interest of the society should have priority over hers.

The basis of the decision, that of imputing an intention to a person on the basis of what that person would have intended had she thought about it, is suspect, in that it is not normally the case when considering issues relating to ownership of the house that one imputes intentions to parties which they might have formed had thought been given to the matter. Instead, the normal judicial role is to seek to infer what the parties actually did intend.[96] Nevertheless, the reasoning has been tacitly approved by the House of Lords,[97] although a better explanation of the decision is probably to say that a person in Mrs Henning's position is, as against the mortgagee, estopped from asserting her right.[98]

Whatever the precise rationale of the judgment, however, the result is eminently justifiable. It is one thing to argue that the occupation rights of a co-owner should be protected when the house in which she lives is mortgaged without her knowledge; it is rather different to say that such rights should be capable of assertion against a

---

[94] [1995] 1 W.L.R. 778; *Paddington Building Society v. Mendelsohn* (1995) 50 P. & C.R. 244. See M.P. Thompson (1986) 49 M.L.R. 245; [1986] Conv. 57.

[95] The couple were not, in fact, married. It is important to appreciate that, in cases of this nature, the marital status of the beneficial co-owner is immaterial.

[96] See Intention at acquisition, pp. 320–321.

[97] *Abbey National Building Society v. Cann* [1991] A.C. 56 at 94 *per* Lord Oliver of Aylmerton.

[98] *Skipton Building Society v. Clayton* (1993) 25 H.L.R. 596 at 602 *per* Slade L.J. Se also *Thompson v. Foy* [2009] EWHC 1079 (Ch.) at [142]–[143] *per* Lewison J., and the detailed analysis of this issue in *Bank of Scotland v. Hussain* [2010] EWHC 2812 (Ch.) at [96]–[111] *per* Newey J.

mortgagee when that mortgage is, to her knowledge, created in order for the house to be bought at all. That said, the rather questionable theoretical basis of the decision was used to arrive at a less justifiable result in *Equity and Law Home Loans Ltd v. Prestidge.*[99]

Subrogation

A couple bought a house together, the legal title being in the sole name of Mr Prestidge but he and his partner, Mrs Brown, were beneficial co-owners of it. £30,000 of the purchase price was provided by the Britannia Building Society who took a mortgage over the property. Some time later, he negotiated a further mortgage with the plaintiff, the sum to be borrowed being some £42,875. He told the plaintiff of Mrs Brown's interest in the home and the company were satisfied with his assurance that, although she had not yet consented to the mortgage, he was confident that she would do so. No questions were addressed to her. Of the sum borrowed, part of it was used to redeem the mortgage in favour of Britannia and the remainder was used by Mr Prestidge for his own purposes. When default occurred on the mortgage, the plaintiff sought possession and this action was defended by Mrs Brown, who argued that her interest was binding on the mortgagee. The Court of Appeal held that the mortgagee was entitled to possession and, on a sale of the property, would be entitled from the proceeds of sale to the first £30,000. Thereafter, Mrs Brown would receive a sum equivalent to her share in the property and the balance would then go to the mortgagee in respect of the remainder of its loan.

The starting point in the judgment was to recognize that, had the second mortgage never occurred and it had been Britannia which had brought possession proceedings, its claim would have succeeded. The case would have been indistinguishable from *Henning*. As part of the money borrowed from Equity and Law had been used to pay off that mortgage, the conclusion was reached that it should stand in the same position as Britannia and so, as against Mrs Brown, have priority to the same extent as Britannia. While plausible, it is suggested that this is dubious. Equity and Law should only have been able to assume the position of the first mortgagee if the purpose of the loan had been to redeem the first mortgage, such a situation not being uncommon when a borrower wishes to change a mortgage because another lender is offering a more attractive rate of interest than that which pertains under the existing mortgage.[100] In such cases, the second lender is subrogated to the rights of the first lender.[101] In the present case, it might be thought that the position of Mrs Brown was not prejudiced in any way by the solution arrived at; if default had been made on the Britannia mortgage, the result would have been the same as that which was actually arrived at. This, however, is not necessarily true. As the second mortgage was for a larger amount

---

[99] [1992] 1 W.L.R. 137. For criticism, see M.P. Thompson [1992] Conv. 206. This decision was entirely overlooked in *Midland Bank plc v. Cooke* [1995] 4 All E.R. 562, and should have led to a different result. See Priority of interests, p. 344.

[100] See *Walthamstow Building Society v. Davies* (1990) 22 H.L.R. 60.

[101] See *Anfield (UK) Ltd v. Bank of Scotland Plc* [2010] EWHC 2374 (Ch.).

than the first mortgage, the repayment figures would also have been higher and it may transpire that it is an inability to meet the higher payments which causes the mortgage default and that the default might not have occurred had the repayment schedule not altered. As such, although *Prestidge* provides further support for the *Henning* principle, it represents an undesirable extension of it by, in effect, extending the doctrine of subrogation, when such an extension would not seem to be justified. The principle is, however, firmly established.[102]

The registration gap

The decision in *Henning* represents an important restriction on the potential applicability of *Boland*. There cannot be many instances where a beneficial co-owner does not know that a house is being bought with the help of finance provided by a mortgagee,[103] and if the co-owner does know this, she cannot claim to have an interest which is binding upon the mortgagee. This removes a considerable part of the concern felt by lending institutions concerning the potential impact of the decision in *Boland*. The related concern focused on what is termed the registration gap. This concern centred on the gap in time between the execution of the transfer document and the mortgage and the subsequent application for registration. As it is the latter event which vests the legal title in the transferee,[104] it was generally thought that, if a person with a beneficial interest in the property was in actual occupation at this, later, date, she would then have established an overriding interest binding upon the mortgagee.[105] In *Abbey National Building Society v. Cann*,[106] however, the House of Lords considered such a result to be an absurdity and so construed the statutory provisions in such a way that, for the purpose of section 70(1)(g) of the Land Registration Act 1925, the relevant time at which the person claiming to have an overriding interest must be in actual occupation of the property is the date of the transfer and creation of the mortgage and not the date when application is made for registration. The conclusion arrived at in *Cann* was based upon a purposive interpretation of the 1925 Act. The same position is arrived at explicitly by the 2002 Act: Schedule 3, paragraph 2 makes clear that the rights of a person in actual occupation, if they are to override a registered disposition, must exist at the time of the disposition. The upshot is that, when a mortgage is created contemporaneously with the transfer of the land, which is the normal situation when the mortgage is being used to finance the purchase of the house, a co-owner will only be able to establish an interest binding upon the mortgagee if, first, she was unaware that a mortgage was being created and, secondly, she had gone into actual occupation prior to the execution of the mortgage deed. It is highly unlikely that a beneficial co-owner can satisfy both conditions, and so mortgagees who lend money for an acquisition

---

[102] See *Le Foe v. Le Foe* [2001] 2 F.L.R. 970 at 983–984 *per* Mr Nicholas Mostyn Q.C.

[103] For a rare example of such a situation, see *Lloyds Bank plc v. Rosset* [1991] 1 A.C. 107.

[104] Land Registration Act 1925, s. 20.

[105] For an argument to the contrary, see P. Sparkes [1986] Conv. 309.

[106] [1991] A.C. 56. See S. Baughen [1991] Conv. 116; P.T. Evans [1991] Conv. 155. For the same position with regard to leases, see *Cook v. The Mortgage Business Plc* [2012] EWCA Civ. 17.

mortgage can view the potential problems caused to lenders by the decision in *Boland* with equanimity.[107]

Non-acquisition mortgages

As has been seen, a mortgagee is only likely to be affected by the interest of a co-owner if the mortgage is created some time after the property has been acquired, that is when the house is used as security for further borrowing. When there is only one legal owner of the property, then the mortgagee must make enquiries of any adults[108] who are in actual occupation of the property. Where there is co-ownership at law, the position is different.

Legal co-ownership

In *City of London Building Society v. Flegg*,[109] a married couple were registered proprietors of a house which they held on trust for themselves and her parents. Without informing the parents, the legal owners created a number of mortgages over the house until, finally, they created a mortgage in favour of the plaintiffs, the money borrowed[110] being used to redeem the existing mortgages. No enquiries were addressed to the parents who, when the mortgagee sought possession, argued that, as beneficial co-owners who were in actual occupation, they had an overriding interest binding upon the mortgagee. Reversing a highly controversial decision of the Court of Appeal[111] in favour of the parents, the House of Lords held in favour of the society and made an order for possession.

This decision very much reflected orthodox opinion as to the effect of a mortgage executed by two legal owners, that being to overreach the beneficial interests existing behind the trust.[112] It was apparent, also, that the House of Lords were strongly motivated by the perceived conveyancing implications of the case, and considered that a decision in favour of the occupiers would have the consequence that 'financial institutions [would] face hitherto unsuspected hazards';[113] a prospect which was not viewed with equanimity.

While one can appreciate the force of this argument, it is not, perhaps, compelling. The rationale behind the decision in *Boland* is to prevent occupiers of property, who

---

[107] If the mortgage is contemporaneous with the transfer, it will also be very difficult to establish the existence of a beneficial interest in the property prior in time to the mortgage.

[108] Persons under the age of 18 are not regarded as being in actual occupation of the property and so, even if they have a beneficial interest in the property, will not have an overriding interest: *Hypo-Mortgage Services Ltd v. Robinson* [1997] 2 F.L.R. 422, although see The protection of occupiers, p. 151.

[109] [1988] A.C. 54. See M.P. Thompson [1988] Conv. 108.

[110] It is immaterial if the mortgage was created but no capital money was paid. *State Bank of India v. Sood* [1997] Ch. 276. See C. Harpum [1980] C.L.J. 277; M.P. Thompson [1997] Conv. 134.

[111] [1986] Ch. 605. For strong criticism, see D.J. Hayton (1986) 130 N.L.J. 208. For a lone defence, see M.P. Thompson (1986) 6 L.S. 140.

[112] See, e.g. H. Forrest [1978] Conv. 194 at 199–201; M.D.A. Freeman (1981) Fam. Law 37 at 40; J. Martin [1980] Conv. 361; W.T. Murphy (1979) 42 M.L.R. 467. For an unsuccessful argument to the contrary, see M.P. Thompson (1986) 6 L.S. 140.

[113] [1988] A.C. 54 at 72 *per* Lord Oliver of Aylmerton.

have a beneficial interest in it, from losing their homes as a result of the actions of the legal owner in mortgaging the property for his own financial purposes without consulting the other co-owner. From the perspective of the occupier, it is doubtful if the significance of the mortgage being executed by two, as opposed to one, legal owner would be fully appreciated. When one considers that the type of mortgage in question involves a situation where a home is being used as security for future borrowing, a case can be made that it is not unreasonable to expect the lender to consult all the occupants of the house before lending the money by way of mortgage.

Such arguments found favour with the Law Commission who, in contrast to the view taken of the decision in *Boland*, recommended that the decision in *Flegg* be reversed by legislation.[114] This recommendation has not, however, been implemented.[115] Although it has been argued that *Flegg* has been overruled by the provisions of the Trusts of Land and Appointment of Trustees Act 1996,[116] this argument, which has been considered earlier,[117] seems unlikely to prevail and it seems that the decision in *Flegg* will remain the definitive determination of this issue. For dispositions occurring after the Land Registration Act 2002 came into force, this matter is made clear by section 26, which provides that, insofar as a disponee is concerned, a person's right to exercise owner's powers in relation to a registered charge or estate is to be taken free from any limitations affecting the validity of the disposition thereby, *inter alia*, confirming the result in *Flegg*.

Vitiating factors

The decisions in *Boland* and *Flegg* were concerned with the competing interests of lenders prepared to lend money against the security of people's homes and the rights of beneficial co-owners of the home. The essential problem involved balancing the interests of co-owners, whose names were not on the legal title, against the interests of the legal owner or owners and of the mortgagee. An issue which has recently come to prominence is the potential conflict of interest between the legal co-owners, both of whom must be party to the mortgage deed. The situation which arises is when A and B are legal owners of the property and, therefore, the signature of both of them is necessary to effect the mortgage. In getting B to sign, A commits some wrong, either misrepresentation or the exercise of undue influence, both being regarded as vitiating factors to the transaction.[118] The question which arises is to determine the circumstances when the existence of such a vitiating factor will cause the mortgage to be set aside as against B, the mortgagee not, itself, having committed this wrong.

[114] (1989) Law Com. No. 188.
[115] See the comments in *State Bank of India v. Sood* [1987] Ch. 276 at 290 *per* Peter Gibson L.J. See also M.P. Thompson in Meisel and Cook (eds), *Property and Protection: Essays in Honour of Brian Harvey* (Oxford: Hart Publishing, 2000), 157 at 171–172.
[116] G. Ferris and G. Battersby [1998] Conv. 168.   [117] See Registered land, pp. 299–300.
[118] Although the two concepts are distinct, the presence of either can lead to the transaction being set aside. See *Annulment Finance Co. Ltd v. Cowey* [2010] EWCA Civ. 711 at [61]–[64] *per* Morgan J.

At one time, it was thought that a mortgage would be liable to be set aside in one of two situations. The first situation involved the use of the agency principle. This involved the person who was seeking the loan being entrusted with the task of obtaining the signature of the other co-owner to the mortgage deed. If that person, when obtaining the signature of the other, had either misrepresented the nature of the transaction or had exercised undue influence to obtain the signature, then the mortgage would not be valid against the victim of the wrong. The co-owner who obtained the signature was regarded as the agent of the mortgagee and the wrong committed by that agent was attributed to the lender.[119] Alternatively, if undue influence had actually been used to obtain the signature and the mortgagee, or its agent, had notice of this, then the mortgage would also be void.[120] Otherwise, it seemed that the position of the mortgagee would be safe, notwithstanding that undue influence, or some other wrong, had been employed to obtain the signature of the co-owner.[121]

The O'Brien defence

A different approach to this issue was taken, however, in the landmark decision of the House of Lords in *Barclays Bank plc v. O'Brien*.[122] This decision sought to lay down a sound conceptual base for the law's intervention in this area and to provide principled guidelines to enable a proper balance to be struck between the competing interests of commercial lenders on the one hand and residential occupiers on the other. Unfortunately, the attempt to do this was far from being an unmitigated success. A torrent of litigation followed on from the decision and this led to the House of Lords, to a considerable extent, recasting the law in what is now the leading case of *Royal Bank of Scotland v. Etridge (No. 2)*.[123] To understand the issues which arose in *Etridge*, however, it is necessary to explain the basis of *O'Brien* and some of the resulting difficulties which emanated from it.

Mr and Mrs O'Brien were joint legal owners of their matrimonial home. Mr O'Brien was closely involved with a company which had an overdraft facility with the bank. He agreed with the bank that he would stand surety for the company's indebtedness and create a mortgage over the matrimonial home to provide security for this undertaking. When discussing this with his wife, he told her that the level of debt was in the region of £60,000 and would be repaid within three weeks. The agreement to mortgage

---

[119] See *Avon Finance Co. Ltd v. Bridger* [1985] 2 All E.R. 281; *Kingsnorth Trust Ltd v. Bell* [1986] 1 W.L.R. 119.

[120] *Bank of Credit and Commerce International SA v. Aboody* [1990] 1 Q.B. 923. An additional requirement of this case, that the transaction be to the manifest disadvantage of the co-owner, is no longer good law. *CIBC Mortgages plc v. Pitt* [1994] 1 A.C. 200 at 208 *per* Lord Browne-Wilkinson.

[121] See, e.g., *Coldunell Ltd v. Gallon* [1986] Q.B. 1184; *Midland Bank plc v. Perry* (1988) 56 P. & C.R. 202; *Lloyds Bank plc v. Egremont* [1990] 2 F.L.R. 351.

[122] [1994] 1 A.C. 180. For the fullest accounts of the issues pertaining to this area of the law, see Fehlberg, *Sexually Transmitted Debt: Surety Experience in English Law* (Oxford: Clarendon Press, 1997); Pawlowski and Brown, *Undue Influence and the Family Home* (London: Cavendish Publishing Ltd, 2002); Enonchong, *Duress, Undue Influence and Unconscionable Dealing* (London: Sweet & Maxwell, 2006), Chapters 6–12. See also M.P. Thompson in Cooke (ed.), *Modern Studies in Property Law, Volume 2* (Oxford: Hart Publishing, 2003), Chapter 7.

[123] [2001] 4 All E.R. 449.

the house was not implemented straightaway. When the mortgage was created, the level of debt was £135,000 and the mortgage included an 'all moneys clause': that is the mortgage was to secure open-ended liability, so that whatever the company owed was to be secured by the mortgage. At the time when the bank sought possession under the mortgage, the company's debt was £154,000.

When the mortgage was signed by the O'Briens, the bank official did not follow the official bank policy, which was to explain to a person in Mrs O'Brien's position the nature and effect of the mortgage and to recommend to her that she obtain independent legal advice prior to signing it. Instead, she simply signed the mortgage deed and a side letter acknowledging that she had had the mortgage deed explained to her and that she had understood it. This was not the case and she believed that the mortgage was to secure a short term loan of £60,000, rather than to secure open-ended liability. The House of Lords held that the mortgage was void against her.

It was clear on the evidence that Mrs O'Brien, although not a victim of undue influence,[124] had, as a result of a misrepresentation made to her by her husband, misunderstood the document which she had signed. The issue was to determine the circumstances in which a person in such a position could avoid liability under the mortgage. In deciding this question, Lord Browne-Wilkinson adverted to a familiar dilemma in cases of this nature; that one's instinctive sympathy for a wife threatened with the loss of her home at the suit of a rich bank should not be allowed to obscure a competing need that wealth locked up in a matrimonial home should not be made economically sterile.[125] One must strike a balance between the competing interests of residential occupiers and institutional lenders, it being in his view 'essential that a law designed to protect the vulnerable does not render the matrimonial home unacceptable as security to financial institutions'.[126]

To determine how the balance between the two competing interests should be struck, Lord Browne-Wilkinson sought to tackle the problem by the application of first principles. First, he rejected the argument which had prevailed in the Court of Appeal[127] that there was a special rule of equity that, where a wife was acting as surety for her husband, the creditor owed a duty to ensure that she fully understood the transaction and had been separately advised.[128] Neither did he accept the previous line of authority which had adopted the agency principle, where the person in the position of Mr O'Brien was regarded as the mortgagee's agent. True cases of agency he regarded as being likely to be very rare.[129] Instead, he focused on the nature of the relationship between the parties and the scope of the doctrine of undue influence.

---

[124] An argument based upon undue influence which had originally been raised was not pursued: [1994] 1 A.C. 180 at 187 per Lord Browne-Wilkinson.
[125] Ibid., at 188.   [126] Ibid.   [127] [1993] Q.B. 109.
[128] This doctrine was based to a large extent on *Yerkey v. Jones* (1939) 63 C.L.R. 649, an approach which has been continued in Australia: *Garcia v. National Australia Bank Ltd* (1998) 72 A.J.L.R. 1243. See P.J. Clarke [1998] All E. Rev. 271. For criticism, see M.P. Thompson [1992] Conv. 443.
[129] [1994] 1 A.C. 180 at 195.

Undue influence

In considering the role of undue influence, Lord Browne-Wilkinson adopted the classification which had previously been employed by the Court of Appeal in *Bank of Credit and Commerce International S.A. v. Aboody.*[130] This categorization put cases of undue influence into either Class 1 or Class 2. Class 1 undue influence was where one party to a transaction established that undue influence had actually been used by the other. In such a case, the complainant is entitled to have the transaction set aside. It is not necessary to prove as an additional factor that the transaction was to her manifest disadvantage.[131] The other category is Class 2, which was sub-divided into Class 2(A) and Class 2(B).

Class 2(A)

The first category involved a situation where, because of the relationship between the two parties, the law will presume that one of them has exerted undue influence over the other. This type of relationship is narrow and includes doctor and patient, solicitor and client, and spiritual adviser and penitent. Where there is such a relationship between the parties, the person in the vulnerable position can set aside the transaction unless the other is able to show that undue influence was not used.

Class 2(B)

The second category, Class 2(B), was the more important of the two. In this category, the complainant must prove the *de facto* existence of a relationship under which she generally reposed trust and confidence in the wrongdoer. Once the existence of that relationship has been established, its existence raises the presumption of undue influence and the onus of proof then shifts to the alleged wrongdoer to show undue influence has not occurred.[132] Lord Browne-Wilkinson said:

'In a Class 2(B) case, therefore, in the absence of evidence disproving undue influence, the complainant will succeed in setting aside the impugned transaction *merely by proof that the complainant reposed trust and confidence in the wrongdoer without having to prove that the wrongdoer exerted actual undue influence or otherwise abused such trust and confidence in relation to the particular transaction impugned.*'[133]

The essential difference between Class 2(A) and Class 2(B) was that, as between the parties, in the first category of case, the relationship is such that the law will presume that, in the absence of evidence to the contrary, the stronger party has exerted undue influence on the weaker; in Class 2(B), the weaker party must first establish a relationship of trust and confidence. Once that has been done, the law will make the same presumption with regard to undue influence.

---

[130] [1991] Q.B. 923 at 957 *per* Slade L.J.

[131] The actual decision on this point in *Aboody*, which required the complainant to establish that the transaction was to her manifest disadvantage was overruled in *CIBC Mortgages plc v. Pitt* [1994] 1 A.C. 200.

[132] *Barclays Bank plc v. O'Brien* [1994] 1 A.C. 180 at 189 *per* Lord Browne-Wilkinson.

[133] *Barclays Bank plc v. O'Brien* [1994] 1 A.C. 180 at 189–190. Emphasis supplied.

In *O'Brien*, Lord Browne-Wilkinson accepted that a Class 2(B) relationship existed. The mortgage was void against her because, owing to the conduct of the bank official in obtaining her signature to the mortgage, the bank was fixed with constructive notice of the presence of the vitiating factor.

Relationship of trust

The basis upon which the Court of Appeal had approached the problem in *O'Brien* was to hold that, as between husband and wife, there is a special doctrine of equity whereby, if a wife acts as surety for her husband, then it is incumbent upon the creditor to take steps to ensure that she understands fully the transaction which is being entered into. If the creditor does not do this then the transaction would only be valid to the extent of her understanding. This doctrine was rejected in the House of Lords. Lord Browne-Wilkinson did not accept that, as between husband and wife, there was a legal presumption that, in a transaction between them, he had exerted undue influence upon her;[134] this relationship does not come within Class 2(A). Instead, it must be established that there is a relationship of trust and confidence. Such relationships are not confined to married couples. They include all emotional relationships, such as homosexual and other non-marital relationships,[135] including brother and sister[136] and also, in admittedly unusual circumstances, employer and employee.[137]

The position of the mortgagee

In a case such as *O'Brien*, Mrs O'Brien was not seeking to set a transaction aside against her husband. She was arguing that the mortgagee could not enforce the mortgage as against her. Lord Browne-Wilkinson considered that this issue could be solved by the application of the doctrine of notice, a doctrine he regarded as being at the heart of equity.[138] The key issue for him was whether the bank had notice of her right to set aside the mortgage and the fact that the mortgage was against the matrimonial home was not, of itself, sufficient to put the bank on enquiry. For this to be the case, it was necessary that there was something in the nature of the transaction to alert the mortgagee that the consent to the mortgage may not have been freely given.

In *CIBC Mortgages plc v. Pitt*,[139] a couple were the joint owners of their matrimonial home, in which there was a very large equity. Mr Pitt was keen to borrow money against the security of their home in order to speculate on the stock market. Mrs Pitt was very reluctant for him to do this but succumbed to pressure from him to sign the mortgage. When the mortgage was applied for, the purpose of the loan was said to be to pay off the small existing mortgage on the house and to enable them to buy a holiday home.[140]

---

[134] For a position where the roles were reversed, see *Barclays Bank plc v. Rivett* [1999] 1 F.L.R. 730.

[135] [1994] 1 A.C. 180 at 198. See *Massey v. Midland Bank plc* [1995] 1 All E.R. 925.

[136] *Northern Rock Building Society v. Archer* (1998) 78 P. & C.R. 65.

[137] *Credit Lyonnais Bank Nederland N.V. v. Burch* [1997] 1 All E.R. 144.

[138] [1994] 1 A.C. 180 at 195.   [139] [1994] 1 A.C. 200.

[140] Curiously, the loan was not to be secured by a mortgage against the holiday home; a matter on which no comment was made: ibid., at 205.

The company lent £150,000 to the Pitts, who executed a mortgage against their home. He then used the money to engage in a number of speculative investments which, while initially successful, turned out to be disastrous, and he was unable to service the mortgage repayments. The company sought possession and Mrs Pitt argued that the mortgage was void as against her because her signature to it had been secured by the use of undue influence, and that the bank had neither explained the mortgage to her, nor urged her to seek independent legal advice prior to signing it.

Notice

The House of Lords accepted that undue influence had been used but, nevertheless, upheld the validity of the mortgage. The reason for this was that there was nothing in the transaction, as it was presented to the lender, to alert it to the fact that this was not a loan for the mutual benefit of the husband and wife. As this appeared to be a perfectly normal joint venture, the mortgagee did not have constructive notice of the presence of a vitiating factor. That notice was a critical factor was stressed by Lord Browne-Wilkinson, who said:

'Even though, in my view, Mrs Pitt is entitled to set aside the transaction as against Mr Pitt, she has to establish that in some way the plaintiff is affected by the wrongdoing of Mr Pitt so as to be entitled to set aside the legal charge as against the plaintiff.'[141]

This point about notice had been stressed also in *O'Brien*. There Lord Browne-Wilkinson said:

'A wife who has been influenced to stand surety for her husband's debts by his undue influence, misrepresentation or other legal wrong has an equity as against him to set aside that transaction. Under the ordinary principles of equity, her right to set aside that transaction will be enforceable against third parties (e.g. against a creditor) if either the husband was acting as the third party's agent or the third party had actual notice of the facts giving rise to her equity.'[142]

Notice clearly was a key issue and the mortgagee in *O'Brien* was held to have notice of the vitiating factor while in *Pitt*, it did not. The circumstances when a lender would be fixed with constructive notice were stated in *O'Brien* as follows:

'a creditor is put on inquiry when a wife offers to stand surety for her husband's debts by the combination of two factors: (a) the transaction is on its face not to the financial advantage of the wife; and (b) there is a substantial risk in transactions of this kind that, in procuring the wife to act as surety, the husband committed a legal or equitable wrong that entitles the wife to set aside the transaction.'[143]

The difference between the two cases was that, in *O'Brien*, the purpose of the loan was to provide finance for a company with which her husband was involved, whereas in *Pitt*, the stated purpose appeared to be for their mutual benefit. In the former case,

---

[141] Ibid., at 210.   [142] *Barclays Bank plc v. O'Brien* [1994] 1 A.C. 180 at 195.
[143] [1994] 1 A.C. 180 at 196.

the bank was put on notice that undue influence may have been exercised, and so if a mortgage granted to Mrs O'Brien was to be valid, it was necessary for the bank to take certain precautions to ensure, so far as possible, that this had not occurred.[144] As there was nothing on the facts, as presented to the company in *Pitt*, to alert it to the possibility that undue influence might have been exerted, there was no need for it to take any special precautions before accepting Mrs Pitt's signature to the mortgage.

The impact of O'Brien

Various related themes emerged from *O'Brien*, all of which occasioned subsequent difficulty,[145] both conceptually and practically. Central to the decision is that it is not on every occasion when a family home is used as the security for a loan that the mortgage is liable to be set aside on the ground of undue influence.[146] For the mortgage to be open to attack, it was necessary for the lender to be put on notice of the possible existence of a vitiating factor, and the source of notice was the ostensible reason given for the loan. If this was not on its face to the financial advantage of the wife, this would apparently establish both the Class 2(B) relationship and also serve to put the lender on notice of the possibility of there being a vitiating factor.

On a conceptual level, it is quite clear that Lord Browne-Wilkinson saw the resolution of disputes of this nature as being dependent upon the application of orthodox principles of Property Law. To him, the question was whether a mortgagee was to be regarded as having notice of a wife's equity to set aside a transaction as against her husband. This reasoning is, however, flawed, and is based upon a false analysis of the nature of the transaction. Inherent in the reasoning is that there are two transactions. The first is between the husband and the wife where, because of the surrounding circumstances, she has, as against him, an equity to set aside. There then follows the mortgage between the husband and wife on the one hand and the mortgagee on the other. The issue then, according to the House of Lords, is whether the mortgagee has notice, actual or constructive, of her equity.[147] If it does, the mortgage will be void as against her.

A principal difficulty of this analysis is that in cases such as *O'Brien* and *Pitt*, it is simply not true to say that there are two transactions. There is but one, which is the mortgage which the couple created. Consequently, there is no prior equity of which the bank can be affected. Any equity to set the mortgage aside arises because the mortgagee is regarded as being privy to the impropriety of the husband.[148] The reasoning in *O'Brien* obscured this fact, and it soon became clear that the notice in

[144] For the nature of these precautions, see Precautions, pp. 506–510.
[145] See B. Fehlberg (1996) 59 M.L.R. 675; M. Oldham (1995) 7 C.F.L.Q. 104.
[146] For an argument in favour of such a position, see Fehlberg, loc. cit., at 682.
[147] For a debate as to the proper role of notice, see M.P. Thompson [1994] Conv. 140; C. Harpum and M. Dixon [1994] Conv. 421; P. Sparkes [1995] Conv. 250; G. Battersby (1995) 15 L.S. 315. It has become apparent that, although the words actually used by Lord Browne-Wilkinson support the view taken by Thompson and Sparkes, the correct analysis is that by Harpum and Dixon.
[148] See Harpum and Dixon, loc. cit., at 423.

this context was not being used in the sense in which this concept is ordinarily used in Land Law.[149]

The nature of the transaction

A vital element in the analysis in *O'Brien* is that the mortgagee is put on notice of the potential for undue influence to have been exerted. In Class 2(A) transactions, the presumption of undue influence arises automatically because of the nature of the relationship. In terms of the *O'Brien* analysis, if the mortgagee has notice of the particular relationship, he should be regarded as having notice of the presumed undue influence. So if a bank is approached by a solicitor and his client to borrow money secured by a mortgage against the client's house alone, then it would be regarded as having notice of the undue influence, regardless of what the purpose of the loan is said to be. In the case of Class 2(B), however, the relationship between the parties does not, of itself, give rise to any presumption of undue influence. Ordinarily the bank will not know what the actual relationship between the parties is between the couple seeking the loan: the bank official will not know whether she reposes trust and confidence in him. For the mortgagee to be affected with notice, it is the nature of the transaction which puts him on notice. So, in Class 2(A) cases, one is put on notice of undue influence affecting the transaction by the nature of the relationship; in Class 2(B) cases, it is the nature of the transaction which gives notice of a particularly close relationship from which the presumption of undue influence arises.

Leaving this aside, it is clear that it is not every transaction which will alert the mortgagee to the possibility that undue influence might be exerted and the consequent need to take precautions. The transaction must, on its face, not be to the financial advantage to the wife.[150] This has proved to be a difficult test to apply. This has particularly been the case when the purpose of the loan is to secure the debts of one of the parties to the mortgage or to provide finance for a business venture. The particular difficulty is that the loan may appear to benefit both parties, who may each benefit if the business is successful.[151] This led the courts subsequently to consider the degree of involvement of the complainant in the business; the greater the involvement in the business, the more unlikely the transaction would be seen as not, on its face to the financial advantage to the wife,[152] and *vice versa*.[153] Paradoxically, the less obvious it was from the outset that the relationship between the parties was one of trust, such as where they were respectively employer and employee, the court may be more willing

---

[149] See *Barclays Bank plc v. Boulter* [1999] 4 All E.R. 513 at 518 *per* Lord Hoffmann; M.P. Thompson [2000] Conv. 43 at 47–48.

[150] This requirement meant that the debate as to whether the transaction must also be manifestly disadvantageous to the claimant became somewhat arid: see M.P. Thompson [2000] Conv. 444.

[151] See Anthony Mann Q.C. speaking to the Chancery Bar Association, comments reported at [1994] Conv. 339.

[152] *Britannia Building Society v. Pugh* [1997] 2 F.L.R. 551; *Bank of Scotland v. Bennett* [1999] 1 F.L.R. 1115.

[153] *Goode Durrant Administration v. Biddulph* [1994] 1 F.L.R. 551; *Northern Rock Building Society v. Archer* (1998) 78 P. & C.R. 65.

to find the existence of the requisite relationship because, unless such a relationship exists, it is difficult to see why else the employee would agree to act as a guarantor of her employer's debts.[154]

All moneys clauses

One particular factor was likely to cause a court to consider that a transaction had been entered into as a result of undue influence. This was where the mortgage contains an 'all moneys' clause. The effect of such a clause is that the mortgage will secure unlimited borrowing by one of the parties and is not to secure an initially agreed sum. Such a clause is now contrary to the voluntary Code of Banking Practice,[155] and its effect is that it enables the husband, 'without recourse to the wife, to subject the house to much greater financial risks than she could ever have known'.[156] Such clauses should always be regarded as alerting the mortgagee to the possibility of undue influence.

The decisions in *O'Brien* and *Pitt* represented attempts by the House of Lords to strike a balance between the ability of commercial lenders to be able, safely, to lend money against the security of the family home, confident in the knowledge that, in the event of non-payment, they will be able to enforce their mortgages, while at the same time seeking to prevent one co-owner from exploiting the other. To achieve this balance, recourse was had to the law relating to undue influence and the doctrine of notice. If the bank was alerted to the fact that undue influence may have been exerted, then the courts laid down guidelines as to what precautions lenders must take to avoid these mortgages, subsequently being held to be void as against one of the co-owners. Unfortunately, the manner in which this was done led to considerable conceptual and practical difficulties. The appeals in *Royal Bank of Scotland v. Etridge (No. 2)*[157] gave the House of Lords another opportunity to consider both the appropriate principles to be applied to this area and also to consider the practical issues facing lenders and legal advisers.

Recasting the law

The decision in *Royal Bank of Scotland v. Etridge (No. 2)* involved eight conjoined appeals. In seven of them, wives who, along with their husbands, had been a party to a mortgage, argued that the mortgage should be held to be void as against them on the basis of undue influence. In the eighth, a wife was suing her solicitor in negligence, in respect of advice given to her before she signed the mortgage. In each case, the purpose of the mortgage was principally for the benefit of the husband. The stage was set for a major review of this area of law,[158] and, although a number of speeches were given, the

---

[154] *Credit Lyonnais Bank Nederland N.V. v. Burch* [1997] 1 All E.R. 144.

[155] See *Royal Bank of Scotland v. Etridge (No. 2)* [1998] 4 All E.R. 705 at 716 *per* Stuart-Smith L.J.

[156] *Barclays Bank plc v. Coleman* [2000] 1 All E.R. 385 at 401 *per* Nourse L.J.

[157] [2001] 4 All E.R. 449.

[158] Unsurprisingly, the decision has already generated considerable academic comment: see, e.g. R. Bigwood (2002) 65 M.L.R. 435; M. Haley (2002) 14 C.F.L.Q. 93, and (2010) 61 N.I.L.Q. 141; M. Oldham [2002] C.L.J. 29; M.P. Thompson [2002] Conv. 174 and in Cooke (ed) *Modern Studies in Property Law* (Volume 2) (Oxford: Hart Publishing, 2003) Chapter 7; P. Watts (2002) 118 L.Q.R. 337.

leading speech was that of Lord Nicholls of Birkenhead, it being made clear by Lord Bingham of Cornhill that, whatever differences in nuance there might be between the various speeches, 'it is plain that the opinion of Lord Nicholls commands the unqualified support of the House'.[159]

Policy issues

The competing policy issues underlying this area of law were clearly articulated by Lord Nicholls. He pointed out that bank finance is the most important form of external finance for small businesses with less than ten employees. These businesses make up about 95 per cent of businesses in this country and are responsible for nearly one-third of all employment. Finance raised by second mortgages on homes is an important source of capital for these businesses. It is important, therefore, that:

'If the freedom of home-owners to make economic use of their homes is not to be frustrated, a bank must be able to have confidence that a wife's signature of the necessary guarantee and charge will be as binding upon her as is the signature of anyone else on documents which he or she may sign. Otherwise banks will not be willing to lend money on the security of a jointly owned house or flat.'[160]

As against this, it was recognized that the marriage relationship is normally characterized by a high degree of trust and confidence and that there is scope for that trust and confidence to be abused. In particular, a husband, anxious, or even desperate, for finance may misstate the financial position or mislead his wife and it was considered that the 'law would be seriously defective if it did not recognise these realities'.[161] The task, therefore, as had been the case in *O'Brien*, was to strike a balance between the desire to protect potentially vulnerable parties in respect of financial transactions affecting their homes while, at the same time, not making the degree of protection such that financial institutions were no longer prepared to advance finance against the security of a family home. As Lord Bingham put it:

'The law must afford both parties a measure of protection. It cannot prescribe a code which will be proof against error, misunderstanding or mishap. But it can indicate minimum standards which, if met, will reduce the risk of error, misunderstanding or mishap to an acceptable level. The paramount need in this important area is that these minimum requirements should be clear, simple and practically operable.'[162]

Undue influence and notice

The combined effect of *O'Brien* and *Pitt* was to identify situations where, on a mortgage of a jointly owned home, the circumstances were such that the mortgagee should be regarded as having notice that the signature of one of the co-owners to the mortgage may have been obtained as a result of undue influence or some other vitiating factor. If the lender was put on notice, then it was required to take certain precautions

---

[159] [2001] 4 All E.R. 449 at [3] *per* Lord Bingham of Cornhill.
[160] Ibid., at [36] *per* Lord Nicholls of Birkenhead.   [161] Ibid.   [162] [2001] 4 All E.R. 449 at [2].

if the mortgage was not, subsequently, to be set aside as against the complainant. The basis of doing this was if the mortgagee was on notice that the relationship fell within Class 2(B). The mortgagee had notice of this if the transaction was not, on its face, to the financial advantage of the complainant.

This classification of undue influence was considered to be unhelpful by the House of Lords in *Etridge*. For Lord Clyde, the various classifications added mystery rather than illumination; Lord Hobhouse of Woodborough considered it not to be a useful forensic tool and Lord Scott of Foscote thought the adoption of this classification had set the law on the wrong track.[163]

Establishment of a vitiating factor

Lord Nicholls analysed the doctrine of undue influence at some length. The normal scenario is that after a transaction is entered into between two parties, one of them, the complainant, seeks to have it set aside on the basis of undue influence exerted by the wrongdoer. The onus of proof, normally, is then on the complainant to establish that undue influence occurred. Proof that there was a relationship of trust between the two[164] and that the transaction is such that it calls for an explanation is normally sufficient to discharge the onus of proof, so that the onus then shifts to the alleged wrongdoer to show that undue influence has not taken place.[165] In the case of certain relationships, however, which, it was accepted does not extend to husband and wife, the courts are prepared to assume that, because of the position in which one party stood to the other, undue influence was exerted to bring about the transaction.[166] In these cases, which fall into Class 2(A), it is the relationship itself that gives rise to the presumption of undue influence. To then ascertain whether the transaction calls for an explanation is problematic.

In cases such as *O'Brien*, instead of starting with a position of the establishment of a relationship of trust and confidence, and then a transaction between the two which calls for an explanation, one was starting from the other end. As Lord Nicholls observed, this has involved judge after judge grappling with the baffling question as to whether a wife's guarantee of her husband's overdraft was a transaction manifestly to her disadvantage.[167] In many cases where a wife is prepared to do this, there may be good and sufficient reasons as to why she should have agreed so to do. She may be an enthusiastic participant in the business venture; alternatively she may not be. The fact that she has agreed to act as a guarantor for her husband did not necessarily call for an explanation.

---

163   Ibid., at [92], [107], and [158] respectively.
164   The relationship of trust and confidence is not limited to trust and confidence in financial affairs: see *Thompson v. Foy* [2009] EWHC 1076 (Ch.) at [100] *per* Lewison J.
165   *Royal Bank of Scotland (No. 2) v. Etridge* [2001] 4 All E.R. 449 at [459]. See also *Turkey v Awadh* [2005] EWCA Civ. 382 at [38]–[39] *per* Chadwick L.J.
166   See, generally, *Allcard v. Skinner* (1887) 36 Ch.D. 145 at 181 *per* Lindley L.J. (Mother Superior and novitiate).
167   [2001] 4 All E.R. 449 at [27].

A further problem with the reasoning in *O'Brien* lay in the fact that it had been accepted that relationships other than those between married couples could involve trust and confidence, and that trust and confidence could be abused. It was not considered to be possible to compile a finite list of the types of relationships where one party reposed trust and confidence in the other. Lord Nicholls thought that there was 'no rational cut-off point, with certain types of relationship being subject to the *O'Brien* principle and others not'.[168] Accordingly the analysis based on there being a Class 2(B) category of presumed undue influence was abandoned. The person seeking to have the mortgage set aside must establish the existence of some vitiating factor.[169]

Although the most common vitiating factors will be undue influence or misrepresentation, a transaction may be called into question on other grounds. In *Hewett v. First Plus Financial Group Plc*,[170] a husband persuaded his reluctant wife to sign a mortgage deed, the purpose of which was to secure his credit card debts. When doing so, he did not reveal to her that he was, at the time, having an affair, the non-disclosure of which was held to be a significant breach of trust and confidence. The result was that the mortgage was set aside as against her, the bank admitting that it had failed to take adequate precautions to see that she had been property advised prior to entering into the transaction.[171]

What must be made clear, however, is that the person seeking to set aside the transaction has been the victim of some wrongdoing. First, it can be established that undue influence has been used. If this is done, it is not necessary to argue that the nature of the relationship and the type of transaction gives rise to any presumption of a wrong having been committed.[172] To establish this as a fact, it is not enough to show simply that the parties were under external financial pressure, as this will commonly be the case in situations such as this. Some misconduct must be shown.[173] If the purpose of the mortgage is to finance the other co-owner's business, an over-optimistic assessment of that business's prospects,[174] or an underestimate of the amounts needed to be invested,[175] will not amount to a sufficient wrong to cause the transaction to be set aside. Neither will a promise honestly made at the time of the transaction, but subsequently reneged upon, have that effect.[176] Where the presence of a vitiating factor cannot be established by direct evidence, and it is necessary to rely on a presumption arising from the nature of the relationship and the transaction in question, this presumption is rebuttable. Should the evidence rebut

---

[168] Ibid., at [87].

[169] Ibid., at [87] *per* Lord Nicholls of Birkenhead; at [93] *per* Lord Clyde; at [146] *per* Lord Hobhouse of Woodborough; at [146] *per* Lord Scott of Foscote. See also *Habib Bank Ltd v. Tufail* [2006] EWCA Civ. 374 at [21] *per* Lloyd L.J.

[170] [2010] EWCA Civ. 312.   [171] For the nature of these precautions, see Precautions, pp. 506–510.

[172] See *Annulment Funding Co. Ltd v. Cowey* [2010] EWCA Civ. 711.

[173] Ibid., at [60] *per* Morgan J.

[174] *Royal Bank of Scotland v. Etridge (No.2)* [2001] 4 All E.R. 449 at [33] *per* Lord Nicholls of Birkenhead.

[175] *Royal Bank of Scotland Plc v. Chandra* [2011] EWCA Civ. 192.

[176] *Thompson v. Foy* [2009] EWHC 1076 (Ch.) at [112] *per* Lewison J.

any such presumption, then the argument that the transaction should be set aside will, of course, fail.[177]

Notice

Central to Lord Browne-Wilkinson's analysis in *O'Brien* was that a mortgage would be set aside as against the complainant, if the mortgagee had notice of her equity to set the transaction aside as against the complainant. He then explained what steps a mortgagee should take to avoid being fixed with constructive notice of that equity. As has already been pointed out, however, this is a strange use of the doctrine of notice, in that, prior to the creation of the mortgage, there is no transaction to set aside, and so notice is not being used in its conventional sense.[178] This was accepted by Lord Nicholls, who also made the point that the precautions that a mortgagee should take were not, as Lord Browne-Wilkinson had suggested, to prevent the mortgagee being fixed with notice of a pre-existing wrong. They were designed to prevent the wrong occurring in the first place.[179] Consequently, references to the doctrine of notice were not seen as being helpful.

From property to contract

The underlying theoretical basis of *O'Brien*—that a mortgage would be set aside as against a complainant, if the mortgagee had notice of a trusting and confidential relationship, whereby the wrongdoer could exert undue influence—was effectively rejected in *Etridge*. The House of Lords was concerned, however, that the law should provide protection to a person who agrees to a mortgage in order to secure the debts of another or to allow that other person to raise capital for what seems to be his own purposes. To that end, it may be said that the underlying philosophy of *O'Brien* was retained, but it was given a different theoretical underpinning.

O'Brien proceeded on a property-based approach: the issue was regarded as being to determine in what circumstances a mortgagee should be considered to have notice of a prior equity to set aside a transaction. In *Etridge*, the House of Lords analysed the matter on the basis of the law of contract. In cases where the family home is mortgaged to provide finance for one of the parties, this is a tripartite contract between the lender, the borrower, and the guarantor. It is, so far as the guarantor is concerned, a one-sided contract, in that she generally derives no benefit from it. Accordingly, the view was taken that, as a matter of contract law, for the contract to be valid as between the lender and the guarantor, the lender is required to take certain steps to seek to ensure that that person is fully aware of the risks involved in entering the transaction and is properly, and independently, advised before she does so. Accordingly, the view which was adopted was that in *every* case where a wife is standing surety for her husband's

---

[177] See *Turkey v. Ahmad* [2005] EWCA Civ. 382.

[178] See The position of the mortgagee, pp. 496–500. For a surprising use of the traditional language of notice, see *UCB Corporate Services Ltd v. Williams* [2003] 1 P. & C.R. 12 at para. 100 *per* Jonathan Parker L.J.

[179] [2001] 4 All E.R. 449 at [41].

debts, the lender must take precautions designed, so far as possible, to ensure that she was not induced to enter into the contract as a consequence of undue influence or misrepresentation.[180]

This statement of the need for the mortgagee to take precautions is essentially to provide guidance for lending institutions. As was recognized in *Etridge*, the threshold as to when a bank is alerted of the need to take precautions is lower than that which is necessary for a presumption of undue influence to arise.[181] A situation may occur when a bank is put on notice of the need to take precautions and fails to do so. That alone, however, should not necessarily mean that the mortgage will be set aside. The bank may be lucky, and it may transpire that, on the facts, there was no vitiating factor present. A consideration of the issues which arose in *Annulment Funding Co. Ltd v. Cowey*[182] may illustrate this.

A cohabiting couple, Mr Cowey and Ms Cowlam, owned a house as tenants in common in equal shares, each share being worth £215,000, the equity in the house being double that sum. He was declared bankrupt, with debts in excess of £120,000. The effect of his bankruptcy was that his beneficial share in the house vested in the trustee in bankruptcy, and the normal situation would then be that he would seek a sale of the house and, in the absence of exceptional circumstances, such a sale would be ordered a year after the bankruptcy.[183] I Ltd, a mortgage broker, was approached. In return for a fee it introduced the couple to the claimant. It was prepared to lend £138,000 as a short-term loan to provide bridging finance. This would enable the bankruptcy to be annulled and, the plan was, to allow a longer term mortgage to be obtained. The money was advanced and a second charge on the house was executed. Subsequently, as a consequence of his credit rating and the changed financial climate, a long term mortgage was not available, and the claimant sought possession. This was resisted by Ms Cowlam who argued, successfully, that the mortgage should be set aside as against her.

The claimant conceded that it had not taken the precautions as laid down in *Etridge*. This, however, was not the end of the appeal. It was argued that there was no vitiating factor, and so the mortgage should stand. This failed on the facts. The trial judge had found that he had exercised undue influence on her: that he had caused her to follow him blindly into a transaction which was very much against her interests.[184] Moreover, it was found that Mr Cowley did not fully understand the nature of bridging finance, and so it followed that when he explained it to her he was misrepresenting the transaction. Either of these findings would, of course, have been fatal to the claimant's case. It is not difficult to envisage a situation where neither of these factors would have been present. Faced with the prospect of a forced sale at the behest of the trustee in bankruptcy, admittedly to pay off his debts, it is not difficult to see a person in Ms Cowlam's position freely agreeing to the course of action which was embarked upon. In such

---

[180] [2001] 4 All E.R. 449 at [44].   [181] Ibid.   [182] [2010] EWCA Civ. 711.

[183] Insolvency Act 1986, s. 335A; Trusts of Land and Appointment of Trustees Act 1996, s. 15(4). See Insolvency Act, pp. 392–396.

[184] [2010] EWCA Civ. 711 at [32] *per* Morgan J.

circumstances, despite the lender not taking the requisite precautions, the mortgage would have been valid. It is, of course, very foolish of a lender not to follow the guidance given by Lord Nicholls, thereby leaving itself open to the risk of being unable to realize its security.

Mutual transactions

The type of transaction with which the House of Lords was concerned was where the family home is mortgaged to provide security for the husband's debts, or to provide finance for his company. In all such cases, it is now incumbent on the banks to take precautions before the creation of the mortgage. These precautions, which will be considered shortly, involve the taking of legal advice. The House did not wish to impose these obligations in every case where a family home was being mortgaged. If, as was the case in *CIBC Mortgages plc v. Pitt*,[185] the purpose of the loan appeared to be for a mutual enterprise such as the purchase of a holiday home, or to finance an improvement to the house, it will not be necessary for any particular precautions to be taken before granting the mortgage.[186] If, however, the loan is to support a business activity then, regardless of whether the wife has any involvement in that business, precautions must be taken.[187]

Other relationships

In *O'Brien*, itself, it was recognized that relationships of trust and confidence could exist in relationships other than married couples. To establish that the case was a Class 2(B) instance of presumed undue influence, one had to have regard to the nature of the transaction to ascertain if it pointed to this type of relationship. With the abandonment of this classification of undue influence, the House in *Etridge* was able to put the law on a much simpler footing. In the case of all transactions which are not mutual in the sense described above, unless the relationship between the borrowers is a commercial one, the lenders, to ensure that the mortgage will not be susceptible to later challenge, must take precautions to ensure that the guarantor is properly advised before signing the mortgage.[188]

Precautions

The central problem in cases such as *O'Brien* and *Etridge* is that a home is mortgaged in circumstances where one of the parties to it may have been subjected to undue influence or misrepresentation by the person who is the principal beneficiary of the

---

[185] [1994] 1 A.C. 200. See also *Bank of Scotland v. Hussain* [2010] EWHC 2812 (Ch.), where a mortgagee providing finance to D2 to purchase a house had no reason to suspect that the transfer from D1 to D2 had been secured by undue influence exerted by D2 on D1, and the mortgage was, therefore, binding on D1 despite the transfer to D2 being set aside.

[186] See also *Chater v. Mortgage Agency Services Number Two Ltd* [2003] H.L.R. 61 at [67] *per* Scott-Baker L.J.

[187] [2001] 4 All E.R. 449 at [49]. Cf *Royal Bank of Scotland Plc v. Chandra* [2011] EWCA Civ. 192.

[188] [2001] 4 All E.R. 449 at [88].

loan. To avoid the complainant subsequently being able to challenge the validity of the mortgage, it became incumbent on the mortgagee to take certain precautions before the mortgage was created. The nature of these precautions has been the subject of much debate since the decision in *O'Brien*.

Obligations of the mortgagee

In *O'Brien*, Lord Browne-Wilkinson set out requirements to be followed by mortgagees who were put on notice that one of the mortgagors may be subject to undue influence. In his view,

'a creditor will meet these requirements if it insists that the wife attend a prior meeting (in the absence of the husband) with a representative of the creditor at which she is told the extent of her liability as a creditor, warned of the risk she is running and urged to take legal advice.'[189]

Following this decision came a veritable deluge of litigation principally concerned with whether the precautions taken by the bank had been adequate. Although this litigation was complicated by the fact that most of the transactions pre-dated *O'Brien* and Lord Browne-Wilkinson had stated that his guidelines were intended to apply to future transactions, it soon became clear that the courts were diluting those guidelines.[190] In particular, despite what had been said in *O'Brien*, in none of the subsequent litigation had an official of the bank conducted a private meeting with the wife. What became a central feature of the litigation was the independence of the legal advice and the quality of it.

Independent legal advice

In much of the post-*O'Brien* litigation, the issue concerned the precautions taken by the mortgagee and, in particular, the role of the solicitor who acted in the transaction. It soon came to be established that, provided that a solicitor was prepared to certificate that he had provided legal advice to the wife before she signed the mortgage, then, in virtually every case, the bank's interest would be protected. This was so, even if the solicitor was acting for the potential wrongdoer,[191] the company with which the wrongdoer was associated,[192] or even, so it seemed, for the mortgagee, itself.[193] The only exceptions to this appeared to be if the mortgagee was privy to information concerning the transaction which it does not communicate to the solicitor,[194] or the transaction is so manifestly disadvantageous that a solicitor

---

[189]   *Barclays Bank plc v. O'Brien* [1994] 1 A.C. 180 at 196.
[190]   See S. Wong [1998] Conv. 457 at 458. See also *Royal Bank of Scotland v. Etridge (No. 2)* [2001] 4 All E.R. 449 at [113] *per* Lord Hobhouse.
[191]   *Midland Bank plc v. Serter* [1995] 1 F.L.R. 1034.
[192]   *Banco Exterior International v. Mann* [1995] 1 All E.R. 936, criticized by A. Dunn [1995] Conv. 325 at 330–332.
[193]   *Halifax Building Society v. Stepsky* [1997] 1 All E.R. 46; *Barclays Bank plc v. Thomson* [1997] 4 All E.R. 816, criticized by M.P. Thompson [1997] Conv. 216.
[194]   *Northern Rock Building Society v. Archer* (1998) 78 P. & C.R. 65; M.P. Thompson [1999] Conv. 510.

should refuse to act for her if she insists on going ahead, although such a situation will obviously be rare.[195]

The Etridge guidelines

One effect of *Etridge* was to lower the threshold as to when a mortgagee must take precautions to ensure that the potential complainant is protected from the possibilities of undue influence or misrepresentation being exercised from that which had previously existed, in that it is no longer necessary to demonstrate that a particular transaction is not to her financial advantage. It will suffice simply to show a non-commercial relationship and that the transaction is not for a mutual purpose. The opportunity was also taken to review the precautions the bank must take when that threshold has been crossed.

Private meeting

It was accepted that, despite what had been said in *O'Brien*, banks did not have a private meeting with the wife prior to her signing the mortgage. Provided that the mortgagee 'has taken reasonable steps to satisfy itself that the wife has had brought home to her in a meaningful way, the practical implications of the proposed transaction',[196] it will be protected and it is not essential that the mortgagee conduct this private meeting.

Independence of advice

In the past, it was considered to be acceptable for the same solicitor to act for both parties to the transaction. Lord Nicholls could see arguments on both sides with regard to the acceptability of this. On one side, there is the potential for a conflict of interest, and his advice to her may be less robust than would be the case if he was not also acting for him. On the other is the issue of cost. Obviously, it would add to the expense of the transaction if, in every case, the bank, to protect its own interests, had to insist that a different solicitor represent the two parties. On balance, he felt that the latter point outweighed the former and he considered it to be acceptable for the same solicitor to act for both parties. He stressed, however, that the solicitor must be clear that, when advising the wife, he is acting solely in her interests and that if he feels at any stage in that advice that there is a conflict of interest he must cease to act for her.[197]

Provision of information

Lord Nicholls was aware that, although a certificate from a solicitor that he had advised the wife was sufficient to protect the mortgagee, on many occasions the advice which had been given was of poor quality and amounted to what Sir Anthony

[195] See *Credit Lyonnais Nederland N.V. v. Burch* [1997] 1 All E.R. 144.
[196] *Royal Bank of Scotland v. Etridge (No. 2)* [2001] 4 All E.R. 449 at 467 *per* Lord Nicholls.
[197] Ibid., at [74]. See also at [96] *per* Lord Clyde.

Mason had described as the 'ritual reliance on the provision of legal advice'.[198] In an effort to make this advice more useful, he laid down a practice which the lending institutions should follow to protect their position. In so doing, he made it clear that these guidelines were to operate prospectively.[199] 'In respect of past transactions, the bank will ordinarily be regarded as having discharged its obligations if a solicitor who was acting for the wife in the transaction gave the bank confirmation to the effect that he had brought home to the wife the risks she was running by standing surety.'[200]

When security is being sought from a wife in respect of her husband's debts, the bank should communicate directly with her. In that communication, the mortgagee should made clear that it will require written confirmation from a solicitor, acting for her, that the transaction, its effects and practical implications have been explained to her and that the effect of this confirmation will be that she will not be able, subsequently, to dispute the validity of the mortgage. She will be asked to nominate her solicitor, and that solicitor may be the same person who is acting for her husband. Until an appropriate response is received from her, the mortgagee should not go ahead with the transaction. This procedure would preclude the mortgagee from using its own legal department to advise the wife, and it is also inadequate for a bank to instruct a solicitor to attend to the formalities of the transaction on its behalf. The solicitor will then be seen as the agent of the bank and any deficiencies in the advice given will be attributed to the mortgagee.[201]

The duties of the mortgagee do not stop there. Once a solicitor has been nominated, the bank must furnish him with sufficient information for him to be in a position to advise her fully. To this end, the bank must supply the solicitor with financial information concerning the husband and a copy of the mortgage application. This information is, as between the bank and the husband, confidential and the bank cannot release it without his consent. If that consent is not forthcoming, however, then the mortgagee should not proceed further with the proposed transaction.[202]

These precautions are designed to strike an acceptable balance between the interests of the mortgagee and the wife and would seem so to do. They are to be applied in normal cases of mortgage applications. Where the potential complainant is, to the knowledge of the bank, particularly vulnerable, however, this should be made

---

[198] Cited by Sir Peter Millett (1998) 114 L.Q.R. 214 at 220.

[199] It is unusual for judgments to operate in this way. The normal position is that they state what the law has always been. For a striking example, see *Kleinwort Benson Ltd v. Lincoln City Council* [1999] 2 A.C. 349. See M.P. Thompson [1999] Conv. 40. For a full discussion of prospective decisions, see *In re Spectrum Plus Ltd (in liquidation)* [2005] 2 A.C. 680.

[200] [2001] 4 All E.R. 449 at 474. See also *Bank of Scotland v. Hill* [2002] EWCA Civ. 1081; *First National Bank plc v. Achampong* [2003] EWCA Civ. 487. See M.P. Thompson [2003] Conv. 314.

[201] *National Westminster Bank plc v. Amin* [2002] 1 F.L.R. 735 at 741–742 *per* Lord Scott of Foscote. See M. Haley [2002] Conv. 499.

[202] [2001] 4 All E.R. 449 at [79].

known to the solicitor acting for her, so that additional care may be taken in advising her.[203]

The role of the solicitor

Provided that the mortgagee follows the guidelines laid down by Lord Nicholls, and receives a certificate from the solicitor to the effect that the wife has been fully advised, the complainant will not be able to argue that the mortgage is liable to be set aside. It may, however, be the case that there is a cause of action against the solicitor if, contrary to the certificate, this is not actually the case. Guidance was given by Lord Nicholls as to what the role of the solicitor is. He should see her separately from her husband and explain the transaction to her in non-technical language. He should explain the consequences which will follow if the mortgage payments are not met. He should also explore with her the financial position of her husband and the amount being borrowed and, above all, make it clear to her that she has a choice as to whether to proceed with the transaction. She should be asked if she is happy for the solicitor to confirm to the mortgagee that she has been fully advised and wishes to proceed, or whether she wishes the solicitor to negotiate on her behalf with the mortgagee. If she is, then the solicitor can go ahead and give the requisite confirmation to the bank.[204]

The effect of a vitiating factor

An important issue, particularly when the vitiating factor is misrepresentation rather than undue influence, is whether the effect of the misrepresentation is that the mortgage can be avoided entirely by the misrepresentee, or whether it will be upheld up to the limit of that person's understanding of the transaction. The point is now settled that the mortgage will be regarded as voidable.[205] In *TSB Bank plc v. Camfield*,[206] the husband's company needed an overdraft of £30,000. This was agreed to, provided that security was given for the loan. Mrs Camfield, as a result of an innocent misrepresentation made to her by her husband, thought that, if she signed the mortgage, her personal liability under it would be limited to £15,000, whereas, in fact, her liability was unlimited. It having been accepted by the bank that it had constructive notice of the misrepresentation,[207] it was argued that the mortgage should be enforceable against her to the extent of her understanding of the transaction: that is a liability of £15,000. This was rejected by the Court of Appeal,[208] who held that the effect of the misrepresentation was, as against her, to render the mortgage void.

---

[203] See *National Westminster Bank plc v. Amin* [2002] 1 F.L.R. 735. Here, the parents of the mortgagor spoke no English. This is not a very good example, however, as surely this fact would have been obvious to the solicitor.

[204] [2001] 4 All E.R. 449 at 470.

[205] *Bank Melli Iran v. Samadi-Rad* [1995] 2 F.L.R. 367. If the mortgage is tainted by a vitiating factor, a second mortgage to redeem the first is also tainted: see *Yorkshire Bank plc v. Tinsley* [2004] 3 All E.R. 463; M.P. Thompson [2004] Conv. 399.

[206] [1995] 1 W.L.R. 430. See A. Dunn [1995] Conv. 325; P. Ferguson (1995) 111 L.Q.R. 555.

[207] On the facts, this concession was almost certainly made wrongly.

[208] Applying *Allied Irish Bank plc v. Byrne* [1995] 2 F.L.R 325.

THE RIGHTS AND REMEDIES OF THE MORTGAGEE

The previous section considered the obstacles that a mortgagee may encounter when seeking to realize his security; the obstacles being the rights of persons other than the borrower. This section is concerned with the actions available to the mortgagee to recover the money owed to him. These actions can be divided into personal actions and proprietary actions; the former being the rights that the mortgagee has, personally, against the mortgagor, and the latter, which is the more important, concerns the rights and remedies exercisable against the mortgaged property.

The covenant to repay

A mortgage is granted to secure a loan. One option for a mortgagee is, simply, to sue the mortgagor, personally, for repayment of that loan. Ordinarily, the mortgagee does not do this, it being preferable to utilize his more favourable position as a secured creditor. There are two situations, however, where the mortgagee may wish to pursue his personal remedy against the mortgagor either in conjunction with his rights as a secured creditor or as an alternative to such rights.

Cumulative remedies

The remedies of a mortgagee have always been regarded as being cumulative; that is, subject to the nature of the remedy which has been pursued, the mortgagee may avail himself of more than one remedy in order to secure the repayment of what is owed. So, if the mortgagee has secured a sale of the property and the proceeds of sale are insufficient to discharge the debt, the mortgagee can pursue a personal remedy against the mortgagor in respect of the balance.[209] In cases of negative equity, this is an additional option available to mortgagees if a sale of the property has failed to realize sufficient money to repay in full all that is owed.

The second situation where the availability of a personal action against the mortgagor will potentially be of value to the mortgagee is where he is unable to pursue his rights as a secured creditor. This will be because a third party has rights in the property with priority to his, an example of such a situation occurring in *Williams and Glyn's Bank Ltd v. Boland*.[210] In that case, the bank was unable to obtain possession of the property because it was established that it was bound by an overriding interest. The remedy open to the bank in this situation would seem to have been to have sued Mr Boland on his personal covenant to repay the loan. If, as is probable, he would be unable to pay this sum, then a petition for bankruptcy could be lodged and, if granted, upon the adjudication of bankruptcy, the trustee in bankruptcy would

---

[209] *Rudge v. Richards* (1873) L.R. 8 C.P. 358; *Palk v. Mortgage Services Funding plc* [1993] Ch. 330 at 337 *per* Sir Donald Nicholls V.-C.
[210] [1981] A.C. 487.

then petition the court for a sale of the property. Unless there were exceptional circumstances, this petition would almost certainly be granted a year after the date of the bankruptcy.[211] While it is true that the wife would be entitled, first, to her share of the proceeds of sale, the bank would still be able to recover a significant amount of that which was owed.

Such an action was brought by a mortgagee in *Alliance & Leicester plc v. Slayford*.[212] The mortgagee had failed in action for possession, because an *O'Brien* defence raised by Mrs Slayford had been successful. A money judgment was then sought against Mr Slayford, the object of which was that, if he could not meet it, he would be declared bankrupt and the trustee in bankruptcy would petition for a sale. The argument which had been successful at the county court, that this was an abuse of the process of the court,[213] was rejected. The view of the Court of Appeal was that the personal action for the money owed was a quite separate action from the previous action for possession, and that it would also be absurd if a secured creditor should be in a worse position that an unsecured one.[214] The money judgment was therefore awarded, a further argument that this contravened the right to a fair trial within a reasonable period of time as provided by Article 6 of the European Convention on Human Rights was also rejected.

Possession

The most usual way in which a mortgagee will enforce his security is by procuring a sale of the property. Prior to doing so, however, it will almost invariably be the case that possession will be obtained. It will be difficult, otherwise, to sell the property if it remains occupied by the mortgagor. The normal prelude to a sale of the property is an action for possession brought by the mortgagee.

The right to possession

Although it is easy to see the taking of possession by the mortgagee as a remedy available to him as a secured creditor, juridically, this is not correct. It is a right and not a remedy. This was put in stark terms by Harman J. who said, in an oft-quoted passage:

'…the right of a mortgagee to possession in the absence of some contract has nothing to do with default on the part of the mortgagor. The mortgagee may go into possession before the ink is dry on the mortgage unless there is something in the mortgage, express or by implication, whereby he has contracted out of that right.'[215]

---

[211] See Bankruptcy, pp. 392–396.
[212] [2001] 1 All E.R. (Comm.) 1. See M.P. Thompson [2002] Conv. 53. See also *First National Bank plc v. Achampong* [2003] EWCA Civ. 487.
[213] See *Henderson v. Henderson* (1843) 3 Hare 100.
[214] See *Cheltenham & Gloucester Building Society v. Grattidge* (1993) 25 H.L.R. 454 at 457 *per* Hoffmann L.J.
[215] *Four-Maids Ltd v. Dudley Marshall (Properties) Ltd* [1957] Ch. 317 at 320. See, generally, M. Haley (1997) 17 L.S. 483.

At one time, the courts sought to modify this position by invoking an inherent jurisdiction to adjourn possession proceedings so that, 'in proper cases the wind was tempered for the shorn lamb, time being given for payment and so forth'.[216] This claimed jurisdiction did not, however, command general assent. The traditional perspective that the possession was a right and not a remedy was considered to be too well-established to be overturned and it became clear that the only jurisdiction to postpone possession was to allow the mortgagor a relatively short period of time in which to redeem the mortgage in full.[217]

Although the mortgagee was entitled as of right to possession of the mortgaged property, irrespective of whether or not the mortgagor was in default on the mortgage, in practice, possession would only be sought if there was default. The position of a mortgagor could then be seen to be less favourable than that of a tenant who was in arrears with the rent. In such a case, if the landlord sought to forfeit the lease, the tenant had considerable scope on paying off the arrears to obtain relief against forfeiture.[218] There was no such jurisdiction in the case of mortgage arrears. To rectify this anomaly, the Payne Committee[219] recommended legislation to give a court discretion to suspend or postpone possession proceedings if there appeared to be a realistic chance of the mortgagor being able, within a reasonable period of time, to pay off the arrears while continuing to service the mortgage payments or, in other words, to allow a financially embarrassed mortgagor some breathing space in order to get his financial affairs back onto an even keel. Unfortunately, as it has been graphically put, 'however clear the goal of this promised land, the meanderings of the law towards it have made the wanderings of the children of Israel in the wilderness look almost direct'.[220]

The Administration of Justice Acts[221]

Under section 36 of the Administration of Justice Act 1970, where a mortgagee under a mortgage of land, which consists of or includes a dwelling-house,[222] brings an action for possession, the court is given the power to adjourn the proceedings or, on making an order for possession, stay or suspend execution of the order or postpone the date for delivery of possession for such period or periods as the court thinks reasonable. These powers may be exercised if it appears to the court that the mortgagor is likely to be able, within a reasonable period of time, to pay any sums due under the mortgage or to remedy a default[223] consisting of any breach of any other obligation arising under or

[216] *Redditch Benefit Building Society v. Roberts* [1940] Ch. 415 at 420 *per* Clauson L.J.
[217] *Birmingham Citizens Permanent Building Society v. Caunt* [1962] Ch. 863. See R.E.M. (1962) 78 L.Q.R. 171.
[218] See Non-payment of rent, pp. 455–456.
[219] Enforcement of Judgment Debts (1969), Cmnd. 3909.   [220] See S. Tromans [1984] Conv. 91.
[221] See M. Haley (1997) 17 L.S. 483; M. Dixon (1998) 18 L.S. 279.
[222] The date to determine whether the property consists of a dwelling-house is the date of the hearing: *Royal Bank of Scotland v. Miller* [2002] Q.B. 225.
[223] It has since been held that the court has jurisdiction under the Act even if the mortgagor is not in default: *Western Bank Ltd v. Schindler* [1977] Ch. 1.

by virtue of the mortgage. Although it has been argued that this statutory discretion to postpone the making of an order for possession means that it is no longer true to describe the taking of possession as being a right as opposed to a remedy,[224] this argument has been rejected.[225] This result seemed inevitable, however, as the property had been sold after peaceful possession had been taken, and so no mortgage was in existence, and the possession action was not being brought by a mortgagee, so it is difficult to see how the Act could apply.[226]

Default clauses

Although the aim of the Act was tolerably clear—to allow a mortgagor who had got into arrears with his mortgage repayments a reasonable time in which to clear those arrears—one potential problem had not been foreseen. This problem involved clauses in mortgages, known as default clauses, whereby, if the mortgagor defaulted on his repayments, the whole capital sum would become payable forthwith. Such clauses, not unlike some others contained in mortgages, are not, normally, intended to be taken literally, but are inserted to ensure that the mortgagee's statutory power to sell the property arises.[227] Nevertheless, in *Halifax Building Society v. Clark*,[228] such a clause was interpreted so as to deprive a mortgagor of the protection which the Act was intended to give.

In this case, under the terms of the mortgage, if the mortgagor defaulted on the payment of two mortgage instalments, the whole sum borrowed became payable immediately. The effect of this was that, although the arrears under the mortgage amounted to some £72.97, the effect of the default clause was that the amount owing under the mortgage was £1,420.58. The issue to be decided was whether, for the purposes of the Act, the sum due under the mortgage was the actual arrears, or the whole sum which had been borrowed. It was held that the latter amount was the one to which regard should be had and, as there was no prospect of this sum being paid in what the judge considered to be a reasonable period,[229] there was no jurisdiction to postpone possession.

This approach, which stultified the purpose of the Act,[230] led directly to the passing of the obscurely drafted section 8 of the Administration of Justice Act 1973. Section 8(1) provides that:

'Where...the mortgagor is entitled or is to be permitted to pay the principal sum secured by instalments or otherwise to defer payment of it in whole or in part, but provision is also made for earlier payment in the event of any default by the mortgagor or of a demand by

---

[224] See A. Clarke [1983] Conv. 293.

[225] *Ropaigelach v. Barclays Bank Plc* [1999] 4 All E.R. 235. See A. Dunn [1999] Conv. 263.

[226] See also *Horsham Properties Group Ltd v. Clark* [2009] 1 W.L.R. 1255.

[227] See Power arising, p. 524.   [228] [1973] 2 All E.R. 33.

[229] Even adopting this analysis, the result could have been avoided by taking a reasonable period to mean the anticipated length of the mortgage: see *First Middlesbrough Trading and Mortgage Co. Ltd v. Cunningham* (1974) 28 P. & C.R. 29.

[230] See H.L. Deb., vol. 338, col. 398 *per* Lord Hailsham L.C.

the mortgagee or otherwise, then, for the purposes of section 36 of the Administration Act 1970...a court may treat as due under the mortgage on account of the principal sum secured and of interest on it only such amounts as the mortgagor would have expected to be required to pay if there had been no such provision for earlier payment.'

Section 8(2) then goes on to make it clear that the court shall not exercise its powers under the 1970 Act unless, in addition to paying off, within a reasonable time, the arrears which have accumulated, the mortgagor is also able to meet the payments which he would ordinarily have expected to make under the mortgage. In other words, the payment schedule must be such as will meet the normal repayments had there been no default and such additional sum as is necessary to clear the arrears within a reasonable period.

Mortgages to which the Acts apply

Once again, while the aim of this provision is clear—that in assessing what sums are due under a mortgage, default clauses should be ignored—the wording is not. In particular, it is not clear what is meant by 'being permitted to defer payment'. In *Habib Bank Ltd v. Tailor*,[231] Mr Tailor had a bank overdraft secured by a mortgage against his house. It was a term of the mortgage that the overdraft was repayable on demand. When he exceeded the agreed overdraft limit, the bank called in the loan and sought possession under the mortgage. He argued that the loan was an indefinite loan and, so, the demand for payment in full by the bank operated in the same way as a default clause. The consequence of this, it was contended, was that the court should regard the case as being within section 8 of the Act, the result being that, in the exercise of its discretion, the court should allow him a reasonable period to pay off the sum by which his borrowing exceeded the agreed overdraft. This was rejected, the Court of Appeal being of the view that section 8 was not applicable to this type of loan. The phrase 'is to be permitted...otherwise to defer payment' must, it was held, refer to a date from which payment was to be deferred. This could mean either, as Mr Tailor contended, the date of the mortgage or, alternatively, the date upon which the mortgage envisaged repayment being made. It was held that the latter view was correct. As there was no provision for payment to be deferred after the bank had demanded repayment, section 8 was irrelevant and so the issue was whether he could repay the whole sum borrowed within a reasonable time, which he could not, and so possession was ordered.

Endowment mortgages

While the case is clearly correct on the facts, it occasioned concern, in that its effect might be that the section was inapplicable to endowment mortgages.[232] The reason for this concern was that, with endowment mortgages, the capital sum is not repayable until the end of the agreed mortgage term. There is no provision for the deferment of payment after that date. If, therefore, owing to some default on payments

---

[231] [1982] 1 W.L.R. 1218.
[232] For a valuable discussion of this issue, see S. Tromans [1984] Conv. 91.

of interest or on the endowment policy, the capital sum becomes payable at a date earlier than the end of the mortgage period, section 8 would not appear to be applicable, because the mortgage was not one where the mortgagor had been permitted to defer payment. This point was argued by the mortgagee in *Bank of Scotland v. Grimes*,[233] but rejected by the Court of Appeal. While accepting the result in *Habib Bank Ltd v. Tailor* as being correct, its reasoning was not applied in the instant case, which was regarded as being markedly different. As the court found itself unable to come to any conclusion as to the meaning of the words in the section referring to the deferment of payment,[234] it felt able to construe the section purposively. The view was taken that, as a matter of common sense, a mortgage which is not to be repaid for twenty-five years is one where the mortgagor is entitled to defer payment. If there was provision whereby the mortgagor could be required to pay the capital sum, in full, before that date, then section 8 applied and the court could exercise its discretion under section 36 of the Administration of Justice Act 1970. A distinction was drawn, therefore, between mortgages to be repaid, either by instalments or through an endowment policy, over a prolonged period, and mortgages where it is actually envisaged that the loan borrowed is, in reality, to be repayable on demand. In other words, the Administration of Justice Acts will apply to all mortgages commonly used to finance the purchase of a home.

Parties to the action

Under section 30(3) of the Family Law Act 1996, payment by a spouse of payments under a mortgage is to be regarded as being as good as payment by the other spouse. By virtue of the statutory right of occupation, therefore, the spouse without an interest in the dwelling-house is empowered to take over the mortgage payments. If the mortgagee seeks to enforce its security, the spouse is entitled to be made a party to the proceedings, if the court sees no special reason against it and the court is also satisfied the spouse could be expected to make such payments as would affect the outcome of such proceedings or that the expectation of it should be considered under section 36 of the Administration of Justice Act 1970.[235] A practical problem which arose was that the courts were of the view that the mortgagee was under no obligation to inform the spouse of the institution of proceedings and, so, by the time she discovered this, the arrears that had arisen may be such that she may not be in a financial position to exercise her rights.[236] This position has been alleviated to an extent by a requirement on the mortgagee to serve notice on the spouse of possession proceedings. That requirement, however, applies only if the spouse has protected her statutory right of occupation in the appropriate manner by registration.[237]

[233] [1985] Q.B. 1179.
[234] Ibid., at 1188 *per* Sir John Arnold P. See also *Royal Bank of Scotland v. Miller* [2002] Q.B. 225.
[235] Family Law Act 1996, s. 55. For the rights of connected persons, see ibid. and ss 33, 35.
[236] See *Hastings & Thanet Building Society v. Goddard* [1970] 1 W.L.R. 1544.
[237] Family Law Act 1996, s. 56(1)(2).

The exercise of discretion under the Act

How the court will exercise its discretion will, to a considerable extent, depend upon the facts of individual cases which may, themselves, be influenced by the different practices of lending institutions, who display quite varied reactions to instances of mortgage default in terms of how readily they will seek to enforce their rights as secured creditors. This variety of attitudes as to how to respond to mortgage default has been criticized,[238] although the position has been improved by the introduction of the Pre-Action Protocol for Possession Claims based on Mortgage or Home Purchase Plan Arrears in Respect of Residential Property[239] promulgated in November 2008. The Protocol describes the behaviour that the court will normally expect of the parties prior to the start of a possession action, although its existence does not alter the parties' rights and obligations.[240] The overall aims of the Protocol are to ensure that the lender and borrower act fairly towards one another, and to encourage more pre-action contact between the parties.[241] In particular, the lender should then provide the borrower with information pertaining to the mortgage arrears, and be prepared to consider proposals from the borrower in respect of changes to manner of repayments.[242]

As has already been noted, in the exercise of its discretion under the legislation, much will depend on the facts of individual cases, although some general principles have emerged. First, the court should not grant an open-ended postponement of a possession order; a finite period must be stipulated by the end of which the arrears should be paid off, together with the payments which would normally be expected under the mortgage.[243] Secondly, any counterclaim that the mortgagor might have against the mortgagee is to be disregarded, the two actions being seen as independent of each other.[244] A third point is that the court should look realistically at the mortgagor's financial situation. In particular, it should not sanction the postponement of a possession order which is not based upon a realistic assessment of the situation. It is improper either for the court to make an order for payments which, while it would clear the arrears and meet the ongoing payments, is one which the mortgagor cannot afford, or, alternatively, make an order which the mortgagor could afford but would not, within a reasonable period of time, enable the arrears to be cleared, while also servicing the normal mortgage repayments.[245] In assessing the financial situation of the mortgagor, regard should not be had to speculative windfalls, such as winning

---

[238] For arguments in favour of greater harmonization of the practices of lenders and greater publicity to be given to the fights of borrowers, see L. Whitehouse in Jackson and Wilde, *The Reform of Property Law* (Dartmouth: Ashgate, 1997), Chapter 9 and in Bright and Dewar, *Land Law: Themes and Perspectives* (Oxford: Oxford University Press, 1998), Chapter 7.

[239] 48th update to the Civil Procedure Rules.   [240] Ibid., paras 1.1–1.2.   [241] Ibid., para. 2.1.

[242] Ibid., para. 5.   [243] *Royal Trust Co. of Canada v. Markham* [1975] 1 W.L.R. 1416.

[244] *Citibank Trust Ltd v. Ayivor* [1987] 1 W.L.R. 1157; *National Westminster Bank plc v. Skelton* [1993] 1 W.L.R. 72n. Cf. *Ashley Guarantee plc v. Zacaria* [1993] 1 All E.R. 254 and *Banfield v. Leeds Building Society* [2007] EWCA Civ. 1369 at [66] *per* Lawrence Collins L.J.

[245] *First National Bank plc v. Syed* [1991] 2 All E.R. 250 at 255 *per* Dillon L.J.

the pools (or, nowadays, the lottery) or receiving a large legacy,[246] or the hope, at some time in the future, of securing highly paid employment.[247]

Reasonable period

A key issue in the exercise of discretion under the Act was the period of time which a court was prepared to accept as being reasonable in which to pay off the accumulated arrears. Although in one case,[248] the Court of Appeal accepted that this was essentially a matter for the judgment of county court judges and that their exercise of discretion would not be interfered with unless it was clearly wrong, in the leading case of *Cheltenham and Gloucester Building Society v. Norgan*[249] clear guidelines were laid down as to how this discretion should be exercised. This is far preferable to the earlier approach of allowing trial judges a wide general discretion, the consequence of which would be to lead to different results being reached in essentially similar cases.

Mrs Norgan had experienced constant difficulty in meeting the mortgage payments and, on several occasions, actions for possession had been brought and orders had been made but, in the exercise of the statutory discretion, postponed. Finally, although the amount of the arrears was disputed, another action for possession was brought and this time was granted. Mrs Norgan appealed.

Whole term

It was recognized that a practice had developed, whereby a period of two to four years had been accepted as being the maximum which would be allowed to the mortgagor to pay off the arrears.[250] The opportunity was taken to introduce a new policy. It was accepted that, in assessing what is a reasonable period by which to postpone a possession order to enable arrears to be paid off, the starting point should be the agreed length of the mortgage term, that being the period when the mortgagee would expect to be paid, in full, the capital sum with interest. To obtain relief, the mortgagor should present a detailed financial plan which, if implemented, would result in the loan itself, including the arrears, being paid off by the term date of the mortgage.[251] Because, in the instant case, the judge had not considered the prospects of Mrs Norgan being able to achieve this in the remaining thirteen years of the mortgage, the matter was

---

[246] *Hastings & Thanet Building Sociey v. Goddard* [1970] 1 W.L.R. 1544 at 1548 *per* Russell L.J.

[247] *Town & Country Building Society v. Julien* (1991) 24 H.L.R. 261. Cf. *Cheltenham and Gloucester Building Society v. Grant* (1993) 24 H.L.R. 48.

[248] *Cheltenham and Gloucester Building Society v. Grant* (1993) 24 H.L.R. 48, criticized by M.P. Thompson [1995] Conv. 51.

[249] [1996] 1 All E.R. 499. See M.P. Thompson [1996] Conv. 118.

[250] [1996] 1 All E.R. 449 at 456 *per* Waite L.J. See also Judge Parmiter (1992) 16 L.S.G. 17 referring to a Judicial Studies Board 'recommendation' of two years. Cf. *Citybank Trust v. Ayivor* [1987] 1 W.L.R. 1157 at 1164 *per* Mervyn-Davies L.J., who considered 18 months to be an appropriate period. This must now be considered to be unduly restrictive.

[251] Had this approach been established when the 1970 Act was passed, there would have been no need for the amendment brought in by the Administration of Justice Act 1973, s. 8.

remitted for this matter to be determined, there being insufficient evidence before the Court of Appeal for a final decision to be made.

The decision in *Norgan* is to be welcomed.[252] First, authoritative guidelines were laid down, which should lead to a greater consistency of approach at county court level to an important issue. Secondly, it would seem, while giving adequate protection to the mortgagee,[253] to offer greater prospects for the mortgagor to be able to remain in the home, in that, financially, it will clearly be easier to meet the additional payments necessary to clear the arrears and meet the ongoing payments if such payments are spread out over the whole period of the loan rather than having to be made within a set, and somewhat arbitrary, period.

One reason for the court taking as a reasonable period the entire length of the mortgage was that, as this was the most favourable view so far as the mortgagor was concerned, further litigation could be avoided.[254] If a possession order has been postponed once, on the basis of the mortgagor's financial plan being considered to be acceptable, and the mortgagor fails to comply with the terms of that plan, thereby falling into arrears again, then it was said that there would be a presumption, if a further possession action was brought, against there being any further postponement. This is because one of the aims of introducing the new guidelines was to avoid serial litigation relating to possession actions, such a multiplicity of actions being a feature of *Norgan*, itself.

Sale

The decision in *Norgan* is of relevance to a situation where a mortgagor is in a financial position to make payments additional to those which he would have been expected to make had default not occurred. He must make the normal payments together with such additional amount as would, over the life of the mortgage, also pay off the accumulated arrears. If the mortgagor is not in receipt of sufficient income to be able to produce a financial plan which, if implemented, would enable this to be done, an alternative position for the mortgagor to take is to seek to argue that possession should be postponed to allow him to sell the property in order to discharge the debt. The question which will then arise, in these circumstances, is as to how long a postponement a court will countenance.

The normal judicial position in cases such as this is that any postponement of the sale will be only for a relatively short time and the court will require quite strong evidence that an early sale of the property is likely.[255] The mere fact that the mortgagor has put the property in the hands of estate agents will not, of itself, be convincing

---

[252] For an account of the more hostile reaction to the decision in Northern Ireland, see L. McMurtry (2007) 58 N.I.L.Q. 194.

[253] For the importance of the position of the mortgagee being safeguarded, see *Realkredit Danmark v. Brookfield House* (1999), unreported.

[254] [1996] 1 All E.R. 449 at 459–460 *per* Waite L.J.

[255] *Royal Trust Co. of Canada v. Markham* [1975] 1 All E.R. 433; *National and Provincial Building Society v. Lloyd* [1996] 1 All E.R. 630.

evidence that a sale is imminent, even if the agent is quite bullish as to the prospects of a quick sale. The reason for this is that such optimism might be misplaced, it having been said that 'the estate agency profession . . . would win by a distance any competition between members of different professions for optimism'.[256]

The reluctance of the courts to grant a prolonged possession order to a mortgagor in order to allow him to sell the property and repay what is owed is understandable, particularly if the level of indebtedness is continuing to rise as the mortgagor is unable to meet the ongoing mortgage repayments. A more interesting problem occurred in *Bristol and West Building Society v. Ellis*.[257] Arrears of some £16,000 had accrued on an initial loan of £60,000 amounting to a total indebtedness of £76,000. The mortgagor, Mrs Ellis, was in a position to pay the mortgagee a lump sum of £5,000 and meet the normal repayments and also to pay £10 per month towards clearing off the arrears. On these facts alone, she would have succeeded in paying off the arrears in ninety-eight years, which nobody argued could be seen as a reasonable period within the meaning of the Act. She argued, however, that the position was that the debt was stabilized. She then proposed that the sale of the property should be postponed for a period of five years to allow her son to finish his education and that, when the house was sold in five years' time, enough would be realized on the sale to discharge, in full, her debt to the mortgagee. The Court of Appeal rejected her argument and awarded the mortgagee possession.

Although possession was ordered, the Court of Appeal did not accept that there was a rule that the mortgagor must necessarily show, in cases of this type, that a sale would take place imminently, or even within a short space of time. Regard must be had to two criteria. In a case such as this, Auld L.J. stressed that:

'the critical matters are the adequacy of the security for the debt and the length of the period necessary to achieve a sale. There should be evidence, or at least some informal material . . . before the court of the likelihood of a sale the proceeds of which will discharge the debt and of the period in which such a sale is likely to be achieved.'[258]

While it is true that the second criterion, the likelihood of a sale, points to a sale in the near future, this may be coloured by the adequacy of the security. In *Ellis*, the value of the property was disputed and the equity in the house was small. To postpone a sale for a five-year period, even though the arrears were not increasing, might prejudice a mortgagee if house prices started to fall, the result of that being that there might no longer be full security for the loan. In cases such as *Ellis*, however, where there is a larger equity in the house, the postponement of possession to allow a sale in a few years' time may be an attractive solution, protecting, to an extent, the mortgagor's use of the property as a home without endangering unduly the position of the mortgagee.

---

[256] *Target Home Loans Ltd v. Clothier* (1992) 25 H.L.R. 48 at 53 *per* Nolan L.J.
[257] (1996) 73 P. & C.R. 158. See M.P. Thompson [1998] Conv. 125.
[258] (1996) 73 P. & C.R. 158 at 162.

Who sells the property?

The previous section was concerned with arguments put by the mortgagor that the arrears can be cleared by means of a sale of the property at some time in the future. A further argument relating to the sale of the property has emerged, except on this occasion, the argument being put is that the mortgagor wishes for the property to be sold against the wishes of the mortgagee, this situation usually occurring in cases of negative equity.

Under section 91(2) of the Law of Property Act 1925, in any action, whether for foreclosure, for redemption, or sale, or for the raising of any payment in any manner of mortgage money, the court, on the request of the mortgagee or any person interested either in the mortgage money or in the right of redemption, may direct a sale of the property on such terms as it sees fit. It may make such an order notwithstanding that any person dissents to the sale.

This section has attracted attention in situations where the mortgagor wishes the property to be sold and either the mortgagee is opposed to a sale, or wishes to conduct the sale itself rather than leave this matter to the mortgagor. In *Palk v. Mortgage Services Funding plc,*[259] the mortgagee brought a possession action in respect of a house in which there was a negative equity. Its purpose in obtaining possession was not, however, as a prelude to the exercise of its power of sale. Instead, it intended to rent out the property with a view to selling it some years later, by which time it was confident that the value of the house would have risen sufficiently to enable the mortgagors' debt to be recouped in full. The mortgagors argued that the house should be sold straight away as, under the mortgagee's scheme, their indebtedness would increase progressively as the projected rental income was less than they would be expected to pay each month under the mortgage. The Court of Appeal accepted this argument and directed a sale of the property.

Negative equity

The facts of the case were unusual, in that the mortgagee was seeking to speculate on the recovery of the property market at the risk of the mortgagors, who would remain liable on the personal covenant to repay if, subsequently, the house could not be sold at a price sufficient to recoup what was owed. Moreover, the level of indebtedness of the mortgagors would continue to increase while, if possession was granted, they would be unable actually to occupy the property, a result which, potentially, would cause them considerable hardship. The unusual nature of the facts in *Palk* was stressed in *Cheltenham and Gloucester plc v. Krausz,*[260] where, again, a mortgagor sought an order for the sale of a mortgaged property, on this occasion when the mortgagee had obtained a warrant for possession and had yet to execute that warrant. The proposed sale price would not have produced sufficient funds to pay off what was owed. The

---

[259] [1993] Ch. 330.
[260] [1997] 1 All E.R. 21. See also *Cheltenham and Gloucester plc v. Booker* (1997) 29 H.L.R. 634; A. Kenny [1998] Conv. 223.

Court of Appeal refused to order a sale and instead allowed the warrant for possession to be enforced.

The opportunity was taken to address the matter as one of principle: can a mortgagor, in a position of negative equity, resist a possession action by the mortgagee on the basis that he should be allowed to remain in possession in order to sell the property at a price which will not clear the debt, but may be a better price than the mortgagee could get when selling a property which is physically vacant, a possession order having been obtained? The answer to this was in the negative. It was pointed out that, to create such a state of affairs could allow a mortgagor, understandably reluctant to lose his home, to conduct the sale in such a way as to allow him to spin matters out and delay the conclusion of any sale; a state of affairs which is potentially unfair to the mortgagee.[261] In normal cases, a mortgagor will not be able to obtain a sale of the property against the will of the mortgagee when the proposed sale of the property will not discharge the amount which is owed.[262]

Duty on taking possession

The mortgagee will normally only seek possession of the mortgaged property in order to be able to sell the property. Ordinarily, the mortgagee will not wish to take possession as an end in itself because of the potential liability imposed by equity. In equity, the mortgagee is under a liability to account strictly in respect of any profits, such liability being on the basis of wilful default. An example of this principle is provided by *White v. City of London Brewery Co.*,[263] where the mortgaged property was a public house which had been let as a 'free house'. The mortgagee, which was a brewery, took possession of the property and let it as a tied house. It was held liable to the mortgagor for the additional rent which could have been obtained had the property been let as a 'free house'. In cases where the mortgaged property is used for commercial purposes, it is likely, if possession is being sought, that that business is in difficulty. In such circumstances, a mortgagee who has taken possession should seek, either, to sell the property as expeditiously as possible, or, alternatively, not seek to run that business himself but appoint a receiver to do so.[264]

Appointment of a receiver

The potential liability of a mortgagee who has gone into possession is a disincentive for him to take this course of action unless he has done so with a view to an expeditious sale of the property. If it is not envisaged that the property will be sold in the short term, but the mortgagee wishes to derive the benefit of any income generated

[261] [1997] 1 All E.R. 21 at 27 *per* Phillips L.J. *Barrett v. Halifax Building Society* (1995) 28 H.L.R. 634, which seemed to adopt this course, was strongly doubted: at 31 *per* Millett L.J.

[262] But see *Polonski v. Lloyds Bank Mortgages Ltd* [1998] 1 F.L.R. 896, where *Krausz* was not cited and is, it is submitted, wrongly decided. See also M.P. Thompson [1998] Conv. 125 at 130–132.

[263] (1889) 42 Ch.D. 237.

[264] Cf. *AIB Finance Ltd v. Debtors* [1998] 2 All E.R. 929; M.P. Thompson [1998] Conv. 391 at 395.

by the property, a more attractive alternative to going into possession is to appoint a receiver.

The mortgagee may appoint a receiver provided that his power of sale has become exercisable.[265] If the criteria, to be considered shortly, enabling the power to be exercised are satisfied, then an appointment of a receiver must be in writing. The advantage of appointing a receiver is that, by section 109(2) of the Law of Property Act 1925, the receiver is deemed to be the agent of the mortgagor. This means that, although the receiver will collect money derived from the property and use that money to pay the interest due under the mortgage, the mortgagee will escape the strict liability which would be imposed upon him had he taken possession of the property himself.[266] A further advantage is that, if the income takes the form of the payment of rent by an occupying tenant, receipt of the rent by a receiver will not, of itself, amount to the adoption of the tenancy by the mortgagee. If the mortgagee receives rent directly from the tenant, then that tenancy will be adopted, with the result that, assuming the creation of that tenancy was unauthorized, the mortgagee will be bound by the tenancy and may not be able, subsequently, to obtain possession from the tenant, whereas previously he would have been able so to do.[267]

Foreclosure

The right of the mortgagor to redeem the mortgage after the contractual date of redemption has passed is a right conferred by equity; it is the equitable right to redeem. What equity has given, equity can also take away. The removal of the equitable right to redeem is effected by foreclosure. Before 1925, when the legal title was vested in the mortgagee, the effect of foreclosure was to remove the equitable right to redeem and, thereby, to extinguish the equity of redemption. After 1925, an order is necessary to vest the legal fee simple, which was formerly vested in the mortgagor, in the mortgagee.

Foreclosure, which can occur only when the contractual date of redemption has passed, involves a two-stage process: the foreclosure *nisi* and the foreclosure absolute. The former requires the mortgagor to repay the money borrowed, and so redeem the mortgage, within a finite period, normally of six months. A failure to do so will lead to the foreclosure being made absolute. Under section 91 of the Law of Property Act 1925, the court may, at the instance of the mortgagee or any person interested, order a sale of the property rather than grant a foreclosure order. As the effect of foreclosure may well be to overcompensate the mortgagee by vesting in him property worth more than the debt, 'foreclosure actions are almost unheard of today and have been so for many years. [Mortgagees] usually appoint a receiver or exercise their powers of sale.'[268]

---

[265] Law of Property Act 1925, s. 109(1).

[266] The receiver may, however, be liable to the mortgagor if he fails to exercise reasonable care in the management of the property: *Medforth v. Blake* [1999] 3 All E.R. 97; A. Kenny [1999] Conv. 434.

[267] See Adoption, pp. 484–485.

[268] *Palk v. Mortgage Services Funding plc* [1993] Ch. 330 at 336 *per* Sir Donald Nicholls V.-C.

If a foreclosure action is actually brought, it would be anticipated that the mortgagor would petition for the property to be sold.

Sale

The most potent remedy available to the mortgagee is to sell the property, this normally occurring after the mortgagee has obtained possession. With respect to sales of the property, various issues arise. These concern the question of when the property can be sold and the effect of the sale, the duties imposed upon the mortgagee when selling the property, and, finally, determining what is to happen to the proceeds of sale. This issue may be affected by the existence of more than one mortgage having being created over the property, when questions of priority may arise.

Power of sale

Since 1925, the legal fee simple remains vested in the mortgagor. When selling the mortgaged property, therefore, the transfer by the mortgagee will operate to transfer something which he does not actually own. For him to be able to do this, it is essential that the statutory power of sale has arisen. A further matter which then becomes relevant is whether the power of sale is exercisable. There is an important difference between the power arising and it becoming exercisable.

Power arising

For the mortgagee to have the power to sell the mortgaged property, the criteria set out in section 101 of the Law of Property Act 1925[269] must be satisfied. These are:

(a) that the mortgage is made by deed; and

(b) that the mortgage money has become due.

In the case of legal mortgages, these must be created by deed and so the first condition will always be satisfied.[270] It is the second requirement, that the mortgage money becomes due, that has caused mortgage deeds to convey a misleading impression. To ensure that the mortgage money is due, with the result that the power of sale arises, it is common for the mortgage deed to stipulate either that the whole sum borrowed will be repaid within six months of the creation of the mortgage, or to insert a clause that if there is a default in the payment of any instalment, the whole sum borrowed becomes payable.[271] It is unfortunate that the need to ensure that the statutory power of sale arises necessitates the insertion of clauses

---

[269] The provisions relating to the power of sale may be varied or excluded by the mortgage deed: Law of Property Act 1925, s. 101(3)(4).

[270] This may not always be the case for equitable mortgages and it is preferable that such mortgages are also created by deed.

[271] It would seem that this is unnecessary as, if there is default in the payment of an instalment, the courts are prepared to accept that the mortgage money is due: *Payne v. Cardiff Rural District Council* [1932] 1 K.B. 241. See H.P. (1932) 48 L.Q.R. 158.

of this nature into mortgages, as both clauses are artificial and distort the apparent nature of the transaction.

The effect of a sale

On a sale of freehold property by a mortgagee exercising the power conferred by the Act, the purchaser will acquire the fee simple freed from all estates rights and interests and rights to which the mortgagee has priority, but subject to all estates, interests, and rights which have priority to the mortgage.[272] This means that the purchaser will take subject to any third party rights, including mortgages, which were binding upon the mortgagee, but free from all other rights including, most importantly, the mortgagor's equity of redemption, which is overreached. If a mortgagee exercises the power of sale without first taking possession, this, although it pre-empts any defence to a possession action under the Administration of Justice Acts, does not infringe the European Convention of Human Rights.[273]

For overreaching to occur, the mortgagee must exercise the power conferred by the Act or by the terms of the mortgage contract. If the power of sale has not arisen, then all that the mortgagee can convey is his own interest in the property, that is, his own mortgage. So, if there is a £40,000 mortgage on a property and the mortgagee sells the property for its actual value, say £80,000, but the power of sale has not arisen, then all the purchaser will acquire is a mortgage worth £40,000. To avoid such a catastrophic result, it is therefore imperative that the purchaser satisfies himself that the power of sale has arisen. For this reason, the purchaser's task is easier if the mortgage stipulates that the money is repaid within six months of the creation of the mortgage, rather than if the mortgage contains a default clause. One can easily tell if the contractual date for redemption has passed; it is less easy to be sure that the default clause has been activated.[274]

Power becoming exercisable

For the power of sale to arise, the criteria laid down in section 101 of the Law of Property Act 1925 must be satisfied. Once the power of sale has arisen, it only becomes exercisable if one of the criteria laid down in section 103 are fulfilled. The power is not exercisable unless either:

(a) notice requiring payment of the mortgage money has been served on the mortgagor and default has been made in payment of the mortgage money, or of part thereof, for three months after service of such notice; or

(b) some interest under the mortgage is in arrears and unpaid for two months after becoming due; or

(c) there has been breach of some provision in the mortgage other than the payment of the mortgage money or interest.

[272] Law of Property Act 1925, s. 104(1).
[273] *Horsham Properties Group Ltd v. Clark* [2008] EWHC 2327 (Ch.).   [274] See H.P., op. cit., 159.

There is a significant difference between the mortgagee purporting to exercise the power of sale when that power has not arisen and him selling the property when the power of sale is not exercisable. As has been seen, if the power of sale has not arisen then the mortgagee lacks capacity to transfer the fee simple and can transfer only his own mortgage. If the property is sold before the power of sale has become exercisable, the consequence is less drastic. It is provided by section 104(2) of the Act that when a conveyance is made in exercise of the power of sale, the title of the purchaser shall not be impeachable on the ground that the power of sale is not exercisable and the purchaser is not concerned to make enquiries as to whether the power is exercisable. If the purchaser, however, is actually aware that the power of sale is not exercisable, then the sale will be set aside,[275] but such a situation is likely to be very rare, particularly as the purchaser is exonerated from making any enquiry as to this. The sanction for selling the property before the power of sale has become exercisable is that the mortgagee is liable to pay damages to any person who suffers loss by the improper exercise of the power of sale.[276]

Duties on sale

In practical terms, the exercise of the power of sale is the most fundamental remedy of the mortgagee and will, in most cases, bring to an end the relationship between the mortgagor and the mortgagee. Given the nature of the remedy, it has a considerable impact upon the mortgagor. In the residential sector, the effect will be, of course, that the mortgagor will lose his existing home and have to seek alternative accommodation. In addition, the mortgagor will retain a financial interest in the transaction. If there is equity in the house then, after the sale occurred, the mortgagor will be entitled to the balance of the proceeds of sale after the debt to the mortgagee has been discharged. Conversely, if there is negative equity, the mortgagor will remain personally liable to the mortgagee for the shortfall after the property has been sold. The conduct of the sale is, therefore, a matter of considerable importance to the mortgagor and, as one would expect, certain duties are imposed upon the mortgagee with respect to the exercise of the power of sale.

Genuine sale

The first point to make is that the sale must be a genuine one. This means that the mortgagee cannot buy the property himself, or through an agent.[277] Where this principle has been infringed, the mortgagor is entitled to set the transaction aside and does not have to prove that there was any fraud involved, the courts being of the view that a sale by the mortgagee to himself is not really a sale at all.[278] Unless the sale is under the

---

[275] *Waring v. London and Manchester Assurance Co. Ltd* [1935] Ch. 310 at 318 *per* Crossman J. See also *Jenkins v. Jones* (1860) 2 Giff. 99.

[276] Law of Property Act 1925, s. 104(2).

[277] *Martinson v. Clowes* (1882) 21 Ch.D. 857 at 860 *per* North J.

[278] *Farrar v. Farrars Ltd* (1888) 40 Ch.D. 395 at 409 *per* Lindley L.J.

direction of the court,[279] or the mortgagee is expressly permitted by statute to buy the mortgaged property,[280] the rule prohibiting the mortgagee from buying the property appears to be absolute.

Associated persons

While it is clear that the mortgagee cannot buy the mortgaged property himself the position with regard to a sale to an associated person is more flexible. There is no rule that such a sale cannot take place[281] but, depending on the circumstances, the sale may be liable to be set aside. In *Tse Kwok Lam v. Wong Chit Sen*,[282] the mortgagee sold the mortgaged property at an auction. The only bidder was the mortgagee's wife, whose bid matched exactly the reserve price. Subsequently the mortgagor sought to have the sale set aside. The Privy Council held that, while the close relationship between the seller and the buyer did not entitle the mortgagor automatically to set the sale aside, the existence of the relationship meant that the onus of proof was thrown onto the purchaser to show that the sale was in good faith and at the best price reasonably obtainable at the time. On the facts, this onus was not discharged, and, had it not been for the excessive delay on the part of the mortgagor in seeking to impugn the sale, the transaction would have been set aside.

Where, as in this case, the mortgagee is knowingly selling to a closely associated person, then the shifting of the normal burden of proof from the mortgagor to the parties to the sale seems entirely appropriate. If the mortgagee is unaware of the identity of the buyer, however, this will not be the case. In *Corbett v. Halifax plc*,[283] the Halifax were exercising their power of sale. It was the strict policy of the company that under no circumstances could staff of the Halifax group of companies or agents' staff or their families purchase a property in possession. Notwithstanding this policy, a Mr Deakin, who was employed by the Halifax, and who was aware of the policy, contrived a plan, whereby his uncle bought the property and then re-sold it to him and his wife. As the Halifax was unaware of this deception, the sale was not challengeable by the mortgagor on the basis of the sale being to an associated person. Even had the Halifax been aware that the real buyer was Mr Deakin and his wife, however, it is thought that the sale would still have been unimpeachable. He had had nothing to do with the conduct of the sale, and derived no advantage from his association with the mortgagee.[284] An even clearer situation where a sale to an associated person would be free from subsequent challenge by the mortgagor is where the sale is conducted in accordance with instructions given by him.[285]

---

[279] See *Palk v. Mortgage Services Funding plc* [1993] Ch. 330 at 340 *per* Sir Donald Nicholls V.-C.

[280] See Housing Act 1985, s. 452, Sched. 17, para. 1, as amended by Housing and Planning Act 1986, which avoids the difficulty relating to this issue highlighted in *Williams v. Wellingborough B.C.* [1975] 1 W.L.R. 1327.

[281] *Newport Farm Ltd v. Damesh Holdings Ltd* [2003] UKPC 54 at para. 25 *per* Lord Scott of Foscote.

[282] [1983] 1 W.L.R. 1349.   [283] [2003] 4 All E.R. 180; M.P. Thompson [2004] Conv. 49.

[284] See Thompson, loc. cit., at 59–60.   [285] *Newport Farm Ltd v. Damesh Holdings Ltd, supra.*

Conduct of the sale

Assuming that the sale is not open to objection on the basis of the identity of the purchaser, the next issue to consider is what duties are owed to the mortgagor by the mortgagee when exercising the power of sale.

It has long been accepted that the exercise of the power of sale was subject to some judicial control, although the extent, and indeed the juridical basis, of that control was less certain. In some cases, it was said that the mortgagee would only incur liability if the sale was not exercised in good faith.[286] In other decisions, however, the standard was pitched somewhat higher, it being said that the mortgagee owed a duty to the mortgagor to obtain the best price reasonably obtainable.[287] The conflict between these differing formulations was settled by the Court of Appeal in *Cuckmere Brick Co. Mutual Finance Ltd*.[288] In this case, after the property had been sold, the mortgagor sued the mortgagee alleging that the sale price achieved was too low, the result, it was said, of the extent of the planning permission attached to the land not being properly advertised.

Although the court was divided as to the application of the law to the facts of the case, it was unanimous as to the standard of care to be expected of a mortgagee. It was agreed that the mortgagee was under a duty to take reasonable care to obtain the true market price for the property. This was explained on the basis that:

'The proximity between them could hardly be greater. Surely they are "neighbours". Given that the power of sale is for the benefit of the mortgagee and that he is entitled to choose the moment that suits him, it would be strange indeed if he were under no legal obligation to take reasonable care to obtain what I call the true market value at the date of the sale.'[289]

Tort or equity?

The dichotomy of view as to whether the obligation imposed on the mortgagee was to act in good faith, or was the higher duty to take reasonable care to obtain the true market value of the property, was solved by holding that the mortgagee owes both duties to the mortgagor.[290] With regard to the former, this will add little to the higher duty of care imposed on the mortgagee. Provided that the power of sale is not exercised for reasons other than the recovery of the debt, it will not be considered to have been wrongly exercised.[291] It will, of course, be extremely difficult to establish this.[292]

The language used in *Cuckmere* in respect of the duty of care imposed upon the mortgagee is redolent of the application of tortuous principles. Since then, however, the opportunity has been taken to stress that it is the province of equity and not tort

---

[286] See, e.g., *Kennedy v. De Trafford* [1897] A.C. 762; *Warner v. Jacob* (1882) 20 Ch.D. 220; *Reliance Permanent Building Society v. Harwood-Stamper* [1944] Ch. 362.

[287] See, e.g., *McHugh v. Union Bank of Canada* [1913] A.C. 299; *National Bank of Australia v. United Hand-in-Hand Band of Hope* (1879) 4 App. Cas. 391; *Farrar v. Farrars Ltd* (1888) 40 Ch.D. 395; *Colson v. Williams* (1889) 58 L.J. Ch. 539.

[288] [1971] Ch. 949.   [289] [1971] Ch. 949 at 966 *per* Salmon L.J.   [290] Ibid.

[291] See *Meretz Investments NV v. APC Ltd* [2006] EWHC 74 (Ch.) at para. 314 *per* Lewison J.

[292] Although, in the context of an action for possession, see *Quennell v. Maltby* [1979] 1 W.L.R. 318.

to regulate the exercise of the mortgagee's power of sale.[293] The practical consequence of this, in the context of the standard of care to be expected of the mortgagee is not great, however, as it is clear that that standard which was laid down in *Cuckmere* is the appropriate standard to be imposed by equity, so that it is now well established that the mortgagee is under a duty to obtain the best price reasonably obtainable when selling the mortgaged property.[294]

The main significance of the debate as to whether the source of the mortgagee's liability lay in tort or in equity related to whether or not the mortgagee could be liable in respect of the timing of the sale. For a long time, it has been established that the mortgagee need not wait until the market is favourable before exercising the power of sale.[295] Indeed, provided that power of sale is exercisable, the mortgagee could sell the property at the least advantageous time for the mortgagor.[296] In the aftermath of *Cuckmere*, it was thought to be arguable, on the supposition that the position was governed by the law of tort, that this position might need reconsideration, so that it might be the case that the mortgagee should exercise reasonable care as to when the property is put onto the market.[297] This argument was rejected, however, in *China and South Sea Bank Ltd v. Tan Soon Gin*,[298] where the Privy Council held that a mortgagee could not be liable for failing to exercise its power of sale when market conditions were more favourable than they subsequently became, as the timing of the sale was a matter entirely for the mortgagee.

The current position was recently restated by the Court of Appeal in *Silven Properties Ltd v. Royal Bank of Scotland plc*.[299] Lightman J., giving the judgment of the court, said:

'When and if the mortgagee does exercise the power of sale, he comes under a duty in equity (and not tort) to the mortgagor (and all others interested in the equity of redemption) to take reasonable precautions to obtain "the fair" or "the true market" value of or "the proper price" for the mortgaged property at the date of the sale and not ... the date of the decision to sell.... The remedy for breach of this duty is not common law damages, but an order that the mortgagee account to the mortgagor and all others interested in the equity of redemption, not just for what he received but for what he should have received.'

---

[293] *Downsview Nominees Ltd v. First City Corporation Ltd* [1993] A.C. 295 at 315 *per* Lord Templeman; *Yorkshire Bank plc v. Hall* [1999] 1 W.L.R. 1713 at 1728 *per* Robert Walker L.J.

[294] See *Medforth v. Blake* [2000] Ch. 86 at 102 *per* Sir Richard Scott V.-C.; *Glatt v. Sinclair* [2011] EWCA Civ. 1317 at [12] *per* Kitchin L.J. The duty was, in respect of building societies, for a long time statutory: see Building Societies Act 1986, Sched. 4, replacing earlier legislation. The position is now governed by the general law; Building Societies Act 1997, s. 2.

[295] See *Warner v. Jacob* (1882) 20 Ch.D. 220 at 224 *per* Kay J., *Bank of Cyprus (London) Ltd v. Gill* [1980] 2 Lloyd's Rep. 51.

[296] See *Duke v. Robson* [1973] 1 W.L.R. 267.

[297] *Standard Chartered Bank Ltd v. Walker* [1982] 1 W.L.R. 1410 at 1415 *per* Lord Denning M.R.

[298] [1991] 1 A.C. 531. See also *Silven Properties Ltd v. Royal Bank of Scotland plc* [2004] 4 All E.R. 484 at 491–492 *per* Lightman J.

[299] Ibid., at 492–493.

It will be observed that, in this passage, Lightman J. refers to the duty being owed to others interested in the equity of redemption. Thus, it has been held that the duty is owed to a surety of the loan,[300] and to a subsequent mortgagee,[301] but, perhaps surprisingly, not to an equitable co-owner of the property.[302]

Breach of duty

The question of whether a mortgagee is in breach of his duty to take reasonable care is essentially one of fact, and in determining whether the mortgagee has fallen below the requisite standard, the court will consider whether the sale was within a bracket of reasonableness,[303] and if the house is immediately re-sold for a considerable profit, this will provide strong evidence that the original sale was at an undervalue.[304] If it was not, the measure of damages is the diminution in value of the equity of redemption.[305] An issue relevant to this is whether or not the mortgagee owes a duty to the mortgagor to gazump, that is to accept a higher offer than one which has previously been accepted, subject to contract.[306] In *Corbett v. Halifax plc*,[307] it emerged that the policy of the Halifax, when selling mortgaged property, was not to entertain a higher offer, unless it exceeded a previous offer by more than 5 per cent. This was not commented on in the Court of Appeal, but in principle, it would seem that the mortgagee's duty to the mortgagor should override any considerations of commercial ethics.[308]

In assessing whether the mortgagee is in breach of its duty, some general principles have emerged. First, to escape liability it is not sufficient to show that the property has been put into the hands of a reputable agent. Any negligence on the part of the agent will be attributed to the mortgagee.[309] Secondly, when selling the property it must be properly exposed to the market. If a lower price is obtained than would otherwise have been the case, because the property was sold on a 'crash sale' basis, the mortgagee will be liable to the mortgagor in respect of the shortfall.[310] On the same basis, as it is generally perceived that a lower price for a house can be obtained when it has been repossessed, than would be the case if the sale were conducted in the normal way by

---

[300] *Standard Chartered Bank Ltd v. Walker* [1982] 1 W.L.R. 1410. 'Equity intervenes to protect a surety': *China and South Sea Bank Ltd v. Tan Soon Gin* [1991] 1 A.C. 536 at 544 *per* Lord Templeman.

[301] *Downsview Nominees Ltd v. First City Corporation Ltd* [1993] A.C. 295 at 311 *per* Lord Templeman. See also *Adamson v. Halifax plc* [2003] 4 All E.R. 423 at 425 *per* Sir Murray Stuart-Smith.

[302] *Parker-Tweedale v. Dunbar Bank* [1991] Ch. 12.

[303] *Michael v. Miller* [2004] 2 E.G.L.R. 151 at 160 *per* Jonathan Parker L.J. A margin of error of 10%, suggested at first instance, in *Corbett v. Halifax plc* [2003] 4 All E.R. 180 seems unduly generous. See M.P. Thompson [2004] Conv. 49 at 54.

[304] See *Glatt v. Sinclair* [2011] EWCA Civ. 1317. (Re-sale at a 38% uplift in price).

[305] *Adamson v. Halifax plc* [2003] 4 All E.R. 423.   [306] See Gazumping, pp. 185–187.

[307] [2003] 4 All E.R. 180.

[308] See *Buttle v. Saunders* [1950] 2 All E.R. 193; Thompson, loc. cit., at 54–56.

[309] *Tomlin v. Luce* (1889) 43 Ch.D. 191 at 194 *per* Collins L.J.; *Cuckmere Brick Co. Ltd v. Mutual Finance Ltd* [1971] Ch. 949; *Francis v. Barclays Bank plc* [2004] EWHC 2787 (Ch.) at para. 13 *per* Rattee J.; *Glatt v. Sinclair* [2011] EWCA Civ. 1317 at [52] *per* Kitchin L.J.

[310] *Predeth v. Castle Phillips Ltd* [1986] 2 E.G.L.R. 141. See also *Skipton Building Society v. Stott* [2000] All E.R. 779; *Michael v. Miller* [2004] 2 E.G.L.R. 151 at 160.

the owners of it, the property should not, it is thought, be marketed on the basis that it is a forced sale.

It is open to the mortgagee to exclude liability in respect of his duty on a sale of the property, although any exclusion clause will have to be very clearly drafted in order to be efficacious.[311]

Proceeds of sale

While the mortgagee is not a trustee of the power of sale,[312] he is a trustee of the proceeds of sale. When the property has been sold, the mortgagee is required by section 105 of the Law of Property Act 1925 to apply the proceeds of sale in the following order:

(a) the discharge of any prior incumbrances free from which the property was sold;

(b) the payment of expenses properly incurred in the sale;

(c) the discharge of any money due under the mortgage; and

(d) payment of any balance to a subsequent mortgagee and, if there is none, to the mortgagor.

The existence of subsequent mortgages can be discovered by searching in the land charges register or the land registry, as appropriate. The mortgagee will have notice of subsequent mortgages if they are either registered as a land charge or protected by the entry of a notice on the register,[313] so the mortgagee exercising its power of sale should make the requisite searches. If the mortgagee sells the property, because he holds the balance of the proceeds of sale on trust for subsequent mortgagees, they have proprietary interests in that money. In *Buhr v. Barclays Bank plc*,[314] it was held that when the mortgagor sells the property to discharge the first mortgage, the interests of subsequent mortgagees in the balance of the proceeds of sale are also proprietary.

PRIORITY OF MORTGAGES[315]

The principal advantage of being a secured creditor is that, when the property is sold, the creditor is paid what is owed to him, in full, from the proceeds of sale. Where there is more than one secured creditor, then they do not share the proceeds of sale proportionately; they are paid on the basis of the priority of their securities. Thus, if a house is mortgaged, first, to A for £60,000 and, secondly, to B for £50,000 and then sold

---

[311] See *Bishop v. Bonham* [1988] 1 W.L.R. 742.

[312] *Walker v. Jacob* (1882) 21 Ch.D. 220 at 224 *per* Kay J.   [313] Land Registration Act 2002, s. 54.

[314] [2001] EWCA Civ. 1223. See L. McMurtry [2002] Conv. 53.

[315] See, generally, R.E. Megarry (1940) 7 C.L.J. 243.

for £100,000, A, assuming that his mortgage has priority, will receive £60,000 from the proceeds of sale. B will then receive £40,000 but will be an unsecured creditor in respect of the remaining £10,000. If, as in the example just considered, the property is mortgaged for more than it is worth when it is actually sold, the issue of priority will become of central importance. Unfortunately, the law regulating this matter is complicated and unsatisfactory, involving the need not only, as is commonly the case, to distinguish between registered and unregistered land, but also to have regard to the pre-1925 law concerning this matter. The account of this issue will be confined to the priority of legal mortgages.

Unregistered land

Before 1925, the usual method of creating a legal mortgage was by the mortgagor conveying the land to the mortgagee as security for a loan. This could only be done once, so that one would not normally find more than one legal mortgage affecting the property. If having created a legal mortgage, the mortgagor purported to create a further legal mortgage then, being unable to convey what he has not got, the second purported legal mortgage would operate as an equitable mortgage and the question of priority would be between a prior legal mortgage and a later equitable mortgage. After 1925, there is no such restriction on the mortgagor's ability to create legal mortgages: '[t]he mortgagor can mortgage the property again and again'.[316] In each case, the question was to determine the circumstances when the holder of a legal estate would lose the priority, which the ownership of that estate would normally confer, to the holder of a later estate. To answer that question it is necessary to distinguish between mortgages which are registrable and those which are not.

Non-registrable mortgages

A mortgagee is entitled to possession of the title deeds to the property. This type of mortgage is not then registrable as a land charge. Where difficulties arise is where the mortgagee subsequently parts with the title deeds. As will be seen, a mortgage which is not protected by the deposit of title deeds is registrable as a land charge. If the mortgagee parts with the title deeds, it is generally accepted that the mortgage does not then become registrable; were the position otherwise, the mortgage would oscillate between being registrable or not depending upon the current possession of the deeds. Instead, where there is a mortgage which is initially protected by the deposit of title deeds, and the mortgagee subsequently parts with possession of them and a subsequent mortgage is created, then the issue of priority is governed by the pre-1925 rules.

Under the pre-1925 law, a legal mortgagee could lose priority to a subsequently created mortgage either by a failure to take possession of the title deeds or by subsequently parting with possession of them. A simple failure to have possession of the deeds was not, of itself, sufficient for the first mortgagee to lose priority.[317] For priority

---

[316] *Downsview Nominees Ltd v. First City Corporation Ltd* [1993] 1 A.C. 295 at 311 *per* Lord Templeman.
[317] See, e.g., *Grierson v. National Provincial Bank of England Ltd* [1913] 2 Ch. 18.

to be lost, the mortgagee must either allow the mortgagor to present himself as the unencumbered owner of the property, a form of estoppel,[318] or, 'it must be shown that he left [the deeds] in the hands of the mortgagor, either fraudulently, or what is called for want of a better expression, gross negligence'.[319] Although *dicta* exist which seem to draw a distinction between an initial failure to take deposit of the title deeds and a subsequent failure to retain them,[320] the better view is that the level of culpability required for the legal mortgagee to lose priority to a subsequent mortgagee should be the same in both situations, the test in each case being that of fraud or gross negligence.[321]

For post-1925 mortgages, the result is this. If the mortgagee fails to take possession of the title deeds, then the mortgage will be registrable as a land charge and the issue of priority will fall to be resolved by an application of the principles contained in the provisions of the Land Charges Act 1972. If, however, the mortgage was originally protected by the deposit of title deeds, then priority will be lost if the mortgagee, as a result of gross negligence, fails to retain the title deeds and another mortgage is subsequently created.

Registrable mortgages

Section 2(4) of the Land Charges Act 1972 provides that a puisne mortgage is a Class C(i) land charge. A puisne mortgage is defined by section 2(4)(i) of the Act as being a legal mortgage which is not protected by a deposit of title deeds relating to the legal estate affected.

By definition, this type of land charge refers to a legal interest affecting land and an immediate query might be as to why a legal interest which, as a matter of general principle, is binding upon a purchaser regardless of notice should be registrable at all, registration being the means of providing notice of equitable interests.

The reason is pragmatic. Take as an example a house which is worth £100,000, which is subject to a mortgage of £60,000 and so is good security for a further loan of £40,000. If a potential lender is approached, he will know of the existence of the first mortgage because that mortgagee will have possession of the title deeds. Armed with this information, he will discover the amount of money which has been secured by that mortgage and will know how much it is prudent to lend against the security of the house. Because only the first mortgagee will have possession of the title deeds, however, unless subsequent mortgages were made registrable, there would be no way for potential lenders to discover if there was already in existence a second, or even a third mortgage and it would, therefore, be very unsafe for them to lend money against the security of the house. To avoid this problem, a legal mortgage which is not protected by a deposit of title deeds—a puisne mortgage—is made registrable as a C(i) land charge.

[318] See *Perry-Herrick v. Attwood* (1857) 2 De G. & J. 21 at 39 *per* Lord Cranworth L.C.
[319] *Colyer v. Finch* (1882) 5 H.L. Cas. 905 at 924 *per* Lord Cranworth L.C.
[320] *Northern Counties of England Fire Insurance Co. Ltd v. Whipp* (1884) 26 Ch.D. 482 at 487 *per* Fry J.
[321] *Oliver v. Hinton* [1899] 2 Ch. 264 at 274 *per* Lindley L.J.

Legislative conflict

Ordinarily, when a particular interest in land is made registrable, the consequence of non-registration is clear; the interest in question is rendered void against a particular type of purchaser.[322] Although this is generally true in the case of mortgages, complications can arise in certain circumstances where, because of conflicting legislative provisions, the resolution of certain problems of priority is problematic.

Section 4(5) of the Land Charges Act 1972 provides that:

'a land charge of Class C...shall be void as against a purchaser of the land charged with it, or any interest in such land, unless the land charge is registered in the appropriate register before the completion of the purchase.'

Section 97 of the Law of Property Act 1925 provides that:

'Every mortgage affecting a legal estate in land...(not being a mortgage protected by the deposit of documents relating to the legal estate affected) shall rank according to its date of registration pursuant to the Land Charges Act [1972].'

The conflict between the two provisions is best shown by an example:

On 1 January, a puisne mortgage is created in favour of A.

On 8 January, a puisne mortgage is created in favour of B.

On 10 January, A registers his mortgage.

On 12 January, B registers his mortgage.

According to the Land Charges Act, the priority is B then A, because A's mortgage is void against B for non-registration. Under section 97 of the Law of Property Act 1925, however, the mortgages rank in order of registration and the order should therefore be A then B.

Support exists for both solutions. In favour of the first solution is that the effect of the Land Charges Act is to make the mortgage void and it is not generally the case that something which is void for non-registration can be resuscitated by subsequent registration.[323] As against that, the point can be made that section 97 deals specifically with the issue of the priority of mortgages and, unless allowed to prevail, has no discernible meaning or function.[324]

Although there is clear force in the latter view, it is suggested that the former argument is to be preferred. This is for the practical reason that A was in a position to protect himself by the simple expedient of registration, whereas B could not have discovered the existence of A's mortgage and, prior to lending the money, may well have relied on having obtained a clear certificate of search against the mortgagor. Although the comparison is not exact, the position of A could be seen to be similar to that of

---

[322] See The effect of non-registration, pp. 100–104.
[323] Cf. *Kitney v. MEPC Ltd* [1977] 1 W.L.R. 981. See also Harpum, Bridge, and Dixon, op. cit., 1192–1193.
[324] Farrand, *Emmet on Title* (19th edn) (London: Sweet & Maxwell, 2000, Looseleaf), para. 25.105.

a person who, through gross negligence, has failed to take or retain the title deeds, thereby enabling the mortgagor to present himself as the unencumbered owner of the property. This problem, and the even more intractable difficulties when there are more than two mortgages,[325] has yet to be resolved and it does little credit to the law that this important issue remains clouded in obscurity.

Registered land

When title is registered, a mortgage is created by a registered charge. The priority of charges is governed by section 48 of the Land Registration Act 2002,[326] which provides that the charges rank between themselves in the order on which they are shown on the register. Until a charge is registered it operates only in equity. If there are two such charges, the priority is the order in which they were created.[327] This can be illustrated by an example.

A charge over registered land is created in favour of A. Two weeks later another charge is created in favour of B. Neither has yet applied for registration of their charges. The priority order is A then B, the order of their creation. B then registers his charge. The effect of this is that A's charge, which has yet to be registered will be postponed to that of B,[328] so the priority order will now be B then A.

Subrogation

This result will occur unless the remedy of subrogation is available, as occurred in *Anfield (UK) Ltd v. Bank of Scotland Plc.*[329] In September 2000, a charge was registered in favour of the Halifax. A registered charge was created in June 2007 in favour of LSL and, in October of that year, a unilateral notice was registered in respect of a pending land action, and, in April 2008, an equitable charge was created, these two registrations being by Anfield. In April 2009 a charge was registered in favour of the Bank of Scotland. Ordinarily, the order of priorities would have been, first, LSL, second Anfield, and finally the Bank of Scotland. The 2009 charge was, however, registered in respect of a mortgage granted by the Bank in 2006, and the purpose of that mortgage was to pay off the mortgage in favour of the Halifax. It was held that the Bank of Scotland had priority over the other charges. This was because, as the purpose of the loan was to pay off that mortgage, it was subrogated to the rights of the Halifax, whose charge clearly had priority over the subsequent charges.

Tacking

The process of tacking involves a mortgagee granting a further loan to the mortgagor and adding that loan to the amount which is already secured by the existing

[325] See Harpum, Bridge, and Dixon, op. cit., 1104.
[326] For the position prior to the 2002 Act coming into force, see 1st edn, pp. 380–381.
[327] Land Registration Act 2002, s. 48.   [328] Ibid., s. 30.
[329] [2010] EWHC 2374 (Ch.). See also *Cheltenham & Gloucester plc v. Appleyard* [2004] EWCA Civ. 291.

mortgage. The ability to do this may, of course, impact upon the rights of subsequent mortgagees who may, as a result, find that their loans are no longer fully secured. Because of this, restrictions are imposed upon the right to tack and it is again necessary to distinguish between registered and unregistered land.

Unregistered land

The right to tack, where title is unregistered, is governed by section 94 of the Law of Property Act 1925 and can be done in three situations.

Consent of intervening mortgagee

If property is mortgaged, first to A, and then to B, A may tack a loan to the existing mortgage if B consents to this being done. This is unsurprising as it is, in any event, open to mortgagees, if they wish, to agree to change the normal order of priorities.[330]

No notice of intervening mortgage

A mortgagee may tack a further loan to an existing mortgage if he has no notice of an intervening mortgage. If the property is mortgaged first to A and then to B, A cannot tack if he has notice of B's mortgage. A will have notice of B's mortgage if B has registered the mortgage as a land charge. If the mortgage to A is to secure further advances, then A will not be deemed to have notice of B's mortgage merely because it has been registered as a land charge.[331] To avoid any difficulties, B should inform A of the existence of his mortgage.

Obligation to make further advances

If the first mortgagee is, under the terms of the mortgage, obliged to make further advances to the mortgagor, he is entitled to tack the loan to the original mortgage regardless of whether he has notice of a subsequent mortgage.

Registered land

The right to tack is governed by section 49 of the Land Registration Act 2002, which reproduces the conditions contained in the 1925 Act and adds one further situation when tacking can occur. It also puts onto a statutory footing what had been the previous practice of lenders.

Under section 49(1) of the Act, the proprietor of a registered charge may tack a further advance if he has not received from a subsequent chargee notice of the creation of a subsequent charge. This puts on a statutory footing the previous practice of lenders. Tacking may also occur if under the charge, the proprietor is obliged to make further advances and this is noted on the register.[332] He may also tack if a subsequent chargee agrees.[333] These two provisions replicate the previous law.[334]

---

[330] *Cheah Theam Swee v. Equitcorp Finance Group Ltd* [1992] A.C. 472.
[331] Law of Property Act 1925, s. 94(2).   [332] Land Registration Act 2002, s. 49(3).
[333] Ibid., s. 49(6).   [334] Land Registration Act 1925, s. 30.

Under the 2002 Act, one new situation when tacking can occur has been introduced. Under section 49(4), if the parties to a charge have agreed a maximum amount for which the charge is created, tacking can occur up to that limit. If A creates a charge in favour of B to secure borrowing of up to £100,000 and, at the time when the charge is created, only £50,000 has been lent, then further advances up to the £100,000 limit can be tacked to the charge. For this to happen, the agreement in relation to the maximum amount must be entered on the register.

13

Easements

The first part of this book had been concerned largely with ownership rights. The previous chapter on mortgages dealt with an important third party right, although the origins of this right lay also in ownership of the property and it is still the case that a mortgagee is regarded as the purchaser of a legal estate in land. In the course of the consideration of the law relating to land ownership, the enforceability of third party rights has been considered. The remainder of the book is concerned with the substance of those rights. This chapter is concerned with the form of third party right categorized as an easement. The remaining chapters will deal with freehold covenants and licences. For reasons of space, neither rentcharges nor *profits à prendre*, which today are of relatively little importance, will be considered in any detail.

THE NATURE OF AN EASEMENT

The essential nature of an easement is that it is a right over another person's land. These rights are very important, and it has recently been said that, 'Without easements it may be very difficult if not impossible to enjoy the benefits of land ownership';[1] an observation attested to by the fact that at least sixty-five per cent of registered freehold titles are subject to at least one easement.[2] Classic examples of such rights are rights of way and rights of light. These are only examples. Others abound. Rights which have been recognized as falling within the legal definition of easements include the right to use a washing line on a neighbour's land,[3] the right to use a neighbour's lavatory,[4] and the right to park a car on another person's land.[5] This, of course, is not an exhaustive list. These are simply examples of rights which have been afforded the status of easements. What it is necessary to do is to identify the characteristics common to all easements.

---

[1] *Wall v. Collins* [2008] 1 All E.R. 122 at [58] *per* Hooper L.J.
[2] (2008) Law Com. Consultation Paper No. 186, para. 1.3.
[3] *Drewell v. Towler* (1832) 3 B. & Ad. 735. See also *Mulvaney v. Gough* [2002] EWCA Civ. 1078.
[4] *Miller v. Emcer Products Ltd* [1956] Ch. 304.
[5] See *Patel v. W.H. Smith (Eziot) Ltd* [1987] 1 W.L.R. 853 at 859 *per* Balcombe L.J. See Car parking, pp. 546–548.

The most authoritative exposition of the nature of easements was given by the Court of Appeal in *Re Ellenborough Park*,[6] where, for the first time, the right of householders to walk freely in a nearby park was recognized as satisfying the requirements to qualify as an easement, thereby adding a new example to the list of rights recognized as being interests in land within this overall class of rights.

Dominant and servient tenement

For a right to exist as an easement, that right must affect two plots of land, or tenements, it being 'an essential element of an easement that it is annexed to land, and that no person can possess an easement otherwise than in respect of land and in amplification of his enjoyment of some estate or interest in a piece of land'.[7] If the easement in question is a right of way, then the person claiming the right does so in his capacity as the owner of a tenement over another plot of land. The land which enjoys the benefit of the right is termed the dominant tenement and the land over which the right is exercised is the servient tenement. If a person claiming to have a right to cross another person's land does not own land himself, then the right may be either a licence or even a public right of way, but it cannot be an easement. The easement must exist for the benefit of land or, putting the same point another way, an easement cannot exist in gross.[8]

The rule that an easement cannot exist in gross has been subject to criticism. It has been argued that, in a modern society, it should be possible to possess an easement without them having to be a dominant tenement.[9] On the other hand, a complementary requirement for an interest to be recognized as an easement is that, not only must there be a dominant tenement, but the right in question must also accommodate that tenement. To abandon the need for a dominant tenement may lead to a number of new rights being found to burden land, and this is not something which the law has been keen to encourage.[10] The Law Commission, having explored the pros and cons of this issue, provisionally concluded that there should be no change in the existing law,[11] and this conclusion was supported after consultation;[12] a proposal which seems sensible.

---

[6] [1956] Ch. 131 at 163 *per* Sir Raymond Evershed M.R., adopting a passage in Cheshire, *The Modern Law of Real Property* (7th edn) (London: Butterworths, 1954), 456. See also *Mulvaney v. Gough* [2002] EWCA Civ. 1078.

[7] *Alfred F. Beckett v. Lyons* [1967] Ch. 449 at 483 *per* Winn L.J.L., and includes an incorporeal interest such as a fishing right: *Hanbury v. Jenkins* [1901] 2 Ch. 401 at 422–423 *per* Buckley L.J.

[8] See *Hawkins v. Rutter* [1892] 1 Q.B. 668; *London and Blenheim Estates Ltd v. Ladbroke Retail Parks Ltd* [1994] 1 W.L.R. 31 at 36 *per* Peter Gibson L.J.

[9] See M.F. Sturley (1980) 96 L.Q.R. 557.

[10] See A. Lawson in Tee (ed.), *Land Law: Issues, Debates, Policy* (Cullompton: Willan Publishing, 2002), 64 at 69–74.

[11] (2008) Law Com. Consultation Paper No. 186, para. 3.18.

[12] (2011) Law Com. No. 327 para. 2.24.

Once an easement has been created, it will run automatically with the dominant land and can be enjoyed by any occupier of that land. If there was no need for there to be a dominant tenement, the passing of the benefit of easements may present problems.

The right must accommodate the dominant tenement

An easement exists to benefit land. As such it is necessary, but not sufficient, that the person claiming the right in question must own land; it is also a requirement that the right claimed actually benefits his land or, again, putting the same point in a different way, the right must accommodate the dominant tenement. The right must benefit the owner of the land in that capacity and not simply confer a personal benefit on him incidental to his ownership of the land. The fact that the easement benefits one plot of land does not mean that the owner of that land can use the easement for the benefit of other plots of land which he owns but which do not have the benefit of that easement.[13] In general, with regard to this matter, two issues arise. These are the mutual proximity of the two plots and the nature of the advantage claimed.

Proximity

For a right over one tenement to confer a benefit on another, common sense would dictate that the two plots of land need to be reasonably close to each other. So, as was once famously commented, if the owner of an estate in Northumberland granted a right of way over that land to the owner of an estate in Kent, there would be no link between the two estates and so the right could not take effect as an easement.[14] This is not to say, however, that the two plots must necessarily be physically contiguous as a right may exist over land which is separated from the dominant plot by other land. So, for example, in *Re Ellenborough Park*,[15] it was held that the right to walk in a park could be enjoyed as an easement by the owners of property on an estate when those properties did not physically adjoin the park. There was sufficient connection between the right in question and the particular properties. Clearly, however, whether the two tenements are sufficiently proximate to each other so that the right really does benefit the dominant tenement, is essentially one of fact and, the greater the physical separation of the two plots in question, the more difficult it will be to establish that the right actually does accommodate the dominant tenement.

Nature of the claim

Leaving aside the question of physical proximity, the other main aspect of whether the right claimed accommodates the dominant tenement concerns the nature of the right claimed; whether it has some natural connection with the estate,[16] or whether it

---

13 *Peacock v. Custins* [2001] 2 All E.R. 827.
14 See *Bailey v. Stephens* (1862) 12 C.B. (N.S.) 91 at 115 *per* Byles J.
15 [1956] Ch. 131. See also *Pugh v. Savage* [1934] 1 Ch. 631.
16 *Bailey v. Stephens* (1862) 12 C.B. (N.S.) 91.

confers merely a personal advantage for the current owner of that estate. This, again, is essentially a question of fact and the essential test to determine this matter is whether the right makes the occupation or use of the dominant tenement more convenient.

Business use

If the dominant tenement is used for business purposes, a right which facilitates that business use can exist as an easement. In *Moody v. Steggles*,[17] the dominant tenement was a pub. The right to place a sign on neighbouring land in respect of that pub was accepted as accommodating the dominant tenement and recognized as being an easement. Conversely, in *Hill v. Tupper*,[18] the tenant of land on a canal bank had been given the exclusive right by the freeholder to put pleasure boats on the canal. The defendant put rival boats on the canal and so the tenant sued, his claim being based on the argument that the defendant was interfering with his easement to put the boats on the canal. The claim failed, it being held that this right did not amount to an easement because it did not accommodate the dominant tenement. The difference between the cases, which both involved business use, would seem to be that, in the former, the right being claimed was supportive of the business use of the dominant tenement, whilst, in the latter, the right being claimed as an easement was the business itself. While the existence of the exclusive right to put boats onto the canal would have been an advantage to the owner of the land, it did not benefit the land itself. This argument gains support from the decision in *P. & S. Platt Ltd v. Crouch*,[19] where it was accepted, seemingly without argument to the contrary, that a right to moor boats on an island close to the dominant land which was used as an hotel accommodated the dominant tenement. The right to moor boats could be seen as an advantage to the existing use of the benefited land.

The tenements must be owned by different people

An easement is a right over another person's land. The rule that the two tenements must be owned by different people is, therefore, at first sight at least, an almost self-evident proposition. So, if a person owns a house and a nearby field and he uses the field as a convenient means of access to a main road, there is no easement. His use of the field is as the owner of it. The field is being used in a subordinate way to the house and, had the two tenements been separately owned, the right of way would exhibit the essential characteristics of an easement. In recognition of this, the use of the field in these circumstances is described as a quasi-easement. While the land is in common ownership, the existence of a quasi-easement is of little importance. It may become very important, however, if the land is subsequently sold off separately.[20]

---

[17] (1879) 12 Ch.D. 261. See also *Wong v. Beaumont Property Trust Ltd* [1965] 1 Q.B. 173.
[18] (1863) 2 H. & C. 121.   [19] [2003] EWCA Civ. 1110.
[20] See Section 62 of the Law of Property Act 1925, pp. 556–560.

Somewhat counterintuitively, although persuasively, the Law Commission provisionally recommended, insofar as registered land is concerned, a relaxation of this rule to enable a person to create an easement in respect of land which he also owns. The situation that the Commission had in mind is one where a developer builds a housing estate and sells individual houses. Then, it will be necessary to grant easements over the various plots but, as the law currently stands, he cannot do this while he still owns the relevant land. Consequently, it was provisionally proposed that, provided that the plots are registered with separate titles, a person should be able to create easements over land which he owns.[21] This proposal was described by one consultee as the single most important proposal in the Consultation Paper,[22] and met with general support. Consequently it has been recommended that, provided that title to the benefited and burdened land is registered, the fact that they are in common ownership and possession shall not prevent the creation or existence of easements or profits.[23]

Leasehold property

The rule that an easement cannot exist if the two tenements are owned by the same person admits of one important exception. If the one person owns the freehold of two properties and lets one of them, there is no objection to the tenant of that property owning an easement over his landlord's other property. Such an easement exists for the benefit of the leasehold estate and so will end on the termination of the lease.

The right must be capable of being the subject matter of a grant

An easement is capable of existing as a legal interest in land. As such, it is a prerequisite that it is capable of being granted by deed. This entails that there must be both a capable grantor and a capable grantee. In addition to this, the right claimed must be sufficiently definite. This requirement has defeated claims to an easement entitling a landowner to a good view,[24] a passage of air through an undefined channel,[25] and the right to drain water through an undefined channel.[26]

Recognition of new easements

In considering this final criterion for the recognition of easements, the need for the right claimed to have sufficient certainty to form the subject matter of a grant is not the only matter to which the courts will pay regard. Although it has been said that there was a tendency in the past to freeze the categories of easements, the decision in

---

[21] See (2008) Law Com. Consultation Paper No. 186, paras 3.56–3.66. See also, in respect of restrictive covenants, Schemes of development, pp. 587–588.

[22] (2011) Law Com. No. 327, para. 4.24.   [23] Ibid., para. 4.44.

[24] *William Aldred's Case* (1610) 9 Co. Rep. 57b.   [25] *Harris v. De Pinna* (1886) 33 Ch.D. 231.

[26] *Home Brewery plc v. William Davis & Co. (Loughborough) Ltd* [1987] Q.B. 339; *Palmer v. Bowman* [2000] 1 All E.R. 22. A right to the supply of water through a defined channel can be an easement. See *Rance v. Elvin* (1985) 50 P. & C.R. 9.

Re Ellenborough Park,[27] where the right to use a park for recreational purposes was, for the first time, recognized to be an easement, has been said to have been a defrosting operation,[28] so that the courts are prepared to accept new rights as being capable of being easements.[29] In so doing, the courts are prepared to accept that the law should be prepared to adapt to changing social conditions, hence the comparatively recent acceptance that the right to park a car anywhere in a defined area can exist as an easement.[30] As against this, the courts have traditionally been wary of allowing novel rights to be attached to land because to allow this would place impediments on a person's subsequent ability to deal with the land.[31] As part of the resolution of these tensions, certain types of right are unlikely to be recognized as capable of being easements.

Negative rights

Subject to two well-established exceptions, it is highly unlikely that the courts will recognize as an easement a claim which restricts the use to which the owner of the servient land can put his land.[32] The exceptions to this general principle concern a right to light, the existence of which was recognized by statute in the nineteenth century,[33] and the right to the support of buildings.[34] In the case of the first easement, the effect of the existence of the easement is that the owner of the servient tenement is restricted as to how he can build upon his own land. In the case of the latter, the tenement owner cannot demolish structures on his own land if the effect of so doing would be to undermine buildings on the dominant land.

Other than that, negative easements will not be recognized. Hence, a right to privacy,[35] or to an interrupted flow of air over an undefined area[36] have been held not to be easements. More recently, it was argued in *Hunter v. Canary Wharf Ltd*,[37] that there could be an easement in respect of the uninterrupted receipt of a television signal. Such a claim failed, however, on the basis that no such easement could exist.[38] Should it be sought to restrict the user of servient land, an easement is not the most apt means of so doing. Instead, this can be achieved by the use of an appropriately drafted restrictive covenant.[39]

Expenditure of money

The essential nature of an easement is that it enables the owner of the dominant tenement to do something on the servient tenement. A 'positive obligation on the owner

---

[27] [1956] Ch. 131.

[28] *Dowty Ltd v. Wolverhampton Corporation (No. 2)* [1976] Ch. 13 at 22 *per* Russell L.J. (right to use an airfield).

[29] See also *Dyce v. Hay* (1852) 1 Macq. 305 at 312 *per* Lord St Leonards L.C.

[30] See *Patel v. W.H. Smith (Eziot) Ltd* [1987] 1 W.L.R. 853 at 859 *per* Balcombe L.J.; *London and Blenheim Estates Ltd v. Ladbroke Retail Parks Ltd* [1992] 1 W.L.R. 1278 at 1287 *per* Judge Baker Q.C., see Car parking, pp. 546–548. See also *Horton v. Tidd* (1965) 196 E.G. 697 (right to retrieve cricket balls).

[31] *Keppell v. Bailey* (1834) 2 My & K. 517 at 535 *per* Lord Brougham L.C.

[32] For an historical, and critical, approach to this issue, see I. Dawson and A. Dunn (1998) 18 L.S. 510.

[33] Prescription Act 1832, s. 3.   [34] See *Dalton v. Angus* (1881) 6 App. Cas. 740.

[35] *Browne v. Flower* [1911] 1 Ch. 219.   [36] *Bryant v. Lefever* (1879) 4 C.P.D. 172.

[37] [1997] A.C. 655.   [38] Ibid., *per* Lord Hoffmann.   [39] See Chapter 14.

of the servient tenement owner to do something is inconsistent with the existence of such an easement'.[40] A court is, therefore, unwilling to recognize as an easement a right which requires the owner of the servient tenement either to spend money or to do some positive act and, on this basis, has declined to accept that a claim to have one's property protected from the weather could exist as an easement.[41] Similarly, a claim to use a neighbour's swimming pool is unlikely to be recognized as an easement, because it would impose on the owner of the servient tenement an obligation to keep it filled.[42] An exception exists to this general rule, in what has been described as being 'in the nature of a spurious easement',[43] and is the obligation to maintain fencing to keep in livestock.[44] This exception is limited to fences for the purpose of enclosing livestock and does not apply to the erection of fences in general, so that an agreement between neighbours that one of them is responsible for maintaining a boundary fence is enforceable as between them but the burden of that obligation will not run with the land.[45] Recognizing the spurious nature of such easements, the Law Commission has recommended that it should not be possible to create an easement of fencing, and that any such obligation would need to be expressly created as a land obligation, a new legal right in land which it has proposed should be created.[46]

Access to neighbouring land

If there exists an easement, the owner of the servient tenement is under no obligation to do any repairs or maintenance to enable the dominant owner to enjoy the easement but the owner of the dominant land may enter the land to effect necessary repairs.[47] This is only a limited right of access and, together with the fact there is no easement to protect one's property from the elements, this created problems for a person who needed to go onto his neighbour's land to effect repairs and maintenance to his own property. To meet this problem, the Access to Neighbouring Land Act 1992 was passed. Under section 1, a landowner may apply to a court for an order to enable access to adjoining or adjacent land. Such an order will be made if the court is satisfied that a landowner needs to go onto that land to do work which is reasonably necessary for the protection of his own land and that the work can only be done, or would be substantially more difficult to do, without entering the servient land. This access order will be binding upon a purchaser of the servient land if protected by registration: in

---

[40] *Rance v. Elvin* (1985) 50 P. & C.R. 9 at 13 *per* Browne-Wilkinson L.J.; *William Old International Ltd v. Arya* [2009] EWHC 599 (Ch.). See also *Jones v. Price* [1965] 2 Q.B. 618 at 644 *per* Winn L.J.

[41] *Phipps v. Pears* [1965] 1 Q.B. 76. Contrast *Sedgwick Forbes Bland Payne Group Ltd v. Regional Properties Ltd* (1979) 257 E.G. 64 at 70 *per* Oliver J. (property divided horizontally, i.e. flats, rather than vertically).

[42] *Moncrieff v. Jamieson* [2007] 1 W.L.R. 2620 at [47] *per* Lord Scott of Foscote.

[43] *Lawrence v. Jenkins* (1873) L.R. 8 Q.B. 274 at 279 *per* Archibald J.

[44] *Bolus v. Hinstorke* (1670) 2 Keb. 686. See also *Crow v. Wood* [1971] 1 Q.B. 77.

[45] See *Jones v. Price* [1965] 2 Q.B. 618 at 637 *per* Willmer L.J. See also at 639 *per* Diplock L.J., where the existence of the easement in respect of livestock is described as 'anomalous'.

[46] (2011) Law Com. No. 327, para. 5.94. See Chapter 14.

[47] See *Jones v. Prichard* [1908] 1 Ch. 630 at 637–638 *per* Parker J. See also *Bond v. Nottingham Corporation* [1940] Ch. 429 at 438–439 *per* Sir Wilfrid Greene M.R.; *Carter v. Cole* [2006] EWCA Civ. 398.

the case of unregistered land, by the registration of a writ or order affecting the land and, where title is registered, by the registration of a notice.[48]

Excessive claims

A further ground on which it was thought that a claim to an easement could be defeated was if the claim amounted to an excessive user of the servient tenement.[49] Thus, in *Copeland v. Greenhalf*,[50] a person claimed to have an easement to store vehicles on adjoining land. Although a right to deposit trade goods on another person's land had previously been recognized as being an easement,[51] in the instant case the claimed failed because, on the facts, it was regarded as being too extensive a use of the servient land to amount to an easement.[52] On the other hand, in *Wright v. Macadam*,[53] not cited in *Copeland v. Greenhalf*, the right to store coal in a shed was held to be an easement. The cases were not easy to reconcile.[54] An attempt at reconciliation was made in *London and Blenheim Estates Ltd v. Ladbroke Retail Parks Ltd*,[55] where Judge Baker Q.C. concluded that the matter was one of degree and that the more extensive the use, the less likely it is that the claim would be upheld as being an easement.

Before exploring this issue further, one related matter can first be considered. In *Copeland v. Greenhalf*, the easement was claimed on the basis of prescription, that is long user,[56] and the judge thought that the claim should really have been based on adverse possession, whereas in *Wright v. Macadam*, the right of storage had been the subject of an express grant. It was thought that the courts might be more willing to recognize that extensive use of the servient land could be an easement if there was an express grant rather than a claim based on long user.[57] Any such distinction was rejected, however, in *Moncrieff v. Jamieson*,[58] where Lord Scott of Foscote expressly stated that there was no difference between the characteristics of an easement created by prescription and one created expressly.

To return to the main issue, recent case law had accepted, as a general proposition, the notion that if a right amounted to an extensive use of the servient land, it could not be an easement. In *Mulvaney v. Gough*,[59] the Court of Appeal, while prepared to accept that the right to cultivate flower beds on adjoining land could be an easement, was concerned that this right was not focused on a particular part of the servient land. If it had been, then this would have been a claim to the exclusive use of part of

[48] Access to Neighbouring Land Act 1992, ss 4, 5.
[49] See M. Haley and L. McMurtry (2007) 58 N.I.L.Q. 490; A.Hill-Smith [2007] Conv. 223.
[50] [1952] Ch. 488.
[51] *Dyce v. Hay* (1852) 1 Macq. 305. See also *Attorney-General of Southern Nigeria v. John Holt & Co. (Liverpool) Ltd* [191] A.C. 599 at 617 *per* Lord Shaw of Dunfermline.
[52] [1952] Ch. 488 at 498 *per* Upjohn J.   [53] [1949] 2 K.B. 744.
[54] See the general observations on the confused state of the authorities concerning easements in *McAdams Homes Ltd v. Robinson* [2004] 3 E.G.L.R. 93 at [1] *per* Neuberger J.
[55] [1992] 1 W.L.R. 1278 at 1285–1286, affirmed at [1994] 2 K.B. 744.
[56] See Prescription, pp. 565–573.   [57] See J.R. Spencer [1973] C.L.J. 30 at 32.
[58] [2007] 1 W.L.R. 2620 at [59].   [59] [2002] EWCA Civ. 1078. See M.P. Thompson [2002] Conv. 571.

the servient land which, it was felt, was inconsistent with the nature of an easement.[60] This consensus has, however, been cast aside by far-reaching *dicta* in *Moncrieff v. Jamieson*.[61]

Car parking

The question of excessive user has arisen on a number of occasions when consideration has been given to the question of whether the right to park a car can exist as an easement, an issue which has been described as being very important in practice.[62] Although the judicial consensus appeared to favour the acceptance that it could,[63] it was initially considered to be important as to how the right was to be exercised. In *Batchelor v. Marlow*,[64] a claim to the exclusive right to park cars on a particular strip of land between 8.30 a.m. and 6.30 p.m. on Mondays to Fridays was considered to amount to too extensive a use of the servient land to be capable of being an easement, whereas in *Hair v. Gillman*,[65] the court held that a right to park one car on any part of a forecourt which could accommodate four cars could be an easement. The reasoning underlying this line of cases was disapproved, however, by the House of Lords in *Moncrieff v. Jamieson*.[66]

The case concerned whether a person who had a right of way over adjoining land also had an implied right to park on that land. Given the topology of the two plots of land, it was not possible to park on the dominant land, and it was held, applying *Jones v. Prichard*,[67] that the grant of an easement is, *prima facie*, also the grant of such ancillary rights as are reasonably necessary to its exercise and enjoyment. In this case, if there was no such right to park, the owners of the dominant tenement would have had to walk 150 yards in all weathers from where they parked their car to their own property,[68] and it was held that such a right was ancillary to the right of way. In so doing, the House confirmed that the right to park a car is capable of being an easement.[69] Of wider significance are the *obiter* remarks concerning the nature of easements.

---

[60] See also *Grigsby v. Melville* [1972] 1 W.L.R. 1278 at 1285–1286 *per* Brightman J., affirmed without reference to this point at [1974] 1 W.L.R. 80. Cf. J.R. Spencer, loc. cit., at 34, who considers *Copeland v. Greenhalf* to have been wrongly decided, although it was approved in *Hair v. Gillman* (2000) 80 P. & C.R. 108 at 113 *per* Chadwick L.J.

[61] [2007] 1 W.L.R. 2620.   [62] *Waterman v. Boyle* [2009] EWCA Civ. 115 at [24] *per* Arden L.J.

[63] *Newman v. Jones* (1982), unreported (a decision of Sir Robert Megarry V.-C.); *Patel v. W.H. Smith (Eziot) Ltd* [1992] 1 W.L.R. 1278 at 1287 *per* Balcombe L.J.; *London & Blenheim Estates Ltd v. Ladbroke Retail Parks Ltd* [1992] 1 W.L.R. 1278 at 1287 *per* Judge Baker Q.C. (affirmed at [1994] 1 W.L.R. 31). Cf. *Saeed v. Plustrade Ltd* [2002] P. & C.R. 19 at [22], where Sir Christopher Slade left this point open.

[64] (2001) 32 P. & C.R. 36.

[65] (2000) 80 P. & C.R. 108. See also *P. & S. Platt Ltd v. Crouch* [2003] EWCA Civ. 1110, where the right to moor boats in a specific place on an island was accepted as being an easement, this issue being considered to be one of fact and degree: ibid., at [45] *per* Peter Gibson L.J.

[66] [2007] 1 W.L.R. 2620.   [67] [1908] 1 Ch. 630 at 638 *per* Parker J.

[68] [2007] 1 W.L.R. 2620 at [34] *per* Lord Hope of Craighead. Contrast the view of Lord Rodger of Earlsferry at [83].

[69] Lord Hope reserved his opinion as to whether the right to park which is not ancillary to a right of way could be an easement: ibid., at [22]. No such doubts were expressed by other members of the panel.

Nature of use

Both Lord Scott of Foscote and Lord Neuberger of Abbotsbury rejected as a test that one determined whether the use was too excessive as being one of fact and degree, and disapproved *Batchelor v. Marlow*.[70] Lord Scott, who was prepared to accept that *Copeland v. Greenhalf* was correctly decided on the facts,[71] was minded 'to reject the test that asks whether the servient owner is left with any reasonable use of his land, and substitute for it a test which asks whether the servient owner retains possession of, and subject to the reasonable exercise of the right in question, control of the servient land'.[72]

It is envisaged that the application of this test will be difficult to apply. Lord Scott was prepared to say that sole user of a shed to store coal by the owner of the dominant tenement would not mean that the owner of the servient tenement had not retained possession of it, as he could use the shed for any other purpose which did not interfere with the storage right,[73] although he cast no light on what realistically this might entail. Lord Neuberger arguably went further, as he said that 'as at presently advised, I am not satisfied that a right is prevented from being a servitude or an easement simply because the right granted would involve the servient owner being effectively excluded from the property'.[74] One difficulty with this is that, where there is no express grant but the claim is based upon long user, it is difficult to distinguish between the type of use referred to and a claim for adverse possession. As the owner of land now has, effectively, a power of veto over claims to a possessory title,[75] the *dicta* in *Moncrieff* may lead a person who would, in the past, be regarded as a squatter to now argue, provided that the period of use has been long enough, that he has an easement.

A real problem with the *dicta* in *Moncrieff*, it is suggested, is that it makes it difficult to distinguish between a use which amounts to adverse possession and use to support a claim to an easement. A further difficulty lies in distinguishing some forms of easements from a lease. In the light of Lord Scott's comments concerning an easement of storage, it is clear that a right to park a car in a garage can be an easement.[76] The difficulty here is that such a right would normally be granted by a lease.[77] If, in return for a lump sum, a document grants a person a right to park a car for a period of a year in a garage then, provided that the grantee has land nearby which would benefit, it is now very difficult to say whether this is an easement for a year, or a lease. If the former, it would be required to be registered; if the latter it would not.[78]

A further point which can now arise is the enforceability of easements against third parties. Prior to the coming into force of the Land Registration Act 2002, easements

---

[70] Ibid., at [60] and, more tentatively, at [143], respectively.   [71] Ibid., at [56].

[72] Ibid., at [59].   [73] Ibid., at [55].   [74] Ibid., at [139].

[75] See The new limitation regime, pp. 261–268.

[76] The view expressed by M. Haley and L. McMurtry, loc. cit., at 502–503 that an exclusive right to park in an allocated space cannot be an easement has now been overtaken by events, and does not represent the law.

[77] See, e.g., *Kling v. Keston Properties Ltd* (1989) 49 P. & C.R. 212.

[78] Land Registration Act 2002, ss 4(1)(c), 27(2)(d).

were overriding interests.[79] Quite deliberately, the range of easements which were to be overriding was reduced by the 2002 Act to those easements created by implication or by prescription. An easement created by express grant or reservation is required to be registered.[80] Now that the House of Lords has accepted that an easement can exist whereby the owner of it can occupy the servient land, this raises the possibility that an expressly granted easement may override a registered disposition of the servient land, as a person in actual occupation of that land.[81] While the decision itself is to be welcomed in providing confirmation that a right to park a car is capable of being an easement, some of the wider *dicta* have, it is suggested, disturbed some quite well settled principles underlying the law of easements, and may give rise to considerable difficulty in the future.

The Law Commission considered this matter and concluded that the law must continue to distinguish between arrangements which confer exclusive possession and those which do not. If exclusive possession is granted, then this should entail the grant of a freehold or a lease, but should not amount to an easement.[82] It went on to say, however, that the law should continue to recognize as an easement a use that stops short of exclusive possession, even if it deprives the owner of the servient land all reasonable use of it.[83] This seems regrettable, in that it will make the distinction between an easement and other legal concepts difficult, and also recognize as a third party interest in land a right which, to most intents and purposes, is exclusionary in nature and is something which goes beyond what has traditionally been recognized as an easement.

EASEMENTS AND RELATED CONCEPTS

The essential nature of an easement is that it is a right to do something on or over another person's land. Rights of a similar nature can arise in other ways and it is useful, briefly, to consider some of those rights by way of comparison.

Natural rights

The law implies certain natural rights for landowners, the interference with which will make the neighbour liable in nuisance. There are two such rights: the right of support and the right to water.

Right of support
The right of support exists to protect the land itself but, not entirely logically, this right does not extend to any buildings on the land. In respect of support for the land itself the owner of the adjoining land is liable for his action which causes neighbouring land

---

[79] Land Registration Act 1925, s. 70(1)(a).   [80] Land Registration Act 2002.
[81] Ibid., Sched. 3, para. 2. See M.P .Thompson [1986] Conv. 31 at 36.
[82] (2011) Law Com. No. 327, para. 3.206.   [83] Ibid., at 3.208.

to subside.[84] So, if by excavation[85] or the removal of underground salt[86] damage is caused to neighbouring land, this is actionable.

The obligation with regard to support extends to acts of omission as well as to acts of commission. In *Holbeck Hall Hotel Ltd v. Scarborough Borough Council*,[87] the plaintiff owned a hotel which stood on a cliff overlooking the sea. The land between the hotel and the sea was owned by the defendant. After two minor slips caused by coastal erosion, there was a massive slip which caused the ground under the hotel's seaward wing to collapse and the issue arose as to the defendant's liability. It was held that the duty of support extended to omissions as well as to commissions. That duty is not, however, absolute. Liability will only arise in such cases if the landowner is aware, or should be aware, of the danger. Moreover, in cases of omission, regard must also be had to the extent of the duty and, in particular, whether it is fair and reasonable to impose potentially huge expense on a landowner in respect of geological problems which are not his fault.[88] In the instant case, while the authority was aware that there was a problem of erosion, it was not aware of the scale of the problem. Given the cost of any remedial work, it was considered, also, that the scope of its duty may have been limited to sharing its knowledge of the danger with affected parties.[89]

There is no natural right to the support of buildings, although such a right can be obtained as an easement.[90] If the damage to the buildings is caused by withdrawal of support for the land itself, however, then the loss caused by the damage to the building is also recoverable.

Water

There is a natural right to water which flows through a natural channel.[91] Where water does not flow through a defined channel but percolates naturally through the land, the owner of the lower land does not have the right to receive that water.[92] In the case of water which accumulates naturally on land, there is a natural right of drainage onto adjoining land,[93] so that the owner of the land on which the water accumulates is not liable for any flooding caused to the land onto which that water drains. Whether the owner of the lower land can take steps to prevent that drainage in order to protect his own land is unclear.[94] There is authority to favour this view,[95] which leads to the

---

[84] There is no cause of action unless the withdrawal of support causes damage: *Darley Main Colliery v. Mitchell* (1886) 11 App. Cas. 127. See, generally, T.H. Wu [2003] Conv. 237.

[85] *Redland Bricks Ltd v. Morris* [1970] A.C. 652.

[86] *Lotus Ltd v. British Soda Co. Ltd* [1972] Ch. 123.

[87] [2000] 2 All E.R. 705; *Leakey v. National Trust* [1980] Q.B. 485. See M.P. Thompson [2001] Conv. 177.

[88] See also *Goldman v. Hargrave* [1967] 1 A.C. 645 at 663 *per* Lord Wilberforce.

[89] [2000] 2 All E.R. 705 at 726 *per* Stuart-Smith L.J.

[90] See *Dalton v. Angus & Co.* (1881) 6 App. Cas. 740.

[91] *Swindon Waterworks Co. Ltd v. Wilts and Berks Canal Navigation Co.* (1875) L.R. 7 H.L. 697.

[92] *Chasemore v. Richards* (1859) 7 H.L.C. 376.   [93] *Palmer v. Bowman* [2000] 1 All E.R. 22.

[94] The point was left open in *Palmer v. Bowman* [2000] 1 All E.R. 22 at 35 *per* Rattee J. (a Court of Appeal authority).

[95] *Home Brewery plc v. William Davis & Co. (Loughborough) Ltd* [1987] Q.B. 339 at 349 *per* Mr Piers Ashworth Q.C.

slightly odd proposition that the owner of the higher land has the right of drainage but the owner of the lower land is not under a duty to receive the water, but this nevertheless, seems reasonable.

Public rights

An easement is a private right which one landowner owns and which is enforced against another person's land. Some rights are exercisable by the public at large, the most common of those rights being a public right of way.[96] Such rights can be created expressly by statute, or under common law. The common law method is by a process known as dedication and acceptance. The essence of this method is long user, the general presumption being that a public right of way can be established after twenty years' uninterrupted use.[97]

Profits à prendre

A *profit à prendre*, or as it is more commonly known, a profit, is similar to an easement in that it gives a person the right to go onto another's land. The essential aspect of the profit, however, is the right to take something off that land, that something being either the natural produce of the land, such as crops, or the animals existing on it. The right to fish another's land, known as a right of piscary, can exist as a profit. A profit can be appurtenant to land, that is, exist for the benefit of a dominant tenement, or, unlike an easement, it can exist in gross, that is, it can be owned independently of land.

Restrictive covenants

As has been seen, the law is highly reluctant to recognize as an easement a claim which restricts the use of the servient tenement, such rights being limited effectively to rights of light and rights of support. This gap in the law is catered for by the law relating to restrictive covenants, an equitable development modelled closely on the law of easements. Whereas easements can be either legal or equitable, restrictive covenants are entirely an equitable construct. It is an important area of law which will be considered in Chapter 14.

Licences

The essence of a licence is that it makes lawful what would otherwise amount to a trespass. It is a permission to use another's land. A licence may display some, or indeed all, of the characteristics of an easement but nevertheless not qualify as one. If

---

[96] For a major extension of public rights, see Countryside and Rights of Way Act 2000.
[97] Highways Act 1980, s. 31(1).

a person is given permission to cross another's land but does not own land, himself, then this right of way cannot be an easement because there is no dominant tenement. The right can therefore only be a licence. If a landowner allows his neighbour to cross his land, then this does display the characteristics of an easement, but will not be one if all that was intended was to give that neighbour a personal permission to use the land in this way. Again, the right in question would be a licence. The law relating to licences is an area which has, in recent years, assumed considerable importance and forms the subject matter of Chapter 15.

LEGAL AND EQUITABLE EASEMENTS

An easement may be either legal or equitable. To be legal, an easement must come within the terms of section 1(2) of the Law of Property Act 1925. This means that it must exist for the equivalent of a fee simple absolute in possession or a term of years absolute. It follows from this that an easement for life must necessarily be equitable. In the case of easements for the equivalent of a term of years, this will normally arise when a tenant enjoys an easement, the duration of that easement, so far as the tenant is concerned, being coterminous with the lease. This is not necessarily the case, however, so that if the tenant acquires the title to the reversion, thereby causing the lease to merge with the freehold,[98] the easement will continue to exist for the time originally envisaged.[99]

Legal easements

A legal easement can be created in one of three ways: by statute, by deed, or by prescription. Easements created by statute are relatively unimportant and tend to involve local Acts of Parliament creating a particular right, such as a right of support. The latter two methods of creating legal easements are important and will be discussed fully below.

Equitable easements

Equitable easements can arise in a number of ways. First, if the owner of the dominant land has only an equitable estate, which will be the case if he holds an equitable lease, then any easement will itself take effect only in equity. Secondly, if the easement does not come within the definition of legal easement provided by section 1(2), then it can only be equitable. Finally, where title is unregistered, if a purported

---

[98] See Merger, p. 459.   [99] *Wall v. Collins* [2008] 1 All E.R. 122.

grant of an easement is not by deed, then no legal easement can arise and any easement can only take effect in equity. In the case of registered land, the creation of a legal easement must be completed by registration. This means noting the benefit of the easement on the title of the dominant tenement and the burden on that of the servient tenement. If this is not done, the transaction will only operate in equity.[100]

If a deed is not used, the purported grant may not be entirely ineffectual. Provided that the purported grant complies with the formal requirements of section 2 of the Law of Property (Miscellaneous Provisions) Act 1989, then it may take effect as a contract to create an easement. Provided, as will normally be the case, that this contract is specifically enforceable, then, on the principle that equity looks on that as done which ought to be done, an equitable easement will arise.[101]

The effect of easements

If a legal easement is created, then, if title is unregistered, a purchaser will automatically take subject to it, precisely because it is a legal interest. In the case of registered land, the position was that legal easements would be binding on purchasers because they were overriding interests.[102] If an equitable easement is created, if title is unregistered, to bind a purchaser, it must be registered as a land charge.[103] If title was registered, provided that the equitable easement was exercised openly, it took effect as an overriding interest.[104] Under the Land Registration Act 2002, only legal easements will override a registered disposition.[105] Subject to transitional provisions, the intention was that only easements created by implication[106] or by prescription will override a registered disposition, and only then if it was either within the knowledge of the purchaser, or would have been obvious on a reasonably careful inspection of the land, save where the easement has been exercised within a year of the disposition.[107] It would now seem to be the case that some easements may override, because the owners of them are in actual occupation of the servient land.[108]

---

[100] Land Registration Act 2002, s. 27.

[101] See, generally, *E.R. Ives Investment Ltd v. High* [1967] 2 Q.B. 379 at 397 *per* Danckwerts L.J.; at 403 *per* Winn L.J.; *R (on the application of Beresford) v. Sunderland City Council* [2004] 1 All E.R. 160 at 172 *per* Lord Scott of Foscote.

[102] Land Registration Act 1925, s. 70(1)(a).   [103] Land Charges Act 1972, s. 2(2).

[104] *Celsteel Ltd v. Alton House Holdings Ltd* [1985] 1 W.L.R. 204 (reversed in part on another point [1986] 1 W.L.R. 31); *Thatcher v. Douglas* (1996) 146 N.L.J. 282.

[105] Land Registration Act 2002, Scheds 1, para. 3, and 3, para. 3.

[106] This includes easements created by the operation of the Law of Property Act 1925, s. 62. See Registered dispositions, p. 152.

[107] Land Registration Act 2002, s. 27, Sched. 3, para. 3. See Registered dispositions, p. 152.

[108] See Nature of use, pp. 547–548.

THE CREATION OF EASEMENTS

Legal easements are commonly created by the parties themselves by an express act. To do this a deed is essential. The usual, although not invariable, occasion when this occurs is when a person is selling some of his land and retaining the rest. In this circumstance, it is important to know whether the vendor has retained rights over the land which he has sold or, alternatively, given rights to the purchaser over the land which he has retained. The former process is known as reservation and the latter a grant. In either case, this may be express or implied.

Express reservation

If the vendor of land wishes to retain rights over property which he is selling, it is normally necessary for him to do so expressly. This is because the law is reluctant to imply rights in favour of a grantor who, if he wishes to retain such rights, should expressly stipulate for them.[109] So, if A owns a house and a field, and sells the field to B, and he wishes to retain the right to cross that field as he had done when he owned both properties, then he must take care to ensure that this right is expressly reserved. If he fails to do so, it is very unlikely that the law will imply such a right in his favour.

In the example given above, the only person who has the right to grant an easement over the field is the purchaser of it, B. In a situation such as this, until 1926, B would have had formally to grant to A the requisite easement. This was inconvenient. To simplify matters, section 65 of the Law of Property Act 1925 provides that the reservation of a right will operate as a regrant by the purchaser[110] without the need for him to execute the conveyance by a regrant. So, in the example being considered, if A conveyed the field to B and, in the conveyance, reserved the right to cross the field, this would be sufficient to create a legal easement in favour of A without the need for B to execute the conveyance. As an alternative method, if A conveys the field subject to a right of way over it, this will operate to create an easement in his favour.[111]

The effect of this provision is that the reservation operates as a regrant of an easement by the purchaser. Applying the *contra proferentem* principle, whereby, in cases of ambiguity, a document is construed against the grantor and in favour of the grantee, it has been held that any ambiguities should be resolved in favour of the vendor.[112] This has rightly been condemned as being illogical because the reality is that the terms of the easement will have been drafted by the vendor and, consequently, any ambiguities should be construed against him.[113]

---

[109] See *Ray v. Hazeldine* [1902] 2 Ch. 17 at 19 *per* Kekewich J.
[110] See *Johnstone v. Holdway* [1963] 1 All E.R. 432.
[111] Law of Property Act 1925, s. 65(2); *Wiles v. Banks* (1984) 50 P. & C.R. 80.
[112] *St Edmundsbury & Ipswich Diocesan Board of Finance v. Clark (No. 2)* [1975] 1 W.L.R. 468.
[113] (2008) Law Com. Consultation Paper No. 186, para. 4.21.

Implied reservation

As has already been observed, when one person transfers land to another, the law is very reluctant to imply rights over that land in favour of the grantor. In the present context, easements over land which has been transferred will, in the absence of an express reservation, arise in favour of the grantor in two situations, these being where the law is prepared to imply such a grant.

Necessity

It may happen that, when a person sells off part of his land and retains another plot, he has so arranged matters that he has not reserved to himself any access to or from the retained plot. The land has now become landlocked. When this occurs, the court will be prepared to imply an easement of necessity in favour of the grantor.[114] For an easement of necessity to be implied, the case must really be one of necessity. The fact that the proposed right will form a much more convenient means of access will not be sufficient for an easement to be implied.[115] In *Titchmarsh v. Royston Water Co.*,[116] land had been sold and the only means of access to the retained land was by means of a road which was some twenty feet below the land itself. It was held that, while this means of access was undeniably inconvenient, it was not impossible and, consequently, no easement of necessity was implied.

The prerequisites for a claim to an easement of necessity to be successful were spelled out by the Privy Council in *Manjang v. Drameh*,[117] as being that:

'There has to be, first, a common owner of a legal estate in two plots of land. It has, secondly, to be established that access between one of those plots and the public highway can be obtained only over the other plot. Thirdly, there has to be found a disposition of one of those plots without any specific grant or reservation of a right of access.'

If these criteria are met, the basis upon which the courts will imply an easement of necessity is that this is taken to be what the parties intended, it not being supposed that either party intended the grantor of the land to be left marooned on the retained land. If, however, it is clear that there was no intention to create an easement, then the courts will not invoke the doctrine of public policy, which is against land being sterilized in this way, to impose an easement of necessity against the will of the grantee.[118] While such a situation is likely to be very rare, it is nevertheless clear that a claim to an easement of necessity is extremely hard to establish.

---

[114] See *Pinnington v. Galland* (1853) 9 Exch. 1. See L. Crabb [1981] Conv. 442.

[115] See *Peckham v. Ellison* (1998) 31 H.L.R. 1031 at 1036–1037 *per* Cazalet J.

[116] (1900) 81 L.T. 673. For a more recent, if less extreme, example, see *M.R.A. Engineering Ltd v. Trimster Co. Ltd* (1987) 56 P. & C.R. 1.

[117] (1990) 61 P. & C.R. 194 at 197 *per* Lord Oliver of Aylmerton.

[118] *Nickerson v. Barraclough* [1981] Ch. 426. See also *Adealon International Proprietary Ltd v. The Mayor and Burgesses of the London Borough of Merton* [2007] EWCA Civ 362. One suggestion put forward by the Law Commission is that, subject to the expression of a contrary intention, public policy should favour the grant of an easement of necessity: (2008) Law Com. Consultation Paper No. 186, para. 4.133.

Notwithstanding clear authority that indicates that easements of necessity are only to be implied very sparingly, in *Sweet v. Sommer*,[119] Hart J. felt able to imply a right of vehicular access as an easement of necessity. This seems to be wrong. To prevent the property being landlocked, a right of access by foot is all that is necessary, and to imply a greater right than this is not justified. The Court of Appeal, while upholding the decision on an alternative ground, declined to comment on this aspect of the case,[120] which, it is suggested, should be treated with considerable caution, it having been said more than 150 years ago that 'A grant, arising out of the implication of necessity, cannot be carried further than the necessity of the case requires...'[121]

Implied intention

Although the creation of easements is said to be based upon the intention of the parties,[122] there can also be an implied reservation of an easement if the court is satisfied that this was the mutual intention of the parties. Such an intention can be implied when there is no actual necessity but, again, the person arguing in favour of an implied reservation will face a difficult task.[123] The most common situation where there will be an implied easement on the basis of mutual intention is where a person sells a house and retains a house next door. A mutual easement of support is then likely to be implied.[124]

With regard to other easements, the courts are reluctant to imply a reservation but the Court of Appeal was prepared to do so in the recent case of *Peckham v. Ellison*.[125] In this case, the facts were exceptional, and in particular all concerned thought at the relevant times that a right of way, which had been in fact exercised for a considerable number of years, actually existed in law and it was accepted that, had thought been given as to the need for a reservation of the right, both parties would have accepted that this should be done. It was made clear, however, that the onus that the person claiming an implied reservation must discharge is a heavy one. The court does not approach the issue on the same basis that it would when the issue is what terms should be implied into a contract.[126] What is necessary to infer a common intention to reserve an easement across the land being transferred is 'that the facts are not reasonably consistent with any other explanation—it is not enough that they are simply consistent with such an explanation'.[127] So, the fact that the owner of the quasi-dominant plot exercised the right at the time of the conveyance is not sufficient for the court to imply a common intention to reserve an easement over the servient land;[128] neither is it sufficient that

---

[119] [2004] EWHC 1504 (Ch.).   [120] [2005] EWCA Civ. 227.

[121] *Holmes v. Goring* (1824) 2 Bing. 76 at 84 *per* Best C.J.

[122] For strong, and justified, criticism of the process of discerning the intentions of the parties, see (2011) Law Com No. 327, para. 3.45.

[123] See *Re Webb's Lease* [1951] Ch. 808.

[124] See *Jones v. Prichard* [1908] 1 Ch. 630 at 638 *per* Parker J.

[125] (1998) 31 H.L.R. 1031. See L. Fox [1999] Conv. 353.

[126] (1998) 31 F.L.R. 1031 at 1044 *per* Cazalet J.   [127] Ibid., at 1043 *per* Cazalet J.

[128] *Re Webb's Lease* [1952] 1 Ch.D. 808 at 828 *per* Jenkins L.J.

the use of the right is physically apparent.[129] In short, it will only be in the clearest cases that the court will feel able to imply a common intention that an easement is to be reserved over the land which is being transferred.[130] Somewhat surprisingly, the view of the Law Commission is that an implied reservation of an easement should occur on the same basis as an implied grant.[131] This would represent quite a shift as the law has consistently, and rightly, been very reluctant to imply rights in favour of a grantor. The proposed changes to the law will be considered later in the chapter.[132]

Express grant

Little need be said about the situation where one person expressly grants an easement to another. Care should be taken in drafting such a grant in order to avoid later disputes. So, if a right of way is being granted, it is preferable to stipulate whether this includes access by car or lorry as well as pedestrian use. Similarly, if the right in question is a right of light and more light is required than is necessary for domestic use, as might be the case where the dominant land is being used as a market garden, then this should also be stipulated in the grant.[133] What requires rather more consideration is the effect of section 62 of the Law of Property Act 1925, the effect of which, paradoxically, can be to cause the express grant of an easement to occur when there is no actual mention of the right in the deed itself.

Section 62 of the Law of Property Act 1925

Until the enactment of the Conveyancing Act 1881, it was necessary, when conveying land, to include expressly all rights appurtenant to that land. So, if land had the benefit of an easement, for that right to pass, the conveyance had not only to convey the land but also expressly to transfer the benefit of that easement. With a view to shortening conveyances, first, section 6 of the 1881 Act and latterly section 62 of the Law of Property Act made this unnecessary. Section 62 provides that:

'A conveyance of land shall be deemed to include and shall by virtue of this Act operate to convey, with the land, all...liberties, privileges, easements, rights, and advantages whatsoever, appertaining or reputed to appertain to the land, or any part thereof, or, at the time of the conveyance...enjoyed with, or reputed or known as part or parcel of or appurtenant to the land or any part thereof.'

This section, which is subject to the expression of a contrary intention in the conveyance,[134] is obviously sufficient to pass the benefit of an existing easement. So if A has been granted an easement over B's land and then conveys his land to C, C will, by operation of section 62, obtain the benefit of that easement notwithstanding that there is no mention of it in the conveyance. Rather less obviously, the effect of section 62 can

---

[129] *Wheeldon v. Burrows* (1879) 12 Ch.D. 31.
[130] See *Chaffe v. Kingsley* [2000] 1 E.G.L.R. 104. See also *Shrewsbury v. Adam* [2006] 1 P. & C.R. 27.
[131] (2011) Law Com. No. 32, para. 3.30.   [132] See Law reform proposals, pp. 563–564.
[133] Cf. *Allen v. Greenwood* [1980] Ch. 119.   [134] Law of Property Act 1925, s. 62(4).

be to convert licences and certain quasi-easements into full legal easements. This was explained in *Campbell v. Banks*,[135] by Mummery L.J., who said:

'On a conveyance by a vendor selling part of his land, the land conveyed may become a dominant tenement and the land retained by him, or sold by him to a different purchaser, may become a servient tenement. In this fashion a facility previously enjoyed over part of the vendor's land may be transformed into a legal easement for the benefit of dominant land now in different ownership.'

A good illustration of this occurred in *International Tea Stores Co. Ltd v. Hobbs*.[136] A tenant was given permission by his landlord to use a roadway. Some time later, the landlord sold the reversion of the tenancy to the tenant. It was held that what had previously been a licence to use the roadway on the landlord's land had now become a full legal easement. As the licence was a liberty or privilege existing at the time of the conveyance,[137] the effect of the section was to include in the conveyance of the property words to the effect that the premises were sold together with the right to use the roadway. In other words, the effect of the predecessor to section 62 was to operate to create an easement by an express grant.

It should be appreciated that in this case, prior to the conveyance, the landlord would have been entirely free to have revoked the tenant's licence, so that his right to use the roadway was precarious. It has been argued that the section should have been construed in such a way as not to enlarge the licensor's right, so that if the right was revocable before the conveyance, it should remain revocable after it.[138] While there is force in this argument, this is not the approach which the courts have taken, so that, provided certain conditions are met, if a licensor conveys land to a licensee, section 62 will operate to upgrade a licence into an easement over land retained by the licensor.[139] The 'key to the operation of [section 62] is enjoyment in fact, not title'.[140] As such, the section can operate as a trap for the unwary[141] and the conditions when the section will operate in this way must now be considered.

Competent grantor

For the section to operate, the person who conveys the land must have the power to grant an easement: there must be a competent grantor.[142] This, seemingly obvious point, can sometimes be overlooked.[143] Where the section will be relevant is where a

---

[135] [2011] EWCA Civ. 61 at [2]   [136] [1903] 1 Ch. 165.

[137] It is essential that the claimed right was being exercised at the time of the conveyance. See *Campbell v. Banks* [2011] EWCA Civ. 61.   [138] See L. Tee [1998] Conv. 115; C. Davis (2000) 20 L.S. 198 at 210.

[139] See, e.g., *Goldberg v. Edwards* [1950] Ch. 247; *Wright v. Macadam* [1949] 2 K.B. 744. See also *Graham v. Philcox* [1984] Ch. 747 (a case on the enlargement of an easement) noted by P. Todd [1985] Conv. 60.

[140] *Wall v. Collins* [2008] 1 All E.R. 122 at [15] *per* Carnwarth L.J.

[141] This is the view of the Law Commission, who recommend that this aspect of the law should be changed: (2011) Law Com. No. 327, para. 3.64. This view does not sit easily, however, with its proposals to change the law regarding the implication of easements. See Law reform proposals, p. 564.

[142] Law of Property Act 1925, s. 62(5).

[143] Cf. *M.R.A. Engineering Ltd v. Trimster Co. Ltd* (1987) 56 P. & C.R. 1 at 5 *per* Dillon L.J.; at 7 *per* Nourse L.J.

vendor owns land and sells off part of it to a purchaser. Any licence granted to the purchaser prior to the conveyance to him is then, potentially, liable to be upgraded into an
easement. The essential point is that, prior to the conveyance, the two plots must have
been in common ownership.[144]

Right capable of being an easement

For an easement to be created as a result of the operation of section 62, the right in
question must be capable of being an easement. It must satisfy the criteria laid down
in *Re Ellenborough Park*.[145] In *Green v. Ascho Horticulturist Ltd*,[146] a tenant had been
given a licence to use a passageway on his landlord's property whenever it was convenient to the landlord. The landlord then conveyed the reversion to the tenant and
the issue arose as to whether the licence had become an easement. It was held not. The
licence was of too intermittent a nature to be the subject matter of a grant and, consequently, section 62 did not operate to convert it into an easement.

The rule in Long v. Gowlett

In *Long v. Gowlett*,[147] two plots of land had at one time been in common ownership.
The owner of plot 1 used to go onto plot 2 to clear weeds from the river. The person who
acquired plot 1 claimed to have an easement to go onto plot 2 to clear the weeds. The
claim failed. According to Sargent J., before an easement can be acquired under section 62 there must be a prior diversity of occupation of the dominant land prior to the
conveyance. This means that there must have been a licensee or a tenant in occupation
of the dominant land, owned by the owner of the servient land, prior to the dominant
land being conveyed to him.

Quasi-easements

The existence of this rule was the subject of some debate.[148] The reason for this debate
was the decision of the Court of Appeal in *Broomfield v. Williams*.[149] In this case,
there was a quasi-easement of light and the vendor sold the quasi-dominant plot to
a purchaser and it was held that he acquired, under the statutory predecessor to section 62, a full legal easement of light. In this case there was not, prior to the conveyance, a diversity of occupation; both plots were occupied by the vendor. There was,
however, in existence a quasi-easement and this was continuous and apparent, that
is, one could see from an inspection of the two properties that the quasi-dominant
plot enjoyed access to light over the quasi-servient plot. The result is that section 62
operates to convert into easements either licences enjoyed prior to the conveyance,

---

[144] See *Odey v. Barber* [2008] Ch. 175 *per* Silber J.   [145] [1956] Ch. 131.
[146] [1966] 1 W.L.R. 889. See also the discussion of this issue in *P. & S. Platt Ltd v. Crouch* [2003] EWCA
Civ. 1110 at paras 43–46 *per* Peter Gibson L.J.
[147] [1932] 2 Ch. 177.
[148] P. Jackson (1966) 30 Conv. (N.S.) 340; P. Smith [1978] Conv. 449. For a convincing, and instructive,
defence of the rule, see C. Harpum [1979] Conv. 113.
[149] [1897] 1 Ch. 602.

the situation where there is a prior diversity of occupation, or quasi-easements which are continuous and apparent. In short, there are two, alternative, aspects to the rule in *Long v. Gowlett*.

The primary aspect of the rule that prior to the conveyance there must be diversity of occupation was confirmed, *obiter*, by the House of Lords in *Sovmots v. Secretary of State for the Environment*,[150] where Lord Edmund-Davies said, 'the section cannot operate unless there has been some diversity of ownership or occupation of the quasi-dominant and quasi-servient tenements prior to the conveyance'.[151] This *dictum* is a little misleading, in that before the section can operate at all, the two plots of land must have been in common ownership. It does, however, confirm the main plank of the rule. *Broomfield v. Williams* was, misleadingly, disregarded on the basis that it concerned an easement of light, which was considered to involve different considerations.

It is wrong to seek to distinguish *Broomfield v. Williams* in this way. It overlooks that there are two limbs to the rule, which are that, for the section to operate, then prior to the conveyance there must have been either a diversity of occupation, or there was in existence a continuous and apparent quasi-easement. That this is so is illustrated by a number of decisions, not involving light, where the section was held to operate to convert a continuous and apparent quasi-easement into a full legal easement,[152] and it is unfortunate that, in *Payne v. Inwood*,[153] this point was not made as unambiguously as it could have been.[154] That section 62 will operate to convert a quasi-easement into a full legal easement was, however, made clear in *Alford v. Hannaford*,[155] where Patten L.J said:

'But where there has not been diversity of occupation prior to the sale, the generally held view is that s. 62 can only operate to grant easements over the land retained by the vendor when the exercise of the relevant rights has been continuous and apparent....'

Rationale of the rule

The underlying basis of the rule in *Long v. Gowlett* is to allow the section to operate in a way which might be supposed to accord with the implied intention of the parties: hence the section is not operative in the case of a compulsory purchase.[156] If a person is allowed into occupation of land prior to the conveyance, and is given a licence to use other land owned by the vendor, it is not unreasonable to suppose that he might be expecting to enjoy that right after the conveyance. Similarly, if it is evident from

---

[150] [1979] A.C. 144.   [151] Ibid., at 176.

[152] See *Watts v. Kelsen* (1870) 6 Ch. App. 166 (a case where general words were used in the conveyance); *Kay v. Oxlye* (1875) L.R. 10 Q.B. 360, especially at 365 *per* Blackburn J.; *Bayley v. G.W.R.* (1884) 26 Ch.D. 434.

[153] (1996) 74 P. & C.R. 42; M.P. Thompson [1997] Conv. 453.

[154] See (1996) 74 P. & C.R. 42 at 47 and at 51 *per* Roch L.J.

[155] [2011] EWCA Civ. 1099 at [36]. See also *P. & S. Platt v. Crouch* [2003] EWCA Civ. 1110 at [42] *per* Peter Gibson L.J., and *Campbell v. Banks* [2011] EWCA Civ. 61 at [4] *per* Mummery L.J.

[156] *Sovmots v. Secretary of State for the Environment* [1979] A.C. 144. The position is different in respect of leasehold enfranchisement: see *Kent v. Kavanagh* [2006] EWCA Civ. 162.

looking at the two properties that the quasi-servient land was used for the advantage of the quasi-dominant plot, it is not unreasonable to suppose that it was intended that the purchaser might acquire as a right that which had previously existed only as a quasi-easement. When neither of these factors is present, it would occur to neither party that the purchaser might acquire rights over land retained by the vendor. The rule in *Long v. Gowlett* operates to prevent section 62 being more of a trap than it potentially already is.

Conveyance

Section 62 only operates if there has been a conveyance. A conveyance is a document which operates to transfer a legal estate or charge in land.[157] This includes an assent or a written lease of less than three years, a transaction which is not required to be created by deed.[158] Such a lease can, in fact, be created orally, but such a lease is not a conveyance.[159] Neither is a document which creates an equitable lease.[160]

Contrary intention

Section 62 is subject to a contrary intention. If a vendor is selling part of his land and has let a purchaser into possession prior to the conveyance, he should take care to revoke any licences he has given prior to conveying the property. This is a matter which should, in any event, be dealt with in the contract of sale. It is the case, however, that the section operates to give effect to the intention of the parties, and if it is clear that both of them are aware that no such right is intended to be created, the section will not operate to create an easement.[161] There is, however, a heavy burden of proof on the vendor to establish that this is the case.[162]

Implied grants

There are three situations when the grant of an easement will be implied.

Necessity

The same principles apply in the context of an implied grant as in the case of an implied reservation.[163]

Mutual intention

Again, similar principles apply as in the case of reservations, save that the task of persuading the court that the grant of an easement was intended is a little easier than is the case when the grantor is seeking to establish an implied reservation. In

---

[157] Law of Property Act 1925, s. 205(1)(ii).
[158] Ibid., s. 54. See *Wright v. Macadam* [1949] 2 K.B. 74.   [159] *Rye v. Rye* [1962] A.C. 496.
[160] *Borman v. Griffith* [1930] 1 Ch. 493.
[161] See *Birmingham, Dudley and District Banking Company v. Ross* (1888) 38 Ch.D. 295.
[162] See *P. & S. Platt Ltd v. Crouch* [2003] EWCA Civ. 1110.
[163] See Implied reservation, pp. 554–556.

Wong v. Beaumont Property Trust Ltd,[164] a property had been let as a restaurant. To comply with health regulations, it was necessary for there to be adequate ventilation. An easement to install a ventilation duct on the landlord's property was implied.

The rule in Wheeldon v. Burrows

The rule in *Wheeldon v. Burrows*[165] is similar, but not identical to, the operation of section 62 of the Law of Property Act 1925. In this case, the vendor owned two plots of land. On one plot, there was a shed which had three windows overlooking the other plot. There was a quasi-easement of light over that plot. In 1875, he sold the quasi-servient plot to the defendant and, a year later, sold the quasi-dominant plot to the plaintiff. When the defendant erected hoardings which blocked the light to the plaintiff's windows the issue arose as to whether the plaintiff had an easement of light. He did not. The reason was that it was the quasi-servient plot which had been sold first and there was no implied reservation of an easement.[166] Had it been the case that it was the quasi-dominant plot which had been sold first, then there would have been an implied grant. Of this, Thesiger L.J. said:

'on the grant by the owner of a tenement or part of that tenement as it is then used and enjoyed, there will pass to the grantee all those continuous and apparent easements (by which, of course, I mean *quasi*-easements), or, in other words, all those easements which are necessary for the reasonable enjoyment of the property granted, and which have been and are at the time of the grant used by the owners of the entirety for the benefit of the part granted.'[167]

There are three aspects to the rule. The first is that this is an implied grant. It must be the quasi-dominant part of the land which is sold first. Secondly, the quasi-easement must be continuous and apparent. This means that there is some visible sign, such as a marked track, across the quasi-servient land,[168] and the finding in *Donaldson v. Smith*,[169] that to be continuous and apparent there needs be neither a made-up track, nor any discernible traces of the use on the quasi-servient land, appears to be clearly wrong. In the case of light, the fact that adjoining land is uncovered, so that the quasi-dominant plot enjoys an uninterrupted flow of light, means that this is continuous and apparent. The fact that the quasi-dominant plot enjoys access to light over the quasi-servient plot is visible by looking at the two plots of land.[170] Thirdly, the right must be necessary for the reasonable enjoyment of the land.[171]

This last aspect of the rule is problematic. It does not mean that the right in question is essential for the enjoyment of the land, as is the case for an easement of necessity.

---

[164] [1965] 1 Q.B. 173.   [165] (1878) 12 Ch.D. 31.   [166] See also *Ray v. Hazeldine* [1902] 2 Ch. 17.
[167] Ibid., at 49.
[168] See the discussion of this in *Ward v. Kirkland* [1967] Ch. 194 at 224–226 *per* Ungoed-Thomas J.
[169] (2006), unreported, at [23] *per* Mr David Donaldson Q.C.
[170] See *Phillips v. Low* [1892] 1 Ch. 47.
[171] See *Millman v. Ellis* (1995) 71 P. & C.R. 158 at 162–163 *per* Sir Thomas Bingham M.R.

On the other hand, it appears to mean more than that the right accommodates the dominant tenement.[172] This distinction was made by Mummery L.J. in *Campbell v. Banks*,[173] as being the difference between a right necessary for the reasonable enjoyment of the land, which can be created by implication, and those which are convenient and can be created by section 62. This is hopelessly imprecise and, for this reason, as indicated by the above comment, much the better view is that any continuous and apparent quasi-easements pass on a conveyance of the quasi-dominant land due to the operation of section 62 of the Law of Property Act 1925. Under that section, there is no need to show that the right claimed is necessary for the reasonable enjoyment of the land; merely that the right in question satisfies the normal requirements of easements. This would leave the rule in *Wheeldon v. Burrows* scope to operate only in situations where there is no conveyance, for example when there is a document which has created an equitable lease.[174]

LAW REFORM PROPOSALS

The Law Commission has recently made proposals which, if implemented, would change considerably the law relating to the implied acquisition of easements. The reform proposals also include easements currently created as a result of section 62 of the Law of Property Act 1925. Although it was recognized that, strictly speaking, such easements are created by express grant, and not by implication, because the operation of the section overlaps to a considerable extent with the rule in *Wheeldon v. Burrows*, it was appropriate to consider this section as part of its work on the implied creation of easements,[175] an approach which seems sensible.

Reform of section 62

The Law Commission was impressed with the criticisms of the manner in which section 62 can operate to upgrade precarious rights into full legal easements. It has, therefore, been proposed that the section shall no longer operate to transform precarious benefits into legal easements on a conveyance of land.[176] While many critics of the current law might welcome this proposal, if it and the complementary proposals with regard to the law relating to the implication of easements are enacted there may be, in fact, very little change in substance to the law.

---

[172] See, generally, *Wheeler v. J.J. Saunders Ltd* [1996] Ch. 19, criticized by M.P. Thompson [1995] Conv. 239.

[173] [2011] EWCA Civ. 61 at [32].

[174] See *Borman v. Griffith* [193] 1 Ch. 493; *Donaldson v. Smith* (2006), unreported.

[175] (2011) Law Com. No. 327, paras 3.57–3.58.   [176] Ibid., at para. 3.64.

Implication of easements

At the heart of the Law Commission's approach to this matter is the replacement of the current circumstances when an easement is created by implication with one unified test. This test is not to be based on any attempt to discern the intentions of the parties but is, instead, to be underpinned by an objective test based on what is necessary for the reasonable enjoyment of the land.[177] To this end, it is proposed 'that an easement should be implied as a term of a disposition where it is necessary for the reasonable use of the land at that date, bearing in mind:

(1) The use of the land at the time of the grant;

(2) The presence on the servient land of any relevant physical features;

(3) An intention for the future use of the land, known to both parties at the time of the grant;

(4) So far as relevant, the available routes for the easement sought; and

(5) The potential interference with the servient land or inconvenience to the servient owner.'[178]

Implied reservation

An initial point to make about this proposal is that the various criteria to which regard is to be had in determining whether an easement is to be implied appear to be alternatives, and this view is reinforced when regard is had to clause 20 of the draft Law of Property Bill which is appended to the Report, which makes clear that the criteria to which regard is to be had in determining whether a particular easement is necessary for the reasonable enjoyment of the land includes the items listed above. The first two criteria quoted seem to indicate the current requirements that the right which is to be implied was, first, in use at the time of the disposition and, secondly, was continuous and apparent, or at least apparent, in current terminology. Under the existing law, both criteria had to be satisfied; under the proposal, they would seem to be alternatives.

A second important feature of this proposal is that it applies to all dispositions of land, and not, as is presently the case, to dispositions of the quasi-dominant tenement. This will enable easements to be implied in favour of a grantor on the same basis as is currently the case for a grantee. This is a significant change. As has been seen, the current position is that the law is highly reluctant to imply any rights in favour of the vendor of land, and will do so only in a case of necessity, which is narrowly defined, and where the implication is necessary to give effect to the implied intention of the parties. The rationale for this approach is that, if a vendor wishes to retain rights over land which he is selling, he should expressly reserve them.[179] Under this proposal the law would change, and one result would be that the actual decision in *Wheeldon v. Burrows* would now be different.

---

[177] Ibid., at paras 3.39–3.43.   [178] Ibid., at para. 3.45.

[179] See Express reservation, pp. 553–556.

In that case, it will be recalled, there was a quasi-easement of light, and it was the quasi-servient land which was then sold first. It was held that no easement was implied in favour of the vendor, precisely because the law is reluctant to imply easements in favour of the grantor, and against the grantee; had it been the quasi-dominant plot which had been conveyed first, the law would have implied an easement in favour of the purchaser. Under the proposed new law, a right to light would be implied in favour of the vendor; it was in use at the time of the grant, and that use would have been apparent on an inspection of the servient land and also, it would seem, it was necessary for the reasonable enjoyment of the land. One would have anticipated rather more justification for such a major change than is present in the Report.

Repeal of section 62

The Law Commission, as has been seen, proposed to reform the current position whereby section 62 of the Law of Property Act 1925 allows precarious rights to be upgraded into easements. Unfortunately, it seems to be overlooked that the new proposal on the implication of easements would, if enacted, reintroduce the substance of the existing law in another guise. In *International Tea Stores Co. Ltd v. Hobbs*,[180] a tenant had been given permission to use a roadway on the landlord's land. On the conveyance of the reversion to the tenant, this precarious licence was due to the operation of the statutory predecessor of section 62,[181] converted into a legal easement. Despite the recommendation of the Law Commission to prevent section 62 from operating in this way, the proposal for the implication of easements would seem to produce the same result: as the right was exercised at the time of the disposition then, assuming that it was necessary for the reasonable enjoyment of the land, that fact would cause an implied easement to be created.

Necessary for the reasonable enjoyment of the land

The overarching criterion for the implication of easements is to be that the right in question is necessary for the reasonable enjoyment of land. This currently is a requirement for an easement to be implied under the rule in *Wheeldon v. Burrows*, but is not a separate requirement for the operation of section 62. In that context, it is sufficient that the right claimed accommodates the dominant tenement. This additional requirement is one of some uncertainty, and its introduction as the guiding criterion is not to be welcomed.

Conclusion

While the implementation of the Law Commission's proposal would appear to simplify the law, in that it would provide a unified test for the implication of easements,

180 [1903] 1 Ch. 165.   181 Conveyancing Act 1881, s. 6.

thereby doing away with the old law concerning easements of necessity and the position when an easement will be implied to give effect to the intentions of the parties, it does so at a price. In particular, it shifts the law a long way from the present, justifiable, state whereby the law is reluctant to imply rights in favour of a person who is disposing of part of his land. Secondly, while at first sight, the trap inherent in section 62 of the Law of Property Act 1925 is removed, that is likely to prove to be illusory. Finally, the emphasis on the need for the right in question to be necessary for the reasonable enjoyment of land is likely to be the subject matter of litigation, it being unclear what, if anything, it adds to the requirement that the right in question accommodates the dominant tenement.

PRESCRIPTION

The final method by which an easement can be acquired is by prescription. The basis of prescription is that a right has been enjoyed for a long period of time. Unlike the position with adverse possession, where the law operates negatively to extinguish the title of the paper owner of the land,[182] prescription works positively. It enables a person to make a positive claim to a right over another person's land, and it has been said that 'Any legal system must have rules of prescription which prevent the disturbance of long-established de facto enjoyment.'[183]

As one would expect, before any right can be acquired by prescription, it must display the general characteristics of an easement. A number of issues then arise. These relate to the nature of the user of the right and the length of time that the use has been enjoyed. Unfortunately, this latter issue is complicated by the fact that there are three separate forms of prescription, a matter which reflects little credit on the law.

Nature of the use

To establish a claim to an easement by prescription, the claimant must be able to show user as of right. This is traditionally summed up in the Latin phrase that the use must be *nec vi, nec clam, nec precario*. This means that it must be used neither by force, by stealth, or by permission, or 'putting the point more positively: the user must be peaceable, open and not based on any licence from the owner of the land.'[184] If the

---

[182] See Chapter 7.

[183] *R. v. Oxford County Council, ex p. Sunningwell Parish Council* [2000] 1 A.C. 335 at 349 *per* Lord Hofffmann. For interesting discussions of the merits of prescription, see C. Sara [2004] Conv. 13; F. Burns [2007] Conv. 133.

[184] *R (on the application of Lewis) v. Redcar and Cleveland Borough Council* [2010] EWSC 11 at [87] *per* Lord Rodger.

claimant establishes such use, nothing further is required; no further criterion need be established.[185]

Force

Generally speaking, the issues as to whether the use has been occasioned by force will not be difficult to establish, so, if the claimant demolishes barriers to enjoy a right of way,[186] then this will amount to forceable use. Physical force is not necessary, however to defeat a claim to an easement, so that if the use is contentious, then it will also be regarded as being forceful use.[187]

Secrecy

The question of secrecy can give rise to more subtle issues. If the user of the right is not obvious as, for example, if underground rods are used to support a structure, then no easement will be acquired by prescription, on the basis that the use was secret.[188] Potentially a more difficult problem arose in *London Tara Hotel Ltd v. Kensington Close Ltd*.[189] In 1973 Tara granted a personal licence to KCL, who were then the owners of the Kensington Close Hotel, to use a roadway from year to year, and provision was made for payment of £1 per annum, although this was never collected. The ownership of the hotel changed hands in 1980, although Tara was not aware of this. This caused the licence to terminate, although the use of the roadway continued and, indeed, increased. It was argued that the use for the requisite period of time after 1980 was secretive because Tara did not know of the change of the ownership and consequent revocation of the licence. This argument failed. Although it was accepted that, had there been some deception as to the change of ownership the continued use of the roadway may have been regarded as secretive, this was not the case here.[190] The use was open, and it was immaterial if the owner of the servient plot mistakenly believed that the use was under a licence granted in the past.

Permission

Because the requirement is that the user is of right, a claim to an easement by prescription will fail if it is shown that the right was enjoyed with the permission of the servient owner.[191] This does not entail that the person exercising the right believes that he has the legal right to do so,[192] as the claimant's beliefs are generally irrelevant to the issue

---

[185] Ibid., at [20] *per* Lord Walker; *London Tara Hotels Ltd v. Kensington Close Hotel Ltd* [2011] EWCA 1356 at [74] *per* Lewison L.J.

[186] *Newnham v. Willison* (1987) 56 P. & C.R. 8.

[187] *R (on the application of Lewis) v. Redcar and Cleveland Borough Council* [2010] EWSC 11 at [87] *per* Lord Rodger. See *Smith v. Brudenell-Bruce* [2002] 2 P. & C.R. 2.

[188] *Union Lighterage Co. v. London Graving Dock Co.* [1902] 2 Ch. 557. See also *Liverpool Corp. v. Coghill & Son Ltd* [1918] 1 Ch. 307 (surruptitious discharge of effluent); *Ironside v. Barefoot* (1981) 41 P. & C.R. 326 (intermittent use of right not sufficient).

[189] [2011] EWCA Civ. 1356.   [190] Ibid., at [37] *per* Lord Neuberger M.R.

[191] *Gardner v. Hodgson's Kingston Brewery Co. Ltd* [1903] A.C. 229.

[192] See *R v. Oxfordshire County Council, ex parte Sunningwell Parish Council* [2000] A.C. 335.

of prescription.[193] If, however, the owner of the servient land simply tolerates the use without expressly consenting to it, this use will be sufficient to establish a prescriptive right to an easement.[194] 'A landowner who wishes to stop the acquisition of prescriptive rights must not acquiesce and suffer in silence.'[195] This is illustrated by the decision of the Supreme Court in *R (on the application of Lewis) v. Redcar and Cleveland Borough Council.*[196] The issue was whether a person was entitled to apply to register land as a town or village green. He was entitled to do this, if he could establish that a significant number of the inhabitants in the locality had indulged as of right in lawful sports and pastimes on the land for a period of at least 20 years.[197] The meaning of 'as of right' was accepted as being the same as is required to establish a prescriptive easement. In this case the claimant was one of a group of walkers, who would follow their pursuit across a golf course. On the facts, it was clear that it was overwhelmingly the case that the walkers would defer to the golfers so that, if a person was taking a shot, the walkers would wait until the path was clear. These acts of deference, it was held, did not make the acts of walking across the course permissive. It was merely the give and take inherent when two groups of people are using the same land. As Lord Walker put it:

'I have great difficulty in seeing how a reasonable owner would have concluded that the residents were not asserting a right to take recreation on the disputed land, simply because they normally showed civility (or in the inspector's word, deference) towards members of the golf club who were out playing golf.'[198]

If, however, the owner of the servient land gives an unsolicited permission for a person to use his land, then the user is not of right, and a claim to an easement by prescription will be defeated.[199] Such permission will normally need to be express, however, as the courts will not readily accept that inaction on the part of the servient tenement owner will amount to permission. What appears to be necessary is 'some overt act which is intended to be understood, and is understood, as permission to do something which would otherwise be an act of trespass.'[200]

Finally, it should be noted that use which was originally permissive may cease to be so. This may be because the original licence was revoked, either by the act of the parties or by law. The use may also be in excess of what was originally permitted, for example by vehicular use as opposed to pedestrian use, in which case the fact that the original use was permissive will not prevent the creation of an easement.[201]

---

[193] *R (on the application of Lewis) v. Redcar and Cleveland Borough Council* [2010] EWSC 11 at [34] *per* Lord Walker. See also *Bridle v. Ruby* [1989] QB 169.

[194] *Davies v. Du Paver* [1953] 1 Q.B. 184; *Mills v. Silver* [1991] Ch. 271.

[195] *R (on the application of Beresford) v. Sunderland City Council* [2004] 1 All E.R. 160 at [77] *per* Lord Walker of Gestingthorpe.

[196] [2010] EWSC 11.   [197] Commons Act 2006, s. 15.   [198] Ibid., at [37].

[199] *Odey v. Barber* [2008] Ch. 175, applying *Rafique v. Trustees of the Walton Estate* (1992) 65 P. & C.R. 356.

[200] *R (on the application of Beresford) v. Sunderland City Council)* [2004] 1 All E.R. 160 at [75] *per* Lord Walker of Gestingthorpe; *London Tara Hotels Ltd v. Kensington Close Hotel* [2011] EWCA Civ.1356 at [86] *per* Lewison L.J.

[201] See *London Tara Hotels Ltd v. Kensington Close Hotel* [2011] EWCA Civ. 1356.

User in fee simple

An easement can only be acquired by prescription if the use is by a fee simple owner against another fee simple owner.[202] Any claim made to an easement by a tenant can only be made on behalf of the owner of the reversion. Similarly, if the servient land is in the possession of a tenant, any claim to an easement by prescription will fail, unless it can be shown that the freehold owner of the land was able to prevent the user. In this respect, it is important whether the user preceded the grant of the tenancy. If it did, it is then easier to establish the requisite acquiescence on the part of the freeholder to base a claim to a prescriptive easement.[203]

Prescription periods

It is unfortunate that the position is that there are three different periods of prescription.

Common law

The common law rule was that to establish a claim to an easement by prescription the claimant had to show that the right had been enjoyed from time immemorial. For historical reasons, this date, the date of legal memory, was set at 1189. Evidently, such a task would be very hard to accomplish, and so to alleviate the difficulty, the courts were prepared to make the presumption that, if a right had been enjoyed for twenty years, it had been enjoyed since 1189. As with all presumptions, however, it is rebuttable. If it could be shown that the right could not have been enjoyed from 1189, then a claim to an easement at common law would fail.[204] This meant, for example, that a claim to an easement of light would fail at common law if the buildings which were to enjoy the light were erected after 1189. In reality, prescription at common law is effectively obsolete.

Lost modern grant

Clearly, the task of establishing a prescriptive claim to an easement at common law was nigh on impossible. To overcome this difficulty, the courts invented a fiction that, if there had been enjoyment of a right for a prolonged period, set at twenty years, then the presumption would be made that an easement had, in the past, been granted but that the grant had been lost.

'Juries were first told that from user, during living memory, or even during twenty years they may presume a lost grant or deed; next they were recommended to make such presumption; and lastly, as the final consummation of judicial legislation, it was held that a jury should be told, not only that they might, but also that they were bound to presume the existence of such

---

[202] *Kilgour v. Gades* [1904] 1 K.B. 457 at 460 *per* Sir Richard Henn Collins M.R. Despite the strong criticism of this rule by Lord Millett in *China Field Ltd v. Appeal Tribunal (Buildings)* [2009] UKCU 1650 (a decision of Hong Kong's Court of Final Appeal), the Law Commission has proposed the retention of this rule: (2011) Law Com. No. 327, para. 3.150.

[203] See *Williams v. Sandy Lane (Chester) Ltd* [2006] EWCA Civ. 1738 at [22] *per* Chadwick L.J.

[204] See *Hulbert v. Dale* [1909] 2 Ch. 570 at 577 *per* Joyce J.

a lost grant, although neither judge nor jury, nor anyone else, had the shadow of a belief that any such instrument had ever really existed.'[205]

This fiction, for such it is, was endorsed by the House of Lords in *Dalton v. Angus*.[206] Because the basis of the doctrine is fictitious, it is entirely irrelevant that evidence exists that no such grant was ever made.[207] A claim to an easement based upon the fiction of the lost modern grant will only be defeated if it is shown that it was actually impossible for a grant to have been made.[208] Other than this restriction on the fiction, if the claimant can show twenty years' user as of right, and this, unlike the position under the Prescription Act 1832, does not have to be twenty years' user immediately connected with the adjudication of the claim,[209] then that claim will succeed. It appears to be the case, however, that to succeed under the doctrine of lost modern grant, stronger evidence of user as of rights is required than would be the case if the claim is made at common law.[210] If the evidence shows that the right claimed could not have been enjoyed throughout the twenty-year period, as where a claimed right of way would have been obstructed by a wall, the argument based on prescription will fail.[211]

Illegal use

A claim to an easement through a lost modern grant cannot be sustained, if the use is illegal,[212] the reason being that 'a lawful grant to do an act or acts which if done would be illegal cannot be made'.[213] This rule is not, however, absolute. So, in the welcome decision in *Bakewell Management Ltd v. Brandwood*,[214] it was held that the driving of a vehicle without lawful authority across land subject to rights of common, which is an offence unless authorized by the owner of the land,[215] could give rise to an easement by prescription. Because the owner of the land could have authorized the activity, a lost modern grant was a legal possibility.

Statutory prescription

A legal doctrine which is based squarely upon a fiction, as is the case with the doctrine of lost modern grant, is inherently unattractive. One possibility would be to replace that doctrine by legislation. That, however, has not been done. Although the Prescription Act 1832 does enable prescription to occur on a statutory basis, the Act operates in

---

[205] *Bryant v. Foot* (1867) L.R. 2 Q.B. 161 at 181 *per* Lord Cockburn C.J.   [206] (1881) 6 App. Cas. 740.

[207] *Tehidy Estate Ltd v. Norman* [1971] 2 Q.B. 528.

[208] *Neaverson v. Peterborough Rural District Council* [1902] 1 Ch. 557, where such a grant was prohibited by statute.

[209] See *Mills v. Silver* [1991] Ch. 221.

[210] See *Tilbury v. Silva* (1890) 45 Ch.D. 98 at 123 *per* Bowen L.J.

[211] See *Jones v. Scott* [2006] EWHC 2908 (QB).   [212] *Cargill v. Gotts* [1981] 1 W.L.R. 441.

[213] *Bakewell Management Ltd v. Brandwood* [2004] 2 A.C. 519 at 541 *per* Lord Scott of Foscote.

[214] [2004] 2 A.C. 529. *Henning v. Top Desk Travel Group* (1993) 68 P. & C.R. 14, to the contrary, was overruled. Although the decision has been criticized, M. Templeman (2005) 121 L.Q.R. 200, the better views are the supporting arguments by D. Fox [2004] Conv. 173, anticipating the decision, and C. McNall [2004] Conv. 517, supporting it.

[215] Law of Property Act 1925, s. 193(4).

tandem with the common law doctrines. Moreover, the Act is not particularly well drafted: the Law Reform Committee having said of it that it 'has no friends. It has long been criticised as one of the worst drafted Acts on the Statute Book.',[216] and its continued existence on the statute book after a period of over 75 years has been described as providing some support for the adage that only the good die young.[217] Moreover, the situation is complicated by the fact that a different regime exists in respect of easements of light than with other forms of easement, which means that there is a need to consider the different types of easement separately.

Easements other than light

To acquire an easement under the Act, it must be shown that there has been either twenty or forty years' continuous user next to, that is immediately before, the action. The reason for there being two different periods will be addressed shortly. The latter requirement means that, subject to the requisite period of interruption, the requisite period of user must occur prior to the matter being litigated. If, for example, a person has exercised a right of way for twenty-five years, but that use stopped two years prior to the action being brought, then a prescriptive claim under the statute will fail. Instead, a claim will have to be made under the doctrine of lost modern grant,[218] where there is no requirement that the use continues up until the date of the action.

Interruptions

The Act requires the user to have been without interruption. Section 4 of the Act requires the court to disregard an interruption unless it has been acquiesced in or submitted to for one year. This means that a claim to an easement can be made under the Act even where there has not been the full twenty years' user. If a person has used a right for nineteen years and one day and that use is then interrupted then, provided that the action is brought precisely 364 days after the interruption, the claim to an easement under the Act will succeed. The two periods will be added together to make up the requisite twenty-year period.[219] In the same way that acts of adverse possession can be added together by different squatters,[220] user by different owners can be accumulated to make up the requisite period under the Act.[221] The action cannot, however, be brought before that date, as taking the two periods together, there will not have been twenty years' user as of right. Neither can the action be brought after that

---

[216] (1966) Law Reform Cttee, Cmnd. 3100, para. 40.
[217] *London Tara Hotels Ltd v. Kensington Close Hotel Ltd* [2011] EWCA Civ. 1356 at [20] *per* Lord Neuberger M.R. For an interesting historical critique, see *Housden v. The Conservators of Wimbledon and Putney Commons* [2008] 1 All E.R. 397 at [33]-[69] *per* Mummery L.J.
[218] See *Mills v. Silver* [1991] Ch. 221.
[219] See *Flight v. Thomas* [(1841) 8 Cl. & Fin. 231 at 241 *per* Lord Cottenham L.C.
[220] See Limitation under the 1980 Act, pp. 237–238.
[221] *Midtown Ltd v. City of London Real Property Co. Ltd* [2005] EWHC 33 (Ch.), a product of the Law of Property Act 1925, s. 62.

date, because then the interruption will have lasted for more than one year, which will defeat a claim under the Act.[222]

Overriding status

The Land Registration Act 2002 has curtailed the possibility of easements taking effect as interests which override registered dispositions.[223] Easements created by the operation of section 62 of the Law of Property Act 1925,[224] or the rule in *Wheeldon v. Burrows*, or by prescription, continue to have overriding status. Because, under the Prescription Act the use must be before the action, it was thought that claims could no longer be made under the Act against a purchaser, because the long use would not, until the action was brought, have caused an easement to arise, and so there would not be anything to bind the purchaser.[225] This argument has, however, been refuted on the basis that the time simply runs against the new owner of the land, against whom the action can then be brought.[226]

Different time periods

Section 2 of the Act, in setting out the prescription periods, stipulates two different periods, these being twenty years and forty years next to, that is immediately before, the action. The distinction is then made that a prescriptive claim based upon forty years' user prior to the action will only be defeated if it was shown that the right was enjoyed by written consent or agreement, or that the owner of the servient land lacks the capacity to grant an easement.[227]

At common law, to acquire an easement by prescription, the user must be *nec vi, nec clam, nec precario*, that is without force, stealth, or permission. These requirements apply also in the case of prescriptive claims under the Act, except that the final requirement, that the use is without permission, is modified in the case of prescription based upon user for forty years. The effect of the Act is this. If, prior to the use commencing, oral permission was given to the person exercising the right, then the use will be *precario*, that is permissive, and a claim to an easement based upon twenty years' use will fail. If, however, the use continues for forty years, then the fact that its origin was permissive will not matter. It is only if the permission was in writing that the claim will fail. If, however, permission is given to use a particular right, and this permission is repeated periodically, an easement will not be acquired whether the use be for twenty or forty years, because the user has not been of right.[228] The provision with regard to the forty-year period allows the first, verbal, permission to be disregarded. It will not affect the position if the permission is repeated periodically.

---

[222] See *Reilly v. Orange* [1955] 1 W.L.R. 616.
[223] See Easements and *profits à prendre*, pp. 151–153.
[224] Land Registration Act 2002, s. 27(7).   [225] P.H. Kenny [2003] Conv. 304 at 312.
[226] G. Battersby [2005] Conv. 195 at 205.
[227] *Housden v. Conservators of Wimbledon and Putney Commons* [2008] 1 All E.R. 397.
[228] *Gardner v. Hodgson's Brewery Co. Ltd* [1903] 2 A.C. 229.

Easements of light

Easements of light are governed, principally, by section 3 of the Act. If enjoyment of access to light has occurred without interruption for twenty years, that right will become absolute, unless it was enjoyed with written permission. As is the case with prescription in respect of other easements, the use must be next to, that is immediately, before an action. The same rule applies also in respect of interruptions. There are, however, some important differences between a prescriptive right to light and the acquisition of other easements.

Interruption to the enjoyment of light

It is relatively easy to obstruct, physically, a right of way. One simply blocks it by the erection of a gate or a fence. It is less easy to prevent the enjoyment of a flow of light. To do this would require the owner of the servient tenement to build upon his land in such a way as to obstruct the flow of light. This may cause problems, either because planning permission cannot be obtained for the building or, simply, the owner of the servient land does not want to build at the present time. He may, nevertheless, be concerned that, by inertia, an easement of light is not acquired over his land. To alleviate this difficulty, a procedure exists under the Right to Light Act 1959, whereby, the owner of the servient land can register a notional obstruction to the flow of light, and this will suffice to interrupt the enjoyment of the light, thereby preventing the acquisition of an easement by prescription. If there is an actual obstruction, as is the case when the windows are boarded up, no easement will be acquired, because light is not being enjoyed, as all that is happening is the illumination of the back of a panel.[229]

Written consent

In the case of easements of light, there is only one relevant time period, that period being twenty years. A claim to an easement of light which has been enjoyed for twenty years next to an action will fail if, and only if, there was written permission to enjoy the right. The wording of section 3 does not insist that the user was as of right. It is sufficient if access to the light was actually enjoyed throughout the period. Thus, if an annual payment is made in respect of the enjoyment of the right to light, this will not, after twenty years, prevent the right maturing into an easement.[230]

It is not necessary for the writing to refer expressly to an easement of light for it to amount to written permission sufficient to prevent a right of light being acquired. In *RHJ Ltd v. FT Patten (Holdings) Ltd*,[231] one of the terms of a lease reserved the right of the landlord to build on the land adjoining the tenant's property. This had the effect that, pending any building, the tenant was enjoying the light over the landlord's land with his written permission, thereby preventing an easement being claimed under the Act.

---

[229] *Tenures (Vincent Square) Ltd v. Fairpoint Properties (Vincent Square) Ltd* [2006] EWHC 3589 (Ch.).
[230] See *Plasterers' Co. v. Parish Clerk's Co.* (1851) 6 Exch. 630.
[231] [2008] EWCA Civ. 151.

No grant

The easement of light does not rest upon any presumed grant. The section provides for the right to become absolute after the expiry of the requisite period. This has been held to mean that, unlike other cases of prescription, a tenant can acquire an easement by prescription.[232]

Prescription rules reform

Unsurprisingly, in its review of the law relating to easements, the Law Commission considered the rules governing prescription to be ripe for reform. Having considered, but rejected, the idea of abolishing this means of acquisition altogether,[233] changes to the existing law were recommended. Underlying the proposals were the laudable aims of simplifying the law, avoiding litigation, ensuring compatibility with land registration principles, and ensuring that the scope for prescription was not extended.[234]

What is proposed is, first, to abolish the three existing methods of prescription and to replace them with a single prescription period of twenty years of continuous qualifying use, this period to apply to all types of easement. To count as qualifying, the use must, as is the case at present, be without force, stealth or permission. The use must also not be contrary to the criminal law, unless such use can be rendered lawful by the dispensation of the servient owner.[235]

This proposal would retain a good deal of the substantive law, while making welcome changes to remove some of the confusing and anomalous variations between different types of easement, and different time periods. One substantive change which is recommended is that the twenty year use need no longer be next before action, as is currently the case. This aspect of the existing statutory regime is, apparently, exceptionally unpopular,[236] and is, of itself, a principal reason for the continued application of the common law fiction of the lost modern grant, where no such requirement is imposed. It was recognized, however, that this recommendation, if implemented, would potentially cause some risk to purchasers of registered land, in that prescriptive easements can take effect as interests which override registration.[237] This risk is nevertheless small, as such easements will only override if either the easement was within the actual knowledge of the person to whom the disposition was made, or would have been obvious to him on a reasonably careful inspection of the land, or, alternatively, the easement had been exercised within the period of a year ending with the date of the disposition. The proposed reforms would bring a good deal of improvement to an unnecessarily complicated area of law.

---

[232] *Morgan v. Fear* [1907] A.C. 429.   [233] (2011) Law Com. No. 327, paras 3.74–3.80.
[234] Ibid., at para. 3.116.   [235] Ibid., at para. 3.123.   [236] Ibid., at 3.131.
[237] Land Registration Act 2002, Sched. 3, para. 3(1). Expressly granted easements cannot take effect as overriding interests: ibid., s. 27(2)(d).

14

Covenants between Freeholders

In a previous chapter, the enforceability of covenants between landlord and tenant and their respective successors in title was considered.[1] The principal concern of this chapter is with covenants made between freeholders and the circumstances in which successors in title to the original parties to the covenant can either acquire the benefit of a covenant or take subject to the burden of it.

People at large are generally aware that, if they wish to develop their land, or build upon it, planning permission is necessary. Applications for planning permission are publicized and people who may be affected by the development are given the opportunity to make representations. The law governing this area involves the public control of land use. It is a highly complex body of law and no attempt will be made in this book to enter into any discussion of it save to say that the fact that planning permission has been granted will not override a private right to restrict a particular activity.[2] Instead, this chapter is concerned with the private control of land use. This involves landowners seeking to regulate how land is used within a particular locality. The arrangements which people make take the form of covenants and these covenants may affect not only the parties who make them but can also affect successors in title. The person who makes the covenant is termed the covenantor and the person who obtains the benefit of that covenant is termed the covenantee.

These covenants can operate to prevent the development of land, even when planning permission has been granted by the requisite authority. As such, they form a type of private planning law, operating in tandem with regulations affecting the public control of land. It is with these covenants that this chapter is concerned.

PRIVITY OF CONTRACT

As a general proposition, landowners are perfectly free to enter into any contractual relationship they see fit with regard to their respective properties. So, for example, if A contracts with B, his neighbour, to paint the outside of B's house every year, then this

---

[1] See Chapter 11.

[2] See *Margerison v. Bates* [2008] EWHC 1211 (Ch.) at [58]–[59] per Mr Edward Bartley Jones Q.C. See also Wheeler *v. J.J. Saunders* [1996] Ch. 19 at 26–30 *per* Staughton L.J., and *Watson v. Croft Promo-Sport Ltd* [2009] EWCA Civ. 15 at [32] *per* Sir Andrew Morritt C., in the context of the law of nuisance.

is a perfectly enforceable contract and if A does not do the painting, he will be liable to B for breach of contract. Again, if one house owner covenants with his neighbour that he will only use his property as a private residence then, as between the parties to the covenant, this contract is fully enforceable. The question of principal interest to a property lawyer is not so much the enforceability of the covenants between the original parties. The main issue is, if A sells his land to C and B sells his land to D, whether D has acquired the right to sue on the covenant and whether C is subject to the obligation created by A, his predecessor in title. This issue is determined by considering whether the benefit of the covenant has run with the land and, also, whether the burden has run. These questions raise different issues and will be addressed shortly. First, however, attention will be paid to the extended notion of privity of contract and how it operates in this context.

Statutory extension of privity

In the context of Land Law, a key statutory provision which extended the notion of privity of contract was section 56 of the Law of Property Act 1925, which enables a person who is not a party to a covenant to sue upon it. The section provides that:

'A person may take an immediate or other interest in land, or other property, or the benefit of any condition, right of entry, agreement over or respecting land, although he may not be named as a party to the conveyance or other instrument.'

The scope of this section was, at one time, highly controversial. In particular, it was used as authority in an attempt to outflank the common law doctrine of privity of contract, at least so far as it affected property.[3] This expansive view of the section did not, however, survive the decision of the House of Lords in *Beswick v. Beswick*.[4] Although the case did not fully resolve all the difficulties pertaining to the section, it did leave matters tolerably clear as to its scope in the context of covenants relating to land.

The way that the section operates is to allow a person to sue on a covenant to which he is not a party if the covenant purports to be made with him.[5] It was not sufficient if the covenant simply purported to confer a benefit on the third party.[6] So, if A and B entered into a covenant and that covenant purported to be made also with C, then C, although not actually a party to the covenant could, because of the operation of section 56, sue on it because he was regarded as being privy to it.[7] If, however, the covenant between A and B was expressed to be for the benefit of C, but did not purport to be made with him, then C could not sue on the covenant. The need for the covenant to purport to be made with the third party meant, also, that that person had to be identifiable at the time when the covenant was made. If, therefore, a covenant purported

3 See, e.g., *Drive Yourself Car Hire Co. (London) Ltd v. Strutt* [1954] 1 Q.B. 250 at 274 *per* Denning L.J.
4 [1968] A.C. 58.
5 *White v. Bijou Mansions Ltd* [1937] 1 Ch. 610 at 625 *per* Simonds J.; *Lyus v. Prowsa Developments Ltd* [1982] 1 W.L.R. 1044 at 1049 *per* Dillon J.
6 See *Re Ecclesiastical Commissioners for England's Conveyance* [1936] Ch. 430.
7 See *Stromdale & Ball Ltd v. Burden* [1952] 1 Ch. 223 at 234 *per* Danckwerts J.

to be made with future landowners, such people, when they acquired their land, could not sue directly upon the covenant as, at the time when it was made, they were not identifiable and existing people.[8]

Relaxation of privity

In the case of covenants made after May 2000,[9] the distinctions made with regard to section 56 will cease to be relevant. Under section 1(1) of the Contracts (Rights of Third Parties) Act 1999, a third party may sue on a contract to which he was not a party if, either, the contract expressly provides that he may or, a term in the contract purports to confer a benefit on him. The distinction which previously existed between a contract purporting to be made with a third party and one purporting to confer a benefit on him will disappear as now, in both cases, the third party will be able to enforce the covenant directly. Also gone is the rule that the third party must be an identifiable person at the date of the contract, if he is to benefit from it. This change was effected by section 1(3) of the Act, which provides that the third party must be expressly identified in the contract by name, as a member of a class or as answering a particular description, but need not be in existence when the contract was made.

THE TRANSMISSION OF COVENANTS

Once one has established who is able to sue directly on the covenant because they are party to it, or it was made for their benefit, the next issue to arise is to consider the circumstances when the benefit of that covenant has passed to a successor in title to the covenantee and when the burden of the covenant passes to a successor in title to the covenantor.

It will usually be necessary to consider these issues separately. If the issue in a given case is whether A can sue B on a covenant to which neither was party, two questions will need to be answered. These are whether A has acquired the benefit of the covenant and whether B has taken subject to the burden. It is also necessary to distinguish between the approach taken by the common law and that adopted by equity.

COMMON LAW

In considering the position at common law, care must be taken to distinguish between the benefit and the burden of covenants.

---

[8] For covenants made with existing neighbouring landowners, see *Forster v. Elvet Colliery* [1909] A.C. 98.

[9] Contracts (Rights of Third Parties) Act 1999, s. 10(2).

The burden

It is a general rule of the law of contract that only a person who is a party to that contract can be sued upon the obligations created by it. While the doctrine of privity of contract has been considerably relaxed by the enactment of the Contracts (Rights of Third Parties) Act 1999, that relaxation relates to the acquisition of contractual rights. It does not allow a person who is not a party to a contract to be sued upon that contract. The law relating to landlord and tenant represents a significant exception to this principle, in that the burden of covenants can affect assignees of either the lease or the reversion, the basis of this liability being privity of estate.[10] Other than that, the rule is largely inviolate. There is no question of the burden of a covenant running at law so as to adversely affect a successor in title to the covenantor.[11]

The benefit

Unlike the position with regard to the running of contractual burdens, the common law has never had a problem with the benefit of covenants being transmitted. Contractual rights, such as a debt, can readily be assigned to others. If A owes B £100, B can sell that debt to a debt collecting agency, who will then have the right to enforce the obligation against A. In the case of covenants relating to land, the benefit of the covenant can pass to a successor in title without the need for the right to be expressly assigned.

The leading case is *Smith & Snipes Hall Farm Ltd v. River Douglas Catchment Board*.[12] The defendants covenanted with various freeholders that they would maintain the banks of the Eller Brook. One of the landowners then conveyed land to the first plaintiff, expressly with the benefit of the covenant. The first plaintiff then created a lease in favour of the second plaintiff. The river then burst its bank causing extensive flooding and the action was brought by both plaintiffs, who argued that they had acquired the benefit of the original covenant and were therefore entitled to sue for its breach. The Court of Appeal held in favour of both plaintiffs.

It was held that for the benefit of a covenant to run at common law various criteria had to be satisfied. First, before the benefit of the covenant will pass, the covenant must touch and concern the land, that is 'it must either affect the land as regards mode of occupation, or it must be such as per se, and not merely from collateral sources, affects the value of the land'.[13] Secondly, the successor in title must have a legal estate in the land, although not necessarily the same estate as the predecessor in title so that, in the present case, the second plaintiff, who was a tenant, acquired the benefit of a covenant made with a predecessor in title, who was a freeholder.[14] Thirdly,

---

[10] See The enforceability of covenants, pp. 447–453.
[11] *Austerberry v. Corporation of Oldham* (1885) 29 Ch.D. 750; *Rhone v. Stephens* [1994] 2 A.C. 310. See Restrictive covenants, pp. 580–581.
[12] [1947] 2 K.B. 500.   [13] [1947] 2 K.B. 500 at 506 *per* Tucker L.J.
[14] See also *Williams v. Unit Construction Co. Ltd* (1955) 19 Conv. (N.S.) 262 at 266–267 *per* Lord Tucker.

the land to be benefited must, from the deed containing the covenant, be reasonably identifiable, although such identification need not be express, and extrinsic evidence is admissible to identify the land in question.[15] Finally, the parties must intend that the benefit of the covenant runs with the land.

This last requirement was held to have been satisfied by the operation of section 78 of the Law of Property Act 1925. This section, which became controversial in the context of the running of the benefit in equity,[16] provides that:

'A covenant relating to any land of the covenantee shall be deemed to be made with the covenantee and his successors in title and the persons deriving title under him or them, and shall have effect as if such successors and other persons were expressed.'

The effect of the section was that the covenant made by the covenantor was read as if it said that the covenant was made for the benefit not only of the covenantee, but also with his successors in title. This, together with the other criteria having been met, meant that the plaintiffs had acquired the benefit of the covenant and could sue upon it.

Nature of the covenant

Provided that the criteria referred to above are satisfied, the benefit of the covenant will run at common law. With regard to the running of the benefit, while it is essential that the covenantee owns land to be benefited by the covenant, it is immaterial as to whether the covenantor owns land himself.[17] Neither is it relevant, insofar as the running of the benefit is concerned, as to the type of covenant involved: whether it is positive or negative. While, as will be seen, this is a highly relevant consideration when regard is had to the running of the *burden* in equity, the *benefit* of either positive or negative covenants is capable of running at law.

Landlord and tenant

A recent example of the running of the benefit of a covenant at common law is provided by *P. & A. Swift Investments (A Firm) v. Combined English Stores Group plc.*[18] The defendant had stood surety for the rent payable by a tenant to the original landlord. The landlord subsequently assigned the reversion to the plaintiff and the tenant then got into financial difficulties and was unable to pay the rent, whereupon the plaintiff sued the surety upon the contractual guarantee given to the original landlord. The issue was, therefore, whether the benefit of this covenant had passed to the plaintiff upon the assignment of the reversion.

Because there had never been a relationship of landlord and tenant between the plaintiff and the defendant, the rules concerning the running of covenants in leases were of no assistance to the plaintiff. Instead, the argument was that the benefit of the

---

[15] [1949] 2 K.B. 500 at 508 *per* Tucker L.J.   [16] See Statutory annexation, pp. 585–587.

[17] *Smith & Snipes Hall Farm Ltd v. River Douglas Catchment Board* [1947] 2 K.B. 500 at 517–518 *per* Denning L.J.

[18] [1989] A.C. 632.

covenant had run at common law. The House of Lords held that it had done so. The covenant touched and concerned the land because, first, it was only of benefit to the holder of the reversion for the time being, it being of no use to him after the reversion had been assigned; secondly, it affected the nature and quality or mode of user of the land or its value and, thirdly, the covenant was not expressed to be personal to the original contracting parties.[19] So, the benefit of the surety covenant ran at common law, it not being material that the surety did not own land and that the land benefited by the covenant was a freehold reversion.

To sum up, therefore, the position at common law is that the benefit of certain covenants can run with the land but the burden cannot. In equity, however, a quite different approach has developed.

EQUITY

A central feature of the common law approach to covenants was that the obligations imposed by such covenants were personal to the parties who were privy to their creation. Put another way, the burden of such covenants do not run with the land. Equity, however, took a different view, the starting point of the development of this branch of the law being the decision in *Tulk v. Moxhay*,[20] a case which is the foundation stone of the modern law of restrictive covenants.

The burden of covenants

In *Tulk v. Moxhay*, Tulk, in 1808, sold a vacant plot of land in Leicester Square to Elms. Elms covenanted on behalf of himself, his heirs, and assigns that he would, at all times, keep and maintain the said piece of ground in an open state, uncovered with any buildings. The land then passed through various pairs of hands until, finally, it was conveyed to Moxhay, who admitted that he had notice of the existence of the covenant. Notwithstanding his knowledge of this covenant, he then threatened to build upon the land and Tulk sought and obtained an injunction to restrain him from building.

In granting the injunction, the reasoning of Lord Cottenham L.C. was quite general. He said:

'That the question does not depend on whether the covenant runs with the land is evident from this, that if there was a mere agreement and no covenant, this court would enforce it against a party purchasing with notice of it; for if an equity is attached to the property by the owner, no one purchasing with notice of that equity can stand in a different situation from the party from whom he purchased.'[21]

---

[19] [1989] A.C. 632 at 642 *per* Lord Oliver of Aylmerton.   [20] (1843) 2 Ph. 773.
[21] (1843) 2 Ph. 773 at 778.

It should be observed that the judgment in this case does not rest upon the premise that the type of covenant he was considering was a form of interest in land, the burden of which is then capable of binding a purchaser of that land. To the contrary, the basis of the decision is that, if a purchaser buys land with notice of some prior undertaking relating to that land, then it is inequitable for him to act in a way which is inconsistent with that obligation. Put in such broad terms, all sorts of different obligations could become enforceable against successive owners of land. This is something against which the law has traditionally set its face: to allow this to happen could make certain land virtually unsellable as it might be affected by a multitude of different obligations. So, although the decision in *Tulk v. Moxhay* is still regarded as the foundation of the modern law, the actual rationale of the judgment is not. Instead, the courts have taken care to fashion a new interest in land, the nature of this right being modelled closely on the law of easements.

RESTRICTIVE COVENANTS

In *Tulk v. Moxhay*, the covenant to keep and maintain the ground in an open state, uncovered with buildings, reads, at first sight, as a positive covenant. The words 'keep' and 'maintain' tend to indicate an obligation to do something. In substance, however, the covenant is negative, or restrictive, as its effect is to prevent the covenantor from building upon his own land. The reasoning in the passage quoted above does not, however, lay any emphasis upon whether the covenant was to do something or to refrain from certain conduct. The issue seemed to be, simply, whether or not the successor in title had notice of the covenant. If he did, he was bound by it. This led to a view that both positive and negative covenants could be enforced as against purchasers with notice[22] and, for a time, judicial support could be found for such a proposition.[23] It soon came to be settled, however, that the only covenants which were capable of binding a successor in title to the covenantor were negative covenants. In the leading case of *Haywood v. Brunswick Permanent Building Society*,[24] it was held that a mortgagee of an assignee was not bound by a covenant to build and keep in repair houses on the land, it being made clear that 'only such a covenant as can be complied with without the expenditure of money will be enforced against the assignee on the ground of notice'.[25]

Ever since this decision, it became the received wisdom that only restrictive covenants were capable of running with the land. That wisdom was directly challenged in the House of Lords in *Rhone v. Stephens*,[26] where it was held, confirming the rule

---

[22] See C.D. Bell [1981] Conv. 52 at 57–60. For a strong counter-argument, see R. Griffith [1983] Conv. 29.

[23] See *Morland v. Cook* (1868) L.R. 6 Eq. 252; *Cooke v. Chilcott* (1876) 3 Ch.D. 694; *Luker v. Dennis* (1877) 7 Ch.D. 227.

[24] (1881) 8 Q.B. 403.   [25] Ibid., at 410 *per* Lindley L.J.

[26] [1994] 2 A.C. 310. See N.P. Gravells (1994) 110 L.Q.R. 346. See also *Thamesmead Town v. Allotley* [1998] 3 E.G.L.R. 97.

established in *Haywood v. Brunswick Building Society*, that a covenant to maintain a roof was not binding upon a successor in title to the covenantor. In reaching this conclusion, considerable stress was laid, in the field of Property Law, on the need to maintain certainty and, in particular, not to upset established rights. Lord Templeman said:

'It is plain from articles, reports and papers to which we were referred that judicial legislation to overrule the *Austerberry* case would create a number of difficulties, anomalies and uncertainties and affect the rights of people who have for over 100 years bought and sold land in the knowledge, imparted at an elementary stage to every student of the law of real property, that positive covenants affecting freehold land are not directly enforceable except against the original covenantor.'[27]

The House of Lords, therefore, confirmed the long-established rule that it is only restrictive covenants which can be made to run directly with freehold land, and attempts to make positive covenants binding on successors in title have been described as 'hopeful rather than realistic'.[28] In the previous chapter on easements, it was noted that the law was highly reluctant to recognize as an easement a right which restricts the use to which the servient owner can put his land.[29] Any problem caused by this reluctance is largely met, however, by the development of the law relating to restrictive covenants, whereby constraints on land use can be imposed by the creation of a suitable covenant. There is, however, a similar reluctance to recognize as an easement any right which will involve the expenditure of money by the owner of the servient land. Here, the law concerning covenants relating to freehold land does not provide an alternative means of imposing such a liability. This lack of a direct means of providing for the enforceability of positive covenants does cause problems. These problems, and the means of circumventing them, will be considered at the end of this chapter.

Land to be benefited

As the law of restrictive covenants developed, increasingly the interest in land which was created began to take on the characteristics of a negative easement affecting land.[30] If a right is to be recognized as an easement, there must exist a dominant tenement. Before the burden of a restrictive covenant will run with the land the same requirement exists. The person seeking to enforce that covenant must retain land to be benefited.

This rule is exemplified by the decision in *Formby v. Barker*.[31] F sold all of his land subject to various covenants restricting its use. The defendant acquired part of that land with notice of the covenants. The administratrix of F's estate then sought an

---

[27] Ibid., at 321.   [28] *Davies v. Bramwell* [2007] EWCA Civ. 821 at [8] *per* Lloyd L.J.
[29] See Negative rights, p. 543.
[30] See *London and S.W. Railway Co. v. Gomm* (1882) 20 Ch.D. 362 at 382–383 *per* Sir George Jessel M.R.
[31] [1903] 2 Ch. 539.

injunction to restrict the building on that land which, it was alleged, would infringe the covenant. The action failed on two grounds. First, it was held that the proposed building would not actually amount to a breach of covenant. More importantly, the burden of the covenant did not run because the person seeking to enforce it did not have any land which would be benefited by the covenant. This rule was confirmed in *London County Council v. Allen*,[32] where a local authority sought to enforce covenants made in its favour. The relevant land was later conveyed and the attempt to enforce the covenant failed because the authority did not own land to be benefited by the covenant and so the burden of it was held not to have run.

This decision confirms the general rule that, for the burden of a restrictive covenant to run, there must, in effect, be a dominant tenement. The consequence of the rule in the present context was, however, potentially awkward and so, in favour of local authorities, the rule has been modified, to allow them to enforce such covenants despite not having land to be benefited.[33] The basic rule, however, remains.

Allied to the rule that the person seeking to enforce the covenant must have land to be benefited by that covenant is the requirement that the land retained does benefit from the covenant. This means two things. First, that the covenant touches and concerns the land and, secondly, that the two plots of land are sufficiently proximate to each other for the dominant land to be benefited. So, as is the case with easements, that a right of way in Kent does not exist for the benefit of land in Northumberland,[34] covenants relating to land in Hampstead will not be regarded as benefiting land in Clapham.[35] The covenant must accommodate the dominant tenement.

Intention that burden will run

It is not compulsory that restrictive covenants entered into by two landowners will necessarily create an interest in land binding upon successors in title to the covenantor. The covenant may be intended to be personal to the parties making it. For the burden of the covenant to run with the land, the parties must intend this to happen. This matter is governed by section 79 of the Law of Property Act 1925, which provides that:

'A covenant relating to any land of a covenantor or capable of being bound by him, shall, unless a contrary intention is expressed, be deemed to be made on behalf of the covenantor on behalf of himself his successors in title and the persons deriving title under him or them and, subject as aforesaid, shall take effect as if such successors and other persons were expressed.'

The expression 'relating to the land' is the familiar concept that the covenant must touch and concern the land. The reference to 'capable of being bound' would seem

---

[32] [1914] 3 Q.B. 642.
[33] Town and Country Planning Act 1990, s. 106(3), replacing earlier legislation.
[34] See *Bailey v. Stephens* (1862) 12 C.B. (N.S.) 91 at 115 *per* Byles J.
[35] *Kelly v. Barrett* [1924] 2 Ch. 379 at 404 *per* Pollock M.R.

to be sufficient to prevent the burden of a positive covenant running with the land, as such covenants are not capable of binding the servient land.[36] Provided that the other criteria discussed above are met, then unless a contrary intention is expressed, the burden of the covenant will run with the land. In terms of finding the requisite contrary intention, while an express statement to this effect is preferable,[37] the court is prepared to construe the document as a whole to see if it was intended that the covenant is to be personal to the covenantor.[38]

Equitable right

The restrictive covenant is an interest in land which was developed by equity. Unlike legal interests in land, equitable interests will not automatically bind a purchaser of the servient land and, subject to some exceptions, its enforceability will depend upon registration. It is necessary to deal separately with unregistered and registered land.

Unregistered land

A restrictive covenant is, except for two types of covenant, registrable as a Class D(ii) land charge. If registered, all subsequent purchasers will be deemed to have actual notice of it and, therefore, be bound by it.[39] If it is not registered, it will be void against a purchaser of a legal estate for money or money's worth.[40] An unregistered restrictive covenant will be binding upon a squatter, who is not, of course, a purchaser for money or money's worth.[41]

There are two classes of restrictive covenant which are not registrable as land charges. These are covenants created before 1926 and covenants between landlord and tenant. The determination of whether a purchaser has notice of such covenants and, therefore, is bound by them, is dependent upon the old doctrine of notice which, in this context, will mean whether or not they could be discovered by a proper investigation of title.[42]

Registered land

A restrictive covenant is not capable of overriding a registered disposition and, if it is to bind a purchaser for value, it must, unless it is a covenant between landlord and tenant, be protected by the registration of a notice.[43]

---

[36] See *Rhone v. Stephens* [1994] 2 A.C. 310 at 322 *per* Lord Templeman.

[37] See *Gregg v. Richards* [1926] Ch. 521.

[38] *Re Royal Victoria Pavilion, Ramsgate* [1961] Ch. 581; *Morrells of Oxford Ltd v. Oxford United F.C. Ltd* [2001] Ch. 459.

[39] Law of Property Act 1925, s. 198.   [40] Land Charges Act 1972, s. 4(6).

[41] See *Re Nisbett and Pott's Contract* [1906] 1 Ch. 306.

[42] See Investigation of title, pp. 53–54.   [43] Land Registration Act 2002, ss 32 and 33.

The benefit of restrictive covenants

The application of the rules derived from *Tulk v. Moxhay* indicate when the burden of a restrictive covenant has run with the land, so that one knows if a particular purchaser is bound by it. The second, independent, question then arises as to whether there is anybody who can enforce that covenant; whether the benefit of the covenant has also run. As the common law developed rules concerning the running of the benefit of covenants, so, too, did equity. In practice, the equitable rules are more important than their common law counterparts because if a person is seeking to enforce a covenant, the burden of which has passed in equity, he must establish, if he is not the original covenantee, that the benefit of that covenant has passed to him under the equitable rules.[44] If this cannot can be established, then despite the burden of the covenant having run, the position will be that there is nobody in a position to enforce it.[45] In the case of registered land, the register can then be altered to remove the entry relating to the burden of the covenant.[46]

In equity, the benefit of a covenant can run in one of the three ways, set out by Sir Charles Hall V.-C. in *Renals v. Cowlishaw.*[47] These are:

(i)   annexation;

(ii)   assignment; and

(iii) a scheme of development.

These three methods will be considered in turn.

Annexation

Annexation involves the permanent attachment of the benefit of a restrictive covenant to the land. Once the benefit has been annexed, it will pass automatically on a transfer of the land without specific mention. It was previously the case, and still is with regard to pre-1926 covenants,[48] that the law concerning how annexation was effected was highly complex, with meticulous attention being paid to the precise wording of a particular covenant to establish that the requisite intention had been shown to annex the covenant to the dominant land.[49] It was also necessary for the land in question to be clearly identified. There was a further complication in that, once it had been shown that the benefit of a covenant had been annexed, it was regarded as annexed to the land as a whole. Unless when the benefit of the covenant was annexed, it was annexed to

---

[44] See, e.g., *Re Union of London & Smith's Bank Conveyance, Miles v. Easter* [1933] Ch. 611.

[45] See, e.g., *Seymour Road (Southampton) Ltd v. Williams* [2010] EWHC 111 (Ch.).

[46] See *Southwark Roman Catholic Diocesan Corporation v. South London Church Fund &. Southwark Diocesan Board of Finance* [2009] EWHC 3368 (Ch.).

[47] (1878) 9 Ch.D. 125 at 129.

[48] See *Shropshire County Council v. Edwards* (1982) 46 P. & C.R. 270; *J. Sainsbury plc v. Enfield London Borough Council* [1989] 1 W.L.R. 590; *Southwark Roman Catholic Diocesan Corporation v. South London Church Fund &.Southwark Diocesan Board of Finance* [2009] EWHC 3368 (Ch.).

[49] See, e.g., *Rogers v. Hosegood* [1900] 2 Ch. 388.

each and every part of the dominant land, on a sale of only part of the land, the benefit of the covenant would not pass.[50] Happily, a good deal of the complexity affecting this branch of the law was swept away as a result of the decision of the Court of Appeal in *Federated Homes v. Mill Lodge Properties Ltd.*[51]

Statutory annexation

One of the issues which arose in *Federated Homes* was whether the benefit of a covenant restricting the amount of building which could take place on a neighbouring plot had been annexed to the land and had, therefore, passed to the plaintiff. Despite the fact that there were no express words of annexation in the conveyance, the Court of Appeal held that section 78 of the Law of Property Act 1925 had the effect of annexing the benefit of the covenant. This section, it will be recalled, provides that a covenant relating to the land of the covenantee shall be deemed to have been made with the covenantee, his successors in title, and persons deriving title under him. Brightman L.J. held that, providing that the covenant in question related to the covenantee's land, the effect of the section was to annex the benefit of the covenant to the land. He held, further, that the section annexed the covenant not just to the land as a whole, but to each and every part of it, thereby removing the difficulty adverted to earlier.[52]

The decision in *Federated Homes*, although advocated by some writers in the past,[53] was controversial.[54] Strong exception was taken by one specialist practitioner in the field[55] to the interpretation of section 78 that, provided that the covenant touched and concerned the land, the benefit of the covenant became annexed to the land. Before appraising the merits of the decision, one important matter must be addressed. In *Federated Homes*, Brightman L.J. left open the question whether, for annexation to take place, the covenant must identify the land to be benefited.[56] In *Crest Nicholson Residential (South) Ltd v. McCallister,*[57] Chadwick L.J. confirmed that this was a necessary requirement. As well as being supported by authority, there is a good practical reason for insisting upon this requirement, as it facilitates the task of a purchaser of the burdened land to discover which land has the benefit of the covenant in question.[58]

Although the decision has been criticized, in defence of it, it can be pointed out, as Brightman L.J. did himself, that at common law the benefit of covenants will, as a result of this section, run with the land without the need for the intention that it should do so being expressed.[59] It would be odd for equity to take a less relaxed, more

---

[50] *Re Ballard's Conveyance* [1937] Ch. 473.   [51] [1980] 1 W.L.R. 594.

[52] Although see the somewhat odd remarks in *City Inn (Jersey) Ltd v. Ten Trinity Square Ltd* [2008] EWCA Civ. 156 at [33] *per* Jacob L.J.

[53] Se, e.g., H.W.R. Wade [1972B] C.L.J. 94.

[54] See D.J. Hayton (1980) 43 M.L.R. 445. For a supportive reaction, see D.J. Hurst (1982) 2 L.S. 53.

[55] G.H. Newsom (1981) 97 LQ.R. 32, perhaps vindicating the view that the decision would be more popular with academics than with practitioners: A. Sydenham [1980] Conv. 216 at 217.

[56] [1984] 1 W.L.R. 594 at 604.   [57] [2004] 1 W.L.R. 2409. See J. Howell [2004] Conv. 507.

[58] [2004] 1 W.L.R. 2409 at 2422.

[59] [1980] 1 W.L.R. 598 at 605, referring to *Smith & Snipes Hall Farm Ltd v. River Douglas Catchment Board* [1947] 2 K.B. 500; *Williams v. Unit Construction Ltd* (1955) 19 Conv. (N.S.) 262.

formalistic, approach to an issue such as this than did the common law. Moreover, the decision should be welcomed for having consigned to history some of the arcane learning that had been allowed to develop around this branch of the law. It is now clear that, provided that the land to be benefited is identified, whether by the conveyance or by admissible extrinsic evidence, and provided that the covenant touches and concerns the land, the benefit of it will run with the land. It will not also be necessary to show, by express words in the conveyance, the specific intention that it should pass to successors in title.[60]

Contrary intention

One of the criticisms levelled at *Federated Homes* was that, unlike section 79 of the Act, which relates to the passing of the burden of restrictive covenants, section 78 is not expressed to be subject to the expression of a contrary intention.[61] So, it was argued, if the covenant in question touched and concerned the land, the effect of section 78 would be to make annexation compulsory, whatever the intention of parties. This fear was dispelled in *Roake v. Chadha*.[62] This concerned a covenant which was expressed 'not to enure for the benefit of any owner or subsequent purchaser of the…estate unless the benefit of the covenant shall be expressly assigned'. The effect of this wording was held to be that the covenant did not relate to the land and was not, therefore, annexed to it. The effect of the decision is that annexation will occur unless a contrary intention is expressed and the statement that the benefit can pass only by express assignment was a sufficient statement of a contrary intention.

The finding of a contrary intention is a matter of construction, and 'the parties may restrict the ambit of the benefit of a restrictive covenant to the original covenantee and whether or not they have done so is a question of construction of the instrument as a whole.'[63] In *City Inn (Jersey) Ltd v. Ten Trinity Square Ltd*,[64] various restrictive covenants were entered into for the benefit of the Port of London Authority on a transfer by it of land. The covenant referred to the Authority as 'the transferor', that term being used twenty-eight times in the conveyance. On a couple of occasions reference was made to the transferor and its successors in title. This led to the conclusion that the benefit of the covenant was intended to be personal to the Authority, and so did not run to a successor in title. The same reasoning was employed in *Margerison v. Bates*,[65] where, on some occasions, the conveyance referred simply to the vendor, and on others, to the vendor and her successors in title. In a professionally drawn legal document, this was seen as deliberate, with the result that the covenant which was expressed to be made with the vendor was made with her personally, and there was no intention that the benefit of it should run. What is key to these decisions is the deliberate use of the

---

[60] *Mohammadzadeh v. Joseph* [2008] 1 P. & C.R. 6 at [46] *per* Etherton L.J.
[61] See also *Morrells of Oxford Ltd v. Oxford United F.C. Ltd* [2001] Ch. 459 at 466 *per* Robert Walker L.J.
[62] [1984] Ch. 40. See also *Crest Nicholson Residential (South) Ltd v. McAllister* [2004] 1 W.L.R. 2409.
[63] *Rees v. Peters* [2011] EWCA Civ. 836 at [9] *per* Sir Andrew Morritt C., a case involving a highly ambiguous document.
[64] [2008] EWCA Civ. 156.   [65] [2008] EWHC 1211 (Ch.).

expression 'successors in title' in some references and not in others. If there is simply a reference to the transferor, the intention that the benefit will run will, as a result of section 78, readily be found.[66]

Assignment

If a covenant has not, at the time of its creation, been annexed to the land, then it is possible, on a subsequent conveyance, for the benefit of that covenant to be assigned with the land. For assignment to take place in equity, the assignment of the covenant must be coupled with a transfer of the land and the conveyance and assignment must be simultaneous.[67] The assignment must identify the land to be benefited, although such identification can be done through surrounding circumstances.[68]

Once the benefit of the covenant has been assigned, the better view is that, on subsequent conveyances, further assignments should not be necessary. This view is based on the idea that an assignment should operate as a 'delayed annexation' so that the benefit of any covenants should, thereafter, pass automatically.[69] Such authority as there is on this point is, however, against this view. It would appear, therefore, to be necessary for there to be an express assignment of the benefit of the covenant each time that the land is conveyed, so that there is an unbroken chain of assignments from the covenantee to the person seeking to enforce the covenant.

Schemes of development

The final method of ensuring that the benefit of a covenant passes with the dominant land is to establish a scheme of development. The essence of such a scheme is that land, at one time owned by a single person, is divided up into lots and then sold off to various purchasers. The idea is that the covenants entered into, which are for the benefit of the estate, become mutually enforceable between the various owners of the different plots of land. Although the existing rules could have been employed to achieve the required result, a different set of rules was devised with the result that, when the existence of a scheme is established, a local law is created with regard to this area of land. It should be borne in mind, however, that it has been said that: 'It may be, indeed, that this is one of those branches of equity which work best when explained least.'[70]

Origins of the doctrine

When the courts began to develop this branch of the law, quite stringent criteria were adopted which had to be met before the courts would accept that a scheme of

---

[66] See *Mahon v. Simms* [2005] 3 E.G.L.R. 67.

[67] *Re Union of London and Smith's Conveyance, Miles v. Easter* [1933] Ch. 611.

[68] *Newton Abbot Co-operative Society Ltd v. Williamson v. Treadgold Ltd* [1952] Ch. 286; *Marten v. Flight Refuelling Ltd* [1962] Ch. 115.

[69] P.V. Baker (1968) 84 L.Q.R. 22.

[70] *Brunner v. Greenslade* [1971] 1 Ch. 993 at 1006 *per* Megarry J.

development had been created. Four conditions were laid down in *Elliston v. Reacher*[71] which had to be satisfied. These were:

(i)   the land must have been disposed of by a common vendor;

(ii)   prior to the sale the land had to be laid out in lots subject to common obligations;

(iii)   the common vendor must have intended the benefits of the covenants to be for the benefit of all the owners and not merely for himself; and

(iv)   the land must have been bought on the footing that the restrictions were to be enforceable by the owner of other lots.

A more relaxed approach

In more recent times, the courts have been prepared to relax the criteria established in *Ellliston v. Reacher* and find there to be a scheme of development to have been created when one or other of these conditions has not been met.[72] Nowadays, the courts are concerned to see that two conditions are satisfied. The first is that the area to be affected by the scheme has been properly identified.[73] Secondly, and of paramount importance, is that it is shown that it was clearly intended to set up a scheme for the reciprocal enforcement of obligations. In order to establish such an intention, it is helpful if the land is laid out in lots, as this gives rise to a presumption that there is such a reciprocal intention.[74] It is not, however, essential to do this, as such an intention can be established by extrinsic evidence and the fact that the various covenants are identical is strong evidence to this effect.[75] No such intention to establish a reciprocal scheme will be found to exist unless its existence is brought to the attention of prospective purchasers.[76]

REMEDIES

A restrictive covenant is an equitable right and, as such, the remedies available in respect of any breach of covenant are equitable. The principal remedy which is sought is the injunction. The type of injunction sought may vary. If the breach has not actually occurred, but is merely threatened, then the plaintiff will seek a *quia timet* injunction. This is a remedy to prevent conduct which if carried out, will, it is envisaged, amount to an infringement of the plaintiff's rights, and so prevents that infringement from occurring, thereby restraining the anticipated breach. Alternatively, the breach may

---

[71]   [1908] 2 Ch. 374.

[72]   See Gray and Gray, *Elements of Land Law* (5th edn) (London: Oxford University Press, 2009), 283–286.

[73]   See *Lund v. Taylor* (1975) 31 P. & C.R. 167.

[74]   See *Baxter v. Four Oaks Properties Ltd* [1965] 1 Ch. 816; *Re Dolphin's Conveyance* [1970] Ch. 654.

[75]   See *Brunner v. Greenslade* [1971] 1 Ch. 993.

[76]   See *Jamaica Mutual Life Assurance Society v. Hillsborough Ltd* [1989] 1 W.L.R. 1101.

have occurred and the injunction is sought to prevent the continuation of the breach. Finally, a mandatory injunction may be sought to undo what has been done, such as the demolition of a building erected in breach of contract.[77]

As with all equitable remedies, the grant of an injunction is discretionary but that discretion is exercised in accordance with settled principles,[78] so that, for example, delay in bringing an action may cause the injunction to be refused.[79]

Damages in lieu

Because a breach of a restrictive covenant is the infringement of an equitable, as opposed to a legal, right, there is no right to damages. The court has, however, since the time of Lord Cairns' Act 1858,[80] had the power to award damages in lieu of an injunction. As the effect of the award of damages is, in effect, to allow the wrongdoer to pay for a right to do that which he was not entitled to do, it is a jurisdiction which is used sparingly.[81] The principles on which damages are payable in lieu of an injunction were laid down in *Shelfer v. City of London Electric Lighting Co.*[82] They are that the injury to the plaintiff's legal right is small; it is capable of being estimated in money; that damages would be adequate compensation; and that it would be oppressive to the defendant to grant an injunction. This latter consideration is likely to be an important consideration when, in breach of covenant, buildings have been constructed and the remedy sought would involve a mandatory injunction requiring their demolition. In such circumstances, the award of an injunction may be seen as oppressive, although if the person who is infringing the claimant's right took a calculated risk that the building may have that effect, this consideration will have considerably less weight.[83] The damages which are awarded are then assessed on the basis of what could reasonably have been charged for the release of the covenant.[84]

DISCHARGE OF COVENANTS

Some restrictive covenants affecting land may have been imposed many years in the past, when conditions were very different from those currently pertaining. Yet, they remain binding upon successive purchasers of the land, despite serving little

---

[77] See *Wakeham v. Wood* (1982) 43 P. & C.R. 40; *Mortimer v. Bailey* [2004] EWCA Civ. 1514.

[78] See, generally, Hanbury and Martin, *Modern Equity* (18th edn) (London: Sweet & Maxwell, 2009), Chapter 25.

[79] See *Chatsworth Estates Co. v. Fewell* [1931] 1 Ch. 224.

[80] Chancery Amendment Act 1858, s. 2. See now Supreme Court Act 1981, s. 50.

[81] It has been said that this jurisdiction should only be used in 'exceptional circumstances': *Watson v. Croft Promo-Sport Ltd* [2009] EWCA Civ. 15 at [44] *per* Sir Andrew Morritt C.

[82] [1895] 1 Ch. 287 at 322–333 *per* A.L. Smith L.J.

[83] See *Regan v. Paul Properties Ltd* [2006] EWCA Civ. 1391 at [74] *per* Mummery L.J. (easement of light). See, in the context of easements of light and remedies, P. Chynoweth [2007] Conv. 175.

[84] *Wrotham Park Estate Co. Ltd v. Parkside Homes Ltd* [1974] 1 W.L.R. 798; *Jaggard v. Sawyer* [1995] 1 W.L.R. 269. See D. Halpern [2001] Conv. 453.

purpose in modern society. It may also be the case that their continued enforceability is socially detrimental, preventing socially desirable development of the land. Such considerations led the Law Commission's Conveyancing Standing Committee[85] to canvass various options to curb the effect of restrictive covenants, the most radical being to abolish them altogether, although, perhaps more reasonably, less drastic proposals were also mooted, such as putting a legislative lifespan on their effect. Nothing came of this consultation paper and the only way to mitigate the sometimes doleful effect of restrictive covenants is to utilize the statutory jurisdiction conferred on Lands Tribunals to modify or discharge restrictive covenants, either with or without compensation.

Application may be made to the Lands Chamber of the Upper Tribunal (formerly the Lands Tribunal) under section 84 of the Law of Property Act 1925[86] for a covenant to be modified or discharged. Such an order can be made on one of four grounds:

(i)   that the covenant has become obsolete;

(ii)   that the continued enforcement of the covenant would be obstructive to some public or private use of the land and that the covenant confers no practical benefit or is contrary to the public interest and any loss can be adequately compensated by money;

(iii) with the consent, either express or implied, of all persons of full age entitled to the benefit; and

(iv)   the discharge or modification would confer no injury on the person entitled to the benefit.

While the Law Commission has recommended that the jurisdiction of the Lands Chamber should be extended to easements, profits, and its proposed new interest, the land obligation, it did not advocate any changes to the grounds on which such modifications could be made.[87]

POSITIVE COVENANTS

In *Rhone v. Stephens*,[88] the House of Lords confirmed that the burden of covenants in respect of freehold land does not run either at law or in equity. This rule causes distinct practical problems. These problems run from the fairly mundane, to some very serious matters. To take the former matter first, it is hardly satisfactory that, under English law, it 'remains impossible to use a simple legal structure to manage

---

[85] (1986) Law Commission Conveyancing Standing Committee, *What Should We Do About Old Restrictive Covenants*, 11–12.

[86] As amended by Law of Property Act 1969, s. 28.   [87] (2011) Law Com. No. 327, paras 7.54–7.55.

[88] [1994] 2 A.C. 310.

responsibility for mending a fence between properties, or a single facility shared by a few properties.'[89] This is a matter of some inconvenience because, apparently, every time there is a major storm, the Land Registry is inundated with enquiries about the ownership and maintenance of boundaries and the callers are disappointed to learn that the Registry cannot say who owns them or is liable for their repair.[90] With regard to more important matters, where flats are concerned, one needs to be able to impose binding positive covenants in respect of matters such as contribution to the common parts of a building. Because it is impossible to achieve this where the flats are owned on a freehold basis, this is one of the reasons why flats are held on long leases, as covenants in leases, be they positive or negative, can bind assignees of both the lease and the reversion.

Commonhold

The position with regard to positive covenants is far from ideal,[91] and, following the publication of the Aldridge Report,[92] the position was reformed by the invention of a new legal regime by the Commonhold and Leasehold Reform Act 2002. The Act introduced a new form of landholding, termed copyhold, whereby a collective group of people can own the freehold of a property and also own individually the freehold of their own parts of it. The scheme introduced by the Act is highly complex.[93] The system will in practice apply only to new buildings, generally blocks of flats, and will entail a collaborative system of control to be exercised over the building and the individual units within it. The new scheme has had a very low take-up rate, however, so that as of 2008, there had only been fourteen such schemes registered.[94]

Indirect enforcement

With regard to freehold land, it is not possible, by direct means, to make the burden of positive covenants run with the land. This position has long been considered to be problematic, and has led to a number of proposals for reform,[95] the most recent of which will be considered shortly. The absence of a direct method of imposing a positive burden on land has led, however, to various indirect methods, of varying efficacy, of achieving this result.

---

[89] (2011) Law Com. No. 327, para. 5.42.   [90] Ibid., para. 5.21, n. 31.

[91] For an excellent discussion of the legal problems associated with communal living, see D.N. Clarke in Bright and Dewar (eds), *Land Law: Themes and Perspectives* (Oxford: Oxford University Press, 1998) Chapter 15.

[92] (1987) Cmnd. 279.

[93] See generally D.N. Clarke, *Commonhold, The New Law* (Bristol: Jordans, 2002).

[94] See (2008) Law Com Consultation Paper No. 186, para. 11.4.

[95] See (1965) Cmnd. 2719 (The Wilberforce Committee); (1984) Law Com. No. 127. See also H.W.R. Wade [1972B] C.L.J. 157.

Chain of covenants

One not very effective way of seeking to impose continuing liability in respect of posi-tive covenants is to employ a chain of covenants. If A covenants with B to maintain a fence between their two properties, A will be liable if the fence falls into disrepair. This liability remains even after A has sold the land to C. On the occasion of that con-veyance A can obtain a covenant from C to indemnify him in respect of any liability resulting from the failure to maintain the fence. When C conveys the land to D he then obtains a similar indemnity from him, and so on. The covenant is enforced by B suing A, who then seeks an indemnity from C who, in turn, seeks an indemnity from D. Fairly obviously, such a chain of covenants will soon break down and this is an unsatisfactory method of seeking to impose liability.

Enlargement of a long lease

In the case of certain long leases, the tenant has the right, under section 153 of the Law of Property Act 1925, to have that lease enlarged into a freehold. If this is done, the freehold is subject to the same obligations as was the lease. Positive covenants contained in the lease would, therefore, appear to be binding on the freeholder. This method of making positive covenants binding on the freehold is regarded as artificial and has not been tested in the courts.

Rentcharges

A rentcharge is an annual payment of money charged upon land. This is enforced by a right of re-entry if the money is not paid: a means of terminating the estate. The rent-charge is made subject to the performance of various terms, which can include the performance of positive acts which, if not performed, give the holder of the charge the right to enter the land and perform those acts, charging the cost to the freeholder. The creation of new rentcharges after 1977 was, in general, prohibited by section 2 of the Rentcharges Act 1977, but an exception was made for a rentcharge imposed to enforce the performance of positive obligations.[96] This is the most effective method of making positive covenants enforceable against a freeholder.

Mutual benefit and burden

In *Halsall v. Brizell*,[97] a purchaser of land was given the right to use various roads on an estate, it being a requirement that he contributed to their upkeep. It was held that so long as he elected to avail himself of that right, he must take subject to the correla-tive burden. From this decision, the principle, termed 'the pure principle' of benefit and burden, was extracted that, if one took the benefit of a conveyance, one must take

---

[96] Rentcharges Act 1977, s. 2(4).   [97] [1974] Ch. 169.

subject to any burdens which that conveyance sought to impose.[98] The adoption of such a principle would, effectively, have ended the rule that positive covenants cannot be made to run with freehold land and it was rejected by the House of Lords in *Rhone v. Stephens*.[99] It was made clear that for the principle of benefit and burden to operate there must, as in *Halsall v. Brizell*, be a clear reciprocity between the enjoyment of a particular benefit and the correlating burden, in the sense of using a road and contributing to its upkeep.[100] Moreover, the person on whom the burden is sought to be imposed must have a real choice as to whether he wishes to accept the benefit to which the burden is sought to be imposed.[101] It is evident that this principle is very narrow in scope and not an acceptable way in which to seek to make positive covenants run with freehold land.

Reform proposals

If, as is clearly the case, it is desirable that, in certain circumstances, the burden of a positive obligation should be able to run with the land, it is clearly preferable for the law to allow this to be achieved directly rather than forcing people to use indirect methods. The Law Commission is of this view[102] and has recommended the creation of a new land obligation to enable this objective to be achieved.

This new form of obligation is to include what have previously been referred to as positive and negative covenants. This new obligation is intended to supersede the old law on restrictive covenants, so that those already in being would continue to exist and to be governed by the prevailing law, new negative obligations would take the form of land obligations, and old-style restrictive covenants would no longer be capable of creation.[103] In order to take the form of a land obligation, it must touch and concern the land. This would permit a distinction to be drawn between an obligation to mend a fence, which does touch and concern the land, and so could run with it, and an obligation to to walk a neighbour's dog, which would not.[104]

Legal interest

It is proposed that this new form of obligation should take the form of a new legal interest in land, and that section 1(2) of the Law of Property Act 1925 be amended accordingly. The principal reason for advocating that this new interest be legal is to facilitate the discovery of who would hold the benefit of such a covenant. By making the obligation a legal right, it would enable the benefit of it to be registered as appurtenant to the dominant land, which currently it cannot be.[105] In the case of

---

[98] *Tito v. Waddell (No. 2)* [1977] Ch. 106 at 289–311 *per* Sir Robert Megarry V.-C.

[99] [1994] 2 A.C. 310.

[100] Ibid., at 322–323 *per* Lord Templeman. It is now not clear whether the use of this principle as a ground for decision in *E.R. Ives Investment Ltd. v. High* [1967] 2 Q.B. 379 is correct.

[101] See also *Thamesmead Town Ltd v. Allotley* [1998] 3 E.G.L.R. 97; *Davies v. Jones* [2009] EWCA Civ. 1164 at [27] *per* Sir Andrew Morritt C.

[102] (2011) Law Com No. 327, para. 5.37.   [103] Ibid., at 5.89.   [104] Ibid., at 5.50.

[105] Land Registration Act 2002, s. 2. (2011) Law Com. No. 327, para. 5.62.

registered land, the recommendation is that this right could not take effect as an overriding interest and would, in order to bind a purchaser, need to be protected on the register.[106] Where title is unregistered, despite the normal rule being that a legal right would bind a purchaser, regardless of notice, it is recommended that it become registrable as a land charge.[107]

This latter recommendation is sensible. While it is true that, where title is unregistered, a legal easement will bind a purchaser regardless of notice, in practice, the existence of the more common easements are frequently apparent on an inspection of the servient land. In the case of covenants, this is not so. Accordingly, for pragmatic reasons,[108] it is desirable that this new legal right should be registrable, and if not registered it would be void as against a purchaser of the burdened land, or of any interest in that land.[109]

These proposals represent a sensible solution to a long-standing problem. It remains to be seen whether they will share the fate of earlier proposals, which have been left to gather dust, or whether they will be implemented to effect an overdue reform of this area of law.

---

[106] Ibid., para. 6.67.   [107] Ibid., at 6.57.

[108] There is a precedent for this in the case of certain legal mortgages: see Class C(i): A puisne mortgage, pp. 89–90.

[109] (2011) Law Com No. 327, para. 6.57.

15

Licences and Estoppel

This chapter is concerned with licences. This is a subject where, in recent times, there has been considerable development in terms of seeking to ascertain how rights in land can be created and the circumstances in which such rights can affect purchasers of land. As such, they occupy something of an amorphous position; licences are not admitted to the category of full proprietary rights but provide an interesting area where the law seeks to afford protection to licensees against both the licensor and, in certain circumstances, a purchaser. It is an area of law where the courts have had to come to terms with informal relationships and seek to accommodate the conflicting pressures of the satisfaction of legitimate expectations, on the one hand, and the desire for security of transactions, on the other.

THE NATURE OF LICENCES

To date, the concept of a licence has been encountered mainly as an alternative to a lease. This concerns an occupancy right where, because the rights given by the agreement do not fulfil the necessary criteria requisite to the creation of a lease, usually because exclusive possession has not been given to the occupier, the law considers that the status of that occupier is not that of a tenant. This is not, however, the only context in which licences can be encountered. While a licence can be occupational in nature, this is not necessarily the case. Another type of licence can involve a person, the licensee, being given a right of access to another's property. Such a right can entail the creation of what is accepted to be a fully fledged proprietary right, an easement; if it does not, then it will be a licence. In this type of situation, two essential questions arise. The first relates to the position as between the licensor and the licensee. The second concerns what, if any, rights the licensee has against a purchaser of the land. In considering both issues, much will depend upon how the licence was created.

Typically, but not inevitably, a licence involves a relationship between two people which does not, for some reason, qualify as an orthodox interest in property. For this reason, the starting point in a consideration of the nature of licences is the statement of principle made in *Thomas v. Sorrell*[1] that, '[a] dispensation or licence properly passes no interest nor alters or transfers property in anything, but only makes an action lawful, without which it would have been unlawful'.

This statement is now no longer totally accurate but serves as a useful starting point in a consideration of licences. The essential nature of a licence is that it is a personal permission given by the licensor to another person, the licensee, to use the licensor's land in some way. What is done is lawful because permission has been given to do it; were that not the case, the act in question would amount to trespass. What becomes important is the source of that permission, this being the principal means of classifying the different types of licence. Licences fall into one of four essential categories,[2] each of which must be considered in turn. The two fundamental questions which must be considered in each case are the effect of the licence as between the original licensor and licensee and then the effect, if any, of that licence upon a successor in title of the licensor.

Gratuitous licences

A gratuitous licence is, as its name suggests, a licence to occupy, or otherwise use, land which is given without consideration. Such licences are extremely common and would include social invitations, such as an invitation given to friends to come round for dinner, or a more functional example, such as when a householder tells one of his neighbours' children not to ask for permission to retrieve a football every time it is kicked over the garden fence but simply to let himself in and get it.

Obviously, such licences are given without consideration and, consequently, they can be revoked by the licensor. If the dinner guests cause offence, they can be asked to leave and, if the householder tires of the children repeatedly entering the garden to retrieve errant footballs, the permission to enter can be withdrawn. The only remaining question is how much time the licensee is to be given to leave the property. The test is then one of reasonableness[3] and this will depend upon the facts surrounding the licence. In the case of dinner guests who have outstayed their welcome, a reasonable time will be short. In the case of a long-time cohabitee who, on the termination of a relationship, is found to have no interest in the house in which she lived and whose status is, therefore, that of a gratuitous licensee,[4] then a reasonable period in order to find alternative accommodation could be a number of weeks.[5]

---

[1] (1673) Vaugh. 330 at 351 *per* Vaughan C.J.

[2] For a classification into eight groups, see Dawson and Pearce, *Licences Relating to the Occupation or Use of Land* (London: Butterworths, 1979), 21–49.

[3] See *Greater London Council v. Jenkins* [1975] 1 All E.R. 354 at 357 *per* Lord Diplock. For a detailed discussion, see J. Hill [2001] C.L.J. 89.

[4] See, e.g., *Burns v. Burns* [1984] Ch. 317.

[5] In the unusual, but instructive, case of *Macclesfield v. Parker* [2003] EWHC 1846 (Ch.) a reasonable period was held to be two years. See M.P. Thompson [2003] Conv. 516.

Because it is always open to the licensor to revoke a gratuitous licence, then it must be the case that a successor in title to the licensee cannot be in any worse position than the person from whom he derives title. It follows, therefore, that just as the licensor could have revoked a gratuitous licence, so can a purchaser from him. There can be no question of such a licence being binding in any way upon a purchaser of the licensor's land.

Licence coupled with a grant

This type of licence is a right to enter land which is a necessary corollary to the existence of a property right, an example of such rights being the right to take game or minerals from another person's land.[6] This type of right is known, generically, as a *profit à prendre*, the right to take and carry away. To exercise such a right, it is necessary that the holder of it has the right to go onto the other person's land. The licence is, therefore, inextricably linked to the property right in question and will, as a consequence, be irrevocable and bind purchasers to the same extent as the property right in question.

Contractual licences

Contractual licences to use another person's land are extremely common. As their name suggests, they are licences given for consideration. Common examples of such licences occur when a person buys a ticket to go to the theatre or to the cinema. Similarly, when a person books a room in a hotel, the guest has a contractual licence to occupy the room. Because of the degree of control exercised by the owner of the hotel, the guest does not have exclusive possession and is termed a lodger,[7] or licensee.

Contractual licences, such as those instanced above, are clearly situations where the relationship is commercial in nature. At one time, there was an attempt made by the courts to fit domestic arrangements into a contractual analysis. In *Tanner v. Tanner*,[8] a married man formed a relationship with another woman, who adopted his name. After she gave birth to twins, he bought a house for her to live in. She did not contribute to the purchase of the house but she did put some £150 towards furnishing it. When the relationship broke down, the Court of Appeal felt able to imply a contractual licence whereby she was to be permitted to live in the house until the children had come of age. As she had, at the time of the hearing, moved into alternative accommodation, she was awarded £2,000 damages for breach of contract.

The obvious difficulty with this analysis is that it is hard to see the normal constituents of a contract—offer, acceptance, and consideration—being present. In the

---

[6] See, e.g., *Frogley v. Earl of Lovelace* (1859) Johns. 333.

[7] *Street v. Mountford* [1985] A.C. 809 at 818 *per* Lord Templeman.

[8] [1975] 1 All E.R. 776. See also *Chandler v. Kerley* [1978] 1 W.L.R. 693, but cf. *Hardwick v. Johnson* [1978] 1 W.L.R. 683.

factually similar case of *Horrocks v. Foray*,[9] no contract was found to exist. Megaw L.J. stressed the need for the court to be able to find the normal consensus and considera- tion necessary in the general law of contract[10] and found that not to be the case, on the facts. *Tanner v. Tanner* was distinguished but it seemed clear that there was little judi- cial enthusiasm to try to apply a contractual analysis to informal, family relationships. Such cases are now argued on the basis of estoppel without attempting to construct a contract when, on normal principles, such a contract would not be found to exist.

Estoppel licences

Equitable estoppel is a doctrine of considerable antiquity and flexibility. In the con- text of Land Law, it is frequently, if a little misleadingly,[11] referred to as proprietary estoppel. Its principal role is to enable rights to be acquired in another person's land. The underlying ethos of the doctrine is that one person, A, acts in the expectation that he either already has rights in the land of another person, B, or that he will obtain such rights in the future. A will obtain rights in equity if he has relied upon that expectation in circumstances when it would be unconscionable for B to deny some effect to that expectation.[12] It is then a matter for the court, in the exercise of its discretion, to determine what remedy is most appropriate to give effect to the expec- tation which has been acted upon. The central issues of the circumstances when an equity will arise and the nature of the rights which have been acquired will be con- sidered shortly.

CONTRACTUAL LICENCES: THE LICENSEE'S RIGHTS

Having sketched the general nature of the different types of licence, one can now consider more closely the rights which the licensee obtains and the circumstances in which those rights may bind a successor in title to the licensor.

The revocability of licences

The question whether it is open to a licensor to revoke a contractual licence has met, at different periods of time, with rather different responses. The approach of the

---

[9] [1976] 1 All E.R. 737, described as '*Tanner v. Tanner* in a middle-class setting': M. Richards (1976) 40 Conv. (N.S.) 351 at 364.

[10] [1976] 1 All E.R. 737 at 742.

[11] By terming this form of estoppel proprietary, this assumes that it operates to create an interest in prop- erty, a point which is not uncontroversial, although, see now Land Registration Act 2002, s. 116, Estoppel and third parties, pp. 640–644.

[12] See *Taylors Fashions Ltd v. Liverpool Victoria Trustees Co. Ltd* [1982] Q.B. 133n at 154–155 *per* Oliver J.

common law was robust and straightforward. In *Wood v. Leadbitter*,[13] the plaintiff had bought a ticket to attend Doncaster races. On the instruction of the stewards, he was evicted, no more force than was necessary being used to achieve this result. He then brought an action for assault. The action failed. This was because it was held that, as the licence was not an interest in land, it was always open to a licensor to revoke a licence. The effect of such a revocation was that the licensee became a trespasser and it is then open to the licensor to use such force as is reasonable to evict the licensee from his land.

A rather different approach was taken in *Hurst v. Picture Theatres Ltd*.[14] The plaintiff had bought a ticket to watch a film and, because it was thought, wrongly, that he had not paid for admission, he was forcibly evicted, whereupon he brought an action for damages, the basis of his claim being assault. On this occasion, the majority of the Court of Appeal held in his favour. There were two reasons for this. The first was that the licence in question was a licence coupled with a grant, the grant in question being the right to watch the performance. This is manifestly wrong. As was pointed out in an Australian case, 'Fifty thousand people who pay to see a football match do not obtain fifty thousand interests in the football ground.'[15] No property right is created, the reason being that the transaction of buying a ticket for an entertainment does not create anything other than a contractual right in the buyer against the seller.[16] It is, however, the nature of that contractual right which is central to the question as to whether the licence can be revoked.

The intervention of equity

The second reason for the decision in *Hurst*, and this reason did have a lasting influence on the development of the law, was the intervention of equity. *Wood v. Leadbitter* was seen as a case decided entirely at common law. Since the passing of the Judicature Acts 1873 and 1875, the court should have regard to equity as well as law. The view was taken that equity would have granted an injunction to restrain the defendant from breaching his contract with the plaintiff. Because equity would have done this, it followed that the eviction in breach of contract was unlawful and, consequently, the use of force to evict the plaintiff was wrongful, with the result that damages were payable. The fact that an injunction had not actually been obtained was immaterial. Were the position otherwise, a person could improve his position by acting wrongfully and this is not correct.[17]

This reason for the decision proved to be influential. In *Millennium Productions Ltd v. Winter Garden Theatre (London) Ltd*,[18] the owners of a theatre purported to revoke a licence given to the plaintiffs to use it. The Court of Appeal granted an injunction

---

[13] (1835) 13 M. & W. 838.

[14] [1915] 1 K.B. 1. For strong contemporary criticism, see J.C. Miles (1915) 31 L.Q.R. 217.

[15] *Cowell v. Rosehill Racecourse Co. Ltd* (1937) 56 C.L.R. 605 at 616 *per* Latham C.J.

[16] Ibid., at 617.   [17] Ibid., at 651 *per* Evatt J. (dissenting).   [18] [1946] 1 All E.R. 678 at 685.

restraining this action. Lord Greene M.R. held that there was an implied term of the contract that it would not be revoked and, to restrain a breach of contract, granted an injunction. The House of Lords[19] reversed this decision on the basis that, on the proper construction of the contract, no such term precluding revocation of the licence should be implied. If, however, the proper construction of the contract had been that it was not to be revoked, then it was considered that injunctive relief would have been appropriate. The House of Lords considered that the propositions of law stated by Lord Greene were clearly correct and, indeed, unanswerable;[20] the decision of the Court of Appeal was reversed simply because the House of Lords disagreed with how those propositions had been applied to the facts of the case.

Construction of the contract

The House of Lords accepted, *obiter*, the proposition that, depending upon the proper construction of the contract, a contractual licence may be irrevocable. Unfortunately, an earlier Court of Appeal decision to the contrary, although cited in argument, was not referred to in the speeches. In *Thompson v. Park*,[21] a schoolmaster had entered into a contract, whereby he was permitted to share a school building with the plaintiff, who was the licensor. After a disagreement, the defendant was evicted and he responded by effecting a forcible re-entry, the manner of that entry, according to Goddard L.J., having the effect that he would have been 'guilty at least of riot, affray, wilful damage, forcible entry, and, perhaps, conspiracy'.[22] The plaintiff was then granted an injunction requiring the defendant to vacate the property.

In holding for the plaintiff, two reasons were given. One was that, given the egregious conduct of the defendant, and the impossibility of making an order which would require two people, who were clearly at loggerheads with each other, to share the same premises, it would be wrong to grant the defendant equitable relief. This reasoning is uncontroversial and, as an exercise of the judicial discretion inherent in the award of any equitable remedy, manifestly correct. What was more controversial was the reiteration of the rule laid down in *Wood v. Leadbitter*, that it is always open to a licensor to revoke a contractual licence, even in circumstances where such a revocation would amount to a breach of contract.

One of the grounds of the decision in *Thompson v. Park* is inconsistent with later *dicta* in the House of Lords in the *Winter Gardens* case and this inconsistency occasioned Megarry J. some discomfort in *Hounslow London Borough Council v. Twickenham Garden Developments Ltd*,[23] where the issue of the revocability of a contractual licence arose again. After an extensive review of the authorities, he decided to follow the *dicta* in *Winter Gardens* and held that the decision as to whether or not a contractual licence can be revoked depends upon the construction of the contract and, as a matter of construction, some such licences are irrevocable.

---

[19] [1948] A.C. 173.   [20] Ibid., at 202 *per* Lord Uthwatt.   [21] [1944] K.B. 408.
[22] Ibid., at 409.   [23] [1971] Ch. 233.

Irrevocable licences

This analysis was followed by the Court of Appeal in *Verrall v. Great Yarmouth Borough Council.*[24] The council, when under the control of the Conservative Party, entered into a contract to allow the National Front to hold its annual conference in the town's conference hall, the period of the hire being two days. After the election, control of the council passed to the Labour Party, who refused to allow the National Front to hold its conference there. It was conceded that this would amount to a breach of contract but the council argued that the plaintiff should be left to a remedy in damages, that it was always possible for a licensor, albeit wrongly, to revoke a licence. Specific performance was ordered because damages would not have been an adequate remedy.

The argument was put, based upon *Thompson v. Park*, that a licensor could always effectively, even if unlawfully, revoke a contract. It was held that that decision could not stand with the *dicta* of the House of Lords in *Winter Gardens* and could no longer be regarded as good law. Certain contractual licences cannot be revoked and, in appropriate cases, may be enforced by a decree of specific performance. Such an order will not, of course, be appropriate in all cases; damages must be an inadequate remedy. In the present case, the National Front would not, had the council been allowed to revoke the licence, have been able to hold their conference anywhere and, consequently, damages would not have provided them with adequate compensation. Whether or not a contractual licence can be revoked will therefore depend upon the proper construction of the contract. Some such licences may be irrevocable;[25] others revocable only upon the giving of a substantial period of notice.[26]

Enforcing the contract

Although none of these authorities were referred to in the Supreme Court decision in *Berrisford v. Mexfield Housing Co-operative Ltd,*[27] the conclusion reached in that case is entirely consistent with the view taken in *Verrall*. In *Berrisford*, the occupier had been granted a periodic occupancy agreement. Under the terms of that agreement, the freeholder could only terminate the agreement on certain, limited, grounds. Although the Supreme Court held that a valid lease had been created,[28] consideration was also given as to what the position would have been had that not been the case. According to Lord Clarke,

'It follows that... even if the contract does not create a tenancy, it creates rights and obligations between the parties, so that in an appropriate case Ms Berrisford could in principle gain an injunction against Mexfield for a threatened breach of contract.'[29]

The position would appear to be settled.

---

[24] [1981] Q.B. 202.

[25] See *Hardwick v. Johnson* [1978] 1 W.L.R. 683 (perhaps an extreme construction).

[26] *Chandler v. Kerley* [1978] 1 W.L.R. 693 (twelve months).   [27] [2011] UKSC 52.

[28] See Leases for life, pp. 401–403.   [29] [2011] UKSC 52 at [110] See also at [60] *per* Lord Neuberger.

CONTRACTUAL LICENCES AND THIRD PARTIES

One of the reasons for the view that a contractual licence was always revocable, even if to revoke it would amount to a breach of contract, was the traditional position that such a licence could create only personal rights and was not a proprietary right. While it is not necessary, when deciding whether, as between the parties to the licence, to determine whether or not the licence had any effect on a purchaser of the land, this, as has been seen, did have a significant impact. Conversely, once it came to be decided that, as between the original licensor and licensee, the licence could not be revoked, the view was propounded that, if the original licensor could not revoke the licence, then neither could a person claiming through him. The effect of this reasoning would be to elevate an irrevocable contractual licence to the status of being an interest in land. As will be seen, this line of authority has now been discredited, but problems still remain in deciding the effect, if any, that a contractual licence may have against purchasers of land.

Denial of proprietary status

The issue of whether a purchaser of land was bound by a contractual licence was considered by the House of Lords in *King v. David Allen & Sons, Billposting Ltd.*[30] King contracted to allow David Allen the right to affix posters on the wall of his cinema for a period of four years. King then leased the cinema to a third party, who refused to allow David Allen to display his posters on the cinema wall, whereupon he sued King for breach of contract. In holding King to be liable, an essential part of the reasoning was that the tenant was not bound by the contractual licence which had created rights personal to the parties to the contract. If the tenant had been bound by the licence, then David Allen would have been able to continue to fix his posters on the wall and King would not have been in breach of contract. This decision[31] then, provided a formidable obstacle to the development of the idea that a contractual licence could be regarded as an interest in land.

A new interest in land?

Notwithstanding the decision in *King v. David Allen*, a theory began to take root that an irrevocable contractual licence was an interest in land which was therefore capable of binding third parties. This development started in the controversial decision in *Errington v. Errington and Woods.*[32] A father bought a house and gave permission to

[30] [1916] 2 A.C. 54.
[31] See also *Clore v. Theatrical Properties Ltd* [1936] 3 All E.R. 483, which reached the same conclusion with regard to a licence giving front of theatre rights.
[32] [1952] 1 K.B. 90. Cf. *Ramnarace v. Lutchman* [2001] 1 W.L.R. 1651, where there was no payment to the freeholder.

his son and daughter-in-law to live in it, provided that they paid the mortgage instalments. When the mortgage had been paid in full, he promised to convey the house to them. The father then died and his widow sought to evict her daughter-in-law from the property, her son having left the home to return to live with his mother.

In considering the status of the couple, it was decided that, although they had exclusive possession, they were not tenants. This conclusion seems correct as, under the terms of their agreement, they were free to leave at any time and were not bound to continue to make any payments to the father whereas, provided that they did make the payments, he, it was held, could not evict them from the property. Such an arrangement is neither a fixed term tenancy, a periodic tenancy nor a tenancy at will and is, therefore, one of the rare situations where exclusive possession is granted to residential occupiers but no lease is created. The couple were therefore licensees and were regarded as being contractual licensees.[33]

Intervention of equity

Denning L.J. then reviewed the authorities dealing with the question as to whether contractual licences could be revoked and concluded that, because of the intervention of equity, certain licences were irrevocable and that, in this case, if the couple continued to pay the mortgage instalments, their licence could not be revoked. He then went on to say:

'This infusion of equity means that contractual licences now have a force and validity of their own and cannot be revoked in breach of contract. *Neither the licensor nor anyone who claims through him can disregard the contract except a purchaser for value without notice.*'[34]

In the italicized part of this passage, Denning L.J. makes the considerable leap from holding that, because, as between the licensor and the licensee, the terms of the contract mean that the licence is irrevocable, this means that its status has changed and such licences should now be regarded as equitable interests in land. Not surprisingly, this was controversial.[35] The creation of new interests in land appears to be precluded by statute,[36] and it is also not easy to see how this *dictum* can be reconciled with the decision in *King v. David Allen*.[37] Again, the point can be made that certain relationships are classified as licences precisely because they do not qualify as other recognized interests in land, such as leases and easements. To admit contractual licences to the category of interests in land undermines the law's efforts to restrict the ability of

---

[33] For a different analysis, see A.D. Hargreaves (1953) 69 L.Q.R. 466 and The return to orthodoxy, pp. 605–609.

[34] [1952] 1 K.B. 290 at 299. Emphasis supplied.

[35] For criticism, see H.W.R. Wade (1952) 68 L.Q.R. 337. For more sympathetic reactions, see G.C. Cheshire (1953) 16 M.L.R. 1; L.A. Sheridan (1953) 17 Conv. (N.S.) 440 at 446–449.

[36] Law of Property Act 1925, s. 4(1).

[37] See the comments made in *National Provincial Bank Ltd v. Ainsworth* [1965] A.C. 1175 at 1239–1240 *per* Lord Upjohn; at 1251 *per* Lord Wilberforce. For a more overtly hostile approach, see *National Provincial Bank Ltd v. Hastings Car Mart Ltd* [1964] Ch. 665 at 697–698 *per* Russell L.J.

individuals to create new interests in land.[38] If parties were free to create such interests, then land could become encumbered with an ever-increasing variety of rights, the effect of which would be to make the process of transferring land more precarious than is currently the case.

Life interest

Despite these objections, the attempt to elevate the contractual licence to the status of a proprietary right continued. *Binions v. Evans*[39] was a case where the merits lay entirely on one side but where it was difficult to find a convincing reason to reach the conclusion that those merits dictated so that, in the end, 'the law is as it ought to be'.[40] Mr Evans had been, like his father and grandfather before him, a longstanding employee of Tredegar Estates and lived with his wife in a cottage owned by the Estate. On his death, the Estate entered into an agreement with his widow, who at that time was seventy-three, that she could remain living in the cottage for the rest of her life, rent free, provided that she kept it and the garden in good order. Tredegar Estate then sold the cottage to Mr and Mrs Binions, expressly subject to the right of Mrs Evans' right of occupation and the price which was paid reflected this agreement. Shortly afterwards, Mr and Mrs Binions brought an action for possession, arguing that she occupied the cottage as a tenant at will. Unsurprisingly, but for different reasons, the Court of Appeal held in favour of Mrs Evans.

Megaw and Stephenson L.JJ. held that the agreement between the Estate and Mrs Evans created a life interest,[41] the effect of which was to constitute her as a tenant for life under the Settled Land Act 1925.[42] As the purchasers had notice of this, they took subject to her interest. Lord Denning M.R., mindful that the consequence of this reasoning would be to vest in Mrs Evans all the statutory powers conferred upon the tenant for life, including the power of sale, dissented from this. Instead, he regarded her as occupying the cottage under an irrevocable contractual licence. Although on this occasion he referred to *King v. David Allen*, he reiterated the view that he had expressed in *Errington* to the effect that a licence of this type will take effect as an equitable interest in land.[43] Alternatively, in his view, because under the contract, Mr and Mrs Binions had expressly agreed to give effect to Mrs Evans' interest, for them to renege on this would be inequitable and, to prevent this, a constructive trust would be imposed under which her licence would be protected.[44]

---

[38] See the comments in *Keppell v. Bailey* (1833) 2 My & K. 517 at 533 *per* Lord Brougham L.C.

[39] [1972] Ch. 359.   [40] Ibid., at 373 *per* Stephenson L.J. See R.J. Smith [1973] C.L.J. 123.

[41] Had a nominal rent been charged, the subsequent difficulties would have been avoided as the transaction would have taken effect as a determinable ninety-year tenancy: Law of Property Act 1925, s. 149(6). Cf. *Skipton Building Society v. Clayton* (1993) 66 P. & C.R. 223.

[42] See Accidental settlements, pp. 285–287.   [43] [1972] Ch. 359 at 369.

[44] This view continues to have some judicial support. See Constructive trusts p. 210.

The retreat from Errington

Lord Denning's views on the proprietary effect of contractual licences, while remaining controversial, had an impact, being applied, with evident reluctance, in other cases.[45] In *Re Sharpe*,[46] an elderly lady had what was held to be a contractual licence[47] to occupy a house owned by her bankrupt nephew. The trustee in bankruptcy had contracted to sell the house and, in order to obtain vacant possession, sought possession. His action failed. While taking pains not to decide what the position would have been had the contract been completed and the action been brought by the purchaser, for whose plight Browne-Wilkinson J. expressed considerable sympathy,[48] the judge felt constrained by authority to hold that the licence conferred some sort of equity or equitable interest under a constructive trust. His lack of enthusiasm was evident, as he commented that:

'I do not think that the principles lying behind these decisions have been fully explored and on occasion it seems such rights are found to exist simply on the ground that to hold otherwise would be a hardship to the plaintiff.'[49]

He concluded by expressing:

'the hope that in the near future the whole question can receive full consideration in the Court of Appeal, so that, in order to do justice to the many thousands who never come to court at all but who wish to know with certainty what their proprietary rights are, the extent to which these irrevocable licences bind third parties.'[50]

The return to orthodoxy

Within ten years, this plea was answered. In *Ashburn Anstalt v. Arnold*,[51] the question was whether an occupancy agreement took effect as an overriding interest and was, therefore, binding upon a purchaser. Fox L.J., giving the judgment of the court, wrongly[52] held the agreement to be a lease, and therefore binding. Mindful that this conclusion could be wrong, however, a full review of the proprietary status of contractual licences was undertaken. As a result of this review, it was concluded that, although the actual decisions in *Errington v. Errington* and *Binions v. Evans* were

---

[45] Although see *D.H.N. Food Distributors Ltd v. Tower Hamlets London Borough Council* [1976] 1 W.L.R. 852. A contractual licence was assumed to be an interest in land in *Midland Bank Ltd v. Farmpride Hatcheries Ltd* [1981] E.G.L.R. 147, criticized on this point by R.E. Annand [1982] Conv. 67.

[46] [1980] 1 W.L.R. 219.

[47] For the persuasive view that this was really a case on estoppel, see J. Martin [1980] Conv. 207 at 213–214.

[48] [1980] 1 W.L.R. 219 at 226. In reliance on the contract he had sold his own house and, at the time of the action, was living in a small motorized caravan on, or near, Hampstead Heath: ibid., at 224.

[49] Ibid., at 223.   [50] Ibid., at 226.

[51] [1989] Ch. 1. See A.J. Oakley [1988] C.L.J. 353; P. Sparkes (1988) 104 L.Q.R. 175; J. Hill (1988) 51 M.L.R. 226; M.P. Thompson [1988] Conv. 201.

[52] The decision on this point was overruled in *Prudential Assurance Co. Ltd v. London Residuary Body* [1992] A.C. 386. That the case was overruled on this point does not affect the authority of the *dicta* on the proprietary effect of contractual licences.

correct, the statement in *Errington* that contractual licences were binding upon all but a purchaser without notice was *per incuriam* (that is, decided without reference to binding authority to the contrary) and wrong. It is now quite clear that the view that contractual licences are to be regarded as interests in land is heretical[53] and that *dicta* asserting that they are will no longer be followed, it now seeming to be axiomatic that a contractual licence, while quite capable of binding the parties to it, 'is not capable of binding their respective successors, as no interest in land or proprietary interest would subsist.'[54] What remains is to explain the results, if not the reasoning, in *Errington v. Errington* and *Binions v. Evans*.

The decision in *Errington* was regarded as being clearly correct. Two of the reasons are connected. First, the agreement was seen as being an estate contract: a unilateral contract by which the couple would have been entitled, on the payment of the entire purchase money, to have had the legal estate conveyed to them. Although this had not been registered, this would not have been void against the mother as she was not a purchaser for value. While plausible, the problem is that, if for some reason they chose not to complete the payments, they would not have had the right to the conveyance. The second reason is that, by paying each instalment, which went towards the purchase of the property, they acquired a corresponding beneficial interest in it under a resulting trust. This seems correct. Finally, the view was expressed that the true explanation as to why the offer could not have been revoked once the couple had embarked upon acceptance of it was estoppel.[55]

Estoppel

This final reason relates to the reason why an offeror, in cases of unilateral contracts, is not allowed to revoke an offer once the offeree has begun acceptance.[56] The difficulty is that, in such cases, no contract is created until the acceptance of the offer is complete; the offeree is free to abandon the acceptance if he chooses to do so and it is not obvious why the offeror cannot revoke the offer once acceptance has begun. One theory is that there is a collateral contract that the offer will not be revoked once the offeree has begun to accept it and the consideration for this is that of partial acceptance.[57] An alternative view is that the preferable explanation is that the offeror was estopped from revoking the offer.[58] The basis of this argument is that the offeree, with the encouragement of the offeror, has relied on his expectation that the offer will not be revoked, with the result that the estoppel arises. In *Ashburn Anstalt*, Fox L.J. did not consider

---

[53] See *I.D.C. Group Ltd v. Clark* [1992] 1 E.G.L.R. 187 at 189 *per* Browne-Wilkinson J., affirmed [1992] 2 E.G.L.R. 184. See also *Canadian Imperial Bank of Commerce v. Bello* (1991) 64 P. & C.R. 48 at 52 *per* Dillon L.J.

[54] *Berrisford v. Mexfield Housing Co-operative Ltd* [2011] UKSC 52 at [60] *per* Lord Neuberger.

[55] [1989] Ch. 1 at 17.

[56] See the discussion of this issue in Law Reform Committee's 6th Interim Report (1937), para. 39.

[57] See Peel, Treitel's *The Law of Contract* (12th edn) (London: Sweet & Maxwell, 2007), 41, who accepts that this analysis is artificial. See also *Daulia v. Four Millbank Nominees* [1978] Ch. 231 at 239 *per* Goff L.J.; A. Briggs [1983] Conv. 285 at 287.

[58] See R.H. Maudsley [1956] Conv. 281 at 287–288; M.P. Thompson [1983] Conv. 50.

either argument in detail but simply offered the suggestion that the true explanation of *Errington* was that it was an estoppel licence which, he appeared to assume, was binding upon the third party. While it is suggested that it is correct that *Errington* is best seen as an estoppel case, the further assumption, that it necessarily binds a third party is not uncontroversial.[59] Although section 116 of the Land Registration Act 2002 declares that, for the avoidance of doubt, an equity by estoppel is capable of binding successors in title, the position of purchasers requires some scrutiny. Certainly, in *Errington* itself, the plaintiff should have been held to have been bound by the rights of the licensee. As she was not a purchaser for value, she should not be in any better position than her husband, who could not have revoked the licence. The general effect of estoppel licences on third parties will be considered in more detail below.

Constructive trusts

In *Ashburn Anstalt*, attention was given to the role of the constructive trust in this context. Reference was made to *Binions v. Evans* where, as one of the grounds for his decision, Lord Denning M.R. held that Mr and Mrs Binions held the property on a constructive trust, this trust being imposed to give effect to their contractual obligation that they would take the property subject to the rights of Mrs Evans. Fox L.J. accepted that this was justified but was clearly anxious that such a trust should not be imposed too lightly, because the effect of so doing would be to upset titles to land. He accepted that a constructive trust should be imposed when a purchaser expressly undertakes to give effect to a particular interest.[60] A constructive trust should not be imposed, however, merely because a purchaser agrees to take subject to a particular interest.[61]

The restricting of the circumstances when a constructive trust will be imposed is welcome but, even in the limited situations where it is considered to be right to impose such a trust, there are problems with this solution.[62] When a trust is created, the normal situation involves the separation of the legal and equitable estate. Yet, in a situation such as *Binions v. Evans*, it is not easy to see what estate is actually held by Mrs Evans, unless it is a life estate, which would bring the case back within the confines of the Settled Land Act 1925. This difficulty would be more acute if the licence in question was an irrevocable right to cross another person's land rather than to occupy it. In such a situation, it is difficult to see how, on orthodox principles, a constructive trust could be imposed to give effect to a right of way.

A second difficulty with the constructive trust approach is that, although the trust will only be imposed when a purchaser has expressly agreed to give effect to a particular right, the enforceability of that trust against a subsequent owner of the land will not

---

[59] See *Habermann v. Koehler* (1996) 73 P. & C.R. 515 at 523 *per* Peter Gibson L.J.

[60] Applying *Lyus v. Prowsa Developments Ltd* [1982] 1 W.L.R. 1044. See also *Lloyd v. Dugdale* [2002] 2 P. & C.R. 13, at [52], [55] *per* Sir Christopher Slade. See M. Dixon [2002] Conv. 584.

[61] [1989] Ch. 1 at 25–26. See also *Chattey v. Farndale Hodings Ltd* (1996) 75 P. & C.R. 298 at 317 *per* Morritt L.J.

[62] See M.P. Thompson [1988] Conv. 201 at 205–206.

rest upon that purchaser agreeing to give effect to the interest in question. Because a constructive trust has been imposed, then, in principle, it would appear to be enforceable against a subsequent purchaser on the same basis as any other equitable interest in land. It is not clear that the courts would be prepared to hold that this is the case.

Privity of contract

Another objection to the use of the constructive trust in cases such as *Binions v. Evans* is that it appears to run contrary to the doctrine of privity of contract. The essential reasoning appears to be that, if A and B enter a contract under which B agrees to give effect to rights in favour of C, then C, owing to a contract to which he was not a party, will acquire enforceable rights against B through the medium of a constructive trust. As such, the use of the constructive trust appears to run contrary to the common law principle of privity of contract.[63]

This objection has become academic, however, in respect of contracts entered into after the coming into force of the Contracts (Rights of Third Parties) Act 1999. Section 1(1) of the Act provides that:

'a person who is not a party to a contract...may in his own right enforce a term of the contract if—

(a) the contract expressly provides that he may, or

(b) ...the term purports to convert a benefit on him.'

This provision now seems to provide a ready solution to cases such as *Binions v. Evans* and is likely to mean that cases of this type will be decided by reference to it and the constructive trust will not be used. This is to be welcomed, as the trust was being used in an unorthodox way, largely to provide a remedy in hard cases, without paying too close a regard to normal trust principles.

The economic torts

A final matter which must be considered when discussing the potential effect of a contractual licence is the role, if any, of the economic torts.[64] The use of tort was suggested as a possible solution to the problem in *Binions v. Evans*, itself.[65] Under the tortious doctrine of interference with contractual relations, if there is a contract between A and B, and C, with knowledge of that contract, induces A to break that contract, C commits a tort. To prevent this, an injunction may be granted. In *Binions v. Evans*, if Mr and Mrs Binions had succeeded in evicting Mrs Evans from the property, the result would have been to cause Tredegar Estates to be in breach of their contract with her. As the couple had, prior to their purchase of the property, actual knowledge of her contractual right to stay in the cottage, there seems to be no reason in principle why

---

[63] For a more sympathetic approach to this argument which, however, understates the privity problem, see B. McFarlane (2004) 120 L.Q.R. 667.

[64] For an excellent discussion of the potential impact of the economic torts on Land Law, see R.J. Smith (1977) 41 Conv. (N.S.) 318.

[65] [1972] Ch. 359 at 371 *per* Megaw L.J.

an injunction would not lie against them to restrain them from action which would necessitate Tredegar Estates committing a breach of contract. Such a solution would have the merit of avoiding the imposition of an ill-defined constructive trust, while producing a result which the merits of the case would seem to demand.

As yet, there has been little judicial discussion of the role of the economic torts in this context and it is possible, especially since the coming into force of the 1999 Act, that the courts will be unwilling to use this method of enforcing contractual licences against third parties, particularly as the effect of utilizing the economic torts in this way could have very wide-ranging consequences.[66] To allow tort to play a role in this way would enable rights which have not been admitted to the rank of property interests to be enforced indirectly, on the basis that a purchaser had prior knowledge of certain contractual rights affecting the property prior to purchasing it and such a result may be seen to be subversive of Property Law principles.

Conclusions

The development of the law relating to contractual licences represented an interesting, albeit unsuccessful, attempt to fashion a new interest in land. The attempt to do this could be seen to be motivated by two considerations; a desire to achieve what was perceived to be fair results in individual cases and a wish to give effect to informal transactions when, with proper legal advice, the parties involved could have ordered their affairs in such a way so as to avoid any subsequent problems.[67] On the other hand, the competing interest was the weight given to certainty and security in conveyancing transactions; a factor which clearly influenced Browne-Wilkinson J. in *Re Sharpe*. Ultimately, this latter consideration, together with the weight of authority, prevailed. That said, however, the failure of the attempt started in *Errington* to create a new interest in land, the contractual licence, does not mean that other informal transactions may not give rise to rights against third parties. Many of the cases involving licences arise in informal situations where it may be difficult to construe the relationship as being contractual in nature. It is in these types of situations where the flexible doctrine of equitable estoppel has an important role to play.

EQUITABLE ESTOPPEL

Equitable estoppel is a doctrine of considerable antiquity[68] which, while the subject of considerable judicial development in the nineteenth century,[69] lurked in a degree of obscurity until interest in the subject was revived comparatively recently, as witnessed

---

[66] See Smith, *Property Law* (7th edn) (London: Longmans, 2011), 484–485.

[67] For example, in *Binions v. Evans*, subsequent problems would have been avoided had Mrs Evans been granted a non-assignable ninety-nine-year lease at a low rent, determinable on death.

[68] For early examples, see *Hunt v. Carew* (1649) Nels. 47; *Hobbs v. Norton* (1682) Vern. 137; *Huning v. Ferers* (1711) Gilb. Rep. 85.

[69] See D.C. Jackson (1965) 81 L.Q.R. 84, 223.

by the production of a number of monographs devoted to it.[70] Equitable estoppel is seen as having two main forms. In the law of contract, it is seen principally as having a defensive function, operating to modify the doctrine of consideration to prevent one party to a contract from enforcing, fully, his contractual rights against the other.[71] In the law of contract, this doctrine, termed promissory estoppel, is seen traditionally as being defensive in nature, it being seen as a shield and not a sword. Although this traditional view has been challenged,[72] this is not an issue of major importance in Land Law, in which context, it has long been accepted that equitable estoppel can operate, directly, to found a cause of action. When operating in this way, the doctrine is frequently referred to as proprietary estoppel.

This nomenclature is, perhaps, unfortunate. First, it tends to obscure the similarities which exist between promissory and proprietary estoppel;[73] a matter of some theoretical significance, but beyond the scope of this book.[74] The second reason is that the word 'proprietary' carries the assumption that rights which arise through the medium of estoppel are equitable interests in land in much the same way as, for example, a restrictive covenant. This latter issue is, however, contentious and will be addressed below. With these caveats in mind, proprietary estoppel is a widely used expression and will be used to describe the form of estoppel whereby a cause of action can be acquired with respect to another person's land.

The origins of the doctrine

Although cases of proprietary estoppel can be traced back to the seventeenth century,[75] the doctrine did not really begin to take shape until somewhat later. In *Plimmer v. The Mayor of Wellington*,[76] the plaintiff's predecessor in title had built a jetty on his land. Later, at the request of the Government, and at considerable expense, he extended it onto Government land. The land in question then passed to the defendant and the issue was whether the plaintiff had an interest in land sufficient to qualify him for compensation under the relevant statute. The Privy Council held that he did.

In upholding his claim to compensation, it was held that the Government had encouraged him to spend money on extending the jetty in circumstances when it was clear that he had an expectation of obtaining some interest in the land. Because of

---

[70] See Pawlowski, *The Doctrine of Proprietary Estoppel* (London: Sweet & Maxwell, 1996); Spence, *Protecting Reliance: The Emergent Doctrine of Equitable Estoppel* (Oxford: Hart Publishing, 1999); Cooke, *The Modern Law of Estoppel* (Oxford: Oxford University Press, 2000).

[71] *Central London Property Trust Ltd v. High Trees House Ltd* [1947] K.B. 130. The main authorities relied upon were *Hughes v. Metropolitan Railway Co.* (1877) 2 App. Cas. 349 and *Birmingham and District Land Co. v. London and North Western Railway Co.* (1889) 40 Ch.D. 268.

[72] See Jackson, loc. cit., M.P. Thompson [1983] C.L.J. 257.

[73] 'I do not find helpful the distinction between promissory and proprietary estoppel': *Crabb v. Arun District Council* [1976] Ch. 179 at 193 *per* Scarman L.J.

[74] For contributions to this debate which are supportive of a more unified approach, see M.P. Thompson [1983] C.L.J. 257; M. Halliwell (1994) 14 L.S. 15; M. Lunney [1992] Conv. 239. For a different, highly conservative view, see P.T. Evans [1988] Conv. 346.

[75] See *Hobbs v. Nelson* (1649) Nels. 47.   [76] (1894) 9 App. Cas. 699.

this encouragement, and his action in reliance on that expectation, it would be quite inequitable for him to be denied some relief. In satisfying the equity which had arisen, it was held that he was entitled to an indefinite licence to occupy the land on which he had extended the jetty and that this licence was, for the purposes of the statute in question, a sufficient interest in the land to entitle him to compensation when that land had been compulsorily acquired.

A number of important features emerge from this case. First, the actual expenditure was undertaken by the plaintiff's predecessor in title. The benefit of the equity which had arisen then passed with the land to the plaintiff. Secondly, this was a case where there had been active encouragement by one person to another to do work on the implicit understanding that he would, thereby, acquire an interest in the land. In such cases, it is often easier to establish that an equity has arisen than in cases, to be considered shortly, where one person is mistaken as to what the true position is and acts on the faith of that belief. A third important point is that, in the case itself, it was clear that the plaintiff had an expectation of acquiring an interest in the adjoining land but that the full extent of that interest had not been articulated. This was not a problem, because:

'there is good authority for saying what appears to their Lordships to be quite sound in principle, that the equity arising from expenditure on land need not fail merely on the ground that the interest to be secured has not been expressly indicated'.[77]

In other words, unlike the position in the law of contract, a claim in estoppel will not fail on the ground of uncertainty;[78] it is sufficient if the claimant can establish that he has some expectation in respect of another person's land. It is not essential that the metes and bounds of that expectation are precisely articulated. This is important, in that estoppel cases frequently arise in informal situations when it is not entirely clear what the intentions of each party are.

A stringent test of certainty

This position, which appeared to be firmly established,[79] was undermined, however, by what was said by Lord Scott of Foscote in *Yeoman's Row Management Ltd v. Cobbe*.[80] This was a commercial case where the claimant had agreed with the defendant that he would, at his own expense, apply for planning permission for the demolition of an existing property owned by the defendant and the construction of terraced houses in its place. Once planning permission had been obtained, it was agreed between the parties that they would enter into a second agreement, whereby

---

[77] (1894) 9 App. Cas. 699 at 713 *per* Sir Arthur Hobhouse.

[78] See also *Ramsden v. Dyson* (1866) L.R. 1 H.L. 129 at 170 *per* Lord Kingsdown (dissenting on the application of the law to the facts).

[79] See, e.g., *Turner v. Jacob* [2007] EWHC 317 (Ch.) at [81] *per* Patten J.; *James v. Thomas* [2007] EWCA Civ. 1212 at [18] *per* Sir John Chadwick.

[80] [2008] EWHL 1139. See also, on similar facts, *Capron v. Government of Turks and Caicos Islands* [2010] UKPC 2.

he would purchase the site for £12 million, and would be entitled to fifty per cent of the gross proceeds of sale of the new houses if the sales of them realized more than £24 million. A number of terms of this second agreement were, however, left outstanding. After he had done a considerable amount of work to secure planning permission, the defendant refused to enter this second agreement. Reversing the decisions below, the House of Lords held that he had no rights through estoppel, but was only entitled to a sum to compensate him for the value of his work, the basis of this being *quantum meruit*.

That the claim to an interest in the property failed is not really surprising. This was because the parties were experienced practitioners in property transactions, and were aware that the original agreement was binding in honour only. The claimant was, therefore, taking the risk that there might not ever be a concluded contract between them.[81] Nevertheless, Lord Scott decided that no right had arisen through estoppel on wider grounds.

Having noted that the second agreement was insufficiently certain to amount to a contract because not all the terms had been agreed, he considered that this was also a fatal objection to a claim based on estoppel. He referred to a passage in *Ramsden v. Dyson*,[82] where Lord Kingsdown referred to an agreement that a person should have a certain interest in land, and took this to mean that there must be certainty as to what that interest was to be.[83] With respect, this seems quite contrary to principle, and flies in the face of the passage just cited from *Plimmer v. The Mayor of Wellington*. As is the case with the word 'quite', 'certain' is a word which admits of more than one meaning, and that meaning is dependent upon the context in which it is used. The word 'quite' can be comparative or emphatic. An example of the former is to describe an argument as being 'quite persuasive'; an instance of the latter is to describe an argument as being 'quite compelling'. In the latter instance the word 'quite' is synonymous with the word 'utterly'. So, too, in the case of the word 'certain'. If one says that a person should be given a certain latitude, one is not seeking to define, in advance, what degree of latitude is being given; whereas, if one refers to a 'term certain' one is saying that the length of the term must be precise. It seems clear that in *Plimmer*, the word 'certain' is being used in the former sense of the word.

Emasculation of estoppel

The narrow meaning of the expectation expressed by Lord Scott is also quite inconsistent with the leading case of *Jennings v. Rice*,[84] to which he did not refer. In that case Robert Walker L.J., in discussing what remedy was appropriate,[85] distinguished

---

[81] See also Lord Neuberger [2009] C.L.J. 537 at 540–542.

[82] (1866) L.R.1 H.L. 129 at 170. He treated a passage in *Taylors Fashions Ltd v. Liverpool Victoria Trustees Co. Ltd* [1982] Q.B. 133n at 144 *per* Oliver J. in the same way.

[83] [2008] UKHL 55 at [19]–[22]. For similar remarks in the context of promissory estoppel, see *Woodhouse A.C. Israel Ltd SA v. Nigerian Produce Marketing Co. Ltd* [1972] A.C. 741 at 757 *per* Lord Hailsham L.C.; and at 762 *per* Lord Pearson, explained by M.P. Thompson [1983] C.L.J. 257 at 263–264.

[84] [2003] 1 P. & C.R. 8.   [85] See Satisfaction of the expectation pp. 631–638.

between two types of case. The first is where the arrangement between the parties is of a 'consensual nature falling not short of an unenforceable contract'.[86] The second is where 'the claimant's expectations may not be focused on any specific property',[87] let alone any specific interest in it, because 'the claimant's expectations are uncertain (as will be the case with many honest claimants)...'[88] More importantly, if followed, his reasoning would limit the application of the doctrine of eqitable estoppel so severely as, effectively, to emasculate it.[89] Writng extra-judicially, Etherton L.J., who had heard this case at first instance, commented that if Lord Scott's approach was applied in its entirety, it would be difficult to see any scope left for the doctrine. This is because either there is a contract which is complete in all its terms and complies with the formalities prescribed by section 2 of the Law of Property (Miscellaneous Provisions) Act 1989, in which case there is a legally binding contract and no need to rely on any estoppel, or there is not, in which case there is neither an enforceable contract nor scope for proprietary estoppel.[90]

The return to principle

The better view was that Lord Scott's remarks should be read in the context of the particular facts of the case, where a claimant was arguing that he had rights under an agreement which had yet to be fully negotiated and was, itself, 'subject to contract'. That they should not be applied, generally, to defeat a claim in estoppel where the claimant's expectation was imprecise[91] was re-established by the House of Lords in *Thorner v. Major*.[92] The case involved two cousins, David and Peter Thorner. David began to work on Peter's farm in 1976, and continued to do so for the next 29 years. David hoped to inherit the farm, and this hope became a firm expectation when, in 1990, Peter handed him a bonus notice on two life assurance policies and told him that these were for death duties. David continued to do a considerable amount of unpaid work at Peter's farm, and did not pursue a number of opportunities which were open to him. Peter did in fact make a will in David's favour, but subsequently revoked it, and died intestate in 2005. David then brought an action against Peter's personal representatives. Reversing the Court of Appeal, and restoring the judgment at first instance, the House of Lords held David to be entitled to a transfer of the land, together with other assets of the farming business.

The problems in raising an estoppel argument related, first, to the fact that both men were taciturn individuals, and it was not easy to identify quite what it was that had been promised, and, secondly, to the fact that the identity of the farm had changed over the years. This was because between 1990, when the conversation

---

[86] [2003] 1 P. & C.R. 8 at [45].

[87] Ibid., at [46]. See also *Powell v. Benney* [2007] EWCA Civ. 1283 at [25] *per* Sir Peter Gibson.

[88] Ibid., at [47].   [89] See B. McFarlane and A. Robertson [2008] LMCLQ. 449.

[90] T. Etherton [2009] Conv. 104 at 120. See also Lord Neuberger [2009] C.L.J. 537 at 546.

[91] See *Sutcliffe v. Lloyd* [2008] EWHC 1329 (Ch.) (expectation of a share in profits); *Hopper v. Hopper* [2008] EWHC 228 (Ch.) (some beneficial interest in a farm).

[92] [2009] UKHL 18. For a somewhat muted reaction, see M. Dixon [2009] Conv. 260.

about death duties had occurred, and 2005, when Peter died, some of the fields making up the farm had been sold, and the proceeds reinvested in other land. In short, there appeared to be a lack of certainty which, in the light of what had been said in *Yeoman's Row*, might have been thought to have been fatal to the claim. In holding that this was not the case, Lord Walker of Gestingthorpe stressed that, while the assurance must be clear, what amounts to sufficient clarity is hugely dependent upon context.[93] He also observed, making reference to Lord Scott's comments on certainty in *Yeoman's Row* that: 'All the 'great judges' to whom Lord Kingsdown referred [*sc* in *Ramsden v. Dyson*] thought that even where there was some uncertainty an equity could arise and could be satisfied, either by an interest in land or in some other way.'[94]

Lord Neuberger took the view that statements made by Peter could have reasonably been understood to indicate that he intended to leave the farm to his cousin, which he regarded as sufficiently clear to form the basis of an estoppel claim.[95] He accepted that, to found such a claim, there must be some sort of assurance which is clear and unequivocal. He went on to say, however, that this was subject to three qualifications. First, it is important that any words or actions must be considered in the context in which they were made. Secondly, he stressed that it would be quite wrong for a court to search for uncertainty or ambiguity, and it is sufficient for the person invoking the estoppel to establish that he reasonably believed the statement or action to be an assurance on which he could rely. Thirdly, even if the assurance could reasonably be understood as having more than one meaning, and the facts would otherwise satisfy all the requirements of estoppel, he thought that that ambiguity should not deprive a person who reasonably relied on that assurance of all relief, and that it might be right to afford relief on the basis of the interpretation least favourable to him.[96]

It now seems clear, notwithstanding what was said in *Yeoman's Row*, that it is not necessary in order to raise an estoppel that the precise ambit of what the claimant expects to receive has been spelled out.[97] Provided that the promise or assurance is sufficiently clear to justify reliance, it is not necessary that the actual interest to be acquired should be defined with precision.[98] What is common to all estoppel cases is the resolution of three questions:

'First, is there an equity established? Secondly, what is the extent of the equity if one is established? And, thirdly, what is the relief appropriate to satisfy the equity?'[99]

These questions will be considered in turn.

---

[93] Ibid., at [56].   [94] Ibid., at [64].   [95] Ibid., at [67].   [96] Ibid., at [84]–[86].

[97] As to whether any assurance must relate to specific property, see Testamentary expectations, pp. 619–622.

[98] *McDonald v. Frost* [2009] EWHC 2276 (Ch.) at [11] *per* Ms Geraldine Andrews Q.C.

[99] *Crabb v. Arun District Council* [1976] Ch. 179 at 193 *per* Scarman L.J. See also *Macclesfield v. Parker* [2003] EWHC 1846 (Ch.) at [207] *per* Lewison J.

Establishing an equity

In *Thorner v. Major*,[100] Lord Walker, while recognizing that there is no comprehensive and uncontroversial definition of proprietary estoppel, said that 'most scholars would agree that the doctrine is based on three main elements, although they express them in slightly different terms: a representation or assurance made to the claimant; reliance on it by the claimant; and detriment to the claimant in consequence of his (reasonable) reliance....' While this statement does encapsulate the general gist of proprietary estoppel, it should not be taken as a literal template. This is because, as Lord Walker himself recognized,[101] the assurance element of this statement has to be taken to include cases of passive acquiescence, where the person against whom the estoppel has arisen has stood by when a person has acted in reliance on an expectation which has been acted upon by another. Although an estoppel can arise as a result of reliance on a direct assurance, it can do so in other situations as well, and so, for that reason, it is better to talk of an expectation as opposed to an assurance.

Active encouragement

In estoppel cases there are two paradigm situations where an equity can arise. The first is the case where one person, A, actively encourages another person, B, to believe that he either has, or will acquire, an interest in A's land. B then relies upon that expectation and an equity arises in his favour.[102] *Plimmer v. The Mayor of Wellington*[103] is an example of such a case. So, in more recent times, is *Inwards v. Baker*,[104] where a father suggested to his son that, instead of trying to buy land on which to build a bungalow, when this option was too expensive, he should build a larger bungalow on land owned by the father. The son did this and was living in the property when his father died leaving the land to trustees on trust for someone other than the son. The trustees sought possession. The Court of Appeal held that, as the son had a clear expectation of being able to stay in the bungalow indefinitely, that expectation having been created by his father, and he had relied upon that expectation, an equity arose in his favour which was satisfied by holding that he had an indefinite right to remain in the property. The trustees' possession action therefore failed.

Passive acquiesence[105]

The other paradigm is where the landowner does not actively encourage the other person to do anything but allows that person to act upon an expectation that he

---

[100] [2009] UKHL 18 at [29].

[101] Ibid., at [55]. This is recognized in the slightly wider formulation by Lord Neuberger [2009] C.L.J. 537 at 538.

[102] Once such encouragement has been given, the onus is on the person giving the encouragement to disprove reliance: *Greasley v. Cooke* [1980] 1 W.L.R. 1306, criticized by M.P. Thompson (1981) 125 S.J. 418. But see *Hammersmith and Fulham London Borough Council v. Top Shops Ltd* [1990] Ch. 237 at 262 *per* Warner J; and Presumption of reliance, pp. 624–625.

[103] (1884) 9 App. Cas. 699.

[104] [1965] 2 Q.B. 29. See, also *Dillwyn v. Llewelyn* (1862) 4 De G.F. & J. 517.

[105] See, generally, K.F.K. Low (2012) 128 L.Q.R.63.

has rights in the land, without disabusing him of his mistaken view. In cases such as this, it is difficult to establish the existence of an equity. What it is necessary to establish is that the landowner is actually aware of the other person's error[106] and consciously does not stop him from relying on that mistake. In *Ramsden v. Dyson*,[107] Lord Wendsleydale said of this type of situation:

'If a stranger build upon my land, supposing it to be his own, and, I knowing it to be mine, do not interfere but leave him to go on, equity considers it dishonest in me to remain passive and afterwards to interfere and take the profit. But if a stranger build knowingly on my land, there is no principle of equity which prevents me from insisting on having back my land, with all the additional value which the occupier has imprudently added to it. If a tenant of mine does the same thing, he cannot insist on refusing to give up the estate at the end of the term. It was his own folly to build.'

The five probanda

The emphasis in cases of passive acquiescence is that one party has made a mistake as to what the legal position is and the other, knowing of that mistake, allows the former to rely on his mistaken view of what the position is. Although in *Plimmer v. The Mayor of Wellington*,[108] it was pointed out that cases of active encouragement and passive acquiescence involve quite different considerations, the explanation of the law came to be dominated by statements apposite only to the latter situation.

Willmott v. Barber[109] was a case where, if any rights were to be acquired through the medium of estoppel, they would arise through the landowner's passive acquiescence in the other's mistaken behaviour. Fry J. however, spoke in quite general terms of what is required for rights to be obtained. While stressing that the underlying basis of proprietary estoppel, admittedly not an expression which he actually used, is fraud, he listed five criteria, or *probanda*, which had to be satisfied before a claim could be established. The five *probanda*, or things which had to be proved, were:

(i)   the plaintiff must have made a mistake as to his legal rights;

(ii) he must have spent some money or relied on his mistaken belief;

(iii) the defendant must be aware of the true position;

(iv) the defendant must know of the plaintiff's mistake; and

(v)   he must have encouraged the plaintiff in his expenditure or other act of reliance.[110]

Unconscionability[111]

Although the criteria listed by Fry J. may be apposite in cases of passive acquiescence, they are not appropriate to all cases where estoppel may arise. In particular, it should

---

[106] See *Dann v. Spurrier* (1802) 7 Ves. 232 at 235–236 *per* Lord Eldon L.C. See also *Pilling v. Grant* (1805) 12 Ves. 78 at 84 *per* Sir William Grant M.R.; *De Busche v. Alt* (1878) 8 Ch.D. 286 at 315 *per* Thesiger L.J.

[107] (1866) L.R. 1 H.L. 129 at 168.   [108] (1884) 9 App. Cas. 699 at 712 *per* Sir Arthur Hobhouse.

[109] (1880) 15 Ch.D. 96.   [110] Ibid., at 105–106.

[111] See K.R. Handley [2008] Conv. 382; H. Delaney and D. Ryan [2008] Conv. 401.

be pointed out that not all cases will fall into the paradigm examples given earlier. What may occur is a situation where both parties are mistaken as to the correct legal position. The leading case of *E.R. Ives Investment Ltd v. High*[112] provides a good illustration of such a situation.

Mutual mistake

Mr High and Mr Westgate were neighbours. Mr Westgate built a block of flats, the foundations of which, it was later discovered, encroached onto Mr High's land. The two then agreed that, in return for no objection being made to this continuing trespass, Mr High should have a right of way over Mr Westgate's land. This contract was an agreement to create an easement and, as it was specifically enforceable, gave rise to an equitable easement and, consequently, was registrable as a land charge. No such registration took place. The effect of non-registration was that, when Mr Westgate sold the land to Mr and Mrs Wright, the equitable easement was void against them. Nobody seemed to be aware of this and matters continued as if Mr High did have a right of way. Relying on his belief that he had such a right, Mr High constructed a garage in such a way that the only way he could access it was by using the right of way over the land owned by the Wrights. They were perfectly well aware of this and complimented him on his work. In addition, when the yard over which the right of way was enjoyed came to be re-surfaced, Mr High contributed to the cost. The Wrights then sold and conveyed the land to Ives Investment, expressly subject to his right of way. Ives Investment, relying on the fact that the equitable easement was void for non-registration, sought an injunction restraining him from using the yard. The action failed.

In deciding in favour of Mr High, one of the grounds for the decision[113] was estoppel. It was held that, as against the Wrights, Mr High had acquired an equity arising out of estoppel and that this right was binding upon Ives Investment. The latter issue, the binding effect of the equity on a purchaser, is an important one, which will be considered below. Of present interest is how the equity arose in the first place. This was not a case where the Wrights encouraged Mr High to believe that he had a right. He believed he had this right prior to them becoming owners of the land. Neither was it a case where the Wrights knew of his mistake and watched while he relied upon his mistaken belief. They, too, thought that he had the right to use the yard. What caused the estoppel to arise was their encouragement of, and acquiescence in, his acts of reliance, so that had it been them who had sought to restrain his use of their yard, it would have been regarded as inequitable for them to do so. He would, through proprietary estoppel, have acquired an equity against them.

---

[112] [1967] 2 Q.B. 379.

[113] The other ground was the principle of benefit and burden. See Mutual benefit and burden, pp. 592–593.

Abandonment of the probanda

The five *probanda* were not considered in *Ives v. High*. Had they been applied, Mr High would have lost because they were not satisfied. The Wrights were not aware of the true position and were therefore unaware that he was acting under a mistaken view of the legal position. The supposed importance of the *probanda* was stressed in argument, however, in what has rightly been described as being 'a watershed in the development of proprietary estoppel',[114] in the leading case of *Taylors Fashions Ltd v. Liverpool Victoria Trustees Ltd*,[115] where it was held that it was not necessary in order to acquire an equity through estoppel that the five *probanda* must be met. Having conducted an extensive review of the authorities, Oliver J. concluded that to establish an equity one should apply 'the broad test of whether in the circumstances the conduct complained of is unconscionable without the necessity of forcing those incumbrances into a Procrustean bed constructed from some unalterable criteria'.[116]

The application of a broad test of unconscionability has not gone uncriticized. It has been described as 'unhelpful'[117] and, in rather more trenchant terms, it was said that if one was to apply such a test of unconscionability, 'one might as well forget the law of contract and issue every judge with a portable palm tree. The days of justice varying with the size of the Lord Chancellor's foot would have returned.'[118] Such criticism is, however, misplaced[119] and, save for the occasional and unwelcome re-emergence of the five *probanda* as a template against which any claim must be measured,[120] the broad test of unconscionability introduced has attracted judicial approval, and is now widely accepted.[121] The reason it is preferable to the more rigid formula of the five *probanda* is that it is applicable to the wide range of differing situations which may occur and, when properly applied, does not lead to arbitrary or unprincipled results. 'It is not a sort of joker or wild card to be used whenever the Court disapproves of the conduct of a litigant who seems to have the law on his side.'[122] Neither is it 'penicillin for all types of ailments... the last plea of desperate and the treatment of choice for a court looking for a remedy for a deserving litigant,'[123] nor 'a sort of moral US fifth cavalry riding to the rescue every time a claimant is left worse off than he anticipated as a result of the

[114]   Gray and Gray, *Elements of Land Law* (5th edn) (Oxford: Oxford University Press, 2009), 1209.
[115]   [1982] Q.B. 133n.
[116]   Ibid., at 154. For a broadly similar analysis, see *Ward v. Kirkland* [1969] Ch. 194 at 239 *per* Ungoed-Thomas J.
[117]   Peel, op. cit., 161.
[118]   *Taylor v. Dickens* [1998] 3 F.C.R. 455 at 471 *per* Judge Weeks. Contrast the comments of the same judge in *Jennings v. Rice* [2003] 1 P. & C.R. 8 at para. 14, cited by Aldous L.J.
[119]   Although see the interesting attempt to conceptualize unconscionability by M. Balen and C. Knowles [2011] Conv. 176.
[120]   See *Coombes v. Smith* [1986] 1 W.L.R. 808 at 818–820 *per* Jonathan Parker Q.C.; *Matheru v. Matheru* (1994) 68 P. & C.R. 93 at 102 *per* Roch L.J.
[121]   See, e.g., *Habib Bank Ltd v. Habib Bank A.G. Zurich* [1981] 1 W.L.R. 1265 at 1285 *per* Oliver L.J.; *Lim Teng Huan v. Ang Swee Chuan* [1992] 1 W.L.R. 113 at 117 *per* Lord Browne-Wilkinson; *Gillett v. Holt* [2000] 2 All E.R. 289 at 301–302 *per* Robert Walker L.J.
[122]   *Yeoman's Row Management Ltd v. Cobbe* [2008] UKHL 55 at [46] *per* Lord Walker of Gestingthorpe.
[123]   M. Dixon (2010) 30 L.S. 408 at 410.

defendant's behaving badly, and the common law affords him no remedy.'[124] Rather it is a flexible and principled equitable doctrine of long standing.

It is, of course, easy to see why a test based on a broad principle of unconscionability should be viewed with some suspicion; it may be seen as providing scope for judges to apply idiosyncratic notions of fairness to different factual scenarios, the result being uncertainty. This is not, however, the case. For the test of unconscionability to be satisfied, the claimant must be able to bring his case within the broad principles enunciated in *Re Basham*.[125] These were stated as being:

'where one person, A, has acted to his detriment on the faith of a belief, which was known or encouraged by another person, B, that he either has or is going to be given a right over B's property, B cannot insist on his strict legal rights if to do so would be inconsistent with A's belief. The principle is commonly known as proprietary estoppel.'

There are a number of elements in this statement which need elaboration.

Expectation

The starting point for any claim in estoppel is that the claimant must have the expectation of some right over or to another person's property. This element does not often cause difficulty but can do in some situations. Problems can arise if an expectation is considered to be unjustified. One such situation is where parties have entered into 'subject to contract' negotiations but one of them spends money, or does some other act of reliance, in the belief that the contract will be entered into but the other side later withdraws from the transaction. In this situation, it is very difficult to claim any right arising through estoppel. This is because the effect of negotiating 'subject to contract' is generally well known and so, usually, there is no justification for any expectation that the other side is in some way committed to going ahead with the contract.[126]

Testamentary expectations

A second area where problems have arisen has concerned situations where assurances have been given that property will be left to a person on death, and that person then acts on that assurance.[127] The problems have centred on the certainty of the property to be left to the claimant, and the issue of testamentary freedom.

---

[124] Lord Neuberger [2009] C.L.J. 537 at 540.

[125] [1986] 1 W.L.R. 1498 at 1503 *per* Edward Nugee Q.C. See also *Wayling v. Jones* [1995] 2 F.L.R. 1029.

[126] See *Attorney-General for Hong Kong v. Humphreys Estates (Queen's Gardens) Ltd* [1987] A.C. 114; *Regalian Properties plc v. London Docklands Development Corporation* [1995] 1 W.L.R. 212; *Edwin Shirley Productions Ltd v Workspace Management Ltd* [2001] 3 E.G.L.R. 16 at 22 *per* Lawrence Collins J; *Yeoman's Row Management Ltd v. Cobbe* [2008] UKHL 55. Cf. *Salvation Army Trustee Co. Ltd v. West Yorkshire County Council* (1980) 41 P. & C.R. 179 where, on unusual facts, such a claim succeeded. See Subject to contract agreements, pp. 213–216.

[127] See, generally, M. Davey (1988) 8 L.S. 72. For a comparative discussion of this issue, see S. Nield (2000) 19 L.S. 85 and, further, S. Nield (2007) 58 N.I.L.Q. 287.

Certainty of property

At the outset, the need to identify the precise property which was to be left on death did not appear to be a particular issue. Although in *Layton v. Martin*,[128] Scott J. had declined to hold that an assurance of financial security could, of itself, form the basis of an estoppel claim, in *Re Basham*,[129] a promise, in effect, to leave the residuary estate to the claimant was sufficiently certain, when relied upon, to give rise to an estoppel right. Subsequently, Robert Walker L.J. pointed to the difficulty in reconciling these approaches,[130] but appeared to favour the latter decision, noting that it had subsequently been cited with approval.[131] Given his previous approach, it is a more than a little curious that in *Thorner v. Major*[132] he expressed himself rather differently. Echoing the approach taken by Lord Hoffmann that, to acquire an estoppel interest the claimant must prove a promise or assurance that he would acquire a proprietary interest in a specific property,[133] he also said that the assurance 'must relate to *identified property* (usually land) owned (or, perhaps, about to be owned) by the defendant'.[134]He then proceeded to cast doubt on *Re Basham*. Taking the view that, in the instant case, the reference to the farm was sufficiently certain in referring to what constituted the farm at the time of death, he expressly contrasted that with the more general assurance in *Layton v. Martin*, which he appeared to approve. As to *Re Basham*, he stated that it was not necessary to determine whether or not it was correctly decided so far as it extended to the residuary estate, and expressly reserved his opinion as to this.[135] Given this ambivalence, it is not surprising that, subsequently, in *McDonald v. Frost*,[136] Ms Geraldine Andrews Q.C. should state that *Re Basham* should be treated with the utmost caution and could not be regarded as laying down any general principle to the effect that assurances given about inheriting a residuary estate would be sufficient to give rise to a proprietary estoppel.

It is regrettable that this complication has been introduced. As a matter of first impression, it is difficult to see why if one person gives a specific assurance that he will leave his house to another, and that assurance is relied upon, this could give rise to a cause of action, whereas if the promise was to leave everything that is owned at the time of death, and that was similarly relied upon, it could not. Leaving first impressions aside, the principled argument in favour of such a distinction would appear to be that, in the first case, the person has an assurance of a proprietary right in specific property, whereas in the second case, because of the uncertainty in identifying the property which is to be subject to the right, he does not. This analysis is, however, seemingly predicated on the notion that the role of proprietary estoppel is limited to the informal creation of interests in land. Such an analysis is not consistent, however, with decisions whereby the courts have satisfied an equity which has arisen with a monetary award, and declined to award the claimant any interest in the property

---

[128] [1996] 2 F.L.R. 227.   [129] [1987] 1 W.L.R. 1498.   [130] *Gillett v. Holt* [2001] Ch. 210 at 226.
[131] Ibid. See also *Jennings v. Rice* [2003] 1 P. & C.R. 8 at [45].   [132] [2009] UKHL 8.
[133] Ibid., at [2].   [134] Ibid., at [61]. Original emphasis.   [135] Ibid., at [62]–[63].
[136] [2009] EWHC 2276 (Ch.) at [19].

which had been promised,[137] a solution which is particularly evident in a case such as *Wayling v. Jones*,[138] where, at the time of death, the person who had made the promise no longer owned the property he had promised to leave by will. It is submitted that, in principle, there is no reason why a promise to leave ill-defined property should not be capable of giving rise to an estoppel right, although it may well be the case that the courts will not be prepared to accept this.

Testamentary freedom

A second potential stumbling block to the operation of estoppel in the present context might be seen to relate to testamentary freedom. In *Taylor v. Dickens*,[139] an elderly woman promised her gardener that she would make a will in favour of him and his wife leaving virtually all her property to them. He then offered to work for her for nothing, which he did. Having made a will in accordance with what she had said, she later, without telling the couple, revoked it and left the property elsewhere. On her death, he argued that he had rights against the estate arising from estoppel. This claim was rejected. Judge Weeks took the view that the claimant's expectation was that the lady would make a will in his favour; not that she would not, subsequently revoke such a will. As she had, in fact, made a will which she subsequently revoked, any expectation which he may have had, had been fulfilled.

This reasoning is highly artificial and was regarded as wrong by the Court of Appeal in *Gillett v. Holt*,[140] and in a number of cases, including, of course, *Thorner v. Major* itself, a claimant who expected a will to be made in his favour has been able to enforce an equitable right against the estate after the will had been revoked.[141] It is, however, true that it is well known that a will, once made, can be revoked, and 'it is notorious that some elderly persons of means derive enjoyment from the possession of testamentary power, and from dropping hints as to their intentions, without any question of an estoppel arising.'[142] Because of this, it is necessary that the assurance must be in such terms, or in such circumstances,[143] that it is clear that property is to be left to the claimant,[144] and that it is reasonable for the person to whom the assurance is made to rely on that assurance,[145] and it may be that the less precise the description of the property to be left, the less reasonable it becomes for the person to whom the assurance is addressed to rely on it.

---

[137] See *Campbell v. Griffin* [2001] EWCA Civ. 990; *Jennings v. Rice* [2003] 1 P. & C.R. 8. See Restitution, pp. 629–630.

[138] (1993) 69 P. & C.R. 179.

[139] [1998] 1 F.L.R. 806. For strong criticism of this decision, see M.P. Thompson [1998] Conv. 210; W. Swadling [1998] R.L.R. 220. Contrast M. Dixon [1999] Conv. 46.

[140] [2001] Ch. 210. See also, dealing with the same point, *Sledmore v. Dalby* (1996) P. & C.R. 196 at 203 *per* Roch L.J. See M.P. Thompson [2001] Conv. 78.

[141] *Wayling v. Jones* (1993) 69 P. & C.R. 170; *Henry v. Henry* [2010] UKPC 3.

[142] *Gillett v. Holt* [2001] Ch. 210 at 228 *per* Robert Walker L.J.

[143] See *Thorner v. Major* [2009] UKHL 8 at [24] *per* Lord Rodger of Earlsferry.

[144] For a claim which failed due to considerable ambiguity as to this, see *McDonald v. Frost* [2009] EWHC 2276 (Ch.).

[145] See *Thorner v. Major* [2009] UKHL 18 at [17] *per* Lord Scott of Foscote.

A related point which can arise is what is to happen to the property pending the death of the person making the assurance. In this type of case, it would appear that the person making the assurance is not precluded from dealing with his property until death. So, in *Thorner v. Major*, the physical configuration of the farm changed during the lifetime of its owner, as some fields were sold, and others bought. Nevertheless, it was held that the equity which had arisen was still enforceable against the estate. The question which can arise is what the position would be if it became apparent prior to the death, either by proposed dealings with it, or the manifestation of a clear intention that the property was not to be left in the way in which it had been promised. This latter situation occurred in *Gillett v. Holt*,[146] where despite the fact that the promisor had not died, as it was clear from the facts that he was not going to leave the property as promised, the court awarded a remedy prior to the death, when it was envisaged that the property would be transferred. This would appear to be the approach to be adopted if it appears that the property is to be substantially disposed of prior to the death,[147] so that in a case 'where a claimant has a clear right to expect that a property will be left to him by another, an attempt to circumvent a promise to that effect by changing the will or by selling the property may give rise to enforceable rights even before the death of the promisor.'[148] If, however, as in *Thorner v. Major* some of the farm has been sold, and the proceeds spent, that, in itself, should not allow the equity to be enforced prior to death. The degree of dissipation necessary to enable the promisee to secure an early enforcement of the equity will, it is thought, be a matter of degree.

Reliance and detriment

That a person has an expectation of acquiring an interest in property is, of itself, insufficient to raise an estoppel. Before any equity can arise in his favour, it is necessary that the claimant has acted on the faith of that expectation and, in the sense to be explained, that that reliance is to his detriment.

An obvious form of reliance is to spend money. Such a form of reliance occurred in *Plimmer v. The Mayor of Wellington*,[149] where the reliance involved spending money on the extension of a jetty. While this may be the clearest form of reliance, other forms of conduct will suffice. For example, in *Crabb v. Arun District Council*,[150] the plaintiff, in reliance upon an assurance that he would enjoy a right of way over the defendant's land, sold part of his own land with the result that, when the defendant resiled from his assurance, he was left with no means of access to the property. The act of selling land was, in these circumstances, seen as a clear act of reliance. Similarly, in *Jones v. Jones*,[151] although the acts of reliance on an assurance that a house would be his included the expenditure of money, the act of giving up a job and moving from existing accommodation was also regarded in the same way.

---

146 [2001] Ch. 210.
147 See *Thorner v. Major* [2009] UKHL 18 at [18] *per* Lord Scott; at [88] *per* Lord Neuberger.
148 *Clarke v. Meadus* [2020] EWCA 3117 (Ch.) at [74] *per* Warren J.   149 (1884) 9 App. Cas. 699.
150 [1976] Ch. 178.   151 [1977] 1 W.L.R. 438. See also *Watts v. Story* (1983) 134 N.L.J. 631.

Family disputes

A not untypical situation where claims are based upon estoppel is where the parties are in a relationship and, on the breakdown of that relationship, one party, usually the woman, makes a claim to the other's property. Quite commonly, in such situations, an assurance has been given that the person making a claim will always have secure accommodation and the difficulty is to establish an act of reliance on that assurance.[152] The nub of the problem is that the claimed acts of reliance can be seen as conduct which is an integral part of the relationship, rather than behaviour based upon the assurance which has been given.[153] The case law reveals a disparity in judicial attitude.

In *Maharaj v. Chand*,[154] a woman who had secure accommodation of her own, was asked to move in by her partner. Before doing so, she sought and received an assurance that she would have a secure home in the house into which she was to move. Some years later, the relationship broke down and he sought to evict her from the property. The Privy Council held that she had, through the operation of estoppel, a personal and indefinite right to remain in the house. Her act of giving up secure accommodation of her own was regarded as being a sufficient act of reliance. In stark contrast is the case of *Coombes v. Smith*.[155] In this case, a married woman left her husband to live in a house bought by her new partner, who was also married, after being assured that she would always have secure accommodation. She also had his child. On the breakdown of their relationship, it was held that she had no right to remain in the property.

The estoppel claim was considered primarily on the basis of whether or not she could satisfy the five *probanda*, considered earlier, which the judge considered that she could not. There had been no mistake as to her legal rights. Although this approach to estoppel cases is no longer appropriate, the judge, in any event, considered that she had not relied to her detriment on the assurance which she had been given. In his view, her leaving her husband and having their child was an inherent part of their relationship. She had not done anything which could be attributed to the assurance of security in the house which she had been given.

While such a view is understandable, it is not necessarily convincing. It is true, as the judge pointed out, that to hold that the woman in this case had an equity in the house would mean that, in most cases where there is a dispute between an unmarried couple and the woman has left secure accommodation of her own to move in with her partner, quite a common event, she would be able to claim an interest in the house, or at least the right to remain in it.[156] That, however, may be no bad thing and could lead to fairer results than those which can occur when a longstanding non-marital relationship breaks down and a dispute occurs as to occupancy rights in the home.

These two cases are not easy to reconcile, and display a very different approach to what can constitute reliance. Latterly, it is becoming increasingly clear that a more

[152] See, e.g., *Vaughan v. Vaughan* [1953] 1 Q.B. 762.
[153] For an excellent discussion, see A. Lawson (1996) 16 L.S. 218. [154] [1986] A.C. 898.
[155] [1986] 1 W.L.R. 808. See also *Negus v. Bahous* [2008] 1 F.L.R. 381 at [54]–[55] *per* Mr Roger Kaye Q.C.
[156] [1986] 1 W.L.R. 808 at 816 *per* Jonathan Parker Q.C.

liberal approach is the one which is favoured. In the increasingly influential decision in *Wayling v. Jones*,[157] a homosexual couple began to cohabit in 1971, and this continued until 1987, when the elder of the two died. When the cohabitation began, W was 21 and J was 56. They lived in a hotel owned by J. W worked in the hotel, but received very little money. What he did receive was regarded as akin to pocket money. When he mentioned that he would need more money, J promised him that he would leave everything to him. The arrangement then continued as before, and the promise was repeated. On J's death, it transpired that the will by which he had intended to implement his promise was ineffective to do so. W then brought an action against the estate, basing his claim on estoppel.

Presumption of reliance

The difficulty was not establishing the expectation; it was showing reliance. In evidence, W said that, had no promise ever been made, he would have stayed with his partner on the same basis as before. At first instance, this statement was held to be fatal to the estoppel claim, it being considered to have shown that no reliance had taken place. Reversing this decision, the Court of Appeal held the claim to have been substantiated. Starting from the premise that once a clear promise had been made it was for the promisor to disprove reliance by the promisee,[158] it was held that this had not been done. This was because of the further evidence given that, had J told him that the promise was being withdrawn, then J would have left. This was sufficient to establish reliance,[159] and the court ordered that he be paid by the estate the value of what had been promised.

Mixed motives

This decision is significant in that it establishes that reliance can be established when a person acts with more than one motive, in this case affection for his partner and the expectation of inheritance, and when a person does not change his conduct in reliance on a promise, but would do so if the promise was subsequently withdrawn.[160] This was followed in *Campbell v. Griffin*.[161] A young man of 30 moved into lodgings with a couple who were then in their late seventies. After five years living in the house, the relationship between him and the couple grew increasingly affectionate. He stopped paying rent and, more and more, took on the role of a carer, as they became increasingly frail. He was promised that he could live in the house for the rest of his life after the couple had both died. When that occurred, it transpired that he had been left nothing and he, too, brought an action against the estate. Again, the principal problem was to show reliance. Relying on *Wayling v. Jones*, however, the Court of Appeal found in

---

[157] (1983) 69 P. & C.R. 170. See E. Cooke (1995) 111 L.Q.R. 389 at 391, where the disparity between the two preceding decisions is commented upon.

[158] See *Greasley v. Cooke* [1986] 1 W.L.R. 1306.

[159] See also *Clarke v. Meadus* [2010] EWHC 3117 (Ch.) at [54] *per* Warren J.

[160] See also *Ottey v. Grundy* [2003] EWCA Civ. 1113; M.P. Thompson [2004] Conv. 137.

[161] [2001] EWCA Civ. 990; M.P. Thompson [2003] Conv. 157.

his favour. Although he was acting in a caring capacity before the promise was made, and continued to do so afterwards, this conduct was still considered to amount to reliance. The court was prepared to accept that the promise did influence his decision to stay in the house to care for an increasingly infirm couple. The fact that he was genuinely fond of them and said that, for that reason, he would not have left them on their own to suffer did not negate reliance. As was recognized, his motives may well have been mixed, and he should not lose his claim because he insisted that he was motivated by affection and altruism as well as the prospect of gain.[162]

Detriment

The underlying basis of equitable estoppel is unconscionability. Essential to this is that the claimant has acted in reliance, in the sense explained above, on having some expectation of acquiring some right over another person's land, in circumstances where it would be inequitable to deny some effect to that expectation. This means that the acts of reliance have to be detrimental to the claimant. This requirement can easily be misunderstood to mean that the acts relied upon must, themselves, be harmful in some way to the claimant, in the sense that they put him in a worse position than he was in before.[163] This is not so. The proper meaning of detriment is that the claimant's position would be damaged if the expectation or assumption which formed the basis of his reliance were to be departed from.[164] So, to return to the facts of *E.R. Ives Investment Ltd v. High*,[165] the claimant's act of building the garage in such a way that it could not be used without being able to cross his neighbour's land was not, in itself, detrimental to him; the detriment would have been caused if the assumption on which he acted, that he did have a right of way, was departed from.

An holistic approach

The more relaxed view of what constitutes reliance, coupled with a principled view of what constitutes detriment, offers scope for solutions to be arrived at in cohabitation cases where the claimant seeks some remedy when her behaviour has not been of a purchasing behaviour, which are more favourable to the claimant than an application of the law of trusts would suggest.[166] In *Gillett v. Holt*,[167] a young boy moved into a farm owned by a much older man, with whom he had a platonic relationship for over forty years. He gave up his education, and worked on the farm, having been promised on a number of occasions that he would eventually inherit the property. When the owner of the farm sought to renege on these undertakings, the claimant was held to be entitled to a remedy in estoppel. In addressing the issue of what constituted detriment,

[162] Ibid., at para. 19 *per* Robert Walker L.J.
[163] See, e.g., *Coombes v. Smith* [1986] 1 W.L.R. 808 at 819–820 *per* Jonathan Parker Q.C.
[164] See *Grundt v. Great Boulder Pty Gold Mines Ltd* (1937) 59 C.L.R. 641 at 674–675 *per* Dixon J.; *Gillett v. Holt* [2001] Ch. 210 at 232–233 *per* Robert Walker L.J.
[165] [1967] 2 Q.B. 379.
[166] See Chapter 9, and M.P. Thompson in Jackson and Wilde (eds), *Contemporary Property Law* (Dartmouth: Ashgate, 1999), 120 at 135–137.
[167] [2001] Ch. 210. See R. Wells [2001] Conv. 13; M.P. Thompson [2001] Conv. 78.

Robert Walker L.J. made it clear that this need not consist of the expenditure of money. Rather, the case must be looked at in the round as part of a broad enquiry as to whether it would be unconscionable to go back on assurances which had been given. On the facts of the case, the giving up of his education and alternative career prospects was seen as detrimental reliance.[168] Similarly, in *Ottey v. Grundy*,[169] it was held that staying to look after an ill partner, following assurances of inheritance, at the expense of the possible continuation of a career in show business, also amounted to detrimental reliance. In the light of these developments, it seems very arguable that the giving up of a career to look after children in a family home can, and should, form the basis of a claim in estoppel.

The correctness of this approach was recently confirmed by the Privy Council in *Henry v. Henry*.[170] In this case, the claimant had been promised that he would be left land. He worked that land for many years. He gave some of the produce to the landowner and sold the remainder, this in large part amounting to his livelihood. At first instance, the trial judge had held that he had not established detrimental reliance, because, for decades, he had enjoyed rent free accommodation on the land. While the Privy Council considered this to be relevant, the Board also took the view that the position had to be looked at in the round, and regard should be had to the disadvantages which he had suffered, such as the forgoing of opportunities to move on elsewhere,[171] as well as the advantages he had enjoyed. Having undertaken this exercise, it was held that, overall, there had been detrimental reliance.

Mutuality

For the claimant to acquire a right through proprietary estoppel, he must have acted in reliance on an expectation that he either has, or will acquire, rights in another person's property. Such acts, it may be said, raise an equity in his favour. For it to be unconscionable for the other person to deny some effect to that expectation he must be in some way responsible for that action, so that an equity arises against him. This was explained in *Sledmore v. Dalby*,[172] where it was said that:

'The party asserting the estoppel must be able to show that his own conduct was attributable to an expectation or mistake *contributed to by the conduct (including inaction) of the affected party*.'

Finding such responsibility on the part of the person against whom the claim is made will depend to a considerable extent on the facts of each case but will be easier to find

---

[168] Ibid., at 232–235.

[169] [2003] EWCA Civ. 1176. Contrast *Lissimore v. Downing* [2003] 2 F.L.R. 308, where the giving up of a job behind the counter of a pharmacist's shop to live with a member of the band Judas Priest was not considered to be detrimental reliance, as there was no sense that she was giving up a career: ibid., at 322 *per* Judge Norris Q.C.

[170] [2010] UKPC 3.

[171] Ibid., at [53] *per* Sir Jonathan Parker. See also *Malik v. Kalyan* [2010] EWCA Civ. 113, where such a foregoing of opportunities was not established on the facts.

[172] (1996) 72 P. & C.R. 196 at 207 *per* Hobhouse L.J. (emphasis supplied), citing *Commonwealth of Australia v. Verwayen* (1990) 95 A.L.R. 321 at 322 *per* Mason C.J.

when there has been some contribution to the claimant having an expectation than will be the case where the expectation derives from a shared mistake.

In *Crabb v. Arun District Council*,[173] a council representative led the plaintiff to believe that, if he sold off a plot of land, he would have a right of way over land owned by the council. He duly sold that land and, when the council refused to allow him access, the effect was to leave his property landlocked. The Court of Appeal held the plaintiff to be entitled through estoppel to an easement. As the council had been responsible for the creation of the expectation, it was straightforward to find that, when the plaintiff had relied upon it, an equity arose against them.

Mutual mistake

In cases of positive encouragement, finding that an equity has arisen against the person affected is straightforward. In cases where a mutual mistake is made as to the legal position, such a finding is more difficult and can require a close analysis of the facts. Such an analysis occurred in *Taylors Fashions Ltd v. Liverpool Victoria Trustees Ltd*,[174] a decision which is illustrative of cases where an estoppel can arise where there is never an express assurance given by one party to the other.

The first plaintiff was granted a twenty-eight-year lease which contained an option to renew it for a further fourteen years. This option was, unbeknown to the parties for a considerable period of time, void against the defendants, who had purchased the freehold, because it had not been registered as a land charge, it not being appreciated for some time that an option to renew a lease was registrable.[175] The second plaintiff took a lease of adjoining property for a period of forty-two years, that lease being determinable by the landlords if the option to renew the first lease was not exercised. In other words, it was intended to synchronize the running of the two leases. When the first plaintiff sought to exercise the option, the objection was made that it was void. The first plaintiff sought a declaration that, through estoppel, the option was valid, despite non-registration, and the second plaintiffs sought a declaration that the defendants could not determine the lease. The first plaintiff failed and the second plaintiff succeeded.

Responsibility for reliance

In both cases, the tenants had a mistaken belief that the option to renew the first lease was valid. That belief was not created by the defendants; it was a case of mutual mistake. The reasons why the first plaintiff failed were, first, that it could not show reliance on that mistaken belief and, secondly, even if it could show reliance, there was, on the facts, nothing to make it unconscionable for the defendants to deny any effect to the expectation. The reliance alleged by the first plaintiff was the installation of a lift in the property. Although the defendants' representatives were aware of this work, the difficulty was that the installation of the lift was contemplated by the lease itself; there was nothing to show that its installation was done on the basis that

---

[173] [1976] Ch. 179.   [174] [1982] Q.B. 133n.
[175] It was decided that such options were registrable in *Beesly v. Hallwood Estates Ltd* [1961] Ch. 105.

there was an option to renew the lease for a further fourteen years from the date of its determination. Indeed, installing a lift into commercial property when there was still eighteen years remaining on the original lease would be a normal thing to have done, regardless of whether there existed an option to renew.[176] The second problem was that the work which was done was done on property controlled by the first plaintiff. While the defendants were aware of what was being done, they did not encourage it and were powerless to stop it. Accordingly, even if the work had been regarded as reliance on the expectation that the option was valid, it was not unconscionable for the defendants to rely on the strict legal position, which was that the option was void.

As regards the second plaintiff, the position was different. The whole basis upon which its lease was negotiated with the defendant was that the option in the first lease was valid. While it was true that the risk was run that the first plaintiff might choose not to exercise the option, so that the defendants could then determine the second lease, what was not the case was that the lease was being entered into on the basis that the option could never be exercised, thereby giving the defendants the unfettered right to determine the lease. As the defendants had been party to the act of reliance of the second plaintiff, the entry into the lease, they could not take the point, as against the second plaintiffs, that the option was void and could not, therefore, determine the lease.

What emerges is that, in cases of active encouragement of the expectation, for example, saying that 'the house is yours',[177] once reliance is established, there is no further difficulty in holding that an equity has arisen against the creator of the expectation. In cases where the expectation arises owing to a mutual mistake as to what the true position is, for an equity to arise against the person against whom the claim is made, it would seem that that person must either actively encourage the acts of reliance,[178] or be a party to it, as in *Taylors Fashions*. If he does neither of these things, then it is probable that an equity will only arise if he is aware of the mistake, and of the action in reliance, and does nothing to stop the other person from acting in reliance upon his mistaken expectation.

The extent of the equity

The second aspect of equitable estoppel identified by Scarman L.J. was to identify the extent of the equity which has arisen. This means, quite simply, determining the ambit of the expectation. Where there has been an actual representation, then the expectation is defined by that representation. If, as may happen, any such representation is imprecise in scope, then it is for the court, as best it can, to infer what the actual scope of the expectation was.[179] The less formal the understanding between the parties, the

---

[176] [1982] Q.B. 133n at 156 *per* Oliver J.   [177] See *Pascoe v. Turner* [1979] 1 W.L.R. 431.

[178] See *E.R. Ives Investment Ltd v. High* [1967] 2 Q.B. 379.

[179] See *Plimmer v. The Mayor of Wellington* (1884) 9 App. Cas. 699 at 713–714 *per* Sir Arthur Hobhouse. See also *Thorner v. Major* [2009] UKHL 18 at [84]–[86] *per* Lord Neuberger.

more difficult will be the task of determining the full extent of the equity, and this may impact on the remedy which has been arrived at.[180]

Satisfaction of the equity

The final aspect of an estoppel claim is the determination of the remedy to be afforded to the claimant. From quite early times, judges have stressed that, once an equity has arisen, it is for the courts, in the exercise of their discretion, to decide how the equity should be satisfied.[181] The greatest remedy available is the complete satisfaction of the expectation;[182] It is not possible to award a claimant a remedy greater than his expectation.[183] That, however, is not a necessary conclusion, and the courts have shown considerable flexibility in determining the appropriate remedy.[184] There are various possibilities, the first being in the nature of compensation, and the alternative being the enforcement of the expectation.[185]

Compensation

In terms of compensating the claimant as a result of his reliance upon the expectation, such compensation can be designed to reflect different types of loss. The claimant may, as a result of his reliance, have incurred expenditure, but the expenditure incurred does not benefit the other party to the action. In such cases, any compensation simply reflects the cost of the reliance.[186] An example of this would be a claim for pre-contractual expenditure when it is anticipated that a binding contract will subsequently be entered into.[187] It is not, however, easy to establish such a claim. Moreover, in cases involving land, this may not been seen as the most appropriate response. If someone's reliance on an assurance of security in a home is to give up existing secure accommodation, while it might be possible to quantify this in terms of reliance loss, a more appropriate response may be to seek to enforce the expectation and protect the security of that accommodation.[188]

Restitution

Situations can arise when the claimant's act of reliance does not only involve him in expenditure but also confers a benefit on the other party. Such cases normally involve

[180] See *Jennings v. Rice* [2003] 1 P. & C.R. 8.
[181] See *Plimmer v. The Mayor of Wellington* (1884) 9 App. Cas. 699 at 713–714 *per* Sir Arthur Hobhouse.
[182] See *Macclesfield v. Parker* [2003] EWHC 1846 (Ch.); *Wormall v. Wormall* [2004] EWHC 1643 (Ch.). The comment in *Jennings v. Rice* [2003] 1 P. & C.R. 8 at [21] that a remedy greater than the expectation has been awarded is wrong. See M.P. Thompson [2004] Conv. 225 at 231–232.
[183] See *Jules v. Robertson* [2011] EWCA Civ 1322 at [24] *per* Warren J.
[184] See *Roebuck v. Mungovin* [1994] 2 A.C. 224 at 235 *per* Lord Browne-Wilkinson.
[185] See, generally, L.L. Fuller and W.R. Purdue (1936) 46 Yale L.J. 52.
[186] For an argument advocating reliance damages as the normal starting point, see A. Robertson (1998) 18 L.S. 360, an argument which takes a very wide view of the role of such damages.
[187] See, e.g., *Regalian Properties plc v. London Docklands Development Corporation* [1995] 1 W.L.R. 212, where such a claim failed on the facts.
[188] See *Maharaj v. Chand* [1986] A.C. 898.

the claimant effecting some sort of improvement to the other's land, this being done in reliance on an expectation of having an interest in that land. While, again, it may be the case that the court may seek to give effect to the expectation, there may be reasons why this is not practicable. In such circumstances, a restitutionary remedy can be effected by ordering the return of the money expended upon the land.[189] This can be done by granting the claimant a lien over the other's land as security for the amount to be repaid,[190] or, more simply, allowing the claimant to remain in the property until the amount which has been expended upon it has been repaid.[191]

Similarly, the reliance may take the form of conferring a benefit on a person, rather than on property. Such cases tend to involve the claimant acting as a form of unpaid help or carer for the other person.[192] In such cases, the courts can, again, choose to award the claimant a restitutionary remedy, ordering a payment to be made, the quantum of that payment representing a rough approximation of the value of the work which has been done.[193]

Expectation

As will be seen, it is quite common in cases of equitable estoppel for the court to make an order which gives effect, at least in part, to the claimant's expectation. This may not be possible, however, and, instead, the court may make a monetary order to compensate for the loss of the expectation.[194] In *Wayling v. Jones*,[195] the plaintiff had been assured by his lover that he would be left a particular hotel in his will. A will in these terms was in fact made but prior to his death that hotel had been sold and another purchased and no testamentary provision was made with regard to that property. The plaintiff, having been held to have relied upon the assurance made to him,[196] sought, and obtained, a judgment that he was entitled from the estate to the proceeds of sale of the first hotel. In other words, although his expectation could no longer be satisfied *in specie*, he was awarded a financial payment to compensate him for his expectation interest. Such instances of money payments being awarded are rare,[197] but are indicative of the willingness of the courts, in cases of equitable estoppel, to seek to satisfy the claimant's expectation.

---

[189] See *Sledmore v. Dalby* (1996) 72 P. & C.R. 196 at 208 *per* Hobhouse L.J. For an interesting discussion of the relationship between estoppel and restitution, see N.W. Hopkins in Cooke (ed.), *Modern Studies in Property Law, Volume 2* (Oxford-Portland, Oregon: Hart Publishing, 2003), Chapter 8.

[190] *Unity Joint Stock Mutual Banking Association v. King* (1858) 25 Beav. 72.

[191] *Dodsworth v. Dodsworth* [1973] E.G.D. 223. See also *Re Sharpe* [1980] 1 W.L.R. 219.

[192] See *Campbell v. Griffin* [2001] EWCA Civ. 990; *Jennings v. Rice* [2003] 1 P. & C.R. 8.

[193] See *Jennings v. Rice* [2003] 1 P. & C.R. 8 at [48] *per* Robert Walker L.J.

[194] See C. Davis [1995] Conv. 409 at 414–416; S. Bright and B. McFarlane [2005] Conv. 14.

[195] (1993) 69 P. & C.R. 170.

[196] This aspect of the decision was controversial. See the discussion by E. Cooke (1995) 111 L.Q.R. 389; C. Davis [1995] Conv. 409.

[197] See *Holiday Inns Inc. v. Broadhead* (1974) 232 E.G. 951; *Baker v. Baker* [1993] 2 F.L.R. 247. This may, also, be the best explanation of *Tanner v. Tanner* [1975] 1 W.L.R. 1346, although the case was actually decided on a different basis.

Satisfaction of the expectation

Although any equity which has arisen can be satisfied by financial compensation, commonly the remedy which is obtained involves the actual satisfaction of the claimant's expectation. In *Pascoe v. Turner*,[198] a man purported to give a house and its contents to his partner. In reliance on this purported gift, she spent a significant amount of her savings, consisting of several hundred pounds, effecting improvements to it. He, having formed a relationship with another woman, then sought to evict her from the house. His claim failed and, instead, he was ordered to convey the house to her.

The result of the case lends support to the thesis that the role of equitable estoppel is to perfect an imperfect gift,[199] or, put another way, that the role of estoppel is, in general, a medium through which the claimant's expectation is fulfilled.[200] There is force in this argument; indeed, were it not valid, the actual decision in *Pascoe v. Turner* would appear to represent a remarkable windfall for the woman in the case who, for the expenditure of a relatively modest sum, was awarded the house for nothing.[201] Nevertheless, the reasoning in the case itself and in other decisions does not support such an analysis.

In *Pascoe v. Turner*, it was apparent to the Court of Appeal that the remedy awarded to satisfy the equity which had arisen might appear to be extreme and the court regarded the choice as being between giving her an indefinite licence to occupy the property or ordering a conveyance of it to her.[202] In arriving at the conclusion that a conveyance was the appropriate result, Cumming-Bruce L.J. had regard to a number of factors, which included their relative financial positions, in that he was wealthy and she was not. Moreover, it was felt that, given the nature of the relationship at the time of the trial, if she were to be afforded some lesser remedy, then the likelihood was that he would pester her in the future, an undesirable outcome which the 'clean break' solution arrived at would avoid. This was a family case,[203] where the solution arrived at was much the same as one might expect to have occurred if the couple had been married and this had been a case of reallocation of property on divorce. Because of the nature of the expectation encouraged by him, the court was able to arrive at a solution in a cohabitation case consistent with that which would have been arrived at if the couple had been married.[204]

---

[198] [1979] 1 W.L.R. 431. See also *Dillwyn v. Llewelyn* (1862) 4 De G.F. & J. 517; *Jiggins v. Brisley* [2003] EWHC 841 (Ch.).

[199] See D.E. Allen (1963) 79 L.Q.R. 238; S. Moriarty (1984) 100 L.Q.R. 376. For an argument against this view, see M.P. Thompson [1986] Conv. 402.

[200] See E. Cooke (1997) 17 L.S. 258; S. Gardner (1999) 111 L.Q.R. 438. Both writers recognize, however, that this is not the invariable outcome of estoppel cases. See A. Robertson [2008] Conv. 295.

[201] The case has been criticized precisely on this basis. See Hanbury and Martin, *Modern Equity* (18th edn) (London: Sweet & Maxwell, 2009), 935.

[202] [1979] 1 W.L.R. 431 at 438 *per* Cumming-Bruce L.J.

[203] For the relevance of this in a related situation, see E. Cooke (1995) 111 L.Q.R. 389 at 393–394.

[204] For a discussion of this tendency, see M.P. Thompson [1984] Conv. 103.

Practicalities

In determining to what extent the claimant's expectation should be fulfilled, although it has been said that it is often appropriate to satisfy the equity by granting the claimant the interest that he was intended to have,[205] it has also been recognized that the solution to the dispute must always depend upon the circumstances of the particular case.[206] In particular, a relevant factor will be the practicalities of the situation. If the estoppel arose in a situation which involves the claimant and the other party living together in the same house, then an order is unlikely to be made which will require people, whose relationship has broken down, to continue to live together in the same house.[207] The way that the equity is then satisfied may then take a wholly different form from that which was envisaged and is likely to involve compensation for reliance.[208]

Conduct

A further factor which is relevant to the exercise of the court's discretion is the conduct of the parties.[209] A good example of this is provided by *Crabb v. Arun District Council*.[210] The plaintiff had been encouraged by the defendants to believe that, if he sold off part of his land, he would enjoy a right of way over the defendants' land. Having sold off the land, the defendants refused him access and he sought a declaration that he enjoyed such a right. In the Court of Appeal, his claim was upheld and it was held that he was entitled to an easement, which was the full extent of his expectation.

Although this case provides an example of the equity being satisfied in full, it is clear from the judgments that the obstructive behaviour of the defendants in the period after the equity had arisen, which occurred when the plaintiff sold his land, was a highly significant factor in the way that the discretion was exercised. Because of the defendants' obstructive attitude, the plaintiff's land had been rendered useless for a period of six years. Were it not for this, the plaintiff would only have been granted the remedy he sought on terms, those terms being that he be required to pay for the right.[211] As Scarman L.J. put it,

'Had matters taken a different turn, I would without hesitation have said that the plaintiff should be put on terms to be agreed if possible with the defendants, and, if not agreed, settled by the court.'[212]

---

[205] *Burrows and Burrows v. Sharp* (1989) 23 H.L.R. 82 at 92 *per* Dillon L.J. See also *Chalmers v. Pardoe* [1963] 1 W.L.R. 677 at 681 *per* Sir Terence Donovan.

[206] *Voyce v. Voyce* (1991) 62 P. & C.R. 290 at 293 *per* Dillon L.J.

[207] Although see *Stallion v. Stallion* [2009] EWHC 1950 (Ch.) at [138] *per* Ms Sarah Asplin Q.C.

[208] *Burrows and Burrows v. Sharp* (1989) 23 H.L.R. 82 at 92 *per* Dillon L.J. See also *Dodsworth v. Dodsworth* [1973] E.G.D. 233.

[209] See M.P. Thompson [1986] Conv. 406 at 411–414.

[210] [1976] Ch. 179. See also *The Mayor of London Borough of Bexley v. Maison Maurice* [2006] EWHC 3192 (Ch.).

[211] Ibid., at 189 *per* Lord Denning M.R.; at 192 *per* Lawton L.J.   [212] Ibid., at 199.

Misconduct by the claimant

Crabb v. Arun District Council provides an excellent illustration of a situation where the conduct of the person against whom the right is sought has an influence upon how the court satisfies the equity which has arisen. In the converse situation, where it is the claimant who has been guilty of misconduct prior to the court adjudicating on how the equity should be satisfied, then this will affect the exercise of the discretion and, in extreme cases such as where part of the claimant's case is based upon perjured evidence, may cause the court to decline to give the claimant any relief at all.[213] If, as in *Williams v. Staite*,[214] the misconduct occurs after the equity has been satisfied, then its effect would seem to depend upon the order which the court had made previously when deciding how the equity should be satisfied. If, for example, the court had previously ordered the property to be conveyed to the claimant, then such an order is clearly final and no order will be made for the land to be reconveyed. If, however, the order is for some sort of indefinite right of occupation then, it is thought, it may be, if the misconduct is of a sufficiently egregious nature, that the protection given by equity may subsequently be withdrawn.

Occupation

Estoppel cases often arise in a residential setting, with the claimants being given varying degrees of assurance as to the security of their occupation in a house. In such situations, when it comes to satisfying any equity which has arisen, a principal concern, where this is practicable, is to make an order which seeks to preserve the security of that occupation. So, in *Inwards v. Baker*,[215] where a father had encouraged his son to build a bungalow on the father's land, the Court of Appeal, in satisfying the son's equity, held that he had an indefinite right to remain in the bungalow, for the rest of his life should he so wish.

The perceived problem with this solution, and one which was considered to have been overlooked in *Inwards v. Baker*,[216] was that such a right could be perceived to be a life interest. The consequence of this, at that time, was that the life tenant would then be endowed with all the statutory powers, including sale, conferred by the Settled Land Act 1925,[217] an outcome considered to be undesirable. In *Griffiths v. Williams*,[218] a grandmother had relied on a representation by her granddaughter that she could live in a house, rent free, for the rest of her life. Regarding the task of the court as being 'to see, having regard to all the circumstances, what is the best and fairest way to secure protection for the person who has been misled by the representations made to [her] and subsequently repudiated',[219] the parties were prevailed upon to agree that the granddaughter should grant the grandmother a non-assignable lease,

---

[213] *J. Willis & Son v. Willis* [1986] 1 E.G.L.R. 62. See also *Gordon v. Mitchell* [2007] EWHC 1854 (Ch.).
[214] [1979] Ch. 291.   [215] [1965] 2 Q.B. 25.
[216] See *Dodsworth v. Dodsworth* [1972] E.G.D. 233 *per* Russell L.J.   [217] See Chapter 8.
[218] (1978) 248 E.G. 947.   [219] Ibid., at 950 *per* Goff L.J.

determinable upon death, at a rent sufficiently low to avoid the statutory protection conferred by the Rent Acts.

This decision shows a degree of creative flexibility on the part of the courts in seeking to achieve an appropriate solution to the problem. Now that it is no longer possible to create a strict settlement, a life interest taking effect under a trust of land,[220] a court need no longer be concerned with such complications when seeking, in appropriate cases, to allow a claimant an indefinite right of occupation. It may be anticipated that when a person has assured another that he will be able to stay in a house indefinitely, and this assurance has been relied upon, an order giving effect to that expectation is a likely outcome.[221]

Wider considerations

Pascoe v. Turner,[222] where the claimant was granted her expectation in full by the order that the house be conveyed to her, is considered by some to be a very generous response in the light of her rather limited acts of reliance.[223] The Court of Appeal was aware of this, but nevertheless considered on the facts that this was the fairest solution, a factor in that conclusion being the relative wealth of the two parties. He was considered to be a rich man and she was in straitened financial circumstances so that, to her, the expenditure of several hundred pounds was a significant outlay.[224]

The attention paid to what has been regarded as redistributive factors has been criticized,[225] yet, within a flexible jurisdiction, the needs and resources of the parties seem to be a legitimate criterion to which the court should have regard in the exercise of its discretion. Such considerations can also work against the claimant, so that although the essential elements of equitable estoppel are satisfied, in the circumstances, no remedy is considered to be appropriate.[226] The decision of the Court of Appeal in *Sledmore v. Dalby*[227] is interesting in this context.

Changing circumstances

Mr and Mrs Sledmore bought a cottage in 1962. In 1965, Mr Dalby married their daughter and they moved into the cottage as tenants of the Sledmores. Rent was paid until 1976, when the daughter became seriously ill and Mr Dalby became unemployed. Between 1976 and 1979, Mr Dalby carried out extensive improvements to the house and was encouraged to do so by the Sledmores. Mrs Sledmore knew that her husband intended to leave the cottage to the couple and had told them of this intention. In 1979, Mr Sledmore transferred his interest in the cottage to his wife, who made a will to ensure that her daughter would inherit the cottage. In 1983, Mrs Dalby died and her husband continued to live in the cottage and refused to pay rent. In 1990,

---

[220] Trusts of Land and Appointment of Trustees Act 1996, ss 1, 2.

[221] See *Maharaj v. Chand* [1986] AC 898. But see *Campbell v. Griffin* [2001] EWCA Civ. 990, [34] *per* Robert Walker L.J.

[222] [1979] 1 W.L.R. 431.   [223] See n. 151.   [224] [1979] 1 W.L.R. at 439 *per* Cumming-Bruce L.J.

[225] See S. Gardner (1999) 115 L.Q.R. 438 at 459–460.

[226] See *Appleby v. Cowley* (1982), *The Times*, 14 April.   [227] (1996) 72 P. & C.R. 196.

Mrs Sledmore sought possession of the cottage. At the time, Mr Dalby was employed and lived in the cottage on only a couple of nights a week, spending the rest of the time with his new partner. One of his daughters, who was twenty-seven and in employment, lived in the cottage. On the other hand, the house in which Mrs Sledmore lived was in need of repair. She was on income support and the interest on the mortgage on that house was being paid by the Department of Social Security. The Court of Appeal ordered possession.

It was clear that an equity had arisen in favour of Mr Dalby, but the view was taken that, although he had clearly assumed that he would be able to stay rent free in the cottage for the rest of his life, this was a case where he had to be satisfied with something less than that expectation.[228] A principal reason for awarding him nothing to satisfy the equity which had arisen was that he had already enjoyed considerable benefit in satisfaction of the equity, in that he had lived, rent free, in the property for a considerable number of years and so, in the circumstances, he had received sufficient satisfaction of the equity which had arisen in his favour.[229]

Although this decision has received a mixed reaction,[230] it seems to be correct in principle, in that, in deciding how the equity is to be satisfied, the court has a discretion to exercise. It can make an order which will result in the expectation being satisfied in full, but need not do so. Regard must be had to all the circumstances, including 'the subject-matter of the dispute, what was said and done by the parties and what has happened since'.[231] As has been seen, the conduct of the parties after the equity has arisen can be a material factor in how the court will satisfy any equity which has arisen;[232] there seems to be no reason, in principle, why material changes to the circumstances of the parties pending resolution of the dispute should not also be considered relevant: 'equitable estoppel [by contrast with contract] ... does not look forward into the future [; it] looks backwards from the moment when the promise falls due to be performed and asks whether in the circumstances which have actually happened, it would be unconscionable for the promise not to be kept.'[233] This retrospective can include a consideration of the changed circumstances of the parties.

Proportionality

An important factor which is relevant in the consideration of whether the satisfaction of an expectation in full is appropriate is whether to do so would, given the nature of both the expectation and the reliance, amount to something of a windfall to the claimant. This issue exercised the Court of Appeal in *Crabb v. Arun District Council*, and

---

[228] (1996) 72 P. & C.R. 196 at 204 *per* Roch L.J.

[229] Cf. *Campbell v. Griffin* [2001] EWCA Civ. 990 at [32]–[33] *per* Robert Walker L.J.

[230] It is supported by M. Pawlowski (1997) 113 L.Q.R. 232 at 236–237, but criticized by J.E. Adams [1996] Conv. 458.

[231] *Voyce v. Voyce* (1991) 62 P. & C.R. 290 at 296 *per* Nicholls L.J.

[232] *Crabb v. Arun District Council* [1976] Ch. 179. See Misconduct by the claimant, p. 633.

[233] *Walton v. Walton* (14 April, 1994, unreported), at [21] *per* Hoffmann L.J. cited in *Thorner v. Major* [2009] UKHL 18 at [101] *per* Lord Neuberger.

led to the initial view of the court being that the plaintiff's expectation should only be partially fulfilled: that is, he could have an easement, but only on the terms that he paid something for it. That he was held to be entitled to an easement without having to pay anything for it was a direct result of the obstructive behaviour of the defendant. The appreciation that to order satisfaction in full might lead to the overcompensation of the claimant has led the courts to consider only the partial fulfilment of the expectation either by effectively remodelling the understanding of the parties,[234] or simply by awarding less than the claimant expected.[235] The matter was fully ventilated in the leading case of *Jennings v. Rice*.[236]

Mr Jennings, and latterly his wife, did a lot of unpaid work for a Mrs Royle. That work progressively included some personal services. She made a number of promises to Mr Jennings to the effect that, one day, all this would be his. When she died, she had not left them anything in her will and he sued her estate. One issue which arose was what his expectation actually was. Her estate was worth in excess of £1.2 million, whereas the house and contents were valued at £435,000. At first instance neither expectation was fulfilled as the trial judge awarded him a payment of £200,000. He appealed, arguing that he was entitled to a larger award, but the Court of Appeal affirmed the original decision.

Extent of reliance

Central to the appeal was the argument that the normal role of estoppel is to satisfy, in full, the expectation of the claimant. In approaching this question Robert Walker L.J. expressed initial sympathy with the view that the courts should not exercise an unfettered discretion as to remedy, and that the starting point should be to fulfil the claimant's expectation.[237] He nevertheless upheld the original award. To do otherwise, on the facts of the present case, would be to run the risk of substantially overcompensating the claimant for the work he had done. He, therefore, concluded that the appropriate remedy was the £200,000 awarded by the trial judge, on the basis that this amounted to a rough approximation of the value of the work which had been done. The role of the court was to craft a remedy, which is 'the minimum equity to do justice to the plaintiff',[238] an approach which 'does not require the court to be constitutionally parsimonious, but... does implicitly recognise that the court must also do justice to the defendant'.[239]

---

[234] See *Morritt v. Wonham* [1993] N.P.C. 2, discussed by M.P. Thompson [1994] Conv. 233.

[235] See *Gillett v. Holt* [2001] Ch. 210 at 227 *per* Robert Walker L.J., commenting on *Taylor v. Dickens* [1998] 1 F.L.R. 806. Seee W. Swadling [1998] R.L.R. 220 at 221; M.P. Thompson [1998] Conv. 210 at 217. See also *Campbell v. Griffin* [2001] EWCA Civ. 990 (lump sum rather than a life interest awarded).

[236] [2003] 1 P. & C.R. 8; *Powell v. Benney* (2007) EWCA Civ. 1283. See M.P. Thompson [2004] Conv. 225; S. Gardner (2006) 115 L.Q.R. 438.

[237] [2003] 1 P. & C.R. 8 at para. 42, citing with approval articles by E. Cooke (1997) 17 L.S. 258 and S. Gardner (1999) 115 L.Q.R. 438.

[238] *Crabb v. Arun District Council* [1976] Ch. 179 at 198 *per* Scarman L.J.

[239] *Jennings v. Rice* [2003] 1 P. & C.R. 8 at [48]

The approach to be taken in satisfying the equity is to have regard to both the nature of the expectation and to the degree of reliance. Having done that:

'There is a clear line of authority from at least *Crabb* to the present day which establishes that once the elements of proprietary estoppel are established an equity arises. The value of that equity will depend upon all the circumstances including the expectation and the detriment. The task of the court is to do justice. *The most essential requirement is that there must be proportionality between the expectation and the detriment.*'[240]

This is a principled approach, reflecting both the discretionary nature of the remedies available in estoppel cases, and the need to consider all aspects of the case when arriving at an appropriate remedy, a feature which will, it is thought, lead in many, albeit not all, cases to an order which seeks to compensate the claimant for the reliance.[241] It should be stressed that the courts do have, in estoppel cases, considerable flexibility in arriving at a just solution to a particular dispute. So, in *Henry v. Henry*,[242] where the claimant had lived rent free for many years on property which he had been promised he would inherit, this was a key criterion in awarding him only a half of the property. In deciding whether to enforce the expectation in full, regard was had to the benefits he had enjoyed following the assurance, together with the detriment he had suffered.[243]

Flexibility

Such flexibility in awarding only partial fulfilment of a claimant's expectation is consistent with the flexible approaches to other, not unconnected, areas of law. If a person has overpaid another and, subsequently, seeks restitution, then the person against whom that remedy is sought can rely upon the defence of change of position. This is a flexible defence and avoids the conclusion that, if a person has relied upon a representation that he is entitled to money which has wrongly been paid to him, the fact of reliance precludes restitution. Such a conclusion would allow the recipient of the money to retain an amount which he had been mistakenly paid, when his reliance did not equate to that overpayment,[244] a result which would result in unjust enrichment.[245] Similarly, when the reliance on an expectation is significantly less than the value of the expectation, the enforcement of the expectation in full may be an excessive response to the equity which has arisen so that, although seen by some as

---

[240] Ibid., at [36] *per* Aldous L.J. Emphasis supplied. See also *Malik v. Kalyan* [2010] EWCA Civ. 113 at [31] *per* Rimer L.J.; *Ashby v. Kilduff* [2010] EWHC 2034 (Ch.) at [73]–[74] *per* Mr Bernard Livesey Q.C.

[241] See also *Murphy v. Burrows* [2004] EWHC 1400 (Ch.) at [124] *per* Mr Richard Sheldon Q.C.

[242] [2010] UKPC 3.

[243] See also *Clarke v. Meadus* [2010] EWHC 3117 (Ch.) at [68] *per* Warren J.

[244] See *Avon County Council v. Howlett* [1983] 1 W.L.R. 605; a case of estoppel by representation at common law.

[245] See *Lipkin Gorman (A Firm) v. Karpnale Ltd* [1991] 2 A.C. 548 at 580 *per* Lord Goff of Chievely; *Scottish Equitable plc v. Derby* [2000] 3 All E.R. 793 at 804 *per* Harrison J., affirmed [2001] 3 All E.R. 818; *Philip Collins Ltd v. Davis* [2000] 3 All E.R. 808 at 826–840 *per* Jonathan Parker J. See M.P. Thompson [2000] Conv. 548.

unprincipled,[246] it seems that the better view is that, once rights have arisen through equitable estoppel, it is true to say that the courts have a very wide and flexible discretion as to how to satisfy the resultant equity.

ESTOPPEL AND OTHER CONCEPTS

It is quite uncontroversial that, in Land Law, equitable or proprietary estoppel operates to give rise directly to a cause of action. It is instructive to compare and contrast, albeit briefly, the underlying basis of this cause of action with other similar concepts.

Contract

A feature of some estoppel cases is that one person encourages another to believe that he will gain a right over another's property; for example, when one person promises that he will leave the other property in a will. The effect of reliance on such a promise is that the claimant will, as a result, acquire rights in equity. This has led to the argument that such cases, properly understood, are actually contract cases, the argument being that foreseeable reliance on a promise amounts to consideration, so that the promise becomes contractually binding.[247] There are two main problems with this analysis. The first is that, while it may be clear the claimant has an expectation of acquiring some interest in the property, the full nature of that expectation may lack the clarity sufficient to form the basis of a contract. The second reason is closely related to the first and relates to the question of remedy. If the existence of a contract is established, then the claimant is entitled to have his expectation interest fulfilled. This is because there is a bargain, and he is, in general, entitled to get what he bargained for. In estoppel cases there is no such bargain, and, as a result, the same level of remedy may not be appropriate. So, in estoppel cases, the 'remedy is at the discretion of the court; the plaintiff will obtain what it is just to give him, which is not necessarily the same as what he expected to receive'.[248]

The inherent flexibility of estoppel is a feature which distinguishes it from contract. In estoppel cases, the expectation may be imprecise and the consequent reliance, while foreseeable, may vary in degree. These factors lead to a necessary difference in approach as to remedy. There are, therefore, important features which distinguish this equitable cause of action from the law of contract.

---

[246] Gardner, op. cit., at 463.

[247] See P.S. Atiyah (1976) 92 L.Q.R. 174, commenting on *Crabb v. Arun District Council* [1976] Ch. 179. For a fuller discussion of this issue, see P.S. Atiyah, *Consideration in Contracts* (Canberra: Australian National University Press, 1971), 45–59.

[248] See P.J. Millett (1976) 92 L.Q.R. 342 at 346, where Atiyah's argument is effectively refuted.

The constructive trust

In a previous chapter concerned with the acquisition of an interest in the home, the role of the constructive trust was considered.[249] The type of situation where such a trust is imposed occurs when a house is being acquired and the legal title is put into one person's name, usually the man's, but, prior to this happening,[250] there is some sort of agreement that the beneficial ownership is to be shared. This agreement can be an actual agreement,[251] or one that is inferred from the fact that some pretext is given as to why the property is not being put into their joint names.[252] While such an agreement can be sufficient, where personal property is concerned, to create a trust,[253] it would be insufficient in the case of land because the formal requirements necessary to create such a trust have not been complied with.[254] If, however, relying on that agreement, the woman contributes to the acquisition of the house, it is fraudulent on the part of the holder of the legal title to plead the lack of writing and to claim sole beneficial entitlement and, to prevent this, a constructive trust is imposed to give effect to that agreement.[255]

The underlying basis of the imposition of a constructive trust in this situation is the prevention of unjust enrichment. Were the legal owner to be allowed to use the lack of writing required by the statute to deny the existence of the trust, then he, having received the benefit of her contribution to the acquisition of the house, would be unjustly enriched at her expense. To prevent this, a constructive trust is imposed which has the effect of enforcing the oral agreement between them.

More recent cases involving the imposition of a constructive trust have downplayed the aspect of unjust enrichment and, instead, treated the issue to be decided as being whether the claimant has relied upon the agreement to share the beneficial ownership of the house. This, in turn, has led to judicial statements to the effect that the role of constructive trust and equitable estoppel is the same.[256]

While it is evident that there are similarities between the constructive trust and equitable estoppel, they are separate doctrines and should not be regarded as a fused concept.[257] The constructive trust is predicated upon the basis that there is an

---

[249] See Chapter 9.

[250] In some cases, the agreement occurs after the house has been acquired by one of the parties. See *Austin v. Keele* (1987) 61 A.J.L.R. 605 at 609 *per* Lord Oliver of Aylmerton.

[251] See *Re Densham* [1975] 1 W.L.R. 1519.

[252] See, e.g., *Eves v. Eves* [1975] 1 W.L.R. 1338; *Grant v. Edwards* [1986] Ch. 638.

[253] See *Paul v. Constance* [1977] 1 W.L.R. 527; *Rowe v. Prance* [1999] 2 F.L.R. 787, criticized by S. Baughen [2000] Conv. 58.

[254] Law of Property Act 1925, s. 53(1)(b). See *Lloyds Bank plc v. Rosset* [1991] A.C. 107 at 129 *per* Lord Bridge of Harwich.

[255] See *Re Densham* [1975] 1 W.L.R. 1519. This line of authority derives from *Rochefoucauld v. Boustead* [1897] 1 Ch. 196.

[256] See *Grant v. Edwards* [1986] Ch. 638 at 656 *per* Sir Nicolas Browne-Wilkinson V.-C.; *Lloyds Bank plc v. Rosset* [1991] 1 A.C. 107 at 132 *per* Lord Bridge of Harwich.

[257] For an argument favouring fusion, see D. Hayton [1990] Conv. 370. For a different view, see P. Ferguson (1993) 109 L.Q.R. 114.

agreement to share the beneficial ownership of property. While in an estoppel case, the expectation may be to acquire beneficial ownership of land, it may be to have some lesser right, such as a right of occupation.[258] Further, the expectation may be to have a quite different type of right, such as an easement.[259] It is difficult on orthodox trust principles to see how the expectation of the acquisition of an easement can be achieved through the medium of a constructive trust. Thirdly, the theoretical bases of the two doctrines are different. The rationale of the constructive trust is to prevent unjust enrichment; that of estoppel is to prevent unconscionability, which is a wider concept. In principle, to acquire an interest under a constructive trust the conduct must have contributed to the acquisition of the house in question, while reliance is a much wider concept. Finally, the role of the constructive trust is to give effect to the agreement reached. In estoppel cases, the court has a discretion as to how the equity which has arisen is to be satisfied, such remedy being tailored so as to meet the justice of the case. So while there are undeniable similarities between the two doctrines, it is preferable to see them as separate but related reactions by equity to the question of how interests in land can be acquired informally. This view has since been endorsed in *Stack v. Dowden*.[260]

ESTOPPEL AND THIRD PARTIES

In the context of contractual licences what was a vexed question for some considerable time was whether or not such a licence would bind a purchaser, whether it was a new interest in land. This issue has now been resolved, it having been determined that it is not.[261] In estoppel cases, a similar issue arises; if A has, through the medium of estoppel, acquired an equity against B, will that equity be binding on a purchaser of B's land?[262]

When an equity has arisen, it is at the court's discretion as to how that equity should be satisfied. It is also the case that, until a decision is made as to how that equity is to be satisfied, the equity is inchoate in nature. How the discretion is exercised may then be affected by events occurring after the equity has arisen; indeed, in some situations, the circumstances may be such at the time of the trial that a decision not to afford any remedy at all might be seen to be the most appropriate outcome to the dispute.[263]

---

[258] See *Maharaj v. Chand* [1986] A.C. 898.   [259] See *Crabb v. Arun District Council* [1976] Ch. 179.

[260] [2007] A.C. 432 at [35] *per* Lord Walker of Gestingthorpe, recanting his earlier views in *Yaxley v. Gotts* [2000] 1 All E.R. 711 at 721–722. See also *Q. v. Q.* [2008] EWHC 1879 (Ch.) at [113] *per* Black J. Contrast *Thorner v. Major* [2009] UKHL 18 at [20] *per* Lord Scott, who is advocating a new, remedial, constructive trust rather than the more conventional model referred to here.

[261] See *Ashburn Anstalt v. Arnold* [1989] Ch. 1.

[262] See S. Baughen (1994) 14 L.S. 147; B. McFarlane [2003] C.L.J. 661.

[263] See *Sledmore v. Dalby* (1996) 72 P. & C.R. 196.

Because the equity is uncertain in scope, this has led some to argue that rights arising from estoppel are not capable of being proprietary in nature.[264]

In cases of equitable estoppel, the claim that is made is normally to be entitled to an interest in land and such claims are frequently vindicated. As such, the status of the claim seems to amount to more than a mere equity such as the deserted wife's equity, if such a claim could properly be described as an equity at all.[265] Certainly, there are a number of authorities where the courts have accepted that an estoppel claim is binding upon third parties. Thus, where property has been bought for value, and the purchaser has actual notice of the estoppel right, the courts have been quite prepared to hold him to be bound by that right.[266] Similarly, in cases where the person against whom the claim is made is not a purchaser for value at all, the courts have been fully prepared to enforce the claim against that person.[267] Cases such as these have led to the view being expressed in *Lloyds Bank plc v. Carrick*[268] that, at least so far as the Court of Appeal was concerned, the matter was settled that an estoppel interest gave rise to an interest in land. On the other hand, more recently the view was expressed by Peter Gibson L.J. in *United Bank of Kuwait plc v. Sahib*,[269] that estoppel would only affect a purchaser for value who had, himself, acted unconscionably. The matter is not, therefore, as clear as it might be.

The weight of authority would seem to suggest that there are circumstances when an equity which has arisen can adversely affect a third party[270] but that the circumstance surrounding the acquisition of the property by the purchaser may be a relevant factor in the resolution of the dispute.

Unregistered land

Where title is registered, the first issue to determine is whether the claimant has a right which is capable of affecting a purchaser and, if so, the circumstances when he will be bound by it. The final issue which should then be considered is, if the purchaser is bound, what is the appropriate remedy to be granted?

In *E.R. Ives Investment Ltd v. High*,[271] the defendant, Mr High, and his neighbour, Mr Westgate, agreed that, in return for Mr Westgate being allowed to keep the foundations of a building encroaching on the defendant's land, Mr High should have a right of way over Mr Westgate's land. This agreement created an equitable easement and, when Mr Westgate sold his land to the Wrights, this equitable easement became

---

[264] See T. Bailey [1983] Conv. 99 at 100; S. Bright in Bright and Dewar (eds), *Land Law: Themes and Perspectives* (Oxford: Oxford University Press, 1998), 529 at 544.

[265] See *National Provincial Bank Ltd v. Ainsworth* [1965] A.C. 1175.

[266] See *E.R. Ives Investment Ltd v. High* [1967] 2 Q.B. 379; *Williams v. Staite* [1979] Ch. 291.

[267] See *Inwards v. Baker* [1965] 2 Q.B. 29; *Voyce v. Voyce* (1991) 62 P. & C.R. 290, especially at 294 *per* Dillon L.J. See also *Errington v. Errington* [1952] 1 K.B. 290.

[268] [1996] 4 All E.R. 630 at 642 *per* Morritt L.J.

[269] [1997] Ch. 107 at 142. Interestingly, Peter Gibson L.J. sat in *Carrick* and agreed with the judgment of Morritt L.J. For a valuable discussion, see P. Critchley [1998] Conv. 502.

[270] See also G. Battersby in Bright and Dewar, op. cit., 487 at 504–505.   [271] [1967] 2 Q.B. 379.

void for non-registration. Neither the Wrights nor Mr High were aware of this and Mr High, believing he had a right of way over the Wrights' land, did various acts in circumstances in which had a dispute then arisen, it would have been unconscionable for the Wrights to have denied some effect to his expectation of having a right of way. The Wrights then sold the land to the plaintiff, the conveyance stating that the land was sold subject to the defendant's right of way. The plaintiff, arguing that the right of way was void for non-registration, sought an injunction to restrain the defendant from using the claimed right.

The injunction was refused for two reasons. First, as the foundations remained on the defendant's land, under the principle of benefit and burden,[272] the plaintiff could not continue to retain the benefit of having his building encroach on the defendant's land with taking subject to the corresponding burden. Secondly, however, the Court of Appeal held that the plaintiff took the land subject to the defendant's equity which had arisen through estoppel. The Court of Appeal held that this equity was binding upon successors in title[273] and was not registrable as a land charge.[274] Whether the purchaser was bound depended, therefore, upon notice and, obviously, on the facts, the plaintiff had express notice of the equity.

This was a case where the plaintiff had the clearest notice of the defendant's equity. To explain the case in the terms used by Peter Gibson L.J., that the equity was enforceable because the plaintiff had behaved unconscionably is, however, unsatisfactory because the defendant had not relied in any way upon the plaintiff's behaviour. No new equity arose after the plaintiff had acquired the land. He must, therefore, have been bound by the equity which had arisen previously. The case is, therefore, clear authority that the equity which arises through estoppel is capable of binding a purchaser. Whether or not he is bound by it should depend, therefore, on the application of the orthodox principles of notice.

Position of the purchaser

That, however, does not conclude the matter. As in all estoppel cases, once it is clear that the claimant has an equity, the question remains as to how that equity should be satisfied and it is in determining this matter that it is suggested that the circumstances surrounding the acquisition of the land become relevant. How the equity is to be satisfied is a matter for the discretion of the court and, in determining this issue, regard can be had to any relevant factors from the date when the equity arose to the time when the question as to how that equity is to be satisfied is to be answered. The fact that the relevant property has changed hands, so that the equity is being claimed against someone other than the person who was privy to its creation, would seem to be a relevant factor, as would the capacity of the purchaser and the state of his mind when he acquired the property. On this basis, it is argued that, if the purchaser has not given value, or has actual notice of the equity, then it is reasonable to satisfy the equity

---

[272] See Mutual benefit and burden, pp. 592–593.
[273] [1967] 2 Q.B. 379 at 394 *per* Lord Denning M.R.   [274] Ibid., at 405 *per* Winn L.J.

in the same way as it would have been had the purchase not taken place. Where, however, a purchaser for value has only constructive notice of the equity, he would still, on principle, be bound by the equity but the remedy afforded to the claimant may not be as extensive as would be the case if he had had actual notice of the right.[275]

Registered land

Where title is registered, the position has now, to a considerable extent, been clarified by section 116 of the Land Registration Act 2002. This section declares that, for the avoidance of doubt, an equity by estoppel has effect from the time the equity arises as an interest capable of binding successors in title (subject to the rules about the effect of dispositions on priority). Plainly, therefore, it is the case that a purchaser of registered land can be affected by an equity arising from estoppel, although the questions will remain as to the circumstances in which he will be bound and as to how the equity which has arisen will be satisfied. Before considering this, the point can also be made that, although this section applies only to registered land, it would seem to be inevitable that a court would now hold that, when title is unregistered, an equity arising from estoppel will have proprietary effect.

For an equity arising from estoppel to bind a purchaser, it will be necessary that it is either protected by the registration of a notice or that it takes effect as an interest which overrides a registered disposition. Given that estoppel rights arise in informal situations, the prospect of the holder of such a right protecting it by registration is remote. If it is to bind a purchaser, therefore, it will be on the basis that the holder of the right is in actual occupation of the land, within the meaning of paragraph 2 of Schedule 3 to the Act. If the purchaser is bound by the equity on this basis, the question will still remain as to how it should be satisfied and, again, the state of mind of the purchaser when the land was acquired would appear to be relevant. This was explicitly recognized by the Privy Council in *Henry v. Henry*,[276] where Sir Jonathan Parker said:

'The Board does not rule out the possibility that cases may arise in which the particular circumstances surrounding a third party purchase may, notwithstanding the claimant's overriding interest, require the court to reassess the extent of the claimant's equity in the property.'

Given that the court has a discretion as to how any equity that has arisen should be satisfied and, as the fact that the person against whom the equity is to be enforced was not a party to its creation, this seems clearly to be correct. As, however, to be an interest overriding a registered disposition, the occupation has to be obvious on a reasonably careful inspection of the land,[277] it may well be the case that the equity will be satisfied in the same way as it would have been against the person who was privy to its creation. Even if that is the case, however, if the transfer has been made by two legal owners,

---

[275] See the comments in *Re Sharpe* [1980] 1 W.L.R. 219 at 226 *per* Browne-Wilkinson L.J.
[276] [2010] EWPC 3 at [56].   [277] Land Registration Act 2002, Sched. 3, para. 2(c).

and the right claimed under estoppel is to a beneficial interest in the property, then, in principle, the estoppel right should not be binding on the transferee. This is because, if there had been in existence a beneficial interest under a trust, a transfer by two legal owners would overreach that right.[278] It would be a quite remarkable result if a full beneficial interest under a trust would be overreached in such circumstances, whereas the more precarious equity arising from estoppel would not be.[279]

Easements

Where the right claimed is, as in *E.R. Ives Investment Ltd v. High*, to an easement, it could, in the past, have been argued that the right would take effect as an equitable easement under section 70(1)(a) of the Land Registration Act 1925. This will still be the case in respect of rights arising before the 2002 Act comes into force.[280] Where such a right arises after the Act comes into force, it is difficult to see how it could take effect as an interest overriding registration, because only legal easements can have this status.

Conclusions

The law relating to licences is a fascinating chapter in the development of the law, as the courts have struggled to come to terms with competing interests with regard to land. On the one hand, there is the desire to maximize the security of land transactions and, on the other, to seek to protect informally created expectations affecting property. In the case of contractual licences, the attempt to develop a new proprietary right, binding upon all but the bona fide purchaser, has failed, although in certain, tightly defined circumstances, such licences will be binding on a purchaser. The development of estoppel has seen the courts fashion a flexible and principled response to situations where it would be unconscionable to deny one person rights as against another. The very flexibility of the doctrine does give rise to problems, in that the outcome of cases remains unpredictable but this can be seen as an acceptable price to pay to avoid patently unjust results to particular disputes. The effect of estoppel rights against third parties remains unclear, although it is suggested that to pay attention to the circumstances of the purchaser as a relevant consideration in the resolution of disputes affords a reasonable compromise between the two competing tensions mentioned above.

---

[278]   *City of London Building Society v. Flegg* [1988] A.C. 54.
[279]   See *Birmingham Midshires Mortgages Ltd v. Saberwal* (2000) 80 P. & C.R. 256 at 262 *per* Robert Walker L.J. Cf. *Campbell v. Griffin* [2001] EWCA Civ. 990 at [37], *per* Robert Walker L.J., where this point was overlooked. See M.P. Thompson [2003] Conv. 157 at 165–167.
[280]   Ibid., Sched. 12, para. 9.

Index